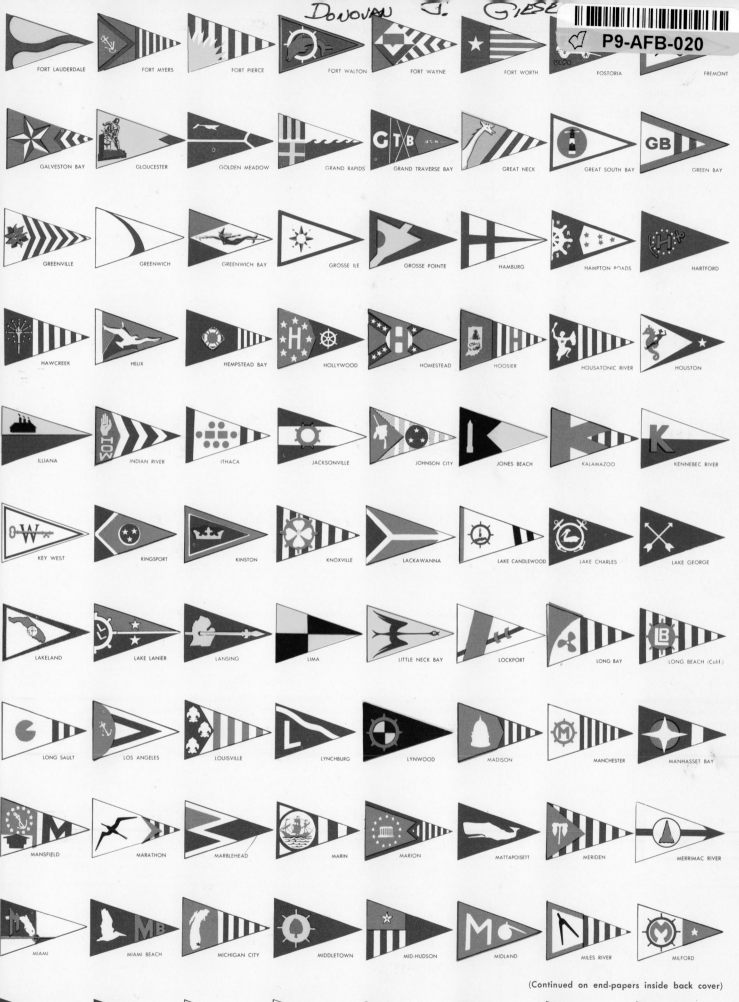

FORT LAUDERDALE · FORT MYERS · FORT PIERCE · FORT WALTON · FORT WAYNE · FORT WORTH · FOSTORIA · FREMONT

GALVESTON BAY · GLOUCESTER · GOLDEN MEADOW · GRAND RAPIDS · GRAND TRAVERSE BAY · GREAT NECK · GREAT SOUTH BAY · GREEN BAY

GREENVILLE · GREENWICH · GREENWICH BAY · GROSSE ILE · GROSSE POINTE · HAMBURG · HAMPTON ROADS · HARTFORD

HAWCREEK · HELIX · HEMPSTEAD BAY · HOLLYWOOD · HOMESTEAD · HOOSIER · HOUSATONIC RIVER · HOUSTON

ILLIANA · INDIAN RIVER · ITHACA · JACKSONVILLE · JOHNSON CITY · JONES BEACH · KALAMAZOO · KENNEBEC RIVER

KEY WEST · KINGSPORT · KINSTON · KNOXVILLE · LACKAWANNA · LAKE CANDLEWOOD · LAKE CHARLES · LAKE GEORGE

LAKELAND · LAKE LANIER · LANSING · LIMA · LITTLE NECK BAY · LOCKPORT · LONG BAY · LONG BEACH (Calif.)

LONG SAULT · LOS ANGELES · LOUISVILLE · LYNCHBURG · LYNWOOD · MADISON · MANCHESTER · MANHASSET BAY

MANSFIELD · MARATHON · MARBLEHEAD · MARIN · MARION · MATTAPOISETT · MERIDEN · MERRIMAC RIVER

MIAMI · MIAMI BEACH · MICHIGAN CITY · MIDDLETOWN · MID-HUDSON · MIDLAND · MILES RIVER · MILFORD

(Continued on end-papers inside back cover)

MILWAUKEE · MINNETONKA · MISSION BAY · MISSISSIPPI COAST · MOBILE · MOHAWK-HUDSON · MORGANTOWN · MORICHES BAY

DONOVAN J. GIESB

PILOTING, SEAMANSHIP
AND
SMALL BOAT HANDLING

PILOTING, SEAMANSHIP
AND
SMALL BOAT HANDLING

A complete illustrated course
prepared especially to develop skill, pleasure and safety
in the navigation of small boats on coastal and inland waters

1969-70 EDITION
47th YEAR

By CHARLES F. CHAPMAN, M. E.

Published by

THE YACHTSMAN'S MAGAZINE

959 Eighth Avenue, New York, N.Y. 10019

PRINTED IN THE UNITED STATES OF AMERICA
BY AMERICAN BOOK—STRATFORD PRESS, INC., N.Y.

from a painting by Terése McGinnis

Again, Happy Piloting!

This, the 1969/70 edition of Chapman's, is the 48th printing of this famous book, dating back to the days when yachtsmen joined the U.S. Navy, during World War I.

Year by year, from the days when boating was in its infancy, to the present time, with boats numbered in the millions, every edition has been enlarged and revised.

May the contents of this present edition add to the enjoyment of your boating.

Charles F. Chapman

ABOUT THE AUTHOR   CHARLES FREDERIC CHAPMAN completed half a century of distinguished service to Motor Boating magazine and to the boating public on May 9, 1962.

For 48 of these 50 years "Chap" served as Editor of Motor Boating, and for the last seven as Publisher and Vice President. He established the editorial policies and objectives which have made Motor Boating great.

Never an "armchair" editor, Chap, from the earliest days delved deeply, mentally, physically and with his whole being, into anything that promised to be of interest to boatmen or that might somehow help boating.

Relatively few people know that Chap is a Connecticut Yankee, born in Norwich, Connecticut in 1881 Graduating from Norwich Academy in 1900, he entered Cornell University where he majored in Mechanical and Marine Engineering and Naval Architecture, earning an M.E. degree.

Settling in New York City, he joined the New York Motor Boat Club at 147th Street on the Hudson River. This club, a member of the American Power Boat Association, soon found use for Chap's helpfulness and elected him Commodore. From this beginning Chap went on to serve as Chairman of the APBA Racing Commission, sanctioning body for all motorboat races in the country, and Secretary—a post he held for 25 years. He was the first to be elected to the Honor Squadron of the APBA.

Pioneering long-distance racing, Chap initiated many contests for motorboats. On two occasions he organized races between crack trains and Gar Wood's famous speedboats. The boats beat the trains—in 1921 from Miami to New York, and in 1925 from Albany to New York. Chap himself was the navigator on these runs. In addition, Chap drove speedboats himself, finishing second in the Gold Cup classics of 1924 and 1927, and in the Duke of York race in England in 1926.

And in that latter year Chap helped organize the National Outboard Racing Commission, serving as its Chairman until World War II called a halt to racing. The first "outboard racing rules," written by Chap in the late twenties, have been used basically ever since.

Chap was a leader in organizing the U.S. Power Squadrons in February 1914. He holds USPS Certificate #A 1. Chap conducted the first national tests for USPS members; he designed the USPS ensign which 60,000 or more members proudly salute today; he served as Treasurer, Chairman of the Committee on Rules and Vice Commander. And when he could no longer deny demand of the membership, he served two terms as Chief Commander—1946-1947. As Chairman of the Flag and Etiquette Committee and Member of the Governing Board, he still actively helps the USPS in every way he can.

In each World War, Chap authored, out of his store of lore and knowledge, a compact instruction manual on small boat seamanship for young men aiming at the Navy, Coast Guard or Merchant Marine.

Chap's "extra-curricular" efforts have also included officerships in the Columbia and Manhasset Bay Yacht Clubs (Commodore 1941-1944) and honorary life membership in Larchmont Yacht Club, as well as civic responsibilities for the village of Plandome, Long Island where he has served as Water Commissioner, Fire Commissioner, Police Commissioner, and Acting Mayor!

But one we can't omit—because its paraphrasing of a Churchillian classic expresses so perfectly how his friends feel about Chap. In 1955 the Ole Evinrude Boating Foundation, in recognition of "long contributions to recreational boating" awarded Chap (its initial award) a silver bowl with a citation which said:

"No other man deserves so much from so many of us in the World of Boating."

The Editors of Motor Boating
January 4, 1968

FOREWORD   The compilation of *Piloting, Seamanship and Small Boat Handling* has been a work of some magnitude. It has entailed not only the gathering, editing and processing of authoritative materials from many sources, but perpetual revision to keep it abreast of developments in the sport of boating. Techniques and materials change, regulations are never static. When Bill Koelbel joined the staff of Motor Boating in 1928, the major portion of this effort fell on his shoulders. In those days, Chap's "bible" was an unpretentious book of less than 200 pages, but over the past four decades it has steadily kept pace with the phenomenal growth of boating. By 1964, the volume had more than tripled in size, and Bill had written or revised a large part of the content, to which Chap in autographing a copy for Bill paid tribute: "... for his unsurpassed knowledge of boating and whose skill alone and untiring energy have made possible the publication of this book."

In 1965, a long-range project was initiated, envisioning the total reconstruction of the "blue book" into a completely new volume—new in concept, new in content, new in format. Now, as we launch this 1969-70 edition, the work is rapidly nearing completion, with 21 new chapters, a few awaiting anticipated changes in federal Pilot Rules, and a few others requiring little more than re-styling in the new format. This 1969-70 edition of nearly 700 pages marks the fourth in as many years since embarking on this program. Each has been personally edited and coordinated by Bill Koelbel. Surveying progress already made in two short years, Chap, his hand still steady on the helm, reflected in his autograph of Bill's copy in June 1967: "...If the volume is to have a place in posterity, he deserves a large share of the credit, not only for this particular edition, but for many of (those) which have preceded (it)."

John R. Whiting
Publisher, Motor Boating
October 1, 1968

PREFACE TO THE 1969-70 EDITION
(47th Year)

FOR ALMOST FIFTY YEARS, *Piloting, Seamanship and Small Boat Handling* has been widely acclaimed as the acknowledged authority on subjects of vital interest to all who love boats—those who own, handle or cruise as guests aboard them...whether driven by wind or motor. Its unique reputation as the "bible of boating" has been earned only through dedicated year-by-year editing for technical accuracy, enlargement of the scope of its content to embrace newest developments in the field, (while retaining other worthwhile features which have been completely updated), and adoption of a totally new format, organized for clarity and legibility.

Even with the annual addition of voluminous new material, the original page numbering system has been basically preserved by the addition of lettered pages in proper sequence to retain valuable references used in the past.

Because of the continuing nature of revisions required to keep it strictly up-to-date, a piloting text, unlike a novel, can never be said to be quite "finished." Any reader or student, however, familiar with the radical transformation that has taken place in *Chapman's,* especially in several recent editions, will appreciate that the 1969-1970 edition is a *new* book.

This 1969-1970 edition is a far cry, indeed, from the first (1922) edition of only 120 pages. In recent years it has grown, annually, to its present size of more than 690 pages. During these years, *Piloting, Seamanship and Small Boat Handling,* the "blue book," has been the text used in free instruction courses given by the U.S. Power Squadrons and the USCG Auxiliary. It has also been used extensively in courses given by branches of the Navy, Coast Guard, and Army, as well as many nautical schools and colleges.

Acknowledgment is due several contributing editors who have prepared new chapters for recent editions. All have made significant contributions to the educational work of the United States Power Squadrons. In the 1966-67 edition, new material included Marlinespike Seamanship by H. D. DaBoll, Weather by Gardner Emmons, the Mariner's Compass by John Wilde, and Electronic Equipment by Elbert S. Maloney. Included in that edition was a revised chapter on Flag Etiquette by the author.

Special recognition must be given the outstanding work of Mr. Maloney who, in 1966-67, prepared a complete four-chapter section on charts and piloting, followed in 1968-69 by Seamanship, Aids to Navigation, Government Publications, and Signaling. This 1969-70 edition includes his new chapters on Safety, Customs and Etiquette, and Clothing and Uniforms. William Koelbel's Anchoring chapter has been fully updated, revised and put in the new format.

This edition also includes many additional features. Among the 28 pages devoted to color plates, the newly authorized U.S. Coast Guard Auxiliary Insignia are fully illustrated. The Signaling chapter (including an illustrative page in color) has been revised to reflect late changes in the International Code. Proposed new Rules of the Road for United States waters have been briefly summarized. As in all previous editions, full recognition has been given to recent changes in Government rules and regulations. Expansion of four chapters has required enlargement of the edition by 24 pages.

Originality is not claimed for all the contents of this book, representing as it does a compilation of data from many sources. The publishers are indebted to many members of the armed forces and the U.S. Power Squadrons for their invaluable suggestions. The unqualified cooperation of the U.S. Coast Guard, the U.S. Coast and Geodetic Survey, Army Engineers and their U.S. Lake Survey, the author gratefully acknowledges. The U.S. Navy and its Oceanographic Office have been particularly helpful. To all who have contributed so generously toward the success *Piloting, Seamanship and Small Boat Handling* has achieved, the author expresses his sincere thanks and appreciation.

At no time has the author ever claimed that seamanship or navigation can be mastered from the printed page alone. But the experienced boatman will surely acknowledge that a careful study of the principles of good small-boat seamanship, as presented in the following pages, will be generously repaid. By application of these principles in practice, he will reap a three-fold reward: increasing his own enjoyment of boating, he will make a major contribution to the cause of safety afloat, and be welcomed, in due course, to the ranks of "seasoned skippers."

—C. F. C.
November 1, 1968

CONTENTS, 1969-70 EDITION

NOTE: The high folio on the last page of the general index of this book is not a true total of the actual number of pages. In order to add much valuable up-to-date material in proper sequence by chapter and subject without destroying earlier references, lettered pages (a, b, c, d, etc.) have been inserted with a minimum of change in original page numbers. A total of 166 lettered pages have been added to the present edition, bringing the total to approximately 690 exclusive of end-papers. The General Index, starting on page 509, includes both numbered and lettered pages. Readers will find it invaluable as a frequent reference in locating specific subjects.

PENNANTS OF THE UNITED STATES POWER SQUADRONS......See end papers

REFERENCES FOR USPS INSTRUCTION COURSES

REFERENCES FOR USCG AUXILIARY STUDY COURSE

FLAGS

When and How
to Fly Them

This illustration shows the Union Jack flying at the port yardarm. Correct practice dictates that this flag can be flown only on Sundays or Holidays.

Diagrams illustrating how to fly various flags on a yacht club mast ashore will be found on page 360.

NOTE:—While it is true that no naval or other authority can be quoted for the display of the Union Jack on a yacht club mast ashore, a long-standing precedent has been established in its widespread use by the better yacht clubs.

To be rated a 100% boatman—in other words, a "Seasoned Skipper" — the owner or captain of a boat must know flags, what they mean, and how to fly them.

In this connection, it has always been my feeling that yachtsmen would gladly comply with the protocol associated with the display of flags if they understood it.

With these thoughts in mind, the editors of Motor Boating have prepared this special section containing illustrations of flags in full color and authoritative information concerning their use.

There is a right way to fly every flag. Following this guide, you can be sure you are displaying your flags correctly.

As a long-time proponent of propriety in the flying of flags aboard ship, it gives me considerable pleasure to recommend this feature to our readers.

Charles F. Chapman

WHEN AND WHERE TO FLY FLAGS ON BOATS

FLAG CODE OF THE UNITED STATES POWER SQUADRONS

FLAG	WHEN FLOWN	Power Boat with Bow and Stern Staffs Only	Power Boat with Bow and Stern Staffs and Signal Mast	Single-Masted Sailing Yacht	Power Boat or Sailing Yacht With Two Masts
U.S. ENSIGN OR U.S. YACHT ENSIGN[1]	0800 to Sundown	Stern Staff	Stern Staff	At Anchor or Under Power Alone: Stern Staff[3] Under Way: From Peak or Leech of Mainsail	At Anchor or Under Power Alone: Stern Staff[3] Under Way: From Peak or Leech of Aftermost Sail
USPS ENSIGN[1]	0800 to Sundown	Stern Staff	Stern Staff or Starboard Yardarm[2]	At Anchor or Under Power Alone: Stern Staff[3] Under Way: From Peak or Leech of Mainsail	At Anchor or Under Power Alone: Stern Staff[3] Under Way: From Peak or Leech of Aftermost Sail
SQUADRON PENNANT OR YACHT CLUB BURGEE	0800 to Sundown	Bow Staff	Bow Staff	At Bow Staff If Yacht So Equipped; Otherwise At the Truck	Foremost Truck
PRIVATE SIGNAL OR USPS PAST OFFICER'S SIGNAL	0800 to Sundown	Not Flown	At the Truck	At the Truck	Aftermost Truck
FLAG OFFICER'S (RECTANGULAR)	Day and Night While Boat Is In Commission	Not Flown	At the Truck Instead of Private Signal	At the Truck Instead of Squadron Pennant or Yacht Club Burgee	Aftermost Truck, Instead of Private Signal
APPOINTED OFFICER'S (SWALLOWTAIL)	0800 to Sundown	Not Flown	At the Truck Instead of Private Signal	At the Truck, Instead of Squadron Pennant or Yacht Club Burgee	Aftermost Truck, Instead of Private Signal
UNION JACK	0800 to Sundown, At Anchor Only, On Sundays and Holidays or When Dressing Ship	Not Flown	Not Flown	Not Flown	Jack Staff
ABSENT FLAG	0800 to Sundown When Owner Is Absent	Not Flown	Starboard Yardarm	Starboard Spreader	Starboard Main Spreader
GUEST FLAG	0800 to Sundown When Owner Is Absent, But Guests Are on Board	Not Flown	Starboard Yardarm	Starboard Spreader	Starboard Main Spreader
OFFICER-IN-CHARGE (OIC) PENNANT	See USPS By-Laws Art. XVI, Sec. 9	Not Flown	At the Truck, Above Officer's Flag or Private Signal	At the Truck, Above Officer's Flag or Private Signal	Aftermost Truck, Above Officer's Flag or Private Signal

Footnotes:

[1] A USPS Member has the Option of Flying the U.S. Ensign, the U.S. Yacht Ensign or the USPS Ensign.

[2] If the USPS Ensign is Flown from the Yardarm, the U.S. Ensign or the U.S. Yacht Ensign should be Flown from Stern Staff.

[3] On Sailing Yachts with Overhanging Booms, the Stern Staff should be located on the Starboard Side of the Boom.

Where the Same Hoist Is Indicated for More Than One Flag or Signal, the Choice Is Optional. The Flying of Two Flags or Signals From the Same Hoist Is Not Authorized, Except In the Case of the OIC Pennant or International Code Flags.

NOTE — When a motor yacht with mast and gaff is under way, the ensign (U.S., USPS or U.S. Yacht) should be flown at the gaff instead of the stern staff. A mastless boat may display, on a staff erected on the superstructure, the flag designated by this code to be flown from the truck of single-masted yachts.

U.S. GOVERNMENT and ARMED SERVICES FLAGS

Except for those of the Army, Navy and Coast Guard, the flags illustrated on this page won't often be seen flying from small craft. Nevertheless, they are presented here with the thought that every American will want to be able to identify whatever flag he may see afloat—or ashore. For a complete discussion of flag etiquette, see pages 354-371.

PRESIDENT OF THE UNITED STATES

NATIONAL
ENSIGN AND MERCHANT FLAG

VICE PRESIDENT

SECRETARY OF STATE

SECRETARY OF TREASURY

SECRETARY OF DEFENSE

ATTORNEY GENERAL

COAST GUARD ENSIGN

JOINT CHIEF OF STAFF

POSTMASTER GENERAL

SECRETARY OF LABOR

COAST GUARD COMMANDANT

SECRETARY OF THE NAVY

SECRETARY OF THE ARMY

SEC. OF AGRICULTURE

SEC. HEALTH, ED. & WELF.

COAST GUARD REAR ADMIRAL

ADMIRAL, U. S. NAVY

CORPS OF ENGINEERS
(U. S. Army)

SEC. OF INTERIOR

FISH AND
WILD LIFE SERVICE

BOW
PENNANT

U. S. CUSTOMS

NAVAL RESERVE
YACHT PENNANT

U. S. ARMY TRANSPORT

SEC. OF COMMERCE

COAST & GEODETIC SURVEY

U.S. I.S.
UNITED STATES
IMMIGRATION SERVICE

U. S. MARINE CORPS

SECRETARY, AIR FORCE

NOTE—Caption, third flag, third row, should read CHAIRMAN, JOINT CHIEFS OF STAFF. Fifth flag, sixth row—Army Transport not in current use.

YACHTING FLAGS

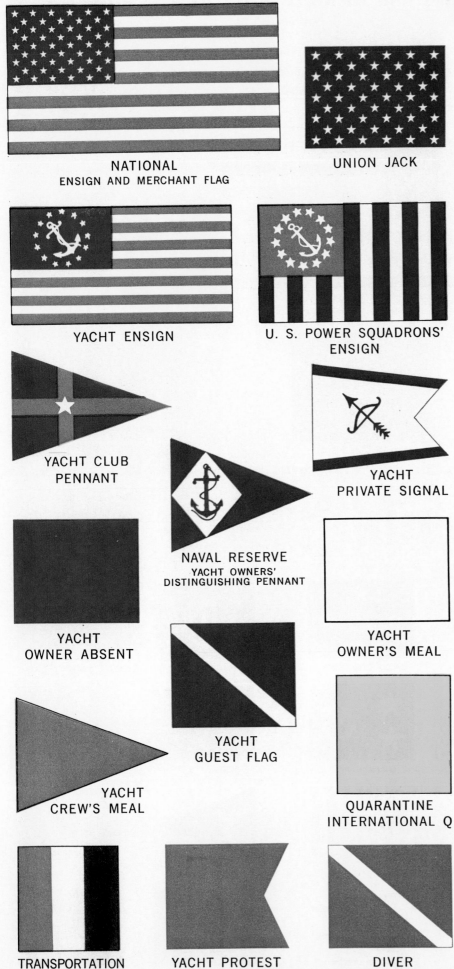

NATIONAL
ENSIGN AND MERCHANT FLAG

UNION JACK

YACHT ENSIGN

U. S. POWER SQUADRONS' ENSIGN

YACHT CLUB PENNANT

YACHT PRIVATE SIGNAL

NAVAL RESERVE
YACHT OWNERS' DISTINGUISHING PENNANT

YACHT OWNER ABSENT

YACHT OWNER'S MEAL

YACHT GUEST FLAG

YACHT CREW'S MEAL

QUARANTINE INTERNATIONAL Q

TRANSPORTATION

YACHT PROTEST

DIVER

NOTE: Navy Department regulations provide that the Union Jack should be the same size as the union of the ensign flown from the stern. See page 360 on two types of Naval Reserve pennant.

GENERAL COMMENTS

COLORS: Though the term "colors" is frequently used to include all flags on a boat, a strict interpretation would restrict its use to the national flag which identifies the nation to which the boat belongs. The term "colors" or "making colors" is also used to refer to the ceremony of hoisting the boat's flags at 8 A.M. and lowering at sunset.

WHEN TO FLY FLAGS: A boat's flags should be flown from 8 A.M. to sundown, except as otherwise noted in the chart opposite. At sundown flags should be lowered, whether the boat is underway, at anchor, or made fast. However, if you *enter* or *leave* port *before* 8 A.M., it is permissible to hoist your flags while there is sufficient light for them to be seen. Likewise, if you are *entering* or *leaving* port after sundown, the same holds true. During bad weather at sea, flags may or may not be flown, at the captain's discretion.

At 8 A.M. the national ensign should be hoisted first, followed by the USPS ensign (*if* you are a member of the U.S. Power Squadrons in good standing, and in command of the boat), the yacht club burgee, officer's flag, and/or private signal. For C.G. Auxiliary vessels the same procedure holds, but C.G. Auxiliary blue ensign and officer's flag are substituted for yacht club flags. Flags are hoisted smartly, but lowered ceremoniously. Flag officers' flags, though displayed day and night, may be temporarily lowered and hoisted at colors.

At U.S.P.S., C.G. Auxiliary, or Club rendezvous, marine parades, etc., on order of the Commanding Officer, flags may be flown after sundown but must be lowered at or before midnight, as ordered.

SIZE OF FLAGS: The national ensign, yacht ensign, USPS ensign, whichever is flown (See Footnote 1, opposite), should be a minimum of 1″ on the fly per foot of overall length of boat. The hoist should be two-thirds the fly. The burgee, private signal, and flag officer's flag should be a minimum of ½″ on the fly for each foot of the highest truck above the water on sailing yachts, and ⅝″ on the fly for each foot of overall length for motorboats.

When the USPS ensign is flown from the starboard yardarm on motorboats, the fly should be ⅝″ per foot of overall length of boat.

SALUTING: Never salute, or answer a salute, by dipping the U.S. national ensign. Salute by dipping the yacht ensign, or the USPS ensign, when flown at the stern or gaff of motor craft, stern staff of sailing vessels, under power or at anchor. Never salute by dipping a flag flown from the yardarm or spreader.

MISCELLANEOUS

CHARTER: When a boat is chartered, use flags of the charterer.

DISTRESS: Though not official, flying the U.S. Ensign upside down is universally recognized as a distress signal.

OPTIONAL: Flags authorized by naval, military, government, or yachting organizations, may be displayed at option, providing the procedure for flying such flags specified by these organizations is followed. No other flag should be displayed, except when making signals with international code flags or when dressing ship.

COCKTAIL: The cocktail flag, etc., being signals, may be flown where best seen.

QUARANTINE: The square yellow quarantine flag is a signal meaning "I request pratique." Fly entering foreign port—or return to U.S.

TRANSPORTATION: Code flag "T" is used to call club tender.

PROTEST: For sailors who race. See illustration.

DIVERS: Display when diving is in progress. See illustration. Do not fly underway.

STRIKING: "Striking colors" is a naval term meaning surrender. *Never* use in yachting.

USPS PAST OFFICERS' SIGNALS

PAST CHIEF COMMANDER

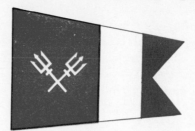

PAST VICE COMMANDER

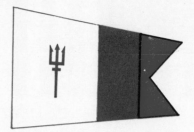

PAST REAR COMMANDER

PAST STAFF COMMANDER

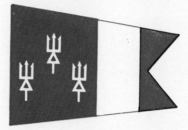

PAST DISTRICT COMMANDER

PAST SQUADRON COMMANDER

PENNANTS OF CANADIAN POWER SQUADRONS

CANADIAN NATIONAL ENSIGN

CANADIAN POWER SQUADRONS ENSIGN

NATIONAL OFFICERS	DISTRICT OFFICERS	SQUADRON OFFICERS
 C/C Chief Commander (in command of fleet)	 D/C District Commander	 Cdr. Squadron Commander
 V/C Vice Commander	 D/Lt/C District Lieutenant Commander	Lt/C Squadron Lieutenant Commander
 R/C Rear Commanders (as defined in by-laws)	 D/Lt District Lieutenant	1st/Lt Squadron Elected First Lieutenant
 Stf/C Staff Commanders (as defined in by-laws)	 D/Stf/Lt District Staff Lieutenant	 Lieut. Squadron Lieutenant

(See CPS by-laws for detailed information on what Canadian officers are permitted to fly officers' pennants.)

NEW ZEALAND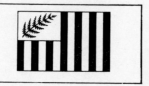

CANADIAN PAST OFFICER'S PENNANT

Red block letter "R" is positioned on upper left quadrant of appropriate pennant.

See additional U.S. Power Squadrons' Flags on next page

IXd

U.S. POWER SQUADRONS' FLAGS

U. S. POWER SQUADRONS' ENSIGN

The USPS ensign, at left, is flown as an outward and visible signal to other craft that the boat is commanded by a member of the USPS in good standing, one who is an able seaman, with a knowledge of things nautical, and competent to handle his craft. Other flags which may be seen on Power Squadron craft are shown below. The table on page IXa covers where to fly these flags. Initials preceding the identifying captions represent abbreviations designating rank as used in the U.S. Power Squadrons.

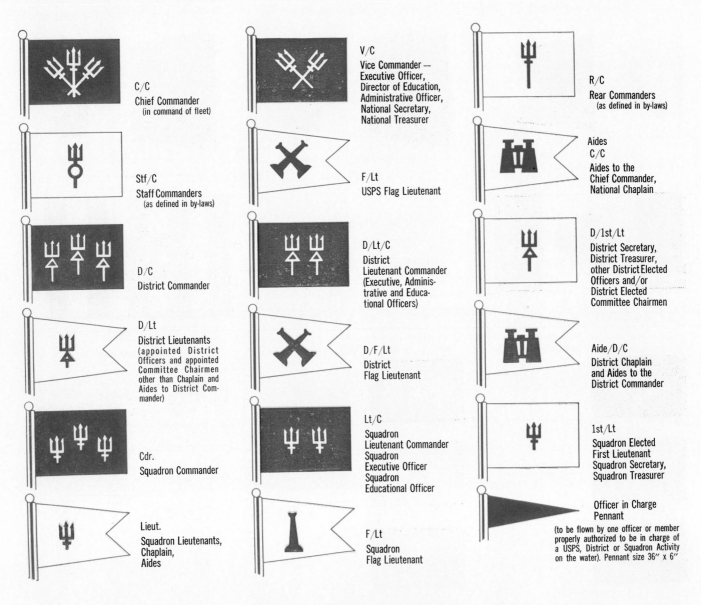

C/C
Chief Commander
(in command of fleet)

Stf/C
Staff Commanders
(as defined in by-laws)

D/C
District Commander

D/Lt
District Lieutenants
(appointed District Officers and appointed Committee Chairmen other than Chaplain and Aides to District Commander)

Cdr.
Squadron Commander

Lieut.
Squadron Lieutenants, Chaplain, Aides

V/C
Vice Commander —
Executive Officer,
Director of Education,
Administrative Officer,
National Secretary,
National Treasurer

F/Lt
USPS Flag Lieutenant

D/Lt/C
District Lieutenant Commander (Executive, Administrative and Educational Officers)

D/F/Lt
District Flag Lieutenant

Lt/C
Squadron Lieutenant Commander
Squadron Executive Officer
Squadron Educational Officer

F/Lt
Squadron Flag Lieutenant

R/C
Rear Commanders
(as defined in by-laws)

Aides C/C
Aides to the Chief Commander, National Chaplain

D/1st/Lt
District Secretary, District Treasurer, other District Elected Officers and/or District Elected Committee Chairmen

Aide/D/C
District Chaplain and Aides to the District Commander

1st/Lt
Squadron Elected First Lieutenant Squadron Secretary, Squadron Treasurer

Officer in Charge Pennant
(to be flown by one officer or member properly authorized to be in charge of a USPS, District or Squadron Activity on the water). Pennant size 36" x 6"

INTERNATIONAL CODE FLAGS

ALPHA BRAVO CHARLIE DELTA ECHO FOX TROT GOLF HOTEL INDIA

JULIET KILO LIMA MIKE NOVEMBER OSCAR PAPA QUEBEC ROMEO

SIERRA TANGO UNIFORM VICTOR WHISKEY X-RAY YANKEE ZULU CODE AND ANSWERING PENNANT

For use of code flags in signaling, see pages 383-395. For USPS pennants, see end papers. For USPS insignia, see page 495. Current spelling of flags: A, Alfa—F, Foxtrot (one word)—J, Juliett.

IXe

U.S. COAST GUARD AUXILIARY FLAGS

COAST GUARD ENSIGN

COAST GUARD AUXILIARY

THE AUXILIARY FLAG, known as the "Blue Ensign" (at left), is flown only from 8 A.M. to sunset when a qualified Auxiliarist is in charge of an approved facility. Here's how:

On a vessel without a mast—at the bow staff.

On a vessel with one mast—at the truck.

On a vessel with two or more masts—at the main truck.

Never in place of the national ensign.

AN OFFICER'S PENNANT, or a past officer's burgee (same design except swallow-tail shape), flies day and night when officer is on board:

On a vessel without a mast—at the bow staff in lieu of the Auxiliary flag.

On a vessel with one mast—at starboard spreader.

On a vessel with two or more masts—at main starboard spreader.

Only **one** officer's pennant or burgee may be flown at one time. An incumbent officer's pennant takes precedence.

When the Blue Ensign is displayed, it is improper to hoist a guest, owner absent, meal, cocktail, or novelty flag.

NATIONAL COMMODORE

NATIONAL VICE COMMODORE

DISTRICT COMMODORE

DISTRICT VICE COMMODORE

DISTRICT REAR COMMODORE

DIVISION CAPTAIN

DIVISION VICE CAPTAIN

DIVISION TRAINING OFFICER

FLOTILLA COMMANDER

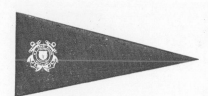

FLOTILLA VICE COMMANDER

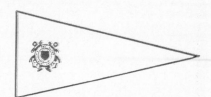

FLOTILLA TRAINING OFFICER

U.S. COAST GUARD AUXILIARY STAFF OFFICERS' BURGEES AND PENNANTS

Staff Flags, both pennants and burgees, will have a gold field and the standard blue Auxiliary emblem. Vertical blue bars designate the echelon of the officer. The system follows elected officer procedures except National Staff Officer Flags have three bars. Because of design considerations, the bars are slightly different from Elected Officer Flags.

STAFF OFFICER PENNANT

No Bars—FLOTILLA STAFF OFFICER

One Bar—DIVISION STAFF OFFICER
Bar located ⅞ of hoist from hoist on center.

Two Bars—DISTRICT STAFF OFFICER
Second Bar located ½ of fly on center.

Three Bars—NATIONAL STAFF AUFFICER
Third Bar located 1⅛ of hoist from hoist on center.

PAST STAFF OFFICER BURGEE

No Bars—PAST FLOTILLA STAFF OFFICER.

One Bar—PAST DIVISION STAFF OFFICER.
Bar located ⅛ of hoist on center, to left of reference point (5/6 of hoist from hoist).

Two Bars—PAST DISTRICT STAFF OFFICER
Second Bar located 5/6 of hoist from hoist on center.

Three Bars—PAST NATIONAL STAFF OFFICER
Third Bar located ⅛ of hoist on center, toward the fly from second bar.

See USCG Auxiliary flag code, pages 463 and 496, and new insignia, page x.

U.S. COAST GUARD AUXILIARY INSIGNIA

OFFICER	METAL COLLAR and SHOULDER INSIGNIA 1.	SHOULDER BOARDS 2.	SLEEVE 3.
National Commodore			
National Vice Commodore District Commodore			
District Vice Commodore With Red "A": Department Chief			
District Rear Commodore With Red "A": Division Chief			
Division Captain With Red "A": Branch Chief Division Staff Officer			
Division Vice Captain Flotilla Commander With Red "A": Aide			
Flotilla Vice Commander			
Flotilla Staff Officer (Red "A")			

Notes: 1. Large metal shoulder insignia is worn on blue raincoats; the same insignia in smaller size is worn on khaki, blue flannel, and khaki tropical shirts.

2. Shoulder Marks are worn on khaki coats, blue overcoats, and white tropical shirts.

3. Sleeve Grade stripes are worn on blue coats; braid goes only halfway around the sleeve.

CAP DEVICE

SHIELD
Current Officer

SHIELD
Staff Officer

SHIELD
Past Officer

Silver Collar
Insignia-Member

AUXILIARY AVIATOR

CHAPTER I

Equipment and Government Regulations

Equipment Required by The Motor Boat Act; Other Equipment Which Should be Aboard; Requirements for a U. S. Coast Guard Auxiliary Seal of Safety; Equipment Carried by U.S.C.G. Aux. Facilities; The Federal Boating Act of 1958; Documenting; Tonnage; Licensing; Inspection; Customs and Immigration Regulations.

A COMPREHENSIVE knowledge of piloting, seamanship and the proper handling of small boats embraces many subjects. Perhaps the first and most important is an understanding of what constitutes the proper equipment of a motor boat. This includes not only the equipment required by the Motor Boat Act, which specifies what equipment *must* be carried, but also a consideration of other equipment without which the boat cannot be safely, properly and efficiently operated.

Logically considered with this is a study of those regulations which have been drafted to govern the operation of certain types of boats which require licensed operators, licensed officers and crew, and inspection of hull and machinery. As will be pointed out later in greater detail, the motor boat which is operated for pleasure only is primarily concerned with equipment and collision regulations, since she requires no licensed operator, officers or crew, nor is any inspection of her hull and machinery prescribed. She may, however, in the discretion of appropriate officials (primarily the Coast Guard), be boarded for inspection of the equipment required by law.

Division of Motor Boats Into Classes

Under the Motor Boat Act of 1940 (*see text of the act, page 500*) motor boats are divided into four classes according to length. Equipment prescribed by law varies somewhat according to the class. Class A covers boats less than 16 feet in length. Class 1 comprises those of 16 feet or over, but less than 26 feet. Class 2 takes in those from 26 to less than 40 feet, and Class 3 motor boats of 40 to 65 feet in length.

Lights

The following few paragraphs relating to lights are only a brief resumé of the type of lighting equipment prescribed for the four classes of motor boats in the Motor Boat Act. Chapter II discusses in detail the lighting requirement for all vessels.

Lights are required on all classes, to be displayed from sunset to sunrise. Motor boats under 26 feet (embracing Class A and Class 1) carry forward a combination red-and-green bow light arranged to show a red light on the port side and a green light on the starboard side. Each colored light shows through 10 points (see page 32) from dead ahead to two points abaft the beam on its respective side. Aft they carry a bright white light showing all around the horizon (32 points), arranged higher than the combination light forward.

Lights prescribed for motor boats from 26 to 65 feet (embracing Class 2 and Class 3), and operating on the navigable waters of the United States, are different from those just described. Forward they carry a 20-point white bow light showing from dead ahead to two points abaft the beam on either side. On the port side a separate red 10-point light shows from dead ahead to two points abaft the port beam. On the starboard side a separate green 10-point light shows from dead ahead to two points abaft the starboard beam. Aft, a 32-point white light, higher than the white bow light, shows all around the horizon.

Other Lighting Requirements

On boats of Class 2 and Class 3 the colored side lights must be fitted with inboard screens of sufficient height or mounted on the cabin sides so as to prevent the lights from being seen across the bow.

For all classes, white lights prescribed by the act must be visible for at least two miles. Colored lights must be visible for at least one mile.

Motor boats of Class 2 and Class 3, when under motor and sail, show the same lights as when they are under motor only (white bow light, red and green side lights and white stern light). Under sail alone, they carry red and green side lights and 12 pt. white stern light.

Motor boats of Class A and Class 1, when under motor and sail, show the lights of their class as a motor boat (red and green combination light forward, and 32-point white light aft). Under sail alone, they carry the red and green combination light and 12 pt. white stern light.

Note, however, that motor boats and auxiliaries not more than 65 feet in length, may on "inland" waters optionally, elect to carry lights prescribed for their respective classes on the high seas by International Rules. (*See pages 16, 32 and 40.*)

When at anchor, on other than the high seas, motor boats (like all other power-driven vessels under 150 feet) must show a white light less than 20 feet above the hull and visible around the horizon for at least two miles. The only exception is in waters designated by the Secretary of the Army as "special anchorage areas", where anchor lights are not required on boats 65 feet and smaller.

Since the regulations prescribe that lights must be shown "from sunset to sunrise" when under way, no penalty is incurred for failure to carry them by day between sunrise and sunset.

Whistle and Bell

Boats of Classes 1, 2 and 3 must carry an efficient whistle or horn. This is used to give both passing signals and fog signals. A fog horn is not required on motor boats and should not be used in place of a whistle.

On Class 1 the whistle or horn may be hand-, mouth-, or power-operated, and must be audible at least ½-mile. On Class 2, it must be hand- or power-operated, audible at least 1 mile. On Class 3, it must be power-operated, audible at least 1 mile.

In every case the whistle must be capable of producing a blast of 2 seconds or more duration.

The whistle is not required on Class A (less than 16 feet).

Boats of Class 2 and Class 3 must also carry an efficient bell, used when the boat is at anchor in a fog. When struck, it must produce a clear bell-like tone of full round characteristics.

Fire Extinguishers

With the exception of outboards under 26 feet, not carrying passengers for hire, and whose construction will not entrap explosive vapors, all motor boats must carry the means for promptly and effectually extinguishing burning gasoline. The number, size and type of fire extinguishers necessary for each class of motor boat to cover this requirement has been prescribed by law. The law stipulates that they must be kept in condition for immediate and effective use and must be placed so as to be readily accessible.

Fire extinguishers are classified as to type and size and a minimum number is prescribed by the Coast Guard for each class of motorboat. The classification and requirements are shown in the tables below.

Fire Extinguisher Classification

Classification type-size	Foam, gallons	Carbon dioxide, pounds	Carbon tetrachloride	Dry chemical, pounds
B-I	1¼	4	Not approved	2
B-II	2½	15		10

Fire Extinguisher Requirements

Class of motor-boat	Length, feet	Minimum number of B-I hand portable fire extinguishers required [1]	
		No fixed fire extinguishing system in machinery space	Fixed fire extinguishing system in machinery space
A	Under 16	1	0
1	16 and over, but under 26	1	0
2	26 and over, but under 40	2	1
3	40 and over, but not over 65	3	2

[1] One B-II hand portable fire extinguisher may be substituted for two B-I hand portable fire extinguishers.

Special regulations apply to motor vessels over 65 feet in length and to motor boats and motor vessels of more than 15 gross tons carrying freight or passengers for hire. Generally speaking, they are required to carry a minimum number, size and type of portable extinguishers plus additional protection for machinery spaces. Specific requirements vary with the tonnage of the vessel.

Approved types of fire extinguishers are identified by make and model number. When purchasing be sure to buy only approved equipment. Toxic vaporizing liquid type fire extinguishers (carbon tetrachloride and chlorobromomethane types) are not approved.

Life Preservers

All motor boats are required to carry one life-saving device for every person on board, including children and babies. The devices must be readily accessible.

Motor boats up to 40 feet in length (Classes A, 1 and 2) may carry either regulation approved life preservers, buoyant vests, ring buoys, buoyant cushions, or special purpose water safety buoyant devices.

On Class 3 boats, buoyant vests and cushions are not acceptable. Life-saving devices on Class 3 motor boats must be regulation approved life preservers or ring buoys.

Note that life preservers, buoyant vests and cushions, ski jump vests, horseshoe life rings, and ring buoys must all be of a type approved by the Coast Guard.

Approved lifesaving devices carry markings such as stamps of approval, tags, etc. to indicate that they meet Coast Guard requirements. Details concerning these markings for life preservers, buoyant cushions, ring buoys, and buoyant vests are contained in Coast Guard pamphlet CG-340 outlining all legal requirements for motorboats. (Extracts from this are given on page 16.)

Motor boats which carry more than 6 passengers for hire, and those of over 15 gross tons carrying freight for hire are required to be inspected and certified by the Coast Guard. Required life-saving equipment for these vessels would be as prescribed by the Coast Guard at the time of inspection.

Motor boats which carry 6 or less passengers for hire, even though not inspected and certificated, must carry an approved life preserver for each person on board. If the owner desires, however, these boats may carry approved ring buoys, buoyant vests, cushions, or special purpose water safety buoyant devices in addition to the required life preservers.

Approved inflatable life rafts are now available. Other pneumatic devices or appliances filled with granulated cork are not acceptable as required equipment.

Exemption of Racing Outboard Boats

Outboard-powered motor boats while competing in a race previously arranged and announced, or engaged in tuning up for such a race, are exempt from the need of carrying bells, fire extinguishers and whistles.

No motorboat should ever leave her berth on a cruise, however short, without a check to see that all required equipment is aboard and in compliance with applicable law, including federal and local regulations. The list includes other items, not necessarily required by law, but essential to safe operation of the boat. (Photo by Peter R. Smyth)

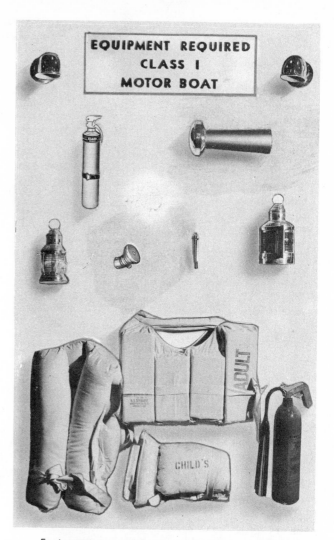

Equipment required by law on motor boats of Class A (under 16′) and Class 1 (16 to less than 26′). Note that a bell is not required and that a combination bow light is used instead of the separate bow and sidelights of the larger classes. One fire extinguisher of approved type covers the law on boats under 26 feet. (See p. 16)

Flame Arresters

The carburetors on inboard (and stern-drive) gasoline engines must be fitted with an approved device for arresting backfire. Installations made before November 19, 1952, may be used as long as they are in good condition.

Ventilation

Motor boats built or decked over since April 25, 1940, using gasoline or any other liquid fuel having a flash point of less than 110 degrees Fahrenheit must be equipped (by June 1, 1967) with provision for ventilating the bilges of every engine and fuel tank compartment.

The minimum requirement specifies at least "one exhaust duct installed so as to extend from the open atmosphere to the lower portion of the bilge and at least one intake duct installed so as to extend to a point at least midway to the bilge or at least below the level of the carburetor air intake. The cowls shall be located and trimmed for maximum effectiveness so as to prevent displaced fumes from being recirculated." *See pages 494a–d.*

Exempt from ventilation requirements are "those motorboats or motor vessels with all engine and fuel tank compartments and other spaces to which explosive or flammable gases and vapors from these compartments may flow, open to the atmosphere so as to prevent the entrapment of such gases and vapors within the vessel."

Equipment On Lakes and Certain Other Waters

Motor boats operating on other than federal waterways, that is, on inland lakes which do not form part of the boundary line between two states or between this country and Canada, are not required to carry the equipment required by the Federal Government. Boats operating on such inland lakes must comply with state law. Always check your state laws; equipment prescribed on some coastal waters goes beyond minimum federal requirements.

Inspection of Equipment

The United States Coast Guard is charged with the duty of seeing whether the proper Government equipment is aboard every motor boat while under way. Inspectors or members of the U. S. Coast Guard or customs officials are authorized to make such inspections.

A boat must be operated or navigated to incur an equipment penalty. A boat hauled out on shore therefore, is not subject to these requirements. However, a boat temporarily at anchor with persons aboard, which was navigated to the anchorage and will subsequently be operated, must have all required equipment. If tied to a wharf or at anchor with no persons aboard, no equipment (except an anchor light when called for) is required.

A boat of an inspection officer or having an inspection officer on board will fly the flag of the U. S. Coast Guard.

Motorboats Rented by Liveries

Motorboats (including outboards) rented by launch liveries must, of course, comply with the Motor Boat Act as to equipment, etc. On motor boats carrying passengers for hire, a penalty of $200 may be imposed on the owner, operator, or both, for violations having to do with life preservers, fire extinguishers, or licensed operators.

13

EQUIPMENT REQUIRED
CLASS II
MOTOR BOAT

Class 2 boats (26 to less than 40') carry a separate white 20-point bow light, red and green 10-point side lights properly screened, 32-point white stern light, a bell, hand or power-operated whistle or horn, a life preserver for each person on board, at least two fire extinguishers and a flame arrester on the carburetor of each inboard gasoline engine. At least two cowl ventilators and ducts to the bilges are required. Note that a box-type buoyant cushion is acceptable in lieu of a life preserver on boats up to 40 feet

NOTE: Under a new law (P.L. 89-476), effective September 27, 1966, tonnage measurement has been simplified by permitting a computation which uses the product of length, breadth, depth and appropriate coefficients.

* How Tonnage Is Measured

Persons unfamiliar with the term tonnage as it is used in connection with the measurement of vessels are likely, in error, to think only of the common ton which is a measure of weight—either 2,000 or 2,240 pounds, depending on whether it is a short or a long ton.

The law repeatedly refers to vessels of a certain tonnage, as for example when it states that a yacht of 5 net tons or over may be documented. Gross tons are not measurements of weight, but of volume.

Gross and Net

Gross tonnage is the total enclosed space or internal capacity of a vessel, calculated in terms of tons of 100 cubic feet each. This has been agreed upon as an average space or volume required by a ton of general merchandise. Gross tonnage includes all spaces below the upper deck as well as permanently closed-in spaces on that deck.

Net (or registered) tonnage is a measurement of the earning power of a vessel when carrying cargo. Therefore, to arrive at a net tonnage figure it is necessary to deduct from the gross the volume of such spaces as would have no earning capacity or room for cargo. For example, from the gross would be deducted engine room, boiler and shaft alley spaces, also fuel compartments and the space required for the steering and working of a vessel, crew's quarters, etc. Many charges against vessels such as canal tolls, harbor dues, etc., are based on the net.

Displacement and Deadweight

Displacement tonnage is the actual weight in tons of 2,240 pounds which a vessel displaces when floating at any given draft. This naturally varies with the draft. The displacement is calculated by figuring the volume of the vessel under water in cubic feet and dividing by 35, since 35 cubic feet of sea water weigh one ton (2,240 pounds).

Deadweight tonnage is the carrying capacity of a vessel, figured by weight in terms of tons of 2,240 pounds. If her displacement were calculated when the vessel was light (but with fuel and stores aboard) and again when she was loaded (with the same fuel and stores aboard), the difference would express the deadweight tonnage.

Very roughly, considering a modern freighter as an example, the gross tonnage would be about 1½ times the net, the deadweight carrying capacity about 2½ times the net, and the loaded displacement about 2¼ times the gross.

Yachts Not Required To Be Inspected or Carry Licensed Officers

The Government does not require that the *owner* of a motor boat or yacht of any size whatever shall have any knowledge of his boat or navigation or the handling of his boat. Neither does the Government require that a motor boat or motor yacht under 300 gross tons not engaged in trade or not carrying passengers for hire should have on board a licensed officer. Nor are boats of this kind subject to inspection.

No licensed officers are required on motor vessels documented as yachts except on those of 200 gross tons and over when navigating the high seas.

Licensed Officers and Crew

Motor vessels of above 15 gross tons carrying freight or passengers for hire, but not engaged in fishing as a regular business, and sea-going motor vessels of 300 gross tons and over, shall not be navigated unless there are on board such complement of licensed officers and crew as are required by the certificate of inspection.

In the case of such motor vessels, above 15 gross tons, but not more than 65 feet in length, the only licensed officer required by the certificate of inspection shall be a person duly licensed as described in the Motor Boat Law.

In the case of such motor vessels, of above 15 gross tons, and more than 65 feet in length, there will be required by the certificate of inspection at least one pilot and one licensed engineer.

The licensing of pilots and engineers for boats of over fifteen tons gross or over 65 feet in length engaged in trade should not be confused with the operator's license which is required for motor boats of under 65 feet in length or under sixteen tons carrying passengers for hire. On motor boats of this size carrying passengers for hire only an operator's license is required.

Fishing vessels and vessels propelled by machinery not more than 65 feet in length, except tugboats propelled by steam, will not be required to carry licensed officers, except a licensed operator on such vessels carrying passengers for hire.

Inspection of Hull and Machinery

All motor vessels of above 15 gross tons, carrying freight or passengers for hire, but not engaged in fishing as a regular business, and all sea-going motor vessels of 300 gross tons and over, are subject to inspection by the Officer in Charge, Marine Inspection, of the U. S. Coast Guard.

Such vessels may not be navigated without having on board, and posted in a conspicuous place in the vessel, framed under glass, where it will be most likely to be observed by passengers and others, an unexpired certificate of inspection.

The machinery of a motor boat over 40 feet in length, if propelled by steam, would be subject to inspection.

Under the provisions of the Ray Act (Public Law 519) which became effective May 10, 1956, inspection is required, at least every three years, of all vessels carrying more than six passengers. Types of vessels specifically affected include sailing vessels of 700 gross tons or less; barges of 100 gross tons or less; and mechanically-propelled vessels of 15 gross tons or less (thus affecting, for example, the usual types of charter fishing boats, etc.). For detailed regulations, which became effective June 1, 1958, consult the Officer in Charge, Marine Inspection, U. S. Coast Guard. *(See also page 494)*

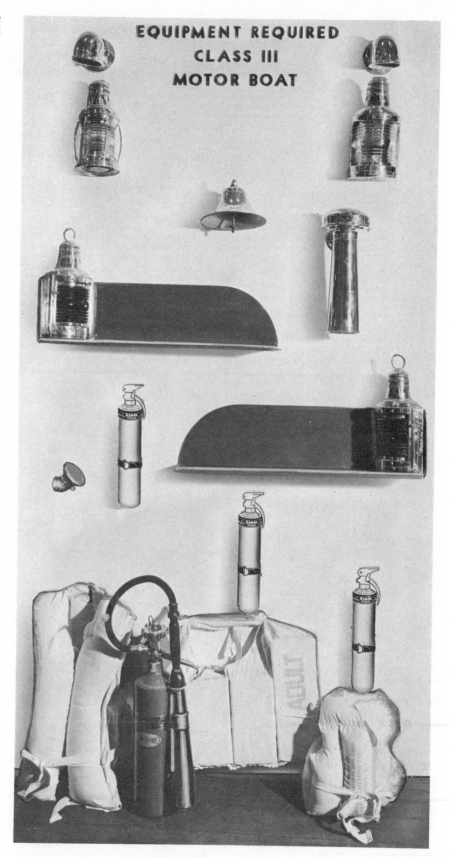

EQUIPMENT REQUIRED CLASS III MOTOR BOAT

Equipment for Class 3 (40 to 65 feet) is the same as that required for Class 2 motor boats with a few exceptions. The whistle or sound-producing device on Class 3 must be power-operated. Buoyant cushions are not allowed as life preservers on Class 3, although ring buoys (not shown) are. Not less than three B-1 type fire extinguishers or one B-1 plus one B-II extinguisher. Lights, bell, flame arresters and proper ventilation are also required, as on Class 2. The table on p. 16 summarizes differences in each class

Minimum Required Equipment

EQUIPMENT	CLASS A (Less than 16 feet)	CLASS 1 (16 feet to less than 26 feet)	CLASS 2 (26 feet to less than 40 feet)	CLASS 3 (40 feet to not more than 65 feet)
BACK-FIRE FLAME ARRESTER	One approved device on each carburetor of all gasoline engines installed after April 25, 1940, except outboard motors.			
VENTILATION	At least two ventilator ducts fitted with cowls or their equivalent for the purpose of properly and efficiently ventilating the bilges of every engine and fuel-tank compartment of boats constructed or decked over after April 25, 1940, using gasoline or other fuel of a flashpoint less than 110°F.			
BELL	None.*	None.*	One, which when struck, produces a clear, bell-like tone of full round characteristics.	
LIFESAVING DEVICES	One approved life preserver, buoyant vest, ring buoy, special purpose water safety buoyant device, or buoyant cushion for each person on board or being towed on water skis, etc.			One approved life preserver or ring buoy for each person on board.
WHISTLE	None.*	One hand, mouth, or power operated, audible at least ½ mile.	One hand or power operated, audible at least 1 mile.	One power operated, audible at least 1 mile.
FIRE EXTINGUISHER— PORTABLE — When NO fixed fire extinguishing system is installed in machinery space(s).	At least One B–I type approved hand portable fire extinguisher. (Not required on outboard motorboat less than 26 feet in length and not carrying passengers for hire if the construction of such motorboats will not permit the entrapment of explosive or flammable gases or vapors.)		At least Two B–I type approved hand portable fire extinguishers; OR At least One B–II type approved hand portable fire extinguisher.	At least Three B–I type approved hand portable fire extinguishers; OR At least One B–I type *Plus* One B–II type approved hand portable fire extinguisher.
When fixed fire extinguishing system is installed in machinery space(s).	None.	None.	At least One B–I type approved hand portable fire extinguisher.	At least Two B–I type approved hand portable fire extinguishers; OR At least One B–II type approved hand portable fire extinguisher.
	Fire extinguishers manufactured after 1 January 1965 will be marked, "Marine Type USCG Type —— Size —— Approval No. 162.028/EX . . ." **			

*NOTE.—Not required by the Motorboat Act of 1940; however, the "Rules of the Road" require these vessels to sound proper signals.

**NOTE.—Toxic vaporizing-liquid type fire extinguishers, such as those containing carbon tetrachloride or chlorobromomethane, are not accepted as required approved extinguishers on uninspected vessels (private pleasure craft).

LIGHTS REQUIRED

ON BOATS UNDERWAY

BETWEEN SUNSET AND SUNRISE

FOR POWER BOATS UNDER 65 FEET

AND ALL SAILING VESSELS

* * *

Vessels at anchor must display anchor lights except those under 65 feet in "special anchorage area"

Lights Used Where Inland, Western Rivers and Great Lakes Rules Apply

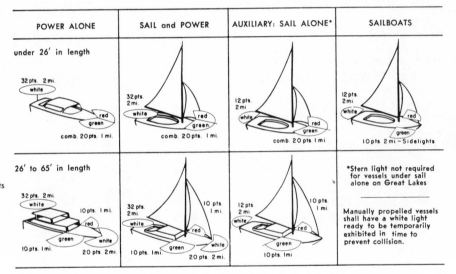

POWER ALONE	SAIL and POWER	AUXILIARY: SAIL ALONE*	SAILBOATS

*Stern light not required for vessels under sail alone on Great Lakes

Manually propelled vessels shall have a white light ready to be temporarily exhibited in time to prevent collision.

INTERNATIONAL RULES.—

required on high seas, may be used inland

POWER ALONE	SAIL and POWER	AUXILIARY: SAIL ALONE*	SAILBOATS

The tables on this page, taken from the "Recreational Boating Guide," CG-340, U. S. Coast Guard, for sale by the Superintendent of Documents, U. S. Government Printing Office, Washington, D. C. 20402, at 45 cents per copy, are a brief resumé of equipment required on motorboats. For detailed information, see pages 11–15 and 28–46.

A motor boat on the waters of the United States may carry the lights prescribed by the Motorboat Act of April 25, 1940 (above) or it may carry the lights prescribed by the International Rules (left).

A motorboat on the high seas "must" carry the lights prescribed by the International Rules, and "only" these lights.

On the high seas, "all" equipment on a motorboat must meet requirements for vessels under International Rules.

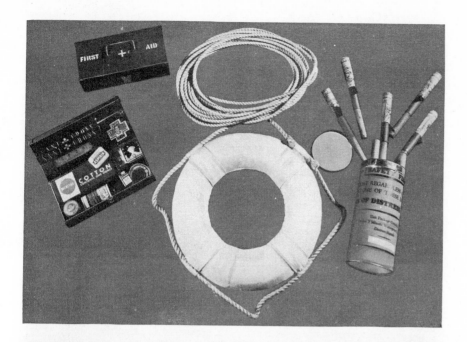

Left—To cover the law, a boat may carry regular life preservers or box type cushions for her life saving devices, but in addition, at least one ring buoy should be aboard. On boats not carrying passengers for hire it passes as a life preserver. Attached to it should be a length of strong light line (preferably a bright-colored floating-type synthetic) and it should be so mounted that it can be thrown quickly to a person in the water. First aid essentials are packed in regular kits. With it there should be a good first aid manual. One of the most effective means of summoning aid is the use of flares which can be purchased in a small watertight container, convenient to stow. More elaborate equipment consists of a pistol that shoots a parachute type of flare

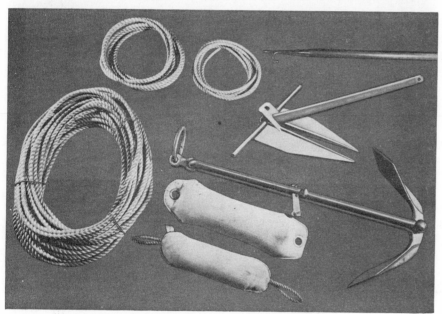

Left—Carry at least two anchors, preferably three. For brief stops, a light anchor is sufficient. Overnight stops and all-around service require one of greater holding power. A heavy spare should be aboard for emergencies. Anchors should be selected on the basis of holding power, not by weight alone. Anchor lines should be manila or nylon, generous in length, not necessarily thick in diameter, but strong. An extra long new unused line should be aboard for use with the spare anchor. Large craft often use chain. A couple of dock lines and a few extra lines for spring lines and general use should also be carried. For picking up mooring lines, the boat hook is useful. A number of fenders will be essential for the protection of the hull

OTHER ARTICLES OF EQUIPMENT WHICH SHOULD BE ABOARD EVERY WELL-FOUND BOAT, THOUGH NOT REQUIRED BY LAW

THE Motor Boat Act prescribes that motor boats must carry certain equipment for the safety of those aboard. This includes life preservers, lights, whistle, bell, fire extinguishers, flame arresters on carburetors, ventilating cowls and ducts for the bilges, and the certificate of registration. These requirements vary with the class of boat, and certain exceptions are made in some classes.

In addition to this required equipment, however, there are other things which should be aboard before a boat may be considered to be well-found. The extent of cruising the boat does will determine the amount and kind of equipment.

The items illustrated here should not be taken as a complete and detailed inventory. Rather they emphasize some of the more important articles of equipment; others will suggest themselves to the boatman from time to time.

Illustrated are such items as anchors and lines, boat hook, fenders, bilge pump, tool kit, spare engine parts, piloting equipment, auxiliary lighting equipment, and such special safety equipment as ring buoys, flares, and a first aid kit.

In the same category with tools and spare parts we might include a few good carpenter's tools, extra pieces of line of several sizes, a ball of marlin, an assortment of nails, screws, bolts, washers, wire, caulking cotton, paint, etc. On boats equipped with sails a small repair kit should be added containing twine, wax, needles, palm, fid, and similar articles. All should be properly stowed to keep it accessible and in good condition.

Other miscellaneous items would be a deck mop, pail (some prefer a canvas bucket), a chamois for cleaning windows, brass polish, a supply of oil for engine, grease (both the regular and waterproof varieties as required), some light machine oil and penetrating oil for rusted parts, vaseline petroleum jelly, distilled water, a hydrometer, some clean rags and several rolls of paper towels. An emergency tiller is often carried.

Club burgee, ensign and owner's private signal or officer's flag are usually found aboard, together with any

Left—Every boat should be equipped with a good bilge pump, one that will really throw quantities of water without effort. Its intake should be screened to prevent its being clogged by chips and other matter in the bilge. Don't use a supply line from pump to strainer that may collapse with suction. A good set of mechanic's tools, though seldom required, should always be aboard. Some spare parts for the engine are desirable. An extra coil, a condenser, breaker points for the distributor, some spark plugs, extra wire, tape, gasket material, etc., are among the more important items

Below—Essentials of piloting equipment would include a good compass, parallel rules or course protractor, a timepiece, dividers, pencil and log book, lead line, charts, pelorus or bearing finder, and up-to-date charts. A barometer and good pair of binoculars are very useful. Certain publications are particularly valuable in piloting, such as Tide and Current Tables, Tidal Current Charts, Light Lists and the Coast Pilot. All should be kept up-to-date by means of corrections published in Notices to Mariners. For general information the Yachtsman's Guide is very helpful. The compass should be properly installed and with it should be a deviation card showing its error. Some boats have a patent log to record distance run, and a marine type of speedometer is excellent. A tachometer to record engine revolutions may be used to determine speed, from which distance may be computed. The lead line, preferably, should be of synthetic type, like braided dacron

other flags that might be desired. A set of signal flags would be a good investment. Slickers or some other form of wet weather clothing will be required at times.

The galley will be stocked with utensils of the owner's selection, together with the usual food supplies when cruising. Lay aside in a locker some canned foods and pilot biscuits in air-tight tins as an emergency reserve.

Modern radio equipment is a source of great satisfaction. A good receiving set for entertainment and weather reports is fine and the radiotelephone is becoming increasingly popular. The radio direction finder is a valuable adjunct to piloting equipment.

Right—Provide your boat with plenty of lighting equipment, entirely independent of the boat's electrical system. A waterproof hand flashlight would be a minimum. Some types of battery-operated portable flashlights can be carried like a lantern. A trouble light that can be clipped directly on the terminals of the boat's storage battery is a fine thing when working around an engine. A built-in searchlight is invaluable for picking up aids to navigation at night and when maneuvering around docks and moorings. The more powerful the better, but don't play it on other craft. Sailing craft and other boats without a storage battery may use a portable searchlight mounted directly on a battery. Another handy light is the portable searchlight which can be held in the hand but operated from the boat's regular battery. Spare bulbs should be carried for all of the boat's lighting equipment, and fuses as well

EQUIPMENT REQUIRED FOR AWARD OF A C.G. AUXILIARY SEAL OF SAFETY

Coast Guard Auxiliary decal displayed on a boat shows she meets high standards of safety, above minimum legal requirements. Free examinations of equipment, never compulsory, given by Auxiliary members on boat owner's request

Have you ever wondered about the significance of those attractive shield-shaped decalcomanias prominently displayed by some of the boats in your area? Perhaps you have guessed they were the symbol of membership in some boating club or organization. They're not, as such, but rather identify the owner as one who maintains his boat according to a relatively high standard outlined by the U. S. Coast Guard Auxiliary.

Practically everyone is, or should be, aware of the fact that all motorboats must meet certain minimum safety standards by complying with regulations outlined in the Motorboat Act, specifying the equipment each is to carry, according to its class. When a motorboat is inspected by the Coast Guard, these are the minimums which have been set to avoid citation for violation of this Act. These legal requirements have been discussed elsewhere, so we will not repeat here.

In the interest of a high degree of safety on the water, the Coast Guard Auxiliary has specified certain other additional conditions which, though not legally required, must be met if a boat is to earn the Coast Guard Auxiliary's Courtesy Examination decal.

Courtesy examinations—they are not "inspections"—are made by qualified members of the Coast Guard Auxiliary, a civilian group. They are performed strictly as a courtesy to the boat owner, upon his request, with a view toward making boating more enjoyable through safety, education and knowledge. Examinations are never forced on an owner.

After a boat has been examined, the decal for the current year will be awarded if the boat meets all requirements. Display of the decal on a boat generally means that the Coast Guard will not board that boat for a formal inspection unless a violation in operation or required equipment is

The Shield of Safety

apparent. If the courtesy examination reveals any deficiencies, they are not reported as violations but are brought to the attention of the owner so he will have an opportunity to correct them.

Suppose, then, that we have equipped our boat so that she complies with every legal requirement of the Motorboat Act, as to life preservers, lights, fire extinguishers, whistles, bells, ventilation, flame arresters, etc. Just what more will the C.G.A. Courtesy Examiner expect before he considers that the boat rates a decal? Here's the gist of what the official Vessel Examiners Guide (CG-289) has to say about each point.

Amplification of Legal Requirements

LIGHTS—Though the Motorboat Act does not require lights to be aboard during daylight hours, the decal will not be awarded unless the boat is so equipped, the lights are operative, and visible through the required arc.

LIFESAVING EQUIPMENT—There must be at least as many approved devices on board as there are berths, with two as a minimum, even if there are less than two berths.

FIRE EXTINGUISHERS—Class A and 1 motorboats having a fixed CO-2 system in the engine room must also have at least one portable extinguisher. Outboard boats, of open construction, less than 26 feet in length not carrying passengers for hire, are not required by law to carry extinguishers, but class 1 outboards must have at least one hand portable extinguisher to qualify for the decal.

FLAME ARRESTERS—Carburetors must be equipped with flame arresters, regardless of when the engine was installed.

NUMBERS—Must be of correct size and style, properly applied.

Other Items Checked

The paragraphs above amplify the legal requirements. Other points the examiner will check are as follows.

GALLEY STOVES—These must be installed so they cannot shift, and located so no flammable material nearby can be ignited. Any of the common types of stove fuel may be used, except gasoline. Decals will not be awarded to boats equipped with gasoline stoves.

FUEL TANK FILLER PIPE—The fuel tank filler pipe must be connected to a filler plate on deck, outside the cockpit, to prevent vapors from getting inside the boat and to assure that overflow when fueling will run overboard. If the cockpit is self-bailing, filling pipes may connect to plates in the deck of such cockpits.

FUEL TANK VENTS—Vent pipes of fuel tanks must lead outboard, and never discharge into enclosed spaces.

CARBURETOR DRIP PAN—Downdraft carburetors, because of their construction, require no drip pan. Updraft carburetors, however, must have a drip pan installed beneath them, equipped with fine mesh wire screen to prevent gasoline in the pan from catching fire. Preferably, drip pans should be connected by thin copper tube to the intake manifold to empty them automatically. If not so equipped, the owner should empty the pan frequently to prevent accumulation of gasoline. Some updraft carburetors have a vacuum sump which prevents leakage; these do not require a drip pan.

General Condition of Boat

GENERAL CONDITION—Boats, to earn a decal, must be in good overall condition. Bilges must be clean and free from oil, grease and water. Fuel lines must be intact and preferably lead from the top of the fuel tanks. Electrical wiring and fittings must comply with good marine practice, be in good condition, and installed to minimize danger of short circuits. The hull must be generally sound. In fact, the boat as a whole must, in the examiner's opinion, be shipshape and seaworthy.

CLASS A BOATS—Class A boats (those under 16 feet in length), whether inboard or outboard, must meet the same basic requirements as outlined, but must in addition carry certain other equipment before a decal may be awarded. This includes a distress flare, one paddle or oar, anchor and line suitable to the locality, and an adequate pump or bailer.

RADIOTELEPHONE CHECK—While the presence or absence of a radiotelephone, or its condition, has no bearing on the award of a decal, a boat owner may request a check of his equipment. The examiner will do this as a further courtesy, and will not report any violations to enforcement officials, but merely bring them to the owner's attention for correction.

EQUIPMENT CARRIED BY U.S. COAST GUARD AUXILIARY FACILITIES

Special requirements regarding equipment applicable to boats enrolled in the Coast Guard Auxiliary, flying the Auxiliary flag—the boats used by Auxiliary members in making courtesy examinations preliminary to award of a decalcomania

As the guiding thought behind all United States Coast Guard Auxiliary operations is safety, it is only logical that standards set for equipment of C.G.A. vessel facilities are even higher than requirements for award of a decalcomania to a pleasure boat operator.

An Auxiliary vessel must be one of the safest boats afloat. To this end, in its Vessel Examiners Guide (CG-289), the Coast Guard outlines certain minimum requirements for different types of craft flying the Auxiliary flag.

Auxiliary facilities of the conventional pleasure boat type, for example, must carry at least two *anchors* and *lines*—a medium weight anchor for service conditions and a heavier one for use in emergencies. Length and diameter of anchor lines will depend on a number of variables such as the length and weight of boat, normal depths of water, the type of fiber used, etc.

For signaling they must carry a *distress flare* and the means of producing a *flashing light* at night. *Bilge pumps* must be in good order. Class 2 and 3 boats must have at least two means of pumping bilges.

Storage batteries must be secured against shifting, and covered to minimize danger from sparks should a tool or metal object be accidentally dropped across terminals. Terminals must be soldered lug type, and additional recommendations are given as to location of batteries for safety.

High standards are set for the installation of *wiring* and electrical connections, *fuel systems, auxiliary generators, stoves* and *heaters*. Gasoline is not acceptable as fuel in stoves in any Auxiliary facility.

The items noted above are those specifically mentioned as applicable to all Auxiliary facilities of the pleasure motorboat type. Beyond that, an additional list of equipment is required; this varies, naturally, with the type and size of boat and its location. The Director of Auxiliary in each District advises Examiners which items must be carried by vessels in his particular District.

A typical listing of such additional (mandatory) equipment is given below, as it applies to Auxiliary boats enrolled in the Third Coast Guard District, Southern Area. Pleasure boatmen in general will find it helpful as a guide.

Equipment Req—Required NR—Not required Opt—Optional	Sailboats of open design (used primarily for racing)	Class A and Class I (open boats)	Class I and II (except Class I open boats)	Class III and Facilities over 65' in length
1. Charts	Opt	Opt	*	*
2. Light List	NR	NR	NR	NR
3. Lake Survey Bulletin	NR	NR	NR	NR
4. Coast or River Pilot (Sandy Hook to Cape Henry)	NR	NR	Req	Req
5. Deviation table	NR	NR	Req	Req
6. RPM table (except outboard)	NR	NR	Req	Req
7. First aid kit	Req	Req	Req	Req
8. Means of taking bearing	NR	NR	Req	Req
9. Auxiliary ensign	Preferable if a regular member			
10. National ensign	Opt	Opt	Opt	Opt
11. Compass	NR	NR	Req	Req
12. Dividers	NR	NR	Req	Req
13. Ring buoy (or one spare approved buoyant cushion)	NR	NR	Req	Req

Equipment Req—Required NR—Not required Opt—Optional	Sailboats of open design (used primarily for racing)	Class A and Class I (open boats)	Class I and II (except Class I open boats)	Class III and Facilities over 65' in length
14. Fenders	Opt	Opt	Opt	Opt
15. Boathook	Req	Req	Req	Req
16. Water lights	NR	NR	Opt	Opt
17. Searchlight	Opt	Opt	Opt	Opt
18. Hand lead and lines	Opt	Opt	Req	Req
19. Mooring lines	Req	Req	Req	Req
20. Heaving lines	Opt	Opt	Req	Req
21. Tools	Req	Req	Req	Req
22. Extra oil lamp or flashlight	Req	Req	Req	Req
23. Spare running light bulbs	Req	Req	Req	Req
24. Course protractor or parallel rules	NR	NR	Req	Req
25. Aircraft emergency procedure	Req	Req	Req	Req

* Local and coast charts

THE FEDERAL BOATING ACT OF 1958

First drastic revision of nation's small-boat registration system since 1918 provides new regulations for numbering undocumented vessels by states—requires report of accidents—and makes provision for civil penalties for violations, imposed by Coast Guard

(See text of the act, page 502, and regulations, page 505)

THE intent of the Federal Boating Act of 1958 is defined by the subtitle of the document itself: "An act to promote boating safety on the navigable waters of the United States, its Territories, and the District of Columbia; to provide coordination and cooperation with the States in the interest of uniformity of boating laws; and for other purposes." That "coordination and cooperation" are key words for the law provides that the states were to have first crack at setting up its legislation. The limit to the provision is that the state-enacted legislation be within the federal framework.

States had to: (1) Institute a system of numbering in accordance with the Federal Act; (2) provide for the renumbering of boats at least every three years; (3) agree to a reciprocity period of 90 days in recognizing numbers awarded by another state, and (4) require that reports be made to the state concerning accidents involving vessels numbered by the state under its numbering system. These four points are the principal requirements a state must have met to comply with the Act.

They are broad requirements, though, allowing plenty of room for modification. States were able, for instance, to lower or eliminate the 10-horsepower exemption (explained below) to include all types of pleasure craft, from dinghies to sailboats.

WHAT GETS NUMBERED: The Act calls for the numbering of every undocumented * vessel propelled by machinery of more than 10 horsepower, whether or not such machinery is the principal source of propulsion, using the navigable waters of the United States, its territories and the District of Columbia, and every such vessel owned in a state and using the high seas. Exceptions are:

(1) foreign vessels temporarily using the navigable waters of the U.S., its territories, etc.;

(2) public vessels of the U.S.;

(3) state and municipal vessels;

(4) ships' lifeboats;

(5) certain vessels specifically desig-

HIGHLIGHTS

In substance, this Act requires that the operator of any boat involved in an accident causing death, personal injury, or property damage, must stop, render aid, offer identification, notify authorities, and file a written report.

It provides for the publication by the Coast Guard of statistics based upon the accident reports.

It amends the Motorboat Act of April 25, 1940, to permit the imposition of a civil penalty by the Coast Guard for reckless or negligent operation, failure to obey the Rules of the Road, failure to comply with the regulations, etc. (Note: the new Law makes NO CHANGE IN THE REQUIREMENTS of the Motorboat Act of 1940 respecting lifesaving equipment, fire extinguishers, lights, or other equipment.)

It requires the numbering of all undocumented vessels on the navigable waters of the United States, propelled in whole or in part by machinery of more than 10 horsepower (in the aggregate), regardless of the vessel's length. Numbers issued under this act are for identification only and do not authorize any vessel to engage in trade.

Boats are numbered according to the state of principal use, and that state may, at any time, by the enactment of a suitable law, assume the numbering functions.

Until April 1, 1960, the Coast Guard continued to issue numbers in accordance with the Numbering Act of 1918 *except* in those states that assumed the numbering functions under the Federal Boating Act of 1958. This necessitated issuance, as of April 1, 1960, of new numbers by the Coast Guard to all boats subject to this new act and principally used in states which, by that date, had not assumed the numbering functions.

---

nated by the Secretary [of the Treasury] as being exempt;

(6) Undocumented vessels used exclusively for racing; and

(7) Undocumented vessels operating under valid temporary certificates of number.

That "10 horsepower" terms as used here means the total of all propellant machinery on a vessel. In general, the Coast Guard will accept as evidence of the horsepower of the machinery in question, the manufacturer's rated horsepower at a stated maximum rpm as given on the nameplate attached to the engine, or as described in a "book of instructions" or other literature issued for the engine.

States administering their own system will probably do the same. If a state has not acted by April 1, 1960, the Coast Guard must administer the program, collect the fees ($3 for first numbering, $3 for renewal, $1 for reissue of lost or destroyed certificate of number), and register the state's boats that come under the Act's provisions.

WHERE IT GOES: The Act says: "The number awarded shall be required to be painted on, or attached to, each side of the bow of the vessel for which it was issued, and shall be of such size, color, and type, as may be prescribed by the Secretary." And prescribed it has been. On March 10, 1959, the following regulation, one of several passed to implement the Federal Boating Act,* became effective:

"The numbers shall be placed on each side of the forward half of the vessel in such position as to provide clear legibility for identification. The numbers shall read from left to right and shall be in block characters of good proportion not less than 3 inches in height. The numbers shall be of a color which will contrast with the color of the background and so maintained as to be clearly legible; i.e., dark numbers on a light background, or light numbers on a dark background."

WHAT YOU GET: The actual certificate of number—and remember, we are talking about the Federal Government's system now—includes: name, address,

---

* "Undocumented Vessel" here means any vessel not required to have, and does not have, a valid Marine Document.

* See *Federal Register*, December 25, 1958.

date of birth, and present citizenship of owner; state in which the vessel is principally used; hull material (wood, steel, aluminum, plastic, other); length of vessel; make and year built (if known); type of propulsion; type of fuel; declaration as to use (pleasure, livery, dealer, manufacturer, commercial-passenger, commercial-fishing, commercial-other); ownership certification by the applicant; number awarded to vessel; expiration date of certificate; and the owner's signature.

Also included on the certificate of number, which, incidentally, is pocket size (approximately 2½″ x 3½″) and water resistant, is a notice to the owner that he (1) report within 15 days changes of ownership or address, and destruction or abandonment of vessel; (2) report every accident involving injury (personal injury causing incapacitation for more than 72 hours) or death to persons, or property damage over $100; (3) stop and give aid if involved in a boating accident; and (4) always carry this certificate on the vessel when it is in use.

NUMBERING MANUFACTURERS' BOATS: Provision has been made to meet the requirements of boats operated by manufacturers and dealers. The description of the boat will be omitted from the certificate of number because the numbers and the certificates of number awarded may be transferred from one boat to another. In place of the description, the word "manufacturer" or "dealer" will be inserted on each certificate.

The manufacturer or dealer may have the awarded number printed upon or attached to a removable sign or signs to be temporarily mounted upon or attached to the boat being demonstrated or tested so long as the display meets the requirements (see previous section "Where It Goes").

The certificate of number of livery boats will be marked "livery boat" and the description of the motor and type of fuel will be omitted where the motor is not rented with the boat.

One more point concerning the certificate of number needs clearing. If a vessel is to be principally used on the high seas, it will be assigned a number for the state in which the vessel is usually docked, moored or berthed.

ABOUT CHANGES: When the owner of a vessel numbered by the Coast Guard changes the state in which the vessel is principally used, he must within 90 days surrender the certificate of number to the Coast Guard, and apply for another original number to the office issuing numbers for that state.

If only the address is changed but not the state, the owner must within 15 days notify the Coast Guard of his new address.

It may be fruitful to remind the reader that most of the above is in effect only in states which have not enacted their own legislation under the Federal Boating Act. Even so, however, the requirements will be similar to those listed here. And regardless of whether the state or the Coast Guard is administering the system, one thing is certain: every inboard and outboard boat powered by an engine of more than 10 horsepower must carry an assigned number on its bows if it operates on waters under federal control (navigable waters).

ACCIDENT REPORTING: The new accident-reporting program *in force on all federal waters* throughout the nation stipulates that whenever a death results from a boating accident, a written report shall be submitted within 48 hours. For every other reportable boating accident a written report shall be submitted within five days after the accident.

The written reports must be submitted to the Coast Guard Officer in Charge, Marine Inspection, nearest the place where the accident occurred or nearest to the port of first arrival after the accident. If more than one boat is involved, a separate report must be submitted by the operator of each boat. If the operator is not physically capable of making the report it should be made by the boat owner or other person familiar with the facts of the accident. Every written report must give the following information:

(1) The numbers and names of vessels involved.

(2) The locality where the accident took place.

(3) The time and date of the accident.

(4) Weather and sea conditions at time of accident.

(5) The name, address, age, and boat operating experience of the operator of the reporting vessel.

(6) The names and addresses of operators of other vessels involved.

(7) The names and addresses of the owners of vessels or property involved.

(8) The names and addresses of any person or persons injured or killed.

(9) The nature and extent of injury to any person or persons involved.

(10) A description of damage to property (including vessels) and estimated cost of repairs.

(11) A description of the accident (including opinions as to the causes).

(12) The length, propulsion, horsepower, fuel and construction of the reporting vessel, and

(13) Names and addresses of known witnesses.

The Coast Guard Form CG-3865 (Boating Accident Report) may be used for the written accident report required.

Photograph by U. S. Coast Guard—UPI

Administration of the Federal Boating Act is under the jurisdiction of the U. S. Coast Guard. In the dramatic illustration above, the Coast Guard is shown engaged in one of its activities centered about the safeguarding of life and property at sea, as a patrol boat crosses an inlet bar against a breaker—no place for any but Coast Guard boats. (See Chapter 27, pp. 396-415, Seamanship in Breaking Inlets.)

DOCUMENTATION

Not all vessels come within the provisions of the Numbering Act. For example, those vessels which are documented as vessels of the United States by the United States Coast Guard are not subject to the requirements for numbering as motorboats. The documents which are issued to vessels are of five forms, namely: register, enrollment and license, license, yacht enrollment and license, and yacht license.

Marine documents are also described as permanent, granted to vessels at their home ports; and temporary, granted to vessels at ports other than their home ports.

A vessel under a register which is not limited by a prohibitive endorsement on its face may engage in any trade, including the foreign trade, the coastwise trade, and the American fisheries. Registered vessels, however, may be subject to the requirement for payment of certain pilotage fees and other charges upon arrival in a port of the United States to which other documented vessels are not generally subject.

An enrollment and license may be issued to a vessel of 20 net tons or more and, if the vessel is entitled to be so documented, may authorize it to engage in the coasting trade, the mackerel fishery, the cod fishery, the whale fishery, or the coasting trade and mackerel fishery. A vessel so authorized to engage in the mackerel fishery may be used in the taking of fish of any description. Special enrollments and licenses are issued on the frontiers, authorizing vessels to engage in the foreign and coasting trades. Vessels of 5 net tons or more may be granted an enrollment and license for navigating the waters of the northern, northeastern, or northwestern frontiers.

A license may be issued to a vessel of 5 net tons or over but of less than 20 net tons and, if the vessel is entitled to be so documented, may authorize the vessel to engage in any one of the employments for which an enrollment and license may be issued.

A yacht enrollment and license may be issued to a vessel used exclusively for pleasure of more than 20 net tons and a yacht license may be issued to such a vessel of 5 net tons or over but of less than 20 net tons. Important privileges extended by documentation of vessels as yachts are: (1) authority to fly the yacht ensign, which authority is not granted other boats; (2) right to voyage to a foreign port without clearing the vessel through United States customs; (3) in the case of yachts of 15 gross tons or less, the right to return to a port of the United States from a foreign port or ports without entering * the vessel through United States customs; (4) the privilege of recording bills of sale, mortgages, and other instruments of title for the vessel in the office of the collector of customs at the vessel's home port, giving constructive notice to all of the effect of such instruments and permitting the attainment of the status of preferred mortgages by mortgage instruments which are so recorded, thus giving additional security to the mortgagee and facilitating financing and transfers of title for such vessels.

The master of a documented vessel, other than one under register, must renew the document annually and any changes of master (except in the case of a licensed ferryboat) must be reported to a collector of customs.

The name of every documented vessel, yachts excepted, is required to be marked in full upon each bow and upon the stern and the hailing port is required to be marked upon the stern. A yacht is required to have its name and hailing port marked on some conspicuous part of its hull.

However, the documentation of yachts is not mandatory and it is entirely discretionary with the owner as to whether he should document his craft as a yacht. If the

* However, any vessel having dutiable merchandise aboard must report to customs.

vessel is not documented, however, as indicated above, it may become subject to the requirements for numbering.

Vessels which are documented are not permitted or required to have a number issued under the Federal Boating Act.

On the other hand, vessels which are engaged in trade and which are of 5 net tons or over will become subject to penalties provided by law if not documented for the employment in which they are engaged.

Foreign-built vessels, except in special circumstances, may be documented only to engage in the foreign trade, in trade with certain island possessions of the United States, or as yachts when used exclusively for pleasure. Such vessels may not be documented for the coastwise trade nor the American fisheries. In addition, vessels sold foreign or placed under foreign flag cannot thereafter be documented, as a general proposition, for the coastwise trade but are otherwise unrestricted as to documentation.

Before a vessel may be issued a document, it must be "admeasured" for gross and net tonnage. A procedure has been adopted under which the owner of a boat used exclusively for pleasure may file an "Application for Simplified Admeasurement" with the Officer in Charge, Marine Inspection, in his local Coast Guard District. He may take his own length, breadth and depth measurements and complete the transaction by mail, quickly and without cost.

LICENSES TO OPERATE MOTORBOATS CARRYING PASSENGERS

(For legislation affecting vessels carrying more than six passengers, see page 494)

(For legislation affecting vessels carrying more than six passengers, see page 494)

Since June 9, 1910, persons wishing to operate a motorboat carrying passengers *for hire* have required a license. This is not to be confused with those held by licensed pilots and engineers on vessels over 15 tons gross, or more than 65 feet in length, engaged in trade. Nor should it be implied that any license is required of a person who operates his motorboat for pleasure only. As a matter of fact licensed officers are required on yachts or other motor vessels used exclusively for pleasure *only* if they are seagoing and exceed 300 gross tons.

Motorboats under 65 feet in length carrying freight for hire are not required to have licensed pilots and engineers.

The terms of the Motor Boat Act of 1940 and Executive Order No. 9083 empower the Commandant, U. S. Coast Guard, to draft any regulations necessary to implement the Act and make it effective.

Section 7 of the Act itself exempts from the need of having a license operators of motorboats engaged in any fishing contest previously arranged and announced.

Licenses to operate motorboats for hire are not granted to anyone under 18 years of age.

The license is required regardless of whether passengers carried for hire are aboard the motorboat or are carried on another non-self-propelled vessel towed or pushed.

Who Issues Licenses

Licenses are issued by the Officers in Charge, Marine Inspection, U. S. Coast Guard. These officers are located in the ports listed in Table I-B (p. 25).

The applicant must submit a sworn application on Form 866 to an Officer in Charge, Marine Inspection, who examines him concerning his character and fitness to hold the license. He investigates the proofs submitted concerning his character and ability and determines whether his "capacity, knowledge, experience, character and habits of life" qualify him to hold such a license.

The applicant must also submit documentary evidence of at least one year's experience in operating motorboats.

The oral examination is based upon subjects which any person operating a motorboat carrying passengers should

United States Coast Guard

License to

Operate or Navigate Motorboats Carrying Passengers for Hire

This is to certify that _____ *has given satisfactory evidence to the undersigned Officer in Charge, Marine Inspection for the district of* _____, *that he can safely be intrusted with the duties and responsibilities of operator of motorboats as defined in the Act of April 25, 1940, when carrying passengers for hire, on the navigable waters of the United States, and is hereby licensed to act as such operator for the term of five years from this date.*

Given under my hand this _____ *day of* _____, 19_.

_____
OFFICER IN CHARGE, MARINE INSPECTION.

The form of license required by the Motor Boat Act of those who operate motorboats carrying not more than six passengers. A special license is provided for small vessels carrying more than six passengers. (See page 494.) A limited license may be issued to operators of tenders of less than 30 feet in length at marinas and yacht clubs. Applicants for licenses may get detailed information from the Officer in Charge, Marine Inspection, U.S. Coast Guard

When License Is Lost

In case of loss, except where the license has been suspended or revoked, a certificate may be obtained from the Officer in Charge, Marine Inspection, on presentation of satisfactory evidence of loss. The certificate is then as valid as the license for the unexpired term.

When an Officer in Charge, Marine Inspection, learns that a license has been lost or stolen, he in turn notifies the District Coast Guard Officer and supplies him with all available information concerning the case.

Suspension and Revocation

If any operator is found guilty of incompetency, misbehavior, negligence, unskillfulness, endangering life, or wilfully violating any provision of law or safety regulations, his license may be suspended or revoked. When revoked, it automatically expires. If revoked or suspended, the license must be surrendered to the hearing officer before whom the hearing was held. If an appeal is made to the hearing officer, a temporary certificate for the period of the appeal may be issued upon request.

Specimen Questions

The following sets of specimen examinations are not intended to present the exact questions which will be asked by the marine inspectors, but are given only to serve as a guide so that an applicant may have a general understanding of the type of questions he is likely to be asked.

know before being entrusted with its operation and navigation.

Questions deal generally with regulations governing motor boats, collision regulations on the waters the applicant operates in, fire protection, life-saving equipment, safe operation of gasoline engines, methods of operating and navigating boats carrying passengers for hire, and elementary first aid.

Collision regulations differ in various parts of the country. Consequently, if the holder of a license ever operates elsewhere than on the waters for which he was examined, it is his duty to familiarize himself with the collision regulations applicable to the new locality.

Physical Examination

Applicants must be physically fit. In the case of persons who have held a license prior to April 25, 1941, a physical examination may not be required, if it appears to the inspectors that the applicant's color sense, vision, hearing and physical fitness are not badly impaired.

Those who have not held a license prior to April 25, 1941, must be examined by a U. S. Public Health surgeon or reputable physician. Bad hearing or eye-sight, color blindness, use of narcotics, insanity or presence of certain diseases are grounds for rejection of the applicant. The applicant must be able to read and write.

The License

Licenses are issued and signed by Officers in Charge, Marine Inspection. Every license (or certificate of lost license) must be signed by the person to whom it is issued, who also places his fingerprint upon the back. It is good for five years, after which it can be renewed by application on form CG-866. There is no charge.

To renew the license one must present it to an Officer in Charge, Marine Inspection, together with a certificate of color sense, within one year after the date of its expiration. If more than a year elapses after expiration, the operator will have to take another examination. Except under extraordinary circumstances, renewal cannot be made more than 90 days in advance of the date of expiration.

I

1. What is the meaning of two short blasts of the whistle?
2. What signal would you display while at anchor during the night?
3. What is the rule concerning speed during foggy weather?
4. Suppose you see a red light on your starboard bow, what would you judge it to be and what would you do?
5. In keeping clear of another vessel what must you avoid doing?
6. What motor boats are included in Class 2?
7. What person must hold a motor boat operator's license? Under what conditions would a license as operator of a motor boat be subject to suspension or revocation?
8. Explain how a life preserver is worn and how it is adjusted.
9. Must fire extinguishers used on motor boats be approved?
10. Outline briefly the features of the fixed CO_2 system. What boats are required to be equipped with it?
11. What precaution would you take in regard to the bilges of the engine and fuel tank compartments of motorboats (except open boats) using as fuel any liquid of a volatile nature?
12. What should you do after refueling?
13. What precautions do you take with oily rags and waste?
14. What would you watch out for in regard to wiring?
15. When passengers are aboard how must you handle your motor boat with regard to their safety?
16. Suppose a person falls overboard and is recovered in an unconscious state, how would you go about reviving him?

II

1. You are anchored in a fairway in a fog. What signals must you give and how often?
2. What is the meaning of one short blast on the whistle?

3. You are navigating in foggy weather. What signals must you give? What duration and at what intervals?

4. Suppose you saw a red pennant displayed from a Coast Guard station, or a lighthouse, or yacht club, what would it mean to you?

5. In narrow channels, on which side shall vessels navigate, if safe and practicable?

6. What does the word "motorboat" include according to the Motor Boat Regulations?

7. Describe the lights carried on Class 3 motor boats.

8. What would you look for before purchasing a life preserver?

9. What type, size and number of fire extinguishers are accepted for use on motor boats? How are they operated?

10. If gasoline is spilled, what immediate steps should be taken?

11. What safety measures must be observed when refueling?

12. Before starting an engine, which is located in a cabin or other enclosed space, what would you do first?

13. Where should the vent from the gasoline tank terminate?

14. What precaution must be taken to prevent back-fire of the engines (except outboard motors) of motor boats, the construction of which, or the replacement of the engines of which was commenced subsequent to April 25, 1940?

15. When carrying passengers for hire, what provision must be made for one's safety?

16. Name the points of the compass.

*When a Motor Boat Is Carrying Passengers for Hire

There are many obvious cases where a motor boat, normally used for pleasure only, might carry passengers for hire. The owner, for example, might charge a group of persons a definite amount for taking them on a day's outing, fishing or cruising. It is clear that in cases of this kind the boat is carrying passengers for hire, and must be equipped in accordance with all the regulations for such boats, including a life preserver of approved type for every person on board. The operator of such a boat must have a license to carry passengers for hire.

However, there are other border-line cases where the status of the motor boat owner may be in doubt. For example, consider the following examples:

1. When he (the ordinary yachtsman) invites guests on his boat, and a guest brings a gift of food or liquor to be used on the trip.

2. When arranging a cruise with guests, and the guests agree to pay their proportionate part of the expenses, including gasoline and other supplies.

3. Or, in the extreme case, where the cruise guest takes the owner ashore for dinner and entertainment.

4. Supposing a yachtsman takes business associates on a cruise, perhaps with the intent of creating good will and friendship in negotiating business not relating to the yacht or the cruise.

According to a ruling of the former Bureau of Marine Inspection and Navigation, and reaffirmed by the Commandant, U. S. Coast Guard, a motor boatman would *not* be considered to be carrying passengers for hire in cases 1, 3, and 4.

When There Is An Agreement in Advance

However, in case 2 if there was a prearranged plan or agreement *in advance* that the guests agree to pay their proportionate part of the expenses of the cruise, then the boat would be considered to be carrying passengers for hire, the operator would have to be licensed, and the equipment as explained above would have to be in conformity with regulations for boats carrying passengers for hire.

If, on the other hand, the owner of a motor boat invites guests to accompany him on a cruise and while on the cruise one or more of the guests offers to pay for gasoline or food in return for the hospitality extended them, then the owner would not be regarded as carrying passengers for hire, would not require a license, and his ordinary equipment carried on a motor boat operated for pleasure only would be adequate.

In April 1953, the following clarification was made, in an opinion expressed by the Commandant of the Coast Guard: "It is possible, of course, for the owner of any vessel to operate on a share-the-expense basis if all guests are willing to enter into a written agreement that the voyage will be a joint venture and that all parties to the contract will share all liabilities as well as benefits. In this situation the owner would not be considered as transporting passengers for hire. Expenses could then be shared. In case of a casualty all parties to the contract would be jointly responsible in case of suit."

At the same time, the opinion was given that "In a case where the owner of a vessel competes in a regatta for cash prizes or trophies and has on board a paid driver or mechanic, this is not considered carrying passengers for hire as no passengers are being transported. The driver, mechanic or operator of the vessel is considered part of the crew necessary to man the boat . . ."

When An Owner Charters and Supplies the Crew

Subsequently the former Bureau was asked for a decision on the following:

5. In the event an owner of a motorboat, under 65 feet in length, which is in complete commission with a paid crew aboard, elects to charter this boat for a definite period of time for the exclusive use of another individual, the charter to include the furnishing by the owner of his crew to operate the vessel during the period of charter.

In such a case it was the former Bureau's opinion and reaffirmed by the Commandant, U. S. Coast Guard, that the boat would be regarded as carrying passengers for hire and accordingly would have to be in charge of a licensed operator.

6. Supposing the same situation as 5 (above) but with a vessel of more than 65 feet in length.

Here again the former Bureau's ruling, and reaffirmed by the Commandant, U. S. Coast Guard, was to the effect that the vessel is carrying passengers for hire and if she is over 15 gross tons, she must be in charge of the necessary complement of licensed engineers and pilots as prescribed by the Officer in Charge, Marine Inspection.

When the Owner Does Not Supply the Crew

7. In the event of an owner of a motor boat under 65 feet in length which has not as yet been commissioned and on which there is no crew elects to charter this boat for a period of time to another individual who will hire and place upon it his own crew at his own expense.

8. The same situation as 7 (above) but considering a motor boat over 65 feet in length.

In both cases 7 and 8, the former Bureau's ruling, and reaffirmed by the Commandant, U. S. Coast Guard, was that if such a vessel, regardless of its length, is used exclusively for pleasure, it would *not* be considered to be carrying passengers for hire. Therefore no licensed operators would be required.

Coast Guard in Charge of Licenses and Inspection

The U. S. Coast Guard has charge of the granting of all licenses and the inspection of hull and machinery of those motorboats where this is required. A list of the offices of the Officers in Charge, Marine Inspection, will be found below.

Application should be made to any of these for information relative to obtaining certificates, examinations, etc.

These local offices (ports) are grouped into districts under the direction of district Coast Guard commanders:

District No. 1. BOSTON—Portland, Me., Providence, R. I. 2. ST. LOUIS—Cairo, Dubuque, Cincinnati, Louisville, Memphis, Nashville, Pittsburgh, Pt. Pleasant. 3. NEW YORK—Bridgeport, Albany, Philadelphia. 5. NORFOLK—Baltimore. 7. MIAMI—Charleston, Savannah, Tampa, San Juan. 8. NEW ORLEANS—Mobile, Port Arthur, Galveston, Houston, Corpus Christi. 9. CLEVELAND—Buffalo, Oswego, Detroit, Duluth, Toledo, St. Ignace, Chicago, Ludington, Milwaukee. 11. LONG BEACH, CALIF. 12. SAN FRANCISCO. 13. SEATTLE—Portland, Ore., Ketchikan. 14. HONOLULU, T. H.

* NOTE: See page 494 for information on Ray Act affecting vessels carrying more than six passengers.

CUSTOMS AND IMMIGRATION REGULATIONS

When an American yacht crosses the national boundaries of the United States to visit a foreign port, or a foreign yacht visits an American port, certain customs and immigration regulations must be complied with. Due to various provisions and exemptions applying to yachts, not engaged in trade, the procedure has been made so easy that there is nothing in these legal requirements to deter a pleasure craft from enjoying a cruise outside the limits of United States waters. Severe penalties are provided for failure to observe regulations, however.

It should be noted that customs and immigration inspections are two separate functions even though, in some of the smaller ports, they may be administered by a single official or his office. Separate offices handle these duties where traffic across the border is heavy.

Clearing and Entering

The terms clearing and entering are commonly used in connection with a vessel's voyage to a foreign port. Clearing involves the obtaining of permission to sail by presenting the ship's papers to a customs official. Entering relates to arrival, when the owner or master enters his vessel by having his ship's papers accepted by customs authorities. Thus a vessel might be required to clear from an American port, enter at a Canadian or other foreign port, and then, on returning, clear from the foreign port and enter at the American port.

Under provisions of an Act of September 1, 1954, neither a licensed yacht nor an undocumented American pleasure vessel (not engaged in trade nor in any way violating the customs or navigation laws of the United States) is required to clear upon departure from the United States for a foreign port or place. Similarly, a licensed yacht of any size and an undocumented American pleasure vessel (not engaged in trade nor in any way violating the customs or navigation laws of the United States and not having visited any hovering vessel) are exempted from entry.

Foreign vessels are not only subject to the requirements of entry and clearance on foreign voyages but must also enter and clear when proceeding between U. S. ports.

If desired, bills of health may be secured free of charge before leaving for a foreign port. This is not compulsory and is used chiefly by vessels going to tropical countries, where epidemics are more prevalent.

Canadian boatmen with craft of less than five tons can now enter the border waters of the United States for a day's outing without applying for admission at a U. S. port of entry. The new Canadian Border Landing Card (Form 1-68) doesn't require advance application and is good for repeated 24-hour visits throughout the navigation season. It is good only for border waters. If the boatman wants to go further into the U. S., he still must apply at a port of entry and submit to inspection.

Report on Arrival

On arrival at the foreign port the owner or captain of a yacht (any size) should report at once to the customs and immigration authorities. When reporting, crew and guests must remain aboard the boat until it has passed inspection. Any additional regulations to be complied with, including any details in connection with clearing from there, will be supplied by the customs and immigration authorities of the port.

Every vessel, whether documented or not, arriving in the United States from a foreign port or place must come into a port of entry and, within 24 hours, must report to the customhouse at that port. The crew and guests of all vessels arriving within the United States should remain aboard and no baggage or merchandise should be removed until the customs and immigration officials have made their inspection.

All boats regardless of size must report to the immigration authorities on return to a United States port. Any alien passengers aboard must be reported and a heavy penalty attaches to failure to detain passengers and crew, if ordered to do so by the authorities. A report giving names and other informaton concerning any paid hands aboard must be made on a crew manifest.

Charges

There is no charge for the documentation of a vessel, but nominal fees are charged for the recording of instruments of title presented to the collector of customs in connection with any application for documentation and, if the vessel is outside a port of entry or a customs station at

A Coast Guard mobile boarding team, showing safety equipment alongside the boat. This team, and others like it, travel to inland waters under Federal jurisdiction carrying out Coast Guard boarding and rescue duties and promoting safety afloat. (U.S. Coast Guard official photo)

the time of admeasurement, certain charges are made to defray the cost of sending an admeasurer to the vessel.

Vessels of less than 100 net tons which are entered must pay an entry fee of $1.50. The fee for vessels of 100 net tons or over is $2.50. The same fees are charged upon the clearance of a vessel for a foreign port. Payment of entry and clearance fees is not required in the case of a vessel proceeding between Canada and the northern, northeastern or northwestern frontiers of the United States otherwise than by sea.

Free Permits

Yachts going into Canada may secure cruising permits with privileges of free entry and clearance for the period from May 1 to October 1. This is issued free of charge by the Canadian customs authorities at the Canadian port where the yacht first reports and must be surrendered to the issuing authority when leaving that country. Provided the yacht does not leave Canadian waters, she is then free to visit other Canadian ports until the permit is surrendered, though reports are to be made at any port called at where a customs officer is located.

Under special statute, qualified foreign yachts may receive from customs authorities in the United States a cruising license granting them special treatment in United States waters.

A documented yacht, belonging to a regularly organized and incorporated yacht club, may be issued a commission to sail for pleasure on a foreign voyage. Application therefor may be made to any collector of customs in the United States. The commission serves primarily as an identification of the owner and the vessel. It must be surrendered upon return from the foreign country.

Tonnage Tax

Regular tonnage tax is assessed upon the entry from a foreign port or place of a vessel engaged in trade. Special tonnage tax at the rate of 50 cents per net ton and light money at the same rate, or a total of $1 per net ton, are assessed upon the entry from a foreign port or place of an American or foreign undocumented vessel of 5 net tons or over which is engaged in trade. The rate of special tonnage tax is reduced to 30 cents per net ton if the undocumented foreign vessel was built in the United States. Undocumented American vessels which are documented as vessels of the United States prior to their departure from the first port of arrival are exempt from the payment of special tonnage tax and light money.

General

For detailed information with regard to customs requirements, see your nearest customs officer.

Log Books and Records May Be Inspected

Regulations provide that the owner, charterer, agent, master, or other licensed officer of any vessel involved in a marine casualty or accident shall retain the voyage records of the vessel, including both rough and smooth deck and engine room logs, bell books, navigation charts, navigators' work book, compass deviation cards, stowage diagrams, records of draft, aids to mariners, radiograms sent and received and the radio log and crews' and passengers' lists, which upon request shall be produced for the inspection of the U. S. Coast Guard Examiners whenever required.

The Shipping Act of 1916

Section 37 of the Shipping Act of 1916, as amended (46 U. S. C. 835), became effective upon Presidential Proclamation 2914, dated December 16, 1950 (15 F. R. 9029). Accordingly, this proclamation has brought into operation, among others, the statutory provisions prohibiting the transfer of any interest in an American owned vessel or shipbuilding plant to foreign ownership without prior Maritime Administration approval.* The prohibition extends to sales, charters, leases, and other transfers of interest in such vessels and plants; in agreements to effect such transfers; to agreements and understandings whereby the controlling interest or a majority of the stock of a corporation, organized in the United States and owning such vessels or facilities, would be vested in or for the benefit of a noncitizen; and to related activities. Accordingly, sales of undocumented and numbered vessels by American citizens to aliens without the consent of the Maritime Administration, U. S. Department of Commerce, *under such regulations as are prescribed by that agency cannot be consummated.*

[Ed. note: Undocumented vessels of less than 65 feet overall length and less than 600 horsepower are granted blanket approval provided the purchaser is not a citizen of any of the following: Cuba, Hong Kong, Macao, Albania, Bulgaria, Communist China (including Manchuria), Communist-controlled area of Viet Nam, Czechoslovakia, East Germany, Estonia, Hungary, Latvia, Lithuania, North Korea, Outer Mongolia, Rumania, and the Soviet Union. Exception to the blanket approval of such small craft would include those having a displacement of more than 45 tons, hydrofoil craft, and vessels equipped with certain types of navigational gear or munitions equipment requiring special licenses.]

* Approval was granted April 12, 1961 on undocumented pleasure boats of 65 feet in overall length and/or 500 rated horsepower, or less, sold to any Canadian citizen, living in Canada, and importing it for registration or license under Canadian law. Approval is required on undocumented pleasure boats of 40 feet overall length or more, and/or of 50 rated horsepower or more, to Canadian citizens living outside of Canada when the boat is neither imported into nor registered or licensed in Canada, nor intended to be imported into Canada or registered or licensed under Canadian law.

U.S. Coast Guard Photo

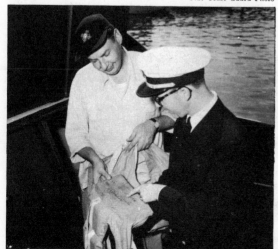

Left: A Coast Guard Auxiliary member, making a free courtesy examination of equipment, checks the Coast Guard approval stamped on a life preserver. Below: This boat has passed inspection and has a decal applied to the windshield

For All Classes of Boats

(See pages 36-46, and Chapter IV, pages 61-78)

NOTE

White *bow lights* mentioned in this article are 20-point, showing from dead ahead to two points abaft the beam on each side.

White *stern lights* are 32-point lights showing all around the horizon.

Red (port) *side lights* are 10-point, showing from dead ahead to two points abaft the port beam.

Green (starboard) *side lights* are 10-point, showing from dead ahead to two points abaft the starboard beam.

Side lights must be screened so as not to shine across the bow.

Red-and-green *combination lights* show red from dead ahead to two points abaft the port beam, and green from dead ahead to two points abaft the starboard beam.

NO matter how the subject is presented, there often seems to be some misunderstanding as to how certain classes of small vessels are to be lighted at night—particularly auxiliaries. Most of the confusion is caused by the fact that regulations governing lights are to be found both in the Pilot Rules, which cover all water craft on federal waters generally, and also in the Motor Boat Act, which, though also applicable on federal waters, is concerned *only* with boats up to 65 feet in length, "propelled by machinery."

More than one interpretation might reasonably be taken from that phrase "propelled by machinery" so a further element of doubt enters into the picture. Fortunately, an amendment (June 4, 1956) to the Motor Boat Act goes a long way toward making the rules more consistent and logical, particularly with respect to auxiliaries.

At the outset is it important to note that the Pilot Rules govern the navigation of vessels on harbors, rivers and "inland waters" of the United States, separate rules being provided for the Great Lakes and connecting and tributary waters as far East as Montreal, and for the Red River of the North and certain rivers emptying into the Gulf of Mexico and their tributaries.

When the Pilot Rules say "inland waters" they do not mean inland lakes lying wholly within the boundaries of one state; such waters are subject only to state or more local jurisdiction. Inland waters are all other waters lying inland and inshore of lines that have been laid down to separate them from the high seas on which International Rules apply.

Left: Vessels under sail only and without engines are lighted according to the Pilot Rules which require red and green side lights and (except on the Great Lakes) a white stern light. Provision is made, however, in all rules for small vessels (under 10 gross tons on Inland Waters) which cannot accommodate fixed lights while under way in bad weather. The general provision is to the effect that under such circumstances, they must keep portable colored side lights lighted, ready at hand, to show on the approach of or to other vessels. An "electric torch or lighted lantern" may be shown in place of a fixed white stern light on small vessels unable to accommodate the latter.

Right: An outboard motor boat, being "propelled by machinery", is a motor boat and at night must carry the lights prescribed for a motor boat. Under 26 feet in length, it would have a combination red-and-green bow light and a white stern light. White stern lights should be placed on the centerline or as near to the centerline as practicable.

In 1968, a table of recommended lamp numbers was prepared to enable operators of boats and other vessels to comply more easily with requirements as to distance of visibility of navigation lights. The numbers given below provide the minimum requirement of candlepower outside the lenses.

Distance of Visibility, in nautical miles	Color	Lamp number for specified voltage systems					
		With fresnel lens			Without fresnel lens		
		6	12	32	6	12	32
1	Red	82	90	1226	1130	1142	1230
1	Green	88	94	1228	—	—	—
2	White	64	68	1224	82	90	1226
3	White	82	90	1226	1130	1142	1230

Disregarding, for the purposes of our discussion here, all special types such as pilot vessels, ferry boats and other types for which specific lights are prescribed, the big, broad classifications of "vessels" in the Pilot Rules would be—steam vessels (motor boats) and sailing vessels. So far as these rules are concerned, a steam vessel includes any vessel propelled in whole or in part by machinery. Furthermore a steam vessel under sail and not under steam is considered a sailing vessel. Every vessel under steam, whether under sail or not, is considered a steam vessel.

The Motor Boat Act

Now, on "navigable" (Federal) waters of the United States, vessels propelled by machinery, not over 65 feet in length (except tug boats and tow boats propelled by steam) are classed as motor boats. They come within the provisions of the Motor Boat Act of 1940, which divides them into four classes (A, up to 16 feet; 1, 16 to 26 feet; 2, 26 to 40 feet; and 3, 40 to 65 feet) and contains provisions prescribing the equipment to be carried by each class. Included in this equipment are the lights which must be exhibited by every motor boat in all weathers from sunset to sunrise when under way. (A vessel is under way when not at anchor, aground or made fast to the shore.) The law does not require lights to be aboard during the day.

"Navigable" waters of the United States are those navigable to the sea or which cross state and international lines. Outside these waters (on the high seas) a motor boat would comply with International Law. On lakes and other waterways lying wholly within the boundaries of one state, motor boats would not be under Federal jurisdiction and would, therefore, comply with the motor boat law of that state, if any statutes have been passed. (Several states do have regulations regarding the lighting of motor boats on state waters.)

When Is a Vessel "Propelled by Machinery"?

Now, in order to determine whether a certain vessel should be lighted in accordance with the Motor Boat Act or according to the Pilot Rules, it is necessary to determine whether she is "propelled by machinery" and whether she is under or over 65 feet.

According to an opinion given originally by the former Bureau of Marine Inspection and Navigation, when asked about the status of auxiliaries, a vessel (under 65 feet) is considered to be a motor boat when the motor is connected to the shaft and propeller, regardless of whether the engine is actually in operation or not. Thus, they say, in the case of a sailing vessel carrying an outboard motor, the vessel is an auxiliary (and would be classed as a

Above: Sailboats (without an engine) are not lighted according to the Motor Boat Act but as provided by the Pilot Rules, which require a 10-point red side light to port and a 10-point green side light to starboard. They must also carry a 12-pt. white stern light showing 6 points from right aft on each side. Under the Inland Pilot Rules (excepting the Great Lakes and Mississippi River), vessels under 10 gross tons, in bad weather, when the side lights cannot be fixed, may keep separate red and green side lights (properly screened) at hand ready to show to approaching vessels.

Below: An inboard motor boat of Class 1 (16 to less than 26'). Forward she carries a combination red-and-green light, each showing through 10 points, and aft a 32-point (all around) white light.

motor boat) when the outboard motor is attached to the stern. A sailing vessel is also an auxiliary when it has an inboard motor aboard connected with the shaft and propeller. (This definition or ruling is also important from the angle of the Federal regulations which require undocumented "motor boats" to carry a number assigned by the state or by the Coast Guard.)

In the light of this interpretation, any auxiliary—whether its engine is running or not—is subject to the light requirements specified in the Motor Boat Act of April 25, 1940 for motor boats under sail alone or under sail and power. A recent amendment to the act clarifies rules in respect to lights to be carried by auxiliaries, eliminating much confusion on the subject.

Left: This motor sailer, when running under sail only, carries separate red and green side lights. She must also carry a 12-pt. white stern light showing aft, visible for at least two miles

Above: The same motor sailer, driven by her engine alone, or sail and engine both, carries, in addition to separate red and green side lights, a 20-point white bow light and a 32-point white stern light

Lights for the various types of boats under way differ from anchorage requirements and the remainder of this article is concerned entirely with the lights carried at night by boats *under way.*

Sailboats

Consider first the out-and-out sailboat that has no motive power of any kind aboard (or perhaps may have an outboard motor stowed away somewhere in a locker for emergency): since she is not "propelled by machinery" it makes no difference whether she is under or over 65 feet. She does not come under the definition of a motor boat and is not subject to the Motor Boat Act, but should carry the lights specified by the Pilot Rules. The vessel mentioned parenthetically above, with outboard stowed away, would be considered an auxiliary only when the outboard was attached to the hull in its propelling position.

Now the Pilot Rules specify, for sailing vessels, a red 10-point side light to port and a green 10-point side light to starboard. Formerly they carried no fixed white lights. Under present rules, they carry a 12-pt. fixed white stern light (except on the Great Lakes where the stern light is not required. Great Lakes rules do, however, have a provision that sailing vessels at all times, on the approach of any steamer at night shall "show a lighted torch upon that point or quarter to which such steamer shall be approaching.")

When small sailboats are under way in bad weather it may not be feasible to fix the required red and green colored

At Anchor and Under Way

All boats under 150 feet in length at anchor are required to display one white 32-point light forward where it can best be seen. This must be visible at least 2 miles. In special anchorage areas designated by the Secretary of the Army, however, no anchorage light is required on vessels 65 feet or less in length.

Vessels 150 or more feet in length at anchor show one white 32-point light forward, not less than 20 feet above the hull. In addition, they also show another white 32-point light aft at least 15 feet lower than the forward light. These, too, must be visible at least 2 miles.

Special Rules

Special rules are applicable to barges, canal boats, scows and other nondescript craft of 150 feet or more in length when anchored within special anchorage areas and to several such craft anchored as a unit.

Above: This cruiser, in Class 2 (26 to less than 40 feet), carries a 20-point white bow light, 32-point white stern light, and separate red and green side lights, each showing through 10 points

Right: Here is an auxiliary. Having an engine, she is lighted according to the Motor Boat Act. When she is under sail only, she carries separate red and green side lights, and a 12-point white light aft. If her engine were running, whether or not her sails were up, she would carry side lights and the white bow and stern lights of a motor boat. If she were less than 26 feet in length, under sail alone, she would carry a combination red-and-green light forward and 12-point white light aft. With engine running, she would carry a combination light and a white 32-point light aft

side lights (these frequently are attached to the standing rigging). To provide for such conditions, the rules are nearly uniform in providing that whenever small vessels are under way in bad weather and cannot keep the side lights fixed in the normal way, they may keep portable lights lighted and ready at hand to be shown at the approach of or to other vessels in time to prevent collision. Obviously, when shown, the lights would be displayed on their proper respective sides, red to port and green to starboard and in such a way as not to show the wrong color across the bow.

To make the use of portable colored side lights more certain, they must be painted on the outside with their respective (red or green) colors and fitted with proper screens.

Under both Great Lakes and Western River Rules, it is stipulated that these provisions for portable lights are for "small" vessels. The Inland Rules, while probably just as comprehensive, use a vessel of "less than 10 gross tons" to illustrate what is meant by a "small vessel."

As for the 12-point white stern light required on inland waters and on Western Rivers, the alternative to a fixed light on a small vessel is an "electric torch or a lighted lantern" to be shown as required to prevent collision.

Some years ago rulings had been made with respect to certain exceptions made for small open sailboats less than 18 feet in length. Under one such ruling, such a boat was at that time regarded as a "rowboat under sail" and accordingly was excused from carrying the colored side lights, but no authority can be found under present rules for the validity of such an exception.

Motor Boats—Not Under Sail

Now we turn to the out-and-out motor boat, having no sail. It is propelled by machinery and is, by definition, of necessity under 65 feet. It is lighted according to the Motor Boat Act, and the nature of the lights varies with the class of the boat. Let's examine the classes again:

Class A, under 16 feet; Class 1, 16 to less than 26 feet; Class 2, 26 to less than 40 feet; Class 3, 40 to 65 feet.

Classes A and 1 (including all motor boats up to 26 feet) carry a combination lantern forward which shows red from dead ahead to two points abaft the port beam and green from dead ahead to two points abaft the starboard beam. Aft they carry a white 32-point light, higher than the red-and-green combination light forward.

Classes 2 and 3 (including all motor boats from 26 to 65 feet) carry a 20-point white light forward showing from dead ahead to two points abaft the beam on each side, and a white 32-point light aft, showing all around the horizon, higher than the white bow light. Separate red and green side lights are prescribed, the red showing 10 points from dead ahead to two points abaft the port beam, and green showing from dead ahead to two points abaft the starboard beam.

Motorboats—Under Sail Only
(See Fig. 4, page 37)

There are times when a motorboat may be driven by sail only, as for example when a motor sailer is sailing while her engine is not in operation.

In such cases motorboats of classes 2 and 3 (26 to 65 feet) carry the separate red and green side lights and a 12-point white stern light, showing aft.

Motorboats of classes A and 1 (under 26 feet) under sail only, carry a red-and-green combination bow light and 12-point white stern light.

Small boats, in bad weather, may carry in lieu of the fixed white stern light a white lantern or flashlight which is shown in time to avert collision.

Auxiliaries—Under Sail Only

Like the motor sailer illustrated in Figure 4, page 37, the auxiliary subject to the Motor Boat Act (under 65 feet) shows a white stern light and colored side lights, when driven by sail alone.

This means that the auxiliary from 26 to 65 feet (classes 2 and 3) carries separate 10-point red and green side lights.

The auxiliary under 26 feet (classes A and 1) shows a combination red-and-green light forward in addition to her stern light.

Like small motor boats, small sailboats in bad weather may have a white lantern or flashlight at hand to be shown in time to avert collision.

Auxiliaries—Under Motor Only or Motor and Sail
(See illustrations, pages 30 and 31)

Auxiliaries, when driven by motor only, or motor and sail both, are lighted like motorboats of their respective classes driven by motor only. Thus, auxiliaries of 26 to 65 feet (classes 2 and 3) carry their separate red and green 10-point side lights, a 20-point white bow light, and the 32-point white stern light.

Auxiliaries less than 26 feet in length (classes A and 1) carry the red-and-green combination light forward and white 32-point stern light aft.

Amendment to Motor Boat Act

From the foregoing sections, it will be seen that there is now a consistency in the provisions for lights, requiring the craft under sail to be lighted as a sailboat, and the craft driven by motor to be lighted as a motorboat, whether or not she is using sails. These provisions are contained in an amendment which became effective June 4, 1956 (Public Law 552).

Optional Lighting Under Motor Boat Act

Public Law 552 also provides a new optional arrangement of lights which eliminates the necessity of changing lights when motorboats of any class operate from inland waters to the high seas.

On Inland Waters, the Great Lakes, and Western Rivers, between sunset and sunrise, motorboats of classes A, 1, 2 and 3 may continue to carry the lights prescribed for their respective classes in the Motor Boat Act. However, they now have the option of carrying, instead, the lights prescribed in International Rules for the high seas.

Thus motorboats of 65 feet or more lighted under International Rules should carry the regular seagoing lights prescribed for power-driven vessels. (See item 31, page 40.) Motorboats under 40 feet classify as power-driven vessels which may carry their white light forward at a height of less than 9 feet above the gunwale, but at least 3 feet higher than their sidelights or combination light. (See item 27, page 40.)

Caution in Night Piloting

At night good practice necessitates that no other lights outside of the specified navigation lights be shown anywhere on the deck of a vessel. Not only are extraneous lights disconcerting to the pilots of other vessels, but the glare of nearby lights on a boat will interfere with the vision of its own pilot. The visibility at night is at its best when the pilot is in absolute darkness.

Visibility Requirements

Every white light under the Motor Boat Act must be visible at least two miles; every colored light, at least one mile.

Lights installed on new boats or replacements on old ones must be constructed to comply with legal requirements.

Basic Rules

Colors are used to differentiate one light from another; they have distinct and separate meanings. White, red and green lights are used and these are arranged to show in four different ways. There are 10-, 12-, 20- and 32-point lights indicating the arc of the compass through which they would be visible—the 32-point light being visible from every point in the compass. (A point equals 11¼°; hence 32 points equals 360°.)

Red and green side lights show through 10 points for all classes of vessels. White lights which are designed to show only ahead are always made to show through 20 points. Lights which show through 32 points are of course visible from ahead also.

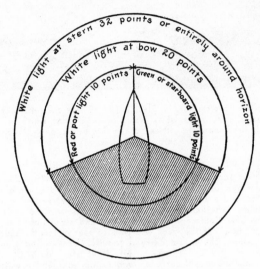

Diagram showing the arc covered by various lights. The 32-point white stern light shows all around the horizon, the white bow light ahead through 20 points (10 points each side) and the colored side lights 10 points on their respective sides

Side Lights Should Be Screened
(See illustrations, pages 14 and 15)

The regulations provide that the red and green side lights shall show from dead ahead to two points abaft the beam. The manufacturers of the light will generally provide a lens which will produce this angle.

It may be necessary for screens to be fitted so that the lights will not show across the bow. The light itself must necessarily be a small distance from the screen and the size of the lamp and reflected light all tend to make the light show across the bow. Care should be exercised and tests made to prevent this. Formerly the size of light lenses and light screens for Classes 2 and 3 was prescribed and lenses were also required to be of fresnel or fluted type. However, the Motor Boat Act of 1940 did away with these requirements. Under the law the side lights on boats of Class 2 and Class 3 must be fitted with inboard screens, but instead of a prescribed size the law merely mentions that they must be of sufficient length and height so as to prevent these lights from being seen across the bow. As an alternative they may be mounted on the cabin sides.

It is interesting to note that the Navy discovered, after World War II, that red and green paint on side light screens was not satisfactory, as it permitted, by diffuse reflection, the colored lights to be seen across the bow. Dull black was tested but, strangely, glossy black was found to be best. The Navy adopted the latter and subsequently the Coast Guard required it on merchant vessels.

Rowboats

Under Inland Rules a rowboat, under oars or sail, merely shows a white light at the approach of another vessel. This does not have to be permanently fixed. A lantern showing a white light may be kept at hand and displayed in sufficient time to avert collision. A similar provision ("electric torch or a lighted lantern") is made for rowboats under the International Rules.

Inland Steamers

Inland steamers are lighted at night in exactly the same way as motor boats of Classes 2 or 3. A white light forward will show through 20 points of the horizon. The port and starboard lights will show over 10 points of the horizon, while the white range light aft will show through 32 points. The range light aft must be carried at least 15 feet higher than the forward white light; on the Great Lakes the "15-foot" minimum applies only to steamers over 100 feet.

Ocean-Going Power-Driven Vessels
(See Fig. 31, page 41)

The lights prescribed for power-driven vessels under International Rules are shown not only by ocean liners, but also by seagoing yachts and other vessels which navigate the high seas, i.e., outside the limits delineated for inland waters.

They show a white 20-point bow light 20 to 40 feet above the hull, visible 5 miles. Their red and green 10-point side lights are visible 2 miles and are fitted with "inboard screens projecting at least 3 feet forward from the light."

The sea-going power-driven vessel carries a white 20-point range light at least 15 feet higher than the foremast light, visible 5 miles. The two white masthead lights must be in line with, and over, the keel. Horizontal distance between them must be at least 3 times the vertical distance. The range light is optional on vessels under 150 feet.

A fixed white 12-point stern light is now mandatory, except on towing vessels which may use a small white towing light not visible forward of the beam.

Power-driven vessels under 65 feet (see Fig. 27, p. 41) may, optionally, carry a 20-point white light forward, 10-point red and green side lights, and 12-point white light aft.

Government Vessels
(See item 18, Table 1, page 38)

Vessels of the U. S. Government are required to display the same lights as other vessels. However, the exhibition of any light on board a vessel of war of the United States or on vessels of the U. S. Coast Guard may be suspended whenever, in the opinion of the Secretary of the Navy, the Commander-in-Chief of a Squadron, or the Commander of a vessel acting singly, the special character of the service may require it.

Similarly, special lights may be prescribed for use on Naval and other vessels of the Government when found necessary. Differences in the lighting of certain types of naval vessels are necessitated because of their military function or special construction. Aircraft carriers are one example. The special lights shown by some naval craft may be displayed in combination with navigational lights, and sometimes naval vessels will appear to have an unorthodox arrangement of lights.

The inland steamer shown above carries lights similar to a Class III motor boat. Note the 20-point white bow light, 32-point white stern light, and 10-point red and green side lights

Range Lights

(See illus. below, also Fig. 6, p. 37 and Fig. 31, p. 41)

When a vessel's lights are visible in the distance there may be reasonable doubt as to its course. The *relative* location of the range lights will be the key. Where only one of the side lights is seen it can be assumed that you are within the 10-point sector of the other boat's side light.

Whether the relative courses of the two vessels will bring them together or not will be determined by the location of the range lights. Should the lower forward range light be to the left or right of the after range light the distance between them will indicate the approximate angle of the other vessel with your line of sight.

Should the range lights be directly over one another then it can be assumed that the other vessel is approaching head on and danger of collision exists. When the course is changed the range lights will separate and a shift to starboard will show by the lower light moving to your left while a shift to port will show by the lower light moving to your right.

Of particular value when the port light of a vessel shows is the relative location of these range lights. It can be assumed that the other vessel is in your danger zone and has the right of way.

Naturally, the relative speeds of the two boats must be taken into consideration. Also, the angle of alignment of range lights of an approaching vessel off on the beam may change rapidly, closing together and then opening again, indicating that you are safely crossing ahead of her.

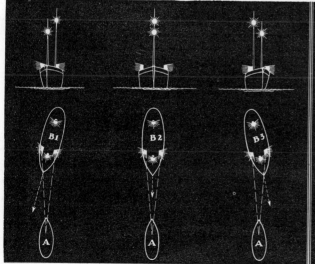

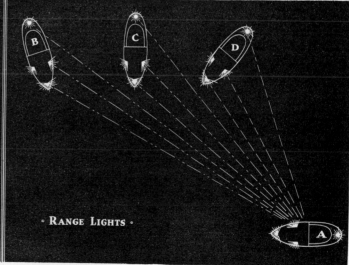

· RANGE LIGHTS ·

At the left, above, range lights one above the other indicate a vessel (B 2) approaching A head on. In B 1 and B 3 the position of the forward lower bow light to the left or right of the aft (upper) range light shows her course directed to port or starboard of A's course.

At right, above, A knows the other vessel (at B, C or D) is in her danger zone. Although the relative positions of range lights and side lights here are similar, they aid A in changing course to keep clear

Ferry Boats
(See Fig. 7, page 37)

Special provision has been made in the Inland Rules for the type of craft generally termed double-ended ferry boats. They are provided with two central white range lights at the same height above the water line and generally placed on top of the pilot houses on each end of the vessel. These show through 32 points.

A special light, which may be colored, carried amidships, designates the line to which the ferry belongs. Red and green 10-point side lights are of course also carried. Ferries not of the double-ended type carry the same lights as inland steamers.

Vessel Not Under Control
(See Fig. 38, page 41)

There are other cases which call for special lights. A vessel which is not under control, for example a steamer which may have lost a rudder, can operate to some extent by means of its twin screws. Under International Rules, and it would indicate the fact by showing two red lights vertically arranged, at least 6 feet apart, and the customary red and green lights. If she is not making headway through the water the red and green lights are not used.

Cable-Laying Vessels

A cable-laying vessel, under International Rules, displays three 32-point lights, vertically arranged, 20 to 40 feet above the hull. They are spaced at least 6 feet apart and must be visible at least 2 miles. The upper and lower lights are red, the middle one white. She carries no side lights unless under way with way on, when the regular red and green 10-point side lights would be carried. (This now includes vessels working on navigation marks, surveying and underwater operations.)

Pilot Vessels

When operating on their station and not at anchor steam pilot vessels will indicate their character by carrying in addition to the red and green lights two other lights on their main mast showing completely around the horizon. Of these the upper one is white and the lower one is red.

When at anchor the pilot vessel continues to display the special distinguishing lights but extinguishes the red and green side lights. When not engaged in pilot service the vessel will carry the customary lights for boats of her size.

Fishing Boats

Under Inland Rules fishing craft of 10 gross tons or more, "when under way without nets, trawls, dredges, or lines in the water," must carry the same lights as conventional vessels under way. Such fishing vessels *under* 10 gross tons need not carry side lights but must show an appropriately colored lantern (red to port, green to starboard) to approaching or approached vessels.

All vessels trawling, dredging or fishing must exhibit "from some part of the vessel where they can be best seen" two 32-point lights, separated vertically by not more than 12 or less than 6 feet and horizontally, if at all, by not more than 10 feet. The upper light must be red and visible for at least 2 miles, the lower one white and visible for at least 3 miles.

Under International Rules fishing vessels not engaged in fishing must show the lights for conventional vessels of the same length. The term "engaged in fishing" means fishing with nets, lines or trawls "but does not include fishing with trolling lines." Vessels engaged in trawling (i.e., dragging a dredge or similar apparatus through the water) must carry two lights arranged vertically, not less than 4 or more than 12 feet apart, each 32 points and visible for at least 2 miles, the upper green and the lower white.

All other vessels engaged in fishing must carry the same lights as the trawling vessel except that the upper light must be red instead of green.

When making way through the water all fishing vessels must carry the appropriate stern and side or combination lights. When not making way through the water they must not show either a stern light or side lights.

Tugs (Inland Rules)
(See illustrations, pages 37, 39 and 44)

Tugboats, under Inland Rules, if they have *no tow,* are lighted the same as ordinary steam vessels. In addition to red and green 10-point side lights, they have a 20-point white light forward and a 32-point white range light at least 15 feet higher than the foremast light.

If the tug has a *tow alongside,* the tug carries her red and green side lights as usual, and if one side light should be obscured by the tow, it is transferred to the outside of the tow. The tug also carries two (three if more than one vessel is being towed astern) white towing lights, vertically arranged, at least 3 feet apart. Optionally these may be 20-point foremast lights or 32-point lights carried where her white range light would be if running without a tow. When the tow is *pushed ahead* she now carries at the stern two 12-point amber lights showing aft, vertically arranged, with two 20-point white towing lights forward, vertically arranged, and the usual red and green side lights.

Whether her tow is alongside or astern, if her towing lights are carried forward, she may carry a 32-point white light aft as a range. If the towing lights are carried aft, she may display a 20-point white light forward.

Ocean-Going Tugs
(See Fig. 41, page 41 and page 43)

The ocean-going tug is lighted according to International Rules. If she has *no tow,* she has a white 20-point light forward, 20 to 40 feet above the hull, visible 5 miles. Her red and green 10-point side lights must be visible for at least 2 miles. Aft she carries a white 12-point light showing astern, visible 2 miles. A white 20-point range light is also carried, at least 15 feet higher than the foremast light, and visible 5 miles. When towing, the range light is optional. Horizontal distance between masthead lights must be at least 3 times the vertical.

An ocean-going tug with a *vessel in tow* carries, in addition to the red and green side lights, two white 20-point lights in a vertical line on the foremast, not less than 6 feet apart; if the length of the tow, measuring from the stern of the towing vessel to the stern of the last vessel towed, exceeds 600 feet, the towing vessel must carry three rather than two vertical white lights. Either a fixed 12-point stern light or a small white light is carried aft for the tow to steer by. This must not be visible forward of the beam.

Regardless of the length of her tow, authorities agree that she should carry the optional 20-point white range light aft.

Red 32 Points

White 32 Points

The commercial fishing vessel at the left, when under way and engaged in fishing on inland waters, carries a red 32-point light above a white 32-point light. (See Table II, page 40, for various lights prescribed for fishing vessels under International Rules)

Vessel Towing Submerged Object

Sometimes, when a vessel has a submerged or partly submerged object (such as wreckage, etc.) in tow, it is not feasible to display lights on the object towed. In such cases, under the Pilot Rules, the towing vessel carries her regular red and green 10-point side lights, but in lieu of the regular white towing lights she displays four lights in a vertical position not less than three feet nor more than six feet apart, the upper and lower of which are white, and the two middle lights red, all of the same character as prescribed for regular towing lights.

Inland rules permit the option of carrying these four special lights as 20-point lights forward, with a 32-point white light aft; or as 32-point lights aft, with a 20-point white light forward. The object of the extra white light, forward or aft, as the case may be, is to provide a range.

The vessel above at work on a wreck shows a white 32-point light at bow and stern, and two red 32-point lights in a vertical line. Steamers, derrick boats, lighters and any other vessels so engaged are lighted in this manner.

Vessels Working on a Wreck

Under the Pilot Rules steamers, derrick boats, lighters, or other vessels made fast to a wreck which is on the bottom or partly submerged or drifting, show a white 32-point light from the bow and stern of each outside vessel, not less than 6 feet above the deck. In addition, two red 32-point lights are displayed in a vertical line not less than 3 feet nor more than 6 feet apart, and not less than 15 feet above the deck.

Dredges

Lights for dredges which are held in position by moorings or spuds are also provided for in the Pilot Rules. They show a white light at each corner not less than 6 feet above the deck. In addition, they show two red 32-point lights in a vertical line not less than 3 feet nor more than 6 feet apart, and not less than 15 feet above the deck.

When scows are moored alongside such dredges they show a white light on each outboard corner, not less than 6 feet above the deck.

Canal Boats and Barges

(See illustrations, pages 37 and 39)

Canal boats and barges when operating on inland waters are provided with particular types of lights which will indicate their character. It is important to note that the general regulations for these types of craft for inland waters do not apply on the Hudson River and adjacent waters and on Lake Champlain. The Great Lakes, the Red River of the North, and certain rivers emptying into the Gulf of Mexico are also excepted. By recent amendment of the Inland Rules, tows on the Gulf Intracoastal Waterway are lighted according to Western River rules.

Inland Waters

Under the general Inland Rules, when barges and canal boats are towing singly or in tandem astern of steam vessels, each boat in tow carries a green light on the starboard side and a red light on the port side and a white light on the stern, except

that the last vessel of the tow must carry two white lights on the stern, athwartship, horizontally arranged, showing through 32 points. The colored lights are 10-point.

When two or more boats are towed abreast, the colored lights are carried at the outer sides of the bows of the outside boats. Each of the outside boats in the last tier of a hawser tow carries a white light on the stern.

The white stern lights carried by barges and canal boats which show red and green side lights are 12-point lights, showing right aft and 6 points on each side.

When barges, canal boats or scows are towed alongside a steam vessel, when the deck, deckhouse, or cargo of the towed boat should obscure the side lights of the towing boat, then the colored side light of the towing boat is carried on the outer side of the barge or canal boat. If there is more than one barge, canal boat or scow abreast alongside, the colored lights are displayed from the outer side of the outside boats.

Scows carry a white light at each end of each scow, except that when they are massed in tiers, astern, two or more abreast, each of the outside scows carries a white light on its outer bow, and the outside scows in the last tier carry in addition a white light on the outer part of the stern. White lights for scows are 32-point.

When scows, barges or canal boats are pushed ahead of the tug, the head boat carries red and green 10-point side lights on the outer bows. If there are more than one abreast, these colored lights are shown from the outer bow of outside boats.

Nondescript vessels, not otherwise provided for, are lighted like scows.

Hudson River and Lake Champlain

The following special regulations apply to barges and canal boats in tow of steam vessels on the Hudson River, its tributaries from Troy to the boundary lines of New York Harbor off Sandy Hook, the East River, and Long Island Sound (and the waters entering thereon, and to the Atlantic Ocean) to and including Narragansett Bay, Rhode Island, and Tributaries, and Lake Champlain.

On these waters barges and canal boats towing singly astern of steam vessels carry a white light on the bow and a white light on the stern. When towing in tandem, close up, each boat carries a white light on its stern, and the first or hawser boat carries in addition a white light on its bow. When towing in tandem with intermediate hawser between the separate boats of the tow, each boat carries a white light on the bow and a white light on the stern, except that the last vessel in the tow carries two white lights on her stern, athwartship, horizontally arranged. When towed at a hawser, two or more abreast in one tier, each carries a white light on the stern and a white light on the bow of each of the outside boats. When in more than one tier, each boat carries a white light on its stern and the outside boats in the hawser or head tier carry in addition a white light on the bow.

The white lights specified above are 32-point lights showing all around the horizon.

Nondescript vessels known as scows, car floats, lighters, barges, or canal boats and vessels of similar type when towed alongside the steam vessel show a white light at the outboard corners of the tow.

Garbage scows navigating on the Hudson or East River or tributary waters when towed in tandem carry, instead of the white lights previously required, red and green side lights in addition to the white lights shown by an overtaken vessel.

Seagoing Barges

Seagoing barges towed in tandem carry red and green side lights on each barge. The last one in the string also carries two white lights horizontally arranged to show all around the horizon, while the others show small white steering lights at the stern. When towed alongside they carry the red or green lights on the proper side if their height obscures the tow boat's side light.

When seagoing barges come into the waters covered by the Hudson River rules they are not required to change their seagoing lights except that the last vessel of the tow must carry two white 32-point lights on her stern athwartship, horizontally arranged.

Note—Illustrations, tables and additional data on lights will be found on the following eleven pages.

LIGHTS FOR VARIOUS TYPES OF CRAFT—INLAND RULES

TABLE I

Note: Vessels lighted according to the International Rules are not required to change their lights when navigating waters subject to other Rules of the Road.

		Bow (Foremast or Forward)	Side	Range	Remarks or Additional Lights
1	MOTOR BOATS Class A—under 16' Class 1—16' to less than 26'	None	Combination red and green each color showing 10 pts.*	White 32 pt.[1] Visible 2 mi.	[1]Placed higher than combination *Visible 1 mi.
2	Class 2— 26' to less than 40'	White—20 pts. Visible 2 mi.	Red—10 pt. Green—10 pt. Screened so as not to show across bow.†	White 32 pt. ‡Visible 2 mi.	†Visible 1 mi. ‡Placed higher than bow light
3	Class 3— 40' to 65'	White—20 pts. Visible 2 mi.	Red—10 pt. Green—10 pt. Screened so as not to show across bow.†	White 32 pt. ‡Visible 2 mi.	†Visible 1 mi. ‡Placed higher than bow light

4 Motorboats and auxiliaries driven by *sail only,* as in illustration 4, show the colored side lights appropriate to their class, and are now required to carry a *fixed white 12 pt. stern light showing aft, visible 2 miles, carried as nearly as possible at the level of the side lights. Motorboats and auxiliaries, under *motor and sail,* are lighted as motorboats of their respective classes.

Note:—Under Motor Boat Act, motorboats of any class, may, optionally, carry lights prescribed by International Rules while operating on other than the high seas; on the high seas they must carry such lights. (See pages 32, 40 and 41.)

		Bow (Foremast or Forward)	Side	Range	Remarks or Additional Lights
5	Sailing vessel or vessel in tow (except barges, canal boats, scows, etc.)	None	Red—10 pt. Green—10 pt.	None	*12 pt. white showing aft, visible 2 mi., at level of side lights (See note bottom of page)
6	Steam or motor vessels over 65' in length (except those vessels falling in classifications noted below)	White 20 pt. Vis. 5 mi.	Red—10 pt. Green—10 pt. Vis. 2 mi. 36 in. screens	White—32 pt.[2]	[2]At least 15 feet higher than foremast light
7	Double-ended[3] ferry boat	White—32 pt.[4]	Red—10 pt. Green—10 pt. Vis. 2 mi. 36 in. screens	White—32 pt.[4]	[3]If not of double-ended type, carries same lights as inland steamer [4]On both pilot houses at same height. Special light amidships designates line
8	Steam pilot vessel on station[5] on pilotage duty and underway[6]	None	Red—10 pt. Green—10 pt.	None	White 32 pt. at masthead 8' above red 32 pt., each vis. 2 mi. Shows flares at intervals of not more than 15 min. [5]If not on station, carries same lights as other steam vessels [6]On station at anchor, side lights are extinguished
9	Fishing vessel underway engaged in commercial fishing[7]	None	None	None	Red 32 pt. 6' to 12' above white 32 pt. not more than 10' apart horizontally. White vis. 3 mi. red 2 mi. [7]If underway, but not fishing carries usual lights of her class except vessel under 10 gross tons may show combination red and green lantern to other vessels, in lieu of fixed side lights
10	Inland[10] tug without tow[8]	White 20 pt.	Red—10 pt. Green—10 pt.	White 32 pt.[9]	[8]Lighted same as ordinary inland steam vessel [9]At least 15' higher than foremast light [10]For lights of ocean-going tug on inland waters, see International Rules, Table II
11	Inland tug with tow alongside or pushed ahead	Two white 20 pt. vertically arranged, at least 3' apart *or* lights mentioned in fourth column	Red—10 pt. Green—10 pt. If side light is obstructed by vessel towed, light is transferred to outside of tow	Two white 32 pt. vertically arranged, at least 3' apart *or* foremast lights mentioned in second column	With 20-pt. towing lights forward, may carry 32-pt. white range light aft May carry small white light aft for tow to steer by, not visible forward of beam. With 32-pt. towing light aft, may carry 20-pt. white light forward. When pushing tow ahead and using 20 pt. white towing lights forward, carries two amber 12 pt. lights aft (vertically) not visible forward of beam
12	Inland[10] tug with tow astern	Three white 20 pt. vertically arranged, at least 3' apart *or* lights mentioned in fourth column	Red—10 pt. Green—10 pt.	Three white 32 pt. vertically arranged, at least 3' apart *or* foremast lights mentioned in second column	
13	Rowboat (under oars or sail)	None	None	None	White light shown on approach of another vessel
14	Vessels working on a wreck	White 32 pt.[11] (each outside vessel)	None	White 32 pt. stern light[11] (each outside vessel)	Two red 32 pt. in vertical line, 3' to 6' apart, at least 15' above decks [11]White lights at least 6' above decks

NOTE:—Small sailing vessels under way in bad weather, if they cannot keep their side lights fixed, may keep side lights at hand ready to show in time to avert collision. *In bad weather, small boats may, if necessary, show an electric torch or lighted lantern to overtaking vessels.

11 and 24

2

6

4

5

7

13 and 21

LEBER
FAGANS

LIGHTS FOR VARIOUS TYPES OF CRAFT—INLAND RULES
TABLE I (Continued)

		Bow (Foremast or Forward)	Side	Range	Remarks or Additional Lights
15	Dredge (held in position by moorings or spuds)	None	None	None	White 32 pt. each corner at least 6' above deck. Two red 32 pt. in vertical line 3' to 6' apart, at least 15' above deck. Scows moored alongside show white 32 pt. on each outboard corner, at least 6' above deck
16	Dredge (self-propelling suction type, underway, with suction on bottom)	White 20 pt.	Red—10 pt. Green—10 pt.	White 32 pt.	Two red 20 pt. under the white 20 pt. foremast light, 3' to 6' apart. Upper red light 4' to 6' below white light. At stern two red 4 pt. showing aft, in vertical line 4' to 6' apart
17	Vessel towing wreck	Carries lights same as described for inland tug with tow astern (see No. 12) except that in lieu of the regular 3 white towing lights she shows 4 lights vertically arranged, 3' to 6' apart, upper and lower white, two middle lights red, 20-point if carried on the foremast, 32-point if carried aft			
18	Naval and other U.S. Government vessels[12]	[12]	[12]	[12]Both the Inland and International Rules provide, in Article 13, that these rules shall not interfere with special rules made by the Government of any nation with respect to additional station and signal lights for two or more ships of war or for vessels sailing under convoy, or with exhibition of recognition signals adopted by ship owners, properly authorized by their respective Governments	
19	At anchor—vessel under 150' in length	One white 32 pt. forward, vis. 2 mi. where best seen	None	None	In specially designated anchorage areas, vessels under 65' need no anchor light.
20	At anchor—vessel 150' in length or over	One white 32 pt. forward at least 20' above hull.	None	None	One white 32 pt. aft, at least 15' lower than forward light. Vis. 2 mi.

LIGHTS FOR BARGES, CANAL BOATS AND SCOWS IN TOW ON INLAND WATERS
TABLE IA

Except Great Lakes, east to Montreal—Red River of the North—Mississippi River and tributaries above Huey P. Long Bridge—that part of the Atchafalaya River above its junction with the Plaquemine-Morgan City alternate waterway—Gulf Intracoastal Waterway and certain connecting waters, from the Rio Grande to Cape Sable—Hudson River (Troy to Sandy Hook)—East River and Long Island Sound—Narragansett Bay—Lake Champlain—and other tributaries.

		Bow	Side	Stern	Remarks or Additional Lights
21	One barge or canal boat towed astern of tug	None	Green—10 pt. Red—10 pt. Vis. 2 mi.	Two white 32 pt. athwartship horizontal. At least 5' apart and at least 4' above deckhouse	None
22	More than one barge or canal boat towed astern in tandem	None	Green—10 pt. Red—10 pt. Vis. 2 mi.	[13]One white—12 pt. Vis. 2 mi.	[13]Except last vessel of tow which carries instead, two 32 pt. white athwartship horizontal at least 5' apart and at least 4' above deckhouse
23	More than one barge or canal boat towed astern abreast (one tier)[14]	None	Green—10 pt. Red—10 pt. Vis. 2 mi. (carried at outer sides of bows of outside boats)	[14]One white—32 pt. on each outside boat.	[14]If more than one tier, white stern lights are placed on outside boats of last tier only
24	Barges, canal boats or scows towed alongside of tug	None	Colored side lights carried on outer side of outside barge if side lights of towing vessel are obstructed by barge	None	None
25	Scows towed singly or tandem	White 32 pt.	None	White 32 pt.	Lights to be carried at least 8' above surface of water. Vis. 5 mi.
26	Scows massed in tiers, two or more abreast, astern	White 32 pt. on outer side of all outside scows	None	White 32 pt. on outer side of outside scows in last tier only	Lights to be carried at least 8' above surface of water. Vis. 5 mi.

NOTE:—When barges, canal boats or scows are *pushed ahead* of the tug, head boat carries red 10-pt. and green 10-pt. side lights on outer bows, or if more than one abreast, they are shown from outer bow of outside boats.

12 and 22

10 PT. LT.
20 PT. LT.
32 PT. LT.

11 and 24

19

20

12 and 23

12 and 25

LIGHTS FOR VARIOUS TYPES OF CRAFT—INTERNATIONAL RULES

TABLE II

		Bow (Foremast or Forward)	Side	Range	Remarks or Additional Lights
27	Power - driven vessels less than 65 feet in length[17] NOTE—In illustration 27, opposite page, bow light, often rigged as shown on inland craft, should be higher to comply with 9' minimum requirement. Small power-driven boats may carry white light forward at height less than 9 feet but it must be carried not less than 3 feet above the side lights or combination red and green light.	White—20 pt. at least 9' above gunwale. Vis. 3 mi.	Red—10 pt. Green—10 pt. Vis. 1 mi. or combination red and green, each color showing 10 pts. At least 3' below foremast light	None	12-pt. white showing aft. [17]Instead of the lights called for here these vessels may optionally carry those lights intended for larger power-driven vessels (see item 31)
28	Vessels under oars or sails under 40 feet	None	Combination red and green, each color showing 10 pts. shown to approaching vessels	None	May optionally carry on top of foremast two 20-pt. lights, upper red, lower green, visible 2 mi., sufficiently separated for distinction
29	Rowboats, under oars or sails	None	None	None	Show electric torch or lighted lantern to prevent collision
30	Sailing vessel or vessel in tow	None	Red—10 pt. Green—10 pt. Vis. 2 mi. 36 in. screens	None	12 pt. white light showing aft. Vis. 2 mi.
31	Power - driven vessels (ocean liners, sea-going yachts, etc.)	White 20 pt. 20' to 40' above hull. Vis. 5 mi. Both (see "range") 20-pt. white lights must be in line with, and over, the keel.	Red—10 pt. Green—10 pt. Vis. 2 mi. 36 in. screens	White 20 pt. at least 15' higher than foremast light vis. 5 mi. Optional on vessels under 150 feet, and vessels towing. Horizontal distance between white lights at least 3 times the vertical distance	White 12 pt. showing astern. Vis. 2 miles. Carried at, or near, level of side lights
32	Pilot vessels (power-driven)	On station, under way, carry white 32-pt. masthead light not less than 20 ft. above the hull, and 8 feet below it a red 32-pt. light, both vis. 3 mi.			Show flare or intermittent 32-pt. white light at 10-minute intervals
33	Vessels engaged in trolling	[18]	[18]	[18]	[18]Show only lights appropriate for power-driven or sailing vessel
34	Vessels engaged in fishing but not trolling or trawling	None	When making way through the water same side lights as under items 27 or 28 above	Two vertical 32-pt. lights, upper red, lower white, 4' to 12' apart. Boats under 40' may show the white 3' under red and not less than 9' above gunwale; larger craft must show it at height above side lights of at least twice distance between vertical lights	12-pt. white stern light. If outlying gear extends more than 500', another 32-pt. white light 6' to 20' away from vertical lights toward outlying gear and neither higher than white light nor lower than side lights
35	Vessels engaged in trawling	None	Same as item 34	Same as item 34 except that upper of two vertical lights is green	Same as item 34
36	Vessels at anchor	32-pt. white light at or near bow, vis. 2 mi. On boats 150 feet or more, at least 20' above hull, vis. 3 mi.	None	None	At or near stern of vessels 150' or more, a 32-pt. white light at least 15' lower than forward one and vis. for 3 mi.
37	Vessel aground	Same as in item 36	None	None	Same as in item 36 plus two red vertical 32 pt., at least 6' apart. Vis. 2 mi.
38	Vessel not under control	None	None, unless under way with way on, when side and stern lights are carried	None	Two red 32 pt. in vertical line at least 6' apart. Vis. 2 mi.
39	Cable-laying vessel	Three 32-pt. in vertical line at least 6' apart. Upper and lower red; middle white. Vis. 2 mi.	None, unless under way with way on, when side and stern lights are carried	None	Same rules now apply to vessels laying or picking up a navigation mark, or engaged in surveying or underwater operations
40	Tug without tow	White 20 pt. 20' to 40' above hull. Vis. 5 mi.	Red—10 pt. Green—10 pt. Vis. 2 mi. 36 in. screens	White 20 pt.	White 12 pt. showing astern. Vis. 2mi.
41	Power-driven vessel with one vessel in tow, or more, if tow is less than 600' in length	Two white 20 pt. in vertical line not less than 6' apart	Red—10 pt. Green—10 pt. Vis. 2 mi. 36 in. screens	White 20 pt. optional	Must show either the fixed white 12-pt. stern light, or small white light aft for tow to steer by, not visible forward of beam
42	Power - driven vessel with tow over 600' in length	Three white 20 pt. in vertical line at least 6' apart. Third light may be not less than 14' above hull	Red—10 pt. Green—10 pt. Vis. 2 mi. 36 in. screens	White 20 pt. optional	Must show either the fixed white 12-pt. stern light, or small white light aft for tow to steer by, not visible forward of beam

CHARACTERISTICS OF LIGHTS
USED ON LIGHTHOUSES, LIGHTSHIPS, BUOYS AND OTHER AIDS TO NAVIGATION

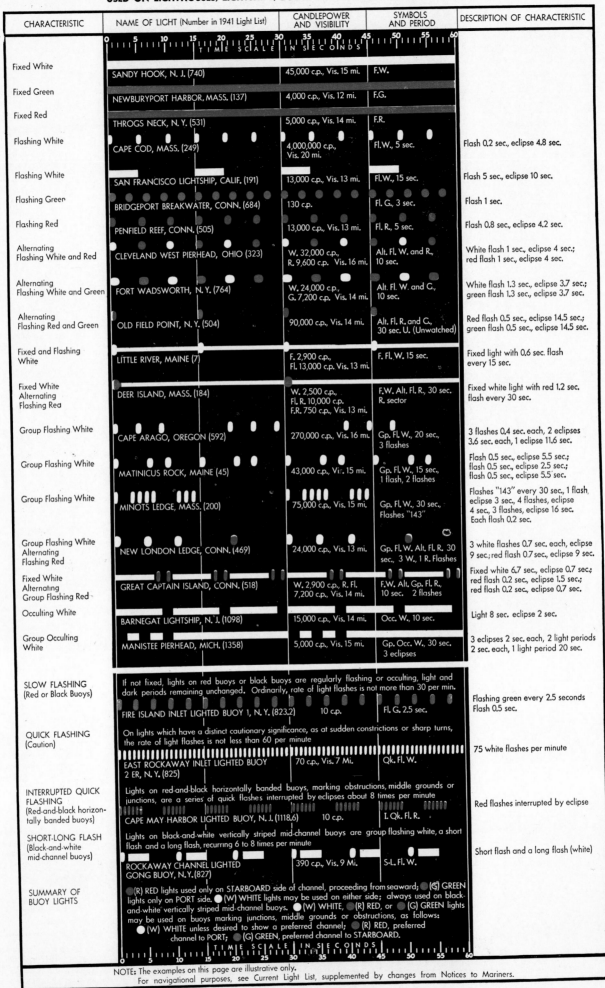

CHARACTERISTIC	NAME OF LIGHT (Number in 1941 Light List)	CANDLEPOWER AND VISIBILITY	SYMBOLS AND PERIOD	DESCRIPTION OF CHARACTERISTIC
	TIME SCALE IN SECONDS 0 5 10 15 20 25 30 35 40 45 50 55 60			
Fixed White	SANDY HOOK, N. J. (740)	45,000 c.p., Vis. 15 mi.	F.W.	
Fixed Green	NEWBURYPORT HARBOR, MASS. (137)	4,000 c.p., Vis. 12 mi.	F.G.	
Fixed Red	THROGS NECK, N. Y. (531)	5,000 c.p., Vis. 14 mi.	F.R.	
Flashing White	CAPE COD, MASS. (249)	4,000,000 c.p. Vis. 20 mi.	Fl.W., 5 sec.	Flash 0.2 sec., eclipse 4.8 sec.
Flashing White	SAN FRANCISCO LIGHTSHIP, CALIF. (191)	13,000 c.p., Vis. 13 mi.	Fl.W., 15 sec.	Flash 5 sec., eclipse 10 sec.
Flashing Green	BRIDGEPORT BREAKWATER, CONN. (684)	130 c.p.	Fl. G., 3 sec.	Flash 1 sec.
Flashing Red	PENFIELD REEF, CONN. (505)	13,000 c.p., Vis. 13 mi.	Fl. R., 5 sec.	Flash 0.8 sec., eclipse 4.2 sec.
Alternating Flashing White and Red	CLEVELAND WEST PIERHEAD, OHIO (323)	W. 32,000 c.p., R. 9,600 c.p. Vis. 16 mi.	Alt. Fl. W. and R., 10 sec.	White flash 1 sec., eclipse 4 sec.; red flash 1 sec., eclipse 4 sec.
Alternating Flashing White and Green	FORT WADSWORTH, N. Y. (764)	W. 24,000 c.p., G. 7,200 c.p. Vis. 14 mi.	Alt. Fl. W. and G., 10 sec.	White flash 1.3 sec., eclipse 3.7 sec.; green flash 1.3 sec., eclipse 3.7 sec.
Alternating Flashing Red and Green	OLD FIELD POINT, N. Y. (504)	90,000 c.p., Vis. 14 mi.	Alt. Fl. R. and G., 30 sec. U. (Unwatched)	Red flash 0.5 sec., eclipse 14.5 sec.; green flash 0.5 sec., eclipse 14.5 sec.
Fixed and Flashing White	LITTLE RIVER, MAINE (7)	F. 2,900 c.p., Fl. 13,000 c.p. Vis. 13 mi.	F. Fl. W. 15 sec.	Fixed light with 0.6 sec. flash every 15 sec.
Fixed White Alternating Flashing Red	DEER ISLAND, MASS. (184)	W. 2,500 c.p., Fl. R. 10,000 c.p. F.R. 750 c.p. Vis. 13 mi.	F.W. Alt. Fl. R., 30 sec. R. sector	Fixed white light with red 1.2 sec. flash every 30 sec.
Group Flashing White	CAPE ARAGO, OREGON (592)	270,000 c.p., Vis. 16 mi.	Gp. Fl. W., 20 sec., 3 flashes	3 flashes 0.4 sec. each, 2 eclipses 3.6 sec. each, 1 eclipse 11.6 sec.
Group Flashing White	MATINICUS ROCK, MAINE (45)	43,000 c.p., Vis. 15 mi.	Gp. Fl. W., 15 sec., 1 flash, 2 flashes	Flash 0.5 sec., eclipse 5.5 sec.; flash 0.5 sec., eclipse 2.5 sec.; flash 0.5 sec., eclipse 5.5 sec.
Group Flashing White	MINOTS LEDGE, MASS. (200)	75,000 c.p., Vis. 15 mi.	Gp. Fl. W., 30 sec., Flashes "143"	Flashes "143" every 30 sec., 1 flash, eclipse 3 sec., 4 flashes, eclipse 4 sec., 3 flashes, eclipse 16 sec. Each flash 0.2 sec.
Group Flashing White Alternating Flashing Red	NEW LONDON LEDGE, CONN. (469)	24,000 c.p., Vis. 13 mi.	Gp. Fl. W. Alt. Fl. R. 30 sec., 3 W., 1 R. Flashes	3 white flashes 0.7 sec. each, eclipse 9 sec.; red flash 0.7 sec., eclipse 9 sec.
Fixed White Alternating Group Flashing Red	GREAT CAPTAIN ISLAND, CONN. (518)	W. 2,900 c.p., R. Fl. 7,200 c.p., Vis. 14 mi.	F.W. Alt. Gp. Fl. R., 10 sec. 2 flashes	Fixed white 6.7 sec., eclipse 0.7 sec.; red flash 0.2 sec., eclipse 1.5 sec.; red flash 0.2 sec., eclipse 0.7 sec.
Occulting White	BARNEGAT LIGHTSHIP, N. J. (1098)	15,000 c.p., Vis. 14 mi.	Occ. W., 10 sec.	Light 8 sec. eclipse 2 sec.
Group Occulting White	MANISTEE PIERHEAD, MICH. (1358)	5,000 c.p., Vis. 15 mi.	Gp. Occ. W., 30 sec. 3 eclipses	3 eclipses 2 sec. each, 2 light periods 2 sec. each, 1 light period 20 sec.
SLOW FLASHING (Red or Black Buoys)	If not fixed, lights on red buoys or black buoys are regularly flashing or occulting, light and dark periods remaining unchanged. Ordinarily, rate of light flashes is not more than 30 per min. FIRE ISLAND INLET LIGHTED BUOY 1, N. Y. (823.2)	10 c.p.	Fl. G. 2.5 sec.	Flashing green every 2.5 seconds Flash 0.5 sec.
QUICK FLASHING (Caution)	On lights which have a distinct cautionary significance, as at sudden constrictions or sharp turns, the rate of light flashes is not less than 60 per minute EAST ROCKAWAY INLET LIGHTED BUOY 2 ER, N. Y. (825)	70 c.p., Vis. 7 Mi.	Qk. Fl. W.	75 white flashes per minute
INTERRUPTED QUICK FLASHING (Red-and-black horizontally banded buoys)	Lights on red-and-black horizontally banded buoys, marking obstructions, middle grounds or junctions, are a series of quick flashes interrupted by eclipses about 8 times per minute CAPE MAY HARBOR LIGHTED BUOY (1118.6)	10 c.p.	I. Qk. Fl. R.	Red flashes interrupted by eclipse
SHORT-LONG FLASH (Black-and-white mid-channel buoys)	Lights on black-and-white vertically striped mid-channel buoys are group flashing white, a short flash and a long flash, recurring 6 to 8 times per minute ROCKAWAY CHANNEL LIGHTED GONG BUOY, N. Y. (827)	390 c.p., Vis. 9 Mi.	S-L. Fl. W.	Short flash and a long flash (white)
SUMMARY OF BUOY LIGHTS	(R) RED lights used only on STARBOARD side of channel, proceeding from seaward; (G) GREEN lights only on PORT side. (W) WHITE lights may be used on either side; always used on black-and-white vertically striped mid-channel buoys. (W) WHITE, (R) RED, or (G) GREEN lights may be used on buoys marking junctions, middle grounds or obstructions, as follows: (W) WHITE unless desired to show a preferred channel; (R) RED, preferred channel to PORT; (G) GREEN, preferred channel to STARBOARD.			
	TIME SCALE IN SECONDS 0 5 10 15 20 25 30 35 40 45 50 55 60			

NOTE: The examples on this page are illustrative only.
For navigational purposes, see Current Light List, supplemented by changes from Notices to Mariners.

See also page 296(a)

Lights for Steam Vessels, Towing

THE International, Inland and Pilot rules are none too explicit as to the white lights displayed by a towing vessel.

Briefly, Article 3 of the Inland Rules states that a steam vessel towing shall, *in addition to her side lights, carry two* (when pushing ahead or towing alongside) *or three* (towing astern) *bright white lights in a vertical line,* one over the other. These may be placed forward, in which case they are to be 20-point, or they may be carried aft (except by seagoing vessels), in which case they are to be 32-point.

If Article 3 of the Inland Rules is read alone, without reference to other articles, it would appear that the 2 or 3 vertically arranged white lights, in addition to the red and green side lights, are all the lights to be carried by a towing vessel.

However, even though Article 3 is the only Article of the Inland Rules which refers specifically to lights for a towing vessel, yet as the Rules are enacted chiefly to prevent collisions, they should apply as a whole, rather than any specific part or article. Some authorities feel that lights provided by Article 3 alone do not provide sufficiently for the safety of navigation and therefore other Articles should be applied.

Article 2 of the Inland Rules, while it makes no mention of towing vessels, provides that a steam vessel under way shall carry red and green side lights, a white 20-point light forward and, for seagoing steam vessels, optionally a white 20-point light aft of the forward one. Article 2 (f) provides that (except on seagoing vessels and ferry boats) the after light shall be a 32-point range light.

Consequently, when Articles 2 and 3 are read together, range lights would be required of the steam vessel towing. On this theory, on the East Coast most tugs carry both masthead and after towing lights.

Other authorities contend that Article 3 is complete in itself, so that the towing vessel should display only side lights and towing lights, without the range. Thus, in most West Coast ports, the masthead light forward is seldom seen with after towing lights.

The Steamboat Inspection Service (functions of which are now discharged by the Coast Guard) for many years *required* the after range light with forward towing lights, and *permitted* the forward masthead light with after towing lights.

According to an opinion expressed in the Proceedings of the Merchant Marine Council of the U. S. Coast Guard, "it appears that range lights may be carried by steam vessels towing in inland waters . . . but that to make such lights compulsory an amendment to Rule 3, Inland Rules, would be necessary."

If *both* the forward and aft range lights specified by Article 2 were added to the white towing lights specified by Article 3, one of the added white lights would be useless. Therefore, it appears that a practical solution would be that if the towing lights are carried forward, one of the towing lights is in lieu of the forward light required by Article 2 (a) and all are 20-point lights. If carried aft, one of the lights is in lieu of the range light required by Article 2 (f) and all are 32-point lights. Thus a range is established.

Where the Rules provide that the after range light *may* be carried, it is recommended that it should be.

As to whether two or three towing lights should be carried, the Inland and International Rules differ slightly. Under the latter, in order to carry three lights, the total length of the tow must be over 600 feet.

In the case of the Inland Rules when towing alongside or pushing ahead, only two towing lights are required regardless of the number of vessels towed. When towing astern, three towing lights are used regardless of the length of the tow or the number of vessels towed.

Of course in addition to the two or three towing lights and the forward light (if the towing lights are 32-point lights carried aft) and the after range light (if the towing lights are 20-point lights carried forward) the towing vessel must carry 10-point red and green side lights. In addition, the towing vessel may carry a small white light aft * for the towed vessels to steer by, but such light shall not show forward of the beam. On the high seas, she might, optionally, carry a fixed white 12-point stern light.

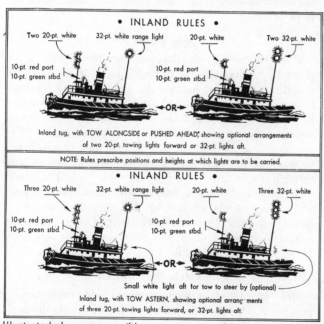

• INLAND RULES •

Two 20-pt. white — 32-pt. white range light — 20-pt. white — Two 32-pt. white

10-pt. red port
10-pt. green stbd.

10-pt. red port
10-pt. green stbd.

←OR→

Inland tug, with TOW ALONGSIDE or PUSHED AHEAD, showing optional arrangements of two 20-pt. towing lights forward or 32-pt. lights aft.

NOTE: Rules prescribe positions and heights at which lights are to be carried.

• INLAND RULES •

Three 20-pt. white — 32-pt. white range light — 20-pt. white — Three 32-pt. white

10-pt. red port
10-pt. green stbd.

10-pt. red port
10-pt. green stbd.

←OR→

Small white light aft for tow to steer by (optional)

Inland tug, with TOW ASTERN, showing optional arrangements of three 20-pt. towing lights forward, or 32-pt. lights aft.

Illustrated above are possible arrangements of lights on a towing vessel, according to Inland Rules,* showing optional 20-point or 32-point towing lights, with range lights, in each case. Inland Rules are not explicit, so that in some localities the single white 32-point range light aft or the single 20-point white foremast light is not carried. It is usual to carry the towing lights aft.

The seagoing tug, under International Rules, carries her 20-point white towing lights forward. Red and green side lights are required; the 20-point white range light aft is optional. White stern light may be fixed 12-point or small towing light

• INTERNATIONAL RULES •

Two 20-pt. white — 20-pt. white range light (optional)

10-pt. red port
10-pt. green stbd.

Small white light aft for tow to steer by or fixed 12-pt. white stern light

Seagoing tug with one vessel in tow, or more than one, if tow does not exceed 600 feet in length.

NOTE: INLAND Rules permit the seagoing vessel to continue to carry her 20-pt. optional white range light, instead of the 32-pt. after range light prescribed by the Inland Rules.

• INTERNATIONAL RULES •

Three 20-pt. white — 20-pt. white range light (optional)

10-pt. red port
10-pt. green stbd.

Small white light aft for tow to steer by or fixed 12-pt. white stern light

Seagoing tug when tow exceeds 600 feet in length.

* NOTE:—*Under an amendment to Inland Rules, effective Aug. 14, 1958, when tow is pushed ahead and 20-pt. white towing lights are carried forward, the tug must carry two 12-pt. amber lights aft in vertical line, showing aft. In illustration, top left, they would be carried below the optional 32-pt. white range light. Amber lights are not required when 32-pt. white towing lights are carried aft. The small white light aft for tow to steer by, which formerly could be carried regardless of position of towing lights, may now be carried only when towing lights are carried forward.*

International Rules of the Road Revised

First major changes in rules for the high seas since 1948,
drafted in 1960, became effective September 1, 1965

BACK in the 1800's the United States first codified a set of rules for navigation upon the high seas, giving the force of law to what had been largely custom. These rules have been revised and expanded since then, of course, the most recent change taking effect September 1, 1965.

The "high seas" with which the International Rules are concerned should be distinguished from the "high seas" which limit a nation's sovereignty. The latter begins at least a marine league (3 nautical miles) out from the coast, and often much farther than that. The former begins all over the place, now touching the coast, now a mile or so off shore. To the U.S. Coast Guard goes the chore of designating these rules-of-the-road boundaries; a call to your District Office will tell you just where the "inland seas" end and the "high seas" begin. So will U.S. Coast and Geodetic Survey charts. By determining this information you will know with what set of Rules to comply. In an accident "the liability for damages is upon the ship or ships whose fault caused the injury. But where . . . a ship at the time of a collision is in actual violation of a statutory rule intended to prevent collision" there is a presumption it is at fault. That from the United States Supreme Court.

The new revisions have not changed the provision which permits a skipper to deviate from the rules, but first be sure you have a clear, compelling reason for doing so. Changes that have taken place—nothing drastic insofar as recreational boating is concerned—reflect updating in concept—the use of radar is treated—and wording. Gross tonnage descriptions, for instance, used to designate classifications of boats, have been discarded in favor of boat length. Rule 20 probably makes the most significant change in substance, removing some of the sailboat's priority over motorboats in certain circumstances. The following is a breakdown of the more important changes in the International Rules.

Lights, Day Signals

Rule 1 (scope and definitions) adds a provision that running lights may be shown, besides between sunset and sunrise, "in all other circumstances when it is deemed necessary." Too, the definition of "whistle" has been changed from "whistle or siren" to "any appliance capable of producing" the prescribed blasts.

Rule 2 (running lights) has dropped "bright" from all "bright white light" references. Inasmuch as minimum visibility requirements are set out for required lights the use of "bright" is unnecessary.

Rule 3 (towing or pushing) has been modified but the changes, affecting largely long tows, will have little application to pleasure boats.

Rule 4 (seaplanes, minesweepers, etc.) has little application to pleasure boats.

Rule 5 (sailboats) adds that sailboats under sail *may* carry two vertical lights "on the top of the foremast," the upper light red, the lower one green, and "sufficiently separated so as to be clearly distinguished."

Rule 6 (bad weather) makes no substantial change.

Rule 7 (substitute lights for small vessels) changes "40 tons" to "65 feet" and "20 tons" to "40 feet" and adds that vessels under power and less than 40 feet in overall length may carry their forward white light "not less than 3 feet above the sidelights or the combined lantern . . ." Other changes affect small boats being towed or pushed.

Rule 8 (pilot vessels) has little application to pleasure boats.

Rule 9 (fishing vessels) will exclude vessels trolling lines from the category of a vessel engaged in fishing.

Rule 10 (sternlights) no longer requires that the sternlight be on the same level as the sidelights; the designation now reads simply that the 12-point white light be carried "at her stern."

Rule 11 (anchored or aground) will permit vessels smaller than 150 feet to show, at their option, a second 32-point white light at or near the stern but "not less than 15 feet lower than the forward light."

Rule 12 (other lights) remains substantially unchanged.

Rule 13 (war ships) has no application to pleasure boats.

Rule 14 (under both sail and power) reverses the direction in which the black cone must be displayed during the day on vessels proceeding under power and sail simultaneously; the cone must now point down instead of up.

Fog Signals

Rule 15 (sound signals) provides the signals to be given by trolling vessels during conditions of restricted visibility—fog, mist, heavy rain, etc. These are identical to signals required of motorboats and sailboats under way in conditions of limited visibility, namely: power-driven vessels under way must sound "a prolonged blast" (4 to 6 seconds) at 2-minute or shorter intervals; power-driven vessels "under way, but stopped and making no way through the water," must sound two prolonged blasts separated by a 1-second interval every 2 minutes or less; and sailing vessels, at intervals of 1 minute or less, must sound one blast (1 second duration) if on a starboard tack, two blasts if on a port tack, and three successive blasts if running with the wind abaft their beam.

Caution in Thick Weather

Rule 16 (speed in thick weather) adds the following provision: "A power-driven vessel which detects the presence of another vessel forward of her beam before hearing her fog signal or sighting her visually may take early and substantial action to avoid a close quarters situation but, if this cannot be avoided, she shall, so far as the circumstances of the case admit, stop her engines in proper time to avoid collision and then navigate with caution until danger of collision is over."

Under a section subheaded "Annex to Rules" the following new statutes have been enacted, all bearing heavily on Rule 16:

(Continued on page 46)

ANY POWER-DRIVEN VESSEL

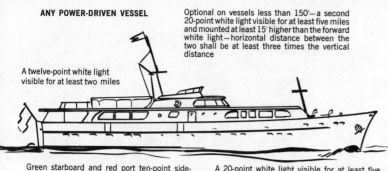

Optional on vessels less than 150'—a second 20-point white light visible for at least five miles and mounted at least 15' higher than the forward white light—horizontal distance between the two shall be at least three times the vertical distance

A twelve-point white light visible for at least two miles

Green starboard and red port ten-point sidelights visible for at least two miles from dead ahead to two points abaft the beam

A 20-point white light visible for at least five miles and mounted not less than 20' above the hull but nor more than 40' above the hull

POWER-DRIVEN VESSELS LESS THAN 65'—OPTION 1

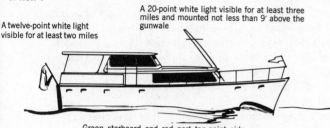

A 20-point white light visible for at least three miles and mounted not less than 9' above the gunwale

A twelve-point white light visible for at least two miles

Green starboard and red port ten-point sidelights visible for at least one mile from dead ahead to two points abaft the beam

ANY VESSEL UNDER SAIL—OPTION 1

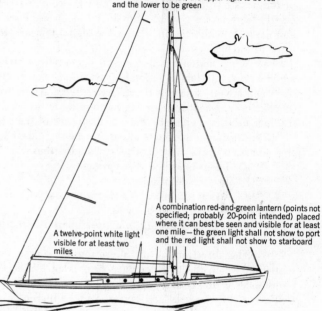

Optional—two 20-point lights sufficiently separated as to be clearly distinguished and visible for at least two miles, the upper light to be red and the lower to be green

A twelve-point white light visible for at least two miles

A combination red-and-green lantern (points not specified; probably 20-point intended) placed where it can best be seen and visible for at least one mile—the green light shall not show to port and the red light shall not show to starboard

POWER-DRIVEN VESSELS LESS THAN 65'—OPTION 2

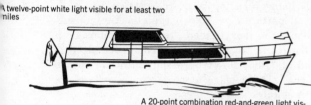

A 20-point white light visible for at least three miles and mounted not less than 9' above the gunwale

A twelve-point white light visible for at least two miles

A 20-point combination red-and-green light visible for at least one mile from dead ahead to two points abaft the beam and mounted not less than 3' below the 20-point white light

POWER-DRIVEN VESSELS LESS THAN 40'—OPTION 1

A 20-point white light visible for at least three miles and permitted to be mounted less than 9' above the gunwale but not less than 3' above the combination light

A twelve-point white light visible for at least two miles

A 20-point combination red-and-green bow light visible for at least one mile from dead ahead to two points abaft the beam

ANY VESSEL UNDER SAIL—OPTION 2

Optional—two 20-point lights sufficiently separated as to be clearly distinguished and visible for at least two miles, the upper light to be red and the lower light to be green

POWER-DRIVEN VESSELS LESS THAN 40'—OPTION 2

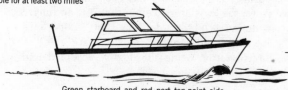

A 20-point white light visible for at least three miles and permitted to be mounted less than 9' above the gunwale but not less than 3' above the sidelight

A twelve-point white light visible for at least two miles

Green starboard and red port ten-point sidelights visible for at least one mile from dead ahead to two points abaft the beam

A twelve-point white light visible for at least two miles

Green starboard and red port ten-point sidelights visible for at least two miles from dead ahead to two points abaft the beam

"(1) Assumptions made on scanty information may be dangerous and should be avoided.

"(2) A vessel navigating with the aid of radar in restricted visibility must . . . go at a moderate speed. Information obtained from the use of radar is one of the circumstances to be taken into account when determining moderate speed. In this regard it must be recognized that small vessels, small icebergs and similar floating objects may not be detected by radar. Radar indications of one or more vessels in the vicinity may mean that "moderate speed" should be slower than a mariner without radar might consider moderate in the circumstances.

"(3) When navigating in restricted visibility the radar range and bearing alone do not constitute ascertainment of the position of the other vessel under [Rule 16] sufficiently to relieve a vessel of the duty to stop her engines and navigate with caution when a fog signal is heard forward of the beam.

"(4) When action has been taken under [Rule 16] to avoid a close quarters situation, it is essential to make sure that such action is having the desired effect. Alterations of course or speed or both are matters as to which the mariner must be guided by the circumstances of the case.

"(5) Alteration of course alone may be the most effective action to avoid close quarters provided that—

"(a) There is sufficient sea room.

"(b) It is made in good time.

"(c) It is substantial. A succession of small alterations of course should be avoided.

"(d) It does not result in a close quarters situation with other vessels.

"(6) The direction of an alteration of course is a matter in which the mariner must be guided by the circumstances of the case. An alteration to starboard, particularly when vessels are approaching apparently on opposite or nearly opposite courses, is generally preferable to an alteration to port.

"(7) An alteration of speed, either alone or in conjunction with an alteration of course, should be substantial. A number of small alterations of speed should be avoided.

"(8) If a close quarters situation is imminent, the most prudent action may be to take all way off the vessel."

Sailboats, Right of Way

Rule 17 (sailboats approaching each other) has been simplified by removing references to tacks to determine right of way. It now reads:

"(a) When two sailing vessels are approaching one another, so as to involve risk of collision, one of them shall keep out of the way of the other as follows—

"(i) When each has the wind on a different side, the vessel which has the wind on the port side shall keep out of the way of the other.

"(ii) When both have the wind on the same side, the vessel which is to windward shall keep out of the way of the vessel which is to leeward.

"(b) For the purposes of this section the windward side shall be deemed to be the side opposite to that on which the mainsail is carried or, in the case of a square-rigged vessel, the side opposite to that on which the largest fore-and-aft sail is carried."

The old and often harsh provision that burdened the sailboat with the wind aft has been dropped.

Rule 18 (power-driven vessels meeting end on) makes no substantial change.

Rule 19 (power-driven vessels crossing) makes no substantial change.

When Sailboat Must Give Way

Rule 20 (power and sail meeting) has this new provision: "This section [giving the sailboat right of way over the motorboat when the two are on a collision course] shall not give to a sailing vessel the right to hamper, in a narrow channel, the safe passage of a power-driven vessel which can navigate only inside such channel." *

Rule 21 (whatever necessary to avert collision) remains substantially unchanged.

Rule 22 (burdened vessels) adds to the duty of a burdened boat—that is, a boat not having right of way—the necessity to "take positive early action to comply with" the obligation to keep out of the way of the privileged vessel and, if practical, to avoid crossing ahead of her.

Rule 23 (duty to slow, stop or reverse) makes no substantial change.

Rule 24 (overtaking) makes no substantial change.

In Narrow Channels

Rule 25 (in narrow channels) newly provides that in a narrow channel a power-driven vessel smaller than 65 feet "shall not hamper the safe passage of a vessel which can navigate only inside such channel." *

Rule 26 (right of way of fishing vessels) makes no substantial change affecting pleasure boats.

Rule 27 (departure from rules), while making no substantive change, is now headed "Special circumstances requiring departure from rules to avoid immediate danger" instead of "Departure from requirements in special circumstances." This change more pointedly reflects the intent of the statute.

Optional Visual Signal

Rule 28 (signals to indicate course) adds a provision for an optional visual signal to be used with the prescribed sound signals. It reads: "Any whistle signal . . . may be further indicated by a visual signal consisting of a white light visible all round [sic] the horizon at a distance of at least 5 miles, and so devised that it will operate simultaneously and in conjunction with the whistle-sounding mechanism and remain lighted and visible during the same perod as the sound signal."

Rule 29 (additional precautions) is substantially unchanged.

Rule 30 (authority for local rules) is substantially unchanged.

Distress Signals

Rule 31 (distress signals) adds to the list of recognized distress signals a hand flare (red), an orange-smoke signal, and the repeated raising and lowering of one's outstretched arms.

Rule 32 (orders to helmsmen) has been omitted from the revised rules, the legislators feeling that it is no longer necessary to define "right rudder" or "left rudder" as meaning "put the vessel's rudder to starboard" or "to port," the interpretation being thoroughly accepted and practiced where the terms are used.

* By Public Law 89–764, effective 2/3/67, a similar rule applies under Inland, Western River and Great Lakes Rules.

CHAPTER III
Rules of the Road, Right of Way, Whistle Signals

(See also pages 44-46, 60, Chapter IV, pages 61-78, and Special Western River Rules, page 438.)

ALL of us on land have had the experience upon walking down the street of meeting another pedestrian, turning to the right and having him turn to his left, then turning to the left and having him turn to his right and finally bumping him. To the pedestrian on the sidewalk, such action and such a collision is comical but between two boats on the water, it is serious, yet boats often behave like human beings and do that very thing.

Besides, in the case of pedestrians on the sidewalk and even in the case of automobiles in the street, it is a fairly simple matter to keep clear of such approaching danger as both pedestrians and motor cars follow fairly well defined paths or channels and by keeping to their own right, the danger of collision is eliminated. However, on water it is a far different matter. Except in a very limited number of cases, there are no narrow paths or channels to follow. Boats as a rule have a wide expanse of water on which to navigate, with their paths or courses constantly crossing those courses of many other craft which may be in the immediate vicinity. Therefore, the caution which must be observed on the water, even if the traffic may be much more limited than it is on land, is far more serious and important than on the sidewalks and streets.

To prevent such things and collisions, very carefully considered rules have been laid down so that the duty of the skipper in charge of any boat under any meeting, overtaking or crossing situation is pretty definitely prescribed. The rules which prescribe such duties and actions are of three general classes: First, there are the International Rules of the Road adopted at conventions among maritime nations. The second type is the Inland Rules of the Road. These rules are enacted by the Congress of the United States and are law. The Inland Rules authorize the Commandant, U. S. Coast Guard, to issue regulations based upon the Inland Rules and these regulations are issued in what is commonly known as the Pilot Rules.

The Pilot Rules are not necessarily laws but are more in the form of interpretations by the proper officials and regulations issued to make the Inland Rules of the Road effective. Such regulations can be upset in proper court proceedings and the courts have not hesitated to upset certain of the pilot rules as being unwarranted by the Inland Rules passed by the Congress of the United States.

Piloting

Piloting in the usual sense of the word might be defined as the art of conducting a boat or vessel through the channels and harbors and along the coasts, where landmarks and aids to navigation may be properly identified and are available for fixing one's position and where the depth of the water and the dangers to navigation are such as to require a constant watch to be kept upon the boat's course and frequent changes to be made therein.

Piloting is a most important part of navigation and perhaps the part requiring the most experience and best judgment. An error in position on the high seas may be subsequently corrected without serious result but an error in position while piloting usually results in disaster. Therefore, the boatman should make every effort to be a good pilot.

Requisites for a Good Pilot

It will be seen that a study of piloting embraces a knowledge of a wide range of subjects which are allied to the proper handling of one's boat. This includes a knowledge of the Rules of the Road, rights of way, whistle signals, lights for the various types of craft, fog signals, both under the Inland and International Rules and a study of where these are applicable, whether on the high seas, Great Lakes or inland waterways.

Other important subjects which should be included in the study of piloting are a knowledge of the buoyage and lighthouse system of the United States, the necessary equipment to have aboard, including both that equipment required by law and for one's own safety, the compass and the chart and the use of each, piloting instruments, and a knowledge of tides and currents, as well as many other lesser allied subjects. Good seamanship and particularly a knowledge of the regulations of safety at sea are most important. Weather sense and the fundamentals of ground tackle and anchoring are important requisites.

Only One Way to Learn Boat Handling

There is only one way for one to learn how to handle his boat correctly. That way is by practice alone. No amount of printed matter or rules can accomplish this. However, it is a fact that a knowledge of the basic principles which compose successful boat handling goes a long way, especially in conjunction with an equal amount of experience.

Perfection cannot be obtained unless the skipper becomes familiar with his duties upon the water. He must practise them. He should practise them upon every occasion whether his fellow boatman does or not.

Duty of Man at Wheel

It should be remembered as the first principle to learn, that the man at the wheel while he is on watch has but one duty in life—the safe guidance of his ship. Everything else should be absolutely out of his mind until his boat is brought to her destination or the command is turned over to another person.

A Captain or person in charge is absolute authority over the guidance of his ship as well as being responsible not only for her safety but for the safety of all on board. Under ordinary conditions the judgment, instructions and commands of the Captain must be complied with and may not be questioned.

Safety First

The Golden Rule for small boat handling is Safety First and Keep to the Right. Indecision of action or those actions having an obscure motive may mislead the other vessel and confusion may result. Time should never be considered wasted if safety is at stake. When there are alternate methods of avoiding danger, the safer of the two should be selected.

Rules of Road Applicable to All Types of Vessels

The rules of the road are applicable to all types of vessels being used afloat. Therefore, they apply with equal force whether a boat has headway or sternway. They apply to craft which are adrift or not under control. They apply to boats driven by motor or sail, to ferry boats, pilot boats, tugs and tows, to sailing vessels and, to some extent, to a vessel propelled by hand power and the current.

When Is a Vessel Under Way?

A boat is considered under way when she is not at anchor, aground or made fast to the shore. Under all other conditions except these three, a boat is considered under way and the Rules of the Road are applicable.

Where Inland and International Rules Prevail

The Inland Rules are those applicable to the navigation of all vessels on all harbors, rivers and inland waters of the United States, including coastal waters inshore of the lines established by Congress or the Coast Guard as dividing the inland waters from the high seas. Upon the high seas, that is, waters outside of these established boundary lines, the International Rules apply. The inland rules also apply (generally speaking) at all buoyed entrances from seaward to bays, sounds, rivers etc. for which specific lines are not prescribed by the Pilot Rules, inshore of a line drawn approximately parallel with the general trend of the shore, drawn through the outermost buoy or other aid to navigation of any system of aids. The Pilot Rules list in detail the lines of demarcation which have been established between the inland waters and high seas.

Generally speaking, waters contained within any one state are not federal waters but are under the jurisdiction of the State. For example, Lake Champlain located on the boundary between the states of New York and Vermont is Federal water and the Inland Rules of the Road prevail. However, Lake George, wholly within the State of New York, and Lake Hopatcong, wholly within the State of New Jersey, are not Federal waterways. The former is controlled by the navigation laws of the State of New York while Lake Hopatcong is under the jurisdiction of the State of New Jersey.

As a rule the state navigation laws are similar to those of the Federal government; in certain respects the laws of the states may differ considerably from those of other states and with the Inland Rules.

The International Rules prevail on waters outside the inland waters of the United States. In many instances the Inland and International Rules are identical. In others they differ. (On pages 60 and 178 will be found tables giving comparisons of the International and Inland Rules. See also Chapter IV.)

Purpose of the Rules
(See Figs. 1 and 7)

The fundamental purpose of the Rules of the Road is to prevent collision. Risk of collision can often be ascertained by watching the compass bearing of an approaching vessel. "If the bearing does not appreciably change," the Rules dictate, "such risk should be deemed to exist." Boatmen are cautioned, however, against presuming the absence of any risk when there is an appreciable change in bearing. Such a presumption, it has been held (112 F. 161), might under some circumstances be unwarranted. Each situation must be scrutinized on its own merits.

The phrase "risk of collision" has been judicially defined as *not* meaning "immediate danger" but rather "chance," "peril," "hazard" or simply "danger of collision"; this court ruled (199 F. 299) that there is risk of collision whenever it is not *clearly* safe to go on.

The failure of a vessel to take special precautions during the constant-bearing approach of an oncoming vessel constitutes negligence. Furthermore, as the United States Supreme Court has reiterated on several occasions (see for example 73 U.S. 225 and 76 U.S. 146), those precautions required by the Rules to be taken when risk of collision exists must be taken in time to be effective against such risk or they will furnish no defense to the charge of negligence.

When there is doubt about the risk of collision, vessels should slow or stop or reverse, whichever is the safest course.

Boats Coming Out of Slip
(See Fig. 2)

In the case of boats coming out of a slip or moving from docks or piers the Rules of the Road passing signals do not apply until such vessels are entirely clear of the slip or pier. On the other hand, passing craft may not block the entrance to or exit from any pier or slip.

As a boat leaves her pier or slip, she must sound one long blast on her whistle (this signal is not considered a passing whistle signal). As soon as a boat is clear of such obstruction, the ordinary Rules of the Road passing signals and rights of way apply. *See River Rules, p. 440v*

Overtaking
(See Figs. 3, 10 and 11)

A boat is considered to be overtaking another boat when she is approaching the course of (and is gaining on) the leading boat from more than two points abaft the beam of the leading boat. In such a case, the privileges rest with the leading boat, the overtaking vessel having the duty not to pass until it can be done safely.

Even though a sailing vessel, which under almost all other conditions has the right of way over motor vessels, may be overtaking a motor vessel, such sailing vessel has no rights. In all instances, an overtaking vessel must keep clear of an overtaken vessel.

In Case of Accident
(See Fig. 4)

In case of collision or other accident between vessels, it is the duty of the person in charge of each vessel to stand by the other vessel until he has ascertained that she is in no need of further assistance. He must render to the other vessel, her master, crew and passengers such assistance as may be practicable and necessary so far as he can do so without danger to his own vessel or persons aboard. He must also give the name of his own vessel and her port when requested. (See also p. 22.)

When boats are involved in a marine casualty or accident either to hull or machinery, causing property damage in excess of $100, or when any persons are injured or any lives lost, immediate notice thereof must be forwarded to the nearest Local or District Officer of the United States Coast Guard or to Coast Guard Headquarters, Washington, D. C., unless an accident report is required to be filed with the state.

Fig. 1. Above: Rules of the Road, intended to prevent collision, set out measures to be taken by vessels in various situations whenever risk of collision exists, a condition which must be individually determined in each situation. If the tug and the ships here are on a collision course the tug, approaching from within the ship's "danger zone," becomes the privileged vessel with right-of-way over the ship. If the speed of the ship is such as to insure that she will clearly pass the tug without danger of collision, she may hold her course and speed, using extreme caution to keep clear and avoid damage caused by wake or wave

Fig. 2. Above: Boats coming out of a slip must exercise particular caution. They should sound one long blast on their whistle as a warning. They may not sound passing whistle signals or exercise any rights of way until entirely clear of the slip or pier. Passing boats must not block or prevent exit or entrance from or to slips or piers

Fig. 4. Above: In case of collision or other serious accident between boats, it is the duty of each to stand by and give any necessary assistance. Boats shall not leave the scene of an accident until no further assistance to crew, passengers or boat is necessary. In assisting, one is not expected to endanger his own craft or any of the persons aboard.

Fig. 3. Below: A vessel overtaking another is deemed a burdened vessel until free and clear of the overtaken vessel. The overtaking vessel may ask permission to pass to starboard by sounding one blast of her whistle or to port by sounding two blasts. If the leading vessel thinks it is expedient for the overtaking vessel to pass, she will answer with the same number of whistle signals. However, should the leading boat think it not expedient for the overtaking boat to pass, she should sound the danger signal of four or more blasts. The following boat must then stay astern until given permission to pass by exchange of proper signals

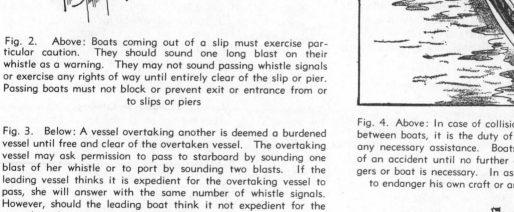

SEE TABLE OF
WHISTLE SIGNALS, PAGE 60
AND RIVER RULES, PAGE 438

Boats on Parallel Courses
(In Same Direction)
(See Fig. 5)

Neither the Inland Rules nor the Pilot Rules have anything to say about two boats on parallel courses heading in the same direction, since no danger of collision is involved and no whistle signals are necessary.

Figure 5 illustrates a situation which might conceivably develop, as for example if two vessels were to leave adjacent docks at the same time. If their courses are parallel or if the courses are diverging, even slightly, there is no necessity to exchange signals.

However, their courses may have been laid so that they gradually converge, resulting in a crossing situation. On crossing courses, the vessel which has the other on her own starboard side must keep out of the way of the other. Thus the vessel on the starboard side may exercise her right of way, signal with one blast, and expect to receive a one-blast reply indicating that the boat to port will slow down and pass astern. An exchange of two blasts would indicate that the boat to starboard (the privileged vessel) intends to slow down and go astern of the other.

Boats on Opposite Parallel Courses

When two boats are on parallel courses heading in opposite directions but each course so far to the starboard of the other that no change of course is necessary in order to allow the boats to clear, two blasts of the whistle should then be given by one boat, which should then be acknowledged by two blasts from the other boat. Each boat will hold its course and speed and should pass clear of the other, starboard side to starboard side. This is the only meeting or crossing situation where it is allowable to use a two-whistle signal in passing.

Rights of Way of Fishing Vessels
(See Fig. 6)

Boats of all types while underway must keep out of the way of boats fishing, including fishing boats at anchor or with nets, lines and trawls. No vessel is permitted to engage in fishing in a channel or fairway nor to obstruct navigation in any way. The boats underway should give all boats fishing a wide berth in order not to disturb them by their wash.

Duties of Privileged and Burdened Vessels
(See Figs. 8, 13 and 17)

In the eyes of the Rules of the Road, that is, the laws to prevent collision between two vessels, one of the two vessels must necessarily be considered to have the right of way. This vessel is called the privileged vessel. The other, which is the vessel which must give way, is known as the burdened vessel. In all of the rules, no matter to what phase of boating they refer, the privileged vessel must hold her course and speed. The burdened vessel must adopt all reasonable means to keep out of the way of the privileged vessel.

When a Departure from Rules Is Allowable

The precautions to prevent collision which are spelled out by the Rules of the Road are mandatory and in all probability competent to safely meet every risk of collision the recreational boatman is apt to encounter. Still, because of the impossibility of legislators to foresee every conceivable danger pattern, the Rules of the Road include what is termed the General Prudential Rule which allows a departure from ordinary Rules of the Road procedures when it is "necessary in order to avoid immediate danger." This latitude should not be resorted to lightly; there must be a clear, pressing need to depart from the ordinary procedures.

Also affording some discretion is the rule that "When in consequence of thick weather or other causes, the vessel which has the right of way finds herself so close that a collision cannot be avoided by the action of the giving way vessel alone, she also shall take such action as will best aid to avert collision."

Both Vessels May Be Responsible

By the above two rules, to a greater or lesser degree, the responsibility for an accident is up to the masters of both boats. If for any reason an accident cannot be prevented by one of two boats, namely the boat which is supposed to give way, then the other boat must do all in her power to prevent a collision. In the case of motor boats which are, or at least should be, able to stop within almost their own length as well as to maneuver readily there is little to relieve them of some of the responsibility for an accident, especially when a commercial or vessel of large size is the other party to the situation.

The Danger Zone
(See Figs. 9 and 15)

The area around one's boat located clockwise from dead ahead to two points abaft the starboard beam might well be called the Danger Zone. It is this area which should give the skipper the greatest concern. Other boats located in this Danger Zone which are approaching the course of your boat have the right of way over your boat. Consequently your boat must keep clear of boats in the Danger Zone.

Boats located outside of your Danger Zone which are approaching your course must give way to you. You have the right of way over all such boats.

The fact that the Danger Zone is located in the area from dead ahead to two points abaft the starboard beam is an excellent reason to locate the steering wheel on the starboard side of one's boat instead of on the port side if the wheel has to be located on one side or the other. With the steering being done where the best and an unobstructed view of the Danger Zone can be obtained, it works out for the greatest safety. Should the steering wheel be located to port, there would be danger that deck obstructions, persons on deck, etc., would hide, to a greater or lesser extent, this important Danger Zone.

At night, boats in your Danger Zone show you their red side light—the danger signal for you to give way. Boats outside the Danger Zone show their green side light—the clear signal to you that they must give way.

Meeting Obliquely or Crossing
(See Figs. 9, 10, 11 and 17)

If the courses of two motor vessels are such that the two are approaching each other at right angles or obliquely, so as to involve risk of collision (other than overtaking) the motor vessel which has the other on her own port side shall be the privileged vessel and shall hold her course and speed. The motor vessel which has the other on her own starboard side is the burdened vessel and shall keep out of the way of the other vessel, using whatever means are necessary to do so. They exchange one short blast of the whistle. Though the privileged vessel should blow first, either may.

Visual Signal

An amendment to the pilot rules for boats operating on Western Rivers requires that, after January 1, 1945, whistle signals must be further indicated by a visual signal consisting of an amber colored light visible one mile all around the horizon. The light must operate simultaneously and in conjunction with the whistle, and be visible during the same period as the whistle blast.

This rule does not apply to Class A and Class 1 motor boats. Class 2 and Class 3 motor boats are also exempt from this regulation if not engaged in trade or commerce.

Fig. 5. Above: In the illustration above it would appear that the ferry and tug were on parallel courses, a situation concerning which neither Inland Rules nor Pilot Rules have anything to say, since no danger of collision exists, and no whistle signals are required. If the courses in reality are diverging, there is still no risk of collision and no need for whistle signals. However, if the courses are actually converging, we have a crossing situation in which the tug (in the ferry's danger zone) has the right of way. Exchanging one blast of the whistle, the ferry would properly slow down and pass astern of the tug. If two blasts were exchanged, the tug would slow down and go astern of the ferry

Fig. 6. Below: The rights of fishing craft must be respected by other craft underway. Boats have a right to fish in all waters other than in channels and fairways and while they are not obstructing navigation. Passing craft should give fishermen a wide berth

Fig. 8. Left: As the motor vessel has the tug on her port bow, and the motor vessel is in the tug's danger zone, the motor vessel technically has the right of way and it would ordinarily be the tug's duty to keep clear. To exercise her rights as the privileged vessel, the motor vessel would sound one blast, hold her course and speed and pass ahead of the tug. However, even though the rules give no special rights to the tug, the motor vessel is so much easier to maneuver that good judgment in this case would dictate that she sound two blasts, slow down, and pass astern of the tow

Fig. 7. Below: Give whistle signals only when danger of collision exists. In the situation illustrated, both boats would pass clear, without either changing her course or speed; signals are unnecessary

Fig. 9. Right: The danger zone of the boat in the center of the illustration is shown by the shaded section. Therefore, she has the right of way over all other vessels except the one in the shaded zone which has the right of way over the boat in the center. Thus the boat at the lower right may pass ahead of the center craft. As will be seen in the illustration, the boat in the center has the right of way over the one which is crossing her stern and also over the small boat which is overtaking

When in Doubt as to Whether One or Two Blasts Should Be Given

As to the action called for by one or two blasts of the whistle, there is a simple rule to help you remember whether you are to pass to port or starboard, ahead or astern of the craft initiating the signal. The rule will also hold good when you wish to indicate to the other craft what action you intend to take, and the course you wish to follow, providing you are the right-of-way (privileged) boat.

Keeping in mind the two sides of the boat—that is, port and starboard—we note that "port" has one syllable and "starboard" two. If you simply remember that the word of *one* syllable is always associated with *one* blast of the whistle and the word of *two* syllables with *two* blasts of the whistle, you will have no difficulty in giving and obeying the passing whistle signals. If the oncoming boat gives you one blast of her whistle, it is your duty to answer with one blast of the whistle, provided all is well. The exchange of one blast is an indication that the boats must pass port side to port side. If two whistles are given and answered, associate this signal with the word of two syllables, and the boats will then pass starboard side to starboard side. This rule holds good in all instances of meeting and crossing.

Cross Signals

Motor vessels are forbidden to use what is known as cross signals; that is, answering one whistle with two or answering two whistles with one. In cases where a whistle is correct according to the rules but with which signal it is deemed injudicious to comply, instead of answering with a cross signal, one should at once sound the danger signal of four or more short and rapid blasts. In such a case, both boats should be stopped or reversed and neither should proceed again until the proper whistles have been exchanged.

Method of Giving Signals

The method of giving the various sound signals under different conditions of navigation is fully described in the rules. Whether the signal must be given by whistle, horn or bell is important. Promptness in giving signals is also important. The navigator of any boat, big or small, whether it be the smallest motor boat or the largest ocean liner, who fails to promptly give and answer signals, may be subject to a penalty.

Differences Between International, Inland and Great Lakes Rules
(For a complete analysis, see pages 60-78)

The International Rules prescribe that passing whistle signals should be given only when (and always when) there is a change of course if any other vessel is in sight. The signals must be accompanied by a change of course. Limits of risk of collision are the visibility limits in fair or thick weather.

The Inland or Pilot Rules prescribe that in fog, mist, falling snow, or heavy rainstorms when vessels *are not in sight of each other,* fog signals and not passing whistle signals must be given. Passing signals are to be given when proposing how to pass and are to be given whether or not accompanied by a change of course, and always when risk of collision is involved.

The Great Lakes rules prescribe that passing whistle signals shall be given in all weathers regardless of visibility and are to be sounded whether or not accompanied by a change of course and are to be given when risk of collision is involved.

The signals of one short blast and two short blasts have practically identical significance in the International, Inland and Great Lakes Rules. Three short blasts indicate that "my engines are going astern" under International and Inland Rules, yet three short blasts are recognized officially by the Great Lakes Rules only as a steamer fog signal when underway.

The signal of four or more short blasts (five or more on the Great Lakes) is recognized as a danger signal in the Inland Rules. In general, this danger signal is used to indicate that the other vessel's course or intention is not understood, is an alarm signal in emergency, to indicate to an overtaking vessel that the overtaken vessel considers it unsafe to pass as requested and to indicate that conditions prevent immediate compliance with the signals. On the high seas, five or more short and rapid blasts may be used when a power-driven vessel, required to hold her course and speed, is in doubt that another vessel is taking sufficient action to avert collision. A whistle signal of one long blast is a signal specified in the Inland and Great Lakes Rules to be given by a vessel navigating a channel where visibility is less than ½ mile because of a bend in the channel and high banks and to be given by a vessel leaving the dock or berth. In both of these instances, this one long blast is a warning (not passing) signal and should be answered by approaching vessels with the same signal. A recently added International Rule requires a power-driven vessel, when within ½ mile of a bend, to give a "prolonged" (4- to 6-second) blast.

When Crossing and Overtaking Rules Conflict
(See Fig. 11)

When one vessel is both overtaking and crossing another, the overtaking rule prevails. Once an overtaking vessel, always an overtaking vessel, until free and clear.

A crossing vessel which has come up from more than two points abaft the beam of the leading vessel must keep clear even though she is on the starboard side of the leading boat. She is not free from this obligation even after she draws ahead on the beam and bow of the other vessel until she is free and clear of her.

Sailing Vessels Have Right of Way Over Motor Craft
(See Fig. 12)

A sailing vessel has the right of way over a motor craft in all situations except when the sailing vessel is overtaking the motor vessel, or when in a "narrow channel" exercising right of way would hamper "the safe passage of a power-driven vessel which can navigate only inside such channel." A sailing vessel is not required to stand in stays, tack or wear or jibe to allow another vessel to pass. A sailing vessel must observe the difficulties under which the burdened vessel may be and give due attention thereto. A motor vessel must observe any condition which would prevent a sailing vessel from finishing its tack and must be prepared for a sailing vessel accidentally missing stays, jibing, etc. A sailing vessel must not endanger a motor vessel by tacking suddenly in a narrow channel or fairway, directly in the path of the motor vessel, without due warning, when an alternative action may be safely taken by the sailing vessel.

Whistle Signals as Salutes

Yachts should never exchange salutes by means of whistle signals. Commercial craft often salute by the whistle; those on the east coast by three long blasts and on the Great Lakes by three long followed by two short.

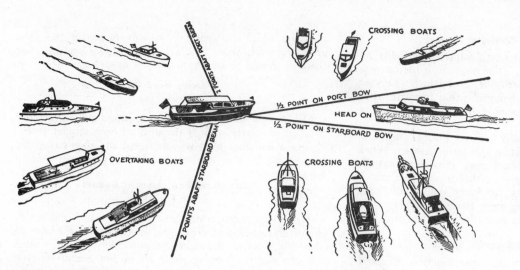

CROSSING BOATS

2 POINTS ABAFT PORT BEAM

½ POINT ON PORT BOW

HEAD ON

½ POINT ON STARBOARD BOW

OVERTAKING BOATS

2 POINTS ABAFT STARBOARD BEAM

CROSSING BOATS

Fig. 11. Below: A boat approaching the course of another from a position of more than two points abaft the beam of the leading boat is considered to be an overtaking vessel, and remains such until free and clear of the overtaken vessel

Fig. 10. Above: The three situations—meeting head on, crossing and overtaking. Boats are considered meeting head on when their masts seem to be in line or nearly in line. They are overtaking when one boat is approaching the course of another from a point more than two points abaft the beam of the leading boat or when at night her side lights, if correctly placed, cannot be seen. In all other cases where the courses intersect either at right angles or obliquely, the situation is said to be crossing. Only those boats shown in the lower right-hand corner of the illustration should hold their course and speed relative to the boat in the center. All boats in the other positions must alter their progress to keep clear

Fig. 12. Right: A sailing vessel, that is, one propelled by wind power alone without the assistance of any kind of motor or mechanical power, has the right of way over every form of motor or steam vessel in all situations except when overtaking or when in a narrow channel subject to International Rules and exercising a right of way would hamper a power-driven vessel which can safely navigate only within that channel. Sailing vessels under power are deemed motor vessels

Fig. 13. Left: The privileged vessel, that is, one having the right of way, must hold her course and speed. It is not permissible fo. the right of way vessel in crossing ahead or attempting to cross ahead, to steer a crooked course. The burdened vessel, that is, the one not having the right of way, must keep clear by any efficient means

Caution When Piloting at Night

Take care to see that your boat's colored side lights are not showing across the bow. The position of the lamp as a whole, which must necessarily be several inches at least from the inboard screen, and the reflection from the after side of the light-box tend to make the lights show across the bow.

The white range lights, if properly placed, are useful in determining the position of an approaching vessel. When the lights are directly over each other, it is clear that the vessel is approaching dead head-on, but when her course is changed even in the slightest the range lights will "open out," the lower one drawing away from the upper in the same direction in which the boat's bow is changing.

Rules Prohibit Excessive Speed

The rules of the road make little mention of speed, other than when a steam vessel becomes a burdened one, in which case it must slacken speed or stop or reverse if necessary to keep out of the way of the privileged vessel, and when navigating in fog, mist, snow or heavy rainstorms, in which case it must go at a "moderate speed, having careful regard to the existing circumstances." Despite the absence of an express Rule for speed during other times, good seamanship and the general laws of negligence require that the speed of a boat be reasonable for the time, place and surrounding conditions. Court rulings have upheld these statements even though the statutes are silent on these points. Excessive speed is a fundamental cause of collision or capsize. A speed reasonable in open waters, free from traffic, would be unreasonable in crowded waters, harbors, narrow channels and particularly where yachts and motor boats are anchored. Excessive speed near any other vessel should be avoided. A vessel is responsible for injury caused by her wash or suction.

Generally speaking, the speed of a boat should not be greater than would enable her to change seasonably from headway to sternway should danger present itself.

The Motor Boat Act of 1940 provides that anyone who operates any vessel in a reckless or negligent manner shall be guilty of a misdemeanor, punishable by a fine not exceeding $2,000, or by imprisonment for not over one year, or both.

Port Helm and Starboard Helm

The orders of "port your helm" or "starboard your helm" are confusing and should never be used.

The helm is neither the boat's steering wheel nor rudder. It more closely refers to the tiller which was the method of steering boats in days gone by. When the tiller was moved to port the boat's bow swung to starboard and when the tiller was put over to starboard the boat's bow went to port.

Most steering wheels on modern craft are rigged so that the boat's bow swings in the same direction that the steering wheel moves. One occasionally finds, however, steering wheels rigged so that the boat's bow swings in the opposite direction from that in which the steering wheel is turned. In the former case, when an order is received to "port your helm" or "port helm" the wheel must be moved to "starboard" but when a steering wheel is rigged to turn in the opposite direction from the rudder, then to "port your helm," you must turn your wheel to port, etc. Avoid these ambiguous orders.

Right Rudder and Left Rudder

The expressions "port helm" and "starboard helm" have been replaced by "right rudder" and "left rudder." "Right rudder" always means to turn the steering wheel in that direction which will swing the bow of the boat to the right or to the starboard. Similarly "left rudder" means that the bow should be swung to the left or to port.

Meeting Head On
(See Fig. 14)

When two motor vessels are approaching each other head-on or nearly so, it is the duty of each skipper to exchange a short one-blast whistle signal and then swing the bow of his boat to starboard and thus pass port side to port side.

Points on the Bow, Beam or Quarter
(See Fig. 15)

Directions and bearings between dead ahead and astern are given names, first depending upon whether they are on the boat's starboard (right) or port (left) hand. Then the 180 degrees between dead ahead and astern on each side are divided into 16 equal parts (11¼ degrees each) called points. The first point to the right of dead ahead is known as 1 point on the starboard bow; then 2 points on the starboard bow; 3 points on the starboard bow. The 45 degree direction is called 4 points or broad on the starboard bow. The next point aft is called 3 points forward of the starboard beam, then 2 points forward of the starboard beam; one point forward of the starboard beam. Then on the starboard beam.

Working further aft the points become, in order, 1 point abaft the starboard beam; 2 points abaft the starboard beam; 3 points abaft the starboard beam; then 4 points or broad on the starboard quarter. The next point aft is known as 3 points on the starboard quarter; 2 points on the starboard quarter; 1 point on the starboard quarter, and astern.

The similar points on the port side have corresponding names.

Rights of Way of Sailing Craft
(See Fig. 16)

Sailing vessels do not indicate their course or intended action in passing either another sailing vessel or a motor vessel by any whistle signal. The rights of way between two sailing vessels are determined solely by the direction of the wind in reference to the boats' sailing directions at the time. A sailing vessel running free must give way to a close-hauled sailing vessel. When both sailing vessels are close-hauled, the one on the port tack (having the wind over her port bow) must keep clear of the sailing vessel on the starboard tack. In cases where both sailing vessels are running free but with the wind on different sides, that one which has the wind on her port side must keep clear. If both are running free with the wind on the same side, the boat to windward shall keep clear of the vessel which is to leeward. A sailing vessel having the wind aft shall keep out of the way of other sailing craft.

The International Rules have revised (effective September 1965) and in so doing simplified the steering and sailing rules of sailing vessels approaching one another. They now read:

"(i) When each has the wind on a different side, the vessel which has the wind on the port side shall keep out of the way of the other.

"(ii) When both have the wind on the same side, the vessel which is to windward shall keep out of the way of the vessel which is to leeward."

For these purposes the International Rules define the "windward side" as "the side opposite to that on which the mainsail is carried or, in the case of a square-rigged vessel, the side opposite to that on which the largest fore-and-aft sail is carried."

Fig. 14. Above: When two vessels are meeting head on, it is the duty of the skipper of each boat to give one blast on the whistle, and swing his bow to starboard, boats passing port side to port side

Fig. 15. Below: Diagram illustrating the proper way in which directions and bearings are named on shipboard. The unit is the "point" which is 1/32 of a complete circle or 1/16 of the angular distance from dead ahead to dead astern. Each point has a distinct name. These names are dependent upon the angular distance and the particular direction from the bow, the beam and the stern of the boat. The word starboard or port is always used with the name of the point to indicate to which particular side of the boat it refers. The black zone of the illustration below, from dead ahead to two points abaft the starboard beam, is known as the danger zone. Approaching boats in this zone have the right of way over you and you must keep clear. Boats approaching your course from outside your danger zone must give way and keep clear of you

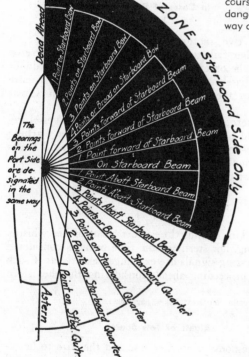

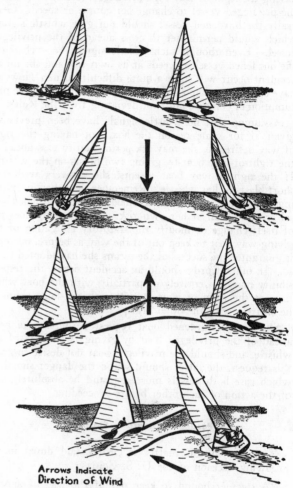

Arrows Indicate Direction of Wind

Fig. 16. Above: The rights of way between two strictly sailing vessels is determined by the direction of the wind in reference to the boats' sailing directions. A sailing vessel which is running free must keep out of the way of the one which is close-hauled. A sailing vessel which is close-hauled on the port tack must keep out of the way of a vessel which is close-hauled on the starboard tack. If both sailing vessels are running free, with the wind on different sides, the one which has the wind on the port side shall keep out of the way of the other. If both sailing vessels are running free, with the wind on the same side, the vessel which is to windward shall keep out of the way of the vessel which is to leeward. A sailing vessel having the wind aft shall keep out of the way of other sailing craft. The International Rules no longer use references to "tack" to determine rights of way

Fig. 17. Right: In the crossing situation, the boat having another on her own port bow has the right of way; she is the privileged vessel. Her action is to give one blast on her whistle, maintain her course and speed and pass ahead of the other boat. The other craft, the burdened vessel, having the privileged vessel in her danger zone, must take any timely action to keep clear. The privileged vessel should signal first, but either may

Crossing Ahead of Privileged Vessel

Every vessel which is directed by the rules to keep out of the way of another vessel must, if the circumstances of the case admit, avoid crossing ahead of the other.

This is probably the rule which is most violated. It should be remembered that under no ordinary circumstances is it permissible for the vessel not having the right of way (the burdened vessel) to pass ahead of the vessel having the right of way (the privileged vessel) or to cause the privileged vessel to change her course or speed. Generally the burdened vessel should not give whistle signals which would permit her to cross ahead of the privileged vessel. Even though such whistle signals be exchanged, the burdened vessel proceeds at its own risk and should an accident occur will have a quite difficult burden (lawyers have called it an impossible burden) of overcoming the presumption of being at fault for deviating from the Rules.

Assuming that no whistle signals have been previously given, if for some reason the boat not having the right of way desires to, she may ask permission to pass ahead of the right-of-way boat by giving two blasts on the whistle. If the right-of-way boat assents, she answers with two short blasts of her whistle. Remember, however, in granting this permission it is understood that the burdened vessel crosses ahead at her own risk. Such a reply does not of itself change or modify the statutory obligation of the giving-way boat to keep out of the way as before, nor does it guarantee the success of the means she has adopted to do so. In other words, should an accident occur, the responsibility may rest entirely or partially with the boat which has not the right of way, even though the fault seems to lie entirely with the other craft.

Should the burdened boat request permission to cross ahead of the privileged boat by giving two blasts of her whistle, and should the privileged boat not desire to grant this request, the latter should sound the danger signal, in which case both vessels must stop and be absolutely sure of the action of each other before proceeding.

Passing Starboard to Starboard

The law in this matter is clearly laid down in the following decision of the U. S. Courts:

"A steamer bound to keep out of the way of another steamer by going to the right, has no right, when under no stress of circumstances, but merely for her own convenience, to give the other steamer a signal of two whistles, imparting that she will go to the left unless she can do so safely by her own navigation, without aid from the other, and without requiring the other steamer to change her course or speed. Otherwise she would be imposing upon the latter steamer more or less of a burden and the duty of keeping out of the way which by statute is imposed on herself. When two blasts are given under such circumstances, the steamer bound to keep out of the way thereby says in effect to the other: 'I can keep out of your way by going ahead of you to the left and will do so if you do nothing to thwart me; do you assent?' A reply of two whistles to this means nothing more than an assent to this course, at the risk of the vessel proposing it. Such a reply does not of itself change or modify the statutory obligation of the former to keep out of the way as before, nor does it guarantee the success of the means she has adopted to do so."

(See "The City of Hartford," Federal Reporter 23, page 650.)

Indicate Your Course
(See Fig. 18)

In addition to the sounding of the proper whistle signal, it is essential that the helmsman of each boat should indicate what his course is to be by the swinging of the bow of his boat sharply to port or starboard, as the case may be, for a moment, as in many instances the whistle signals of a small boat cannot be heard at a great distance. When the helmsman of an approaching boat sees its bow swing to one side or the other, he immediately recognizes what the action of this boat is to be, even if he has failed to hear or to understand the whistle signals.

When Does Danger of Collision Exist?

Danger of collision may be deemed to exist when the bearing between two approaching vessels does not change. If there is no change of bearings as the boats proceed on their course and at a uniform speed, a collision will ultimately result. If the bearings change materially they will pass clear.

Whether there is a change of bearing may be easily determined by noting a range or bearing on some part of the boat's structure, such as a stanchion, or from the boat's compass to the other craft.

In Cases of Doubt
(See Fig. 19)

Whenever two motor vessels are approaching each other and either fails to understand the signals, course or intentions of the other for any reason, the vessel in doubt should immediately give the danger signal of four or more short blasts of the whistle (five or more on the Great Lakes).

Under International Rules, a power-driven vessel required to hold her course and speed may give a warning signal of five or more short (1-second) and rapid blasts if she is in doubt that another vessel is taking sufficient action to avert collision.

Boats Backing
(See Fig. 21)

A boat backing sounds three short blasts of her whistle. While backing, her stern for the time being is considered her bow. Passing signals are exchanged exactly as if such a boat were proceeding ahead, considering that her stern is her bow.

Note: See exception on Great Lakes, page 60.

Rights of Tow Boats

A tug is responsible for her tow and they are to be regarded as one vessel. A tug with a tow has no special privileges under the rules. Moreover, as such an outfit is unwieldy, a tug has increased responsibilities and is not excused from obeying all the rules applicable to it. Steam and motor vessels, upon passing a tow when there is a chance that their wash or waves will cause damage, must slow down. (*But see also caption, Fig. 8.*)

Rights of Way of Ferry Boats

While there is no express provision of the Rules giving special privileges to ferry boats, the courts have repeatedly ruled that ferry boats are entitled to a reasonable freedom of entrance to and exit from their slips. The same is true in regard to other boats using slips or piers. Vessels should avoid passing close to piers, wharves, etc.

Fig. 19. Below: When a power-driven boat fails to understand the course or intention of an approaching vessel, the danger signal (four or more short and rapid blasts) should be given immediately. When the danger signal is blown, it is the duty of every vessel to stop immediately and not proceed until the situation has cleared itself or until the proper whistle signals have been given, answered and understood. In no case should cross signals be given, that is, answering one signal by two and vice versa. If such signals are given, it should be followed by the danger signal and both boats should stop

(See p. 56 for danger signals on the high seas.)

Fig. 18. Above: It is very essential, especially in the case of small motor craft, that they indicate what their course is to be, not only by giving the correct whistle signal, but by swinging the boat's bow sharply in one direction as an indication of what course and action they intend to take. The chances are that this action will be much more readily recognized and understood than if reliance is placed solely on whistle signals for the proper execution of the law

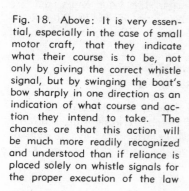

LESTER FAGANS

Fig. 21. Right: In case of a boat backing, she should sound three blasts on her whistle. When the vessel has sternway on, her stern must be considered as her bow for the time being, and crossing and passing whistle signals given accordingly. In the situation illustrated, the boat at the right is backing and therefore her stern is considered her bow, putting her in the danger zone of the boat at the left. Consequently the backing boat has the right of way and may back across the bow of the other boat. Her proper passing signal would be one blast, this to be answered by one blast by the other boat

Fig. 20. Left: The Inland Rules provide that the duty to exhibit lights aboard any "vessel of war of the United States or a Coast Guard vessel" may in the discretion of the Secretary of the Navy be suspended. Give them a wide berth

Definition of Motor Boat

Under the Motor Boat Act of 1940, which superseded the Motorboat Act of 1910, any boat propelled by machinery and not more than 65 feet in length, with the exception of tugs propelled by steam, is designated as a motor boat. Motor craft of a greater length fall into the class of steamers.

For purposes of the Rules of the Road every vessel propelled by machinery is a "steam vessel" regardless of whether the engine burns gasoline, diesel fuel or coal. Evidencing a more updated terminology, the International Rules label any vessel propelled by machinery a "power-driven vessel."

Operating Under Both Sail and Power in Day Time

(See Fig. 23)

For a boat (motor) having a length of more than 65 feet, a special day mark is specified when the boat is under both sail and power. For a motorboat (less than 65 feet in length) there is no such provision. It will be realized that there are times when it is difficult if not impossible to determine from even a short distance even in the daytime whether a boat which has the outward appearance of a sailing vessel is using power in addition to her sails. Should she be a sailing craft her rights will generally be superior to those of every other type of craft but should she be an auxiliary, with motor running, she will have no more rights than if she had no sails.

The situation just described may lead to confusing and hence dangerous complications. A certain action may be planned on the assumption that the oncoming vessel is strictly a sailing vessel. Should she be an auxiliary (with motor running and sails up), which would call for an entirely different response, her identity might not be discovered until the execution of the action based upon the first assumption was well under way. In the meantime, the crew of the auxiliary, inasmuch as there is no reason for doubt to exist in their minds as to the proper action of the other (motor) vessel as well as their own, may have changed their own course (probably correctly) in a manner contrary to the expectations of those on the vessel carrying no sails. Both boats might give way in the same direction at the same instant, presumably to allow the (assumed) right-of-way boat to hold her course and speed. A collision under such circumstances is almost inevitable.

A reasonable precaution where in the daytime one of two approaching boats is operating under power alone and the other under both sail and power, is for the latter to be prompt with her passing whistle signals and take whatever action is possible in order to make her status known. Strictly speaking, neither of such boats has the right of way if only the types of the boats are considered. The relative position of the boats must decide which is to hold her course and speed and which is to keep clear. Both craft are motor boats under the law. However, the crew of the vessel carrying sail in addition to her power must be careful to take no action which will confuse the other craft.

Under Sail and Power by Night

(See Fig. 22)

Figure 22 illustrates a situation in which a sailboat and a motorboat are on crossing courses at night. The sail-

boat—*if her engine is not running*—has the right of way and the motorboat must keep clear.

The motorboat knows the other is under sail only, as the latter does not show a white light forward. If the sailboat were to start her engine and run under both sail and power, the rules require her to show the lights of a motorboat (that is, the white bow and stern lights, in addition to her colored side lights). With motor running, whether her sail were up or not, she would be subject to rules for motor vessels, and would become the burdened vessel in Figure 22, giving way to the motorboat approaching in her danger zone.

"Steam Vessel" Defined

The Pilot Rules all provide that every vessel under steam, whether under sail or not, is to be considered a steam vessel. These Pilot Rules define the term "steam vessel" as including any vessel propelled by machinery. Motorboats under sail and power thus fall within the definition of steam vessels in the Pilot Rules and are therefore subject to all the provisions of the Pilot Rules except as the Pilot Rules are modified by other statutes.

When Not to Give Passing Signals

(See Fig. 24)

Passing signals provided by Inland Rules are never to be given except when the vessels are in sight of each other and the course of each can be determined by the sight of the vessel itself or at night by seeing the running lights. In fog, mist, falling snow or heavy rainstorms, when vessels cannot see each other, fog signals only must be given. Whistle signals are not to be given unless danger of collision exists. If there is doubt or uncertainty as to whether danger of collision does exist, then it should be assumed to exist. Whistle signals between a motor boat and sailing vessel or between two sailing vessels should never be given.

Meeting in Winding Channel

(See Fig. 25)

When two boats are approaching each other in a winding channel, they must be considered as meeting head on and not as meeting obliquely or crossing. Each boat should keep to the starboard side of the channel. Good judgment provides that when two boats are to meet at a narrow bend in the channel, the one which is navigating against the current shall stop until the boat navigating with the current has safely passed.

Rights of Way of Row Boats

Row boats should take into consideration their ability to maneuver in tight spaces more readily than motor or sailing craft, and when they can keep out of the way of larger craft by a few strokes they should do so. When row boats are in distress or where there is any uncertainty of their movements, a motor or sailing vessel should keep clear of them. Small boats capable of being propelled by oars should be equipped with them even when their usual power is either sail or motor.

Fig. 22. Left: A boat under sail only has the right of way over a motorboat except when overtaking, and in certain "narrow channel" situations. Until the Motor Boat Act was changed by an amendment in 1956, confusing and dangerous situations often developed when the sailboat was operating at night as an auxiliary, with sail up and engine running. Now, however, the auxiliary with engine running is lighted as a motorboat of her class. Consequently other craft can tell from her lights whether she is under sail only and hence has right of way, or whether she has her engine running and therefore is to be treated as a motorboat

Fig. 23. Right: In the daytime, a vessel under both sail and power is considered a motor vessel and must observe only the rules of the road of motor vessels. The addition of sail power does not change her status over that of the motor vessel in any way. Confusion is likely to result unless the boat under both sail and power is very careful in her navigation and takes the necessary action to make it clear to other vessels that she is following the rules of a motor vessel. This is often not apparent from distant observation unless caution is observed

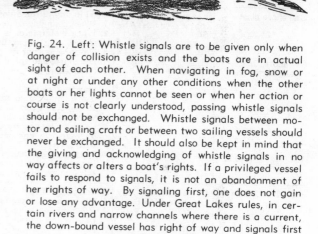

Fig. 24. Left: Whistle signals are to be given only when danger of collision exists and the boats are in actual sight of each other. When navigating in fog, snow or at night or under any other conditions when the other boats or her lights cannot be seen or when her action or course is not clearly understood, passing whistle signals should not be exchanged. Whistle signals between motor and sailing craft or between two sailing vessels should never be exchanged. It should also be kept in mind that the giving and acknowledging of whistle signals in no way affects or alters a boat's rights. If a privileged vessel fails to respond to signals, it is not an abandonment of her rights of way. By signaling first, one does not gain or lose any advantage. Under Great Lakes rules, in certain rivers and narrow channels where there is a current, the down-bound vessel has right of way and signals first to indicate the side she will take

Fig. 25. Right: Boats approaching a bend in a river or channel where other approaching boats cannot be clearly seen, should give one long blast on their whistle. Ordinarily they should keep to the starboard side of the channel and should not depart from this rule either to escape unfavorable currents or to gain any tidal advantage. Boats approaching each other around such a bend should be considered as meeting head on and not as meeting obliquely or crossing. Passing signals are given accordingly. It has been ruled that passing signals should be given as soon as vessels sight each other

See Special River Rules, p. 438.

PASSING WHISTLE SIGNALS

How International, Inland and Great Lakes Rules Differ

	INTERNATIONAL RULES	INLAND OR PILOT RULES	GREAT LAKES RULES
WHEN passing signals are given	Only when (and always when) there is a change of course if any other vessel is in sight. Signals must be accompanied by change of helm. Limits of risk of collision are the visibility limits in fair weather, and the visibility limit also prevails in thick weather.	Prescribe that in fog, mist, falling snow, or heavy rain storms when vessels cannot see each other, *fog* signals only must be given. Passing signals to be given when proposing how to pass and in answer thereto. Signals given whether or not accompanied by change of helm. Signals given when risk of collision is involved. 3-blast signal (engine reversing) required when vessels are in sight of one another. Signals given when passing or meeting at a distance within ½ mile of each other.	*Passing signals* given in all weathers regardless of weather or visibility. Signals given when proposing to pass or in answer thereto. Signals given whether or not accompanied by change of helm. Signals given when risk of collision is involved. Signals given before vessels approach within ½ mile of each other.

SUMMARY of the above, as to WHEN passing signals are given:— *For Western River rules, see page 438.*

GREAT LAKES and INLAND rules similar, except when visibility is bad.
On the GREAT LAKES, passing signals are given not only in clear weather but even in a fog (or other conditions of low visibility) when the situation can be understood, and positions and intentions of vessels made clear, from sound alone, or by sight.
INTERNATIONAL and INLAND rules, on the other hand, provide for passing signals to be given when the other vessel can be seen.
GREAT LAKES and INLAND rules both differ from the INTERNATIONAL in that the latter prescribe passing signals only when (and always when) changing course within sight of another vessel. (*Exception*—At bends, with visibility restricted by banks, vessels may not be in sight of each other when they exchange passing signals, following the long warning blast.)

COMPARISON OF WHAT THE PASSING SIGNALS MEAN

	INTERNATIONAL	INLAND OR PILOT RULES	GREAT LAKES
One short blast (A "short" blast means about one second duration)	I am altering my course to STARBOARD	Used in any of the following situations:— 1. When changing course to starboard. 2. When maintaining a course to starboard which will allow a safe passing on parallel courses, port side to port side. 3. On crossing courses, privileged vessel signifies she will hold her course and speed. 4. On crossing courses, burdened vessel agrees and understands that privileged vessel will hold her course and speed. (This may require burdened vessel to stop, slow down, or change course, in order to give way.) 5. Request by overtaking vessel to pass another on overtaken vessel's starboard side. 6. Granting request by another vessel to overtake you and pass on your own starboard side, and indicating it may be done with safety. 7. If danger signal has previously been sounded to prohibit passing, one blast indicates that overtaken boat now considers it safe for overtaking boat to pass on the former's starboard side.	Same as INLAND (On Great Lakes, blasts are "distinct," not "short".)
Two short blasts	I am altering my course to PORT	Used in any of the following situations:— 1. When changing course to port. 2. When maintaining a course to port which will allow a safe passing on parallel courses, starboard side to starboard side. 3. Request by overtaking vessel to pass another on the overtaken vessel's port side. 4. Granting request by another vessel to overtake you and pass on your own port side, and indicating it may be done with safety. 5. If danger signal has previously been sounded to prohibit passing, two blasts indicate that overtaken boat now considers it safe for overtaking boat to pass on the former's port side.	Same as INLAND (On Great Lakes, blasts are "distinct," not "short".)
Three short blasts (International 1 second) (Inland—short) (Great Lakes—distinct)	My engines are going astern.	My engines are going at full speed astern.	Recognized officially only as a steamer *fog* signal when underway. However, by common use, it is recognized by seamen as indicating sternway and as a request to a passing vessel to slow down.*
Four, or more, short blasts (danger signal)†	Five or more short and rapid blasts used by power-driven vessel required to hold course and speed if in doubt whether other vessel is taking sufficient action to avert collision.	Used in any of the following situations:— 1. To indicate that other vessel's course or intention is not understood. 2. An alarm signal in emergency (failure to understand other vessel's course or intention because of lack of time to effect agreement through exchange of proper signals). 3. To indicate to an overtaking vessel that the overtaken vessel considers it unsafe to pass as requested. 4. To indicate conditions prevent immediate compliance with signals.	Danger signal requires not less than five short blasts.
One long blast (A "long" blast means about 10 to 12 seconds duration)	One "prolonged" (4- to 6-second) blast given by power-driven vessel within ½ mile of bend in channel where approaching vessel cannot be seen	1. Given by vessel navigating a channel where visibility is less than ½ mile because of bend in channel and high banks. This is a *warning* (not passing) signal and should be answered by approaching vessels with the same signal. Passing signals given only after the exchange of such warning signals. 2. Given by vessel leaving a dock or berth. This is a *warning* (not passing) signal. Passing signals exchanged when vessel is clear of berth and fully in sight of approaching vessels.	Same as INLAND (On Great Lakes, blast is at least 8 seconds.)

* Note:—U. S. and Canadian Government patrol vessels on the Great Lakes signal a vessel to slow down with 3 long blasts of a whistle or horn; order her to stop until further orders are given by the patrol vessel, with 4 long blasts; indicate she may proceed, by 1 long blast followed by 4 short blasts.
† Note:—In many U. S. ports, a signal of five prolonged (4 to 6 second) blasts on the whistle or siren is sounded by ships when afire in port or in the harbor (except when under way) as a supplement to other means of sounding the alarm of fire aboard the vessel.

How Rules of the Road Differ

CHAPTER IV

THE rules of the road governing traffic afloat have been drafted with the express purpose of preventing collision. There is a condition inherent in the system of rules, however, that undoubtedly contributes toward confusion—and therefore possibility of collision—on the part of those who may be earnestly trying to understand and obey the rules.

We refer, of course, to the obvious lack of uniformity that exists in the several sets of rules governing various waters. In justice to the rules it may be said that there is a certain consistency of principle running through all, but the differences in detail are bewildering, especially to the growing number of new boatmen.

Without going into detail as to how the complexity of rules has arisen in the United States, we should point out that a boat cruising along our coastal and inland waters may find herself successively under the jurisdiction of the following different sets of federal rules:

1. *The International Rules*—These apply on the high seas, outside of the limits specified for so-called "inland waters." Boundary lines have been prescribed outside of which the International Rules apply, connecting, in the main, offshore aids to navigation, points of the mainland, islands, etc. At buoyed entrances from seaward to bays, sounds, rivers, or other estuaries for which specific lines are not established, International Rules apply outside of a line roughly parallel with the trend of the shore, drawn through the outermost buoy or other aid to navigation of any system of aids.

2. *Inland Rules and Pilot Rules*—These apply on waters inside the above-mentioned boundary lines of the high seas, except (a) the Great Lakes and connecting and tributary waters, and the St. Lawrence River as far east as Montreal; (b) the Red River of the North; (c) the Mississippi River and its tributaries above Huey P. Long Bridge; and (d) that part of the Atchafalaya River above its junction with the Plaquemine—Morgan City alternate waterway.

3. *Great Lakes Rules and Pilot Rules for the Great Lakes*—These apply on the Great Lakes and connecting and tributary waters, and on the St. Lawrence River as far east as Montreal.

4. *Western River Rules and Pilot Rules for Western Rivers*—These apply on the Mississippi River and its tributaries above Huey P. Long Bridge, the Red River of the North, and that part of the Atchafalaya River above its junction with the Plaquemine—Morgan City alternate waterway.

5. *The Motorboat Act of 1940*—In addition to the rules outlined above for various waters, motorboats must also comply with provisions of the Motorboat Act. Rules in this act apply to motorboats on navigable inland waters of the United States, including the Great Lakes, and rivers emptying into the Gulf of Mexico. Requirements for lights and signals apply to all motorboats, in their respective classes and as defined by the act, when operating in these waters. On the high seas, lights and signals are prescribed by International Rules. Motorboats, like other

INTERNATIONAL, INLAND, GREAT

LAKES, AND WESTERN RIVER RULES

VARY IN SOME WAYS PERTAINING

TO VARIOUS SITUATIONS AFLOAT

vessels, observe the rules of the road governing the particular waters in which they happen to be operating.

Comparison of the rules reveals that, in a given situation, International Rules might, for example, require one signal, Inland Rules another, and Great Lakes Rules and Western River Rules may omit the situation entirely. In other cases, rules to cover a given situation might be entirely different in each of the four jurisdictions.

The publications giving the full text of the rules and regulations include:— 1. CG-169 Rules of the Road—International-Inland; 2. CG-172 Rules of the Road—Great Lakes; and 3. CG-184 Rules of the Road—Western Rivers. (These formerly were commonly referred to as the "Pilot Rules" for these waters. The titles were changed in 1959.)

These are Coast Guard publications, available free from Coast Guard Headquarters, or the nearest Marine Inspection Office of the Coast Guard.

It would take a sizable volume to present in detail all the points of conflict between the various rules. However, a digest of some of the highlights is of considerable interest, emphasizing to all boatmen the existence of such discrepancies, and the necessity of understanding rules applicable to the body of water you happen to be navigating, if collision is to be avoided, and safety afloat assured.

Less than 1 percent of all collisions, reports the Coast Guard, have occurred with both vessels acting in compliance with the rules. They lay stress on certain fundamental ideas which should form the basis of any consideration of the rules. A collision approach, they point out, is not the time or place to study the rules; hence the importance of knowing them before an emergency arises. When a situation is met calling for application of the rules, they must be obeyed until the vessels are finally past and clear.

They cite five important points to be borne in mind: (1) the rules, as a whole, are not optional but mandatory; (2) they must be obeyed promptly; (3) they apply alike to all vessels; (4) court interpretations have modified many of the rules; and (5) vessels are governed by the particular rules which apply in the geographical location where they find themselves at the time of an approaching situation.

And here are four cardinal points in the prevention of collision. Motor boatmen will do well to heed them. (1) Keep proper lookout; (2) take bearings to determine whether risk of collision exists; (3) carry proper lights; and (4) use the prescribed whistle signal. Failure to give whistle signals is one of the commonest causes of collision.

Reduced to simplest terms, there are eight general instances in which the various rules may be said to reflect uniformity in underlying principle:

(1) Approaching steam (power-driven) vessels, in good visibility, may be classified as meeting, overtaking, or crossing.

(2) Right of way as between approaching sailing vessels is determined by their courses relative to the wind direction.

(3) Vessels are said to be meeting when their courses

are opposite, or within a point or two of opposite. Vessels may meet at bends though they first sight each other at right angles. Vessels meeting should pass port to port, except where a starboard-to-starboard passing would be safe without changing course. Before passing port to port, change of course at a safe distance is required.

(4) An overtaking vessel is one proceeding on a course within six points of the same direction as a slower vessel ahead. The overtaking vessel, under all rules, is burdened and must keep clear. The principle of privilege and burden is evident in all rules.

(5) Steam (power-driven) vessels are said to be crossing when one approaches the other on either side in the arc between meeting and overtaking—from a point or two on the bow to two points abaft the beam. All rules require the privileged crossing vessel (having the other on her own port hand) to keep her course and, in three out of the four jurisdictions, to hold her speed, until definite remedial action is imperative. The burdened vessel must keep clear, avoid crossing ahead and, if necessary, slow down, stop or reverse. When in dangerous proximity, both must take positive action to avert collision.

(6) Though differing radically in the fog signals themselves, rules agree that in thick weather signals must be given on the whistle, siren, or fog horn, and these signals must be given at frequent intervals. Speed in fog must be moderate, and collision averted by stopping, not

dodging. When another boat's fog signals are heard ahead, speed must be reduced.

(7) All rules recognize that there may be situations where conditions are such that departure from the rules is necessary. This is covered in the Rule of Special Circumstances, which authorizes departure from the rules, only to avoid imminent danger, and only to the extent that such departure is necessary.

(8) The rules are also uniform in requiring the exercise of good seamanship, covered in a general precautionary rule.

These, then, are the broad points of similarity in principle common to all the rules. What are some of the fundamental differences in detail, which give rise to confusion when passing from one jurisdiction to another? The most important differences are in the use of whistle signals (both clear weather and fog) and in lights and day signals prescribed for certain classes of vessels in the various jurisdictions.

WHAT WHISTLE SIGNALS MEAN (EXCEPT FOG SIGNALS)

Whistle equipment prescribed under International, Inland and Western River Rules consists of a whistle or siren for steam (power-driven) vessels; a fog horn for sailing vessels and vessels towed. On the Great Lakes, steam vessels require a whistle (steam or substitute); sailing vessels, a fog horn. On Western Rivers, a compara-

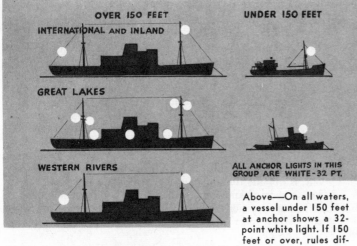

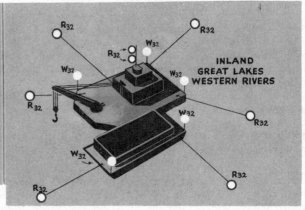

Above—On all waters, a vessel under 150 feet at anchor shows a 32-point white light. If 150 feet or over, rules differ. Under International, Western River and Inland Rules, they display another white light aft. On the Great Lakes, two white lights are carried horizontally, both fore and aft, plus white lights every 100 feet along the deck. Boats 65 feet and under which are anchored in "special anchorage areas" need not show the otherwise required white anchor lights

In addition to lights prescribed for stationary dredges Inland Rules and War Department Regulations prescribe red lights to mark buoys of anchors of a floating plant. Or, the dredge may throw a light on buoys when vessels approach. This applies on all except the high seas and certain waters of New York Harbor. International Rules make no mention of this case, but a dredge could throw a searchlight on the mooring buoys as required

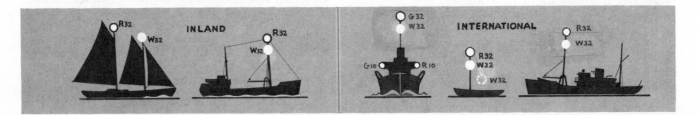

Above—On inland waters vessels trawling, dredging or fishing with nets or lines out show "from some part of the vessel where they can be best seen" a red light 6 to 12 feet vertically above a white light. (At anchor, fishing vessels on inland waters with gear attached, display only white anchor lights, differing from the practice on the high seas, as illustrated at the right. When under way and not fishing, such vessels show the same lights as other vessels under way

Above—On the high seas, vessels trawling (left) carry a 32-point green light above a 32-point white light, 4 to 12 feet apart. (20-point white light showing forward is optional.) When making way, they also carry usual red and green side lights and 12-point stern light. Vessels other than trawlers, engaged in fishing (right) carry identical lights except that the upper light is red. Boats under 40 feet in length (center) may carry these lights lower. On all fishing boats an additional white light is displayed in the direction of outlying gear extending more than 500 feet into the seaway

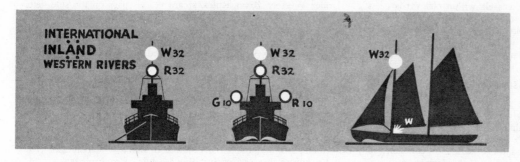

INTERNATIONAL
INLAND
WESTERN RIVERS

W32 · R32 · G10 · R10 · W32 · W

Left—Under International, Inland and Western River Rules, the steam (power-driven) pilot vessel on station shows a white light above a red light. When not at anchor, she also shows side lights. Sailing pilot vessels have a white masthead light and exhibit a flare-up at short intervals. Great Lakes Rules do not provide for pilot vessels. International Rules require all pilot vessels at anchor to show anchor lights also

Below—Western River rules make special provision for "river steamers", that is, a river-type steam vessel with two smokestacks in an athwartship line. They may carry, in lieu of the usual lights of a steam vessel underway, a red light on the outboard side of the port smokestack and a green light on the outboard side of the starboard smokestack. These lights show forward, aft and abeam on their respective sides. Under Western River rules, a seagoing steamer carries the lights required of her by International Rules, and steam vessels in general, other than those specially provided for, are lighted as under Inland Rules.

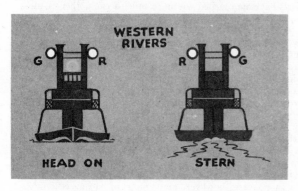

WESTERN RIVERS

G · R · R · G

HEAD ON · **STERN**

Right — Except on the high seas, vessels moored or anchored, laying pipe or operating on submarine construction or excavation, show three red lights in vertical line. Under the new International Rules, three vertical lights (upper and lower red; middle one white) are shown by a vessel laying cable, working on aids to navigation, or on surveying or underwater operations. Appropriate anchor lights are also shown, when at anchor

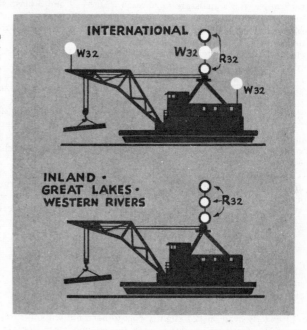

INTERNATIONAL

W32 · W32 · R32 · W32

INLAND · GREAT LAKES · WESTERN RIVERS

R32

tively new requirement (from which motor boats used for pleasure are exempt) is an amber visual signal synchronized with the whistle blasts. Motorboats, under the terms of the Motor Boat Act, carry a whistle, horn, or other sound-producing mechanical device. Class A (less than 16 feet) is exempt; regulations specify whether it must be mouth-, hand-, or power-operated in Classes 1, 2, and 3. The bell, when required, is used in fog.

Under the International Rules power-driven vessels, under way, when in sight of one another, must use prescribed signals of one, two, or three short (about 1 second) blasts to indicate their course when taking any action prescribed by the rules. Thus, a power-driven vessel will blow 1 short blast to indicate she is changing her course to starboard; 2 if she is directing her course to port; 3 if her engines are going astern. This applies in meeting, overtaking, and crossing situations, regardless of the bearing of the other vessel and whether or not the other is a power-driven or sailing vessel. One- and 2-blast signals thus are rudder signals to be used each time the vessel changes course. The 3-blast signal is required, not only when engines are going at full speed astern, but at any speed astern, or whenever the vessel is making sternway. As a warning signal, to attract attention, a vessel may use a flare-up light or detonating signal such as a gun.

Under Inland Rules, steam vessels under way when in sight of one another, also blow the 3 short blasts when engines are going at any speed astern, or when the vessel is making sternway. On the other hand the 1 or 2 short blast signals must be given, and answered, when steam vessels approach from any direction within ½ mile of each other, regardless of whether or not courses are altered. Signals for meeting, overtaking, and crossing are prescribed and these will be discussed later. Inland Rules

also provide for an optional warning signal (flare-up light or detonating signal) to attract attention.

The danger signal is now used on all waters in some form, both in clear weather and in fog. It consists of 4 or more short blasts (under Inland and Western River Rules) given when the course or intention of an approaching vessel is in doubt. Under both International and Great Lakes rules, the danger signal is 5 or more short and rapid blasts, and if vessels on the Lakes are within ½ mile of each other, both must reduce speed to bare steerageway and, if necessary, stop and reverse. On the high seas, a power-driven vessel required to hold her course and speed may give 5 short, rapid blasts on the whistle if in doubt as to whether an approaching vessel is taking necessary action to avert collision. All except International Rules have an express provision against cross signals (answering 1 blast with 2, and vice versa) and call for the danger signal in such cases.

No provision is made in Western River Rules for a "long" blast signal, found nearly alike in Inland and Great Lakes Rules. The long blast (8 to 10 seconds) is in the nature of a warning, sounded when nearing a bend or curve where an approaching vessel could not be seen at a distance of ½ mile. The long blast must be answered by any approaching steam vessel within hearing, after which the usual meeting and passing signals are exchanged, when vessels come in sight of each other. Inland and Lake Rules also prescribe the long blast as a warning signal when steam vessels are leaving a dock or berth. When clear of the berth, in sight of other vessels, passing whistle signals are exchanged. If backing out of a berth, the long blast is followed by 3 short blasts, as soon as another vessel is in sight. (On the Lakes, rules now specify not a "long" blast, but one of at least 8 seconds' duration.)

On Western Rivers, the signal for vessels within 600 yards of a bend, or leaving a dock, is three distinct blasts.

International Rules require a "prolonged" (4- to 6-second) blast when a power-driven vessel arrives within ½ mile of a bend, to be answered by other approaching power vessels within hearing around the bend.

WHEN TO GIVE PASSING SIGNALS

IT is important to note that passing whistle signals on the high seas are given only when (and always when) there is a change of course if any other vessel is in sight.

Inland Rules require passing whistle signals to be given only when vessels are in sight of each other, and there is risk of collision; in fog and other cases of low visibility when the vessels cannot see each other, fog signals are to be used. One-, 2- and 3-blast signals may be used in fog only after vessels sight each other. The danger signal, of course, may be used properly in fog or clear weather as necessary. Under Inland Rules, the 1- or 2-blast signal must be exchanged whenever steam vessels approach within ½ mile (or sooner), regardless of the need for a change of course.

On the Great Lakes, passing signals are given in all weathers regardless of visibility, before vessels meet or pass within a distance of ½ mile of each other, if risk of collision is involved. On the theory that a 1-second blast is considered too short for passing signals, Lakes rules now require "distinct" blasts, not "short." Three blasts on the Lakes is not a signal when reversing, it signifies a steam vessel under way in a fog. On the Lakes, signals must be exchanged whether or not either vessel changes her course.

On Western Rivers, as on the Lakes, the passing whistle signals are given in all weathers, regardless of visibility, and care must be used to sound the proper signal if a vessel is not distinctly visible. Where possible, signals must be exchanged before vessels are within ½ mile of each other.

WHEN STEAM (POWER-DRIVEN) VESSELS MEET

THE meeting, overtaking, and crossing situations have already been touched upon in respect to the meaning of the signals under the various sets of rules. Other aspects of each of these situations will now be considered.

Meeting situations should be broken down into five separate cases: (1) exactly head on (2) slightly port-to-port, but without safe clearance (3) port-to-port with course far enough apart for clearance without changing course (4) slightly starboard-to-starboard, but without safe clearance, and (5) starboard-to-starboard, with courses far enough apart for safe clearance without changing course. In the first four cases, all rules require a port-to-port passing. Only in the fifth case is a starboard-to-starboard passing permissible. In cases requiring a turn to starboard it is imperative that, long before any danger of collision exists, the pilot should decide, with the aid of bearings, on which side he is to pass, signal promptly accordingly, and change course upon the return signal. In open water this means a definite and ample change of course which cannot be misunderstood; in narrow channels it means moving promptly to the proper side of the channel as far as safety permits.

In meeting situations, vessels are not required to hold their course and speed. On the contrary, each is required to change course and reduce speed when safety demands it. Danger signals should be blown if a signal is not agreed to, if a vessel repeatedly fails to answer or appears to be making the wrong maneuver, or if the vessel is unable (a jammed rudder, perhaps) to comply with the expected maneuver.

We have previously indicated that short blast whistle signals on the high seas are basically rudder signals, evidencing change of course. When power-driven vessels meet end on, or nearly so, on the high seas, in such a manner as to involve risk of collision, each alters course to starboard and blows one short blast to indicate her change of course. If a second change of course were required, she would signal again. If courses were so far to starboard of each other that no course change was needed, no signal would be given.

Now, under Inland, Lake, and River Rules, the situation is different. Here rules prescribe that when two steam vessels meet head-and-head (end on or nearly so) they shall exchange one short blast and pass port side to port. If the courses are so far to starboard of each other as not to be considered a head-and-head meeting, then they exchange two short whistle blasts and pass starboard-to-starboard. If they pass port-to-port, and do not change course, they still exchange one short blast. In short, except on the high seas, the signals are given, whether or not there is a change of course. (For simplicity, the "distinct" Lakes and River signal is here considered short, though not 1 second.)

Under Western River Rules, steam vessels pass on the side determined by the descending steam vessel.

Meeting in Narrow Channels

INTERNATIONAL and Inland Rules both contain a provision that in narrow channels steam (power-driven) vessels must, when safe and practicable, keep to the starboard side. All Rules hold that power-driven vessels under 65 feet and in a narrow channel must avoid hampering the safe passage of a vessel "which can navigate only inside such channel."

When steamers meet in narrow channels where there is a current, Great Lakes rules give right of way to the (less-maneuverable) descending steamer, and she is required to signal which side she elects to take, before they approach within ½ mile of each other.

On Western Rivers, the rules also give the right of way to the (privileged) descending steamer, but require the ascending (burdened) vessel to signal first, to be answered by the same signal from the descending steamer unless the latter regards passing, on the side indicated, as dangerous. In that case, she blows the danger signal of 4 or more short and rapid blasts, which the ascending steamer must answer, after which both are stopped and backed if necessary, until signals for passing are exchanged. After the danger signal is exchanged, the descending steamer indicates on which side she wishes to pass and the pilot of the (burdened) ascending steamer must govern himself accordingly. Signals, where possible, must be exchanged before the vessels have approached within ½ mile of each other. Unless they do complete their understanding of intended action while still a great distance apart, a hazardous situation is created.

In narrow channels, River rules also provide for the right of way of descending steamers by requiring the ascending steamer to stop below the entrance of a narrow channel till a descending steamer has passed through. If they unavoidably meet in a narrow channel, the ascending steamer signals and then lies at the side of the channel with bare steerageway while the descending steamer is worked carefully by. When meeting near a bridge span, if the descending steamer deems it dangerous to pass between bridge piers, she sounds the danger signal, which the ascending steamer must answer in kind, slowing or stopping until the (privileged) descending steamer has passed through.

When two steam vessels meet at the confluence of two (Western rivers, the steam vessel which has the other to port must give the first signal. In no case, however, may pilots of steam vessels attempt to pass each other until there has been a thorough understanding as to the side which each vessel is to take.

Passing Dredges, Vessels Aground, Etc.

RECENTLY the Pilot Rules for Inland Waters were amended, modifying regulations having to do with whistle signals required when passing floating plants, dredges, etc., working in navigable channels. Similar regulations of the Department of the Army make them effective also on the Great Lakes and Western Rivers.

Essence of the new regulations is to the effect that vessels intending to pass such floating plants, when within 1 mile, shall blow a long blast of the whistle. The dredge responds with the correct passing signal so as to direct the approaching vessel to the proper side for passing, which signal is returned by the approaching vessel. If the channel is not clear, the dredge blows a danger signal, whereupon the approaching vessel must slow down or stop, and await further signals from the dredge.

If the pipe line of a dredge obstructs the channel in such a way that it is not safe for an approaching vessel to pass around it, the dredge will sound the danger signal, open the pipe line and give the correct passing signal.

A special signal is also provided in Great Lakes Rules for St. Mary's River only (See "Special Rules—St. Mary's River" on page 66.) when a vessel is aground in a channel. Such a vessel sounds not less than 5 short and rapid blasts, upon the approach of another vessel bound up or down the channel. If the approaching vessel cannot pass with safety, she must stop and avoid fouling the grounded vessel, and sound the same signal to any vessel coming up astern of her. If additional vessels approach from the same direction, the last vessel in line sounds this signal. When visibility is low, fog signals are also sounded.

THE OVERTAKING SITUATION

AN overtaking vessel may pass the vessel to be overtaken on either side, if safe; the overtaking vessel is burdened and must keep clear by slowing down, stopping, or reversing, while the overtaken vessel is privileged and must hold her course and speed (a privilege she exercises until the other vessel is finally past and clear). In open water a wide berth should be allowed when overtaking; in narrow channels it should not be attempted at all unless clearly safe, having regard for the effect of a vessel's suction in shallow water.

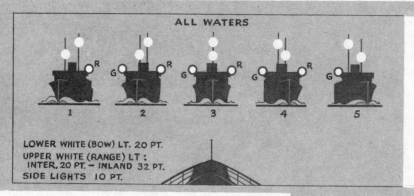

ALL WATERS

LOWER WHITE (BOW) LT. 20 PT.
UPPER WHITE (RANGE) LT:
INTER. 20 PT. – INLAND 32 PT.
SIDE LIGHTS 10 PT.

1   2   3   4   5

Left—Five types of meeting situation: 1. Port to port, with clearance without change of course. 2. Port to port, without safe clearance. 3. Exactly head on. 4. Starboard to starboard, without safe clearance. 5. Starboard to starboard, with clearance without change of course. On all waters, in all cases except number 5, meeting vessels must pass port to port. Range lights indicate approaching vessel's heading. On the high seas, after range light is now mandatory on power-driven vessels, except for those under 150 feet, or vessels towing

Right—Head-on and port side views of a power-driven vessel under way; vessels lighted according to International Rules are not required to change lights when navigating waters tributary to the high seas. Thus, in any waters, the seagoing vessel would be lighted as shown. Her 12-point white stern light is not visible from abeam. On Great Lakes, 32-point white range light is required on vessels over 100 feet

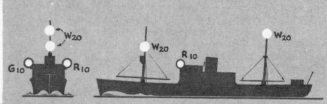

ALL WATERS

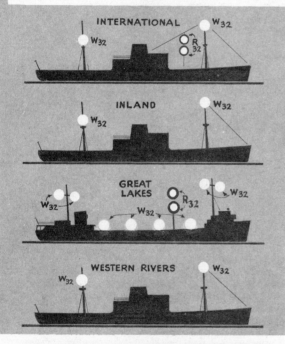

INTERNATIONAL

INLAND

GREAT LAKES

WESTERN RIVERS

Above—A steam (power-driven) vessel (over 150 feet) aground in various waters. She carries lights of a vessel at anchor except for two additional red lights required under International and Great Lakes Rules. All vessels aground use them on the St. Mary's River; vessels over 65 feet on the Lakes. On Western Rivers, lights would be same as in Inland Rules

Above—A moored dredge, under International Rules, shows three lights in vertical line (one white between two red), also appropriate anchor lights. The scow alongside carries a similar white light. The two red lights, shown in other waters by the dredge, are used on the high seas by a vessel not under command

INTERNATIONAL

INLAND
GREAT LAKES
WESTERN RIVERS

Above—A dredge held stationary by moorings or spuds, on all waters except the high seas, displays two vertical red lights in addition to white lights at each corner and white lights at outboard corners of the scow alongside. The red lights are shown 3 to 6 feet apart, and not less than 15 feet above the deck, displayed where they may best be seen

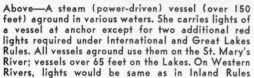

· INLAND· WESTERN RIVERS

· INTERNATIONAL· GREAT LAKES

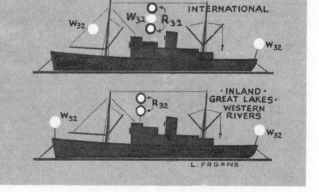

INTERNATIONAL

· INLAND· GREAT LAKES· WESTERN RIVERS

L. FAGANS

Above—Under International Rules, a vessel of less than 40 feet, under oars, would keep at hand a lantern with green glass on one side and red glass on the other, showing it to avert collision. International Rules also provide for "small rowing boats" (as distinguished from a vessel of less than 40 feet under oars) which show a white light. Inland Rules require rowboats, under oars or sail, to show a white light in time to prevent collision

Above—Vessels on all waters except the high seas made fast alongside or moored over a wreck on the bottom, partly submerged or drifting, show a white light from bow and stern of each outside vessel (where several are at work) and two red lights in vertical line. On the high seas, she would display the lights of a vessel engaged in underwater operations—one white between two red, vertically arranged. If not drifting, anchor lights are shown also

A vessel is deemed to be overtaking when she comes up from a direction more than 2 points abaft the beam of another; if there is any doubt, the "overtaking" vessel should conduct herself as an overtaking vessel. Furthermore she must not alter course or speed in such a way as to endanger the overtaken vessel, even after passing.

On the high seas, an overtaking vessel uses her 1- and 2-blast signals in accordance with the general rule which requires 1 blast when she alters her course to starboard, 2 blasts when she turns to port. She does this not only when she makes her initial change of course, but also when she turns to get back on course after passing. The overtaken vessel, holding course and speed, does not reply to the signals, and the overtaking vessel would also remain silent if no course change were required.

Under Inland Rules, when an overtaking vessel, approaching within ½ mile, wishes to pass, whether changing course or not, she sounds 1 short blast if she wishes to pass on the starboard side of the vessel ahead, or 2 short blasts if she wishes to pass on the port side of the vessel ahead. Rules require the overtaken vessel to answer with similar signals if in agreement with the proposed passing. But if she does not think the passing safe, she must not give a cross signal; instead she would use the danger signal which would keep the overtaken vessel astern until passing was safe, and proper signals have been exchanged. Should the overtaken vessel use a danger signal to indicate that she considers passing on the side first proposed unsafe, she may follow it with a contrary signal to indicate that passing on the opposite side is agreeable.

Assent to a passing signal never relieves the burdened overtaking vessel from keeping clear, and when she returns to her course she does not whistle as she would under International Rules.

Essentially, the rules for the overtaking situation are the same on the Great Lakes and Western Rivers as in the Inland Rules except, of course, that use of the danger signal would now require 5 short blasts on the Lakes. There is also a provision in Great Lakes rules which, in channels less than 500 feet wide, prevents a steam vessel from passing another going in the same direction unless the latter is disabled or signifies her assent to the passing.

STEAM (POWER-DRIVEN) VESSELS CROSSING

As an aid in analyzing the crossing situation with a view to understanding it, it is suggested that there are, in essence, only two types of crossing situation. First, where you look to starboard, in any direction from a few degrees on the bow to 2 points abaft the starboard beam, and see another steam (power-driven) vessel crossing your own course from right to left. At night, a red side light would be visible, accompanied by one or more white lights. No green light would be visible. Here you are burdened—you must keep clear; you must not cross the other vessel's bow; if necessary, you must slow down, stop, or reverse. Usually the best action is to swing to starboard and pass well astern of the other vessel; the other alternative would be to slow down so the other vessel may maintain her course across your bow. The burdened vessel must never cross the bow of the privileged vessel. The taking of continuous bearings in a situation like this is of the greatest importance. If the bearing does not change, collision is certain.

The other kind of crossing situation would be one in which you look to port, in any direction from a few degrees on the bow to 2 points abaft the port beam and see another power-driven vessel crossing your own course from left to right. At night, you would see a green light, and one or more white lights, but no red light.

Here you are the privileged vessel. You have the right of way. Under all rules you must hold your course and speed (except on Western Rivers where you must hold your course). It is only by adhering to this regulation that the burdened vessel will know how to act in keeping clear.

We have already explained how, under International Rules, a privileged vessel holding her course and speed has no duty to blow a whistle signal. However, if circumstances arise where a collision would be inevitable if she held on, then she must take action to avert collision. Under the new International Rules, a warning signal is now provided for a power-driven vessel required to hold her course and speed. If she is in doubt that the burdened vessel (which must be in sight) is taking sufficient action to avert collision, she may give at least 5 short (1-second) rapid blasts on the whistle. This calls attention of the burdened vessel to her obligations under the rules. The burdened vessel, in most normal crossing cases, would blow 1 short whistle blast as she altered her course to starboard when passing astern of the privileged vessel, but here too if she alters course a second time or reverses, it must be accompanied by the appropriate whistle signal blast (2 if she turns to port, 3 if she reverses).

In a crossing situation on inland waters, 1 short blast signifies that the (privileged) steam vessel to starboard of the burdened vessel, will hold her course and speed. Though the privileged vessel should blow first, either may. If signals are misunderstood, or if immediate compliance with the signals is not possible, the danger signal (4 or more short blasts) is blown and both vessels stop and back if necessary until proper signals are made and understood. Thus, though the privileged vessel would normally hold her course and speed, she is obliged to take remedial action if signals are misunderstood. When a burdened vessel receives the 1-blast signal in a crossing situation, she properly replies with 1 blast and keeps out of the way by passing astern of the privileged vessel, which may necessitate her changing her course to starboard, slacking speed, stopping, or reversing.

The necessity of exchanging 1-blast signals on inland waters is an aid to the privileged vessel in knowing when the burdened vessel is failing in her duty to give way.

Broadly, Great Lakes Rules are in agreement with Inland Rules on crossing situations. Formerly, on the Great Lakes, the privileged vessel was required to blow "one blast," to be answered by "one short blast" from the burdened vessel. By recent amendment, the signal is now one "distinct" blast. Again, on the Lakes, the danger signal, if used, would be 5 or more short blasts. Though whistle signals are required on the Lakes in fog as well as clear weather, there is no obligation to hold course and speed till vessels are in sight of each other. Rather the obligation is to reduce speed and proceed with caution.

On Western Rivers, either vessel may signal first with one "distinct" blast, which is to be answered with a similar blast. However, a steam vessel with tow descending a river has right of way over any steam vessel crossing the river, and gives, as a signal of her intention to hold on across the bow of the other vessel, 3 distinct blasts, to which the crossing vessel must immediately reply.

SPECIAL RULES—ST. MARYS RIVER

SPECIAL anchorage and navigation requirements for the St. Marys River, in Michigan, supplement the general rules and regulations applicable to vessels on the Great Lakes. These are set forth in a separate section of the Great Lakes Pilot Rules.

UNIFORM REGULATIONS PROPOSED FOR NATIONAL PARKS AND WILDLIFE AREAS

Uniform regulations covering boating in National Parks and Federal wildlife areas have been drafted. Boating groups were consulted before the proposed regulations were issued and no objections were received. In the past, each park has had its own rules with the result that boating is banned or heavily restricted in some places and encouraged in others. When the proposed rules become final, they will apply nationally and uniformly and will parallel Coast Guard regulations pertaining to navigable waters. Houseboat owners will get a break under the prospective changes. In general, houseboats have been banned even where cruisers have been allowed. Since the line of demarcation between houseboats and cruisers is often a narrow one, controversies have arisen. Now houseboats will be considered eligible along with other powered craft. Another alteration is to extend the length limit from 32 to 40 feet. Also, an age minimum of 14 will be established and youthful operators must be accompanied by a competent person at least 18 years old. Among the new requirements are permits to be issued by the park superintendent, and Coast Guard boat numbers on all power craft of more than 10 horsepower.

Right of Way; Distress Signals; Special Circumstances; Day Marks

R ULES governing actions of vessels in fog concern themselves with the proper signals to be given both when under way and at anchor, and the subject of moderate speed. The common theory underlying rules in all jurisdictions is that vessels must run at moderate speed, and avoid collision by stopping, not dodging. Moderate speed, according to the courts, means bare steerageway when visibility ahead is little or nothing; when visibility is an appreciable distance, it means such a speed as will enable a vessel to stop in less than half the distance of visibility. On high seas and inland waters engines must be stopped on hearing a fog signal forward of the beam. On Great Lakes and Western Rivers speed must be reduced to bare steerageway (on the Lakes, if the signal appears to come from within 4 points of ahead).

International and Inland Rules require as fog signal equipment on steam (power-driven) vessels a whistle (sounded by steam or substitute for steam), a fog horn, and bell. Under International Rules the fog horn must be mechanically operated. Sailing vessels of 40 feet or over carry a fog horn and bell. Under Great Lakes Rules steam vessels carry a whistle (sounded by steam or substitute for steam) audible 2 miles, and a bell. Sailing vessels carry a fog horn and bell. On Western Rivers, steam vessels have a whistle or siren, and bell; sailing vessels a fog horn (and bell, if over 20 gross tons).

Motor boats (except Class A, under 16 feet) under the Motor Boat Act, carry an efficient whistle or other sound-producing mechanical appliance. This is used for fog signals as well as passing signals. Motor boats of Class 2 and Class 3 carry an efficient bell. The fog horn is not required on any motor boats under the Act.

Courts have ruled that fog signals are proper when

RULES IN FOG

visibility falls below two miles, the required visibility of side lights. Fog signals are proper not only in fog, but also in mist, falling snow, and heavy rain-storms, by day or night. Under International and Inland Rules, the "prolonged" blast called for in fog signals means from 4 to 6 seconds' duration. With respect to motor boats, however, 2 seconds is considered prolonged. A sailing vessel may use either short or prolonged blasts in fog.

Courts have decided that the danger signal is a fog signal as well as a clear weather signal. In inland waters, therefore, it should be used whenever approaching signals of another vessel would indicate impending collision.

Steam Vessels Under Way

On the high seas, the fog signal for a power-driven vessel under way is 1 prolonged blast of the whistle at intervals of not more than 2 minutes. Under Inland Rules she would sound 1 prolonged blast, but at intervals of not more than 1 minute. On the Great Lakes she sounds 3 distinct blasts

The square flag and ball (above or below the flag) are now (since recent amendments to Great Lakes rules) recognized as a daytime distress signal by all except Inland Rules. However, the International Code Signal NC—illustrated at the right—is not recognized under Great Lakes or Inland Rules, though specifically provided for under International and Western River Rules

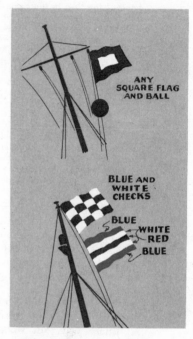

ANY SQUARE FLAG AND BALL

BLUE AND WHITE CHECKS

BLUE
WHITE
RED
BLUE

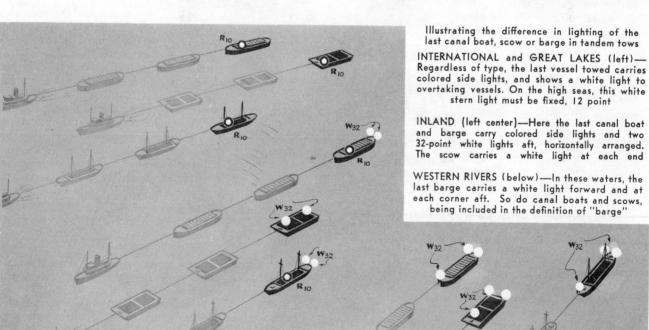

Illustrating the difference in lighting of the last canal boat, scow or barge in tandem tows

INTERNATIONAL and GREAT LAKES (left)— Regardless of type, the last vessel towed carries colored side lights, and shows a white light to overtaking vessels. On the high seas, this white stern light must be fixed, 12 point

INLAND (left center)—Here the last canal boat and barge carry colored side lights and two 32-point white lights aft, horizontally arranged. The scow carries a white light at each end

WESTERN RIVERS (below)—In these waters, the last barge carries a white light forward and at each corner aft. So do canal boats and scows, being included in the definition of "barge"

NOTE:—For the Gulf Intracoastal Waterway and certain adjacent waters, provision is made for vessels in tow in a separate section of the Inland Rules.

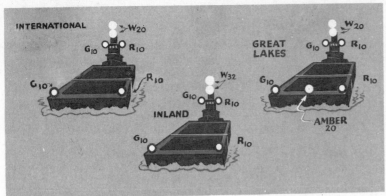

Above: Two tandem barges pushed ahead. Tugs display side lights and towing lights. On Western Rivers, lights of tug and tow are the same as shown for Great Lakes except that, instead of the 20-point white lights, the tug has two amber lights vertically arranged, visible from aft, not forward of the beam. The 20-point amber light at the head of the tow, in the centerline, is required on the Western Rivers and Gulf Intracostal Waterway, optional on the Lakes. Barges are lighted as one vessel. Instead of white 32-point towing lights aft, the inland tug might carry two 20-point white towing lights forward and two 12-point amber lights aft, vertically arranged, not visible forward of the beam

Right: A tug with steamship in tow. In every case, the ship towed shows her side lights and no white lights (except for the white light shown to overtaking vessels, or fixed stern light on the high seas). The ocean-going tug, in addition to side lights, has two towing lights because only one vessel is in tow. The inland tug has three towing lights because her tow is astern. (Optionally, these may be 32 or 20-point, and range lights also are optional.) Vessels towing may carry a small white light abaft the funnel or aftermast for the tow to steer by (not visible forward of the beam). On the high seas, they must carry the towing light or fixed 12-point white stern light

vessels under way. They prescribe, at intervals of not more than 1 minute, 1 blast on the fog horn when on the starboard tack; 2 blasts in succession when on the port tack; and 3 blasts in succession when the wind is abaft the beam. (Great Lakes Rules conform to the above only when the vessel is not in tow.) On Western Rivers sailing vessels give signals prescribed for steam vessels, but use the fog horn.

* Vessels at Anchor

In all waters, the bell is used as a fog signal by vessels at anchor. Under International, Inland and Western River Rules, it is to be rung rapidly for 5 seconds, at intervals of 1 minute. On the Great Lakes it is rung rapidly for 3

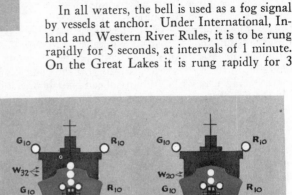

on her whistle at intervals of not more than 1 minute (except when she has a raft in tow). On Western Rivers her signal would be 3 distinct blasts every minute (2 of equal length, followed by a longer one).

International Rules (only) also provide for the power-driven vessel under way, but stopped, and having no way upon her. Here the signal is 2 prolonged blasts (with 1-second interval between)

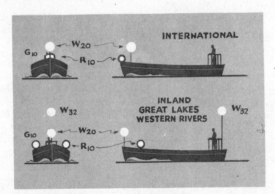

Left: A 40-foot motor launch. Except on the high seas, she carries the lights of a Class 3 motor boat. Being under 40 tons, under International Rules she may carry a combined red-and-green lantern and, above it, a 20-point white light. The fixed white 12-point stern light, now required by International Rules, is not visible from abeam

to 5 seconds at intervals of 2 minutes. In addition, a signal is sounded every 3 minutes on whistle or horn—1 short, 2 long, 1 short blasts in quick succession. (The same signal is used by vessels aground in or near a channel or fairway.) On the high seas, a vessel aground gives 3 strokes on the bell before and after the regular anchor signal.

On the high seas, a vessel at anchor in a fog, in order to give an approaching vessel more definite warning of her position, may give, before and after the usual bell signals, a sound signal of three blasts—1 short, 1 prolonged, 1 short.

Vessels Towing or Towed

On the high seas, a vessel towing, or employed in laying or picking up a telegraph cable or navigation mark, and a vessel under way which is unable to get out of the way of an approaching vessel through being not under command, or unable to maneuver, would sound 1 prolonged blast on the whistle followed by 2 short blasts. A vessel towed gives 1 prolonged blast, followed by 3 short blasts—on the whistle or fog horn. (Despite the provision above for the vessel not under command, it is held that if the vessel broken down is a steam vessel she must use the

Above: Rules for all waters are fairly consistent in requiring sailing vessels under way to show colored side lights, and a white light aft. On the Great Lakes the stern light is a flare-up; on other waters it must be fixed, 12-pt.

at intervals of not more than 2 minutes. This signal must not be used except on the high seas. With respect to the interval between signals, this is a maximum interval; in heavy traffic they should be given more frequently.

Sailing Vessels Under Way

International, Inland, and Great Lakes Rules are fairly uniform with respect to fog signals for sailing

* On Inland Waters and Western Rivers, vessels under 65 feet in length and nondescript craft like barges, scows, etc., need not give fog signal when at anchor in special anchorage areas.

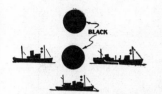

On all waters, a single black ball at least 2 feet in diameter is the day mark of a vessel over 65 feet (any size on high seas) anchored in a fairway or channel. On inland waters it may be shown by a steam vessel under sail only

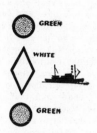

Two black balls, on the high seas, identify the vessel not under command. So too on the Lakes but only on vessels over 65 feet. On Inland Waters, the Lakes and Western Rivers, it is the day mark of a self-propelling suction dredge under way and dredging. Inland Rules provide this day mark for all dredges under way and for a Coast and Geodetic Survey vessel at anchor in a fairway. Three black balls, on the high seas, indicate a vessel aground (on Great Lakes, only for vessels over 65 feet)

Inland Rules only, provide a special day mark for Coast and Geodetic survey vessels under way and engaged in hydrographic surveying. This is a white diamond, and above and below it a green ball

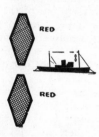

On the high seas day signal for vessels fishing (but not trolling) is 2 black cones with points together. Boats under 65 feet may show basket instead. On inland waters all vessels under way and fishing show a basket

Except on the high seas, steamers, derrick boats, lighters and other vessels made fast alongside, or moored over, a wreck display two bright red shapes, each double frustums of a cone, base to base

2 prolonged blast signal if she loses all headway at sea but does not come to anchor—that is, the signal for steam vessels under way, but having no way on.)

Under Inland Rules, a steam vessel towing also uses the signal of 1 prolonged blast followed by 2 short blasts, and the vessel towed may give the same signal on the fog horn. Analyzing these rules, it will be noticed that, on the high seas, the towing signal is used by either a steam or sailing vessel towing. In inland waters, a sailing vessel towing would give the customary signals of a sailboat without a tow.

On the Great Lakes a steamer towing a raft sounds at intervals of not more than 1 minute a screeching or Modoc whistle for from 3 to 5 seconds. Any vessel being towed sounds 4 bells at intervals of 1 minute (2 in quick succession, followed by 2 more after an interval, in the manner that 4 bells would be struck to indicate time).

On Western Rivers, a steam vessel towing sounds 3 distinct blasts of equal length, at intervals of not more than 1 minute.

Miscellaneous Craft

International Rules provide that "a rowing boat," seaplanes, and boats less than 40 feet in length are not obliged to give the regularly prescribed fog signals but, if they do not, they must make some other efficient sound signal at intervals of not more than 1 minute. Vessels engaged in fishing, under way or at anchor, sound at 1-minute intervals 1 prolonged and 2 short blasts. Vessels under way with trolling lines out sound the same signals as other non-fishing vessels under way.

In the case of a power-driven vessel the signal is given by a whistle; if a sailing vessel, on her fog horn. Vessels being towed may give the prescribed signals on the whistle or fog horn. Fishing vessels and boats of less than 40 feet need not make these signals but, if they do not, they must make some other efficient sound signal at intervals of not more than 1 minute.

Inland Rules contain a provision for rafts and other water craft navigating by hand power, horse power, or the current of a river. They sound a blast on a fog horn, or equivalent signal, at intervals of not more than 1 minute.

On the Great Lakes, vessels under 10 registered tons need not give prescribed signals but, if they do not, must make some other efficient sound signal at intervals of not more than 1 minute. Produce boats, fishing boats, rafts, and other craft navigating by hand power, horse power or by current of the river, or anchored or moored in or near a channel or fairway and not in any port, not otherwise provided for in the rules, sound a fog horn or equivalent signal at intervals of not more than 1 minute.

An old regulation requiring miscellaneous nondescript craft on Western Rivers to sound a foghorn, "which shall make a sound equal to a steam whistle" has been omitted in new Rules.

On Western Rivers, steamers lying to during fog or thick weather, when another steamer is heard approaching, give 1 tap on the bell if lying on the right bank (facing down-stream), 2 taps if lying on the left bank, at intervals of not more than 1 minute. The signals are continued until the approaching steamer has passed.

On the Great Lakes and Western Rivers, signals for meeting and passing are also used in foggy weather, in addition to the special fog signals prescribed.

Lower left: Day marks are not provided in the rules for minesweepers, but the naval services in all waters use three black balls, one each at the masthead and spreader ends

Right: Except on the high seas (and certain waters in and adjacent to New York Harbor) barrels or buoys are used to mark bow, stern, and breast anchors of floating plant moorings

On all waters except the high seas, two red balls are the day mark of a dredge being held stationary by moorings or spuds

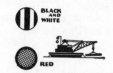

Except on the high seas, a vessel moored or anchored and laying pipe or operating on underwater construction or excavation displays two balls, the upper one having black and white vertical stripes, the lower one red

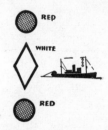

On the high seas, the day mark shown above (white diamond between red balls) is used by vessels laying or picking up telegraph cable, working on aids to navigation, or engaged in surveying or underwater operations

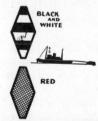

On waters other than the high seas, a vessel with submerged object in tow uses a day mark consisting of two shapes; these are double frustums of a cone, base to base. The upper has alternate horizontal black and white stripes; the lower is bright red

RIGHT OF WAY

Rules of the road recognize the basic idea that risk of collision in any given situation will be minimized if one of two vessels is privileged and the other burdened, the privileged vessel being under obligation to continue exactly what she is doing until the vessels are past and clear, the burdened vessel to take positive action to keep out of the way. However, though a vessel may be "privileged," her obligation to hold course and speed is as definite as that of the burdened vessel to keep clear, reduce speed, and avoid crossing ahead.

Circumstances may sometimes arise, due to thick weather or other causes, when a collision would be inevitable if the privileged vessel continued to hold her course and speed too long. Consequently, when a privileged vessel finds herself in such a situation, she is required to take any other action

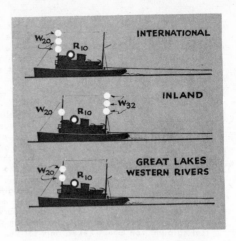

Below: A tug with tow (not over 600 feet in length) astern. The ocean-going tug is shown with side lights, two 20-point towing lights forward and (optional) range light (20-point). Stern light is not visible from abeam. The inland tug is carrying side lights and three 32-point towing lights, and (optionally) a 20-point range light forward. On Great Lakes and Western Rivers, she is shown with side lights and two 20-point white lights forward

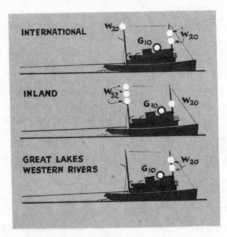

Above: A tug with more than one vessel in tow (length of tow over 600 feet). The ocean-going tug carries three towing lights in addition to her side lights. (Optional after range light is not showing here.) Stern light is not visible from abeam. The inland tug, since the tow is astern, is lighted the same as when her tow is under 600 feet. On Great Lakes and Western Rivers, too, the fact that her tow is over 600 feet in length does not change her lighting

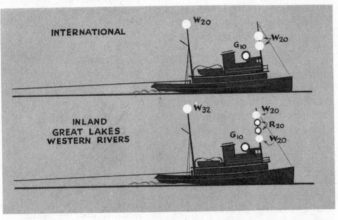

Above: A tug with submerged tow. On the high seas her lights are the same as though her tow were on the surface. Her 12-point white stern light or towing light is not visible from abeam. In other waters, she carries two red lights between two white lights in vertical line, in place of her usual towing lights, and also side lights. On inland waters, she may also carry the optional range light aft (shown)

that will best help to avert collision, and this action must be taken just as soon as she sees that the giving way of the burdened vessel alone will not of itself prevent collision. This is the rule in all waters.

In the matter of right of way, International and Inland Rules are identical in intent, if not exactly in terminology. Under both sets of rules, in any situation where one vessel is directed to keep out of the way, the privileged vessel must keep her course and speed, while the burdened vessel keeps clear by slackening speed, stopping, or reversing, not by crossing ahead.

On the high seas and inland waters alike, when power-driven vessels are on crossing courses, the vessel which has the other on her own starboard side is burdened and must keep clear. Overtaking vessels are burdened.

When two sailing vessels approach, so as to involve risk of collision, right of way on all except the high seas is determined as follows: (1) A vessel running free keeps out of the way of a vessel close-hauled. (2) A vessel close-

hauled on the port tack keeps out of the way of a vessel close-hauled on the starboard tack. (3) When both are running free, with the wind on different sides, the vessel which has the wind on the port side keeps out of the way of the other. (4) When both are running free, with the wind on the same side, the vessel to windward keeps out of the way of the vessel to leeward. (5) Except on the Great Lakes, a vessel with the wind aft keeps out of the way of the other vessel.

Revised (1965) International Rules, while producing the same result, have simplified the language: (1) when each sailboat has the wind on a different side, the one with the wind to port keeps clear of the other, and (2) when both have the wind on the same side the vessel which is to windward keeps clear of the other. The "windward side" for these purposes is deemed to be the side opposite to that on which the mainsail is carried or, for square-riggers, the side opposite to that on which the largest fore-and-aft sail is carried.

Sailing vessels invariably have right of way over steam vessels, except in the rare case when the sailing vessel is overtaking. All vessels must keep out of the way of fishing vessels, though fishing vessels have no right to obstruct fairways.

Seaplanes on the high seas are subject to International Rules, though it should be remembered that they may not be able to change their intended actions promptly.

On the Lakes and Western Rivers

On the Great Lakes, the rules governing right of way are substantially the same as those outlined above for both the high seas and inland waters. The privileged vessel holds her course and speed and the burdened vessel keeps out of the way, slackening speed, stopping or reversing as necessary. The special provision in Lakes rules, giving right of way to a descending steamer in narrow channels with a current, is discussed on page 64.

Western River Rules differ from all others in that they require a privileged vessel to hold her course but not her speed. In fact, *every* steam vessel approaching another vessel so as to involve risk of collision is obliged to slacken her speed or if necessary stop and reverse.

NOTE—In narrow channels, under all rules, neither sailboats nor motorboats have the right to hamper the passage of larger vessels which can operate only within such channels.

The provision granting right of way on Western Rivers to a descending steamer has also been mentioned in the discussion of whistle signals. (See page 64.) In other than the cases just noted, River Rules are practically in agreement with the International with respect to the principle of right of way.

SPECIAL CIRCUMSTANCES

ONE point where all four sets of rules are in agreement is in the general prudential rule, or rule of special circumstances, which authorizes (in fact, requires) departure from the rules in order to (but only to) avoid immediate danger. The rule reads: "In obeying and construing these Rules due regard shall be had to all dangers of navigation and collision, and to any special circumstances, including the limitations of the craft involved, which may render a departure from the above Rules necessary to avoid immediate danger."

Courts have laid emphasis on the words "immediate danger" in rendering their decisions, the principle being that rules must not be abandoned whenever perceptible risk of collision exists, but only when imperatively required by special circumstances in order to avoid immediate danger.

The courts have recognized five cases where the rule of special circumstances is properly invoked, as follows:

(1) Where vessels get so close that collision is inevitable unless preventive action is taken by both.

(2) When physical conditions prevent compliance with the rules. The example cited is that of a tug with tow astern running down a river in a swift current, meeting a free vessel crossing the river. The tug and tow, in such an unusual circumstance, would necessarily be granted the right of way, regardless of ordinary rules.

(3) When more than two vessels are involved in an approaching situation. In such a case, one or more of the vessels might be unable to obey the regular rules, as there may be a conflict between her duty to one vessel and her duty to another. Prompt, intelligent use of whistle signals is often a solution in such cases, with care that one vessel does not accept a signal intended for another. At the first evidence of confusion, every vessel must slow down and take any other action that will help to avert collision.

(4) Where a situation is not covered in the rules, as when one vessel is backing toward another. International and Inland Rules provide only for the 3 short blast whistle signal when a vessel is backing, and say nothing of passing signals for vessels going astern. In practice, the stern is usually regarded as the bow in such a case as it enables a vessel to determine what passing signals she should propose in inland waters. When one or both vessels approach on a collision course stern first, the rule of special circumstances replaces regular rules for meeting and passing.

(5) When one steam (power-driven) vessel proposes an action contrary to the rules and the other vessel agrees to the proposal. Examples of this would be a crossing situation where vessels exchanged 2 blasts and the burdened vessel attempted to hold her course across the bow of a privileged vessel, or a starboard-to-starboard passing when vessels meet head-and-head. Out of such cases have arisen the following decisions: A proposal to proceed contrary to law is not binding on the other vessel. Unless and until such a proposal is agreed to, both vessels must proceed in accordance with the regular rules. When such a proposal has been agreed to, neither vessel has right of way and both are equally bound to proceed with caution under the rule of special circumstances.

GOOD SEAMANSHIP

THE rule of good seamanship, binding on all vessels on all waters, states that "Nothing in these Rules shall exonerate any vessel, or the owner, master or crew thereof, from the consequences of any neglect to carry lights or signals, or of any neglect to keep a proper look-out, or of the neglect of any precaution which may be required by the ordinary practice of seamen, or by the special circumstances of the case."

Good seamanship requires the exercise of any required precaution in addition to mere observance of the rules. With regard to maintaining a proper lookout recent court decisions have held: the performance of lookout duty is an inexorable requirement of prudent navigation (Maryland Ct. of Appeals, 1962); a vessel navigating in congested waters is under a prime duty to provide an effective lookout (Virginia District Ct., 1963); although no specific location aboard is prescribed for a lookout he should be where he can best see and hear whatever may be in the vessel's way (Maryland District Ct., 1961).

DISTRESS SIGNALS

INTERNATIONAL Rules provide the following methods of indicating that a vessel is in distress:

(1) A gun or other explosive fired at intervals of about 1 minute.
(2) Continuous sounding of any fog signal apparatus.
(3) Rockets or shells, throwing red stars fired one at a time at short intervals.
(4) Signal by radiotelegraphy, or other method, consisting of the group . . . — — — . . . in the Morse Code.
(5) Signal by radiotelephony consisting of spoken word "Mayday."
(6) The International Code signal N.C.
(7) A signal consisting of a square flag and above or below it a ball, or something resembling a ball.
(8) Flames on the vessel (as from a burning oil or tar barrel).
(9) A rocket parachute (or hand) flare showing a red light.
(10) An orange smoke signal.
(11) Slowly and repeatedly raising and lowering arms outstretched to each side.

NOTE: Radio signal (12 dashes sent in one minute—each dash 4 seconds, each interval 1 second) has been provided to actuate auto-alarms of other vessels. *(See also page 78a)*

Inland Rules combine (1) and (2) above in prescribing, as a daytime signal, the continuous sounding of any fog signal apparatus, or the firing of a gun. These two signals are also recognized in Inland Rules as acceptable by night, as well as flames on the vessel, as from a burning tar or oil barrel, as in International Rule (8) above.

Great Lakes Rules provide for (1), (2) and (7) of the International Rules (above) by day; and, at night, (1), (2), (3) and (8).

Western River Rules provide for (1), (3), (6) and (7) of the International Rules (above) by day; and, at night, (1), (3), and (8). In addition to the use of a fog signal apparatus, by day or night, Western River Rules include the continuous sounding of a steam whistle.

All recognize the day signal of slowly and repeatedly raising and lowering arms outstretched to each side.

Special distress signals for airplanes down at sea and for submarines are used by the Navy both on the high seas and in inland waters. While these are not statutory, they should be understood, so that proper assistance may be rendered—by going immediately to the aid of an airplane, or by communicating at once with the nearest Coast Guard Air-Sea Rescue or Naval Station in the case of a submarine.

A submarine unable to surface fires a bomb which, at an altitude of 100 to 200 feet above the surface, explodes and releases a parachute with a red smoke bomb. A yellow smoke bomb (not a distress signal) warns surface vessels when a submarine is about to surface.

Very signals are used by airplanes forced down on navigable waters, with the following significances: White—"Slight damage, no assistance needed." White and green—"Stand by, may need assistance." Green alone—"Need mechanic and tools, stand by." Red—"Send assistance to save personnel."

MISCELLANEOUS RULES

THERE are a number of special rules which are specifically written into Inland, Great Lakes, and Western River Rules, and, though not expressly provided for in International Rules, vessels on the high seas would nevertheless observe them in following the rule of good seamanship. Among these are the following:

When passing floating plants, vessels are required to reduce speed to insure safety (not more than 5 mph when passing within 200 feet). Passing over lines of such plants, engines must be stopped, while light draft vessels are required to keep outside buoys marking the ends of mooring lines of a plant working in the channel.

Flashing the rays of a searchlight or other blinding light onto the bridge or into the pilot house of any vessel under way is prohibited. Lights not required by law, which would interfere with distinguishing the signal lights, must not be shown. Unnecessary whistling within any harbor limits of the United States is also prohibited. Violation of any of these rules may lead to revocation or suspension of a pilot's license or certificate.

Failure to have the required "Rules of the Road" pamphlet (which replaced old "Pilot Rules" as of May 1, 1959) on board and readily available (when practicable) on vessels and craft over 65 feet in length while on Inland Waters and Western Rivers, or two copies of the placard form CG-807 while on the Great Lakes, may be grounds for assessment of a $500 penalty.

In all waters, in case of collision, vessels must stand by to render assistance. Masters or persons in charge are required to give the vessel's name, her port, and ports from and to which she is bound.

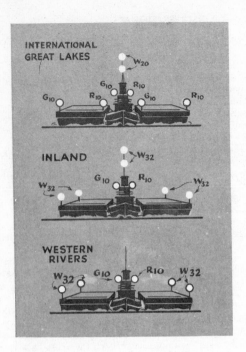

INTERNATIONAL
GREAT LAKES

INLAND

WESTERN
RIVERS

Vessel at Anchor or Aground

Lights displayed by a tug with one scow on each side. Note that each scow, on the high seas, carries both red and green lights, as distinguished from practice on Western Rivers. The fixed white stern lights on tug and tow are not visible from ahead. On inland waters, the scow's lights are white; the tug is shown with two 32-point white lights, the usual practice, though optionally the towing lights might be 20-point. Optionally, she might in the illustration also have a 20-point white range light forward, though it is neither required nor forbidden. Tows on the Gulf Intracoastal Waterway carry the same lights as they do under Western River rules. The tug, on Western Rivers, has two amber lights aft, vertically arranged, not visible forward of the beam

Lights for Vessels—
On the High Seas,
Inland Waters,
Great Lakes,
And Western Rivers

Steam (Power-driven) Vessels Under Way

Under International Rules, a power-driven vessel under way carries a white 20-point (225°) light forward (20 to 40 feet above the hull); red and green 10-point (112½°) side lights (with 36-inch screens); and a white 20-point (225°) range light aft (at least 15 feet higher than the foremast light). Horizontal distance between masthead lights (which must be in line with, and over, the keel) must be at least 3 times the vertical distance. A fixed 12-point (135°) stern light, showing aft, is now mandatory. (The 20-point white masthead light aft is optional on vessels under 150 feet, and vessels towing.)

Under Inland Rules, a steam or motor vessel under way (excepting seagoing vessels, ferry boats and motor boats) shows a 20-point white light forward; 10-point red and green side lights (with 36-inch screens); and a 32-point white range light aft at least 15 feet higher than the foremast light. Overtaken vessels, except steam vessels with 32-point after range light, show a white light or flare-up.

On the Great Lakes, a steam vessel under way carries the

WITH respect to the carrying of lights at night, rules are fairly uniform in requiring them to be carried in all weathers from sunset to sunrise. International Rules add "and in all other circumstances when it is deemed necessary." The word "visible" as applied to lights means visible on a dark night with a clear atmosphere. No other lights which can be mistaken for the prescribed lights may be exhibited.

In all waters a vessel at anchor, if less than 150 feet in length, displays one 32-point white light. It must be visible at least 2 miles on Inland Waters and Western Rivers, 1 mile on the Great Lakes. Under International Rules for vessels under 150 feet it is 2 miles, over 150 feet 3 miles. The single anchor light is carried forward where it can best be seen.

On larger vessels requiring two lights, the forward light is carried at least 20 feet above the hull, the second at or near the stern at a height not less than 15 feet lower than the forward light.

On the Great Lakes a vessel over 150 feet in length at anchor would carry two white 32-point lights forward (at the same heights as mentioned above) and two white 32-point lights aft. These are horizontally arranged athwartships (at least 10 feet apart) in such a manner that one or both will be visible from any direction at a distance of 1 mile. In addition, at intervals of 100 feet, she carries white 32-point deck lights not less than 2 feet above the deck.

In anchorage areas specially designated by the Secretary of the Army vessels 65 feet and smaller need not show anchor lights. The rules make special provision for barges, canal boats, scows and other nondescript craft at anchor in such areas.

With a few exceptions, a vessel aground shows the lights prescribed for her when at anchor. Under International Rules, in addition to the anchor light (or lights) she would also show the two vertically arranged red 32-point lights of a vessel not under command. Great Lakes Rules provide that vessels aground, over 65 feet in length, must show the two red vertical lights, except on the St. Mary's River where they are shown regardless of boat length.

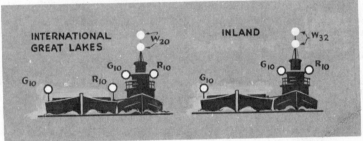

INTERNATIONAL GREAT LAKES

INLAND

A tug with barge or canal boat alongside, her side light not obscured by the tow. Though Inland Rules do provide for white lights for scows alongside, no lights are specified for canal boats and barges alongside unless they obscure the tug's side light. It is held that, in such a case, it is proper for the tow to be lighted the same as though the tug's side light were obscured. On the Great Lakes, a canal boat shows only the outer side light, whereas a barge shows both. On Western Rivers, lights would be the same as shown for Inland Waters, except that the tug's white lights would be replaced by 12-pt. amber ones, not visible forward of the beam and tow would show white lights on outboard corners, as on the Intracostal Waterway

20-point white light forward, and 10-point red and green side lights (with 36-inch screens). The forward light is carried higher than the side lights. Steam vessels under 100 feet in length also carry a 32-point bright white light aft, in line with the keel and higher than the white light forward. Steamers over 100 feet carry a 32-point white range light (at least 15 feet higher than the bow light and at least 50 feet abaft it). Optionally, the range light may be replaced by two lights not more than 30 inches apart horizontally, "one on either side of the keel," arranged so that one or both will be visible from any angle.

Ocean-going steamers, when under way on Western Rivers, carry the lights required by International Rules.

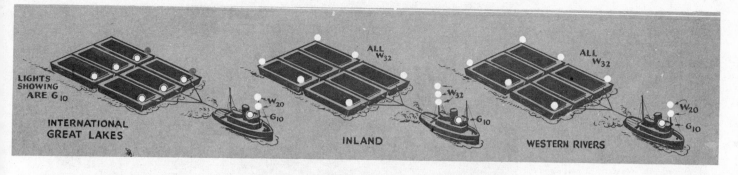

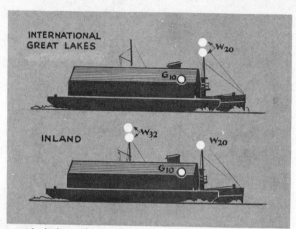

Above: A tug with scows astern, three abreast in two tiers. Note colored side lights on the tow on the high seas and Great Lakes, white lights on other waters. Three towing lights on the inland tug indicate tow is astern. (Optional range lights not shown)

Right: A tug with tow alongside, her side light obscured. On the high seas and Great Lakes, the tow is also carrying a 10-point red light on the port side, not visible here. In all waters, a side light must show on the outer side of the tow. Inland tug is showing optional range light. (White stern lights required on high seas not visible in these views.) On Western Rivers, white lights are carried on outboard corners of tow, side lights only if tug's colored side lights are obscured.

Above: On Western Rivers, the tug carries side lights and, aft, two red lights, vertically arranged, not visible forward of the beam

Left: Except on the high seas, double-ended ferries carry a central range of two white 32-point lights at equal height fore and aft, in addition to side lights. On the high seas, they use a set of range and side lights each way, and 12-point stern light

larger craft. If they do not, then they are lighted as follows:—

Power-driven vessels under 65 feet carry forward (at least 9 feet above the gunwale) a 20-point white light and red and green side lights, or in lieu of separate red and green lights a combined red-and-green lantern, carried not less than 3 feet below the white light. Small motor craft, such as are carried aboard sea-going vessels, may carry the white light less than 9 feet above the gunwale, but in that case rules specify it must be above the combined red-and-green lantern.

Vessels under oars or sails and less than 40 feet carry ready at hand a lantern with green glass on one side and red glass on the other shown, with the colored lights on the proper sides, at the approach of other vessels.

Small craft on the high seas, if unable to carry a fixed white 12-point stern light showing aft, may show an electric torch or lighted lantern to approaching vessels. Rowboats on the high seas show a white lantern in time to prevent collision.

Great Lakes Rules also have a provision for open boats, which are permitted to carry, instead of regular side lights, a lantern with red and green slides, to be shown when other craft approach. They show a white light at anchor, and may use a flare-up if necessary.

Lights Required by Motor Boat Act

Motor boats (including auxiliaries) on the navigable waters of the United States must be lighted in accordance with the Motor Boat Act of 1940, rather than Pilot Rules pertaining to any one of the four geographical jurisdictions thus far discussed. "Navigable" waters, under Federal jurisdiction, are those navigable to the sea, or waterways crossing state or international boundaries.

Briefly, under the terms of the Act, motor boats (vessels propelled by machinery not more than 65 feet in length, excepting tugs and towboats driven by steam) are divided into four classes determining, among other things, how they are to be lighted. Classification is by length, as follows:

Class A, under 16 feet; Class 1, 16 to under 26 feet; Class 2, 26 to under 40 feet; and Class 3, 40 to 65 feet.

Classes A and 1, instead of a white bow light, carry a combination red-and-green light forward (each color showing through the customary 10 points), and a 32-point white light aft higher than the combination light.

Classes 2 and 3 carry a white 20-point bow light, screened separate 10-point red and green side lights, and 32-point white light aft higher than the bow light.

A motor boat under sail is lighted as a sailboat,

River steamers navigating waters subject to Western River Rules carry a red light on the outboard side of the port smoke pipe and a green light on the outboard side of the starboard smoke pipe, showing forward and abeam on their respective sides.

Steam vessels, other than those expressly provided for, are required under Western River Rules to carry lights similar to the usual lights of a steam vessel on inland waters.

There is no provision in Rules of the Road for the Great Lakes to permit seagoing vessels to display lights required by International Rules while navigating the Lakes.

International and Inland Rules both provide that a vessel may, if necessary to attract attention, show a flare-up or use any detonating signal that cannot be mistaken for a distress signal.

Small Vessels Under Way

All rules uniformly provide that on small vessels when, due to bad weather, it is impractical to keep side lights in their fixed positions, they may be kept lighted and at hand, ready to be displayed at the approach of other vessels.

Under International Rules, power-driven vessels under 65 feet, vessels under oars or sails of less than 40 feet in length, and rowboats need not carry the lights required of

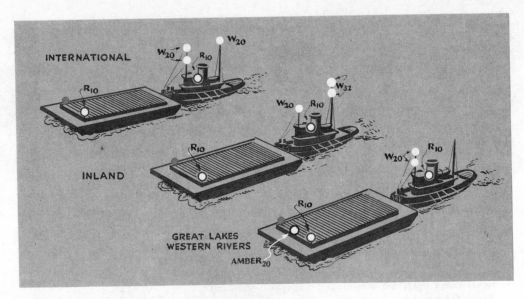

On inland waters, a tug pushing her tow ahead must now carry two white towing lights the same as if her tow were alongside. She is shown here with optional 20-point range light. The ocean-going tug is also shown carrying the optional 20-point range light, but her required white stern light is not visible in this view. In all cases, the tow displays colored side lights forward. The amber bow light is now required on Western Rivers and Gulf Intracoastal Waterway, and optional on the Great Lakes

showing colored side lights and she is now required to carry a 12-pt. white light aft. Motorboats under sail and power both are now lighted like motorboats of their respective classes. Under the amended Motor Boat Act, motorboats may, optionally, carry lights prescribed by International Rules.

White lights prescribed for motor boats must be visible at least 2 miles, colored lights at least 1 mile. Outboards are required to carry the appropriate lights of their class, depending on length. At anchor, motor boats show a single white 32-point light, the same as other vessels. On the high seas motor boats would be lighted according to International Rules.

Steam (Power-driven) Vessels Towing

A power-driven vessel towing, on the high seas, carries red and green side lights and two white 20-point towing lights forward in vertical line not less than 6 feet apart, the lower not less than 14 feet above the hull. She must carry either a small white light aft (not visible forward of the beam) for the tow to steer by, or a fixed 12-point

(135°) white stern light. She may also carry the 20-point after range light provided for a power-driven vessel under way. If carried, it should be high enough above the towing lights so as not to be mistaken for another towing light.

If the length of tow from the stern of the tug to the stern of the last vessel exceeds 600 feet, she carries three white 20-point towing lights instead of two.

On inland waters vessels towing, in addition to side lights, carry two vertical white towing lights if the tow is alongside or ahead, and three if the tow is astern (regardless of the length of the tow or number of vessels composing it). The towing lights may be 20-point, carried forward, or 32-point, carried aft. Range lights are neither required nor forbidden, but when 20-point towing lights are carried forward, a 32-point range light aft is desirable, not only because it provides a range but because it is visible from aft. To prevent confusion, a range light (whether it is carried forward or aft) should be placed so that the vertical distance between it and the towing lights is at least twice as much as the interval between towing lights. Otherwise it might be mistaken (when seen from dead ahead) as a third towing light, when in fact only two are being carried.

Tugs showing a 32-point light aft (either towing lights or range light) are not required to show the white light or flare-up light usually required of overtaken vessels.

On the Great Lakes a steam vessel with a tow (other than a raft) carries, in addition to her side lights, two 20-point white towing lights forward in vertical line (at least 6 feet apart). Aft she carries a small white light (not visible forward of the beam) for the tow to steer by. On the Lakes she is similarly lighted when towing a raft, except that the two towing lights forward are 32-point, and are carried in a horizontal line athwartships (at least 8 feet apart).

On the Lakes, harbor tugs under 100 tons net register, when not towing, carry red and green side lights, and a 20-point white light at the foremast head or on top of the pilot house. When towing (except a raft) they carry an additional 20-point white light at least 3 feet vertically above or below the 20-point headlight. When towing a

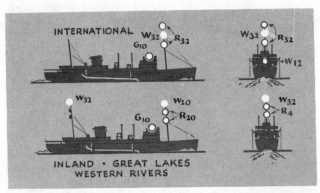

Above: On the high seas, a self-propelling suction dredge under way with suction on bottom would show in addition to side lights, three vertical lights (one white between two red), and a 12-point white stern light. On other waters, besides running lights, they have two red 20-point lights below the 20-point white masthead light, and two red 4-point lights showing astern

Right: The distinguishing lights of the minesweeper are the three green 32-point lights at the masthead and spreader ends. She also shows towing light. Optionally, she might show a range light

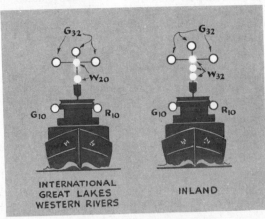

raft, the two headlights are 32-point instead of 20-point, horizontally arranged athwartships not less than 4 feet apart.

On Western Rivers, steam vessels towing one or more vessels on a hawser astern carry in addition to their sidelights two 20-point white lights on the foremast, vertically arranged. When the tow is alongside or ahead, they show, instead of the white lights, two amber lights aft, vertically arranged, not visible forward of the beam.

When the tow is submerged, towing vessels on the high seas are lighted the same as when their tow is on the surface. On all other waters, Inland Rules and War Department Regulations require her to substitute for the white towing lights four 32-point lights vertically arranged—the upper and lower white, the two middle ones red.

Sailing Vessels Under Way

ON all waters, sailing vessels under way carry the red and green side lights, and show a white light aft. Under Inland and Western River Rules, this white light must be a fixed 12-point light showing aft except that small boats, in bad weather, may show an electric torch or lighted lantern to overtaking vessels. Under Great Lakes Rules sailing vessels under way show "a lighted torch on that point or quarter to which such steamer shall be approaching." On the high seas, a fixed white 12-point stern light is now mandatory.

Vessels Being Towed

WITH the exception of barges, scows, and canal boats (for which special lights are prescribed) vessels in tow are almost uniformly lighted like the sailing vessel—with side lights and the white light shown aft. The special lights for barges, scows, and canal boats are prescribed by the Commandant of the Coast Guard. Since these regulations are applicable only on inland waters, the Great Lakes and Western Rivers, it follows that on the high seas every vessel in a tow (whether she is steam, sail, or not self-propelled) must show red and green side lights. The last vessel in a tow, under International Rules, must carry a fixed white 12-point light aft. Others may carry the fixed light or a small white towing light.

A special section of the Inland Rules is devoted to lights for barges, canal boats, scows and other vessels of nondescript type in tow on the Gulf Intracoastal Waterway.

Barges and Canal Boats, Towed Astern—Inland Waters
(Except New York Harbor and Vicinity, Hudson River, Lake Champlain, East River, Long Island Sound, and Certain Gulf Intracoastal Waters)

ON inland waters, with the exceptions noted above, barges and canal boats, towed astern singly or in tandem, each carry red and green side lights and a 12-point white light on the stern. The last vessel in the tow (or the only one, if there is but one) carries, instead of the 12-point light, two white 32-point lights horizontally arranged athwartships. When two or more boats are abreast, the colored side lights are carried on the outboard bows of outside boats, and each outside boat in the last tier carries a 32-point white light on the stern. White stern lights for boats other than the last are 12-point.

Under Inland Rules, tows on the Gulf Intracoastal Waterway now carry the same lights as prescribed for Western Rivers.

Barges, Canal Boats, and Scows, Alongside
(Obscuring Side Lights)

WHEN the side lights of a towing vessel are obscured by such a craft alongside, the towed vessel carries a green side light if towed on the starboard side, a red side light if on the port side. If there is more than one towed boat abreast, the colored side light is displayed from the outer side of the outside boat.

In this situation (towing alongside and obscuring the towboat's side lights) and also when pushed ahead of the towboat, barges, canal boats and scows are lighted alike. When the tow is astern, scows are lighted differently from barges and canal boats.

Barges, Canal Boats, and Scows, Pushed Ahead

WHEN pushed ahead of a towboat, barges, canal boats, and scows show a red light on the port bow and green light on the starboard bow of the head boat. If there is more than one abreast, the lights are displayed from the outer sides of the outside barges. A tow boat pushing her tow in inland waters now carries the same towing lights she would show with tow alongside.

Barges, Canal Boats, and Scows, in Tow
(In New York Harbor and Vicinity, Hudson River, Lake Champlain, East River, Long Island Sound, and Narragansett Bay)

IN these waters, to which special rules apply, all nondescript vessels such as barges, canal boats, scows, car floats, lighters, etc. are lighted alike.

When towed astern, singly, they carry a white light on bow and stern. In tandem, close up, each boat carries a white light on the stern and the first boat also carries a white light on the bow. In tandem, with intermediate hawser between boats in tow, each carries a white light on bow and stern, except the last which carries two white lights on the stern, horizontally arranged.

Seagoing barges are not required to change their seagoing (red and green) lights on entering these waters except that the last vessel in tow must display two white lights on the stern, horizontally arranged athwartships.

When towed at a hawser, two or more abreast, in one tier, each boat has a white light on the stern, and each outside boat has a white light on the bow. In more than one tier, every boat carries a white light on the stern and the outside boats in the head tier also carry a white light on the bow.

(All the white lights mentioned above are 32 point.)

When towed alongside, a white light is displayed at each outboard corner of the tow. When pushed ahead, a 10-point red light is carried on the port bow and a 10-point green light on the starboard bow of the head barge or barges.

Dump scows carrying garbage from New York Harbor waters to the high seas when in tandem carry red and green side lights and show a white light to overtaking vessels.

Barges and canal boats in tow, correctly lighted according to the rules of waters in which they are usually employed, need not change their usual lights if merely passing through the waters governed by these Inland Rules.

Canal Boats in Tow—Great Lakes

CANAL boats towed astern on the Great Lakes, singly or in tandem, carry colored side lights and a small bright white light aft. At a hawser in one or more tiers, two or more abreast, the starboard boat in each tier carries a green light on her starboard side, and the port boat in each tier carries a red light on her port side, and each outside boat in the last tier carries a small white light aft. Towed alongside, a canal boat on the starboard side of a steamer carries a green side light; towed on the port side, she carries a red side light. With one boat on each side, the starboard boat carries a green light, the port boat a red light. The side lights mentioned, of course, are 10-point; the white light must not be visible forward of the beam.

On the Great Lakes specific provision is made as above for canal boats, but not for barges, scows, lighters and other nondescript craft in tow. Thus, they would carry the lights provided generally for vessels in tow which means colored side lights and a small bright white light aft.

When a tow is pushed ahead on the Great Lakes, red and green side lights mark the maximum projections to port and starboard, and a 20-point amber light may be carried forward, in the center line.

Rafts in Tow or Drifting or at Anchor in a Fairway

UNDER Inland Rules, vessels propelled by hand power, horsepower, or river current (except rafts and rowboats) carry one white light forward. Rafts of one crib in width carry one white light at each end. Rafts of more than one crib in width carry 4 white lights, one at each outside corner. Unstable log rafts of one bag or boom in width carry 2 to 4 white lights in a fore-and-aft line, one of which is at each end. If more than one bag or boom in width, they carry a white light on each outside corner. The white lights are all 32-point, carried at least 8 feet above water.

Barges, Canal Boats and Scows—Western Rivers

IN the new Western River rules (effective January 1, 1949) a "barge" is taken to include not only barges, but canal boats, scows, and nondescript vessels not otherwise provided for. In a tow of one or more barges pushed ahead, a 20-point amber light must now be carried at the extreme forward end of the tow, at the centerline, visible 2 miles.

In addition to the amber light, barges towed ahead carry colored side lights—red on the port bow, green on the starboard bow—to mark the outermost projections of the tow. Towed alongside, barges carry white lights at outside corners of the tow, colored side lights only if the side lights of the tug are obscured by deckhouses, etc. A single barge, towed astern, has a white light at each corner. With two or more astern, with intermediate hawsers, the first barge has a white light at each corner of the bow, and one at the stern, amidships. Intermediate barges carry a white light bow and stern, amidships. The last barge has a white light forward, amidships, and a white light at each corner of the stern. For tows astern in tandem, close up, the arrangement is much the same except that intermediate barges have a single light aft, amidships. When in tiers astern, each outside barge in each tier has a white light at the outboard corner of the bow; in addition, outside barges in the last tier carry white lights at the outboard corners of the stern.

Naval Vessels

RULES are, broadly, in agreement in providing that nothing shall interfere with the operation of special rules made by the government of any nation with respect to additional station and signal lights for war vessels and ships in convoy, or with the exhibition of recognition signals by shipowners, authorized by their respective governments. Compliance with them is proper on all waters navigable by seagoing vessels, in accordance with terms of the enacting clause of International Rules. Under the provisions of this rule special lights have been prescribed for such craft as minesweepers which carry, in addition to side lights and towing lights, three 32-point green lights, one at the foremasthead and one at each yardarm.

The normal navigation lights of submarines could be mistaken for those of a small vessel, whereas in fact they are large deep-draft vessels with limited maneuvering characteristics while operating on the surface. In addition to their regular navigational lights they are authorized to display, above the masthead light, an amber colored rotating light producing 90 flashes per minute, visible all around the horizon.

On PT boats, landing craft and other naval vessels of special construction, where it is impossible to carry lights in prescribed positions, they are displayed in accordance with regulations issued by the Secretary of the Navy. Under such provisions the masthead light of a PT may be located in the after part of the vessel rather than forward.

Under all rules except the International, a special provision permits suspension of the exhibition of lights aboard vessels of war or Coast Guard cutters whenever, in the opinion of the Secretary of the Navy, the commander-in-chief of a squadron, or the commander of a vessel acting singly, the special character of the service may require it.

Pilot Vessels

ALL except Great Lakes Rules provide special lights for pilot vessels. A steam (power-driven) pilot vessel under way on station on pilotage duty carries a 32-point white light at the masthead and, 8 feet below it, a 32-point red light. These are in addition to the red and green side lights. At anchor, or course, side lights are extinguished.

A sailing pilot vessel carries a 32-point white light at the masthead and shows a flare-up at short intervals. (On the high seas, instead of a flare, a bright intermittent white light may be used on power-driven pilot vessels.) Side lights, when under way, are shown at the approach of other vessels.

If the pilot boat is of a type designed to go alongside a vessel to put a pilot aboard she may show the white light instead of carrying it at the masthead and also have a red-and-green lantern at hand to be shown as necessary.

Pilot vessels not engaged on station on pilotage duty carry the same lights as other vessels of their tonnage.

Revised International Rules specifically provide that all pilot vessels on station on duty at anchor must carry anchor lights in addition to their special lights.

On the Great Lakes no special rule is provided, so pilot vessels are lighted the same as other vessels of their class.

Fishing Vessels

UNDER the International Rules, vessels engaged in fishing (vessels fishing with trolling lines are expressly deemed to be *not* vessels "engaged in fishing") must, whether at anchor or under way, show two vertical 32-point lights, the upper red, the lower white unless the boat is trawling, i.e., dragging a dredge net or similar equipment, in which case the upper light must be green. If outlying fishing gear extends more than 500 feet horizontally an additional 32-point white light must be shown "not less than 6 feet nor more than 20 feet away from the vertical lights in the direction of the outlying gear." All fishing vessels under way must show the conventional side lights, or lantern, as appropriate, and a stern light.

Under Inland Rules, fishing vessels of less than 10 gross tons, under way with no lines, nets, trawls, or other gear out, need not carry side lights but may have ready at hand a lantern with red glass on one side and green glass on the other to show to approaching vessels. Such a vessel over 10 tons must carry the usual lights of a vessel of her class under way.

When trawling, dredging, or fishing with any kind of dragnets or lines, fishing boats on inland waters exhibit a red light over a white light (6 to 12 feet apart vertically, and the horizontal distance, if any, less than 10 feet). These are 32-point lights.

On the Great Lakes and Western Rivers fishing boats navigating bays, harbors, or rivers by hand power, horsepower, or river current, or at anchor in a channel, carry one or more white lights.

Law Enforcement Vessels

LAW enforcement vessels of the United States, a State, or its political subdivisions, including municipalities, having administrative control over use of navigable waters, may display in addition to prescribed lights and day signals a distinctive blue rotating light of low intensity. It is carried forward, wherever effective.

Seaplanes

SEAPLANES on the water on the high seas are subject to International Rules. Seaplanes under way on the water carry forward, amidships, a 220° white light showing 110° on each side from right ahead (visible 3 miles); on the starboard wing tip a 110° green light and on the port wing tip a 110° red light, each showing from right ahead to 20° abaft the beam on its respective side (visible 2 miles); and at the stern a white 12-point (135°) light showing 6 points (67½°) each side from right aft (visible 2 miles), carried at the approximate level of the side lights.

Vessel Not Under Command

UNDER International Rules (and Great Lakes, if vessel is over 65 feet) a vessel not under command, that is, not maneuverable, carries two red 32-point lights vertically arranged.

On other waters vessels not under command cannot show the same signal, as two red lights in Inland Rules and War Department Regulations are reserved for a different use.

Vessel Working on Telegraph Cable

VESSELS laying or picking up telegraph cable on the high seas carry three 32-point lights in vertical line (at least 6 feet apart) —the upper and lower red, and the middle white. When making way through the water they also carry side lights.

On other waters, they carry three red lights in vertical line, 3 to 6 feet apart, with the lowest light carried at a height of at least 15 feet above deck.

Vessels Working on Buoys, Underwater Operations, Etc.

IN the revision of the International Rules, effective September 1, 1965, provision is made for types of vessels engaged in operations which would prevent their getting out of the way of approaching vessels.

On the high seas, a vessel engaged in laying or in picking up a navigation mark or an underwater cable, or a vessel engaged in surveying or underwater operations, when from the nature of her work she is unable to get out of the way of approaching vessels, carries 3 lights in a vertical line, the upper and lower red, the middle one white—and each visible all around the horizon for at least 2 miles. When making way through the water, they also carry side lights. At anchor, they carry appropriate anchor lights as well as the distinguishing lights.

On inland waters, Western Rivers and the Great Lakes vessels engaged in such operations show three red lights in a vertical line, 3 to 6 feet apart, with the bottom one "not less than 15 feet above the deck."

Fixed White Stern Lights Required

PRIOR to August 14, 1958 some vessels, like sailboats under sail alone, were permitted the choice of showing a flare-up light to overtaking vessels. Since that date, Inland Rules and Western River Rules both require *all* vessels not otherwise required to carry a light visible from aft, to carry when under way a *fixed* 12-point white stern light showing aft. It is carried as nearly as possible at the level of side lights. *Only exception* is in the case of small vessels unable to do so, as in bad weather. They may show an electric torch or lighted lantern to overtaking vessels.

Proposed New Rules of the Road for United States Waters

A bill was introduced in Congress in mid-July 1968 which would establish a single set of rules of the nautical road to replace the existing Inland, Great Lakes, and Western Rivers Rules. The new regulations would be known as the "United States Nautical Rules."

Basically the proposed rules would be patterned after the International Rules of the Road, in many cases using identical language. In other instances, certain requirements, such as the height of lights or required distance of visibility, have been somewhat relaxed or modified.

Rules relating to lights

Navigation light requirements are derived from the International Rules, but contain some exceptions and options. Lights for power-driven vessels are based on the international requirement for a single 225° white light forward on craft less than 150 feet in length and a central range of such lights for longer vessels. A 360° after range light would continue to be permitted, and would be required on the Great Lakes. Lights for towing vessels would be changed in many details from those now prescribed by the Inland and Western Rivers Rules.

The lights and shapes for vessels not under command and vessels engaged in operations restricting their ability to maneuver, found in International Rule 4, would be made applicable to U.S. waters. The minimum vertical light separation would be reduced from the 6-foot spacing of the International Rules to the 3-foot spacing found in inland waters.

The international requirements for lights carried by sailing craft and vessels being towed would be incorporated in the new U.S. Rules, as would the optional red-over-green lights for sailboats.

International Rule 7, lights for craft under 65 feet in length, would be modified to allow white lights visible 2 miles rather than 3; the minimum height of masthead lights would be reduced to 3 feet above the sidelights in lieu of 9 feet above the deck. All lights prescribed by the 1940 Motorboat Act would be permitted.

Distinctive shape for craft under sail and power

The proposed new Rule 14 parallels the International Rule of the same number and would require craft propelled by sail *and* machinery to show a distinctive shape of a black cone, point down.

Changes in fog signals

Fog signals would be revised to conform more nearly to the International Rules including the two-minute interval between signals, except on the Great Lakes.

Right-of-way for sailboats

The right-of-way rules for sailboats would be changed to parallel the simpler and clearer International Rules. The vessel on a starboard tack would be privileged over

one on a port tack; or if both were on the same tack, the leeward boat would have the right of way over the windward craft.

Danger signal changes

The danger signal on the whistle would be increased from a minimum of four blasts to at least five in accordance with high-seas procedures. The meaning of one- and two-blast signals, however, would remain as they presently are in the Inland Rules—intended action in meeting or passing rather than changes of course.

PRACTICAL EFFECT OF THE NEW PROPOSALS

Although the stated intent of the legislation is to replace three existing sets of rules of the road with a "single unified set of rules," the draft bill contains many exceptions and special provisions for the Great Lakes. The result is a complex document of much greater length than would be necessary for a truly "single" set of rules.

NOT EFFECTIVE YET

It is emphasized that this is **proposed** legislation, *not yet an effective change* in the regulations. As 1968 was an election year, the late introduction of the bill prevented complete Congressional action in that session. It is expected that the measure will be reintroduced in the 91st Congress (where it will get a new number) early in 1969, with committee hearings thereafter, and passage later in the year. Although some individual provisions may be modified as the rules progress through Congress, it is a near-certainty that the United States Nautical Rules will come into being. The proposed effective date would be one year after enactment into law.

Moored Dredges

ON INLAND waters, Great Lakes and Western Rivers dredges held stationary by moorings or spuds show, at least 6 feet above the deck, a white light at each corner and, "where they can best be seen," two 32-point red lights, arranged vertically 3 to 6 feet apart and at least 15 feet above the deck. Scows moored alongside such a dredge must show a white light on each outboard corner, at least 6 feet above the deck.

Vessels Moored at Wrecks

INLAND, Great Lakes and Western River rules require a vessel moored alongside or over a wreck (whether stationary or drifting) to show a white light from bow and stern of each outside vessel (not less than 6 feet above deck) and, where they can best be seen, two 32-point red lights vertically arranged (3 to 6 feet apart) not less than 15 feet above deck.

Vessels Engaged in Submarine Construction

EXCEPT on the high seas, vessels moored or anchored and engaged in laying pipe or cable, or operating on bank protection, submarine construction or excavation, show three 32-point red lights in vertical line (3 to 6 feet apart) not less than 15 feet above deck.

Survey Vessels

ON INLAND WATERS a vessel of the Coast and Geodetic Survey at anchor in a fairway, engaged in surveying, would display two red lights vertically arranged (6 feet apart—or 3 feet, if necessary, on small craft). Coast Guard vessels handling or servicing aids to navigation also use two red lights in vertical line as a warning signal. Speed of boats passing within 200 feet of such Coast Guard vessel, must not exceed 5 mph.

Suction Dredges

ON GREAT LAKES and Western Rivers self-propelling suction dredges under way and engaged in dredging operations carry regular running lights. In addition, they carry two red 20-point lights vertically arranged under the 20-point white masthead light and aft two red 4-point lights to show astern. The same lights are shown under Inland Rules for all self-propelled dredges under way while dredging.

Floating Plant Moorings

UNDER INLAND RULES, excepting certain waters in and adjacent to New York Harbor, anchors of a floating plant in navigable channels are marked at night by throwing a searchlight on their buoys when a vessel is passing, or the buoys may be lighted by red 32-point lights. The same rule applies to the Great Lakes and Western Rivers. On the high seas, with no specific rule to cover the situation, white anchor lights on buoys would be proper and the beam of light may also be used, though not required.

Double-Ended Ferries

DOUBLE-ENDED FERRIES, on all except the high seas, carry a central range of two white 32-point lights at equal height fore and aft. In addition, they carry the usual red and green side lights. Amidships, 15 feet above the range lights, they may show an extra white or colored light designating the line. Single-ended ferries are lighted like other steam vessels. On the high seas a double-ended ferry would use one set of range and side lights each way, similar to the lights of other steam vessels under International Rules.

To Attract Attention

INTERNATIONAL and Inland Rules provide that any vessel may, to attract attention, show in addition to required lights a flare-up light or use any detonating signal (which cannot be mistaken for any otherwise authorized signal) that cannot be mistaken for a distress signal. This would be proper on any waters navigable by seagoing vessels.

DAY MARKS

JUST AS special lights characterize various types of vessels at night, so day marks prescribed by the rules indicate to other craft the nature of a vessel or the kind of work she is engaged in. There is a considerable difference in rules to be observed in waters under the various jurisdictions, the principal difference being between the International and all other rules.

Vessels over 65 feet in length, *anchored in a fairway* or channel,

use a day mark consisting of one black ball or shape at least two feet in diameter. This is uniform on all waters except that on the high seas, this day signal is used by vessels at anchor regardless of length.

On inland waters, a *steam vessel under sail only* may use one black ball as a day mark.

On the high seas, a power-driven *vessel* when *propelled by both sail and machinery* carries forward a black conical shape, point downwards.

On the high seas a *vessel not under command* carries, in vertical line, two black balls or shapes, each 2 feet in diameter. They are also carried on the Great Lakes but only by vessels over 65 feet.

On all waters except the high seas two black balls (at least 2 feet in diameter and 15 feet above the deckhouse) are the day mark of a self-propelling *suction dredge under way* while dredging.

Under Inland Rules only, two black balls (in vertical line 6 feet apart) are also used as a day mark by *survey vessels* of the Coast and Geodetic Survey at anchor in a fairway on surveying opertions. If under way and engaged in hydrographic surveying they may carry three shapes in vertical line, the highest and lowest globular in shape and green in color, the middle one diamond in shape and white.

On the high seas, three black balls in vertical line are the day mark for a *vessel aground*. They are also shown on the Lakes, but only by vessels over 65 feet.

Boats or *vessels fishing* with nets, lines, trawls, or other gear out when under way on inland waters display a basket. If at anchor with gear out they show the basket toward the nets or gear. On the high seas, the basket is also used but only by vessels under 65 feet (larger boats show two black cones); in cases where lines or nets extend more than 500 feet, they show another black conical shape, apex upward. When a fishing vessel gets her gear fast to a rock or other obstruction, International Rules require her to haul down the basket (day mark) and carry forward a black ball not less than 2 feet in diameter, the day mark of a vessel at anchor.

Steamers, derrick boats, lighters and other *vessels fast to a wreck*, alongside or moored over it, display two red shapes in vertical line, except when more than one vessel is at work, when the shapes are displayed from one vessel on each side of the wreck. These shapes are double frustums of a cone, base to base. The rules are uniform except on the high seas.

On all waters except the high seas *dredges held stationary* by moorings or spuds display two red balls in vertical line 3 to 6 feet apart, 15 feet above the deckhouse.

Under all rules except the International, a *vessel* moored or anchored and *engaged in laying pipe* or operating on submarine construction or excavation displays two balls in vertical line, the upper painted in black and white vertical stripes 6 inches wide, and the lower ball solid red.

A *vessel laying or picking up telegraph cable* on the high seas carries three shapes in vertical line, the highest and lowest globular in shape and red in color, the middle one diamond in shape and white. This International rule has been extended to apply to *vessels engaged in laying or picking up a navigation mark, or engaged in surveying or underwater operations.*

On waters other than the high seas, a Coast Guard vessel handling or *servicing aids to navigation* displays two orange and white vertically striped balls in vertical line. On the high seas she would show three shapes—a white diamond between two red balls in vertical line.

Except on the high seas the day mark for a *vessel with submerged object in tow* is two shapes in vertical line. The shapes are in the form of double frustums of a cone, base to base. The upper is painted in alternate horizontal stripes of black and white 8 inches wide and the lower is solid red. Shapes are 2 feet in diameter (8 inches at the end of cones) and 4 feet from end to end. This case is not covered in International Rules.

Special provision is made for a *vessel towing a "dracone"* (a sausage-shaped envelope of strong woven nylon fabric coated with synthetic rubber). Strings of these dracones used as flexible "barges" to carry cargoes of petroleum products are towed astern on long hawsers, almost entirely submerged. The towing vessel uses a black diamond shape as a daymark and the dracone tows a float also showing a black diamond shape. At night the vessel carries ordinary towing lights and an all-around blue light; the float or last dracone in line shows an all-around white light.

Bow, stern and breast anchors of *floating plant moorings* working in navigable channels (except on the high seas) are marked by barrels or buoys. Certain New York Harbor waters also excepted.

Special Day Signals for Survey Vessels

By day, surveying vessels of the Coast and Geodetic Survey, under way and engaged in surveying, may carry in vertical line, not less than 6 feet apart, where best seen, three shapes not less than 2 feet in diameter. The highest and lowest are green and globular; the middle one white and diamond-shaped.

These signals do not relieve them from complying with rules regarding right of way; and, at night, when surveying under way, they carry the regular lights prescribed by the rules.

At anchor in a fairway, when surveying, they show by day two black balls in vertical line 6 feet apart; at night, two red lights in the same manner. A flare-up is shown if necessary.

When necessary, small survey boats also carry these special signals but the distance between the balls or lights may be reduced to 3 feet.

Signals for Minesweepers

The maneuverability of a minesweeper is hampered by its sweeping operations. To indicate the nature of their work they display special signals, and all vessels are cautioned to keep out of their way.

By day, all vessels towing sweeps show a day signal consisting of a black ball at the fore masthead and a black ball at each yardarm. At night, 32-point green lights are used in place of the black balls, exhibited in the same positions. The lights are shown only to warn friendly ships.

Pilot Signals

A pilot may be obtained by displaying: By day—(1) International Code Signal G, (2) International Code Signal P. T. (3) the Pilot Jack hoisted at the fore. Either G or P. T. means "I require a pilot," (see H. O. Pub. No. 103). By night—(1) The pyrotechnic light (blue light) every 15 minutes, (2) a bright white light, flashed or shown at short or frequent intervals just above the bulwarks for about a minute at a time, (3) the International Code Signal P. T. by flashing light.

Signals for Drawbridges

Signals for the opening of drawbridges vary in different localities. A common signal is three blasts of the whistle, as on the Harlem River, New York. If the draw is ready to be opened, the bridge answers with three blasts; if not, two blasts. Always consult the Coast Pilot for specific regulations.

Distress Signals—Inland Rules

By Day:—(1.) A continuous sounding with any fog signal apparatus, or firing a gun.

(2.) Slowly and repeatedly raising and lowering arms outstretched to each side.

By Night:—(1.) Flames on the vessel, as from a burning tar or oil barrel, etc. (2.) Continuous sounding with any fog signal apparatus, or firing a gun.

Distress Signals—International Rules

(1) A gun or other explosive signal fired at intervals of about 1 minute.

(2) Continuous sounding of any fog signal apparatus.

(3) Rockets or shells, throwing red stars fired one at a time at short intervals.

(4) Signal by radiotelegraphy, or other method, consisting of the group ...———... in the Morse Code.

(5) Signal by radiotelephony consisting of spoken word "May-day."

(6) The International Code signal N.C.

(7) A signal consisting of a square flag and above or below it a ball, or something resembling a ball.

(8) Flames on the vessel (as from a burning oil or tar barrel).

(9) A rocket parachute flare showing a red light.

(10) An orange smoke signal.

(11) Slowly and repeatedly raising and lowering arms outstretched to each side.

NOTE:—Radio telegraph alarm signal (12 dashes sent in one minute—each dash 4 seconds, 1 second interval between 2 consecutive dashes) has been provided to actuate auto-alarms of other vessels.

Lifesaving signals adopted by the International Convention for the Safety of Life at Sea (SOLAS) recognize vertical motion of a white light or flare from the beach as an indication to a vessel in distress that "this is the best place to land"

The Square-and-Ball and Orange-Red Flag Signals

The Coast Guard has recently recognized two new distress signals, particularly well adapted to the needs of small craft. One is an excellent signal, developed by the Canadian Coast Guard, which any boat owner could make. It consists simply of a 45" × 72" rectangular fluorescent orange-red cloth on which are displayed a black 18" square and black 18" circle separated by an 18" space, symmetrically placed with a 9" space at each end. It is based on the International rule [Art. 31 (vii)] which recognizes "a signal consisting of a square flag having above or below it a ball. . . ." It could be displayed horizontally across a cabin top.

The other is a simple orange-and-red flag of any size, waved from side to side.

Submarine Distress Signals

A submarine of the United States Navy which may be in need of assistance releases a red smoke bomb.

A submarine which may be compelled to surface in the vicinity of surface craft releases a yellow smoke bomb. Surface vessels should keep clear of the yellow smoke bombs.

A yellow marker buoy, telephone-equipped, may be released by a submarine in distress on the bottom.

Any person sighting a red smoke bomb rising from the surface of the water or a yellow distress marker buoy (about 3 feet in diameter) should report the time and location immediately to the nearest Naval authority or Coast Guard unit.

Aircraft Distress Signals

When an aircraft desires to call upon a surface craft to render assistance to survivors or planes in distress, the aircraft will: (1.) Circle the vessel at least once, (2.) Fly across the bow of the vessel at a low altitude, opening and closing the throttle, or changing propeller pitch, when possible, (3.) Head in the direction of the rescue scene. This is repeated until the vessel acknowledges by following. An Aldis lamp, radio or dropped message is used, if possible, to explain the situation.

The surface craft should follow the aircraft or indicate that it is unable to comply by hoisting the international flag NEGAT, or by other visual or radio means.

Radar Search

A wooden boat that may be the object of a search by Coast Guard patrol or rescue craft should hoist a large metallic object aloft to aid in detection by radar, which is effective by night and in periods of low visibility as well as by day. Collapsible metal radar detection devices, inexpensive and easy to stow, are being marketed. Metallic objects below decks are likely to be shielded by hull or bulwarks.

Fog Signals

GIVEN, DAY OR NIGHT, IN FOG OR

THICK WEATHER, SUCH AS MIST,

FALLING SNOW, OR RAIN STORMS

Fig. 53

Right: In a fog, a steam or motor vessel (this includes motor boats) under way on inland waters sounds a prolonged blast (4 to 6 seconds) on the whistle at intervals of not more than 1 minute. On the high seas, under International Rules, the signal is also 1 prolonged blast, but at intervals of not more than 2 minutes. On the Great Lakes, she sounds 3 blasts in rapid succession every minute (except when towing a raft)

Fig. 54

Left: Under International Rules, vessels "engaged in fishing" (the term is restricted to fishing with nets, lines or trawls but excludes trolling lines) must at intervals of not more than 1 minute sound 3 blasts in succession—1 prolonged and 2 short. Vessels using trolling lines sound the signals appropriate for non-fishing vessels. Vessels smaller than 40 feet may, instead of the above signals, give some other efficient signal at 1-minute intervals. Inland Rules and Great Lakes Rules do not make special provisions for such craft

Fig. 55

Right: The International Rules (only) also provide for the power-driven vessel under way, but stopped and having no way on. She gives two prolonged blasts on the whistle at intervals of not more than 2 minutes (1 second between blasts). Such a signal is given when a vessel is navigating in a fog and headway is stopped so that the navigating officers can more readily listen for the fog signal on some aid to navigation. It is also used when two vessels approach each other, giving the usual fog signals for vessels under way, and have come so close that it is necessary for safety for one or both to stop headway. Two blasts then indicate headway has been stopped; 1 blast that she still has way on

Fig. 56

Left: Vessels at anchor or not under way (when in a fairway) ring a bell rapidly for 5 seconds at intervals of not more than 1 minute, under both Inland and International Rules. On the Great Lakes, they would ring the bell rapidly for 3 to 5 seconds at intervals of not more than 2 minutes, followed by four blasts in quick succession, every 3 minutes on whistle or horn—1 short, 2 long, 1 short. The same signal is prescribed for a vessel aground in or near a channel or fairway on the Great Lakes. On the high seas, a vessel over 350 feet in length at anchor or not under way, in addition to the bell which she sounds forward, strikes a gong aft at 1 minute intervals
(See footnote, p. 78d)

Fig. 57

Left: On the high seas a vessel laying or picking up telegraph cable or a navigation mark, or a vessel which is under way but not under command or unable to maneuver, sounds 1 prolonged blast on the whistle followed by 2 short blasts. This signal is given at 1-minute intervals

Fig. 58

Right: Courts have held that, even though vessels aground and vessels at anchor are, under Inland Rules, in the same category as far as lights are concerned, it would be proper for a vessel aground in a fog to give a distress signal (continuous sounding of the whistle) as a fog signal to distinguish her from a vessel at anchor, which rings a bell at 1-minute intervals. (See Fig. 56.) A vessel aground, under International Rules, gives the signal for a vessel at anchor, and three strokes on the bell before and after it. Great Lakes rules prescribe that vessels aground *must* give the same signal as a vessel at anchor (ringing bell for 3 to 5 seconds at 2-minute intervals, followed by 1 short, 2 long, 1 short blasts in quick succession, every 3 minutes, on whistle or horn)

Fig. 59

Left: A vessel towing, on inland waters or the high seas, gives a prolonged blast on the whistle followed by 2 short blasts, at intervals of not more than 1 minute. Under Inland Rules, the vessel towed may give the same signal as the vessel which is towing, except on a fog horn. On the high seas, the vessel towed sounds 1 prolonged blast followed by 3 short blasts, on the whistle or fog horn. On the Great Lakes a vessel being towed strikes a bell 4 times (twice in quick succession, then twice in quick succession again) at 1 minute intervals. The vessel towing gives the usual Great Lakes signal for a vessel under way of 3 blasts on the whistle in rapid succession every minute, except that steamers towing a raft sound every minute a screeching or Modoc whistle for 3 to 5 seconds

Fig. 61

Below: A sailing vessel on the starboard tack sounds a fog signal of 1 blast on the fog horn at intervals of not more than 1 minute

Fig. 60

Below, right: A sailing vessel on the port tack sounds 2 blasts in succession on the fog horn every minute. Fog signals for sailboats are the same under Inland and International Rules, and on the Great Lakes also (unless being towed)

Fig. 62

Above: When the wind is abaft the beam the fog signal for a sailing vessel is 3 blasts on the fog horn in succession, at 1 minute intervals

FOG SIGNALS

(See Figures 53–62)

(To be given, whether by day or night, in fog or thick weather, such as mist, falling snow, or heavy rain storms)

A COMPARISON OF INTERNATIONAL, INLAND, GREAT LAKES AND WESTERN RIVER RULES

NOTE: A prolonged blast means a blast of 4 to 6 seconds' duration.

	International Rules	Inland Rules	Great Lakes Rules	Western River Rules
How signals are given when *under way*	Steam vessels:—Whistle Sailing vessels and Vessels towed:—Fog horn	Same as International	Steam vessel:—Whistle Sailing vessel (not in tow):—Fog horn (See special cases below)	Steam vessel:—Whistle or siren Sailing vessel:—Fog horn
Fog signal equipment required (For MOTOR BOATS, see special regulations below)	Power-driven vessels:—Whistle sounded by steam, or substitute for steam; fog horn (mechanical); bell Sailing vessels (20 gross tons or over):—Fog horn and bell	Same as International	Steam vessels:—Whistle, sounded by steam or substitute for steam, audible 2 miles; bell Sailing vessels:—Fog horn and bell	Steam vessels:—Whistle or siren Sailing vessels:—Fog horn (Sailing vessels over 20 gross tons also carry a bell)
Steam (power-driven) vessel under way (See Fig. 53)	1 prolonged blast at intervals of not more than 2 minutes	1 prolonged blast at intervals of not more than 1 minute	3 blasts at intervals of not more than 1 minute (except when towing raft)	3 blasts at intervals of not more than 1 minute (2 of equal length, last one longer)
Steam (power-driven) vessel under way but stopped and having no way on (See Fig. 55)	2 prolonged blasts (1 second between) at intervals of not more than 2 minutes	Not mentioned	Not mentioned	Not mentioned
Sailing vessels under way (See Figures 60, 61, 62)	Starboard tack, 1 blast Port tack, 2 blasts in succession Wind abaft the beam, 3 blasts in succession Intervals in each case not more than 1 minute	Same as International	If not in tow, same as International	Same as steam vessel, but uses fog horn
Vessels at anchor or not under way (See Figures 56, 58)	Ring bell rapidly for 5 seconds at intervals of not more than 1 minute* Vessel aground, in addition to anchor signal, gives 3 strokes on bell, before and after	Same as International **	At anchor or aground, ring bell rapidly 3 to 5 seconds at 2-minute intervals. In addition, every 3 minutes, sound signal on whistle or horn—1 short, 2 long, 1 short blasts in quick succession.	Same as International **
Vessels at anchor or not under way (over 350 ft.)	In addition to bell in forepart of vessel, sound gong in after part, at intervals of not more than 1 minute*	Not mentioned	Not mentioned	Not mentioned
Vessels towing or towed (See Figures 57, 59)	Vessels when towing, laying or picking up a submarine cable or navigation mark, or under way but not under command or unable to maneuver:— 1 prolonged blast (on whistle) followed by 2 short blasts, at intervals of not more than 1 minute Vessel towed gives 1 prolonged blast, followed by 3 short, on whistle or fog horn	1 prolonged blast (on whistle) followed by 2 short blasts, at intervals of not more than 1 minute. Vessel towed may give same signal (on fog horn)	Steamer towing raft:—Sounds at intervals of not more than 1 minute, a screeching or Modoc whistle for 3 to 5 seconds Vessel towed:—At intervals of 1 minute strikes bell four times (twice in quick succession, followed by a little longer interval, then twice in quick succession again)	Vessel towing sounds 3 distinct blasts of equal length at intervals of not more than 1 minute
Small craft or craft not otherwise provided for	Vessels of less than 40 feet, rowboats, and seaplanes on the water, if they do not give regular signals prescribed above, make some other efficient sound signal at intervals of not more than 1 minute (On small seagoing vessels, gong may be used instead of bell)	Rafts and other watercraft not provided for above navigating by hand power, horse power, or river current, sound 1 blast of fog horn or equivalent signal at intervals of not more than 1 minute	Vessels under 10 registered tons, if they do not give regular signals prescribed above, make some other efficient sound signal at intervals of not more than 1 minute. Produce boats, fishing boats, rafts, or other watercraft navigating by hand power or river current, or anchored or moored in or near channel or fairway, not in port, sound fog horn or equivalent signal at intervals of not more than 1 minute	Not mentioned
Vessels engaged in fishing (but not with trolling lines) (See Figure 54)	1 prolonged blast followed by 2 short blasts, at 1 minute intervals (whistle if power-driven; fog horn if sail). Vessels fishing with trolling lines and under way sound the same fog signals as vessels not fishing	Not mentioned	Not mentioned	Not mentioned
Speed in fog or thick weather	Moderate speed, with regard to circumstances and conditions. Power-driven vessel hearing, forward of beam, fog signal of vessel, position of which is not ascertained, must stop and then navigate with caution until danger of collision is past	Same as International	Moderate speed. Steam vessel hearing, from direction not more than 4 points from right ahead, fog signal of another vessel, must reduce speed to bare steerageway, then navigate with caution until vessels have passed.	Moderate speed. Steam vessel hearing, forward of beam, fog signal of another vessel, must reduce speed to bare steerageway, then navigate with caution till vessels have passed

FOG SIGNAL EQUIPMENT FOR MOTOR BOATS

WHISTLE	Motor boats, under way, give their fog signals on the whistle, not on a fog horn. Boats of Class 1, 16'–26'; Class 2, 26'–40'; and Class 3, 40'–65' carry an "efficient" whistle or other sound-producing mechanical appliance. With respect to motor boats, a blast of at least 2 seconds is considered a prolonged blast. A mouth whistle capable of producing a 2-second blast that can be heard at least ½ mile, has been held to be in compliance with the law, on Class 1 only. However, an efficient electric or air horn is preferable, especially on boats with deckhouses. On Classes 2 and 3, whistle must be audible 1 mile. On Class 3, it must be power-operated; on Class 2, hand or power; on Class 1, hand, mouth or power.	BELL	Class 2 and Class 3 carry an efficient bell.
		FOG HORN	NOT required on MOTOR boats.
		EXEMPTIONS	OUTBOARD MOTOR BOATS competing in a race previously arranged and announced or tuning up for such a race are exempt from carrying the above equipment. All boats of Class A, under 16', are also exempt.

* International Rules now authorize, in addition to bell signals at anchor, a warning signal of three blasts (1 short, 1 prolonged, 1 short)
** On Inland Waters and Western Rivers, vessels under 65 feet in length and nondescript craft like barges, scows, etc., need not give fog signal when at anchor in special anchorage areas.

HOW many times have you heard a boatman, in describing his boat to a friend, remark that "she made 10 knots per hour on a measured mile," or perhaps, that his run from port to port was a distance of 12 knots? Often, no doubt.

As a matter of fact, a strict interpretation of his terms would be the equivalent of "she made 10 nautical miles per hour per hour." You see, the knot is a measure of speed, equal to one nautical mile per hour. Similarly, the second statement is not according to the best usage. The speaker should have said "12 nautical miles" because the knot isn't a measure of distance, in this sense.

Landsmen's terms grate hard sometimes on the ear of one trained to speak the language of the sea, who thinks naturally in nautical terms. When the guest who unnecessarily remarks that he doesn't know "the front from the back" of the boat, goes "downstairs" into what he is pleased to call the "kitchen" and adds insult to injury by calling the chart a "map," the boatman's reaction must be akin to that of the well-bred English professor who must listen to "ain'ts" and "he don'ts" hurled with reckless abandon into his learned conversation.

Landsmen are not the only offenders in the use of incorrect nautical terminology as our first reference to knots and miles shows. Few persons speak absolutely pure English—few are always precisely right in their seafaring language. The words carline and beam are often used interchangeably by men with a broad background of nautical knowledge, yet a distinction could be drawn in their meanings.

Within the limits of our space here, we hope to cover just as many as possible of the more common terms used aboard boats. We do not pretend to offer verbatim definitions as might be taken from a dictionary. Rather the sense will be condensed into the briefest possible terms for the benefit of those to whom sea language is still a jargon. This is done at the risk of being taken to task by hair-splitting "sea lawyers" who might feel that brevity leaves the explanation vague. Glossaries are available to those who wish precise, long-winded definitions.

The landsman guest previously referred to might have incurred less of his host's displeasure had he called the front and back of the boat, the *bow* and *stern,* respectively. *Port* and *starboard* (starb'd) are terms in constant use—port designating the left; starboard, the right side, facing the bow or, to express it otherwise, facing *forward.* Turning around and facing the stern, we look *aft.* The bow is the *fore* part of the boat, the stern the *after* part. When one point on the boat is further aft than another it is said to be *abaft.* Thus we might say that the deckhouse is abaft the main cabin. When an object lies on a line parallel to the keel we refer to it as *fore-and-aft,* as distinguished from *athwartships,* which is at right angles to the keel line. Planks in a deck run fore and aft; the beams supporting deck planks run athwartships.

The term *amidships* has a double meaning. In one sense, it refers to an object in the line of the keel, midway between the sides, as an engine is mounted amidships in the centerline over the keel. Often, however, it relates to something mid-way

CHAPTER V

Nautical Terms

(See also Nautical Dictionary, Chapter XXXI)

between bow and stern. The galley, for example, might be located amidships, though off to the port or starboard side. The *midship section* would be the view of a boat presented by cutting it transversely through the middle.

To express the idea upward, overhead, or above the deck, one says *aloft. Below* means below deck. A seaman goes aloft in the rigging, below to his berth in the cabin.

We never say that a person is on or in a boat—rather, he is *aboard,* though *on board* is an alternate expression. *Inboard* and *outboard* draw a distinction between objects near or toward amidships and those which are out from the boat, away from the centerline. Inboard engines are those permanently installed within the hull; outboards being temporarily attached at the stern, outside the hull.

To convey the idea opposite or at right angles, we say *abreast.* An object at right angles to the centerline (keel) of the boat is *abeam.* If we draw ahead to a point where that object is midway between its position abeam and another directly astern, then it is *broad on the quarter,* starboard or port as the case may be. *Dead ahead,* of course, refers to any point which the boat is approaching directly on a straight course. Midway between dead ahead and a point abeam, an object is *broad on the bow* (port or starboard).

To express the direction of another vessel or any object relative to our position we say it *bears* so-and-so. Directions through 360 degrees around the horizon are divided into 32 *points.* Each point or direction is named. Thus a lighthouse might be said to bear two points *abaft the starboard beam, broad on the port bow,* etc.

Windward means toward the wind, the direction from which the wind blows; *leeward,* away from the wind, or

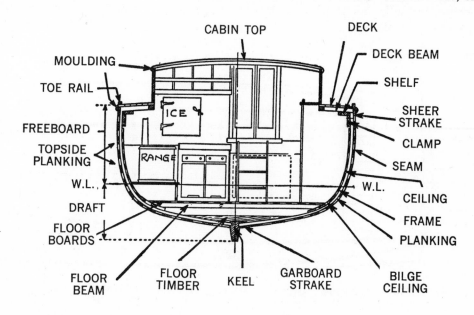

the direction toward which the wind blows. The *lee* side of a boat or island is protected; the *windward* or *weather* side is exposed, unprotected. Note, however, that while one runs into the lee of an island or point for an anchorage protected from the wind, a *lee shore* refers to a shore line to leeward of a vessel, consequently a dangerous one exposed to the wind. While this may seem confusing at first, the logic of it is apparent with a little thought.

Some of the common terms by which the dimensions of a vessel and characteristics of her design are expressed are obvious in their meanings. Others baffle the tyro. The length of a boat is often given in two dimensions: on the *waterline* (W. L.), the meaning of which is apparent; and *over-all* (O.A.), measuring from the fore part of the stem to the after part of the stern. The breadth of a vessel is its *beam; draft,* the depth of water required to float it. This is not to be confused with the term *depth* as applied to larger vessels, which is measured vertically inside the hull from deck to bottom or floors. *Headroom,* in a small boat, is the vertical space between floor boards or deck and the cabin or canopy top, or other overhead structure.

Sheer is the term properly used to designate the curve or sweep of the deck of a vessel. The side planking of a boat between the waterline and deck or rail is called the *topsides.* If they are drawn in toward the centerline away from a perpendicular, as they often do at the stern of a boat, they are said to *tumble home.* Forward they are more likely to incline outward to make the bow more buoyant and keep the hull dry by throwing spray aside. This is *flare. Flam* is that part of the flare just below the deck. The height of a boat's topsides from waterline to deck is called the *freeboard.* The significance of the term *deadrise* can be appreciated by visualizing a section transversely across a hull. If the bottom planking were flat, extending horizontally from the keel, there would be no deadrise. In a round or vee bottom boat, when the bottom rises at an angle to such a horizontal line, the amount of rise is the deadrise.

The *bilge* is the turn of a boat's hull just below the waterline. *Bilge water* accumulates in the *bilges,* the deepest part of the hull inside along the keel. Aft where the lines converge toward the stern, under the overhang, is the *counter.* The lines converging toward the stern post are called the boat's *run.* The *buttock* is the rounding part of a boat's stern; *buttock lines,* drawn by the architect, may be visualized if one pictures longitudinal saw cuts vertically through a boat's planking at a distance

from the keel, parallel to the plane of stem and keel.

We have been talking about the *hull,* but haven't defined it. This term refers generally to the principal structure of the boat whereas cabins, deckhouses, etc., built above the deck are referred to as the *superstructure.* The main longitudinal timber in a hull, first laid in construction, is the *keel.* When another timber is fastened along the top of the keel to strengthen it, or as a necessary part of the construction, this is the *keelson,* sometimes *apron.* One-piece timbers running the full length of the keel are not always available. In this case, shorter pieces are bevelled and bolted together in a joint called a *scarph. Deadwood,* in small boats, is usually the solid timber above the keel at the stern. The *propeller post* stands vertically behind the deadwood, is joined to it and also to the keel.

The *frame* is the skeleton of a hull, comprising its principal structural members. The transverse members to which the planking is fastened are called *frames*—in some instances *ribs,* though some contend that a boat has frames, an animal ribs. The *stem* is one of the main frame members, at the bow. When the stern is shaped like the bow, drawing to a point as in a canoe, the boat is a *double-ender.* The *transom* type of stern is more common.

Knees reinforce the joints between members butting or intersecting at or near a right angle. *Clamps* and *shelves* are the longitudinal members joining the frames on which the deck beams rest. Misunderstanding often exists in connection with the use of the term *floor.* A *floor* in boat construction is one of the transverse frame members tying the lower ends of frames together at the keel. It has nothing to do with the decking. *Limber holes* are cut in the lower edge of frames to allow bilge water to flow into the deepest part of the hull from which point it can be pumped out.

Planks are applied to the outside of frames in constructing the hull, each continuous line of planks from bow to stern being called a *strake.* If short planks are used in one strake, the ends are *butted* and joined on *butt blocks.* The lowest strake, next to the keel, is called the *garboard.* Strakes between the bottom and topsides are called *wales,* and the *gunwale* (pronounced gun'l) is the upper part of the sheer strake or top plank of the *topsides.* When the topsides are carried above the deck, they are called *bulwarks;* the top of the bulwarks, the *rail.* The *taffrail* is the rail at the stern, furthest aft. Spaces between planks are called *seams;* to make them watertight, these are *caulked* by rolling or driving cotton

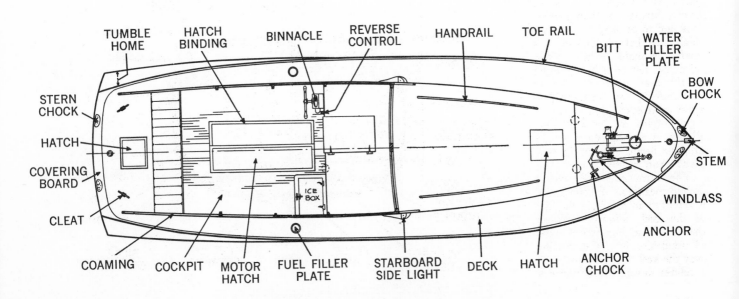

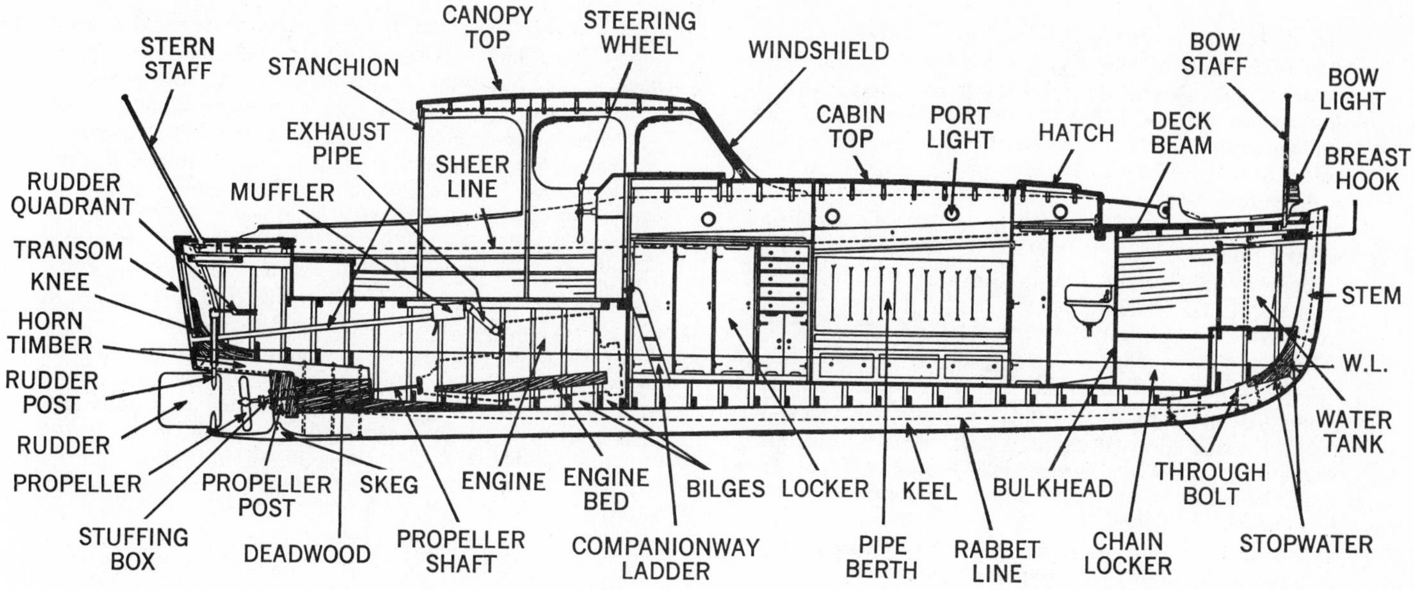
STERN STAFF
STANCHION
CANOPY TOP
STEERING WHEEL
WINDSHIELD
BOW STAFF
BOW LIGHT
EXHAUST PIPE
SHEER LINE
CABIN TOP
PORT LIGHT
HATCH
DECK BEAM
BREAST HOOK
RUDDER QUADRANT
MUFFLER
TRANSOM
KNEE
HORN TIMBER
RUDDER POST
RUDDER
STEM
W.L.
WATER TANK
PROPELLER
PROPELLER POST
SKEG
ENGINE
ENGINE BED
BILGES
LOCKER
KEEL
BULKHEAD
THROUGH BOLT
STUFFING BOX
DEADWOOD
PROPELLER SHAFT
COMPANIONWAY LADDER
PIPE BERTH
RABBET LINE
CHAIN LOCKER
STOPWATER

into them (*oakum* in large boats) after which the seams are *payed* (filled) with white lead or seam composition.

Frame members such as the keel and stem are *rabbetted* to receive the edges and ends of planks. This rabbet is merely a longitudinal recess or cut into the wood of proper size to take the plank. Plank ends at the stem and stern are the *hood ends.* We have already referred, in passing, to *beams* and *carlines. Deck beams* are the thwartship members which carry the decks; *carlines,* properly, are fore-and-aft timbers placed between the deck beams.

Vertical partitions, corresponding to the walls in a house, in a boat are called *bulkheads. Scuppers* are holes permitting water to drain overboard from decks and *cockpits,* the latter of course being the open space outside the cabins and deckhouses, not decked over flush. *Flush decks* are unbroken by either cockpits or deck erections such as the cabin or other houses.

Coamings (often misspelled combings, probably through confusion with the word *comber,* which is the name for a long curling wave) are vertical members around cockpits, hatches, etc., to prevent water on deck from running below. Deck openings are commonly referred to as *hatches. Companion ladders* are stairways or steps leading below from the deck. These are also referred to as *companionways.*

Another misunderstood term is *ceiling.* For this the landsman would be inclined to look overhead; as a matter of fact, this is actually a light sheathing of staving or planking applied to the inside of frames, for strength and interior finish.

On deck, lines are made fast to *cleats* or *bitts* (*samson posts*) and led through *chocks,* either open or closed, to reduce chafing. In larger craft *hawse pipes* are often provided in the bow through which the anchor chain runs, and into which the anchor is hauled.

The *forecastle* (pronounced fo'c's'l), if any small boat may properly be said to have one, is the compartment furthest forward, in the bow. In olden days, the forecastle head was an elevated structure forward, providing a platform from which men could fight. As construed today, it generally is considered to mean the crew's quarters forward.

Berths and *bunks* are the seagoing names for beds aboard a boat. *Lockers* are closets or chests to provide space for stowage. Afloat one does not pack or put away; he *stows.*

When a vessel is hauled out of the water she is *shored* up with supports to hold her upright. If she is not supported properly, so that she is held amidships while bow and stern settle, the boat will assume a shape described as *hogged.*

Helm is a term relating to the tiller, by which some sailboats are steered. More loosely, the term covers a wheel aboard a motor boat or any other method of steering. In the old days, the command *port your helm* meant put the tiller to port, thus throwing the rudder and the boat's head to starboard. Universal practise today dictates the command *right rudder* to carry the same meaning, *left rudder* the opposite. This eliminates much confusion.

Compasses are mounted near the helm, in boxes or other protective casings which are known as *binnacles.* Compasses are swung in *gimbals,* or pivoted rings, which permit the compass bowl and card to remain level regardless of the boat's motion. To enable the helmsman at the wheel to steer a compass course, a *lubber line* is painted on the inner side of the compass bowl to indicate the boat's bow.

We've spent considerable time getting familiar with the proper names for various parts of the boat and its construction, so let's pass to a consideration of more general terms dealing with the action and behavior of boats, the handling of lines and anchors, the action of water, navigational terms, etc.

When a boat moves through the water she is said to be *under way* (or *weigh*). According to the Pilot Rules she is under way when not aground, at anchor, or made fast to the shore. The direction in which she is moving may be made more specific by stating that she makes *headway* (when moving forward), *sternway* (backward), or *leeway* (when she is being set off her course by the wind). The track or disturbance which she leaves in the water as a result of her movement is called the *wake.* When she is not made fast to the bottom, shore, a dock

A GENERAL EXPLANATION OF THE MEANING OF

SOME OF THE MORE COMMON NAUTICAL TERMS

WHICH SHOULD BE FAMILIAR TO ALL BOATMEN

or any other fixed object, she is said to be *adrift*. She *grounds* when she touches bottom, and is then *aground*.

Trim relates to the way in which a boat floats in the water. When she floats properly as designed, she is on an *even keel,* but if inclined to port or starboard she *lists*. *Heel* (not keel) conveys the same idea as list, that is, a sidewise inclination from the vertical. If she is too heavily loaded forward, she trims *by the head,* whereas if her draft is greater than normal aft, she trims *by the stern*.

A *stiff vessel* returns quickly to her normal upright position; if she rolls in a seaway without quick action or sudden movement, her roll is *easy*. When a boat's center of gravity is too high and stability low, she is *tender; crank* conveys the same idea. Sidewise motion in a seaway is called *roll;* while the vertical motion as the head rises and falls in the waves is *pitch*. Quick upward motion in pitching is *scending*. She *yaws* when she runs off her course as a vessel might if she didn't steer properly in a following sea. If she yaws too widely and is thrown broadside into the *trough of the sea* (between crests of the waves and parallel with them) she *broaches to,* a situation which should always be carefully avoided. When subjected to heavy strains in working through a seaway, a vessel is said to *labor*.

A boat *scuds* when she runs before a gale; is *driven* when she is pressed hard with much sail. A ship may *capsize* without *foundering*—in the first instance she turns over; in the latter she is overwhelmed by a heavy sea, fills and sinks. Before she is reduced to such straits, the wise skipper *heaves to,* in order to enable a vessel to ride the seas more comfortably, generally head to the wind, or near it, with shortened sail and possibly lying to a *sea anchor* which prevents the head from falling off from the wind. The sea anchor does not go to the bottom, merely serves as a drag.

Generally speaking, the word *rope* is used but little aboard a boat, being referred to rather as *line*. *Hawsers* are heavy lines, in common use on larger vessels, but rarely aboard small pleasure craft. *Heaving lines* are light lines with a knot or weight at the end which helps to carry them when thrown from one boat to another or to a dock. *Heave* is the nautical term for throw. The knot which encloses the weight at the end of a heaving line is a *monkey's fist*. *Painters* are lines at the bow of the boat for the purpose of towing or making fast. Thus dinghies are usually equipped with painters. The line by which a boat is made fast to her mooring is called a *pennant*. *Spring lines* are among those used at docks, leading from the bow aft to the dock or from the stern forward to the dock, to prevent the boat from moving ahead or astern.

The *bitter end* of a line is the extreme end, the end made fast to a *bitt* when all line is paid out. *Belay* has a double meaning. A line is belayed when it is made fast; as a command it signifies stop, cease. Ends of lines are *whipped* or *seized* when twine is wrapped about them to prevent strands from untwisting. Ragged ends of lines are said to be *fagged*. When a line is made fast with light line or twine to another or any other object, it is *seized* or *stopped*. Joining two ends to make one continuous line by tucking strands under without knotting is called *splicing*. When an end is worked back into the line itself to form a loop, it is called an *eye-splice*. One does not tie a line to another aboard a boat; he *bends* it on. Line is coiled down on deck, each complete turn being a *fake* or *flake*.

When a line is let out, one *pays* it out; it is *cast off* when let go. *Blocks* (pulleys) are provided with *sheaves*. These are the wheels or rollers of the block and the term is pronounced as though spelled shiv. When a line is passed through a block or hole it is *reeved; render* indicates that it passes freely through the block or hole. If a strain is put on a line heavy enough to break it, then it *parts*. Lines have *standing parts* and *hauling parts,* the standing part being the fixed part, that is, the one which is made fast; the hauling part, that part of a tackle which is hauled upon. A *bight* is any part within the ends of a line, that is to say, a bend. Lines are *foul* when tangled, *clear* when in order ready to run.

Ground tackle is a general term embracing anchors, lines, etc., used in anchoring. On small boats, the anchor line is a *rode*. *Moorings* are the permanent anchorages at which boats lie, consisting of a heavy anchor (usually *mushroom* type), chain, shackles, swivels, a mooring buoy, and pennant of nylon or manila. Larger vessels are said to be moored when lying with two anchors down. They may also be moored to piers when made fast with stout mooring lines. *Grapnels* are light anchors with claw-like hooks or prongs. A *kedge* is a light anchor often used for getting off a

shoal. The kedge is carried out in the dinghy and power to haul the boat off is then applied either by man power or *winch* (a device for raising the anchor). This is called *kedging*. *Warping* consists of turning a boat at a dock by applying power to lines fast to the dock. *Bowers* are heavy anchors carried forward; the heavier one, the *best bower*. Years ago *sheet anchors,* the heaviest aboard, were carried in the *waist* of a ship (amidships) for emergencies. *Stream anchors* are heavier than kedges, lighter than bowers.

Various terms are used to describe specific water movements or conditions of the surface. *Rips* are short, steep waves caused by the meeting or crossing of currents. The confused water action found at places where tidal currents meet is also called a *chop*. *Sea* is a general term often used to describe waves and water action on the surface but, properly, it should be applied only to waves produced by the wind. *Swell* is the long heavy undulation of the surface resulting from disturbances elsewhere on the sea. *Surf* is produced when waves leave deep water, breaking on the shore as the *crests* curl over. A *following sea* is one which comes up from astern, running in the same direction as the boat's course; a *head sea* is just the opposite, where the progress of the waves is against that of the boat, the boat meeting them bow on. *Cross* seas are confused and irregular.

The word *tide* has probably been misused as much as any nautical term, so much so that its misuse has come to be accepted without question as a matter of course. Commonly it has been used to describe the inflow and outflow of water caused by the gravitational influence of the moon and sun. Better usage would restrict the term to the vertical rise and fall of water produced by these causes. *Current* is the proper term for a horizontal flow of water. Thus a current resulting from tidal influences is a *tidal current*. It is better to say two-knot current than two-knot tide.

The incoming tidal current running toward shore is the *flood;* the retreating current flowing away from the land is the *ebb*. The direction in which the current flows is the *set; drift,* its velocity. (The amount of leeway a vessel makes is also called its drift.) *Slack* is the period between flood and ebb when the current is not flowing; *stand* the period with no rise or fall in tide level.

Reversing currents are those in rivers, straits, and channels which flow alternately in opposite directions. Offshore, where there is no restriction, the current may be *rotary,* flowing continually with no period of slack, but changing direction through all points of the compass during the tidal period. *Hydraulic* current is the type of reversing current in a strait resulting from a difference in the tidal head of water at the two ends of the passage.

Spring tides are those produced when the moon is new or full, and have a greater *range* (difference between the heights of high and low water) than average. *Neap* tides, caused when the positions of sun and moon relative to the earth are such as to offset each other in effect, have a smaller range than average. Too often every huge wave is referred to as a *tidal wave*. Generally, it is used in the wrong sense, as this term should be limited to waves resulting from tidal action, rather than indiscriminately applied to the great waves which build up as a result of wind storms.

Range, mentioned above, is also a navigational term and is used when two or more objects are brought into line to indicate a safe course. The distinction between *knots* and *miles* has already been made. A *fathom* is six feet; this is a measure of depth. One *heaves a lead* to determine depth, the process being known as *sounding*. The lead (a weight at the end of the lead line) is *armed* by greasing the bottom with tallow or some other sticky substance to bring up a sample at the bottom. In navigation, one *plots* a course on the chart (never map), takes *bearings* to determine his position (*fix*), takes a *departure* to establish an exact point from which to commence his *dead reckoning* (calculation of courses and distances sailed), has an *offing* when he is well to seaward, though yet in sight of land.

Entries are made in a *log* (book) to record all events during a cruise; the *patent log* is an instrument to record distance travelled. One *raises* a light or landmark when it first becomes visible, makes a *landfall* when land is first sighted coming in from sea. *Passage* is generally construed to mean a run from port to port; *voyage* includes both the outward and homeward passage. *Watches* are four-hour periods of duty aboard ship; *dog watches* are two-hour periods between 4:00 and 8:00 P.M. A period of duty at the wheel is a *trick*.

When any part of the vessel's gear or equipment breaks or gives way, it *carries away;* an object goes *by the board* when it goes

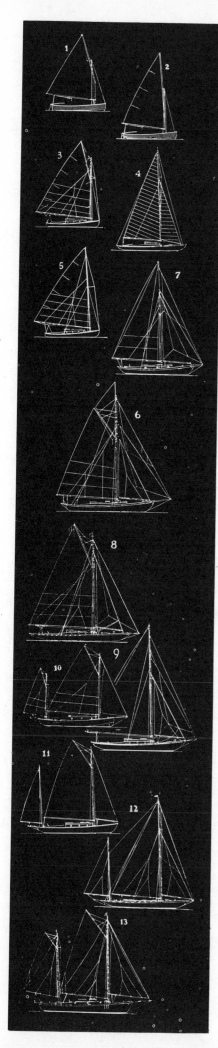

The Rigs
of
Sailing Craft

Here's a chance to test your knowledge of the rigs of various types of sailboats, or to learn them if you've never been able to distinguish a sloop from a cutter, or a yawl from a ketch. How many can you identify?

1—Standing lug rig—strictly small boat sail plan.

2—Sliding gunter—"gaff" fits snug against mast. Used on small boats.

3—Gaff cat rig.

4—Marconi-rigged knockabout—features are jib and mainsail and no bowsprit. Is also seen gaff-rigged, of course.

5—Marconi cat rig.

6—Gaff-rigged cutter. Usual definition of cutter is: single-masted yacht with mast placed about 2/5 of the waterline length abaft the forward termination of the waterline.

7—Marconi-rigged cutter.

8—Gaff-rigged sloop. The placing of the mast further forward distinguishes the sloop from the cutter. Otherwise, there is little difference.

9—Marconi-rigged sloop.

10—Gaff-rigged yawl. Usual distinction between yawl and ketch is that yawl's mizzen is stepped aft of the rudder post and mizzen is generally not over 20 percent of the total sail area in size.

11—Gaff yawl, with jib-headed or Marconi mizzen. Not usual rig.

12—Marconi-rigged yawl.

13—Gaff-rigged ketch.

14—Marconi-rigged ketch.

15—Staysail ketch, or "main trysail-rigged" ketch.

16—Staysail schooner. Main staysail (lower sail between spars) sets on boom.

17—Gaff-rigged schooner. Schooners can also have three or more masts, all fore-and-aft rigged.

18—Marconi mainsail and gaff foresail schooner (most usual schooner rig today).

19—Topsail schooner, or square topsail schooner.

20—Hermaphrodite brig, *not* brigantine, though often termed such. If vessel has three or more masts, square-rigged throughout on the foremast and schooner-rigged on all the rest, she is called a barkentine.

21—Ship. A ship-rigged vessel has three (or more) masts, all square-rigged.

22—Bark. This example is a four-masted bark (Hussar). Bark is a vessel with three or more masts, square-rigged on all but the aftermost mast.

Illustrations courtesy of Marine Facts, 1954, by Peirce & Kilburn Corp., New Bedford, Mass.

A brig (not illustrated) is two-masted, square-rigged on both fore and main. A brigantine is like a brig, but the mainsail (only) is fore-and-aft.

For a complete treatise on the subject of sailing craft and sailing, see Basic Sailing published by Motor Boating.

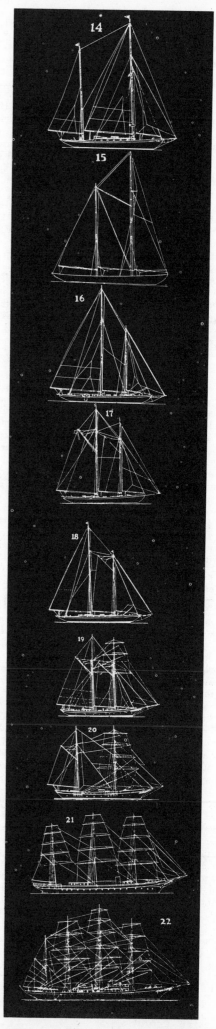

overboard. If a boat is *stove* (planking broken in from outside) the boat *springs a leak,* or *makes water.* When water is dipped out of a small boat, the process is called *bailing.*

By general usage, the term *Corinthian* has come to mean amateur sailor. A boat is *ship-shape* when everything is in good order, *well found* if well equipped. One *swabs* the deck when he washes it down with a mop (called a swab aboard ship). *Clean* is a term applied, not to a ship's condition, but rather to her lines. If the lines are *fine,* so that she slips easily through the water, the lines are clean.

The term *clear* has many meanings. Before leaving for a foreign port, a ship must be cleared through the Customs authorities. She clears the land when she leaves it, clears a shoal when she passes it safely. The bilges may be cleared of water by pumping it out. Tangled (*foul*) lines are cleared by straightening them out and getting them ready for use.

The meaning of the word *lay* also depends on its usage. One lays aft, when he goes to the stern of the boat; lays down the lines of a boat full size before building; lays up the boat when putting her out of commission. A vessel lays her course if, in sailing, she can make her objective without tacking. When an oarsman stops rowing, he lays on his oars. *Lay to* is synonymous with heave to, previously defined. Referring to cordage, lay is the direction and tightness of the twist (right-hand or left-hand, hard or soft).

A boat *stands by* when she remains with another vessel prepared to give her assistance if necessary. When used as a command, stand by means to be prepared to carry out an order. A vessel is said to *hail* from her home port. One hails a vessel at sea to get her attention, *speaks* her when communicating with her.

SPACE does not permit a long discussion of sails, wind, and the rigs of vessels, but a few of the more common terms will be touched on briefly. Wind *veers* when it shifts, changing its direction clockwise; it *backs* when it shifts in a counter-clockwise direction. Wind changing from abeam forward, *hauls;* from abeam aft, *veers.* A vessel is sailing *off the wind* when her *sheets* (lines controlling the sail, not the sail itself) are slacked off (*eased*). She is *on the wind* when sailing *close-hauled,* as close to the wind as possible. When *before the wind,* the wind comes from aft and is called a *fair, free* or *leading* wind. A *following* wind blows in the direction of the ship's course. Sailing *down the wind,* a vessel sails to leeward. A *beam wind* obviously is one which blows athwart the boat's course. An *offshore* wind blows from the land; an *onshore* wind, toward it,

Canvas is a general term for a boat's sails. Sails *draw* when they fill with the wind providing power to drive the boat through the water. One *makes sail* when the sails are set; *shortens sail* when the amount of sail set is reduced; *reefs* it by partly lowering the sail and securing it so that its area is reduced; *dowses* it when it is lowered quickly; *furls* it when it is rolled up and secured to a boom or yard.

A sailboat *tacks* by sailing in a zig-zag direction to make good a course directly into the wind. This is also called *beating.* If the wind comes from the starboard side, she is on the *starboard tack;* from the port side, the *port tack.* Tacking, she *goes about.* If she attempts to tack and the head does not fall off on the other tack she is *caught in* (or *misses*) *stays,* or is said to be *in irons.* When preparing to tack the order is given, *ready about;* then, as the helmsman puts the helm over to change the boat's course, *hard alee. Wearing ship* is another means of bringing a vessel on the other tack, but in this case she does it by changing course so that the wind is brought astern, from one side to the other. As the boom swings from one side to the other as the wind comes dead aft in this maneuver (sometimes it occurs accidentally when running before the wind) she *jibes.*

When the wind comes from abeam or forward of the beam, the boat is *reaching; running* when she is sailing dead before the wind. A vessel is *sailing free* when the wind is well aft; *full and by* or *close hauled* when all sails are drawing and her course is as close to the wind as she can sail. She is *pinched* when she is brought so close to the wind that the sails shiver. A vessel is *luffed* when she is brought up into the wind so as to spill some of it out of the sail, thus relieving the pressure and *easing* her. Sailing *before the wind,* sails are sometimes set on opposite sides of the boat; this is called *wing and wing.* One boat *blankets* another when, being just to windward, she takes the wind out of the other's sails. She *outfoots* another by sailing faster, *outpoints* her by sailing closer to the wind.

Catboats have a single mast and sail. *Sloops* have one mast but, in addition to the mainsail, have *headsails,* forward of the mast. Sometimes additional sails are set from *bowsprits,* projecting over the boat's bow. A sloop without a bowsprit, in which the jib sets from a stay at the stem, is a *knockabout.* A *cutter* is a sloop in which the

single mast is stepped further toward amidships than in the conventional sloop. *Yawls* have two masts, the after one of which is much the shorter and stepped abaft the rudder post. A *ketch* is rigged somewhat like a yawl, except that the short after mast is stepped forward of the rudder post instead of aft of it as in the case of the yawl. *Schooners* are *fore-and-aft* rigged (as distinguished from *square-rigged*) and have two or more masts. Unlike yawls and ketches, the after mast is never the shorter. *Rig* is the general term applying to the arrangement of a vessel's masts and sails. The term *slutter rig* (not in general use) is a British term used to distinguish a sailing craft that uses a masthead genoa, reaching jib or ballooner.

In *trunk cabin* cruisers (see Fig. 703, p. 112), the cabin is built up from the deck in such a manner as to provide a deck forward and at the sides of the cabin. The *raised deck* cruiser (See Fig. 820, p. 122) has its forward cabin provided by extending topsides upward from the normal sheer line and decking over the raised portion for the full width of the boat. It may have a small cockpit forward. *Deckhouses* may be built up as superstructures on both the trunk cabin and raised deck (Fig. 2204 p. 355) types. On small boats, the trunk cabin may be modified to provide relatively larger areas of glass as in the *sedan* type (Fig. 2203, p. 354). Many small skiffs have a somewhat similar *shelter cabin* forward, consisting of a light permanent windshield, top and side wings, frequently open aft, or perhaps enclosed by canvas curtains.

Some confusion has arisen in use of the term *skiff.* It has been defined as a flat bottom, shallow draft open boat of simple construction, with sharp bow and square stern, propelled by motor, sail or oars, and used often as a pleasure boat in sheltered water. This is a general term, often loosely used. The *Seabright skiff,* native to the New Jersey beach, was originally a dory type, its flat tapered bottom merging into rounded lapstrake topsides, the garboards shaped aft into a boxed deadwood construction. Later, *sea skiffs* evolved from this type, retained the lapstrake construction (though they have been built smooth, or carvel, as well) but used a conventional keel instead of the flat keel. In recent years, many craft have been loosely referred to as "skiffs" or "sea skiffs" when referring to the modern fast fisherman-type of seaworthy design developed from the Jersey boats.

Motor sailers are a cross between the motor cruiser and the sailboat or auxiliary driven principally by her sails. Motor sailers perform well under power but generally do not carry sail enough to do as well under sail alone as the conventional sailboat. See illustrations, page 30.

THE term *spars* is used generally to cover masts, booms, gaffs, yards, etc. *Masts,* of course, are the principal vertical spars from which sails are set. They are *stepped* when set in position, *raked* when the mast is not plumb, but inclined aft at an angle. *Gaffs* are spars supporting the *head* (upper edge) of a fore-and-aft sail. Triangular sails requiring no gaff, in which the head of the sail is a point, are *Marconi* sails (jib-headed). *Yards* are the horizontal spars supporting the head of square sails. The *foot* (lower edge) of fore-and-aft sails is usually attached to a *boom.* If no boom is used, or if the sail is not laced or otherwise secured to it, the sail is *loose-footed.* The *luff* is the forward edge of a fore-and-aft sail; the *leach* the after edge. *Roach* in a sail is curvature of its edge. The *peak* is the upper aft corner of a gaff-rigged sail; the *tack,* the lower forward corner; the *clew,* the lower aft corner; the *throat,* the forward part of the head. *Bolt rope* is the rope sewed around the edge of a sail to reinforce it. *Battens* (thin, flat wooden strips) are placed in *pockets* along the leach of a sail to flatten the edge and give it shape.

Gear is the general term for miscellaneous lines, spars, sails and similar items. *Rigging* refers to all the lines aboard a boat, used in connection with setting and handling sail. Lines or wire staying the masts comprise the *standing rigging;* the lines used in setting and furling sails, the *running rigging. Halyards* are lines or tackles used to hoist sails; *shrouds* stay the mast at the sides. The wire ropes commonly used to support the mast from a point forward are called *stays.* Those supporting the mast from aft are *backstays.* When the slack in stays and shrouds is taken up, the rigging is said to be *set up.*

One could go on indefinitely defining a multitude of terms that constitute the vernacular of the sea, but space forbids. What has been covered here will serve as framework. As the novice gains experience in sailing and handling boats, his vocabulary will broaden proportionately and naturally. We hope, however, that his enthusiasm for the subject will not cause him to toss indiscriminate Avasts, Ahoys and Belays into every conceivable nook and corner of his conversation. The natural, proper use of correct terms is much to be desired; strained efforts to affect a salty lingo are conspicuously inappropriate.

conventional bow. The stem is a vertical member set up on the forward end of the keel. It is commonly of white oak in wooden construction and may be straight or curved, depending on the shape desired. It is *plumb* if set up perpendicular to the waterline, but is often *raked* at an angle for better appearance. *Ring bolts,* having a ring through the eye of the bolt, are fitted through the stems of many small boats, and often at the stern as well.

Deadwood is solid timber placed on the keel to connect

W HAT'S the difference between a sheer plank and the plank sheer? Do the terms carvel and clinker have any special significance to you? Do you know the distinction between a keel and a keelson?

In the first part of this chapter on nautical terms, we have explained the meaning of many of the more common nautical terms. In it special emphasis was laid on those which should be part of every motor boatman's vocabulary, including correct terminology applying to various parts of a motor boat.

Sailing and rowing craft, too, have their special nomenclature, some of the terms seldom being encountered by the motor boatman not concerned with sailing. The terms applicable to sailing and rowing craft are of particular interest to men going into the Navy, Coast Guard and other branches of the service. Knowledge of the correct technical terms to use in connection with the whaleboats, cutters, dinghies, wherries and other small craft they will handle will stand them in good stead.

There must of necessity be some overlapping in the terms discussed here and those covered in the foregoing pages. Certain parts are common to all types of boat, whether propelled by motor, sail or oars. In such cases some repetition is unavoidable.

To begin at the logical beginning, let's consider some of the terms identified with the boat's hull construction. The *keel* is the principal frame member of the boat, usually the first one laid when construction is begun. Almost invariably it is on the outside of the hull, though in cases (as in some P.T. boats) the keel is inside. Often an extra piece is fastened to the bottom of the main keel to protect it. This is a *false keel*.

Ordinarily a timber or stringer, bolted inside as a reinforcing member to the keel, is called a *keelson* (pronounced kelson). Between the keel and keelson, blocks are fitted *athwartship* (at right angles to the fore and aft centerline of the keel). These blocks are called *filling pieces.*

Keel blocks are used to support the keel of a boat during construction. When boats are stowed in *cradles* aboard a vessel, a *keel stop* is fitted at the after end of the keel to locate the boat in a fore and aft position on the cradle. The keel stop is a small metal fitting.

A *stem* is common to all boats with the conventional type of bow, whereas the square-nosed *pram* or *punt* type has a bow resembling its square stern. Flat planking across the stern is called the *transom,* but in a *double-ender* the stern construction is pointed, resembling the

the end timbers. Most of it is found at the stern of a boat, though it may also be used forward, in which case it may take the form of a *stem heel.* Timbers connecting the *stem knee* to the keel are often called *sole* pieces. An *apron* (sometimes called *stemson*) is an inner stem fitted abaft (behind) the stem to reinforce it. It gives added surface on which the *hood ends* of the planking can land, the hood ends being those ends which fit into the *rabbet,* cut into the stem to receive them.

Stem bands of metal are usually fitted on the forward edge of the stem for protection. The spars which project out over the bow on sailing craft to take the *stays* from which jibs and other *head sails* are set, are called *bowsprits.* *Breast hooks* are reinforcing knees set horizontally behind the stem.

Various kinds of *knees* are used throughout the hull construction to connect members joined at an angle to each other. They may be of metal, though often a natural growth of wood is selected—hackmatack, for example—in which the grain runs in the desired shape for maximum strength. There are *bosom* knees and *carling* knees, *dagger* knees and *hanging* knees, *lodging* knees, *panting* knees, *thwart* knees, etc., each designating the special part of construction in which it is employed, or its relative position.

Going *aft,* now to the *stern* of the boat, we have *horn timbers,* used to fasten the *shaft log* to the *transom knee.* The transom has already been defined. Shaft logs are timbers between keel and deadwood through which the propeller shaft (if the boat is motor driven) passes. At the stern the principal vertical member is called the *stern post,* set up on the after end of the keel or shaft log, to which it is attached by the *stern knee.* A *stern hook* is not a hook at all but, in a double-ended boat, is that reinforcing member which corresponds to the *breast hook* at the bow. Breast hooks at the stern are also called *crutches.* If the boat has a transom stern, she would have *quarter knees* at each side of the transom instead of the one stern hook.

Frames are the timbers set up on the keel, providing the skeleton over which the *planking* is laid. The frames may be curved as in a round bottom boat or straight as in certain types of V-bottom design. Sometimes they are *sawn* to shape; otherwise they are *steam bent*.

Floors, nautically speaking, are not laid as in a house to be walked upon. In a boat they are important transverse structural members, tying together the keel and the lower ends of the frames.

The *gunwale* (pronounced gun'l) of an open boat is the upper edge of the side. *Inwales* are the longitudinal members fastened inside a canoe or small boat along the gunwales. Sometimes they are referred to as *clamps*. The ends of *deck beams,* on which decking is laid, rest upon the clamps, although a horizontal *shelf* may be used above the clamp. Then deck beams rest upon the shelf.

Sometimes boatmen speak of deck or cabin *carlines* when they really mean beams. The beams run *thwartships* (at right angles to a center line passing through the keel) whereas carlines, or carlings, are short pieces of timber running *fore and aft* (lengthwise, parallel to the keel) between deck beams. Carlines, for example, would be found at the port and starboard sides of *hatch* openings in a deck.

Stringers are longitudinal members fastened inside the hull for additional structural strength. If they run along the *bilge*

(the turn of the hull below the waterline) they are called *bilge stringers.* There are other types.

Open boats often have a finishing piece which runs along the gunwale, lying on top of the clamp or inwale and covering the top edge of the planking and heads of frames. This is a *capping.* In many small boats, capping is omitted, so that there is nothing to catch dirt and water when the boat is turned over to be emptied instead of bailing. Such a boat would be said to have *open gunwales.*

Planking, laid over the outside of frames in *strakes* (continuous narrow lengths from stem to stern), provides the outer shell of the *hull,* which is the general term describing the main structure of the boat. Planking is called *carvel* if the surface finishes smooth with *caulked seams* between the strakes to make the hull watertight. It is *clinker* or *lapstrake* if the successive strakes lap each other as the clapboards of a house are lapped. Hulls are sometimes *double planked,* in which case there is commonly an inner *skin* or layer of planking laid diagonal to the keel, and an outer skin fore and aft, with waterproof glue, or glue and fabric, between layers. Sometimes the two layers of planking are run diagonally at an angle of forty-five degrees from keel to gunwale, planks of the two layers being at right angles to each other. Frames are omitted in this type of construction.

The *sheer* line is the line, as seen in profile, along the hull defined by the gunwale or top edge of the topmost strake of planking, the *sheer strake.* Sheer strakes are sometimes thicker than other strakes of planking. When a second plank, next below the sheer strake, is fitted thicker than the others, it is called a *binding strake.*

Bilge strakes would be the heavier planks fitted at the turn of the bilge, though the term might be applied to ceiling inside in the bilge. *Ceiling* is not overhead, as ashore; it is planking laid inside the frames. The *garboard* (pronounced garb'd) strake is the lowest strake of planking, fitted next to the keel.

Strakes of planking between the bottom and *topsides* are called *wales.* Topsides refers to the portion of the hull between the waterline and the rail or gunwale. The term wales is also used to describe heavy strakes (*rubbing strakes*) below the gunwale. Longitudinal timbers, extending outside the exposed faces of planking, usually metal-shod to protect the topsides, are referred to as *side fenders* or *fender guards.* In pleasure boating, the term *fenders* commonly calls to mind the cork-filled canvas devices, or those of rope or rubber, suspended over the side to take shocks when lying against a dock or another boat.

We have already used the term *bilge* in speaking of the "turn of the bilge" and in its

Some of the terms applicable to the rig of a small knockabout, with jib-headed (Marconi) mainsail. On the preceding page, a section through the centerboard trunk

MAST-HEAD
MAIN HALYARD SHEAVE
MAIN HALYARD (Leads down mast to belaying pin in mast bench)
HEAD
SAIL TRACK AND SLIDES
MAST
LUFF
MAST CLEAT FOR SHROUD
MAST CLEAT FOR HEAD STAY
JIB HALYARD BLOCK
STAYSAIL OR JIB HALYARD
STAYSAIL OR JIB
BATTENS (IN POCKETS)
SHROUD
LEACH
HEAD STAY
REEF BAND
REEF POINTS
STAYSAIL OR JIB BENT TO STAY WITH SLIDES OR SNAPS
MAIN SAIL
CLEW OUTHAUL THRU SHEAVE TO CLEAT ON BOOM
CLEW
TURNBUCKLE
WIRE BRIDLE OR HORSE
FOOT
MAINSHEET
TILLER
BOOM
TACK
GOOSENECK
MAST BENCH
BOW PLATE
RUDDER
WATER LINE
STAYSAIL SHEET
TURNBUCKLE
CHAINPLATE
BELAYING PINS FOR MAIN AND STAYSAIL HALYARDS

86

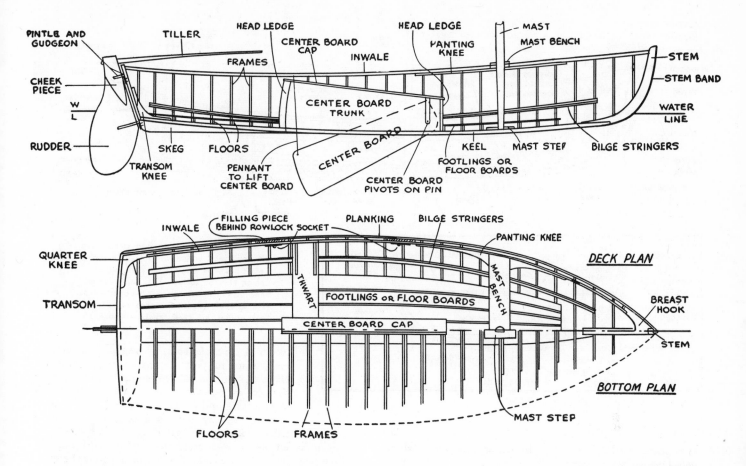

association with "bilge strakes." However the bilge is also the lowest part of the hull inside where *bilge water* accumulates. Boats carried out of water on larger craft must have *boat plugs,* usually of metal, which can be removed to drain water which might otherwise collect inside.

The sheer plank has been defined as the topmost strake along the hull where the deck joins the topsides. *Plank sheer,* on the other hand, means the outermost plank of the deck. Sometimes called a *covering board,* it covers the tops of frames and upper edge of the sheer strake in a decked boat, as capping does in an open boat. Covering boards are usually wider than any of the narrower deck planks.

Chain plates are strips of bronze or iron bolted to the side of a boat, to which rigging is attached, such as the shrouds or shroud whips (to be defined later). *Bottom boards* (sometimes *foot boards*) are those laid in the bottom of the boat to walk upon. In small boats they are often removable. Where there are no deep *floors,* previously defined, boards may be laid directly upon the inside of the frames to walk on. These are *footlings.*

The transverse seats in small craft are called *thwarts.* On them, oarsmen sit when rowing. When two men pull one oar, the oars are *double-banked,* but the boat is also double-banked if two men pull from one thwart. To support the thwart, a vertical piece is often fitted under it amidships, called a *thwart stanchion.* A man who is *sculling* would stand in the stern and propel the boat by working a single oar back and forth, using either one or two hands. The term sculling is also applied to the rowing of light racing *shells.*

Stretchers (also called *foot boards,* although this creates confusion with the alternate term for bottom boards) are sometimes fitted in small boats, athwartships, for the oarsmen to brace their feet against. The ends of thwarts land on *risers,* or *risings,* which are fore and aft pieces or stringers fastened to the inside of the frames.

Side benches, running fore and aft, are fitted at the sides of a boat over the air tanks which float the boat if capsized. The benches protect the tanks. Planking over tanks is also called *ceiling.* Instead of decks, some small boats have *platforms* at the level of the thwarts forward of the foremast. A *gang-board* runs down the centerline of the boat from the forward platform to the after thwart.

The terms *rowlock* and *oarlock* are synonomous. These are the fittings which hold the oars when rowing. In place of oarlocks, wooden *thole pins* are sometimes driven into holes or sockets. In certain types of boats, like surf boats and whaleboats, used in rough water where a rudder might be out of water so much as to destroy its effectiveness, a *steering oar* is used at the stern, *shipped* (put or held in place) in a swiveled *steering rowlock,* sometimes called a *crutch.* *Trailing lines* are attached to oars to keep them from going overboard. When oars are *muffled* to prevent noise, pieces of canvas with strands of rope yarn attached are placed between the oars and the oarlocks. These are *thrum mats.* *Sweeps* are long oars.

Oars are very simple in their construction, yet they have a special nomenclature to designate their respective parts. The *handle* of course is the part gripped in the hand when rowing. At the other end, in the water, is the flat *blade.* *Spoon* oars, for racing, have curved blades. The round part of an oar between handle and blade is usually called the *loom,* although the term loom may properly be applied to the part from handle to oarlock, in the boat when rowing. The loom tapers as it approaches the blade. Where loom and blade meet is the *neck;* at the end of the blade is the *tip,* sometimes protected with a strip of sheet copper.

Oars is a command given to oarsmen to order them to stop pulling, holding the oars horizontally with blades *feathered* (parallel with the water to reduce wind resistance.) *Out oars* is a preliminary command given when the oars are to be made ready in the oarlocks for pulling

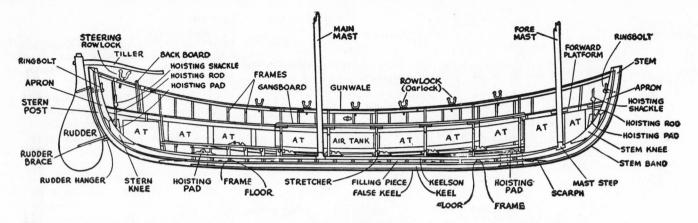

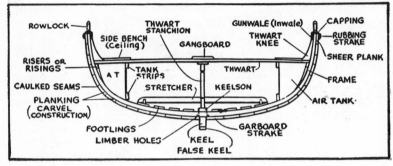

Technical terms designating parts used in the construction of a double-ended whaleboat. A flagstaff and awning stanchion may be set up abaft the foremast, and also in the stern abaft the backboard. Along each side is a row of air tanks (A T) with other air tanks at bow and stern

—in other words, to ship them in the *oars* position. *Give way* means start pulling.

Trail is an order to let go the oars while the boat is under way, allowing them to swing around in a fore and aft position, with blades trailing alongside. (Hence the term trailing line, defined above.) If there are no trailing lines, the handle of the oar is held in the hand to execute this order. To check the *way* (movement through the water) of a boat—either *headway* if going forward, or *sternway*, if going backward (some old salts might prefer to say *sternboard* instead of "backward")—the command is *hold water*. The command hold water is executed by holding the blades vertically in the water with oars at right angles to the keel.

To go astern, the command to oarsmen is *stern all*, whereupon they will *back water*, using the oars in a manner just opposite to that when pulling to give the boat headway. To make a turn the order is *back starboard* or *back port* depending on whether the turn is to be made to starboard or port. A quick turn to starboard can be made, provided the boat does not have too much headway, by ordering *back starboard, give way port*. *Back port, give way starboard* will result in a quick turn to port, as the port oarsmen are backing water while the starboard oarsmen are pulling ahead. *Stand by to give way* calls for the position at the beginning of a stroke as oarsmen, leaning forward, prepare to row.

When coming alongside a vessel, the command *toss oars* is given to order the the oarsmen to place their oars in a perpendicular position, blades fore and aft, handles resting on the footlings. Commonly the command is preceded by a cautionary *stand-by to toss*. Whenever a warning to the crew is desirable, before issuing any command, the expression is *stand by to. . . .* For example, a preparatory or warning command for the order or position *oars* is *stand by to lay on the oars*.

Boat the oars means place them in the boat on the thwarts, blades forward. When a boat has grounded, the order is *point the oars,* whereupon the oarsmen, standing, set the oars at an angle, blade tips on the bottom, ready to shove the boat off on command. *Way enough* means stop pulling and boat the oars.

Stand by the oars is a command given when shoving off from a ship or going alongside, when the oarsmen grasp the handles of the oars and see that the blades are clear of other oars. Blades are laid flat on the gunwale, handle over the thwart. At *up oars,* they are raised vertically, blades trimmed fore and aft, handles on the footlings. These commands make a boat ready for duty alongside a ship.

At the command *shove off* the bowman lets go the painter and shoves the bow off from a vessel's side with the boat hook while the *coxswain* aft, in charge of the boat, *sheers* the boat off with the tiller. The duty of various oarsmen in such a maneuver varies with their position in the boat. The order *let fall* is a command given when the boat is clear of a vessel's side. This is an intermediate order between *up oars* and *oars* as the blades are dropped outboard into the rowlocks. *In bows* is ordered as a landing is made to instruct bowman to toss oars at a forty-five degree angle, boat them, pick up boat books and stand holding them vertically in readiness for the landing or ready to receive lines.

The coxswain (pronounced cox'n), as explained, is the officer in charge of a boat. He stands aft at the *tiller* to steer and issues the orders. The tiller of course is the bar or handle on the *rudder head* by which the rudder is moved to steer the boat. Sometimes the tiller is not shipped. Instead a thwartship piece of wood or metal may be fitted on the rudder head. This is a *yoke*. Then the boat is steered by means of lines called *yoke ropes* or *lanyards* attached to the yoke. In order to provide sufficient thickness for a slot for the tiller to be shipped in, *cheek blocks* may be bolted on the sides of the rudder.

Pintles and *gudgeons* are commonly used to hang the rudder of small boats. The pintle is in the form of a hook or pin on the rudder, point downward. This fits into the gudgeon on the stern post, which has an eye to receive the pintle. In other boats, *rudder hangers* are used, providing a vertical rod of metal for attachment to the stern post with *rudder braces* to fit over the hanger.

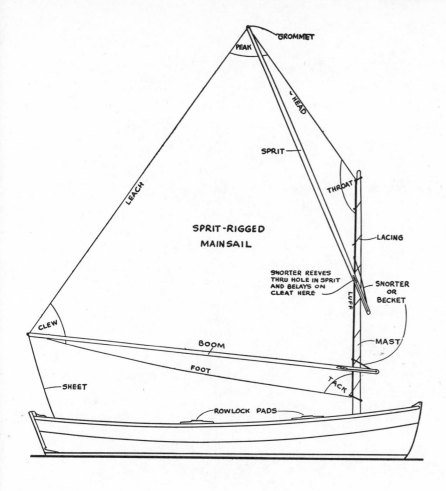

Labels on diagram: GROMMET, PEAK, HEAD, SPRIT, THROAT, LEACH, LACING, SPRIT-RIGGED MAINSAIL, SNORTER REEVES THRU HOLE IN SPRIT AND BELAYS ON CLEAT HERE, SNORTER OR BECKET, LUFF, CLEW, MAST, BOOM, FOOT, TACK, SHEET, ROWLOCK PADS

NAUTICAL TERMS USED IN CONNECTION WITH

THE RIGGING AND HANDLING OF SAILING

CRAFT. VARIOUS TYPES OF SAILS AND RIGS

WE have covered in the preceding pages many of the nautical terms relating to parts of the construction of rowing and sailing craft. Most of these terms are applicable alike to the whaleboats, cutters, and other small craft used by the Navy and Coast Guard, and to many types of small pleasure craft. Proceeding now to the terms used in the rigging and handling of sailing craft, we encounter a jargon quite unintelligible to the landsman.

For example, consider some of the *rigs* which distinguish various types of sailboats by the arrangement of their masts and sails. Simplest of all is the *catboat,* with its single heavy mast stepped well forward, and one sail. The original type of catboat had a *gaff-headed* mainsail and no *bowsprit* or *shrouds.* (These terms will be defined later.)

The *sloop* also has one mast, stepped further aft so that, in addition to its *mainsail* abaft the mast, there is room for *jibs* and other *headsails* forward of the mast. Properly, the sloop has a bowsprit. Without a bowsprit, the rig is described as a *knockabout* or *stem-head sloop.*

The *cutter,* like a sloop, has one mast but this is stepped more nearly amidship so that the total *sail area* is almost equally divided between mainsail and headsails. (A cutter is also a type of ship's boat.)

Ketches have two masts. Of these the taller (the *mainmast*) is forward. The *mizzen mast* (the after one) is stepped forward of the rudder post. *Yawls* resemble ketches, except that the mizzen mast or *jigger* is abaft

the rudder post. **Yawls have** proportionately less of their total sail area in the mizzen, and the rig of the ketch is said to be *inboard* because it does not project much beyond the stern of the boat as in a yawl.

Schooners have two or more masts, with the *fore-and-aft* rig which distinguishes practically all modern sailing craft from the *square* rigs of the old windjammers. In the latter, the square sails were set from *yards* set horizontally across the mast. Unlike yawls and ketches, the after mast (mainmast) of a schooner is always as tall as, or taller than, the *foremast.*

Schooners are sometimes *staysail rigged* with triangular fore and aft *staysails* between the fore and mainmast, jib-headed triangular (*Marconi*) mainsail and the usual headsails. Schooners without *topmasts* above the lower masts are *baldheaded.*

A *sprit* rig is used on some dinghies and other small craft. In this type of rig the upper aft corner (*peak*) of the fore and aft sail is held *aloft* by a light *spar* called a sprit, inserted in an eye called a *grommet.* The sprit at its lower end is supported by a *snorter* or *becket* consisting of a light line about the mast with an eye in the lower end to take the sprit. Although the sail is quadrilateral, no *gaff* at the *head* of the sail or *boom* at the *foot* is required, though a boom is sometimes used, as in the illustration, its forward end held in a becket, the same as the sprit above it.

Lug rigs are of various types and their use is also confined to small craft. The *standing lug* has a yard which crosses the mast obliquely while the *tack* (forward lower corner) of the sail is made fast to the mast. If there is no boom, the sail is said to be *loose-footed.* The *balance lug* differs in that the boom projects somewhat forward of the mast. In a *dipping lug* the tack is made fast to the stem, or ahead of the mast, so that the yard must be *dipped* around the mast when tacking.

A *sliding gunter* has a triangular jib-headed sail, with topmast sliding aloft as an extension of the lower mast. This is popular on many small racing dinghies.

Whale-boats are double ended pulling lifeboats, 24 to 30 feet in length, used by the Navy. They often have a standing lug rig on two masts, but no jib. *Cutters* are double-banked ships' boats, with transom sterns, used for general duty. (See also previous definition of cutter rig.)

Wherries are a type of small pulling boat, 12 to 14 feet in length, used generally by officers of Navy craft. *Dinghies* are not only the small boats towed by pleasure craft, and propelled by oars, sails, or outboard motors. Dinghies used by the Navy are 16 to 20 feet in length, have four oars, single-banked, and a sprit rig for sailing. *Gigs* are ships' boats used by captains or commanding officers.

From bow to stern, the mast of a four-masted schooner would be named the *fore, main, mizzen,* and *jigger.* The principal (lower) sails set on these are the *foresail, mainsail, mizzensail* and *spanker,* the latter being the after sail of a schooner having more than three masts.

Topsails may be set above lower sails from *topmasts,* with names corresponding to the masts on which they are set. A *bowsprit* projects out from the stem and a jib-boom may be rigged out beyond the bowsprit.

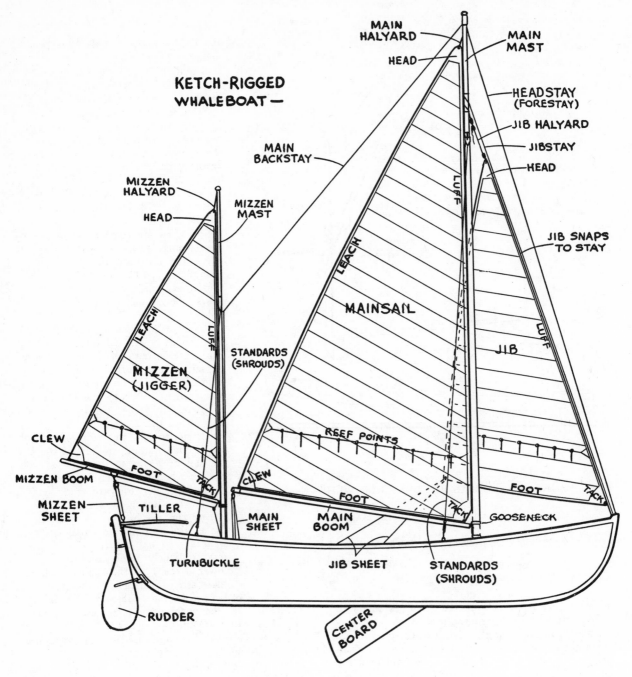

KETCH-RIGGED WHALEBOAT —

Jibs are usually triangular sails set before the fore-mast, although in recent years the *clew* (aft lower corner) has been cut off certain jibs, making them quadrilateral. Some jibs are large, like the *Genoa* and *balloon jib,* overlapping the mainsail.

If a schooner has four principal *headsails* before the foremast, they are, working aft, the *flying jib, outer jib, inner jib,* and *fore staysail.*

Staysails, as previously mentioned, are triangular jib-shaped sails set from the *stays* which support the masts. *Spinnakers* are large triangular sails set from booms called *spinnaker poles* on the opposite side of the main or fore boom when running before a *fair wind.*

Canvas is a term used in speaking about all sails in general. *Plain sails* are the ordinary *working* sails, not including the lighter jibs and staysails. *Storm canvas,* on the other hand, includes jibs, staysails, or *trysails* of extra heavy canvas for use in heavy weather.

The *head* of a quadrilateral sail is its upper side, *bent* (made fast or secured) to a *gaff;* in a jib-headed sail, the head is the upper corner. The *foot* is the lower edge, bent to a *boom.* The forward side of a fore-and-aft sail is the *luff,* bent to the mast by means of *hoops,* or the more modern *sail track* and *slides.* In either case the method of bending the sail to the mast is such as to permit *hoisting* and *lowering.* The small pieces of manila used to secure mast hoops to the luff of a sail are called *robands.* The *leech* is the after side of a fore-and-aft sail.

In a gaff-rigged sail, the upper aft corner is the *peak;* the forward upper corner where gaff and mast meet, the *throat* (also called *nock.*) The lower corner forward where mast and boom meet is the *tack;* the lower corner aft, the *clew.*

Bolt rope is sewed to the edges of a sail to strengthen it. *Tabling* is the re-enforced part of the sail to which the bolt rope is sewed. The leech of a fore-and-aft sail (and the foot of a square sail) is usually cut with a curve called the *roach.* To support the roach and preserve its shape by flattening the leech, wooden *battens* (thin flat strips of wood) are inserted in *pockets* in the sail along the leech. *Brails* are lines running from the leech to the mast, used to aid in gathering sail in and securing it.

Sails today are usually *cross-cut*—that is, the cloths or strips which are seamed together to make the sail are laid out so that the seams are perpendicular to the leech.

(See illustration of ketch-rigged whaleboat.) Cross-cut sails allow a freer flow of wind across their surface. A variation of this practice is found in *mitered* sails. In loose-footed sails, the general practice is to run the cloth strips two ways, perpendicular to both leech and foot, joining at the *miter* which runs from the clew to a point on the luff.

When wind pressure is too great on a sail, sail area is reduced by *reefing,* which is accomplished by gathering in canvas along the boom as the sail is lowered part way. Parallel to the foot of the sail, strips of canvas called *reef bands* are sewed for reenforcement and short pieces of line are attached. These are *reef points,* passed around the foot of the sail and secured. A *reef cringle* is an eye in the leech or luff of a fore-and-aft sail in line with the reef points. *Reef earings* (or *pendants*) are short pieces of line spliced into the cringles to permit the latter to be secured to the boom.

The masts, gaffs, booms, yards, etc., from which sails are set are referred to generally as *spars.* The mast, of course, is the principal vertical spar, supporting the gaffs, booms, sails, etc. On larger craft there may be a *topmast* above the lower mast, and even *topgallant* masts above the topmast. A *jury* mast is any spar rigged temporarily as a mast in the event that the mast itself is carried away.

The *boom* has already been spoken of as the spar to which the foot of a fore-and-aft sail is bent; the *gaff,* the one to which the head is bent. At the mast end, *jaws* of the boom and gaff encircle the mast to keep these spars in place. *Goosenecks* (also called *Pacific irons*) are swiveled metal fittings used on many booms instead of jaws. Light spars used on a staysail or topsail or foot of the jib are not booms, but *clubs.*

Square sails are set from *yards,* a term applied also to the light spars used at the head of a lug rig sail. *Bowsprits* have been defined elsewhere as spars projecting from the stem. Short spars sometimes project from the stern, particularly on boats of the yawl type, where the mizzen boom overhangs the stern considerably. These are *boomkins.*

The foot of a mast—that is to say, its lower end—is called the *heel;* it fits in a *step* on the keel. Its topmost end is the *masthead,* often capped by a *truck,* a flat circular piece of wood. Hence the expression "from truck to keel," including everything in a ship from top to bottom. At the masthead, a *sheave,* the grooved wheel of a block, may be let into the mast to take *halyards* by which sails are hoisted.

Mast cleats of wood are sometimes attached to masts at the point where shrouds and stays (see definitions under rigging) are attached. Horizontal spars fitted on the mast to spread the shrouds and stays are *spreaders. Tangs* are metal plates attached to a mast where rigging is to be made fast. They distribute the strain over a considerable area.

A *mast hole* in a deck or the thwart of a small boat is the hole through which the mast is passed when stepped. When the primary function of a thwart is to serve as a support for the mast, rather than as a seat, it is often spoken of as a *mast bench.* Instead of a hole in the thwart, a semi-circular metal band is sometimes hinged at the edge of a thwart to hold the mast. This is called a *gate,* sometimes *mast clamp.*

All the various ropes of a vessel which secure masts and sails, taken together, are referred to as *rigging.* The *standing rigging* includes that part, like shrouds and stays, which is permanently secured, whereas the *running rigging* embraces the part which is movable, such as the sheets, halyards, etc., running through *blocks.*

Masts are supported by *stays* forward (*headstays, jibstays, forestays,* etc.), usually of wire rope, with *shrouds* at the sides, and *backstays* from aft. A *spring stay* is one running between a schooner's mastheads. *Turnbuckles,* as previously indicated, may be used in rigging to *set it up. Deadeyes* (round blocks of lignum vitae with holes through them and a groove around the edge) are used for the same purpose. They are found between the shrouds and chain plates on the vessel's side. *Lanyards* of rope *reeve* (pass) through the holes of the deadeyes and provide a method of adjusting tension in the shrouds. *Shroud whips* are also used to set up the shrouds.

While a mast is *stayed* in a vertical position, bowsprits are *guyed* horizontally (or at an angle) by *bowsprit shrouds* at the sides and a *bob-stay* from below. *Steeve* is the term that describes technically the angle the bowsprit makes with the horizontal.

Sheets are *not* sails. Sheets, of rope, are made fast to booms or the clew of loose-footed sails to control the angle at which the sail sets, relative to the wind directions.

While a simple single sheet is used on some small sailboats, on larger craft it is customary to provide additional power for handling the sails by reeving the sheet through blocks, constituting a *tackle* (*purchase*). A *gun tackle,* as used in shroud whips, is a purchase having

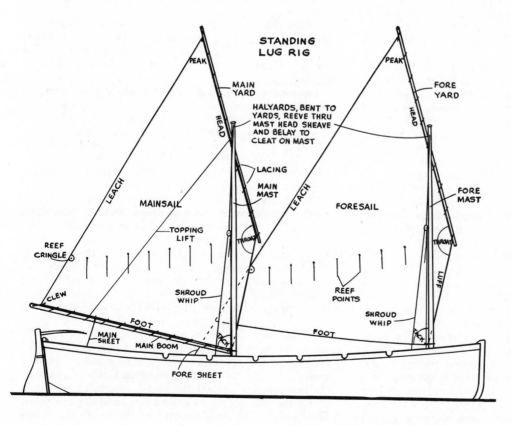

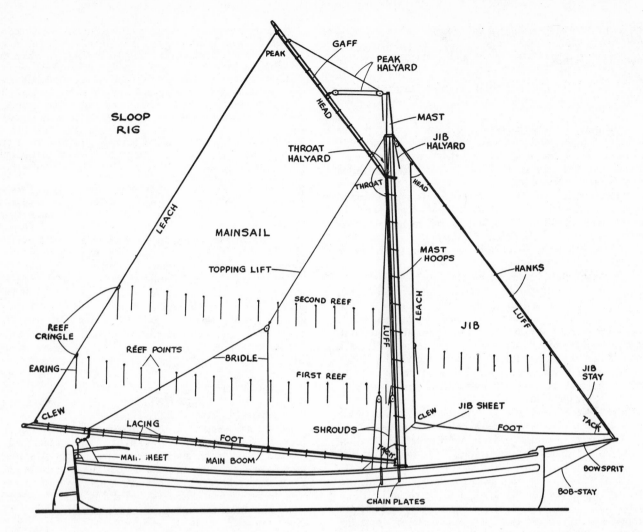

SLOOP RIG

MAINSAIL — PEAK, GAFF, PEAK HALYARD, HEAD, MAST, JIB HALYARD, THROAT HALYARD, THROAT, HEAD, LEACH, MAST HOOPS, TOPPING LIFT, SECOND REEF, HANKS, LEACH, JIB, LUFF, REEF CRINGLE, REEF POINTS, EARING, FIRST REEF, BRIDLE, LUFF, JIB STAY, CLEW, LACING, CLEW, JIB SHEET, TACK, FOOT, FOOT, SHROUDS, MAIN SHEET, MAIN BOOM, BOWSPRIT, BOB-STAY, CHAIN PLATES

two single blocks. There are *main sheets, jib sheets,* etc., depending upon what particular sail the sheet is used to control.

A metal rod called a *deck horse* or *boom horse* is commonly bolted to the deck and on it the ring of a *sheet block* can travel from side to side as the boom swings over. This is the *traveller.* On small boats, a wire bridle often takes the place of a deck horse. Ordinarily today one speaks of the deck fitting (horse) or wire bridle on which the sheet block runs, as the traveller. Running rigging is secured to *belaying pins* of metal or wood set in *pin rails* (*fife rails*) and is said to be *belayed,* when made fast. *Cleats* are also used on small craft in place of belaying pins. In small boats it is good judgment never to belay the sheets, as sudden squalls may make it necessary to let them go in a hurry, to prevent capsizing (turning over).

Halyards (also spelled halliards), another part of the running rigging, are the ropes or tackles used to hoist sails or yards, while the tackle or rope that hauls them down is called a *downhaul.* *Outhauls* haul the corner of a sail, the clew for example, out to the end of a spar. *Topping lifts* are lines used to support or hoist the outer end of a boom. Down from the topping lifts, light lines lead, in the form of bridles, to the boom. These are *lazy jacks,* which control the sail as it is taken in, preventing the sail from falling on deck.

Whereas a motor boat has only to lay her course, regardless of wind and weather, (except under unusual conditions), a sailboat's course is governed to a large extent by the wind direction. For example, a sailboat can never go *dead to windward* or into the *wind's eye* (in the direction from which the wind is blowing) but would be said to *point well* if she could sail within four or five points of the wind. Therefore, to reach an objective to windward, she must *tack* along a zig-zag course, each leg of which is a *board.* Thus she goes alternately on the *starboard tack* (when the wind comes over the starboard bow) and the *port tack* (wind on the port bow) and is then said to be *beating* (or *working*) to windward.

When she is sailing as close to the wind as possible, a boat is *close-hauled, on the wind,* or *by the wind.* *Full and by* is a synonymous expression indicating that all sails are full (*drawing*) and the boat is *pointing* as *high* as possible.

Opposed to the idea of sailing as close to the wind as possible is the expression *sailing free,* associated with the condition when the wind is aft. Or, under similar conditions, if she is sailing with sheets well *eased off* (not hauled in close) she may be said to be *sailing large* or *off the wind.* She *runs before the wind* when sailing free with the wind well aft, that is, over the stern or quarter.

Sheets taken in as much as possible are *hauled flat.* Sails are *trimmed in* when they are brought in more nearly parallel with the boat's fore and aft centerline, but to allow the sails to swing off away from that centerline, the sheets are *started.*

In changing from one tack to another the boat *goes about* or *comes about.* To prepare his crew to execute such a maneuver, the coxwain orders *Ready about!* Then, putting the tiller *down* (away from the wind, toward the *lee* side of the boat), he calls *Hard alee!* and brings her about.

As the sails belly out, catching the wind as it shifts across the bow, they *fill away,* or the boat is said to fill away as it gathers headway on the new tack. To *miss stays* is to attempt to come about and fail to complete the maneuver. Then if the boat is caught in a position where she will not fill away on either tack, she is *in irons.* Should the wind catch the sails on the wrong side while she is in irons and start to drive the boat astern, sails are said to be *aback*.

One *fetches* a given objective if he is running a course to windward and reaches the mark without tacking. When working to windward, each *leg* or tack is a *board* and, depending on the length of each leg, there may be *long boards* and *short boards*.

If a gust of wind comes along, threatening to capsize the boat, the coxswain must ease the pressure of wind on his sails, so he puts the tiller *down* (away from the wind, toward the *lee* side). He is *luffing* then as the boat's bow swings into the wind and the luffs of the sails shake so that wind is spilled. If he attempts to sail too close to the wind, causing all the sails to shake, and spill wind, the expression is *all in the wind*.

A *reach* is a course that can be made good when sailing off the wind, that is, sailing free, not close-hauled. The wind then is nearly abeam. With the wind forward of the beam, it is a *close reach*; abaft the beam, a *broad reach*.

Running before the wind, sails are sometimes set with booms on opposite sides, *wing and wing*. It is considered the most dangerous point of sailing to have the wind *dead aft* because of the risk, to an inexperienced boatman, of having the boom accidentally swing across the stern to the opposite side. This is a *jibe* (or *gybe*) and at the least can cause considerable damage to spars and rigging. If the maneuver is executed deliberately, with the sail and boom kept under control, there is no danger and this is exactly what happens when *wearing*. Instead of tacking, with the bow passing through the wind, the stern in wearing is brought through the wind.

Another point that must be watched in running before the wind in a tendency to *yaw*, or *veer* suddenly off course. The boat is said to *broach to* if, through bad steering or the force of a heavy sea, she is allowed to slew around with a possibility, as she swings into the wind, of being caught broadside *in the trough*.

To *bring to* is to stop a boat by throwing her head into the wind, (or to come to an anchorage). To *heave to* is to lay the boat with helm to leeward and sails trimmed so that the boat alternately *comes to* and *falls off*, keeping out of the trough. Vessels often heave to in heavy weather. Motor boats heave to when the boat's head is brought into the wind or sea and held there by means of her engines. Larger ships sometimes are allowed to drift in whatever position they will assume relative to wind and sea, with wind on the quarter or even with the ship lying in the trough. That may be their method of heaving to, depending on how the ship will be most comfortable under stress of weather.

A SAILBOAT *lies to* when, without anchoring, she is held in one position with no way on. The bow *pays off* when it swings away (falls off) from the wind. She is kept a *rap full* when sails are filled, not quite close-hauled, and is *pinched* when sailed so close to the wind that the sails shiver. If a boat is *carrying* a heavy *press* of canvas, the helmsman may *ease her* by luffing a little. Lines are eased off when slacked.

Sails are *bent* to spars; lines belayed to cleats or bitts when made fast or secured. Lines *reeve* through blocks or *fairleads* (which guide them in the desired direction). Sails *draw* when they fill with wind and drive a boat; *bag*, when they set too full, with *taut* (tight) leaches and canvas slack. *Slack* is the opposite of taut. One *looses sail* when *unfurling* it. To *furl* sail is to roll it up and secure it to a yard or boom, and unfurl conveys the opposite idea when the sail is made ready for use.

A boat is under *easy* sail if she is not laboring or straining, but when the wind *freshens* it may be necessary to *shorten sail* (reduce the amount of canvas carried). *Douse* and *strike* are synonymous terms used when sail is shortened.

Reefing (spoken of elsewhere in connection with the parts of a sail) consists of reducing the area of a sail by lowering it part way, gathering the foot of the sail along the boom, and securing it with the *reef points*. There are usually several bands of reef points; to *close reef* means to shorten down to the last band, rather than just a *single* or *double reef*. When no sail is set, as happens on occasion when a vessel *scuds* (drives) before a gale, she is under *bare poles*.

MOST confusing are some of the terms having to do with directions relative to the wind. As previously indicated, *windward*

(pronounced windard) means toward the wind, the direction from which the wind blows. A boat goes to windward, but in speaking of the side of a vessel and the parts on that side on which the wind is blowing, it is better to refer to the *weather* side.

Opposed to windward is *leeward* (pronounced looard), the direction away from the wind, toward which it is blowing. The *lee side*, therefore, is away from the wind, and a boat makes *leeway* when blown sideways off her course. A *lee shore* is a good one to *give a wide berth* (keep well clear of it). Many use this term in a mistaken sense, thinking that there is protection from the wind under a lee shore. But since it is one on which the wind is blowing, it is dangerous. When a vessel is caught on a lee shore and has to work her way clear, she is *clawing off*.

As a boat *heels* (*not* keels) to the wind in sailing, the weather side is *up*, the leeward side *down*. Hence the expression, putting the helm or tiller up or down. A boat *carries weather helm* if the tiller must be kept to windward in order to hold her course; *lee helm* if it must be kept to leeward. In a good breeze it is well for a sailboat to carry a little weather helm. Then if the tiller is let go the boat will tend to come up into the wind instead of falling off. The *trim* of the boat, determined by the distribution of the weight of crew and ballast, has much to do with what helm the boat will carry.

Other Terms

FEW will require to have the distinction between *cabin* and *cockpit* pointed out in their application to small boats. Many small rowing and sailing craft are entirely open or partly decked. On small decked boats a cabin is the enclosed space, the cockpit open. In sailing vessels the cockpit is usually a small well aft where the steering wheel is located.

A lot of misunderstanding revolves about the use of the term *sheets*. When speaking of the parts of a boat—not sails—the *foresheets* indicate that space forward of the foremast thwart. The *sternsheets* is the space abaft the after thwart.

When small boats are fitted with sails, the keel is usually not deep enough to provide good sailing qualities so they are fitted with either *centerboards* or *daggerboards*. Their function is the same, but the construction differs. The centerboard lies in a vertical well, its long dimension fore and aft. It can be hoisted or lowered as required, being pivoted at the forward end. The well or box which houses the centerboard in its raised position is watertight and is called a *trunk*. The trunk has *head ledges* (vertical members) at each end and a *cap* on top. Dagger-boards fulfill the same function as a centerboard by increasing the keel area, but are raised and lowered vertically in the trunk, not pivoted.

A PAINTER is a line at the bow of the boat, used for towing or *making* the boat *fast*. (One does not "tie a boat up.") A painter at the stern is called a *stern fast*. A *sea painter* is used in life boats when launching them at sea. This is a long line attached to a thwart by means of a *toggle* so that it can be cast off easily, the line being led well forward on the ship, outside all stanchions, etc.

Chocks are metal fittings through which mooring or anchor lines are passed so as to lead them in the proper direction toward a dock, other vessel, etc. *Cleats*, of metal or wood, are fittings with two arms or horns on which lines can be made fast, or *belayed*.

When boats are to be lifted from the water on *davits* or hoists, metal fittings must be attached to the hull, usually the keel, to provide an eye into which hoisting gear can be hooked. These are *hoisting pads*, though on small pleasure boats it is often the practice to use *lifting rings* on deck, with rods passing down to the keel. Cleat and lifting ring may be designed as a combined fitting. *Hoisting shackles* are bolted to *hoisting rods* or pads; into these shackles the lower block of the *boat falls* is hooked.

Boat falls are the blocks and tackle used to hoist and lower boats on davits. A *block* consists of a wood or metal frame or shell containing one or more *sheaves* (pronounced *shivs*) or rollers in the *sheave hole* (space) between the *cheeks* of the block. Power to pull or hoist anything is greatly multiplied when a line is passed continuously around the several sheaves of a pair of blocks. The blocks with the line constitute a *tackle* (pronounced by seamen *taykle*). Boats, like fishermen's dories, are *nested* when thwarts are removed and the boats stowed one inside the other. Half a dozen boats, or more, may be so nested.

Cleats and Bitts

While cleats are satisfactory for making lines fast, wooden or metal *bitts* are often preferred where heavy strains are to be carried. These are vertical posts, sometimes single, sometimes double. They may take the form of a fitting bolted securely to the deck but often, as in the case of the wooden *samson post*, pass through the deck and are securely *stepped* at the keel or otherwise strongly fastened.

Towing bitts are also called *towing posts*. Where feasible, towing bitts on a towboat are located as near amidships as possible to permit the stern of the towing boat to swing for better maneuvering. Sometimes round metal pins are fitted through the head of a post or bitt to aid in belaying the line. Such a pin is a *norman pin*. They are also used to secure rudder heads.

Slings of wire rope or chain are used when handling boats on *booms* or *cranes*. Booms are also rigged out from a ship's side for small boats to ride to when alongside. When a boat handled on davits aboard a ship is to be secured at the *davit heads*, it is held in position by *gripes* against *strongbacks*, which are spars lashed between davits. Gripes may be of canvas or tarred hemp with a wood mat backed with canvas. If the boat is secured in a *cradle* or *chocks* on deck the gripe may be of chain or metal, tightened down by means of *turnbuckles*. These are threaded metal devices having left- and right-hand threads so that the eyebolts, hooks or shackles at either end may be drawn together as the turnbuckle is screwed up. Turnbuckles are commonly spliced into rigging on sailing craft so *shrouds* and *stays* can be *set up*. When rigging is set up, the slack is taken out.

Boat hooks, mentioned elsewhere, hardly need definition. They are simply poles with metal hook fittings on the end used when a boat comes into a dock to *fend off* (prevent hitting) or to pick up a mooring. *Fenders*, of various kinds, have already been defined.

Docks, Piers and Harbors

Speaking of docks and related subjects, a distinction must often be drawn between terminology technically right when applied to ships and commercial craft and that which is more appropriate for small pleasure craft. For example, *marina* and *yacht basin* come to mind when the average yachtsman thinks of a protected basin offering facilities for the berthing (tie-up) of pleasure craft. A shipmaster might think of a *dock* as an artificial basin, protected perhaps by jetties and breakwaters, with facilities for loading and unloading his vessel. A boatman, on the other hand, usually thinks of a dock as the structure he builds at the edge of the bank or shore in protected waters for his boat to lie to, as distinguished from the situation where a boat lies to a permanent *mooring* in an *anchorage*, away from the shore.

Piles, that is, substantial stakes, are often driven into the bottom at marinas to form individual *slips* in which boats can be berthed. When piles are used to support structures such as bridges, they are referred to as *piers*. A *wharf* is a structure built on the shore of a harbor extending into deep water so that vessels may lie alongside to load or unload cargo or passengers. In the United States, a wharf running at an angle to the shore line may also be referred to as a pier. One makes fast *to* a pile, but *alongside* a wharf. Whether he makes fast to or alongside a pier depends on what kind of pier he has in mind. Fishermen in small boats often make fast under a bridge *to* the piers supporting it, but if it is the wharf-like pier that is under discussion then the vessel makes fast *alongside*.

Boats are *hauled out* of the water on inclined planes at the water's edge called *ways* (marine way or marine railway), the framework which supports her as she is hauled out being called a *cradle*.

Jetties are dikes or embankments connected to the land; when these are used to protect a harbor, and have no connection with the land, they are generally referred to as *breakwaters*. *Groins* are jetty-like dikes built out at roughly a 90-degree angle from the shore to prevent erosion of the shore line.

A *harbor* is an anchorage which affords reasonably good protection for a vessel, with shelter from wind and sea. Strictly speaking, it applies to the water area with whatever breakwaters, jetties, etc., are needed for its protection. *Port* is a more comprehensive term,

including not only the harbor but, collectively, all the facilities for freight and passengers as well, such as docks, wharves, piers, warehouses and similar structures.

Miscellaneous Terms

Here are a few miscellaneous terms you may use more or less frequently. *Bilge keels* are narrow keels sometimes applied at the turn of a vessel's bilge to help reduce her rolling. *Ground plates* are sheets of anti-corrosive metal secured to the bottom below the water line, to which electrical ground wires are attached. *Teredos* are a type of shipworm which may bore into a boat's bottom if unprotected by copper paint. A *stuffing box* is a metal fitting (usually bronze) which fits around the propeller shaft to prevent water from entering the hull. The *shaft*, of course, connects the engine and propeller.

Secure, in nautical terms, does not mean obtain, but rather to make fast, or safe. One *secures for sea* when he puts extra lashings on movable objects to prevent their shifting. *Scope* is the length of anchor line paid out from hawse pipe, or bow chock, to anchor, often expressed as a ratio to the depth of water. A *round turn* is taken when a line is passed completely around a spar, bitt, rope or other object. *Two-blocks* is the term used when a tackle has been hauled up so that the blocks meet. *Signal halyards* are light lines used for hoisting flags and signals to spreaders, yard arms, etc.

Galley smoke pipes are sometimes called *Charley Nobles*. Closets, aboard a boat, are called *lockers* and a *hanging locker* is one deep enough for full-length garments. When something is put away in its proper place aboard ship, it is *stowed*; *lazarettes* are compartments in the stern of a vessel used for stowage. *Overhead* is a nautical term for ceiling or roof. Properly, you have no roof on a boat, and *ceiling*, in nautical use, is the sheathing or planking inside the frames, as distinguished from the outer planking. When the stem or stern of a boat *rakes* (is not perpendicular), the term *overhang* describes the projection of the upper part of bow or stern beyond a perpendicular from the waterline. A *jumper* is a preventer rope, wire or chain used to prevent a spar from giving way in an upward direction. A job is done *smartly* when done quickly, in a neat, efficient, shipshape manner.

Some Terms Relating to Courses, Bearings, etc.

A *great circle* is a circle on the surface of a sphere made by intersection of a plane through the sphere's center. A *meridian* is a great circle of the earth, passing through its poles. *Magnetic meridians* are irregular lines on the earth's surface, passing through the magnetic poles. They indicate the direction of the earth's magnetic field.

A *course* is the direction of movement prescribed for a vessel from one place to another. A *true course* is one taken from the chart with reference to true north. (The angle between a vessel's keel and the geographic meridian, when the vessel is on course.) The *magnetic course* is the angle between a vessel's keel and the magnetic meridian passing through her position. A *compass course* is the course as indicated by a vessel's compass. (The angle between a vessel's keel and the direction indicated by the north point of the compass card when the vessel is on course.) The *course steered* is the direction in which a vessel is steered, and may be given a true, magnetic or compass value. The *heading* is the direction a vessel's bow points at any given time. This may not coincide with her course. A *track* is the *course made good*, that is, the actual path of the vessel over the bottom. (Usually given a true value.) A *bearing* is the direction of a terrestrial object from an observer, and may be given a true, magnetic or compass value. A *relative bearing* is the direction of a terrestrial object from an observer, relative to the vessel's heading, best measured in degrees from 000 to 360.

Variation is the angle between true north and the direction of north as indicated by a magnetic compass unaffected by deviation. (It is easterly if the north point of such a compass points to the east of true north, westerly if it points west of true north.) *Deviation* is an error in a magnetic compass caused by magnetic influences on the vessel. (Easterly if the north point of the compass points east of magnetic north, westerly if it points west of magnetic north.) *Compass error* is the algebraic sum of variation and deviation.

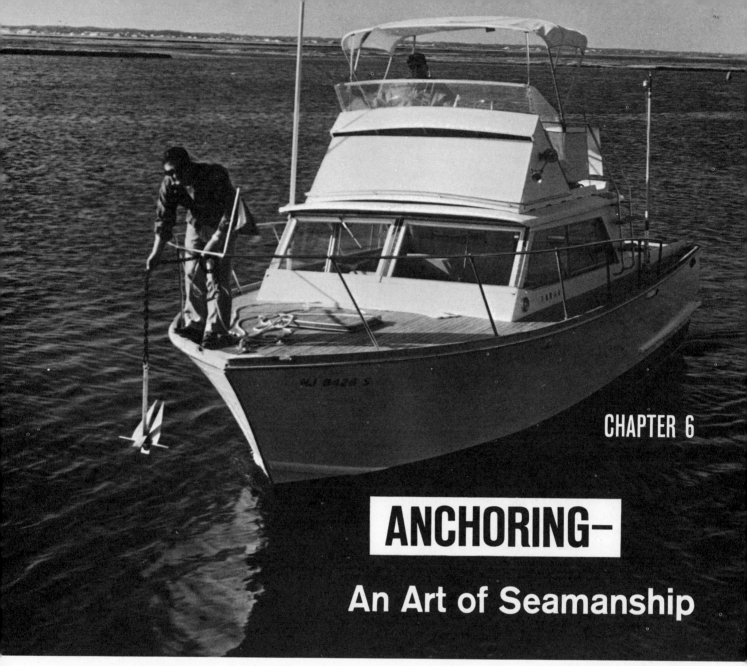

Photograph by Peter Smyth

CHAPTER 6

ANCHORING—

An Art of Seamanship

Of all the skills involved in seamanship, the art of anchoring is one the boatman must master if he is to cruise with an easy mind. Perhaps he is just getting by with inadequate gear, despite bad practices acquired in home waters. Sooner or later, carelessness and ignorance will lead to difficulty—probably inconvenience, possibly danger.

The essence of successful anchoring is to "stay put," without dragging, whenever the anchor is let go. Corollary to this is the need to respect the rights of nearby boats which could be fouled or damaged by your dragging.

Though the art may not be learned from the printed page alone, this chapter should help the tyro to get off to a good start, the seasoned boatman to round out and update his technique.

In quiet anchorages, in familiar surroundings, *ground tackle* (the gear we use) and the methods used are seldom put to test. Cruising into strange waters, find inadequate shelter in an exposed anchorage during a hard blow, and the elements will surely take the measure of both tackle and technique. The ultimate test, of course, would come in deep water on a lee shore with nothing between you and breakers on the beach except dependable gear. Ask yourself *now*, in a situation like that, would I hold . . . or hope?

The problem, then, breaks down into two principal parts—(1) the equipment we should carry, and (2) knowledge of how to use it. It is in this sequence that we treat the subject here, however anxious the reader may be to plunge headlong into the "how" aspect before he is quite familiar with the "what."

Conditions vary

In approaching the subject, it is imperative to have a sense of perspective, impossible to achieve if one is so wedded to the lore of one locality (no matter how good or effective) as to be blinded to practices proved in other areas. Lay down universal rules based on experience solely with one type of anchor in one kind of bottom, and the gale that would test your "rules" would be but a breeze compared to the storm of controversy you might raise in other knowledgeable quarters.

When we realize that the gear we see aboard that visiting boat from a distant port may have been dictated by proved and practical experience foreign to our own, we will have gone a long way toward broadening that perspective we need . . . and, who knows, perhaps improving our own anchoring skill as well.

Some of the variables

The man who has cruised in many areas, over many years, knows he can list nine or ten important variables. To cite a few: the size and type of boat; whether she is of light or heavy draft; the size and design of anchor; the nature of the bottom in which the anchor is bedded; the protection afforded by the anchorage; and the amount of sea running.

To say that any one kind of ground tackle would be ideal under all conceivable conditions for all boats of a given length is to discount the combined knowledge of the saltiest boatmen in waters all up and down our coastline. To rule out completely the value of certain specialized equipment is to overlook the fact that many a seasoned skipper has his own well-founded preferences . . . or prejudices.

FIG. 601 A century ago, wooden stock anchors were still in use. This one snagged the net of a dragger in the late 1940's, off Chatham, Cape Cod, offshore of Pollock Rip Lightship. It's likely that it was lost by a four- or five-masted coastal cargo schooner.
(From Kodachrome by Wm. H. Koelbel)

Evolution of the modern anchor

It is beyond the scope of this chapter to delve deeply into the history of anchors, interesting though that may be. Touching on it briefly, however, we get an insight into the evolution from ancient to modern design, and what lies behind the quest for an anchor that will *bury*, not drag. At this point it will be helpful to refer to the sketches, fig. 602, and labeled diagram, fig. 604, which, later, will clarify the meaning of terms used to describe the anchor's parts.

Going back to primitive times, the earliest "anchor" of which we have record was a simple stone used with a crude rope. Though it may have served under ideal conditions to prevent the drift of an ancient watercraft, dragging at times was inevitable, when sheer weight was unable to hold against the pull of wind and current.

Obviously what was needed was a device to engage the bottom, giving rise to the addition of simple wooden (and later, iron) hooks, forerunner of the arms and flukes found in later developments. To this day, survivors of this early anchor concept may be found Down East in Nova Scotia, where fishermen still fashion by hand their "killicks" of wood, stone and manila. Colloquially, we drop a "hook" when we lower an anchor.

Modifications of the hooking type of anchor evolved and, roughly 4,000 years ago, the Chinese added a stock at the crown end of the shank, perpendicular to the plane of the hooking arms, to put them in position to get a bite in the bottom. Junks still use this type today. In an ancient Greek design (about 750 B.C.) the stock had moved to the ring end of the shank.

In due course, in an effort to increase holding power, broad triangular flukes were added to the arms, giving rise to the old-fashioned kedge, fig. 603, often with a wooden stock, fig. 601, at the ring end of the shank, as used on naval vessels well into the 19th century. In 1821 the first of a series of stockless (patent) Navy anchors was invented Elimination of the stock permitted the shank to be drawn up into the hawsepipe of a vessel, flukes lying flat against the topsides.

Toward the middle of the 19th century, the mushroom anchor appeared, its design restricting its principal value to use in permanent moorings. Though their holding power is low, very small craft often use them for brief stops in light weather.

The principle of placing the stock at the crown end was brought to a relatively high state of development in the Northill design, where short, broad, thin flukes provided better penetration, and a folding stock improved stowage characteristics.

In 1933, a radical innovation in design was introduced in England—the plow, a stockless type in which conventional flukes were replaced by a casting resembling a plow, pivoted at its point of attachment to the shank.

Supplanting mass and weight with scientific design, R. S. Danforth in 1939 developed what has been referred to by the U.S. Navy as the *lightweight-type* anchor in which broad pivoted flukes, stabilized by a stock, not only penetrate the bottom but bury completely until firm holding ground is reached. It is this feature, primarily, which distinguishes the *burying* anchor from a type that is prone to drag.

So much for history.

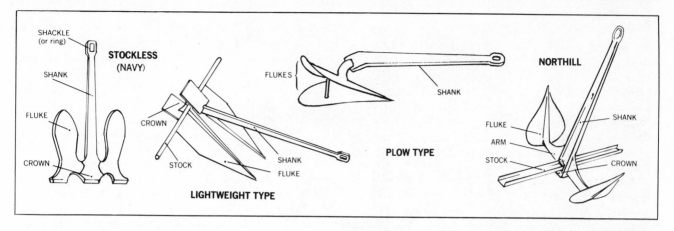

FIG. 602 How several anchor types differ. Principal parts of each are shown. All have shanks; not all have stocks.

Ground Tackle

Some terms and definitions

To prevent possibility of confusion in the use of terms, refer again to the labeled illustration of the parts of an anchor, fig. 604, and the more general definitions in Table 6-1. A popular version of the kedge was chosen to illustrate the parts, because it is a type frequently visualized as a conventional anchor. Subsequently we shall see how the proportioning and placement of parts have varied with the introduction of later designs. Many otherwise well-informed boatmen have often spoken of the shank and

stock as though the terms were interchangeable. In fact, however, most anchors (with few exceptions) have shanks, but some are stockless.

To illustrate graphically the basic fundamentals in anchoring, one authority sketches, in fig. 605, what has been referred to as *the anchoring system*. Though *scope* has been defined in Table 6-1 as a relation between length of rode and depth of water, there are other vital considerations in determining the length of rode to be paid out—the height of bow, range of tide, etc. This will be dealt with more fully later, as scope is one of the most important of all factors in determining holding power.

Finally, to forestall argument as to the validity of the term *rode*, it should be noted that the word has, on rare occasions, been challenged. Without going to its defense here, we can say that our best boating authorities have long accepted its usage in nautical jargon, and it is unlikely that it will ever be lost to the language.

TYPES OF ANCHORS IN USE

Lightweight type (LWT)

Scan a marine hardware catalog and, without experience, you may be confused by the diversity of designs offered today. What you should be buying, essentially, is holding power; sheer weight is no index of that. On the contrary, scientific design is the key to efficiency and a lightweight type, *if properly manufactured,* unquestionably stands at the top of the list today on a holding power-to-weight basis.

The lightweight type was originated just prior to World War II by R. S. Danforth. Its efficiency in war service was so high that it made possible the retraction of amphibious craft in assaults on enemy-held beachheads. Its versatility in sand and mud bottoms quickly won widespread popularity among yachtsmen as models were developed specifically for convenience aboard pleasure craft. Generally, with a little caution, the lightweight anchor can even be hooked in rocky bottoms.

In the Danforth anchor, flukes are long and sharp, designed so that heavy strains bury the anchor completely. Tests have proved that it tends to work down through soft bottoms to firmer holding ground below, burying part of

---

TABLE 6-1. SOME BASIC DEFINITIONS

Anchor—A device designed to engage the bottom of a waterway and through its resistance to drag maintain a vessel within a given radius.

Anchor Chocks—Fittings on the deck of a vessel used to stow an anchor when it is not in use.

Anchor Rode—The line connecting an anchor with a vessel.

Bow Chocks—Fittings, usually on the rail of a vessel near its stem, having jaws that serve as fairleads for anchor rodes and other lines.

Ground Tackle—A general term for the anchor, anchor rodes, fittings, etc., used for securing a vessel at anchor.

Hawsepipe—A cylindrical or elliptical pipe or casting in a vessel's hull through which the anchor rode runs.

Horizontal Load—The horizontal force placed on an anchoring device by the vessel to which it is connected.

Mooring Bitt—A post or cleat through or on the deck of a vessel used to secure an anchor rode or other line to the vessel.

*Scope—The relation between the length of an anchor rode and the depth of the water in which a vessel is anchored.

Vertical Load—The lifting force placed on the bow of a vessel by its anchor rode.

*Definitions adopted by the American Boat and Yacht Council in drafting a code of recommended practices and standards covering ground tackle.   *See caption fig. 605.*

the rode as well, fig. 609(b).

In place of a stock through the head, the lightweight type has a round rod at the crown end to prevent the anchor from rolling or rotating. This placement of the stock does not interfere with its being drawn into the hawse-pipes of larger craft for stowage. (Many yachtsmen slip protective rubber tips over the stock ends.)

The lightweight-type Danforth is made in two models, the Hi-Tensile and Standard, fig. 606. They bear a close family resemblance but differences in materials and manufacture permit the Hi-Tensile to achieve maximum holding power on a given weight. In selecting any anchor, remember that all manufacturers have their individual concepts of design and "look-alikes" do not necessarily hold alike.

While not put forth as a size recommendation for boats in general, one impressive evidence of holding power is the experience of a 40-foot auxiliary cruising sloop which held in all bottoms, including soft mud six feet deep in 25-mile winds, with a 5-pound Danforth!

The success of the lightweight type anchor manufactured by Danforth has prompted other manufacturers to offer their own versions, varying in efficiency with details of design and construction, as in fluke angle and welding practices. Finishes vary, too; some are rubber-covered or enamelled instead of hot-dip galvanized. Some are good; others cannot compare with the efficiency of the original.

The plow

The plow anchor is unique in design, resembling none of the other types. It originated in England as a result of a challenge to Professor G. I. Taylor of Cambridge University from a cruising companion to invent an anchor of greater holding power on lower weight. He called it the CQR (secure). It found wide acceptance because of its demonstrated efficiency in a variety of bottoms. Opinions vary as to its effectiveness in heavy weed, which is not surprising in that certain weed growths resist penetration by any anchor. Some European versions of the plow failed to equal the efficiency of the original. The Plowright, fig. 608, is an improved model recently developed and manufactured in this country.

When a plow is lowered, the anchor first lies on its side

on the bottom. See fig. 609(a). Then when a pull is put on the rode, it rights itself, driving the point of the plow in, and finally burying the plow completely. The Plowright is claimed to hold up to 300 times its weight, depending naturally on the kind of bottom. CQR suggested catalog weights vary from 10 pounds for a 20-footer to 75 pounds for 75–125-footers.

Because of the pivoting feature of the shank, the tendency of the plow is to remain buried when the angle of pull is changed by wind or current. There is no projecting fluke to foul the rode and it breaks out easily when the pull is vertical, in position to bring the anchor up on deck.

Kedges

In discussing kedges it is important to make a sharp distinction between the more massive ancient types and later versions which have been designed for yacht use. In glossaries, "kedge anchors" as a rule are light anchors (of any design) carried out from a vessel aground to free her by winching in on the rode. Here, however, we refer to the kedge as an anchor with the more conventional type of

FIG. 604 Wilcox Crittenden's Yachtsman anchor, with parts labeled. The stock can be folded to lie along the shank.

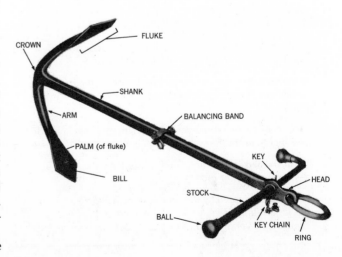

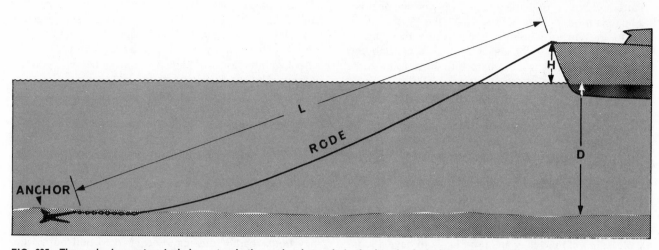

FIG. 605 The anchoring system includes not only the anchor but rode L, the length of which is referred to in terms of scope. In practice, however scope may be defined, the boatman must make due allowance for height (H) of his bow chocks above water, and any increase a rising tide may add to depth (D).

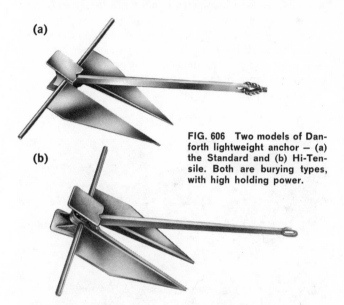

FIG. 606 Two models of Danforth lightweight anchor — (a) the Standard and (b) Hi-Tensile. Both are burying types, with high holding power.

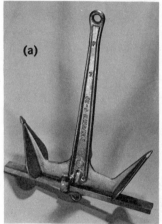
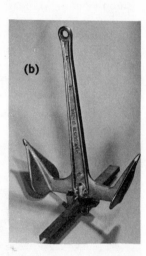

FIG. 607 Newest Danforth is the Utility model shown (a) with stock folded and (b) with stock set up in position ready for use.

arms, flukes and stocks as distinguished from newer lightweight types.

The earliest kedges, aside from their mass, were characterized by roughly triangular flukes and relatively dull bills. See fig. 610. The shoulders on the flukes, being nearly square with the arm, invited fouling of the rode as a vessel swung at her anchorage with shifts in wind and current. The dull bills made it difficult to bite in hard bottoms. Other kedges, like sand and trawl anchors, designed for use primarily on hard bottoms, had very small flukes and sharp bills. Both of these types left much to be desired for general yacht use, though often right for special purposes.

Yachtsman and Herreshoff anchors

Types of anchor which evolved from earlier kedges include the Yachtsman, fig. 604, and Herreshoff, fig. 611(b), designs. Though varying in details of construction, the principle used in both was a redistribution of the weight, a different proportioning of the length of stock to the chord measured from bill to bill, and a drastic change in the shape and size of fluke relative to the arm.

A major distinguishing feature of these modified kedges is the diamond-shaped fluke, embodied in the design to reduce risk of fouling, on the theory that the rode would slip off an exposed fluke where no squared shoulder was presented. At the same time, sharpening of the bill permitted better penetration in hard bottoms.

Neither of these kedges is claimed to be a "burying" type, as the shank lies on the bottom and one fluke remains exposed. On the other hand, its "hook" design recommends it, probably above all other types, on rocky bottoms where one fluke can find a crevice, and retrieval, with proper precautions, is not too difficult. (More about this later.)

The Northill

The concept of light weight was first brought to kedge design with the introduction of the Northhill, fig. 612. Originally made in stainless steel, the current model is fabricated of rugged malleable iron, hot-dip galvanized for resistance to corrosion.

The Northill is also unique, resembling the kedge only to the extent that it is a "hooking" type. Here, however, for the first time in our modern anchors, the stock has moved to the other end of the shank, square with the arms, but movable to fold against the shank for better stowage.

Patterned after a principle utilized on wooden anchors in Malaysia through thousands of years, the Northill stock adds to the anchor's holding power when the fluke is buried. Arms are at right angles to the shank, and the broad reinforced flukes with sharp bills are set at a carefully computed angle to assure a quick bite. See fig. 613. Narrow fluke arms allow the anchor to penetrate well.

The Northill has demonstrated its efficiency in sand and mud, and has performed well even in heavy kelp and on rocky bottoms.

Other types

All the anchors discussed thus far have been of the so-called *stock-type,* though the stock, as we have seen, may be placed at either the ring or crown end of the shank. Although some stock anchors are made with a fast stock, for pleasure boat use they are more likely to have a loose stock which can be folded for better stowage. Frequently, a key is required to pin the stock of a kedge in its open position when set up ready for use, the key in turn being lashed in its slot to hold it in place.

Some anchors, however, are *stockless.* Frequently these are cataloged as Navy-type anchors. Inexperienced boatmen, seeing them on large vessels, sometimes jump to the conclusion that they are consequently the best for all vessels, including boats. Nothing could be further from the truth. Ships use them because stockless anchors can be hauled up with power into hawsepipes. On pleasure boats, the ratio of weight to holding power is so great that, if it is heavy enough to hold, it is a back-breaker; if weight is held within reason, holding power is far below the limits of safety. The Sea-Claw is an improved version of the Navy anchor, with a different proportioning of its parts, and round stock at the crown. See fig. 614.

When we speak of *folding anchors,* we think not so much in terms of a Yachtsman's kedge with movable stock as a highly specialized design in which, at some sacrifice of holding power, all parts fold against the shank into the smallest possible space for most convenient stowage. In one stockless type, the Norwegian SAV (imported by Canor Plarex) there are two pairs of flukes at right angles to each other, almost in the manner of a grapnel. In rocky bottoms, they hook readily and may be rigged to pull out easily, crown first. See fig. 646.

Grapnels, though used more extensively by some commercial fishermen than many boatmen realize, are not recommended for general anchoring service aboard pleasure boats. These are also stockless models with, as a rule, five curved sharp-billed claw-like prongs symmetrically arranged around the crown end of the shank. Eyes may be cast in both ends of the shank—at the head in lieu of a ring for attachment of a rode (if used as an anchor) and at the

FIG. 608 Woolsey's Plowright anchor has plow-shaped flukes, causing the anchor to bury deep. The shank is pivoted.

FIG. 609 How burying anchors work when an anchoring strain is put on the rode. In (a) below, a plow lands on the bottom on its side (1) gets a quick bite (2) and rights itself (3), digging deep. In (b) a lightweight anchor lands with flukes flat (1), penetrating (2) as the strain comes on the rode, and (3) burying in the holding position.

FIG. 610 Early kedges used aboard yachts had dull bills and shoulders on flukes that often fouled the rode when the boat swung in a complete circle at an anchorage.

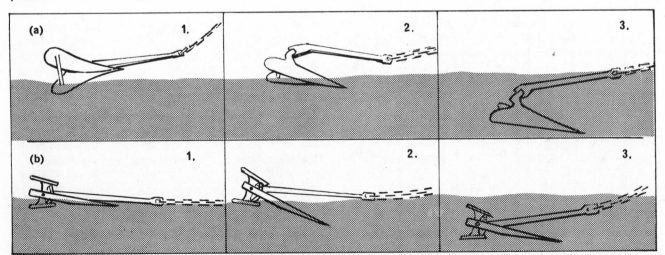

FIG. 611 (a) Flukes of this sand anchor are relatively small, the bills sharp, to penetrate hard bottoms. In soft bottoms holding power is low. (b) The Herreshoff version of the kedge. Note difference in fluke area.

FIG. 612
The Northill Utility anchor combines the hooking action of a kedge with relatively high holding power.

crown end for a buoyed trip line. By dragging a small grapnel back and forth, a boatman may *grapple* for a piece of equipment lost on the bottom. See fig. 615.

Discussion of *mushroom* anchors, fig. 652, will be reserved till later as, properly, their principal use is in conjunction with permanent moorings, at anchorages. Modified versions of the mushroom are manufactured for small craft like canoes and rowboats, but their efficiency as "anchors" is at the lowest end of the scale.

All the anchors under discussion in this chapter are devices designed to keep a boat from drifting, by engagement with the bottom. *Sea anchors* do not fall in this category. These are intended to float at or just below the surface, serving merely as a drag to hold a boat's bow (or stern) up toward the seas to prevent her from lying in the trough. Sea anchors are rarely used aboard pleasure boats, and then only in the heaviest weather offshore, where there is room to drift to leeward. See chapter 9, Seamanship (pages 157-158) for a discussion of sea anchors and their use. *Drogues*, like the highly effective Fenger-type, are devices made up with planks, chain, weights and rode, to serve the purpose of a conventional sea anchor which, in some cases, they are reported to have bettered in efficiency.

THE RODE

All of the gear, taken collectively, that lies between a boat and her anchor is called the *rode*—whether it be synthetic fiber (like nylon), vegetable fiber (like manila), chain, wire, or a combination of fiber and chain. When his rode is nylon or manila, a knowledgeable boatman will not refer to his anchor "rope," as rope in a coil becomes "line" when cut for specific uses. Thus, with fiber rodes, it is quite appropriate to refer to the "anchor line."

Nylon

Since the introduction of synthetics, a quiet revolution has been taking place in the choice of material for anchor rodes. Good quality manila was once the accepted type of line. Synthetics, however, have brought new properties that make them even better adapted to the boatman's use.

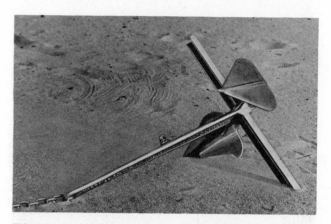

FIG. 613 Pitch of the flukes of a Northill causes it to penetrate and dig in quickly. Here the anchor is already turning to its ultimate horizontal position. The stock is at the crown end.

Because other synthetics, such as dacron, polypropylene, polyethylene, etc., have little elasticity, they are not recommended for anchoring and towing. Nylon, on the other hand, has high elasticity and is the outstanding choice today.

Any differential in cost between nylon and manila is more than made up by differences in strength and longer life, both on the side of nylon. (See Table 11-1, breaking strengths, page 198.) Several times the strength of manila, nylon can be used in smaller diameters, light and easy to handle. See fig. 616. Though it can be damaged by rust from iron fittings or rusty chain, it is highly resistant to the rot, decay and mildew that attack vegetable fibers.

For anchoring purposes, nylon's greatest asset is its elasticity, stretching a third or more under load. Its working elasticity of 15 to 25% is several times greater than that of manila. When a boat surges at anchor in steep seas, there is a heavy shock load on fittings and ground tackle unless provision is made to absorb it gradually. Nylon's elasticity does exactly that.

Some boatmen unwittingly lose part or most of the advantage inherent in nylon by buying too strong a line. Within the limits of safe working loads, the smaller the diameter the better the elasticity for given conditions. A

101

FIG. 614
The Sea-Claw is an improved version of the Navy type, with parts proportioned differently, and stock added.

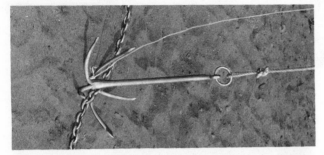

FIG. 615 A grapnel, shown here as it might be used in grappling to recover a mooring chain.

FIG. 616 Nylon (a) and manila (b). Nylon's great elasticity makes it popular for anchor rodes. A 3/8-inch diameter nylon line (breaking strength 3650 lbs.) will replace 9/16-inch manila (3450 lbs.).
(Gordon S. Smith photo)

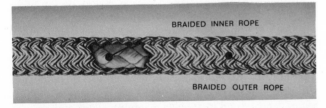

BRAIDED INNER ROPE

BRAIDED OUTER ROPE

FIG. 617 Because of its construction, braided synthetic line has no tendency to twist. Braided nylon, for anchor rodes, retains high elasticity; braided polyester, with little stretch, is better for sheets and halyards.

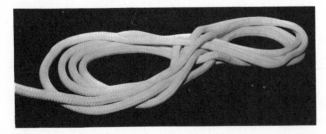

FIG. 617 (a) Braided line coils best when faked (or flaked) down in a figure 8.

FIG. 618 On this large yacht, *wildcats* in the winch engage the links of the all-chain rodes. Chain, leading down to the anchors through hawsepipes, is shown here *stoppered*, held by split-hook *devil's claws*.

practical limit is reached when small diameters (though rated high enough for breaking strength) are not convenient to handle. Some of the most experienced boatmen use nylon as light as ³/₈-inch diameter on the working anchors of their 30- to 40-foot cruisers.

Braided synthetic line

Most of the nylon currently in use today for anchor rodes is the type that is laid up by twisting three strands, in the same manner as manila. Synthetics, however, may also be laid up by braiding. For anchoring, mooring and towing, a braided outer cover of nylon surrounds a braided inner synthetic core. See fig. 617. The result is a line of exceptional stability with no inherent tendency to twist because of the nature of its lay. Consequently, it can be fed down into rope lockers without fear of kinking.

When braided nylon is handled on deck, it is advisable to fake it down in figure-8 pattern, rather than the conventional clockwise coil used with twisted fibers to prevent kinking. Because of the relatively smoother surface of braid, with more fibers exposed, chafe is less of a problem than it is with the twisted three-strand lay. Braided nylon retains a high degree of elasticity (14% at working loads, as against 25% for twisted nylon).

For sheets and halyards, where it is preferable to eliminate the stretch, an outer cover of polyester is used. Double-braided nylon is becoming increasingly popular for mooring pennants.

Double-braided synthetic rope is a quality product, its smooth, soft handling characteristics recommending it highly as a "yacht" line. Obviously it requires a special splicing technique, covered in detail in Samson Cordage Works' Splicing Manual.

Manila

Most of the arguments that could once have been advanced for the selection of manila have quite generally been settled with the increasing trend toward nylon. It is a fact that manila is still in common use on many lighter anchors and in some areas it survives among boatmen of

FIG. 619 Manila line, badly chafed on a rough coral bottom. A fathom of chain, shackled between the anchor and fiber rode, would have prevented this.

FIG. 620 A thimble, shackle and eye splice are commonly used to secure fiber rodes to the anchor ring. Lashings hold the key when inserted into the stock as the anchor is set up.

the old school who are not yet ready to give up the line they've grown up with. They find it easy to handle, light in weight (for required strength), comparatively inexpensive, and capable of enough stretch to absorb some shock load. Above all, it holds knots and splices better than the more slippery synthetics. Even at that, the experience of some of the hardest working commercial craft, like the charter fishermen who anchor day in and day out in open water in all weathers, is hard to deny. They've turned to nylon.

Chain

Nylon in diameters up to 1 inch is used on boats up to 50 or 60 feet in length—even larger, under normal conditions. Any fiber line, however, more than 1½ inches in diameter, is hard to handle, so chain is often chosen for larger craft. BBB chain is recommended (its size designated by the diameter of material in the links). To handle it, the boat should be equipped with a winch having a *wildcat* to fit the chain. See fig. 618.

From this it should not be inferred that chain is not also in use on smaller craft. On boats that cruise extensively and have occasion to anchor on sharp rock or coral, chain is often preferred—in cases, regarded as indispensable, as it stands chafing where fiber won't. Some boatmen with wide cruising experience have used four or five fathoms of chain shackled between the anchor and fiber line. Others prefer chain throughout.

In the larger diameters, the weight of chain tends to produce a sag in the rode which cushions shock loads due to surging. Once the sag is out, it is quite generally agreed that the shock on both boat and anchor is greater than with nylon or even manila. Too much emphasis should not be placed on the cushioning effect of a chain's sag, in small sizes. One test made in a moderate wind with generous scope of 10-to-1 revealed not a single link of chain resting on the bottom. On the other hand, in larger sizes, exhaustive tests on a 104-footer with ½-inch and ⅝-inch chain showed the weight of chain to be beneficial, reducing the maximum load on the anchor to as little as 5% of that recorded in a similar test with wire rope. Wire cable has

been used on some larger craft; though strong, it has no elasticity.

Nylon-and-chain

Today the concensus appears to be that for most average conditions, the ideal rode consists of a combination of nylon and short length (a fathom, more or less) of chain between the nylon and anchor. The only exception to this is in the very softest bottoms where one authority claims that the lightweight anchor bites best without chain.

The effect of chain in a combination rode is to lower the angle of pull, because chain tends to lie on the bottom. Of equal, perhaps greater, significance is the fact that modern lightweight anchors often bury completely, taking part of the rode with them. Chain stands the chafe, fig. 619, and sand has less chance to penetrate strands of the fiber line higher up. Sand doesn't stick to the chain, and mud is easily washed off. Without chain, nylon gets very dirty in mud.

Chain used in this manner may vary roughly from ¼-inch diameter for 20-footers up to ⅜-inch for 50-footers. It should be galvanized, of course, to protect against rust. Neoprene-coated chain is an added refinement, as it will not mar the boat.

SECURING THE RODE

To the ring

Various methods are used in securing the rode to the anchor ring. With fiber line, the preferred practice is to work an eye splice around a thimble and use a galvanized shackle to join the thimble and ring. See fig. 620. Using manila, the common galvanized wire-rope thimble is satisfactory; with nylon more care must be taken to keep the thimble in the eye. A tight, snug splice will help and seizings around the line and the legs of the thimble, near the V, will keep the thimble in the eye splice when the line comes under loads that stretch the eye. A better thimble, fig. 621, is available in bronze alloy or plastic for use with synthetic rope. This is designed to hold and protect the line.

FIG. 621 Improved types of Newco thimble in plastic or bronze alloy for use with synthetic rope prevent line from jumping out of the thimble when an eye splice stretches under load.

TABLE 6-2 ANCHOR WEIGHT* (pounds)			
BOAT LENGTH (Maximum)	Lunch hook	Working anchor	Storm anchor
20'	4 (10)	5 (20)	12 (40)
30'	5 (15)	12 (30)	18 (60)
40'	12 (20)	18 (40)	28 (80)

*Bold-face figures based on modern lightweight burial-type anchors of efficient design. Figures in parentheses show how weights would be increased, using a formula of ½, 1 lb. and 2 lbs. per foot for certain kedges.

FIG. 622 Some boatmen prefer to make the rode fast to the anchor ring with an anchor bend. For added security, the free end may be seized to the rode. Line illustrated is braided nylon.

With this kind of rig, it is a good idea to put a bit of silicone spray, Lubriplate or graphite grease on threads of the shackle pin. This will keep the threads from seizing. Wire the pin to prevent its working out accidentally. For convenience, and to prevent loss of the pin, many prefer to bend a piece of marline to the eye of the pin, so that it can be lashed to a link of the chain. Watch for corrosion if different metals are used in thimbles, shackles and rings. Also beware of rust stains on nylon; cut out and resplice on new thimbles if the line is rust-stained.

With a thimble and shackle, a ready means is provided of backing up your line with a length of chain, if desired, shackling the chain in turn to the anchor ring. Shackles should be large enough so as not to bind the fiber against the ring and cause chafing.

When an anchor has an eye cast into the head of the shank, but no ring, it is generally convenient to use a shackle in the eye, even if the rode is to be bent to the anchor without an intermediate length of chain.

Anchor bends and bowlines

Some boatmen would rather bend their line directly to the ring using an anchor bend, fig. 622, seizing the free end to the rode. In the Chesapeake, and elsewhere, they use a bowline with an extra round turn around the ring, fig. 623, pointing out that this makes it easy to turn the line end-for-end occasionally or to remove the line from the anchor for easy handling when stowing.

Turning a line end-for-end greatly extends its useful life, as the lower end which has chafed on the bottom becomes the inboard end. Shackles and eye splices may be used at both ends of the rode, or may be added as necessary when the rode is turned.

Another convenient rig on small craft is merely to work a big eye splice in the end of the line, pass it through the ring, over the anchor while the stock (on stock types) is folded along the shank and then tighten the eye by hauling it up on itself at the ring.

Even where the regular working anchor is kept made-up with a combination of line and chain, it is well to know how to bend a line directly to the anchor. Often this is the handiest way to drop a light "lunch hook" for a brief stop, or to make up a second anchor when a bridle or stern anchor is needed.

Shackles, fig. 624, must be used to secure chain cables to the anchor, stout swivels, fig. 625, being an added re-finement on combination rodes. As swivels are a weak point, they must be large. On an all-chain rode, they are a *must*. Swivels, however, should *not* be used with twisted soft-laid synthetic lines; a hockle, fig. 626, may be the result. Double-braided synthetic lines will not hockle, even though subjected to very heavy strains.

At the bitter end

To guard against loss in case the anchor goes by the board accidentally, the bitter (inboard) end of an anchor cable should preferably be made fast to some part of the boat. Sometimes this is accomplished by leading the line below, perhaps through a deck pipe, and securing to a Samson post or other strong timber. On sailboats, it may be secured to a mast. On small boats where the entire length of rode is carried on deck, it is usually feasible to have an eye splice in the bitter end to fit the post. Run this down close to the deck and use a clove hitch above the eye splice to adjust the scope.

HOW MANY—AND HOW HEAVY?

The number of anchors to be carried aboard will be conditioned upon several things—the size of boat, whether she is used only in sheltered waters or cruises extensively offshore and, to some extent, the type of anchor.

Though some small boats, like runabouts and utilities, are occasionally found with only a single anchor, this can by no stretch of the imagination be considered adequate. Even discounting the possibility of fouling one anchor so badly that it cannot be retrieved, there are many occasions when it is desirable to lie to two. Again, one anchor heavy enough for extreme conditions could be a nuisance in ordinary weather.

Many boats carry two anchors, proportioning the weight in the ratio of about 40 percent in one, 60 percent in the other. For cruising boats, three are undoubtedly better. This allows for two to be carried on deck—a light *lunch hook* for brief stops while some one is aboard, and a *working anchor* for ordinary service, including anchorages at night in harbor. The third might well be a big spare *storm anchor*, carried below, selected with an eye to its holding no matter what else lets go, even under extreme conditions of wind and weather. Break this out when you find it necessary to anchor overnight in an exposed anchorage, and you will sleep better. On long cruises, some experienced yachtsmen carry four.

Anchor size and holding power

Down through the years there have been repeated attempts to reduce anchor weights to a simple formula or table based on boat length or tonnage. Recommendations varied widely, up to as high as 3 or 4 pounds per foot for the heavy spare on cruising boats, assuming this would be a kedge type.

With the introduction of new anchors of lightweight design, it becomes obvious that the older figures no longer apply. Recognizing further that inefficient copies of a well

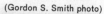
(Gordon S. Smith photo)

FIG. 623 The anchor bowline, an alternate method of bending the rode to the anchor ring. Note the extra round turn around the ring.

TABLE 6-3 SUGGESTED RODE AND ANCHOR SIZES*

For Storm Anchor (Winds up to 60 knots)

L.O.A.	BEAM		RODE		ANCHOR		
	SAIL	POWER	NYLON	CHAIN	NORTHILL	STANDARD	HI-TENSILE
10'	4'	4'	100'-1/4"	3'-3/16"	12 lb. (6-R)	8-S	5-H
15'	5'	5'	125'-1/4"	3'-3/16"	12 lb. (6-R)	8-S	5-H
20'	6'	7'	150'-3/8"	4'-1/4"	27 lb. (12-R)	13-S	12-H
25'	6'	8'	200'-3/8"	4'-1/4"	27 lb. (12-R)	22-S	12-H
30'	7'	10'	250'-7/16"	5'-5/16"	46 lb. (20-R)	22-S	20-H
35'	8'	12'	300'-1/2"	6'-3/8"	46 lb. (20-R)	40-S	35-H
40'	10'	14'	400'-5/8"	8'-7/16"	80 lb. (30-R)	65-S	60-H
50'	12'	16'	500'-5/8"	8'-7/16"	105 lb. (50-R)	130-S	60-H
60'	14'	19'	500'-3/4"	8'-1/2"	105 lb. (50-R)	180-S	90-H

For Working Anchor (Winds up to 30 knots)

L.O.A.	BEAM		RODE		ANCHOR		
	SAIL	POWER	NYLON	CHAIN	NORTHILL	STANDARD	HI-TENSILE
10'	4'	4'	80'-1/4"	3'-3/16"	6 lb. (3-R)	4-S	5-H
15'	5'	5'	100'-1/4"	3'-3/16"	6 lb. (3-R)	8-S	5-H
20'	6'	7'	120'-1/4"	3'-3/16"	12 lb. (6-R)	8-S	5-H
25'	6'	8'	150'-3/8"	3'-3/16"	12 lb. (6-R)	8-S	5-H
30'	7'	10'	180'-3/8"	4'-1/4"	27 lb. (12-R)	13-S	12-H
35'	8'	12'	200'-3/8"	4'-1/4"	27 lb. (12-R)	22-S	12-H
40'	10'	14'	250'-7/16"	5'-5/16"	46 lb. (20-R)	22-S	20-H
50'	12'	16'	300'-1/2"	6'-3/8"	46 lb. (20-R)	40-S	35-H
60'	14'	19'	300'-1/2"	6'-3/8"	80 lb. (30-R)	65-S	35-H

For Lunch Hook

L.O.A.	BEAM		RODE		ANCHOR		
	SAIL	POWER	NYLON	CHAIN	NORTHILL	STANDARD	HI-TENSILE
10'	4'	4'	70'-1/4"	3'-3/16"	6 lb. (3-R)	2½-S	5-H
15'	5'	5'	80'-1/4"	3'-3/16"	6 lb. (3-R)	2½-S	5-H
20'	6'	7'	90'-1/4"	3'-3/16"	6 lb. (3-R)	2½-S	5-H
25'	6'	8'	100'-1/4"	3'-3/16"	6 lb. (3-R)	4-S	5-H
30'	7'	10'	125'-1/4"	3'-3/16"	6 lb. (3-R)	4-S	5-H
35'	8'	12'	150'-1/4"	3'-3/16"	12 lb. (6-R)	4-S	5-H
40'	10'	14'	175'-3/8"	4'-1/4"	12 lb. (6-R)	8-S	5-H
50'	12'	16'	200'-3/8"	4'-1/4"	12 lb. (6-R)	8-S	12-H
60'	14'	19'	200'-3/8"	4'-1/4"	27 lb. (12-R)	13-S	12-H

*Suggested sizes assume fair holding ground, scope of at least 7-to-1 and moderate shelter from heavy seas.

PLOW ANCHORS—Woolsey, manufacturer of the Plowright anchor, makes the following recommendations for winds up to 30 knots: for *working anchors*, 10'-21', 6 lbs.—22'-32', 12 lbs.—32'-36', 18 lbs.—36'-39', 22 lbs.—39'-44', 35 lbs. For *lunch hooks*, they advise stepping down one size. For *storm anchors*, up one size.

KEDGES—Holding powers vary widely with the type. Best to consult manufacturer for individual recommendations.

FIG. 624 A shackle is used at the anchor to secure a short piece of chain in a nylon-chain rode.

FIG. 625 Swivels are required on all-chain rodes to prevent snarls.

designed anchor may vary tremendously in holding power, it is equally evident that a hard-and-fast table of anchor weights could easily be an over-simplification. With this caution, Table 6-2 is offered, merely as a point of departure, to be modified as necessary in individual cases. This same caution applies to Table 6-3, giving suggested rode and anchor sizes for boats from 10 to 60 feet in length.

Horizontal loads as criteria for anchor sizes

In a recent project to establish an advisory code of safety standards for all kinds of small craft up to 65 feet in length, the equipment division of the American Boat and Yacht Council took a different tack in recommending practices and standards for ground tackle. They have set up a Table (6-4) specifying, for boats of 10 to 60 feet in length, typical minimum *horizontal loads* (in pounds) which an anchor should be able to hold, assuming freedom to swing and moderate shelter from seas proportionate to hull size. This, too, is broken down into three sizes of anchor—lunch hooks, working anchors, and storm anchors. Armed with these figures, you can consult the recommendations of the manufacturer of the particular anchor you prefer.

STOWAGE

The boatman's seamanship is often measurable by the amount of common sense and foresight he displays in every-day boating practice. It shows up, for example, in the attention he gives to stowage of his ground tackle. Exactly how he goes about it depends to some extent on the kind of boating he does, the size of his boat, and the way it is equipped. In any case, unless his deck is uncluttered, with gear ready for immediate use, yet secured so that it cannot shift, he will never rate high as a seaman.

Ordinarily a cruising boat will carry one, sometimes two, anchors on deck, made up ready for use. On some small boats, where it is not feasible to leave anchors on deck at all times, or in cases where lines are stowed below at the home anchorage, one anchor and line at least should be prepared and made ready before getting under way from the dock or mooring. Engines have been known to fail and, when they do, it's likely to be at an embarrassing moment, with wind or current setting you down on a shoal or reef. Then it's too late to think about breaking out gear that should have been ready at hand.

An anchor lying loose on deck is a potential hazard. If the boat happens to roll deep in a seaway or be caught by the heavy wash of a passing boat, it may slide across the deck, leaving in its wake scars on woodwork and damage

TABLE 6-4	TYPICAL HORIZONTAL LOADS (pounds)		
Length over all	Lunch hook	Working anchor	Storm anchor
10'	40	160	320
15'	60	250	500
20'	90	360	720
25'	125	490	980
30'	175	700	1,400
35'	225	900	1,800
40'	300	1,200	2,400
50'	400	1,600	3,200
60'	500	2,000	4,000

to equipment, conceivably going over the side, and taking line with it, at the risk of fouling a propeller. To forestall this, every anchor on deck should be stowed in chocks. See fig. 627. These are available at marine supply stores to fit standard anchors. Lashings hold them down to prevent their jumping out of the chocks. Hardwood blocks, prop-

FIG. 627 Anchors stowed on deck should be lashed down in chocks.

FIG. 628 A short "pulpit" on this motor sailer provides for the housing of a plow anchor.

FIG. 626 To avoid a hockle, swivels should not be used with twisted soft-laid synthetic lines.

FIG. 629 Hawsepipes are commonly seen on large vessels, and may also be used on some yachts. The planking is protected by a circular pad.

erly notched, have often been used in lieu of metal chock fittings. Rubber caps should be fitted over the round stock ends of lightweight type anchors.

As an alternate to chocking on deck, anchors carried aboard auxiliaries may be lashed to shrouds, off the deck, where there is no risk of their getting underfoot, and less risk of their fouling running rigging. In one Dutch yacht, a foreign-built lightweight type anchor is carried in hooks provided in the bow rail. Some cruisers and motor sailers equipped with bowsprits or pulpits have a roller at the outboard end so that a plow can be carried in this outboard position as a regular working anchor. See fig. 628. There are devices that combine the anchor with a kind of well fixture to be let in flush with the deck. In considering such equipment, be sure the anchor weight and design are such as to meet the boat's requirements as to holding power. On some yachts provision is made to haul the anchor into a hawsepipe fitted into the topsides forward. See fig. 629.

Stowing the storm anchor

As the big spare storm anchor is used only on rare occasions, it is customary to carry it in some convenient location below. Frequently this will be a lazarette or in stowage space below a cockpit deck, accessible through a hatch. Chocks here should be arranged to carry the weight on floors or frames, never on the planking. If the big anchor gets adrift, it could easily loosen a bottom plank and start a leak.

The big risk in stowing a spare anchor away in some out-of-the-way corner is the possibility that other gear may be allowed to accumulate over and around it. Guard against that. Its sole value may some day depend upon your being able to get that big hook over quickly, bent to a long and strong spare rode that must be equally accessible.

Lunch hooks are small and seldom needed in a hurry, so there's justification for stowing them in some convenient

locker. Keep them away from the compass, however, as they can be a potent cause of deviation. That goes for all anchors and any ferrous metal that might inadvertently be left too close to the compass.

Rope and chain lockers

Though small craft frequently carry their lines coiled on a forward deck or in an open cockpit, many cruising boats are built with rope lockers in the forepeak. Nylon dries quickly and can be fed down into lockers almost as soon as it comes aboard. Manila, on the other hand, must be thoroughly dried on deck before stowing below. Gratings are sometimes provided as an aid to drying lines on deck before stowage. Lockers must be well ventilated and arranged to assure good air circulation at all times. See fig. 630. Dark, wet lockers are an invitation to dry rot. A hatch over the rope locker will permit exposure to sun and air.

The rode should always be ready to run without fouling. Line is often passed below through a deck pipe, slotted so that it can be capped even when the line is in use. Slots must face aft to prevent water on deck from finding its way below. Caps are usually connected with a length of chain, preferably of brass, as galvanized chains may rust out too quickly. Some cast mooring bitts are also made with an opening on the after face, through which line can be passed below.

Chain won't soak up moisture like manila and is easy to stow in lockers. Where weight of chain in the bow of a small offshore cruising boat is objectionable, this can be overcome by splitting a long cable into two or three shorter lengths, stowed where convenient and shackled together as necessary. The chain portion of a combination nylon-and-chain rode is ordinarily shackled in place for regular use, but small-diameter nylon, if left on deck, should preferably be shaded from the sun to protect surface fibers from damage by ultraviolet rays.

SCOPE

Later, in a discussion of anchoring techniques, we will go into the matter of holding power but at this point it seems appropriate to cover, in advance, the subject of *scope*. See fig. 631. Once an anchor of suitable design and size has

FIG. 630 Lightweight anchors chocked on deck, their round stock-ends fitted with rubber tips. A grating provides ventilation to the forepeak. Inboard ends of the nylon dock lines are *flemished* in spiral mats.

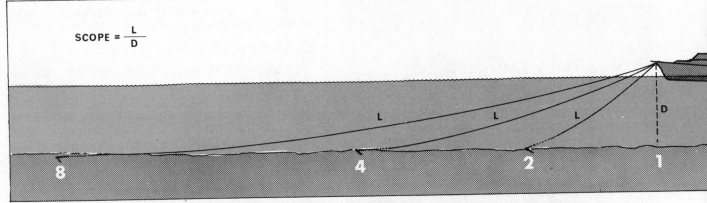

$$SCOPE = \frac{L}{D}$$

FIG. 631 Scope is the ratio of length of rode (L) to depth of water (D), plus allowance for height of bow above water. At (1) length of rode equals the depth. At (2) rode length is twice the depth, at (4) four times the depth. Note how the angle between rode and bottom decreases. At (8) the scope is 8:1 and the short length of chain at the anchor lies flat on the bottom.

been chosen to provide adequate holding power, scope is the factor that will determine whether you will, in fact, hold or drag. Too short a scope can destroy the efficiency of the best anchor.

Although definitions may be found that would refer to scope as "the length of cable from hawespipe to anchor," and others that roughly call it the ratio between length of rode paid out (between boat and anchor) and depth of water, two important factors are frequently overlooked: the height of bow chocks above water and the range of tide.

Let's assume we anchor in 10 feet of water with 60 feet of rode paid out. Theoretically, one might suppose this is a reasonable scope of 6:1. Our bow chock, however, is 5 feet above the surface. Immediately the ratio is cut to 4:1 (60:15). Six hours later the tide has risen another 5 feet. So now we have an actual scope of 3:1 (60:20), exactly half of the original theoretical ratio.

What is a proper scope? Under favorable conditions, 5:1 might be considered a *minimum*; under average conditions, 7 or 8:1 is regarded as satisfactory. Government tests have indicated that proper scope ratios will range between 5:1 and 10:1, the latter for heavy weather. Even in a very hard blow, in an exposed anchorage, the chances are that you will never need a scope of more than 15:1 with an anchor of suitable holding power. Boatmen who carry more than one kind of anchor have found that effective scope required under a given set of conditions may vary with the type.

In our hypothetical example above, the length of rode paid out should have been 140 (7:1) to 160 (8:1) feet; 100 feet (5:1) might be regarded as a minimum.

To provide maximum efficiency, all anchors require a low angle of pull—preferably less than 8 degrees from the horizontal. With short scope, holding power is reduced because the angle of pull is too high, tending to break the anchor out. As the pull is brought down more nearly parallel with the bottom, flukes dig in deeper with heavier strains on the line. Surging, as a boat pitches in a sea, throws a great load on the anchor, particularly on short scope. With long scope, the angle of pull is not only better, but the elasticity of a long nylon line cushions the shock loads materially.

FIG. 632 A plastic marker used to indicate the scope of anchor line paid (or veered) out.

Marking a rode for scope

Granting that we know how much scope is required, how do we know when we have paid out enough? Estimates are risky. Plastic cable markers, fig. 632, may be bought in sets to mark 30, 50, 70, 100, 125 and 150 feet. These are attached simply by inserting them under a strand of the line. In daylight, when the figures are legible, these are fine. Some saltier yachtsmen, harking back to traditional methods of marking lead lines, have improvised markings using strips of leather, white cotton and red flannel rags, and pieces of marline with knots in them. These can be identified by touch in the dark.

For all practical purposes, five or six marks at intervals of 20 feet (say 60-140 feet) should be adequate. One practical method would be to paint wide and narrow bands of a red vinyl liquid called Whip-End Dip at significant points, calling wide bands 50 feet, narrow ones 10. On chain rodes, as a measure of scope, some boatmen have painted links white at intervals.

One method that has proved successful on a 150-foot line with an additional 8 feet of chain is to whip the line at 50 and 100 feet from the chain with red sail twine. This gives an exact measure of 58 and 108 feet; other lengths can easily be estimated with sufficient accuracy.

Anchoring Techniques

HOW TO ANCHOR

Thus far we have discussed only equipment, or ground tackle. Let's consider now the technique—the art of anchoring. As a matter of fact, good equipment is more than half the battle; anyone can easily learn to use his gear correctly.

If, on the other hand, your anchors are of doubtful holding power, and your lines too short, then you can never escape the uneasy feeling associated with wondering whether, some day, you'll find yourself dragging on a lee shore. No part of your boat's equipment is more important, so don't stint here.

Before you can think about *how* to anchor, you must decide *where* you'll anchor, and here, as in all other phases of seamanship, a little foresight pays off handsomely.

Selecting an anchorage

There will be times, of course, when you will stop briefly in open water, coming to anchor for lunch, a swim, to fish, or perhaps to watch a regatta—but, in the main, the real problem of finding an anchorage comes down to choice of some spot where there's good holding bottom, protection from the wind, and water of suitable depth. Such an anchorage is the kind you'd look for in which to spend the night, free from anxiety about the weather.

Use the chart

The chart is the best guide in selecting such a spot. Sometimes you will be able to find a harbor protected on all sides, regardless of wind shifts. If not, the next best choice would be a cove, offering protection at least from the direction of the wind, or the quarter from which it is expected. As a last resort, anchorage may be found under a windward bank or shore—that is, where the wind blows from the bank toward the boat. In this case, watch for wind shifts, which could leave you in a dangerous berth on a lee shore.

Anchorages are sometimes designated on charts by means of an anchor symbol. Areas delineated on the chart by solid magenta lines, marked perhaps by white buoys, are often shown as special anchorage areas, where lights are not required on vessels less than 65 feet in length. See fig. 633. Never anchor in cable areas or channels, both indicated by broken parallel lines.

Shallow depths are preferred for an anchorage, because a given amount of scope will then provide better holding and reduce the diameter of the circle through which the boat will swing. Consideration, however, must be given to the range of tide, so that a falling level does not leave you aground, impaled perhaps on the exposed fluke of your own anchor, or bottled up behind a shoal with not enough water to get out at low tide.

Characteristics of the bottom

Character of the bottom is of prime importance. While the type and design of anchor fluke has a direct bearing on its ability to penetrate, as already noted, it may be stated broadly that mixtures of mud and clay, or sandy mud, make excellent holding bottom for most anchors; firm sand is

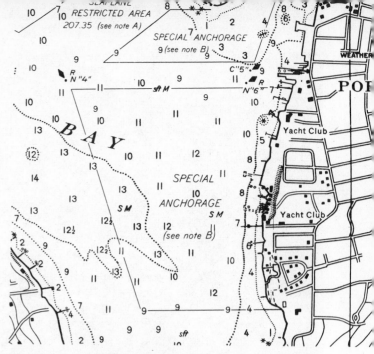

FIG. 633 In special anchorage areas shown on the chart, lights are not required on boats less than 65 feet in length.

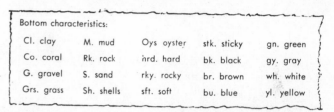

Bottom characteristics:				
Cl. clay	M. mud	Oys oyster	stk. sticky	gn. green
Co. coral	Rk. rock	hrd. hard	bk. black	gy. gray
G. gravel	S. sand	rky. rocky	br. brown	wh. white
Grs. grass	Sh. shells	sft. soft	bu. blue	yl. yellow

FIG. 634 Abbreviations of some bottom characteristics as shown on charts.

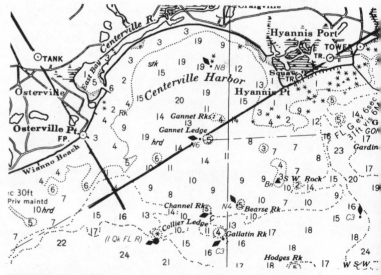

FIG. 635 How ranges may be used to select an anchorage by lining up visible charted objects. At the intersection of one range through the tank and flagpole, and another through two towers, the boat has 14 feet of water (at low tide) in hard bottom, clear of rocks, with room to swing outside of shoal water.

good *if* your anchor will bite deep into it; loose sand is bad. Soft mud should be avoided if possible; rocks prevent an anchor from getting a bite except when a fluke is lodged in a crevice; grassy bottoms, while they provide good holding for the anchor that can get through to firm bottom, often prevent a fluke from taking hold.

Sometimes bottoms which ordinarily provide reasonably good holding will be covered with a thick cabbage-like

FIG. 636 In this crowded anchorage, there's risk that the swinging circles of boats may overlap.

growth that positively destroys the holding power of any anchor. Even if you happen to carry one of the fisherman's sand-anchor types, with its thin spidery arm and small flukes, expect it to pick up half a bushel of this growth. All you can do is clean it off and try elsewhere.

Characteristics of the bottom are always shown on charts. By making a few casts with the hand lead, a check can be had on the depth, and if the lead is armed with a bit of hard grease or tallow, samples of the bottom will be brought up as a further check. Abbreviations for some bottom characteristics are shown in fig. 634.

Approaching the anchorage

Having selected a suitable spot, try to run in *slowly* on some range ashore, selected from marks identified on the chart, crossing ranges, fig. 635, or referring your position to visible buoys and landmarks to aid you in locating the spot. Later these aids will also be helpful in determining whether you are holding or dragging, especially if the marks are visible at night and it comes on to blow after dark.

If there are rocks, shoals, reefs or other boats to consider, give them all as wide a berth as possible, keeping in mind a possible swing of 360 degrees about the anchor with wind shifts or current changes.

Remember, too, that large yachts nearby may swing to a much longer scope than you allow—and, conversely, that you may swing much further than a smaller boat nearby lying on short scope. See fig. 636. Such conditions bring about an overlapping of the swinging circles.

The risk of fouling a neighboring craft is aggravated when, in a current, the deep-draft vessel holds her position while a light-draft boat swings to a shift of wind not strong enough to influence the other. Keel sailboats may lie one way in a light current, power boats another.

The boat that has already established her location in an anchorage has a prior claim to the spot and can't be expected to move if you later find yourself in an embarrassing position. Consequently, allow room enough so that you can pay out more scope if necessary in case of a blow, without being forced to change your anchorage, perhaps at night.

The way other boats lie, together with the set of nearby buoys, will help to determine how you should round up to the chosen spot. Estimate the relative effects of wind and current on your own boat and come up, *slowly*, against the stronger of these forces—in other words, heading as you expect to lie after dropping back on the anchor. Running through the anchorage, take care that your way is reduced to a point where your wake cannot disturb other boats.

FIG. 637 With its stock set up, this anchor can be let go quickly by casting off the lashing. Chain leads outboard through a hawsepipe up to the ring. Davit tackle can be hooked into the ring of the balancing band on the shank. On the port side of the winch a gipsy is provided for use with fiber rode.

Letting the anchor go

These preliminaries disposed of, you are ready to let the anchor go. Unless you are forced to work single-handed, one man should be stationed on the forward deck. Enough line should be hauled out of the locker and coiled down so as to run freely without kinking or fouling. If previously detached, the line must be shackled to the ring, stock set up (if of the stock type) and keyed. See fig. 637. Many an anchor has been lost for failure to attach the rode properly. Rodes, too, have gone with the anchor when not secured at the bitter end. Lightweight anchors are always ready for use and do not have to be set up, but always check to see that the shackle is properly fastened.

Despite the fact that in certain localities some experienced boatmen have adopted the practice of letting go while the boat has headway, depending on way to snub the anchor and give it a bite, the amateur motor boatman would do well to make it a standing rule *never* to let go while his boat has any way on.

In a motorboat, or auxiliary under power, the bow should be brought *slowly* up to the spot where the anchor is to lie, and headway checked with the reverse gear if necessary. Then, just as the boat begins to gather sternway slowly in reverse, the anchor is lowered easily over the side till it hits bottom, crown first.

Never stand in the coils of line on deck and don't attempt to "heave" the anchor by casting it as far as possible from the side of the boat. Occasionally, with judgment, a light anchor in a small boat can be carefully thrown a short distance—taking care that it lands in its holding position—but the best all-around rule is to *lower* it as described. That way, the possibility of fouling is minimized.

Setting the anchor

With the anchor on bottom and the boat reversing slowly, line should be paid (sometimes spoken of as *veered*) out as the boat takes it, preferably with a turn of line around the bitt. When a scope of about 7 or 8 times the depth has been paid out, *snub* the line by holding and the anchor will probably get a quick sure bite into the bottom, after which the line can be shortened if the anchorage is so crowded that such a scope would be excessive. Snubbing too soon may cause the anchor to drag.

In setting lightweight burial-type anchors, a little more care is required, particularly in soft mud bottoms where the anchor shank and chain can sink through the mud and cause the anchor to skid. This skidding can be readily avoided by lifting the chain and shank out of the mud with a short two-to-one scope, starting the plow or flukes to dig in, then backing down to lay out full scope.

Regardless of the type of anchor, after full scope has been paid out, a back-down load in excess of any anticipated loads should be applied. This is particularly important if the boat is to be left unattended.

Sometimes the anchor may be shod with a clod of mud adhering to flukes, in which case it is best to lift it, wash it off and try again.

When you must work single-handed, you can get your ground tackle ready to let go, long before you arrive at the anchorage, bring the boat up to the chosen spot, and then lower the anchor as the boat settles back with wind and current, paying out line as she takes it.

Making fast

After the anchor has gotten a good bite, with proper scope paid out, the line can be made fast and the motor shut off.

On small boats equipped with a Samson post, the best and easiest way to secure is with a clove hitch, similar to that usually thrown when making fast to a pile. The principal objection to the clove hitch on a small post is that it will sometimes jam pretty tight, especially when wet, if the strain is heavy.

On winches, three or four round turns can be taken on the gipsy, belaying the end on a cleat or on the winch itself with a clove hitch. Where a stout cleat is used to make fast, take a round turn around the base of the cleat, one turn over each horn crossing diagonally over the center of the cleat, and finish with another round turn around the base. Some boatmen prefer to finish with a half-hitch on one horn. Clove hitches have also been used on cleats in cases where the proportion of rode diameter to clearance under the horns has been such as to obviate risk of jamming. On small metal cleats it could be risky.

The fundamental idea in making fast is to secure in such a manner that the line can neither slip nor jam. If the strain comes on top of a series of turns on a cleat, fig. 638(a), then it will be practically impossible to free if you want to change the scope, without first taking the strain off it by using power.

If it becomes necessary to shorten scope, clear the bitt

FIG. 638 The wrong way (a) to cleat a line. With a strain (arrow) on the half hitch, it could be difficult to clear the line from the cleat. At (b) a round turn is first taken on the base of the cleat, the strain properly taken in the direction of the arrow. A turn over each horn and a half hitch on one will finish the job.

(Gordon S. Smith photos)

first of old turns or hitches. Don't throw new ones over the old.

A trick worth using when the sea is so rough that it is difficult to go forward on deck—especially if you are single-handed—is to set up the anchor in the aft cockpit, lead the line forward on deck through a closed chock, and back aft to the cockpit. If there are stanchions for life lines, the lead of the rode from chock to anchor must obviously be outside any such obstructions. When you're ready to let go it can be dropped on the weather side from the cockpit, and the line secured on a bit or cleat aft.

Anchoring without power

When anchoring under sail you don't have the same maneuverability that power supplies and, of course, there is no positive way to dig your anchor in. Here it is best to approach your anchorage with wind abeam so that you can spill most of the wind out of your sails, thereby slowing the boat down. If necessary trim your sail in to gain more headway as needed. Approach the anchorage with all sails down except the mainsail and with enough headway to keep the boat under control. Just before you are ready to let the anchor go, you should have steerageway, but no more. Let your sheet run and, with tiller hard-alee, shoot your bow directly into the wind and drop the mainsail. As your boat loses headway her bow will fall off and the boat will begin to drift to leeward; now lower your anchor.

Pay out scope as the boat drifts back and, occasionally, give a few jerks on the line. This usually helps to set the anchor. Hand-test the line by pulling it. You will be holding when the boat is drawn toward the anchor. Then pay out the usual scope of 7 or 8:1.

Hand signals

Anchoring, like docking, is one of the situations where it's a great help to have another hand aboard. The problem is communication between the anchor man on deck and the skipper at the wheel. With engine and exhaust noise, it's usually difficult for the skipper to hear, even though the man on deck can. Wind often aggravates the problem. If the skipper is handling the boat from a flying

bridge, he can usually hear better and, from his higher position, can see the trend of the anchor line.

In any case, it helps to have a pre-arranged set of hand signals. There is no need for standardization on this, as long as the helmsman clearly understands the crew's instructions. Keep the signals as simple as possible. Motion of the hands, calling for the helmsman to come ahead a little, or back down, can take the most obvious form. Pointing ahead or aft accomplishes the same purpose. A simple vertical wave of the hand may be used to signal "stop."

WHEN THE ANCHOR DRAGS

Let's assume now that you have anchored with a scope of 8:1, have inspected the rode, and taken bearings, if possible, as a check on your position. Though the wind has picked up, you turn in, only to be awakened at midnight by the boat's roll. Before you reach the deck you know what has happened—the anchor's dragging and the bow no longer heads up into the wind.

This calls for instant action—not panic. A quick check on bearings confirms what the roll indicated. You're dragging, with the wind abeam. Sizing the situation up swiftly, you note that danger is not imminent; there is still plenty of room to leeward and no boats down-wind to be fouled. Otherwise you would have to get under way, immediately.

The first step in trying to get the anchor to hold is to pay out more scope. Don't just throw over several more fathoms of line; pay it out, with an occasional sharp pull to try to give it a new bite. If you're dragging badly and can't handle the rode with your hands, take a turn around the bitt and snub the line from time to time. If this doesn't work, start the engine and hold the bow up into the wind

FIG. 639 Two schools of thought on the use of sentinels (kellets). In (a) below, the traditional use of a weight (about 25 pounds) or light anchor sent down the rode by means of a shackle over the rode, with light line to control the scope between sentinel and boat. In (b) below, a buoy rather than a weight has been proposed as a superior method, utilizing the principle commonly found in permanent mooring systems.

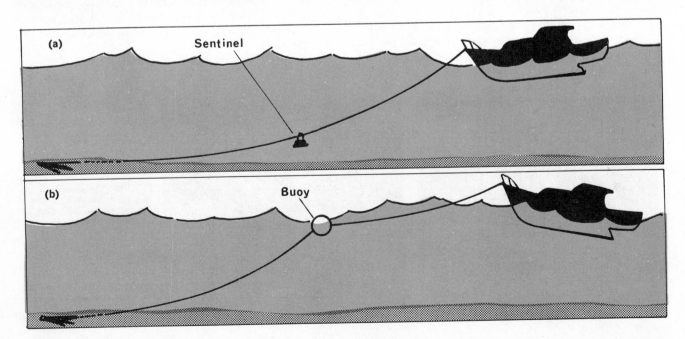

with just enough power to take the strain off the rode. This gives the anchor a chance to lie on the bottom and perhaps get a new bite as you ease the throttle and let the boat drift back slowly. If you haven't held when the scope is 10:1, get the anchor back aboard and try again with your larger storm anchor.

Sentinel—or buoy?

Suppose, now, that we have no spare storm anchor to fall back on. Can anything be done to increase our holding power? Here we enter an area of controversy with weight of experience on two opposing sides. We'll present both views.

For generations, seasoned cruising boatmen have known of the device known as a *sentinel*, or kellet. See fig. 639(a). Many have reported using it successfully; few have challenged its effectiveness. In principle, the sentinel is nothing more than a weight sent more than half-way down the rode to lower the angle of pull on the anchor and put a sag in the rode that must be straightened out before a load is thrown on the anchor. Working only with what came readily to hand in such a case, boatmen have shackled or snapped their light anchor to the main anchor rode, and sent it down the main rode with a line attached to the ring of the lunch hook, to be stopped at a suitable distance. A pig of ballast or other weight would do as well, provided it could be readily attached.

The other school of thought claims that when this principle is used with short scope in order to limit swinging room, it has proved inadvisable and dangerous, on the theory that, under storm conditions, a resonant condition

FIG. 640 A plastic foam buoy. Note how the strain is transmitted by solid rod through the buoy.

may be encountered which could quickly snap the line. Their alternative would be to use a buoy, fig. 639(b) rather than a weight, claiming that, properly used, the buoy can carry most of the vertical load in an anchoring or mooring system, limiting the basic load on the boat to the horizontal force required to maintain the boat's position. The argument is advanced that the buoy permits the boat's bow to ride up easily over wave crests, rather than being pulled down into them, with excessive loads on both rode and anchor.

What to watch

From these opposing views, certain conclusions may be drawn. To be most effective, a buoy, if used, should preferably be of the type found in a permanent mooring system, fig. 640, where its efficiency is undoubted. Its connection into the system should be as positive as it would be in a

mooring buoy, all strain being carried directly by the rode —in short, no "weak link" here! Provision should be made for carrying it as part of the "emergency" equipment, rather than trusting to a makeshift device improvised under stress of weather.

On the other side of the picture, if the sentinel is to be used, it should be done *with ample scope*, and every precaution taken to avoid a chafing condition on the main rode.

In support of advocates of the sentinel, we cite the scientific test made under controlled conditions aboard a 104-footer in which a *30-pound* weight, suspended from $5/8$-inch wire cable used as the main rode, cut the maximum anchor load practically in half. Obviously, wire rope is less suited to the average pleasure boat than it was to this test boat, it has no stretch and stands chafe of the sentinel's shackle, but figures on reduction of the load are irrefutable.

An alternate system

We offer a compromise. Carry a boat-length of substantial chain and a 25-pound pig of lead with a ring bolt cast in it. Stow them away somewhere in lieu of ballast. When the chips are down, with breakers to leeward, shackle the chain to your biggest and best anchor, and the chain in turn to your best and longest nylon rode, with the ring of the pig lead shackled in where chain and nylon join. It cannot be anything but an improvement over the same long scope of nylon without benefit of the extra scope of chain and added weight. This would seem to eliminate the twin problems of chafe (at the sentinel) and any tendency to hold the boat's bow down in the surge of pitching seas.

GETTING UNDER WAY

When you are ready to *weigh anchor* and get under way, run up to the anchor slowly under power, so that the line can be taken in easily without hauling the boat up to it. Ordinarily the anchor will break out readily when the line stands vertically.

As the line comes in, it can be whipped up and down to free it of any grass or weed it may have picked up. This clears the line before it comes on deck. If the anchor is not too heavy, mud can be washed off by swinging it back and forth near the surface as it leaves the water. With care, the line can be snubbed around a bitt and the anchor allowed to wash off as the boat gathers way, preferably astern. Two things must be watched: don't allow the flukes to hit the topsides, and be careful that water flowing past the anchor doesn't get too good a hold and take it out of your hands.

Manila, if used, must be coiled loosely on deck and allowed to dry thoroughly before stowing below. When the anchor is on deck, the stock (if there is one) can be folded and the anchor lashed down securely in its chocks.

On larger craft, equipped with a davit, the anchor is brought up with the winch to a point where a light tackle can be hooked into a ring in the balancing band on the anchor's shank. With the anchor suspended over the side, mud can be washed off with a hose.

In all this anchor handling, try to avoid letting the anchor hit the hull at any time as planking is soft and will get badly gouged and dented. Fiberglass finishes and metal hulls can also be marred. Guests often are eager to "help" by getting the anchor up, but unless they have had some experience, it's better to handle this part of the job your-

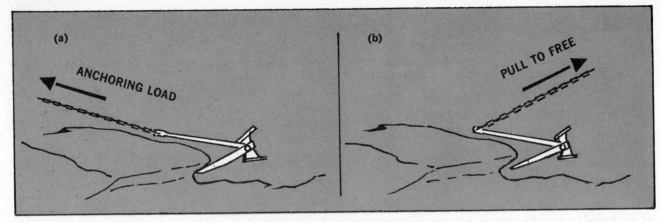

FIG. 641 In rocky bottoms when an anchor fouls, the first attempt to clear it should be made by reversing the original angle of pull (a), with moderate scope, so as to draw it out as shown in (b).

self. Handle and stow lines carefully. If a bight or end of line slips over the side it is almost certain to run back under the bottom and get hopelessly fouled in the propeller.

In a boat under sail alone, have your mainsail up before you break the anchor loose. The same procedure is used as stated above but there is no motor to help. However, it is possible to use your sails to assist.

Clearing a fouled anchor

If an anchor refuses to break out when you haul vertically on the line, snub it around the bitt and go ahead with the engine a few feet. If it doesn't respond to this treatment, it's an indication that the anchor may have fouled under some obstruction. To clear it, try making fast to the bitt and running slowly in a wide circle on a taut line. Changing the angle of pull may free it, or a turn of line may foul an exposed fluke (if it's a kedge) and draw it out.

Sometimes a length of chain can be run down the anchor line, rigged so that another boat can use her power to haul in a direction opposite to that in which the anchor line tends, thus changing the angle of pull 180 degrees. With kedges, if one fluke is exposed, a chain handled between two dinghies can occasionally be worked down the rode to catch the upper arm and draw the anchor out, crown first.

If the anchor is not fouled in something immovable, it may be broken out by making the line fast at low water and allowing a rising tide to exert a steady strain. Or, if there is a considerable ground swell, the line may be snubbed when the bow pitches low in a trough. There's some risk of parting the line this way, in case the fluke is fouled worse than you think.

In rocky bottoms, the first thing to try is reversing the direction of pull, opposite to that in which the anchor was originally set, using a moderate amount of scope. See fig. 641.

There is a type of anchor in which the ring is free to slide the full length of the shank. Properly rigged, it is claimed to be virtually snag-proof. More about this later.

If you have been anchored for a day or two in a brisk wind, the anchor may be dug in deep. Don't wait till you're ready to sail; 20 minutes before departure shorten the scope—*but keep a sharp watch*. Motion of the boat will tend to break the anchor out and save a lot of work.

HOLDING POWER

Before getting into some of the special techniques of anchor use, some understanding of holding power is in order. We have already seen how important anchor design and scope are in determining relative holding power, assuming of course that we are comparing anchors of equal weight. To understand just how critical design can be, remember that a change of as little as 1 degree in fluke angle may cause as much as a 50 percent reduction in efficiency. Lacking equipment to make individual scientific tests, one can readily appreciate how essential it is to rely on the reputability of the manufacturer.

Some factors involved

Tests have shown that the normal strain on an anchor due to wind and current in average weather is comparatively small. Current is a relatively small factor as compared with the pressure exerted by wind on exposed surfaces. Surge when a boat pitches in a seaway may throw a tremendous strain on the boat and all her ground tackle. Weight of the boat is also significant.

In calculating holding power required under average conditions, manufacturers have taken into account all of these factors, including such boat dimensions as length, beam, hull depth, draft, displacement, and height of superstructure. One has tabulated it as a percentage of gross

TABLE 6-5 HORIZONTAL HOLDING POWER DANFORTH ANCHORS (pounds)

Hi-Tensile	Soft Mud	Hard Sand	Standard	Soft Mud	Hard Sand
5-H	400	2,700	2½-S	140	800
12-H	900	6,000	4-S	230	1,600
18-H	1,250	8,750	8-S	480	3,200
28-H	1,600	11,000	13-S	720	4,900
60-H	2,400	17,000	22-S	1,200	8,000
90-H	2,900	20,000	40-S	1,500	10,000
200-H	5,000	35,000	65-S	2,300	15,000
500-H	7,500	50,000	85-S	2,700	19,000
3000-H	21,000	140,000	130-S	3,100	21,000

weight—for centerboard sailboats 5%; small motorboats 6%; larger cruisers 7%; keel-type sailboats 10%. As wind pressure varies as the square of the velocity, the same manufacturer has suggested another formula for extreme conditions where a boat is anchored in a gale. For sailboats, the formula says that pull (in pounds) = $AV^2/186$, for motorboats $AV^2/220$. (V is wind velocity in miles per hour, A a factor derived by multiplying height, from waterline to deckhouse top, by overall beam.) An added safety factor of one-third should be allowed.

Varies with bottom

In preparing tables of holding power for specific anchor sizes, the manufacturer must give proper consideration to the kind of bottom in which his tests are run. Table 6-5 illustrates how wide the discrepancy can be between results in soft mud and hard sand. The figures also bring into sharp focus the variation in holding power between different models of equal weight offered by the same manufacturer.

One test the boatman can make

A simple test that any boatman can make has been suggested by the owner of a 40-foot auxiliary sloop. He found that a well-powered boat can use her engine to throw a load on an anchor greater than she will normally register when riding to that anchor.

The pull of an engine can be approximated by multiplying the horsepower by 20, a value that works out about right for a fairly heavy-duty propeller. With a high-speed propeller of small diameter, the pull is reduced somewhat.

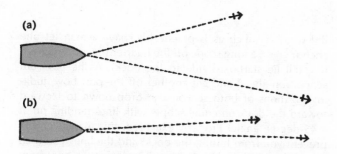

FIG. 642 Using two anchors out ahead, it is better to have the rodes form an angle as at (a), instead of in line as at (b).

The anchor to be tested is let go astern and scope of 7 or 8:1 paid out before making fast. Then the engine is speeded up till the anchor drags. Sufficient speed is maintained to drag the anchor at one or two knots, meanwhile noting the engine rpm. Testing other anchors the same way provides a basis for comparison in the varying rates of rpm required to move each.

Actual test readings of the load can be made by using spring scales in the line, rigged if necessary to permit a small scale to register heavy loads. If a lever-operated winch is available, the scale can be attached at the end of the lever. The scale's reading is then multiplied by the ratio of the radius of the lever arm to the radius of the drum on which the chain or rope is carried.

The originator of this idea determined that his 40-footer, powered with a 52 hp engine driving a 20-by-12 propeller through 2:1 reduction, under full power pulled about 1,000 pounds. Under normal conditions of anchoring, he found that the boat would rarely surge to a value higher than 400 pounds, especially if generous scope were paid out.

When making a comparison of holding powers it is interesting to note that holding power is proportional to the area of buried fluke multiplied by the distance it is buried in the bottom. Consequently, for given areas of fluke, the design which permits deepest penetration is the most effective.

USING TWO ANCHORS

Two anchors are sometimes laid for increased holding power in a blow. If your working anchor drags, you can run out your spare storm anchor, without picking up the working anchor. The important thing to remember is to lay them out at an angle, not in line, to reduce the risk of having one that drags cut a trough in the bottom for the other to follow. See fig. 642.

To stop yawing

Deep-draft sailboats lie well head to the wind but motorboats often "tack" back and forth at anchor. Skiffs, with high freeboard and little draft forward, are among the worst offenders in this respect.

You can stop this yawing by laying two anchors, lines leading out from either bow, making an angle of about 45 degrees between them. To do this, get one anchor down first and have a man tend the line carefully as you maneuver the bow off to one side before letting the other go. Then you can settle back on both lines, adjusting scope as

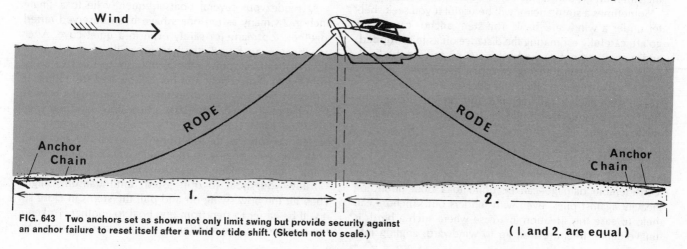

FIG. 643 Two anchors set as shown not only limit swing but provide security against an anchor failure to reset itself after a wind or tide shift. (Sketch not to scale.)

(1. and 2. are equal)

necessary. *Fouling the wheel in slack line under the boat in maneuvers like this is disastrous.*

With good handling, it is possible to get two anchors down single-handed. The easiest way is to settle back on one anchor, making fast when the proper scope has been paid out. Then go ahead easily with the propeller, rudder over enough to hold the line out taut so you can keep an eye on it at all times. When the line stands out abeam, stop your headway, go forward and let the other anchor go, then drop back and adjust the lines to equal scope.

If a dinghy is available, the second anchor can be carried out in it, lines being adjusted as required after both anchors are set.

To guard against wind or current shifts

When anchoring overnight, or if the boat is to be left unattended, a wise precaution is to lay two anchors, made fast forward but set as shown in figure 643. It provides an extra measure of security against the risk of having a single anchor break out with a 180-degree wind shift and failure to reset itself again. See fig. 644.

If the two-anchor technique is used in a crowded anchorage to limit swinging radius, remember that other nearby boats may lie to one anchor only, so risk of having the swinging circles overlap is increased. Use of three anchors cuts the swinging circle to a minimum.

When setting a second anchor for use as described above, set the up-wind anchor in the conventional way and then back down till double the normal scope is out. After the down-wind anchor is set, adjust the scope at the bow chocks till both are equal. In ranging ahead, with a rode tending aft, take every precaution to prevent its fouling in the propeller.

Stern anchors

In some anchorages, boats lie to anchors bow and stern. The easiest way to get these down is to let the bow anchor go first, and then drop back with wind or current on an extra long scope (15-18 times the depth), drop the stern anchor, and then adjust the scope on both as necessary, taking in line forward. In tidal waters make allowance for increasing depth as the tide rises. The value of this arrangement is pretty well restricted to areas where permanent moorings are set explicitly for this purpose, as in narrow streams, or on occasions where there is no risk of getting a strong wind or current abeam. Under such conditions, the strain on ground tackle could be tremendous.

Sometimes a stern anchor will be useful if you seek shelter under a windward bank. The stern anchor can be let go aft, carefully estimating the distance off as it is dropped, and scope paid out as the boat is run up toward the bank or beach. A second anchor can then be bedded securely in the bank, or a line taken to a dock or tree ashore.

The stern anchor will keep the stern off and prevent the boat from ranging ahead. But, again, *watch that stern line, while the propeller is turning!*

At docks

A berth on the weather side of a dock is a bad one, as considerable damage can be done to a boat pounding heavily against piles, even with fenders out. Anchors can help to ease the situation in a case where such a berth is unavoidable. Keeping well up to windward, angling into

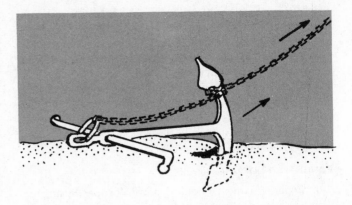

FIG. 644 When a boat swings with wind or current about an anchor, fouling a line around an exposed arm, holding power is destroyed.

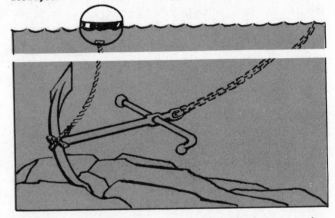

FIG. 645 A buoyed trip line to the crown will permit an anchor fouled in rocky bottom to be hauled up fluke first.

the wind as much as is practicable, have a man let one anchor go on a long scope off the quarter (the port quarter, if you'll lie starboard side to the dock). As he pays out scope, run ahead and get another off the port bow, judging positions of both so you can drop down to leeward toward the dock on equal scope, with lines tending off at a 45-degree angle. Properly executed, this maneuver will prevent you from hitting the dock, and the lines you then carry ashore will be needed only to prevent the boat from moving ahead or astern.

RAFTING

At rendezvous several boats frequently lie to a single anchor. As many as ten boats have been observed rafted together, too many for safety even in a quiet cove. After one boat is anchored, the second pulls alongside with plenty of fenders out on both. Stay six to ten feet away from the anchored boat and heave bow and stern lines. If this can't be done, run up to the anchored boat's bow at an angle of about 45° and pass a bow line first, then your stern line. Make sure you have no headway when lines are passed. As soon as the bow line is aboard the anchored boat, stop your engine so that there will be no chance of going ahead, breaking the anchor out.

Allow your boat to drift astern until transoms align. Then let the bow swing off and pull the sterns in close so it will be easier to step from one boat to another. To keep the transoms in line and fenders in position a spring line

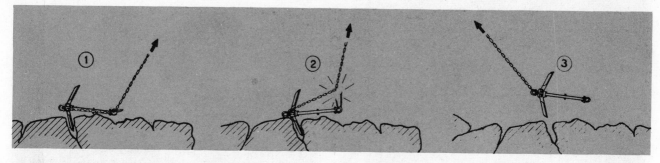

FIG. 646 Scowing an anchor. The rode to this Norwegian SAV folding anchor is attached to the crown and led back along the shank, to be lashed at the ring. When it fails to release at (1), an upward strain (2) parts the lashing and the anchor is drawn out as shown at (3).

must be run from the stern of the second boat forward to the anchored boat.

If a third boat ties up, the anchored boat should be in the middle; if more tie up always alternate them, port and starboard of the anchored boat. Each succeeding boat should use the same technique, always with a spring from the stern of the outboard boat forward to the one next in-board. Keels of all boats in the group should be nearly parallel. Naturally boats should raft only when there is little wind and a relatively smooth surface. When four or more are tied together, it is a good precaution for the outboard boats to carry anchors out at a 45° angle. When it's time to turn in for the night, every boat should have its own separate anchorage.

OTHER TECHNIQUES

On rocky bottoms

Earlier we spoke of certain steps that could be taken to clear a fouled anchor. Hazardous at best, rocky bottoms should preferably be avoided, regardless of the type of anchor used. Before leaving a boat unattended, a load should be applied to the anchor, after setting, well in excess of any expected load.

If you normally anchor in rocky bottoms or suspect that the bottom is foul in the area where you must anchor, it is better to forestall trouble. One time-tested device is the *buoyed trip line*. See fig. 645. Make a light line fast to the crown (in some anchors an eye is provided). This trip line should be long enough to reach the surface (with allowance for a rising tide) where it is buoyed with any convenient float—a block of wood, ring buoy or plastic disposable bottle. If the anchor doesn't *trip* readily at the first pull on the rode, haul in the trip line and the anchor will be withdrawn, crown first.

An alternate scheme is to *scow* the anchor, fig. 646, by bending the rode to the crown, leading it back along the shank, and stopping it to the ring with a light lashing of marline. With sufficient scope, the strain is on the crown and not on the lashing. When hove up short, the strain is on the lashing. When this parts, the anchor comes up crown first.

There are anchors (the Sure-Ring, fig. 647, is typical) that have a slotted shank in which the ring can travel freely from end to end. If the anchor should snag, the theory is that when the boat is brought back over the anchor, the sliding ring can slip down the shank so the anchor will be drawn out backwards. The Sure-Ring has an added refinement—a unique ring design that permits the rode to be

bent to an eye in the shank for overnight or unattended anchoring. In the Benson anchor the shank is formed of round rod, along which the ring slides when the anchor is to be backed out.

Kedging off a bar

The term *kedging* is often, and properly, applied to the use of a light anchor (not necessarily kedge-type) carried out to deep water in a dinghy to haul a stranded boat off a shoal. If you ever have to resort to this, coil the line down carefully in the dinghy, so that it pays out freely from the stern as you row. The dink might well become unmanageable in a wind or strong current if an attempt is made to pay the line out from the deck of the stranded boat.

Anchoring at night

Anchoring at night, you must display a white 32-point light, visible at least 2 miles, rigged forward where it can be best seen. Vessels over 150 feet in length show a white light forward at least 20 feet above the hull, and another aft at least 15 feet lower than the forward light. Vessels over 65 feet at anchor display a black ball as a day mark.

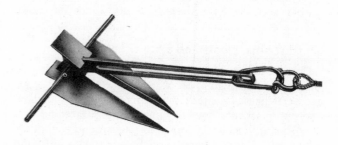

FIG. 647 In the Danforth Sure-Ring anchor, a ring slides in a slot down the shank so the anchor can be drawn out backwards if it snags. For overnight use, the line can be shackled through the eye in the shank.

In certain specially designated anchorage areas, fig. 633, no lights need be displayed at night on vessels less than 65 feet in length.

When anchoring overnight, if you have no ranges to check your position (or if those you have are unlighted) you can rig a *drift lead* (the lead line will do). Lower it to the bottom, leave some slack for swinging, and make fast. If it comes taut, you've dragged. Don't forget to pick it up before getting under way.

FIG. 648 Salisbury plastic Chafe-Gard protects mooring lines from abrasion at the bobstay of this auxiliary.

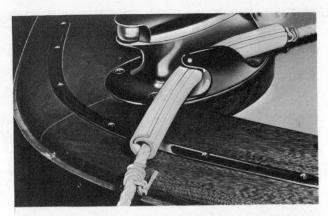

FIG. 649 Chafe-Gard is lashed by thongs to the rode to hold it in place to protect against chafe at the chock.

FIG. 650 The drum of an electric windlass and, behind it, a substantial well-rounded wooden Samson post. The horizontal Norman pin keeps line from slipping off the top. At lower left, a deck pipe through which the rode is passed below.

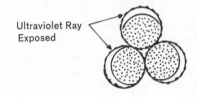

Ultraviolet Ray Exposed

FIG. 651 Small-diameter nylon line must be protected from damage by exposure to ultraviolet rays of the sun.

SOME CAUTIONS

Guard against chafe

Every possible precaution must be taken to avoid chafe on fiber lines. Wherever the line comes in contact with chocks or rails and rubs back and forth under continuous strain, outer fibers may be worn to such an extent as to seriously weaken the line. Mooring pennants, fig. 648, are particularly susceptible to this.

When lying at anchor, you can *freshen the nip* by paying out a little more scope from time to time, or parcel the line at the point of chafe with strips of canvas wrapped around it. Modern chafing gear is available in the form of plastic or rubber sleeves, fig. 649, which can be snapped over the line, centered in a chock and seized with thongs to prevent shifting. Chafing gear also comes in the form of a white waterproof tape, to be applied around the line at bitts, chocks and other points of contact.

The increasing use of relatively light anchor rodes of small diameter (frequently ³/₈ inch) points up the necessity of preventing chafe. The chafe that a ³/₄-inch line could tolerate might render a ³/₈-inch line unsafe.

Chocks, bitts, cleats and other fittings

Chafe is aggravated wherever a fitting has a rough surface to accelerate abrasion of the fiber. Even small nicks and scratches in a chock can damage a line by cutting fibers progressively, one at a time. Serious weakening of a line develops when it is forced to pass around any fitting with relatively sharp corners, such as a square bitt with only a minimum chamfering of the edges, especially when the bitts are too small for the job they have to do. Theoretically the ideal bitt is round, of generous diameter. The best chocks are those of special design with the largest possible radius at the arc where the line passes over it.

Mooring bitts especially must be fastened securely. The best bitt is the old-fashioned wooden bitt, fig. 650, long enough to have its heel fastened deep in the boat's frame. If a cast fitting must be used on deck, it should be through-bolted, the deck below reinforced with husky partners. Bitts have been torn completely off the decks of boats anchored in open water with chain rode.

All fittings playing a part in the use, handling or stowage of ground tackle should be designed and installed not with an eye to just getting by in fair weather, but proof against failure in the worst blow the vessel will ever encounter.

Damage from ultraviolet rays

The outer layers of all types of rope are subject to some degree of damage from ultraviolet rays of the sun. See figure 651. With nylon line of relatively large diameter (upwards of ³/₄ inch) damage from this cause is probably negligible. As the diameter decreases, the problem becomes proportionally more serious. In ³/₈-inch nylon it is an important factor to be reckoned with. Every possible precaution should be taken to shield such lines from unnecessary exposure to direct sunlight. Often the rode can be fed down into a locker. If it must be carried on deck, it pays to shade it.

CARE AND INSPECTION

Anchors and chain

Galvanized anchors are usually coated by the hot-dip process which leaves a tough protective finish, normally requiring no care except ordinary washing off of mud that may be picked up in use. Occasionally, they are freshened up in appearance by a coat of aluminum paint.

On soft bottoms chain may come up fouled with mud

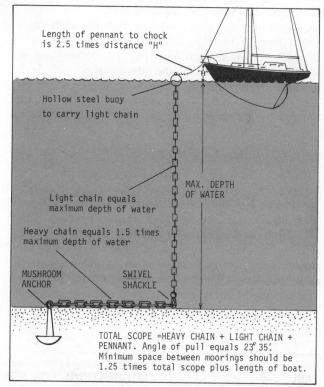

FIG. 653   This mushroom anchor has a heavy bulb cast into the shank at the shackle end.

FIG. 652   A small permanent mooring system consisting of mushroom anchor, chain, buoy and pennant, with necessary swivels, shackles, thimble and eye splices. Rigged as shown, no strain is carried by the buoy.

because its weight has caused it to lie on the bottom, where even a light strain would keep all but a few feet of fiber line from touching bottom. Obviously, the chain needs thorough cleaning and on some larger yachts a hose is carried on deck for the purpose.

Fiber Lines

Fiber lines should be kept free from sand and grit; manila must be dried before stowing. A low-pressure hose can be used to wash off grit or you can slosh the line overboard, tied in a loose coil. Throwing a strain on a kinked fiber or wire line can be fatal. To a lesser degree, short bends are injurious.

Good practice dictates the need for one long spare rode in good condition. Too often this is an "old but new" unused manila line, which has rotted in its locker. This might fail in the emergency for which it is broken out.

Lengths of line in regular use may be turned end-for-end periodically, as most of the chafe and wear come on the anchor end. On small boats it is often feasible to standardize on one size of line for all uses. A new one can be laid by in the spring as a spare and the old spare is then put into regular service.

Nylon should be unreeled from the coil like wire, not up through the coil like manila. Neither should it be towed like manila when new to take out the kinks. When splicing, tape and fuse the ends with a hot knife or flame. Strands should be kept twisted, and an extra tuck taken, the ends to be left a little longer, when trimming, until the splice is well set under strain. Use synthetic rope thimbles or splice thimbles in tightly to prevent them from dropping out when the nylon stretches. On deep-sea tugs the "legs" of thimbles are seized to the line. All whipping and seizings should be made tightly so they cannot slip.

Periodic inspection

Periodic inspection of all lines, particularly anchor lines, pays big dividends. Look for and appraise the effect of abrasion, cuts, rust on nylon, broken or frayed yarns, variations in strand size or shape, burns, rot and/or acid stains, and fiber "life." Rotten manila fibers have little or

Length of pennant to chock is 2.5 times distance "H"

Hollow steel buoy to carry light chain

MAX. DEPTH OF WATER

Light chain equals maximum depth of water

Heavy chain equals 1.5 times maximum depth of water

MUSHROOM ANCHOR

SWIVEL SHACKLE

TOTAL SCOPE = HEAVY CHAIN + LIGHT CHAIN + PENNANT. Angle of pull equals 23° 35'. Minimum space between moorings should be 1.25 times total scope plus length of boat.

FIG. 654   Diagram of mooring practice recommended by the Lake Michigan Yachting Association and approved by the U.S. Coast Guard. A weight added at the shackle between lengths of heavy and light chain would increase holding power.

no strength when broken individually. Nylon line may fuzz on the surface although the yarns are not broken. This seems to act as a cushion, reducing further outside abrasion.

Consider the remaining cross-sectional area as compared to new rope. Untwist and examine the inside of strands. They should be clean and bright as in new rope. If powder or broken fibers appear, the line has been overloaded or subject to excessive bending. Nylon may be fused or melted, either inside or out, from overloads.

Most old-timers in yachting know cordage. If you are in doubt, replace your line or get an expert's opinion. For a more detailed discussion of marlinespike seamanship, see Chapter 11.

Permanent Moorings

Permanent moorings, as distinguished from ordinary ground tackle in daily use, consist of the gear used when boats are to be left unattended for long periods, at yacht club anchorages, for example. See fig. 652. The traditional system has often consisted of a mushroom anchor, chain from the anchor to a buoy and a pennant of stainless steel or nylon from the buoy to a light pick-up float at the pennant's end.

Mushroom anchors, especially the type with a heavy bulb cast in the shank, fig. 653, have been able through suction to develop great holding power under ideal conditions if they are allowed time enough to bury deep in bottoms that will permit such burying. Unfortunately ideal bottom conditions are not always present.

Complicating the problem is the fact that anchorages are becoming increasingly crowded so that adequate scope cannot be allowed each boat because of overlapping swinging circles. Add to this the threat of abnormally high hurricane tides, reducing scope to a ratio allowing no safety factor and you have the explanation for devastation wrought by several hurricanes along the Atlantic Coast, beginning in 1938.

Systems used by typical yacht clubs

The problem faced by the Manhasset Bay Yacht Club at Port Washington, N. Y., is typical of that existing in numerous anchorages. Here about 200 boats are moored in a limited space. If it were possible to permit each boat to use a length of chain equal to 5 to 7 times the depth of water (maximum 30 feet), safety would be assured, but this would require a swinging radius of several hundred feet for each boat, which is not possible. After exhaustive study, they prepared a set of recommended standards, given in Table 6-6.

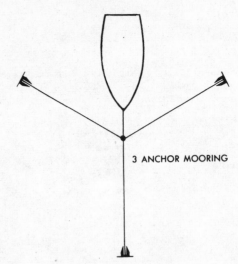

FIG. 655 A modern permanent mooring system scientifically designed as a vast improvement over single-mushroom systems. Three lightweight anchors are bridled 120 degrees apart. From the intersection a relatively short rode limits swing.

A similar system was adopted by the Lake Michigan Yachting Association, their standards approved by the U.S. Coast Guard. See figure 654.

Guest moorings are often available at yacht clubs. The launch man will know which of those not in use for the night will be heavy enough to hold your boat. As a rule, it's easier and safer to pick up such a mooring. In some places, a charge may be made.

A multiple anchor system

One hurricane that ravaged the North Atlantic Coast swept through an anchorage in the New York area and tore almost every boat from her moorings. Only two survived. What these two had in common was an "unconventional" mooring system—multiple (3) anchors bridled to a common center, with chain and pennant leading from that point to the boat. The principle is diagrammed in fig. 655.

TABLE 6-6- SUGGESTIONS FOR PERMANENT YACHT MOORINGS
For Wind Velocities Up to 75 M.P.H.

Boat Length Overall	Mushroom Anchor (Min. Wt.)	Heavy Chain		Light Chain		Length (Minim.)	Pennant			Total Scope (Chocks to Mushroom)
		Length	Diameter	Length	Diameter		Manila	Nylon	Stainless Steel	
—FOR MOTOR BOATS—										
25	225	30	7/8	20	3/8	20	1	7/8	9/32	70
35	300	35	1	20	7/16	20	1-1/4	1	11/32	75
45	400	40	1	20	1/2	20	1-1/2	1-1/4	3/8	80
55	500	50	1	20	9/16	20	2	1-1/2	7/16	90
—FOR RACING TYPE SAILBOATS—										
25	125	30	5/8	20	5/16	20	1	7/8	9/32	70
35	200	30	3/4	20	3/8	20	1-1/4	1	11/32	70
45	325	35	1	20	7/16	20	1-1/2	1-1/4	3/8	75
55	450	45	1	20	9/16	20	2	1-1/2	7/16	85
—FOR CRUISING TYPE SAILBOATS—										
25	175	30	3/4	20	5/16	20	1	7/8	9/32	70
35	250	30	1	20	3/8	20	1-1/4	1	11/32	70
45	400	40	1	20	7/16	20	1-1/2	1-1/4	3/8	80
55	550	55	1	20	9/16	20	2	1-1/2	7/16	95

NOTE:—Heavy chain to be shackled to mushroom anchor, light chain shackled to end of heavy chain.
With stainless steel pennants, use special bow chocks and mooring bitts to eliminate sharp bends.

TABLE 6-7   SUGGESTED ANCHOR SYSTEMS FOR PERMANENT MOORINGS — (Winds up to 75 knots)

LENGTH O.A.	BEAM		PENNANT NYLON	*RODE (COMBINATION)		RODE CHAIN⊕ ONLY	ANCHOR				
	SAIL	POWER		NYLON	CHAIN		†MUSHROOM	NORTHILL	DANFORTH		
									STANDARD	HI-TENSILE
10'	4'	4'	4'-⅜"	⅜"	5'-¼"	¼"	250 lb.	12 lb. (6-R)	8-S	5-H
15'	5'	5'	6'-⅜"	⅜"	6'-⁵⁄₁₆"	⁵⁄₁₆"	400 lb.	27 lb. (12-R)	13-S	12-S
20'	6'	7'	8'-⅜"	⅜"	6'-⁵⁄₁₆"	⁵⁄₁₆"	550 lb.	27 lb. (12-R)	22-S	12-H
25'	6'	8'	10'-⅞"	⁷⁄₁₆"	8'-⅜"	⅜"	750 lb.	46 lb. (20-R)	40-S	20-H
30'	7'	10'	12'-⁷⁄₁₆"	⁷⁄₁₆"	8'-⅜"	⅜"	1050 lb.	80 lb. (30-R)	65-S	35-H
35'	8'	12'	14'-½"	½"	10'-⁷⁄₁₆"	⁷⁄₁₆"	1350 lb.	105 lb. (50-R)	85-S	60-H
40'	10'	14'	16'-½"	½"	10'-⁷⁄₁₆"	⁷⁄₁₆"	1800 lb.	105 lb. (50-R)	130-S	60-H
50'	12'	16'	18'-¾"	¾"	12'-½"	½"	2400 lb.	—	180-S	90-H
60'	14'	19'	20'-1"	1"	14'-⅝"	⅝"	3000 lb.	—	300-S	90-H

NOTE: *Total scope with combination rode to be a minimum of 7:1. ⊕Scope with chain only to be a minimum of 5:1. Buoy with each system to have lifting power (in pounds) of 1½ times the submerged weight of total rode. †Suggestions offered (by Danforth) in table above may sound excessive to those accustomed to lighter tackle. Experience, however, under storm conditions has proved the wisdom of providing for loads of unexpected severity. Sizes suggested assume fair holding ground, scopes as recommended, and moderate shelter from heavy seas.

A casual inspection of figure 655 reveals the obvious advantages of the system. Regardless of how the wind shifts, the boat swings through a small circle, despite the advantage of a relatively long total scope from boat to anchor. The short rode up from the three-way bridle minimizes any "tacking" tendency. Always there will be one or two anchors to windward, the strain tending in the same direction. Using modern lightweight anchors instead of mushrooms, the greater the load the deeper they bury. Mushrooms often need a relatively long period to bed in securely, but lightweight anchors will dig in almost immediately. Using a safety factor of 1.5, each anchor in the 3-anchor system should have a holding power equal to the design holding power of the moorings.

A scientific 3-anchor system of this kind overcomes all of the weaknesses inherent in poor systems using inadequate scope and concrete blocks, railroad car wheels and old engines, all categorized as "dragging" types of "anchor."

Mooring buoys

To comply with new uniform state waterway regulations (applicable on waters under state control), mooring buoys should be white with a horizontal blue band. Buoys used in any mooring system should be of a type that transmits strain directly through chain or rod. See fig. 640. Buoys perform a useful function in removing much of the vertical load, the pennant is under a more nearly horizontal load, and the boat's bow is freer to lift to heavy seas.

Pennants of stainless steel have often been preferred because failures frequently were traceable to chafing of fiber pennants. When fiber is used for the pennant, it should be carefully protected with chafing gear, especially if there is a bobstay against which it can saw. See figure 648.

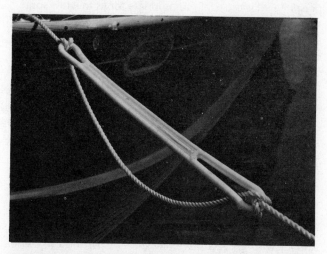

FIG. 656 The Rubbermaid snubber, bent into a mooring line with clove hitches as shown, leaving a loop of slack, absorbs heavy shock loads on line and fittings. Tensile strength is 2000 pounds.

Annual inspection necessary

Because ordinary moorings often depend for holding power on a period of time to silt in, annual inspection of chain, links, shackles and pins should be made early in the season—never disturbed just about the time storm warnings are issued. On the other hand, it is also wise to give the pennant from buoy to boat a double-check in mid-season, just before the August-September months when hurricanes most often strike.

Table 6-7 includes figures suggested for Danforth and Northill anchors when used in place of mushroom anchors in a permanent mooring system.

CHAPTER 7

THE SKIPPER

His Duties and Responsibilities

The yachtsman is properly interested in the pleasure and comradeship that he obtains with his boat; the rigorous routine of a battleship has little, if any, place on the bridge of a 40-foot cruiser. However, we amateurs can learn from Navy practices. As many of these practices have as their sole purpose insurance of the safety of the ship and her personnel, it is especially appropriate for us to know something of them and apply to our own cruising those that will contribute to our own safety. *The first responsibility of a skipper is the safety of his ship and his people.*

LEADERSHIP AND DISCIPLINE

Suppose we think first about leadership and discipline. These are subjects that are rarely considered by the yachtsman but in them we find much that can be of value in that sudden emergency for which all of us who cruise must always be prepared.

Discipline; shades of a hickory stick. But, discipline is not subservience, discipline is self-control. It means prompt and cheerful obedience to necessary laws and regulations, laws and regulations designed for the sole purpose of our safety. It also means a square deal to our shipmates; the skipper who expects discipline of his crew must likewise discipline himself. A well-disciplined boat is a secure and safe boat.

Discipline does not mean a long string of commands with a crew constantly scurrying about the deck. Gold braid is not necessary to discipline. Discipline does not mean that all the joy is gone out of the job. There can be discipline on board the smallest yacht without there being any apparent show of it. Real discipline is a function of leadership and leadership can be exercised in dungarees on board a 20-foot sailboat; it is a characteristic that all of us should cultivate and practice.

Leadership is based on three things: (1) each man must know himself, his abilities and his limitations; (2) he must know his job, know it so well that he doesn't have to think about the details of doing it; (3) he must know his men and his boat and what he can reasonably expect of them in an emergency.

Authority and obligations

From the lowest third class Petty Officer to the Admiral of the Fleet, every man of the Navy charged with authority has two functions to perform: (1) his function as a military leader; (2) his function as a specialist in some technical phase of his profession. It is relatively easy for any of us to become technically skilled in shaping a course, making

FIG. 701 The primary responsibility of every skipper is the safety of his boat and crew.

a mooring, even swabbing a deck. All of these have to do with our technical ability and are equally applicable in the Navy and in amateur cruising.

But there usually comes a time, and it is always an emergency when seconds count, when there are too many jobs for even the most skillful of us to handle them all. This is the time when our capacity for leadership will bring us to port or put us aground. In one way, leadership on a motor cruiser is even more important than it is on an aircraft carrier; our friends on board may not be skilled in the operation of a boat. We have to make up for their lack of technical ability.

Let's look at it another way. There is an old saying that you get more out of a job when you have to work at it; the average guest on board should more quickly feel at home and should have pleasanter memories of his cruise if he has some of the boat's work to perform, if he must coordinate his efforts with those of his shipmates. As skippers, we all welcome the guest who is eager to turn to and do his share.

Assignment of tasks

A good skipper will privately catalog in his own mind the abilities of his guests and think ahead to the tasks that he will request them to do should an emergency arise. See fig. 702. He may and should go one step further; without making it obvious, he should see to it that all on board are given various jobs to do not only so that he can find the best spot for each but also so that they are able to do more than one thing. *Our first obligation is the safety of our boat and her people.*

One good U. S. Power Squadron skipper makes it a practice to have "informal formal" watches, which amount to Navy watch, quarter, and station bills. From the stories told of cruises in his schooner, everyone on board has a bang-up good time, as well as a safe cruise. This man is a real leader and he doesn't hesitate to work at it.

Let's not try to define leadership; there have been as many definitions of this word as there have been writers. Any intelligent man thoroughly understands the meaning and significance of the term. Taking honesty and integrity for granted, it is the first characteristic that a man should develop. Out of leadership comes confidence, pride, emulation on the part of our associates; out of it will come the pleasant cruise that all of us want.

FORESIGHT

Next to leadership comes forehandedness or foresightedness. A first class skipper doesn't wait for an emergency to arise; he has long before formulated several solutions to any emergency with which he may be faced. Commander Frost, one of the foremost destroyer captains in the Navy, put it something like this: "The most expert captain is the first to admit how often he has been fooled by some trick of wind or current. Dangerous situations develop with startling suddenness so even when things look easiest, watch out. Have an answer to every threat and a trick to take you out of every danger." An officer must always look ahead, a minute, an hour or a day as the circumstances of his situation dictate. And, whether we like it or not, a yacht skipper is an officer, good or bad.

VIGILANCE

Next in importance to forehandedness is vigilance. In no position more than that of the skipper is "eternal vigilance the price of safety." He must see intelligently all that comes within his vision, outside and inside the ship. And his vigilance must extend beyond this to the faculty of foreseeing situations as well as seeing them. The rule of the airlines that a pilot must be able to get into alternate fields as well as the airport of his destination holds meaning for the boat skipper too.

COMMON SENSE

One more check point; it is common sense. The successful skipper has a sense of proportion and of the fitness of things; let us adjust ourselves to our situation. For example, it is obviously ridiculous to dress in white flannels and blue coat when kedging off, although we might do so when the ladies are on board of a quiet Sunday afternoon. Yet we all probably can recall cases where, through a failure to exercise common sense, we did things as silly as that suggested above. The old adage "use your head" applies equally well on shipboard.

One more quotation from Commander Frost. He has defined the art of handling a ship: "Systematic application of knowledge and skill, acquired by study, observation and experience, in effecting the safe, smart, effective and economical operation of your ship." Think it over.

COURTESY

There is a courtesy extended by large ships that is worthy of attention: dipping the ensign when passing a ship of the Navy. Pleasure craft frequently do not do this but it is a mark of respect that is highly desirable for all to show. As your bridge draws abeam the bridge of the Naval vessel, dip the ensign and immediately hoist it two-blocks. All persons on board except the helmsman should face the warship and stand at attention. Any in uniform should salute.

DUTIES AND RESPONSIBILITIES

We come now to the duties and responsibilities of a skipper, of those activities with which you must be familiar while on the bridge.

Approximately in the order of their importance, the responsibilities of the skipper or of the man having the watch are as follows:

• Safe navigation of his boat.

• Safe and efficient handling of the boat in company with or in the presence of other boats. See fig. 703.

• Safety of personnel and materiél on board.

• Rendering assistance to all in danger or distress.

• Smart handling and smart appearance of the boat.

• Comfort and contentment on board.

• A good log.

These are some of the instructions that the U. S. Navy gives to watch officers, men who are charged with the

FIG. 702 The good skipper will catalog in his mind the abilities of guests and crew, assigning tasks accordingly.

responsibility for the ship. They form a pattern that all of us, whatever the size of our craft, can follow with benefit. They presuppose that a man know himself, his job, his crew, and his ship. Let's see what they mean in terms of actual practice.

Check of equipment

Before a boat can be gotten under way, it is important that a check-up be made to determine if she is ready to sail. Not alone should the equipment required by law be on board and in proper condition for use but all navigational and other equipment should be at hand. See fig. 704. Water and gasoline tanks should be sounded, the ground tackle inspected, stores checked, and all those other little odd jobs that can be done at the mooring, but not at sea in an emergency, completed. These things sound elementary and worthy of little consideration but all of us can recall results that might have been different had the proper attention been given in advance to such minor details.

The Navy provides each ship with a check list that the officer must use before he takes charge or gets the ship under way. The yachtsman could profitably make up his own check list and either actually or mentally go over it as he steps from the dock to the deck. The whole subject of safety is so important that every yachtsman should consider himself disqualified until he so thoroughly knows the requirements that he executes them as second nature.

Physical condition of the skipper

Another point in the safe navigation of a ship has to do with the physical condition of the skipper. The constant vigil which is necessary requires the complete possession of all faculties as well as a sense of physical well-being. No man should expose his boat or his people to danger, except in an extreme emergency, unless he is in good physical and mental condition.

Avoidance of risk

The good skipper will not permit any of his personnel to take needless risks. If a dangerous job that may result in a man's being swept overboard has to be done, he will insist that that man wear a life jacket. This may not be customary in yachting circles but that omission does not justify contempt for danger. In this connection, the state of the weather should be carefully observed and every effort made before getting under way to ascertain what the weather will be for the period of the cruise. A little foresight in this regard may save a ship or a life.

In conclusion, for those of us who wish to cruise tomorrow as well as today, let us think first of the things that spell safety; then the fun will take care of itself.

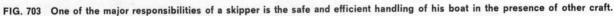

IMPORTANT THINGS TO DO

Here is a short check list of things to do:

• Frequently check and plot the boat's position when in sight of land or aids to navigation; be certain of the identification of the objects used to fix position.

• Take soundings and heed their warning.

• Note the effect on the boat of wind and current, especially in close waters or when maneuvering with other boats.

• Do not follow other boats blindly; steer a safe course and do not assume that the other fellow is on a safe course.

• When in doubt as to position, slow down promptly; do not wait until the last minute.

• Remember that the other fellow may not see us and always be alert immediately to take such steps as will prevent a collision.

FIG. 703 One of the major responsibilities of a skipper is the safe and efficient handling of his boat in the presence of other craft.

Maintenance of a lookout

A small cruiser cannot readily utilize the lookout routine of the large vessel but the implication of vigilance and caution of that routine should be acknowledged. We should make it a matter of pride that we, as skippers, will observe any danger before any other person on board sights it; this is definitely our responsibility.

Regarding Refuse The admonition (see item below) against throwing refuse overboard is more than a matter of etiquette alone—it is based on law. Complaints received by both the Coast Guard and Army Engineers concerning refuse in coastal waters have fostered an official appeal by both agencies to the public. While asking each citizen to do his part voluntarily the appeal pointed out that "throwing, discharging, or depositing either from or out of any floating craft or from the shore refuse matter of any kind into any navigable waters of the U.S. or into any tributary of any navigable waters from which the same shall float or be carried into such navigable water is a violation of federal law (33 USC 407)." And for any who might take the warning lightly the appeal adds that such violation is punishable by a fine not exceeding $2500, not less than $500 or by imprisonment for not more than one year nor less than 30 days, or by both fine and imprisonment.

Official U.S. Coast Guard photo.

FIG. 704 The skipper must take full responsibility for seeing that all essential equipment, including that required by law, is aboard (and in proper condition for use) before casting off.

YACHT_____

Glad To Have You On Board

The Skipper and Mate welcome you on board. We look forward to your company during our cruise and ask

Please

DO make yourself at home. The mate will show you your locker. There is no lock on the refrigerator and the berths are said to be comfortable. Decks are usually swabbed down at 0900.

DO be informal. Old clothes are fit companions for swabbing decks, weighing anchor, and securing from chow.

DO ask us all the questions you wish—while we are not handling the boat. If you have a yen for rope-work or other ship's business, let us know. Too, you may find a helpful magazine or book on board.

DO locate your life-belt and learn how to use it. We will show you how to toss a life-ring, if you do not know. Not looking for trouble, but we want to be ready for it.

DO the same for the fire extinguishers. In case of fire, the Skipper will tell you what to do—and not to do.

DO report any danger or unusual occurrence to the Skipper at once: what it is, where it is, what it is doing.

DO go swimming at every opportunity. Swim upstream, keeping an eye on your shipmates and on the boat.

DO fish too, if you wish. But watch out for fouling the propeller and mooring lines, watch out for that fish-hook.

DO conserve fresh water. Use all that you need but remember, the supply is limited.

DO likewise conserve electricity. Lights out on the bridge when under way at night.

DO learn to work the "head." The Skipper or Mate will gladly show you.

DO stand clear of dock lines and anchor rode, of all boat controls.

DO remember that sound carries far over the water especially late at night.

Please

DO NOT smoke or strike a match or cigarette lighter or touch off the galley stove while fueling or starting the engines.

DO NOT take chances on deck, especially if the sea kicks up. Remember, rubber-soled shoes often slip on a wet deck.

DO NOT fall overboard or cause another to do so, while under way or at anchor.

DO NOT use any equipment with which you are not familiar. See the Skipper or Mate.

DO NOT jump from deck to dock without watching your footing. Landing on a rope-end usually results in a sprained ankle.

DO NOT jump into the dinghy; it isn't built to "take it."

DO NOT let go the dinghy painter until you are ready to clear.

DO NOT jump over the side while wearing a life-belt; your chin may be the worse for wear.

DO NOT throw refuse overboard without instructions from the Mate. Puncture cans at both ends; fill bottles with sea water and jettison only in deep water.

DO NOT use the "head" for cigarettes, matches, chewing gum or bulky articles; plumbers are scarce afloat.

DO NOT wear hard-soled or high-heeled shoes on deck; a good varnish job is too hard to come by.

DO NOT use the Skipper's binoculars or chart without permission; he may need them in a hurry.

DO NOT intrude on the privacy of others.

Morning colors at 0800—Evening colors at sunset—Recognition Signal—COOPERATION

_____Mate   _____SKIPPER

CHAPTER 8
BOAT HANDLING

"The art of handling a vessel may be defined as the systematic application of knowledge and skill—acquired by study, observation and experience—in effecting its safe, smart, effective and economical operation."—COMDR. H. H. FROST, USN

Without a doubt some of the finest exhibitions of skill in the art of handling motor boats are often given by men who may never have read a printed page on the subject of seamanship. Their facility at the helm of a motor boat is their sheepskin from the sea's school of experience – in which the curriculum, admittedly, may be tough.

Witness, for example, the consummate skill some commercial fisherman might display in maneuvering his skiff into a tight berth under adverse weather conditions, finally to bring her up against the wharf in a landing that wouldn't crack an egg. Such proficiency, developed over long years of meeting every conceivable kind of situation, eventually manifests itself almost as an instinct, prompting the boatman to react right whether he has time to think the problem out in advance or not.

Sometimes the old-timer's methods might appear, to a novice, to verge on carelessness, but that's probably be-

cause the old salt in a practical way understands exactly what the minimum requirements are for the safety of his craft and therefore doesn't waste any time on non-essentials. Consequently if he uses three lines where the text book says six, don't jump to the conclusion that he wouldn't know how to use more if they were needed.

So, in approaching a study of the principles of boat handling, it's helpful to keep in mind that the goal is not so much to be able to repeat verbatim definitions or the prescribed answers to a set of questions for the sake of passing a quiz as it is to understand the "why" of some of the curious capers your boat may cut when you're out there handling her. If she stubbornly refuses to make a turn under a given set of conditions, or persistently backs one way when you want her to go the other, you will be less likely to make the same mistake twice when you understand the reasons behind her behavior.

First Principles

The paragraphs above lead up to a very fundamental thought. Learn all you possibly can about the principles according to which average boats respond under normal conditions; supplement this with all the experience you

can get aboard your own boat and other types as well, and then learn to act so that controlling elements aid you rather than oppose you.

Some of the ideas to be developed later may seem applicable only to larger vessels, but remember that some day you may be at the wheel of a craft double the size of your own familiar 30-footer. Then the significance of these points will be more apparent.

No two boats will behave in identical manner in every situation, so great is their individuality. This applies even to "standardized" craft which to outward appearances may be alike as two peas in a pod. Exactly how the boat will perform depends on many things—among them the design; the form and shape of the hull's underbody; the construction; the shape, position and area of the rudder; the trim; speed; the weight; load; strength and direction of wind and current; and the nature of the sea, if any.

EFFECT OF WIND AND CURRENT

Wind and current are particularly important factors in analyzing a boat's behavior as they may cause her to respond precisely opposite to what you would expect without these factors to reckon with. As a case in point, many motor boats have a tendency to back into the wind despite anything that can be done with the helm.

Given two boats of roughly the same size, one of which (A) has considerable draft forward but little aft, and another (B), with relatively greater draft aft but more superstructure forward—you will find radical differences in their handling qualities. What governs is the relative area presented above water to the wind as compared with the areas exposed to the water, both fore and aft.

The former (A), with wind abeam, might hold her course reasonably well when the bow of the latter (B) would persistently pay off, requiring considerable rudder angle to hold her up. On the other hand, with wind and sea aft, B might go along about her business with little attention to the helm while A insisted on "rooting" at the bow and yawing off her course despite the best efforts of the helmsman.

As a general rule, the boat with low freeboard and superstructure but relatively deep draft tending toward the sailboat type, fig. 801, will be less affected by wind and more by current than the light draft motor boat, fig. 802, with high freeboard and deckhouses. The latter floats relatively high in the water and has little below the waterline to hold her against wind pressures acting on areas exposed above water to drive her to leeward.

In the type of motorboat where the greatest draft and least freeboard are aft, the greatest exposure to windage is presented by the relatively higher bow and cabin forward. Obviously her bow will be affected by wind pressures more than the stern. With wind abeam, the tendency would be for her bow to be driven to leeward more than the stern. To offset that, she would need a certain amount of rudder angle to hold her on her course and compensate for leeway.

For the same reason if she is drifting in a smooth sea with engine stopped, wind pressure on her bow will make the bow pay off so that the wind finally is brought abaft the beam. The action might also be compared to that of a sailboat in which a flattened jib, but no other canvas, is set.

But, just as an illustration to show how boat behavior may vary, suppose it is raining and cockpit curtains are buttoned down on that same cruiser. Here a new factor is introduced and the windage aft is increased to such an extent that it may more than offset the effect of the windage forward. Under such conditions she might be very hard to handle in close quarters because of the great amount of total windage compared to her draft.

Although flying bridges, fig. 803, on modern cruisers tend to add to the windage, they have an undeniable ad-

FIG. 803 A modern cruiser being brought up to a finger pier. The flying bridge and twin screws are a great advantage in handling, from the standpoint of visibility and control. Crew tends bow line.

vantage in better visibility when maneuvering, and running at night or in strange waters.

Some boats require humoring under certain conditions. For example, because of a combination of excessive superstructure forward and little draft at the bow, it may be practically impossible to turn a boat in close quarters by the conventional technique.

HELMSMAN MUST DEVELOP JUDGMENT

From these and many other variations in boat behavior it begins to be evident that the boatman must develop judgment, based on understanding of the individual boat he is handling and the forces acting upon her. Combina-

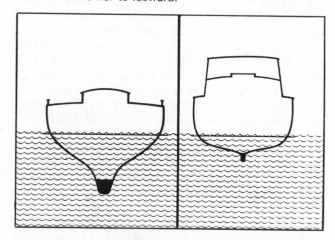

FIG. 801 Section of a deep-draft sailboat with relatively low freeboard, as compared with a typical motorboat.

FIG. 802 In this motorboat the draft is small compared to the height of superstructure exposed to windage.

FIG. 804 Approaching a bridge. At this point the helmsman waits for the span to open. When about to enter the opened span, he will square away parallel with the center line.

tions of conditions are infinite, so he must be able to appraise the situation and act promptly, with decision.

A good helmsman will be prudent and try to foresee possibilities, having a solution in mind for the problem before it presents itself. On that basis, it's likely that he'll never meet an "emergency." To cite a simple example, if you're running down a narrow channel with a strong wind abeam, and you have a choice as to which side to take, the windward side is the better bet. If the engine should stop, you'll probably then have a chance to get an anchor down before going aground on the leeward side.

By the same token, you wouldn't skirt the windward side of a shoal too closely. To leeward, in case of engine failure, you would drift clear, but to windward you'd be driven down on the shoal. A strong current might have the same effect, and would have to be taken into account.

As another example of how the helmsman should try always to be prepared for possibilities, suppose you are approaching a bridge, fig. 804, having a narrow draw opening with a strong wind or current setting you down rapidly on it. If you were to approach the opening at an angle,

and power or steering gear failed, you'd be in a jam. On the other hand, if you are prepared and straighten out your course while still some distance off so you will be shooting down the center of the opening in alignment with it, the chances of doing any damage are practically nil because her straight course will tend to carry her through in the clear in any case.

In developing your boat sense, draw from as many sources as possible. Observe the way experienced yachtsmen, fishermen and Coast Guardsmen handle their boats, making due allowance for differences in your own boat when you try similar maneuvers.

TERMINOLOGY OF BOAT HANDLING

Before getting too deep into discussion of actual problems of maneuvering it is necessary in advance to get some of the correct terminology fixed in mind.

The *port* side of a boat is the *left* side facing forward; the *starboard* is the *right* side. This is easy to visualize while the boat has headway but when the boat is reversing the operator may face aft and get all mixed up when the terms right, left, starboard and port are used.

Therefore, bear in mind that the port side is the port side *no matter which way the boat is going*. When we speak of the boat's going to port it means that her bow turns to port when she has headway and her stern to port when she has sternway. Figure 805 makes this clear. At A the boat has headway and her bow is turning to port. At B she is going astern and her stern is going to port.

The old terms of port helm and starboard helm have now given way to new terms which prevent misunderstanding. In Figure 805 the boat has *left rudder* in both cases and with headway, as at A, her bow goes to port. *Right rudder*, which is not illustrated, is just the opposite. The rudder is then on the starboard side of the boat's centerline and her bow goes to starboard when the boat has headway.

A *balanced rudder*, fig. 806, is one in which the area of the blade surface is distributed so that part of it lies ahead of the rudder stock. An unbalanced rudder would have the stock attached at the edge of the blade.

While the proportion of this balanced area may be only

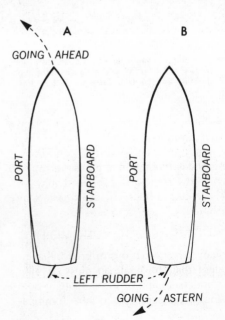

FIG. 805 With left rudder in a boat going ahead (A) the stern is thrown to starboard, bow to port. Going astern, left rudder throws stern to port.

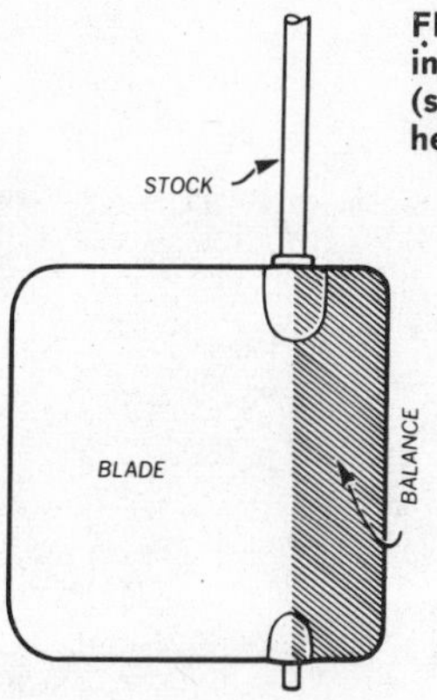

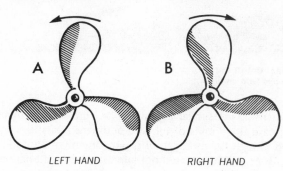

FIG. 806 A balanced rudder, in which part of the blade area (shaded section) projects a-head of the rudder stock.

STOCK

BLADE

BALANCE

FIG. 807 Left-hand and right-hand propellers. This is how they turn when you stand astern of them, looking forward at the aft side of the blades.

A
LEFT HAND

B
RIGHT HAND

20 per cent of the total rudder area, it exerts considerable effect in taking strain off the steering gear and making steering easier, though it may slow the boat on a turn more than the unbalanced type.

RIGHT- AND LEFT-HAND PROPELLERS

Propellers are right-handed or left-handed, depending on the direction of their rotation. It is vital that the difference be understood because this has a great bearing on how a boat maneuvers, especially when reversing. To determine the hand, stand outside the boat, astern of the propeller, and look forward at the driving face of the blades, fig. 807. *If the top of the propeller turns clockwise when driving the boat ahead, it is right-handed; if counter-clockwise, left-handed.* A is left-handed; B, right-handed.

Most propellers on marine engines in single-screw installations are right-handed although some are left-handed. In any maneuvering problems which follow, the assumption is that the propeller on a single-screw boat under dis-

cussion is right-handed unless specifically noted to the contrary.

In twin-screw installations the ideal arrangement is to have the *tops of the blades turn outward* for better maneuvering qualities. In fig. 807 the port engine swings a left-hand wheel, the starboard engine a right-hand wheel.

Don't be confused by the term right- and left-hand as applied to the engines that are driving the propellers. If you stand inside the boat, facing aft toward the engine, fig. 808, and the flywheel turns *counter-clockwise* (as in most marine engines) it is a *left-handed engine* and requires a *right-hand propeller*. A right-hand engine takes a left-hand wheel.

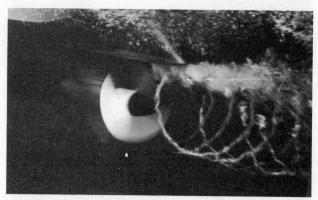

FIG. 809 The discharge screw current from a propeller is given a spiral twist by the propeller blades, as this view of an outboard lower unit shows. A left-handed inboard engine, driving a right-hand propeller, would create an opposite (clockwise) spiral.

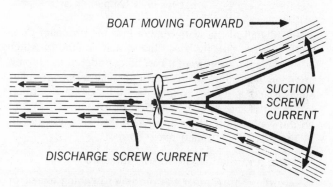

BOAT MOVING FORWARD →

SUCTION SCREW CURRENT

DISCHARGE SCREW CURRENT

FIG. 810 The screw current which drives a boat through the water. Here the boat has headway. Suction current is shown leading into the propeller, the discharge current driven out astern.

FIG. 808 Direction of rotation is marked on this marine engine flywheel housing. This is a left-hand engine, as shown by the counterclockwise direction of the arrow. It takes a right-hand propeller.

FIG. 811 The lower unit of an outboard motor which, unlike the inboard engine, pivots to provide steering control.

FIG. 812 The inboard-outboard, like the inboard boat, has an inboard engine. Unlike the inboard, it has an outboard drive unit which pivots like the outboard. This boat has twin engines.

HOW THE PROPELLER ACTS

Motor boats are driven through the water by the action of their propellers which act almost like a pump, drawing in a stream of water from forward (when going ahead) and throwing it out astern. This stream moving astern reacts on the water around it to provide the power for propulsion. Sometimes an analogy is drawn between propeller action and a screw thread working in a nut, but this fails to give a correct picture of what really is happening at the propeller.

Actually all of the water drawn into the propeller does not flow from directly ahead like a thin column of water but for our purposes here it can be considered as coming in generally parallel to the propeller shaft. The propeller ejects it and as it does so imparts a twist or spiral motion to the water, fig. 809, its direction of rotation dependent on the way the propeller turns. This flow of water set up by the propeller is called *screw current*.

Suction and discharge screw currents

Regardless of whether the propeller is going ahead or reversing that part of the current which flows into the propeller is called the *suction screw current*. The part ejected from the propeller is the *discharge current*, fig. 810. The latter is not only spiral in motion but is also a more compact stream than the suction current and exerts a greater pressure than the suction current.

By locating the rudder behind the propeller in this discharge current a greater steering effect is possible than if it were to be placed elsewhere, to be acted upon only by water moving naturally past the hull. For that reason a twin-screw cruiser is likely to have twin rudders, one behind each propeller, thus keeping their blades at all times more directly in the propeller's discharge current. Exactly what the effect of each part of the screw current on the boat's behavior will be will depend upon what part of the boat it is acting upon.

In boats driven by outboard motors, steering action results from rotation of the lower unit, fig. 811, around a vertical axis, so that the propeller's discharge current acts at an angle to the boat's keel. (See Chapter 27, Outboard

Seamanship.) A similar action results from control of the outboard drive units of inboard-outboard boats, fig. 812, even though the motor itself is permanently mounted inboard. As will be pointed out later, the inboard boat gets its steering effect from the action of the propeller's discharge current on a movable rudder.

There is also a *wake current*. This is a body of water carried along by a vessel with her as she moves through the water due to friction on her hull. This has its maximum effect near the surface, is practically of no consequence at the keel.

Unequal blade thrust

Finally, there is another factor of some moment that needs to be understood in analyzing a boat's reaction to propeller rotation. While this has been sometimes referred to as sidewise blade pressure, it is more properly an unequal thrust exerted by the ascending and descending blades of the propeller, fig. 813.

Here we are looking at the starboard side of a propeller shaft, inclined, as most shafts are, at a considerable angle to the water's surface and to the flow of water past the propeller blades. The actual pitch of the blades as manufactured, of course, is the same, but the water flows diagonally across the plane in which the blades revolve.

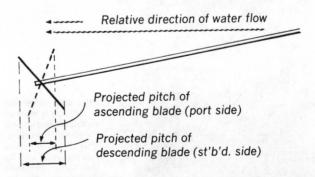

Relative direction of water flow

Projected pitch of ascending blade (port side)

Projected pitch of descending blade (st'b'd. side)

FIG. 813 With rudder amidships, bow of boat with right-hand propeller may swing to port. Angularity of the propeller shaft has the effect of increasing the pitch of the descending blade relative to that of the ascending blade, so greater thrust is exerted on starboard side.

Figure 813 shows clearly how the effect of this is to increase the pitch of the descending starboard blade as compared with the ascending port blade, when considered relative to the direction of water flow past the propeller.

The importance of this factor is reduced as the shaft angle is decreased, and naval architects, taking cognizance of this, sometimes take pains to have the engine installed as low as possible to keep the propeller shaft nearly parallel to the water's surface and the flow of water past the blades. This naturally contributes to propeller efficiency, and is a worth-while factor to be considered wherever consistent with other requirements of the design. Limitations in some designs, however, make it necessary for the engine and shaft to be installed at a considerable angle.

Effect of unequal blade thrust

The relatively greater pitch of the blade on the starboard side has the effect of creating a stronger thrust on this side with the result that the bow of the boat tends to turn to port. Putting it another way, insofar as this single factor is concerned, there is a natural tendency for the stern of a single-screw boat with right-hand propeller to go to starboard when the propeller is going ahead, and for the stern to go to port when it is reversing.

Again, when such a boat has headway, the bow apparently wants to turn to port if the rudder is held amidships, so a certain amount of right rudder may be necessary to maintain a straight course. To correct it, shafts are sometimes splayed to port, fig. 814, or a small trimming tab may be attached at the after edge of the rudder blade, on the side toward which the boat tends to pull.

The effect is a great variable, so small in some cases as to be negligible; quite pronounced in others.

HOW INDIVIDUAL BOATS DIFFER

We have seen how the helmsman has many things to consider when handling boats, due partly to individual characteristics which cause them to respond differently under identical conditions of wind, weather and current.

We have dealt too with the effect which draft and freeboard have on a boat's behavior, showing how high freeboard creates windage which acts to drive a boat to leeward whereas deep draft gives her a grip on the water with which to oppose that tendency.

The general principle is easily observed in the case of a deep keel sailboat, where deep draft acts to hold her on her course, and minimum freeboard is designed into her to reduce the windage factor.

Not only the draft, but the trim, has a bearing on a boat's handling qualities. Later we will see how the effect of rudder action in steering is to cause a boat to pivot about a point near the bow. But if she trims by the stern, that is,

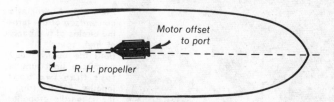

FIG. 814 Ordinarily engines are installed on the center line, but unequal blade thrust tends to make stern go to starboard, bow to port (assuming a right-hand propeller). Sometimes shaft is splayed to one side of the center line as illustrated to offset that tendency.

FIG. 815 Boats under sail only have no propeller discharge current to increase the rudder's effect in steering. Their maneuverability is limited, and there are many tight places into which a motor boat could be worked where the sailboat (without power) could not.

deeper than normal aft, the tendency is for that pivoting point to move aft.

The tendency to stray off course

Different boats require varying degrees of rudder angle to compensate for any tendency to fall off from a straight course. Depending on differences in construction, arrangement of rudder blade, and the hand of the propeller, the bow may tend to fall off to port or starboard. These are all factors that the helmsman should understand before attempting maneuvers with a boat.

Using a concrete example to make the significance of the last point more clear, a certain group of boats of almost identical design were found to have a strong tendency to pull off course to port. In some of these, the condition was corrected by the simple expedient of lowering the rudder blade, without changing its size or shape but merely by lengthening the stock an inch or two.

Before correcting that condition, these boats would make a quick and easy turn to port but would be obstinate in turning to starboard. As a matter of fact, unless steering controls were rigged with worm and gear to hold the wheel against pressure on the rudder, the boat would immediately swing into a short circle to port the instant the wheel was left unattended. While this is an exaggerated condition, far from normal, it does illustrate the handling characteristics the helmsman must pay attention to, especially in an unfamiliar boat.

Then again, the state of the sea will have an effect on a boat's performance. A heavy, deep-draft boat or one which is heavily loaded will carry her way through the water longer than a light one when the propeller is disengaged by throwing the reverse gear level into neutral. This is likely to be even more marked in a seaway, the light displacement boat losing her way against the sea much sooner than a heavier craft would.

HOW THE RUDDER ACTS

Although there are some boats, like fast hydroplanes, which have bow rudders, the conventional arrangement for steering on most inboard boats is by means of a vertical rudder blade at the stern pivoted in hangers or on its stock so that movement of the steering wheel or tiller throws it to port or starboard of the boat's centerline.

In a sailboat, or auxiliary, fig. 815, when the engine is not driving a propeller, when the boat has headway water flows past the hull and if the rudder is moved to one side of the keel a resistance on that side is created together with a current at an angle to the keel. The combined effect is to throw the stern to port with right rudder, to starboard with left rudder.

But note that *any control from the rudder is dependent on the boat's motion through the water.* Even if she is drifting, with motion relative to the bottom, but none so far as the surrounding water is concerned, her rudder has no effect. Only when the water flows past the rudder and strikes it at an angle does the boat respond. The faster she is moving, the stronger the rudder effect. It makes no difference how her headway has been produced—she may even be in tow—there is control as long as there is motion relative to the water.

Propeller current's action on rudder

In a motor boat the situation is different from that encountered in a sailboat. Here the rudder blade is almost invariably directly in the discharge current of the propeller which is pumping a strong stream of water astern. Moving the rudder to one side of the keel deflects the stream to that side. The reaction which pushes the stern in the opposite direction is much stronger than it would be in the absence of that powerful jet.

At very slow propeller speeds the boat's headway may not be sufficient to give good control over the boat if other forces are acting upon her at the time. For example, with a strong wind on the port beam, even with rudder hard over to port, it may not be possible to make a turn into the

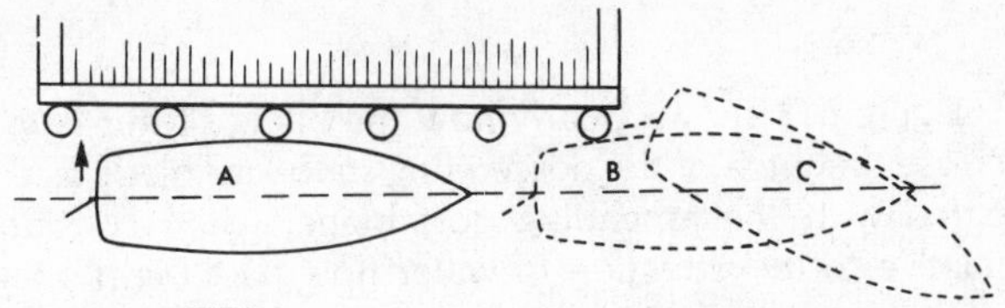

FIG. 816 With right rudder, as boat moves from A to B to C, stern is driven against piles, with risk of damage. Rudder should be amidships till boat is clear.

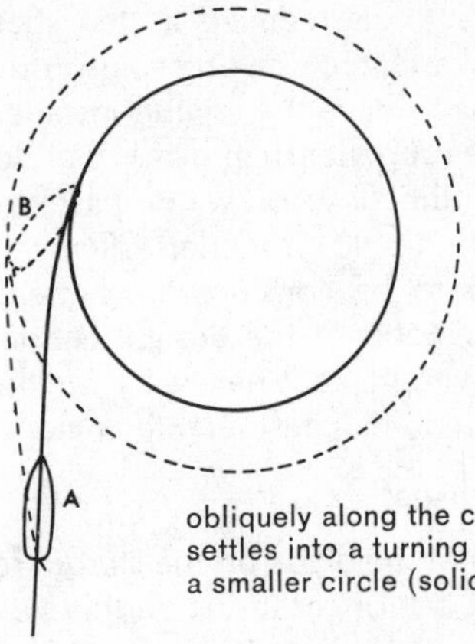

FIG. 817 When a boat's rudder is put over to make a turn, her stern is kicked away from the direction in which the rudder moves. Then, after sliding obliquely along the course (as shown from A to B) she settles into a turning circle in which the bow describes a smaller circle (solid line) than the stern (dotted line).

wind until the propeller is speeded up enough to exert a more powerful thrust against the offset rudder blade.

Here is a fundamental principle to remember in handling motor boats. In close quarters a motor boat can often be turned in a couple of boat lengths by judicious use of the power. If, for example, the rudder is set hard to starboard (that is, right rudder) while the boat has no headway and the throttle is suddenly opened, the stern can be kicked around to port before the boat has a chance to gather headway. The exact technique of turning in limited space will be described in detail further along.

KEEP STERN FREE TO MANEUVER

As soon as the boatman understands the underlying difference between the steering of a boat and a car, he will always be conscious of the need to keep the stern free to maneuver in close quarters. Furthermore, when he lies alongside a dock, a float or another boat, and wants to pull away, he will never, automobile-fashion, throw the wheel over until the stern is clear.

To set the rudder to starboard, for example, while lying port side to a dock and then attempt to pull away by going ahead, fig. 816, would only throw the port quarter against the dock piles and pin it there, to slam successively into one pile after the other as the boat moves ahead, with the

FIG. 818 A dramatic comparison of the turning circles of two boats at high speed. At "a" (left) the outdrive unit permits a tight turn in less than two boat lengths. At "b" (right) the inboard's propeller is fixed, and she responds only to rudder angle for steering.

FIG. 819 On inland waterways, boats may get into shoal water. This reduces the speed and also affects their handling qualities, response to the rudder being sluggish.

likelihood of doing damage.

Steering gears on motor boats are almost invariably rigged today so that they turn with the rudder, that is, turning the top of the wheel to port throws the rudder to port. Consequently, with the usual rig, the boat having headway, putting the wheel over to port gives her left rudder which kicks the stern to starboard so that the bow, in effect, moves to port. Conversely, turning the wheel to starboard gives her right rudder, throwing the stern to port so that the boat turns to starboard.

TURNING CIRCLES

When the boat has headway and the rudder is put over to make a turn (to starboard, let us say), the stern is first kicked to port and the boat then tends to slide off obliquely, "crab-wise." Due to its momentum through the water it will carry some distance along the original course before settling into a turn, in which the bow describes a smaller circle than the stern, fig. 817. The pivoting point about which she turns may be between one-fourth and one-third of the boat's length from the bow, varying with different boats and changing for any given boat with the trim.

The distance a vessel moves in the direction of her original course, after the helm has been put over, is called the *advance*.

While there is always a loss of speed in making a turn, the size of a boat's turning circle will vary but little with changes in speed, assuming a given rudder angle. Whether she makes it at slow speed or at wide open throttle, the actual diameter of the turn is about the same.

There is, however, a great difference in the size of turning circles for single-screw inboards as compared with outboards or inboard-outboards because, as has been noted, the shaft and propeller of the inboard are fixed on the center line and cannot be rotated. This is dramatically illustrated in fig. 818. The twin-screw inboard, on the other hand, provides excellent maneuverability, as will be seen later.

Stops are invariably put on a rudder to limit its maximum angle. Beyond that point an increase of rudder angle would result, not in a smaller turning circle, but a larger one. That's why Naval vessels usually have a maximum rudder angle of 35 degrees.

When the boat has sternway (reversing) the rudder normally would be turned to port (left rudder) to turn the stern of the boat to port, while right rudder should normally tend to turn the stern to starboard in backing. However, the subject cannot be dismissed as easily as that and we shall see later how, under certain circumstances, the effect of the reversing propeller may more than offset the steering effect of the rudder.

Just as the speed of a boat is cut down in shallow water, fig. 819, so the depth has an effect on a boat's steering. Even though the keel may not actually be touching the bottom, it will be noticed that the boat's response to rudder action in shallow water is almost always sluggish.

Response of Boat to Propeller and Rudder

Let us consider now a number of typical situations to see how the average inboard motor boat will respond to propeller and rudder action *(assuming a single-screw boat with right-hand propeller)*.

NO WAY ON, PROPELLER TURNING AHEAD

Picture her first without any way on, engine idling and rudder amidships. Being dead in the water there is no wake current to act on the propeller blades. Now the clutch is engaged and the propeller starts to turn ahead.

Until she gathers headway, the unequal blade thrust (refer back to fig. 813) tends to throw her stern to starboard. As she gets headway, wake current enters the picture, increasing pressure against the upper blades (remember wake current is strongest at the surface, has little effect at the bottom of the keel) and this tends to offset the effect of unequal blade thrust.

What happens under identical conditions, except that the rudder is hard over at the time the propeller is engaged? In this case the propeller's discharge current strikes the rudder and exerts its normal effect of kicking the stern to port with right rudder, or stern to starboard with left rudder. With right rudder the kick to port would be much stronger than the effect of unequal blade thrust.

WITH HEADWAY, PROPELLER GOING AHEAD

After the boat has gathered normal headway, with rudder amidships, the average boat tends to hold her course in a straight line fairly well. From a purely theoretical standpoint, the unequal blade thrust, with a right-hand wheel, should tend to move the stern to starboard, and bow to port. In most cases, however, this is a relatively unimportant consideration.

It is only in a comparatively few cases that the unequal thrust of the propeller blades has a pronounced effect.

Now, the boat having headway, assume the rudder is put to starboard. The water flowing past the hull hits the rudder on its starboard side, forcing the stern to port. The propeller's discharge current intensifies this effect by acting on the same side and the boat's bow turns to starboard, the same side on which the rudder is set. With rudder to port the action would naturally be just the opposite.

WITH HEADWAY, PROPELLER REVERSING

A boat has no brakes as does a car, so she depends on reversing the propeller to bring her to a stop. Assuming that the boat has headway, rudder amidships, and the propeller is reversed, the effect is to throw the stern to port as the boat loses headway. The rudder has no steering effect in this case, and unequal blade thrust of the propeller (which, remember, is reversing) tends to throw the stern to port. At the same time the propeller blades on the starboard side are throwing their discharge current in a powerful column forward against the starboard side of the keel and bottom of the boat, with nothing on the port side

to offset this pressure. The stern, of necessity, is thrown to port.

This principle explains why a boatman will bring his boat up to a landing port side to the dock, if he has a choice. The stern then is thrown in toward the dock by the reversing propeller instead of away from it.

With rudder to port

Going back now to the case where the boat has headway and the propeller is reversed—this time with rudder over to port, let us say. Here the situation is more complicated. As before, we have the unequal blade thrust and propeller discharge current both driving the stern to port.

In addition there are two opposing factors. If the boat has much way on (ahead) her left rudder tends to throw the stern to starboard. However, her propeller suction current is being drawn in from astern in such a manner that it strikes the back of the rudder blade, tending to drive the stern to port.

Which combination of factors will be strongest depends on the amount of headway the boat has, fig. 820. If she has been running at some speed, the steering effect of left rudder will probably be the dominant factor and her stern would be thrown to starboard at first. As this steering effect weakens with reduced headway, the propeller slowing her down, then the effect of the suction current is added to help the tendency of the stern to port until eventually, with all headway killed, even the steering tendency to starboard is lost and all factors combine to throw the stern to port.

NO WAY ON, PROPELLER REVERSING

Now if the boat is lying dead in the water with no headway, rudder amidships, and the propeller is reversed, we again have that strong tendency of the stern to port as the

FIG. 820 Factors governing a boat's response to propeller and rudder depend, in part, on the amount of headway she has. Here, in close quarters, the helmsman slows down and keeps his boat under control. Effect of wind must be considered.

discharge current strikes the starboard side of the hull. You see, in each of the cases where the discharge current of the reversing propeller is a factor, the strong current on the starboard side is directed generally toward the boat's bow but upward and inward in a spiral movement. The descending blade on the port side, on the other hand, tends to throw its stream downward at such an angle that its force is largely spent below the keel. Therefore, the two forces are never of equal effect.

Until the boat gathers sternway from her backing propeller it would not matter if the rudder were over to port or starboard. The discharge current against the starboard side is still the strong controlling factor and the stern is thrown to port. (Come back to this later when we discuss the matter of turning in a limited space.)

WITH STERNWAY, PROPELLER REVERSING

Now visualize the boat gathering sternway as the propeller continues to reverse. Here arises one of the seemingly mystifying conditions that baffle many a helmsman during his first trick at the wheel. The novice assumes that if he wants to back in a straight line his rudder must be amidships, just as it must be when he goes ahead on a straight course. Under certain conditions his boat may even respond to *right* rudder as he reverses by going to *port*, which is exactly what he doesn't expect, and if he is learning by trial-and-error he comes to the conclusion that it depends on the boat's fancy, while rudder position has nothing to do with control.

Let's analyze the situation, however, to see if he's right and whether there is anything that can be done about it. Fortunately, there is.

Backing with left rudder

At the outset we can rule out any effect of wake current as that force now is spent at the bow. Considering first the most obvious case, let's assume we have left rudder. Here there are four factors all working together to throw the stern to port. Unequal blade thrust is pushing the stern to port; the discharge current of the propeller is adding its powerful effect; and now we add the steering effect of the rudder acting on the aft side of the rudder blade, against which the suction current of the propeller is also working.

Remember this condition well for it is the answer to why *practically every single-screw vessel with right-hand propeller naturally backs to port* easily when she may be obstinate about going to starboard when reversing, fig. 821.

Backing with rudder amidships

Now, while backing to port, let's bring the rudder amidships and see what happens. Here we have eliminated the effects of suction current and steering from the rudder, leaving unequal blade thrust and the discharge current to continue forcing the stern to port.

Backing with right rudder

Assuming further that we have not yet gathered much sternway, let's put the rudder to starboard and see if we can't possibly make the boat back to starboard as you might expect she should with right rudder. The forces of unequal blade thrust and discharge current still tend to drive her stern to port, but the suction current of the pro-

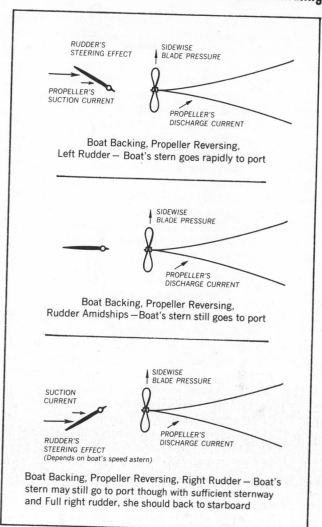

Boat Backing, Propeller Reversing, Left Rudder — Boat's stern goes rapidly to port

Boat Backing, Propeller Reversing, Rudder Amidships — Boat's stern still goes to port

Boat Backing, Propeller Reversing, Right Rudder — Boat's stern may still go to port though with sufficient sternway and Full right rudder, she should back to starboard

FIG. 821 Three different situations where a boat is backing, her propeller reversing, with rudder set in various positions. Some boats back to port no matter how the rudder is set, but usually with right rudder and good sternway, they can be turned to starboard, though the turn to port is much better.

peller wants to offset this. The effect of the discharge current is stronger than the suction so the tendency is still to port. Now, with sternway, the steering effect of right rudder is to starboard, but as yet we haven't way enough to make this offset the stronger factors.

STEERING WHILE BACKING

Just about the time we are about to give it up on the assumption that she can't be made to back to starboard, we try opening the throttle to gain more sternway. This finally has the desired effect and with full right rudder we find that the steering effect at considerable backing speed is enough (probably) to turn her stern to starboard against all the opposing forces. How well she will back to starboard—in fact, whether she will or not—depends on the design.

All of this means that if the boat will back to starboard with full right rudder, she may also be made to go in a straight line—but not with rudder amidships. There's no use trying. She will need a certain amount of right rudder depending both on her design and the speed. Some boats, while their backing to port is always much better than to starboard, can be controlled with a reasonable degree of precision by one who understands the particular boat he is handling.

In cases, boats may even be steered backwards out of crooked slips or channels—not, however, without a lot of backing and filling if there is much wind to complicate the situation. Generally the trick is to keep the boat under control, making the turns no greater than necessary so as to prevent the boat from swinging too much as a result of momentum and making it correspondingly difficult to get her straightened out again.

In maneuvers of this kind it is best to set the rudder first and then get added maneuvering power by speeding up the propeller in the desired direction, instead of trying to swing the rudder after the propeller is turning fast either ahead or astern.

WITH STERNWAY, PROPELLER TURNING AHEAD

There is one other situation to be considered, where we wish to kill our sternway by engaging the propeller to turn ahead. Regardless of rudder position, unequal blade thrust with the propeller going ahead now tends to throw the stern to starboard while the suction current is of no consequence. Unequal blade thrust may or may not be offset by the steering effect and the discharge current.

With rudder amidships, there is no steering effect and the discharge current does not enter our calculations. Therefore the stern will go to starboard. Now if you throw the rudder to port the discharge current of the propeller hits the rudder and drives the stern to starboard—even though the normal steering effect of left rudder would be to send the stern to port, with sternway. The powerful discharge current from the propeller going ahead is the determining factor.

If the rudder is put to starboard, the steering effect works with the unequal blade thrust tending to move the stern to starboard but the discharge current strikes the starboard side of the rudder and acts to kick the stern to port. Application of enough power so that the force of the discharge current outweighs the other factors will result in the stern's going to port.

PROPELLER ACTION GOVERNS

From this analysis it will be seen that in a single-screw inboard boat one must constantly keep in mind what the propeller is doing in order to know how to use the rudder to best advantage. What the propeller is doing is even more important than whether the boat at the time may have headway or sternway.

To cite an example to make this clear, let's suppose you are backing in a direction that brings your port quarter up toward a dock. The tendency if you were to try to steer away from it would be to use right rudder. But the efficacy of that would be doubtful, because of the boat's inclination to back to port.

Therefore, we plan to kick the stern away by going ahead with the propeller so we set the rudder to port (left rudder, *toward* the dock), throw the reverse gear lever into the forward position and go ahead strong with the engine. The discharge current checks the sternway and, striking the rudder, throws the stern to starboard, clear of the dock.

It takes a lot of experience with any given boat to learn all her whims and traits—to know her strong points and use them wisely to overcome the weak ones. But boats, like individuals, do respond to understanding treatment.

Practice at the helm

Proficiency in motor boat handling is a matter of 10 percent principles, 90 percent application of these principles in practice. Therefore, the sooner we get afloat and start experimenting, the better. We've absorbed enough of the theory to have a broad idea of what to expect in practice; the next step is to get at the helm of a boat and actually learn by doing.

POINTS TO REMEMBER

Here are a few basic ideas to keep in mind, summarized from what has gone before.
• Remember that *the boat is always under better control with headway* than when she has sternway, because of the effect of the propeller's discharge current on the rudder when steering.
• Until the boat has gathered headway the stern has a tendency to swing (to starboard, with right-hand propeller) even with rudder amidships, as the propeller starts to turn ahead. *With good headway, rudder angle is the principal factor affecting control.*

• *Backing, there is a strong tendency to go to port* regardless of rudder angle, except (ordinarily) with full right rudder and considerable sternway. To back in a straight line you need a certain amount of right rudder varying, probably, with the speed.
• *With no way on there is no rudder control,* yet the stern can be kicked rapidly to port or starboard by putting the rudder over and applying plenty of power before the boat has a chance to gather way.
• *With left-hand propeller, the boat's reaction will be contrary to that outlined for the right-hand propeller.*

THE FIRST TIME OUT

The first step in applying these principles will be to take the boat out in open water—preferably on a day when there is little wind and no current. These factors should be ruled out at first and studied separately later, after the boat's normal reactions are fully understood.

With unlimited room to maneuver and no traffic to worry about, try putting the boat through all the maneuvers already discussed. Practice with every combination of

FIG. 822 In channels like this, speed must be held down to avoid damage to other craft and discomfort to their passengers. A boat is liable for damage caused by her wake.

conditions—with headway, sternway, and no way on; with right-rudder, left rudder and rudder amidships; with propeller turning in the direction of the boat's way, and also those cases where the propeller is turning opposite to the direction of the boat's way.

In each of these maneuvers note whether the rudder or propeller has the greater effect; note, too, how changing the speed alters the boat's response. Put the rudder hard over each way and see what happens when considerable power is applied before the boat has any way on.

Practice turns to determine the size of the boat's turning circle and the space required to bring the boat to a full stop with varying amounts of way, up to full speed.

GAINING EXPERIENCE

Later, when these fundamentals are mastered, go out again and observe how wind and current and sea alter the situation. Note how she tends to back into the wind until good steerageway is reached. How, if she is lying in the trough in a seaway, she tends to stay there with rudder amidships, because wave action is stronger than her natural tendency in smooth water to back to port.

Watch too how her stern starts to settle, and the bow comes up, when you get into shoal water. If there's just enough water to permit her to run without grounding, a wave will pile up on her quarter, steepest on the shallower side, as the natural formation of the wake is disturbed.

You should, of course, pick your maneuvering grounds from the chart to avoid danger of grounding, but if you see the first wave of your wake stretching away on the quarter in a sharp inverted V, tending to break at the top, beware of shoal water on that side.

GETTING UNDER WAY

Whenever you are about to get under way, assuming that you are starting a cold motor, don't spend too much time at the dock or mooring "warming up." There are a few things to check before getting under way and by the time these have been taken care of you will be ready to cast off and let the warming up of the motor be accomplished under load, at about half speed. Long periods of idling are bad for the clutch and the motor will warm up

better and quicker with the propeller engaged.

Before casting off, check the oil pressure and see that the cooling water is circulating. In most all marine installations sea water is circulated through the engine water jackets. Leaving the jackets, part or all of this water goes into the exhaust to be discharged overboard. Until this water flows from the exhaust pipe it is unsafe to get under way.

If the water doesn't circulate, investigate at once as overheating can cause much damage, especially if the cold water is suddenly picked up and pumped into the hot cylinder block. Cracking of the casting might result.

Never race the motor as it idles, especially when cold. If the propeller is the right size and the throttle stop properly set, the motor should be able to take the propeller when the clutch is engaged at idling speeds. Boats don't require transmissions with a change of speeds as in cars, because the propeller slip automatically takes care of picking up the load gradually as the clutch is engaged.

After the clutch is in, the throttle (which almost invariably is hand-operated) can be opened gradually. Roughly speaking, normal cruising should be done at about two-thirds or three-quarters throttle. The extra few hundred revolutions available at wide open throttle seldom yield an increase in speed proportionate to the extra power required and the corresponding increase in fuel consumption. In congested waterways speed should be moderate, taking care that no damage is done by the wake, fig. 822.

One caution to observe when first learning to maneuver the boat is to avoid operating at too high a speed. Later, after you have become more familiar with the boat and its response to wheel and throttle, you will be able to use more power in certain situations—to accomplish a quick turn, for example—without getting into a jam.

CHECKING HEADWAY

Before attempting the maneuver of picking up a mooring you will want to experiment with the technique of checking the boat's headway while she is out in open water. Having no brakes, you must reverse the propeller to bring the boat to a stop. In by-gone days when many boats had no reverse gears the engine itself had to be stopped, permitting the boat to coast up to a landing, and it was often quite a trick to estimate exactly when the ignition should be cut. Reverse gears make the problem relatively simple.

Your experiments will show how effective the propeller is in killing the boat's headway. Generally speaking the larger diameter propellers, acting on a large volume of water, will exert the greatest effect. Small propellers, poorly matched to heavy hulls, may churn up much water before they are able to overcome the boat's momentum.

Many fast boats can be stopped in an incredibly short distance. When their throttles are closed, the boat changes her trim suddenly and headway is quickly lost, even before the propellers are reversed.

Whenever it is necessary to go from forward into reverse or vice versa, close the throttle to slow the engine down while going through neutral. If you make a practice of cracking the reverse gear from full ahead to full astern, look out for trouble. This is hard on the gear even if it doesn't fail—which it might do just when you're counting on it most.

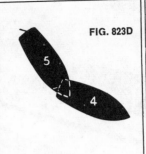
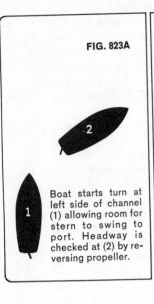
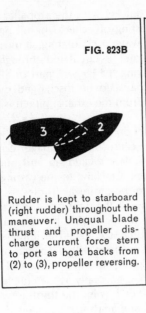

FIG. 823A

Boat starts turn at left side of channel (1) allowing room for stern to swing to port. Headway is checked at (2) by reversing propeller.

FIG. 823B

Rudder is kept to starboard (right rudder) throughout the maneuver. Unequal blade thrust and propeller discharge current force stern to port as boat backs from (2) to (3), propeller reversing.

FIG. 823C

Going ahead again, sternway is checked at (3) and propeller turning ahead kicks stern to port as shown at (4) before the boat has had a chance to gather headway.

FIG. 823D

Reversing once more, headway is checked at (4) and boat backs to (5). If necessary, alternate going ahead and backing can be repeated. Space available for the turn governs this. Turning in two boat lengths is easy.

FIG. 823E

At (5) boat is in a position to go ahead with right rudder, bringing it amidships at (6), where she is ready to proceed, having reversed her course 180° from her original position at (1).

TURNING IN CLOSE QUARTERS

Turning a boat in a waterway not much wider than the boat's length often seems a bugbear to the novice but, once he has mastered the technique, it's no more difficult than turning a car on a narrow road.

Take a look at fig. 823. The situation sketched might apply in many cases. Perhaps you've run to the head of a dead-end canal and must turn around. Or possibly the waterway is a narrow channel, flanked by shoals. In the former case you must allow room so the swinging stern doesn't hit the canal bulkhead; in the latter, a similar allowance must be made to avoid throwing the stern up on shoal water.

Referring to fig. 823A, we start at (1), on the left side of the channel, running at slow speed. Putting the rudder hard over to starboard, the boat swings toward position (2), her headway being checked by reversing. *Always* execute this maneuver (if the propeller is right-handed) by going ahead to starboard, backing to port, to take advantage of the boat's natural tendency, as explained before.

Now (see 823B) *leave the wheel hard over to starboard* (right rudder). Normally you would expect to use left rudder in backing from (2) to (3), but this is unnecessary as the boat has no chance to gather sternway. As the reversing propeller stops the boat at (2), open the throttle for an instant and the stern will be kicked around to port to position (3).

Any attempt to shift from right rudder while going ahead to left rudder while going astern only results in extra gymnastics at the wheel at a time when you want your hands free for the throttle and reverse gear lever.

Throttling while we engage the clutch to go ahead, the sternway is checked at (3). Opening the throttle again, just for an instant, keeps the stern swinging to port toward position (4)—see fig. 823C. Now the operation described in 823B is repeated, backing from position (4) to (5) as shown in 823D.

If this happens to be a bulkheaded slip you are maneuvering in, allow plenty of room so that the port quarter is not thrown against the head of the slip as you go ahead

again at (5)—see 823E. The stern will continue to swing to port as the boat straightens away toward (6). At this point the rudder can be brought amidships, the boat having executed a 180-degree turn.

Backing around a turn

Fig. 824 illustrates the successive steps required to work out another practical problem in boat handling. Suppose (see 824A) you are in a narrow slip or canal at position (1) and want to back around a sharp turn, to starboard.

Reversing with full right rudder, you will not be able to turn short enough to steer around the 90-degree angle. Most likely you will back to a position about as indicated at (2), gaining a little to starboard. Now (see 824B) by going ahead with left rudder the stern is kicked over to starboard, placing the boat at (3).

Reversing once more, with full right rudder, the boat backs to (4), necessitating our going ahead once more with left rudder. This puts the boat at (5) (824D) in a position to back down on the new course.

Note that if she is expected to back down in a straight line from (5) she will need right rudder, though not necessarily hard over.

Backing to port from a slip

Fig. 825 illustrates a variation of the maneuver just described. Suppose the boat is lying in a slip, at A, and wishes to back out into the channel, space being limited. Fig. 824 showed how it would be necessary to work her around if the turn were to starboard. In fig. 825 her problem would be exactly the same if she had to back around in the direction of C.

However, if there is a choice, and she can back out to port, the probability is that with left rudder she will work around from A to B without any special maneuvering. To do it, her initial position in the slip must be about as shown at A with some clearance on her port side, but considerably more on the starboard side.

Clearance on the port side is needed because in reversing her stern immediately starts to move to port. More clearance on the starboard side is necessary because the

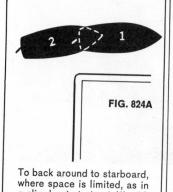

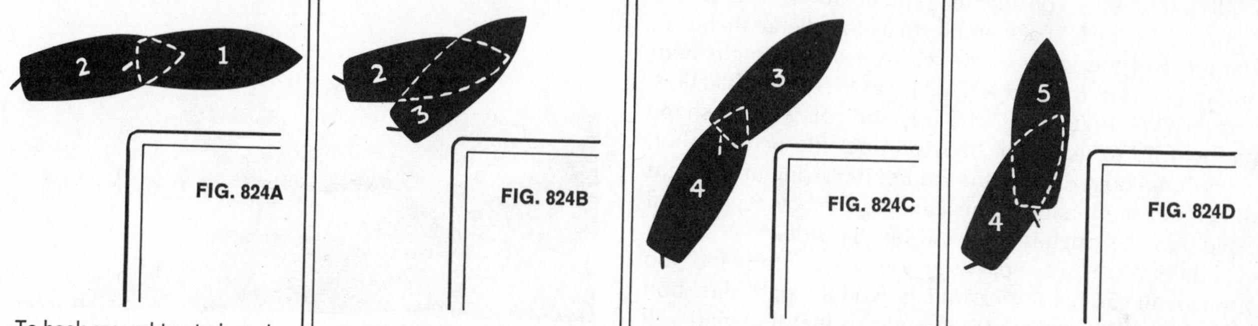

FIG. 824A

To back around to starboard, where space is limited, as in a slip, boat starts at (1) with right rudder, and backs to (2). She cannot turn short to starboard.

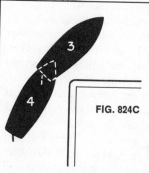

FIG. 824B

At (2) rudder is shifted to port and, with full left rudder, stern is kicked around to starboard by going ahead strong for a few revolutions of the propeller.

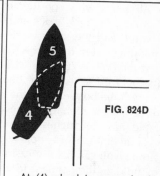

FIG. 824C

From position (3) boat can be backed down to (4) by reversing with full right rudder. Boat may back nearly in a straight line or gain a little to starboard.

FIG. 824D

At (4) wheel is swung hard over again, to give left rudder, while propeller, turning ahead, moves boat to (5). Backing down from (5) she will need right rudder to hold a straight course.

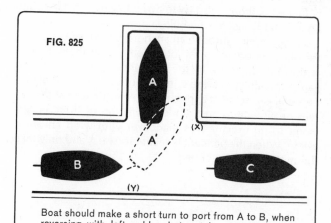

FIG. 825

Boat should make a short turn to port from A to B, when reversing with left rudder, but watch points X and Y.

bow will swing over toward point (x) as she backs.

In fact, points (x) and (y) are the ones to watch in executing this maneuver. If the boat shouldn't turn as short as expected, and doesn't swing directly from A to B, but takes a position as shown by the dotted lines at A', the starboard bow is in danger of touching at (x) and the starboard quarter at (y). This could be corrected at A' by going ahead with the propeller a few revolutions, using right rudder, to kick the stern over to port. This must be done carefully as there is no latitude here for much headway.

Having straightened her up, you could then back with left rudder to B and finally square away with rudder amidships to proceed toward C.

LEAVING A MOORING

For permanent berths, boats lie either at docks or moorings. Most yacht clubs have anchorages for members' boats, using mushroom anchors and mooring buoys to which the boat is secured by a pennant or mooring line over the forward bitt.

Getting away from the mooring when you are about to start a cruise is among the simplest of maneuvers, yet there is a right and a wrong way to go about it. The principal hazard in doing it wrong is the possibility of getting either the mooring line or dinghy painter fouled in the propeller. Handling of the boat is dictated by whatever is necessary

to accomplish this with a minimum of fuss.

As soon as the motor is running, shorten up the dinghy painter so that the reversing propeller cannot pull any slack down into it, to be hopelessly fouled around the shaft and wheel. See that any boarding ladders, fenders or boat booms are aboard and send a man forward to let the mooring line go. The pennant usually has a small block of wood or metal buoy to float the end, making it easy to pick up again on return to the mooring.

In a river or stream where there is a current, the boat will lie head to that current (unless the wind is stronger). But in a bay on a calm day there may be neither wind nor current to move the boat even when the mooring line is let go. To go ahead under such conditions would almost certainly result in fouling the propeller.

To avoid this, back away a few boat lengths, far enough so you can keep the buoy in sight and allow sufficient room to clear it when you go ahead, with particular regard for any swinging of the stern. Whether you back away straight or turn as you reverse depends largely on the position of neighboring boats in the anchorage.

Until you are clear of the anchorage, run well throttled so as not to create a nuisance with your wake. Then, as you open up to cruising speed, the dinghy can be dropped back near the crest of the second wave astern. If she is astern of that crest, she will tow too hard, running "uphill" with bow too high. Shorten the painter from this point until the pull on it lessens as she flattens out to a better trim, but don't have her run "down-hill" either, if there is any tendency for her to yaw off the course. Exactly how you trim the dinghy by the length of the painter will depend largely on boat speed and sea conditions, fig. 826.

When there is wind or current

When your mooring is in a stream or if a tidal current flows past it, the boat will be set back when the mooring line has been let go. This usually simplifies the problem of getting away; reversing may not be necessary.

In a wind (assuming the current is not stronger) the boat will be lying head to the wind. As she drops back from the mooring, whether or not the reverse gear is used, the bow will pay off to one side and shape the boat up to get away without additional maneuvering.

All boats with considerable freeboard have a strong tendency to "tack" back and forth as they lie at anchor in a wind, and the same is true to an extent at permanent moorings unless the gear is so heavy as to retard this action.

If the bow is "tacking" this way and you want to shape the boat up to leave the buoy on one side or the other, wait till the boat reaches the limit of her swing in the right direction and then let the pennant go. The bow will pay off rapidly as she catches the wind on that side.

Sometimes, if the boat isn't too big or the wind too strong, you can help to cast the bow in the right direction by holding the pennant to one side so that the wind will catch that side and cause her to pay off toward the other.

PICKING UP A MOORING

Returning to the anchorage when the cruise is finished, approach your mooring at slow speed, noting carefully how other boats are lying at their buoys. They are heading into the wind or current (whichever is stronger) and your course in approaching the buoy should be roughly parallel to the way they align up-wind or against the current. Shorten the dinghy painter as necessary.

Now slip the clutch into neutral when you estimate that you have just way enough to carry you up to the buoy. A man should be stationed on the bow with a boathook to pick up the pennant float when it comes within reach. If you see that you are about to overshoot the mark, reverse enough to check the headway as the bow comes up to the buoy. If you fall short, a few extra kicks ahead with the propeller should suffice.

FIG. 826   Length of the dinghy painter will determine how well she tows.

Don't expect the man forward to do the work that the engine should accomplish in holding the boat in position until the signal is given that the pennant eye has been secured on the bitt. Watch especially that the boat doesn't tend to drop astern while the man forward tries to hang on with the boathook. Also try to avoid having the buoy chafe unnecessarily against the hull.

When running through an anchorage keep an eye peeled for other moorings so as not to foul or cut them. If yours is the only mooring in the anchorage, you will have to gauge the effect of wind and current on your own boat as best you can so as to approach up-wind or against the current or directly against any combination of these factors. Don't try to execute this maneuver with wind abeam or astern. When the pennant is secure forward, and only then, the motor can be stopped.

Landing at a Dock

The knowledge you have already acquired in turning a boat where space for maneuvering is limited will stand you in good stead when you tackle the next problem of bringing her in neatly to a dock or float.

The factors involved here are, in part, the same as in coming to a mooring, with certain modifications. For example, when you pick up a mooring you have wind and current to consider, generally determining the angle of your approach. Wind and current must also be reckoned with at docks, but there are many occasions when the angle of approach to a dock is not a matter of choice.

With no wind or current to complicate the situation, landing, with a right-handed propeller, can be accomplished most effectively by bringing the boat in port side to the dock. Our previous analysis of propeller action when reversing makes the reason for this clear.

Keep boat under control

Don't come in with a grand flourish at high speed but throttle down gradually to keep the boat under control, fig. 827. When you see that you have way enough to reach the dock, slip the clutch into neutral and use the reverse gear as and when necessary to check headway as the boat goes into her berth.

If your speed has been properly estimated you will be several boat lengths from the dock when the clutch is thrown into neutral. Coming in at too high a speed you will be forced to go into neutral a long way from the dock (losing maneuverability with the propeller disengaged) or face the alternative of trusting the reverse gear to check excessive headway.

This is a good time to exercise judgment, keeping the way necessary for good maneuverability, yet using no more

FIG. 827   This boat, properly, is being maneuvered near her berth at slow speed.

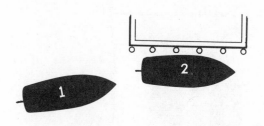

FIG. 828 When landing port side to a dock, approach at an angle of 10 to 20 degrees as shown. Discharge current of the reversing propeller (if R.H.) will set the stern to port, as at (2), even though rudder is amidships.

than required. Remember that just because a destroyer does her maneuvering at 15 knots it doesn't follow that it would be good seamanship to do the same with a little cruiser where 15 knots represents her maximum speed.

As the reversing propeller throws its discharge current against the starboard side aft, the stern is carried to port. For this reason it is customary to approach, not exactly parallel with the dock, but at a slight angle—say 10 to 20 degrees. Then as she comes up to the dock her stern will be brought alongside, fig. 828, with the boat parallel to the dock, properly berthed.

In docking, lines should be kept ready to run fore and aft and fenders placed if necessary to keep the boat from chafing against unprotected piles.

WIND OR CURRENT PARALLEL TO DOCK

When the dock happens to be on the shore of a river or bank of a tidal stream so that the current flows parallel to it, it is best to govern the direction of approach by the current flow, even though this puts the starboard side toward the dock. Heading into the current will enable you to keep the propeller turning over slowly—right up to the moment of reaching the dock, if the current is strong enough.

The same is true if wind is the force you are opposing. If your course puts the wind over the stern you will have to make a wide swing, starting far enough from the dock to permit you to round up to leeward of it, coming in against the wind. To miscalculate here by not allowing room enough for the turn would be embarrassing, as you head for the bank with wind or current sweeping you downstream. Hence the importance of preliminary practice in open water, noting the size of turning circles under various conditions, before attempting the actual docking maneuvers.

In starting a turn like this, even at some distance from the dock, it will be necessary to throttle down long before the dock comes abeam. Otherwise the wash the boat throws may carry along and leave you wallowing in your own wake just when you're trying to come alongside.

In coming up against wind or current, you use that force to check your headway, instead of the reverse. Therefore, allowance usually need not be made for the effect of a reversing propeller.

LANDINGS DOWN-WIND OR WITH CURRENT

Avoid, if you can, the landing in which wind or current is setting you down towards the dock in the direction of

your course. In cases of this kind you are dependent on your reverse gear and even though they are practically 100 percent dependable an error in judgment or minor motor ailment would put you on the spot.

However, you will meet such situations, where space does not permit a turn before docking. For example, suppose you are coming in to a canal lock with a strong wind astern. Hold the speed down to a minimum consistent with adequate control and by all means take the port side of the lock, unless there is no choice.

Plan to get a line out from the stern or port quarter as soon as headway is checked. If necessary, the boat would lie well enough temporarily to this line alone, whereas to get a bow line fast first and then miss making the stern line fast would be to risk being turned end-for-end by the wind. This has happened repeatedly to inexperienced boatmen on their first cruise through canals, to the embarrassment of other boats already berthed along the lock walls.

Handling the lines

If you have a couple of hands aboard, assign one to the bow and one to the stern to handle lines, with instructions not to make fast until headway is checked. The seriousness of checking the boat's way by means of a snubbed bow line instead of reversing the propeller is only too obvious. If single-handed, you will have to work smartly, with a stern line fast to the after bitt coiled ready to carry ashore, and a bow line, preferably run in advance along the deck back to the cockpit. Such lines of course would have to be led outboard of all stanchions, to be clear when taken ashore.

The problem is no different if you are making your landing with a fair current. In either case you must be ready with the reverse on the approach, using it as strongly as necessary to hold the boat against its momentum and the push of wind or current. The propeller ordinarily should be turning over slowly in reverse for the last boat length or two of headway, the throttle being opened gradually and as needed to kill all headway at the right instant.

WHEN BOATS LIE AHEAD AND ASTERN

Let's vary the problem by assuming that boats are already lying at the dock, leaving you little more than a boat length to squeeze into your berth. The technique is decidedly not the one you are accustomed to in parking a car at a curb.

Referring to fig. 829, boats A and B are already in their berths astern and ahead, respectively, of the berth we, in

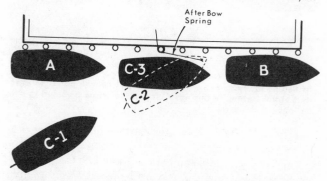

FIG. 829 Landing at a dock between boats (A) and (B), C approaches at an angle. At (C-2), a spring line is run aft to dock from forward bitt. Going ahead with propeller and right rudder, boat swings into berth at (C-3).

boat C, want to slip into. The position of boat A necessitates our going in at a greater angle than if the dock were clear, and there is no room to go either ahead or astern once we have nosed up to position C-2.

Consequently a man is stationed forward to take a line (in this case technically called an after bow spring) leading aft from the forward bitt to a pile or bollard on the dock. He takes a turn around the pile and holds fast while we go ahead with the propeller, setting the rudder to starboard. The spring prevents the boat from going ahead and the stern is thrown in toward the dock until she assumes her final position against the dock, as at C-3.

As the boat swings in, the spring must be slacked off a little and often a fender or two will be necessary at the point of contact.

USING WIND OR CURRENT

In a case such as that covered by fig. 829, with conditions the same except for a wind from the south (assume boats A and B are headed east) we could have used the wind to advantage in bringing the boat in.

Under such conditions the boat could be brought up parallel to her final position at C-3, allowing the wind to set her in to her berth at the dock. The bow, probably, would come in faster than the stern, but this would not matter.

During this maneuver, the engine would be idling and, if there were any tendency for the boat to go ahead or astern, it could be offset by a turn or two of the propeller as needed, to maintain her position midway between A and B.

Balancing current against propeller action

A variation of this problem is sketched in fig. 830, where a current is flowing east. Here the boat is brought up to a position C-1 parallel to her berth at C-2. The propeller will have to be turning over very slowly in reverse (perhaps at the engine's idling speed) to hold her at C-1 against the current.

Now if the rudder is turned slightly to port the boat will tend to move bodily in toward the dock, though the stern is likely to come in first. An after quarter spring should be

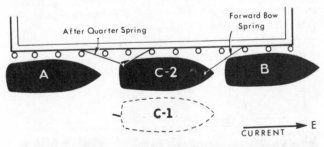

FIG. 830 The boat can be worked into her berth, using the current, by setting the rudder to port and using just enough power to offset drift of the current. In this case, propeller must be reversed to hold her against the current.

run first, to hold the boat against the current as the propeller stops turning.

Only enough rudder and power should be used to work the boat slowly sidewise. Too much power will put her out of control and too much rudder may cause her stern to go to port too fast, permitting the current to act on the boat's starboard side.

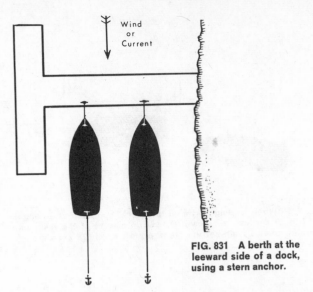

FIG. 831 A berth at the leeward side of a dock, using a stern anchor.

Under identical conditions, except for a current setting west instead of east, the propeller would be allowed to turn slowly ahead, just enough to hold the boat against the current. Then, with rudder slightly to port, the boat would edge off sidewise to port, the bow coming in slightly ahead of the stern. The forward bow spring would be the first of the mooring lines to make fast in this case.

LANDING ON THE LEEWARD SIDE

Sometimes you will run into situations where a pier juts out into the water, with wind blowing at right angles to it, giving you a choice of sides on which to land. If there is much wind and sea, the windward side can be uncomfortable as the boat will pound against the piles.

The rougher it is, the more important it becomes to take the leeward side. The wind will then hold her clear, at the length of her mooring lines. If there is much wind you will have to work smartly when bringing the boat up to such a berth and it will help to have men ready at both bow and stern to run the mooring lines.

Bow line first

The bow line of course must be run first and made fast. The stern line may present more of a problem since the boat has had to approach at an angle to allow for the wind's tendency to blow the bow off. The stern line can be heaved ashore by the man aft to the other on the dock, after the latter has made his bow line fast. The bow line, if necessary, can be used as a spring to bring the stern in by going ahead with rudder to starboard, on the principle sketched in fig. 829.

This maneuver, single-handed, would be difficult. It could be accomplished by getting a bow line off to use as a spring, working the stern up to the dock with the power, and lashing the wheel (unless you have a worm-and-gear steerer) to keep the rudder to starboard while you get a stern line fast.

Often it is a question of just how smartly the boatman works as to how much maneuvering he must go through. If he knows his boat and his crew know their job, he probably will get his lines ashore fast enough so that the spring line may not be needed to get the stern in.

STERN ANCHOR TO LEEWARD

Fig. 831 illustrates a method by which boats often line up at a dock beam to beam. Each has a secure berth on the leeward side of the dock and a maximum number of

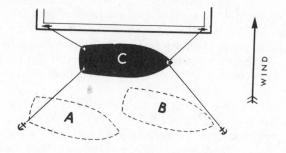

FIG. 832 Laying anchors to windward from the bow and quarter to keep a boat from pounding on the windward side of a dock.

boats are accommodated for a given amount of dock space. The principal objection is the difficulty of stepping ashore from the bow.

The arrangement shown makes a snug berth even in a hard blow but a shift of wind might necessitate a shift of berth if the wind came abeam, throwing a heavy strain on the stern line and anchor.

The principle of getting into a berth like this is obvious from the sketch. Simply run up against the wind or current, propeller turning over just fast enough to give steerageway, and have a man let the anchor go over the stern, paying out line until the bow is close enough to get a line on the dock. The stern line is available as a check though the helmsman should make it his business to bring the bow up as required without over-shooting his mark and hitting the dock.

After passengers have been discharged the bow line can be slacked and the stern anchor line shortened, though this means that one person must be aboard. If all are to go ashore, adjust the stern line so that it just checks the boat from touching the dock. Then if there is room, carry the bow line off at an angle to another pile. This increases the clearance at the bow, and the wind or current acting on one side will help to hold her clear.

The sketch is not to scale. Often the scope of the anchor line astern will need to be much greater than that indicated to provide holding power in a given depth. Seven times the depth of water is a rough-and-ready rule to determine the scope of anchor lines though this is qualified by dozens of factors.

USING ANCHORS TO WINDWARD

If you see that a berth on the windward side of a dock is inevitable and there is reason to believe that the hull will suffer even with fenders strategically placed, plan in advance to get anchors out to windward. This trick is not used nearly as often as it should be, especially if the boat is to occupy such a berth for a considerable time.

You will need a man on the bow and another on the stern to handle anchor lines, though in a pinch the helmsman can handle the stern line if he takes every precaution to keep slack lines from fouling the propeller. Referring to fig. 832, the stern anchor is let go from the quarter when the boat is at A, moving slowly ahead, to be checked at B, when the man forward lets his anchor go. If someone is tending the line aft, the helmsman can back a little as necessary to place the boat as the wind carries her down to her berth at C.

Tend lines carefully

On the other hand, if the helmsman must leave his wheel and tend the stern line, then the boat can be jockeyed into position merely by adjusting the length of the various lines. This probably will necessitate hauling in some of the stern line while the bow line is slacked away. Throughout, the lines should be carefully tended. Dock lines can be run from the port bow and quarter.

Note that at A and B the boat is not parallel to the dock, but has been headed up somewhat into the wind. As she drifts in, after the engine is put in neutral at B, the bow will come in faster than the stern.

This plan should be used with a full understanding of the great strain the anchor lines are carrying with the wind hitting the boat abeam, especially if there is some sea running as well. The stronger the wind and the rougher the sea, the longer the scope required if the anchors are to hold without dragging.

If you plan to land on the windward side of the dock without using anchors to hold her off, make due allowance for leeway on the approach and keep the bow somewhat up to windward if possible, checking headway while abreast of the berth you will occupy. Then have fenders handy as she drifts in.

WHEN CURRENT SETS TOWARD DOCK

Let's suppose now a situation in which the boat must find a berth off a dock in such a position that the current will be flowing from the boat toward the dock, fig. 833.

In this hypothetical case it may be assumed that the outside of the dock, which ordinarily would be the natural choice for landing, must be kept clear for ferries, perhaps, or other boats, while the lower side of the dock is also restricted for some reason. The only remaining berth is above it, at A in the illustration.

This situation should be sized up to determine exactly where the anchor is to be let go, with certainty that you will have sufficient scope. If your anchor drags here, you will be in a bad spot as the current will set the boat down on the dock. Therefore make sure that the anchor really gets a bite.

The spot where the anchor is to be let go may be approached from any direction as long as the boat is rounded up into the current. The procedure, if we wish to land bow to the dock with a stern anchor out, has already been outlined in fig. 831. This, however, is not feasible above the dock because of the difficulty of backing away into the current when leaving.

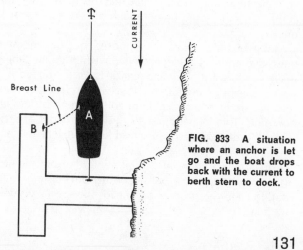

FIG. 833 A situation where an anchor is let go and the boat drops back with the current to berth stern to dock.

Tending scope of anchor line

After the anchor has been let go, the boat can be dropped back toward her berth at A, simply by paying out more scope on the anchor line. The current will do the work though the engine could be used to help control the

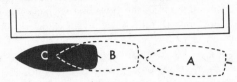

FIG. 834 Making a landing with starboard side of the boat toward the dock. Approaching slowly at (A), nearly parallel with the dock, rudder is shifted to full left at (B), swinging stern to starboard. At this point, give the boat a kick ahead with the propeller (if necessary) to swing the stern. Then reverse to check headway.

FIG. 835 A forward bow spring restrains this boat from moving astern. Clearance at her stern may be limited.

boat's position if wind tended to throw her out of line.

Just before the stern reaches the dock, a stern line can be made fast to a pile, after which the boat's position can be adjusted by the lines as desired. If the anchor is holding securely (and the berth should be left if it isn't) the stern can be brought close enough to the dock for passengers to step comfortably ashore.

The boat should not be left unattended in this position as she may safely be if berthed as in fig. 831. In fig. 833, where a convenient wing of the dock is available alongside the boat, a breast line could be run as shown. Then, before leaving the boat, the anchor line could be shortened to give ample clearance at the stern. Slacking the stern line would permit stepping ashore at B, after which the stern line could be adjusted from the dock.

The breast line is left slack but is available to haul the boat back in to B when boarding again after slacking the stern line. If the breast line is made fast too far aft it would be difficult to haul the stern in because of the "tacking" action of the boat in the current. Made fast forward of amidships, the boat will come in readily.

LANDING STARBOARD SIDE TO DOCK

Though a dock on the port side is preferable, as already explained, a good landing at a dock on the starboard side can be made, if care is exercised.

Referring to fig. 834, the boat is approaching the dock at (A), nearly parallel to it, engine idling or turning over just enough to insure control.

Just before it is necessary to reverse to check the headway, the rudder is shifted to full left (at B) to swing the stern in toward the dock. If she does not respond, give the propeller a kick ahead while the rudder is full left. This definitely kicks the stern in and, as she swings, the reverse can be used to kill the headway.

The Use of Springs and Mooring Lines

Lines play an important part in the handling of vessels at a dock. Obviously, the larger the craft the more lines are likely to be called into play. It would be absurd for the motor boatmen to burden his 30-footer with a spider-web of breasts, springs and other lines that would be appropriate only on a large vessel.

TERMINOLOGY

Nevertheless, it is well to be familiar with correct terms and the functions of lines that may be used. They may come in handy some time—though not necessarily all at once.

Motor boatmen often speak loosely of bow and stern lines—and little else—depending on whether the line is made fast forward or aft and regardless of the direction in which it leads or the purpose it serves. To be strictly correct, according to nautical terminology, there is *only one bow line*. This is made fast to the forward bitt and run along the dock as far as practicable to prevent the boat from moving astern.

Conversely, a *stern line*, properly, leads from the after bitt to a distant pile or bollard on the dock astern of the boat, to check her from going ahead. The special virtue of

such lines as applied to small boats is the fact that, with but little slack, they may allow for considerable rise and fall of the tide.

Breast lines, on the other hand, lead athwartships nearly at right angles to the vessel and to the dock, to keep her from moving sidewise away from her berth. Large craft may use bow, waist or quarter breasts, depending on whether they are made fast forward, amidships or aft.

Naturally breasts on large vessels are more important than on small craft. If a vessel has a 100-foot beam, her bow is 50 feet from the dock and the bow breast must be somewhat longer than that. On a small boat with 10-foot beam, the bow is only 5 feet from the dock, and other lines may serve to keep her from moving away from the dock.

Another point to remember is the fact that a majority of small pleasure boats have only two bitts or cleats—one forward and one aft—to make fast to and no other cleats amidships or elsewhere, to which waist lines can be made fast.

As we shall see later, a small boat might be adequately moored with springs alone, using no breasts. Sometimes boatmen attempt to make fast to a dock with bow and stern breasts only and get into trouble because slack must

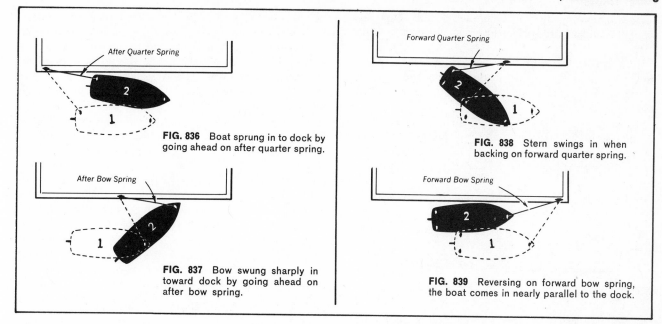

FIG. 836 Boat sprung in to dock by going ahead on after quarter spring.

FIG. 837 Bow swung sharply in toward dock by going ahead on after bow spring.

FIG. 838 Stern swings in when backing on forward quarter spring.

FIG. 839 Reversing on forward bow spring, the boat comes in nearly parallel to the dock.

be left in the line to allow for tide. If adjusted right for low water, they may be entirely too slack at high water and the boat gets a chance to catch in some stringer or projection of the dock when her bow or stern swings in.

KINDS OF SPRINGS

Springs are not as long as bow and stern lines, but they lead forward and aft to check motion astern and ahead, respectively. There may be four springs—the *forward bow spring,* the *after bow spring,* the *forward quarter spring,* and the *after quarter spring.* Bow springs are made fast to the vessel at the bow, quarter springs at the quarter.

Forward springs lead forward from the vessel to the dock, so the forward bow spring, fig. 835, and forward quarter spring check motion astern. After springs lead aft from the vessel to the dock. Thus the after bow and quarter springs check motion ahead.

To keep this clear in mind, remember that the terms *forward* and *after* applied to such lines relate to the *direction* in which the line runs *from* the vessel, not to where it is made fast, the latter being indicated by the terms *bow, waist* and *quarter.*

We have already seen, fig. 829, how, by means of an after bow spring, the stern can be brought in to a dock by going ahead with rudder set away from the dock. In this case the boat lay obliquely to the face of the dock, with bow against it.

Now if the boat lay parallel to the dock but some distance off, she could be breasted in bodily by hauling in on bow and stern breasts, but with a vessel of any size this might require considerable effort.

Effect of after springs

If it were possible to secure an after spring at the boat's center of gravity, she could be sprung in bodily to the dock and her parallel alignment (or any other position) could be held by means of the rudder as the propeller goes ahead, because the stern would be free to swing as the discharge current acts on the rudder.

Actually this is not feasible as we probably have only the bow and stern (or quarter) bitts to make fast to, while the center of gravity may be nearly amidships. Now if we rig an after quarter spring, and go ahead with rudder amidships, the combination of forces is such that the boat will be sprung in nearly parallel to the dock. Her stern will come in till the quarter touches the dock, while the bow may stand off somewhat, fig. 836.

If the rudder were put to port at position (1) in fig. 836, in the expectation that the bow would thus be thrown to port, it would be seen that the effect is negligible, as the stern is prevented from being kicked to starboard by the taut spring. Putting the rudder to starboard would throw the stern in to port fast, however.

Turning to fig. 837, let's rig the after spring from the bow and see what happens.

With rudder amidships, going ahead on this bow spring will cause the bow to be swung abruptly in toward the dock, as the bit describes an arc of a circle, the length of the spring its radius. With left rudder, the bow turns in even faster as the stern is thrown to starboard further away from the dock. With right rudder some of the bow's sharp turn inward to port toward the dock is offset but probably not enough to bring the boat in parallel—unless the spring is made fast further aft.

REVERSING ON A SPRING

The action is just the opposite if we reverse on a spring. Turning to fig. 838, note how the stern is swung sharply in toward the dock by the action of the forward quarter spring when reversing. Compare this action with that illustrated in fig. 837, picturing the boat turned end for end.

Now note what happens, as in fig. 839, when backing on a forward bow spring. The turning effect of the spring on the boat is not important here, and she springs in nearly parallel to the dock in an action which might be compared with that in fig. 836—once again considering the boat turned end for end.

ALLOW FOR TIDAL RANGE

Boatmen located on fresh water streams and lakes have no tidal problem confronting them when securing to a dock with mooring lines, but failure to take this action into account in tidal waters can part lines, and even sink the boat.

Springs provide an effective method of leaving a boat free to rise and fall, while preventing her from going ahead or astern or twisting in such a way as to get caught on dock projections.

The longer a mooring line can be, the more of a rise and fall of tide it can take care of with a minimum of slack,

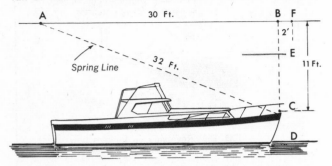

FIG. 840 How long spring lines act with great changes in tidal level. If water level drops 11' from E to D, a 30' spring line (A to B) would cause the boat to move about 2' astern of the position shown. Using a 32' spring (AC), cleat C is at F at the higher level. Principle is a right triangle ($32^2 = 30^2 + 11^2$) approximately. Advantage of long springs is obvious.

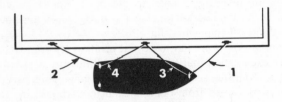

FIG. 841 Usual method of mooring a small vessel to a dock with springs. Lines required are (1) bow line, (2) stern line, (3) after bow spring, and (4) forward quarter spring.

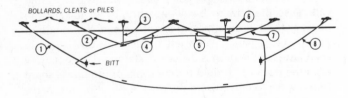

FIG. 842 When a vessel is large enough to justify the use of breasts in addition to springs, her mooring lines may be used as shown—(1) bow line, (2) forward bow spring, (3) forward (bow) breast, (4) after bow spring, (5) forward quarter spring, (6) after (quarter) breast, (7) after quarter spring, (8) stern line. Don't burden a small boat with them all. Aboard ships, mooring lines are numbered from the bow aft, depending on where they are secured aboard ship.

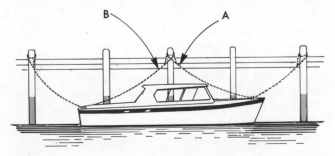

FIG. 843 Use of mooring lines at a dock. Note eye splice of after bow spring (A) run up through eye (B) of forward quarter spring. Either can be cleared without removing the other.

fig. 840. Yet every line must be allowed slack enough so that all do not come taut together at either extreme stage of the tide.

Manila lines are left slack, too, to allow for shrinkage when wet or, if "made up" wet, must be checked when dry for excessive stretch. When nylon is used, generally the lines are "made up" taut, as they don't change much with the weather and will stretch to take up changes in wind strength. This point must be carefully observed in narrow slips or close quarters. Better tight than so loose the boat will move too far.

As a general rule, where space permits, a bow line should be run well ahead of the boat to the dock, and a stern line well aft. If these two lines are run off at an angle of about 45 degrees to the centerline of the boat, they will often prove sufficient for small pleasure boats, breasts being entirely unnecessary and the springs (one or two) resorted to only if the necessary slack of bow and stern lines allows the boat to move about too much at her berth.

MOORING A YACHT

What might be considered a typical satisfactory arrangement of mooring lines on the average cruiser or yacht—even up to 80-footers—is illustrated in fig. 841. Only three cleats, piles or bollards are required on the dock to make fast to, the middle one of which comes about amidships. Both the after bow spring and the forward quarter spring can be run to this, while bow and stern lines run forward and aft, respectively, to the two other points on the dock.

Breast lines here would be superfluous, serving no useful purpose, and therefore should be omitted. In the service, 110-foot sub-chasers have found this arrangement adequate and there is no point in burdening smaller craft with more, except under unusual conditions. Some yachtsmen prefer to run the stern line to the outboard bitt.

Fig. 842 illustrates eight mooring lines that could be used on a large vessel.

If two lines are used anywhere with the idea of getting double the strength of one, they must be of equal length when strain is put upon them. Otherwise one carries the load first and parts, and then the other follows suit.

A boat moored as shown in fig. 841 will lie comfortably at her berth, regardless of changes in tide level, shifts of wind or current, or the wash of passing boats. This last factor can be a serious matter if lines are laid in such a manner that the boat is free to surge fore and aft because of too much slack.

Two lines on one bollard

Frequently, mooring lines may have an eye splice of suitable size in the end which goes ashore, to be dropped over the pile or bollard. Fig. 841 shows both the after bow spring and the forward quarter spring secured to a single bollard about amidships. If these are dropped one over the other, the upper one must first be cleared in order to get the lower one free.

Inasmuch as one or the other of these springs may be needed to get clear of the dock, depending on wind and current conditions at the time, it is well to rig these so that either can be freed without disturbing the other.

Assuming that the eye splice of the forward quarter spring has been placed on the pile first, take the splice of the after bow spring and run it up from below through the eye of the quarter spring and then drop it down over the pile, fig. 843.

This way either line can be cleared without disturbing the other, though it may be necessary to use a little power to ease the strain on one if its eye happens to nip the other line between itself and the pile.

If a boat has much freeboard, the tide is high, and dock piles are relatively short, so that a mooring line leads down at a fairly sharp angle from deck to dock, there may be some risk of its slipping up over the top of the pile. An extra round turn of the eye splice taken over the pile will prevent this, fig. 844.

HEAVING LINES

Part of the essence of good seamanship lies in knowing when a certain method of procedure is applicable to the size of vessel one is handling. Use of big ship technique on small motor boats is amusing to a seasoned boatman. Application of motor boat principles aboard a big vessel may be distressing to a ship captain.

So it is with heaving lines. When a pleasure boat is brought up smartly to a dock, there is rarely any need for springs or heaving lines, though a spring is often helpful in getting clear when leaving.

On small boats the mooring lines are properly kept neatly coiled until needed and then broken out of the locker for use in docking just before required. Manila lines of even 50- and 60-foot yachts are relatively light—say between 1-inch and 1½-inch diameter—and can be handled easily as the boat is brought alongside. Or, if nylon is used, ⅝" or ¾" diameter is an easy size to handle. A diameter of ½" or ⅝" is good for 30- to 40-foot yachts. Sending out any unnecessary springs or sending lines out too soon is not in order.

Messengers and monkey's fists

The lines of a big vessel are heavy hawsers, hard to handle, and impossible to heave. Therefore they make use of heaving lines, which are light lines weighted at the end by a "monkey's fist" (an intricate woven knot which encloses the weight). This heaving line is bent to the hawser near the eye splice—not in the loop where it might be jammed when a strain is thrown on the hawser—and the line is sent from ship to dock, dock to ship, or ship to ship as soon as possible as a messenger, fig. 845.

FIG. 844 An extra round turn in the eye splice of a mooring line should be taken around a pile if the lead is high from dock to deck. This prevents it from slipping up.

On small boats this is more of a principle to remember for possible use than a precept to practice in ordinary run-of-the-mill docking maneuvers. Generally your crew can step ashore with necessary lines and there is no need for getting lines out at some distance from the dock, as in ship-docking procedure.

Even if necessary to heave your regular mooring lines on a small boat, they will carry some distance if properly coiled, half held loosely in the left hand and the remaining half heaved by the right, fig. 846, all uncoiling naturally in the air, without fouling up into a knot and falling short. If necessary, a weight can be added at times to carry a line but this is seldom used.

If, in passing a line for towing purposes, for example, you had to send a heavier line a long distance, then break out the heaving line principle and use it to good advantage.

TURNING AT A DOCK

Turning a boat at a dock—called *winding ship* in the case of a large vessel—is easy if wind or current is used as an aid, or if the engine is used in the absence of these factors.

Fig. 847 illustrates a boat lying, at position (1), with her stern toward the current and the problem is to turn her to head into the current. The first step is to let all lines go except the after bow spring.

Normally the effect of the current will then be sufficient to throw her bow in toward the dock and her stern out into the stream toward the position sketched at (2). If any factor, such as a beam wind, tends to keep her stern pinned against the dock, the stern can be kicked out by going ahead easily with right rudder. A fender should be kept handy as a protection to the starboard bow.

FIG. 845 A monkey's fist carries this light heaving line to a lightship from a Coast Guard cutter. The end will be bent to a heavier line or hawser.

FIG. 846 Mooring lines on pleasure boats are usually light enough to heave, if held properly coiled.

Some steps should be taken to prevent the bow from catching on the dock as she swings, thus exerting a great leverage on the spring. A small boat may roll the fender a little and the boat can be eased off by hand, but in larger craft it is customary to reverse the engine just enough to keep the bow clear, as shown at (3).

As she swings in with the current, the fender should be made ready near the port bow as shown at (4). At this point she may tend to lie in this position, depending on just how much strain there is on the bow spring. If she does not come alongside readily, perhaps helping her by going ahead a little with right rudder, a forward quarter spring can be rigged. Then, by taking a strain on the quarter spring, and easing the bow spring, she will set in to her new berth.

Larger vessels executing this maneuver would get a forward bow spring out on the port bow when the ship reaches position (3), rigging it not from the extreme bow but a point further aft. Going ahead easily with right rudder on this spring alone (the first one having been cast off), the ship could be kept under control and eased in nicely.

In turning a boat this way it is always easier and better to make the turn with the bow to the dock rather than the stern. The procedure would be the same as outlined in a case where wind is blowing in the direction in which the current sets in the illustration.

Turning with power

Considering a problem similar to that sketched in fig. 847, except that we assume there is neither wind nor current to assist in turning, the power of the engine can be used to swing her.

Going ahead on an after bow spring with right rudder (starboard side being toward the dock as in the figure) would throw the stern out away from the dock, a fender being used as in the previous illustration to protect the bow. In this case the stem is allowed to nose up against the dock, using another fender if necessary to cushion it.

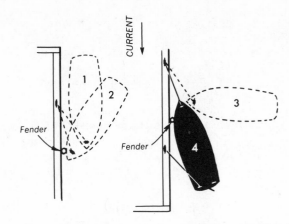

FIG. 847 Turning a boat at a dock, using the current and springs.

As the boat swings toward a position at right angles to the dock, the spring will have to be eased. With the bow against the dock, engine going ahead slowly, and rudder amidships, the boat can be held in this position while the bow spring is cast off from the dock and re-rigged as an after bow spring on the port side. With right rudder again, the stern will continue to swing all the way around, fenders being shifted once more to protect the port bow.

[CAUTION: If nylon springs and lines are used, remember that they stretch and can store energy enough to snap the boat back when power is removed. If nylon is stretched to the breaking point, it can snap back with lethal effect.]

This principle has many applications and will be found useful in dozens of situations when the theory is understood. In a berth only inches wider than the overall length of the boat, without room to go ahead and astern, she can be turned end for end with no line-hauling or manual effort of any kind.

If there happens to be wind or current holding her against the dock, the first half of this maneuver may be used to get the stern out into the stream, preliminary to backing away when ready to get clear of the dock.

Getting Clear of a Dock

When the master of a ship takes his vessel out of her berth at a dock, he speaks of "undocking," a term the appropriateness of which may be questioned when speaking of small pleasure boats. To some boatmen, "undocking" a 20-footer sounds affected.

As a matter of strict terminology, in fact (especially where ships are concerned) purists never refer to a "dock" when, technically, they mean "pier" or "wharf." The reader may decide as to whether he wants to refer to his "2-by-4" structure as a "wharf."

Elsewhere we have discussed the technique of backing a boat out of her slip, turning either to port or starboard, preparatory to getting under way. A variation of this is illustrated in fig. 848, where the boat is pictured lying in a slip at right angles to the outer side of a dock.

BACKING AROUND

The problem may be to back her around so as to have her lying along the outside of the dock, or the principle

might be used as a method of backing clear of the slip, preliminary to getting under way, especially if there is little

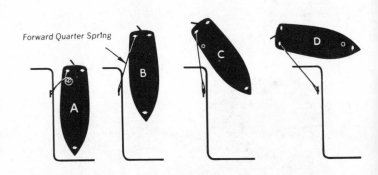

FIG. 848 Use of a forward quarter spring when backing a boat out around the end of a dock. When spring is taut, boat reverses with full right rudder.

room for maneuvering. The idea in this case is to use a forward quarter spring.

At (A) in the illustration, the boat is shown lying starboard side to the dock. The first step is to make the spring ready from a point near the corner of the dock to the after bitt, either amidships if there is only one, or the bitt on the starboard quarter, if there are two.

With the spring ready, but left slack and tended, the bow line is cast off, or slacked away and tended by a man on the dock and the boat is backed easily with full right rudder. At (B), a strain is taken on the spring to prevent her from backing further and this causes her to pivot as the stern is pulled around to starboard, as at (C). As she continues to back toward (D), the boat assumes a position parallel to the outer face of the dock.

At (D), the spring can be cast off the bollard and carried further up the dock to be made fast elsewhere as a stern line, if the boat is to remain in this new berth. The bow line in turn can be used to control the bow and prevent the boat's swinging too far; then made fast as necessary, perhaps to the bollard formerly used to secure the spring.

This method is especially useful when there is a breeze off the dock that would tend to blow her away if maneuvering without lines. No manpower is required and it can be accomplished leisurely in a seamanlike manner.

GETTING UNDER WAY

In the event that the maneuver is used preparatory to getting under way, the bow line is not required. When the boat has pivoted far enough, with starboard quarter near the corner of the dock, the engine can be idled while the spring is cast off the bollard and brought aboard. Getting under way from such a position, the rudder must be set amidships till the quarter clears the dock, then full left rudder turns her bow out into the stream.

Spring lines used this way should have a loop of convenient size in the end, formed either by an eye splice or a bow line so as to slip quickly and easily off the pile, bollard or cleat, yet stand the strain of holding the boat against application of power, without slipping. The eye splice is best; the bowline is quickly turned into the end of a line having no splice.

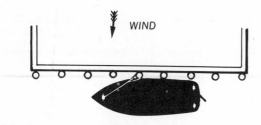

WIND

FIG. 849 Making a brief stop on the leeward side of a dock, boat can be held in position by going ahead on an after bow spring with rudder hard over (in this case, to port).

In this or any other maneuver involving the application of engine power against the spring, it is obvious that strain must be taken up slowly, easily. A sudden surge of power puts a shock load on deck fittings that they were never designed to carry—may even tear cleats right out by the roots, so to speak. If the fastenings hold, the line may part —perhaps with a dangerous snap, as the parted ends lash out.

Once the strain has been taken up easily, proper deck

fittings and good line of adequate size will stand the application of plenty of power, in those cases where the power is really needed. Bear this principle in mind when you are preparing to tow or in passing a line to a stranded boat with a view toward hauling her off.

HOLDING WITH ONE SPRING

While we are talking of springs there is another trick worth remembering that deserves to be used more often, fig. 849.

In the illustration we assume that you have run up along the leeward side of a dock, to remain there for a short time while you pick up guests or perhaps put some one ashore. Instead of getting lines out to make fast fore and aft as you would for a longer stop, or expect the crew to hold the boat against the wind's pressure, try using one line as an after bow spring, as illustrated.

After coming alongside, rig the line and go ahead easily till it takes a strain; then go ahead, with left rudder, with power enough to hold the stern up against the dock. This is a maneuver that you can accomplish single-handed without too much difficulty, by having your spring fast to the forward bitt as you come in, with the end ready to pass ashore for someone on the dock to drop over a pile.

Doubling the spring

Single-handed, you might prefer to use the spring double, with the bight of line around the pile and both ends of the line fast to your bitt. Then, when your guests are all aboard, you can slip the engine into neutral, cast off one end and haul the spring back aboard without leaving the deck. This would be helpful if the wind were of some force, the bollard well back from the dock edge, and no one ashore to assist. This way there would be no risk of the boat's being blown off as you step ashore to cast off the line.

In any case, when the line has been cast off forward, the wind will cause the boat to drift clear of the dock, the bow ordinarily paying off faster than the stern. Whether you go ahead or reverse to get under way will be dependent on the proximity of other docks and boats, etc., and whether your course is to be up- or down-stream. The same maneuver would be applicable if current were setting in the direction that the wind is blowing in the illustration.

FROM A WINDWARD BERTH

When either wind or current tends to set the boat off the dock as shown in fig. 849 there is little difficulty in getting clear when you are ready to get under way. In fig. 850, however, we have assumed a situation in which the wind (or current) tends to hold the boat in her berth against the windward side of the dock. This is a bad berth if there is wind enough to raise much of a sea.

If the principle of the spring is not used in a case like this there may be a great deal of effort expended with boat hooks and manpower doing a lubberly job, with the possibility, even, of damage to the boat. Correct use of an after bow spring is the seamanlike solution.

Referring to fig. 850 (A), all mooring lines have been cast off except the after bow spring. If the boat has been lying to bow and stern lines only, the stern line can be cast off and the bow line transferred to a position on the

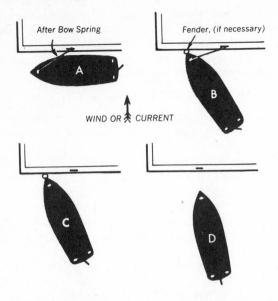

FIG. 850 How an after bow spring is used to leave the windward side of a dock. Boat goes ahead on the spring with rudder set toward dock, then backs away into the wind.

FIG. 851 Rigging an after bow spring.

dock as shown in fig. 851 to convert it into a spring.

Going ahead easily on the spring with right rudder tends to nose the bow in and throw the stern up into the wind away from the dock. If it does not respond with the rudder hard over, open the throttle to provide the kick necessary to work the stern around against wind pressure. Depending on the nature of the dock and type of boat, you may need a fender or two at the critical spots between dock and boat.

Ease the spring

At (B), fig. 850, it is evident that the continued turning of the stern would throw a great strain on the spring. Therefore, it is generally necessary to ease the spring, yet keep the stem from slipping along the dock. One of the best ways to accomplish this is to have the spring made fast on the bitt by means of several round turns and a half hitch. With the half hitch cast off, the turns can be allowed to slip a little to ease the spring as necessary.

Here, again, remember the stretch of nylon with the possible reversal of direction when power is removed. In addition, if sufficient load is placed on a nylon line wound around a cleat or bitt the first turn or two may seize and grab the cleat so the line cannot be eased or slipped if there is a strain or load on the line. It may "jump" loose when turns are removed, causing a rapid and sudden change in control of the vessel by the line.

At (C), the boat has turned far enough so that the stem is not likely to slip, though the boat could be allowed to turn further till her stern was squarely into the wind. At this point the spring and fender can be gotten aboard and the boat backed away with rudder amidships.

When single-handed

This is another of those maneuvers that can be accomplished single-handed with little effort if done in a seamanlike manner. If single-handed, the rudder must be set amidships when the stern has worked up into the wind, giving the helmsman a chance to go forward and cast off

the spring. Furthermore, it will not be easy for him to go forward and ease his spring, but this can sometimes be done by momentarily going into neutral, which allows the spring to pull the stem toward the bollard. This, however, may not be expedient with much wind, requiring the help of a man forward to handle it properly.

When the boat lies with head to the dock and rudder amidships, there may be a natural tendency for her to work her stern around to starboard, because of the effect of unequal blade thrust (with a right-handed wheel). This usually is of little consequence as it takes but a moment to get forward and cast off.

With a worm-and-gear type steerer, which holds its position against pressure on the rudder, or any other type of control that will maintain rudder angle without a hand on the wheel, it can be set in a case like this for just enough right rudder to compensate for the effect of unequal blade thrust.

WITH WIND OR CURRENT ASTERN

The procedure just outlined can be used in getting away from a dock if the wind or current comes from astern—which is along the lines of the technique described in connection with fig. 847 for turning a boat at a dock.

Instead of merely casting off all lines and going ahead in such a situation, it is better to get the maneuverable stern out away from the dock, shaping the boat up to go astern first, before going ahead on the course. The reason, obviously, is that this technique gets the boat away from the dock where there is no risk of scraping her topsides as you pull away—especially if the rudder is not exactly amidships.

Turning again to fig. 850, but assuming the wind is east or that the current sets westward (top of diagram being north) the after bow spring allows her stern to go out into the stream, to be kicked out if necessary by power, going ahead with right rudder. Often in such a case the stern swings out without aid from the power.

When the boat has swung anywhere from 45 to 90 de-

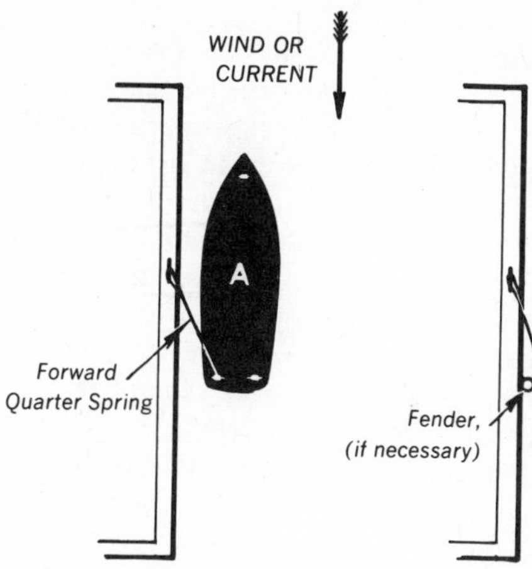

WIND OR CURRENT

A

B

Forward
Quarter Spring

Fender,
(if necessary)

FIG. 852 When wind or current is ahead, backing on a forward quarter spring turns the stern in and bow out, shaping the boat up to get clear by going ahead.

grees, depending on circumstances of the particular case, the spring is cast off and the boat reverses far enough to clear the dock nicely when you go ahead with left rudder.

WIND OR CURRENT AHEAD

Now, referring to fig. 852, let's consider the boat as lying with her bow toward the north. There is a wind from the north or a current which sets south so that its effect is in a line parallel to the dock and opposite to the direction in which the boat is heading.

If, in attempting to get clear of this berth, all lines were cast off immediately, the boat might drift bodily back along the dock or, if power were applied ahead, the helmsman would have to exercise care that the boat was kept exactly parallel in order to pull away without damage.

Again, it is more seamanlike to use a spring (unless the boat is so small that a person stepping aboard at the bow can merely push her bow out enough). This time we need a forward quarter spring on the port side. It is likely that this is already in use as one of the dock mooring lines, so all other lines can be cast off.

If the bow does not swing out at once with the effect of wind or current, backing easily on the spring will pull the stern in toward the dock, probably necessitating use of a fender on the port quarter to protect the hull.

In maneuvers where the bow swings in toward the dock, the fender is not always important if the bow has a good metal rub strip and the topsides are well flared. On the

other hand, in cases like the one under discussion, the stern comes in against the dock and a fender is usually in order, especially if the topsides tumble home. Good stout metal-shod rubrails are a fine thing on any boat that has occasion to maneuver much around docks.

In fig. 852, when the bow has swung out as sketched at (B), the boat has been shaped up to pull directly away by casting off the spring and going ahead with rudder amidships.

MAKE USE OF FENDERS

We have noted from time to time in the foregoing illustrations the necessity of protecting the hull with fenders in maneuvering around rough dock piles, or in lying alongside other craft, fig. 853. Articles on equipment have repeatedly pointed out the desirability of carrying plenty of good fenders, but often the equipment actually provided falls far short of being adequate.

The standard types of yacht fenders are satisfactory if large enough and provided in sufficient number. When a boat lies at a dock with no motion, except the rise and fall of tide and the flow of current, even the lightest of guardrails may be alright. But you can't count on these ideal conditions to prevail at all times.

The combination of topsides that are heavily flared forward, tumble home aft, high superstructure that reaches out practically to the deck edge, and comparatively light guard moldings, possibly of wood not even metal-shod with half-oval, all make for potential damage when the boat starts to roll and pound against piles, either as a result of the swell created by passing craft from the wind or a ground swell.

The ordinary fenders (not "bumpers") for pleasure boats are of several types of construction—canvas covers filled with ground cork for small craft; woven manila or cotton covers, also cork-filled; and all manila rope, braided so that no central core or filler is required. Newer types, fig. 854, include those of synthetic or rubber construction containing air or minute gas-filled cells; others have canvas covers enclosing sponge rubber, shredded rubber or cork and rubber. Kapok is also used as a filling.

The smallest of these fenders sometimes have a grommet, eye or rope ring at one end only, to take the pennant by which it is suspended from fender hooks on the boat. Better practice is to have an eye at each end so that the fender can be rigged horizontally as well as vertically, sometimes by hanging it over the pile, instead of from the

FIG. 853 Rafted boats properly protected by substantial fenders.

FIG. 854 Light-weight pneumatic fenders which can be inflated to various pressures for the service required. Lines may be run through them lengthwise to hang them horizontally.

boat where it moves as the boat moves. Some modern fenders have a longitudinal hole through which a line can be run, especially convenient when the fender is used horizontally.

Half a dozen substantial fenders are not too many to carry and if the boat is equipped with few, or no, hooks, go over it with a critical eye to see that stout fender hooks are placed where needed.

Sideboards or fenderboards

The solution to many problems of protecting the hull has been found in the use of sideboards or fenderboards,

carried aboard in addition to a full complement of good heavy fenders. Yachtsmen have carried such boards in some cases but, due to lack of stowage space or other considerations, they have not always been of suitable size.

If fenders are hung vertically from the boat's side, they give protection in cases where there is a horizontal string-piece to bear against as the boat moves fore and aft. If there are vertical piles to lie against, vertical fenders cannot be expected to stay exactly in place. Movement of the boat fore and aft shifts them between the piles and their value is destroyed. Hanging the fender horizontally by both ends is only a slight improvement and then only if hung on the pile where it is independent of the boat's movement fore and aft. As a matter of fact, even this

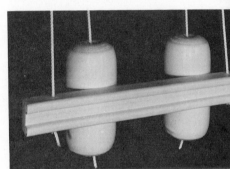

FIG. 855 A side board or plank used in conjunction with ordinary fenders proves invaluable in cases where adequate protection to the hull cannot be provided by fenders alone. The rubber cushion-board illustrated is encased in a thick cover of tough white Nordel rubber with two rubber cushions to absorb the shock of impact.

doesn't provide well for rise and fall of the tide.

The applicability of sideboards and fenders to boats lying side by side is easily seen. If each craft suspends several fenders over the side with a horizontal sideboard to bear directly against the board of the other, each is as comfortable as though moored to a dock and there is no possibility of damage even to high rolling superstructures because the hulls are held well apart.

The method of rigging sideboards is illustrated in fig. 855.

Maneuvering at Slips in Tight Quarters

Some berths provide for piles to tie to, lying off a dock so that boats lie beam to beam, each occupying its own individual slip. In one variation of this, catwalks are provided between the various boats to allow more convenient access to each.

A BERTH BETWEEN PILES

Figure 856 illustrates a problem where a boat must be backed into such a berth in a basin. Complicating the situation is a bulkhead along the east (leeward) and south sides, which prevents approach from any direction except west, down-wind.

If the space between piles and the south bulkhead is sufficient to allow the boat to make a turn, going ahead with right rudder, as in 2-3-4-5, she may round up this way, until, as in (5), she has headed partly into the wind.

If space, turning power, or wind prevent her from getting around any further than the position sketched at (4), her position is awkward as the wind will tend to blow her bow down to leeward faster than the stern so that her angle of approach will not conform with the path sketched

at 6-7-8. In that case, she would have to work out another technique.

Assuming that she can round up under power to position (5) with right rudder, she has been placed so that she can back along the line 6-7-8 without shifting her rudder. Remembering that the stern normally tends to port, and that with full right rudder she might back practically in a straight line, it can be seen how her position at (5) allows

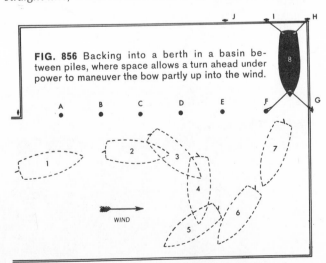

FIG. 856 Backing into a berth in a basin between piles, where space allows a turn ahead under power to maneuver the bow partly up into the wind.

WIND

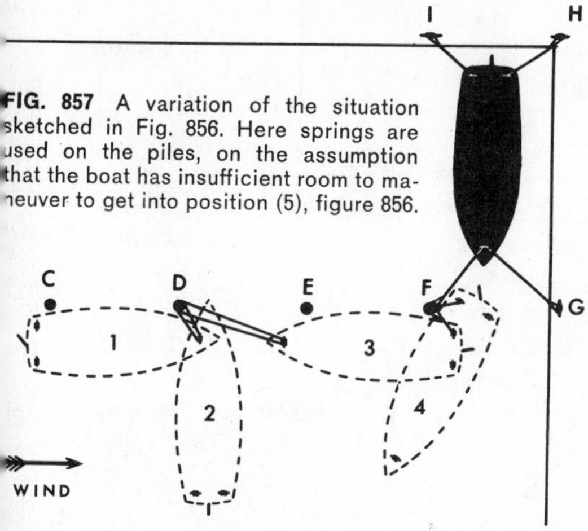

FIG. 857 A variation of the situation sketched in Fig. 856. Here springs are used on the piles, on the assumption that the boat has insufficient room to maneuver to get into position (5), figure 856.

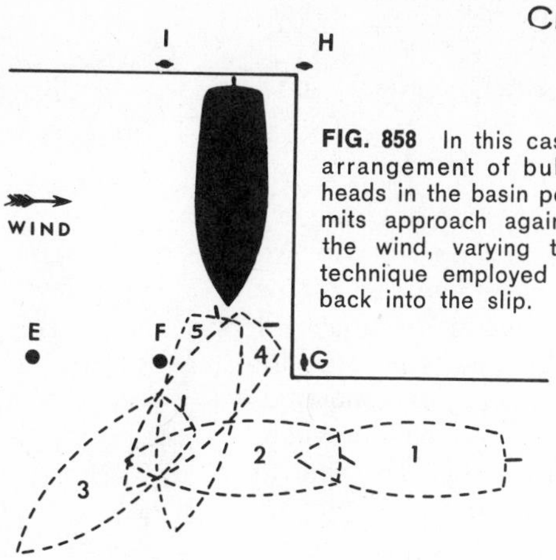

WIND

WIND

FIG. 858 In this case, arrangement of bulkheads in the basin permits approach against the wind, varying the technique employed to back into the slip.

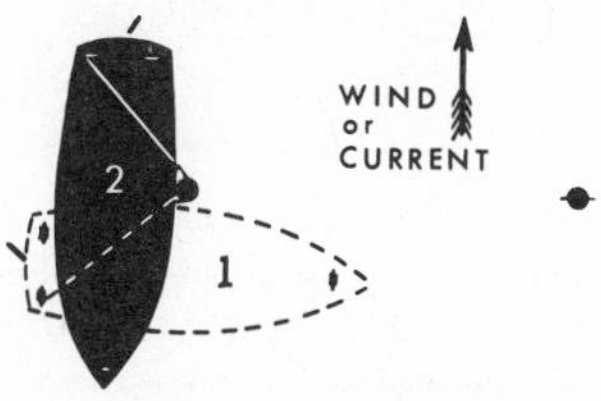

WIND or CURRENT

FIG. 859 How to get clear of a pile when pinned against it by wind or current.

for the wind to blow the bow down to leeward.

At (7) her bow should still be somewhat up into the wind, and her starboard quarter close to the pile (F). Having her head up into the wind more than is shown at (7) is alright as a kick ahead with left rudder will straighten her out to exactly the right angle. If that kick throws her stern too close to the pile (F), idling a moment allows the wind to carry her down into position.

As she passes pile (F), a line should be passed to it—or picked up if one is attached to the pile—and made fast forward when a man at the stern has been able to get another line on cleat (I). Lines to cleats (G) and (H) can be run at leisure.

Before the line to (G) is fast, backing easily draws the stern close enough for a man to step ashore from the stern. Adjusting and securing the line at (G) after all are ashore prevents the boat from going too far astern.

Using springs to the piles

With a good breeze, it might be impossible to get the bow around as shown at (5). In that case there is an alternative, using springs. You might approach close to the line of piles A B C D with the intent of bringing her up alongside piles (C) and (D), heading east, as at position (1), fig. 857. Now run an after bow spring, doubled, from the bitt around pile (D) and back to the bitt. Going ahead easily with left rudder will cause the stern to swing around to the south as at (2). Engine idling, she will swing completely around and if the spring is slacked a little she will lie starboard side against piles (E) and (F), as at (3). It may be necessary to back a little between positions (2) and (3).

Next rig a forward quarter spring on the starboard side to pile (F) and cast off the bow line to (D). The reason why this was doubled is now evident, as you can get the line back aboard by casting off the second hitch.

Reversing on the quarter spring throws her bow to the south and her stern in toward her berth as at (4). This spring can be carried forward by a crewman walking along the starboard side to the bow, where it becomes the forward bow spring to (F) when secured to the forward bitt.

Approaching up-wind

In fig. 856 and 857, if this were not a closed basin, so that approach could be made against the wind, heading west, it would be comparatively easy to swing up into a position approximately as shown at (7) in fig. 856, heading perhaps more closely into the wind—say a 45-degree angle

from the line of piles—with starboard quarter close to pile (F). This would have been accomplished by turning with left rudder as the berth came abeam.

Fig. 858 illustrates such a case. At (2) left rudder, while the boat is still moving ahead, throws the stern in toward the slip and pile (F) as at (3). Backing with right rudder brings her down to position (4), the bow sagging off to leeward somewhat, while the rudder is set to port and the propeller given a strong kick ahead. This throws the stern up to windward as at (5), shaping the boat up to back in with right rudder.

Between positions (4) and (6) it may be necessary to go ahead and back several times but in any case the combination of the engine kicking the stern to windward while the wind blows the bow to leeward can be used effectively to work her in neatly.

Another alternative, at (3), would be to pass a line around the pile (F) and hold on while the wind blew the bow to leeward just enough to shape the boat up, as at (5), to back in. A little reversing between positions (3) and (5) might be indicated. At (5), of course, the line from the starboard quarter is cast off and carried forward to become the forward bow spring on the starboard side, secured to pile (F) for mooring.

Getting clear of a pile

In your maneuvering around piles, as outlined in foregoing illustrations, there is a possibility that you may sometime be caught in a position where the wind or current or both will act to pin the boat against the pile and hold her there so that she is temporarily unmaneuverable.

The solution to this predicament is to rig a forward spring from the pile to a bitt aft, preferably on the side of the boat away from the pile, as shown in fig. 859. Then, by reversing with left rudder, the boat can be wound around the pile and her bow brought into the wind or against the current as in position (2), properly shaped up to draw clear by going ahead with the power as the spring is cast off the pile.

In getting clear from this point, it may be necessary to use a little left rudder to keep the stern clear of the pile, but not enough to throw her stern so far over that the starboard quarter is in danger of hitting the other pile.

As a matter of fact, at position (2) the wind may catch the bow on the port side, easing the boat away from the pile, so that you will be in a position to pull directly away with rudder amidships—always alert, however, to throw the stern one way or the other if needed by proper use of the rudder.

MAKING A TIGHT TURN

Earlier in this chapter when we were discussing the general principles of a boat's response to rudder action, we observed that speed has little effect on the size of the turning circle. The general rule is that the rudder angle will control the diameter of the turning circle; the faster the speed, the shorter the time in which the turn is completed.

While this is theoretically true, there are situations where a burst of speed for a short period may help the boat to turn within the limits of a channel or stream where she couldn't turn at low engine speeds.

Consider the following case in point. In fig. 860, we have a boat bound south in a narrow canal or stream with a strong northerly wind, her dock being on the west side. The south end of the illustration may represent the dead end of a canal or the stream may continue further. This is irrelevant except that if the stream widens further on it would be wise to go on down-stream and take advantage of the greater width for turning, then come back upstream against the wind to dock.

Preferably, if there is room, the helmsman should wait till he is beyond the dock before he starts his turn as this would allow more room for straightening out at the dock. Referring to the illustration, he has slowed down, the boat is under control and he gauges his distance from the east bank so that there is just sufficient room for the stern to swing to port with right rudder at (B) without hitting the bank.

From experience in this maneuver he knows that in the absence of wind he can round up nicely through track A-B-C-D-E-F with full right rudder at low speed. Now if he tries the same thing at low engine speed with the northerly wind, instead of moving from (C) to (D), the wind catches him abeam and tends to hold the bow down to leeward as at (D').

Using power at slow speed

At (D') he would be in a bad way, forced to reverse to avoid hitting the west bank and fortunate if he could back

FIG. 861 A boatman's skill is often quickly revealed by the way he handles his lines.

out quickly enough to prevent his bow from being driven down by the wind on the south bank, if this is a dead end.

Therefore at (B), if the boat is moving slowly, a sudden burst of power at the propeller acting on the full right rudder will bring her around quickly. At (D) the helmsman must be ready to close his throttle in order to prevent the boat from gathering so much way that landing at the dock is difficult.

This is not a maneuver to be guessed at, but if you have occasion to make the same one repeatedly in bringing her in to her usual berth, you will soon get to know whether the strength of the wind will allow you to use these tactics or whether you must resort to some other procedure such as landing down-wind and allowing her to turn at the dock on a spring.

PLAN MANEUVERS IN ADVANCE

In previous pages we have outlined most of the basic ideas or principles by means of which the average single-screw motor boat can be handled when maneuvering around docks and moorings. Obviously the number of possible situations, considering the differences in boats, and the strength, direction, and effect of wind and current is almost infinite. Usually, however, the application of one of the principles we have mentioned, modified perhaps to suit conditions, will permit a seamanlike handling of the problem.

Understanding these principles as a background, you will be less likely to work in opposition to the forces of the elements and will use the control you have over the boat with propeller, rudder, and lines to best advantage. The seamanlike solution usually requires the least manpower and is accomplished with a minimum of confusion, fuss, shouting of orders, and other unnecessary hindrances to an orderly accomplishment of the task.

Even though you know the principles you are to use in executing a maneuver, you will find that it pays to think

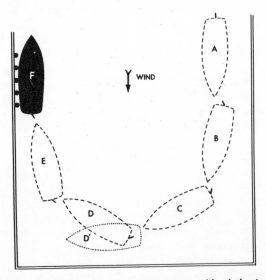

FIG. 860 Turning downwind in close quarters with wind astern. As boat approaches slowly at (B), a sudden short burst of power will turn her, when she may not be able to get around at slow speed.

out in advance the steps you will take, and their succession. With a plan of action clearly worked out, you can take each step slowly and easily, and have time to keep the boat under perfect control. This does not conflict in any way with the truth that there will be occasions that call for bold, swift, and decisive action. Rather, under such circumstances, the need for calm ordered judgment is accentuated.

The lubberly handling of a situation may eventually achieve the end that is sought, but often at the expense of strained lines, fittings, and equipment, not to mention the nerves, muscles, and temper of both skipper and crew.

Common sense in executing the plan

If your planned line of action requires amendment or even complete abandonment because of unforeseen conditions, don't hesitate to act accordingly. If, for example, your plan for a clean approach to a dock has been upset by a freak current you couldn't calculate, back off and square away for another attempt. That in itself is good seamanship and good judgment regardless of how others may judge your apparent "miss" on the first try.

Common sense, if you act with deliberation, will enable you to work out a solution for any combination of conditions. Sometimes, understanding the idiosyncrasies of your own boat, you may put it through evolutions never mentioned in the books but if it achieves your end better than conventional practice, it's still good seamanship.

When you are at the helm and you have men on deck handling lines, fig. 861, issue the necessary orders to each so that all action is coordinated and under your control, instead of having two or three acting independently to cross purposes. This is especially imperative when your crew is not familiar with boats or your method of handling one.

ORDERS TO THE CREW

On larger vessels here are some of the orders used in connection with the handling of lines at a dock. You can be the judge as to whether you consider them appropriate on your own boat, having due regard for its size and the number of men in the crew. The giving of such orders presupposes that crewmen will understand what they mean.

When docking, the order *"Stand by to dock"* puts the crew in readiness, each standing by his respective line, seeing that it is properly coiled ready to heave. If no men are available on the dock to receive lines, others aboard stand ready to step ashore to receive the lines.

At the command *"Heave——(bow line, stern line, or whatever line is named)"* deck men heave the line named to the dock.

"Take in slack on——" requires deckmen to take a turn on the cleat or bitt and pull in slack.

"Take a strain on——" means that deckmen are to pull lines named up tight, taking an extra turn if necessary on the cleat or bitt, but allowing it to slip.

"Ease off on——" means that the line should be allowed to slip off more freely.

"Hold (or snub)——" means to check the line temporarily.

"Secure lines" means to make fast permanently, adjusting to proper length and rigging chafing gear if necessary.

In each case the blanks above imply that a line or lines

will be named to complete the order.

On leaving a dock, the order *"Stand by the lines"* prepares men on the dock to stand by bollards ready to cast off lines and men on deck to take them in when ready. This is followed by the order, *"Cast off the lines"* at which dock men clear the lines from the bollards and toss them to deck men, keeping them clear of the water, if possible.

Easy does it

As previously explained, the procedure is so simplified on a small boat that docking may involve only the stepping ashore of one man each at bow and stern with their respective lines, others to be passed as and if required after these are secured.

One mistake that crewmen often make in helping to handle lines on a small boat is that, in their eagerness to assist, they insist on snubbing them immediately when as a matter of fact the skipper wants them merely to be tended and left slack so that his boat is free to be maneuvered further with the power. A case in point is where the boat is coming in to a landing at a dock and the bow man snubs his line instead of allowing the boat to ease up and draw alongside as the skipper intended.

One caution that cannot be emphasized too strongly is that, in handling lines, whether they are mooring lines, anchor lines, or any other kind, they must not be allowed to get over the side in such a way that they will be sucked down into the propeller and wrapped around the shaft and wheel.

RESUME OF FACTORS AFFECTING CONTROL OF SINGLE-SCREW BOAT

To sum up all the effects which the skipper of a single-screw (R. H.) boat must have in mind as he maneuvers his craft, the following will provide a condensed summary.

I—ENGINE
  (1) *Going ahead*—No effect (or slight tendency of bow to port).
  (2) *Going astern*—Stern goes to port, bow to starboard.

II—RUDDER
  (1) *With headway*
    (a) Left rudder turns stern to starboard, bow to port.
    (b) Right rudder turns stern to port, bow to starboard.
  (2) *With sternway*
    (a) Left rudder turns stern rapidly to port, bow to starboard.
    (b) Right rudder usually turns stern to starboard, bow to port, if sternway is sufficient. With little sternway, boat may back in a straight line, or stern may even go to port.

III—CURRENT
  (1) Sets boat bodily in direction of its flow.
  (2) Other factors interacting (boat held, for example, by waist breast), current normally acts with greater effect on the stern because of deeper draft here.

IV—WIND
  (1) Usually affects bow more than stern, throwing it to leeward.
  (2) Engine backing, boat backs into wind.

V—TWO OR MORE FACTORS COMBINED
  (1) Helmsman must determine relative effects of each on basis of his experience with the boat.

Handling Twin-Screw Boats

It is important to note that practically everything that has been said thus far in regard to the handling of an inboard boat has presupposed a single-screw craft with right-hand propeller, a category which includes a majority of pleasure boats.

Twin screws, however, are increasingly popular, partly because of their superior maneuverability. In the twin-screw boat, the propellers are usually arranged so that the tops of the blades turn outward, so that the starboard wheel is right-hand, the port wheel is left-hand. The effect of this is to give a maximum of maneuverability.

Going ahead with the starboard wheel for a turn to port, the offset of the propeller from the center line is adding its effect by throwing the stern to starboard. Similarly, offset of the port wheel going ahead helps the steering effect when the port propeller is turning ahead for a turn to starboard.

When reversing, the starboard wheel throws its discharge current against the starboard side of the hull to help the turn of the stern to port. Likewise, the port pro-

FIG. 863 Twin-screws give control independent of rudder position. Helmsman here is backing on his port engine, throwing his stern to starboard. Photo, courtesy of Vermont Development Department.

FIG. 862 For maximum maneuverability, twin rudders are placed behind propellers of twin-screw boats, in the discharge currents.

peller reversing throws its stream against the port side of the hull to help the swing of the stern to starboard.

The important factors in turning and steering are thus combined by the outward-turning wheels. The steering effect is exerted in the same direction as the turning moment caused by the off-center location of the propellers.

THE ADVANTAGE OF TWIN RUDDERS

While some boats are rigged with a single rudder between the propellers in the midships line, this arrangement is more common in larger vessels. The trend today in pleasure boats is to use twin rudders, one each directly behind the propellers in the discharge currents, fig. 862. This, too, improves maneuverability by rudder.

It is readily seen that the location of two propellers, one each on the port and starboard sides at some distance from the center line of the keel, gives the operator of such a boat the means of throwing one side or the other ahead or astern, independent of rudder control, fig. 863. In fact, much of the boat's maneuvering at low speed is done without touching the steering wheel as the two throttles

are the principal key to flexibility of control.

If there is only one rudder, a little thought will show that its chief influence in slow-speed maneuvering is felt only when it is placed astern of a propeller going ahead. Its effect behind a propeller reversing is negligible.

Visualize, for example, such a boat making a short turn bow to starboard, by going ahead on the port propeller, and astern on the starboard wheel. If the single rudder is put to starboard (right rudder) nothing is accomplished due to lack of headway. See (A), fig. 864. The rudder is set obliquely behind the reversing starboard wheel and there is no blade behind the port wheel to increase its turning effect. The port engine going ahead is trying to turn the bow to starboard yet it can act on the rudder blade only when the rudder is set for a turn to port, as in (B), fig. 864.

Putting it another way, with a single rudder (neglecting for a moment the action of the starboard propeller) if the port propeller is turned ahead to swing the bow to starboard, turning the rudder to starboard throws it away from and out of the port propeller's discharge current. If the rudder is set to port to get into that current, its steering effect would be to kick the stern to starboard and thus offset the tendency of the port propeller to swing the bow to starboard.

At reasonable speeds, the twin-screw boat can be handled by, and is responsive to, its rudder whether the blade area is all in a single midships rudder or divided between two. Maneuvering in tight corners, the rudder can be set amidships and forgotten while the reverse gear controls are handled to throw the propellers ahead or astern and the throttles are used to control the relative amount of power applied on each.

TURNING IN A BOAT LENGTH

To make a tight turn, a single-screw boat must make a little headway and sternway as the stern is kicked around. Furthermore, it involves going ahead and astern with the propeller, even though the rudder is set to starboard (right rudder) throughout. The throttle, too, must be tended to

Port propeller
going ahead,
starboard propeller
reversing,
in both cases.

Propellers working to turn boat, stern to port, bow to starboard. Right rudder no help without headway because it is out of propeller's discharge current.

Propellers working to turn boat, stern to port, bow to starboard. Left rudder acts to counteract this effect. Therefore turn is best with rudder amidships.

FIG. 864 Why twin-screw boat with one rudder is maneuvered at low speed with propellers, rudder being kept amidships.

makes some sternway as the reversing starboard wheel pulls her around, stern to port.

ONE PROPELLER GOING AHEAD OR BACKING

Again, there is the alternative of casting the stern one way or the other by going ahead or backing on one propeller only without turning the other propeller at all. Some headway or sternway in these cases accompanies the turn.

Referring to (A), fig. 867, a kick ahead on the port propeller throws the stern to port, bow to starboard, as in a single-screw boat with right rudder. If there are twin rudders, right rudder helps this kick. A kick ahead with the starboard wheel throws the stern to starboard, bow to port, as shown at (B). Reversing the port wheel only, pulls the stern around to starboard and vice versa. See sketches (C) and (D).

When reversing with one propeller, the other being stopped, unequal blade thrust, discharge screw current and the offset of the working propeller from the center line all combine to throw the stern in a direction away from the reversing propeller.

FIG. 865 In tight quarters, the twin-screw boat can turn in her own length. Here she backs on the port engine. Under perfect control, she could be made to complete a 180° turn, with starboard engine going ahead. With starboard engine idling, her reversing port engine would probably bring her up to the bulkhead, stern toward the transom of the docked cruiser. (Photo courtesy Palm Beach Isles Sales Corp.)

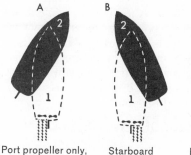

apply sudden bursts of power without allowing the boat to gather way.

In contrast to this, the twin-screw boat can be made to turn in a circle the diameter of which is only a little greater than her length, fig. 865. The turn to port is accomplished as readily as a turn to starboard since such effects as unequal blade thrust on two propellers rotating in opposite directions offset each other.

Turning bow to starboard, the rudder can be set amidships, while the port engine goes ahead and the starboard engine reverses, fig. 866. The engines will probably be turning at nearly, not exactly, the same speed. The boat drives forward more easily than it goes astern and the propeller at a given r.p.m. has more propelling power ahead than astern. Therefore the r.p.m. on the reversing starboard wheel may be somewhat higher than that on the port propeller, to prevent her from making some headway as she pivots.

By setting the throttle for the reversing starboard engine this can be left alone and the port throttle is adjusted till the size of the turning circle is established. A rate of r.p.m. can be found where she is actually turning in her own length. If the port engine is then speeded up a little, the circle is larger and she makes some headway. If the port engine is slowed down, the circle is also larger but she

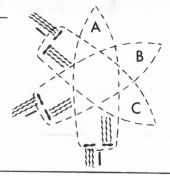

FIG. 866 Turning twin-screw boat, bow to starboard, stern to port, in her own length. Rudder amidships, port propeller going ahead, starboard propeller reversing (probably at somewhat higher r.p.m. than port propeller). Changing r.p.m. can give her headway or sternway as she turns.

A	B	C	D
Port propeller only, going ahead	Starboard only, going ahead	Port propeller only, reversing	Starboard only, reversing

FIG. 867 What happens in a twin-screw boat when one propeller is thrown ahead or astern.

USING SPRINGS WITH TWIN SCREWS

When a twin-screw vessel is lying at a dock and a spring is used to throw the bow or stern out as an aid to getting clear, one engine may be used. For example, with an after bow spring, going ahead on the outside engine only, throws the stern out away from the dock. Or propellers can be turned in opposite directions.

Sometimes a twin-screw vessel is gotten clear of a dock by rigging a forward bow spring and reversing the propeller on the dock side to throw the propeller discharge current on that side forward between the boat and dock as a "cushion." Naturally this is most effective if the dock under water is solidly bulkheaded rather than built on open piling. The discharge current from the inside wheel forces the boat away from the dock and the line is then cast off. Further reversing on the propeller nearest the dock while the other propeller turns ahead, as necessary, shapes the boat up to get the stern clear. The speed of the two motors will vary with conditions of wind and current and the rudder is left amidships till the boat is clear and ready to pull away.

DOCKING A TWIN-SCREW BOAT

Landing at a dock, a twin-screw vessel will approach at slow speed at an angle of 10 to 20 degrees, as is the case with a single-screw boat. When she has just way enough to carry her in nicely, the rudder is swung over to the side away from the dock to bring the stern in as the engines are thrown into neutral. To check headway as she comes up parallel to the dock, the outboard engine is reversed.

Landing either port or starboard side to the dock is accomplished with equal ease because of the starboard propeller turning counter-clockwise as it reverses in a port-side landing, or the port propeller turning clockwise in reverse on a landing starboard side to the dock.

STEERING WITH THE THROTTLES

In maintaining a straight course with a twin-screw vessel, the speed of the motors can be adjusted so that the leeward engine compensates for the effect of leeway. That is, the leeward engine can be turned a little faster to hold the bow up into the wind.

If she happens to sustain some damage to her steering gear, whether it be the rudder(s) or any part of the gear inboard, she can still make port by steering with the throttles. One motor can be allowed to turn at a constant speed—the starboard one, let us say. Then opening the throttle of the port motor will speed up the port propeller and cause a turn to starboard. Closing the throttle of the port motor slows down the port propeller and allows the starboard wheel to push ahead, causing a turn to port. And we have also shown that she is at no great disadvantage when she finally maneuvers into her berth after getting into port as the throttle and reverse gears are adequate for complete control here too.

RESPONSE TO RUDDER WHILE BACKING

A twin-screw vessel starting from a position dead in the water, with both propellers backing at the same speed, is at a great advantage over the single-screw vessel as she can be made to take any desired course by steering with her

FIG. 868 Maneuvering his twin-screw boat, the helmsman can leave his rudders amidships, may even set his throttles, and handle the boat with a touch of one or both of his reverse gear controls.

rudders whereas the single-screw vessel, it will be remembered, is obstinate about backing her stern to starboard. In the twin-screw vessel opposite rotation of the propellers means that the forces which normally throw the single-screw vessel off course are balanced out.

In addition to use of the rudders, the twin-screw vessel offers the possibility of using her throttles to speed up one motor or the other as an aid to steering while maintaining her sternway or she can even stop one propeller or go ahead on it for maximum control in reverse, fig. 868.

While the twin-screw vessel backs as readily to starboard as to port, she is still subject to the effect of wind, waves, and current though the helmsman is in a better position to exercise control over them as we have seen in the case of leeway, offset by different engine speeds instead of holding the rudder offset from the midships line.

OTHER TWIN-SCREW MANEUVERS

If one propeller is stopped while the boat has headway, the bow necessarily turns in the direction of the propeller that is dead. Consequently, if one engine of a twin-screw power plant fails, and the boat is brought in on the other, a certain amount of rudder angle on the side of the operating propeller is necessary in order to maintain a straight course, or some kind of drag must be towed on the side of the working propeller.

A basic principle in the maneuvering of a twin-screw vessel is to use the rudder primarily in relation to the direction of the vessel's movement through the water (that is, whether she had headway or sternway). Elsewhere, it will be recalled, the principle as given for the single-screw vessel was that the rudder should be considered in relation to the direction in which the propeller happens to be turning, regardless of whether the vessel has headway or sternway.

When a twin-screw vessel has headway, both propellers turning ahead, and a quick turn to starboard is desired, the starboard engine is reversed with right rudder. The fact that the vessel has headway in this instance means that the right rudder adds its steering effect to shorten the turn.

With sternway, both propellers reversing, if a quick turn to port is wanted, the port engine is thrown ahead, with left rudder. Again, due to the vessel's sternway, the rudder's effect is added to that of the propellers in causing a short turn to port.

If a twin-screw vessel has considerable headway and her engines are reversed with rudder hard over, the stern will normally swing away from the rudder (to port with right rudder and vice versa) until the headway is overcome by the reversing engines. After she has gathered sternway, her stern tends to work toward the side on which her rudder is set. Then the vessel's stern in the illustration just cited would eventually move to starboard with right rudder, after her headway had changed to sternway.

HANDLING A LARGE YACHT

As a rule, most of our average sized pleasure boats are handled by their owners; the larger yachts are frequently in charge of professional skippers. It's of interest, nevertheless, to note an instruction technique regarded as applicable to craft in the 100-foot category when leaving and returning to a berth alongside other vessels.

In fig. 869 this vessel is the middle one of three tied abreast lying port side to a dock headed toward the beach. Let's call the boats A, B, and C. Our boat is B, the middle one; A is at the dock; C is the outside boat.

The engines are warmed up preliminary to getting under way and when they are ready lines are cleared as follows: First, C's bow breast is cast off from B's bow and run to A, forward of B's stem, with some slack to allow B to maneuver a little.

C now casts off all lines except the bow breast which has been transferred to A and gets a heaving line ready for use after B has pulled out.

B then casts off all lines securing her to A except an after bow spring which is slacked a little to allow B, going ahead, to get the bulge of her bow past that of A's bow and thus permit B to pivot better.

B now goes ahead 1/3 on the outside (starboard) engine and back 1/3 on the inside (port) engine. Two men are standing by with fenders. As B moves slowly ahead a few feet, the spring line takes the strain and the stern works out, to starboard.

Backing clear

C is being swung along with B but no lines secure the two vessels and there is nothing to prevent B from drawing clear as she backs both engines 1/3 after having swung her stern far enough around to starboard.

With B clear, C heaves to A the line she has already prepared. At this point she can either run a stern breast to A and heave in on it or else rig an after bow spring to draw alongside A by using power. In the latter case, she will

go ahead on the inside (port) engine and reverse the outside (starboard) engine. If the bow breast to A tends to check the swing of C's bow, it must be slacked. Back alongside A, C rigs all mooring lines to A as she was formerly secured to B.

B, in the meantime, has backed out into the slip and backs the port engine 2/3 while the starboard engine continues to back at 1/3. The effect of this will be to give her better clearance from the dock and swing her while backing.

Checking sternway and turning

The boat draws well clear of the dock under this maneuver but presently gathers too much sternway so that the starboard engine is thrown ahead 2/3 which checks the sternway and causes her to turn more rapidly, throwing the bow around to port.

When finally straightened out in the slip, both engines are run at 1/3 ahead to gather steerage-way. Then both are stopped (idled in neutral in the case of a boat with reverse gears) while steering with the rudder and a long blast is blown on the whistle as a warning prior to leaving the slip.

Moving out of the slip, the current catches the port bow and tends to set the vessel back toward the dock so she is given a short kick ahead on the starboard engine to offset it. Clear of the dock, she goes ahead 2/3 on both engines.

Returning to her berth

The same craft is now ready to return to her berth alongside another vessel. Keeping well out in the stream till the slip is almost abeam, she turns and passes into the slip about midway between the piers, favoring one side a little to allow for current. No abrupt changes of course will be needed.

Engines are stopped (or, with reverse gears, idling in neutral) passing the pier heads while the vessel is steered to a point just ahead of the other vessel's pilot house. The angle of approach to the other vessel should be small. If it appears that the angle is too wide the helm should be used decisively to place her in position in plenty of time to straighten out.

With reduced speed, the helmsman handles the wheel smartly, using considerably more helm to achieve a given response than he would need if the vessel had good headway. What he does is to get the bow to swing, then shifts the rudder smartly for a moment, then shifts back to the midships position.

Engines are kept stopped (or idling, as the case may be) as she comes in at a moderate angle, her bow about six feet from that of the other vessel. A bow spring is passed, slack taken up and secured. Now the outside (starboard in this case) engine is backed 1/3 while the inside (port) engine goes ahead 1/3. This is just a momentary kick to be repeated if necessary.

The effect of the reversing outside engine is to kill the headway and swing the stern to port toward the other vessel, assisted by the kick ahead on the inside engine. The last of the headway, acting on the spring, also contributes to the same effect. No heaving lines have been used during this maneuver and, under ideal conditions, only the outside engine will be called on for a short kick astern while the inside engine may not be needed at all.

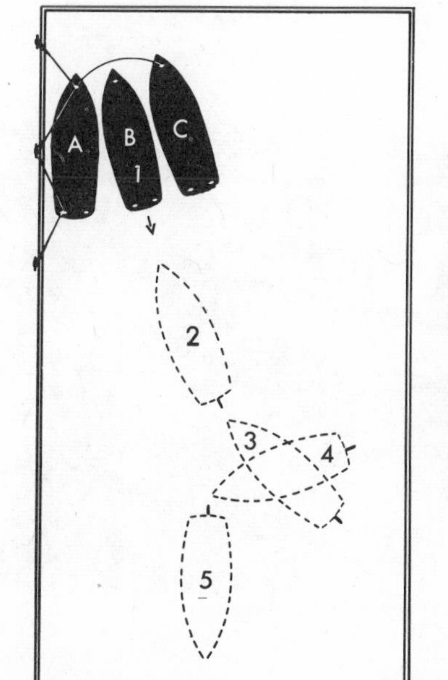

FIG. 869 Large twin-screw vessel leaving berth between two others in a slip. At (1) stern has been sprung out by going ahead on bow spring to (A), starboard engine going ahead, port engine reversing. At (2) spring having been cast off, she has backed clear with both engines reversing. At (3) sternway is checked and stern kicked around to (4) by going ahead on the starboard engine. At (5) she is straightened out and, after headway is gained, responds to her rudder which has been left amidships during the maneuver.

The Fine Art of DOCKING

How large vessels are handled—as adapted to small-boat practice

EVERY DAY, in hundreds of ports the world over, vessels are brought to dock, undocked, and moored. All manner of vessels, from 25,000-ton super-tankers to tiny harbor tugs, are handled expertly—even casually—by men to whom the sea is a profession. From all this, and often from bitter experience and mishap, comes a wealth of knowledge on ship handling which could well be adapted to use by the skipper of a small boat.

The purpose of this article is to bring out several of these ship-handling "kinks" which are particularly adaptable to small-boat maneuvering. They will ease the day-to-day docking of these craft—but, more important, aid during those times when foul weather and adverse seas make docking, more than ever, a matter of judgment and practical skill.

These are by no means *the* ways to dock a boat. But perhaps among them you will find one or two methods which will treat you well, or will be of particular use to your type of boat or waters.

To handle a boat, or a ship, you must first *know* it. Know *what it will do, how fast it will do it,* and *in what space.* No article or text can give you this knowledge—it can come only from actual experience and practice. But attention can be drawn to certain basics which will enable you to get much more from experience. Some of the more important of these. . . .

A. *The propeller controls the direction of a boat when docking, almost as much as the rudder.*

A vessel with a propeller that turns in a clockwise direction when viewed from astern with the engine turning ahead (called a right-handed vessel) is the most common. This vessel's bow will usually swing to port slowly when going ahead, even with the rudder amidships, *but* the stern will swing rather sharply to port when the vessel is going astern, often regardless of where the rudder is. For left-handed vessels the effects are reversed.

B. *This "turning effect" of the propeller is much more pronounced when going astern.*

Since much of a rudder's effect comes from the wash of the propeller rushing past it, if the engine is reversed this wash will be directed in a direction away from the rudder and much of the effect of the helm is lost. The propeller takes over in a pronounced fashion.

C. *Brief spurts of engine power may be*

FIG. 870-a In this case, the slip is on the starboard side of a canal. The helmsman turns to port to place his boat in position to back into the berth.

A Typical Docking Maneuver with a Modern Twin-Screw Cruiser

FIG. 870-b Here he goes ahead easily with the starboard engine, his port engine backing. He turns without making headway and watches clearance at the stern.

148

used to turn the bow or stern of the vessel as desired, without getting the boat under way.

With the rudder to starboard, a brief spurt of the engine (throttle is opened momentarily) will swing the bow to starboard *but,* if the engine is cut off before the vessel gathers way, most of the power of the engine will have gone into turning the vessel rather than getting it moving through the water. The heavier the boat, the more this is so. Don't be afraid to gun your engine briefly to gain maneuverability. A boat's pretty heavy and won't shoot ahead the moment power is applied.

D. *The wind, tide, and current can often be as much help in docking as the engines and helm.*

Nature will often dock your boat for you, if given half a chance. Why waste gas and temper fighting her. A good policy many times is "Ride with the current."

Now to the actual processes of docking. These are presented in outline form to make it easier to grasp details without wading through a lot of text. The word "wind" will be used to cover whichever factor has the most effect on the vessel at the moment, whether it is actually the wind, or whether it may be tide or current. In calm or still water almost any of the methods outlined will work equally well. Boats are shown port side to the docks; for the reverse condition, simply reverse the rudder orders, but maintain the same engine speeds and directions.

LEAVING A DOCK

Alongside Dock; Wind Ahead (Fig. 1)

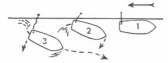

1. Single up to one stern line. No power, no rudder.
2. Let the wind swing the bow out, perhaps helping with boathook or with brief *spurts* ahead against a rudder hard right. (But watch port quarter.)
3. When the bow has swung out 15 or 20 degrees, hard left rudder and spurts ahead to swing stern out clear of the dock. (This is rarely done by small-boat handlers; consequently the stern scrapes along the dock as they pull away. There is no reason for this when a little power and a bit of rudder will get you away without a scratch.)
4. Let go the line when the boat is a few feet off the dock and go ahead slow, steering her *gradually* away from the dock with slight rudder. (Too much rudder will swing the stern right back against the dock and you'll end up no better off than if you had left it there to begin with.)

Wind Off the Dock (Fig. 2)

1. Single up to one stern line and let the wind swing the bow out. Ease off on the stern line and the stern will go out as well. You're now clear of the dock, both bow and stern, without a scratch or a touch of the throttle.
2. Let go the line. Slow ahead and steer her away *easily*.

Wind Astern (Fig. 3)

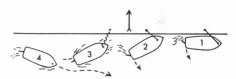

1. Single up to a bow line (spring).
2. Let the wind swing the stern out from the dock or use the engine in spurts against a hard left rudder.
3. Engine astern to back off slowly—cast off line and use rudder to back her off properly.
4. When well clear of dock, engine ahead and easy right rudder to steer her away.

Wind On the Dock (Fig. 4)

1. Single up to one bow line (spring) led well aft onto the dock. Spurts ahead

(continued) ▷

FIG. 870-c Now the transom is centered at the entrance to the slip and the boat is making neither headway nor sternway. Crewman stands ready in the cockpit.

FIG. 870-d With his boat aligned as carefully as wind and current permit, the helmsman starts to back easily. With rudders amidships, he tends the throttles.

If a skipper knows his boat, uses common sense, and plans his maneuvers carefully, he will soon acquire a reputation as a skillful boatman.

against a rudder hard left to swing the stern out.

2. Half to full astern (depending on wind) to back her away from the dock. The stern will swing slowly to port of its own accord. Help it to do so with rudder if desired. When boat is roughly parallel to the dock let go line. . . .

3. Slight right rudder and full ahead. Or (Fig. 5).

(Fig. 5)

1. Single up to one stern line (spring) led well up onto dock.

2. Half to full astern to swing bow out. *No* rudder.

3. Rudder half left and engine slow ahead to swing stern out. When away a bit, let go line and steer her off carefully. Power used here will depend, again, on the force of the wind.

LEAVING A SLIP (Fig. 6)

This method will work on both a walled slip or with a boat moored bow or stern to a dock between two stakes or piles.

1. Single-up to one stern line of a length sufficient to reach from the stern chock forward about ⅔ the length of the vessel. Make the outboard end of this fast to the outer end of the slip.

2. Slow astern till the line is taut, then hard left rudder and the boat will swing her stern to port easily and under *full control*. The line acts as a pivot. This method is especially useful in restricted waters where there is little room to "pull out" from the slip. I know of no method that will get a boat out of a slip in less space or with better control.

3. Cast off when out far enough and slow ahead·giving a *slight* kick of left rudder to swing the stern out clear of the end of the slip or the dock.

This maneuver will do equally well for almost all conditions of wind and sea. More or less power or rudder may be needed but the steps are exactly the same.

This "controlled backing" method keeps you, the slip and your neighbor free from scrapes and gouges, fits of temper . . . and repair bills.

DOCKING

Alongside; Wind Ahead, or Off the Dock (Fig. 7)

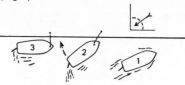

1. Approach slowly at an angle of about 30 to 40 degrees to the dock.

2. Engine astern to stop her about 1 foot off the dock—bow line ashore.

3. Right rudder and spurts ahead to bring the stern in or allow the wind to drift her in.

4. Tie up.

Wind Astern (Fig. 8)

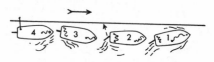

1. Approach *closely* to dock, about 10 to 15 degrees.

2. When near to dock, one or two feet, right rudder and spurts ahead to *start* stern swinging in. As soon as the stern begins to swing in (Boat about parallel to dock). . . .

3. Astern to stop her. This action will keep the stern swinging in toward the dock. (Only practice will tell just where to shift

A Typical Docking Maneuver (continued)

FIG. 870-e   With barely enough clearance on both sides, the helmsman is alert to keep his alignment parallel with the dock, the boat centered as closely as possible.

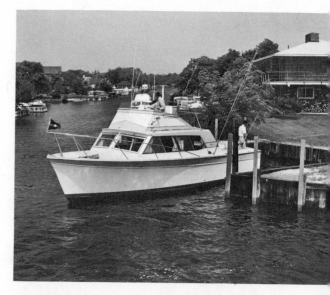

FIG. 870-f   As he backs gently into his berth, the helmsman keeps a sharp eye on his starboard quarter, prepared to kick the stern a little to port if necessary.

from ahead to astern.)

4. Bow should now point about 5 to 10 degrees *outward* from the dock. Stern line onto dock. Let her bow now drift into the dock after stopping engine or help it in with spurts ahead against hard left rudder.

5. Tie up.

Wind On the Dock (Fig. 9)

1. Approach the dock at a *steep* angle (60 to 80 degrees) to allow you to use the engine as a brake on the boat's headway. This is vital in any heavy wind.

2. Astern to stop bow about a foot or two off the dock. Ease her with a boathook if possible. Bow line ashore.

3. Let the wind swing the stern in— braking its speed with the rudder hard right and the engine astern. (This will also help to keep the bow from being forced into the dock.

4. Tie up.

I've had this method succeed where winds were of sufficient force to send other boats crashing into docks in a shower of paint chips and splinters.

ENTERING A SLIP

Wind Anywhere but Astern (Fig. 10)

1. Approach slowly and roughly parallel to end of slip till you are able to pass a line to the cleat or pile nearest your approach.

2. Astern to slow the approach and *stop* her just *short* of the far piling, with the line taut.

3. Rudder hard left and gun ahead on engines to swing her into the slip using the line and the pile as a pivot.

5. Ease her into the slip and tie up.

Wind Astern (Fig. 11)

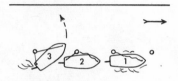

1. Approach as previously described but use enough power astern to stop her positively. Pass a stern line and

2. a bow line, hauling both taut.

3. Using engine, wind and rudder, ease her around and into the slip.

4. Tie up.

This is one of the best methods to use in any reasonably fresh wind as the control you have over the boat is positive and there is little chance that she can get out of control.

TO SUM UP...

- Try to visualize just what conditions will be at the dock *before* you get there.
- Use fenders generously and pad your slip or dock well.
- Keep your engine in good shape and your control cables taut.
- Keep your mooring lines healthy and use chafing gear whenever possible.
- Favor a bight of line around a pile as the last line to let go (as it is an easy matter, when casting off, to let go the end on the vessel).
- Watch lines to see that they don't foul your propeller.
- Remember that a boat will pivot about a point about $\frac{1}{3}$ of her length aft from the bow and will not "follow the front wheels" as does a car. When the bow goes to starboard *the stern will also swing out to port* so that, when turning, a boat cuts a considerably wider path than its beam. It goes around a turn "crab-fashion."

Try the maneuvers (in easy weather first) and see how they treat you. I believe you'll find them kind to your boat, safe under most conditions, and easy to learn and use.

FIG. 870-g As the boat eases astern, the helmsman keeps his eye on the transom, using his controls to turn his propellers ahead just enough to check the sternway.

FIG. 870-h Settled in her berth, the crewman makes fast with docklines, giving attention first to the spring that will prevent the boat's ranging too far astern.

Pacemaker photographs pages 148-151 by Rosenfeld

151(a)

Every good boatman aspires to be known, ultimately, as a good seaman. Perhaps it would be difficult to make a nice distinction between the two. Their skills merge, and overlap. Yet, one may handle his boat effectively in ordinary maneuvers in day-to-day sailing, but lack the inborn instinct of a "good seaman" when faced by a critical situation at sea. The subtle qualities of a seaman can be conveyed neither by word of mouth nor by printed page alone. Instruction can, however, go a long way toward teaching principles based on experience, which the seasoned skipper applies in practice. It is on this premise that the Seamanship chapter which follows has been prepared. Its text is completely new, generous use has been made of illustrations, and both are combined in the new format to which all revised material in recent editions conforms. Its subject matter has been keyed closely to requirements of instruction courses given by the United States Power Squadrons. Studied in conjunction with related chapters which form an integral part of the subject, we believe it constitutes the best and most practical seamanship text ever presented.

SEAMANSHIP

Photograph by Pacific Studio

CHAPTER 9 SEAMANSHIP

The term "seamanship" is a broad one. It encompasses many topics and probably would be defined differently by various persons qualified in the subject. In its broadest scope, *seamanship* for the recreational craft skipper may be considered to cover such areas as knowledge of his craft, its construction and maintenance, its handling under favorable and adverse weather conditions, and the actions to be taken in emergencies. It also covers such subjects as nautical terms and language, and the use of lines, knots, and splices.

Several topics that fall under the general heading of "seamanship" are of such major importance that they are presented as separate chapters. Typical of these are boat handling, anchoring, and marlinespike seamanship. Other subject areas, highly specialized, are also covered separately—seamanship in breaking inlets and outboard seamanship. This chapter will include topics that are not considered elsewhere and thus complete the coverage of this broad but most essential subject area, seamanship.

THE CREW

Recreational boating is usually a family affair—indeed, one of its most pleasing aspects is that essentially the whole family can share in the activities.

One aspect of boating that should not be overlooked is the *training* of the crew. No boat of any appreciable size should depart its slip or mooring for an afternoon's run or a cruise measured in days without an adequately trained crew, especially an alternate for the skipper. The first mate, usually the skipper's wife, should be fully competent to take the helm under all normal conditions of wind and

FIG. 901 In a family crew, the "First Mate"—the Skipper's wife—should be qualified to take the helm and make simple maneuvers, such as coming alongside a pier or anchoring. (Gordon Manning photo)

waves, and hopefully to do so under adverse weather conditions. The mate should be capable of bringing the boat alongside a pier or of anchoring it. A sudden incapacitating illness (heart attack, stroke, etc.) or accident such as a broken arm or leg or blow on the head, may thrust heavy responsibilities upon the mate completely without warning. If that person has been trained ahead of time, the emergency will be significantly less drastic and much more easily handled.

Training the crew

A training program need not be either onerous or unpleasant. It should be planned and carried out on a formal basis so that the skipper can be *sure* that everyone knows what he has to know. The secret to a successful family crew training program is to make it *fun,* and not let it take the pleasure out of pleasure boating. This is not an impossible task; it is not even a difficult one.

With just a little imagination a man-overboard drill can be made into a game without losing one bit of its effectiveness. With patience and adequate opportunities for practice, the mate and older children can be developed into skillful helmsmen. Every member of the crew should know where the fire extinguishers are located *and should have had actual experience in using them.* It is well worth the small price of recharging one or two extinguishers to have had the experience of having put out a fire with one. (By the way, skipper, have *you* ever actually put out a fire with an extinguisher of the type now on your boat?) This practice should not, of course, be carried out on the boat, but it is easily done ashore.

The mate, at least, and preferably several others of the crew, should know how to place the radio set in operation,

how to change channels, which channel is to be used for emergencies, and what to say. All persons aboard, crew or guests, should know where the life preservers are stowed *and how they should properly be worn.*

Instruction plus practice

A proper training program consists of two parts—instruction and practice. The skipper first learns for himself what should be done and how, and then passes this information on to his crew. For routine matters such as boat handling, ample opportunity should be given each crew member to acquire proficiency—it may be quicker and easier on the nerves for the skipper always to bring the boat alongside a pier, but he must have the patience to let others learn how by doing. For emergency procedures, there should be both planned and snap, unannounced drills.

All aboard, *including the skipper,* can be trained to do the right thing instinctively, quickly and unquestioningly should a real emergency ever occur. Not only can they be trained, they must be—this is part of "seamanship" for the crew.

Boat Handling Under Adverse Conditions

Perhaps the greatest test of a skipper's seamanship abilities comes in his handling of his boat under adverse conconditions of wind and waves.

The size of his craft will have little bearing on its seaworthiness. This is fixed more by design and construction. The average power cruiser or sailboat is fully seaworthy enough for all of the conditions that she is likely to encounter in the use for which she is intended. Note carefully that qualifying phrase—"for which she is intended." Don't venture into water areas or weather conditions beyond those for which your boat was obviously designed. It is only good common sense that a craft designed for lake and river use should not be expected to be suitable in all weather offshore.

FIG. 902 Boating is usually a family affair and all members of the "crew" should be given informal training in their duties. Guests should be given a few of the essential "do's" and "don'ts" soon after coming aboard.

FIG. 903 "Rough" seas is a relative term. This ocean-racing sailboat can weather almost any condition of wind and waves if her skipper and crew are good seamen. (Rosenfeld photo)

It is a fact, however, that just what a boat will do is governed to a great extent by the skill of the man at the helm. Thus a good seaman will bring a poor craft through a blow that a novice might not be able to weather in a larger, more seaworthy craft.

"Rough" weather

Rough weather is purely a relative term and what seems a terrible storm to the fair-weather man may be nothing more than a good breeze to the man who has known the sea in all its tantrums.

On large, shallow bodies of water, such as Long Island's Great South Bay, Delaware Bay and River, or Lake Erie, even a moderate wind will cause a steep, uncomfortable sea with crumbling crests because the depth of water is not great enough to permit waves to assume their natural form. Offshore, or in a deeper inland body of water, the same wind force might result in a moderate sea, but the slow, rolling swells would be no menace to a small craft.

Use good judgment—don't panic

Sane small craft skippers don't ask for trouble afloat. Nobody wants to grip the spokes of a wheel when seas are breaking green over the bow or coming over the transom— at least nobody in his right mind. Unfortunately, however, at some time during your cruising career, you may be caught by an unexpected line squall, or obliged to thread your way through an inlet while breakers crash on the bar. *If you apply the fundamentals of good rough weather seamanship, you'll moor at your home berth and have a whopping good yarn to tell.* The casualties stem from those who panic—from boatmen who lose their heads when the going gets rough.

Know your boat

Boat handling under adverse conditions is a quite flexible and individual matter, since no two boats are exactly alike in the same sea conditions. When the going begins to get heavy, each different hull design reacts differently— and even individual boats of the same class will behave differently because of such factors as the way they are loaded and trimmed.

Each skipper must learn his own boat to determine the precise application of general principles to be covered in the following sections. Reading this book and taking courses are important first steps, but they won't be enough when the chips are down. You can pick up the basics of good seamanship by absorbing factual data and principles, but you'll have to pick up the remainder—the elusive quality that makes the "real" skipper—by applying your book and classroom learning on the spot when the wind blows.

Preparations for rough weather

In anticipation of high winds and rough seas, there are certain precautions and preparations that a prudent skipper takes. No single list will fit all boats or all weather conditions, but among the actions that should be considered are these:

1. Secure all hatches; close all ports and windows.
2. Pump the bilges dry and repeat this action as often as required. ("Free" water in bilges adversely affects the

FIG. 904 Each skipper must learn the individual traits of his own boat—how she handles under good and adverse conditions, and what weather she can safely take. Study seamanship, but learn by doing. (Loyd Sandgren photo)

craft's stability.)

3. Secure all loose gear; put away small items and lash down the larger ones.
4. Break out life preservers and have all on board wear them if the situation worsens; don't wait too long.
5. Break out emergency gear that might be needed, such as hand pumps or bailers, sea anchor, etc.
6. Get a good check of your position if possible and update the plot on your chart.
7. Prepare plans for altering course to a protected harbor or sheltered waters if necessary.
8. Reassure your crew and guests; instruct them in what to do and not to do; give them something to do if possible to take their minds off the situation.

HEAD SEAS

Little difficulty should be experienced by the average well-designed power cruiser when running generally into head seas. Spray will be thrown, and in some hull designs there may be a tendency to pound against the waves. If the seas get too steep-sided, or if pounding is encountered, it will be necessary to slow down. This will give the bow a chance to rise in meeting each wave rather than being driven hard into it.

Match speed to sea conditions

Should the conditions get really bad, and there be any danger of "starting" leaks in the planking or tearing loose heavy objects in the bilge, slow down until you're making bare headway, holding your bow at an angle of about forty-five degrees to the swells. The more headway is reduced in meeting heavy seas, the less will be the strain on the hull.

Avoid propeller "racing"

You must reduce speed to avoid damage to either the hull or powerplant for your propeller will "race" as the seas lift the screw clear of the water. It sounds dangerous —and it may be. First, there's a rapidly increasing crescendo of sound as the engine winds up. Then an excessive vibration as the screw bites the water again. Don't panic—simply slow down and change your course till these effects are minimized. Keep headway so that you can maneuver her readily.

Adjust trim

It is possible to swamp your boat if you drive her ahead too fast or if she is poorly trimmed. In a head sea, a vessel with too much weight forward will plunge rather than rise. Under the same conditions, too much weight aft will cause her to fall off. You must give the bow time to rise as she meets the swells instead of driving straight into them. The ideal speed will vary with different boats and power plants —experiment with your craft and discover her best riding speed before you have to utilize the knowledge under storm conditions.

Change the weight aboard if necessary. On outboards, you can shift your tanks and other heavy gear. In any boat, you can direct your passengers and crew to remain where you place them. Under dire emergency situations, you can tow a pail or other form of sea anchor behind you, helping to steer a straight course, slowing your speed forward while enabling you to keep the throttle open wide enough to maneuver. Be careful, however, that you don't foul the line in your propeller.

Meet each wave as it comes

You will be able to make reasonable progress by carefully nursing the wheel—spotting the steep-sided combers coming in and varying your course, slowing or even stopping momentarily for the really big ones. If the man at the wheel is able to see clearly so he can act before dangerous conditions develop, you should be able to weather moderate gales with little discomfort. *Make sure the most experienced seaman aboard acts as helmsman!*

FIG. 905 Close-hauled, with lee rail awash, this yawl is being driven hard. Wind pressure on sails keeps her from rolling as a motor boat would in a beam sea. (Rosenfeld photo)

IN THE TROUGH

If the course to be made good is such that it will require you to run broadside to the swells, bouncing from crest to trough and back up again, you will be rolling heavily, perhaps dangerously. It would probably be wise to resort to what might be called a series of "tacks" much like a sailboat.

Tacking across the troughs

Change course and take the wind and waves at roughly a 45° angle, first broad on your bow and then broad on your quarter. This results in a zig-zag course that makes good the desired objective, while the boat is in the trough for only brief intervals while turning. With the wind broad on the bow, the behavior should be satisfactory; on the quarter, the motion will be less comfortable but at least it it will be better than running in the trough. Make each tack as long as possible for the waters that you are in so as to minimize the number of times that you must pass through the trough when changing tacks.

If you want to turn sharply, allow your powerboat to lose headway for a few seconds, throw the wheel hard over, then suddenly apply power. She will wheel quickly as a powerful stream of water strikes the rudder, kicking you to port or starboard, *without making any considerable headway.* You won't be broadside for more than a minimum length of time. This is the same technique as used in docking in close quarters with adverse current or wind conditions; it is particularly effective with single-screw powerboats.

RUNNING BEFORE THE SEA

Your course may be such that the swells are coming from directly behind you. Running directly before the sea is well enough if the stern of your craft can be kept reasonably up to the seas without being thrown around off course. This is known as *yawing.* But when the seas get too heavy, the boat tends to rush down a slope from crest to trough, and, stern high, the propeller comes out of the water and races. The rudder, also partly out of water, loses its grip, and the sea may take charge of the stern. At this stage, the boat may yaw so badly as to *broach,* to be thrown broadside into the trough out of effective control. This must be avoided through every possible action. Unfortunately, modern cruiser design emphasizes beam at the stern so as to provide a large, comfortable cockpit or afterdeck—this added width at the transom increases the tendency to yaw and possibly broach.

Reducing yawing

Slowing down so as to let the swells pass under the boat usually will reduce the tendency to yaw, or at least will reduce the extent of yawing and so lessen the chances of broaching. While seldom necessary, consideration can be given to towing a heavy line or small sea anchor astern to help check the boat's speed and keep her running straight.

FIG. 906 Sharp lines at the stern of this double-ender make for easier handling in a following sea. Motorboats with wide transoms are much more difficult to keep from yawing as heavy seas pass under the stern. (Rosenfeld photo)

Obviously the line must be carefully handled and not allowed to foul the propeller. Do not tow soft-laid nylon lines which may unlay—even though seized—and cause hockles (strand kinks).

Cutting down the engine speed will reduce the strain imposed on the motor by alternate laboring with stern deep down before an overtaking sea and racing as the head goes down and the propeller comes out at the crest.

Pitchpoling

The ordinary swell off shore is seldom troublesome on this point of running, but the steep wind sea of the lakes and shallow bays makes steering difficult and reduced speed imperative. Excessive speed down a steep slope may cause a boat to *pitchpole,* that is, drive her head under in the trough, tripping the bow, while the succeeding crest catches the stern and throws her end over end. When the going is bad enough to result in risk of this, it helps to keep the stern down and the bow light and buoyant, by shifting weight if necessary.

Shifting any considerable amount of weight aft will reduce a boat's tendency to yaw but too much might cause her to be "pooped" by a following sea breaking into the cockpit. *Do everything in moderation rather than in excess.* Find out if she acts more stable, adjusting her trim bit by bit rather than doing it all at once. Too much speed forward with the incorrect weight distribution might cause a small boat to pitchpole.

Tacking before the seas

Previously, a form of tacking was suggested for avoiding the necessity of running dead into heavy seas or with them directly abeam. This same technique of alternately heading to either side of the base course can also be used when it is desired to avoid large swells directly astern.

Try a zig-zag track so that the swells are off your quarter, minimizing their effects—experiment with slightly different headings to determine the angle at which the waves will have the least tendency to cause your boat to yaw off course. Be careful at all times to keep your craft under control and prevent an unexpected broach.

RUNNING AN INLET

When offshore swells run into shallower water along the beach, they build up a steeper ground swell because of resistance created by the bottom. Natural inlets on sandy beaches, unprotected by breakwaters, usually build up a bar across the mouth. When the ground swell reaches the bar, its form changes rapidly, and a short steep-sided wave is produced which may break where the water is shallowest.

This fact should be taken into consideration when approaching from offshore. A few miles off, the sea may be relatively smooth while the inlet from seaward may not look as bad as it actually is. The breakers may extend clear across the mouth, even in a buoyed channel.

The shoals shift so fast with the moving sand that it is not always feasible to keep buoys in the best water. Local boatmen often leave the buoyed channel and are guided by appearance of the sea, picking the best depth by the smoothest surface and absence of breakers. A stranger is handicapped in such a situation because he may not have knowledge of uncharted obstructions and so may not care to risk leaving the buoyed channel. In a case of this kind,

FIG. 907 Boats that must cross a bar with breaking waves must avoid "pitchpoling"—being thrown end over end if caught driving hard down the face of a steep sea, burying the bow. This double-ended fisherman just misses being caught on the forward face of a breaker. This is no place for pleasure boats.

he should have a local pilot if possible. Otherwise it will sometimes be well to anchor off, if necessary, until you can follow a local boat in.

If it becomes necessary to pick a way through without local help, there are several suggestions which may help to make things more comfortable. Don't run directly in but wait outside the bar until you have had a chance to watch the action of waves as they pile up at the most critical spot in the channel, which will be the shallowest. Usually they will come along in groups of three, sometimes more, but always three at least. The last sea will be bigger than the rest and by careful observation it can be picked out of the successive groups.

When you are ready to enter, stand off until a big one has broken or spent its force on the bar and then run through behind it. Ebb tide builds up a worse sea on the bars than the flood, due to the rush of water out against and under the incoming ground swell. If the sea looks too bad on the ebb, it may be better to keep off a few hours until the flood has had a chance to begin.

This section has concentrated on entering inlets rather than departing through them. This latter action is less hazardous as the boat is on the safe side of the dangerous area and usually has the option of staying there. If the skipper does decide to go out, dangerous areas are more easily spotted from the inside, and a boat heading into surf is more easily controlled than one running with the swells. On the other hand, the skipper of a boat outside an inlet may have little option as to whether or not he can remain in the open sea indefinitely; he may have to enter and can only attempt to do it in the safest possible manner.

For additional information on safely entering a breaking inlet, see Chapter 27.

HEAVING TO

When conditions get so bad offshore that a boat cannot make headway and begins to take too much punishment, it is time to *heave to,* a maneuver that varies in its execution with the type of craft under consideration. Motor boats, both single and twin screw, will usually be most comfortable if brought around head to the seas, or a few points off, using just enough power to make bare steerageway without trying to make any considerable progress through the water. In fact, the boat is likely to be making some sternway or leeway even though kept nearly bow on to the waves.

Sailing craft, when heaving to, will shorten sail, carrying just enough canvas, principally aft, to keep the vessel's head to the sea or nearly so where she can ride comfortably without making progress ahead.

The object always is to lay the craft in such a position that she will take the seas most comfortably, in a manner that is easiest on both the hull and the crew. For some vessels, this may mean allowing her to drift naturally, perhaps with the seas on the quarter, but this is not normal for small craft. For short periods, when the fuel supply permits, the average motorboat will be most comfortable when the propeller is allowed to turn over slowly, giving steerageway enough to keep her head in the desired relationship to the swells as determined by the period of the waves and the natural motion of the boat.

THE SEA ANCHOR

In extreme cases, a *sea anchor* is occasionally used. Normally, this will consist of a canvas cone-shaped bag having an iron hoop to keep it open at the mouth. To this hoop, a bridle and a heavy line is attached which is paid out from the bow and made fast to the forward bitt. A trip line is

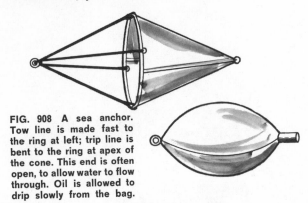

FIG. 908 A sea anchor. Tow line is made fast to the ring at left; trip line is bent to the ring at apex of the cone. This end is often open, to allow water to flow through. Oil is allowed to drip slowly from the bag.

attached to a ring at the end of the cone. This is used to spill the bag and make it easier to haul the anchor back aboard. In use, the theory of the anchor is not to go to the bottom and hold, but merely to present a drag or resistance which will keep the boat's head up within a few points of the wind as she drifts off to leeward. A sea anchor, sometimes called a *drogue,* will usually float a short distance beneath the water's surface.

There are also available on the market, sea anchors made up of a series of plastic floats of a more modern design. These fold compactly for storage and are said to be more effective in holding a boat's head to the sea.

Whatever style of sea anchor is carried on your boat, make sure that it is of sufficient size to be effective. A small one may be easier to stow, but there's no point to having it if it won't do the job.

Improvised sea anchors

In the absence of a regular sea anchor, any form of drag rigged from spars, planks and canvas or other material at hand that will float just below the surface and effectively keep the boat from lying in the trough, would be worth trying. If it could be launched successfully and swamped, with a stout line securely attached, a dinghy could be tried in lieu of the sea anchor, but such procedure is easier to talk about than to accomplish when conditions are bad enough to justify the attempt.

Use of oil with sea anchors

Sea anchors are sometimes equipped with an *oil can* which permits oil to ooze out slowly and form a slick on the surface, thus preventing seas from breaking. The oil might be distributed from a bag punctured with a few holes and stuffed with oakum or waste saturated with oil. (See also the following section on the use of oil.)

Make sure this equipment—sea anchors, trip lines, oil bag lines, lead lines, etc.—is in good condition and not rotten from long disuse or old age. Cotton and manila emergency equipment should be discarded in favor of synthetics.

Sea anchors and lee shores

Sea anchors can be used only if there is sufficient sea room as there is naturally a steady drift to leeward. When a vessel is driven down onto a lee shore and is forced to use her regular ground tackle to ride out a gale, it is imperative that a constant watch be maintained to guard against dragging. Merely having a heavy anchor down doesn't guarantee safety. If ranges are taken on landmarks ashore, dragging can be detected. Engines may have to be used to ease the strain on the anchor during the worst of the blow and a long scope of cable will give the anchor its best chance to hold.

THE USE OF OIL ON ROUGH WATER

Many years of experience at sea have established the value of using oil for the purpose of modifying the effect of breaking seas. Oil is easily dispensed and quickly dispersed; the effect of even small amounts is significant.

The following summary of information on the use of oil on rough waters can guide the small craft skipper should he ever be in a situation requiring its use.

1. On free waves, *i.e.,* waves in deep water, the effect is greatest.

2. In a surf, or waves breaking on a bar, where a mass of liquid is in actual motion in shallow water, the effect of the oil is uncertain, as nothing can prevent the larger waves from breaking under such circumstances, but even here it is of some value.

3. The heaviest and thickest oils are most effectual. Kerosene is of little use; crude petroleum is serviceable when nothing else is obtainable; but all animal and vegetable oils, and waste oil from the engines, will have a useful effect.

4. A small quantity of oil suffices, if applied in such a manner as to spread to windward.

5. In cold water, the oil, being thickened by the lower temperature and not being able to spread freely, will have its effect much reduced. This will vary with the type of oil used.

6. For a boat at sea, the best method of application appears to be to hang over the side, in such a manner as to be in the water, small canvas bags, capable of holding from 1 to 2 gallons of oil, the bags being pricked with a sail needle to facilitate leakage of the oil.

The position of these bags should vary with the circumstances. Running before the wind, they should be hung on either bow and allowed to tow in the water.

With the wind on the quarter, the effect seems to be

FIG. 909 The skipper of this sailboat is a good seaman. Note lifelines around the decks for safety. Note, too, the absence of any clutter of lines or gear on deck.

less than in any other position, as the oil goes astern while the waves come up on the quarter.

Lying-to, the weather bow, and another position farther aft, seem the best places from which to hang the bags, using sufficient line to permit them to draw to windward while the vessel drifts.

7. Crossing a bar with a flood tide, to pour oil overboard and allow it to float in ahead of the boat, which would follow with a bag towing astern, would appear to be the best plan. As noted before, however, under these circumstances, the effectiveness of oil can not always be depended upon.

On a bar, with the tidal current ebbing, it is probably useless to try to use oil for the purpose of entering.

8. For approaching a stranded boat, it is recommended that oil be poured overboard to windward of her before going alongside or close. The effect in this case will greatly depend upon the set of any current and depth of water.

9. For a boat riding in rough water from a sea anchor, it is recommended that the oil bag be fastened to an endless line rove through a block on the sea anchor. By this means, the oil can be diffused well ahead of the boat and the bag can be readily hauled on board for refilling whenever necessary.

10. The general principle involved is to get the oil slick to spread to windward if possible and around the boat in such a way that she stays in the slick. If the oil goes off to leeward or astern, it is of no use.

SEAMANSHIP IN "THICK" WEATHER

Another form of "adverse condition" that will require special skills in seamanship is "thick" weather—conditions of reduced visibility. The cause for this lessoned range of vision may be fog, heavy rain or snow, haze, etc. Of all these, fog is probably the most often encountered and most severe. The general rules and procedures to be considered here are, however, applicable whatever the situation.

Avoiding collisions

Seamanship in fog is primarily a matter of safety, avoiding collisions. Piloting and position determination, the legal requirements for sounding fog signals, and the meterological aspects of fog are all covered elsewhere in this book. Here we will consider only the aspects of boat handling and safety.

The primary needs of safety in fog or other conditions of reduced visibility are to *see and be seen*—to *hear and be heard*. The wise skipper takes every possible action to see or otherwise detect other craft and hazards, and simultaneously takes all steps to ensure that the presence of his boat will be most surely and easily detected by others.

Reduce speed

The detection by sight or sound must be made early enough to allow proper corrective action. All of the Rules of the Road—International, Inland, and others—require a reduction in speed for all vessels in circumstances of low visibility. Specifically, the Rules require that all vessels "go at a moderate speed, having careful regard to the existing circumstances and conditions." Admiralty court decisions over the years have generally established "moderate speed" as that at which the vessel can come to a complete stop in one-half the existing range of visibility. This, obvi-

ously, is subject to varying interpretation rather than precise definition, but it should always be conservatively considered from the viewpoint of safety.

The preferred situation is to be able to stop short in time, rather than having to resort to violent evasive maneuvers to dodge the hazard. The Rules also require that a power-driven vessel hearing the fog signal of another vessel forward of the beam, and not knowing the position of the other vessel, shall insofar as circumstances permit, stop her engines and then navigate with caution until the danger of collision is past.

Lookouts

Equally important with a reduction in speed is the posting of *lookouts*. This, too, is a requirement of the Rules of the Road, but it is also simple common sense. Many, if not most, modern motor and sail boats are designed in a manner such that the helmsman is *not* so located as to be an effective lookout, and thus one or two additional persons are required for this function in thick weather.

Look . . . and listen

Despite the "look" in "lookout," such a person is as much for *listening* as he is for seeing. A person assigned as a lookout should have this duty as his sole responsibility while on watch. A skipper should certainly post a lookout as far forward as possible when in fog, and, if his helmsman is at inside controls, another lookout for the aft sector is desirable. Lookouts should be relieved as often as nec-

FIG. 910 The primary needs of safety in fog are to see and be seen—to hear and be heard. (Bob Ruskauff photo)

essary to ensure their alertness. If the crew is small, an exchange of bow and stern duties will provide some change in position and relief from monotony. If there are enough persons on board a larger craft, a double lookout forward is not wasted manpower. Care should be taken that they do not distract each other from their duties.

A bow lookout should keep alert for other vessels, sound signals from aids to navigation, and hazards in general. In the latter category are rocks and piles, breakers, and buoys—in thick weather, aids to navigation without audible signals can indeed become hazards. A lookout aft should be primarily alert for overtaking vessels, but he may also hear fog signals missed by the man on the bow.

The transmission of sound in fog is uncertain and tricky. It may seem to come from directions other than that toward the true source, and it may not be heard at all at ranges which would be expected as normal. See the discussion of fog signals in Chapter 16.

Stop your engine

When underway in fog in a powerboat, consideration should be given to slowing the engines to idle, or shutting them off entirely, at intervals in order to aid in hearing the fog signals of other vessels and aids to navigation. This is not a legal requirement of the Rules of the Road, but it is an excellent, practical action to take.

During these periods, silence should be maintained on the boat so that even the faintest signal will be heard. These periods of listening should be at least one minute in length in inland waters and two minutes on the high seas to conform with the legally required maximum intervals between the sounding of fog signals. Don't forget to continue to sound your own signal during the listening period —you may get an answer from close-by!

When proceeding in fog at a moderate speed, any time your lookout indicates that he has heard something, immediately cut your engines to idle, or stop them altogether, in order that the lookout may have the most favorable conditions for verifying and identifying what he believes he has heard.

Radar and radar reflectors

Radar comes into its greatest value in thick weather conditions. If you are so equipped, be sure to turn it on and use it; but not at the expense of posting a proper lookout.

Even if you do not have a radar set, you should have a passive radar reflector (see page 382q); then is the time to open it and hoist it as high as possible.

Cruising with other boats

If you are cruising with other boats and fog closes in, you may be able to take advantage of a procedure used by wartime convoys. Tie onto the end of a long, light line some object that will float and make a wake as it moves through the water. A life ring, or a glass or plastic bottle with a built-in handle, will do quite well. This object is towed astern with the boats traveling in column, one object behind each craft except the last.

When the object is kept in sight by the bow lookout on the next boat in column, he knows just where the boat ahead of him is located even though he cannot see her and perhaps cannot even hear her fog signal.

Anchoring and laying-to

If the weather, depth of water, and other conditions are favorable, consideration should be given to anchoring rather than proceeding through conditions of low visibility; but do not anchor in a heavily-traveled channel or traffic lane.

If you cannot anchor, then perhaps laying-to—underway with no way on—may be safer than proceeding at even a much reduced speed. Added quiet will provide increased safety.

Remember that different fog signals are required when you are underway, with or without way on, and when you are at anchor. By all means, sound the proper fog signal and keep your lookouts posted to *look* and *listen* for other craft and hazards.

Helmsmanship

One of the characteristics of a good seaman is the ability to steer well. This is called *helmsmanship*. Here is another quality that cannot be learned entirely from the book, or in a classroom, but there are basic principles that can and should be studied. Knowledge of these, coupled with experience, can make a skipper a better man at the helm than one who has not taken the time and trouble to develop his ability.

Boat's individuality

When considering the general principles of helmsmanship, it must always be borne in mind that these are truly "general" principles. Boats are nearly as individualistic as people, and nowhere is this more noticeable than in their steering characteristics.

Deep-draft and shallow-draft vessels will handle differently. Boats that steer by changing their thrust direction— outboards and inboard-outboards—will respond entirely different than boats steered by rudders. Heavy, displacement hulls will react to helm changes quite unlike light, planing hulls.

FIG. 911 Handling characteristics of various boats are nearly as different as personalities of people. Not all boats will turn as sharply as this fast runabout. A good helmsman knows well the response to the helm of his own craft.

The secret of good helmsmanship is to "know the boat." If you are the skipper of your own craft, this will come relatively quickly as you gain experience with her. If you are invited to take the wheel or tiller of a friend's boat, take it easy at first with helm changes, and make a deliberate effort to get the "feel" of the craft's response.

Steering by compass

At sea and in many larger inland bodies of water, steering is often done by compass. The helmsman must keep the lubberline of the compass (also referred to as the lubber's line; see Chapter 13) on that mark of the card that indicates the course to be steered. If the course to be steered is 100 degrees, and the lubberline is at 95 degrees, the helmsman must *swing the boat's head,* with right rudder, 5 degrees to the right, so that the lubberline is brought around to 100. **Remember, the card stands still while the lubberline swings around it.** Any attempt to bring the desired course on the card up to the lubberline will produce exactly the *wrong* result.

FIG. 912 Steering by compass is a skill that must be acquired by practice. The compass card remains in essentially the same position with relation to the earth and the boat is moved about it.

As a vessel swings with a change in course, there is a tendency for the inexperienced helmsman to allow her to swing too far, due to the momentum of the turn and the lag between turning of the wheel and the craft's response to rudder action. That's why it is necessary to "meet her" so that the vessel comes up to, and steadies on, the new course without over-swinging. This often requires, particularly in larger and heavier cruisers, that the helmsman return the rudder to the neutral, amidships position noticeably before the craft reaches the intended new heading. It may even be necessary to use a slight amount of opposite rudder to check the boat's swinging motion.

A crooked course, yawing from side to side, brands the inexperienced helmsman. A straight course is the goal to shoot at; this can be achieved, after the boat has steadied, by only slight movements of the wheel. It calls for anticipation of the vessel's swing and correction with a little rudder instead of letting her get well off the course before the rudder is applied. A zig-zag course is an inefficient course. The mileage is longer and any offset of the rudder from the center-line tends to retard the craft's progress.

A good helmsman will not only use small amounts of rudder, but he will also turn the wheel slowly and deliberately. The actual manner of steering is again a characteristic of each individual boat and can only be learned by experience with that particular craft.

In piloting small craft, it is often better to pick out a distant landmark, if there is one, or a star at night, to steer by. This helps to maintain a straight course as the compass is smaller and less steady than aboard a larger vessel. The helmsman can then drop his eye periodically to the compass to check his course. Avoid steering on a particular cloud formation as these move with the wind and change shape. In some situations, a boat may be steered for a short time with reference to reflections on the water from the sun or moon, but always remember that these are moving rather than fixed reference points.

EFFECT OF WIND AND SEA

A beam wind will have considerable effect on the steering as the bow, with its relatively greater proportion of freeboard to draft, tends to be driven off more than the stern, and the rudder angle must be sufficient to compensate for this. In a heavy sea, the direction from which the seas are coming will have an effect on the steering. A head sea will be less troublesome than a following sea.

Driving into a head sea, a boat will probably be slowed down to prevent unnecessary pounding, and the swing of the bow will have to be corrected with *slight* rudder changes. In a following sea, the tendency for the stern to be thrown around by overtaking waves (yawing) must be anticipated and checked as much as possible. When the stern is tossed high before an overtaking sea, if it tends to be thrown to starboard, the helmsman must meet her by applying right rudder; a considerable amount of rudder may be required.

Broaching should be avoided at all costs. Ordinarily, if the seas are not too bad, it is possible in handling a small boat to watch astern for the big seas that might cause the boat to yaw excessively. Then by speeding up the engine, with rudder set against the direction of the yaw, the corrective effect of the rudder will be enough to straighten her out and keep the stern up to the sea. As the wave passes the bow, the throttle can be closed again to its previous setting and the rudder brought back to amidships.

SHALLOW WATER

Small craft in heavy following seas such as are built up on inlet bars and in big shallow bodies of water sometimes tend to broach despite anything that can be done by the

FIG. 913 A small steadying sail may be used to advantage to damp the rolling action of a motor cruiser in a beam sea. (F. Raymond Photo)

helmsman. Rudder hard over one way, the boat may run in the opposite direction. When conditions are as serious as that, a drag astern, consisting of a small sea anchor or length of heavy line has been recommended as an aid in keeping the stern up to the sea. The great risk in speeding up too much when the boat has acquired considerable momentum down the descending side of a wave is that of pitchpoling. If she is allowed to trip by running the bow under in the trough between steep seas, the next sea astern may throw her end over end.

Shallow water, besides tending to create a more bothersome steep-sided sea when the wind blows hard, also has a decided effect on the speed and steering of a vessel. A suction is created, the stern settles, and speed is decreased because of the change in the vessel's trim. Propeller and rudder action are both sluggish, so that response to the wheel is not as good as it will be in deep water.

In a small motor boat with exhaust at the stern near the waterline, warning of shallow water is often had before actual grounding, as the exhaust starts to bury under water and a difference in its sound is detected. This happens without any change in the throttle setting.

BEAM SEAS

All craft have what is known as a "natural" period of oscillation, or rolling period, which is the time required by a vessel to roll from one side to the other. If this period happens to coincide with the period of the waves in which she is running, as in a beam sea, the synchronism should be broken by a change of course (and speed, if necessary), to avoid excessive rolling. It is seldom necessary, in such a case, to meet the seas squarely bow-on.

Slight changes of course often damp the rolling enough to make the vessel comfortable. If the craft is disabled, with power not available, then the only way to prevent heavy rolling is to get out a sea anchor or drogue to hold the bow up to the sea, used perhaps in conjunction with storm oil if the waves are breaking.

Occasions may arise, as in preparing to heave to, when a vessel that has been running before a following sea must be brought around head to sea. This calls for skill and judgment and a knowledge of the steering qualities of the particular craft involved. By watching carefully the procession of waves as they pass, taking into consideration their height and the distance between them and space required for the turn, it will usually be possible to avoid having her caught broadside to a dangerous swell.

Invariably a boat is under better control when her engine is going ahead rather than in reverse. The propeller, in the first instance, is throwing a stream of water past the rudder blade. In general, if left to her own devices, with engines stopped, the bow of the average boat will fall off until the wind comes somewhat abaft the beam, because of the relative height of bow and superstructure forward as compared with that aft where the draft is normally greater.

Stranding, Assisting, and Towing

It is an unwritten law of the sea that one should never pass an opportunity to render assistance to any vessel in need of aid. Of course this is one of the primary functions of the Coast Guard, but there are plenty of occasions when a little timely help on the part of a fellow boatman may save hours of labor later after the tide has fallen or wind and sea have had a chance to make up.

As often as not, assistance is likely to take the form of a tow line passed to another skipper to get him out of a position of temporary embarrassment or perhaps to get him to a Coast Guard station or back to port in case of failure of any of his gear.

Or perhaps the situation will be the other way around. If you do a normal amount of boating, and poke your bow into a number of strange places, the chances are that some day *you* may go aground. It is equally possible that some day a balky motor may force you to ask a tow from a passing boat, or you may be on the passing boat from which a tow is requested.

In either case, you should know what to do, and why. Let us consider the problem and possible solutions from each of two points of view—being in need of help yourself, and being the boat that assists another.

STRANDING

Simple stranding, running aground, is more often an inconvenience than a danger and, with a little "know how" and some fast work, the period of stranding may be but a matter of minutes.

If it should happen in that before-mentioned strange harbor, the very fact that it is strange presupposes that you have been feeling your way along and so, probably, have just touched bottom lightly, in which case you should be off again with a minimum of difficulty, *provided* that your immediate actions do not tend to put you aground more firmly.

Right and wrong actions

One's first instinctive act on going aground is to throw one's engines into reverse and gun them to the limit in an effort to pull off; this may be the one thing that you should *not* do.

If in tidal waters, the first thing to consider is, of course, the stage of the tide.

If the tide is rising, and the sea quiet enough so that the hull is not pounding, time is working for you, and whatever you do to assist yourself and the boat will be much more effective after a little time has passed. If, on the other hand, you grounded on a falling tide, you will have to work quickly and do exactly the right things or you will be fast for several hours or more.

About the only thing you know offhand is the shape of the hull, its point of greatest draft, and consequently the part most apt to be touching, but bottom contours may be such that this premise will not be true. If, however, the hull shows any tendency to swing, due to the action of wind or waves, the point about which it pivots is most apt to be the part grounded.

Cautions in getting off

The type of bottom requires immediate consideration. If it is sandy, and you reverse hard, you will be apt to wash a quantity of sand from astern and throw it directly under the keel, with the obvious result of bedding the boat more firmly to the bottom. Always exercise discretion in reversing while aground due to the risk of pumping sand or mud into the engine. If the bottom is rocky and you insist on trying to reverse off, you may drag the hull and do more damage than with the original grounding. Also, if grounded forward, the well known tendency of

the stern to swing to port, when reversing with a single-screw boat having a right-hand wheel, may swing the hull broadside onto exposed pinnacles or to a greater contact with a soft bottom.

How to use a kedge

The one *right* thing to do immediately after grounding is to take out an anchor and set it firmly; this is called a *kedge;* the act of using it is *kedging*.

Unless the boat has really been driven on, the service anchor should be heavy enough. Put the anchor *and* the line in the dinghy, make the bitter end fast to the stern bitts or to something solid and row out as far as possible, letting the line run from the stern of the dinghy as it uncoils. Taken out this way, the oarsman's task will be much easier than if he tries to drag the line from the large boat through the water.

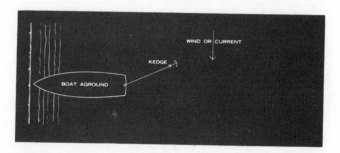

FIG. 914 The most important thing to do after going aground is to get out a *kedge*—an anchor to keep you from being driven further aground and possibly a means of pulling yourself free as waves or the wake from another boat lifts your craft.

If you do not carry a dinghy, it is often possible to swim out with an anchor provided that the sea and weather conditions do not make it hazardous to go into the water. Life preservers or buoyant cushions—one or two of either —can be used to support the anchor out to where you wish to set it. Be sure to wear a life jacket or buoyant vest yourself so as to save your energy for the work to be done.

If there is *no* other way to get a kedge anchor out, you may consider throwing it out as far as possible. Although this is, of course, contrary to the basic principle that an anchor is never thrown over the side, the importance of getting a kedge set is sufficient to warrant the use of this technique under the circumstances. It may be necessary to pull in the anchor and throw again one or more times to get it set firmly.

When setting out the kedge, consider again the sideways turning effect of a reversing single screw and, unless the boat has twin screws, set the kedge at a compensating angle from the stern. If the propeller is right hand, as those of most boats are, set the anchor slightly to starboard of the stern. This will give two desirable effects. When pulling together with kedge line and reverse the boat will have practically a straight pull on it, and when used alternately, first pulling on the line and then giving a short surge with the reverse, the action may give a sort of wiggling action to the stern and the keel, which will be a real help in starting the boat moving.

Getting added pulling power

If you can find a couple of double-sheave blocks (pulleys) and a length of suitable line on board, make up a handy-billy or fall and fasten it to the kedge line. Then you can really pull! Such a handy-billy should be a part of the boat's regular equipment, anyhow.

Whatever else you may do, during the entire period of grounding, persist in keeping that kedge-line as taut as the combined strength of those on board can make it. You may be agreeably surprised by having the boat yield suddenly to that continued pull, especially if a passing boat throws a wake to help lift the keel off the bottom.

Two kedges set out at an acute angle from either side of the stern and pulled upon alternately may give that desired stern wiggle that will help you work clear.

Working off

If the bottom is sandy, that same pull, with the propeller going *ahead* may result in washing some sand *away* from under the keel, with the desired result. If the kedge line is kept taut, you may try it with a clear mind. At least you will not do any harm.

Move your crew and passengers quickly from side to side to roll the boat and make the keel work in the bottom. If you have spars, swing the booms outboard and put men on them to heave the boat down, thus raising the keel line. Shift ballast or heavy objects from over the portion grounded to lighten that section and if you can, remove some internal weight by loading it into the dinghy or by taking it ashore if that is possible.

When to stay aground

All of the above is predicated on the assumption that the boat is grounded, but not holed or strained open. If either of these last has happened, you may be far better off where she lies than you would be if she were in deep water again. If she is badly stove, you may want to take an anchor ashore, to hold her on or pull her further up until temporary repairs can be made. Perhaps, as the tide falls, the damaged portion may be exposed far enough to allow some outside patching; always presupposing that you have something aboard to patch with! A piece of canvas, cushions, bedding, these are all illustrative of items that can be used in an emergency as temporary hull patches.

What to do while waiting

While waiting for the tide to rise, or for the Coast Guard to come, you do not need to sit idle. Take soundings all around the position where the boat lies aground. It is possible that a swing of the stern to starboard or port may do more for you than any amount of straight backward pulling; soundings will reveal any additional depth that may exist to either side to help you out.

If there is another boat present, she may be able to help you even if she is not suitable for pulling. Have the other skipper run his craft back and forth at a speed that will make as much wake as possible. The rise and fall of his wash may lift your boat just enough to permit you to back clear.

Even though the hull is unharmed, and you are left with a falling tide to sit it out for a few hours, you may as well be philosophical and get over the side and make good use of those hours. Undoubtedly you would prefer to do it under happier circumstances, but this may be your chance to get a good check on the condition of the bottom, or do any one of a number of little jobs that you could not do otherwise, short of a haulout.

FIG. 915 If you go aground on a falling tide, you may find yourself "high and dry." If so, try to brace the boat so that she will stay upright; she will refloat easier if you do. While you are out of water, make an inspection of the bottom. (Photo by Charles True)

If she is going to be left high and dry, keep an eye on her layover condition. If there is anything to get a line to, even another kedge, you can make her lie over on whichever side you choose, as she loses buoyancy. If she is deep and narrow she may need some assistance in standing up again, particularly if she lies over in soft mud. Both the suction of the mud and her own deadweight will work against her in that case.

ASSISTING

If, rather than being stranded, you are in a position to render assistance to another skipper who has been so unlucky as to go aground, it is just as important that you know what to do, and what not to do, in the circumstances.

It is of *primary* importance to see that the assisting boat does not join the other craft in its trouble! Consider the probable draft of the stranded vessel in comparison with the draft of your boat. Consider also the size and weight of the boat that is aground in comparison with the power of your engines—don't tackle an impossible job; there are other ways of rendering assistance.

Getting a line over

It may seem easiest to bring a line in to a stranded boat by coming in under engine power, bow on, passing the line and then backing out again, but the maneuver should not be attempted unless one is sure that there will be water enough under the assisting boat, and also, unless the boat backs well, without too much stern crabbing due to the action of the reversed screw. Wind and current direction will greatly affect the success of this maneuver. If all conditions are adverse and tend to swing the boat broadside to the shallows as she backs, it will be best to try to pass the line in some other manner.

Perhaps the assisting boat may back in, with wind or current compensating for the reversed screw, thus keeping her straight and leaving the bow headed out with consequent better maneuverability. In any case, after the line is once passed and made fast, the assisting boat should do the actual pulling with engines going ahead, to get full power into the pull.

If conditions are such that a close approach is unwise, it will be far better for the second boat to drop anchor, or even two anchors, well off the stranded boat and then send the line over in a dinghy, or else buoy the line and attempt to float it in to the grounded boat.

Making the pull

If wind or current or both are broadside to the direction of the pull, the assisting boat would best stay anchored even while pulling. Otherwise, as soon as she takes the strain (particularly if the line is fast to her stern) she will have lost her own maneuverability, and will gradually make leeway, which could eventually put her aground broadside.

If the pulling must be done with the assisting boat under way, the line should be made fast well forward of the stern so that while hauling, she can angle into the wind and current and still hold her own position.

Tremendous strains can be set up, particularly on the stranded boat, by this sort of action, even to the point of carrying away whatever the tow-line is made fast to. Ordi-

nary recreational craft are *not* designed as tug boats! It is probable that the cleats or bitts available for making the line fast are not strong enough for such pulling, and even more likely that they are not located advantageously for such work.

It is far better to run a bridle around the whole hull and pull against this bridle rather than to risk starting some part of the stern by such straining. The assisting boat should also be bridled if there is any doubt of her ability to withstand such concentrated strains.

When operating in limited areas, the stranded craft should have a kedge out for control when she comes off. She should also have another anchor ready to be put over the side if necessary; this may be required to keep her from going back aground if she is without power.

Through all of this maneuvering, it is imperative to see that all lines are kept clear so as not to foul the propeller and that no sudden surge is put on a slack line.

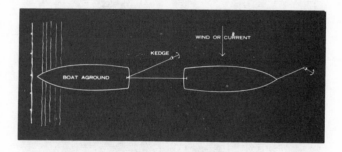

FIG. 917 Most small craft must make the pull with the line made fast near the stern. This restricts maneuverability and, for safe control, a bow anchor should be put out. Slack of the anchor line should be taken up as the stranded boat comes free to prevent the pulling boat from being carried around into shoal water.

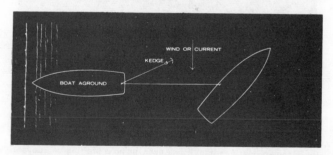

FIG. 918 To aid in maneuverability if a bow anchor cannot be set, the tow line may be made fast to a cleat forward of the stern on the up-wind or up-current side. This cleat *must* be capable of taking heavy strain.

FIG. 916 If a line is to be sent to another boat, you can heave a light line which can then be used to pull the heavier towing line across. A weighted end on the light line will make it easier to throw—this can be a "monkey's fist," as shown.

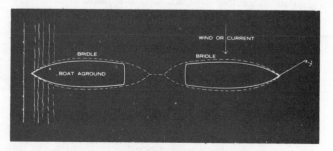

FIG. 919 Tremendous strains are set up when trying to free a stranded boat. Most bitts and cleats on recreational small craft cannot take such a load. It is safer to put a bridle around the superstructure of both boats. Pad pressure points to protect against chafing and scarring.

TOWING

Somewhere in the course of your boating experience you are likely to run up against a situation where you wish to take another vessel in tow. In good weather with no sea running, the problem is comparatively easy, involving little more than the maneuvering of your boat into position in line with, and ahead of, the other boat and the passing of a tow line.

FIG. 920 It is generally desirable to pass a line from the assisting boat to the one being aided. If the weather is rougher than as shown here, or for any reason the other boat cannot be approached, the rescuing boat can float a line over, using a life ring or buoyant cushion.

Generally speaking, it is best for the towing boat to pass her tow-line to the other craft. It may be desirable to emulate large-ship practice and first send over a light line, using that to haul over the actual towing line. Plastic water ski tow lines that float are excellent for use as this initial ("messenger") line to the other boat.

When approaching a boat, dead in the water, with the intention of passing a line, if there is any kind of sea running, do not be dramatic and try to run in too close. Just buoy a long line with several life preservers, tow it astern and take a turn about the stern of the disabled one, but don't foul their propeller in so doing. The occupants will be able to pick it up with a boathook from the cockpit with far less fuss than by any heave-and-catch method.

The forward bitts are usually rugged and so the towed one may make the line fast at that point; then, with someone at the wheel to assist by steering, there is little more

to do than to have an anchor ready to drop if, for any reason, the tow-line parts or is cast loose.

Handling the towing boat

The tow boat, however, requires some real handling!

The worst possible place to make the tow-line fast is to the stern of the lead boat, because the pull of the tow prevents the stern from swinging properly in response to rudder action and thus interferes with the boat's maneuvering ability. The tow-line should be made fast as far forward as practicable, as in tug and tow boat practice. If no suitable place is provided, it is best to make a bridle from the forward bitts, running around the superstructure to a point in the forward part of the cockpit. Such a bridle will have to be wrapped with chafing gear wherever it bears on the superstructure or any corners, and even then, some chafing of the finish is almost bound to occur.

Towing lines

Manila makes a good tow line; nylon is even better because of the spring in it. The "poly" ropes have an added advantage in their floatability. Size and strength must be considered, whatever the choice.

Anything that tends to produce a spring to ease heavy shocks when towing in heavy weather is helpful. It is on this principle that long heavy tow lines are used for easy towing. The sag in the tow line is desirable and can be increased if necessary by bending an anchor to the middle of the line. This will relieve excessive strains on the towing hawser. In rough weather a long tow line should be used, even if the tow is light.

Cautions in towing

The tow-line should be made fast so that it can be cast loose if necessary or, failing that, have a knife or hatchet ready to cut it. This line is a potential danger to anyone near if it should break and come whipping forward. Nylon, when it breaks or lets go, acts like a huge rubber band and there have been some bad accidents. In one case a cleat pulled loose from the deck and came through the air like a projectile. Never stand near or in line with a highly strained line and keep a wary eye out at all times.

If for any reason you have to approach a burning vessel, be sure to approach it in such a manner that the flames are blowing away from you. If there are reasons it must be towed (for instance, to prevent it from endangering other boats or property) your light anchor with its length of chain thrown into the cockpit or through a window could act as a good grappling hook.

Never at any time in the process of towing have people on deck to fend off with hands or feet as even the smallest boats coming together under these condition can cause broken bones or severed fingers. Also never allow anybody to be caught between two large vessels where they will be exposed to this danger. The risk here could be the loss of a whole limb.

Never allow anyone to hold a towing line while towing another vessel regardless of size. Badly torn tendons and muscles could make them cripples for life, or they could be dragged overboard.

Starting the tow

Start off easy! Don't try to dig up the whole ocean with

your screw, and merely end up with a lot of cavitation and vibration without getting anywhere in particular. A steady pull at a reasonable speed will get you there just as fast and with far less strain on boats, lines, and crews.

Towing principles

When towing, boats should be kept "in step," as it were, by adjusting the length of tow line so that the lead boat and her tow are both on the crest or in the trough of seas at the same time. Under certain conditions, with a confused sea, this may be largely a theoretical consideration, but the general principle is to prevent, if possible, a situation where the tow is shouldering up against the back of one sea, presenting a maximum of resistance, while the towing boat is trying to run down the forward slope of another sea. Then when this condition is reversed, the tow alternately runs ahead and surges back on the tow line with a heavy strain. If there is any degree of uniformity to the waves, the strain on the hawser will be minimized by adjusting it to the proper length.

As the tow gets into protected, quiet waters, shorten up on the line to allow better handling in close quarters. Swing as wide as possible around buoys, channel turns, etc., so that the tow will have room to follow.

A small boat in tow should preferably be trimmed a little by the stern because trimming by the head causes her to yaw. In a seaway this condition is aggravated and it becomes increasingly important to keep the bow relatively light.

In smooth water motor boats may at times borrow an idea from tugs which often, in harbor or sheltered waters, take their tow alongside for better maneuverability. If the tow is a big one the tug will make fast on the other craft's quarter.

It is easy for a larger boat to tow a smaller vessel too fast, causing it to yaw and capsize. Always tow at a moderate speed and make full allowance for adverse conditions of wind and waves.

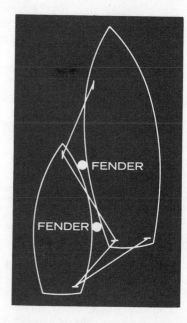

FIG. 921 How springs are used when a boat takes a larger vessel in tow alongside. Fenders are rigged at points of contact, springs made up with no slack. When the towing boat puts her rudder to port or starboard for a turn, both boats respond as a unit.

FIG. 922 A boatman should always be ready to render assistance. In some cases, the best that can be done is to call for assistance and stand by. The Coast Guard 40-footer shown is well equipped to pull a stranded boat free and take her in tow; her crew, too, is better trained and more experienced. (U.S. Coast Guard photo)

When not to tow

Towing can be a dangerous undertaking, as well as an expensive one, if not properly done. If you are not equipped to do a proper towing job, stand by the disabled vessel. It may, however, be feasible to put a line across and assist by holding the other craft's bow into the sea at a comfortable angle while waiting for a more suitable towing vessel.

Call the Coast Guard or other salvage agency and turn the job over to them when they arrive. Don't try to be a hero, as you are more than likely not experienced or trained for this type of work. No boat is worth a life.

Emergency Procedures

The average boatman is a relatively typical person in that he tends to believe that emergencies and accidents happen to "the other guy," and not to him. The seasoned skipper—the good seaman—reasons otherwise. It is not likely to happen to him, but it *could*, and so he prepares himself just in case it does. He also prepares his crew, and, to a lesser extent, the guests aboard his boat.

The best seaman is the one who is prepared for any emergency, before the need arises to meet it.

Value of planning

An emergency is, by definition, not a planned event, but actions to cope with foreseeable ones can be preplanned and rehearsed. Any emergency will be much less severe and much more easily countered if there is a routine to be executed almost instantly when needed.

It must be recognized, of course, that the actual circumstances will surely vary somewhat from those used for planning and practice, but nevertheless a basic approach and assignment of duties will be of immense help in coping with the unexpected. There is nothing more valuable than fast and correct action when something goes wrong.

Need for drills and practice

The best plans are of little value if they have not been tried out and evaluated to the best extent practicable short of having a full occurrence of the emergency.

When the plans have been tried out and modified as needed, the next step is to have periodic drills. This should not be done so much as to become boring or irksome, but there are reasonable minimums that should be met. Every boating family should run through its emergency procedures at the beginning of each boating season, and once again on a staggered schedule later in the season. As mentioned earlier in this chapter, every effort should be made to make the drills enjoyable without reducing their business-like nature.

Guests aboard

Crew training extends, of course, to preparation for emergencies. But do not overlook any guests whom you may have aboard; on most boats, they are at least "temporary crew." You may not be able to train them in drills, but as a minimum they should be shown the location of life preservers and instructed, if necessary, in their use. Do this in a casual, relaxed manner so that they are informed but not alarmed.

If the guests are going to be aboard for an extended cruise, their indoctrination can be correspondingly extended to such items as the location and operation of fire extinguishers, bilge pumps, etc. Use your good judgment as to how far this should be carried with various individuals.

Types of emergencies

The preceding major section of this chapter dealt with what is probably the most common of boating accidents, running aground. Here we will consider emergencies that are more serious, but fortunately much less likely to happen—man overboard, fire, sudden leaking, and abandoning ship.

MAN OVERBOARD

At the cry "Man Overboard" fast—*immediate*—action is of the utmost importance; every second counts, particularly at night, in heavy weather, or in cold water. The actions of the helmsman and other crew members should be automatic and without many shouted orders.

It is helpful to the following action if the cry of "Man Overboard" is supplemented by an indication of which side he went over—Port or Starboard, or even Left or Right. This focuses attention of those who did not see the accident and guides their actions.

Immediate actions

It is customary for the person at the helm to cut the throttle immediately, put the engines in neutral, and swing the stern to the side away from the person in the water. In actual practice, this is of questionable value—a 30-foot boat doing 12 knots moves one boat length in 1½ seconds. Thus even if the person fell off the bow, the stern would be past him before effective action at the controls could be taken. If the victim should fall overboard from

the cockpit, you will be well beyond him almost instantly —don't waste time with throttles or gear shifts, go on immediately with the next steps of the rescue.

Post a lookout

It is imperative that the person in the water be kept in sight at all times, or at least the spot where he was last seen. Heave over some buoyant object *at once*. Preferably, this will be a standard life ring or a buoyant cushion, but throw something over *immediately*. This will serve to mark the spot and perhaps provide assistance to the person overboard. Designate a specific crewman to do *nothing*

FIG. 923 The "Sav-a-Life" plastic ball can be thrown farther and more accurately than a standard life ring or cushion. When it hits the water, it automatically opens and inflates into a buoyant ring that will support a person in the water. Although not an accepted substitute for legally-required life preservers, it can be helpful in man-overboard emergencies.

but watch the person or his last known location. If more than one crew member is available, assign two to this as their *sole* duty. If it is night-time, have a member of the crew man the searchlight and keep it on the person in the water while the boat maneuvers to pick him up.

Throw over a life preserver

Throw overboard a life ring or buoyant cushion even though the person in the water is known to be a strong swimmer. Throw as closely as possible to the person without directly hitting him. He may have had the breath knocked out of him when he hit the water, he may be burdened with clothing and shoes, he may even panic despite his swimming ability—for all these reasons, he should have added buoyancy as soon as possible. A water-activated light attached to a life ring is the most effective nighttime device for man-overboard emergencies.

No "heroes"

Don't let a would-be "hero" jump over the side immediately to rescue the victim—then you would only have two persons rather than one to fish out of the water. The only exception to this would be in the case of a small child or an elderly or handicapped adult. If this must be done, be sure that the rescuer takes with him a life ring or cushion; never let a person enter the water without some added buoyancy.

Maneuvering to return

Whether you turn to port or starboard had best be decided by experiment in advance. Ordinarily a boat with a right-handed propeller turns quickest to port, but practical experience shows that some boats behave otherwise. By this maneuver you should be able to get back to the scene, with boat under perfect control, in less than a minute. You might find that reversing and backing will be more effective for your boat, but the odds are against it. At any rate make a few tests. Throw a paper or cardboard box overboard and experiment in recovering it until you know precisely what to do if the need should ever arise.

If your craft is a sailboat, the maneuvers necessary to return to the location of the accident and recover the victim will vary widely with your point of sailing at the time and the direction of the wind. In some situations, the boat should come about; in others, jibing will result in faster action. If a spinnaker is in use, it will probably have to be gotten down immediately before the boat can maneuver. For sailboats, man overboard drills are far more important than for power craft, and should be executed under a wide variety of situations.

Use additional markers

In some circumstances, particularly at night, it may be desirable to throw overboard additional small objects that will float while the boat maneuvers so as to ensure that the path back to the victim can be retraced. A single marker may be lost to sight; multiple objects increase the probability of returning to the proper location.

Maneuvering for the pick-up

Circumstances will dictate best procedure as to how to approach the man in the water. Although the boat can best be kept under control by approaching from leeward, maneuvering into a position to windward of him will provide a lee as the boat drifts toward him.

The particular maneuver that you use in approaching the victim depends upon common sense and good judgment based on existing conditions such as the sea condition, the temperature of the water, physical condition and ability of the man in the water, boat maneuverability, and the availability of other assistance.

A good procedure is to stop the boat a short distance from the victim in the water, throwing him a light line (such as a skiing tow line of material that floats), and pulling him over to the boat. This will be considerably less hazardous than trying to maneuver the boat right up to him.

Getting the victim on board

While the boat is being maneuvered back to the victim in the water, make all preparations for getting him back on board. Have a member of the crew, who is physically capable, prepare to go into the water, *if necessary*. He should remove any excess clothing and shoes and *always* put on a life jacket. He will need the added buoyancy in order to save his strength to aid the victim. The rescuer should also have a light safety line; it may be useful in transferring it to the accident victim.

Assisting the unlucky victim back into the boat is a highly individualized matter determined by the craft, the person, and the prevailing sea conditions. The availability

of a transom boarding platform if the boat is so equipped will be most helpful. A swimming ladder can usually be quickly rigged if one is carried aboard. Lines with a loop in one end tied with a bowline may be hung over the side for handholds or footholds in climbing back aboard.

Obviously, the propeller should be stopped whenever there is a person in the water near the stern of the boat.

Call for help if needed

If the victim is not immediately rescued, get on the radio with the urgent communications signel "Pan" to summon assistance from the Coast Guard, marine police, and nearby boats. (Do *not* use "Mayday" as your vessel is not in distress.) Continue the search until released by competent authority.

Importance of drills

Man overboard drills are most important. It is not necessary for an individual to go over the side, any floating object about the size of a human head can be used as the "victim." For such drills, one crew member should be told to stand aside and take no part in the "rescue" just as if it were he who was in the water. And don't forget that for some drills this non-participant should be the skipper—some day it just might be he who was the "man overboard" and his rescue had to be effected by the rest of the crew without his guidance.

Always hold a "critique" after each drill. Discuss what was done right and what was done wrong, how the procedures could be done better. Learn from your mistakes, and don't repeat them.

FIG. 924 On every boat, large or small, it is wise occasionally to conduct a "man-overboard" drill. The exact techniques may vary with conditions, but the essence of the idea is: be prepared.

FIRE EMERGENCIES

Fire on a boat can be a serious experience. A person's surroundings are burning, and he is faced with nowhere to go except into the water. In a sense, he is trapped.

Keep in mind that most fires are preventable. A skipper who keeps his boat in shipshape condition, which includes clean bilges and proper stowage of fuel and gear, will probably never be faced with the emergency condition of fighting a fire. This requires constant attention; whenever a condition is observed that might contribute to a fire, it should be corrected at once.

Despite the skipper's best efforts, fires are a possibility and do occur. Every boatman should be foresighted in this regard. Shipshape conditions include the proper stowage and maintenance of firefighting gear. Having this equipment handy and in good working condition is the first step in combating fire.

Explosions and fires

Fires may start with either a "bang"—an explosion—or on a much smaller scale. Should your craft have a gasoline explosion, there usually is little that you can do except grab a life preserver, if possible, and go over the side.

When clear of danger, check about and account for all those who were aboard. Render such assistance as you can to those who may be in the water without a buoyant device and those who may have been burned or injured in the blast. Keep all individuals in the water together in a group for morale purposes and to facilitate rescue by other craft.

Small fires

Should a small fire develop, prompt and effective action will probably control it. Fires require three elements for their existence—fuel, oxygen (air), and heat— remove any one of these and the fire will go out. Thus most fires are fought by smothering them (removing the source of air) or by cooling below the temperature that will support combustion.

FIG. 926 Risk of explosion or fire is greatest when the engines are being started or are running. The helmsman should have an extinguisher within easy reach.

Classes of fires

Fires are classified into three categories:

Class A—fires in ordinary combustible materials such as wood, paper, cloth, etc., where the "quenching-cooling" effect of quantities of water or solutions containing large percentages of water is most effective in reducing the temperature of the burning material below the ignition temperature, and is, therefore, of first importance.

Class B—fires in flammable petroleum products or other flammable liquids, greases, etc., where the "blanketing-smothering" effect of oxygen-excluding media is most effective.

Class C—fires involving electrical equipment where the electrical conductivity of the extinguishing media is of first importance.

Fire extinguishers

Fire extinguishers are classified on the same "A", "B", "C" system as are fires. Some types of extinguishers, however, have a suitability greater than their basic classification. Extinguishers required by law on boats are in the "B" category, but a carbon-dioxide or dry-chemical extinguisher will also have value in fighting an electrical ("C") fire. On the other hand, a foam-type "B" extinguisher is effective on ordinary Class "A" fires but is *not* safe on Class

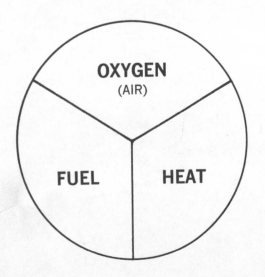

FIG. 925 Three elements are needed to support combustion of a fire—fuel, oxygen (air), and heat. If any one is removed, the fire will go out. Fires can be fought by removal of air (smothering), reduction of heat (cooling), or by shutting off of the flow of liquid or gaseous feul.

"C" electrical fires. Boatmen should remember that for typical Class "A" fires in wood, paper, or bedding, the popular dry-chemical extinguishers are *not* as suitable as an ordinary bucket of water.

Fire extinguishers should be distributed around the boat in relation to potential hazards. One should also be near the boat's control station where it can be grabbed quickly by the helmsman. Another should be mounted near the skipper's bunk so that he can roll out at night with it in his hand. Other locations include the galley (but remember that water is best on a stove alcohol fire!) and any other compartment at some distance from the location of other extinguishers. Fire extinguishers should be mounted where they are clearly visible to all on board as they move about the boat.

Fighting fires

Burning items such as wood, mattresses, and rags are best extinguished by the cooling effect of an agent such as water. For this reason a bailer or bucket can be a most valuable piece of equipment. You will have an unlimited supply of water available on all sides. Throwing burning materials over the side should not be overlooked.

If a fire occurs in a relatively confined space, the closing of hatches, doors, vents, and ports will tend to keep oxygen from fanning the flames. The hatch or door should not be reopened until fire-fighting equipment is ready for use. In addition, should the fire be in a machinery space, shut off the fuel supply and activate the fixed fire-extinguishing system, if your boat is so equipped.

Maneuvering the boat

Now let us consider vessel maneuvers that will assist in extinguishing fires. When underway, wind caused by the boat's motion fans the flames; stopping or reducing speed helps to reduce the wind effect. Also it would make sense to keep the fire downwind—that is, if the fire is aft, head the bow of the boat into the wind; if the fire is forward, put the stern of the boat into the wind. Such action helps to reduce any tendency of the fire to spread to other parts of the boat, and may reduce the hazard of smoke enveloping persons on board.

Stow some life preservers well forward in case of fire aft or the necessity of abandoning ship over the bow.

Summary of actions

The following suggested steps are listed and may be performed, not necessarily in the order shown:
1. If possible, apply the extinguishing agent by:
   a. Using a fire extinguisher,
   b. Discharging fixed smothering system, or
   c. Applying water to wood or materials of this type.
2. If practical, burning materials should be jettisoned (thrown over the side).
3. Reduce the air supply by:
   a. Maneuvering the vessel to reduce the effect of wind, and
   b. Closing hatches, ports, vents, doors, etc. if the fire is in an area where this action will be effective.
4. Make preparation for abandoning ship, which include:
   a. Putting on lifesaving devices, and
   b. Signaling for assistance by radio or any other means available.

LEAKS AND DAMAGE CONTROL

A boat floats properly only so long as the water is kept outside. A small boat with sufficient built-in flotation ability may stay afloat when filled with water, but it will be rather uncomfortable for the crew and passengers. A skipper who is a good seaman prepares a plan of action to be put into effect should his craft suddenly start taking on water as a result of a collision, striking a submerged object, failure of a through-hull fitting, etc.

Planning ahead

The circumstances of suddenly taking on water are so varied as to permit only the most generalized advance planning. Drills are usually not possible for this type of emergency, but a checklist of probably desirable actions can be prepared.

Standard procedures

It should be, to use a military term, SOP (Standard Operating Procedure) to immediately switch on *all* bilge pumps if there is any suspicion of hull damage that might result in taking on water. There are no legal requirements for pumps, as there are for life preservers, fire extinguishers, etc., and many small craft are equipped to handle only a very small inflow of water. The risk of harm to the pumps by running them dry is far less than that of having water in the bilge get a head start on you because of a delay in starting pumping. Remember to turn off the pumps as soon as you are sure that they are not needed.

Actions of the crew

Members of the crew should be assigned immediately to man the manual bilge pump if you have one (and you certainly should have one!). Another crewman should be told to start at once to inspect for leaks; pull up floor boards and check the bilges, don't wait for the water to rise above the cabin sole.

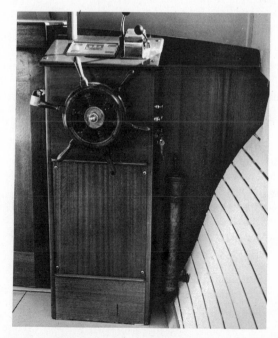

FIG. 927 **In addition to electrical bilge pumps, a boat should be equipped with at least one manually-operated pump. This can be used even if rising water in the bilge shorts out the boat's batteries.**

If it is determined that the boat is taking on water, it is probably advisable for the skipper to turn over the helm to a qualified member of the crew so that he can go below and personally take charge of the damage control actions.

In most situations, the boat should be slowed or brought to a stop to minimize the inflow of water, but it is possible that a hole in the hull could be in such a location that it would be held above the waterline by maintaining speed.

Emergency pumping

It is sometimes possible in grave emergencies, where the regular electric and manual bilge pumps cannot keep up with the inflow of water, to use the water pumps of the main engines. Shut off an engine, close the seacock on the raw water intake, break the connection between the seacock and the hose, and move the latter into the now rising bilge water; restart the engine. Engine raw water pumps have quite a capacity and may make the difference between sinking and staying afloat.

Two precautions must be observed. First, there must be enough water already in the bilge and flowing in to meet the engine's needs for cooling. Secondly, caution must be exercised to keep bilge dirt and trash from being sucked into the engine's intake. To lose power if the engine overheats might be disastrous. These two precautions will usually require that the intake hose be watched and tended at all times by a crew member assigned to that specific duty.

Operating USCG droppable pumps

Coast Guard aircraft are equipped with pumps that can be dropped in floating containers to boats that need them. The following operating instructions are applicable:
1. Make sure suction hose is tight—connect discharge hose.
2. Fill gas tank.
3. Pull stop switch away from spark plug.
4. Close carburetor choke—turn lever in direction of arrow.
5. Open throttle at base of engine.
6. Attach starting cord and spin engine.
7. After engine starts, open choke.
8. Normally, pumps are self-priming—if difficulty arises, prime.
9. When finished, flush out pump with fresh water.

Emergency repairs

Almost anything can be stuffed into a hole in the hull to help stop the inflow of water—cushions, pillows, bedding, spare sails—all of these will have some beneficial effect.

Material used to stop a leak will be more effective if it can be applied from the outside where water pressure will aid in holding it in place. This will, of course, require that the boat be stopped while the temporary patch or plug is positioned and secured. If a hole must be plugged from the inside, the pillow, bedding etc., can sometimes be held in place by nailing a batten or bed slat across it. If no better solution can be found, a member of the crew can be assigned to hold the plug in place. In any event, station a crewman or passenger to watch the patched hole and give immediate alarm if the patch or plug fails to hold.

ASSISTANCE

In any form of emergency, it is well to alert possible sources of assistance without delay. Use your radio with an urgent ("Pan") call to advise the Coast Guard and other craft of your problem. Don't put out a "Mayday" distress call unless you are in obvious danger of sinking, have an uncontrollable fire on board, etc. Don't panic and make a distress call under conditions that do not warrant such action, but also don't fail to alert others to your possible need for assistance soon.

FIG. 928 A radio is probably the primary means of summoning assistance. Do *not* put out a "Mayday" call unless you are in *distress*. If you need help, but are not in danger, use the urgent signal "Pan" on 2182 kc/s or 156.8 Mc/s.

Summoning assistance

A boat's radio is probably the primary means of obtaining assistance, although it is far from being the only method. Use 2182 kc/s and follow the procedures of Chapter 25.

Other distress signals are listed on pages 67 and 78a.

Any signal that will attract attention and bring help is a satisfactory distress signal. However, if your signal is a known or recognized distress signal, your chances of obtaining assistance are enhanced.

Don't overlook the possible use of a small signal mirror equipped with sighting hole and cross-line target. The reflected mirror signals can be seen as flashes of light for many miles and may be just the device that could attract the attention of aircraft.

There are several recently recognized distress signals for small boats on waters of the United States. A simple orange-red flag may be waved from side to side. Even better is a 72-inch by 45-inch fluorescent orange-red panel cloth bearing an 18-inch black square and an 18-inch black circle, 18-inches apart on the major axis of the flag. This could be tied across a hatch or cabin top as a signal to aircraft. A signal may also be made by slowly and repeatedly raising and lowering arms outstretched to each side. This is a distinctive signal, not likely to be mistaken for a greeting. To be as effective as possible, this signal should be given from the highest vantage point on the boat with consideration given to color contrasts.

Helicopter rescue

In more and more instances, Coast Guard assistance is being provided by helicopters rather than patrol craft. This new technique requires new knowledge on the part of the boat skipper and is most effective with advance preparations.

Prior to arrival of helicopter

1. Provide continuous radio guard on 2182 kc/s or specified frequency if possible.
2. Select and clear most suitable hoist area. This must include securing of loose gear, awnings and antenna wires. Trice up running rigging and booms.
3. If hoist is at night, light pick-up areas as well as possible. Be sure you do not shine any lights on the helicopter and blind the pilot. If there are obstructions in the vicinity, put a light on them so the pilot will be aware of their positions.
4. Advise location of pick-up area before the helicopter arrives so that he may adjust for and make his approach as required.
5. Remember that there will be a high noise level under the helicopter, so conversation between the deck crew will be almost impossible. Arrange a set of hand signals between those who will be assisting.

Rescue by hoist

1. Change course so as to permit the craft to ride as easily as possible with the wind on the bow, preferably on the port bow.
2. Reduce speed if necessary to ease the boat's motion, but maintain steerageway.
3. If you do not have radio contact with the helicopter, signal a "Come on" when you are in all respects ready for the hoist; use a flashlight at night.
4. Allow basket or stretcher to touch down on the deck prior to handling to avoid static shock.
5. If a trail line is dropped by the helicopter, guide the basket or stretcher to the deck with the line; line will not cause shock.
6. Place person in basket sitting with hands clear of sides, or strap person in the stretcher. Place a life

jacket on the person if possible. Signal the helicopter hoist operator when ready for hoist. Person in basket or stretcher nods his head if he is able. Deck personnel give "thumbs up."

7. If necessary to take litter away from hoist point, unhook hoist cable and keep free for helicopter to haul in. *Do not secure cable to vessel or attempt to move stretcher without unhooking.*
8. When person is strapped in stretcher, signal helicopter to lower cable, hook up, and signal hoist operator when ready to hoist. Steady stretcher from swinging or turning.
9. If a trail line is attached to basket or stretcher, use to steady. Keep feet clear of line.

ABANDONING SHIP

Many boats involved in casualties have continued to float indefinitely. If it becomes necessary to abandon your boat due to fire, danger of sinking, or other emergency, don't leave the area. Generally a damaged boat can be sighted more readily than a person, and it may help to keep you afloat.

Keep in mind that distance over water is deceptive. Usually the estimated distance is much shorter than the actual distance. Keep your head and restrain your initial impulse to swim ashore. Calmly weigh the facts of the situation such as: injuries to passengers, the proximity of shore, and your swimming abilities, before deciding upon your course of action.

Before abandoning your craft, put on your life preserver and give distress signals. Don't foolishly waste signaling devices where small likelihood of assistance exists. Wait until you sight someone or something. If your vessel is equipped with a radio telephone, a distress message should be sent.

Maintenance

The condition of a boatman's craft can be an indication of his overall seamanship knowledge and abilities. Using a boat is only part of its ownership—maintenance, keeping her shipshape and Bristol Fashion, is the other part.

For most recreational boat owner-skippers, his craft represents a considerable investment of family funds. She must be properly and continuously maintained to keep up the value of this investment. The secret of getting the fullest measure of pleasure from your boat is to make the necessary maintenance effort enjoyable, even fun, and not a grudging chore. The key to this happy situation is proper planning and a low but continuous level of effort.

Don't let your boat get run down; it will not only look worse, but will require more total maintenance than if it had been properly cared for. Deferred maintenance is always more of a burden and more expensive. Maintain the value of your boat—and your pride in her—by continuous attention to maintenance, perhaps peaking in the spring of each year, but not neglected at any time.

USE AND CARE OF EQUIPMENT

A planned maintenance program can start with the use and care of the boat and its equipment. Let us first consider equipment and supplies. To have one's craft in true shipshape condition means a place for everything and every-

FIG. 929 The Coast Guard is making increased use of helicopters for rescue and assistance work. The gas-turbine powered HH-52A shown can land on the water if necessary. Note the hoisting winch above the door. Skippers should know how to cooperate with helicopter crews.   (U.S. Coast Guard photo)

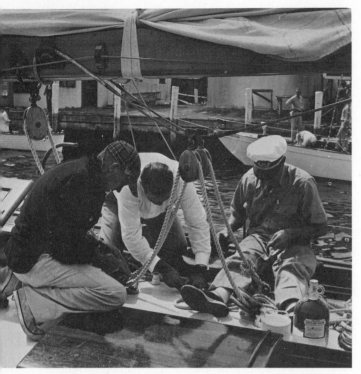

FIG. 930 The key to proper and adequate maintenance, without its becoming a burdensome chore, is a low but continuous level of effort. Do small jobs when they need it—don't put them off. Have a regular schedule for preventive maintenance. (Peter Stackpole photo)

thing in its place; and, too, everything in good working condition.

Lines and sails

There is nothing that we depend upon so much as lines. We use them to anchor, to tie up, and in fact almost everything we do depends upon their use. For our safety, these must be kept in good condition. We must be sure that lines are dry before stowing; if not, they will rot if they are of manila. And, we must be sure that they are stowed in a well-ventilated compartment, for if it is not, we might just as well have not dried them. While synthetic cordage and sail cloth are not subject to rot, mildew can form from deposited spores of fungus unless these items are clean and dry when stowed. The unseamanlike practice of stowing wet ropes and sails below decks will inevitably result in a damp condition, which is uncomfortable.

The same reasoning goes for cotton sails, foul weather gear, and any other materials of the same sort.

Clean, dry, and well-ventilated compartments not only save lines, sails, etc. but contribute to safety of the hull itself. If these compartments, as well as all other parts of the boat, are not well ventilated, dry rot may set in, and this may involve extensive repairs and a big bill. Nothing could be sadder than the boat that at a distance looks fine with a new coat of paint, but which underneath is a rotting shell.

Stowage of supplies

Every item of equipment should be well marked and kept in its specific place. Any article with labels should have the contents painted on the bottle or can proper; it is a good idea even to remove any paper labels, as they may come off in any dampness and cause problems. Some

skippers use adhesive tape on the articles and print the contents on the tape; others merely place a letter on each different item (A means potatoes, B means beans, C means sunburn ointment) and keep a key list on board. The only trouble with the latter method is if you lose the key list you're in trouble.

The new felt-tip marking pens are excellent for labeling cans and other containers. Experiment with different ones until you find the most moisture-resistant type.

Use a checklist

If all equipment is clearly marked and always in its proper place it eases the skipper's mind, to say nothing of adding to his safety. Not only is he sure of having everything, but he doesn't worry for the first day trying to remember what he has forgotten. In order to carry this thought out successfully, it is necessary and good seamanship to have and use a sailing checklist. A sailing checklist is a list of all items that a competent skipper will provide for the boat, her equipment, supplies, stores, and condition prior to shoving off from the mooring. If this list is kept aboard, and if the skipper checks off each item before he shoves off, there will never be any need to worry about being without the necessary equipment.

THE HULL

The hull is, to say the least, a very important part of a boat. No matter how good your superstructure is, if your hull is rotten you just have no boat. In order to preserve a wooden hull, we must keep it well painted. Every year the old coat of paint should be sanded down before new is applied, and every so often, depending on how thick the

FIG. 931 Prepare a checklist to be sure all necessary supplies and equipment are on board before setting out on a cruise. Use it every time, modifying and updating from experience.

old coats of paint are, all paint should be removed, the hull sanded, and seams and scars filled before a new coat of paint is applied.

Selection of paint

The number of different types of paint has expanded remarkably in recent years. While there is nothing wrong with "old fashioned" marine paint as used for many years, the modern skipper should give consideration to some of the new paints with exotic names such as polyutherane, epoxy, acrylic, etc. If you don't feel qualified to make a selection, ask the professionals at your boatyard and talk to other skippers about their experiences with various hull finishes.

Painting techniques

No matter which paint you select, proper surface preparation and application of the paint are *absolutely essential* if the desired results are to be obtained. Follow the manufacturer's directions explicitly from start to finish. Select the proper weather conditions for your work—wait until the morning dew has evaporated, and stop well before sundown.

"Between wind and water," that part of the vessel at or near the waterline, is the most difficult part of the hull to keep protected. This is because it is always getting wet and drying off and also that the water causes a lot of friction at this location. A special quick-drying paint called boot-topping is used here, the principal ingredients of which are varnish and dryer.

Fiberglass hulls

The above comments have been directed to the owners of boats with wooden hulls. If yours is of fiberglass, you will have less maintenance, but some will still be required. Don't neglect the care of your hull just because it requires less attention.

A fiberglass hull should be cleaned as required to keep it free of dirt and oily scum; more cleaning will be needed near the waterline than higher on the topsides. Try to get the job done using only a detergent without an abrasive powder that can dull a high-gloss finish. If you must use a scouring powder to remove marks and greasy streaks, use a mild one and use it with caution.

Liquid cleaner wax is excellent for fiberglass hulls, particularly for mid-season continuing maintenance. Once a year, usually at spring fitting-out, do a more thorough two-step job with a paste cleaner followed by a paste wax. This is also the time to patch up any hair-line cracks that have appeared in the gel (surface) coat of the fiberglass.

After a few years of use, a fiberglass hull may require painting to restore it to top appearance. Many paints are available for this purpose, most of which are two-part products to be mixed just prior to application. Advances in chemical and plastics technology are now resulting in one-part paints for fiberglass surfaces that are easier to use and will give satisfactory results. The problem is to get proper adhesion to the fiberglass plus a high-gloss finish. As with painting a wooden hull, the best procedure is to ask a professional and talk with people who have used various products to get their opinions. Again, too, it is most important that the manufacturer's instructions for surface preparation and paint application be adhered to exactly.

FIG. 932 Two secrets to success in painting are proper preparation of the surface and application of the paint in strict conformity with manufacturer's instructions.

BOTTOM MAINTENANCE

Special attention must be given to the maintenance of the bottom of the boat; this is a most important item as it is usually available for inspection only once or twice a year.

Except for small boats that are taken out of the water after each period of use, the bottom must be kept covered with anti-fouling paint. This type of paint, usually with a copper base, has properties that tend to keep worms out of the bottom as well as to discourage marine growth that attaches itself to the bottom.

Coming into wider use are bottom paints employing other metals and chemicals toxic to marine life. With these, bottom paints are now available in a wide range of colors.

FIG. 933 In most locations, antifouling paint must be applied to a boat's underwater surfaces to protect against worms and marine growth. Bottom finishes are available in many colors as well as the old familiar "copper" paint. (Wm. H. Koelbel photo)

Launching wet or dry

There are two theories about applying bottom paint. Some say that the boat should be put into the water as soon as the paint has been applied, that is, while it is still fairly wet, while others state that the paint should be dry before launching. Follow the manufacturer's directions on the can for the best results.

BRIGHTWORK

Brightwork, natural wood surfaces finished with varnish or similar products, requires special care. Horizontal areas of brightwork should be wiped clear of morning dew each day to prolong their life. All brightwork will require a good sanding at least yearly followed by a fresh coat of varnish. Those parts of the brightwork that receive a lot of wear or spray will need to be given more than one coat each season. Unless varnished areas are kept well covered, moisture will get into the wood and the result will be that

FIG. 934 Varnished surfaces, called "brightwork," require more care than painted or natural wood or fiberglass areas, but to many boat owners their added beauty is worth the effort. Often, care of brightwork can be turned over to the "first mate." (Rosenfeld photo)

it will turn dark, in extreme cases, black.

Wooding down

To keep brightwork looking well is a lot of work, but the beauty of it can make it worthwhile. No matter how much care is taken, it will turn just a little darker each year. Many modern varnishes and synthetic equivalents now include a "filter" to screen out ultraviolet rays of the sun that are most damaging to brightwork. The additive slows down the aging process. Even with this added protection, however, it will be necessary every few years to remove all of the varnish with varnish remover, sand the bare wood, and start with a fresh coat. From four to six separate coats will generally be required.

Reduction of brightwork

In recent years more and more boats have appeared with almost no brightwork at all. The cabins and spars are painted and in fact the only parts left natural may be the handrails, toerails, and trim around hatches.

This move toward little or no brightwork has even invaded interiors. A few years ago this would have been looked upon as sacrilege. No matter how much oldtimers view this trend with alarm, it does have this advantage—it does not reduce the protective qualities which are the main reasons for keeping surfaces covered, and it does make less work. In many cases, natural, unfinished teak is being substituted for mahogany that must be kept varnished.

DECK CARE

Canvas decks present a special problem. They must be kept covered with a good deck paint for protection, but the less paint you put on the better. If you get too much paint on the decks, not only will it crack but they will become smooth. This is not good especially on a small boat, as a smooth deck makes for precarious footing in wet weather. This has been overcome on some boats by sprinkling fine sand on the decks while the paint is still wet. Also, some paint manufacturers are putting out a special paint with a non-skid surface.

Fiberglass decks

Decks of fiberglass require little care other than rinsing off dirt and salt spray. On most boats, anti-slip protection is built in by the manufacturer. In some cases, however, additional non-skid strips or specially painted areas will be required for safety. If it becomes necessary to paint a fiberglass deck, don't fail to provide for continued anti-skid protection where needed.

Teak decks

Decks on large power and sail craft are often made of unfinished teak. Such decks are attractive, quite non-skid, and require little maintenance. They may be allowed to assume a natural, weathered appearance, or they can be periodically bleached to a lighter color, as the individual skipper prefers.

Teak decks should be washed down to keep them free of dirt that might get ground in when walked upon. Salt sea water is excellent for washing down teak decks. A periodic scrubbing with a special teak cleaner is not a difficult chore and will improve overall appearance, but it should not be done too often.

FIG. 935 Teak is an excellent material for decks. The wood can be left unfinished or given a light treatment with special preservatives. It weathers well and provides a non-skid surface.   (Rosenfeld photo)

Decks of teak wood are subject to staining from oily liquids or solids—particularly from some types of food such as bits of potato chips or mayonnaise drippings from sandwiches—but special paste or spray cleaners will efficiently remove these spots.

PAINTING METAL SURFACES

If any metal is to be painted, be sure to use a priming coat of anti-corrosive paint against the metal first. Popular types of such paint include the familiar red lead, zinc chromate, and aluminum. Paints for this purpose will be so labeled on the container; don't use a paint for anti-corrosion protection unless it is so designated.

If your boat has a metal bottom it is specially important that anti-corrosive paint be used before the anti-fouling paint. Ingredients of most bottom paint are oxides of mercury and copper, and if these come in contact with steel, corrosion will result. The anti-fouling paints offer no protection to the hull against sea-water corrosion, but the anti-corrosion paints have no anti-fouling properties, so both must be used.

Painting aluminum

Boats having aluminum hulls may be painted for protection against corrosive attack although this is not generally required with modern alloys properly selected. Underwater anti-fouling paint will be needed for aluminum bottoms under the same conditions as for wood or fiberglass boats.

Aluminum will hold paint very well *provided* that the metal surface has been properly prepared and a suitable primer has been used. Greater care must be taken with this metal than with others commonly used. The aluminum must be *absolutely clean,* free of all oil, scale, dirt, etc., even free of fingerprints. Sand-blasting or wire brushing will be needed to etch the surface slightly in order to make the paint adhere. Zinc chromate is a suitable primer; two

coats should be used to insulate the aluminum hull from any lead-pigmented paint or copper-bearing bottom coating so as to prevent galvanic action between the dissimilar metals.

When patching up the paint job on any area of an aluminum hull, always be sure to prepare the metal surface thoroughly and use a primer coat next to the aluminum.

GENERAL RULES FOR PAINTING

There are a few simple rules for painting. If observed, they will make such work simpler and more satisfactory. These are:

1. Never paint over a wet, dirty, or greasy surface.
2. Never paint during wet weather.
3. Never paint before cleaning and sanding.
4. Do not continuously apply new over old coats.
5. Never apply paint heavily.
6. Paint with reasonable frequency.
7. Use surfacing putty (trowel or brushing cement) to fill nicks and gouges after the prime coat of paint, unless manufacturer's instructions indicate otherwise.
8. Never use a blow torch immediately after applying paint remover.
9. Never scrape or sand near fresh paint.

Sequence for painting

There is a generally preferred order for painting the various parts of a boat as follows:

1. All interiors, including bilge (if painted) and engines.
2. Spars.
3. All deck gear, cockpits, ventilators, hatches, etc.
4. Cabin exterior and decks.
5. Hull topsides.
6. Bottom.
7. Boot-topping.

FIG. 935(a) For boat work, the Black & Decker two-speed belt sander is a versatile tool, eliminating the hard work of hand sanding.
(Photograph by Wm. H. Koelbel)

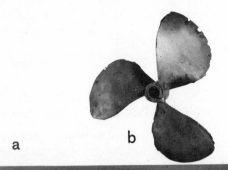

FIG. 936 Whenever your boat is hauled, inspect underwater areas. Zinc blocks and collars, as shown in (a), are used to control galvanic corrosion and must be regularly checked and replaced when needed. Failure to do this may have the results pictured in (b).

INSPECTION NECESSARY

Besides keeping all appropriate surfaces well covered with paint or varnish, there are many other parts that must be inspected regularly. For example, on some boats you must be constantly on the lookout for galvanic corrosion. This chemical reaction is caused when different metals such as brass or bronze and iron come together or in close proximity to each other in salt or impure water. This is often noticeable on boats between an iron rudder and a bronze propeller. Cases have been known where the rudder is just eaten up. This can be checked by placing a zinc plate nearby so that the zinc, in contact with the part to be protected, will be affected instead of the iron. However, if this is done, care must be taken to watch the zinc plate and replace it whenever necessary. Systems may be installed in which a reverse flow of current is used to equalize and offset any destructive current.

Make regular checks

Regular checks of shaft logs, stuffing boxes, bearings, underwater fittings, and the propeller are essential. Your steering system and cables should be gone over often. If your steering system goes wrong in a tight place, you will not only damage your own vessel but may also injure some person or another boat.

Keep your boat clean

All equipment as well as the hull itself must be kept clean at all times. This also includes the bilges. Dirty bilges can result in stopped-up inlets to bilge pumps, and this is sure to happen just when the pump is most needed. There is nothing that gets dirty easier than a boat. Not only is it uncomfortable to try to live on, but it is injurious to the hull and the equipment. Regular cleaning makes for little work to keep your boat spick-and-span; if you let it go, it is a hard job to clean up.

Inspection checklist

Earlier in this section, a sailing checklist was described that all good skippers use before each run. In order to assist the skipper in preventing breakdowns, every boat should have an *inspection checklist* on board and in use. An inspection checklist is a list of all items that the skipper will regularly inspect, and the scheduled periods for such inspections, with a place for the skipper to write in the date of each inspection in order to keep his boat well found.

ENGINE CARE

In a motor boat the engine is the only means of propulsion, and in an auxiliary it is the means of getting in and out of tight places. Therefore, the engine is something that should be in the best of shape at all times and should always start at once. All of us are not good mechanics, but all of us should be able to (1) obtain, read, and follow the manufacturer's instruction book; (2) know enough not to fool with something we are not sure of; and (3) get instruction on simple trouble diagnosis and emergency repairs—U.S.P.S. members can and should take the Engine Maintenance Course.

Routine care

There are, however, a number of things that any skipper can do not only to keep his engine running well for whenever it is needed, but also to keep down the cost of repair bills. All should be done at intervals and in the manner prescribed by the maker's operating manual.

FIG. 937 Regular cleaning makes for little work to keep a boat spick-and-span.   (Rosenfeld photo)

FIG. 938 The average powerboat skipper is not expected to be a mechanic, but he must have an idea of how to maintain his engines. The manufacturer's instruction book should be aboard and its preventive maintenance procedures carried out. (Charles Anderson photo)

Typical routine maintenance items include:
1. Frequently check oil level; change oil regularly.
2. Check cooling system, including intake, regularly.
3. Keep batteries filled and fully charged.
4. Oil starter, generator, and distributor regularly.
5. Keep grease cups filled; turn down and clean regularly.
6. Keep engines clean, especially all filters.
7. Keep fuel lines tight; check for vibration.
8. Check all electric wiring periodically.
9. Do not race a cold motor.
10. Cool down engine before stopping it.
11. Engage clutch only at moderate speeds.
12. Carry spare parts and know how to install them.
13. Carry proper tools.

CARE OF SAILS

Modern sailboats use nearly all synthetic sailcloth—dacron and nylon. These materials have greatly improved characteristics over canvas, but they do require proper use and maintenance.

Care in use

Protect sails from chafing—use wooden or rubber protectors over turnbuckles and at the tips of spreaders. Don't let sails slat needlessly; it wears the stitching and tears batten pockets. Use properly fitted battens and remove them when the sail is furled.

Care in stowage

The greatest enemy of synthetic sailcloth is the sun. Excessive sunlight ultimately causes the material to break down and lose its strength. If sails are left on, they should be furled *and covered*. Water and moisture will not harm dacron and nylon and so such sails can be stored damp if necessary. It is, however, advisable to dry them if you can in order to avoid mildew and the general carrying of mois-

ture below decks.

Wash sails once or twice a season with pure water and soap—no detergents; and never use a washing machine. Hose off, spread to dry, and inspect before folding. Try to keep them as free from salt as possible.

When storing for the winter, wash, clean, and dry. In folding, lay out on the floor, fold lengthwise accordion fashion. When you have a 2- to 3-foot-square bundle, fold head to foot, tie up and store safely or hang to protect from vermin.

Sail maintenance

Although any major repairs should be left to a professional sailmaker, every sailor should be familiar with four basic emergency repairs: the round stitch, the herringbone stitch, the patch, and sail repair tape.

Round Stitch. The round or overhand stitch is used particularly for light sails and in repairing minor tears of from one to four inches. Gather the two sides of the rip, starting about an inch above it. Secure the thread *not* by knotting, but by passing it under the first few stitches; then

FIG. 939 Sails of modern craft are almost entirely synthetic—dacron, nylon, and others. While more resistant to damage from misuse, they still require proper care and maintenance for good service and long life.
(Rosenfeld photo)

179

FIG. 940 When sails are furled on the boom, they should be protected by a cover. Sunshine, more than use, rain, or salt spray, is the greatest enemy of synthetic sails. (Schwarm, Sheldon photo)

sew over it and continue round and round, ending about an inch below the tear. Finish your job in the same turn-under way.

Herringbone Stitch. This is used for more serious repairs. Before placing the two sides of the rip together, fold under a narrow margin on each and "iron" it like a pair of pants by gently scraping the edge of the sailcloth with your knife. Then make alternate long and short stitches to avoid an even line, starting about a quarter-inch from the end of the tear, and finish a quarter-inch below it. Tuck the end of the twine under the final few stitches as in the round job, and cut it. This is a stitch that is best learned from someone who knows how.

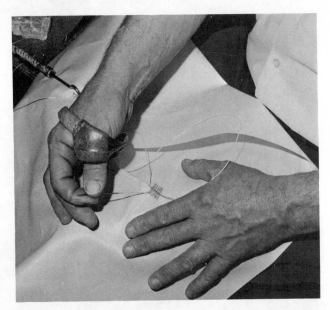

FIG. 941 A sailboat skipper should be able to make minor repairs, but all major maintenance and alteration work should be referred to a professional sailmaker. The herringbone stitch, above, is used for tears too extensive to permit use of the simpler round stitch. Start ¼-inch from the tear and finish below it. (Frank Rohr photo)

Patch. Cut your patch, if possible, from the same weight and type of material as the damaged sail. Allow about one and one-half inches of margin on either side of the tear and turn the patch under a half-inch all the way round, "ironing" folds with knife treatment to keep them manageable, especially with heavier weight cloths. Try to get the weave of the patching cloth to run identically with the sail being repaired. Measuring the approximate area and marking the patch material with pencil before cutting will help.

Miter corners of the patch and, pinning it to sail with extra needles, use the round or overhand stitch to sew your patch to the sail. Pound it into submission with a knife handle; turn the whole lot over; miter the corners of the torn sail itself; sew it to the back of the patch, and hoist away.

Tape. Spinnaker and white rigging tape can be pressed into service swiftly and efficiently to help you finish—even win—a race, or perhaps withstand the wind in some cruising crisis till you reach port.

In making the repair, separate the sticky part from its guard which comes as part of the roll; then, as you unroll the ready tape, press with your fingers on both sides of the rip or seam. It should hold till you can get to it with needle and thread, or bring it ashore to the sailmaker.

Sail repair kit

Various sailmakers can supply emergency repair kits suitable for the sails used on your boat. These include sewing twine, needles, beeswax, a sewing palm, and other useful items, including a booklet of instructions on the care and repair of sails.

WINTER LAY-UP

Perhaps the greatest damage is done to a boat during the long winter months when she is laid up. In the north boats are usually pulled out during the winter, while in the south they are usually left in the water. Of course these call for slightly different techniques.

Storage on land

In general, these are the things to do when laying up for the winter hauled out on shore:
1. Thoroughly clean the bottom, decks, cockpit, bilge, all compartments, and lockers.
2. Apply a coat of good anti-fouling paint to the bottom, and sand down and prime all other marred surfaces.
3. Drain the fuel system, tanks, lines, pumps, and carburetor.
4. Drain and flush out all water systems and tanks; drain the toilets.
5. Winterize the engine in accordance with the manufacturer's instruction manual. This will normally include draining and flushing the cooling system; draining and refilling the crankcase; applying oil to inside of each cylinder through the sparkplug holes; and other preservative actions. Thoroughly clean the exterior of the engine; sand and touch up with paint any scarred areas to prevent rusting.
6. Remove the batteries from the boat; store in an area not subject to freezing temperatures and place on a "trickle" charge.
7. Place a light coating of grease over all chromeplated

metal surfaces.

8. Leave all floorboards up, doors ajar, ports and skylights open, hatches partly open, drawers and lockers open.

9. Carefully fit a well-made winter cover, provided with ventilation ports, if boat is to be stored outdoors.

Storage afloat

When making plans for your boat's winter lay-up, don't fail to give consideration to "wet storage." New ice-protection techniques are coming into wider usage, and more owners are leaving their craft in the water for the winter months—it has many advantages.

The cost is often less, but the real gains are in the better storage conditions for the boat. Water temperatures do not fluctuate so widely or rapidly as do those of the air, and so there is less "sweating" inside the hull. Properly protected with antifreeze, the engine can be periodically started and run, which is better for it than standing idle for several months.

Another advantage of wet storage is that there is less danger of the hull's warping or becoming distorted. A boat's structure is designed to be uniformly supported by water; resting on a few blocks, or even in its own special cradle, is distinctly "unnatural" for it. If protected against ice, covered, in-water storage is the best way for your boat to sit out the winter months until the next boating season.

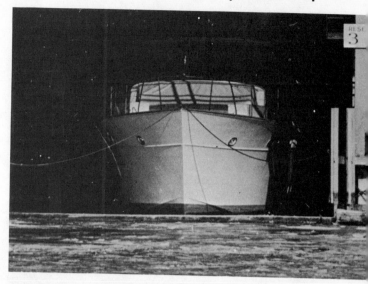

FIG. 943 More and more boats are being kept in the water over the winter season even where ice normally is a problem. Air pumped through pipes on the bottom brings warmer water to the surface and prevents formation of ice near the hull. (Chicago Sun-Times photo)

FIG. 944 Black & Decker's variable speed reversible drill is adaptable to a wide variety of boat construction and maintenance jobs.

Winterizing procedures afloat

The actions to be taken for a winter lay-up afloat will, of course, be somewhat different from those in the list above for when the boat is to be hauled out. The engine should be winterized, but the details, as in connection with the cooling system, will vary. Gas tanks may be filled, to reduce condensation, rather than being drained. Excess gear should be removed from the boat, and all lockers, drawers, etc., should be left open to promote ventilation.

Getting a head start on fitting out

Some annual maintenance chores may be suitable for accomplishment in the fall at the time of laying-up. Any that can be done at this time will reduce the effort required the following spring and so expedite your next boating season.

KEEP YOUR BOAT WELL MAINTAINED

Once a boat is "Shipshape and Bristol Fashion" it doesn't take much work to keep her so. It is only when she is allowed to run down that the work is heavy.

FIG. 942 In northern waters, boats are normally hauled out for dry storage during the winter. Proper blocking and shoring are necessary so that the hull is adequately supported and will not distort in shape. Canvas cover should provide protection and ventilation.

CHAPTER 10

SAFETY AFLOAT

No one should ever be deterred from enjoying the wholesome pleasures of boating by hazards that *might* be encountered; neither should he take safety for granted. No one—skipper, first mate, crew, nor guests—need fear the water and recreational boating if it is approached in a sensible manner.

While not allowing it to detract from the enjoyment of boating, the wise skipper practices safety at *all* times while afloat and studies it frequently ashore. He recognizes its importance, and safety is always in the back of his mind, never forgotten nor ignored. He views safety not as an arbitrary set of rules, but rather as the practical application of knowledge, as commonsense requirements and practices that should be thoroughly understood and followed. If "hazards" of any nature are recognized and respected, they largely cease to be hazards.

It is an established fact that most boating accidents and difficulties arise from ignorance, and could have been avoided. A man does not knowingly put his life, and the lives of others, and the safety of valuable property in jeopardy, but he may do so through lack of knowledge. Serious study and thought toward safety can significantly reduce the problems encountered while on the water.

Safety afloat is a broad topic encompassing essentially all aspects of boating. It is involved in the construction of boats, their equipment, operation, and maintenance. Safety matters are touched on in other chapters of this book in their relationship to government regulations, Rules of the Road, boat handling, seamanship, and other major topics. Here, safety afloat will be the *principal* consideration, with appropriate cross-references to other sections.

SAFETY ORGANIZATIONS

There are a number of public organizations devoted to the promotion of safety in recreational boating. Several of these approach safety as an educational matter; others are concerned with the material and operational aspects of boats and boating. Each plays an important part in enhancing the safety of small craft, their crews and passengers.

Educational organizations

The **United States Power Squadrons** is a volunteer organization of more than 75,000 members organized into over 370 local Squadrons. These units, located throughout the United States and in some overseas areas, offer educational programs of basic boating safety and piloting to the public, and more advanced courses to their membership.

The USPS was founded in 1914 primarily to provide training in the proper operation of power boats (most of the "yachts" of those days were sail). This was accomplished by courses of instruction in winter and boat drills during the summer. Over the years since its founding, membership and activities of the USPS have gradually changed and adjusted to the prevailing interests and needs of boatmen. Today, despite the word "Power" in its name, the USPS includes many sailboat skippers in its membership and teaches a "Sail" course.

Although members may wear uniforms, and various levels of the organization are directed by officers with semi-naval ranks, the United States Power Squadrons is a civilian body in every way, not military. It is a nonprofit, self-sustaining, private membership educational organization dedicated to the teaching of better and safer boating. It also provides cooperation with federal, state, and local governments in the broad interests of boating safety. Boats under command of a member can usually be identified by the USPS ensign with its blue and white vertical stripes; see page IXe.

More than 50,000 boatmen and members of their families attend the free USPS Piloting course every year. Information on local classes is published periodically in *Motor Boating* magazine or an inquiry can be addressed to USPS Headquarters, P.O. Box 510, Englewood, New Jersey 07631.

In Canada, the Canadian Power Squadrons are organized in a manner generally similar to the USPS, with modifications to fit that country's laws and customs. The CPS ensign is illustrated on page IXd. Power Squadron ideals and programs are also spreading to other nations and parallel organizations may be seen in future years.

The **United States Coast Guard Auxiliary** is a voluntary civilian organization of owners of boats, private airplanes, and amateur radio stations; it is a non-military group although administered by the U.S. Coast Guard. Its mission is to promote safety in the operation of small craft through education, boat examinations, and operational activities.

The USCG Auxiliary carries a program of free public in-

FIG. 1001 The United States Power Squadrons is an organization of volunteers dedicated to making boating safer through education. Craft skippered by USPS members are usually identified by the distinctive flag with blue and white vertical stripes, shown here at the starboard yardarm. The "Blue Ensign" of the Coast Guard Auxiliary flies at the truck, the U.S. national ensign at the stern staff.

struction through its 1-lesson Outboard Motorboat Handling Course, 3-lesson Safe Boating Course, and 8-lesson Basic Seamanship Course. Members of the Auxiliary also take courses to increase their knowledge and abilities, advancing through qualifications of Basically Qualified Member, Specialist, and Operationally Qualified Member. Although uniformed and organized along military lines, and closely affiliated with the regular Coast Guard, membership in the Auxiliary remains strictly civil in nature and does not in any way constitute inactive or active military service. The Auxiliary has no law enforcement powers. See pages IXf and X for illustrations of USCGAux (the correct abbreviation for the Auxiliary) flags, pennants, and uniform insignia.

The Coast Guard Auxiliary is well-known for its program of Courtesy Motorboat Examinations, fig. 1002. Specially trained members conduct annual checks of boats only at the owner's request. Boats that meet a strict set of requirements are awarded a decal called the "Shield of Safety." No report to the authorities is made of craft that fail to qualify; the skipper is urged to remedy defects and request re-examination. The CME is provided as a public service for the boat owner's benefit.

Operationally, the Auxiliary promotes safety afloat by assisting the Coast Guard in patrolling marine regattas and

FIG. 1002 The Coast Guard Auxiliary makes Courtesy Motorboat Examinations, but only at the request of the craft's owner. Boats meeting all legal requirements and certain additional safety standards of the Auxiliary are awarded the "Shield of Safety" decal for the current year.
(Official Coast Guard photograph)

FIG. 1003 The Coast Guard Auxiliary is a civilian organization of boatmen closely affiliated with the USCG. Members conduct public instruction classes, make courtesy boat safety examinations, and assist the Coast Guard in near-shore operational missions. The "Blue Ensign" identifies the boat of a USCGAux member. They frequently supplement regular USCG patrol craft at races, regattas, and other marine events. When so functioning in the interest of boating safety, these boats fly the regular Coast Guard flag and carry an identification sign.

racing events. In many areas, the Auxiliary also carries out an extensive program of search and rescue for craft that are in distress, disabled, or reported as overdue. Many lives have been saved and many skippers have been aided by the dedicated members of the Coast Guard Auxiliary.

Information on public classes of the Auxiliary or membership in the organization may be obtained from the Flotilla in your vicinity or by writing to the appropriate Coast Guard District Headquarters; see fig. 1502, page 283.

The **American National Red Cross** has a program of water safety education that includes instruction and the publication of pamphlets. Topics covered by the Red Cross include swimming, outboard boating, and small sailboating. Information on classes and other programs can be obtained from local Red Cross Chapters.

Equipment organizations

In addition to the national volunteer organizations working toward greater safety afloat through education, there are nonprofit groups within and related to the boating industry that promote safety through higher standards for equipment, including its installation and use.

The **American Boat & Yacht Council, Inc.** is a nonprofit, public service organization founded for the purpose of "improving and promoting the design, construction, equipage, and maintenance of small craft with reference to their safety." Membership in the Council is open to anyone interested in furtherance of its objectives. Regular Members may serve in administrative offices and on administra-

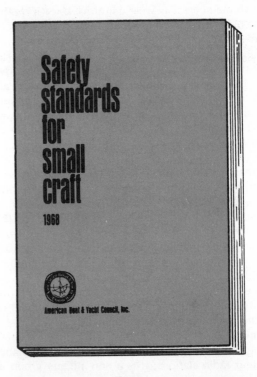

FIG. 1004 The American Boat & Yacht Council, Inc. is a non-profit, public service organization founded to increase safety in the design, construction, equipment, and maintenance of small craft. It periodically publishes a compilation of its "Safety Standards"—worthwhile reading for all skippers.

tive committees, but only Technical Members (highly qualified individuals) may serve on the Council's Technical Board and technical committees.

The American Boat & Yacht Council publishes "Safety Standards." These recommended specifications and practices are intended as good guidance toward making small craft as free from dangerous defect or deficiency as practicable in the interest of minimizing loss of life, injury, and loss of property. Standards are stated largely in terms of desired performance and are not intended to preclude attainment of the desired safety level by other means.

Safety Standards are prepared by Project Technical Committees formed as broadly based groups of recognized authorities with the objective of obtaining a maximum of agreement and acceptance. All technical reports and safety standards are advisory only; the Council has no powers of enforcement.

The AB&YC does not "approve" boats, equipment, materials, or services. Compliance with appropriate standards may be indicated by listings of nationally recognized testing laboratories whose findings may be used as a guide to approval. All standards are reviewed at intervals of three years, or more frequently if necessary because of comments received or advances in technology.

The American Boat & Yacht Council periodically publishes a complete compilation of its "adopted" and "proposed" standards. If needed, supplements are prepared between regular editions of the full publication. Included are standards for such diverse matters as "good visibility from the helm position," "life-saving equipment," "engine exhaust systems," "electrical grounding of DC systems," "lightning protection," "sewerage treatment systems," and "distress signals." The full set of recommended practices is published as "Safety Standards for Small Craft" available for $5 from the Council at 420 Lexington Avenue, New York, N. Y. 10017. The serious skipper can well devote some spare time to reading this volume; it is a good book to have on hand for reference purposes.

The **Yacht Safety Bureau, Inc.** is a nonprofit public service organization under the joint and equal sponsorship of the National Association of Engine and Boat Manufacturers and major marine insurance underwriters. Its primary purpose is inspection, testing, and safety evaluation of products intended for use on, in, or in conjunction with small boats, including hulls and entire boats. The YSB cooperates with and assists the U.S. Coast Guard in matters relating to recreational craft safety.

Simply stated, the Bureau's objective is to see that marine equipment is available to the boating public that has been measured for safety of operation when used as intended. This objective is based on the logic that safety begins with safe products and continues with how they are used.

The Yacht Safety Bureau does not solicit work. Manufacturers voluntarily submit products for evaluation. Extensive laboratory facilities are maintained in New Jersey; field testing is frequently accomplished at other sites.

The word "approved" is frequently misused in connection with YSB product certification. The Bureau does not approve or disapprove anything. What it does is operate a product listing and labeling service.

Satisfactory completion of safety evaluation results in an item's being "listed" by the Yacht Safety Bureau. Listing of a product, with its related privilege of use of the Bureau's label, means that production samples of it have been evaluated and found acceptable under the Bureau's requirements. Listing is an expression of the Bureau's good faith opinion, based on tests, that the item meets minimum applicable safety standards. It is not a warranty of quality or performance, nor are listed products of the same class necessarily equivalent in quality, performance, or merit.

The Bureau's labels include the words "LISTED PRODUCT" in a copyrighted design, fig. 1005. These symbols may be seen in advertisements and on tags, stickers, etc., on products.

The presence of the YSB label on a device or system means that a production sample has been successfully evaluated to related safety requirements, and nothing else. The label may, however, be the basis on which "authorities having jurisdiction" grant approval. Such authorities include individuals making judgments for their own purposes, industry people making judgments for components or original equipment installations, marine surveyors for insurance purposes, and administrators of regulations making judgments required by law.

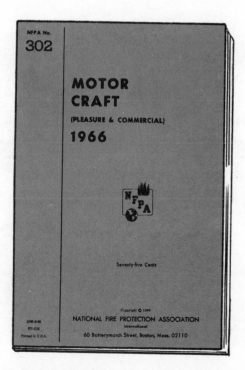

FIG. 1006 Fire Protection Standards for Motor Craft, No. 302, is a small yet valuable safety bulletin issued by the National Fire Protection Association. A copy should be studied by every boat owner and carried aboard as a useful reference document. See text for how a copy may be obtained.

FIG. 1005 Boating products that have passed a safety evaluation are "listed" by the Yacht Safety Bureau. The YSB seal can be used in advertising the items and may be found on it in the form of a sticker, tag, etc. Periodic re-testing ensures the continued safety of all listed products.

Only products commercially available are eligible for listing. New products may be submitted in their model stage for evaluation, but no final listing action is taken until production units are submitted. Continuity of a Bureau listing is provided for by means of its periodic re-inspection service. This is directed only toward confirming that originally tested qualities of listed and labeled products are maintained so long as the listing continues.

The **National Fire Protection Association** is an organization whose activities extend far beyond boating and marine interests to include all aspects of the science and methods of fire protection. NFPA issues codes, standards, and recommended practices for minimizing losses of life and property by fire.

NFPA does not approve, inspect, or certify any installations, procedures, equipment, or materials, nor does it approve or evaluate testing laboratories. It does prepare, by coordinated action of committees of experts, codes and standards for the guidance of all persons in the matter of fire protection. Frequently, NFPA codes and standards are written into law or regulations by various governmental units.

Of interest to boatmen is NFPA Fire Protection Standard No. 302 for Motor Craft (Pleasure and Commercial).

Originally issued in 1925, it has been amended and revised many times. The small booklet, available for 75c from NFPA, 60 Batterymarch Street, Boston, Mass. 02110, is a useful guide to any skipper.

Construction for Safety

In one respect, safety afloat may be considered to start with the design and construction of the craft itself. The average skipper is not likely to build his own boat, but he should be able to recognize proper design features and sound construction characteristics. He should be at least broadly familiar with safe and unsafe aspects of boat construction—the points that should be checked in determining whether or not a particular craft, new or used, should be bought. There is little the average yachtsman can do directly to influence the design and construction of boats, but he can, through knowledge and careful inspection, avoid those that fail to measure up to desirable standards.

A boatman contemplating purchase of a used boat should seriously consider use of the services of a qualified

FIG. 1008 Anti-slip protection on deck walkways and at boarding areas is a must for safety. This can be obtained from the natural qualities of the deck, ingredients added to the deck paint, or by applying special strips of material having a no-slip surface and an adhesive backing.

marine surveyor. He is an expert in determining the condition of the hull, engine, and equipment. He may well discover hidden defects that the would-be buyer overlooked in his enthusiasm. An impartial survey is sound protection for a purchaser; the modest cost involved will be well-justified. Such a survey is often required to obtain insurance, particularly on older boats.

HULL CONSTRUCTION

Modern boats, built by reputable manufacturers, are basically seaworthy because they are honestly constructed to proven designs. This points out the proper course in the selection of a good, sound boat. There is no necessity of trying some freak of questionable worth. If you have no experience in selecting a boat, it is easy enough to avail yourself of the advice and guidance of others who are better qualified; be sure to talk to several persons to avoid personal biases.

Construction materials

For seaworthiness and safety, suitable materials for boatbuilding and highgrade construction are equally essential. Use of fire-retardant materials wherever practicable is suggested. Boats may be built equally well of wood, fiberglass, steel, or aluminum. Combinations of materials may also be used, such as a fiberglass superstructure on a wooden hull.

FIG. 1007 Even an experienced yachtsman should make use of the services of a qualified marine surveyor when considering purchase of a used boat. This expert will make a thorough examination of the craft and its equipment, noting defects, weaknesses, missing safety features, etc. His report should guide the would-be buyer in his decision as to whether to buy. A survey report may also be required for insurance purposes.

FIG. 1009 Lifelines are important on all boats, but are an absolute must on offshore cruising and racing sailboats. The lines must have adequate strength and the stanchions must be securely through-bolted. Note how lines shown above merge into liferails at bow and stern.
(Photograph by Romaine-Skelton)

It should be noted, too, that boats can also be built poorly in any of these materials. Many arguments can be made for and against each hull material, but basically the decision is one for the individual owner, considering the use of the boat, cost factors, maintenance, and not least, his personal preferences.

Water-tight bulkheads (or as tight as practicable) are recommended to isolate bilges of fuel and machinery spaces from those of living quarters. Where feasible, two means of exit should be provided from compartments where persons may congregate or sleep. Thus, in a small craft having only one cabin and cockpit, a forward hatch is a desirable feature.

Safety on deck

A Class 1 or larger boat may have side decks on which individuals move forward to the bow and back. It is essential that four safety features be present. First, these decks must be wide enough for secure footing. People will attempt to pass forward from the cockpit, around the cabin, and to the forward deck. There must be adequate space for their feet to be placed fully on deck, even though the space may be measured in inches and they have to make their way forward sideways. Secondly, if the deck is of a material that is slippery when wet (and most are), anti-slip protection must be provided at critical points. This may consist of a built-in roughness in fiberglass decks, added material to deck paint, or special anti-slip strips attached to the deck with their own adhesive backing. Any place that a person can or has slipped, even once, is a potential area for anti-slip protection.

Thirdly, there must be adequate hand-holds, places to grab and hold on. These must be sufficient in number and so spaced that no one need be beyond a secure grasp of the boat at any time in moving forward and aft, or when coming aboard or leaving the boat. The old saying "one hand for the boat and one for yourself" is an excellent one —even in calm waters; hold on at all times to something strong enough to bear your weight.

Lifelines, also referred to as liferails, are the fourth item of deck security for personnel. No boat large enough for lifelines should be without them. These are often carried forward to join a low rail around the bow. Lifelines are important on most small craft, but are of special value on offshore sailboats, fig. 1009.

Inadequate lifelines are worse than none at all; they may impart a false sense of security. Adequate lifelines, on the other hand, are worth whatever cost and bother they may entail. They are a safety measure against an unpredictable sea, perhaps responsible for the saving of more lives than any other safety feature of boats.

Lifelines must be of adequate inherent strength; even more important, they must be properly installed. Stanchions must be internally strong and through-bolted to the deck. The lines themselves must have the necessary strength and be of a material compatible with that of the stanchions.

Detailed information on non-skid deck materials, lifelines, and handrails will be found in the American Boat & Yacht Council Safety Standard H-12 on the security of personnel on deck. There are also nine other AB&YC safety standards relating to hulls of small craft, all of which will make interesting reading to those seriously concerned with safety afloat.

Superstructure and stability

The mistaken notion that a boat can carry weight anywhere as long as she appears to trim right in the water must be corrected. Addition of more superstructure, such as a flying bridge, is particularly bad, as is the shifting of heavy weights such as motors, ballast, tanks, machinery, etc. Where stability is concerned, no shifts of major weights or changes in design should be considered without the advice of a qualified naval architect. Amateur boatbuilders sometimes ruin boats and reduce their safety factors by deviating from architect's plans in which the proportioning of weights has been given the most painstaking attention.

Through-hull fittings

Fittings which pass through the hull near or below the water line should have sea-cocks installed internally close to the planking to permit positive closing. It is desirable that solid, seagoing metal pipe extend from the sea-cock to a level above the water line, from which point flexible hoses may be run to the pump or other accessory. Where hose is placed over pipe nipples for connections, hose clamps should be used.

There are now available through-hull fittings and sea-cocks that have been safety evaluated by the Yacht Safety Bureau and "listed" by that organization. AB&YC Safety Standard A-2 furnishes additional information on these.

FIG. 1010 Seacocks are important items of safety equipment on boats of all sizes. Every through-hull fitting should have one for cutting off the entry of water in case of hose leakage or for working on equipment. Seacocks should be tested for easy shut-off action at least twice each year; adjust or replace without delay any seacock stuck in the open position.

Engines and Fuel Systems

Probably the first thought that comes to mind in connection with safety afloat is that of preventing fire and explosion. Fire is usually traceable to the engine room or galley where improper equipment, faulty installation, or careless operation is the direct cause. All of these are under the owner's control.

ENGINE INSTALLATION

Engines should be suited to the hulls they power. Extremes of underpowering and overpowering are both bad. Original installations and subsequent changes require the advice of a naval architect or one thoroughly familiar with this phase of boat design.

Conversions of automobile engines for marine duty by amateur mechanics are invariably a source of trouble because of basic differences between the two types. Lubrication and cooling are the chief problems. Selection of an accepted type of marine engine or a commercially-produced conversion is advisable.

Pans, preferably made of copper, are recommended for installation under the engine to catch any oil and grease drippings and prevent these from getting into the bilge. Accumulations should be removed promptly for fire safety.

FUEL SYSTEMS

The primary aspect of fuel system safety is the prevention of fires and explosion. Not to be forgotten, however, are the reliability aspects of the system that will ensure a continuous flow of clean fuel to the engine.

The discussion that follows will be principally concerned with boats using gasoline engines; exceptions and special requirements relating to diesel fuel systems will be covered separately.

Fire prevention

It is of primary importance that the entire fuel system be liquid- and vapor-tight with respect to the hull interior. Gasoline fumes, mixed with air, form an explosive combination. These fumes, several times heavier than air, settle to the bottom of the bilge. A concentration of gasoline in air as low as 1¼% can be exploded by a slight spark with tremendous effect—a half-teacup of gasoline can create enough explosive vapor to totally destroy a large motorboat.

The obvious answer for safety is *prevention*—make it impossible for gasoline, either in liquid or gaseous form, to get into the bilge in the first place. Then keep the bilge clean and ventilate the engine compartment thoroughly, and there will be nothing that can be ignited.

Leakage of liquid gasoline into the bilge can be prevented by proper installation, using strongly built gasoline tanks, copper tubing for fuel lines, leakproof connections, tight fittings, and lengths of flexible metallic fuel hose to take care of vibration. Gasoline vapors created when the tanks are filled must be prevented from finding their way down through open hatches and companionways. Finally, avoidable sparks and flames should not be permitted in the engine room.

Carburetors

Carburetors must be equipped with flame arresters for protection against backfire; see fig. 1011. If not of the downdraft type, they should also have a pan covered with a fine mesh screen attached under the carburetor to collect any drip. Leakage will be sucked back into the engine if a copper tube is run from the bottom of the pan to the intake manifold. Flame arresters should be kept clean both for safety and best engine operation.

Air intakes to the engine compartment should be directed so that any backfires will not tend to blow into the bilges.

Fuel tanks

Fuel tanks should be permanently installed in such a manner as to be secure against moving about in a seaway. The use of portable tanks below decks is not good practice.

Fuel tanks must be constructed of a metal that is compatible both with the fuel and a normal marine environment. Copper and copper alloys of certain specific compositions are used for gasoline tanks. The necessary thickness of metal may vary with capacity of the tank in accordance with standards developed by the American Boat & Yacht Council. Seams of a tank may be welded by any one of several methods as listed in the applicable

AB&YC safety standard. Such tanks should not be painted.

Gasoline tanks must not be integral with the hull. The shape of the tank should be such that there are no exterior pockets that would trap moisture after the tank is in its installed position. Tank bottoms must not have sumps or pockets in which water could accumulate.

Internal stiffeners and baffle plates will normally be used to provide necessary rigidity and resistance to surging of liquid in the tanks. Baffles must meet certain specified design criteria to prevent formation of liquid pockets in the bottom of tanks and vapor pockets in the tops.

There should be no drains or outlets for drawing off fuel from the tank, nor outlets or fittings of any type in the bottom, sides, or ends of tanks. Fuel lines to the engine should enter the tank at its top and internally extend nearly, but not quite all the way, to the bottom.

Fuel filler pipes and vents

One of the most essential requirements in the proper installation of a fuel system is that there be a completely tight connection between the gasoline tank and the filling plate on deck. If the filler is located outside the coaming, spillage will go overboard, while tight pipe connections between deck plate and tank will prevent leakage or spillage below. Fill pipes, at least 1½" inside diameter, should run down inside the tank nearly to the bottom to lessen the production of vapors.

A suitable vent pipe for each tank should lead *outside the hull;* vents should *never* terminate in closed spaces such as the engine compartment or under the deck. Minimum inside diameter of vent pipes should be 9/16". Where a vent terminates on the hull, the outlet should be fitted with a removable flame screen to protect against flash-backs from outside sources of ignition. In boats that normally heel, such as auxiliary sailboats, it may be necessary to have dual vents with the port tank vent led to the starboard side and vice versa.

Non-metallic hose may be used as a coupling between

FIG. 1011 Carburetors on marine engines (other than outboards) must be equipped with a flame arrester. Out of sight beneath the updraft carburetor shown above is a drip pan for further safety. Downdraft carburetors do not need such a pan.

sections of metallic piping. The hose must be reinforced or of sufficient thickness to prevent collapse. A grounding jumper wire must be installed across the non-conducting section so as to provide a complete electrical path from the deck fitting to the fuel tank, which in turn is grounded.

A fuel level indicator, if used, should be of an approved type. If the fuel supply for an auxiliary electric plant is not drawn from the main tank, the separate tank should be installed with fillers and vents similar to those of the main tank.

Fuel lines

Fuel lines should be of seamless copper tubing, run so as to be in sight as much as possible for ease of inspection, protected from possible damage, and secured against vibration by soft non-ferrous metal clips with rounded edges. A short length of flexible tubing with suitable fittings should be used between that part of the fuel line that is secured to the hull and that part which is secured to the engine itself; this will prevent leakage or breakage as a result of vibration.

Reinforced non-metallic hose in the fuel line should be limited to the short flexible section described above, but may be used for the full distance from the tank shutoff valve to the engine if the line is fully visible and accessible for its entire length. Wherever used, non-metallic hose must be dated by the manufacturer and not be used for a period longer than that recommended by the maker.

Tube fittings should be of non-ferrous drawn or forged metal of the flared type, and tubing should be properly flared by tools designed for the purpose, preferably annealing the tube end before flaring.

A shut-off valve should be installed in the fuel line directly at the tank connection. Arrangements should be provided for ready access and operation of this valve from outside the compartment in which tanks are located, preferably from above deck. Where engine and fuel tank are separated by a distance exceeding 12 feet, an approved-type manual stop-valve should be installed at the engine end of the fuel line to stop fuel flow when servicing accessories.

Valves should be of non-ferrous metal with ground seats installed to close against the flow. Types which depend on packing to prevent leakage at the stem should not be used. For fuel, gas, and oil lines a type of diaphragm packless valve is available which is pressure-tight in any position. A YSB-listed electric fuel valve shuts off the flow of gasoline whenever the ignition switch is turned off; it can also be independently turned off in an emergency.

Fuel pumps and filters

Electric fuel pumps, where used, should be located at the engine end of fuel lines. They must be so connected as to operate only when the ignition switch is on and the engine is turning over.

A filter should be installed in the fuel line inside the engine compartment, properly supported so that its weight is not carried by the tubing. Closure of the filter must be so designed that its opening for cleaning will minimize fuel spillage. It should also be designed so that the unit can be disassembled and reassembled in dim light without undue opportunity for crossing threads, displacing gaskets

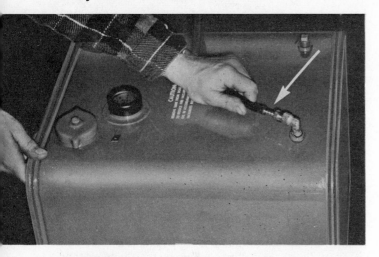

FIG. 1012 Portable gasoline tanks used with outboard motors may have a quick-disconnect fitting on the fuel line. This fitting must be designed so as to minimize leakage of gasoline when it is detached.

or seals, or assembly of parts in an improper order, resulting in seepage of fuel after reassembly. Fuel filter bowls should be highly resistant to shattering due to mechanical impact and resistant to failure from thermal shock.

Fuel systems for outboards

Fuel tanks and systems permanently installed in the hull of outboard-powered boats should be designed, constructed, and installed in accordance with the above principles. No pressurized tanks should be built into or permanently attached to hulls. A quick-disconnect coupling may be used between motor and fuel line but, when disconnected, it must automatically shut off fuel flow from the tank. Arrangements should be provided so that the operation of making and breaking the connection can be accomplished with a minimum of spillage.

Plastic containers for gasoline

Extreme caution must be exercised in the use of plastic containers for storing gasoline. Plastic articles can accumulate a heavy charge of static electricity. As plastic material does not allow the charge to be drained off by grounding connections, a spark could ignite fuel vapors in the container.

Some plastic containers are safe, but a boatman should use *only* those approved by a national listing agency or a major city fire department. In case of doubt, *don't* store gasoline in a plastic container.

Safety first

Every possible precaution must be taken to ensure that not even a single drop of gasoline can find its way into the bilge. Bilge ventilation is most important. It is a strict legal requirement and it is a vital safety measure; see pages 494(a) to 494(d).

Fuel systems of diesel-powered boats

Fuel systems of diesel-powered boats will generally conform to safety standards for gasoline-fueled craft, with a few exceptions as required or permitted by the nature of the fuel and characteristics of diesel engines.

Tanks for diesel fuel may be made of iron or steel as well as nickel-copper. Tanks may be painted if not galvanized externally; iron tanks must not be galvanized internally. Diesel tanks may have a sump or pocket in the bottom for collection of water but, if so, must have a positive means for removal of any accumulations from above deck. Tanks for diesel fuel may be integral with the hull.

Fuel lines for diesel oil may be of iron or steel pipe or tubing in addition to the metals approved for gasoline. A return line to carry excess fuel from the engine back to the tank will be needed.

Additional information

Many additional technical details on gasoline and diesel fuel systems for boats will be found in AB&YC Safety Standard P-2.

The Yacht Safety Bureau has evaluated and accepted for listing a number of fuel tanks, filters, valves, and related equipment by various manufacturers.

EXHAUST SYSTEMS

Exhaust lines and pipes should be installed so that they cannot scorch or ignite woodwork. Where necessary, gratings can be used to prevent gear from touching the line. Exhaust systems must be gas-tight, constructed and installed so that they can be inspected and repaired readily along their entire length. Any leaks must be rectified at once to prevent escape of exhaust gases into various compartments. *Carbon monoxide is a deadly gas.*

A "wet" exhaust system requires a continuous flow of cooling water (from the heat exchanger or the engine block) discharged through the exhaust line, entering as near the manifold as practicable. Exhaust systems of the "dry" type (no cooling water) operate at considerably higher temperatures and their use is relatively rare except on larger yachts.

An exhaust system should be run with a minimum number of bends. Where turns are necessary, long-sweep elbows or 45° ells are recommended. The exhaust system must not result in back pressure at the exhaust manifold greater than that specified by the engine manufacturer. A $1/8$" pipe tap, located not more than 6" from the exhaust-manifold outlet, should be provided for measuring back pressure.

The exhaust system should be designed to prevent undue stress on the exhaust manifold, particularly where an engine is shock-mounted. All supports, hangers, brackets, and other fittings in contact with the exhaust should be noncombustible and so constructed that high temperatures will not be transmitted to wood or other combustible materials to which fittings are secured.

The exhaust piping or tubing should have a continuous downward pitch of at least $1/2$" per foot when measured with the vessel at rest. It must be so designed and installed as to eliminate any possibility of having cooling water or sea water return to the engine manifold through the exhaust system.

Exhaust systems for sailboat engines

Exhaust systems for auxiliary sailing craft should be carefully designed to prevent sea or cooling water from running back into the engines because such engines are usually installed close to or below the water line. A riser must

TYPICAL SAILBOAT EXHAUST SYSTEM

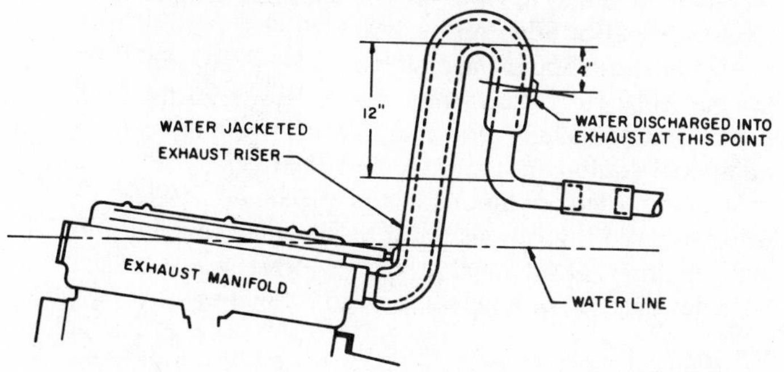

FIG. 1013 The AB&YC Safety Standard for small-craft exhaust systems has special provisions for auxiliary-powered sailboats. Unusual precautions must be taken in such installations as the engine is often below the waterline and a normally-sloping exhaust line cannot be installed.

reach sufficiently high above the water line to allow a steep drop-off of at least 12"; the rest of the piping or tubing should have a downward pitch to the outlet of at least ½" per foot. The high point of the line should form a gooseneck, with cooling water injected aft of this point; see fig. 1015. The vertical dry section must be either adequately insulated and provided with a metallic bellows flexible section or water-jacketed. As an alternate arrangement, a water-trap silencer is recommended.

Flexible exhaust lines

Steam hose or other non-metallic material may be used for exhaust lines where greater flexibility is desired. Every flexible line of this type must be secured with adequate clamps of corrosion-resistant metal at each end. Hose used for this purpose must have a wall thickness and rigidity sufficient to prevent panting (internal separation of plies) or collapse. Full-length nonmetallic exhaust tubing may be used in wet exhaust systems providing it is water-cooled throughout its length and is not subjected to temperatures above 280° F. Tubing used for engine exhaust service should be specifically constructed for that purpose and so labeled by the manufacturer. Tubing should be installed in a manner that will not stress or crimp the inner or outer plies, or permit any local impingement of exhaust gases or cooling water.

Additional information

The AB&YC Safety Standard P-1 provides much additional information on "wet" and "dry" exhaust installations. It should be studied by persons building or rebuilding any boat equipped with an inboard engine.

ELECTRICAL SYSTEMS

The entire electrical installation should comply rigidly with the best and most modern safety practices. Requirements of marine installations are more exacting than other applications where salt- and moisture-laden atmospheres are not prevalent. Wiring and other electrical equipment should be installed correctly in the beginning and kept safe by frequent inspection.

Information on electrical systems will also be found in chapter 25 on pages 377 and 378.

The sources of electrical power for engine starting, lights, pumps, electronic gear, and other electrical accessories are usually lead-acid storage batteries kept charged by a generator or alternator integral with the main engine. Larger craft equipped with electrical cooking and air-conditioning will have a separate engine-driven generator producing AC electrical power similar to shore current. The discussion in this section will be directed to the more-common 12- and 32-volt DC electrical systems found on all boats, even though also equipped with AC power.

All direct-current electrical systems should be of the two-wire type with feed and return wires parallel throughout the system. Conductors should be twisted together where their magnetic field would affect compasses or automatic pilots. Where one side of a DC system is grounded, connections between that side and ground should be used only to maintain that side at ground potential and should not normally carry current.

Wiring diagrams

All boats should be provided with a complete wiring diagram of the electrical system as originally installed. It is recommended that the diagram be enclosed in a suitable plastic envelope and secured to an accessible panel door, preferably near the main switchboard. Diagrams should include an indication of the identification provided for each conductor.

Additions to and/or changes in electrical circuits should be drawn in on the wiring diagram without delay so that it is correct at all times.

Batteries

Storage batteries should be so located that gas generated during charging will be quickly dissipated by natural or mechanical ventilation. They should be located as high as practicable, where they are not exposed to excessive heat, extreme cold, spray, or other conditions which could impair performance or accelerate deterioration. Caution should be taken to avoid locating batteries in areas subject to accumulation of gasoline fumes and also in proximity to any electrical or electronic devices. Engine starting batteries should be located as close to the engine as practicable.

Batteries must be secure against shifting. Care also should be taken to secure a battery against vertical motion which would allow it to pound against the surface on which it is resting while cruising in rough water. Batteries should be chocked on all sides and supported at the bottom by non-absorbent insulating supports of a material that will not be affected by contact with electrolyte. These supports should allow air circulation all around. Where the hull or compartment material in the immediate vicinity of the battery is aluminum, steel, or other material readily attacked by the acid, a tray of lead, fiberglass, or other suitable material resistant to the deteriorating action of electrolyte should be provided.

Batteries should be arranged to permit ready access for inspection, testing, watering, and cleaning. A minimum of 10" clear space above the filling openings should be available.

A non-conductive, ventilated cover or other suitable means should be provided to prevent accidental shorting

FIG. 1014 Storage batteries should have a cover to protect terminals from being shorted by an accidentally dropped tool or other metal object. Such covers must be ventilated to prevent accumulation of gases during charging.

of the battery's terminals; fig. 1014.

An emergency switch capable of carrying the maximum current of the system (including starter circuits) should be provided in each ungrounded conductor as close to the battery terminal connection as practicable. This switch should be readily accessible; a switch with a remote operating handle that can be opened or closed from the bridge or other location outside the compartment containing the batteries is highly desirable.

Generators and motors

Generators, alternators, and electric motors intended for use in machinery spaces or other areas which might contain flammable or explosive vapors must be designed and constructed so as to prevent such devices from becoming a source of ignition of these vapors. These units must be of a type approved for marine service.

Generators, alternators, and electric motors must be located in accessible, adequately ventilated areas as high above the bilge as possible. They must not be located in low or pocketed positions.

Ground connections from battery to starter should be made as close to the starter as possible. It is recommended that all other ground connections to the engine be made at this same point. By making all ground connections at one point, damaging stray-current flow through the metal of the engine will be minimized.

Distribution panels and switches

Switchboards and distribution panels should be located in accessible, adequately ventilated locations, preferably outside of engine and fuel-tank compartments. They should be protected from rain and spray; where necessary, panels should be provided with a drip shield to prevent wetting of terminals or electrical components from overhead dripping.

Totally enclosed switchboards and distribution panels of the dead-front type are recommended. Metal enclosures are desirable, but wood may be used if all terminal strips,

fuse blocks switches, etc., are mounted on non-absorbent, non-combustible, high-dielectric insulating material. It is recommended that the interior of enclosures be lined with asbestos sheet or other fire-resistant material.

All switches should have suitable electrical ratings for the particular circuits on which they are used; distribution panels should have several spare switches to take care of additional equipment that may be added later.

Switches used in fuel-tank and machinery spaces, or other hazardous locations, must be designed so as to prevent ignition of flammable or explosive vapors. Such switches must be of a type approved for marine use.

Wiring

Conductors used for general wiring throughout the boat should be approved for marine use to indicate adequate mechanical strength, moisture resistance, dielectric strength, insulation, and current-carrying capacity for the intended marine service.

The table of wire gauges on page 378, fig. 2504, is for an allowable voltage drop of $1/2$ volt on a 12-volt system. For lighting and other non-critical purposes, the wire size shown there may be reduced slightly (wire gauge number one or two *greater*, as gauge number varies *inversely* with conductor size). For more critical applications, such as for some electronic equipment, the voltage drop should be kept to 3% or less by using slightly larger wire in accordance with fig. 1015.

Current in Amps.	Length of Wire, in feet					
	10	15	20	30	40	50
5	14	12	12	10	8	8
10	12	10	8	6	6	5
15	10	8	6	5	4	3
20	8	6	6	4	2	2
25	8	6	5	3	2	1

FIG. 1015 The table above, extracted from the appropriate AB&YC Safety Standard, specifies the wire gauge to be used versus conductor length for a voltage drop of not more than 3% in a 12-volt system. This small drop is required for some critical electronic installations. For less critical applications, the table in Chapter 25, Fig. 2504, may be used.

All wiring must be routed as high above the bilge as possible with consideration given to protection of wire and connections from physical damage. Wiring should be secured throughout its length, at intervals not exceeding 14 inches, in a manner that will not crush or cut insulation around the conductor. Non-metallic clamps are excellent; if metallic clamps are used, they must be lined with a suitable insulating material. All non-metallic material must be resistant to the effects of oil, gasoline, and water.

Unless absolutely necessary, wire splices should not be made in any circuit vital to the operation of the boat nor in the navigation light circuit. Splices, where made, should be taped to relieve all strain from the joint. If solder is used, it should be a low-temperature resin-core radio solder. Acid-core solder must *not* be used.

Terminal connections

Terminal connections should be designed and installed so as to insure a good mechanical and electrical joint without damage to conductors. Metals used for terminal studs, nuts, and washers should be corrosion-resistant and galvanically compatible with the wire and terminal lug.

Terminals should be of solderless type, preferably with ring-type ends. Solderless terminals should be attached with crimping tools specified by the manufacturer of the terminal. The holes in ring-type terminals should be of a size that will properly fit the terminal stud. Formed and soldered wire terminal connections should not be used. It is recommended that terminal lugs include a means of clamping the wire insulation for mechanical support. A short length of insulated sleeving over the wire at each terminal connection is desirable.

No more than four conductors should be secured to any one terminal stud. Where additional connections are necessary, two or more terminal studs should be used and connected together with copper jumpers or straps.

Wires terminating at switchboards, in junction boxes or fixtures, etc., should be arranged to provide a surplus length of wire sufficient to relieve all tension, allow for repairs, and permit multiple wires to be fanned at terminal studs, etc.

Electrical shock hazards

Voltage is only one factor in determining whether a shock will be fatal or only startling. Many people have received shocks from spark-plugs, where the voltage is 10,000 or more, with no more harm than a few bruised knuckles. The actual factors that determine the extent of harm are: (1) the amount of current that flows through the body, the amperage; (2) the path of the current through the body; and (3) the length of time that the current flows.

The effects of different levels of current are not exact and will vary with the individual victim and the path of current through his body. Unfortunately, there is no way of predicting in advance how much current will flow in any given situation—play safe, work only on de-energized circuits.

Additional information

Further guidance and recommendations for DC electrical systems for boats will be found in Safety Standards E-1, E-3, E-5, E-6, E-9, and E-10 issued by the American Boat & Yacht Council.

AC electrical systems

More and more boats are being wired for 115-volt AC electrical systems so that larger, home-type appliances and equipment may be used afloat. Power may be obtained from dockside connections only or from such sources plus an engine-driven generator for use while under way. From a safety viewpoint, it is important to recognize the increased hazards from this higher-voltage wiring and devices.

All component parts of a 115-volt AC system must be designed, constructed, and installed so as to perform with safety under environmental conditions of continuous exposure to vibration, mechanical shock, corrosive salt atmosphere, and high humidity. The system must provide maximum protection against electrical shock for persons on the boat, in the water in contact with the boat, or in contact with the boat and a grounded object on shore.

Appliances and fixed AC electrical equipment used on boats must be designed so that current-carrying parts of the device are effectively insulated from all exposed metal parts by a dielectric material suitable for use in damp and/or wet locations as determined by location of the item and its intended use.

Further technical specifications for AC electrical systems on boats will be found in AB&YC Safety Standard E-8. Portions of standards E-3, E-5, and E-6 are also applicable.

LIGHTNING PROTECTION

One seldom hears of a boat, power or sail, being struck by lightning, yet cases have been reported. A skipper can add to both his physical safety and his peace of mind by obtaining some basic information and taking a few precautionary actions.

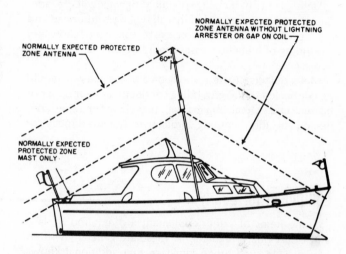

FIG. 1016 Under *certain* conditions, a grounded radio antenna can provide a "cone of protection" from lightning strikes for a boat and its occupants. See text for details. (from A.B. & Y.C. Safety Standards)

Protective principles

A grounded conductor, or lightning protective mast, will generally divert to itself direct lightning strokes which might otherwise fall within a cone-shaped space, the apex of which is the top of the conductor or mast and the base a circle at the water's surface having a radius approximately twice the conductor's height. Probability of protection is considered to be 99.0% within this 60° angle as shown in fig. 1016. Probability of protection can be increased to 99.9% if mast height is raised so that the cone apex angle is reduced to 45°.

To provide an adequately grounded conductor or protective mast, the entire circuit from the masthead to the ground (water) connection should have a conductivity equivalent to a #8 gauge wire. The path to ground followed by the conductor should be essentially straight, with no sharp bends.

If there are metal objects of considerable size within a few feet of the grounding conductor, there will be a strong tendency for sparks or side flashes to jump from the grounding conductor to the metal object at the nearest point. To prevent such possibly damaging flashes, an interconnecting conductor should be provided at all likely places.

Large metallic objects within the hull or superstructure of a boat should be interconnected with the lightning protective system to prevent a dangerous rise of voltage due to a lightning flash.

Protective measures

For power boats, a radio antenna may serve as a lightning or protective mast provided it is equipped with a transmitting-type lightning arrester or means for grounding during electrical storms, and that the antenna height is sufficient to provide an adequate cone of protection for the length of the craft. Antennas with loading coils are considered to end at a point immediately *below the coil* unless the coil has a suitable gap for bypassing lightning current. The size of the grounding conductor, interconnection, and grounding of metallic masses should be in accordance with principles noted above.

Sailboats with metallic standing rigging will be adequately protected provided that all rigging is grounded and a proper cone of protection exists. Interconnection and grounding of metallic masses should be done as on power boats.

Metal objects situated wholly on a boat's exterior should be connected to the grounding conductor at their upper or nearest end. Metal objects within the boat may be connected to the lightning protective system directly or

through the bonding system for underwater metal parts.

Metal objects that project through cabin tops, decks, etc., should be bonded to the nearest lightning conductor at the point where the object emerges from the boat and again at its lowest extreme end within the boat. Spotlights and other objects projecting through cabin tops should be solidly grounded regardless of the cone of protection.

A ground connection for lightning protection may consist of any metal surface, normally submerged, which has an area of at least one square foot. Propellers and metallic rudder surfaces may be used for this purpose; the radio ground plate is more than adequate. A steel hull itself constitutes a good ground connection to the water.

Protection for personnel

As the basic purpose of lightning protection is safety of personnel, the following precautions should be taken by the crew and guests.

Individuals should remain inside a closed boat as much as practicable during an electrical storm.

Persons should avoid making contact with any items connected to a lightning protective conductor, and especially in such a way as to bridge between two parts of the grounding system. For example, it is undesirable to touch either the reverse lever or spotlight control, particularly in contact with both at the same time.

No one should be in the water during a lightning storm.

Equipment for Safety

Some items of safety equipment are required by laws and Coast Guard regulations. These are generally written, however, in such broad language that additional knowledge and guidance are required for the greatest degree of safety afloat.

Additional items of equipment above legal minimums are required to receive the approval decal of the Coast Guard Auxiliary Courtesy Motorboat Examination, see page 19. Still further pieces of equipment are desirable for safety or convenience, or both. Many of these are discussed in Chapter 1 and other chapters. This chapter will supplement rather than duplicate equipment considerations covered elsewhere in the book.

LIFESAVING EQUIPMENT

As noted in Chapter 1, each boat must, by law, have a lifesaving device for each person aboard; few specific details are stated. A wise skipper has, in addition to his regular buoyant devices, several jackets of smaller size to protect children. On boats under 40 feet in length, life "jackets" are not required, but a buoyant cushion is not fully safe for a small child who might lose his grasp on the straps.

Although non-commercial boats under 40 feet may carry buoyant cushions, buoyant vests, or special-purpose buoyant devices (ski vests, racing vests, flotation jackets, etc.), the skipper who is really safety-conscious will carry an adequate number of *life jackets,* the canvas jackets with flota-

tion material (usually kapok) sealed in plastic pouches; fig. 1017. These are identifiable by the figures "160.002" in the Coast Guard approval number on the jacket. Such jackets provide ample buoyancy and, most importantly, float the wearer in the position that will best hold his face clear of the water so that he can breathe adequately even though he may be semi-conscious or unconscious. Jackets of this type (or life rings) are required on Class 3 boats; they are actually of even greater importance on·smaller craft as statistics show that over 97% of all accidents involve boats of the smaller classes. Jackets may be bulkier and harder to stow than vests, and they don't make sitting easier as do cushions (even though these should not be sat upon), but when needed to keep you afloat until help comes, nothing else does the job half so well!

PUMPS AND BAILERS

Oddly enough, there are no federal legal requirements for a boat (if used exclusively for pleasure) to be equipped with a device of any type for removing water that leaks in or comes aboard as spray. Essentially all boats are, of course, equipped with some form of pump or bailer, but too many skippers place their *full* dependence on electrical bilge pumps, and perhaps on only one of those. Once water rises in the bilge to a level sufficient to short out the battery, there is no way to combat the further rise of water. (Incidentally, on most boats the batteries are placed low in the bilge—excellent for stability, but not for safety if the craft starts taking on water.)

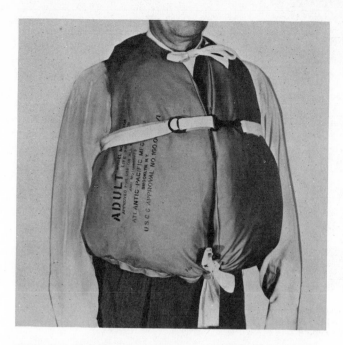

FIG. 1017 Life jackets of the type shown provide a greater measure of safety than other lifesaving devices that may be acceptable on small craft. Properly worn, they will not only provide buoyancy but will float an individual in the best position for breathing. As these are strapped to the person, he cannot lose his grasp as he could with a buoyant cushion. Two children's sizes are also available.
(Courtesy Atlantic-Pacific Mfg. Corp.)

Only the smallest boats should depend on a hand bailer or bucket. Other boats should be equipped with a hand-operated pump of generous capacity. Such an item can be either a fixed installation or a portable pump stowed where it can be quickly and easily reached when needed.

DISTRESS SIGNALING EQUIPMENT

A boat's radiotelephone is probably the most often used means of summoning assistance in an emergency. Use of the radio for this purpose is covered on pages 382(d) to 382(f).

Without special equipment a distress signal can be made to other craft in sight by standing where one is clearly visible and slowly raising and lowering one's arms. Another visual distress signal is a fluorescent red-orange rectangular panel displayed where most visible to boats and/or aircraft. This item of safety equipment is described more fully on page 172.

Signal flares may be projected several hundred feet into the air by a special type of pistol, or to a lesser height from a pocket "tear gas" gun that resembles an old-fashioned fountain pen. The laws of several states regulate possession of these and similar explosive projectile devices; check carefully before putting one aboard, but if permissible, these are effective and desirable items of safety equipment.

There are also hand-held flares of the single- and double-ended types, the latter producing a bright flame at one end for night use and a dense smoke at the other end for day distress situations. Before using any flare, read all instructions carefully so as to avoid personal injury or aggravation of the emergency. Read carefully *before* any emergency arises, you won't have time then!

MISCELLANEOUS ITEMS OF SAFETY EQUIPMENT

There are many small items of equipment that serve to increase safety and convenience.

Every boat should be equipped with several **flashlights** and at least one battery-powered **electric lantern,** fig. 1019. If provided with an adjustable head, the beam can be directed where needed. Flashlights should be distributed so as to be quickly available in an emergency. One should be within reach of the skipper's bunk and the first mate's, too. There should also be a flashlight in the guest cabin, if any, and another on the bridge. The electric lantern should be kept in an accessible place. Batteries in all units should be checked at least monthly to be sure that they have sufficient power.

An installed searchlight of adequate intensity is desirable on medium-sized and large boats operated at night. It is useful both in routine navigation and docking, and in emergencies such as man-overboard situations or assisting another boat in distress. On smaller boats, the electric lantern can serve as a hand-held searchlight.

FIG. 1018 A night distress signal will be seen at much greater distances if projected to a height of several hundred feet. Flare pistols and related devices will do this, but in some states these items of boating safety equipment are subject to firearms laws and regulations.
(Courtesy Abercrombie & Fitch)

FIG. 1019 An electric lantern should be aboard every boat. If provided with adjustable head, it projects a stronger beam of light than most flashlights and has the added advantage of being able to be set down with the light directed where needed, thus making both hands available for working.

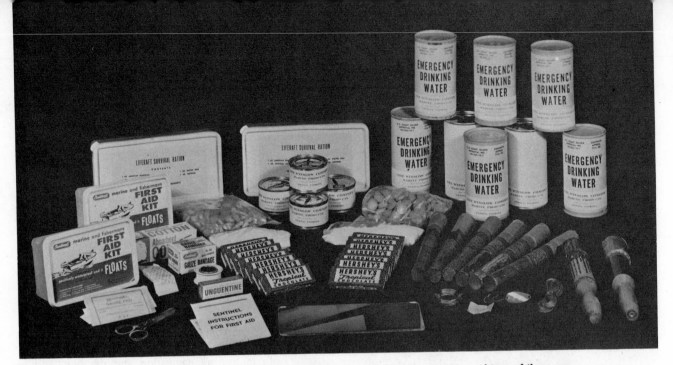

FIG. 1020 Every boat should have aboard some emergency drinking water and food. The quantity and type of these supplies will vary, of course, with the number of persons aboard and the cruising area. Prepared kits of long shelf-life food and water can be purchased, or the boat owner can assemble his own supplies. (Courtesy Winslow Company Marine Products)

Boats of medium or large size should have on board a small **hand axe** to be used in cutting lines in an emergency. The axe should be stowed on deck, where it might be needed in a hurry.

Tools and **spare parts** for the engine and major accessories can be considered parts of a boat's essential safety equipment. Personal experience and conversation with seasoned skippers will offer the best guidance to just what tools and parts should be carried aboard any particular craft. Insofar as practicable, tools should be of rust-proof metal; tools susceptible to rust or corrosion, and all spare parts, should be properly protected from adverse effects of a marine environment.

All but the smallest craft should be equipped with **emergency drinking water** and **food** supplies. The amount will vary with the number of persons normally on board. The type of food is not important—anything will do when you get hungry enough! Non-perishability over a long period is important, but it might be wise once each year to consume your emergency supplies (a shipwreck party?) *after* they have been replaced with a fresh stock. Such items can usually be purchased from marine supply stores or from Army-Navy surplus stores; food should be simple and compact, but sustaining and energy-producing.

First aid kits are essential safety items; they will be considered in more detail later in this chapter.

Navigation equipment, charts, and **ground tackle** are all items of safety equipment, but each is considered in detail elsewhere in this book, see index.

SAFETY ASPECTS OF OTHER EQUIPMENT

Several items generally found on boats are not "safety equipment" per se, but have definite aspects of safety about their design, installation, or operation that must be considered by boat owners.

Galley stoves

All boatmen seem to love to eat, especially when out on the water. Cabin boats will normally have a galley, the de-

gree of size and elaborateness varying with the design and use of the craft.

Galley stoves should be designed, manufactured, and approved for marine use. Types of fuel that are ordinarily used include alcohol, electricity, and liquified petroleum gas (LPG—normally propane or butane). Stoves fueled with kerosene, coal, wood, or canned heat (solidified alcohol) are only rarely seen now. Gasoline is *not* a safe stove fuel and should *never* be used on a boat.

Electricity is probably the safest source of heat for cooking, but an auxiliary generating plant is required to produce the large amounts of AC power required. Because of the inexpensive and simple nature of the equipment,

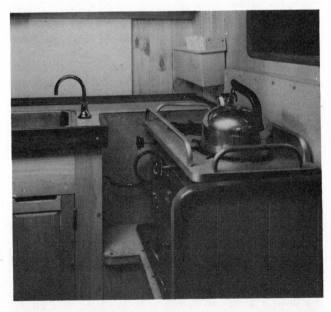

FIG. 1021 This galley stove installation shows the use of insulating board behind, beside, and below the stove to protect woodwork from unsafe high temperatures. The stove also has a drip pan beneath it, another safety feature.

alcohol stoves are widely used on boats despite their rather high fuel costs; with moderate and reasonable precautions, such installations can be quite safe. Plain water will extinguish alcohol fires.

LPG stoves are excellent for cooking, but can present a serious safety hazard unless installed and operated in accordance with strict rules—their use is prohibited on certain classes of commercial vessels.

Stoves should be permanently and securely fastened in place when in operation. Portable stoves are not recommended; if one must be used, it should be secured temporarily while in use. Adequate ventilation should be provided to prevent any excess rise in temperature of an area in which a stove is operated for extended periods of time (for the sake of safety as well as the cook's comfort!). All woodwork or other combustible material directly above or immediately surrounding a stove, including smoke stacks, must be effectively protected with non-combustible sheathing; see fig. 1021. A recommended means is the use of 1/8-inch asbestos board covered with sheet metal.

Fuel for alcohol and kerosene stoves may be supplied to the burners either by gravity or pressure systems provided fuel tanks cannot be filled while the burners are in operation except where the supply tank is remote from burners and the filling operation will not introduce a fire hazard. A removable or accessible liquid-tight metal drip pan at least 3/4" deep should be provided beneath all burners. Pressure tanks should have suitable gauges and/or relief valves.

Refrigeration

Ice is used on many boats as a means of keeping food fresh and for cooling beverages. It offers no safety hazards, but water from melting ice should be piped overboard rather than into the bilge. Fresh-water drip tends to promote dry rot. A collection sump, with pump, may be used if desired.

Mechanical refrigeration will normally be of the electric-motor-driven compressor type similar to units found in the home. Occasionally, a compressor will be belt-driven from a main engine, but this is rare.

Safety aspects of mechanical refrigeration include use of a non-toxic and non-flammable refrigerant, non-sparking motors, safety valves on high-pressure portions of the system, and general construction adequate to survive rigors of marine service.

Kerosene and bottled-gas refrigerators have a constant small open flame. This can produce an explosion hazard, and the use of such absorption-type units is presently excluded from the AB&YC Safety Standard A-6.

Heaters

Cabin heaters are sometimes used on boats in northern waters to extend the boating season or to ward off the chill of a sudden cold snap. Gasoline should never be used as a fuel and portable kerosene or alcohol heaters are not recommended. Built-in electrical heaters are safe; portable electrical heaters should be used only if secured in place while in operation.

Gas-burning heaters should be equipped with an automatic device to shut off the fuel supply if the flame is extinguished. Pilot lights should not be used. Coast Guard regulations prohibit use of LPG fuel for any purpose on certain commercial craft.

Many models of air-conditioning equipment used on boats are of the "reverse cycle" or "heat pump" type and can supply warmth rather than cooling when the former is needed. This is a thoroughly safe method of heating.

Safety in Operations

Safety should be a part of every aspect of the operation of small craft. Boat handling has been covered in Chapter 8. Safety in such operations as stranding and towing was considered in Chapter 9. Navigation and piloting—essential for safety—are discussed in Chapter 21 and other chapters. The aspects of operational safety afloat to be considered here are those that do not fall under other major headings.

FUELING PRECAUTIONS

Certain precautions must be carefully and completely observed *every* time a boat is fueled with gasoline. Step by step, these are:

Before fueling

1. Make sure that the boat is securely tied to the fueling pier. Fuel before darkness, if possible.

2. Stop engines, motors, fans, and other devices capable of producing a spark. Open the master switch if the electrical system has one. Put out all galley fires and open flames.

3. Close all ports, windows, doors, and hatches so that fumes cannot blow aboard and below.

4. Disembark all passengers and any crew members not needed for the fueling operation.

FIG. 1022 Fueling must be accomplished in a safe manner to reduce hazards of gasoline explosion and fire. Refer to the text for a 16-point checklist of actions before, during, and after fueling.

5. Prohibit all smoking on board and in the vicinity.

6. Have a filled fire extinguisher close at hand.

7. Measure the fuel in the tanks and do not order more than the tank will hold; allow for expansion.

While fueling

8. Keep nozzle or can spout in contact with the fill opening to guard against static sparks.

9. Do not spill gasoline.

10. Do not overfill. The practice of filling until fuel flows from the vents is highly dangerous.

11. For outboards, remove portable tanks from boat and fill on shore.

After fueling

12. Close fill openings.

13. Wipe up any spilled gasoline; dispose of wipe-up rags on shore.

14. Open all ports, windows, doors, and hatches; turn on bilge power exhaust blower. Ventilate boat this way *at least* five minutes—time it, don't guess.

15. Sniff low down in tank and engine compartments. *If any odor of gasoline is present, do not start engine;* continue ventilation actions until odor can no longer be detected.

16. Be prepared to cast off lines as soon as engine starts; get clear of pier quickly.

SAFETY IN LOADING

Overloading is probably the greatest cause of accidents in smaller boats and dinghies, and is even a significant factor in medium-size boats such as those of Class 2. Overloading is particularly hazardous as it is not so feared as are fires and explosions. Many a skipper, cautious in his handling of gasoline, will unknowingly load his craft far beyond safe limits. The number of seats in a boat is *not* an indication of the number of persons it can carry safely.

Determining capacity

"Loading" and "capacity" are terms primarily related to the weight of persons, fuel, gear, etc., that can be safely carried. The safe load of a boat in persons depends on many of its characteristics, such as the hull volume and dimensions; the material of which it is built, if it is an outboard hull, whether there is an effective engine well inboard of the transom notch where the engine is mounted; how heavy the engine is; and other factors. Many small boats now carry a "capacity plate," see fig. 1023, placed on the hull in accordance with standards of the Boating Industry Association. Such plates show the recommended maximum weight capacity, usually in number of persons as well as in number of pounds for persons, motor, fuel, and gear.

The BIA standards are accepted by the Coast Guard for boats in classes A and 1. The capacity is determined by the application of two formulas, one quite complex for determination of the boat's cubic capacity and the other simply length times beam divided by 15. The answer in either case is the maximum number of persons to be carried and the smaller of the two results is the one used. This capacity is based on good weather conditions and should be further reduced in rough water. The presence of a capacity plate does not relieve the boatman of the responsibility for exercising individual judgment. This includes knowledge of

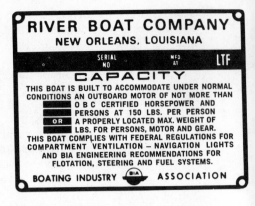

FIG. 1023 The Boating Industry Association has developed standards for safe loading of boats under 23 feet in terms of horsepower and weight-carrying capacity. Boats meeting these standards as determined by an independent testing laboratory will carry the BIA certification plate.

probable future weather conditions as well as those prevailing at the start of a cruise.

The weight-carrying capacity of a small boat having a conventional hull can be computed by multiplying 7.5 x overall length x maximum width x *minimum* effective depth of the boat (the depth of the hull to the lowest point at which water can enter—this penalizes low-cut transoms and recognizes properly designed engine wells). The result is the weight *in pounds* that can be carried; subtract the weight of engine, tanks, fuel, all installed or carried accessories and gear; the remainder is the weight in pounds, of persons that can be safely carried. As between the number of persons computed by weight as above and the number determined from L x B divided by 15, the lower figure should be used.

Safe loading

It must always be remembered that people represent a "live" load (no pun intended); they move about and affect a boat quite differently than a "dead" or static load such as the engine or fuel tank. If the capacity of the boat is fully utilized, or the weather gets rough, distribute the load evenly, keep it low, and don't make abrupt changes in its distribution. Any shifting of human or other weights should be done only after stopping or slowing the boat so that the change can be made safely.

Horsepower capacity

A second aspect of the capacity of an outboard boat is the maximum horsepower motor that can be *safely* put on it. This is exceeded perhaps as often as the weight-carrying capacity. The safe maximum horsepower will also be included on the capacity plate of a boat rated to BIA standards. If a boat does not have such a plate, the maximum horsepower can be determined from the graph and instructions on page 451.

The maximum horsepower that is safe need not be used; most boats will give satisfactory, and more economical, service with motors of less horsepower. A larger engine does not always mean more speed. If the horsepower of the engine is doubled, it does not mean that boat speed will be doubled. It does mean, however, that because of the increased weight of the engine, fuel and accessories it will require, the number of persons that can be safely carried will be significantly reduced.

Boarding a boat

There is a safe way to step aboard a small boat—outboard or dinghy—and an unsafe way. In boarding from a pier, step into the boat as near to the center as possible, keeping body weight low. If you're boarding from a beach, come in over the bow. Keep lines tight or have someone steady the boat.

Never jump into a boat or step on the gunwale (edge of the hull). If you have a motor or other gear to take aboard, pile it on the pier so that you can easily reach it from the center of the boat. Better still, have someone hand it to you after you're aboard.

SAFETY IN THE WATER

Anyone who goes boating regularly should know how to care for himself in the water. Fortunately, most boatmen and their families do know "how to swim," but this is often limited to taking a few strokes in a calm, relatively warm pool, with safety and rest only a few feet away. More attention should be given to staying afloat under adverse conditions of water temperature, waves, etc. Seldom is it necessary, or even desirable, to "swim" any distance; the problem is that of remaining afloat until help arrives. The skipper and crew should all have instructions in "drownproofing."

Safety *in* the water can well start with swimming and/or lifesaving class at the local "Y" or community recreation center. Local chapters of the American Red Cross also give instruction in these subjects.

Lifesaving devices

A person in the water following a boating accident should, of course, have a life jacket or buoyant cushion. It is of extreme importance that these devices be worn or used properly. Buoyant cushions are far from the best flotation device, but are widely used because of their convenience and low cost. Buoyant cushions are *not* intended to be worn. The straps on a buoyant cushion are put there primarily for holding-on purposes and also to aid in throwing the device. Because they must be grasped, cushions are not suitable for small children or injured persons, and are not desirable for non-swimmers. Cushions should never be worn on a person's back since this tends to force his face down in the water.

As mentioned earlier in this chapter, the lifesaving device providing the greatest safety is the canvas jacket with flotation material in sealed plastic pouches. But the real potential of this most important safety item will be realized *only* if several conditions are met. Life preservers should be stored in several locations about the boat so that fire or other disaster cannot cut you off from all of them, and they must be stowed so as to be easily and quickly accessible. Everyone on board, including guests who may be aboard for only a few hours, *must* know where the life preservers are stowed. The skipper and regular crew must have tried them on and must be able to get into them quickly even in the dark (practice wearing a blindfold). Most importantly, the skipper must not delay in ordering everyone into life preservers in advance of their need if the emergency is of the type that builds up rather than striking suddenly without warning. It is far better to put them on, as bulky and uncomfortable as they may be, when trouble first threatens than it is to wait until near-panic develops. At night, anyone on deck should routinely wear a life jacket; non-swimmers, young children, and persons physically handicapped should wear one at all times—a person with a cast on an arm or leg goes down like a rock without added buoyancy.

The wise skipper never carries non-approved, damaged, or condemned lifesaving devices as "extra"—someone might grab one of them in an emergency.

Swimming tips

Even with the best of lifesaving equipment aboard, a boatman may find himself in the water without the aid of a buoyant device. If the boat remains afloat or awash, *stay with it.* Search vessels and aircraft can spot a boat or its

FIG. 1024 Swimming is a fine sport and an excellent capability to have for anyone who goes boating. Every skipper and his crew should know how to stay afloat and swim moderate distances. Take lessons at your local "Y" or Red Cross if you do not have this most desirable ability.

wreckage far easier than an individual whose head only is above water.

A swimmer may find temporary relief from fatigue by floating or by varying his style of swimming. Cold or tired muscles are susceptible to cramps. A leg cramp can often be overcome by moving your knees up toward your chest so that you can massage the affected area. Save your breath as much as possible; call for help only when there is someone definitely close enough to hear you.

PRE-DEPARTURE SAFETY

A worthwhile degree of increased safety afloat can be achieved if certain actions are taken routinely before departing on a short cruise. If it is to be an extended cruise of days or weeks, most of these items should be repeated each day.

Final weather check

Few, if any, boats are of such size for the waters on which they are operated that no heed need be given to possible worsening of weather conditions before return to the home berth or reaching the next port. The wise skipper makes a final weather check just as close as possible to his departure time so as to have the latest weather report of current conditions and most up-to-date forecast. He learns the time of best weather broadcasts, radio and TV, in his home area (such broadcasts vary widely in their scope and suitability for boating); he knows the telephone numbers of agencies that he can call for last-minute information. When away from his home area, he finds on arrival at each overnight stop how he can get early morning forecasts before his departure.

The Coastal Warning Facilities Charts published each year in early summer by the Weather Bureau (see pages 246 and 247) provide information on major radio and TV weather broadcasts as well as the location of day and night storm warning displays. The Weather Bureau also is steadily expanding the number of VHF-FM radio transmitters that broadcast continuous weather information on 162.55 Mc/s.

Pre-departure check list

Each skipper should prepare his own pre-departure checklist *and use it*. The following items are of general applicability; all may not be needed, and others certainly will have to be added for your own boating.

1. All safety equipment is aboard, accessible, and in good working condition, including one Coast Guard-approved life-saving device for each person embarked.

2. The bilge has been checked for fuel fumes and water. Ventilate or pump out as necessary.

3. Horn and all navigation lights operate satisfactorily.

4. All loose gear is stowed securely. Dock lines and fenders should be stowed immediately after getting under way.

5. All guests aboard have been properly instructed in safety and operational matters, both do's and don'ts.

6. Engine oil levels have been checked, both crankcase and reverse/reduction gears; water level has been checked in closed cooling systems. After starting engines, check overboard flow of cooling water.

7. Fuel tanks have been checked for quantity of gasoline or diesel fuel. Know your tank capacity and fuel consumption at various RPMs, thus knowing your cruising radius.

FIG. 1025 Although boating is generally a leisure-time activity, a skipper often leaves his pier or mooring in a hurry. A "pre-departure checklist" will ensure that no essential preparatory step has been left undone. This is especially important for safety when running single-handed and the skipper cannot leave the helm once underway.

FIG. 1026 A "Float Plan" is a handy means of leaving behind on shore essential information when you go out fishing or for a cruise. Should you become overdue and a search must be made, much valuable time may be saved. Be sure, however, to report in when you return so as to avoid needless concern and wasted action.

Make sure there is enough fuel aboard for your anticipated cruising, plus an adequate reserve if you must change your plans for weather or other reasons.

8. There is a second person on board capable of taking over from the skipper should he become disabled or excessively fatigued.

Float plan

Before departing on a cruise, the skipper should advise a responsible relative or friend as to where he intends to cruise and when he expects to make port again; make sure that this person has a good description of the boat. Keep him advised of any changes in your cruise plans. By doing these things, this person will be able to tell the Coast Guard where to search and what type of boat to look for if you are overdue. Be sure to advise this relative or friend when you return so as to prevent any false alarms about your safety.

An excellent means of accomplishing the foregoing is through use of "Float Plan" forms made available by the Marine Office of America, a leading insurer of boats. These forms, fig. 1026, provide a simple and convenient way of filing the necessary information. A pad of forms may be obtained by writing to 123 William Street, New York, N. Y. 10038, or from a local agent of the company.

SAFETY IN WATER SKIING

Water skiing has become an ever more popular sport and its spread brings with it new problems in safety afloat. The following guides should do much to reduce hazards.

1. Allow no one who is not qualified as a basic swimmer to engage in water skiing. A ski belt or vest is intended to keep a stunned or unconscious skier afloat.

2. Water ski *only* in safe areas, out of channels and away from other craft. Some bodies of water will have areas designated for this sport with skiing prohibited elsewhere.

3. Install a wide-angle rear-view mirror or take along a second person to act as lookout. This will permit watching the skier *and* the waters ahead. Some state laws require this mirror or a second person in the boat to assist the operator, or both; check before starting to ski.

4. Make sure that the skier is wearing a proper lifesaving device.

5. If the skier falls, approach him from the lee side; stop your motor before starting to take him aboard.

6. In taking the skier on board, be careful not to swamp the boat. For smaller craft, it is usually safer to take a person aboard at the stern.

Skiing signals

The following set of signals is recommended by the American Water Ski Association; see fig. 1027. Make sure that the skier, boat operator, and safety observer all know and understand the signals.

Faster—palm of one hand pointing upward.

Slower—palm pointing downward.

Speed O.K.—arm upraised with thumb and finger joined to form a circle.

Right Turn—arm outstretched pointing to the right.

Left Turn—arm outstretched pointing to the left.

Return to Drop-off Area—arm at 45° from body pointing down to water and swinging.

Cut Motor—finger drawn across throat.

Stop—hand up, palm forward—policeman style.

Skier O.K. After Fall—hands clenched together overhead.

Pick Me Up or **Fallen Skier, Watch Out**—one ski extended vertically out of water.

FIG. 1027 This simple set of hand signals will allow adequate communication from the skier to the operator or observer on the towing craft. They must all be thoroughly familiar with the full set of signals if maximum safety is to be achieved.
(from the USCG Recreational Boating Guide)

Maintenance for Safety

Safety afloat is achieved, as we have seen in this chapter, by good design, sound construction, proper equipment, and sensible operating practices. The remaining element is continued maintenance for safety. Continual attention is needed for some of the material aspects of safety; for others, periodic checks at weekly, monthly, or annual intervals is sufficient. The important thing is that these checks of safety equipment be made *regularly* when needed.

Keep your boat clean

Cleanliness aboard a boat is an important aspect of safety. Accumulations of dirt, sawdust, wood chips, and trash in the bilge will soak up oil and fuel drippings and become a fire hazard. Such accumulations may also stop up limber holes and clog bilge pumps. Keep your bilge absolutely free of dirt and trash; check frequently and clean out as often as needed.

LIFESAVING EQUIPMENT

Lifesaving equipment usually requires no maintenance, but such items should be carefully inspected at the beginning of each boating season and again near its mid-point. These devices are not permanent; they do slowly wear out. Check for cut or torn fabric, broken stitches, and other signs of deterioration. **Do not delay in replacing below-par lifesaving devices;** attempt repairs *only* where *full* effectiveness can be restored. In case of doubt, ask the Coast Guard.

FIRE EXTINGUISHERS

Portable fire extinguishers and installed systems should be checked at least annually; the best time is at the beginning of the year's activities afloat and again at mid-season if required.

Dry chemical extinguishers

Pressurized dry chemical extinguishers are widely used on boats. These will have a gauge that should be checked every six months for an indication of adequate pressure—needle in center or green area of scale. Do not, however, merely read the gauge; tap it lightly to make sure that it is not stuck at a safe indication. If it drops to a lower reading, take the extinguisher to a service shop for recharging. Even if the gauge reads O.K., take the unit out of its bracket and shake it a bit to loosen the dry chemical inside to keep it from settling and hardening. Any areas on the exterior of the cylinder showing rust should be cleaned and repainted.

CO2 extinguishers

Carbon dioxide—CO2—fire extinguishers are checked annually by weight. Both portable units and built-in systems will have a weight stamped on them at the valve housing. If the weight is as much as 10% below the indicated value, the unit *must* be recharged. Weighing is the only check normally required on CO2 extinguishers, but it must be done accurately. Portable units can be checked by the boat owner if he has access to suitably accurate scales. Built-in systems are best checked by a professional serviceman using his specialized knowledge and equipment.

CO2 cylinders should also have verified the date on which the cylinder was last hydrostatically pressure-tested. This should be done every 12 years if the cylinder is not discharged. If the extinguisher is used, it must be pressure-tested if this has not been done within the preceding five years. If a used CO2 extinguisher is purchased, it should be discharged, hydrostatically tested, and recharged before it is installed aboard. Remember that the pressure confined in these cylinders is tremendous, and if the cylinder has been damaged (through rust or corrosion), it is just like having a time bomb aboard, not knowing when it is set to go off!

Carbon dioxide extinguishers should not be installed where bilge or rain water will collect and cause rust. Any exposed metal should be painted at each annual inspection. If a cylinder becomes pitted from rust, have it hydrostatically tested for safety. Replace any damaged hoses or horns on this type of extinguisher.

Foam-type extinguishers

Foam-type fire extinguishers are acceptable on boats, but are seldom actually installed because they are messy in use and need annual recharging. If you do have one, it must be completely discharged and recharged each year. There is no other method of checking it.

Periodic discharges

It is a good policy to discharge a fire extinguisher periodically even though it is not needed for fighting a fire. An effective way of doing this would be to discharge one of the portable units each year on a regular rotation basis. This should be done in the presence of the whole crew and preferably in the form of a drill, putting out an actual small fire—off the boat, of course—in a metal pan or tub. Probably 99% or more of all persons who go boating have never discharged a fire extinguisher, let alone used one to put out an actual fire! There is no time to read the instructions carefully and practice after a real fire has started on the boat.

A word of warning with respect to CO2 extinguishers— *never* unscrew the hose from the cylinder and then discharge it openly. This would have the same effect as trying to hang onto a rocket. A strong, heavy man would have trouble in hanging onto the cylinder, and if it were to get loose, it could cause a great deal of trouble.

Make sure that when fire extinguishers are removed for testing or practice discharge they are serviced by a competent shop and reinstalled *as soon as possible*. Sitting empty in the basement or garage at home or in the trunk of your car, an extinguisher cannot protect your boat. It is also wise not to denude your boat of fire protection by removing all extinguishers at the same time for servicing; do a half or a third at a time.

Log entries

An entry should be made in the boat's log of all inspections, tests, and servicing of fire extinguishers. This will help keep these essential checks from being overlooked and may prove valuable in the event of insurance surveys or claims.

ENGINE AND FUEL SYSTEM

Frequent safety checks should be made of the engine and fuel system for cleanliness and leaks. Any drippings of oil or grease should be kept wiped up and stopped as soon as possible. Immediate action must be taken in the case of any gasoline leaks—do not use the boat and disconnect the leads from the battery (with all loads turned off so that no spark will jump) in order that the engine cannot be started.

Annually, the entire fuel system should be checked inch by inch, including fuel lines in areas not normally visible. Look for any evidence of weepage of fuel or external corrosion of the lines. If any suspicious joints or lengths of tubing are found, it would be well to call in a qualified mechanic without delay.

ELECTRICAL SYSTEMS

A thorough annual inspection should be made of a boat's electrical system, including all wiring in areas not normally visible. This should be done by a person qualified to evaluate what he finds—the skipper if he has the necessary knowledge and experience, or an outside expert if needed. A search should be made for any cut or chafed insulation, corrosion at connections, excessive sag or strain on conductors, and other visible signs of deterioration. A leakage test should be made by opening each circuit at the main distribution panel and measuring current flow when all loads are turned off. Ideally there should be no current flow; current of more than a few milliamperes indicates electrical "leakage" that should be traced down and corrected without delay.

Bonding systems

If all through-hull fittings, struts, shafts, etc., are electrically connected by an internal bonding system, this wiring should be checked annually. Especially careful checks should be made where connections are made to the fitting or other metal part; connections in the bilge are subject to corrosion and development of poor contacts with high electrical resistance.

The skipper can make a visual check of the bonding system, but an electrical expert with specialized equipment is needed for a thorough evaluation. Should any signs of corrosion at points of connection of bonding wires to through-hull fittings be noted, a complete electrical test is recommended.

With respect to possible electrolysis damage, a bonding system with one or more poor connections is worse than no system at all. Electrolysis can and does cause weakening of through-hull fittings, bolts on struts and rudder posts, etc., that could result in serious safety hazards.

HULL SAFETY MAINTENANCE

Boats that are kept in the water will be hauled out periodically for bottom cleaning and repainting. This occasion should not be overlooked as an opportunity for a *safety* inspection of hull and fittings below the waterline.

Hull planking should be carefully checked for physical damage from having struck floating or fixed objects, and for any general deterioration from age. In general, it is best

to call upon the services of an expert if any suspicious areas are found.

Through-hull fittings

An inspection should be made each time the boat is hauled to see that through-hull fittings and their seacocks are in good condition. This check should include fastenings susceptible to damage from electrolytic action.

Underwater components

Underwater fittings should get an annual inspection. This includes such parts as shafts, propellers, rudders, struts, stuffing boxes, and metal skegs. Stuffing boxes should be repacked as often as necessary to keep them from leaking excessively, shafting checked for alignment and excessive wear at strut bearings, and propellers examined to see if they need truing up.

FOLLOW-UP OF INSPECTIONS

Nothing is gained if prompt and thorough follow-up actions are not taken on findings of periodic safety inspections. *Maintenance related to the safety of the craft and those aboard must not be delayed. Do not operate a boat that has a known safety defect.*

First Aid Afloat

No one who is not educated and properly qualified to practice medicine should attempt to act as a doctor. There are, however, many instances where availability of a first aid kit, some knowledge on the part of the boatman, and a ready reference book have materially eased pain or even saved the life of a sick or injured person on a boat. All skippers should prepare themselves and their craft to render emergency first aid, doing no more than is absolutely necessary while getting the victim to a doctor or hospital as rapidly as possible.

FIRST AID KITS

There are many published guides to the proper contents of a first aid kit. Probably each of these has merit, and the list that follows can, and should, be modified for the size of boat, the number of persons aboard, the length of an average cruise, the area to be cruised, and the hazards likely to be encountered.

The first aid kit must be accessible and each person aboard should be made aware of its location.

Basic first aid materials

There are certain basic first aid materials that should be carried aboard all classes of boats. Bandages should be ready for instant use—each dressing individually wrapped, a complete dressing in itself. Each should be sterilized and designed to provide protection against infection and contamination.

Antiseptic liquids are preferably packaged so that the solution stays at its original strength until used. This type of packaging is available as a swab that contains a sealed ampoule in a sleeve of multi-layered cardboard; when the ampoule is broken there is no chance for the user to be

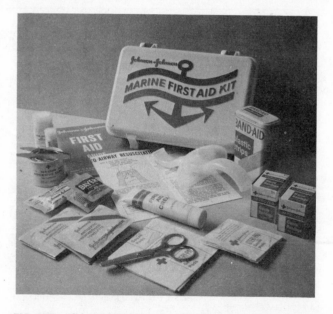

FIG. 1028 All boats should have on board adequate first aid equipment, supplies, and instructions. Kits may be either home-assembled or bought ready-made. See text for recommended items to be included. Skippers should also consider taking a standard first-aid course of instruction.

cut by glass. A close-packed cotton tip saturates instantly and then is applied to the wound area. There is no wasteage, spillage, or deterioration.

Basic first aid materials should also contain burn treatment compounds to take care of sunburn or burns caused by other hazards. Scissors have multiple uses. Forceps, to remove splinters, should be blunt-end, to preclude possi-

Artificial Respiration

Every boatman should have a working knowledge of the principles of artificial respiration. When the need for it arises, there is no time to search for instructions nor to study each step while, at the same time, attempting to apply the treatment. A boatman who has familiarized himself in advance with one of the accepted methods is more likely to work with calm assurance, saving precious minutes that could mean the difference between success and failure.

Through the courtesy of The American National Red Cross, we reproduce below the simplified illustrated methods they advocate. In recent years the mouth-to-mouth method, illustrated in steps 1 to 5, has come into widespread use. Recognizing, however, that some rescuers cannot or will not apply this method, the Red Cross includes instructions for the older manual chest pressure—arm lift (Silvester) and back pressure—arm lift (Holger Nielsen) methods. Study carefully the additional instructions at the bottom of the page applicable to all methods.

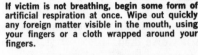

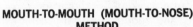

If victim is not breathing, begin some form of artificial respiration at once. Wipe out quickly any foreign matter visible in the mouth, using your fingers or a cloth wrapped around your fingers.

MOUTH-TO-MOUTH (MOUTH-TO-NOSE) METHOD

Tilt victim's head back. (Fig. 1). Pull or push the jaw into a jutting-out position. (Fig. 2).

If victim is a small child, place your mouth tightly over his mouth and nose and blow gently into his lungs about 20 times a minute. If victim is an adult (see Fig. 3), cover the mouth with your mouth, pinch his nostrils shut, and blow vigorously about 12 times a minute.

If unable to get air into lungs of victim, and if head and jaw positions are correct, suspect foreign matter in throat. To remove it, suspend a small child momentarily by the ankles or place child in position shown in Fig. 4, and slap sharply between shoulder blades.

If the victim is adult, place in position shown in Fig. 5, and use same procedure.

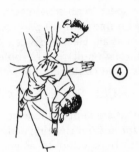

MANUAL METHODS OF ARTIFICIAL RESPIRATION

Rescuers who cannot, or will not, use mouth-to-mouth or mouth-to-nose technique should use a manual method.

THE CHEST PRESSURE-ARM LIFT (SILVESTER) METHOD

Place the victim in a face-up position and put something under his shoulders to raise them and allow the head to drop backward.

Kneel at the victim's head, grasp his wrists, cross them, and press them over the lower chest (Fig. 6). This should cause air to flow out.

Immediately release this pressure and pull the arms outward and upward over his head and backward as far as possible (Fig. 7). This should cause air to rush in.

Repeat this cycle about 12 times per minute, checking the mouth frequently for obstructions.

If a second rescuer is available, have him hold the victim's head so that the jaw is jutting out (Fig. 8). The helper should be alert to detect the presence of any stomach contents in the mouth and keep the mouth as clean as possible at all times.

THE BACK PRESSURE-ARM LIFT (HOLGER NIELSEN) METHOD

Place the victim face-down, bend his elbows and place his hands one upon the other, turn his head slightly to one side and extend it as far as possible, making sure that the chin is jutting out. Kneel at the head of the victim. Place your hands on the flat of the victim's back so that the palms lie just below an imaginary line running between the armpits (Fig. 9).

Rock forward until the arms are approximately vertical and allow the weight of the upper part of your body to exert steady, even pressure downward upon the hands (Fig. 10).

Immediately draw his arms upward and toward you, applying enough lift to feel resistance and tension at his shoulders (Fig. 11). Then lower the arms to the ground. Repeat this cycle about 12 times per minute, checking the mouth frequently for obstruction.

If a second rescuer is available, have him hold the victim's head so that the jaw continues to jut out (Fig. 12). The helper should be alert to detect any stomach contents in the mouth and keep the mouth as clean as possible at all times.

RELATED INFORMATION FOR ALL METHODS

If vomiting occurs, quickly turn the victim on his side, wipe out the mouth, and then reposition him.

When a victim is revived, keep him as quiet as possible until he is breathing regularly. Keep him from becoming chilled and otherwise treat him for shock. Continue artificial respiration until the victim begins to breathe for himself or a physician pronounces him dead or he appears to be dead beyond any doubt.

Because respiratory and other disturbances may develop as an aftermath, a doctor's care is necessary during the recovery period.

bility of doing further injury by probing, which is *not* a first aid measure.

Pre-packed first aid kits, available at most drug stores and marine supply stores, are generally acceptable, but their contents should be checked against recommendations that follow. Consideration should be given to separate purchase of any significant shortages; such items should be stored in or near the kit.

The container

The container for a first aid kit for a boat should not be made of a metal that could rust, nor of cardboard that could soak up moisture. A plastic box such as is often used to hold fishing tackle or tools is a good choice. It should close securely and be moisture-tight. It should *never* be locked, although it may be sealed with tape. Keep it on a high shelf out of the reach of small children. The kit may be lightly secured in place for safety in rough weather, but it must be portable and capable of being quickly unfastened and taken to the scene of an emergency.

Contents (instruments)

First aid kits should contain both simple instruments and consumable supplies. In the first category, the following are recommended:

Scissors—small and sharp; if there is room for two pairs, one should be of the blunt-end surgical type. Also a packet of single-edge razor blades.

Tweezers—small, pointed; tips must meet exactly to pick up small objects.

Safety pins—assorted sizes.

Thermometer—inexpensive oral-rectal type, in case.

Tourniquet—use only for *major* bleeding that cannot be controlled by compresses; follow instructions *exactly*.

Eye-washing cup—small, metal.

Cross Venti-breather—resuscitation device for drowned or asphyxiated person; aids in mouth-to-mouth resuscitation; follow directions on box.

Hot-water bottle and **ice bag**—these items, or a single unit that will serve both purposes, can do much to ease pain. Use with caution, following instructions in the first aid manual or medical advice book; improper use can aggravate conditions, sometimes seriously.

Contents (supplies)

The first aid kit should contain approximately the following types, sizes, and quantities of consumable supplies. Within reasonable limits, substitutions can be made to reflect local availabilities, personal preferences, etc.

Bandages—1", 2", and 4" sterile gauze squares, individually wrapped. Bandage rolls, 1" and 2". Band-aids (or equivalents) in assorted sizes, plus "butterfly closures." A minimum of one unit of each item, more on larger craft with greater number of persons aboard.

Triangular bandage—40" for use as sling or major compress.

Elastic bandage—3" width for sprains or splints.

Adhesive tape—Waterproof, 1" and 2" by 5 or 10 yards.

Absorbent cotton—standard size roll, for cleaning wounds, padding, etc.

Applicators—cotton-tipped individual swabs (Q-tips or equivalent) for applying antiseptics, removing foreign objects from cuts, eyes, ears.

Antiseptic liquid—Tincture of iodine of merthiolate; or zephiran chloride, aqueous solution, 1:1,000. Antiseptic may be in bottle, but preferably in form of individual crushable ampoule applicators. Also a 4 oz. or larger bottle of antiseptic (70% alcohol) solution, or Phisophex solution.

White petroleum jelly—small jar, or preferably tube; plain, not carbolated; for small burns, dressings. An antiseptic burn cream may be substituted. This may be supplemented by a tube or bottle of sunburn remedy and a package of sterile petroleum-jelly-saturated gauze squares.

Antiseptic ointment—1 oz. tube of Bacitracin or Polysporin, or as recommended by your physician (prescription required); for general cuts, abrasions, and infections of the skin.

Nupercainal ointment—1 oz. tube; for local anesthetic purposes—apply to raw surface before cleaning or if painful. Calamine lotion is good for relief from itching.

Pain killer—Aspirin or related compound for ordinary pain. Also Darvon Compound, Codeine, or Demerol tablets or capsules for more severe pain (prescription required).

Sleeping pills—Seconal or equivalent as prescribed by your physician; use with caution as directed. If sleeplessness is related to pain, also give aspirin or Darvon Compound.

Antibiotics—Use *only* if there will be a delay in reaching a doctor and infection appears serious. Use Achroymcin, Eryothromycin, or similar drug as prescribed by your doctor.

Ophthalmic (eye) ointment—small tube of butyn sulphate with metaphen. If necessary to flush out eye, use sterile solution of 1 teaspoon of salt in 1 pint of water; do *not* use sea water.

Antihistamine—Pyrabenzamine tablets or as prescribed by your physician; use for allergies and allergic reactions to stings and insect bites. Also an antihistamine ointment.

Ammonia inhalants—crushable ampoules; for relief of symptoms of faintness or dizziness.

Seasickness remedy—Dramamine, Marezine, Bonamine, or Bonine tablets; may also be obtained in suppository form. Prescription required for all except Bonine. These should be taken before embarking; usually not effective after vomiting starts.

Anti-acid preparation—liquid or tablet, or both, for heartburn and indigestion.

Laxative—one or two forms for variations in personal preferences; Milk of Magnesia is excellent. Also Fleets disposable enemas are desirable items to have on board.

Anti-diarrhea drug—3 oz. bottle of Paregoric (prescription required) or 8 oz. bottle of Kaopectate.

First aid manual

A compact first aid manual should be packed in the top of the first aid kit. A larger medical-adviser and first aid book may be carried in a book shelf, but there should always be a small booklet of instructions in or immediately adjacent to the container of instruments and supplies.

First aid manuals can be obtained from the American Red Cross and other safety agencies. Books relating specifically to medical problems afloat and their management can be obtained through book stores and at many marine supply stores.

Replenishment

A first aid kit missing some items does not provide a full measure of safety afloat. As supplies are used, they should be replenished promptly. Further, some drugs do not last indefinitely. They may lose their strength, become unstable and toxic, or evaporate to increased concentrations that could be harmful. Ask your physician about the safe shelf-life of drugs prescribed by him and other supplies carried in your first aid kit. Replace questionably-old supplies whether used or not.

If instruments, or the first aid manual, become lost or damaged, they, too, should be replaced at the earliest opportunity.

Medicine cabinet

Most cruisers have medicine cabinets in the head where additional first-aid supplies may be found. A word of caution should be sounded here—this cabinet should supplement rather than replace the first-aid kits as outlined above because its contents are not portable to the scene of the emergency. It should contain the items which normally are stocked in a medicine cabinet at home such as aspirin, upset stomach remedies, etc.

ADMINISTERING FIRST AID

It would be highly impractical to attempt the instruction of first aid in the few paragraphs that can be devoted to that topic in this book. It is the skipper's responsibility to his passengers and crew to acquaint himself with the proper first-aid procedures. This can be done through classes given by each Chapter of the American Red Cross in a standard first-aid course. It should be remembered that when you are aboard your boat and at sea, you are out of immediate touch with professional medical attention and thus advance preparedness is necessary.

Rule one. Always take first aid to the victim, not the victim to the first aid. You may well aggravate an injury by attempting to move an accident victim. You will add to a sick person's discomfort by requiring him to move about. Limit movement of the affected individual to that absolutely necessary to get him clear of a hazardous area.

Rule two. When giving first aid, take your time. Usually there is more damage done by the well-meaning amateur than was ever caused by the actual injury. Remember, there are only three instances when speed in giving first aid is required: (1) when the victim has stopped breathing; (2) when there is arterial bleeding; and (3) when the victim has been bitten by a poisonous snake. The measures required in these instances are taught in the standard Red Cross first aid course available locally; get a group of your fellow boatmen together and attend one soon.

It should be noted that we have eliminated splints from the first-aid kit. The average first-aider is not qualified to set a broken limb; it is much safer to place the limb in pillows or blankets, tying them securely around the fractured member so that no further damage will be done. And always remember that first-aid should stop at first aid . . . which is administering aid and comfort to avert further complications until professional medical attention can be obtained.

Radio advice

In many emergency situations, a call to the Coast Guard can bring medical advice for treatment of serious injuries or illnesses. Initial contact should be made on 2182 kc/s, but it is most desirable that the boat be capable of shifting to a Coast Guard working frequency such as 2670 kc/s. On VHF-FM, the initial contact should be on 156.8 Mc/s (Channel 16).

Basic Guides to Boating Safety

1. Carry proper equipment—know how to use it.
2. Maintain boat and equipment in top condition.
3. Know and obey the Rules of the Road afloat.
4. Operate with care, courtesy, and common sense.
5. Always keep your boat under complete control.
6. Watch posted speeds; slow down in anchorages.
7. Under no circumstances, overload your boat.
8. See that life-saving equipment is accessible.
9. Check local weather reports before departure.
10. Inspect hull, engine, and all gear frequently.
11. Keep bilges clean, electrical contacts tight.
12. Guard rigidly against any fuel system leakage.
13. Have fire extinguishers instantly available.
14. Take maximum precautions when taking on fuel.
15. Be sure to allow adequate scope when anchoring.
16. Request a USCG Auxiliary courtesy examination.
17. Enroll in a US Power Squadrons piloting class.

CHAPTER 11
MARLINESPIKE SEAMANSHIP

The Selection and Care of Rope—

Knots, Bends,

Hitches and Splices—

Blocks and Tackles—

The Bosun's Locker—

FIG. 1101 Running rigging on a windjammer. Sails are power on wind-ships; their rigging is as important as the engines of motorboats.

Cordage

Earlier editions of Piloting, Seamanship and Small Boat Handling, before the coming of many types of synthetic cordage, were much concerned with the prevention of rot, which is one of the two worst enemies of natural or vegetable fiber rope. The other is abuse. Abuse rather than proper use, today, is probably the cause of most cordage failure.

In Table 11-1 you will note the variation in weight and strength—size being equal—between ropes made of different fibers. Cordage manufacturers compare ropes of different fibers, or different constructions of the same fiber, by calculating their "breaking length." This simply means the length of rope that would break from its own weight if it were hung on a sky hook. For instance, the "breaking length" of nylon is approximately 100,000 vs. manila at approximately 32,000. The strength of the fiber, the unit weight of the fiber and the rope construction all enter into breaking strength and breaking length.

It would appear that ropes could be substituted on the

basis of strength alone. NOT SO!, except perhaps in some limited applications. A *working* line must have other attributes beyond strength alone. For instance, abrasion resistance; a small line presents less surface area over which to distribute the surface wear. Notice the proportion of cross section area the same size cut or nick makes in two lines of different diameters which might be of the same strength. (Fig. 1102)

FIG. 1102 Relative effect on strength of cuts or nicks in rope of different diameter.

Perhaps as important in size selection, even for large hawsers for ships and tugs, is handling convenience. On a small sailboat a *Dacron 3/16" diameter sheet might be strong enough but it would not be easy to hold or grasp.

Therefore, a 3/8" main sheet and 5/16" jib sheets are about the smallest that can be handled except in very light wind.

SELECTION OF SIZE

Now, to select the size synthetic to substitute for manila or cotton lines, and referring to Table 11-1 of weights and strengths, the following method has worked out in practice:

If nylon is wanted for high stretch, shock-absorbing ability, high strength and abrasion resistance for anchor lines, mooring pennants, tie-up lines, etc., or Dacron is wanted for low stretch and the same other qualities as nylon, for sheets and halyards on sailing vessels or tie-up lines, select the nylon or Dacron size 70 to 75% of the circumference (circ.) of the manila or cotton size in use or recommended. For example a 3/4" diameter, 2 1/4" (2.25") circ. manila rope (16.3 lbs/100ft, 5400 lb strength) could well be replaced by a 9/16" dia. (1 3/4" circ.) or a 5/8" dia. (2" circ.) nylon or Dacron. Added strength and less weight and storage room in addition to long life and the other advantages would be gained. [2.25" x .70 = 1.58"; 2.25" x .75 = 1.69" next larger size 1 3/4" circ. (1.75")

NOMINAL SIZE (inches)		MANILA Fed. Spec. TR 605			NYLON (High Tenacity—H.T.)			DU PONT DACRON or H.T. POLYESTER			POLYOLEFINS (H.T.) (Polypropylene and/or Polyethylene)		
Dia.	Circ.	Net Wt. 100'	Ft. per lb.	Breaking Strength	Net Wt. 100'	Ft. per lb.	Breaking Strength	Net Wt. 100'	Ft. per lb.	Breaking Strength	Net Wt. 100'	Ft. per lb.	Breaking Strength
3/16	5/8	1.47	68	450	1	100	1,000	1.3	77	1,000	.73	137	750
1/4	3/4	1.96	51	600	1.5	66.6	1,700	2.1	47.5	1,700	1.24	80	1,250
5/16	1	2.84	35	1,000	2.5	40	2,650	3.3	30	2,550	1.88	53	1,850
3/8	1 1/8	4.02	25	1,350	3.6	28	3,650	4.7	21.3	3,500	2.9	34.5	2,600
7/16	1 1/4	5.15	19.4	1,750	5	20	5,100	6.3	15.9	4,800	3.9	25.5	3,400
1/2	1 1/2	7.35	13.6	2,650	6.6	15	6,650	8.2	12.2	6,100	4.9	20.4	4,150
9/16	1 3/4	10.2	9.8	3,450	8.4	11.9	8,500	10.2	9.8	7,700	6.2	16	4,900
5/8	2	13.1	7.6	4,400	10.5	9.5	10,300	13.2	7.6	9,500	7.8	12.8	5,900
3/4	2 1/4	16.3	6.1	5,400	14.5	6.9	14,600	17.9	5.6	13,200	11.1	9	7,900
7/8	2 3/4	22	4.55	7,700	20	5	19,600	24.9	4	17,500	15.4	6.5	11,000
1	3	26.5	3.77	9,000	26	3.84	25,000	30.4	3.3	22,000	18.6	5.4	13,000
1 1/8	3 1/2	35.2	2.84	12,000	34	2.94	33,250	40.5	2.5	26,500	24.2	4.1	17,500
1 1/4	3 3/4	40.8	2.45	13,500	39	2.56	37,800	46.2	2.16	30,500	27.5	3.6	20,000
1 5/16	4	46.9	2.13	15,000	45	2.22	44,500	53.4	1.87	34,500	31.3	3.2	23,000
1 1/2	4 1/2	58.8	1.7	18,500	55	1.8	55,000	67	1.5	43,000	39.5	2.5	29,000

FIBER CORDAGE — TYPICAL WEIGHTS AND MINIMUM BREAKING STRENGTHS (POUNDS)

Table 11-1

NOTE:—The figures on synthetics, above, are an average of those available from four large cordage manufacturers. Those for the rope you buy should be available at your dealers. Check them carefully. Also check the rope. In general a soft, sleazy rope may be somewhat stronger and easier to splice but it will not wear as well and is more apt to hockle or unlay than a firm, well "locked-up" rope. Blended ropes, part polyolefins and part other fibers, may be found. Multifilament (fine filament) polypropylene looks like nylon—don't expect it to be as strong or do the job of nylon. (It floats, nylon doesn't.) Braided cordage is used on many small boats and some large ones. The special splicing technique depends on the "Chinese finger" grip. Make sure it doesn't shake out when the rope is relaxed and not under tension. The small surface yarns may abraid faster than the larger yarns in 3-strand rope. Spun, or stapled, nylon and Dacron are not as strong as ropes made from continuous filaments but are less slippery and easier to grasp. Sometimes used for sheets on sailing craft.

*Du Pont registered trademark.

ıs 9/16" dia.] By selecting ⅝" dia., even greater strength and longer life will pay in safety and savings.

By similar method, use 80 to 85% factor to find the polyolefin size to use. (2" circ. ⅝" dia. indicated by previous example). The polys are not as strong and have lower melting points, thus are not as abrasion-resistant. They are, however, the lightest weight and they float which are advantages for "female hands" for tie-up lines and towing, such as dinghies and passing a tow line.

Table 11-3 gives the preferred ropes for different uses. Others may be used if care is taken in the selection, and the limitations are taken into account.

CARE AND PROTECTION OF ROPE

The anchor and mooring lines, standing and running rigging, and similar gear that constitute one of the most important parts of a yachtsman's equipment may be used with intelligent care—to which it will respond with years of useful service—or it may be abused by ignorance and neglect, ruining it in short order.

TEN RULES TO LENGTHEN ROPE LIFE

These ten commandments for the care of rope may not be all-inclusive, but it is safe to say that if they are observed a boatman may very well, in many cases, be able to double the useful life of his rope.

1. Look Out for Kinks

One sure way to destroy the value of a piece of line is to allow it to get a kink in it and then put it under strain. For example, you decide to play the Good Samaritan and break out your new spare line to haul a stranded boat off a bar. The new line is unruly and doesn't handle like the well-used anchor line, so there are a dozen kinks between your quarter bitt and his samson post when you ease the clutch in and open the throttle. In thirty seconds, you'll take more out of that line than you would in thirty weeks of normal service—if you don't shake those kinks out first.

What happens is this: The fibers are overstressed at the sharp bend, weakening fibers of the strands. Rapid wear follows and later the line may part at that spot, right at a critical time—through no fault of its own.

The time to start watching for kinks is in the very beginning when the rope is first taken from the coil or reel. There are right and wrong ways of doing this. The right way is to lay the coil on deck with the inside end down according to direction on the tag attached to the coil. Now reach down into the coil and pull this inner end up through the center, unwinding counter-clockwise. (See fig. 1120.) If it uncoils in the wrong direction, turn the coil over and pull the end out from the other side.

Synthetic rope should be shipped on reels and should be pulled or rolled off, disturbing the lay as little as possible. If it becomes unruly when coiling, try "faking down" in a figure 8. Do not "loop" off over the end of the reel —let it roll.

In natural fiber ropes kinks are most troublesome in wet weather; yachtsmen therefore have more to watch than those who use their rope ashore. Wet manila rope shrinks in length and swells in diameter and the lay shortens, making it more difficult to handle.

Knots have the same effect as a sharp kink. Some knots

Table 11-2

ROPE AND FIBER COMPARISON CHART				
	MANILA	**NYLON**	**DACRON**	**POLY-OLEFINS**
Relative Strength	1	4	3	2
Relative Weight	3	2	4	1
Elongation	1	4	2	3
Relative Resistance to Impact or Shock Loads	1	4	2	3
Mildew and Rot Resistance	Poor	Excellent	Excellent	Excellent
Acid Resistance	Poor	Fair	Fair	Excellent
Alkali Resistance	Poor	Excellent	Excellent	Excellent
Sunlight Resistance	Fair	Fair	Good	Fair
Organic Solvent Resistance	Good	Good	Good	Fair
Melting Point	380° (Burns)	410°F.	410°F.	about 300°F.
Floatability	Only when new	None	None	Indefinite
*****Relative Abrasion Resistance** (*Depends on many factors—whether wet or dry, etc.)	2	3	4	1
KEY TO RATINGS: 1 Lowest—4 Highest				

may take 40 to 50 per cent out of a rope's efficiency. (See table 11-4.) A good splice, on the other hand, will allow a rope to retain 85 to 95 per cent of its original strength. Therefore, if a splice is indicated, don't use a knot.

2. Keep Your Rope Clean

Simple cleanliness in taking care of rope pays big dividends. In the course of use it is bound to pick up mud and sand. When this occurs, the rope should be draped in loose loops over a rail and hosed down gently, with fresh water if available. Don't use a high pressure stream with the intent of doing a more thorough job, as this will only force dirt and grit deeper into the rope. After washing, allow it to dry and then rap or shake it thoroughly to get out any remaining particles of dirt. Grit cuts the fibers.

3. Stow Carefully

Natural fiber rope will rot so it must be dried and carefully stowed in a place with adequate ventilation. This applies to manila, sisal, cotton and, to a lesser extent, linen and flax. Many a yachtman has been embarrassed or worse because of rot. Dry lines on deck before stowing. Hang up light lines. Loosely coil heavier ones on gratings so air can circulate. Don't subject them to intense heat.

Synthetic rope *may* be stowed wet but introduces unpleasant dampness below. Iron rust from rusty chain and thimbles is not good for nylon.

Keep lines away from exhaust pipes and batteries.

4. Guard Against Chafe and Abrasion

Chafe and abrasion are among rope's worst enemies. Heavy coils are sometimes dragged along the ground instead of being carried on the shoulder. Dragging over a rough surface causes the outside fibers to be cut or rubbed off while grit works inside the strands and is equally destructive in cutting inside fibers.

Rope should never be allowed to rub on sharp edges, or one rope chafe against another. Surface wear is accelerated and fraying often starts as a result of it. If it is necessary to have a rope pass over a sharp edge like a rail on the deck edge or a badly designed chock, rig a canvas

Table 11-3

RECOMMENDED ROPE FOR VARIOUS USES								
	Tie-Up or Mooring Lines	Anchor Ropes or Mooring Pennants	Sheets and Halyards	Flag Halyards	Seizing and Whipping	Bolt Rope Synthetic Sails	Towing	Water Skiing
MANILA	✓	✓	✓	✓			✓	
NYLON	✓	✓		✓			✓	
DACRON	✓		✓	✓		✓		
POLYOLEFIN	✓						✓	✓
BRAIDED DACRON			✓	✓				
BRAIDED NYLON	✓	✓		✓	✓		✓	
WIRE (Stainless)		Pennants	✓					
BRAIDED COTTON				✓	✓			
NYLON SEINE TWINE					✓			
LINEN or FLAX			✓	✓	✓			

pad to prevent excessive wear from damaging the fibers.

When riding to an anchor for considerable periods, it is always well to "freshen the nip" by paying out a little line to bring the chafe of chocks in another place.

Chafing gear of canvas will protect the line from this source of trouble; it is particularly desirable on mooring lines where chafing always comes in one spot. Some boatmen carry a split length of rubber hose which can be readily clapped on the line where required. Specially molded rubber and plastic chafing gear is available.

Another trick to lengthen the life of a line like an anchor line or halyard, where most of the wear comes on one end, is to turn the line end-for-end occasionally. Any rope ends that do not terminate in a splice should be whipped to prevent fraying.

When making fast at a dock, select smooth round piles of good diameter to make fast to, and shun square or rectangular timbers with sharp corners. If there is no alternative, pad the sharp edges.

5. Prevent Slipping

When using rope on the drums of winches or hoists it is bad practice to let the rope slip on the drum as it revolves. This not only increases wear on the rope, but the sudden jerks as the rope is snubbed, strain the fibers badly.

Similarly the rope should not be allowed to lie against the revolving drum of a hoist or winch. In addition to objectionable chafe, there is the element of heat from friction to be considered; this may be enough to burn or melt the fibers.

Synthetic ropes that are highly strained and/or repeatedly stretched while around a cleat or winch may melt and grab so they will not run or pay out smoothly.

6. Avoid Small Blocks

There are two sources of trouble when rope is expected to run over too small a block. On the one hand there is excessive internal friction. Wear from such friction is always present when rope runs over the sheaves of blocks and the smaller the sheave diameter, the greater the friction. On the other hand, there is the external wear as the rope chafes against the inside of sheave holes providing insufficient clearance. Faulty alignment of blocks which causes the rope to rub against the sides, or cheeks, of the

blocks is also bad. A combination of this internal friction and external chafe breaks down fibers much faster than would be expected in normal use.

One place where trouble of this kind shows up quickly if installation is faulty is in the use of small sheaves in the steering lines or cables. These get a great deal of hard usage and their life can be extended by the use of sheaves of generous diameter.

In tackles, when matching blocks to rope, use a block with a shell length of at least 3 inches for $3/8$-inch (diameter) rope; 4 inches for $1/2$; 5 inches for $5/8$; 6 inches for $3/4$; 8 inches for $7/8$; 9 inches for 1 inch; and 12 inches for $1\frac{1}{4}$-inch rope. (See table 11-5.)

Care should be exercised to see that sheaves are never allowed to become rough or rusty. See to it that they are well lubricated to reduce friction and to prevent their seizing. A sheave frozen by rust or corrosion on its pin would work havoc on a piece of rope.

7. Don't Lubricate

For natural fiber, the manufacturer has already treated the rope with an oil or solution which preserves it and lubricates internal fibers. This may account for roughly 10 per cent of the rope's weight. Even some synthetics have special fiber treatments.

Users are cautioned not to attempt to improve upon the manufacturer's work by using additional lubricant of any kind upon it. The treatment given the rope originally when manufactured prolongs its life and retains its strength.

8. Beware of Chemicals

Both acids and alkalis attack vegetable fiber rope and some synthetics. See fiber comparison table 11-2. Consequently it should never be stowed any place where it might be brought into accidental contact with chemicals or even be subject to exposure to the fumes. In testing storage batteries with a hydrometer, for example, acid dropped on a rope will burn it badly. Even paint and drying oils, like linseed, should not be allowed to get in contact with it.

Alkalis and acids burn the fibers and kill the life of rope by rendering the fibers brittle. Wet rope is more susceptible to chemical fumes than if it were dry. Rust, too, is bad for rope. If a line must be used around chemicals, it is essential to check it frequently. Spots of discoloration are a danger sign showing when fibers have broken down.

9. Never Overload

An old saw has it that you should never send a boy to do a man's job. So it is with rope. If all available statistics show that you should have a 3/4-inch anchor line, don't try to get away with 1/2-inch. Better be safe than sorry.

Many tables have already been published giving suitable sizes of anchor and mooring lines for motor and sailing craft of all sizes. See Tables 1 and 2, page 103.

Table 11-1 will serve as a guide in this respect. It shows the minimum breaking strain carried by standard brands of manila, and typical synthetic ropes. It should be understood these strengths are for new cordage.

The factor of safety to be allowed in determining the working load on a rope is commonly taken as 5. That is, if a rope must lift 500 pounds, a rope with tensile strength of 2,500 pounds should be selected. With synthetic ropes the same factor of 5 or sometimes 4 (2,000 lbs. in the example above) may be used. The condition of the rope must be considered when making a selection. If the load ever exceeds 75 per cent of the rope's breaking strength the chances are good that it will be permanently injured. In that case, it may fail unexpectedly, without warning.

10. Don't Use Frozen Rope

While this is a problem seldom encountered by the

average yachtsman whose boat is normally laid up in freezing weather, it is still a matter of moment to those such as charter boat fishermen, etc., whose activities often run right through the winter. Manila rope that has been allowed to freeze after a wetting is readily broken and therefore cannot be trusted. Since synthetics absorb very little moisture this is not too much of a problem and is one of the reasons tow boats and fishermen are using synthetics. However, reasonable care should be exercised to prevent internal damage of the rope structure by internal ice formation and subsequent heavy loading while frozen. The only practical solution if this happens is to thaw it out and dry it thoroughly before putting it back into service in extreme weather.

HOW TO INSPECT YOUR ROPE

Careful periodic inspection should, in a practical way, enable you to renew lines long before they have deteriorated to a point where they might be considered unsafe, even though theoretically a scientific breaking test might be insisted upon for some services. Here are things to look out for:

In an external examination of the rope, watch out for abrasion, cuts and broken fibers, variations in size and shape of the strands, and uniformity of the lay. Excessive wear on the outside is revealed when fibers appear to be about half worn out and yarns 1/2 or 2/3 worn through. Then, depending on the rope size and percentage of good yarns remaining, it may be time to down-grade to lighter work loads or time to renew the rope. Acid stains, frayed strands and broken yarns should all be revealed in such an examination, which should include the entire length of the rope.

Now twist the strands so as to open the rope up, revealing the condition of interior fibers. Evidence of powdered or melted or fused fiber is a danger signal warning of excessive internal bending, tension and wear. Repeat this test in several places. If yarns (the twisted fibers inside) appear to be clean, bright and free from spots of discoloration or melting (harsh and brittle) the chances are that the rope is still in good condition—assuming the exterior is also OK.

Signs of damage due to overloading are also found in the interior yarns of the strands. A rope in which these inner yarns have been broken or partly broken or melted by excessive or repeat loading can never be trusted.

Natural fibers should have a certain luster, and evidences of dryness or brittleness should be viewed with suspicion. A good manila rope will have a certain feel that distinguishes it from another out of which the life has gone. The sound rope will have a certain pliability, stretch and flexibility that is never present in a limp, dead worn-out rope. A good rope will be free from splinters of fiber— just another earmark of quality in good rope. A rough and ready breaking test that the owner can apply is to unlay about a foot of one yarn and break it, or fibers taken from it, with the hands. If this single yarn breaks easily, or fibers have little strength, the rope undoubtedly has lost strength from old age or perhaps has rotted.

Again scientists may demand more scientific tests. When black or brown discoloration spots reveal the action of acid or chemical fumes, use this breakage test frequently.

Table 11-4

	% EFF.
HOW KNOTS AND SPLICES REDUCE THE STRENGTH OF ROPE	
Normal rope	**100%**
Anchor or Fisherman's bend	**76**
Timber hitch	**70-65**
Round turn	**70-65**
Two half-hitches	**70-65**
Bowline	**60**
Clove hitch	**60**
Sheet bend or Weaver's knot	**55**
Square or Reef knot	**45**
Eye splice (over thimble)	**95-90**
Long splice	**87**
Short splice	**85**

(KNOTS bracket: Anchor or Fisherman's bend through Square or Reef knot)
(SPLICES bracket: Eye splice through Short splice)

Based on a normal rope strength of 100% (without knots) the figures above show what percentage of strength is left in a straight rope after a knot has been tied in it. Under differing conditions of test and stress, results vary. Therefore the percentages of efficiency tabulated are necessarily approximate, but they do serve as a base for general calculations.

The real problem in advising the boatman as to the knots he should learn to tie and use is to select the few that are of real utility on the average cruiser and exclude the numerous knots which, although serving a special purpose excellently, are of little practical use to the average boatman.

The short list of knots described below and illustrated in the accompanying sketches will meet all ordinary situations. Better know these knots—practice until they can be tied with certainty in the dark or blindfolded—than to have a superficial knowledge of a greater number of knots, including many that are of little practical value.

A knot or splice is never as strong as the rope itself. See table 11-4. Splices are preferred for heavy loads. It may be of some interest to recall that the strength of a rope is derived largely from the friction that exists between the individual fibers, yarn and strands, of which the rope is made. The twisting of these fibers into yarn, then into strands, hawsers and finally cables is always carried out in such a manner as to increase the amount and effectiveness of the friction between the rope elements. In the tying of knots this principle of making use of friction is also applicable, for in this manner, much more can be accomplished by the use of a simple knot, so tied that the strain on the rope adds to the knot's holding power, than will ever develop from a conglomeration of hitches, many of which serve no useful purpose, and which, moreover, make it more practicable in the end to cut the rope than to untie the knots. From the examples which follow it will be evident that wherever possible the most effective use is made of friction between two or more portions of a knot in order to increase its holding power.

Knots, Bends and Hitches

FIG. 1103a   Overhand

The simple overhand knot (fig. 1103a) used to keep the end of a rope from unlaying. This knot jams and may become almost impossible to untie. A better knot for the purpose is shown in fig. 1103b.

FIG. 1103b   Figure Eight

The figure eight knot. This does not jam.

FIG. 1103c   Square or Reef Knot

The square or reef knot (fig. 1103c) perhaps the most useful knot known. The rope manipulated by the right hand (this is the rope leading from the left side of the sketch and terminating in the arrow in A) is turned over the other rope in tying both the first and second half of the knot. Learn to always turn this rope over the other and the knot can be tied with certainty in the dark. If the rope manipulated by the right hand is first turned over and then under the other rope the treacherous granny knot will result.

Do not use the square knot to tie together lines of different sizes, as it will slip. The reef or square knot is used for tying light lines together (not for tying heavy hawsers), for tying awning stops, reef points, cord on packages, and in fact is put to such numerous uses by sailors that many landsmen call it the sailor's knot. The knot has one serious fault. It jams and is difficult to untie after being heavily stressed.

FIG. 1103d   Sheet or Becket Bend

The sheet or becket bend (fig. 1103d) known to landsmen as the weaver's knot, is used for tying two lines together. It will not slip even if there is great difference in the sizes of the lines. To make the knot secure for connecting hawsers for towing, the free ends of the lines should be stopped down with twine in the manner illustrated in fig. 1103j, the reeving line bend.

FIG. 1103e   Bowline

The bowline (fig. 1103e) a knot second in usefulness only to the square knot. The bowline will not slip, does not pinch or kink the rope as much as some other knots, and does not jam and become difficult to untie. By tying a bowline with a small loop and passing the line through the loop the running bowline is obtained. This is an excellent form of running noose.

Bowlines are used wherever a secure loop or noose is needed in the end of a line, such as a line which is to be secured to a bollard in making a boat fast to a pier or wharf. They may also be used in securing lines to anchors where there is no time to make a splice. Hawsers are sometimes connected by two bowlines, the loop of one knot being passed through the loop of the other.

FIG. 1103f   Clove Hitch

The clove hitch (fig. 1103f) is used for making a line fast temporarily to a pile or bollard.

FIG. 1103g   Two Half Hitches

Two half hitches (fig. 1103g) are used for making a line fast to a bollard, pile, timber, or stanchion. Note that the knot consists of a turn around the fixed object and a clove hitch around the standing part of the line.

FIG. 1103h   Correct Method of Making Fast to a Cleat

Correct method of making fast to a cleat (fig. 1103h). The half hitch which completes the fastening is taken with the free part of the line. The line can then be freed without taking up slack in the standing part.

FIG. 1103i   Incorrect Method of Making Fast to a Cleat

Common incorrect method of making fast to a cleat (fig. 1103i). The half hitch is taken with the standing part of the line and the line consequently can not be freed without taking up slack in the standing part. Accidents have been caused by the use of this type of fastening on lines which must be freed quickly.

FIG. 1103j   Reeving Line Bend Free ends must be stopped down with twine

The reeving line bend (fig. 1103j), so called because it is used to connect lines which must pass through a small opening, such as a hawse pipe.

FIG. 1103k   Fisherman's Bend

The fisherman's bend (fig. 1103k), also called the anchor bend, is handy for making fast to a buoy or spar or the ring of an anchor. In some localities it is preferred to the thimble and eye splice for attaching the anchor line to the ring. As is evident from the illustration, it is made by taking two round turns around the ring, then passing the end under both turns to form a half hitch around the standing part of the line. For further security, a second half hitch is taken around the standing part only, or in place of the last half hitch, the end may be stopped down or seized back to the line with twine.

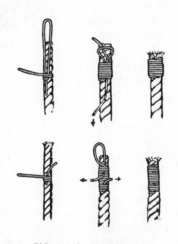

FIG. 1103l   Two Methods of Whipping a Rope End

All butt-ended ropes should of course be whipped to prevent raveling of the strands. Two common methods for doing this are shown in fig. 1103l. While these figures are not strictly to scale this has been done purposely to avoid difficulty in following the several steps involved in either of the two methods.

FIG. 1103m   Sheepshank

The sheepshank (fig. 1103m) is used to shorten a line. Lay the bight in three parts and take a half hitch around each doubled part.

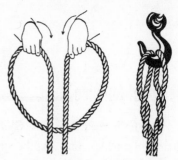

FIG. 1103n   Cat's Paw

The cat's paw (fig. 1103n) used to secure a line to a hook. Make a double loop by twisting two bights of the line as shown.

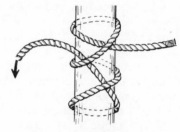

FIG. 1103o   Rolling Hitch

The rolling hitch (fig. 1103o) used to bend a line to a spar or rope. Close turns up tight and take the strain on the arrow-tipped end.

FIG. 1103p   Timber Hitch

The timber hitch (fig. 1103p) temporarily secures a line to a spar or timber, as in towing. The half hitch shown is sometimes omitted. If used, it should be taken first. In both hitches, strain should be kept on the line to make it hold.

FIG. 1103q   Blackwall Hitch

The Blackwall Hitch is easy to make and practical to use when *temporarily* securing a rope to a hook. It will carry a heavy load, *provided* the tension is constant.

The Art of Splicing

EYE SPLICE OR SIDE SPLICE

Start the splice by unlaying the strands, about six inches to a foot or more, or 6 to 10 turns of lay, depending on the size of rope you are splicing. Now whip the end of each strand to prevent its unlaying while being handled. If working with synthetic rope, it is sometimes helpful to use masking or friction tape wrapped around the unlaid strands every 4 to 6 inches to help hold the "turn" in the strand. The ends may be fused with a flame or whipped.

Next form a loop in the rope by laying the end back along the standing part. Hold the standing part away from you in the left hand, loop toward you. The stranded end can be worked with the right hand.

The size of loop is determined by the point X (fig. 1104) where the opened strands are first tucked under the standing part of the rope. If the splice is being made around a thimble, the rope is laid snugly in the thimble groove and point X will be at the tapered end of the thimble. The thimble may be temporarily taped or tied in place until the job is finished.

Now lay the three opened strands across the standing part as shown in fig. 1104 so that the center strand B lies over and directly along the standing part. Left-hand strand A leads off to the left; right-hand strand C to the right of the standing part.

Tucking of strand ends A, B and C under the strands of the standing part is the next step. Get this right and the rest is easy. See fig. 1105.

Start with the center strand B. Select the topmost strand (2) of the standing part near point X and tuck B under it. Haul it up snug but not so tight as to distort the natural lay of all strands. Note that the tuck is made from right to left, against the lay of the standing part.

Now take left-hand strand A and tuck under strand (1), which lies to the left of strand (2). Similarly take strand C and tuck under strand (3), which lies to the right of strand (2). Be sure to tuck from right to left in every case.

The greatest risk of starting wrong is in the first tuck of strand C. It should go under (3), from right to left. Of course, strands (1), (2), and (3) are arranged symmetrically around the rope.

It may help to visualize this by referring to fig. 1106, a cross-section through the rope at X, seen from below.

If the first tuck of each of strands A, B and C is correctly made, the splice at this point will look as shown in fig. 1107.

The splice is completed by making at least two additional tucks in manila rope or 4 full tucks in synthetic rope with each of strands A, B and C. As each added tuck is made be sure it passes over one strand of the standing part, then under the strand next above it, and so on, the tucked strand running against the lay of the strands of the standing part. This is clearly shown in fig. 1108, the completed splice. Note C, C¹ and C², the same strand as it appears after successive tucks.

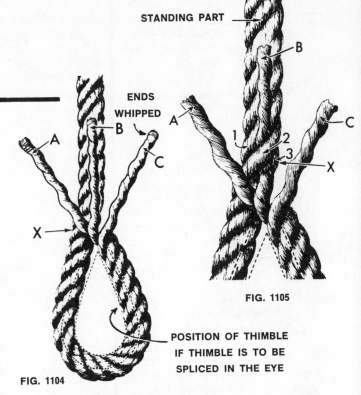

FIG. 1104

FIG. 1105

POSITION OF THIMBLE
IF THIMBLE IS TO BE
SPLICED IN THE EYE

FIG. 1106

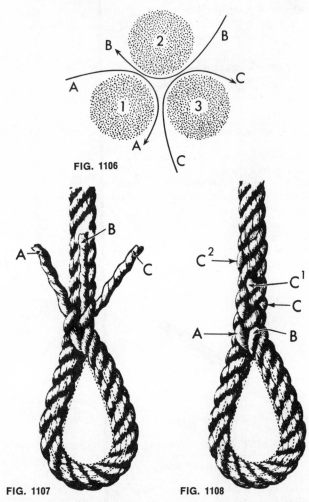

FIG. 1107

FIG. 1108

FIG. 1108 How the eye splice should look when completed. A thimble, if spliced in, would fit as shown by the dotted lines.

Suggestions: The splice can be made neater by tapering. This is done by cutting out part of the yarns from the tucking strands, before the finishing tucks. In any case, the first 3 tucks in manila or 4 tucks in synthetics, are made with the full strands. (Synthetics are slippery and stretchy and thus require at least one extra tuck.) After that, some prefer to cut out one-third of the yarns, make a tuck, then cut out another third of the yarns, and make the last tuck. This produces an even taper. After the splice is finished, roll it on deck under foot to smooth it up. Then put a strain on it and finally cut off the projecting ends of the strands. Do not cut off the "tails" of synthetic rope too short. If possible seat the splice in use or whip down the ends before cutting. The loose fibers may be fused with a match or candle to finish off, but be careful not to melt the rope.

If the rope is heavy or new and cannot be easily opened by twisting in order to make the tucks, use a fid to open the strands. This is a smooth tapered tool of hard wood about 1½ or 2 inches at the butt, tapered to a point in a length of a foot or more. In hard-laid synthetic ropes sometimes a marline spike—a metal fid with a more gradual taper and sometimes a flattened point—is used for easier opening of the rope for tucking.

When unlaid strands tend to untwist, give them a little extra twist as the tucks are made so that the strands keep their strand-like quality and do not appear as a bunch of loose yarns in the finished splice. Do not, however, twist up synthetics too hard. There will be less strain on the fibers if the tucked strands are a little looser than the standing rope strands. Watch this specially after cutting out yarns.

When setting the tucked strands up taut, haul them successively back, toward the loop, not in the direction of tucking. See that each set of tucks leaves all strands neatly in place, not distorted by excessive strain on some strands, too little on others. Keep the tension even and uniform.

In splicing heavy lines, a temporary whipping is sometimes put around the rope itself to prevent strands from unlaying too far.

HOW TO MAKE A SHORT SPLICE

A short splice is used where two ropes are to be permanently joined, provided they do not have to pass through the sheave hole, swallow or throat, of a block. The splice will be much stronger than any knot.

The short splice enlarges the rope's diameter at the splice, so in cases where the spliced rope must pass through a sheave hole, a long splice should be used.

To start the short splice, unlay the strands of both rope ends for a short distance as described for the eye splice. Whip the six strand ends, or fuse or tape them, to prevent unlaying. A seizing should also be made around each of the ropes to prevent strands from unlaying too far. These seizings can be cut as the splice is completed.

Next "marry" the ends so that the strands of each rope lie alternately between strands of the other as shown in fig. 1109. Now tie all three strands of one rope temporarily to the other. See fig. 1110. (Some omit this step; it is not absolutely essential.)

Working with the three free strands, remove temporary seizing from around other rope and splice them into the other rope by tucking strands exactly as described for the eye splice, working over and under successive strands from right to left against the lay of the rope. When first tucks have been made, snug down all three strands. Then tuck two or three more times on that side.

Next cut the temporary seizing of the other strands and the rope and repeat, splicing these three remaining strands into the opposite rope.

Just as in the eye splice, the short splice can be tapered as desired by cutting out yarns from the strands after the full tucks are made. Figure 1111 shows how the short splice would appear if not tapered, after finally trimming off the ends of strands. Never cut strand ends off too close. Otherwise when a heavy strain is put on the rope, the last tuck tends to work out, especially with synthetics.

Another method which some find easier, is to start as in fig. 1109 and tie pairs of strands from opposite ends in an overhand knot. See fig. 1112. This, in effect, makes the first tuck.

Those who may wish to go into this subject intensively are referred to the Encyclopedia of Knots and Fancy Rope Work which contains 3100 examples of knots, ties, splices etc., and other more complete publications on rope work, such as The Ashley Book of Knots.

FIG. 1109

SHORT SPLICE

FIG. 1111

FIG. 1110

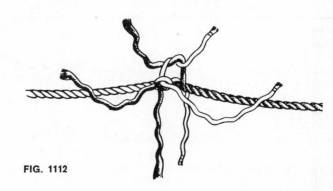

FIG. 1112

HOW TO MAKE A LONG SPLICE

The long splice (fig. 1113) is used where the spliced ropes are to reeve through blocks or sheaves. There are several methods of making this splice. Some splicers unlay both ends, marry as in the short splice and work from the center both ways. But by starting as in fig. 1113 you do not lose any of the lay of strands. For a long splice in a 3-inch circumference line allow not less than 6 feet, or about 2 feet for each inch of *circumference,* as the farther apart the three splices are staggered, the stronger will be the completed splice. In the illustration 2-inch circumference rope was used, but the illustration does not show proper spacing of tucks. After seizing or taping the ends of each strand, to start this splice, unlay one strand of one rope for about 6 feet and cut off, leaving about one foot as in Illustration 1, strand C. Then unlay one strand from other rope and lay in space formerly occupied by strand C, allowing a foot for splicing as in Illustration 1 at A.

When laying the first strand A (1), plan the spacing of splices so that B will be about central in the finished long splice. Next unlay a strand from right hand rope and a strand from left hand rope and lay the left hand strand in the respective space formerly filled by the strand from right hand rope as in Illustration 2. Continue strand C until all three strands are about equal distance as in Illustration 3.

Then with all pairs of strands (for example Illustration 4A) tie an overhand knot with all yarns flat and even. Next take spike and tuck strands over one and under one as in 4B, unlaying or untwisting strands sufficient to allow yarns to lay flat when tucked. The overhand knot at 4A and, after tucking as at 4B, should be as near as possible to an original strand in size and volume of fiber by reducing twist in the tucked strand. Make another full tuck with all strands.

You now have an overhand knot and two full tucks. Halve each strand and tuck as in 4C, again halve the re-

maining yarns and tuck as in 4E. Roll tucks under foot and stretch before cutting off ends. Here, again, do not cut off too short. Much better a little fuzz or whiskers than tucks starting to pull out.

To make a long splice in fishing line, make the same as above, using a sail needle to tuck the strands. The small sail needle, used in fine work, takes the place of the larger fid.

SPLICING WIRE ROPE

In general, wire rope is spliced in a similar way except that tucks are made with the lay rather than against the lay. Splicing vises are used to hold the rope and metal tools and hammers are usually needed.

Splices of wire-to-fiber rope should be left to professional riggers. They can usually be found at sail lofts where wire halyards with rope tails can be made to specification. With the right tools and a lot of practice, you can work out a method yourself.

A FEW TIPS

Practice these knots and splices with a couple of short lengths of line and put them to practical use. Always keep lines dry and clean. Keep ends of lines neatly served or whipped with twine to prevent unlaying. Serving or whipping is preferable to the crown knots or splices sometimes used to prevent unlaying as these knots and splices prevent reeving the line through the openings of a block which would otherwise take the line nicely.

The knots, hitches, bends and splices just described are sufficient for all practical purposes aboard the average pleasure boat. To make them with facility in a seamanlike manner, have some experienced yachtsman, sailor or fisherman show you how he'd do it, especially the bowline, clove hitch and splice.

LONG SPLICE

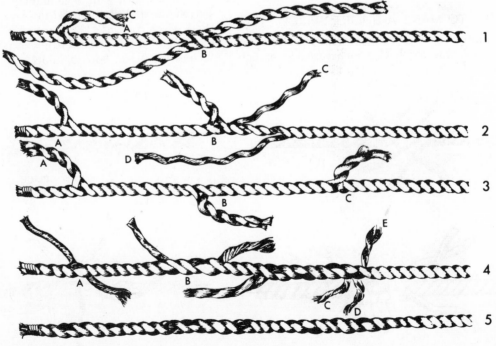

FIG. 1113 While the short splice is excellent for strength and neatness, as compared to a knot, there are times when the spliced line must reeve through a block. In such cases, the long splice should be used. Illustrated above are steps in the making of a long splice.

Blocks and Tackles

The use of blocks and tackle (pronounced tay-kle) or, to use a higher sounding name, mechanical appliances, on board a small cruising type boat is very limited. The competent seaman, however, should have a basic knowledge of them, as their use enables one man to do the work of many.

Blocks and tackle on small boats are almost entirely confined to sailboats where the hoisting of heavy sails, as well as setting them, requires some means for one or two men to match the strength of many. No matter how small the sailboat, the sheets usually run through one or more blocks, which means we have a mechanical appliance.

To see how this aids, go for a sail in a 20-foot boat, in a moderate breeze, and bend a line to the boom. While under way attempt to trim in the sail with your improvised sheet. It will come in but it will be a struggle, so try it with the regular system of blocks and tackle and you will see with what ease the sail comes in. About the most common use on a motorboat is in hoisting your dinghy.

A *block* consists of a frame of wood or metal inside of which is fitted one or more *sheaves* (pulleys—the word is pronounced shiv), and is designated according to the number of sheaves it contains, such as single, double, or triple. The size of the block to be used is, of course, de-termined by the size of the rope to be reeved. If a fiber rope is being used, the size of the block should be *about* three times the *circumference* of the rope and the sheave diameter about twice the circumference. Therefore, if 2-inch rope, $\frac{5}{8}$" diameter, is being used the block could be 6 inches (three times the circumference) and the sheave diameter 4 inches (twice the circumference). This is an approximation. See Table 11-5, block sizes and rope diameter, for recommended sizes.

Wire rope is also used but usually only as halyards on sailboats. Some larger sailing craft use wire sheets and guys. This should be stainless steel and sheaves should be as large as possible for long rope life. Make sure the rope cannot squeeze between the sheave and the cheeks of the block or a "panic party" may ensue.

The term *tackle* is used for an assemblage of *falls* (ropes) and *blocks*. When you pass ropes through the blocks, you *reeve* them and the part of the fall made fast to one of the blocks, or the weight, as the case may be, is known as the *standing part*, while the end upon which the force is to be applied is called the *hauling part*. To *overhaul the falls* is to separate the blocks; to *round in* is to bring them together; and *chock-a-block* or *two blocks* means they they are tight together.

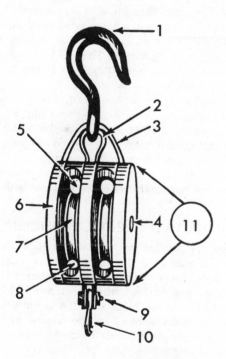

FIG. 1114 PARTS OF A BLOCK

1. Hook
2. Inner Strap
3. Outer Strap
4. Pin
5. Swallows
6. Cheeks
7. Sheaves — either plain, roller, or self-lubricating
8. Breech
9. Becket
10. Thimble
11. Shell

DEFINITIONS:

Block
A frame of wood or metal within which are fitted sheaves or pulleys over which a rope runs. Blocks may be single, double, treble, etc. They are designated by the number of sheaves they contain. The lifting power is multiplied in ratio to the number of sheaves used.

Tackle
A combination of blocks, ropes and hooks for raising, lowering or moving heavy objects. A "tackle" increases lifting power but reduces lifting speed.

Fall Rope
That part of the tackle to which lifting power is applied.

Fall Block or Running Block
The block attached to the object to be moved.

Fled Block or Standing Block
Is fixed to a permanent support.

Standing End
The end of the fall fixed to the tackle.

Running End
The end opposite the standing end.

Return
Each part of the fall between the two blocks or between either end and the block.

Lifting Force
Is in ratio with the number of times the rope passes to and from the fall block.

To Overhaul
Is to separate the blocks.

To Round In
Is to bring the blocks closer together.

Two Blocks
Means the blocks of the fall are in contact.

Shell or Frame
Part which holds sheave or wheel.

(From Columbia Rope Co. rigger's booklet)

KINDS OF TACKLE

Tackles (fig. 1116) are named according to the number of sheaves in the blocks that are used (single, two-fold, three-fold purchases), according to the purpose for which the tackle is used (yard-tackles, stay-tackles, etc.), or from names handed down from the past (luff-tackles, watch-tackles, gun-tackles, Spanish-burtons, etc.). The tackles that may be found aboard cruising boats, and should be known are:

1. Single Whip—A single fixed block and fall—no increase in power. Gain only in height of lift or change in direction of pull.

2. Gun Tackle—Two single blocks. If lower block is movable, double force is gained. If upper block is movable, triple force is gained.

3. Luff Tackle—A double hook-block and single hook-block. Force gained three if single block is movable, four if double block is movable.

4. Two-Fold or Double Tackle—Two double sheave hook-blocks. Force gained four or five, depending upon application.

CALCULATING POWER OF A TACKLE

The force gained as given in all of these tackle combinations is theoretical only, as the friction of the blocks has been ignored. The method of calculating the actual force gained and compensating for this friction is to add

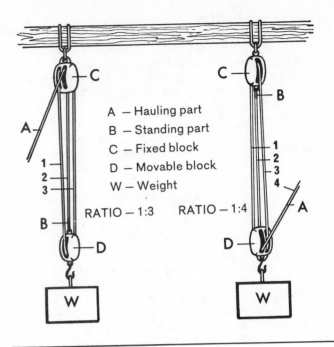

A — Hauling part
B — Standing part
C — Fixed block
D — Movable block
W — Weight

RATIO — 1:3   RATIO — 1:4

FIG. 1115 The number of falls leading to and from the movable block determines the ratio of force to weight necessary for lifting.

10% to the weight W, for each sheave in the tackle before dividing by the number of falls. Thus, in Illustration 4 (fig. 1116) if W is 1000 lbs.: 10% is 100 lbs.; 4 sheaves × 100 = 400 lbs.; total theoretical W then is 1000 plus 400 = 1400 lbs. With 4 falls the force needed on A to lift W would be 1400 ÷ 4 or 350 lbs. rather than an apparent 250 lbs., disregarding friction. This will vary with the type of bearings and pins and lubrication in the blocks and sheave diameter.

There are, of course, a number of other purchases, the heaviest commonly used aboard ship being a three-fold purchase, which consists of two triple blocks. It must be remembered the hauling part reeved through a triple block should be led through the center sheave. If not, the block will cant causing it to bind and, in extreme cases, to break the block. This is especially true with a three-fold purchase.

TO OBTAIN GREATEST EFFICIENCY

To get the greatest mechanical efficiency, the hauling part should lead from the block with the most sheaves, and if both blocks have the same number it is best for the hauling part to lead from the movable block. It is also best to have the block with the greatest number of sheaves the movable block, as the number of falls leading to and from the movable block determines the ratio of force-to-weight necessary for lifting.

In the illustration (fig. 1116) showing two arrangements of luff tackles, in one there are three falls leading from the movable block and ratio of force-to-weight would be 1:3. Now change the blocks—the single block fixed and the double block made movable with the weight attached and the hauling part leading from it. Notice that, counting the hauling part, there are four falls leading to or from the now movable block, and the ratio becomes 1:4, which is quite an increase.

FIG. 1117 The size of rope should be matched to the block it reeves through. Chafe at blocks can cause serious damage. The second and fourth are swivel blocks.

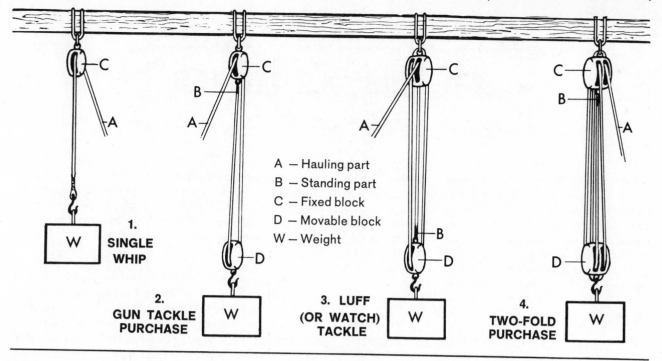

A — Hauling part
B — Standing part
C — Fixed block
D — Movable block
W — Weight

1. **SINGLE WHIP**

2. **GUN TACKLE PURCHASE**

3. **LUFF (OR WATCH) TACKLE**

4. **TWO-FOLD PURCHASE**

FIG. 1116 Some of the common tackles that are found aboard cruising boats.

Table 11-5

BLOCK AND ROPE SIZES *			
Size of Block (Length of Shell)	Diameter of Rope	Size of Block (Length of Shell)	Diameter of Rope
3	⅜"	8	⅞" – 1"
4	½"	10	1⅛"
5	9⁄16" – ⅝"	12	1¼"
6	¾"	14	1⅜" – 1½"
7	13⁄16"	16	1⅝"

*NOTE—Some heavy blocks can accommodate larger rope sizes but the use of smaller blocks for larger rope than recommended reduces rope life. Too small diameter sheaves cause extra strain on outer rope fibers and increase internal friction.

PROPORTIONING BLOCKS TO ROPE SIZE

In using blocks and tackle the utmost care must be taken in having the proper size blocks for the rope used. See Table 11-5. If the rope is too big it will jam and if too small it will slip out of the sheave and jam between the *cheeks* (sides of a block) and the sheave, which will cause untold damage. Also be careful that the proper size of rope and type of tackle is used in reference to the weight to be lifted. There are many tables to give you this. Also your blocks must be lubricated, clean, well painted or varnished (if wooden), and they must be so placed when in use that they will not be crushed or beaten against a spar or other gear.

The entire study of mechanical appliances is a lengthy and technical one, but also immensely interesting. There has been no effort to cover the subject, but only to give a few notes as an introduction. As said before, it allows one man to do many men's work, or it is a case of a "boy doing a man's job."

FIG. 1118 Main sheet tackle rigged with a double block (movable) on the boom, and single block (fixed, with becket) on deck. The extra single block (foreground) does not increase power but serves as a fairlead. Note eye splice around thimble.

THE BOSUN'S LOCKER

There is nothing that distinguishes a seaman from a lubber as much as his proficiency in marlinespike seamanship. There is nothing more pitiful than seeing someone make fast with a multitude of turns around a pile finished off with many fancy loops only to see a puff of wind cause the boat to tug and the entire conglomeration fall apart and the boat begin to drift. Again, it is impossible to keep a boat shipshape and Bristol fashion, if the ends of your lines have "cow's tails" (frayed or untidy ends of rope).

TERMINOLOGY

First let us all make sure that we understand certain terms. Marlinespike seamanship deals with rope and the methods of working it. *Rope* is cordage of all types and sizes: fiber, wire, small cordage. *Small stuff* is small cordage, usually made of tarred hemp, such as spun-yarn, seine twine, either cotton, linen or synthetic, marlin, ratline, houseline, roundline, frequently used as seizing for whipping, worming and serving line. *Line* is a general term applied on board ship to a piece of rope in use.

There are few ropes on shipboard. Here is a good question to ask boating friends or to send to a quiz program: "How many ropes are there aboard ship? Name them." There are but nine principal ropes on board ship. These are bell ropes, man ropes, top ropes, foot ropes, bolt ropes, back ropes, yard ropes, bucket ropes, and tiller ropes. There may be one or two more, of less importance. The main thing to remember is that you don't make fast with a rope, you use a line; you don't trim in a sail with a rope or a sheet-rope, but with a sheet.

KINDS OF FIBER ROPE

There are various types of fiber rope, mainly manila, nylon, polyesters such as Du Pont Dacron or the English Terrylene, and polyolefins such as polyethylene and polypropylene. In addition you may find linen or flax, cotton, sisal, ropes made of two or more fibers in many combinations, and other fibers. New ones seem to come out every year.

Because the *synthetics* have proved themselves, both as to ultimate cost and ease of handling, they are replacing much of the natural fiber rope. The exception seems to be where the rope is lost by accident or theft or rapidly worn out by abuse and where the higher cost, in most cases, of synthetics cannot be recovered by longer life.

Usually the rope is made from three strands but sometimes four-strand rope is made. A cable is made by twisting three ropes together. To keep rope from unlaying easily, each successive step is twisted in the opposite direction. This is done as follows: yarn—right-handed; strands—left-handed; rope—right-handed; and cable—left-handed. It is possible, however, to get left-handed rope and in this case the procedure is reversed. Left-laid genoa jib sheets and others that are winched hard run more freely (without kinks) when spun off the winch and released for tacking.

FIG. 1119 Anchor line neatly coiled, clockwise, on deck. Note the grating below it to aid in drying.

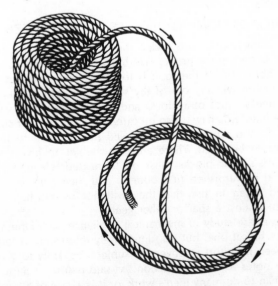

FIG. 1120 Taking line from a new coil, reach down inside and take inner fag end from bottom. Coil clockwise if rope is right-handed.

HOW ROPE IS MEASURED AND SOLD

The size of rope is measured in different ways. Marine fiber rope is measured by its circumference, although most yachtsmen have always designated it by its diameter. On the other hand wire rope is designated by its diameter. Therefore, two-inch wire rope is much thicker than two-inch fiber rope (5/8 inch diameter).

The length of fiber and wire rope may be measured in feet or in fathoms. A fathom is 6 feet. Small stuff is sometimes designated by the number of *threads* it contains. The largest of small stuff is ratline stuff, which is usually 3-stranded, right-handed and may have 8 threads to the strand, in which case it would be 24-thread.

Cordage is sold by the foot or fathom or by the pound. Usually standard coils and reels are sold by the pound and cut lengths are sold by the foot or at a higher price per pound. Your dealer is entitled to increase the price for cuts because of the waste involved in fag ends and his investment and time.

POINTS TO REMEMBER

Vegetable fiber rope will shrink when wet, and because of this fact it is necessary to loosen all standing fiber rigging whenever wet. If this is not done the shrinking will cause an injurious strain on the rope. The rigging should be kept slack until dry.

Rope of natural fiber will deteriorate rapidly from continued dampness and therefore should always be dry before stowed. To dry, it is best to coil down loosely and place where the sun can get at the rope and the air can pass freely all about it. Of course, such rope should never be stowed in a locker that is not well ventilated and dry; for if not, there is not much use in drying the rope as it will rot in the locker.

No attempt should ever be made to put a maximum strain on fiber rope as that will just about ruin a piece of line, even if it is brand new. We well remember a number of years ago we had a house moved and the mover had brand new manila. We said that it was a fine piece of line and would like it afterward. He replied it would be all right, but after they had pulled and hauled on it there was

FIG. 1122 Line is flemished down for neatness by laying it down in close concentric coils, one against the other, in the form of a flat mat, free end at the center. If left long in one spot it may discolor the deck. It does not dry as well as a loose coil. Sunlight may damage nylon and poly ropes.

nothing left but a shell. The rope was ruined by overloading.

Sharp bends are another thing to guard against. It must always be remembered that the safety of the rope decreases after each time it is used and, if care is not taken, all fiber rope will deteriorate rapidly.

One thing not generally understood about synthetic ropes is *cold flow*. Due to the nature of the fiber, a long sustained load may cause the fibers to stretch or elongate permanently with a consequent reduction in rope diameter and ultimate strength. Some synthetics are worse than others in this respect. Temperature affects the flow. In a surging load such as anchoring in moderate weather, the anchor line can recover. But in a hurricane or a long passage at sea the load might be continuous and cold flow could become a hazard. Plenty of safety factors on strength and continual inspection and observation should eliminate much of the hazard.

USE AND CARE OF WIRE ROPE

Wire rope or strand is generally used on board cruising boats as standing rigging. On a number of sailboats, however, it is also used as running rigging. Steel is used almost exclusively in making wire rope. To preserve it from corrosion it is sometimes galvanized. Stainless steel is fine, but expensive. Some wire rope has a hemp core. This greatly increases flexibility and also acts as a cushion against sudden stress or heavy pull.

Great care must be taken of wire rope also. It should always be kept on a reel when not in use and must be

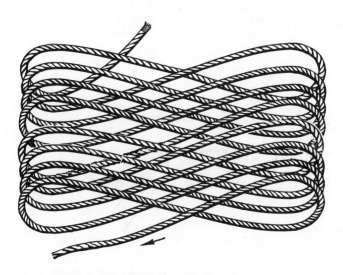

FIG. 1121 Line faked down ready to run out rapidly. Coils, in practice, would lie closer together.

reeled off and not slipped off over the ends of the reel. If kept in a coil it should be rolled off at all times. If a kink ever gets into a wire rope it is a disaster, as this practically ruins it. As with fiber rope, sharp bends will cause an excessive strain and greatly impair the efficiency.

It is important to note that whenever you see broken wires, "meat hooks" that surely cut up the hands, or when the diameter of the outside wires is worn to one-half the original diameter, it is time to condemn the rope as it is no longer safe.

COILING, FAKING AND FLEMISHING

When line is left on deck, or put in a locker, it should never be thrown down in a heap. Not only would this give a lubberly appearance, but if you needed to use the line, especially in a hurry, it might kink or tangle. For safety and good seamanship we always either coil, fake, or flemish down a line.

When it must be kept ready for emergency use, clear for running, a line is generally coiled down (figures 1119-1120) always with the lay (clockwise for right lay rope). To make a straight coil, a circular bight of the secured end is laid and successive bights are placed on top. When all the line has been used, the entire coil is capsized to leave it clear for running.

When the entire length of a line must be run out rapidly it is usually faked down (fig. 1121). To do this a short length of the free end is laid out in a straight line and then turned back to form a flat coil. Successive flat coils are then formed, laying the end of each coil on top of the preceding coils, rather like figure 8s.

When great neatness is desired a line is flemished down (fig. 1122). Successive circles of the line are wrapped about each other with the free end at the center. When it is finished it looks like a mat and with an old piece of line can be used as one.

A disadvantage of coiling down is that you must watch out for kinks. With a flemished-down line care must be taken to prevent coils from falling back and fouling the preceding coil. If a line is flemished down and left on deck

for some time it will mark the deck and remain wet on the under side. On small boats lines are usually either coiled down or flemished down.

KNOTS THE SEAMAN KNOWS

Before a person dares to take a boat out he should be able to make a bowline, two half hitches, clove hitch, square knot and sheet bend. (See figures 1103 c-g.) This is not all he should know, but they are the minimum. The following are those that every competent seaman should know:

A.—Knots in the end of a rope:

1. Overhand
2. Bowline
3. Running bowline
4. Bowline on a bight
5. French bowline
6. Sheepshank
7. Blackwall hitch
8. Figure 8
9. Cat's-paw

B.—Knots for bending two ropes, or two ends of the same rope, together:

1. Square or reef
2. Two bowlines
3. Single and double sheet or becket bend
4. Single and double carrick bend
5. Reeving line bend

C.—Knots for securing a line to ring or spar:

1. Fisherman's bend
2. Timber hitch
3. Timber and half hitch
4. Two half hitches
5. Round turn and two half hitches
6. Rolling hitch
7. Clove hitch
8. Studding sail tack bend
9. Studding sail halyard bend

D.—Knots worked in the end of a rope:

1. Wall knot
2. Wall and crown
3. Single Matthew Walker
4. Lanyard knot

Rope end dip. A new, effective way to treat rope ends is to dip them into a red vinyl liquid called Whip-End Dip. It seals all rope ends in seconds, setting into a tough, flexible permanent finish that eliminates whipping.

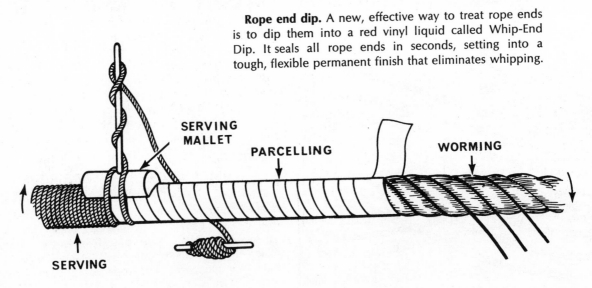

FIG. 1123 Worming, parcelling and serving guards against severe chafe. The rule is: Worm and parcel with the lay; turn and serve the other way.

OTHER ARTS OF THE SAILOR

Besides the general classes of knots and the splices shown earlier, there are other types of work that all seamen should be able to do.

Back Splice: To put an enlarged, finished end on a line.

Stopper on a rope: A length of rope secured at one end used in securing or checking a running line.

Strap on a rope: Turns taken around a standing part with the tackle hooked through the bights.

Mouse a hook: A method of closing the open part of a hook with small stuff to assist in preventing the object to which it is hooked from jumping out.

Grommet strap: A grommet or continuous loop of rope, used to attach a hook to a block permanently.

Seizing: The lashing together of two ends of rope by continuous turns of small stuff. Word sometimes used to mean whipping.

As said before there is nothing more unseamanlike than cow's tails on the end of a line. There are many ways to prevent this such as a back splice, wall knot, etc., but perhaps the best method is by whipping. See fig. 1103-l. Another method, sewed whipping, is preferred as it is easier to get taut and much harder to pull off. Plastic whips that are shrunk on with heat are available but good "fancy" work is preferred over substitutes like friction tape. The advantage of whipping over the other methods of eliminating cow's tails is that it does not increase the size of the rope. This can work as a disadvantage: for example, a sheet can run through all the blocks, making it necessary to re-reeve. Another type, such as a wall and crown, will not allow the end to run through a block.

HOW TO PREVENT CHAFE

There is nothing that wears rope so fast as chafing. In order to prevent this, it is necessary to rig *chafing gear*. When the chafe is of only temporary nature the rope can be protected by wrapping a piece of canvas around it. However, when the chafe will be more or less permanent

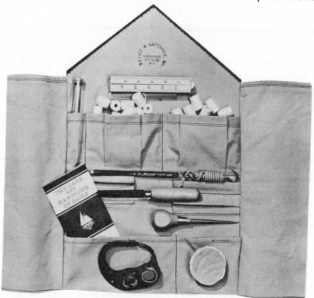

FIG. 1124 This sail repair kit, created by Ratsey & Lapthorn, contains a sailmaker's palm, bench hook, thread, seven needles, awl, knife, wax, rule, pencil and booklet on sail care and handling.

FIG. 1125 Crow's Nest ditty bag contains all the essentials for splicing and sail and canvas repair—palm, assorted needles, marline, sail twine, and 6-inch heavy-duty steel spike.

or severe, the line should be wormed, parceled, and served or molded rubber gear, leather or rawhide, permanently attached.

Worming: consists of following the lay of the rope, between the strands, with small stuff, to keep the moisture out and for filling out the round of the rope.

Parceling: consists of wrapping the rope spirally with long overlapping strips of canvas, following the lay of the rope.

Serving: consists of wrapping small stuff over the parceling opposite to the lay of the rope to form a taut, protective cover. Should be hard-laid marline or seine twine for the best wear.

REPAIRS TO CANVAS

All seamen should be able to work with canvas and a needle. You should provide yourself with a sewing kit consisting of a small canvas kit bag, two or three short and long needles, some beeswax, and some small stuff. The long needle, usually triangular, straight, or curved, is generally used for sewing canvas, while the short needle, usually broad, straight or curved, is generally used for rope work.

There are four main types of stitches used in sewing canvas. Flat is used for seams in sails, tarpaulins, etc.; round is for making duffel bags; baseball, where a snug edge-to-edge fit in canvas is desired; and herringbone is for very stiff or painted canvas.

Have the right cordage for the job and take care of it well—then it will take care of you if you use it correctly.

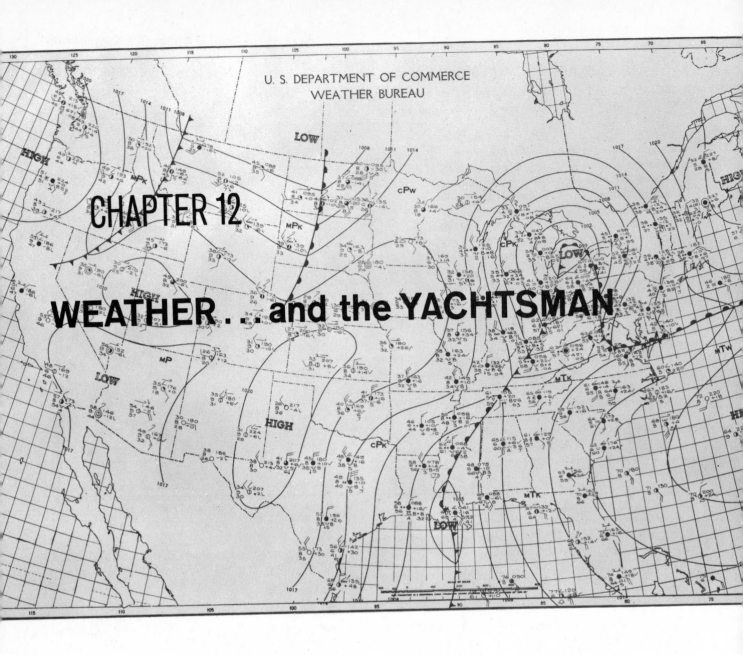

CHAPTER 12

WEATHER...and the YACHTSMAN

How to Read a Weather Map

THE WEATHER MAP provides a bird's-eye view of the weather over a large area. With its many figures, symbols and lines, the map at first appears to be puzzling. But with a little study of these markings and an understanding of their meaning, the map becomes a picture of the weather giving you a good idea of what's in store.

Some boatmen may receive the weekly compilations of daily weather maps mailed to subscribers by the Weather Bureau, Washington, D.C. Most, however, must depend upon newspaper maps for their information. These are drawn from Weather Bureau master weather charts. Four times each day, the Weather Bureau in Washington prepares and analyzes surface and upper air weather charts for the entire Northern Hemisphere.

On surface charts, weather data are plotted as received every six hours from more than 750 reporting stations in North America, more than 200 ships at sea, and 1500 stations in other countries. Each station reports the amount of sky covered by cloud, direction and speed of wind,

visibility distance in miles, present weather, weather during the last three hours, sea level barometric pressure, air temperature, kinds of low, middle and high clouds, dewpoint temperature, character and amount of pressure change in the last three hours, and the character, duration and amount of rainfall in the last six hours. Many of these stations also furnish twelve-hour reports of pressure, temperature, moisture and wind conditions for several levels of upper air. Thus, the central weatherman with his daily surface and several upper air charts has a detailed picture of the weather occurring at the same time over the entire Northern Hemisphere. These charts are used in issuing the daily weather forecasts and warnings of approaching storms.

Over 150 *symbols* are used in entering data on weather maps. Although you may never need know what all the symbols mean, nor have occasion to plot them on a weather map, a knowledge of those most often used will help you to understand and interpret the daily maps appearing in newspapers. See fig. 1201.

THE STATION MODEL

Fig. 1202 shows the "*station model,*" a system weathermen the world over developed for entering data on weather maps. It presents a "model" or picture of the weather at a station, using symbols and numbers, which can be understood in any language. Not only the symbols and numbers but their positions around the station circle tell what each item means. Fig. 1202 represents a typical arrangement.

Study these for a few moments. By referring to fig. 1201 and reading the parenthetical explanations in fig. 1202, you can interpret the weather at this particular station.

For example, starting with the "station circle" itself (the black dot in the middle)—the fact that this circle is solid black indicates that the sky is completely covered with clouds here.

Let's go counterclockwise around the station circle to examine and understand what's shown. Take the wind first. The symbol indicates a pretty windy day, the wind being from the northwest at 21 to 25 mph. The wind

arrows always "fly" with the wind.

Next is temperature in degrees Fahrenheit. As you can see, it was relatively cold, the thermometer registering only 31°.

Since we know the sky was completely overcast, the next two markings—Visibility and Present Weather—begin to give us a picture of conditions at the station. It was a nasty day with a stiff, cold wind blowing light snow all over the place.

PRECIPITATION SYMBOLS

A word about precipitation symbols is in order here. Fig. 1201 shows the symbols used to indicate different forms of precipitation—drizzle, rain, snow, etc. Increasing precipitation is indicated by more than one symbol being plotted, the range being from one to four identical symbols.

In fig. 1202 the use of the two stars (or asterisks) tells you that it is snowing continuously but lightly at this station. If there had been three stars the snow would have

---

SYMBOLS

SKY COVER	WEATHER Present and Past	WIND Miles per Hour

SKY COVER

0 ○ 5 ◒ (quartered)
1 ◍ 6 ◕
2 ◔ 7 ◑
3 ◑ 8 ●
4 ◐ 9 ⊗

WEATHER Present and Past

≡ FOGGY
, DRIZZLING
• RAINING
✳ SNOWING
▽ SHOWERS
↳ THUNDERSTORMS

WIND Miles per Hour

Calm   21-25   50-54
1-4   26-31   55-60
5-8   32-37   61-66
9-14   38-43   67-71
15-20   44-49   72-77

FIG. 1201

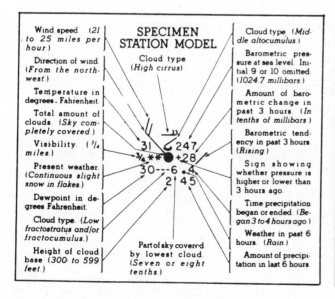

FIG. 1202 Illustrating how symbols in fig. 1201 are used by weathermen to show weather conditions at a station.

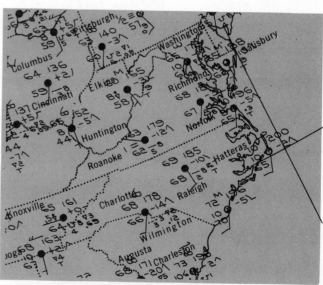

FIG. 1203 A section of the Atlantic coast from a Weather Bureau Surface Chart with data for several stations.

been moderate to heavy. Now, if the *shower* symbol (a triangle) had been shown instead of the star it would have carried a star symbol above it to indicate that the showers were *snow* showers. If the showers were *rain* the shower symbol would have carried a dot (the rain symbol) above it.

Hail is indicated by a small triangle (inverted shower symbol) above the thunderstorm symbol. Fog is represented by three horizontal lines.

Other symbols around the station circle in fig. 1202 are interesting and important to weathermen and anyone wishing to use the information. They are worth studying but since most of them do not appear on the abbreviated maps appearing in newspapers we won't go into a detailed description here. Fig. 1202 does provide a brief explanation of each.

Fig. 1203 shows a small portion of a Weather Bureau surface chart with data plotted for several stations. By re-

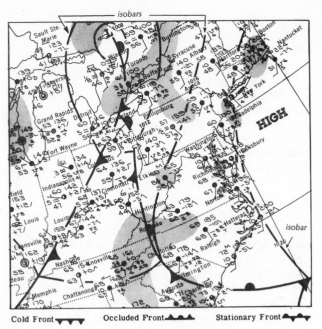

Cold Front ▼▼▼   Occluded Front ▲▲▲   Stationary Front ▬▲▬

FIG. 1205 Section of a weather map with fronts, isobars, HIGHS, LOWS, and direction of fronts plotted on it.

Inches	Millibars	Inches	Millibars
28.44	963	29.77	1008
28.53	966	29.86	1011
28.62	969	29.94	1014
28.70	972	30.03	1017
28.79	975	30.12	1020
28.88	978	30.21	1023
28.97	981	30.30	1026
29.06	984	30.39	1029
29.15	987	30.48	1032
29.24	990	30.56	1035
29.32	993	30.65	1038
29.41	996	30.74	1041
29.50	999	30.83	1044
29.59	1002	30.92	1047
29.68	1005	31.01	1050

FIG. 1204 Conversion table for a weather map's millibars.

ferring to figs. 1201 and 1202 you can tell what the weather conditions at any given station are. Let's take Raleigh, N. C. as a case in point:

You can see that the sky is completely overcast, the wind is south, at 9 to 14 mph, the temperature is 69°F., the dew point is 68°, the numeral 2 indicates the clouds were low, the letter T says that precipitation in the past 6 hours was very slight, T standing for "Trace," the barometer has fallen 1.0 millibar during the past 3 hours, there were thunderstorms at the station during the past 6 hours, and

FIG. 1206 Typical abridged weather map commonly appearing in newspapers.

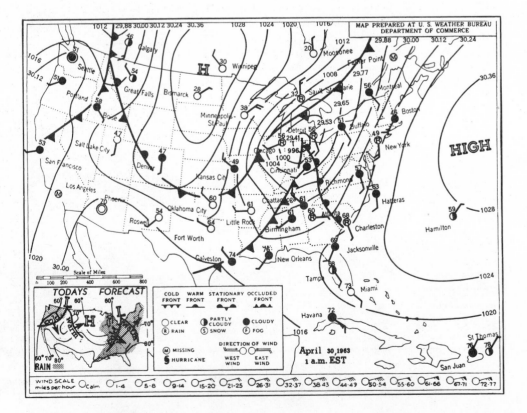

the pressure is 1018.5 millibars or 30.08 inches of mercury.

Fig. 1204 provides a conversion table for changing millibars to inches and vice versa.

ISOBARS AND FRONTS

When data from all stations are entered on the map, the weatherman draws black lines, called *isobars*. These are lines drawn through points having the same ("iso-" means equal) barometric pressure. For example, a 1020 millibar (30.12 inches) isobar is a line drawn through all points having a barometric pressure of 1020 millibars. Ad-

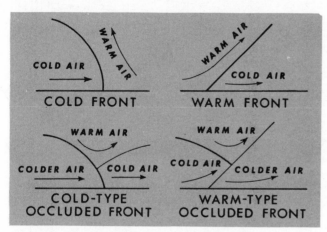

FIG. 1207 Diagrams indicate action of cold and warm fronts and show how their interaction forms occluded fronts.

ditional isobars are drawn for every four millibar intervals. The purpose of the isobars is to position the centers of low and high pressure — the familiar "LOWS" and "HIGHS" which govern our weather. The centers of high pressures are marked "H" or "High" and the low pressures are marked "L" or "Low." It is the movement of these HIGHS and LOWS which enables the weatherman to forecast weather, taking into consideration, of course, the various data supplied by the weather stations.

The heavier lines in fig. 1205 are drawn to indicate *"fronts"* — the boundaries between different air streams. Triangles and half circles are attached to these heavier lines pointing in the direction in which the fronts are mov-,

ing. The triangle indicates a *"cold front,"* the half circle a *"warm front."* (See also fig. 1207.)

A front which is not moving, one which is *"stationary,"* is shown by attaching triangles on one side of the line and half circles on the opposite side. An *"occluded front"* is indicated by attaching both triangles and half circles to one side of the line. Fronts and their significance will be explained later.

WEATHER OFFICES

If you visit a Weather Bureau office you can see the latest surface and upper air weather maps. Maps prepared at the Washington Weather Bureau are sent to the various stations over a picture (facsimile) transmission circuit. Maps prepared by local stations appear much the same as the Washington maps with a few exceptions. The cold fronts, for instance, will be drawn on the map in blue pencil, warm fronts in red, occluded fronts in purple, while the stationary front will be shown by a line of alternating red and blue dashes.

NEWSPAPER WEATHER MAP

Because of their reduced size, it is impossible to include on newspaper maps all of the data usually entered on a map prepared at a Weather Bureau office. To permit easier reading, only sky covered by cloud or other forms of present weather, wind direction and speed, and air temperature are plotted for each station. Barometric pressure at each station is omitted because it can be estimated for any place from the nearest isobar (remember—isobars represent lines of equal barometric pressure). Incidentally, on some weather maps, isobars may be drawn for 3 millibar intervals; for example, 996, 999, 1002, etc., rather than the 4 millibar intervals. Some maps show isobars marked at one end with the millibar pressure and at the other end in inches. Symbols used for entry of all this information, including those for types of fronts, are usually shown in the margin of newspaper maps. See fig. 1206.

Morning newspapers usually contain the weather map prepared from data collected the evening before, while afternoon editions publish the early morning chart. The time is noted on the newspaper chart.

Analysis of the Weather Map

We don't need to know how to draw the isobars and fronts on a weather map in order to be able to read one, but we can review to advantage the method used by the professional weatherman. First, the meteorologist enters on the chart the observations at all stations from which he has received reports. The entries, which include both instrumental and visual observations, are recorded partly in numerical and partly in symbolic form, as illustrated in fig. 1202. Second, he delineates any fronts that may exist, using preceding maps, in addition to present information, as a guide to their locations.

Let's take an actual case as analyzed by the late Dr. B. C. Haynes, Senior Meteorologist with the U.S. Weather Bureau, and published by the Bureau in its booklet "An-

alysis of a Series of Surface Weather Maps." Fig. 1208 is the finished map for 1930 EST Wednesday, 17 April, in the year the analysis was made. Given the observations at each station, how was analysis of the data accomplished?

LOCATING THE FRONTS

Consider first the location of the fronts. A *front* is the boundary between two contiguous bodies, or masses, of air which have come from different geographical regions and traveled along different routes (see fig. 1209) and which, therefore, have different physical properties. The *position of a front* is marked principally by the difference in the temperatures of the two air masses, the difference

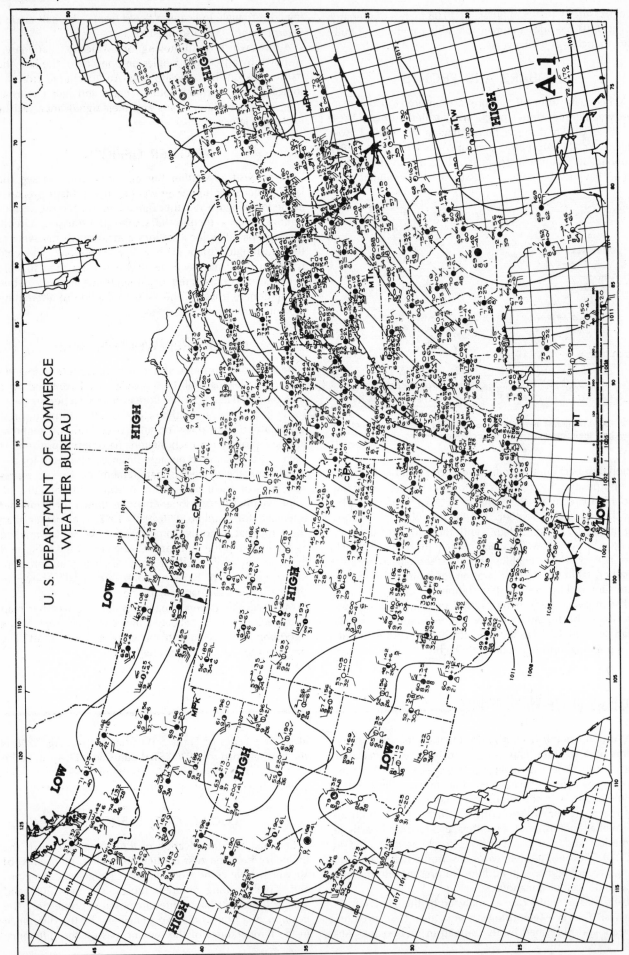

FIG. 1208   The finished weather map for 1930 EST Wednesday, 17 April.

in dew points (the temperature at which the air is saturated with moisture), differences in barometric pressure and pressure tendency, and differences in wind direction and velocity.

To make a start, we examine the plotted data and find that the lowest barometric pressure (998.0 millibars for this map) is at a station in western Indiana. Note that the general wind pattern over Kentucky, Tennessee and the southwestern states is from south to southwest. Over Illinois, Missouri, Kansas and the central plains states the general wind pattern is northwest to north. Different air masses must be over each of these regions and these air masses must be separated by a front. Beginning at our station in western Indiana we will draw this front.

To confirm our finding that a front exists, we look at the next station due west of our starting point; it is located in central Illinois. Here are the salient data at the two stations:

	Western Indiana	Central Illinois
Air temperature	65°	37°
Dew point	60°	36°
Pressure	998.0 mb	1,004.4 mb
Pressure tendency	−2.2 mb	+2.4 mb
Wind direction	SW	N

The differences are sharp; we are on the right track.

We continue southwestward across Illinois, southeastern Missouri, central Arkansas, the northwestern tip of Louisiana, eastern Texas, and into Mexico, all the time comparing the observations at different stations and placing the front between those showing critical contrasts.

Kinds of Fronts

We have drawn a front on our map, but what kind of front is it? To the west and northwest of this front, the observations show relatively colder air moving from the north or northwest; to the east and southeast they show relatively warmer air moving from the south. The colder air is moving toward the front. As it is colder and heavier, it pushes the warmer, lighter air eastward before it, at the same time driving under this warmer air and lifting it off the ground. Cold air is displacing warm; we have a *cold front.*

Are there any more fronts to be found? Starting again at our station in western Indiana, suppose we work eastward this time. Through southern Michigan and northern Ohio we again find differences in wind direction and velocity, in air temperature and dew point. These differences remain quite sharp all the way to western Pennsylvania. We have located another front, a *warm front* this time as the somewhat colder air north of our line is retreating to the northeast and warmer air south of the line is following and replacing the colder.

As we continue eastward from western Pennsylvania, the front becomes more obscure; the differences between the air masses become less pronounced. On the other hand, reports of rain, overcast skies and fog continue. The winds are lighter. We draw in a *stationary front* (neither air mass moving appreciably against the other), all the way across West Virginia, Virginia, and North Carolina to the sea.

Warm fronts and cold fronts are *active* weather factories; a stationary front is a *potential* weather factory. The latter may gradually dissipate or it may resolve itself into an active front.

Taking a final glance at the map, we notice another wind shift and temperature difference in eastern Montana. Applying the same technique, we locate another, a short, warm front in this region. We now have our frontal analysis complete.

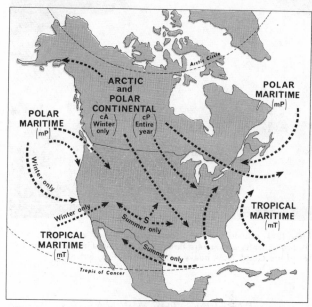

FIG. 1209 **North American Air Masses. Source regions and directions of movement of air masses influencing North American weather are shown. Air remaining in contact with earth's surface gradually acquires properties characteristic of the surface beneath it. Then, as this air mass subsequently moves over the earth, its properties, and its conflicts with other air masses that it may encounter en route, cause changes in weather of the area invaded.** (Reproduced by courtesy of Aviation Training Division, U.S. Navy)

ANALYSIS OF PRESSURE INDICATIONS

The third step is to analyze our map for pressure indications; we need to know the pattern of the *isobars,* where high and low pressure centers exist, *the nature of the pressure field.* Because of the earth's rotation, the wind blows, not directly from high to low pressure, but nearly parallel to the isobars and only slightly across them toward low pressure. The more closely spaced the isobars, the stronger the winds in that area. The closely spaced isobars mean that a greater pressure difference exists, hence the winds are stronger, but the earth's rotation still makes them blow almost along the isobars. Observe the wind direction arrow at each station, then note the direction of adjacent isobars. Compare the velocity of the wind, as indicated by the number of feathers on the arrow, with the spacing of the isobars.

To get back to the map for 17 April, we have a low-pressure center in western Indiana. We find a high-pressure center in northeastern Nevada and another off the coast of Maine. There is a high over the central plains states, another over central Canada, and others off the South Atlantic and Pacific coasts. In addition to our western Indiana low, there are lows in the southwest, off the east coast of Texas, and over western Canada.

As we approach our long cold front, the isobars become more closely spaced; the pressure differences are greater and the winds are stronger. It is not too promising a time for a comfortable cruise along the east coast, the Gulf, Mississippi or Great Lakes.

FIG. 1210 Cumulonimbus cloud, indicative of very unstable air. Strong updrafts and severe turbulence are found in and around center of the cloud. Note heavy rain shower falling out of it.

FIG. 1211 A layer of stratus cloud, typical of moist, stable air. In this picture the stratus is very low; shreds of cloud trailing downward from base of the layer are visible against dark hillside.

LABELING THE AIR MASSES

The fourth step is to determine the *kinds of air masses* on either side of each front. A given air mass has its own individual properties; these properties tell us much about the kind of weather we can expect. Having located our fronts and completed the pressure analysis, we can label these air masses. Look at fig. 1208 again.

In the southeastern United States, the winds and pressure gradient indicate that a broad current of air is flowing from over the warm waters of the Gulf northward across the southeastern states. The high temperatures and high dew points in this area tell us that this air is warm and moist. As this is a late afternoon (1930 EST) map, the air has been further heated for many hours by re-radiation of the sun's heat by the earth, which means that the air probably is unstable. The thunderstorms and showers, cumulus and towering cumulonimbus clouds (see fig. 1210) reported at various stations confirm the diagnosis. We label this air with the symbol mTk, meaning that it is *unstable, tropical maritime air,* air that can result in foul weather.

Looking north of the front along the Atlantic Coast, we note that the winds and pressure gradient indicate an onshore movement of air from over the Atlantic Ocean. Temperatures and dew points are fairly low; fog and low clouds (see fig. 1211) are shown at many stations. These are signs of *maritime, stable polar air* so we label it mPw, the w indicating that it is relatively warmer than the land over which it is moving and hence not given to heating from below. It will lose heat to the earth; more low clouds, fog and light rains are probable.

To the west of our main cold front, we observe northerly winds, low temperatures and low dew points. Many stations report stratocumulus clouds (see fig. 1212) and a few report cumulus clouds. The temperatures recorded tell us that this air mass is being warmed as it moves southward. Again we have unstable air. As it came, however, from the northward over Canada and not from over an ocean, it is

unstable, continental, polar air. We label it cPk.

Studying our map further, we find *stable continental polar air* over the Dakotas (cPw) and *unstable moist (maritime) polar air* (mPk) over the northwestern states.

ESTIMATING EXPECTED CHANGES

We can now make a rough estimate of the changes that will take place during the next 12 hours. The cold front extending from western Indiana to eastern Texas should move eastward in response to the push of the relatively cold northwesterly winds over Illinois, Missouri, Arkansas, Oklahoma and Texas. The warm front across northern Ohio and western Pennsylvania should advance across Lake Erie as the relatively cool air situated to the northeast of the warm front gives way to the moist tropical air flowing from the south. The low-pressure center over western Indiana should be displaced northeastward along the advancing warm front. We should expect this center to move toward the area where the largest negative pressure tendencies are observed, namely, southern Michigan.

A feature of the 1930 EST 17 April map which should not pass unnoticed is the small low-pressure center spotted in the Gulf of Mexico just southeast of the southern tip of Texas. This center appears to be unconnected with the cold front, and its future behavior is hard to judge.

Now let's look at the map for 0730 EST 18 April (fig. 1213). We find that the low-pressure center which was over western Indiana twelve hours earlier has moved in a general northeasterly direction and is situated somewhere between Lake Huron and Lake Ontario. The actual center may be spotted about 100 miles east of the station in eastern Michigan that reports a pressure of 1000.3 millibars, temperature 35°, dew point 35°, and a northwest wind. (Incidentally, twelve hours earlier this same station reported a due north wind, an indication that the cold air there was holding its ground against the advancing warm front. This fact explains why the low-pressure center

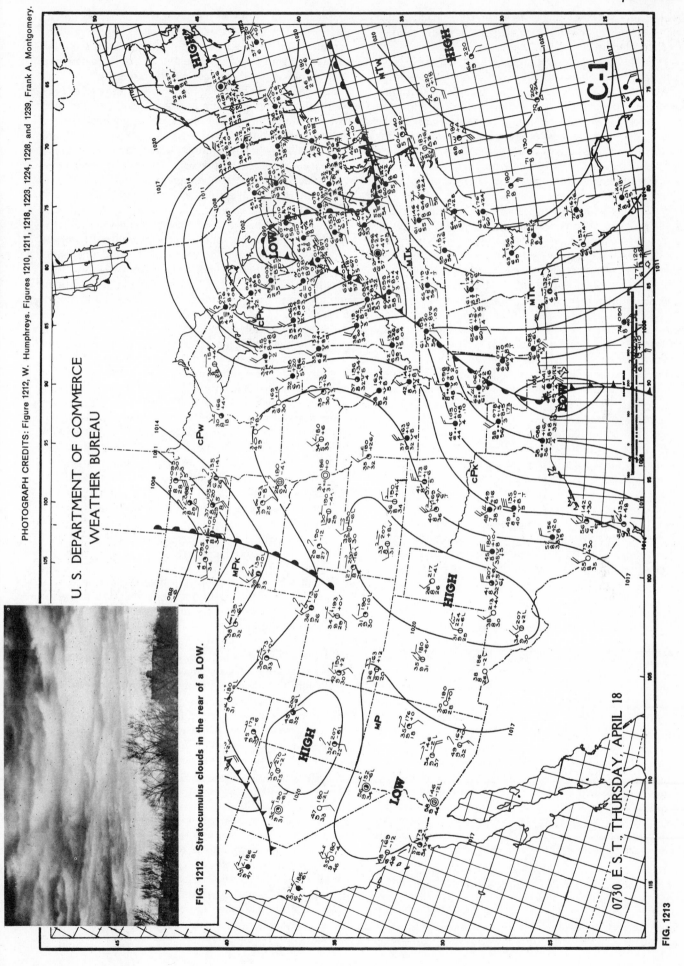

PHOTOGRAPH CREDITS: Figure 1212, W. Humphreys. Figures 1210, 1211, 1218, 1223, 1224, 1228, and 1239, Frank A. Montgomery.

U. S. DEPARTMENT OF COMMERCE
WEATHER BUREAU

C-1

FIG. 1212 Stratocumulus clouds in the rear of a LOW.

0730 E.S.T., THURSDAY, APRIL 18

FIG. 1213

221

moved in a slightly more easterly direction than we had expected from our consideration of the pressure tendencies reported at 1930 EST 17 April.)

From the point of lowest pressure north of Lake Erie we can start our diagnosis of the location of the cold front. The front quite clearly runs southwestward through Ohio and Kentucky, between the stations reporting northwest winds and the stations reporting southerly winds. To the east of the front, temperatures are quite uniformly in the low sixties and dew points in the upper fifties. To the west of it both temperatures and dew points decrease rapidly westward, being in the thirties at a distance of 200 miles from the wind-shift line.

In Tennessee the east-to-west contrasts of temperature and dew point become less sharp, but pronounced differences in wind direction still exist, with winds from the south over eastern Tennessee, Alabama and eastern Mississippi, in contrast to winds generally from the north over western Tennessee, northwestern Mississippi and central and western Louisiana.

If we look at the pressure reports from the region near the Gulf Coast we find a barometric reading at New Orleans of 1004.1 millibars (fig. 1213). This indicates the presence of another low-pressure center, which is almost certainly the same one that we noticed southeast of Texas twelve hours earlier. It has now made connections with the original cold front, and is affecting the movement of this front, as we shall now determine.

In drawing the 1008 millibar isobar northward from the Gulf Coast we find that it no longer can be traced with practically no change in direction all the way to western Pennsylvania, as it could on the preceding map (fig. 1208). It intersects the front in northeastern Mississippi and thence must make a sharp turn to the left, with the result that it returns to the Gulf via western Louisiana. It has become separated from the 1008 millibar isobar to the north, which crosses the front in southwestern Ohio and closes around the northern low-pressure center.

Changes in Wind Pattern

This splitting of the isobaric pattern means that changes in the wind pattern have taken place from Tennessee southward. In eastern Louisiana especially, it can be seen that the winds in the moist tropical air have backed to southeast, while on the other side of the front the winds in the cold air have, in general, veered to a straight northerly, or even north-northeasterly direction. Hence, the winds in the cold air have become more nearly parallel to the front. The result is that the eastward advance of the front has been abruptly stopped; the front has become stationary or is even beginning to reverse its course and to move slowly to the west. Therefore, from the point in Tennessee to just west of New Orleans the front may now be marked a warm front. Southwest of the low-pressure center near New Orleans we assume that the cold air is advancing eastward across the Gulf of Mexico and so we indicate there that the front is acting as a cold front.

RELOCATING THE WARM FRONT

Let us now see how to locate the warm front that extended eastward across northern Indiana, northern Ohio, and thence southeastward to the Middle Atlantic Coast at 1930 EST of 17 April (see fig. 1208). The determination of the position of this front has to be based largely on temperature differences and dew-point differences, since the contrast of wind directions on either side of it are nowhere near as marked as in the case of the cold front.

Beginning at the center of low pressure just east of Lake Huron (fig. 1212), the warm front runs southeastward and may be found in western New York lying between the station that reports a south-southwest wind, pressure 1001.0 millibars, temperature 60°, dew point 58°, and the station in central New York with a southeast wind, pressure 1006.1 millibars, temperature 52°, dew point 45°.

From this point the front extends southward through western Pennsylvania. We determine that it lies between the station in extreme southwestern Pennsylvania (Pittsburgh) which reports a south-southwest wind, temperature 61°, dew point 58°, and the station in central Pennsylvania reporting a southeast wind, continuous light rain, temperature 54°, dew point 47°. (The temperature-dew point combination of 61°/58° observed at Pittsburgh is characteristic, for that latitude, of the moist tropical air that has come from the Gulf of Mexico.)

Beyond this point the position of the front does not show up clearly, owing to the lack of reports from stations in Maryland and northeastern Virginia. We are on safe ground, however, if we draw it between stations reporting south to southwest winds and places where the winds range from northeast to southeast. On this basis we determine that the front intersects the coastline at about latitude 38°. From there we project it eastward out to sea.

We shall not take time to analyze the weather features over the western part of the United States at 0730 EST of 18 April, since little of interest is occurring there. And so we conclude our brief study of the weather map.

SUBSEQUENT DEVELOPMENTS— IN RETROSPECT

The reader, however, may be interested to hear what happened to the principal frontal system and its two associated low-pressure centers during the next four days. During the interval between 0730 EST of 18 April and 0730 EST of 19 April the northern low-pressure area continued its northeastward movement and reached a position just north of the St. Lawrence River. But, meanwhile it weakened considerably, its lowest pressure on 19 April being not less than about 1005 millibars. The northern part of the cold front which extended southwestward from it pushed across Pennsylvania, New York and New England, all the way to the Atlantic. Further south, however, the advance of cold air was slowed by the developing low-pressure center which we noted near New Orleans at 0730 EST of 18 April. During the next 24 hours this center moved north-northeastward to Tennessee, all the while strengthening; by 0730 EST of 19 April it had become more prominent than the northern center.

Subsequently it continued to intensify, as it changed course to a more easterly direction, and eventually it developed into a severe storm. At 0730 EST of 22 April it was located about 250 miles east of Nantucket; the pressure at its exact center had fallen to about 972 millibars (28.70″). It caused exceptionally strong northeast gales off the New England coast during 21 April.

Types of Storms

EXTRA-TROPICAL CYCLONES

The principal source of rain, winds and generally foul weather in the United States is the *extra-tropical cyclone*. There are other storms—the hurricane, the thunderstorm and the tornado—that are usually more destructive but it is a fact that the extra-tropical cyclone is the ultimate cause of most of our weather troubles. Fog is another enemy not to be taken lightly, as we shall see, but let's concentrate on storms right now. If we would take proper and timely precautions for them, we should know something of their characteristics.

A definition of an extra-tropical cyclone in the Northern Hemisphere is: a traveling system of winds rotating counterclockwise around a center of low barometric pressure and containing a warm front and a cold front.

How extra-tropical cyclones develop

We saw what one looked like on the daily weather map. Fig. 1214 is a diagram (plan view) of the birth, development and death of an extra-tropical cyclone. Our thanks are due Captain Charles G. Halpine, USN, for permission to reproduce this diagram from his book "A Pilot's Meteorology," published by D. van Nostrand Company.

In part (a) of fig. 1214, we have a warm air mass, typically moist tropical air, flowing northeastward and a cold air mass, typically polar continental, flowing southwestward. They are separated by a heavy line representing the boundary or front between them. The next stage is shown in part (b). The cold air from behind pushes under the warm air; the warm air rushes up over the cold air ahead of it. A cold front is born on the left, a warm front on the right. Where they are connected, the barometric pressure is lowered and the air starts circulating counterclockwise around this LOW. At the rear of the cold front, a high-pressure area

develops. At the same time, the whole system keeps moving in a general easterly direction. The crosshatched area represents rain. When warm, moist air is lifted, as it is when a cold air mass pushes under it or when it rushes up over cold air ahead, it cools by expansion. After its temperature has fallen to the dew point, excess water vapor condenses to form first clouds and then rain.

In parts (c) and (d) of fig. 1214, the storm matures, the low-pressure area intensifying more and more, the clouds and rain increasing and the winds becoming stronger. In part (e), the cold front begins to catch up with the warm front; an occluded front is formed. The storm is now at its height. It will do about one-half of its mischief while in occlusion. In part (f), it has begun to weaken; after a while, the weather should clear, as the high-pressure area reaches us.

Extra-tropical cyclones often occur in families of two, three or four storms. It takes about one day (24 hours) for this disturbance to reach maturity with three or possibly four days more required for complete dissipation. In winter, these storms occur on the average of twice a week in the USA; in summer they occur somewhat less frequently and are less severe. Their movement is eastward to north of east at a velocity in winter of about 700 miles per day and in summer of perhaps 500 miles per day. Finally, this storm usually covers a large area geographically; it can affect a given locality for two days or more.

Parts of the extra-tropical cyclone

The component parts of an extra-tropical cyclone are:
1. A warm front, with its two conflicting air masses and its weather.
2. A cold front, with its two conflicting air masses, one of which (the warmer) is situated between the cold front and the warm front.

FIG. 1214 Diagram of development of extra-tropical cyclone.
(Reproduced by courtesy of Captain C. G. Halpine, U.S.N., and D. van Nostrand Co., Inc.)

(A)

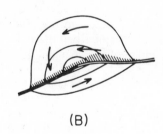

(B)

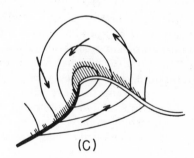

(C)

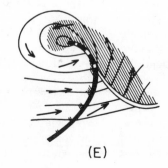

(D)

(E)

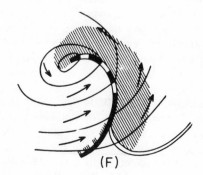

(F)

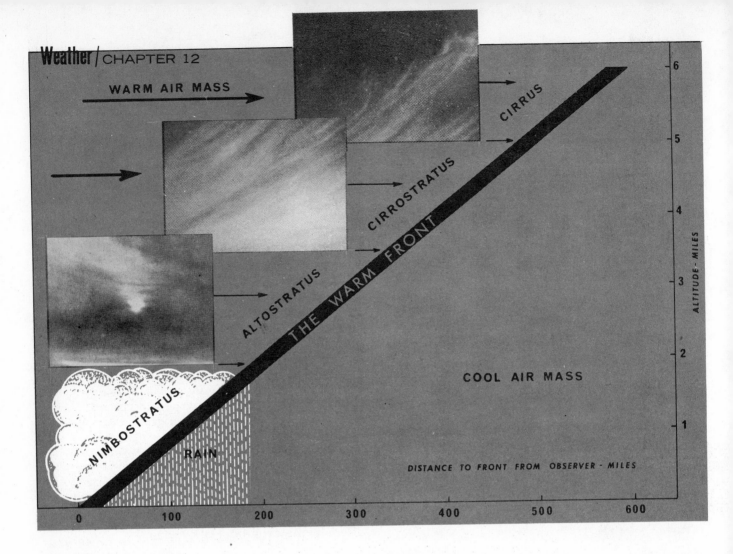

FIG. 1215

3. A center of low barometric pressure with its wind system, at the junction of the fronts.

4. A high pressure area behind the cold front.

A typical cruising experience

In early May a few years ago we were cruising down the Mississippi. We noticed on the weather map that there was an extra-tropical cyclone far to the WSW, its center moving NE along a path that would leave us SSE of it. The warm front, the warm sector between the fronts, and the cold front would pass over us if we continued our cruise. Being stubborn, we kept on but watched carefully for the approaching trouble.

The first day the weather was fine with gentle winds and light fluffy cumulus clouds. The next morning we observed cirrus (Ci) clouds (fig. 1215) to the westward and noted that the barometer was falling. As these slowly thickened, we knew that the warm front was perhaps 500 miles, about one day, away. As the day wore on, the barometer fell more rapidly, the wind blew increasingly strong from the southeast, and the clouds thickened to the cirrostratus (Cs) of fig. 1215. A halo appeared around the sun.

Altostratus (As) clouds (fig. 1215) next were seen approaching from westward. Knowing that these clouds precede a warm front by about 300 miles and that rain can be expected about 200 miles ahead of the front, it required no magician to tell us that we had better begin securing

ship and breaking out the oilskins. We observed that the spread between the air temperature and dew-point temperature was growing less and less; it looked as though we could also expect fog. We decided to anchor until the warm front had passed over.

Next came the low nimbostratus (Ns) clouds and the rain, the barometer continuing to fall and the temperature slowly to rise. The visibility grew worse and worse. The ship's bell began its clamor and we spent a not too comfortable night. By morning, however, the wind had veered to SSW, the clouds had begun to break, the barometer had stopped falling, the rain had ceased. Knowing that it might be 6 to 12 hours before the cold front struck us, we got under way, keeping our eyes peeled for altocumulus (Ac) clouds to the westward. The watch below was set to airing the cabins and our duffle as we ran through the warm sector.

About 1400 the lookout spotted the altocumulus clouds (fig. 1216); the cold front was perhaps 100 miles away. As the day was hot and quite humid, we thought that thunderstorms were probable and that they might be severe. We decided to anchor early, about 1500, and prepare for the worst. The barometer was again falling, the wind was SW and increasing. Nimbostratus (Ns) clouds with cumulonimbus (Cb) (fig. 1216) towering out of them appeared to the west. Rain set in and the wind rose sharply. We had a busy few hours—and were mighty glad that we had known enough to recognize and time the warning signs. By the

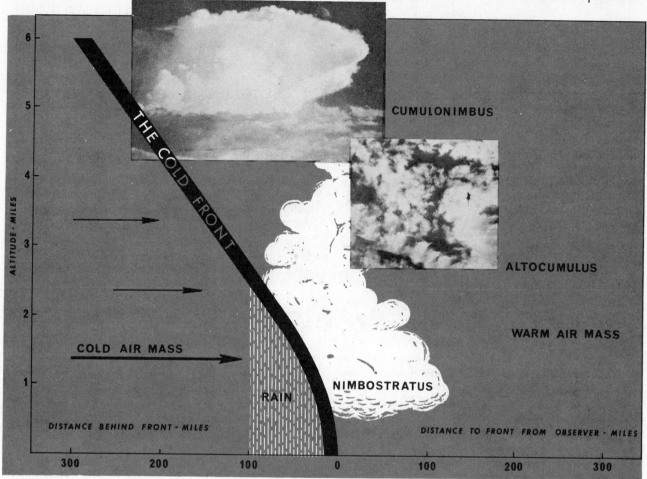

ALTITUDE - MILES

6
5
4
3
2
1

THE COLD FRONT

CUMULONIMBUS

ALTOCUMULUS

WARM AIR MASS

COLD AIR MASS

NIMBOSTRATUS

RAIN

DISTANCE BEHIND FRONT - MILES

DISTANCE TO FRONT FROM OBSERVER - MILES

300   200   100   0   100   200   300

FIG. 1216

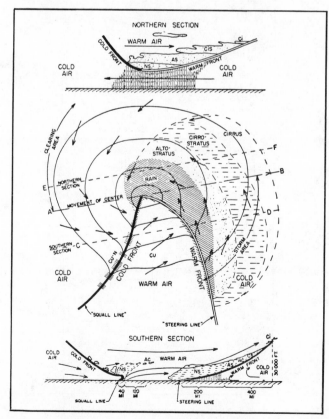

FIG. 1217   Cross-sections of extra-tropical cyclone. (Reproduced by courtesy of Captain C. G. Halpine, U.S.N., and D. van Nostrand Co., Inc.)

next morning the storm was over and we continued our cruise with a blue sky and fair winds.

Thus, we passed through an extra-tropical cyclone. Fig. 1217 is a picture of it, again with acknowledgement to Captain Halpine. The central portion is a plan view of the storm; the lower portion is a vertical cross-section along the line CD, our "course" through the storm. The cloud sequences and the rain are clearly shown (Cb symbol omitted). Had we passed north, instead of south, of the center, the upper diagram would represent the clouds and weather.

HURRICANES

Another type of cyclone which is of concern principally to those of us cruising the Gulf of Mexico and the southeast Atlantic coast is the *tropical cyclone,* which in its most violent (and best known) form is called a *hurricane.* Unlike the extra-tropical cyclone, it does not contain warm and cold fronts, and its occurrence (over waters adjacent to the United States) is restricted to summer and autumn.

The hurricane as a storm type is too well known among sailors to require any description here of the various premonitory signs, the violence of the wind and rain accompanying such a storm and the steps to be taken to minimize the dangers of encounter. These are fully detailed in standard nautical works, such as Bowditch's "American Practical Navigator."

FIG. 1218 Wall cloud around eye of a hurricane, as seen from an aircraft within the eye. Upper edge of wall cloud is at an altitude of nearly 40,000 feet. Note clear space in right foreground.

Over the years much statistical information on the frequency of hurricanes in various regions of the world has accumulated. In the Far East hurricanes (or *typhoons*, as they are called in the western Pacific) may occur in any month, although late summer and early autumn are the preferred seasons. In North American waters, however, the period from early December through May is hurricane-free. August, September and October are the months of greatest frequency; in these months hurricanes form over the tropical Atlantic, mostly between latitudes 8°N and 20°N. The infrequent hurricanes of June and November almost always originate in the southwestern part of the Caribbean Sea.

Development of a hurricane

The birthplace of a hurricane typically lies within a diffuse and fairly large area of relatively low pressure situated somewhere in the latitude belt just mentioned. The winds around the low-pressure area are not particularly strong, and, although cumulonimbus clouds and showers are more numerous than is usual in these latitudes, there is no clearly organized "weather system." This poorly-defined condition may persist for several days before hurricane development commences.

When development starts, however, it takes place suddenly. Within an interval of 12 hours or less the barometric pressure drops 15 millibars or more over a small, almost circular area. Winds of hurricane force spring up and form a ring around the area; the width of this ring is at first only 20 to 40 miles. The clouds and showers become well-organized and show a spiral structure. At this stage the growing cyclone acquires an *eye*. This is the inner area enclosed by the ring of hurricane-force winds, which, by the time the cyclone reaches maturity, has expanded to a width of 100 miles or more. Within the eye we find the lowest barometric reading.

Hurricane eyes average about 15 miles in diameter but may be as large as 25 miles. The wind velocities in the eye of a hurricane are seldom greater than 15 knots and often are less. Cloud conditions vary over a wide range. At times

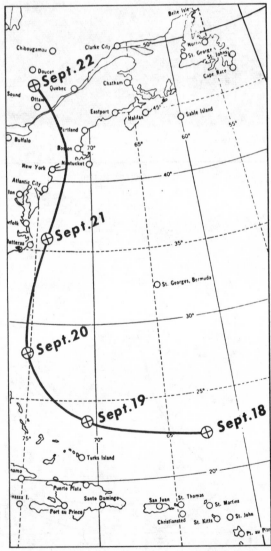

FIG. 1219 Path of the hurricane, showing positions of the center at 0700 EST, 18-22 September 1938.

there are only scattered clouds, but usually there is more than 50% cloud cover. Through the openings the sky is visible overhead and at a distance the dense towering clouds of the hurricane ring can be seen extending to great heights (fig. 1218). This feature has been given the name *wall cloud*.

Hurricane tracks

The usual track of an Atlantic hurricane describes a parabola around the semipermanent Azores-Bermuda high-pressure area. Thus, after forming, a hurricane will move westward on the southern side of the Azores-Bermuda HIGH, at the same time tending to work away from the equator. When the hurricane reaches the western side of this HIGH, it begins to follow a more northerly track, and its direction of advance changes progressively toward the right. Thus, the usual movement of Atlantic hurricanes at first is roughly westward, then northwestward, northward, and finally northeastward. The position where the westward movement changes to an eastward movement is known as the *point of recurvature*.

Occasionally when a hurricane is in a position near the

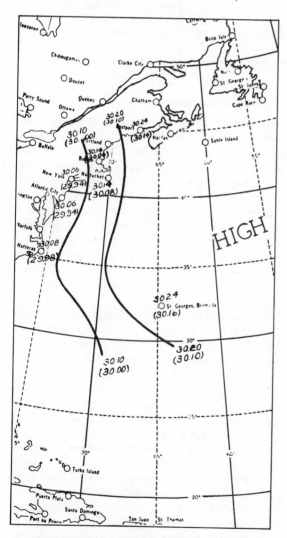

FIG. 1220 Constancy of anticyclonic flow, as shown by unchanged orientation of sea-level isobars from September 19 to September 20. Upper figure of each pair of numbers is barometric reading on September 19, lower figure that on September 20. Although a general fall of pressure took place during the interval, flow pattern remained the same.

southeast Atlantic coast, the Azores-Bermuda HIGH happens to have an abnormal northward extension. In this type of situation the hurricane will fail to execute a complete recurvature in the vicinity of Cape Hatteras. It will skirt the western side of the HIGH and follow a path almost due north along the Atlantic coast, as occurred in the case of the famous New England hurricane of September 1938 (see figs. 1219 and 1220).

The rate of movement of tropical cyclones while they are still in low latitudes and heading westward is about 15 knots, which is considerably slower than the usual rate of travel of extra-tropical cyclones. After recurving they begin to move faster and usually attain a forward speed of at least 25 knots, sometimes 50 to 60 knots, as in the case of the September 1938 hurricane. A small proportion of hurricanes, however, do not recurve at all, and a few of these follow highly irregular tracks which may include a complete loop.

Hurricanes gradually decrease in intensity after they reach middle and high latitudes and move over colder water. Many lose their identity by absorption into the wind circulation around the larger extra-tropical cyclones of the North Atlantic.

THUNDERSTORMS

We stated at the beginning of this section that the extra-tropical cyclone was the ultimate cause of most of our foul weather. We said this advisedly, because in addition to the strong winds and generally wet weather which it generates, smaller-scale storms, such as *thunderstorms* and *tornadoes*, usually are created by the contrasting air masses and conflicting winds within the large-scale, over-all air circulation of the extra-tropical cyclone. Thus, thunderstorms are commonly linked to the cold front of the cyclone. But if the air comprising the warm sector is sufficiently unstable, which is often the case in summer, thunderstorms together with general rain will occur during the approach of a warm front as the warm-sector air ascends over the cold air ahead. They also develop on their own in the middle of an air mass, unaided by frontal activity.

We know a thunderstorm as a storm of short duration, arising only in a cumulonimbus cloud, attended by thunder and lightning, and marked by abrupt fluctuations of temperature, pressure and wind. A *line squall,* now usually referred to in meteorological parlance as a *squall line,* is a lengthy row of thunderstorms stretching for 100 miles or more.

Incidentally, a *shower* (as opposed to gentle, steady rain) is a smaller brother, though the rainfall and wind in it may be of considerable intensity. It characteristically is the product of relatively large cumulus, or small cumulonimbus, clouds separated from one another by blue sky. It is not accompanied by thunder and lightning.

Features of the thunderstorm cloud

In all cases the prime danger signal is a cumulus cloud growing larger. Every thunderstorm cloud has four distinctive features, although we may not always be able to see all four as other clouds may intervene in our line of sight. Fig. 1221 shows these four features; the anvil top is better illustrated in fig. 1222. These three photographs of an anvil were taken from the same position over a period of one-half hour!

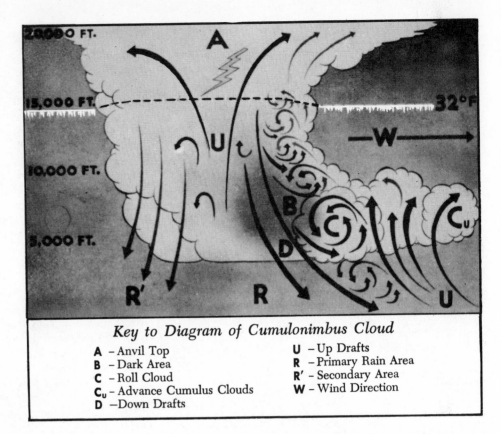

FIG. 1221 Diagram of thunderstorm cloud.
(Courtesy of Aviation Training Division, U.S. Navy)

Key to Diagram of Cumulonimbus Cloud

A – Anvil Top
B – Dark Area
C – Roll Cloud
Cᵤ – Advance Cumulus Clouds
D – Down Drafts

U – Up Drafts
R – Primary Rain Area
R' – Secondary Area
W – Wind Direction

Fig. 1221 is a drawing, by courtesy of the Navy Bureau of Aeronautics from their booklet "Thunderstorms" (Aerology Series Two), of a cumulonimbus cloud; it shows these four features diagrammatically. Starting at the top, we notice the layer of cirrus clouds, shaped like an anvil and consequently called "anvil top," leaning in the direction toward which the upper wind is blowing. This tells us the direction in which the storm is moving.

The next feature is the main body of the cloud; it is a large cumulus of great height with cauliflower sides. It must be of great height, as it must extend far above the freezing level if the cirrus anvil top is to form. Cirrus clouds are composed of ice crystals, not water droplets. The third feature is the roll cloud formed by violent air currents along the leading edge of the base of the cumulus cloud. The fourth and final feature is the dark area within the storm and extending from the base of the cloud to the earth; at the center this is rain, at the edges hail and rain.

Requirements for thunderstorm formation

There are three requirements for the formation of thunderstorms. One, there must be strong upward air currents such as are caused by a cold front burrowing under and lifting warm air or by heating of the air in contact with the surface of the earth on a summer day. Warm, humid air blowing up a mountain slope also can produce a thunderstorm. Two, the air parcels forming the storm must be buoyant relative to their neighbors outside the storm and willing, therefore, to keep on ascending higher and higher until they pass the freezing level. Third, the air must have a large concentration of water vapor. The most promising thunderstorm air is of tropical maritime origin; whenever it appears in our cruising area, especially when a cold front is approaching, we need to be suspicious.

Frequency of thunderstorms

Thunderstorms occur most frequently and with the greatest intensity in the summer over all parts of the USA. While they may strike at any hour, they prefer the late afternoon and early evening over inland and coastal waters. The surrounding land has been a good "stove" for many hours, heating the air to produce strong upward currents. Over the ocean, well away from shore, thunderstorms more commonly occur between midnight and sunrise. Finally, thunderstorms are most frequent and most violent in tropical latitudes; they are less common and less intense in the higher latitudes. The southeastern states experience as many as four thunderstorms per week in summer.

Ahead of a thunderstorm the wind may be either steady or variable, but as the *roll cloud* (fig. 1221) draws near, the wind weakens and becomes unsteady. As the roll cloud passes overhead, violent shifting winds, accompanied by strong downdrafts, may be expected. The wind velocity may reach 60 knots. Heavy rain and sometimes hail begins to fall just abaft the roll cloud. However, the weather quickly clears after the passage of the storm, which brings cooler temperatures and lower humidity.

If the cumulonimbus cloud is fully developed and towers to normal thunderstorm altitudes, 35,000 feet or more in summer, the storm will be violent. If the anvil top is low, say only 20,000 feet or so, as is usual in spring and autumn, the storm will be less severe. If the cumulonimbus cloud is not fully developed, particularly if it lacks the anvil top, and the roll cloud is missing, only a shower may be expected.

We can time the approach of a thunderstorm, once the cumulonimbus cloud is visible, by a series of bearings. If we wish, we can estimate its distance off by another

FIG. 1222 Growth of the anvil of thunderstorm cloud. Top photograph was taken at 1200, the middle at 1220, the lower at 1230 from same position as storm developed.
(Courtesy, U.S. Weather Bureau)

method. The thunder and lightning occur simultaneously at the point of lightning discharge, but we see the lightning discharge much sooner than we hear the thunder. Consequently, time this interval, in seconds. Multiply the number of seconds by 0.2; the result will be the approximate distance off in miles.

TORNADOES

When numerous thunderstorms are associated with a cold front, the storms are apt to be organized in a long, narrow band. The forward edge of this band is usually marked by a *squall line*, along which the cold downdrafts

from a series of thunderstorms meet the warm air (see fig. 1221). Here the wind direction changes suddenly in vicious gusts, and a sharp drop in temperature occurs. The importance of squall lines is that they often spawn a most destructive type of storm, the deadly *tornado*. We should keep firmly in mind the fact that tornadoes have wrecked boats on the Mississippi and elsewhere in the southern part of the USA.

Tornadoes formed at squall lines often occur in families and move with the wind that prevails in the warm sector ahead of the cold front. This wind direction is usually from the southwest. The warm air typically consists of two layers, a very moist one (source: Gulf of Mexico) near the

FIG. 1223 The terrifying "funnel" of a tornado is actually a cloud of water droplets mixed with dust and debris. Close to the ground, dust and debris are plentiful, because greatly reduced atmospheric pressure inside funnel (a lowering of pressure of the order of 50 millibars) causes air to whirl violently inward and upward.

FIG. 1224 Waterspout over St. Louis Bay, off Henderson Point, Mississippi. Note cloud of spray just above sea surface.

ground and a relatively dry layer above. The temperature decreases with altitude relatively rapidly in each layer. When this combination of air layers is lifted along a squall line or cold front, excessive instability develops and violent updrafts are created.

A tornado is essentially an air whirlpool of small horizontal extent which extends downward from a cumulonimbus cloud and has a funnel-like appearance (see fig. 1223). The average diameter of the visible funnel cloud is about 250 yards, but the destructive effects of the associated system of whirling winds may extend outward from the tornado center as much as 1/4 mile on each side. The wind speed near the core can only be estimated, but it undoubtedly is as high as 200 knots. This means almost certain death for the occupants of a boat which might have the misfortune to be in the path of a tornado.

Fortunately, the tornado belt in the USA is in the interior section of the country, but still there are boating areas which can be affected. So, if you live in the Midwest or the southern tier of states, keep your radio tuned to your local station, if weather conditions look threatening. The U.S. Weather Bureau now has a highly refined and reliable system for forecasting the likelihood of tornadoes.

Waterspouts

The marine counterpart of the tornado is the *waterspout*. The conditions favoring the formation of waterspouts at sea are similar to those conducive to the formation of tornadoes over land. Waterspouts are much more frequent in the tropics than in middle latitudes. Although they are less violent than tornadoes, nevertheless they are a real danger to small craft.

A waterspout, like a tornado, forms under a cumulonimbus cloud. A funnel-shaped protuberance first appears at the base of the cumulonimbus and grows downward toward the sea. Beneath it the water becomes agitated and a cloud of spray forms. The funnel-shaped cloud descends until it merges with the spray; it then assumes the shape of a tube that stretches from the sea surface to the base of the cloud (see fig. 1224).

The diameter of a waterspout may vary from 20 feet to 200 feet or more. Its length from the sea to the base of the cloud is usually between 1000 feet and 2000 feet. It may last from 10 minutes to half an hour. Its upper part often travels at a different speed and in a different direction from its base, so that it becomes bent and stretched-out. Finally the tube breaks at a point about one-third of the way up to the cloud base, and the "spout" at the sea surface quickly subsides.

The existence of considerably reduced air pressure at the center of a waterspout can be inferred from visible variations of the water level. A mound of water, a foot or so high, sometimes appears at the core, because the atmospheric pressure on the water surrounding the spout is perhaps 30 to 40 millibars greater than that on the sea surface inside the funnel. This difference causes the rise of water at the center.

Like the tornado, the visible part of a waterspout is composed, on the whole, of tiny water droplets formed by the condensation of water vapor in the air. Considerable quantities of salt spray, however, picked up by the strong winds at the base of the spout, are sometimes carried far aloft. This has been verified by observations of the fall of salty rain following the passage of a waterspout.

FOG

How, Why, Where and When It Forms — Its Distribution in the United States

The essential part is not always to know things; it is to know how to reason about them. This truism applies to fog. The basic causes of fog are few in number and easy to understand. What we want is a working knowledge of these causes; then we can judge if and when fog is likely to upset our plans.

Fog is merely a cloud whose base rests upon the earth, be the latter land or water. It consists of water droplets, suspended in the air, each droplet so small that it cannot be distinguished individually, yet present in such tremendous numbers that objects close at hand are obscured.

If we are to have innumerable water droplets suspended in the air, there must be plenty of water vapor originally in that air. If droplets are to form from this vapor, the air must be cooled by some means so that the vapor will condense. If the droplets are to condense in the air next to the earth, the cooling must take place at the surface of the earth. If the fog is to have any depth, successively higher

layers of air must be cooled sufficiently to cause condensation in them. Fog forms from the ground up. Thus, the land or water must be colder than the air next to it; the lower layers of air progressively must be colder than the layers above them.

If water vapor is to condense out of the air, then the temperature of the air must be lowered to or below the *dew-point temperature,* that is, the temperature at which the air is saturated with water vapor and below which condensation of water vapor will occur.

Air is said to be *saturated* with water vapor when its water-vapor content would remain unchanged if it were placed above a level surface of pure water at its own temperature. The amount of water vapor which is required to saturate a given volume of air depends on the temperature of the air, and increases as the temperature increases. The higher the temperature the more water vapor can the air hold before it becomes saturated, and the lower the temperature the less water vapor can the air hold before it becomes saturated.

If a mass of air is originally in an unsaturated state, it can be saturated by cooling it down to a temperature at which its content of water vapor is the maximum containable amount, that is to say, to the dew-point temperature. Or we can saturate it by causing more water to evaporate into it, thereby raising the dew-point temperature to a value equal to the air temperature. In regard to the latter process, unsaturated air, as it passes over rivers and lakes, over the oceans or over wet ground, picks up water vapor and has its dew point raised. Also, rain falling from higher clouds will increase the amount of water vapor in unsaturated air near the earth.

JUDGING THE LIKELIHOOD OF FOG

In order to judge the likelihood of fog formation, we should periodically measure the air temperature and dew-point temperature and see if the spread (difference) between them is getting smaller and smaller. The Navy, in its Aviation Training booklet "Fog" (Aerology Series 3) has provided us with a diagram of the change in spread; it is reproduced here as fig. 1225.

Fig. 1226 is a graph of a series of air and dew-point temperatures. By recording these temperatures and plotting their spread over a period of several hours, as is indicated by that part of the curve drawn as a solid line, we have a basis for forecasting the time at which we are likely to be fog-bound. The dot-dash portion of the curve represents actual data but it could just as easily have been drawn by extending the solid portion. If an error were made in this extrapolation, it would probably indicate that the fog would form at an earlier hour. This is on the safe side; we would be secure in our anchorage some time before the fifty-ninth minute of the eleventh hour!

Note that the curve is not a straight line. While the average decrease in spread is about one and one-half degrees (Fahrenheit) per hour, the decrease is at a much greater rate in the earlier hours. So long as we do not make unreasonable allowances for a slowing up in the rate of change of the spread, this also will help to keep us on the safe side.

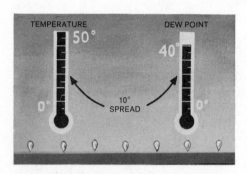

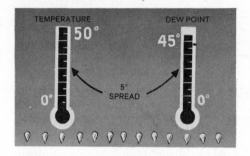

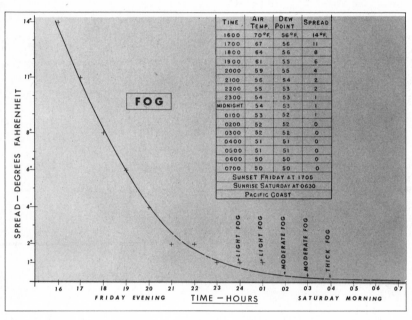

FIG. 1226   Graph of a series of air and dew-point temperatures.

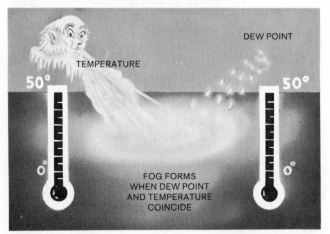

FIG. 1225   Why fog forms.
(Reproduced by courtesy of Aviation Training Division, U.S. Navy)

DETERMINING THE DEW POINT

How do we determine the dew point? By means of a simple-to-operate, inexpensive little gadget known as a *sling psychrometer* (fig. 1227). A sling psychrometer is merely two thermometers, mounted in a single holder with a handle that permits it to be whirled overhead. One thermometer, know as the *dry bulb,* has its bulb of mercury exposed directly to the air. This thermometer shows the actual temperature of the air. The other thermometer, known as the *wet bulb,* has its bulb covered with a piece of gauze. We soak this gauze in water so that the bulb is moistened. If the air is not saturated with water vapor, evaporation then takes place from the wet-bulb thermometer, and the wet bulb is cooled, since the process of evaporation requires the expenditure of heat. The reduced temperature shown by the wet-bulb thermometer, the so-called "wet-bulb temperature," represents the lowest temperature to which the air can be cooled by evaporating water into it.

FIG. 1227   A pocket-type sling psychrometer, having two 5″ etched tubes, 20° to 120° in 1° divisions.
(Courtesy Taylor Instrument Companies)

When we whirl the psychrometer we create a draft around the instrument. The ventilation so produced increases the efficiency of the evaporation process and makes the wet-bulb reading more reliable than it would be if there were little or no air movement past the wet bulb. This is the reason why the psychrometer is designed for whirling.

From the wet-bulb temperature and dry-bulb temperature, the dew point may be determined by referring to a suitable table. As we are far more interested, however, in knowing the *spread, or difference, between the air temperature and dew point,* we will save ourselves some work by using another table (Table 12-1), its use being explained in the next two paragraphs.

If the air is already actually saturated with water vapor, then no water can evaporate from the gauze and both thermometers must show the same value. The dew point then has this same numerical value and so the spread between air temperature and dew point must be zero. But, as explained above, if the air is not already saturated with

water vapor, the wet-bulb thermometer will give a lower reading than the dry-bulb thermometer. We subtract the wet-bulb temperature from the dry-bulb temperature. With this difference and the dry-bulb (the air) temperature, we consult Table 12-1 and find directly the corresponding spread between the air temperature and the dew-point temperature. This is the figure we want.

If, in the late afternoon or early evening, the spread between the air temperature and dew point is less than approximately 6°F, and the air temperature is falling, fog or greatly restricted visibility will probably be experienced in a few hours. These critical values are emphasized by the heavy line above which they lie in Table 12-1. Incidentally, should we ever want to know the dew-point temperature itself, all we need do is to subtract the spread figure given in the table from the temperature shown by the dry-bulb thermometer. Thus, when the dry-bulb thermometer indicates an air temperature of 70°F and the difference between the dry-bulb and wet-bulb temperatures is 11°F, the spread is 19°F and the dew point is 51°F.

FOUR TYPES OF FOG

We can distinguish four types of fog: (a) *radiation fog,* formed in near-calm conditions by the cooling of the ground on a clear night as a result of radiation of heat from the ground to the clear sky; (b) *advection fog,* formed by the flow of warm air over cold sea or lake; (c) *steam fog,* or "sea smoke," formed when cold air blows over much warmer water; and (d) *precipitation fog,* formed when rain coming out of warm air aloft falls through a shallow layer of cold air at the earth's surface.

Radiation fog

There are four requirements for the formation of *radiation fog* (sometimes called "ground fog"). First, the air must be stable, that is, the air next to the earth must be colder than the air a short distance aloft. Second, the air must be relatively moist. Third, the sky must be clear, so that the earth readily can lose heat by radiation to outer space. This enables the ground to become colder than the overlying air, which subsequently is cooled below its dew point both by contact with the ground (conduction of heat) and by radiative loss of heat to the ground.

The fourth requirement is that the wind must be light to calm. If there is a dead calm, the lowest strata of air will not mix with the ones above, and fog will form only to a height of two to four feet. If there is a slight motion of the air (say a wind of three to five knots) and, hence, some turbulent mixing, the cooling is spread through a layer which may extend to a height of several hundred feet above the ground. With strong winds, the cooling effect is distributed through so deep a layer that the temperature nowhere falls to the dew point and fog does not form.

Radiation fog is most prevalent in the middle and high latitudes. It is local in character and occurs most frequently in valleys and lowlands, especially near lakes and rivers where we may be cruising. The cooled air drains into these terrain depressions; the lake or river aids the process of fog formation by contributing water vapor, which raises the dew point.

This type of fog, which may be patchy or uniformly dense, forms only at night. Shortly after sunrise, it will start

TABLE 12-1   AIR TEMPERATURE —— DEWPOINT SPREAD
(All figures are in degrees Fahrenheit at 30″ pressure)

Difference Dry-Bulb Minus Wet-Bulb	Air Temperature Shown By Dry-Bulb Thermometer												
	35	40	45	50	55	60	65	70	75	80	85	90	95
1	2	2	2	2	2	2	2	1	1	1	1	1	1
2	5	5	4	4	4	3	3	3	3	3	3	3	2
3	7	7	7	6	5	5	5	4	4	4	4	4	4
4	10	10	9	8	7	7	6	6	6	6	5	5	5
5	14	12	11	10	10	9	8	8	7	7	7	7	6
6	18	15	14	13	12	11	10	9	9	8	8	8	8
7	22	19	17	16	14	13	12	11	11	10	10	9	9
8	28	22	20	18	17	15	14	13	12	12	11	11	10
9	35	27	23	21	19	17	16	15	14	13	13	12	12
10	-	33	27	24	22	20	18	17	16	15	14	14	13
11	-	40	32	28	25	22	20	19	18	17	16	15	15
12	-	-	38	32	28	25	23	21	20	18	17	17	16
13	-	-	45	37	31	28	25	23	21	20	19	18	17
14	-	-	-	42	35	31	28	26	24	22	21	20	19
15	-	-	-	50	40	35	31	28	26	24	23	21	21

Opposite — Difference Dry-Bulb Minus Wet-Bulb and
Under   — Air Temperature Shown By Dry-Bulb Thermometer
Read   — Value of Spread: Air Temperature minus Dewpoint Temperature

Based on U.S. Weather Bureau Psychrometric Tables

FIG. 1228 Fog bank over Lake Huron. This is basically an advection-type fog which has formed over an area of relatively cold water. When the wind is very light and unsteady, as in this case, fog tends to concentrate in patches, even after it has drifted away from its source.

FIG. 1229 Sea smoke in Great Harbor, Woods Hole, Massachusetts, 0915 EST, 31 December 1962. Water temperature 31.6°F; air temperature (30 feet above sea level) +5°F. Wind NW 20 knots. Height of steaming approximately 15 feet. Rigging of vessel encountering this type of condition will become coated with rime ice. Note frosty deposit on beach grass in lower right corner of photograph.
(Courtesy of P. M. Saunders, Woods Hole Oceanographic Institution)

to evaporate ("burn off") over the land, the lower layers being the first to go. It is slow to clear over water, since the temperature of the water does not vary nearly as much from day to night as does the temperature of the land.

Advection fog

Radiation fog bothers us chiefly in the late summer and early autumn; *advection fog* can be an annoyance at any season. (Advection means transport by horizontal motion.) Winds carrying warm, moist air over a colder surface produce advection fog. The dew point of the air must be higher than the temperature of the surface over which the air is moving. Thus, the air can be cooled below its dew point by conduction and by radiation of heat to the colder surface. Other requirements for the formation of advection fog are as follows: (a) the air at a height of 100 feet or so must be warmer than the air just above the surface; (b) the temperature of the surface—be it land or water—must become progressively colder in the direction toward which the air is moving. Fig. 1230, again by courtesy of the U.S. Navy from its "Flying the Weather," illustrates the formation of advection fog along the coast and fig. 1231

its formation at sea. Advection fog may form day or night, winter or summer, over the sea.

Coastal Fog. For yachtsmen the most bothersome variety is *coastal fog* (fig. 1230). When steady winds blow landward and carry warm oceanic air across cold coastal water, the resulting fog may blanket a great length of coastline and, especially at night, may extend many miles inland up bays and rivers. For example, let's go to the Pacific coast, where the water close to the land is often colder than the water to westward. The prevailing winds in summer are onshore and the air, since it frequently has come from mid-Pacific, usually is nearly saturated with water vapor. Fig. 1230 illustrates the result; the same thing happens when southerly winds carry air across the Gulf Stream and thence northward across the colder Atlantic coastal waters. Advection fog also may form over the larger inland lakes whenever relatively warm and moist air is carried over their colder surfaces.

Advection fog is generally much harder to dissipate than is radiation fog. A wind shift or a marked increase in wind velocity usually is required. Sunshine has no effect on it over the water.

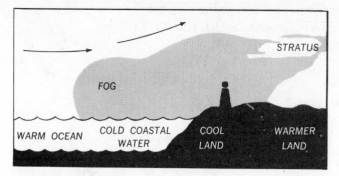

FIG. 1230 Coastal fogs are common along the West Coast—warm ocean, cool coastal water, frequent winds from the sea. (Courtesy Aviation Training Division, U.S. Navy)

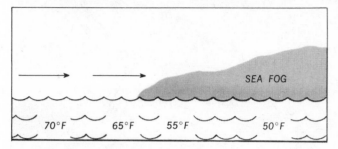

FIG. 1231 Most persistent sea fog is an advection fog that forms when air blows from warm sea to cold sea.

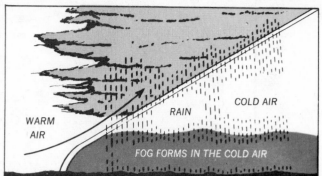

FIG. 1233 Formation of precipitation fog.

American coastal waters are concerned, this variety of steam fog occurs most frequently off the coasts of Maine and Nova Scotia, and in the Gulf of St. Lawrence, where it can be a serious navigational hazard. However, its occurrence is not restricted to the higher latitudes. Off the east coast of the United States it has been observed as far south as Florida and it occurs occasionally over the coastal waters of the Gulf of Mexico.

Steam fog

On the Mississippi and Ohio rivers, a special type of fog, known as *steam fog* is a particular hazard to late evening or early morning cruising in the autumn. When cold air passes over much warmer water, the lowest layer of air is rapidly supplied with heat and water vapor. Mixing of this lowest layer with unmodified cold air above can, under certain conditions, produce a supersaturated (i.e., foggy) mixture. Owing to the fact that the water is much warmer than the air, vertical air currents are created, and we observe the phenomenon of steaming. Hence, this type of fog is called "steam fog"; it forms in just the same way as steam over a hot bath.

Sea Smoke. When, in winter, very cold air (having a temperature less than about 10°F) blows off the land and across the adjacent coastal waters, steam fog may be widespread and very dense. It is then known as *"sea smoke"* (sometimes called *"Arctic sea smoke"*). As far as North

Precipitation fog

As mentioned earlier, we can distinguish a fourth type of fog, which we may call "precipitation fog," or "rain fog." When rain, after descending through a layer of warm air aloft, falls into a shallow layer of relatively cold air at the earth's surface, there will be evaporation from the warm raindrops into the colder air (see fig. 1233). Under certain conditions, this process will raise the water-vapor content of the cold air above the saturation point and fog will form. Its mode of formation is similar to that of the fog produced in the bathroom when one takes a hot shower.

It may be noted that both steam fog and rain fog are basically the result of evaporation from relatively warm water, a process which increases the dew point. These fogs can be placed in the single category of *"warm-surface"* fogs. Likewise, radiation fog and advection fog come under the single heading of *"cold-surface"* fogs.

FIG. 1232 Steam fog forming, then dissipating upwards, over pond near Mount Kisco, N.Y., 0700 EST, 12 October 1964. Air temperature approximately 25°F; water temperature not known, but probably 50°F or higher. Wind less than 1 knot. (Photograph by Caroline S. Emmons)

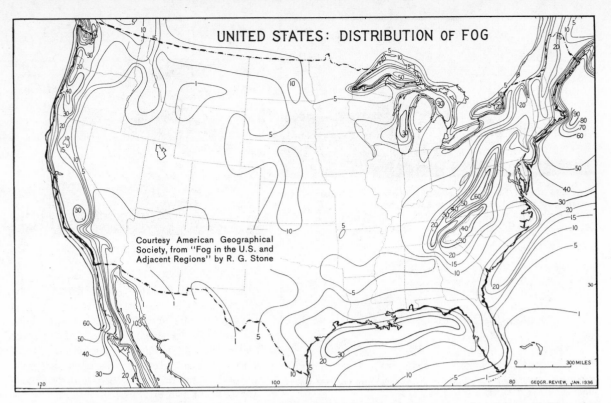

FIG. 1234 Map showing distribution of fog in the United States. Isopleths show mean annual number of days with "dense fog, i.e., fogs obscuring visibility to 1000 feet or less." In order to bring out more detail in the large portion of the country where fogginess is less than 20 days, an interval of 5 days was selected. For regions with more than 20 days of fog a 10-day interval is used.

DISTRIBUTION OF FOG IN THE UNITED STATES

Turning our attention now to the distribution of fog (all types included) in the United States, we find that the coastal sections most frequently beset by fog are (1) the area from the Strait of Juan de Fuca to Point Arguello (Calif.), on the Pacific Coast, and (2) the area from the Bay of Fundy to Montauk Point (N.Y.), on the Atlantic Coast. In these waters the average annual number of hours of fog occurrence exceeds 900, that is, more than 10% of the entire year. In the foggiest parts of these areas, namely, off the coast of Northern California and the coast of Maine, fog is present about 20% of the year.

As we go southward along both the Atlantic and Pacific Coasts the frequency of fog decreases, but it does so much more rapidly on the Atlantic Coast than on the Pacific. Hence, we find that the average annual fog frequency over the waters adjacent to Los Angeles and San Diego is about three times that in the same latitude along the Atlantic Coast.

SEASONAL FREQUENCIES

The *time of maximum occurrence* of fog off the Pacific Coast varies somewhat with the various localities and, of course, with the individual year. In general, however, over the stretch from Cape Flattery (Wash.) to Point Arguello the season of most frequent fog comprises the months of July, August, September and October, with more than 50% of the annual number of foggy days occurring during this period. However, along the lower coast of California, that is, from Los Angeles southward, the foggiest months are those from September through February, and the least foggy from May through July.

On the Atlantic side: Off the coast of New England the foggiest months are usually June, July and August, with a maximum of fog generally occurring during July, in which month fog normally is encountered from one-third to one-half of the time. Off the Middle Atlantic Coast, however, fog occurs mostly in the winter and spring months, with a distinct tendency toward minimum frequency in summer and autumn. Along the South Atlantic Coast (from Cape Hatteras to the tip of Florida) and in the Gulf of Mexico fog rarely creates a problem for the yachtsman. It is virtually non-existent during the summer, and even in the winter and early spring season (December through March), when it has maximum frequency, the number of days with fog hardly anywhere exceeds 20, on the average, during this four-month period.

The *fog regime of the Great Lakes* is essentially like that of the oceanic coastal waters in middle latitudes; the Great Lakes as a whole tend to have more fog in the warmer season. The explanation of this circumstance is to be found in the comparison of the lake temperatures with the air temperatures over the surrounding land. From March or April to the beginning of September the lakes are, on the average, colder than the air. Hence, whenever the dew-point temperature is sufficiently high, conditions are favorable for the formation of advection fog over the water.

The greatest fogginess occurs when and where the lakes are coldest in relation to the air blowing off the surrounding land. On Lake Superior, north-central Lake Michigan, and northwestern Lake Huron the *time* of maximum frequency is late May and June; elsewhere it is late April and May. As to the *location* of maximum fogginess, since the lake temperatures become colder from south to north and from the shores outward, the occurrence of fog increases northward and towards the central parts of each lake.

Observations Afloat—Weather signs

We have already discussed fog and how we can use a sling psychrometer to help us in forecasting its occurrence. There are a few other weather instruments which are practical on shipboard and which provide us with helpful information.

WIND OBSERVATIONS

Every sailor is familiar with the *wind direction indicators* that may be mounted at the masthead. Because a boat, at anchor or under way, can head in any direction all around the compass, a few mental calculations are necessary before we can use this indicator or an owner's flag or club burgee to determine the true direction of the wind. At anchor, the fly will give us the bearing of the wind relative to the boat's head; this must be converted to the true bearing of the wind itself. We can use our compass to obtain these values, provided we know its deviation on our heading and know the variation for our anchorage. Also, we need to remember that wind direction is always stated as the true direction *from* which, not toward which, the wind is blowing.

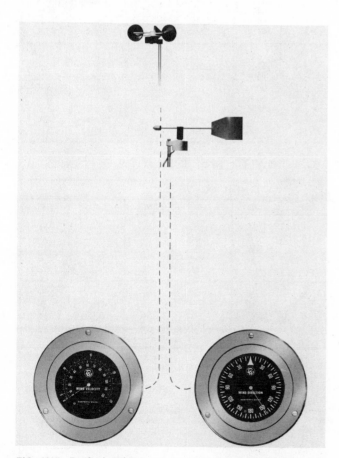

FIG. 1235 Danforth/White's anemometer with flush-mounted wind velocity indicator supplies accurate readings on two scales (0-25 and 0-120 knots). Two-wire conductor leads from indicator to masthead or spreader. Wind direction indicator is a matching unit.

The anemometer

For measuring *wind velocity* we need something else. This is an *anemometer;* the principal parts of the instrument are illustrated in fig. 1235. The anemometer is essentially a speedometer. It consists of a rotor with conical cups attached to the ends of spokes and is designed for mounting at the masthead, where the wind is caught by the cups, causing them to turn at a speed proportional to the speed of the wind. Indications of the rotor's speed are transmitted to an indicator which may be mounted in the cabin.

In the type of instrument illustrated in fig. 1235, the indicator is direct-reading, in two scales from 0 to 25 and 0 to 120 knots for velocity, gusts and variations. Battery drain (.09 amp.) is insignificant. A 60-foot wire cable is supplied to connect the rotor aloft with the illuminated indicator below. At anchor, the reading is the actual or true wind velocity at masthead height.

True and apparent wind

So far we have been considering the determination of the direction and speed of the wind while at anchor. Under way, the determination is more difficult, but the Oceanographic Office of the Navy has worked out the problem, so we may as well use their results. Table 12-2 is based on wind tables formerly published in Bowditch. Using our true course and speed, we can determine from this table the approximate *true* wind direction and velocity, provided we know the *apparent* direction and velocity. Our wind indicator or owner's flag will give us the apparent direction and our anemometer will give us the apparent velocity.

The Beaufort Scale

Another method is to estimate the strength of the wind in terms of the *Beaufort Scale* of Wind Force. Visually we can observe the sea condition and note the Beaufort number to which it corresponds (see Table 12-3). The range of wind velocity represented by each force number on the Beaufort scale is shown in the extreme left-hand column of Table 12-3.

Wind direction can be judged by observing the direction from which the smallest ripples are coming, since these ripples always run with the wind, responding instantly to changes in wind direction.

We don't need to determine wind direction and velocity with great precision, but reasonable estimates are helpful in preparing our own local forecasts. Estimating direction to two points is sufficient; within one Beaufort number is enough for velocity. By observing wind direction and velocity regularly and making a record of them we can obtain clues concerning potential weather developments as the wind shifts direction and changes its velocity.

TABLE 12-2

TRUE FORCE AND DIRECTION OF THE WIND FROM ITS APPARENT FORCE AND DIRECTION ON A BOAT UNDER WAY

APPARENT WIND VELOCITY (Knots)	SPEED OF BOAT							
	5 Knots TRUE WIND		10 Knots TRUE WIND		15 Knots TRUE WIND		20 Knots TRUE WIND	
	Points off Bow	Velocity Knots	Points off Bow	Velocity Knots	Points off Bow	Velocity Knots	Points off Bow	Velocity Knots
I. APPARENT WIND DIRECTION IS DEAD AHEAD								
Calm	D. As.	5 K.	D. As.	10 K.	D. As.	15 K.	D. As.	20 K.
4 K.	D. As.	1 K.	D. As.	6 K.	D. As.	11 K.	D. As.	16 K.
8 K.	D. Ah.	3 K.	D. As.	2 K.	D. As.	7 K.	D. As.	12 K.
12 K.	D. Ah.	7 K.	D. Ah.	2 K.	D. As.	3 K.	D. As.	8 K.
16 K.	D. Ah.	11 K.	D. Ah.	6 K.	D. Ah.	1 K.	D. As.	4 K.
22 K.	D. Ah.	17 K.	D. Ah.	12 K.	D. Ah.	7 K.	D. Ah.	2 K.
30 K.	D. Ah.	25 K.	D. Ah.	20 K.	D. Ah.	15 K.	D. Ah.	10 K.
42 K.	D. Ah.	37 K.	D. Ah.	32 K.	D. Ah.	27 K.	D. Ah.	22 K.
60 K.	D. Ah.	55 K.	D. Ah.	50 K.	D. Ah.	45 K.	D. Ah.	40 K.
II. APPARENT WIND DIRECTION IS 4 POINTS (BROAD) OFF THE BOW								
4 K.	11 pts.	4 K.	14 pts.	8 K.	15 pts.	12 K.	15 pts.	17 K.
8 K.	7 pts.	6 K.	11 pts.	7 K.	13 pts.	11 K.	14 pts.	15 K.
12 K.	6 pts.	9 K.	9 pts.	9 K.	11 pts.	11 K.	13 pts.	14 K.
16 K.	5 pts.	13 K.	7 pts.	11 K.	10 pts.	12 K.	11 pts.	14 K.
22 K.	5 pts.	19 K.	6 pts.	16 K.	8 pts.	15 K.	9 pts.	16 K.
30 K.	5 pts.	27 K.	6 pts.	24 K.	7 pts.	22 K.	8 pts.	21 K.
42 K.	4 pts.	39 K.	5 pts.	36 K.	6 pts.	33 K.	6 pts.	31 K.
60 K.	4 pts.	57 K.	5 pts.	53 K.	5 pts.	51 K.	6 pts.	48 K.
III. APPARENT WIND DIRECTION IS 8 POINTS OFF THE BOW (ABEAM)								
4 K.	13 pts.	6 K.	14 pts.	11 K.	15 pts.	16 K.	15 pts.	20 K.
8 K.	11 pts.	9 K.	13 pts.	13 K.	14 pts.	17 K.	14 pts.	22 K.
12 K.	10 pts.	13 K.	12 pts.	16 K.	13 pts.	19 K.	13 pts.	23 K.
16 K.	10 pts.	17 K.	11 pts.	19 K.	12 pts.	22 K.	13 pts.	26 K.
22 K.	9 pts.	23 K.	10 pts.	24 K.	11 pts.	27 K.	12 pts.	30 K.
30 K.	9 pts.	30 K.	10 pts.	32 K.	10 pts.	34 K.	11 pts.	36 K.
42 K.	9 pts.	42 K.	9 pts.	43 K.	10 pts.	45 K.	10 pts.	47 K.
60 K.	8 pts.	60 K.	9 pts.	61 K.	9 pts.	62 K.	10 pts.	63 K.
IV. APPARENT WIND DIRECTION IS 12 POINTS OFF THE BOW (BROAD ON THE QUARTER)								
4 K.	14 pts.	8 K.	15 pts.	13 K.	15 pts.	18 K.	15 pts.	23 K.
8 K.	14 pts.	12 K.	14 pts.	17 K.	15 pts.	21 K.	15 pts.	26 K.
12 K.	13 pts.	16 K.	14 pts.	20 K.	14 pts.	25 K.	15 pts.	30 K.
16 K.	13 pts.	20 K.	14 pts.	24 K.	14 pts.	29 K.	14 pts.	33 K.
22 K.	13 pts.	26 K.	13 pts.	30 K.	14 pts.	34 K.	14 pts.	39 K.
30 K.	13 pts.	34 K.	13 pts.	38 K.	13 pts.	42 K.	14 pts.	46 K.
42 K.	12 pts.	46 K.	13 pts.	50 K.	13 pts.	54 K.	13 pts.	58 K.
60 K.	12 pts.	64 K.	13 pts.	67 K.	13 pts.	71 K.	13 pts.	75 K.

CONVERSION OF POINTS OFF BOW TO TRUE DIRECTION OF WIND

POINTS OFF BOW	BOAT'S HEADING — TRUE							
	000°	045°	090°	135°	180°	225°	270°	315°
I. WHEN WIND DIRECTION OBTAINED FROM TABLE ABOVE IS OFF STARBOARD BOW								
Dead Ahead	N	NE	E	SE	S	SW	W	NW
4 points	NE	E	SE	S	SW	W	NW	N
8 points	E	SE	S	SW	W	NW	N	NE
12 points	SE	S	SW	W	NW	N	NE	E
Dead Astern	S	SW	W	NW	N	NE	E	SE
II. WHEN WIND DIRECTION OBTAINED FROM TABLE ABOVE IS OFF PORT BOW								
Dead Ahead	N	NE	E	SE	S	SW	W	NW
4 points	NW	N	NE	E	SE	S	SW	W
8 points	W	NW	N	NE	E	SE	S	SW
12 points	SW	W	NW	N	NE	E	SE	S
Dead Astern	S	SW	W	NW	N	NE	E	SE

Abreviations: D. As. = Dead Astern.   D. Ah. = Dead Ahead.   K. = Knots.   pts. = Points off bow.

TO USE THIS TABLE

1. **With Wind Direction Indicator:** Determine Apparent Wind Direction off the Bow.
2. **With Anemometer:** Determine Apparent Wind Velocity, in Knots.
3. **Enter Upper Part of Table:** Use portion for nearest Apparent Wind Direction Opposite Apparent Wind Velocity and under nearest Speed of Boat, read Wind Direction in Points off Bow and True Wind Velocity in Knots. Note whether True Wind Direction is off Starboard or Port Bow.
4. **Enter Lower Part of Table:** Use portion for proper Bow: Starboard or Port. Opposite Points off Bow and under nearest Boat's True Heading, read True Wind Direction.
5. **Log:** Record True Wind Direction as obtained from Lower Part of Table and True Wind Velocity as obtained from Upper Part of Table in Boat's Weather Log.

TABLE 12-3

DETERMINATION OF WIND SPEED BY SEA CONDITION

Knots	Descriptive	Sea Conditions	Wind force (Beaufort)	Probable wave height (in ft.)
0-1	Calm	Sea smooth and mirror-like.	0	—
1-3	Light air	Scale-like ripples without foam crests.	1	¼
4-6	Light breeze	Small, short wavelets; crests have a glassy appearance and do not break.	2	½
7-10	Gentle breeze	Large wavelets; some crests begin to break; foam of glassy appearance. Occasional white foam crests.	3	2
11-16	Moderate breeze	Small waves, becoming longer; fairly frequent white foam crests.	4	4
17-21	Fresh breeze	Moderate waves, taking a more pronounced long form; many white foam crests; there may be some spray.	5	6
22-27	Strong breeze	Large waves begin to form; white foam crests are more extensive everywhere; there may be some spray.	6	10
28-33	Near gale	Sea heaps up and white foam from breaking waves begins to be blown in streaks along the direction of the wind; spindrift begins.	7	14
34-40	Gale	Moderately high waves of greater length; edges of crests break into spindrift; foam is blown in well-marked streaks along the direction of the wind.	8	18
41-47	Strong gale	High waves; dense streaks of foam along the direction of the wind; crests of waves begin to topple, tumble, and roll over; spray may reduce visibility.	9	23
48-55	Storm	Very high waves with long overhanging crests. The resulting foam in great patches is blown in dense white streaks along the direction of the wind. On the whole, the surface of the sea is white in appearance. The tumbling of the sea becomes heavy and shock-like. Visibility is reduced.	10	29
56-63	Violent Storm	Exceptionally high waves that may obscure small and medium-sized ships. The sea is completely covered with long white patches of foam lying along the direction of the wind. Everywhere the edges of the wave crests are blown into froth. Visibility reduced.	11	37
64-71	Hurricane	The air is filled with foam and spray. Sea completely white with driving spray; visibility very much reduced.	12	45

(Courtesy U.S. Weather Bureau)

FIG. 1236 A modern aneroid barometer, graduated in both millibars (inner scale) and inches of mercury (outer scale). Pointer indicates reading at last setting.
(Courtesy Airguide Instrument Company)

THE BAROMETER

Another weather instrument with which we are all familiar is the *aneroid barometer*. The one illustrated (fig. 1236) has several interesting features.

First, there are two *pressure scales*. Not a few of us are accustomed to thinking of barometric pressure in terms of *inches of mercury*, so the outer scale is graduated in these units. Weather maps are now printed with the pressures shown in *millibars* and many radio weather reports specify this value. Consequently, the inner scale is graduated in millibars, and so we don't have to worry about conversions between units.

Second, it is a rugged instrument, a feature not to be despised on board a 40-footer. It has a high order of accuracy.

Third, it has the usual reference hand, so we can keep track of changes in pressure.

The words "Fair—Change—Rain," in themselves, when they appear on the face of an aneroid barometer, are meaningless. It is not the actual barometric pressure that is so important in forecasting; it is the *direction* and *rate of change of pressure*. The words may be misleading if this fact is not clearly understood.

How it is used

Now, a good barometer is a helpful instrument, *provided* a few things: provided we read it at regular intervals and keep a record of the readings; provided we remember that there is much more to weather than just barometric pressure.

An individual reading of the barometer tells us only the pressure being exerted by the atmosphere on the earth's surface at the particular point of observation. But, suppose we have logged the pressure readings at fairly regular intervals, as follows:

Time	Pressure	Change
0700	30.02 inches	—
0800	30.00	−0.02
0900	29.97	−0.03
1000	29.93	−0.04
1100	29.88	−0.05
1200	29.82	−0.06

The pressure is falling, at an increasing rate. Trouble is brewing. A fall of 0.02 inch per hour is a low rate of fall; consequently, this figure would not be particularly disturbing. But a fall of 0.05 inch per hour is a pretty high rate.

Next, there is a normal *daily change in pressure*. The pressure is usually at its maximum value about 1000 and 2200 each day, at its minimum value about 0400 and 1600. The variation between minimum and maximum may be as much as 0.05 inch change in these six-hour intervals (about 0.01 inch change per hour). Thus, when the pressure normally would increase about 0.03 inch (0700 to 1000) our pressure fell 0.09 inch.

Suppose, now, around 1200 we also observed that the wind was blowing from the NE with increasing force and that the barometer continued to fall at a high rate. A rocky lee shore close aboard would not be pleasant to contemplate as a severe northeast gale is on its way. On the other hand, given the same barometer reading of about 29.80, rising rapidly with the wind going to west, we could expect improving weather. Quite a difference.

Barometer rules

A few general rules are often helpful. First, *foul* weather is usually forecast by a *falling* barometer with winds from the *east* quadrants; *clearing* and *fair* weather is usually forecast by winds shifting to *west* quadrants with a *rising* barometer. Second, there are the rules formerly printed on every Weather Bureau daily surface weather map:

"When the wind sets in from points between south and southeast and the barometer falls steadily, a storm is approaching from the west or northwest, and its center will pass near or north of the observer within 12 to 24 hours, with the wind shifting to northwest by way of south and southwest.

"When the wind sets in from points between east and northeast and the barometer falls steadily, a storm is approaching from the south or southwest, and its center will pass near or to the south of the observer within 12 to 24 hours, with the wind shifting to northwest by way of north.

"The rapidity of the storm's approach and its intensity will be indicated by the rate and amount of fall in the barometer."

There are some other generally useful barometer rules.

With our sling psychrometer we can determine the air temperature, so: a falling barometer and a rising thermometer often forecast rain; barometer and thermometer rising together often forecast fine weather. A slowly rising barometer forecasts settled weather; a steady, slow fall of pressure unsettled or wet weather.

Barometric changes and wind velocity

We shall now give some rules relating barometric changes to changes in wind velocity. First, it is generally true that a *rapidly falling barometer* forecasts the development of strong winds. This is so because a falling barometer indicates the approach or development of a LOW, and the pressure gradient is usually steep in the neighborhood of a low-pressure center. On the other hand, a *rising barometer* is associated with the prospect of lighter winds to come. This is true because a rising barometer indicates the approach or development of a HIGH, and the pressure gradient is characteristically small in the neighborhood of a high-pressure center.

The barometer does not necessarily fall before or during a strong breeze. The wind often blows hard without any appreciable accompanying change in the barometer. This means that a steep pressure gradient exists (isobars close together, as seen on the weather map) but that the well-developed HIGH or LOW associated with the steep pressure gradient is practically stationary. In this case the wind may be expected to blow hard for some time; any slackening or change will take place gradually.

It not infrequently happens that the barometer falls quite rapidly, yet the wind remains comparatively light. If we remember the relation between wind velocity and pressure gradient, we conclude that the gradient must be comparatively small (isobars relatively far apart). The rapid fall of the barometer must be accounted for, then, in either one or both of two ways. Either a LOW with a weak pressure gradient on its forward side is approaching rapidly, or there is a rapid decrease of pressure taking place over the surrounding area, or both. In such a situation the pressure gradient at the rear of the LOW is often steep, and in that case strong winds will set in as soon as the barometer commences to rise. (It will rise rapidly under these circumstances.) The fact, however, that the barometer is now rising indicates that decreasing winds may soon be expected.

The barometer and wind shifts

Nearly all extra-tropical cyclones display an unsymmetrical distribution of pressure. The pressure gradients are seldom the same in the front and rear of an extra-tropical cyclone. During the approach of a LOW the barometer alone gives no clue as to how many points the wind will shift and what velocity it will have after the passage of the low-pressure system. This is particularly applicable to situations in which the wind blows from a southerly direction while the barometer is falling. The cessation of the fall of the barometer will coincide with a *veering* (gradual or sudden) shift of the wind to a more westerly direction. Unfortunately, an observer having no information other than that supplied by his barometer cannot foretell the exact features of the change.

In using barometric indications for local forecasting it is most important to remember that weather changes are

FIG. 1237   Forecast—Severe Storm. Squall line clouds mark an advancing cold front; storm will be severe, with sharp, violent shift in wind, rain and probably lightning and thunder. (Courtesy U.S. Weather Bureau)

influenced by the characteristics of the earth's surface in our locality. All rules should be checked against experience in our own cruising waters before we can place full confidence in their validity.

VISUAL WEATHER SIGNS

In addition to our instrumental weather observations there are certain *visual signs* that we can record. First, we should note the *visibility*. Haze, dust and smoke are nearly as important as fog. Many of the tiny particles which are suspended in the air and which reduce the visibility serve as nuclei on which water vapor can condense. Unless the water vapor in the air does condense, we can have no fog nor clouds. If haze thickens to a degree where it restricts the visibility to 3 miles, we have an indication that condensation has begun on the more active condensation nuclei and a warning that fog may soon develop.

Next, we should note the *clouds*. First, we ask ourselves: "What form (or forms) of cloud is (or are) present?" In order to answer this question we need to know the international system of cloud classification. This system resembles the method of classification used in the biological sciences. The different cloud types are given descriptive names which depend mainly upon appearance, but also sometimes upon the processes of formation as seen by an observer on the ground.

Cloud forms classified

Despite an almost infinite variety of shapes and forms, it is possible to define 10 basic types. The following definitions are taken from the 1956 edition of the International Cloud Atlas.

1. Cirrus (Ci)—Detached clouds in the form of white, delicate filaments, or white or mostly white patches or narrow bands. These clouds have a fibrous (hair-like) appearance, or a silky sheen, or both.

2. Cirrocumulus (Cc)—Thin, white patch, sheet or layer of cloud without shading, composed of very small elements in the form of grains, ripples, etc., merged or separate, and

H. T. Floreen

FIG. 1238   Cumulus clouds of fair weather, illustrating situation in which atmosphere is stable a short distance above bases of clouds which, therefore, cannot grow vertically. Appearance of sky indicates fine weather will continue for at least another 6 hours.

more or less regularly arranged; most of the elements have an apparent width of less than one degree.

3. Cirrostratus (Cs)—Transparent, whitish cloud veil of fibrous (hair-like) or smooth appearance, totally or partly covering the sky, and generally producing halo phenomena.

4. Altocumulus (Ac)—White or gray, or both white and gray, patch, sheet or layer of cloud, generally with shading, composed of laminae, rounded masses, rolls, etc., which are sometimes partly fibrous or diffuse, and which may or may not be merged; most of the regularly arranged small elements usually have an apparent width between one and five degrees.

5. Altostratus (As)—Grayish or bluish cloud sheet or layer of striated, fibrous or uniform appearance, totally or partly covering the sky, and having parts thin enough to reveal the sun at least vaguely, as through ground glass. Altostratus does not show halo phenomena.

6. Nimbostratus (Ns)—Gray cloud layer, often dark, the appearance of which is rendered diffuse by more or less continuously falling rain or snow, which in most cases reaches the ground. It is thick enough throughout to blot out the sun. Low, ragged clouds frequently occur below the layer, with which they may or may not merge.

7. Stratocumulus (Sc)—Gray or whitish, or both gray and whitish, patch, sheet or layer of cloud which almost always has dark parts, composed of tessellations, rounded masses, rolls, etc., which are non-fibrous (except for virga) and which may or may not be merged; most of the regularly arranged small elements have an apparent width of more than five degrees.

8. Stratus (St)—Generally gray cloud layer with a fairly uniform base, which may give drizzle, ice prisms or snow grains. When the sun is visible through the cloud, its outline is clearly discernible. Stratus does not produce halo phenomena except, possibly, at very low temperatures. Sometimes stratus appears in the form of ragged patches.

9. Cumulus (Cu)—Detached clouds, generally dense and with sharp outlines, developing vertically in the form of rising mounds, domes or towers, of which the bulging upper part often resembles a cauliflower. The sunlit parts of these clouds are mostly brilliant white; their bases are relatively dark and nearly horizontal. Sometimes cumulus is ragged.

10. Cumulonimbus (Cb)—Heavy and dense cloud, with a considerable vertical extent, in the form of a mountain or huge towers. At least part of its upper portion is usually smooth, or fibrous or striated, and nearly always flattened; this part often spreads out in the shape of an anvil or vast plume. Under the base of this cloud, which is often very dark, there are frequently low ragged clouds either merged

FIG. 1239 Semi-transparent altocumulus clouds. Clouds in this picture clearly show signs of evaporation; edges of individual elements are frayed and indistinct. This indicates continuing fair weather.

FIG. 1240 Altostratus clouds, together with some altocumulus, over Mt. Kisco, New York, 1655 EST, 11 February 1965. (Note aircraft condensation trail in lower left portion of photograph.) At this time a LOW was centered over southeastern Missouri, moving northeastward. Rain began to fall about 7 hours after picture was taken.

(Photograph by Caroline S. Emmons)

with it or not, and precipitation, sometimes in the form of virga (precipitation trails).

Significance of changing cloud forms

Having identified the cloud form (or forms) present in the sky, we should next note whether the clouds are *increasing* or *decreasing* in amount, and whether they are *lowering* or *lifting*. In general, thickening and lowering of a cloud layer, be it a layer of cirrostratus, altocumulus or altostratus, is a sign of approaching wet weather. On the other hand, when a layer of clouds shows signs of evaporation, that is, when holes or openings begin to appear in a layer of altostratus, or the elements of an altocumulus layer are frayed and indistinct at the edges, we have an indication of improving weather or, at least, delay of the development of foul weather.

Finally, we should note the *sequence of cloud forms* during the past few hours. Cirrus clouds are frequently the advance agents of an approaching extra-tropical cyclone, especially if they are followed by a layer of cirrostratus. In this case the problem is to forecast the track the low-pressure center will take to one side or the other, the nearness of approach of the center and the intensity of the low.

As the clouds thicken steadily from Ci to Cs and from Cs to As, we naturally expect further development to Ns with its rain or snow. There are usually contrary indications if such is not to be the case, or if the precipitation will arrive late, amount to little and end soon, or will come in two brief periods separated by several hours of mild, more or less sunny, weather.

If the northern horizon remains clear until a layer of altostratus clouds overspreads most of the sky, the low-pressure center will probably be passing to the south without bringing precipitation. If the northern horizon is slow in clouding up but becomes covered by the time the cloud sheet is principally As, there will probably be some precipitation but not much. If the cloud sheet, after increasing to As, breaks up into Ac and the sky above is seen to have lost most of its covering of Cs, the low-pressure area is either weakening or passing on to the north.

The approach of a squall line accompanied by thunderstorms may be detected an hour or more in advance by observing the thin white arch of the cirrus border to the anvil top of the approaching cumulonimbus cloud. The atmosphere ahead of a squall line is often so hazy that only this whitish arch will reveal the presence of a moderately distant Cb, for the shadowed air under the dense anvil will be invisible behind the sunlit hazy blue air near the observer. Thus this part of the sky will appear to be clear and will resemble the blue sky above the cirrus arch.

THE WEATHER LOG

Although the latest Weather Bureau forecasts are readily available to us via the medium of radio, it is often helpful to keep a record of our own observations of clouds and weather as they develop. This procedure will enable us to check the reliability of the latest prediction. Occasionally the professional forecaster misjudges the future rate of travel of the weather pattern, which may move faster or

TABLE 12-4A Boat Weather Log.

```
                    BOAT WEATHER LOG


Yacht_____At/Passage_____to_____
Day___Date_____Time Zone_____Skipper_____
1.  Latest Weather Map: Date___Time_____Summary of forecast and
    of principal regional weather features:_____
    _____
    _____
    _____
    _____


2.  Radio Weather Reports Received (state source and time):_____
    _____
    _____
    _____
    _____


3.  Local Weather Observations (see over for record)

4.  Remarks and Local Forecast for Next____Hours (state time fore-
    cast effective):_____
    _____
    _____
    _____
    _____
```

TABLE 12-4B Local Weather Observations.

```
                 LOCAL WEATHER OBSERVATIONS


Time -- ZT, Navy Style

Latitude - degrees, minutes
Longitude -    "        "
Course - degrees psc
       -    "     true
Speed - Knots

Barometer - in. or mb.
          - tendency
Clouds - form
       - moving from
       - amount
       - changing to
Sea - condition
    - swells
    - moving from
Temperatures - air, dry bulb
             - dewpoint
             - water
Visibility
Wind - direction, true
     - shifting to
     - velocity, true
     - force (Beaufort)
Weather - present
```

more slowly than anticipated. (This is known as an error of timing.) Or there may occur a new, unforeseen development in the pattern.

Table 12-4 shows a form of *Weather Log* which is similar to that used in the Weather Course of the United States Power Squadrons. Table 12-4 A is the face sheet, Table 12-4 B the reverse side. The first weather items recorded are based on a perusal of the latest weather map (if available to us) and a summary of radio reports received. Then

we use the reverse side to jot down our local observations. Sufficient columns are available to permit the entry of these data six times during one 24-hour day, or at four-hour intervals. Entries may be made using the standard weather code symbols or any other way we choose, provided we use the same system consistently.

From these records we can estimate in what way and to what extent the actual weather during the next few hours is likely to differ from the official forecast.

FIG. 1241 Semi-transparent layer of altostratus clouds over Mt. Kisco, New York, 1445 EST, 14 February 1965, looking south-southwestward. Sun is dimly visible. Later in the afternoon, altostratus layer thickened and lowered. Light snow began to fall about 6 hours after picture was taken.   (Photograph by Caroline S. Emmons)

FIG. 1241-A Squall line approaching Mt. Kisco, N.Y., late afternoon of 27 July 1965. View at left looking toward WNW, center and right toward NW. Time interval between pictures approximately three minutes. Thunderstorm overhead one hour later.   (Photographs by Caroline S. Emmons.)

Appendix

After much preparatory work and consultation with marine groups, yacht clubs, shipping agencies and other coastal interests, a new and simplified system of Coastal Warning Displays was put into effect January 1, 1958 by the U. S. Weather Bureau.

Under this method, only four separate signals are used during the day. During the night, only four comparable lantern signals are used for Small Craft, Gale, Storm, and Hurricane warnings.

The Weather Bureau emphasizes that these visual storm warnings displayed along the coast are supplementary to —and not a replacement for—the written advisories and warnings given prompt and wide distribution by press, radio and television. In most cases, important details of the forecasts and warnings in regard to the time, intensity, duration, and direction of storms cannot be given satisfactorily through visual signals alone.

Following is a detailed explanation of the new signals:

Small Craft Warning: One red pennant displayed by day and a red light above a white light at night to indicate winds up to 38 mph (33 knots) and/or sea conditions dangerous to small craft operations are forecast for the area.

Gale Warning: Two red pennants displayed by day and a white light above a red light at night to indicate winds ranging from 39 to 54 mph (34 to 47 knots) are forecast.

Storm Warning: A single square red flag with black center displayed by day and two red lights at night to indicate winds 48 knots (55 mph) and above *(no matter how high the velocity)* are forecast for the area. NOTE—If winds are associated with a tropical cyclone (hurricane) the *storm warning* display indicates forecast winds of 48 to 63 knots (55 to 73 mph). The *hurricane warning* is displayed only in connection with a tropical cyclone (hurricane).

Hurricane Warning: Two square red flags with black centers displayed by day and a white light between two red

DISSEMINATION OF STORM WARNINGS AND ROUTINE WEATHER INFORMATION

lights at night to indicate that winds 74 mph (64 knots) and above are forecast for the area.

The term *Small Craft Warning* needs some explanation. In the first place, small craft, as defined by the Weather Bureau, consist of "small boats, yachts, tugs, barges with little freeboard, or any other low-powered craft." In the second place, a small-craft warning does not distinguish between the expectation of a general, widespread, all-day blow of 25 knots or more and, for example, a forecast of the occurrence of isolated, late-afternoon thunder-squalls in which winds dangerous to small craft will be localized and of short duration. It is up to the individual skipper to deduce from his own observations, supplemented by any information he can obtain from radio broadcasts about the current over-all weather picture, to which type of situation the warning applies and to plan his day's cruise accordingly.

Storm warnings and storm advisories issued by the U.S. Weather Bureau are broadcast by designated United States Naval and Coast Guard radio stations. A large number of commercial radio stations also broadcast storm warnings, although at somewhat irregular intervals.

In 1945 the display of storm warning signals from lightships was authorized. These signals consist of the standard Weather Bureau flag hoists, displayed by day. No night signals are displayed. The storm warning signals are flown only while the lightships are on station, not while proceeding to and from station.

VHF-FM Broadcasts: The Weather Bureau now has a service at many locations of *continuous* broadcasts on 162.55 MHz of reports and forecasts with particular emphasis on marine use. New tapes are prepared every few hours.

These can be received on regular VHF sets, on inexpensive transistor receivers, and on some newer AM-FM receivers and MF-band radiotelephones. The broadcasts are of excellent quality and are most useful to boatmen.

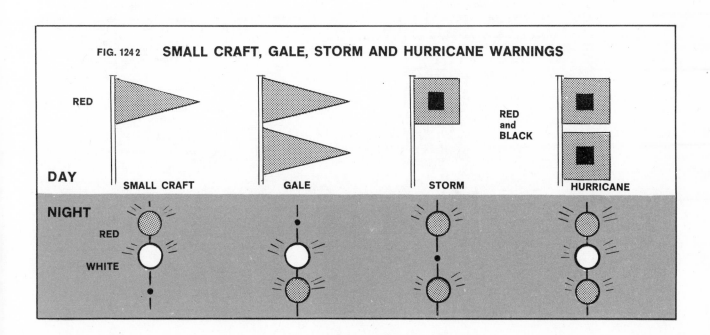

FIG. 1242 **SMALL CRAFT, GALE, STORM AND HURRICANE WARNINGS**

RED

DAY

SMALL CRAFT — GALE — STORM — RED and BLACK — HURRICANE

NIGHT

RED — WHITE

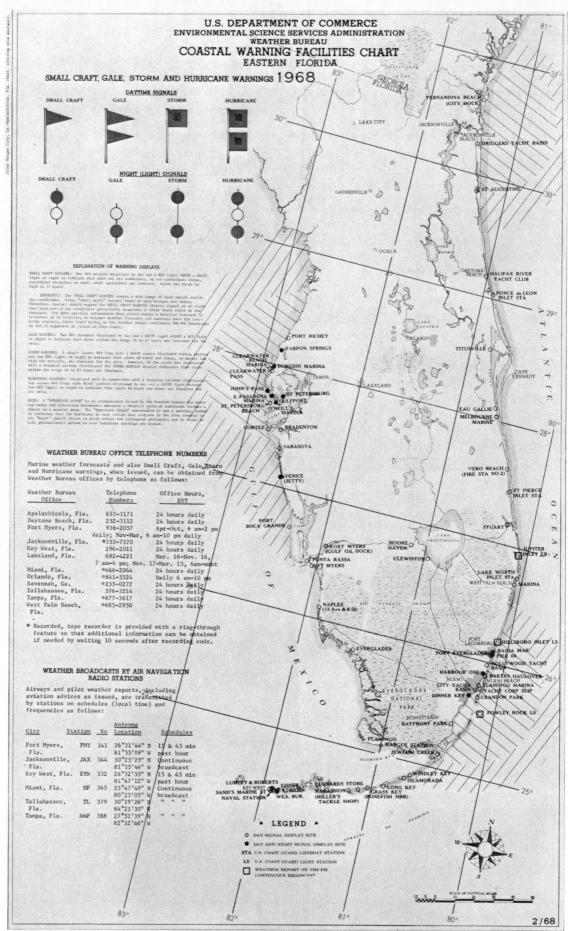

FIG. 1243   Coastal Warning Facilities Chart, Eastern Florida.

(See text page 247)

CLOUDS–How they form–What they mean

Storm warning—the anvil-shaped cumulonimbus cloud associated with thunderstorms. The wind at high altitudes is stronger than lower down, so the top of the cloud is carried ahead of the main body and forms an anvil which points like a finger in the direction toward which the upper wind is blowing. (Photographed, on the Mississippi River, by J. D. Tennison, Jr.)

Out on the water you have a front row seat at one of the greatest shows on earth: the constantly changing and highly instructive spectacle presented by the clouds. The meteorological information that clouds convey can help you to estimate future weather developments and thereby make your boating safer and more enjoyable.

Everyone knows that clouds are composed of water In order to learn how to interpret them, one must first understand how water behaves in the atmosphere.

There is always a certain amount of water in gaseous form ("water vapor") present in the air, even on a perfectly clear day. However, there is a limit to the quantity of water vapor that can exist in a given volume of air.. When the amount of water vapor actually present in the air is equal to the limit, the air is said to be "saturated," because then no more water can evaporate into it from ocean, river, lake or other sources.

Saturated air can be thought of as air that contains its full quota of water vapor. This quota varies with the temperature of the air. The warmer the air, the more water vapor it can take up. Thus, if a volume of saturated air is heated, some additional water can be evaporated into it, because the temperature of the air will be raised and, hence, the allowable proportion of water vapor will be increased.

Suppose, however, the air is cooled, rather than heated, as happens on a clear night. As its temperature is lowered its water-vapor quota is reduced. Eventually the air is cooled to a temperature for which the allowable propor-

tion of water vapor is equal to the actual amount in the air. This temperature is called the "dew point"; the air is now at saturation. If the air is cooled some more, its water-vapor content becomes excessive in relation to its temperature, and condensation results. This leads to the formation of liquid water particles, which form a cloud when the condensation process takes place in the air aloft, or fog when it takes place near the ground.

Air is cooled whenever it rises. As air ascends, the weight of the atmosphere above it decreases, and so the pressure upon the air diminishes. The decrease of pressure permits the air to expand and to cool. If the ascent and accompanying expansion is great enough to cool the air to a temperature below its dew point, clouds appear. (There are several other ways in which air may be cooled sufficiently to produce condensation, but they play a minor part in cloud formation.)

Clouds formed at heights greater than 4 miles, where the temperature is *always* below freezing, might be expected to consist solely of ice particles. However, at these altitudes clouds composed of liquid droplets also are found; such droplets are said to be "supercooled." Although unfrozen water clouds can exist at temperatures as low as −20°F, the introduction of a relatively small number of ice particles into a cloud composed of supercooled water droplets will, by means of a sort of chain reaction, transform it into an ice cloud, out of which snow will fall and produce a trail stretching downward from the underside of the cloud.

The Use of Cloud Observations in Weather Forecasting

It would be naive to believe that anyone can forecast weather 24 hours in advance solely from observations of clouds. Even if such a feat were possible, it would provide no great advantage, since the universality of radio communication makes the official forecasts issued by the government weather service readily available to the boatman.

However, government forecasters, despite the enormous quantity of weather observations at their disposal, have difficulties. Greatest problem is probably that of timing; for example, estimating the time of arrival of a wind-shift line.

Here is where an understanding of the meaning of the clouds can be helpful. Clouds are the visible manifestations of physical processes that are taking place in the atmosphere. Some of these processes cause clouds to form and grow; others cause existing clouds to break up and disappear. The ability to interpret the clouds in terms of the physical processes that are going on aloft often will enable the boatman to decide for himself whether the latest official forecast is working out or not. In many cases he can amend the forecast and thereby still make use of it when the timing or some other feature has been miscalculated.

The formation and growth of a cloud or cloud system means that there is an upward component of motion of the air at the level of the cloud, because the cooling necessary to produce the cloud has resulted from expansion of the air. The general appearance of the growing cloud is determined by the stability of the air in which it forms. If the air is stable, then the upward motion responsible for the cloud is a "forced" one; characteristically it is uniformly smooth and gentle. Therefore, the clouds formed by the expansion and concomitant cooling of air that ascends in this fashion are layered, and they grow or thicken relatively slowly.

The pattern of cloud growth just described is illustrated by Photographs Nos. 5, 9, and 30, viewed in that order. The processes at work often produce long-lasting steady rain and, hence, this sequence of photographs typifies the evolution of the sky during the approach of a widespread rain area.

If the atmosphere is unstable, portions of it will rise spontaneously. The upward motion in this case is irregular and rapid; the clouds that form are of the cumulus type and are separated by clear spaces. The pattern of cloud growth in unstable air is illustrated by Photographs Nos. 15, 16 and 25, viewed in that order. This sequence is typical of pre-thunderstorm weather.

This 4-page insert amplifies the discussion of cloud forms and their significance, which appears on pages 241 and 242.

CIRRUS—These are ice clouds in the form of tufts. Snow is falling out of tuft in upper left portion of photograph. Altitude—above 20,000 feet. The elements are isolated. **1**

CIRRUS—This is a dense ice cloud. If viewed toward the sun it appears greyish. It appears to be the edge of an "anvil" cloud formed from Cumulonimbus. **2**

ALTOSTRATUS — Thin, translucent water cloud sheet, often the forerunner of rain in most parts of the U.S. Small, dark clouds underneath are Cumulus. **7**

ALTOSTRATUS — Translucent sheet cloud with fibrous characteristics. Difference in opacity produces a dark band (bottom). Dark clouds below are Cumulus. Alt—8,000 to 20,000 ft. **8**

CUMULUS — Typical of fine weather. Appearance of sky indicates good weather continuing for 6 hours at least. Altitude—base of cloud 3,000 to 5,000 feet. **13**

CUMULUS—These are less benign than those in Photograph No. 13. However, they do not have a threatening appearance. Altitude of cloud tops about 10,000 feet. **14**

STRATOCUMULUS — Another example of an unbroken sheet of Stratocumulus. The elongation and alignment of the rolls suggest that strong wind is blowing. **19**

STRATOCUMULUS and CUMULUS — Here is cloud-layer formed from decaying Cumulus. Fresh Cumulus are growing underneath. Altitude—base 5,000 to 8,000 feet. **20**

CUMULONIMBUS—This is a "chaotic" sky with Cumulonimbus in the background and growing Cumulus in the foreground. Showers and thunderstorms are occurring nearby. **25**

CUMULUS and CUMULONIMBUS — Cumulus are seen in lower portion. Cloud sheet above is part of a vast Cumulonimbus. Scene is typical of thunderstorm weather. **26**

CLOUDS AND THE BAROMETER—There is very little correlation between individual cloud types and barometric indications. Most clouds shown here can occur in association with either a rising or falling barometer. However, if the sky is filled with Cumulus and the barometer is falling, look for the development of Cumulonimbus and showers. Thickening high-altitude ice clouds accompanying a falling barometer are particularly significant. This combination almost always indicates the approach of wet weather. But *isolated* Cirrus tufts or streaks occur without relation to the barometric trend.

CIRRUS — Ice clouds in the form of 3 both tufts and hooks. The hooks are snow trails which are bent when they encounter changes in wind direction and velocity at lower altitudes.

CIRROSTRATUS — This cloud covers 4 the whole sky. Individual Cirrus tufts appear, but they merge with a sheet of ice filaments. Altitude — above 20,000 feet.

CIRROSTRATUS — Ice cloud in the form 5 of a veil. The halo is caused by refraction of sunlight through the ice crystals composing the veil. The halo is **not** a sure sign of rain.

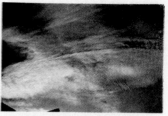

CIRROCUMULUS — Fairly typical in 6 middle section. Cirrus streaks are visible at top. Altitude — above 20,000 feet. This cloud is often difficult to distinguish from Altocumulus.

ALTOSTRATUS — This layer is suffi- 9 ciently translucent to reveal the position of the sun. Dark patches in vicinity of sun probably are remains of Cumulus.

ALTOCUMULUS — This sheet of lightly 10 shaded white to dark grey elements displays the chief characteristics of Altocumulus. Altitude — 8,000 to 20,000 feet.

ALTOCUMULUS — This layer of Alto- 11 cumulus has a wavy appearance. The billows are caused by irregularities in the wind at the altitude of the cloud.

ALTOCUMULUS — This is clearly a 12 water cloud, since it shows no signs of hair-like structure. The elements are ragged and apparently are evaporating.

CUMULUS — The build-up in the left 15 half of the picture appears to be sprouting rather rapidly. However, development of Cumulonimbus is not imminent.

CUMULUS — The Cumulus in the right 16 half of the picture has considerable vertical extent. The bulging upper part indicates strong ascending air currents.

STRATOCUMULUS — Appearance indi- 17 cates localized rising air currents. Stratocumulus is dark cloud in foreground. Cumulonimbus (white cloud). Altitude — base 3,000 to 5,000 feet.

STRATOCUMULUS — This is a solid 18 layer of Stratocumulus formed by the merging of numerous Cumulus clouds. Light showers may fall from it. Often accompanied by gusty winds.

STRATOCUMULUS — Typifies Strato- 21 cumulus formed during the day and evaporating at sunset. Rising currents have stopped; a clear night can be expected.

ALTOCUMULUS — An unusual form of 22 Altocumulus. It might be identified as Cirrocumulus, but absence of streaks means it is a water rather than ice cloud.

ALTOSTRATUS and CUMULUS — This 23 combination and the general appearance of the sky suggest that the weather is beginning to improve following a rainstorm.

CUMULUS and CIRRUS — The white 24 clouds at top are Cirrus (note the streaks). Cumulus below suggest Cirrus have been derived from distant Cumulonimbus.

CUMULONIMBUS — A rain shower can 27 be seen falling from the darkest portion. This feature identifies the cloud as Cumulonimbus even though it is not a thunderstorm cloud.

CUMULONIMBUS — Exhibiting hanging 28 protuberances, called "mamma," caused by the descent of blobs of cloud-filled air. Associated with severe thunderstorms.

CUMULONIMBUS — The heavy rain 29 shower in the distance identifies the cloud as Cumulonimbus. The scene is common over warm ocean waters in summer.

STRATUS — A featureless grey sheet 30 whose base is within a few hundred feet of the ground. If rain falls from it, the cloud is called NIMBOSTRATUS. Note top of tower is obscured.

STABLE vs. UNSTABLE AIR — These terms are best explained by first considering stability in a liquid. A light liquid can float on top of a heavier one without mixing, but a heavy liquid will not float on top of a lighter one. The first arrangement is stable, the second unstable. Heating of a kettle of water from below demonstrates the same fact. The water at the bottom of the kettle is heated and becomes lighter than the water above it. The warmed water rises from the bottom, its place being taken by colder water from above. This action occurs because water is unstable when cold water lies above warm. Because air is compressible, the condition for stability in the atmosphere is — *not* that the temperature shall increase with height, but that the temperature shall not decrease at a rate (*for unsaturated air*) greater than 5.4°F per 1,000 feet. If, due to heating at the earth's surface, the temperature decrease with height exceeds this rate, the air is unstable, or top-heavy, and tends to overturn.

BASIC CLOUD FORMS

Although 10 principal cloud types are defined in the International Cloud Classification (see pages 241-242), there are really only three basic cloud forms: (1) "streak" clouds, (2) "sheet" clouds and (3) "heap" clouds. The streak clouds are composed of tiny ice particles which often form trails, giving rise to the picturesque English name "mares' tails." ("Federwolke" is the German name for the same formation.)

HOW CLOUDS ARE NAMED

In the interest of conformity, however, the cloud designations chosen for international usage are derived from Latin words. Streak clouds are called *cirrus* (a hair or curl). A sheet-like cloud is called *stratus* (a spreading out) and a heap cloud *cumulus* (a heap). When appropriate, other Latin words are joined to these primary ones. Thus, for example, the Latin word *nimbus* (black rain cloud) is combined with *stratus* and with *cumulus* to give *nimbostratus* and *cumulonimbus,* meaning, respectively, "raining cloud sheet" and "raining heap cloud."

SHEET AND HEAP TYPES

Sheet clouds are produced mainly by a slow widespread ascent of stable air, less commonly by radiative cooling of air moving purely horizontally. Heap clouds, on the other hand, are formed in unstable air permeated with localized, strong updrafts created by spontaneous ascent of buoyant "bubbles" of air.

EFFECT OF WIND SHEAR

Numerous modifications of the basic cloud forms are observed. These may be caused by complex motions within the clouds or by the twisting effect of "vertical wind shear," that is, changes in the direction and velocity of the wind from one altitude to another. We have a demonstration of the latter in the not-uncommon sight of curving streaks of ice crystals which trail from a parent cirrus (see photograph No. 3).

IN MIDDLE LATITUDES

In middle latitudes, at elevations greater than about 10,000 feet, the wind velocity generally increases with height but the direction usually remains fairly constant right up to 30,000 feet at least. Tall cumulus clouds in this kind of environment will be bent by vertical wind shear, so that their tops lean forward. A striking example of this is provided in the photograph on page 246 (a). Here the cloud apparently has built up to the base of the stratosphere. At that altitude a temperature inversion has stopped its upward growth, and the stronger wind which exists there has spread the cloud top horizontally off to the right.

IN TRADE-WIND BELTS

In the tropical trade-wind belts, where easterly winds prevail in the lowest 10,000 feet of the atmosphere, cumulus clouds are sometimes seen to lean backwards. This happens because the easterly winds of the tropics ordinarily do not increase in velocity upward as do the westerlies of middle latitudes. It is not uncommon for the wind velocity to decrease with elevation, so that the vertical wind shear is directed from west toward east. If the top of a tall tropical cumulus cloud is seen to be bent sharply backward, perhaps pointing in an almost horizontal direction, it is probable that the cloud top has penetrated an upper layer where the wind is blowing from the west.

ROLLS OR BILLOWS

The roll formations, or billows, that often occur in a layer of middle-level clouds (see photograph No. 11) are usually caused by vertical wind shear. The upper part of the layer is moving faster than the lower part but is flowing in the same direction. The sliding of the upper part over the lower part sets up waves on the boundary between the two, with the result that the cloud deck is shaped into rolls which are oriented approximately at right angles to the direction of the air flow.

CLOUDS AND CLIMATE

The ten cloud types defined in pages 241-242 can be seen the world over. However, the frequency of each type varies considerably from one climate region to another. For example, *cumulus* is far more prevalent in the tropics than in the polar regions, whereas *stratus* occurs more often in middle and high latitudes than in the tropics. Moreover, the predominating cloud types in certain parts of the United States are quite different from those in others.

HEIGHT—RANGES

The table below gives the approximate height-ranges of the bases of the ten principal cloud types. In this table the overlapping of the upper limits of the middle-level water clouds (Ac and As) and the lower limits of the ice clouds is explained by latitudinal, seasonal, and day-to-day variations in temperature, which occur aloft as well as as well as at the earth's surface.

APPROXIMATE HEIGHT-RANGES AT WHICH BASES OF VARIOUS CLOUDS ARE FOUND			
Cloud Type	In polar regions	In middle latitudes	In tropical regions
Ci, Cc, Cs	10,000-30,000 ft.	16,000-45,000 ft.	25,000-55,000 ft.
Ac, As	6,000-15,000 ft.	6,000-23,000 ft.	6,000-25,000 ft.
Ns, Sc, St, Cu, Cb	From near the ground to 8,000 feet		

COASTAL WARNING FACILITIES CHARTS

Coast Guard vessels now display storm warning signals. Headquarters of the Coast Guard are supplied with weather information by the Weather Bureau and Coast Guard vessels receive instructions to fly the proper signals when bad weather is approaching.

The shore stations where storm warning signals are displayed are prominently marked on the *Coastal Warning Facilities Charts,* a series which is published annually by the Weather Bureau. These charts, of which fig. 1243 is an example, also contain detailed information concerning the times of weather broadcasts from commercial stations, the radio frequencies of marine broadcast stations, the specific type of storm warnings issued and the visual display signals (already described and illustrated in the text above) which are used in connection with the warnings. This series consists of fourteen charts, twelve of which cover the coastal waters of the United States and the Great Lakes. The remaining two charts are for (a) the Hawaiian Islands, and (b) Puerto Rico and the Virgin Islands. They can be purchased from the Superintendent of Documents, Government Printing Office, Washington, D. C. 20402.

Yachtsmen will find much interesting weather information on the various Pilot Charts of the North Atlantic and North Pacific Oceans issued by the Oceanographic Office of the Navy Department. The Pilot Charts show average monthly wind and weather conditions over the oceans and in addition contain a vast amount of supplemental data on subjects closely allied to weather.

WIND FORCE—AND ITS EFFECT ON THE SEA

Boatmen, like mariners at sea, frequently use the Beaufort Scale to log wind speed and the condition of the sea. Too often the description of sea conditions relies solely upon a verbal statement like "moderate waves, large waves, moderately high waves" (column 3, Table 12-3) which leaves the boatman pretty much "at sea" in trying to visualize exactly what these relative terms imply.

England's Meteorological Office has solved this problem by issuing a State of Sea card (M.O. 688A) with photographs to accompany each of the descriptions of thirteen wind forces of the Beaufort Scale. Thus the observer has a guide in estimating wind strength (*in knots*) when making weather reports or in logging sea conditions. Fetch, depth of water, swell, heavy rain, tide and the lag effect between the wind getting up and the sea increasing, may also affect the appearance of the sea. Range of wind speed and the mean wind speed are given for each force. By special permission, we are privileged to reproduce (figure 1244, page 249) seven of these photographs (Forces 1, 3, 5, 6, 8, 10, 12). Forces 0, 2, 4, 7, 9, and 11, though not illustrated, may be estimated in relation to those above and below them in the scale.

This table shows the velocity of sound at various air temperatures. Strictly speaking, the table is valid only for dry air, i.e., air containing no water vapor. However, the effect of water vapor on the speed of sound is quite small, so that the values in the table are entirely suitable for use in ordinary, rough calculations.

TABLE 12-5

WIND PRESSURE AT VARIOUS WIND VELOCITIES
(Air temperature 50°F, barometric pressure 1000 mbs.)

WIND VELOCITY (Knots)	WIND PRESSURE (Lbs. Per Square Foot)
0	0.0
5	0.1
10	0.3
15	0.8
20	1.3
25	2.1
30	3.1
35	4.2
40	5.5
45	6.9
50	8.5
55	10.3
60	12.3

This table gives the wind pressure exerted on the windward side of a flat surface oriented at right angles to the wind. The values in the table have been computed for air temperature equal to 50°F and barometric pressure equal to 1000 millibars. At greater barometric pressures and lower air temperature the wind pressure corresponding to a given wind velocity will be somewhat greater; at higher air temperatures and lower barometric pressures, somewhat less.

TABLE 12-6

VELOCITY OF SOUND IN DRY AIR

AIR TEMPERATURE	SOUND VELOCITY	
°F	Feet per second	Knots
100	1160	687
95	1155	684
90	1149	681
85	1144	678
80	1139	675
75	1133	671
70	1128	668
65	1123	665
60	1117	662
55	1112	659
50	1107	656
45	1101	653
40	1096	649
35	1090	646
30	1084	642
25	1079	639
20	1073	635
15	1067	632
10	1062	629
5	1057	626
0	1051	622
−5	1045	619
−10	1040	616
−15	1034	613
−20	1028	609
−25	1022	605
−30	1016	601
−35	1010	598
−40	1004	595

FORCE 1—Wind speed 1-3 kt.; mean 2 kt.

FORCE 3—Wind speed 7-10 kt.; mean 9 kt.

FORCE 5—Wind speed 17-21 kt.; mean 18 kt.

FORCE 6—Wind speed 22-27 kt.; mean 24 kt.

FORCE 8—Wind speed 34-40 kt.; mean 37 kt.

FORCE 10—Wind speed 48-55 kt.; mean 52 kt.

FIG. 1244 — HOW THE SEA LOOKS IN WINDS OF VARYING FORCE

Wind forces used in these illustrations are based on the Beaufort Scale. See column 3, table 12-3, for verbal description of the state of the sea for Forces 0-12.

(All photographs Crown Copyright, by R. R. Baxter, except Force 10, J. Hodkinson, and Force 12, G.P.O. Reproduced by permission of the Controller of Her Brittanic Majesty's Stationery Office.)

FORCE 12—Wind speed 64-71 kt.; mean 68 kt.

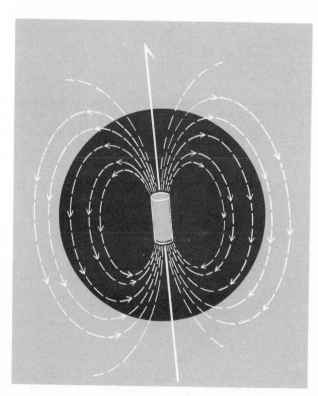

FIG. 1301 Typical spherical compass

CHAPTER 13

*Planning a voyage,
or when under way,
the navigator or the
small boat pilot is always
concerned with direction
and distance.
Methods of determining
and recording distance
are thoroughly
covered elsewhere in
this book. This chapter
is about direction
and, more particularly,
about the most commonly
used direction
indicator afloat,
the mariner's compass.*

THE MARINER'S COMPASS

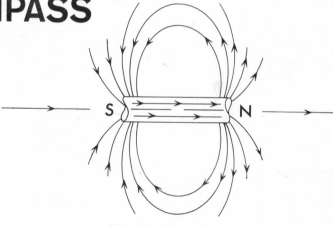

FIG. 1302 Lines of force, bar magnet

Why It Works

The operating principle is the behavior of a freely suspended bar magnet.

A permanent bar magnet has two poles, conventionally labeled north or south, in accordance with usage. The so-called force of the magnet is apparently concentrated at each of these poles. Actually it exists in the three-dimensional space, called the field, around the bar, roughly as shown in fig. 1302 and is presumed to consist of innumerable *lines of force,* a few of which are pictured. Another smaller magnet, brought into this field and free to move, will align itself along a line of force of the larger magnet.

The earth has only some of the properties of a large bar magnet. Fig. 1303. A bar magnet freely suspended in the

FIG. 1303 Lines of force, earth

earth's magnetic field will align itself along one of the earth's lines of force and thus establish a *direction*. As will appear later this direction will not necessarily be north or south, but at any particular point on the earth, for practical navigation, it may be considered relatively constant for periods of several years. It is true that the direction is always changing, has even a diurnal oscillation, but with occasional exceptions *(see the discussion of variation)* these movements are of an order far too miniscule to affect what is indicated by the best of mariner's compasses at any given location. The changes in the indicated direction when the compass is moved many miles to another place will be discussed in due course.

This fact, that a freely suspended bar magnet stably indicates a direction, is the secret of the operation of the mariner's compass. It should be remembered such an indicated direction is generally neither geographic north or south, nor the true direction of the magnetic pole. Nonetheless, it is relatively *constant at a place*. The navigator usually has at hand ready information and rapid means of converting what his compass shows to true directions. He knows that if the magnetic effects of his ship be

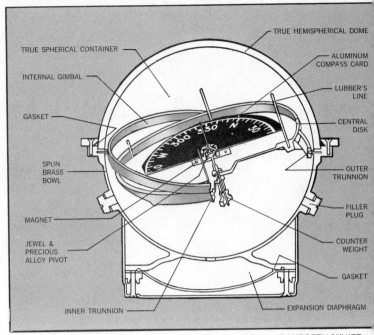

FIG. 1304 Compass with internal gimbal ring

Courtesy DANFORTH/WHITE

FIG. 1305 Navy-type 7½" compass

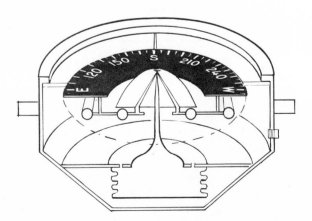

FIG. 1306 Cross section, typical compass

neutralized *(see Chapter 14)* his compass is a magnetic direction finder; that its 'pointer' is aligned with one of the earth's lines of force. This line of force is called the *magnetic meridian* of the place; it will be referred to later.

Construction

Few wearers can describe or need to know the construction of a watch. Some know it contains a motor, an escapement and a gear train. All know it has a dial and hands. A compass has a dial and a hand too. Unlike a watch, the 'hand' of a typical mariner's compass *moves around the periphery of its 'dial.'* The 'hand' is a mark called the *lubber's line,* painted on the inside of the compass bowl or is a stile or a pointer fastened to its upper edge. The 'dial' is the compass card.

Several long thin permanent magnets, each enclosed in a non-magnetic tube, are affixed, parallel to each other, to a light non-magnetic wire frame. Like poles of the magnets are adjacent. In some modern instruments there is a different type of magnetic element. An annular disk, bearing suitable graduations, *the card,* is fastened to the frame above the magnets. Centrally placed under the frame is a bearing. Usually a float is attached to the frame to reduce wear on the pivot and bearing. This whole assembly serves as the dial. The user looks at its peripheral graduations.

The bowl, with its lubberline 'hand,' has a pivot atop a post in its center. See fig. 1306. The frame bearing rests on this pivot. A top of transparent material, either flat or hemispherical, is rigidly fastened with a liquid-proof seal to the top of the bowl. Through a pluggable aperture, the bowl is filled with a non-freezing liquid, formerly alcohol, but now usually a special oil. An expansion chamber is provided to allow for the effects of temperature changes. The sealed unit is mounted in gimbals so as to remain level in a seaway. In some instruments the gimbal mounting is inside the bowl. See fig. 1304.

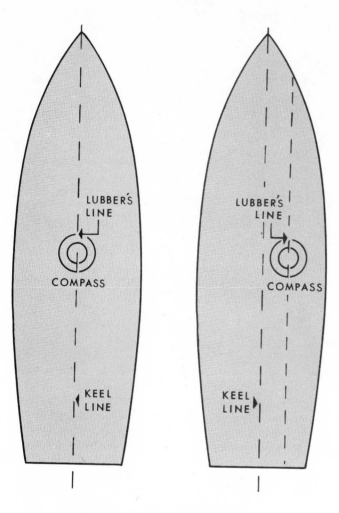

FIG. 1307 Mounting parallel to keel

Mounting

These are principles only. Most strongly is it suggested that pages 269-273 be read before using *any* tools.

The compass should be securely fastened aboard. A line through the lubber's line and the center of the card must be parallel to the keel. See fig. 1307. The instrument should be level, and so placed that it is within easy and unobstructed view of the helmsman. See fig. 1308. It must be lighted for night use with a minimum of illumination, preferably red. Magnetic material in its vicinity should be minimal. Wires near it, carrying direct current, should be twisted. Equipment generating strong magnetic fields should be as far away from it as is practical.

A box compass, fig. 1309, not permanently mounted, should have some permanent receptacle to receive it, so that upon each occasion of use it is correctly positioned.

Ships and larger yachts mount the compass in a stand called the binnacle, fig. 1404 though the term binnacle list does not indicate the need to shore up one side.

Photo by Dale Phillips

FIG. 1309 Box Compass

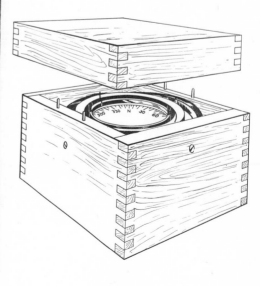

FIG. 1308 Cruiser "bridge" or steering station
showing compass mounted amidships and off centerline

The Card

As previously stated the card serves as a dial; the lubber's line as a hand. A clock has a zero reference point. Time is told by observing the position of two or more hands relative to the twelfth or zero hour. Actually we observe an angle, but long ago each of us learned to ignore the angle, to read immediately what we see as time. The lubber's line indicates an angle, a direction relative to that of the north or zero point of the card, though most of us think not of the angle but of the direction. We think of east as a direction, paying no thought to the fact that it is one-quarter of a single clockwise rotation from north.

Modern compass cards are graduated in degrees, clockwise from north. Marks may be at each degree or for smaller craft at five-degree intervals. Numerals may be printed every ten degrees from 10° to 350°; every fifteen degrees from 15° to 345° or every thirty degrees from 30° to 330°, see figs. 1301, 1310 and 1311.

Still extant are older compasses with cards graduated only ninety degrees to the east and to the west from north and from south. In that system N 90°E means the same as S 90°E, i.e. East.

For many years the card bore only points. There are eight points to a quadrant; thus a point equals 11¼°. As the building of better hulls and the development of the fore and aft rig enabled vessels to hold course with greater accuracy, came need to use smaller units of arc. Each point was divided into fourths, giving rise to quarter-points, about 2¾°. There were various methods of naming these quarter-points. There was a time when no man was a salt unless he could recite them forwards and backwards all around the card starting from any given one. The age of steam brought the ability to hold a course regardless of all but the stronger winds and the need for a smaller division of the 'dial.' So the sexagesimal system came to the helmsman.

The cardinal points, North, East, South and West, and the intercardinals, Northeast, Southeast, Southwest and Northwest are still in common use as rough directions and as descriptions of wind direction. The combination points, as ENE, NNE and so on are but little used and as for the by-points, NxE, NExN, they and their like seem but to embellish (often erroneously) some TV or radio

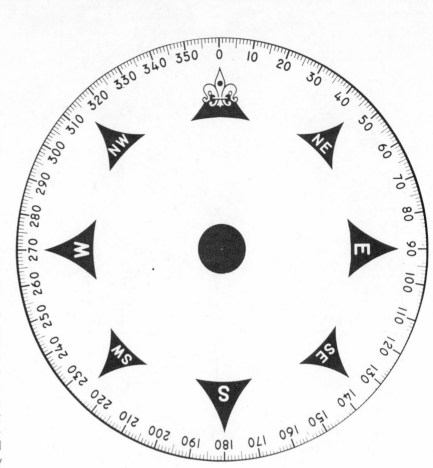

FIG. 1310   Compass Card—degrees, cardinals and intercardinals

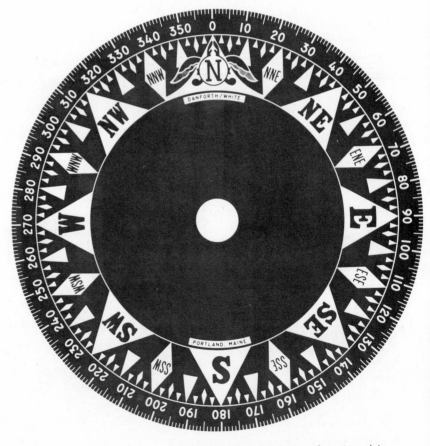

FIG. 1311   Compass Card—degrees, points and quarter points

drama. For those who do not wish to forget the past, and for those neophytes in sail who must learn points for ease in steering their wind-driven craft, there is included a table of comparisons of the various systems of nomenclature, fig. 1312.

Many modern compasses do label the cardinal and the intercardinal points, see fig. 1310, but the ensuing work here will be carried out in degrees.

CONVERSION TABLE—POINTS TO DEGREES

NORTH TO EAST	Points	Angular measure (° ′ ″)	SOUTH TO WEST	Points	Angular measure (° ′ ″)
North	0	0 00 00	South	16	180 00 00
N¼E	¼	2 48 45	S¼W	16¼	182 48 45
N½E	½	5 37 30	S½W	16½	185 37 30
N¾E	¾	8 26 15	S¾W	16¾	188 26 15
N by E	1	11 15 00	S by W	17	191 15 00
N by E¼E	1¼	14 03 45	S by W¼W	17¼	194 03 45
N by E½E	1½	16 52 30	S by W½W	17½	196 52 30
N by E¾E	1¾	19 41 15	S by W¾W	17¾	199 41 15
NNE	2	22 30 00	SSW	18	202 30 00
NNE¼E	2¼	25 18 45	SSW¼W	18¼	205 18 45
NNE½E	2½	28 07 30	SSW½W	18½	208 07 30
NNE¾E	2¾	30 56 15	SSW¾W	18¾	210 56 15
NE by N	3	33 45 00	SW by S	19	213 45 00
NE¾N	3¼	36 33 45	SW¾S	19¼	216 33 45
NE½N	3½	39 22 30	SW½S	19½	219 22 30
NE¼N	3¾	42 11 15	SW¼S	19¾	222 11 15
NE	4	45 00 00	SW	20	225 00 00
NE¼E	4¼	47 48 45	SW¼W	20¼	227 48 45
NE½E	4½	50 37 30	SW½W	20½	230 37 30
NE¾E	4¾	53 26 15	SW¾W	20¾	233 26 15
NE by E	5	56 15 00	SW by W	21	236 15 00
NE by E¼E	5¼	59 03 45	SW by W¼W	21¼	239 03 45
NE by E½E	5½	61 52 30	SW by W½W	21½	241 52 30
NE by E¾E	5¾	64 41 15	SW by W¾W	21¾	244 41 15
ENE	6	67 30 00	WSW	22	247 30 00
ENE¼E	6¼	70 18 45	WSW¼W	22¼	250 18 45
ENE½E	6½	73 07 30	WSW½W	22½	253 07 30
ENE¾E	6¾	75 56 15	WSW¾W	22¾	255 56 15
E by N	7	78 45 00	W by S	23	258 45 00
E¾N	7¼	81 33 45	W¾S	23¼	261 33 45
E½N	7½	84 22 30	W½S	23½	264 22 30
E¼N	7¾	87 11 15	W¼S	23¾	267 11 15
EAST TO SOUTH			**WEST TO NORTH**		
East	8	90 00 00	West	24	270 00 00
E¼S	8¼	92 48 45	W¼N	24¼	272 48 45
E½S	8½	95 37 30	W½N	24½	275 37 30
E¾S	8¾	98 26 15	W¾N	24¾	278 26 15
E by S	9	101 15 00	W by N	25	281 15 00
ESE¾E	9¼	104 03 45	WNW¾W	25¼	284 03 45
ESE½E	9½	106 52 30	WNW½W	25½	286 52 30
ESE¼E	9¾	109 41 15	WNW¼W	25¾	289 41 15
ESE	10	112 30 00	WNW	26	292 30 00
SE by E¾E	10¼	115 18 45	NW by W¾W	26¼	295 18 45
SE by E½E	10½	118 07 30	NW by W½W	26½	298 07 30
SE by E¼E	10¾	120 56 15	NW by W¼W	26¾	300 56 15
SE by E	11	123 45 00	NW by W	27	303 45 00
SE¾E	11¼	126 33 45	NW¾W	27¼	306 33 45
SE½E	11½	129 22 30	NW½W	27½	309 22 30
SE¼E	11¾	132 11 15	NW¼W	27¾	312 11 15
SE	12	135 00 00	NW	28	315 00 00
SE¼S	12¼	137 48 45	NW¼N	28¼	317 48 45
SE½S	12½	140 37 30	NW½N	28½	320 37 30
SE¾S	12¾	143 26 15	NW¾N	28¾	323 26 15
SE by S	13	146 15 00	NW by N	29	326 15 00
SSE¾E	13¼	149 03 45	NNW¾W	29¼	329 03 45
SSE½E	13½	151 52 30	NNW½W	29½	331 52 30
SSE¼E	13¾	154 41 15	NNW¼W	29¾	334 41 15
SSE	14	157 30 00	NNW	30	337 30 00
S by E¾E	14¼	160 18 45	N by W¾W	30¼	340 18 45
S by E½E	14½	163 07 30	N by W½W	30½	343 07 30
S by E¼E	14¾	165 56 15	N by W¼W	30¾	345 56 15
S by E	15	168 45 00	N by W	31	348 45 00
S¾E	15¼	171 33 45	N¾W	31¼	351 33 45
S½E	15½	174 22 30	N½W	31½	354 22 30
S¼E	15¾	177 11 15	N¼W	31¾	357 11 15
South	16	180 00 00	North	32	360 00 00

FIG. 1312

Conversion Table: points and degrees

(From BOWDITCH)

Variation

The point has been made that a freely suspended permanent magnet indicates a direction. That direction is, at any place, the vertical plane of the magnetic meridian. That the magnet may not be strictly horizontal and may dip slightly at one end is of no moment in the use of a mariner's compass.

In his normal day's work the navigator, or the small boat pilot, plotting his track on the chart, has need to know true directions, directions relative to the earth's geographic north. His courses and bearings are recorded with respect to the true north. His directional instrument, his mariner's compass, rarely indicates a direction as an angle referred to true north; always indicates an angle referred to the north point of the compass card, or compass north.

In a non-magnetic ship, one like the now non-existent CARNEGIE, a magnetic compass is subject only to the effect of the earth's magnetic field. In this unusual condition the north point of the compass card lies in the magnetic meridian. In general, the magnetic meridian does not coincide with the true meridian *(which is the direction of the plane passing through the place and the geographic poles)*. There is an angle between them. This angle is termed *variation*. (V or Var)

The variation at any place is the angle there between the true meridian and the magnetic meridian. See fig. 1313. When that part of the magnetic meridian running towards the north magnetic pole lies to the east of the northern half of the true meridian, the variation is termed easterly. When it is to the west, the variation is westerly. Currently variation is expressed in degrees and minutes and labelled east or west, e.g. 7°30'W or 16°45'E. See fig. 1315. Its value may range from 0° to 180°.

Contrary to popular ideas the location of the magnetic poles is of little interest to the pilot or navigator. (Should he cruise in their vicinity he must perforce rely for directions on some instrument other than the magnetic compass.)

Variation is *not* the angle between the direction of the true and the magnetic poles. This supposition, a fictitious construct, useful in helping students to realize that true and magnetic north are usually in different directions, has been accepted by many as truth. Emphatically it is not so. It must be recognized as merely a learning aid, not a factual representation. The magnetic pole does not control the compass. The controlling force, as previously stated, is the earth's magnetic field. The compass magnet does not point to the magnetic pole.

Actually two antipodean points on the earth which are magnetic poles do not exist. There are north and south *magnetic polar areas* containing many magnetic poles, places where a dip needle would stand vertically. If this seems strange, give thought to pin-pointing the pole in the end of a bar magnet having a cross-sectional area of one square inch.

For scientific purposes rough approximate positions of theoretical north and south magnetic poles are computed from a large number of continuing observations made the

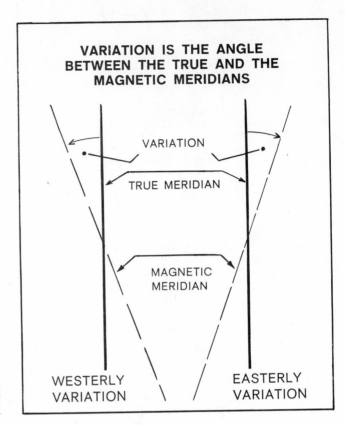

VARIATION IS THE ANGLE BETWEEN THE TRUE AND THE MAGNETIC MERIDIANS

FIG. 1313 Defines Variation

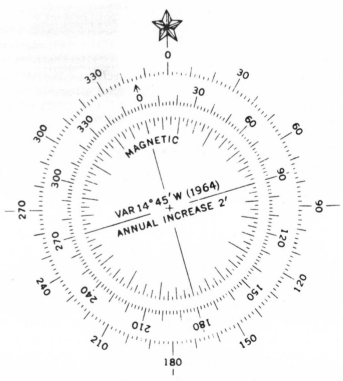

FIG. 1315 Typical chart rose, modern

world over through many years. In 1955 these adopted positions were respectively in latitude 74°N, longitude 101°W and latitude 68°S, longitude 144°E. In 1960 the adopted positions were in latitude 75°N, longitude 101°W and latitude 67°S, longitude 143°E.

Several facts become obvious. A magnetic compass in 79°N, 101°W would show north in a direction to the southward of the instrument! The magnetic poles are not stationary. They are not diametrically opposed as one conceives of the geographic poles. They are far from the geographic poles. A magnetic meridian is generally not a segment of a great circle passing through the magnetic poles, since but one great circle passes through any two surface points not at the end of a diameter. Not so obvious but nonetheless true is that, again generally, the magnetic meridian is not part of a great circle from the place to the adjacent magnetic pole.

Variation changes with location. Cognizance of this is part of the duty of every navigator or pilot. If he neglects it he will be in trouble, see fig. 1314. At any place the amount of the variation is relatively constant, though there is usually a small annual change. The navigator finds this data on the chart he is using. On U.S. Coast and Geodetic Survey coastwise and harbor charts and on Lake Survey charts are printed compass roses suitably spaced for convenient use in plotting. See figs. 1315 and 1316. The rose has two concentric circular scales. The outer one is graduated in degrees and is oriented so that its zero point indicates true or geographic north. The inner one is graduated in degrees and points. Its zero point, identified by an arrow, shows the direction of the northern half of the magnetic meridian at that place. The angle at the center of the rose, between this arrow and the zero point of the outer, or true, rose, is the variation *at that place* for the year stated. This information is printed on the rose to the nearest 15', as "Var 14° 45'W (1964)," together with a further notation on the annual rate of change, to the nearest 1', and whether the variation increases or decreases as "ANNUAL INCREASE 2'," "ANNUAL DECREASE 10' or "NO ANNUAL CHANGE." See fig. 1315.

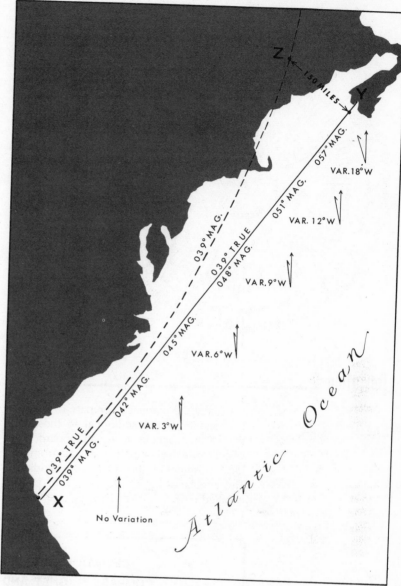

Fig. 1314.

The course from X to Y is 039° true. At X the variation is zero, so the magnetic course is also 039°. Because the variation changes with location, the magnetic course steered must be changed as the vessel enters regions having different variations. This must be done for each 1° change in the variation.

An airplane leaving X headed 039° magnetic for Y and held on this magnetic course would follow the curved track and ultimately be at Z, 150 miles from Y. To remain on the track XY, the magnetic course is altered in successive increments of 1°

On smaller scale charts covering larger areas, variation is shown by labeled *isogonic lines*. Every point on such a line has the same variation. That line joining all the points having zero variation is called the agonic line.

The annual rate of change printed on chart roses permits the chart user to estimate the variation to be expected at some date subsequent to the publishing of the chart. Estimates based on information more than five years old should be used with caution. The annual rate of change is not due to the motion of the magnetic poles. It cannot be predicted accurately. The rate on the chart *is the best guess* of its trend, based upon prior observations of the gradual alterations in the earth's ever-changing magnetic field. Within the suggested time limit the prediction is adequate

for nautical use. It is well to know that there are recorded instances of sudden major changes and indeed reversals in the rate. Here then is another reason for not using old charts. Charts are cheap. Stranding is not.

LOCAL ATTRACTION

In some localities, fortunately few, over relatively small areas, the compass is subject to irregular magnetic disturbances in the earth's field. A striking example is found in Kingston Harbor, Ontario, Canada, where deflection of the compass may be as great as 45° in a distance of a mile and a half. This phenomenon is called local attraction. Charts of the area bear warnings to this effect.

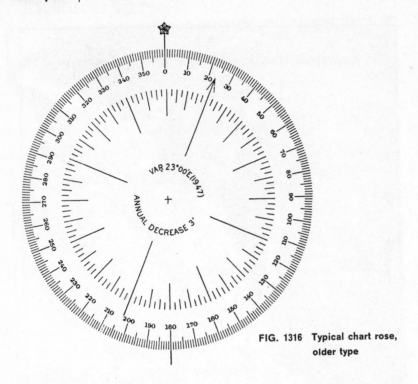

FIG. 1316 Typical chart rose, older type

Deviation is the angle between the magnetic meridian and a line from the pivot through the north point of the compass card. Its amount can range from 0° to 180°, though large values are not to be tolerated. It is described east or west as the compass north lies to the east or west of the north branch of the magnetic meridian, fig. 1317.

It will be recalled that variation changes with geographic position. *Deviation changes with the ship's heading.* The causes will be explained subsequently. To cope with these changes a vessel carries a deviation table, a tabulation of the respective deviations, usually for every 15° of heading by the ship's compass. *(See page 264.)* For added convenience a table is made on the basis of magnetic headings *(page 267),* or the two combined in a direct reading table *(page 267).*

Reducing deviation to a minimum brought into existence professional compass adjusters. A yachtsman may avail himself of their expert services, but with common sense and an understanding of the causes, may *compensate* his compass himself. *(See Chapter 14.)* Note that a compass is not 'corrected'; its deviations are reduced; the process is called *compensating.* Rarely is a compensated compass entirely free of deviation on all headings. As will be seen, there will be residuals, quite possibly of small practical significance.

Deviation

Usually the mariner's compass is subject to magnetic forces additional to those of the earth. Magnetic materials aboard the vessel cause the compass to deviate from its ideal position in the magnetic meridian. This angular swing or rotation on its pivot is called *deviation* (D or Dev) fig. 1317.

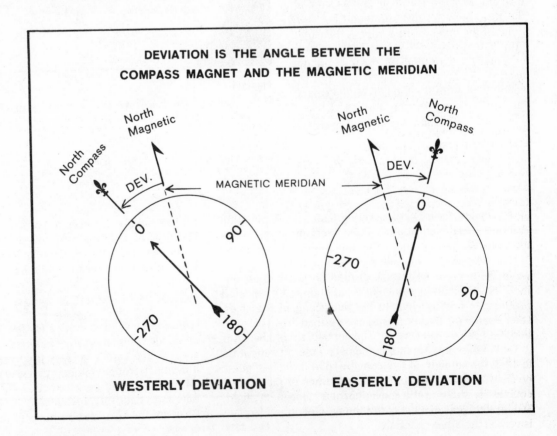

DEVIATION IS THE ANGLE BETWEEN THE COMPASS MAGNET AND THE MAGNETIC MERIDIAN

WESTERLY DEVIATION

EASTERLY DEVIATION

FIG. 1317 Deviation defined

Compass Error

Because variation depends upon location and deviation upon the ship's heading, there are various possible combinations of the two, fig. 1318. The algebraic sum of the variation and the deviation is termed the *compass error,* CE. This is a semantic term. The compass is not in error. It is operating according to the forces that control its behavior. Compass error is merely another angle, that one between the direction of true north and the direction north as shown by the compass. Similarly to variation and deviation it is expressed in degrees and direction, i.e., 5°E or 7°W. The accomplished navigator uses this combined figure frequently in his work.

THE APPLICATION OF VARIATION AND DEVIATION

A course is merely an angle. It is the angle which the keel, or a line on a chart, makes with some other line of reference. Three lines of reference have been established: the direction of true north or the true meridian; the direction of the magnetic meridian; and the direction of the north point of the compass. Thus *there are three ways to name a course,* true, magnetic or compass. Always to be kept in mind, and sometimes this is difficult for the novice, is that no matter how the course be named among these three, *it applies to only one track, one direction,* fig. 1319.

The helmsman steers by compass. Bearings are observed by, or relative to, a compass. On the other hand, the navigator customarily plots and logs his courses, bearings and lines of position as true. Hence there is need for continual interconversion between the three systems of nomenclature.

Like learning to read, to tell time by a watch, to finger a musical instrument, facility in making these conversions comes with practice. At first one reasons out the steps. Later, reasoning is dropped as the process becomes one of habit.

Two of the many mnemonic aids available to help the student master conversion will be described. Both are applicable only when courses are stated in the conventional 0° to 360° system now in most common use. One is verbal, the other pictorial.

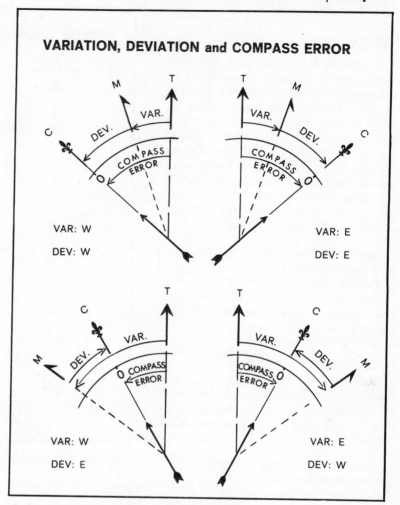

FIG. 1318 Variation, Deviation and Compass Error

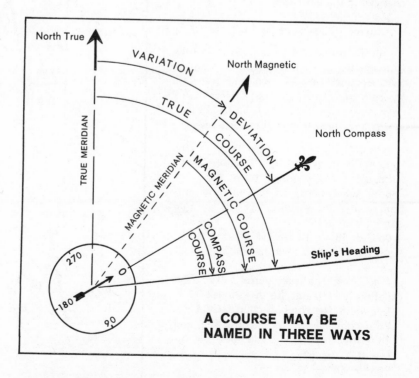

FIG. 1319 Three ways to name a Course

VERBAL AID

Assume the correct method of expressing a course as true, since no variable is involved. See fig. 1320. Assume the magnetic course to be less correct an expression because variation is involved and finally for a similar reason assume the compass course to be the least correct method of expression. Call the conversion of a course from compass to magnetic and from magnetic to true 'correcting.' Then the rule is: *"When correcting, add easterly errors"* which may be shortened to *"Correct add east."*

Example 1. The magnetic course is 061° and the variation is 11°E.

Required: The true course, TC.

The conversion is one of 'correcting' and the variation is easterly, so the basic rule, *"Correct add east"* is used.

061° + 11° = 072°

Answer: TC 072° See fig. 1321.

The rule is easily altered for application to the three other operations of conversion by remembering that *always two and only two* words are to be changed for any application.

Example 2. The magnetic course is 068° and the variation is 14°W.

Required: The true course, TC.

The conversion is 'correcting,' and the variation is westerly. The rule becomes: *"Correct subtract west."* Two words were changed in the basic rule.

068° − 14° = 054°

Answer: TC 054°. See fig. 1322.

Call the process of conversion from true to magnetic, or from magnetic to compass 'uncorrecting.' Now the two other forms of the rule are: *"Uncorrect east subtract"* and *"Uncorrect west add."* Two and only two words have been changed in each case.

Example 3. The true course is 088°. The variation is 18°W and the deviation 12°W.

Required: The compass course, CC.

Both conversions are 'uncorrecting' and both 'errors' are westerly. The rule is: *"Uncorrect west add."*

088° + 18° + 12° = 118°

Answer: CC 118°. See fig. 1323.

Example 4. The true course is 107°. The variation is 14°E and the deviation is 11°E.

Required: The compass course, CC.

Both conversions are 'uncorrecting' and both 'errors' are easterly. The rule: *"Uncorrect east subtract."*

107° − 14° − 11° = 082°

Answer: CC 082°. See fig. 1324.

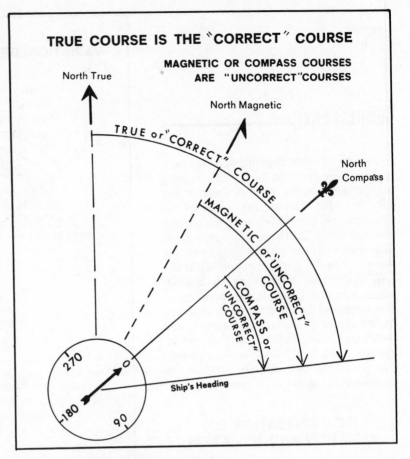

TRUE COURSE IS THE "CORRECT" COURSE

MAGNETIC OR COMPASS COURSES ARE "UNCORRECT" COURSES

FIG. 1320 True Course is the "Correct" Course

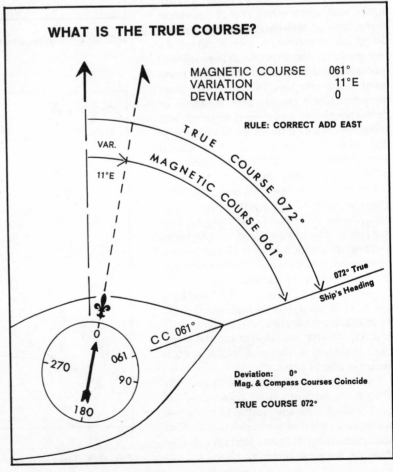

WHAT IS THE TRUE COURSE?

MAGNETIC COURSE	061°
VARIATION	11°E
DEVIATION	0

RULE: CORRECT ADD EAST

Deviation: 0°
Mag. & Compass Courses Coincide

TRUE COURSE 072°

FIG. 1321 Problem What is the True Course Var E

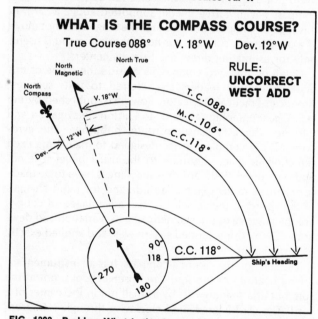

WHAT IS THE TRUE COURSE?

Magnetic Course 068°
Variation 14°W
Deviation 0°

TRUE COURSE 054°
MAGNETIC COURSE 068°
054° True
Ship's Heading
CC 068

RULE:

CORRECT SUBTRACT WEST

Deviation: 0°

Mag. & Comp. Coincide

TRUE COURSE 054°

FIG. 1322   Problem What is the True Course Var W

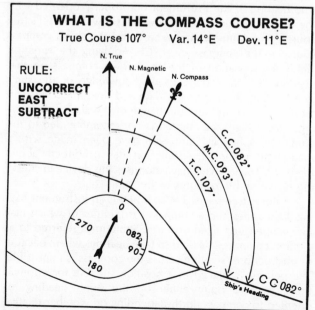

WHAT IS THE COMPASS COURSE?

True Course 088°   V. 18°W   Dev. 12°W

RULE:
**UNCORRECT
WEST ADD**

T. C. 088°
M. C. 106°
C. C. 118°
C.C. 118°
Ship's Heading

FIG. 1323   Problem What is the Compass Course Var W, Dev W

WHAT IS THE COMPASS COURSE?

True Course 107°   Var. 14°E   Dev. 11°E

RULE:
**UNCORRECT
EAST
SUBTRACT**

C.C. 082°
M.C. 093°
T.C. 107°
C C 082°
Ship's Heading

FIG. 1324   Problem What is the Compass Course Var E, Dev E

$$W - \leftarrow \; T \; V \; D \; M \; C \; \rightarrow \; -E$$

PICTORIAL SCHEMA

Vertically arrange the letters representing the three ways of naming a course, true, magnetic and compass, with the respective differences variation and deviation between them. Memorizing the reversal, Can Dead Men Vote Twice, may help to keep this arrangement in mind. On each side of the letters draw an arrow indicating the kind of conversion: on the left true to compass, on the right compass to true. Write in the appropriate arithmetic processes to be used with either easterly or westerly errors. The right side represents what has been called 'correcting' and the left side the reverse process, "uncorrecting." See fig. 1325. Memorize *DAW, DOWN ADD WEST* or WEST DOWN PLUS.

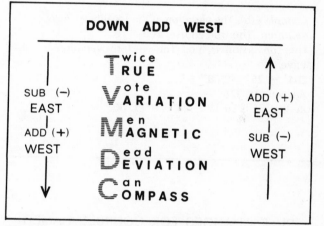

FIG. 1325   Verbal Aid, Down Add West etc

Example 5(a). From the chart the true course is 107° and the variation in the locality is 25°E.

Required: The magnetic course, MC.

The conversion is 'down' the picture. Use the left side. Easterly variation is to be subtracted.

107° − 25° = 082°

Answer: MC 082°. See below.

DOWN	T	107°
SUBTRACT	V	(−) 25°E
EAST ↓	M	082°

Example 5(b). For this magnetic heading the deviation aboard this ship is 11°W.

Required: The compass course, CC.

The conversion is again 'down' the picture. Use the left side. Westerly deviation must be added.

082° + 11° = 093°

Answer: CC 093°. See below.

DOWN	M	082°
ADD	D	(+) 11°W
WEST ↓	C	093°

Note that the so-called *compass error*, CE, the difference between true and compass, is 25°E − 11°W = 14°E. For any bearings taken over the ship's compass, while she is on the compass course 093°, applying the correction of 14°E yields the true bearing to be plotted on the chart.

Example 6(a). A ship is on compass course (CC) 193°. The deviation aboard this ship, for this compass heading is 11°E.

Required: The magnetic course, MC.

The conversion is 'up' the picture. Use the right side. Easterly deviation is to be added.

193° + 11° = 204°

Answer: MC 204°. See below.

ADD	T	178°
EAST	V	(−) 26°W
SUBTRACT	M	204°
WEST	D	(+) 11°E
	C	193°

Example 6(b). The variation in the locality is 26°W.

Required: The true course, TC.

The conversion is 'up.' The westerly variation is subtractive.

204° − 26° = 178°

Answer: TC 178°

Note that CE is 26°W − 11°E = 15°W.

RULE CHANGES FOR COURSES NAMED IN POINTS

When courses are named in points and quarter points, the terms add and subtract should not be used. For this application the shortened rules become:

Correct easterly errors **clockwise**

Correct westerly errors **counter clockwise**

Uncorrect easterly errors **counter clockwise**

Uncorrect westerly errors **clockwise**

The serious student by this time has an understanding of the existence of variation and deviation and the means of making allowances for them in operating his craft. From what has been presented he should know that a chart will give him the variation and that if he has reliable deviation tables he can interconvert courses.

Before explaining why deviation changes with the ship's heading, how to determine the deviations and how to prepare deviation tables it seems well to present a little general information.

Always trust your compass. Failure to do this may be disastrous. The so-called errors of the compass, you have learned, are not errors. A compass does not usually exhibit erroneous behavior. It is subject to natural laws which totally govern its operation. As will be shown, insofar as the small boatman is concerned, its errors are determinable; may be reduced and once determined make the compass an exceedingly accurate instrument. Unless abused or subjected to unusual extraneous magnetic effects caused by wrenches, knives, steel cans, radio or other equipment, it is far more reliable than a watch. For years it will faithfully indicate direction, if properly guarded. No watch is without some rate, which must be allowed for; not so a well treated compass.

No mention has been made of dry compasses. At one time mariner's compasses were dry. The needles were affixed to a card, and the assembly, extremely light in weight, supported on a pivot as in the wet compass. The installation of reciprocating engines in ships caused vibrations which affected the instruments' accuracy. The wet compass, literally damping these vibrations, came into general use.

Do not attempt to use the rules for conversion with a compass having a free needle supported above a card. In this type of compass the card and the magnet do not move as a unit. Such a compass has no lubber's line and is useful only for estimating directions from its center.

Detail on the gyro compass is outside the scope of this book. Interested readers are referred to texts such as: American Practical Navigator, Bowditch, published by the U.S. Oceanographic Office or to Dutton's Navigation and Piloting, The U.S. Naval Institute, publisher. The gyrocompass is a complex device designed to maintain a fixed direction in space. Contrary to the usual belief it is not without "errors." Aboard ship allowances have to be made for changes in geographic latitude and for rapid changes in the speed of the vessel. Its great advantages, of course, are the absence of the magnetic effects, variation and deviation. Gyro error is termed east or west and applied exactly as is deviation.

The sun compass is not a compass. It is an instrument for taking bearings of the sun. The observer looks, not at the sun, but at a shadow cast by a small pin in the center of a card. The card is graduated clockwise through 360° from a zero point at South. Thus the shadow marks the sun's true bearing. If the instrument be properly oriented with the vessel's heading, the shadow will show the vessel's true course. The difference between it and the ship's compass course is the compass error, CE. Applying the variation yields the deviation of the ship's own compass on that heading. Accuracy depends on knowledge of the sun's true bearing. Since latitude, date and time affect this and moreover since the rate of change of the sun's true bearing is inconstant, the method is not recommended to the uninitiate. Spherical compasses have been made with a shadow pin mounted centrally on the card directly above the pivot. The knowing navigator uses this device in checking deviation by azimuths of the sun.

A pelorus *(see pages 334 and 393)* is an instrument having sight vanes and a compass card, either of which may be clamped in a fixed position. Sometimes referred to as a dumb compass, it is used to take bearings when, because of obstructions, sighting across the compass is impossible. The pelorus is placed in a position suitable for observations, its zero point either on the ship's heading, or oriented to compass north depending on whether relative or compass bearings are desired.

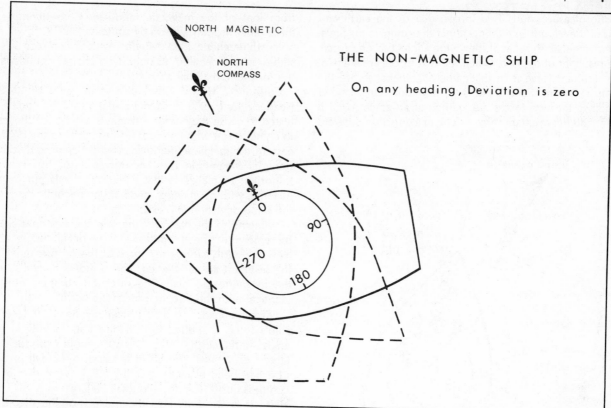

NORTH MAGNETIC

NORTH COMPASS

THE NON-MAGNETIC SHIP

On any heading, Deviation is zero

0

90

270

180

FIG. 1326   The Non-magnetic Ship

WHY DEVIATION DEPENDS ON THE SHIP'S HEADING

Aboard ship the mariner's compass is subject to two magnetic forces, that of the earth and that of the vessel. Were the vessel absolutely free of magnetism, there would be no deviation, regardless of her heading, fig. 1326. The earth's force depends upon geographic location. The compasses of all the ships in a harbor are subject to the same variation. The deviations aboard these ships will be unlike because of the magnetic characteristics of each hull. Further, if all these ships be put on identical magnetic courses, their corresponding compass courses will differ, except in the exceedingly remote circumstance that each compass be completely compensated.

Deviation, it was stated, *varies with the ship's heading,* because of the magnetic material aboard. A little investigation will demonstrate this. Refer again to fig. 1326, the non-magnetic ship. No heading of the vessel affects the compass card; its north point always lies in the magnetic meridian. The compass has no deviation. As the ship changes course, the lubber's line, turning with the ship's head, indicates on the "dial," the card, the magnetic course.

Now put aboard this ship, anchors, chain, rigging, pipe berths, steering gear, galley fittings, gas tanks, water tanks, stanchions, life lines, a host of similar magnetic material, not forgetting the all-important engine. The vessel has acquired a magnetic field of her own. To consider how this may affect the compass, assume the same field is created by fastening a large permanent magnet, slightly askew, in the vessel's stern. This artifact is exceedingly applicable; it simulates the magnetic condition aboard most wood or

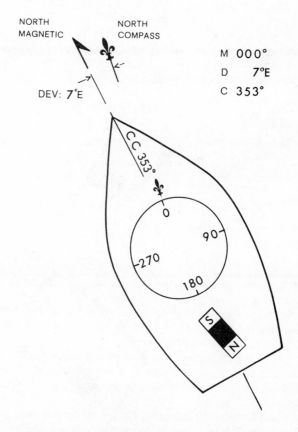

NORTH MAGNETIC   NORTH COMPASS

DEV: 7°E

M 000°
D 7°E
C 353°

CC 353°

0

90

270

180

S
N

FIG. 1327   Heading North Magnetic aboard ANACHRONISM

plastic pleasure craft. Two forces, that of the earth and that of the stern magnet, now affect the compass magnets. The magnets behave as if they were subject to one force, the resultant of the two. When the two forces are aligned, the resultant force is in that same alignment; so are the compass magnets and there is no deviation. On all other headings the two forces are applied at an angle to each other and the resultant force will be in a direction different from that of the magnetic meridian. Consequently, on these other headings, north by compass (000° CC) will not be north magnetic, (000° M), but north by compass will be stable on any specific heading if no changes be made in the magnetic material aboard.

Consider a typical vessel, the yacht ANACHRONISM. Headed North (000°) magnetic, fig. 1327, the forces referred to cause the compass magnets and hence the card, to come to rest with compass north slightly to the right, or east, of the magnetic meridian. There is an easterly deviation. Its magnitude is of no moment in this instance. Important to realize is that whenever she is put on this heading, with no changes made in her magnetic materials, the same deviation will exist.

Swinging to the eastward the ship steadies on a course for which it has been found she has no deviation, fig. 1328. Now the earth's force, the force of the stern magnet and the resultant are all aligned. The compass magnets lie in the magnetic meridian. The direction compass north is identical with the direction magnetic north.

Next she heads East (090°) Magnetic, fig. 1329. Now the ship's force is applied from a direction roughly at right angles to the earth's force. This 90° coupling produces the largest deviations. The effect is just as if a small piece of iron had been brought near the left or west side of the compass north. The deviation will be large. In ANACHRONISM it is westerly. Had the polarity of the theoretical stern magnet been reversed, the deviation on this heading would likewise have been large, but in the opposite direction, to the east.

Coming now to head South (180°) Magnetic, fig. 1330, the stern magnet's force is approaching alignment with the earth's force, but in a direction diametrically opposite to that of the heading 000° Mag. shown in fig. 1327. The large westerly deviation so evident on the heading East mag-

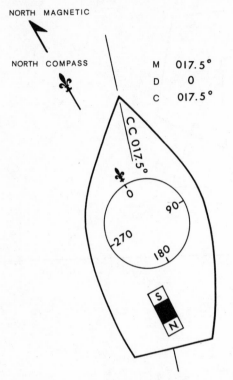

M   017.5°
D   0
C   017.5°

FIG. 1328   Heading with zero deviation aboard ANACHRONISM

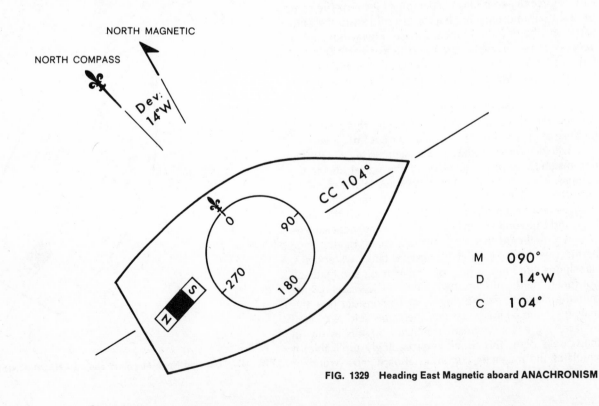

M   090°
D   14°W
C   104°

FIG. 1329   Heading East Magnetic aboard ANACHRONISM

netic is greatly reduced.

As the swing continues there will be a heading on which the two forces and their resultant will be again in line and the deviation zero. (In ANACHRONISM, as will appear later in this chapter, this occurs on the heading 187.5° Mag.)

Heading West (270°) Magnetic, fig. 1331, once more puts the two forces roughly at right angles, but the stern magnet's force is applied from the other side of the compass. The effect, now, is similar to that brought about by putting a small piece of iron close to the right or east side of the compass's north point. Again, as on the heading East, Magnetic, the deviation will be large, but now in the opposite direction, easterly.

Do not assume that on any other vessel these same deviations will exist. A ship's magnetic field does not necessarily lend itself to depiction as that of a single magnet. Indeed, changing the skew of the assumed magnet aboard ANACHRONISM a trifle would have altered the deviations.

To reiterate, were the ship non-magnetic, it would have no magnetic field, no deviation on any heading. Compensating a compass is an endeavor to so neutralize the magnetic field of the ship as to produce this non-magnetic environment for the mariner's compass. It is done by placing small magnets close to the compass in such positions as may be required. For this purpose many modern compasses have small magnets, adjustable as to position, built into their stands or binnacles. By their use and, if necessary, by adding other compensating magnets in the vicinity of the compass, the deviation on small boats is usually reducible to zero on most headings and leaving not more than three or four degrees in the others. Sailing craft, heeling out of the horizontal, frequently require heeling magnets to reduce their deviations. Iron and steel craft

are subject to changes in deviation upon large changes in their geomagnetic latitude. This is outside the scope of this work.

It is not difficult for the small boat operator to ascertain and record the deviations for a number of headings. Such a record becomes a ready reference deviation table good until structural changes or other movements of magnetic material are made aboard.

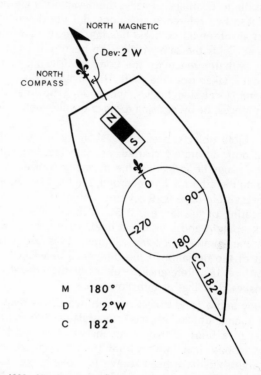

M   180°
D   2°W
C   182°

FIG. 1330   Heading South Magnetic aboard ANACHRONISM

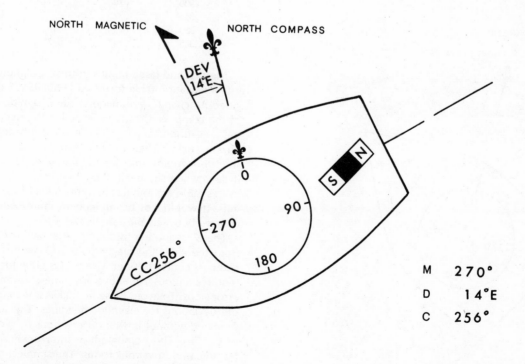

M   270°
D   14°E
C   256°

FIG. 1331   Heading West Magnetic aboard ANACHRONISM

DETERMINING THE DEVIATIONS

Deviation is the angle between the compass card axis and the magnetic meridian, fig. 1317, page 256.

Aboard any craft the direction of compass north is sighted at a glance. Not so the direction of the magnetic meridian or, as it is loosely termed, magnetic north. So it is not possible to compare, visually, the deviation angle between these two reference directions. But the difference between an observed compass bearing, and its magnetic equivalent yields the same angle. The bearing is sighted over, or with reference to, the compass. The magnetic equivalent is taken from the chart. The navigator does this by observing celestial bodies, the piloting boatman by running ranges, or by crossing a range on different headings.

Two visible objects, preferably ashore or fixed to the bottom, both accurately charted, are selected. From the chart the magnetic range, i.e. the magnetic course, from the fore to the after mark is recorded. See fig. 1332. A and B are two visible objects; B is visible behind A. The magnetic bearing of the range is 075°. A vessel sails on the range, keeping A and B visibly in line. While held on this course, the compass heading is noted. It is 060°. The amount of the deviation is the difference between 075° and 060° or 15°. Reference to either of the conversion rules makes clear that its direction is East.

A buoy and a fixed object or even two buoys may be used if a range of fixed objects is unavailable. The charted position of a buoy is that of its anchor. Thus wind, or current, or both may move a buoy from its charted position. Large ships have been known to move buoys inadvertently by collision in thick weather. Steering a visible course from buoy to buoy and noting the heading by compass, will, if the observation be made at the *start of the run*, give reasonably accurate results. (See fig. 1333.) Easiest perhaps is to swing the ship about its compass by sailing different headings across a range, recording the compass bearing of the range on each crossing.

Two prominent objects ashore are on a range bearing 087° from seaward. On a calm day the yacht ANACHRONISM sails across this range on compass headings successively 15° apart. Using sight vanes and an azimuth ring mounted on the compass *(page 393)* the compass bearing of the range is taken at each crossing. The results are recorded and tabulated. *(See below.)*

The navigator, noting the average compass bearing, 086.9°, was unusually close to the magnetic bearing of the range, decided the table was valid.

Ship's Head Compass	Range bears Compass	Range bears Magnetic	Deviation
000°	082°	087°	5°E
015°	086°	087°	1°E
030°	091°	087°	4°W
045°	096°	087°	9°W
060°	100°	087°	13°W
075°	104°	087°	17°W
090°	106°	087°	19°W
105°	106°	087°	19°W
120°	104°	087°	17°W
135°	101°	087°	14°W
150°	097°	087°	10°W
165°	093°	087°	6°W
180°	089°	087°	2°W
195°	085°	087°	2°E
210°	082°	087°	5°E
225°	079°	087°	8°E
240°	076°	087°	11°E
255°	073°	087°	14°E
270°	070°	087°	17°E
285°	069°	087°	18°E
300°	070°	087°	17°E
315°	072°	087°	15°E
330°	075°	087°	12°E
345°	078°	087°	9°E

The first and last columns in this tabulation now constitute a deviation table for ANACHRONISM'S compass provided *no changes are made in the magnetic environment of the compass.* Clearly indicated is the manner in which the deviation changes with the vessel's heading. To paraphrase Lecky, when on the heading 045° *magnetic* the ship's bow points in a direction quite different from where it does when she heads 045° by *compass.* The deviations in this table are applicable immediately to compass headings. It would not be difficult to interpolate visually for courses between the tabular values.

There is another problem. The navigator determines from the chart the magnetic course, wishes to know the compass course to steer. Use of this table for that purpose requires tedious, repetitive and time-consuming trial-and-error steps. To avoid these he makes a second table listing the deviations for *magnetic* headings. The second table is prepared without further observations by plotting a graph of the first. This nomogram or interconversion curve may be prepared in various forms. The simplest to plot and to use is still that of Admiral Sir Charles Napier, R.N., devised early in the nineteenth century, and bearing his name.

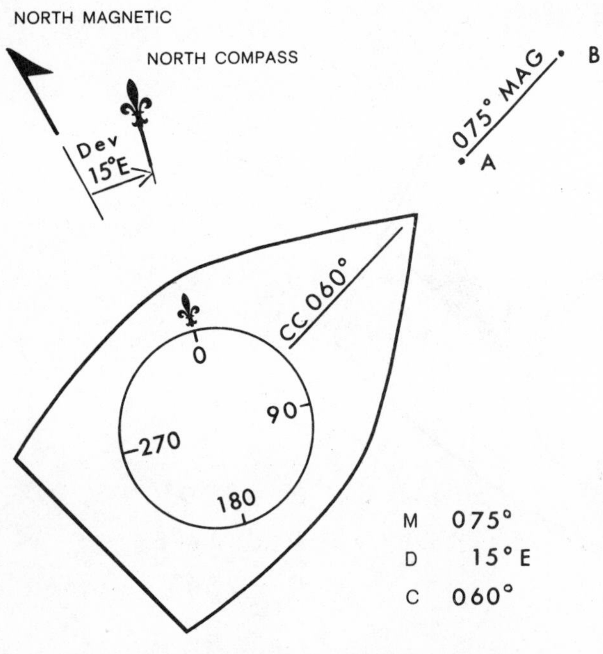

NORTH MAGNETIC

NORTH COMPASS

Dev 15°E

075° MAG. B
• A

CC 060°

0
90
270
180

M 075°
D 15°E
C 060°

FIG. 1332 Determining the Deviation, sailing on a range

The Napier Diagram

The Napier Diagram is used to this day in most of the world's navies, including our own. One cannot now agree with Squire Lecky's statement that "it requires a man who has lived on the same street as a draughtsman to produce" it. Napier arranged his co-ordinates at angles of 60° instead of the usual 90° so that in place of a rectilinear grid, his is a series of equilateral triangles on a common base. This singularly simple device (see fig. 1334) makes the single scale, that of the base line, equally applicable to the in-clined lines. The base line is laid off to represent 360°, with a dot every degree of its length. Every fifth dot is slightly heavier, for ease in identification. Every 15° along the base line is printed an angular value. Through these fifteen-degree stations are drawn the lines of the grid. Those sloping downward to the right are dotted every degree and like the base line, have the fifth dot accented. Those sloping downward to the left are solid.

Note that in the improved form of Napier diagram shown, the base line is not continuous but divided into two sections. To simplify its use for courses near the ends of these sections, this one, prepared by the United States Power Squadrons, has 15° extensions at both ends of each section. When points were in vogue the base and dotted lines were spaced in quarter-points. Perhaps this, the diffi-culty of dividing 11¼° accurately into quarters, may have occasioned Lecky's caustic comment. Deviations for com-pass headings are plotted on the dotted lines, easterly deviations to the right of the base line, westerly ones to its left.

Consider now plotting a Napier curve of ANACHRO-NISM'S deviation table from the observations previously made. For the heading 000° CC the deviation is 5°E. On the dotted line passing through the point marked North or 000° on the base line, circle the fifth dot to the right. For the heading 015° CC the deviation is 1°E. Circle the first dot to the right on the dotted line passing through 015° on the base line. For 030° CC the deviation is 4°W. Circle the fourth dot *to the left* on the dotted line passing through 030° on the base line. Continue in this fashion, plotting each one of the deviations listed in the table. Stations 345°, 195°, 165° and 015° are plotted twice, once in each of their respective positions on the base line.

FIG. 1333 Chart Segment showing magnetic headings from buoy to buoy

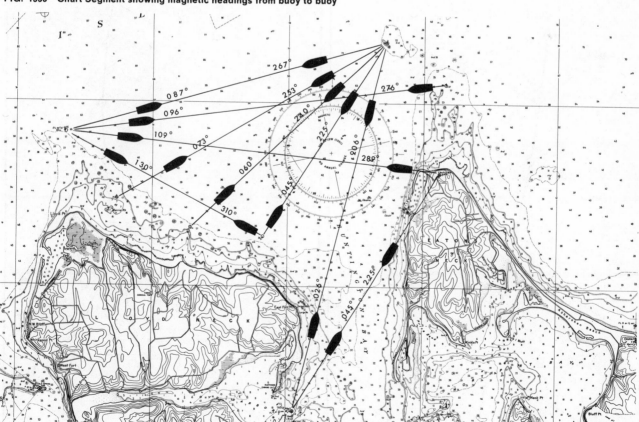

FIG. 1334   Napier Diagram

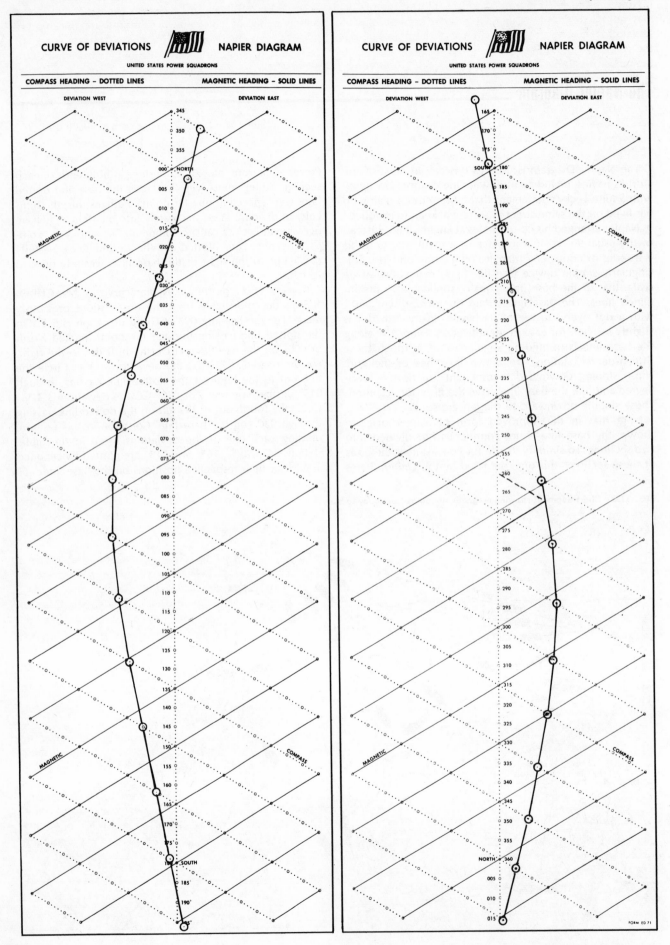

Now draw a fair curve through the plotted points. It may not pass exactly through every point because of observational or other errors, but if most of the points lie on the curve and those few which do not are within ½° of the curve, it will be sufficiently accurate. Should there be larger discrepancies the original observations or their subsequent computations are repeated. This is the conversion curve. All possible deviations of ANACHRONISM'S compass lie between this curve and the base line.

The length, from the base line to the curve, of any line of the diagram's grid, represents, to the baseline's scale, the magnitude of a deviation. Measured on the *dotted* lines are deviations for *compass* headings. Measured on the *solid* lines are deviations for *magnetic* headings. Where the curve is to the east (right) of the baseline, the deviations are east; where it is to the west (left), the deviations are west.

Making the second table, that of deviations for the magnetic headings, is now easy. The lengths of the respective solid lines are measured. Start with north. The curve is east of the baseline, hence this deviation will be east. See fig. 1334. Place one point of a pair of dividers on the center line at 000°. Adjust the dividers so that the other point is on the curve at its intersection with the solid line passing through 000°. Without changing the setting of the dividers' legs and keeping one leg on the base line, swing back to the base line. Record the number of degrees on the baseline between the divider points. It is 7° and the deviation for the heading 000° magnetic is 7°E.

Doing this for stations 15° apart produces the required second table for ANACHRONISM. It looks like this:

Ship's Head Magnetic	Deviation
000°	7°E
015°	1°E
030°	6°W
045°	12.5°W
060°	17°W
075°	19°W
090°	18°W
105°	17°W
120°	14°W
135°	11°W
150°	8°W
165°	5°W
180°	2°W
195°	2°E
210°	4°E
225°	6°E
240°	9°E
255°	11.5°E
270°	14°E
285°	16°E
300°	17.5°E
315°	17°E
330°	15°E
345°	11°E

Reverting to the Napier diagram, note that in swinging the dividers back to the base line it matters not, insofar as the amount of deviation is concerned, which way they are swung. If they be swung so that the two points on the baseline and the point on the curve form an equilateral triangle, the swung leg will indicate not only the deviation, but the corresponding compass course. Direct course conversion

is arrived at this way, or by drawing lines parallel to the grid lines. See fig. 1334 showing the inter-relationship between a magnetic course of 275° and a compass course of 260° aboard ANACHRONISM. This old jingle outlines procedure.

> From compass, the magnetic course to gain,
> Depart by dotted and return by plain.
> But from magnetic, to gain the course allotted,
> Depart by plain and then return by dotted.

From the Napier diagram a third table listing deviations in increments of 1°, applicable to either compass or magnetic headings, may be made. Appended is a portion of such a table, to the nearest integral degree, for ANACHRONISM. It has the advantage that no interpolations are required. For a known magnetic or a known compass course the deviation is immediately available.

Magnetic Heading	Deviation	Compass Heading
017°-018°	0°	017°-019°
019°-021°	1°W	020°-022°
022°	2°W	023°-025°
023°-025°	3°W	027°-028°
026°-027°	4°W	029°-031°
028°	5°W	032°-034°
029°-031°	6°W	035°-038°
032°-033°	7°W	039°-041°
034°-035°	8°W	042°-044°
036°-037°	9°W	045°-046°
038°-039°	10°W	047°-050°

For a compass with deviations as large as those of ANACHRONISM, such a table would be quite extensive, but nonetheless useful. For a compensated compass the table will be shorter because the deviations will be greatly reduced. *See: ANACHRONISM Compensated, Chapter 14.*

Instead of the three tables shown, some pilots prefer a circular deviation card, fig. 1335. The outer rose represents magnetic directions; the inner one directions by compass. Lines are drawn connecting corresponding values, as, for example, one between 275° on the outer rose and 260° on the inner. This really says that to make good 275° magnetic, ANACHRONISM must steer 260° by her compass or, conversely, that when she is steering 260° by compass she is making good 275° magnetic.

Some prefer a columnar arrangement. One column is headed: "For Magnetic"; the other: "Steer, Compass" and the corresponding values tabulated.

Using either of these two, conversion is performed by direct reading. No arithmetic is necessary and, with respect only to courses, not bearings, the user need know neither the amount nor the direction of the deviations.

Let the reader not infer that a Napier diagram or any similar conversion graph is to be used in daily piloting. That would be impractical. The diagram has but one function, to serve as a means of conversion in the preparation of those tables which the pilot chooses to use afloat.

See Chapter 14 for a further discussion of the compass

COMPASS DEVIATION CARD

MAGNETIC COURSE
FROM CHART
ON OUTER
ROSE

COURSE TO STEER
BY COMPASS
ON INNER
ROSE

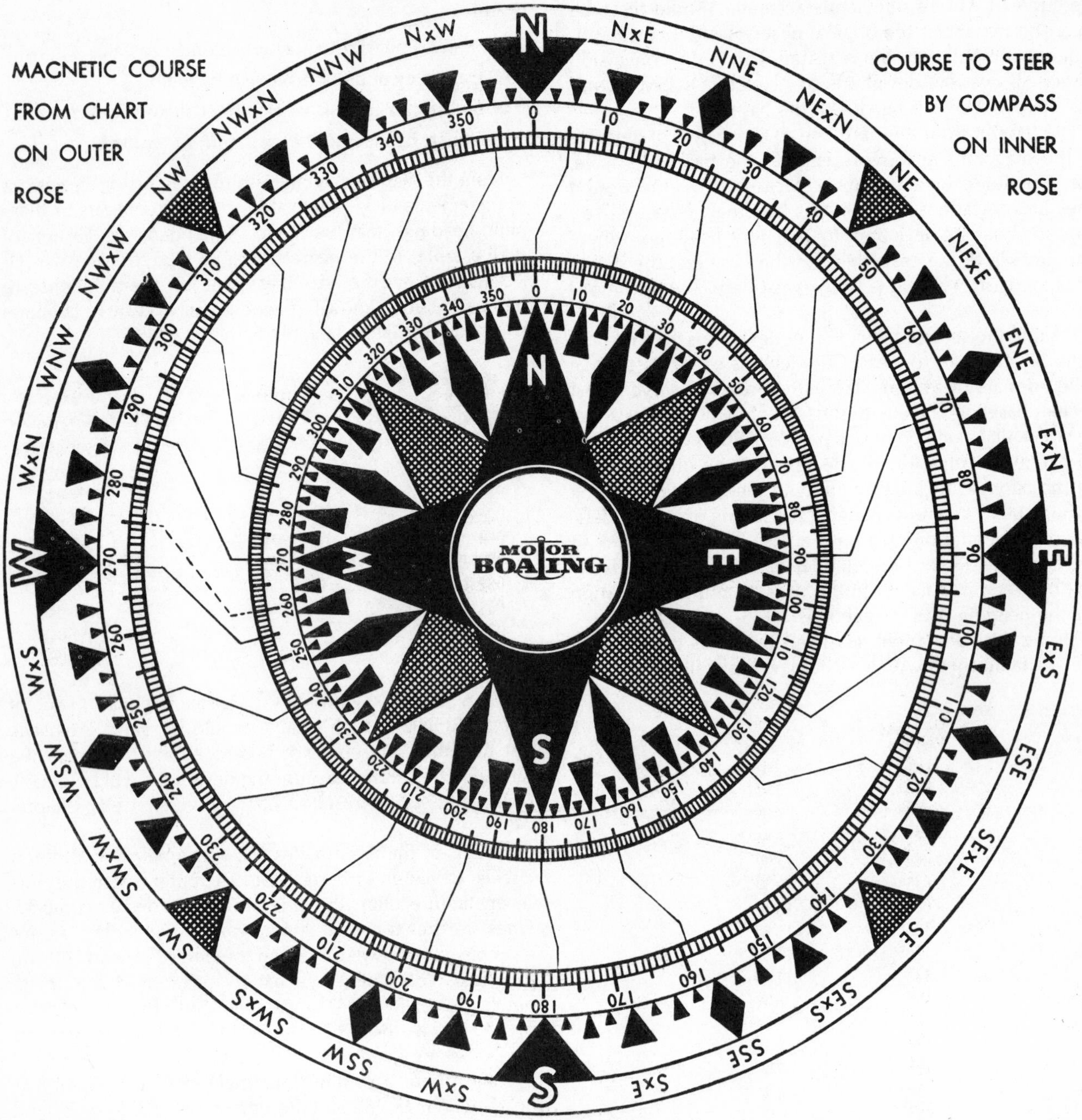

YACHT _____   OWNER _____

PORT _____   DATE _____

Read only MAGNETIC courses on the OUTER rose; only COMPASS courses on the inner one. For each compass heading (inner rose) apply the known deviation and draw a line from that degree or point to the corresponding magnetic heading (outer rose).

TO FIND THE COMPASS COURSE: Locate the magnetic course on the outer rose. Follow the lines to the inner rose and read the compass course.

TO CONVERT COMPASS COURSE TO MAGNETIC COURSE: Locate the compass course on the inner rose. Follow the lines to the outer one and read the magnetic course.

DO NOT CONVERT BEARINGS with this card. To do this find first the deviation for the boat's heading when the bearing was taken. Apply this deviation to the bearing.

FIG. 1335 Deviation Card

CHAPTER 14

THE MARINER'S COMPASS

**SELECTION,
INSTALLATION,
MAINTENANCE
and
COMPENSATION**

A VESSEL'S SAFETY may depend upon her compass. Cruising under conditions of poor visibility, the small craft pilot may have no other means of keeping to his desired track and, crossing a body of open water, no other means of making a good landfall. Running out the time on a given course in thick weather and neither seeing nor hearing the expected aid to navigation is not conducive to peace of mind. There is little comfort in a chain of soundings that does not match what the chart shows in the expected vicinity. Stranding because of unexpected contact with rock, shoal or any bottom is unnerving.

The preceding chapter gave some ways of ascertaining and using variation and deviation. Here will be discussed compensating, the reduction of deviations to a minimum, after some remarks on the choice of a compass and some further details as to its mounting aboard.

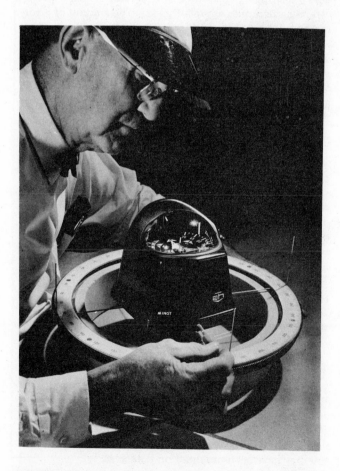

FIG. 1401 Inspecting the pivot action and instrumentally zeroing-in the compensators of a compass, prior to packaging for shipment.

Selecting a Compass

Almost any new compass looks fine in the store, or aboard in the quiet motion of the mooring or the marina slip. Its behavior under way, when the sea makes up and the little ship rolls, pitches and yaws, is of supreme importance. Will the card stick at some angle of heel? Will its apparent motion be jerky or smooth and easy? Are the card graduations legible and different headings easily distinguished? Is the instrument to be subject to large temperature changes? What if under its glass appears a bubble which may distract the helmsman? Answers depend on the quality of the compass.

No aviator will knowingly accept a cheap parachute, no sailor a bargain in life-jackets or fire extinguishers. No boatman should settle for a cheap compass. Select one adequate for your expected needs, erring on the side of luxury. Look at a number of them before buying. Pick them up, tilt and turn them, simulating motions to which they would be subject afloat. The card should have a smooth and stable reaction, come to rest without oscillations about the lubber's line. Reasonable tilting, comparable to the rolling and pitching of your boat, should not materially affect the reading. In fairness to the compass, if it has internal compensators, they must be zeroed-in (see below) before making these tests.

Pay particular attention to the card. Its graduation should be suited to the intended use. That a large craft may be held more easily on course than a small one is axiomatic. Hence the larger the ship, the greater is the number of divisions required on the card periphery. Owners of large ocean-going auxiliaries and cruisers seem to prefer cards which can be read to single degrees. Many of them also use quarter-point cards for long runs under sail.

Except under ideal conditions a small boat cannot long be held on a course with single-degree accuracy. The varying effects of wind, sea and indeed of trim brought about by the movement of a person aboard, swing her off the desired heading. Admittedly in the planning of a voyage, in the chart work, in the application of variation and deviation, accuracy to the nearest degree is essential. It gives the helmsman a goal. The experienced seaman knows little vessels cannot be steered so closely. Their track is an average, made up of headings at times on course, at times off to the right and to the left.

The novice, trying to steer 'too fine,' attempts to achieve the unachievable, to keep constantly on one heading. He cannot do so and, in the endeavor, repeatedly shifting his rudder, he overdoes it, makes steering needlessly laborious and is much less efficient than he would have been in a less effortful and more relaxed operation. Far from the smooth and easy performance of the skilled helmsman, his is that of the learner, most inept and suffering from a self-defeating concentration on precise control.

Steering is a bodily skill. The helmsman's brain, processing information received through his eyes, sends a signal to his muscular system to act in a certain way, to move the wheel or tiller. Lest the boat swing in a circle this muscular action must be stopped and a new one initiated to return the wheel to its previous position. Should the first action be too violent or too long continued, the vessel's head swings past the desired course, causing need for stronger action in the opposite direction in attempted rectification. There is little reason to believe the second action will be less violent than the first. Now the heading is off course in the opposite direction and the whole cycle must be repeated. The ship's head wanders from side to side about the course desired. (The modern science of control, of reducing in many operations this oscillating about a desired end, Norbert Wiener named cybernetics, using Plato's term for the steersman's art.)

Though most machines and electrical circuits respond much faster than man to specific orders, it cannot be denied that man does well when the orders allow him some latitude in performance. Consider attempting to steer 113° for a short 30-minute trick at the wheel using a small compass card. Close to the lubber's line are the graduations representing 111°, 112°, 113°, and 114° not in any way distinguishable from each other, except by position. More easily recognizable, because their marks are somewhat longer and perhaps heavier than the other four, are 110° and 115°. fig. 1402. Under any but the calmest conditions holding on 113° will not be possible. The effort of identifying 113° among the other close and cluttered marks will be difficult. Handling the wheel or tiller to keep the lubber's line on it for 30 minutes will be impossible.

To the best of his ability, the experienced small craft captain will hold the lubber's line midway between the more prominent graduations 110° and 115°, each clearly recognizable, and steer this course with the admonition "nothing to the left," gauging his handling to give her just

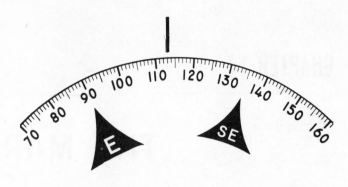

FIG. 1402 Segment of a card graduated in degrees, the lubber's line indicating a course of 113°. Compare fig. 1403.

FIG. 1403 Another card, graduated every 5°. Most helmsmen find this type of graduation easier to use.

"a little to the right." The orders to the operator of the boat's steering mechanism, a man, are not too specific and can be carried out with relative ease. The amount of error, the amount that the track sailed will wander from 113°, will be less than it would have been under rigorous endeavors to keep the lubber's line exactly on that course mark. Moreover the operation will be easier visually when there are no intermediate marks on the card between 110° and 115°. Thus a card graduated only every 5° is ideal for the small boatman's purpose. See fig. 1403.

CRITERIA FOR SELECTION

1. The card should remain level and not stick through reasonable angles of pitch and roll.

2. The card should move but slightly during any course change made by rotating the box or case through 90° or more. Some small motion due to the inertia of the fluid is permissible, but the card should be dead-beat, swinging but once to a steady position, not oscillating about the lubber's line.

3. The card should be easily read and graduated to your preference.

4. Provision should be made for lighting.

5. Hemispherically shaped, rather than a flat top plate.

6. Internally gimballed card and lubber's line.

7. Sturdy waterproof case.

8. Internal compensators, that is, built into the case.

9. Expansion bellows in the assembly to prevent bubbles in the liquid in lowered temperature.

10. For a larger boat a deck-mounted binnacle (fig. 1404), means for taking bearings and frequently for small steel boats soft iron compensators, those hollow iron balls you may have seen mounted on binnacles.

11. Do *not* consider a dry marching compass nor a dry tank compass. This is pure folly, inviting later disaster.

FIG. 1404 Deck-mounted binnacle.

Above all do not be niggardly. Buy an instrument made by a manufacturer of repute and pay his price. Hidden in the construction of a compass are things that make for accuracy and long life. Among them are: precise positioning of the magnetic element or the magnets under the card, so that its 000°-180° axis indicates exactly the direction of the magnetic meridian; the permanency of the markings on the card, of the expansion bellows, of the case seals; the life of the pivot bearing, its resistance to wear or to warping or distention from being, in the case of many little ships, tied up on one heading for five days every week. Here quality will pay off. In the long run the best is the least expensive.

ZEROING-IN

A modern compass having built-in compensators should be zeroed-in before being mounted aboard. If necessary such a compass already installed may be demounted and taken ashore for this purpose. Zeroing-in is nothing more than adjusting the compensators so that they have no effect on the compass. A compass subject only to the earth's field has no need of compensation; there are no deviations to remove. Therefore **before being installed, any deviation caused by improper positioning of the compensators themselves must be removed** and the unit go aboard just as an old-fashioned compass, ready for what magnetic changes may be wrought upon it by the ship's field. Setting the compensators by aligning screws with marks on the case or housing may not be sufficient for accurate navigation. Zeroing-in by trial-and-error is simple and effective, does not require any knowledge of the direction of magnetic North.

Do it in an area well away from any known magnetic influence: iron, steel girders, pipes, and ductwork concealed in walls, floors or ceilings; loud-speakers, radios, motors, refrigerators, freezers and so on. Don't work wearing a steel belt buckle, bracelet or watch band, nor a

yachtsman's cap containing a steel top grommet.

Using non-magnetic screws or tacks mount the compass temporarily on a small board having two parallel edges. Placing the lubber's line closely parallel to these edges is helpful but not essential. On a level flat board—be wary of a table or card table as it may have hidden steel screws or fittings—place a large book and the compass on its small board. Set the compass board with one of its parallel sides firmly against the edge of the book. Turn book and board as a unit until the compass reads North, fig. 1405. Hold the book steady. It serves as a fixed direction marker. Bring the opposite edge of the compass board snugly against the book. The lubber's line is now exactly reversed. If, now, the compass reads South, the N-S compensator is already zeroed-in and needs no adjustment.

If the reading is not South, half the difference must be removed. With a non-magnetic screw driver (a dime may do), slowly turn the N-S screw. Should the card move farther away from South, turn the screw in the opposite direction. With half the difference removed, realign the book and compass board, again as a unit, to the compass heading, South. Then without moving the book, reverse the compass.

If it does not now read North, halve the difference by turning the N-S adjusting screw. Again realign the book and compass on North, reverse the compass and if it does not read South, again halve the difference. Continue this process until the reversal is as nearly perfect as possible. When these adjustments are concluded, the direction of

FIG. 1405 Zeroing-in with book and board. Note that this type of compass is to be mounted so that the lubber's line is between the card and the helmsman.

the magnetic meridian *(see Chapter 13)* is that of the North-South axis of the compass card.

Next adjust the E-W compensators in the same way: line up on either an East or West heading, reverse and if the resultant heading is not exactly opposite, remove half the difference and continue working on East and West headings just as was done on North and South.

If exact reversals are not attainable move to a different

site; some magnetic influence may be at work.

If the adjusting screws are accessible and if the compass fits tightly in its packing box, zeroing-in can be done with the compass in its box instead of mounted on a board. If the compass, however, has to be removed from its box to adjust the screws, it is difficult to halve the differences and the chance of the compass not being exactly reversed is more probable.

Do not discard the temporary mounting board. It may be useful in testing the proposed permanent site aboard.

Installation

Intentionally Chapter 13 made only brief reference to the principles of mounting a compass. Now those should be amplified. There are definite steps to a good compass installation: inspect, test, mount, compensate and maintain.

Look critically at the proposed location. Clearly the compass should be directly in front of the helmsman, placed so that he may view it without bodily stress as he sits or stands in a posture of relaxed alertness. Give thought to his comfort in heavy weather and, in conditions of poor visibility, day or night. His position is fairly well determined by the wheel or tiller he handles. The compass is to be brought into what one might term his zone of comfort. Too far away, he bends forward to watch it. Too close, he rears backward for relief. Much of the time he may be not only the helmsman, but the forward and after lookout. So put the compass where he can bring his eyes back to it with a minimum of bodily movement. A distance of 22 to 30 inches from his eyes with the head tilted forward not more than 20° is about right, see fig. 1406.

Now inspect the site. It should be at least two feet away from engine indicators, bilge vapor detectors, other magnetic instruments and any steel or iron. Six or more feet is better than two, but there may have to be compromise on the small boat. When one or more of these magnetic influences is too close, either it or the compass must be moved. Vertical magnetic material is to be particularly avoided.

When, from this cursory inspection, the location seems satisfactory, test it. There may be magnets or magnetic influences concealed under the cabin top, forward of the cabin's after bulkhead, within the cockpit ceiling or in a wood-covered stanchion. You will test with the compass. If the compass has internal compensators, be sure, before testing, that they have been zeroed-in. If this has not been done, rotary motion of the case will make the card move, nullifying the test procedure.

Move the compass all around the area of the proposed site. Watch the card. One thing only will make it turn, a magnetic influence. Find it with the compass. If it cannot be moved away or replaced by non-magnetic material, test to determine whether it is merely magnetic, a random piece of iron or steel, or is magnetized. Successively bring the North and South poles of the compass near it. Both

FIG. 1406 Consider the helmsman's comfort when installing a compass.

FIG. 1407 Keep magnetic materials away from the compass. This light meter would cause deviation.

poles will be attracted if it is unmagnetized. If it attracts one pole and repels the other, it is magnetized. Demagnetization *(see page 277),* should be attempted.

Next hold or tape down the compass where you expect to mount it. Now the temporary mounting board used in zeroing-in will be helpful. Test everything that might affect the compass. Turn the wheel, switch on and off all the lights, radios, radio direction finder, radio telephone, depth finder and, if there is one, the shipboard intercom. Sound the electric 'whistle,' turn on the windshield wipers. Start the engine, work the throttle, move the gear shift. When there is an auxiliary generator, start it. In short, one at a time test everything that might cause deviation. When, on any one of these tests, the card moves, ideally the compass should be relocated or the cause demagnetized. Some of these things, windshield wipers, for example, you may

have to settle for, making a different deviation table to use when they are operating.

Be sure the site is firm. Vibration not only increases pivot wear, but may initiate that disconcerting phenomenon, a slowly spinning card!

Now prepare to mount the compass, following the principles given on page 251. The line throught he lubber's line and the compass card pivot must be exactly parallel to the boat's keel to forestall an error constant on all courses. Establish the fore-and-aft line of the ship with stout cord or string. Carefully transfer this line to the compass site. If necessary shim the base so that a stile-type lubber's line affixed to the case and not gimballed, is vertical when the ship is on an even keel. Drill one hole, only. If, during compensation, the instrument has to be skewed slightly to counteract disalignment of the card or the fore-and-aft line, more than one hole will present problems.

Maintenance

Maintenance has two aspects. The first is the preservation of the magnetic environment of the compass. Except for occasional testing, no piece of iron or steel is to be brought or installed near it. An ashtray, a beverage can, camera, light meter, freon-powered horn, a portable radio, steel tools and a host of other common magnetic materials must be kept well away from the compass while it is in use. See fig. 1407. They will cause unknown deviations.

The second consists mainly of getting to know your compass. Watch how it appears to swing. Check that its readings are consistent on frequently sailed courses. Note if it appears to become sluggish and above all if it becomes erratic—these two warn you of alien magnetism or a damaged pivot bearing.

Test for a damaged pivot bearing or for undue pivot friction by deflecting the card a few degrees from the lubber's line with a piece of steel. There is need for repair

should the card not return to its former heading.

A bubble is removed by adding some liquid but the liquid must be that with which the compass is filled. No alcohol or water should be added to an oil-filled compass, no oil added to an alcohol-water-filled one lest the card, gaskets and internally painted marks be damaged.

Lightning and electric welding aboard may change the ship's own magnetic field. After exposure to either of these, test to see whether the deviations have changed.

On small welding jobs, placing the ground connection close to the weld limits the electric current flow and the resultant magnetic field to a small area, rendering large changes less likely.

Do read and follow the manufacturer's recommendations for winter storage. They may add years to the instrument's useful life.

PRINCIPLES OF COMPENSATION

It should be understood that what follows applies to compensation in the craft of the average pleasure boat owner. Though in these vessels deviations may be large initially *(see ANACHRONISM, Chapter 13)* and indeed the compass may even lock and swing with the ship after the ill-considered installation of some useful but strongly magnetic article, the causative factors are limited. With common sense, care in procedure and occasional ingenuity, the causes can be removed or their effects largely neutralized by the average boat owner if he will methodically follow the steps laid out in this chapter.

Usually absent in these craft are complications due to permanent hull magnetism acquired during building; the variable transient magnetism induced in vertical iron or steel members: the ship's sides, bulkheads, stanchions, masts; not forgetting those arising from a magnetic cargo. Solution of these and other problems should be left to an expert skilled and experienced in that field, a professional compass adjuster. The reader interested in the magnetic conditions aboard larger steel vessels is again referred to Dutton or Bowditch *(page 260)* or to still more technical treatises.

Compensating a compass is the process of reducing its deviations to a minimum. Deviation is caused by the magnetic field of the vessel. Compensation, then, is the elimination of the effects of this ship's magnetism on the compass. A small magnet very near the compass can negate the effect of more remote large magnetic masses.

In wooden or plastic power craft compensation is usually achieved by firmly fastening two small permanent bar or needle magnets, one parallel to the keel, the other athwartship, close to the compass. These two compensators need not be in the same horizontal plane, but there is one restriction upon their placement. Each must be centered on a line passing through the compass pivot. Thus the one parallel to the keel, called the fore-and-aft magnet, is placed to the right or left of the compass, with its center on a line running accurately athwartship through the compass pivot. The athwartship one is positioned forward or aft of the compass with its center on a truly fore-and-aft line through the pivot.

When, and only when, the compensators are placed that way, a unique condition exists which greatly simplifies the process of compensation. The athwartship compensator will not materially affect the compass on east or west magnetic headings, nor the fore-and-aft one on north or south headings.

A ship is headed east magnetic. An athwartship magnet, centered on a fore-and-aft line through the compass pivot and placed at A or B, fig. 1408, is approximately parallel to the compass's magnetic element. Irrespective of the direction of the compensator's poles, north to starboard or to port, it will exert no force bringing about any practical change in the deviation.

A compensator, centered on an athwartship line through the compass pivot, placed fore-and-aft at D or F, fig. 1409, is roughly at right angles to the compass magnet, exerts a strong torque or turning force upon it, and causes it to move, either increasing or decreasing the deviation.

Obviously similar conditions obtain on a heading of

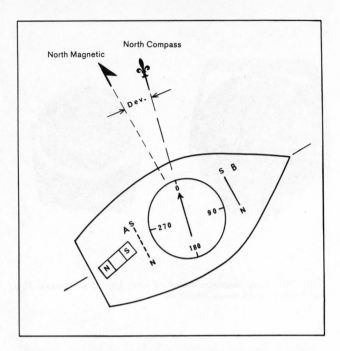

FIG. 1408   On E-W headings athwartship magnets have no effect.

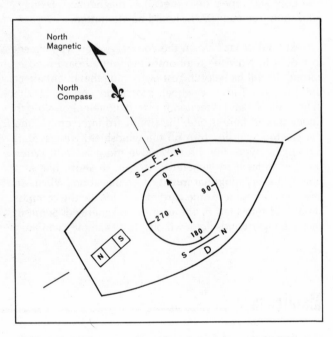

FIG. 1409   On E-W headings fore-and-aft magnets have maximum effect.

west magnetic. In the same way on north-south headings the effectivity of athwartship compensators and the nullity of those placed fore-and-aft could be demonstrated.

Of course both compensators come into use when sailing other than cardinal directions. The great value of the phenomena just explained is that they permit the pleasure craft operator to divide the causes of deviation into only two component parts and, without knowledge of their magnitude, remove each of them separately and uncomplicated by the other.

When the compensators have been fastened in what is found to be their most effective positions they could be replaced by one single horizontal magnet centered exactly under the pivot, at a specific distance from it and fixed at

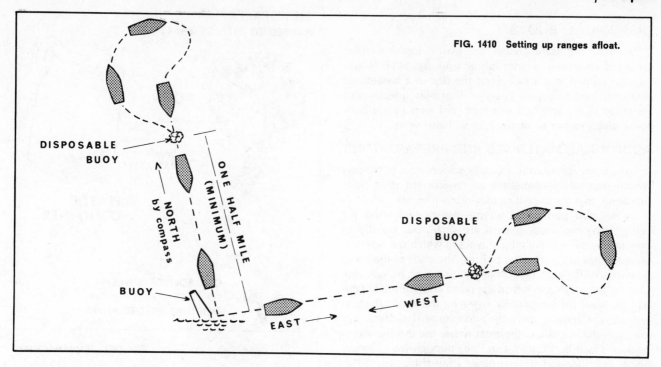

FIG. 1410 Setting up ranges afloat.

some necessary angle to the ship's fore-and-aft line. This, the Admiralty method at one time used in the British Navy, is, to quote Lecky, "very elegant, . . . but somewhat more difficult than the ordinary one in vogue on merchant vessels." For "merchant vessels" read present-day pleasure craft and that understatement made twenty years before the twentieth century began still holds good.

Internal compensators, built in by the manufacturer, are so arranged that when the compass is installed they will be in the proper relative positions previously outlined. They are adjusted, as was shown in the discussion of zeroing-in, by means of a slotted bolt head, usually called a compensating screw. Casual inspection will show that one of the compensating screws is aligned with the lubber's line, the other at right angles to it. On some instruments the screws are marked N-S and E-W. Turning the screw varies the magnet's influence on the compass card from zero to maximum. Aboard many pleasure craft proper setting of these compensators will bring about compensation. When this does not suffice, because of powerful magnetic forces aboard, additional means, to be described later, will be necessary.

The astute reader will have perceived that compensation is analogous to zeroing-in. In zeroing-in, the book and board served to make certain that, at each reversal of the compass, its lubber's line turned exactly 180°. It was as if the compass had been aboard a ship, which, on each reversal, sailed an exactly reciprocal magnetic course.

Zeroing-in ashore began by using an unknown magnetic direction or course, identified only as North (000°) by compass. Zeroing-in was successful because this, or any other unknown magnetic heading, could be accurately reversed. Afloat, compensation may be started in the same way. Afloat, the nub of the problem is achieving accurate reversal, putting and holding the vessel on a course over the bottom, exactly the reciprocal of the original unknown magnetic heading. This, as will be shown, is not as difficult as one might surmise.

SAILING A RECIPROCAL COURSE

Between any two visible marks, or on a range, reversing the magnetic heading is obviously easy. In compensating there is need ultimately to sail at least the four cardinal magnetic directions North, South, East and West. Cardinal directions are seldom defined by aids to navigation or by landmarks in cruising waters. In a yacht anchorage or in waters adjacent to a marina, ranges may be built on these bearings and vessels easily steadied on them.

This then becomes a do-it-yourself project. *The skipper makes his own range.* Departing from a fixed mark (a buoy will do) he sails on a steady compass heading until ready to reverse course, then drops his own disposable buoy clear of the screw, creating the required range. Next he executes a buttonhook turn, lines up the disposable buoy and the original departure point, steadies on this range visually and, ignoring the compass, heads for the starting point, runs down the disposable buoy and continues back toward the mark originally left, fig. 1410. The turn is made as tightly as possible, keeping the buoy in sight, and is completed before the buoy has time to drift. The skipper, knowing the characteristics of his boat, will choose a right or a left turn.

This maneuver has accurately put the ship on a reciprocal course, providing that the buoy remained where it was dropped and that no wind or current sets the ship to either side of her heading on the outward or inward courses. Compensation will be inaccurate if she has moved crabwise over the bottom, going one way, but headed another; therefore the requisite courses are sailed where the current is negligible and when the wind or sea produces no leeway.

The skipper who has qualms about running the buoy down should take it very close alongside, touching it. On a range of ½ nautical mile, 1000 yds, when the buoy is 6¼ feet to one side of the vessel's center line the course error will be 8', less than 1/7 of 1°.

DISPOSABLE BUOYS

Excellent disposable buoys are plastic bleach bottles ballasted about one-quarter full of sand, fig. 1411. Newspapers wadded into a ball about the size of a basketball, tied with light string—no heavy stuff or wire, please—and weighted at the end of a four-foot cord with an old bolt, spark plug, washer or similar gear will also serve.

ADDITIONAL MATERIALS AND PREPARATIONS

For a compass without internal compensators or for one whose internal compensators are insufficient to remove deviation, two compensating magnets will be needed. Each is an encased permanent magnet having two holes for screw fastening. Modern units are small, but equally as effective as the original tubular types in which the magnets were either long steel wires or rods. The ends of the compensators will either be stamped N and S or be colored, blue on the south and red on the north end. Adhesive tape will be ideal for temporarily fastening the external compensators. Carefully mark their longitudinal centers. Lay out carefully in chalk in the areas where the external compensators will be located, two lines through the compass pivot, one fore-and-aft, the other athwartship, fig. 1412.

For the internally compensated compass a non-magnetic screw driver will be needed. A thin coin may do. The compass has been previously zeroed-in.

Every magnetic article of ship's gear should be stowed in its accustomed place, the windshield wiper blades be in their normal position of rest, no magnetic material near the compass, either obviously or hidden in the clothing of the helmsman or others. Realize that steel partial dentures, or the steel grommet of a yachting cap brought within a few inches of the compass may produce deviation. Someone may be working that close to the instrument during compensation. Keep external compensators far from the compass until they are to be installed.

COMPENSATION ON THE CARDINAL HEADINGS

With due regard for the conditions of wind, sea and current already mentioned steer 000° by compass from the

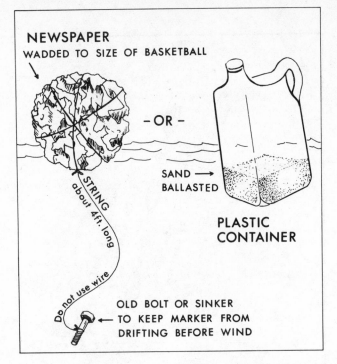

NEWSPAPER WADDED TO SIZE OF BASKETBALL

STRING about 4ft. long

Do not use wire

– OR –

SAND → BALLASTED

PLASTIC CONTAINER

OLD BOLT OR SINKER ← TO KEEP MARKER FROM DRIFTING BEFORE WIND

FIG. 1411 Disposable buoys.

chosen mark, holding rigorously to this course by the compass for half a mile or more. Next, have a crew member drop the disposable buoy over the stern, execute the turn and sail the reciprocal course, fig. 1410. This course, the reader will recall, is not sailed by compass, but by heading for the original departure point. The helmsman must hold this course visually. The compass heading is noted. If it is 180° there is no deviation on either the north or south compass headings. The athwartship internal compensator is not touched and no athwartship external compensator is necessary.

If the compass heading is not 180° compensation is required. Exactly as in the process of zeroing-in, half the difference between 180° and the observed compass course is to be removed. Halving the difference is based on the assumption that the deviation on reciprocal courses is equal and opposite. It may not be exactly so (see again ANACHRONISM, Chapter 13), but it serves well as an approach.

Assume the compass heading is observed to be 200°. Then one half of the 20° difference, or 10°, is to be removed; adjustment is made until 190° is on the lubber's line while the helmsman continues to hold the course by steering for the buoy.

On an internally compensated compass turn the N-S adjusting screw. This controls the concealed athwartship magnet. If the compass course becomes more than 200°, turn the screw in the opposite direction. Move the screw slowly until the compass course is 190°.

For the externally compensated compass the correction will be made by *centering* a compensator athwartship on the chalked fore-and-aft line. If there is room, place a compensator forward of the compass in the position D, A or C, fig. 1413. Should the course become more than 200° the compensator is increasing the deviation and must be turned end-for-end. The card will move in the desired direction.

Should the card stop moving before 190° reaches the lubber's line, the compensator, in a position as at D, is too far from the compass. On the other hand, should the card

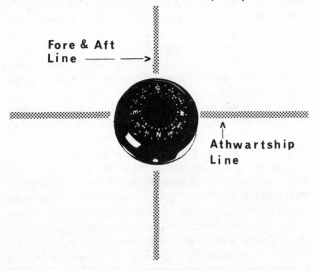

Fore & Aft Line ——→

Athwartship Line

FIG. 1412 Chalk lines for positioning external compensators, laid out through the compass pivot.

swing past 190° the compensator is in the position as at C, too close to the compass. Move the compensator aft or forward as necessary until the course is 190°. Now tape the compensator firmly down; no screws yet. If there is no room for the compensator forward of the compass, place it in the vicinity shown as A'. *Do not place it off the center line as at E.*

In zeroing-in, the compass was next oriented so that 180° was on the lubber's line. This maneuver is not usable here before returning to the buoy because there is no means of laying out a reciprocal course. Return to the buoy, then run either south or north, repeat the procedure: outbound again on 000° (though the track will be 10° away from the original one), drop the disposable buoy, make the turn, head visually for the marker. If the observed course is not now 180° again remove only half the difference by turning the adjusting screw or moving the external compensator, as the case may be. Repeat if necessary until the N-S headings are error-free. Screw down the external magnet in its place, being careful not to move it. Do not touch

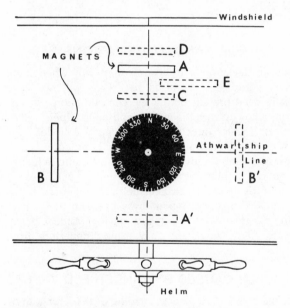

FIG. 1413 How compensating magnets are placed.

the internal compensator screw again. The smallest shift will nullify the careful work and re-introduce some deviation.

A similar method is pursued on east-west headings. Run from a buoy to the eastward on 090° or to the westward on 270°, drop the buoy, make the turn, head back visually for the departure point. Remove half the apparent error. On the internally compensated compass, adjust the E-W screw. With external compensation, place the compensator in a fore-and-aft position and *centered* on the athwartship chalk line, similar to B or B', fig. 1413, following the same techniques as on the north-south headings. When, after sufficient trials, the deviations are zero, *or as near to zero as is attainable,* screw down the external compensator with utmost care. Leave the internal compensator screw alone.

An alternate method of sailing reciprocal courses, credited to Darrach, uses a vertical shadow pin in the center of a horizontal graduated disc, preferably gimbal-mounted.

As the vessel heads north by the compass, the disc is rotated by hand so that the shadow falls on its zero point.

The ship comes about, steadies on a course such that the shadow falls on the opposite edge of the disc, exactly on the 180° mark. Now the course shown on the compass is noted. If it is 180° there is no deviation on N-S headings. If it is not, the procedure for compensation is undertaken, halving the difference and similarly on the E-W headings.

This appears to be simple. The vessel need not run far on any course. No departure mark nor disposable buoy is necessary. Neither wind nor current alters the result. But, reader, wait before you exclaim "this is for me." That shadow is not a fixed direction. The earth turns under the sun. While the ship holds a constant heading for a few minutes, that shadow moves. So time becomes a factor in the operation. Compensators must be adjusted or taped down before the shadow moves appreciably, taking the ship off the reciprocal heading. A navigator knows how to make the needed changes in his course by the shadow pin. The novice would best plan to use this method of course reversal only near the time of the summer solstice when the rate of change of the shadow movement is less than 1° in ten minutes of time, depending on the latitude.

COMPENSATION ON INTERCARDINAL HEADINGS

This is not for the amateur. However, in the average wooden, plastic or aluminum hull after cardinal compensation, the deviations on the intercardinals are usually small, not exceeding 4°.

Steel hulls may present problems whose solution may require installing soft iron spheres on the binnacle, use of Flinders bars and possibly heeling magnets. All this is for the professional, or for the exceptional amateur who, by study and practice in methods not discussed in this book, has achieved professional competence.

RESIDUALS ON INTERCARDINAL HEADINGS

The deviations remaining on the intercardinal headings may be determined by the methods discussed in Chapter 13 or estimated by making reciprocal runs on these headings. In the latter method half the difference between the outward course steered by compass and the observed inward course will be the deviation for the heading. Proper attention should be paid to the direction of the deviation, East or West.

FAILURE TO ACHIEVE COMPENSATION

When compensation cannot be achieved there is a strong magnetic field nearby. If care was used to remove or relocate the more obvious culprits in view of or hidden from the compass as earlier advised, look to the existence of a magnet nearby. Always suspect are tachometer cables and the steering mechanism. Test them with a thin piece of steel; a machinist's thickness gauge .001" thick is ideal. Touch one end to the part being tested and gently pull it away. If the thin piece of steel tends to stick to the part, the latter is magnetized. Test thoroughly. Open the wheel housing and test all its metal parts. Finding a magnet, demagnetize it.

DEMAGNETIZATION

Robert C. Beard wrote: "When the offending part has been located, you can demagnetize it by borrowing from an electronics service shop either his color TV degaussing coil or his magnetic tape bulk erasing coil. Before doing any demagnetizing, *remove the compass from the boat* to prevent accidentally demagnetizing the compass needle.

"Connect the demagnetizing coil to the shore line. Holding it about one foot from the part to be demagnetized, turn it on and keep it on! Do not let it turn off for any reason, until this procedure is finished. Move the coil slowly toward the part until it is in contact with it. Then, still slowly, move it all over the part and around it. Finally, very slowly draw the coil away from the part for about five feet before turning it off. If your finger slipped and allowed the coil to turn off momentarily during the process, you will have to repeat the whole process to be sure of complete demagnetization."

Now test once more, with the thin piece of steel, the previously discovered permanent magnet or magnets. Inaccessibility may have precluded their complete demagnetization. Ideally, such parts should be disassembled, taken ashore, demagnetized and reassembled. Steel used in some linkages may be replaced by non-ferrous metals, aluminum or bronze.

Remount the compass, positioning the lubber's line with care and follow the procedure of compensation.

When the compass has been compensated preserve its magnetic environment as was suggested earlier in this chapter.

WORKING DEVIATION TABLE

Now that the compass has been non-professionally compensated a new deviation table must be made. That of ANACHRONISM is here reproduced.

ANACHRONISM COMPENSATED

Compass Heading	Deviation	Compass Heading	Deviation
000°	2.0°W	180°	2.0°E
015°	2.5°W	195°	2.5°E
030°	3.0°W	210°	3.0°E
045°	3.0°W	225°	3.0°E
060°	3.0°W	240°	3.0°E
075°	2.5°W	255°	2.5°E
090°	2.0°W	270°	2.0°E
105°	1.5°W	285°	1.5°E
120°	1.0°W	300°	1.0°E
135°	0°	315°	0°
150°	0.5°E	330°	1.0°W
165°	1.5°E	345°	1.5°W

From this the direct-reading table in the next column was prepared. Slight discrepancies, due to rounding, have no practical significance.

Either table makes quite evident those courses on which deviations are larger. In planning a voyage and in keeping track of position under way, using accurate deviation is essential. The knowing pilot, seeing at a glance where in ANACHRONISM the deviations are maximum, will be aware of those courses upon which compass bearings differ widely from their magnetic equivalents. Bearings taken on these headings must, before plotting, be converted by applying the deviation for the ship's heading. Bearings taken on headings in the vicinity of 135° and 315° may be plotted immediately as magnetic.

Magnetic	Deviation	Compass
133°-144°	0°	133°-145°
145°-153°	0.5°E	146°-153°
154°-163°	1.0°E	154°-162°
164°-176°	1.5°E	163°-174°
177°-187°	2.0°E	175°-185°
188°-211°	2.5°E	186°-208°
212°-251°	3.0°E	209°-248°
252°-264°	2.5°E	249°-262°
265°-279°	2.0°E	263°-277°
280°-294°	1.5°E	278°-292°
295°-303°	1.0°E	293°-302°
304°-310°	0.5°E	303°-309°
311°-319°	0°	310°-319°
320°-326°	0.5°W	320°-327°
327°-335°	1.0°W	328°-336°
336°-352°	1.5°W	337°-353°
353°-006°	2.0°W	354°-008°
007°-018°	2.5°W	009°-021°
019°-061°	3.0°W	022°-064°
062°-078°	2.5°W	065°-080°
079°-097°	2.0°W	081°-099°
098°-109°	1.5°W	100°-110°
110°-120°	1.0°W	111°-121°
121°-132°	0.5°W	122°-132°

TESTING FOR RANDOM DEVIATIONS

Random deviations are those existent only when some auxiliary equipment is put to use. They will not have normally been present during the compensation process, but may show up with the use of windshield wipers, radio-telephone, radio direction-finder, depth sounder, any lights or other electrical device used intermittently.

Testing is simple. Any single electro-magnetic influence that affects a fully compensated compass will cause a maximum deviation on two diametrically opposed headings. On the two headings midway between these there will be no deviation. A compass having residual deviations, as ANACHRONISM, may exhibit departure from this rule.

DEVIATION CAUSED BY WINDSHIELD WIPERS

Put the ship on a compass heading of 000° for a buoy or a landmark. Hold the course by steering, not by the compass, but visually for the mark. Repeatedly turn on the windshield wipers for five to ten seconds. Watch the compass closely. If the card swings even slightly, the wipers are affecting it. No motion of the card does not, at this point, support the conclusion that the wipers have no magnetic influence. By coincidence this might be the heading of zero deviation.

To continue the test, position the boat so that on a compass heading of 090° or 270° it may be steered visually for a buoy or landmark. Again turn on the wipers repeatedly for five- to ten-second periods. If the card is again motionless, the wipers cause no deviation.

When deviation does occur, the headings of maximum and zero deviations must be found. The opinion of experts is that rarely will these be cardinal points. The wise skipper is concerned with the maximum amount of deviation the wipers may cause. To find the maximum he looks first for a minimum, that heading on which the wiper-caused deviation is zero. Should this be hard to pinpoint he knows the maximum will be small and then hunts for it. He is dealing no longer with the whole 'magnetic mass' of the ship but with one small additional field either present or not present as the wipers are turned on or off.

The magnetic situation is as if, closely enough to affect the compass, a small magnet were sometimes placed in a definite position and orientation. When the wipers are off, the magnet is not there. When the wipers are on, the magnet is there—always in the same place and position, always exerting a deviation force on the compass, constant for any particular heading. Reason says eliminate the magnet. Practice says wipers are necessary; compensating for their magnetic effect is impractical and therefore allowance is to be made for their use. The allowance will be listed in a subsidiary deviation table to be used only when the wipers are running.

Slowly swing the boat, testing with the wipers for deviation on successive headings 15° apart. This is not too tedious. In any quadrant a point of either maximum or minimum deviation must occur. Hunt for a heading of no deviation, a null. Finding it, record the compass heading. If, as may well be, the precise null heading is not determinable, find and record the two headings on which the deviation is respectively 1°E and 1°W or 2°E and 2°W. Now determine arithmetically the mid-point between either of these pairs. Put the ship on a heading 90° from this mid-point. Now turn on the wipers and observe and record the deviation. It should be maximum. Further trial may be necessary to ascertain precisely the heading of maximum deviation.

When the maximum deviations are small, the values for the intermediate headings may be calculated by simple interpolation.

Example. Aboard EVOTZ the deviation is zero on the compass heading 060° and is maximum at 6°W on the compass heading 150°.

Required: The deviations for the intermediate headings at 15° intervals.

Answer. In 90° the deviation changes 6°. Therefore in 15° it will change $\left(\frac{15 \times 6}{90}\right)°$ or 1° and the required deviations will be:

075° 1°W;   090° 2°W;   105° 3°W;   120° 4°W;   135° 5°W

As long as the wiper deviations are small, even though the headings of maximum and minimum are not exactly 90° apart (in the case of a not fully compensated compass), it is safe to estimate the intermediate values. A curve of deviations plotted on a Napier diagram would yield a table more accurate, but only in insignificant fractions of degrees.

A round of observations in ANACHRONISM produces these tables.

WIPERS OPERATING

Compass Heading	Deviation	Compass Heading	Deviation
000°	6°W	180°	6°E
015°	5.5°W	195°	5.5°E
030°	5°W	210°	5°E
045°	3°W	225°	4°E
060°	2°W	240°	2°E
075°	0.5°W	255°	0
090°	1°E	270°	2°W
105°	3°E	285°	3.5°W
120°	5°E	300°	5°W
135°	7°E	315°	6°W
150°	7°E	330°	6°W
165°	6°E	345°	6°W

Magnetic	Deviation	Compass
072°-085°	0°	073°-084°
086°-095°	1°E	085°-093°
096°-103°	2°E	094°-101°
104°-112°	3°E	102°-109°
113°-122°	4°E	110°-117°
123°-130°	5°E	118°-124°
131°-137°	6°E	125°-131°
138°-163°	7°E	132°-156°
164°-201°	6°E	157°-195°
202°-223°	5°E	196°-218°
224°-233°	4°E	219°-229°
234°-239°	3°E	230°-236°
240°-246°	2°E	237°-244°
247°-252°	1°E	245°-251°
253°-259°	0°	253°-260°
260°-266°	1°W	261°-267°
267°-274°	2°W	268°-276°
275°-282°	3°W	277°-285°
283°-292°	4°W	286°-296°
293°-303°	5°W	297°-308°
304°-010°	6°W	309°-015°
011°-028°	5°W	016°-033°
029°-040°	4°W	034°-043°
041°-053°	3°W	044°-055°
054°-062°	2°W	056°-064°
063°-071°	1°W	065°-072°

The existence of other random deviations which cannot be eliminated is unusual in small craft, but tests should be made for them. If present, knowledge of their existence first promotes safety, and second may impel the skipper to remove them.

Using alternate deviation tables is not difficult, particularly if they are made of different colored stock. With a little practice the skipper soon learns those headings on which wipers introduce important changes in deviation or, as in ANACHRONISM, those few headings where the change is slight. Turning on the wipers is an automatic order to recheck the compass course to be steered.

It is well to keep in mind the result of sailing off course. With a 10° error the ship will be set off course 1 mile for every 5.7 miles run. This may be serious when making a landfall in poor visibility. More hazardous are the risks of stranding when running a narrow channel through shallow water in fog or heavy rain. Note the following table.

Error in Course	Number of feet off course after sailing one nautical mile	Miles sailed to be one mile off course
1°	106	57.3
2°	212	28.6
3°	318	19.1
4°	424	14.3
5°	530	11.5
6°	635	9.6
7°	740	8.2
8°	846	7.2
9°	950	6.4
10°	1055	5.7

Properly installed, understood and used, the magnetic compass is the finest, least troublesome, inexpensive direction indicator obtainable by the small-craft sailor. Study and mastery of the principles and methods covered in these two chapters will be richly rewarding. A review of the highlights appears in the following two pages.

COMPASS BRIEFS

→ The heart of the compass is a magnetic element so mounted that on any heading of the ship, it lies in a constant direction in a horizontal plane. A card is rigidly attached to the magnetic element. To the helmsman the card may appear to move, but this is not so. The compass bowl, carrying the lubber's line, the 'hand,' moves around the card, the 'dial,' to mark the course. Except for movements caused by deviation, *the card is stationary*. The ship rotates about the card.

Card graduations are in degrees or points, or in various combinations of the two. Scales read from 000° at North clockwise through 360° or in points logically named by their positions relative to the cardinal or intercardinal points. There are eight points to a quadrant, thus a point is 11¼° and a quarter-point approximately 2¾°.

→ Buy the best compass you can afford or one a little better. A large card makes for easy steering. By virtue of its optical magnification, so does a spherical compass. Card graduations should suit your needs. Many craft sail on only short coastwise, lake or river voyages. On most of these, 'open' cards graduated every 5°, are adequate. Skippers of larger boats or of small ones making blue-water passages prefer graduations in single degrees and points. Many wind sailors still use quarter-points.

→ Before buying, test the compass by simulating the motions of rolling, pitching, yawing and deliberate course change. A good one behaves well under these conditions. It is also 'dead beat,' showing minimum over-swing as the vessel steadies on a new course.

→ Before taking it aboard, zero-in a compass having built-in compensators. Zeroing-in is done by adjusting the compensators so that they do not affect the compass. This is imperative if the unmounted compass is to be moved about its projected site testing for ship's magnetism or magnetic influences.

→ Mount the compass as far as possible from any known shipboard magnetic influences and yet where the helmsman may watch it without strain. There may have to be compromise here. Be sure that a line through the pivot and the lubber's line is parallel to the keel's fore-and-aft direction. See that the instrument is level at cruising speed and *particularly not canted* to port or starboard.

Once mounted, preserve the compass's magnetic environment, except for the adjustments made during compensation.

→ Keep the bowl filled with liquid. Should additions be made, check the tightness of the seals and top-off with nothing foreign to the original contents lest the card, bellows, seals and even the pivot and bearings be damaged. Watch the compass in operation. If it becomes sluggish, test for pivot friction. Should it oscillate in a seaway, look for and consider removing vertical iron aboard.

→ Magnetic meridians are lines of force of the earth's magnetic field. A compass, influenced by this field alone, aligns its N-S axis along a magnetic meridian. Such a compass *does not point to a magnetic pole* but does show accurately the direction of the magnetic meridian. Generally, the magnetic and the true meridians do not coincide. The angle between their similar parts is called variation. It is labelled East or West as the (magnetic) northerly part of the magnetic meridian lies to the east or the west of the true meridian. Variation ranges in amount from zero to 180°.

→ Variation exists where there is no compass. It is an attribute of the earth. Variation changes with geographical position. It is relatively constant in a locality. The small annual changes noted on charts are not persistent. The annual rate of change may itself change. The chart bears at best an educated guess, based on past observations. Therefore do not rely on computations projected from obsolete charts.

→ Magnetic materials aboard ship or alongside cause the compass magnet and card to swing out of the magnetic meridian. The resulting angle between the north-indicating branch of the magnetic meridian and the compass's N-S axis is called deviation. It, too, can range in amount from zero to 180° and, like variation, is termed East or West as the North point of the compass card deviates to the East or West of the magnetic meridian. Deviation exists only where there is a compass and some magnetic force additional to that of the earth. It is an attribute of the compass, not of the earth. Deviation changes with the ship's heading.

Though often so-called, variation and deviation are not errors of the compass, but are simply predictable magnetic effects to be reckoned with in course conversion.

→ A course may be named in three ways: true (TC), magnetic (MC) and compass (CC). A course (or a bearing) is a fixed direction. The scale zero, the line of reference for the angle, may be in one of three directions: the true meridian, the magnetic meridian or the direction of the north point of the compass. Hence courses have to be converted, that is, expressed with respect to the three different reference lines.

Converting courses expressed in degrees is simple.

True	Conversion from true through
Variation	magnetic to compass is in
Magnetic	the rule: *Down Add West* or
Deviation	*DAW*, which should be memorized.
Compass	The changes in the rule are obvious:

Down Subtract East, Up Subtract West, Up Add East.

→ When courses are expressed in points and quarter-points "add" and "subtract" can be confusing instructions. (Try adding ½ pt E to E ¾ N and you will be 1 point in error!) The direction in which the deviation or variation is to be applied is substituted. For 'add' use 'clockwise' and for 'subtract' use counterclockwise. Call conversion from compass to magnetic to true 'correcting' and the reverse conversion 'uncorrecting.' Then a basic rule emerges, Correct Easterly Errors Clockwise, shortenable to *Correct Easterly Clockwise, CEC*. With this in memory, remember further that in any change of this basic, *only two and always two* of the terms are changed. Thus there are UWC, UECC and CWCC. UWC is immediately recognizable as the DAW of the degree system.

→ Deviation changes with the heading because the ship

rotates about the compass card. Hence magnetic material aboard located in the compass's first quadrant while the vessel heads North, will be moved into the compass's fourth quadrant when she heads West. Similarly all the other magnetic material aboard shifts its position relative to the compass on this 90° course change. The compass card, subject to two influences, that of the earth and that of the moved field of the ship, may deviate from its original direction on CC north. Thus it should be seen that any change in heading may change the deviation.

→ Among the methods of determining deviation are running ranges or sailing across one range on different headings. Recording the deviations so observed yields a deviation table for compass headings. Plotting these on a Napier diagram and taking therefrom the deviations for magnetic headings gives a table of deviations on magnetic headings.

Thence for everyday use, deviation cards of various types, pictorial or tabular, are constructible, as the user desires.

→ A word of warning. *Never enter a deviation table with a bearing.* The deviation to be applied to a bearing is that of the ship's head at the time of bearing. For convenience in plotting bearings the proper deviation and the variation are algebraically combined to give one quantity, the so-called compass error (CE). CE = Var + Dev. When the two are in the same direction they are added, when opposite in direction the smaller is subtracted from the larger and the remainder takes the name of the larger.

→ Compensating, often called adjusting, a compass is the act of neutralizing, by small magnets near the compass, the effect on the compass of the ship's own magnetic field. Many compasses are equipped with two small magnets, whose position is adjustable, built into their cases. Adjust-

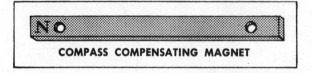

COMPASS COMPENSATING MAGNET

ment or compensation consists of positioning these compensators so that they negate the action of the ship's field. A compass not so equipped is compensated by fastening one or two small magnets near the compass. The proper position of these magnets is most important. Each must be centered on a line passing through the compass pivot. The athwartship magnet is centered on such a line running truly fore-and-aft; the fore-and-aft one on such a line running truly athwartship.

→ A table of deviations may be analyzed to ascertain approximately its components or coefficients and so determine, again approximately, the position of the compensators. This is usually unnecessary in small craft.

→ Compensation in small craft is not difficult. Run from a fixed mark on compass course North, establishing a range with a disposable buoy. Reverse course by sailing the range, ignoring the compass. Now observe the course the compass shows. The difference between 180° and the compass-indicated course is approximately twice the deviation. Remove half of this by adjusting the N-S internal compensator or temporarily taping down an athwartship

external compensator on the fore-and-aft line through the compass pivot. Repeat this operation on N-S and S-N headings until the deviations reach a minimum. Then do the same on the E-W compass headings, adjusting the E-W internal compensator or taping down, on the athwartship line through the pivot, a fore-and-aft external compensator. Permanently fasten the external compensators or leave the internal ones in the optimum positions found.

With a thin piece of steel (.001″) locate any strong magnetic influence which prevents reasonable compensation. Demagnetize it or remove it from the boat and recompensate. *Caution. Do not subject the compass to demagnetization.* Before turning on any demagnetizer unship the compass, take it ashore, well away from the influence of this powerful equipment.

Swing the ship for residuals and make a working deviation table or tables as desired.

Reasonable compensation is obtainable by this method. There may be residuals near the intercardinal points which merit some explanation here.

→ Broadly, deviations may be classified as observational, semicircular and quadrantal. The student need not be fearful of these names.

Observational deviation is that part of the total deviation due to errors in observation. It includes errors caused by lack of parallelism of the pivot-lubber's line axis and the keel. Observational deviation exists when a Napier diagram is symmetrical with respect not to its base line, but to a line parallel to the base line.

Semicircular deviation waxes and wanes, so to speak, in a semicircle. It increases from zero to maximum and decreases again to zero through a course change of 180°.

Quadrantal deviation does the same thing in one quarter of a circle. It increases from zero to maximum and decreases to zero through a course change of 90°.

A plotted curve of deviations includes all these elements. It follows, then, that when a Napier or other curve of deviations is unsymmetrical (i.e. of different shape on the opposite sides of its base line or a base line adjusted for observational error) quadrantal deviation exists. Fore-and-aft and athwartship compensators may not remove all the quadrantal deviations. Those remaining appear as residuals on the intercardinals. Generally, in wooden or plastic craft, they are not large enough to be troublesome.

Removing these residuals by hollow iron spheres, called quadrantal correctors, attached to the binnacle may not be within the competence of the amateur, is best left to the professional.

→ Windshield wipers in operation may cause significant deviations. Test for these. When existent, make a deviation table for use only when they are turned on. In reduced visibility, fog, rain or snow, comes greater need for trying to be sure that the course steered is the one desired to be made good.

→ Preserve the compass's magnetic environment. When it is altered by the installation of a new motor or other equipment, or by electric welding aboard, check the deviations.

→ Know your compass. Know its deviations. Above all, trust it. Not without good reason has it been dubbed the mariner's best friend.   * * *

CHAPTER 15

AIDS TO NAVIGATION

FIG. 1501 The skipper of a boat of any size is highly dependent on aids to navigation to warn him of unseen underwater hazards. He must be able to recognize such aids and know their significance.

Buoyage Systems

Although few mariners or boatmen may be aware of it, directing the movements of a vessel of any size in near-shore waters is closely akin to "flying blind" in an aircraft. It is not the few visible obstacles that are dangerous, but rather the more numerous shoals and rocks that lie unseen beneath the surface.

Natural landmarks may be used as reference points for navigation, but these are often few and far between, and may not be located to best advantage. It is to protect the mariner from these unseen dangers, and to allow him to safely direct his course, that government agencies and private individuals establish and maintain *aids to navigation*.

Figures 1502-1510, 1512, 1514, 1516 and 1517 reproduced from official U.S. COAST GUARD photographs.

The term *aid to navigation* may be applied to any man-made object prepared and located so as to indicate to a mariner the location of his vessel or the safe and proper course on which to proceed. The term includes buoys, day-beacons, lights, lighthouses, lightships, radiobeacons, fog signals, and loran, consolan, and other electronic systems. It covers unlighted objects, floating and non-floating; and visible, audible, and electronic signals and their supporting structures.

The term "aid to navigation" should always be stated thus, and not as "navigational aid". The latter term has been more broadly defined as also including "charts, instruments, devices, methods, etc., intended to assist in the navigation of a craft."

PURPOSE OF AIDS TO NAVIGATION

Aids to navigation are placed at various points along the coasts and navigable waterways as markers and guides to enable mariners to determine their position with respect to the shore and to hidden dangers. They assist mariners in making landfalls when approaching from the high seas, mark isolated dangers, make it possible for pilots to follow natural and improved channels, and provide a continuous chain of charted marks for coast piloting.

Establishment and maintenance of any aid must have economic justification. Aids established by the Federal government must, by law, be needed for the safety of a reasonable amount of water traffic, not just the occasional craft or the coming and going of a few local boats.

Within the bounds of actual necessity and reasonable cost, every aid to navigation is designed to be seen or heard over the greatest practicable area. As all aids serve the same broad purposes, such structural differences as those between an unlighted buoy or beacon, a minor light, or a major lighthouse with radiobeacon, are solely for the purpose of meeting requirements and conditions of the particular location at which the aid is established.

OPERATING AGENCIES

The United States Coast Guard, since 1967 a part of the Department of Transportation, is the agency responsible for maintenance of the system of aids to navigation on waters of the United States subject to Federal jurisdiction. Federal "navigable waters" are legally defined as coastal waters; rivers, bays, sounds, lakes, etc. navigable from the sea; and rivers, canals, and lakes *not* lying wholly within the boundaries of a single state. Such areas include the Atlantic, Gulf, and Pacific coasts of the continental United States, the Great Lakes, the Mississippi River and its tributaries, Puerto Rico, the Hawaiian Islands, and Alaskan waters. Aids to navigation may also be maintained by the Coast Guard at other places where required to serve the needs of our armed forces.

The senior officer of the Coast Guard is its Commandant, with headquarters in Washington, D.C. Functions of planning, procurement, establishment, operation, and maintenance of aids to navigation are carried on under his direction. Because of the wide geographic distribution of such aids on our coasts and inland waters, actual field work is executed by district organization.

There are 12 Coast Guard Districts. They maintain the

system of aids to navigation and carry out other Coast Guard functions. The ten continental Districts are numbered from 1 to 13, omitting 4, 6, and 10; see fig. 1502. Hawaii is in the 14th Coast Guard District, Alaska in the 17th. Each District has its Commander, assisted by a suitable engineering and administrative force. Each District has the necessary supply and buoy depots, and specially designed and equipped vessels for the maintenance of aids to navigation. See fig. 1503.

"Private" aids to navigation

Aids to navigation may, with prior approval, be established in waters subject to Federal jurisdiction by agencies other than the Coast Guard. Information on procedures for obtaining such permission may be obtained from any Coast Guard District office. These aids must be patterned after Federal aids, and if a fixed structure is to be erected in navigable water, a permit must also be obtained from the Army Corps of Engineers.

All such aids to navigation—whether established by an individual, a corporation, a state or local government, or even a Federal agency other than the Coast Guard, such as the Navy—are termed "private" aids. These will have the same appearance as Coast Guard-maintained aids, but will be specially designated in the Light Lists.

State-maintained aids

On bodies of water wholly within the boundaries of a single state, and not navigable to the sea, the state government has the responsibility for the establishment and maintenance of aids to navigation.

Although each state retains authority over its waters, agreement has been reached on a uniform system of aids

FIG. 1502 Maintenance of aids to navigation is a district responsibility in the Coast Guard organization. There are ten districts covering the continental 48 states. District boundaries and headquarters are shown. Note that there are no districts numbered 4, 6, or 10.

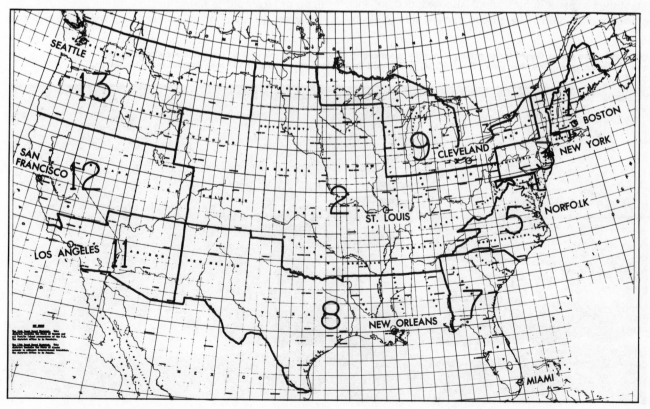

to navigation and regulatory markers. These will be described and discussed in detail later in this chapter.

PROTECTION BY LAW

Whether established by the Coast Guard or by another agency, all aids to navigation are protected by law. It is not only a violation of common sense, but also a criminal offense, to cause any damage or hindrance to the proper operation of any aid. Do not deface, alter, move, or destroy any aid to navigation. Never tie your boat to a buoy, daybeacon, or light structure. Avoid anchoring so close to a buoy that you obscure the aid from the sight of other passing craft.

If you should unintentionally or unavoidably collide with or damage an aid to navigation, this fact must be reported to the nearest Officer in Charge, Marine Inspection, U.S. Coast Guard in full detail and without delay.

For your own safety and that of others, cooperate with the Coast Guard and other agencies by promptly reporting any missing or malfunctioning aid. This will normally be done immediately after returning to port; if the safety of navigation is threatened seriously, the report should be made by radio without delay.

Types of Aids to Navigation

The term "aid to navigation" encompasses a wide range of fixed and floating objects from a single pile with a pointer or a small sixth-class buoy to manned lightships and lighthouses with an array of visible, audible, and electronic signals. Conspicuous shapes and objects on shore, such as mountain tops, radio antennas, smoke stacks, etc., may be charted and used to assist in piloting, but these are generally grouped under the term *landmark* and are excluded from the definition of an aid to navigation. This latter term is applied to objects that have been *primarily* established to assist in navigation. Also excluded are such informal aids as bush stakes placed in many side creeks by local watermen to mark minor natural channels or hazards. These do indeed help the skipper to pilot his boat safely, but they are not a part of the organized system of aids to navigation.

MAJOR TYPES

Buoys are floating objects moored or anchored to the bottom as aids to navigation; lightships fit this overall definition, but they are excluded as they form a separate category of aids. Buoys will have a distinctive shape and color as determined by their location and purpose. They may be equipped with visual, audible, and/or electronic signals.

Daybeacons are unlighted fixed structures established to aid navigation. They may be a single pile or a multiple-pile structure. Clusters of piles are called dolphins. Daybeacons will normally be equipped with a pointer, signboard, or other marker ("daymark"). These pointers or daymarks may be of a distinctive color and shape as determined by the information that they indicate.

Lights are aids to navigation that have active visual signals. These are fixed aids (lighted floating aids are designated as lighted buoys or lightships). Lights are classified by the Coast Guard and other authorities as *primary seacoast lights, secondary lights,* or *minor lights,* as determined by their location, importance, and physical characteristics; the intensity of the light and its visible range will vary with the classification. The shape and color of the structure supporting the light source may be distinctive for purposes of identification, but will not convey information as, for example, in the case of buoys. The term *lighthouse* is often applied to primary seacoast lights and to some secondary lights.

Fog signals are audible signals transmitted to assist mariners during periods of low visibility, primarily fog. Occasionally they may be separate aids, as when located on the end of a jetty, but more often they will be part of a buoy, light, or larger aid to navigation.

Ranges are pairs of unlighted or lighted fixed aids so

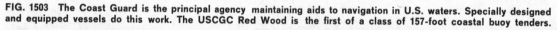

FIG. 1503 The Coast Guard is the principal agency maintaining aids to navigation in U.S. waters. Specially designed and equipped vessels do this work. The USCGC Red Wood is the first of a class of 157-foot coastal buoy tenders.

FIG. 1504 "Super buoys" are now in use at some offshore locations. The one shown, built of high-strength low alloy steel plate, is 40 feet in diameter with a 5,000 candlepower light 33 feet above the water. It replaces the old Scotland Lightship in the approaches to New York Harbor.

located that when observed in line the pilot is on the centerline of a channel. The individual structures may, in some cases, also serve as separate aids to navigation marking a turn in a channel.

Lightships are specially equipped vessels moored or anchored at specific locations to serve as aids to navigation. They are of distinctive shape and color, and will have lights and sound signals, and radiobeacons.

Radiobeacons are transmitters broadcasting a characteristic signal specifically to aid navigation at night, in fog, or at distances exceeding normal visibility. These, too, are usually at another aid, but may at times be located separately.

Electronic navigation systems are radio transmitters, usually in groups, which emit special signals that may be used for assistance in navigation when in fog or otherwise out of sight of land or offshore aids. Such systems include *Loran-A* and *Loran-C*, operated by the Coast Guard, *Consolan* operated by the Federal Aviation Agency, and other systems operated by various government or private interests. Only the USCG and FAA systems will be of general interest and use to boatmen.

Buoys

Buoys are floating objects, other than lightships, anchored or moored to the bottom at specific locations so as to serve as aids to navigation. They are shown on charts by special symbols and lettering that will indicate their shape, color, and visual and/or sound signals. They will vary widely in size from sixth-class buoys projecting only a few feet above the surface of the water to the new "super buoys" that are some 40 feet in diameter with a superstructure rising to 30 or more feet in height; see fig. 1504.

The buoyage system adopted for waters of the United States consists of several different types of buoys, each kind designed to serve under definite conditions. Broadly speaking, all buoys serve as daytime aids; those having lights are also available to aid navigation at night, and

those having sound signals are especially useful in time of fog as well as at night.

The shape, color, and light characteristic, if any, will convey to a pilot information as to his location and the proper guidance of his vessel to remain in safe waters. The size of a buoy does *not* indicate such information and is usually determined by the importance of the waterway and size of vessels using it. The size of a buoy need not be taken into consideration by a skipper, except when estimating distances.

Buoys are normally anchored to the bottom using chain and heavy concrete sinkers weighing from one to five tons, fig. 1505. The length of chain will vary with the location, but will generally be two to three times the depth of water.

FIG. 1505 Buoys are anchored with cast concrete blocks called "sinkers." They range in size from one-ton, shown above, to as heavy as five tons. Normally, only a single sinker of appropriate size is used for any buoy.

BUOY CHARACTERISTICS

Buoys may be subdivided into types as lighted or unlighted, sound buoys, or combination buoys. This latter type is comprised of buoys that have both an audible and a visual signal.

The Coast Guard maintains about 21,000 unlighted and 3,700 lighted and combination buoys in waters under its jurisdiction. Many others are maintained by state and private agencies in non-federal waters.

Buoy shapes

Unlighted buoys may be further classified by their shape.

Can buoys are objects made up of steel plates so that the above-water appearance is cylindrical, like a can or drum floating with its axis vertical and flat end upward; see fig. 1506. Two lifting lugs may project slightly above the flat top of a can buoy, but these will not significantly alter its appearance.

Nun buoys are objects made up of steel plates so that the above-water appearance is that of a cylinder topped

FIG. 1506 Can buoys have a cylindrical shape with a flat top. An older-type, still used, is shown on the left. Newer can buoys have integral radar reflectors as shown in (b) above.

FIG. 1507 Nun buoys have a conical shape coming to a near-point at the upper end. This is a modern nun buoy with radar reflector plates in its upper section.

with a cone, pointed end up, fig. 1507. The cone may come to a point or the tip may be slightly rounded. Smaller nun buoys will have a single lifting ring at the top; larger buoys will have several lugs around the sides.

Unlighted buoys come in standardized sizes. These are designated as classes—first through sixth—and as tall, standard, or special. Knowledge of the various sizes is not important to the boatman, although it may be of general interest to note that the above-water visible portion of a nun buoy may vary from 2'-6" for a sixth-class standard to 14'-0" for a first-class tall. Can buoys are somewhat shorter, ranging from 1'-4" to 9'-9" above the waterline. The smaller buoys are, of course, lesser in diameter also, with a range of 1½ to 5 feet. Pilots should remember that a considerable portion of a buoy is under water, and that they are really much larger and heavier objects than they would appear to be from a casual observation.

The Coast Guard has now eliminated the use of *spar* buoys, but they may be found in some private or foreign systems of aids. These are usually large logs, trimmed, shaped, and appropriately painted; they are anchored from one end with a suitable length of chain.

Special shapes will sometimes be found in use as markers, but these are not regular aids to navigation. Spherical buoys are the most generally used of the special shape category.

Lighted, sound, and combination buoys are described by their visual and/or audible signals rather than by their shape.

Sound buoys

Buoys are often equipped with a characteristic sound signal to aid in their location during periods of reduced visibility, chiefly fog. Several different sound signals are available and are used to distinguish between different aids to navigation that may be within audible range of each other.

Bell buoys are steel floats surmounted by short skeleton towers in which a bell is mounted, fig. 1512. They serve

with considerable effectiveness both by day and night, and especially in fog; they are much used because of their moderate maintenance costs. Most bell buoys are operated by the motion of the sea—four tappers, loosely hung externally around the bell, are readily set in motion. When the buoy rolls as a result of waves, ground swells, or the wake of passing vessels, a single note is heard at irregular intervals. Some bell buoys are operated by electric batteries, their strokes sounding at regular intervals. These are particularly useful in sheltered waters where wave action is often insufficient to sound the signal.

Gong buoys are similar in construction to bell buoys, except that a set of gongs is substituted for the bell, fig. 1512. Gong buoys are used to give a distinctive character-

FIG. 1508 Buoys equipped with both a light and a sound signal are called combination buoys. Shown above in (a) is a lighted buoy with a whistle below the radar reflector. In (b) at the right, the lighted buoy has an electric horn fog signal.

FIG. 1509　This is a late design of lighted buoy without sound signal. Note the straight sides of the tower-like superstructure; older designs had towers that first tapered in and then out near the top.

FIG. 1510　The Coast Guard is experimenting with an atomic power source for a buoy. This buoy is lighted from a strontium-90 thermoelectric system. It is hoped that the use of atomic power will increase the reliability of remote buoys and decrease the number of servicing visits required.

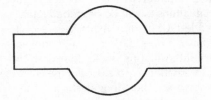

FIG. 1511　The Coast Guard is now equipping lighted buoys with "daylight controls." These electric-eye devices turn off the light during daylight to conserve electric power. Such buoys are marked in white with the symbol shown above.

FIG. 1512　Shown here are models, all to the same scale, of four typical buoys. Note the range of sizes and large mass of the lighted buoys that is below the waterline. The smaller lighted buoy has a bell and the larger one four gongs; both have external "tappers" to strike and sound the fog signal. These are all of the so-called "1962" design, many of which are in use.

istic when there are several sound buoys in one vicinity. In these buoys, four gongs of different tones are mounted, with one tapper for each gong. As the sea rocks the buoy, the tappers strike against their respective gongs, sounding four different notes in an irregular sequence.

Whistle buoys provide yet another distinctive audible signal useful at night or in fog. The whistle is sounded by compressed air produced by the motion of the buoy in the sea. For this reason, such buoys are used principally in open and exposed locations where a ground swell normally exists, fig. 1508.

Lighted buoys

Buoys may be equipped with lights of various colors, intensities, and flashing characteristics (called "phase characterics"). The color and characteristics of the light are used to convey information to the mariner. Intensity of the light will be determined by the distance at which the aid must be detected, influenced by such factors as background lighting, normal atmospheric clarity, etc.

Lighted buoys are constructed as metal floats with a short skeleton tower at the top of which the light is placed; see fig. 1509. The light is powered by electric batteries placed inside the lower body of the buoy below the waterline. Lighted buoys are designed to operate for many months without servicing.

Lighted buoys are now generally equipped with "daylight controls" that automatically turn the light on and off as darkness falls and lifts. Buoys equipped with such electric eye controls are specially marked with a white-paint symbol consisting of a circular spot with horizontal bar running through its center; see fig. 1511.

Lights on buoys, as on other lighted aids, are either red, green, or white. The colors red and green have specific applications as will be discussed later in this chapter. White lights are prescribed for certain specific functions, and may also be substituted for red or green where a greater range of visibility is desired.

Color of buoys

Buoys used for navigation may be painted red, black, red-and-black, or black-and-white. Buoys for special purposes will use these colors and also yellow, green, orange, and blue. The specific meanings of the various colors will be discussed later in this chapter when buoyage systems are considered.

Optical reflectors

Many unlighted buoys are fitted with optical reflectors. These greatly facilitate the locating of the buoys at night when using a searchlight. Optical reflectors may be white, red, or green, and have the same significance as lights of these colors.

Reflective sheeting is used extensively by the Coast Guard for marking buoys. This flexible plastic film is easily attached to any reasonably smooth surface and has improved reflective characteristics over conventional glass reflectors. The reflective material may be in the form of square "patches" or as bands around the buoy.

Although primarily intended to make unlighted buoys more visible at night, reflective material is also placed on lighted buoys to aid in their detection by searchlight between flashes. Numerals of reflective material are now being placed on buoys, and these will aid in their nighttime identification as well as detection.

Radar reflectors

Many buoys are equipped with radar reflectors, vertical metal plates set at right angles to each other in such a manner as to greatly increase the echo returned to a radar receiver on a ship or boat. The plates are shaped and mounted so as to preserve the overall characteristic shape of an unlighted buoy or the general appearance of a lighted buoy. See fig. 1512.

LIGHT PHASE CHARACTERISTICS

The lights on lighted buoys will generally flash in one of several specific patterns. The flashing-light type of operation serves a number of useful purposes:

(1) It conserves the energy source within the buoy by having the light on only a small portion of the total time. Fixed lights, continuously lit with no variation of color or intensity, are not used on Coast Guard buoys, and only occasionally on buoys maintained by other agencies.

(2) Flashing assists in the detection of the lighted aid against a background of other lights.

(3) Flashing allows the signaling during hours of darkness of a limited amount of information, such as the need to exercise special caution at a certain point in a channel.

(4) The flashing characteristic of the light can be selected from a number of available patterns so as to be able to distinguish between several buoys of the same general function that may be within visible range of each other.

Lights are classed as *flashing* when the light comes on for a single brief flash at regular intervals; the period of light is always *less* than the period of darkness. Coast Guard-maintained buoys designated as of the flashing type will flash their light not more than 30 times per minute. This is the more-generally used characteristic for buoys. It is sometimes termed "slow flashing," but the official and correct description is simply "flashing."

Flashing (Fl)

Quick Flashing (Qk Fl)

Interrupted Quick Flashing (I Qk Fl)

Morse Code "A" (Mo A)

FIG. 1513 Buoys show various light phase characteristics which help in conveying information and assist in distinguishing between buoys of the same type located near each other.

Quick flashing lights will flash not less than 60 times each minute. These buoys are used for special situations where they will be more quickly spotted and where particular attention to piloting is required.

Interrupted quick flashing lights are characterized by a series of quick flashes separated by dark intervals of about four seconds' duration. This light characteristic, too, is used in special situations as will be described later.

Morse code "A" flashing lights have a cycle consisting of a short flash, a brief dark interval, a longer flash, and a longer dark interval. This is the "dot-dash" of the letter "A" in the International Morse Code; the characteristic was formerly known as "short-long flashing." The color of the light is always white.

The above light phase characteristics are shown diagramatically in fig. 1513. The *period* of a light is the time required for the completion of one full cycle of flash and dark interval, or flashes and dark intervals. A light de-

FIG. 1514 Buoys should be used with caution because of natural hazards to which they are exposed. A Coast Guardsman is seen here removing ice from a large lighted buoy; such ice may have interferred with the buoy's normal operation.

scribed as "Flashing 4 seconds" has a period of four seconds. One flash and one dark interval lasts just that long before the cycle is repeated.

Standardized flashing rates

As noted earlier, "flashing" lights may have various repetition rates for individual buoy identification, provided that there are not more than 30 flashes each minute. Over the years, the Coast Guard has used various characteristics involving different flash lengths and intervals. Buoys have been operated in the past that flashed at intervals of 2, 2½, 3, 4, 5, and 6 seconds; individual flashes have varied in length from 0.05 to 1.0 second. Standardization has now been introduced into the system of lighted buoys to reduce the number of different light phase characteristics.

Three standard characteristics will be used—flashing at intervals of 2.5, 4, and 6 seconds. These correspond to 24, 15, and 10 flashes per minute. These three light phase characteristics will provide sufficient differences for individual buoy identification and will provide economic battery service periods.

Another part of the Coast Guard's continuing effort to improve the reliability of its aids to navigation is the replacement of motorized mechanical flashers with solid-state (transistorized) electronic equipment having no moving parts. The use of precision moulded acrylic plastic lenses on buoys and minor lights has made possible substantial increases in the candlepower of such aids.

CAUTIONS IN USING BUOYS

A pilot should not rely on floating aids to navigation to always maintain their charted positions, or to constantly and unerringly display their specified characteristics. Obstacles to perfect performance are of such magnitude that complete reliability is manifestly impossible. The Coast Guard makes a continuous effort to keep aids working properly, but cannot be completely successful with all of the many thousands to be checked and maintained.

Buoys are heavily anchored, but they may shift in location, be carried away, capsized, or sunk as a result of violent storms or of having been struck by passing ships. A pilot must be prepared for the possible absence of a buoy he planned to use in his navigation, or its displacement off-station.

Buoys that have been placed to mark shifting shoals may not always be properly located in relation to the hazards they are meant to mark. This is particularly true during and immediately after heavy storms when shoals are liable to shift their positions relative to the buoys.

Lighted buoys may become extinguished, or their control apparatus become broken or deranged causing them to show improper light characteristics. Essentially all audible signals on buoys are operated by action of the sea, and may consequently be silent during periods of calm water. They may fail to sound, regardless of wave activity, due to mechanical defects in their sound-producing mechanism. Even if functioning properly, a sound buoy may not be heard at relatively close range due to erratic transmission of sound in air.

Buoys do not maintain their position directly over their anchors as they must be provided with some scope on their anchor chains; they swing in small circles around the anchor, which is the charted location. (See Chapter 18 for how buoys are charted.) For this reason, buoys are inferior

to fixed aids to navigation when precise bearings are desired.

Moored as they are, buoys have a tendency to yaw about under the influence of wind and current. This action is unpredictable, and a vessel attempting to pass close aboard risks collision with a yawing buoy. In extremely strong currents, buoys may even be pulled beneath the surface.

Buoys are sometimes removed to make way for dredging operations, or for other reasons. In northern waters, buoys may be discontinued for the winter, or smaller unlighted buoys substituted for lighted and combination buoys to prevent damage or loss from ice floes. The dates shown in the Light Lists for seasonal buoys, or seasonal changes in buoys, are only approximate and may vary slightly due to weather or other conditions.

Temporary or permanent changes in buoys may be made between editions of charts. A wise skipper keeps informed of existing conditions through reading Notices to Mariners or Local Notices to Mariners—see Chapter 17.

All buoys (especially those located in exposed positions) should, therefore, be regarded as warnings or guides, and not as infallible navigation marks. Whenever possible, a boat should be navigated by bearings or angles on fixed objects on shore (see Chapter 21), and by soundings, rather than by total reliance on buoys.

FIG. 1515 The simplest daybeacon is a single pile with a pointer or daymark. This one, on a Gulf Coast River Channel, has a numbered black pointer on a white pile with green reflector that will show up brilliantly at night in a boat's searchlight. (Florida State News Bureau photograph)

Daybeacons

Daybeacons are unlighted structures established as an aid to navigation; they are "fixed" rather than "floating" aids. Daybeacons may be located either on shore or in waters up to perhaps 12 to 15 feet deep.

Daybeacons vary greatly in design and construction, depending upon their location and the distance at which they must be seen. A continuing effort is now being made by the Coast Guard to standardize daybeacon structures and markings for easier identification as aids to navigation.

FIG. 1516 Buoys must be periodically hauled out for servicing. A new buoy is placed on station, and the old one is taken in to a depot for scraping and repainting.

FIG. 1517 A minor light may consist of a single-pile structure with the light itself at the top and number identification on the daymark below. The light shown here is receiving periodic maintenance from a Coast Guard crew.

CHARACTERISTICS

The simplest daybeacon is a single pile with a pointer or number sign, called a "daymark," at or near the top, fig. 1515. The pile may be wood, concrete, or metal.

A larger, more visible, and more sturdy daybeacon is the "three-pile dolphin" type. Here the single pile is replaced by three piles separated a few feet at their lower ends, but coming together at their tops where they are strongly held together with wire cables. Such structures are equipped with a daymark at the top, or more likely two daymarks facing in opposite directions. (Some dolphins may be made of five piles, four around one central pile.)

Daymarks and pointers

The daybeacon must be properly identified if it is to serve its purpose as an aid to navigation. Daymarks are widely used for this purpose; in some areas, pointers are placed on single-pile daybeacons in lieu of the daymark.

Daymarks are normally either square or triangular in shape, corresponding to can and nun buoys; see page 292. In some special applications, the daymark may be octagonal (eight-sided) or diamond-shaped. Pointers are all of the same shape, but are painted red or black in accordance with their use. The pointers always point toward the channel, or safe side of the daybeacon.

Daybeacon pointers and daymarks are normally equipped with reflective material to enhance their visibility at night. The reflective material is usually applied to the end of the pointer or around the border of the daymark.

THE USES OF DAYBEACONS

For obvious reasons, the use of daybeacons is restricted to relatively shallow waters. Within this limitation, however, a daybeacon is often more desirable than a buoy. From a navigator's point of view, it is a superior aid to navigation — firmly fixed in position, and more readily seen and identified. From the Coast Guard's viewpoint, a daybeacon is more desirable too—once established, it is in position and requires but little maintenance (buoys must be regularly hauled out for scraping and repainting, fig. 1516).

Daybeacons are used primarily for channel marking and serve in the same manner as buoys in the buoyage systems to be described later in this chapter.

Minor Lights

Just as daybeacons are sometimes substituted for unlighted buoys, so may lighted buoys be replaced with *minor lights*. These are fixed structures of the same overall physical features as daybeacons, but equipped with a light generally similar in characteristics to those found on buoys. Most minor lights are part of a series marking a channel, river or harbor; also included, however, are some isolated single lights if they are of the same general size and characteristics. The term "minor light" does not include the more important lights marking harbors, peninsulas, major shoals, etc.; these have lights of greater intensity and/or special characteristics — these are designated as "secondary" or "primary seacoast" lights and are discussed in detail in Chapter 16.

CHARACTERISTICS

Minor lights are placed on single piles, fig. 1517, on multiple-pile dolphins, fig. 1518, or on other structures in the water or on shore. Daymarks are placed on the structures for their identification, and reflective material is added for nighttime safety should the light be extin-

FIG. 1518 Structures for daybeacons or minor lights may also consist of three or more piles driven in a few feet apart and then bound together at their top. (Morris Rosenfeld photograph)

guished. In general, the description of daybeacons is applicable plus the addition of the light mechanism.

Light characteristics

A minor light will normally have the same color and flash with the same phase characteristics that a lighted buoy would have if the aid were of floating rather than fixed type. Intensity of the light will generally be of the same order as that of a lighted buoy, occasionally somewhat greater, but visibility may be increased by its greater height above water and its more stable platform.

Flashing characteristics of minor lights have been standardized with flashes at intervals of 2.5, 4 and 6 seconds. This is part of the same light modernization program as previously described for lighted buoys.

Sound signals

Minor lights may, in some locations, have an audible fog signal. These cannot, of course, be of a type operated by wave action, as in the case of bell and gong buoys. A bell, horn, or siren will be electrically operated on the structure, in some cases continuously for months during which fog may be expected.

Buoyage Systems

The primary function of buoys is to warn the mariner of some danger, obstruction, or change in the contours of the bottom, and to delineate channels leading to various points, so that he may avoid hazards and continue on his course safely. The greatest advantage is obtained from buoys used to mark specifically defined spots, for if a pilot knows his precise position at the moment and is properly equipped with charts, he can plot a safe course. Such features as shape, coloring, and signaling characteristics of buoys are but means to these ends of warning, guiding, and orienting the navigator.

Most maritime nations use either the *lateral system of buoyage* or the *cardinal system,* or both. In the lateral

system, the buoys indicate the direction to a danger relative to the course that should be followed. In the cardinal system, characteristics of buoys indicate location of the danger relative to the buoy itself. The term "cardinal" relates to cardinal points of the compass, see Chapter 13, page 252.

The Lateral System of Buoyage

In the United States, the lateral system of buoyage is uniformly used in all Federal-jurisdiction areas and on many other bodies of water where it can be applied. In this system, the shape, coloring, numbering, and light characteristics of buoys are determined by their position with respect to the navigable channel, natural or dredged, as such channels are entered and followed from seaward toward the head of navigation. The lateral system is described in detail in the subsequent sections covering each of the basic characteristics.

THE BASIC U. S. SYSTEM

The lateral system of buoyage employs a simple arrangement of shapes, colors, numbers, and light characteristics to indicate the side on which a buoy should be passed when proceeding in a given direction. The system is easily learned and should be known in detail by all boatmen.

As all channels do not lead from seaward, certain arbitrary assumptions must be made in order that the lateral system may be consistently applied. In coloring and numbering offshore buoys along the coasts, the following system has been adopted: proceeding in a southerly direction along the Atlantic Coast, in a northerly and westerly direction along the Gulf Coast, and in a northerly direction along the Pacific Coast will be considered the same as coming in from seaward. This can be remembered as proceeding around the coastline of the United States in a clockwise direction.

On the Great Lakes, offshore buoys are colored and

numbered as proceeding from the outlet end of each lake toward its upper end. This will be generally westerly and northward on the Lakes, except on Lake Michigan where it will be southward. Buoys marking channels into harbors are colored and numbered just as for channels leading into coastal ports from seaward.

On the Mississippi and Ohio Rivers and their tributaries, characteristics of aids to navigation are determined as proceeding from seaward toward the head of navigation, although local terminology describes "left bank" and "right bank" as proceeding with the flow of the river.

Coloring

All buoys are painted distinctive colors to indicate the side on which they should be passed, or their special purpose. In the lateral system, the significance of colors is as shown below.

TABLE 15-1			LATERAL SYSTEM IN U.S. AND CANADIAN WATERS			
Returning from sea*	**Color**	**Number**	**Unlighted Buoy Shape**	**Lights or Lighted Buoys**		**Daymark Shape**
				Light Color	**Light Phase Characteristic**	
Right side of channel	Red	Even	Nun	Red or White	Flashing or Quick Flashing	Triangular
Left side of channel	Black	Odd	Can	Green or White	Flashing or Quick Flashing	Square
Channel Junction or Obstruction	Red-and-black horizontally banded**	Not numbered	Nun or Can**	Red, Green or White**	Interrupted Quick Flashing	Triangular or Square**
Midchannel or Fairway	Black-and-white vertically striped	May be lettered	Nun or Can	White	Morse Code "A"	Octagonal

*or entering a harbor from a larger body of water, such as a lake.
**Preferred channel is indicated by color of uppermost band (shape of unlighted buoy), color of light, if any.

Black buoys mark the left (port) side of a channel when entering from seaward, or the location of a wreck or other obstruction that must be passed by keeping the buoy on the left hand.

Red buoys mark the right (starboard) side of a channel, or the location of a hazard to navigation that must be passed by keeping the buoy to starboard. It is from this color designation that the often-used phrase "Red — Right — Returning" is derived, meaning that *red* buoys should be kept on the *right* side of the boat when *returning* to harbor from the sea or other large body of water.

Red-and-black horizontally banded buoys mark junctions in a channel, or wrecks or obstructions that may be passed on *either* side. If the topmost band is black, the preferred channel will be followed by keeping the buoy on the left (port) hand. If the topmost band is red, the preferred channel is followed by keeping the buoy on the right (starboard) side of the vessel. (Note: When proceeding *toward* the sea, it may *not* be possible to pass such buoys safely on either side. This is particularly true in situations where you are following one channel downstream and another channel joins in from the side, see fig. 1519; always consult the chart for the area.)

Black-and-white vertically striped buoys mark the fairway or midchannel; they should be passed close to, but on either side.

It should be noted that when the areas of color run horizontally, they are "bands"; when they are arranged

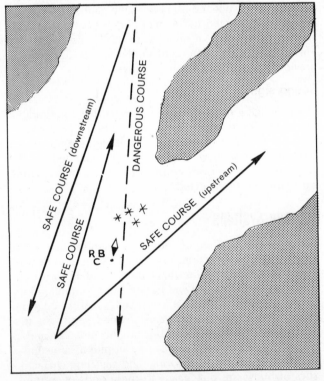

FIG. 1519 When proceeding upstream, a red-and-black horizontally-banded junction buoy may be safely passed on either side. This is not true, however, when going downstream, as examination of the above situation will quickly show.

vertically, they are "stripes." These terms are used in other color combinations in the case of special-purpose buoys.

Shapes of buoys

In the lateral system of buoyage, definite shape characteristics are given to the unlighted buoys to indicate which side of the channel they mark. The use of shapes is particularly valuable when a buoy is first sighted in line with the sun and only its silhouette rather than its color can be distinguished.

Can buoys, painted black, mark the left (port) side of the channel when returning from seaward, or the location of a wreck or shoal that must be passed by keeping the buoy on the left hand.

Nun buoys are used to mark the right (starboard) hand side of channels, or hazards that must be passed by keeping the buoy to starboard.

Channel junction and obstruction buoys may be of *either* can or nun shape. If the uppermost band is *black,* the buoy will be a *can;* if the uppermost band is *red,* it will be a *nun.*

Black-and-white vertically striped midchannel buoys may be either nuns or cans, and in this situation the shape has no significance.

No special significance is to be attached to the shape of spar buoys, bell buoys, gong buoys, whistle buoys, lighted buoys, or combination buoys. The purpose of these is indicated by their coloring, number or the characteristic of the light.

Numbering

Most buoys are given "numbers" that actually may be numbers, letters, or a combination of numbers and letters. These markings facilitate identification and location of buoys on charts.

In the lateral system, numbers serve as yet another indication of which side the buoy should be passed. The system is as follows:

Odd numbered buoys mark the left hand side of a channel leading in from seaward. In accordance with the rules stated above, these will be black buoys, cans if they are unlighted.

Even numbered buoys mark the right (starboard) side of a channel; these will be red (nun) buoys.

Numbers increase from seaward and are kept in approximate sequence on the two sides of a channel by omitting numbers as appropriate if buoys are not uniformly placed in pairs. Occasionally, several numbers will be omitted on longer stretches without buoys in order to allow for possible later additions.

Numbers followed by letters, such as 24A, 24B, 24C, etc., indicate buoys that have been added to a channel with the series not being immediately renumbered.

A buoy marking a wreck will often be designated with a number derived from the number of the buoy next downstream from it, preceded by the letters "WR". Thus, a buoy marking a wreck on the left-hand side of a channel between buoys 17 and 19 would be numbered "WR17A". A wreck buoy not related to a channel may be designated by one or two letters relating to the name of the wrecked vessel or a geographic location.

Letters, without numbers, are applied in some cases to black-and-white vertically striped buoys marking fairways, and to red-and-black horizontally banded buoys marking channel junctions or obstructions.

Numbers followed by letters may be used on some buoys marking offshore dangers. An example of this usage is the buoy marked "2TL" where the number has the usual sequential significance and the letters "TL" indicate the place as a shoal known as "Turner's Lump." This form of marking buoys is now more traditional than necessary.

Color of lights

For all buoys in the lateral system that have lights, the following system of colors is used.

Green lights on buoys are used only on those marking the left-hand side of a channel returning from seaward (black, odd-numbered buoys) or on red-and-black horizontally banded buoys that have the topmost band painted black.

Red lights on buoys are used only on those marking the right-hand side of a channel when entering from sea (red, even-numbered buoys) or on red-and-black horizontally banded buoys having a red topmost band.

White lights on buoys may be used on either side of channels in lieu of red or green. White lights are frequently employed where a greater visible range is desired, such as at a change in the direction of the channel. No special significance is derived from a white light, the purpose of the buoy being indicated by its color, number, or its light phase characteristic.

Light phase characteristics

Fixed lights (lights that do not flash) may be found on either red or black buoys, but are rare.

Flashing lights (flashing at a rate of not more than 30 flashes per minute) are placed only on black or red buoys, or on special purpose buoys.

Quick flashing lights (not less than 60 flashes each minute) are placed only on channel-edge-marking black and red buoys; these are used at points where it is desired to indicate that *special caution* in piloting is required, as at sharp turns or changes in the width of the waterway, or where used to mark wrecks or dangerous obstructions that must be passed only on one side.

Interrupted quick flashing lights are used only on buoys painted with red-and-black horizontal bands. These are the buoys at channel junctions and obstructions that can be passed on either side.

Morse code "A" flashing lights (short-long flashing) are placed only on black-and-white vertically striped buoys that mark a fairway or midchannel; these are passed close to, on either side. The lights are always white.

WRECK BUOYS

Buoys established by the Coast Guard to mark dangerous wrecks are generally placed on the seaward or channel side of the obstruction and as near to it as conditions permit. Wreck buoys are *not* placed directly over a wreck; they must be placed in position by a vessel and it is usually impossible for such vessel to maneuver directly over the hazard without incurring underwater damage to herself.

Caution must be exercised when navigating in the vicinity of buoys marking wrecks because, due to sea action, the wreck may shift in location between the time that the buoy is established and when it is later checked or serviced.

STATION BUOYS

Important buoys, usually large combination buoys, with both light and sound signals, are sometimes accompanied by *station buoys*. These are smaller, unlighted buoys, see fig. 1520, placed in the vicinity of the main buoy on the side away from marine traffic. They are colored and numbered the same as the main buoy. Station buoys are not charted; their existence is noted, however, in the Light Lists in the remarks column for the major aid to which they are related.

The purpose of the station buoy is to mark the location should the main buoy be sunk or carried away for any reason, such as being struck by a passing ship. The station buoy serves as a temporary substitute and aids in the replacement of the main buoy on the correct location.

DAYBEACONS AND MINOR LIGHTS

Although the lateral system of buoyage has been described in terms of unlighted and lighted buoys, the use of comparable daybeacons and minor lights is fully applicable.

Daybeacons with red triangular daymarks or red pointers may be substituted for nun buoys, and structures with black square daymarks or black pointers may replace can buoys where the water is shallow enough to make such installations practicable. Minor lights likewise may be used in place of lighted or combination buoys. It is not unusual to find a channel marked with a mixture of unlighted and lighted buoys, daybeacons, and minor lights.

Occasionally, daybeacons will be used to indicate a channel junction or obstruction. In such a case, the daymark will be red-and-black horizontally banded with the color of the uppermost band indicating the main or preferred channel. The shape of the daymark will be either square or triangular as determined by the color or the top band, similar to the use of a can or nun buoy for this purpose.

Daybeacons used to mark fairways or the middle of a channel will have an octagonal-shaped daymark, painted with the normal black-and-white vertical stripes.

A diamond-shaped daymark has *no* significance in the lateral system. A typical application might be to increase the daytime detectability of a minor light which is not a part of a channel or waterway series.

INTRACOASTAL WATERWAY AIDS

The Coast Guard maintains the system of aids to navigation along the Atlantic and Gulf Intracoastal Waterway (ICW). The coloring and numbering of buoys and daybeacons, and the color of lights on buoys and light structures, is in conformity with the lateral system of buoyage as described above. The system is applied by considering passage from north to south along the Atlantic coast, and from south to north and east to west along the Gulf coast, as corresponding to returning from sea in an entrance channel. Thus, red buoys and fixed aids are on the right side of the channel when proceeding from New Jersey toward Florida and then on to Texas; black aids are on the left hand side of the Waterway when proceeding in the same direction. This rule is applied in a uniform manner from one end of the Intracoastal Waterway to the other, regardless of widely varying compass headings on

FIG. 1520 Station buoys are occasionally used in conjunction with major combination buoys. These are placed near the main buoy on the side away from ship traffic. Such buoys are not separately charted, but they are mentioned in the Light Lists. The older tapered "wasp-waist" design of buoy superstructure is giving way to a newer straight-sided design.

many stretches, and the fact that rivers and other waterways marked by the seacoast system are occasionally followed.

The aids to navigation do differ in one respect, however, in that they carry on additional distinctive marking to identify the ICW route. This special marking is applied to the so-called "inside route" and to those portions of all connecting waterways that must be crossed or followed to make a continuous passage.

Distinctive ICW markings

All buoys, daybeacons, and light structures marking the Intracoastal Waterway have some portion of them painted *yellow*. This is the distinctive coloring adopted for the ICW. Buoys and single piles have a band of yellow at the top; daymarks and pointers have a band or border of yellow. For examples of these markings, see the color illustrations on page 292.

The numbering of Intracoastal Waterway aids follows the same basic rule as for entrance channels, with numbers increasing in the direction from New Jersey toward Florida and Texas. Aids are numbered in groups, usually not exceeding 99, beginning again with "1" or "2" at specified natural dividing points.

Lights on buoys follow the standard system of red or white lights on red buoys, and green or white lights on black buoys. The color of lights on fixed structures follows the same general system. Range lights, not being a part of the lateral system, may be any of the three standard colors.

Dual marking

In order that vessels may readily follow the Intracoastal Waterway where it coincides with another route such as an important river marked on the seacoast system, special *dual markings* are employed. These are applied to the buoys or other aids that mark the river channel for other traffic. Special marks consist of a yellow square or a yellow

continued on page 292 (k)

AIDS TO NAVIGATION ON NAVIGABLE WATERS
except Western Rivers and Intracoastal Waterway

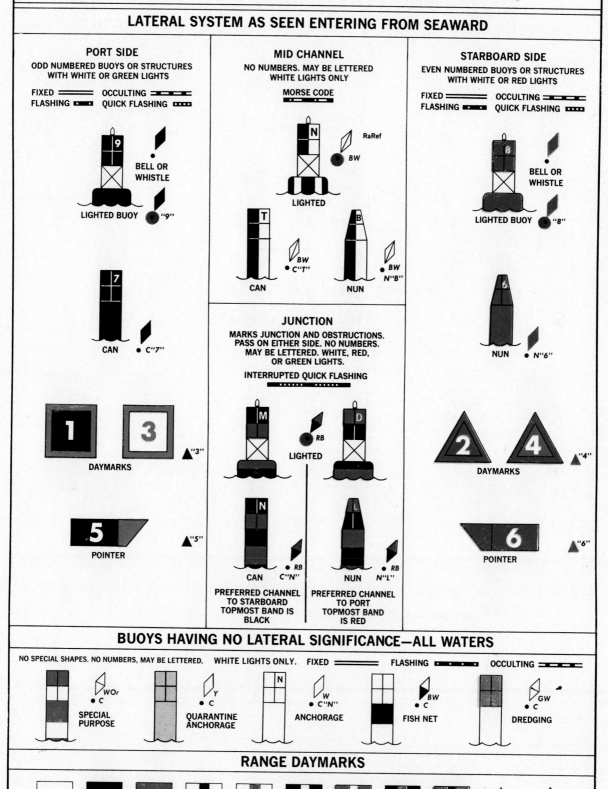

LATERAL SYSTEM AS SEEN ENTERING FROM SEAWARD

PORT SIDE
ODD NUMBERED BUOYS OR STRUCTURES WITH WHITE OR GREEN LIGHTS

FIXED OCCULTING
FLASHING QUICK FLASHING

BELL OR WHISTLE

LIGHTED BUOY "9"

CAN C"7"

DAYMARKS

POINTER ▲"5"

MID CHANNEL
NO NUMBERS. MAY BE LETTERED WHITE LIGHTS ONLY
MORSE CODE

RaRef
BW
LIGHTED

CAN BW C"T"
NUN BW N"B"

JUNCTION
MARKS JUNCTION AND OBSTRUCTIONS. PASS ON EITHER SIDE. NO NUMBERS. MAY BE LETTERED. WHITE, RED, OR GREEN LIGHTS.
INTERRUPTED QUICK FLASHING

RB
LIGHTED

CAN RB C"N"
NUN RB N"L"

PREFERRED CHANNEL TO STARBOARD TOPMOST BAND IS BLACK

PREFERRED CHANNEL TO PORT TOPMOST BAND IS RED

STARBOARD SIDE
EVEN NUMBERED BUOYS OR STRUCTURES WITH WHITE OR RED LIGHTS

FIXED OCCULTING
FLASHING QUICK FLASHING

BELL OR WHISTLE

LIGHTED BUOY "8"

NUN N"6"

DAYMARKS ▲"4"

POINTER ▲"6"

BUOYS HAVING NO LATERAL SIGNIFICANCE—ALL WATERS

NO SPECIAL SHAPES. NO NUMBERS, MAY BE LETTERED. WHITE LIGHTS ONLY. FIXED FLASHING OCCULTING

WOr C
SPECIAL PURPOSE

Y C
QUARANTINE ANCHORAGE

W C"N"
ANCHORAGE

BW C
FISH NET

GW
DREDGING

RANGE DAYMARKS

MAY BE USED IN SPECIAL CIRCUMSTANCES

NOTES: A. Quick flashing lights mark important turns, wrecks, etc., where particular caution is required.   .B. RaRef on chart indicates radar reflector installed.

292(c)

AIDS TO NAVIGATION ON THE INTRACOASTAL WATERWAY

AS SEEN ENTERING FROM NORTH AND EAST AND PROCEEDING TO SOUTH AND WEST

PORT SIDE
ODD NUMBERED BUOYS OR STRUCTURES WITH WHITE OR GREEN LIGHTS

FIXED ═══ OCCULTING ▭▭▭
FLASHING ▭▬ QUICK FLASHING ▭▭▭▭▭

BELL OR WHISTLE

LIGHTED BUOY • "3"

CAN • C"9"

DAYMARKS ▲ "3"

POINTER ▲ "7"

JOINT • C"5"

• N"6"

JUNCTION
MARKS JUNCTION AND OBSTRUCTIONS. PASS ON EITHER SIDE. NO NUMBERS. MAY BE LETTERED. WHITE, RED, OR GREEN LIGHTS.

INTERRUPTED QUICK FLASHING ▬▬ ▬▬

LIGHTED • RB

CAN C"A" • RB

NUN N"S" • RB

PREFERRED CHANNEL TO STARBOARD TOPMOST BAND IS BLACK

PREFERRED CHANNEL TO PORT TOPMOST BAND IS RED

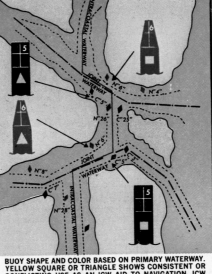

ILLUSTRATING THE SYSTEM OF DUAL PURPOSE MARKING WHERE THE ICW AND OTHER WATERWAYS COINCIDE

BUOY SHAPE AND COLOR BASED ON PRIMARY WATERWAY. YELLOW SQUARE OR TRIANGLE SHOWS CONSISTENT OR CONFLICTING USE AS AN ICW AID TO NAVIGATION. ICW TREATS ▢ AS A CAN AND △ AS A NUN REGARDLESS OF BUOY TYPE OR COLOR.

STARBOARD SIDE
EVEN NUMBERED BUOYS OR STRUCTURES WITH WHITE OR RED LIGHTS

FIXED ═══ OCCULTING ▭▭▭
FLASHING ▭▬ QUICK FLASHING ▭▭▭▭▭

BELL OR WHISTLE

LIGHTED BUOY • "8"

NUN • N"6"

DAYMARKS ▲ "4"

POINTER ▲ "6"

JOINT • N"6"

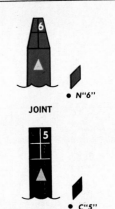

• C"5"

RANGE DAYMARKS

MAY BE USED IN SPECIAL CIRCUMSTANCES

NOTE: The ICW aids are characterized by the yellow border

292(d)

ILLUSTRATING THE SYSTEM OF DUAL PURPOSE MARKING
WHERE THE ICW AND OTHER WATERWAYS COINCIDE

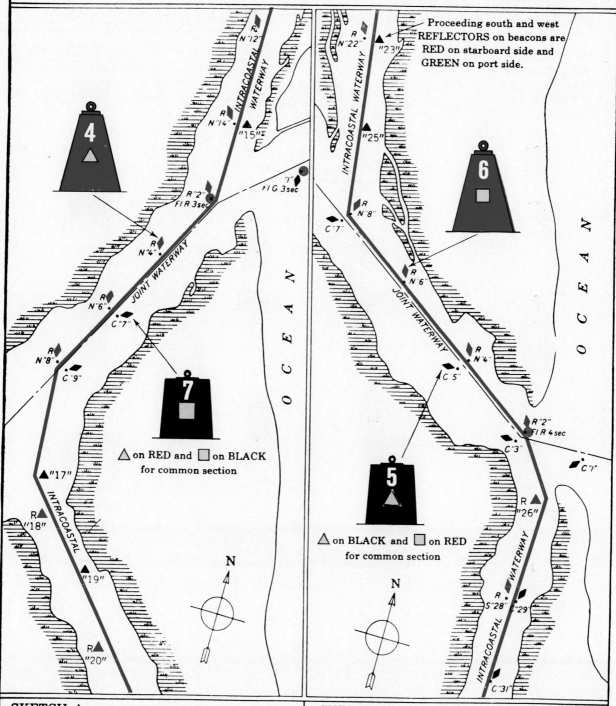

SKETCH A:

ICW joins another waterway, which is numbered from seaward, at buoy No. 2 and is common with it to buoy No. 9. ICW numbers and yellow borders are omitted in this section but the △ or ⬜ is used on the regular aids to designate the ICW.

SKETCH B:

ICW joins another waterway at buoy No. 8 and is common with it to buoy No. 3. This section is numbered in the opposite direction to that of the ICW. The ICW numbers and yellow borders are omitted from the regular aids but a △ or ⬜ is shown to designate the ICW.

In areas where sections of the Intracoastal Waterway join another waterway, ICW numbers and yellow borders are omitted from the regular aids to navigation but yellow triangle or square is used to designate the ICW, thus eliminating any possibility of confusion.

292(e)

AS SEEN PROCEEDING IN THE DIRECTION OF RIVER FLOW (DESCENDING)

LEFT SIDE
WHITE OR RED LIGHTS
GROUP FLASHING (2)
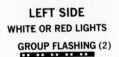

JUNCTION
MARKS JUNCTIONS AND OBSTRUCTIONS.
PASS ON EITHER SIDE.
WHITE, RED OR GREEN LIGHTS.

INTERRUPTED QUICK FLASHING
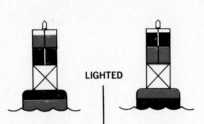

RIGHT SIDE
WHITE OR GREEN LIGHTS
FLASHING

LIGHTED BUOY

LIGHTED BUOY

LIGHTED

NUN

NUN

CAN

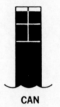

CAN

PASSING DAYMARK
(222)

PREFERRED CHANNEL
TO THE RIGHT
TOPMOST BAND RED
WHITE OR RED LIGHT

PREFERRED CHANNEL
TO THE LEFT
TOPMOST BAND BLACK
WHITE OR GREEN LIGHT

PASSING DAYMARK
111

CROSSING DAYMARK

CROSSING DAYMARK

BUOYS HAVING NO LATERAL SIGNIFICANCE—ALL WATERS

NO SPECIAL SHAPES. NO NUMBERS, MAY BE LETTERED.   WHITE LIGHTS ONLY.   FIXED ═══   FLASHING ▪▪▪▪▪   OCCULTING ═▪═▪═

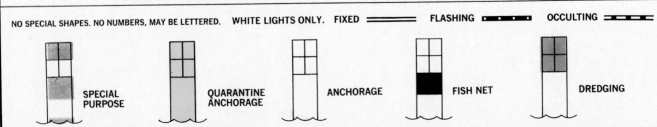

SPECIAL PURPOSE   QUARANTINE ANCHORAGE   ANCHORAGE   FISH NET   DREDGING

GREAT LAKES
CHART SYMBOL INFORMATION

NOTE: WHERE THE TERMS LEFT AND RIGHT ARE USED
THEY ARE SEEN BY A VESSEL PROCEEDING FROM SEAWARD

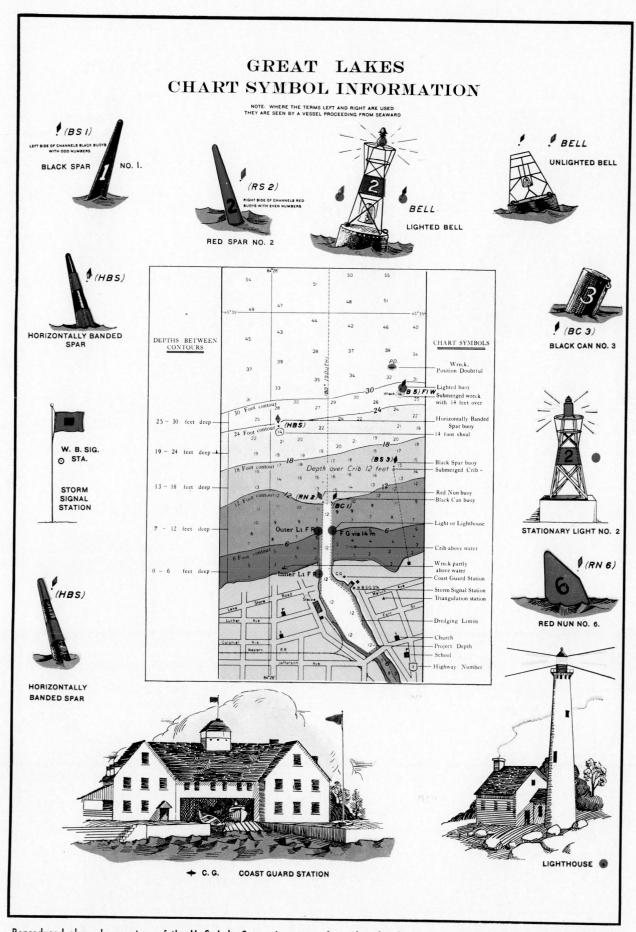

(BS I)

LEFT SIDE OF CHANNELS BLACK BUOYS
WITH ODD NUMBERS

BLACK SPAR NO. I.

(RS 2)

RIGHT SIDE OF CHANNELS RED
BUOYS WITH EVEN NUMBERS

RED SPAR NO. 2

BELL

LIGHTED BELL

BELL

UNLIGHTED BELL

(HBS)

HORIZONTALLY BANDED
SPAR

W. B. SIG.
STA.

STORM
SIGNAL
STATION

(HBS)

HORIZONTALLY
BANDED SPAR

(BC 3)

BLACK CAN NO. 3

STATIONARY LIGHT NO. 2

(RN 6)

RED NUN NO. 6.

DEPTHS BETWEEN
CONTOURS

25 – 30 feet deep

19 – 24 feet deep

13 – 18 feet deep

7 – 12 feet deep

0 – 6 feet deep

CHART SYMBOLS

Wreck,
Position Doubtful

Lighted buoy
Submerged wreck
with 14 feet over

Horizontally Banded
Spar buoy

14 foot shoal

Black Spar buoy

Submerged Crib

Red Nun buoy

Black Can buoy

Light or Lighthouse

Crib above water

Wreck partly
above water

Coast Guard Station

Storm Signal Station

Triangulation station

Dredging Limits

Church

Project Depth

School

Highway Number

C. G.   COAST GUARD STATION

LIGHTHOUSE

Reproduced above by courtesy of the U. S. Lake Survey is a page from their brochure, Charts of the Great Lakes. Symbols show how various navigational aids are identified on charts. In addition to conventional lake charts, the Lake Survey has plans for a series of about 25 recreational-craft charts, in loose-leaf volumes 11" x 17½", each containing about 50 large-scale charts. Four have already been issued. A similar volume covers the N. Y. State Barge Canal System.

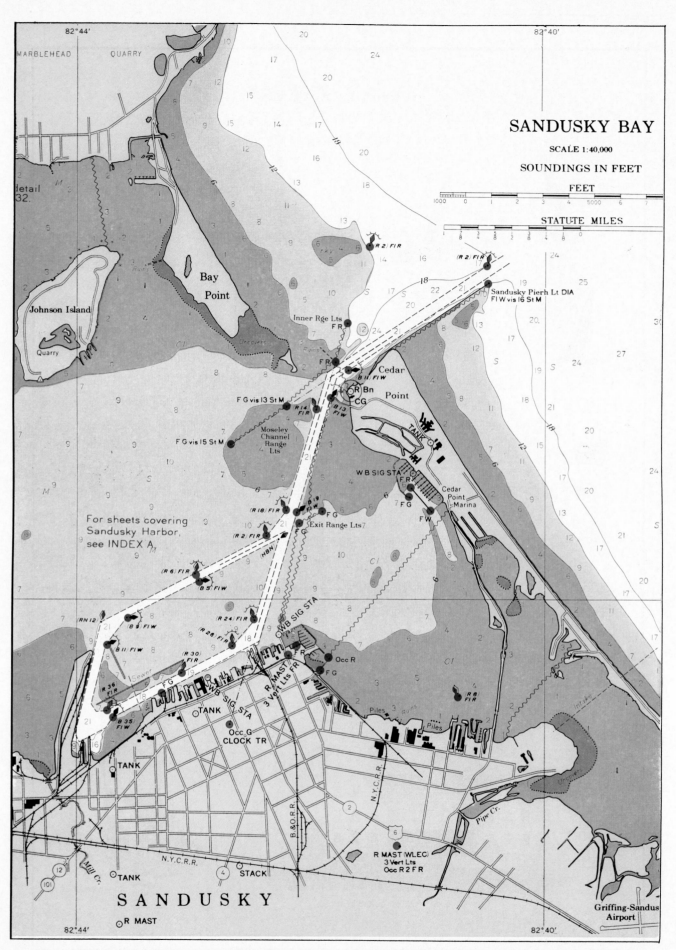

A portion (slightly less than half) of the U. S. Army Engineers' chart for Sandusky Bay (eastern end), south shore of Lake Erie, from the U. S. Lake Survey Recreational Craft Series chart No. 360 — Port Clinton to Sandusky, Ohio. The spiral-bound volume includes 35 charts — lake, rivers, harbors, and islands — and much data of value to the boatman. As reproduced above, the scale differs slightly from that (1:40,000) on which the original chart is drawn. Only charts as published by official sources should be used for navigation.

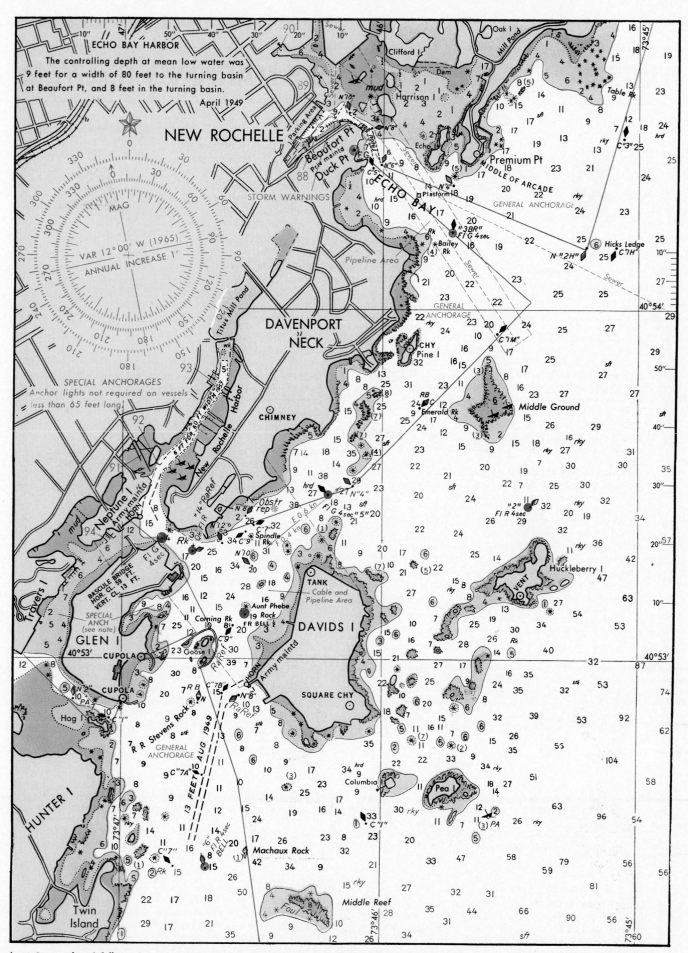

UNIFORM STATE WATERWAY MARKING SYSTEM

AIDS TO NAVIGATION

PORT (left) SIDE

COLOR — Black
NUMBERS — Odd
LIGHTS — Flashing green
REFLECTORS — Green

THE LATERAL SYSTEM—In well-defined channels and narrow waterways, USWMS aids to navigation normally are solid-colored buoys. Though a can and a nun are illustrated here, SHAPES may vary. COLOR is the significant feature. When proceeding UPSTREAM or toward the head of navigation, BLACK BUOYS ← mark the *left* side of the channel and must be kept on the left (port) hand. RED BUOYS → mark the *right* side of the channel and must be kept on the right (starboard) side. This conforms with practice on other federal waterways. On waters having no well-defined inlet or outlet, arbitrary assumptions may be made. Inquire in the locality for further information and charts when available.

STARBOARD (right) SIDE

COLOR — Red
NUMBERS — Even
LIGHTS — Flashing red
REFLECTORS — Red

THE CARDINAL SYSTEM—Used where there is no well-defined channel or where an obstruction may be approached from more than one direction.

BLACK-TOPPED WHITE BUOY indicates boat should pass to NORTH or EAST of it. Reflector or light, if used, is white, the light quick-flashing.

RED-TOPPED WHITE BUOY indicates boat should pass to SOUTH or WEST of it. Reflector or light, if used, is white, the light quick-flashing.

RED-AND-WHITE VERTICALLY STRIPED BUOY indicates boat should not pass between buoy and nearest shore. Used when reef or obstruction requires boat to go *outside* buoy (away from shore). White stripes are twice the width of red stripes. Reflector or light, if used, is white, the light quick-flashing.

MOORING BUOY—White with horizontal blue band. If lighted, shows slow-flashing light unless it constitutes an obstruction at night, when light would be quick-flashing.

NOTE—The use of lights, reflectors, numbers and letters on USWMS aids is discretionary.

LIGHTS—On solid-colored (red or black) buoys, lights when used are flashing, occulting, or equal interval. For ordinary purposes, *slow-flashing* (not more than 30 per minute). *Quick-flashing* (not less than 60 per minute) used at turns, constrictions, or obstructions to indicate *caution*.

REFLECTORS—On lateral-type buoys, *red* reflectors or retro-reflective materials are used on solid-red buoys, *green* reflectors on solid-black buoys, *white* on all others including regulatory markers (except that *orange* may be used on orange portions of markers).

NUMBERS—*White* on red or black backgrounds. *Black* on white backgrounds. Numbers increase in an upstream direction.

LETTERS—When used on regulatory and white-and-red striped obstruction markers, letters are in alphabetical sequence in an upstream direction. (Letters I and O omitted.)

UNIFORM STATE REGULATORY MARKERS

Diamond shape warns of DANGER! Suggested wording for specific dangers: ROCK (illustrated), DAM, SNAG, DREDGE, WING-DAM, FERRY CABLE, MARINE CONSTRUCTION, etc.

Circle marks CONTROLLED AREA "as illustrated." Suggested wording to control or prohibit boating activities: 5 MPH (illustrated), NO FISHING, NO SKI, NO SWIM, NO SCUBA, NO PROP BOATS, SKI ONLY, FISHING ONLY, SKIN DIVERS ONLY, etc.

Diamond shape with cross means BOATS KEEP OUT! Explanatory reasons may be indicated outside the crossed diamond shape, for example SWIM AREA (illustrated), DAM, WATERFALL, RAPIDS, DOMESTIC WATER, etc.

Square or rectangle gives INFORMATION, names, activities. May give place names, distances, arrows indicating directions, availability of gas, oil, groceries, marine repairs, etc.

REGULATORY MARKERS are *white* with *international orange* geometric shapes. Buoys may be used as regulatory markers. Such buoys are *white* with two horizontal bands of *international orange*—one at the top, another just above the waterline. Geometric shapes, colored *international orange*, are placed on the white body of the buoy between the orange bands. When square or rectangular *signs* are displayed on structures as regulatory markers, they are *white* with *international orange* borders. Diamond and circular shapes, when used, are centered on the signboard.

continued from page 292(b)

triangle painted on a conspicuous part of the dual-purpose aid. The yellow square, in outline similar to a can buoy, indicates that the aid on which it is placed should be kept on the left-hand side when following the ICW in the direction from New Jersey to Texas. The yellow triangle, in outline similar to a nun buoy, indicates that the aid should be kept on the right hand side when traveling in the same direction.

The yellow squares may appear on *either* a black can or a red nun of the river channel marks (or comparable daybeacons and light structures). Similarly, the yellow triangle dual markings may appear on any type of lateral aid. These similarly contradictory markings result from the fact that in some situations a southbound ICW route (red nuns on the right side) will be *up* a river channel from seaward (red nuns on the right side); and in other situations, the same ICW route will be down a river toward the sea where black cans will be on the skipper's right side. In both of these situations, however, the yellow triangle will be kept to the right. See page 292A.

Where the yellow squares and triangles are added to regular river or harbor aids to navigation, the ICW yellow band or border is omitted.

Where dual marking is employed, the boatman following the ICW disregards the shape and coloring of the aid on which the yellow square or triangle is placed and pilots his craft solely by the shape of the yellow markings. The numbers on the aids will be those of the river's lateral system, and in some instances where the southward ICW proceeds down a river, the numbers will be temporarily decreasing rather than increasing. See page 292A.

By this system of dual marking, the mariner approaching a body of water such as the Cape Fear River, and realizing that he must follow it for some distance before again entering a dredged land cut of the Intracoastal Waterway, knows that his course lies along such buoys or other aids as are specially marked in yellow. He determines the side of his craft on which these aids should be passed by the shape of the yellow marks, keeping always in mind the basic direction of his ICW travel.

Special Purpose Buoys

In addition to the lateral system of buoyage maintained by the Coast Guard in Federal-jurisdiction waters, several special-purpose buoy characteristics, having no lateral significance, are used to mark dredging areas, anchorages, quarantine areas, fish net areas, race courses, experiments or tests, etc.

The meaning of special-purpose buoys is indicated by their colors as follows:

White buoys mark *anchorage* areas.

Yellow buoys mark *quarantine anchorage* areas.

Note carefully the difference between an *anchorage* buoy and a *mooring* buoy — an anchorage buoy is an aid to navigation marking the boundary of an area in which vessels may be anchored in accordance with prescribed regulations; a mooring buoy is a strong, heavily anchored buoy to which vessels can be made fast in lieu of anchoring.

White buoys with green tops are used in connection with *dredging* and *survey* operations.

White-and-black horizontally banded buoys mark fish

net areas. Particularly, but not exclusively, in the Chesapeake Bay area, such buoys are used to mark the boundaries of areas in which fish nets and traps may be placed; such areas and buoys are indicated on charts. (See fig. 1521.) These buoys may be cans or nuns, the shape has no significance; they carry identification numbers and letters.

White-and-international-orange buoys, with either horizontal bands or vertical stripes, are used for special purposes to which neither the lateral-system colors nor the other special-purpose colors are applicable. (See fig. 1522.)

Special-purpose buoys are illustrated in color at the bottom of page 291.

Yellow-and-black vertically striped buoys mark seaplane operating areas and have no marine significance other than to indicate the need for caution and a sharp lookout for aircraft.

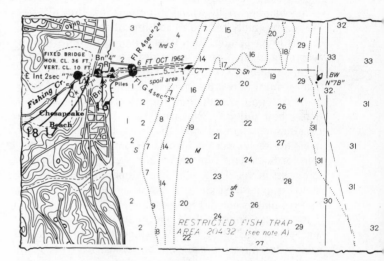

FIG. 1521 A black-and-white horizontally banded buoy is charted here at the intersection of lines (long and short dash) indicating outer limits of a fish trap area.

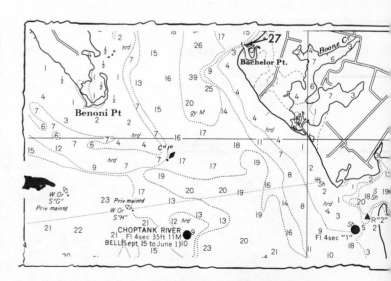

FIG. 1522 Positions of white-and-orange horizontally banded special purpose buoys near Choptank River Light are indicated on this chart. These are lettered for identification and it is indicated that they are privately maintained.

Special-purpose buoys may be lighted or unlighted, and some may have a fog signal. These buoys may be of any shape if unlighted—can, nun, or spherical.

SPECIAL—TYPE BUOYS

Special-type buoys may be encountered in all waters. Typical of these in inland waters are the buoys used in current surveys. The shape, size, color, lights (if any), markings, etc., vary too widely to be described here, but will be completely listed in the public notices that are always published before such buoys are placed in navigable waters.

Offshore boatmen may occasionally encounter large sea buoys used for gathering meteorological or oceanographic data, or those employed in naval defense operations.

Uniform State Buoyage System

Each state has authority over control of navigation on waters that lie wholly within its boundaries. This includes the responsibility for the establishment and maintenance of aids to navigation. Each state is free to mark its waters according to any system that it desires. Initially, the result of this freedom was a considerable variance in the ways that inland waters not subject to Federal jurisdiction were marked. More recently, however, although the states still retain their authority, they have agreed to adopt a single consistent system of markers. With trailer-borne craft traveling freely over the highways from state to state, the gain for boatmen from the uniform system is too obvious to discuss in detail. The rambling skipper no longer has to try to decipher the significance of what had been intended to serve him as an "aid to navigation."

By Act of Congress, the Uniform State Waterway Marking System (USWMS) may be extended to cover waters subject to Federal jurisdiction, but which have not been marked with aids by the Coast Guard. Agreements may be entered into between a Coast Guard District Commander and state officials for the designation of "state waters for private aids to navigation." In such waters, state or local governments may establish and maintain aids to navigation which comply with the standards of the USWMS.

MAJOR FEATURES OF THE USWMS

The Uniform State Waterway Marking System has been developed to provide a means to convey to the small craft operator, in particular, adequate guidance to indicate safe boating channels by indicating the presence of either natural or artificial obstructions or hazards. The USWMS also provides means for marking restricted or controlled areas and for providing directions. The system is suited for use in all water areas and designed to satisfy the needs of all types of small vessels. It supplements and is generally compatible with the lateral system of aids to navigation maintained by the Coast Guard.

The USWMS consists of two categories of aids to navigation:

(1) A system of regulatory markers to indicate to the pilot the existence of dangerous areas as well as those which are restricted or controlled, such as speed zones and areas set aside for a particular use, or to provide general information and directions.

(2) A system of aids to navigation to supplement the Federal lateral system of buoyage.

Regulatory markers

On Federal waters, the boatman can turn to his charts, Light Lists, Coast Pilots, and other publications for information on natural hazards, zoned areas, directions, distances, etc., to supplement the knowledge that he gets from buoys, daybeacons, and other aids. On state waters, he now has a uniform system of water signs or markers that, in themselves, convey their message without reference to any publication — an obvious advantage, especially for inexperienced boatmen.

Just as Intracoastal Waterway markers are distinguished by their special yellow borders or other yellow marks, state regulatory markers are identified by international-orange-and-white colors. On buoys, an orange band will be seen at the top and bottom, and on the white area between these bands, a geometric shape, also in orange, will be noted. An open diamond shape indicates danger. A diamond with a cross inside indicates a prohibited area; vessels are excluded from the area marked by such buoys. A circle signifies zoning or control; vessels operating in such areas are subject to certain operating restrictions. A square or rectangular shape signals the conveying of information, the details of which are spelled out within the shape. (See fig. 1523.)

Where the regulatory marker consists of a square or

FIG. 1523   Uniform state regulatory markers convey their meaning to the boatman without need for reference to charts or other publications.

| **DANGER!** Warns of rocks, reefs, dams, snags, or other hazards. | **BOATS KEEP OUT!** Marks waterfalls, swim areas, rapids, and other restricted areas. | **CAUTION!** Type of control is indicated within the circle such as No ski, speed zone, No anchoring. | **INFORMATION!** Tells distances, locations, other official information. |

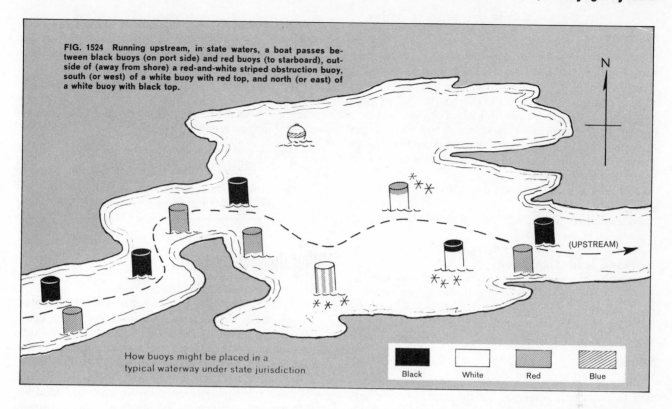

FIG. 1524 Running upstream, in state waters, a boat passes between black buoys (on port side) and red buoys (to starboard), outside of (away from shore) a red-and-white striped obstruction buoy, south (or west) of a white buoy with red top, and north (or east) of a white buoy with black top.

N

How buoys might be placed in a typical waterway under state jurisdiction

(UPSTREAM)

| Black | White | Red | Blue |

rectangular shaped sign displayed from a structure, the sign is white with an international orange border. If a diamond or circular shape is associated with the meaning of the marker, it will be centered on the signboard.

The geometric shape displayed on a regulatory marker is intended to convey the basic idea of danger, or control, etc., so that the boatman can tell at a distance whether he should stay away or may safely approach for more information. To convey a specific meaning, spelled-out words or recognized abbreviations appear within the shape. The sole exception to this is the cross within the diamond shape that is used to absolutely prohibit boats from entering an area, because of danger to the boat, swimmers in a protected area, or for any other reason sufficient to warrant exclusion by law.

To minimize the risk of misinterpretation, initials, symbols, and silhouettes have not been used. In some cases, words may be needed outside the geometric shape to give the reason, authority, or some clarification of the specific meaning.

Aids to navigation

The second category of marker in the USWMS is the aid to navigation having lateral or cardinal meaning. In selecting types of buoys for use on waters not marked by the Coast Guard, the principal objective was to make the state system compatible with the Federal.

On a well-defined channel, including a river or other relatively narrow natural or improved waterway, an aid to navigation of the USWMS is normally a solid-colored buoy. A buoy that marks the left side of a channel viewed *looking upstream* or toward the head of navigation is colored *solid black*. A buoy that marks the *right* side, looking in the same direction, is colored *solid red.* (This, it will be noted, is the same as the Coast Guard lateral system.) On a well-defined channel, solid-colored buoys will be found

in pairs, one for each side of the channel that they mark, and opposite each other, leaving no doubt that the channel lies between the red and the black buoys, and that the skipper should pilot his boat between them.

On irregularly defined channels, solid-colored buoys may be used singly in staggered fashion on alternate sides provided that they are spaced at sufficiently close intervals to clearly inform the skipper that the channel lies between the buoys and that he should pass between them.

Where there is no well-defined channel, or when a body of water is obstructed by objects whose nature or location is such that the hazard might be approached from more than one direction, a *cardinal* system is used. The use of cardinal system aids to navigation is strictly limited to waters wholly subject to state jurisdiction or waters covered by a Coast Guard-state agreement. This restriction is necessary as the Coast Guard's lateral system makes no provision for markers of the cardinal system.

A white buoy with red top indicates that a boat must pass to the *south or west* of the buoy.

A white buoy with black top indicates that the safe water is to the *north or east* of the buoy.

A buoy with alternate red and white vertical stripes indicates that an obstruction extends from the nearest shore to the buoy, and that the boat must not pass between the buoy and that shore. The number of red and white stripes may vary, but the width of the white stripes will always be twice that of the red ones. See fig. 1524.

Characteristics of markers and aids

The size, shape, material, and construction of all markers, fixed or floating, is discretionary with the state authorities. They must, however, be such as to be observable under normal conditions of visibility at a distance such that the significance of the marker or aid will be recognizable before a craft stands into danger.

Numbers

State aids to navigation and regulatory markers may carry numbers, letters, or words. These must be placed in a manner so as to be clearly visible to approaching and passing boats, with characters in block style, well proportioned and as large as the available space permits. Numbers and letters on red or black backgrounds will be in white; on white backgrounds, they will be black. The use of numbers on buoys is optional, but if used will conform to the following system:

Odd numbers will be used on *solid black* buoys and on *black-topped* buoys.

Even numbers will be used on *solid red* buoys and on *red-topped* buoys.

All numbers will *increase* in an *upstream* direction or toward the head of navigation.

Letters only may be used to identify regulatory markers and red-and-white vertically striped obstruction buoys. If used, letters will follow an alphabetical sequence in the upstream direction; the letters "I" and "O" will not be used to prevent possible confusion with numbers.

Reflectors

The use of reflectors or reflective tape is discretionary with the local authorities maintaining the markers and aids. If used, red reflectors or reflective material will be used on solid red buoys, and green on solid black buoys.

All other buoys will have white reflectors or reflective material, as will regulatory markers, except that orange reflectors may be placed on the orange portions of such markers.

Lights

Lights may be used on USWMS regulatory markers and aids to navigation if desired by the state authorities. When used, lights on solid colored buoys will be regularly flashing, regularly occulting, or equal interval. (An "occulting" light is one that is on more than it is off.) For ordinary purposes, the rate of flashing will not be more than 30 times per minute.

When lights have a distinct cautionary significance, such as at sharp bends in a channel, the light may be quick flashing, not less than 60 flashes each minute.

When a light is placed on a cardinal system buoy or a red-and-white vertically striped buoy, it will always be quick flashing.

Red lights are used only on solid red buoys, green lights only on solid black buoys. White lights will be used on all other buoys and on regulatory markers.

Ownership markings

The use and placement of ownership identification is discretionary. If used, such markings must be worded and placed in such a manner that they will not detract from the meaning being conveyed as a regulatory marker or aid to navigation.

Mooring buoys

Mooring buoys in waters covered by the Uniform State Waterway Marking System will be white with a horizontal blue band around them midway between the waterline and the top of the buoy.

A lighted mooring buoy will normally show a slow flashing white light. If, however, its location is such that it is an obstruction to craft operating during hours of darkness, the light will be quick flashing white.

A mooring buoy may carry ownership identification provided that such markings do not detract from the meaning intended to be conveyed by the color scheme and identification letter, if assigned.

Illustration of the USWMS
The Uniform State Waterway Marking System is illustrated in color on page 292F.

Other Buoyage Systems

Buoyage on the "Western Rivers of the United States" (the Mississippi and its tributaries, and certain other designated rivers) conforms to the lateral system, but includes some additional shapes and daymarks not found in other areas. See the color illustration on page 292B.

On these rivers, unlighted buoys are not numbered, while the numbers on lighted buoys have no lateral significance, rather indicating the number of miles upstream from a designated reference point.

Additional details on the buoyage of the Western Rivers will be found in Chapter 28.

Foreign waters

Boatmen who carry their cruising into foreign waters should, prior to departure, fully acquaint themselves with the buoyage systems to be encountered. Significant differences from the U. S. lateral system may be found, and there will be variations between the systems used in different countries.

In Canadian waters, the lateral system of buoyage is essentially the same as in the United States. Minor differences in the physical appearance of buoys may be noted, but these should not be great enough to result in any confusion. Chart symbols, likewise, may be slightly different from those standardized for use on U. S. charts.

In British waters, however, quite a different situation exists. A lateral system of buoyage is employed, but the coloring, light characteristics, etc. are entirely at variance with the U. S. system. The "red-right-returning" rule becomes "black-right-returning." Buoys on the right side of entering channels are conical (nun), but they are painted black or black-and-white checkered; lights will flash in sequences of 1, 3, or 5. On the left side of such a channel, there are can buoys, as an American boatman might expect, but they are painted red or red-and-white checkered; lights will flash in sequences of 2, 4, or 6.

Junction (obstruction) buoys in British waters are spherical in shape and are horizontally banded, red-and-white or black-and-white, according to the general system for indication of the main or preferred channel as used in the United States. Midchannel buoys are of a distinctive shape — a shape other than can, nun, or spherical — and vertically striped in either black-and-white or red-and-white colors.

CHAPTER 16

AIDS TO NAVIGATION —
Lighthouses and Other Aids

The preceding chapter covered the many thousands of aids to navigation that mark rivers and channels for watercraft of all sizes. These constitute the majority in the system of aids in U.S. waters, but there are other, major aids to serve the mariner. These other aids and systems provide guidance to the navigator making a landfall after a sea voyage or piloting his vessel along a coast. Electronic systems serve to help the navigator fix his position when he is out of sight of land because of darkness, fog, or distance. Primary and secondary lights, lightships and offshore tower light stations, fog signals, and ranges and directional lights will be considered in this chapter to complete the topic of aids to navigation. Electronic navigation systems are covered in Chapter 25.

Primary Seacoast and Secondary Lights

Primary seacoast and *secondary lights* are so designated because of their greater importance as aids to navigation. In general, they differ from the minor lights considered in Chapter 15 by their physical size, intensity of light, and complexity of light characteristics. These lights are more individual in nature than minor lights and buoys; only broad, general statements can be made about them as a group.

Primary seacoast lights are maintained to warn the high-seas navigator of the proximity of land. They are the first aids to navigation to be seen when making a landfall (except where there may be an offshore lightship). A coast-wise pilot can use these lights to keep farther offshore at night than if he were using other visual aids. These are the most powerful and distinctive lights in the U.S. system of aids to navigation.

Primary seacoast lights may be located on the mainland or offshore on islands and shoals. When located offshore, they may mark a specific hazard or they may serve merely as a marker for ships approaching a major harbor.

Many primary seacoast lights are so classified from the importance of their location, the intensity of the light, and the prominence of the structure. Other aids will be classed as *secondary lights* because of their lesser qualities in one or more of these characteristics. The dividing line, however, is not clear cut, and lights that may seem to be more properly in one category may be classified in the other group in the Light Lists (see page 301). The difference in classification is of no real significance to boatmen and it can be ignored in practical piloting situations.

STRUCTURES

The physical structure of a primary seacoast light and many secondary lights is generally termed a *lighthouse,* although this is not an official designation used in the Light Lists. The principal purpose is to support a light source and

Figures 1606-1609

from official U. S. COAST GUARD photographs

lens at a considerable height above water. The same structure may also house a fog signal, radiobeacon, equipment, and quarters for the operating personnel. In many instances, however, the auxiliary equipment and personnel are housed in separate buildings nearby; such a group of buildings is called a *light station.*

Lighthouses vary greatly in their outward appearance, determined in part by their location, whether in the water or on shore, the importance of the light, the kind of soil on which it is constructed, and the prevalence of violent storms; see fig. 1601.

Lighthouses also vary in appearance with the distance at which their lights must be seen. Where the need is for a relatively great range, a tall tower with a light of high candlepower is erected. Conversely, at points intermediate to the principal lights, where ship traffic is light, and where long range is not so necessary, a less expensive structure of more modest dimensions is constructed.

The terms, "secondary light" and "minor light," indicate in a general way a wide variety of lights, one class shading imperceptibly into the other. These lights may be displayed from towers resembling the most important seacoast lights, or from a relatively inexpensive structure. The essential features of a light structure where operating personnel are not in residence are: best possible location as determined by the physical characteristics of the site, sufficient height for the requirements of the light, a rugged support for the light itself, and proper shelter for the power source. Many

(Text continued on page 296)

MILE ROCKS LIGHT, at the entrance to San Francisco harbor, was built in 1906. In 1966, its tower superstructure was cut off to provide a landing platform for helicopters. No longer manned, operation is automatic. A horn fog signal is remotely controlled from Pt. Bonita Light.

SULLIVAN'S ISLAND LIGHT at the entrance to Charleston (S.C.) harbor, with 20,000,000 candlepower, is visible 20 miles. Built in 1962, this modern 140-foot structure is one of the world's tallest lights. It is equipped with an elevator.

▲

New and old lights at **CAPE HENRY,** Va., at the entrance to Chesapeake Bay. The old tower, no longer lighted, was the first built by the Federal Government.

On the lower coast of Maine, **CAPE NEDDICK LIGHT** is situated on a small rock islet called The Nubble, separated by a narrow channel from Cape Neddick, a headland which juts out a mile into the Atlantic.

AMERICAN LIGHTS –

▲ **PEMAQUID POINT LIGHT** (Maine) is a secondary light of 10,000 candlepower, visible 13 miles from a white pyramidal tower, 79 feet above water. Originally established in 1827, the rebuilt structure dates to 1857.

◄ **SPLIT ROCK LIGHT,** on a rocky cliff in Minnesota on Lake Superior, is one most frequently visited. Standing 178 feet above water, its 1,000,000 candlepower beam is visible 23 miles.

▲ **EASTERN POINT LIGHT** (Mass.) has guided Gloucestermen for more than a century. Its white brick tower, built in 1890, replaces one built in 1832.

▲ **PORTLAND HEAD LIGHT,** at Cape Elizabeth, Me., guards the entrance to Portland harbor with a 200,000 candlepower beam. The original station dates back to 1791.

◄ Isolated **CAPE SPENCER LIGHT,** 150 miles from a town, marks the northern entrance from the Pacific into the Inside Passage of southeastern Alaska. It is a primary light, fog signal and radiobeacon station.

► **FOWEY ROCKS LIGHT,** a skeleton iron structure, is typical of those used on the Florida Reefs at Carysfort Reef, Alligator Reef, Sombrero Key, American Shoal and Sand Key.

— Safeguards of Coastal Navigation

HOTO CREDITS—Cape Henry, Sullivan's Island, Fowey Rocks, Dry Tortugas, Galveston, and Mile Rocks Official U.S. Coast Guard photos. Portland Head, Cape Neddick and Pemaquid from Kodachromes by Wm. H. Koelbel.

GALVESTON (Texas) **JETTY LIGHT** flashes white and red alternately from a height of 91 feet. Resident personnel attend it. Fog signal is a diaphone. There is a radiobeacon, with special RDF calibration service. ▼

◄ **DRY TORTUGAS LIGHT** on Loggerhead Key in the Gulf of Mexico was established in 1826, rebuilt in 1858. The conical black and white tower is 157 feet high, the light visible 19 miles.

forms of structures meet these requirements—small houses topped with a short skeleton tower, a cluster of piles supporting a battery box and light, and countless others.

Many lights originally tended by resident keepers are now operated automatically because of the availability of commercial electric power and reliable equipment. There are also a great many automatic lights on inexpensive structures, cared for by periodic visits of Coast Guard cutters or by attendants who are in charge of a group of such aids.

The recent introduction of much new automatic equipment means that the relative importance of lights can no longer be judged on the basis of whether or not they have resident personnel; a number of powerful lights in towers of great height are now operated without continuous attention.

Coloring of structures

Lighthouses and other light structures are marked with various colors for the purpose of making them readily distinguishable from the backgrounds against which they are seen, and to make possible the identification of individual lights among others that are in the same general area. Solid colors, bands of color, stripes, and various other patterns are used, fig. 1602.

LIGHT CHARACTERISTICS

Primary seacoast and secondary lights are assigned distinctive light characteristics so that one may be distinguished from another. These characteristics are achieved by using lights of different colors, and by having some that show continuously while others go on and off in regular patterns of great variety. Actually, in these days of modern electronic navigation there is much less need for special distinctive characteristics of major lights—those were necessary when a navigator making a landfall might have been in doubt as to whether he was approaching the coast of Maryland or Virginia, or even farther to the north or south.

The three standard colors used for the lights of major aids to navigation are white, red, and green.

Light phase characteristics

By varying the length of the intervals of light and darkness, a considerable number of individual *light phase characteristics* may be obtained.

The term "flashing" has already been defined in Chapter 15 as a light that is on less than it is off in a regular sequence of single flashes occurring less than 30 times each minute. Some primary seacoast and secondary lights will "flash" in accordance with such a definition although their characteristics will have no relation to the flashes of buoys and minor lights. In general, a flashing major light will have a longer period (time of one complete cycle of the characteristic) and may have a longer flash; for example, Cape Hatteras Light flashes once every 15 seconds with a 3-second flash. On the other hand, some of the newer aids are equipped with xenon-discharge-tube lights that give a very brilliant, but very brief, flash. The intensity of these lights can be varied for periods of good or bad visibility. A few major lights may be "fixed"—a continuous light without change of intensity or color.

Typically, however, the light phase characteristic of a primary seacoast or secondary light will be more complex. These are described below and are illustrated in fig. 1603.

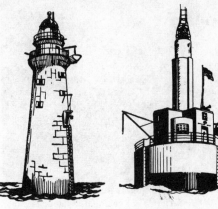

MASONRY STRUCTURE   CYLINDRICAL TOWER SQUARE   SKELETON
HOUSE ON CYLINDRICAL BASE   IRON STRUCT

TYPICAL LIGHT STRUCTURES

FIG. 1601. Primary seacoast and secondary lights are mounted on a wide variety of structures. The location of the light, whether on shore or rising from the water; the degree of exposure to violent storms; the need for great height; and many other factors determine the type of structure. Physical characteristics of the structures are described in the Light Lists.

Group flashing (Gp. Fl.)—the cycle of the light characteristic consists of two or more flashes separated by brief intervals and followed by a longer interval of darkness.

Alternating flashing (Alt. Fl.)—flashes of alternating color, usually white and red, or white and green.

Occulting (Occ.)—the light is on more than it is off. The interval of time that the light is *lighted* is greater than the time that it is *eclipsed*.

Equal interval (Eq. Int.)—the periods of light and darkness are equal; the light will be described in the Light List or on charts in terms of the period, the lighted and eclipsed portions each being just half of that time interval.

Group Occulting (Gp. Occ.)—intervals of light regularly broken by a series of two or more eclipses. This characteristic may have all eclipses of equal length or one may be greater than the others.

Fixed and Flashing (F. and Fl.)—a fixed light varied at regular intervals by a flash of greater intensity. The flash may be of the same color as the fixed light (usually white) or of another color. This characteristic may also appear as *fixed and group flashing (F. and Gp. Fl.)*.

Complex characteristics

The above light phase characteristics may be combined. Examples might include "Group flashing white, alternating flashing red" (Gp. Fl. W. Alt. Fl. R.)—Gay Head Light—with three white and one red flash in each 40-second period; or "Gp. Fl. W., (1 4 3)"—Minots Ledge Light where 1½-second flashes occur at 1½-second intervals in groups of one, four, and three separated by 5-second intervals and followed by a 15½-second longer interval to indicate the proper starting point of the 45-second period; or others of a generally similar nature.

Perhaps one of the most complex characteristics is that of Halfway Rock Light off the Maine Coast where the description is "Alternating fixed white, red, and flashing red" (Alt. F. W., R., and Fl. R.)—in a 90-second period, the light shows fixed white for 59 seconds, fixed red for 14 seconds, a high-intensity red flash for 3 seconds, and fixed red again for the final 14 seconds—this is certainly a distinctive enough characteristic to avoid any confusion.

FIG. 1602. The physical structure supporting a primary seacoast light, usually referred to as a lighthouse, may be painted in a number of different patterns for better daytime identification. The colors are usually black and white. Details are given in the Light Lists.

BOSTON, MASS.   ST. AUGUSTINE, FLA.   CAPE HENRY, VA.   TYBEE, GA.

COLORING OF TYPICAL LIGHTHOUSES

Sectors

Many lights will have *sectors,* portions of their all-around arc of visibility in which the normally white light is seen as red. These mark shoals or other hazards, or warn mariners of nearby land.

Lights so equipped show one color from most directions, but a different color or colors over definite arcs of the horizon as indicated on charts and in the Light Lists. A sector changes the color of a light when viewed from certain directions, but *not* the flashing or occulting characteristic. For example, a flashing white light having a red sector, when viewed from within the sector, will appear as flashing red, fig. 1604.

Sectors may be a few degrees in width, as when marking a shoal or rock, or of such width as to extend from the di-

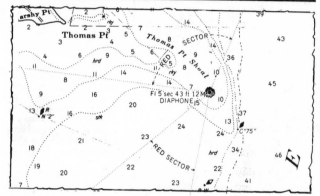

FIG. 1604. Many lights that are basically white in color have one or more **red sectors** to mark areas of shoal water or other hazards. The light will have the same phase characteristics in both the white and red sectors. Red sectors will be indicated on charts and described in the Light Lists.

rection of deep water to the shore. Bearings referring to sectors are expressed in degrees *as observed from a vessel toward the light.*

In the vast majority of situations, water areas covered by red sectors should be avoided, but in all cases the extent of the hazard should be determined from an examination of the chart for the vicinity. A few lights are basically red (for danger) with one or more white sectors marking the direction of safe passage through the hazards. A narrow white sector may also be used to mark a turning point in a channel.

Lights may also have sectors in which the light is *obscured* and cannot be seen. These will be shown graphically on charts and described in words and figures in the Light Lists, fig. 1605.

THE VISIBILITY OF LIGHTS

The theoretical visibility of a light in clear weather depends upon two factors, its intensity and its height above water. The intensity of the light fixes its *luminous range.* The height determines what is known as the *geographic range* which is not affected by the intensity (provided

Illustration	Symbols and meaning		
	Lights which do not change color	Lights which show color variations	Phase description
▭	F. = Fixed . . .	Alt. = Alternating.	A continuous steady light.
▭	F. Fl. = Fixed and flashing	Alt. F. Fl. = Alternating fixed and flashing.	A fixed light varied at regular intervals by a flash of greater brilliance.
▭	F. Gp. Fl. = Fixed and group flashing.	Alt. F. Gp. Fl. = Alternating fixed and group flashing.	A fixed light varied at regular intervals by groups of 2 or more flashes of greater brilliance.
▭	Fl. = Flashing	Alt. Fl. = Alternating flashing.	Showing a single flash at regular intervals, the duration of light always being less than the duration of darkness.
▭	Gp. Fl. = Group flashing.	Alt. Gp. Fl. = Alternating group flashing.	Showing at regular intervals groups of 2 or more flashes.
▭	Gp. Fl. (1+2) = Composite group flashing.	—	Light flashes are combined in alternate groups of different numbers.
▭	E. Int. = Equal interval.	—	Light with all durations of light and darkness equal.
▭	Occ. = Occulting.	Alt. Occ. = Alternating occulting.	A light totally eclipsed at regular intervals, the duration of light always greater than the duration of darkness.
▭	Gp. Occ. = Group Occulting.	—	A light with a group of 2 or more eclipses at regular intervals.
▭	Gp. Occ. (2+3) = Composite group occulting.	—	A light in which the occultations are combined in alternate groups of different numbers.

FIG. 1603. Primary seacoast and secondary lights flash with specific **light phase characteristics.** These permit rapid and positive identification at night. The time for a light to go through one full cycle of changes is called its **period.** See also the color plate on page 42.

296(a)

that the light is bright enough to be seen at the full distance of the geographic range). These ranges are given in the Light Lists in nautical miles; both are important factors about a major light.

As a rule, the luminous range of major lights is greater than the geographic, and the distance from which such aids can be seen is limited only by the earth's curvature. Such lights are often termed "strong"; conversely, a light limited by its luminous range can be called a "weak light."

Often, the glare, or *loom*, of strong lights may be seen far beyond the stated geographic range. Occasionally, under rare atmospheric conditions, the light itself may be visible at unusual distances. On the other hand, and unfortunately more frequently, the range of visibility may be lessened by rain, fog, snow, haze, or smoke.

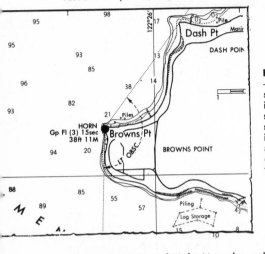

FIG. 1605. Some lights — particularly those on shore—will have sectors in which they cannot be seen at all. The light is said to be "obscured" in these sectors which are indicated on the chart and described in the Light Lists.

The Coast Guard Light Lists show the luminous range of lights when that value is greater than 5 miles in normal clear weather. The Lists also provide means for adjusting the luminous ranges for conditions of exceptional or poorer visibility. The candlepower of the light is also listed. For lights of complex characteristics, candlepowers and luminous ranges are given for each color and/or intensity light.

The geographic range is given in the Light Lists for an observer whose eye level is 15 feet above the water surface. Boatmen should know their eye height when at the controls of their craft. A height of eye of 5 feet decreases the geographic range of a light by 1.8 miles; a height of eye of 10 feet decreases it by 0.8 mile. On the other hand, an eye level height of 20 feet adds 0.7 mile to the geographic range of any light.

Lights on inland waters, where their radius of usefulness is not great, are frequently "weak" lights of insufficient intensity to reach the full limit of their geographic range.

IDENTIFICATION OF LIGHTS

Charts can only briefly describe the characteristics of a primary seacoast or secondary light by means of abbreviations and a notation of the total period of the light cycle. It will often be necessary to consult the Light List for the details of the characteristic that may be needed for positive identification.

When a light is first observed, its color should be noted, and, by means of a watch or clock with a second hand, a check made of the time required for the light to go through its full cycle of changes. If color, period, and number of flashes per cycle agree with the information in the Light

List, correct identification has been accomplished. As a further check, however, the charts and Light List should be examined to see if any other light in the vicinity might have such similar characteristics that there could be a case of mistaken identity. If there is any doubt, a careful timing of the length of all flashes and dark intervals should be made and compared with the Light List entries; this will normally be conclusive.

CAUTIONS IN USING LIGHTS

Complex lights with several luminous ranges may appear differently at extreme distances where, for example, a white fixed (or flashing) light could be seen but a red flash of the same light was not yet within luminous range. Examination of a Light List will show that ordinarily the candlepower of a red or green light is only 1/4 or 1/5 that of a white light from the same aid. Caution must be exercised in light identification under such circumstances.

The effect of fog, rain, snow, haze, etc., on the visibility of lights is obvious. Colored lights are more quickly lost to sight than are white lights under weather conditions that tend to reduce visibility. On the other hand, refraction may cause a light to be seen at a greater distance than would normally be expected.

Caution must also be applied when using light sectors. The actual boundaries between the colors are not so sharp and distinct as indicated on the chart; the lights shade gradually from one color into the other. Allow an adequate margin for safety when piloting by colored light sectors.

The increasing use of brilliant shore lights for advertising, illuminating bridges, and other purposes may cause marine navigational lights, particularly those in densely populated areas, to be outshone and difficult to distinguish from the background lighting.

There is always the possibility of a light's being extinguished. In the case of unattended lights, this condition may not be immediately detected and corrected. If lights are not sighted within a reasonable time after prediction from the course and speed of the boat, a dangerous situation may exist requiring prompt action to ensure the safety of the craft and its crew.

Do not rely on any *one* light, except perhaps for making a landfall. Use several lights *together* as a system, checking each against the others.

At many lights, rip-rap mounds are maintained to protect the structures against ice damage and scouring action, fig. 1606. Skippers should not attempt to pass close to light structures rising out of the water in order to be sure of avoiding collision with uncharted, submerged portions of such rip-rap or with the structure itself.

Standby lights

Standby lights of reduced candlepower are displayed from many light stations when the main light is inoperative. These standby lights may or may not have the same characteristics as the main light. The existence of the standby light, if any, and its characteristics, are noted in the Light Lists.

Fog Signals

Any sound-producing instrument operated in time of fog from a definite point shown on a chart serves as a useful fog signal. To be effective as an aid to navigation, a pilot must be able to identify it and know from what location it is sounded.

The simpler fog signals used on buoys and at minor lights have been covered in Chapter 15. There it was noted that such signals operated by the action of the sea cannot be entirely depended upon and identification might be difficult. At all lighthouses and lightships equipped with fog signals, these devices are operated by mechanical or electrical means and are sounded on definite time schedules during periods of low visibility to provide the desirable feature of positive identification.

SIGNAL CHARACTERISTICS

Fog signal characteristics are described in terms of the length of a total cycle consisting of one or more *blasts* of specific length and one or more *silent intervals,* also of definite lengths. These times are shown in the Light Lists to aid in identification. (Normally, only type of fog signal, without further details, is indicated on charts.) Where counting the number of blasts and the total time for the signal to complete a cycle is not sufficient for identification, reference may be made to the details in the Light List.

Fog signal equipment

The various types of fog signals differ in tone, and this also aids in identification. The type of fog signal for each station is shown in the Light Lists and on charts.

Diaphones produce sound by means of a slotted reciprocating piston actuated by compressed air. Blasts may consist of two tones of different pitch, in which case the first part of the blast is higher pitch and the latter is lower. These alternate-pitch signals are termed "two-tone."

Diaphragm horns produce sound by means of a disc diaphragm vibrated by compressed air or electricity. Duplex or triplex horn units of different pitch are sometimes combined to produce a more musical signal.

Sirens produce sound by means of either a disc or cup-shaped rotor actuated by compressed air, steam, or electricity. These should not be confused with what might be called "police sirens"; these may produce a sound of constant pitch much like a diaphragm horn or a whistle.

Whistles produce sound by compressed air, emitted through a circumferential slot into a cylindrical bell chamber.

Bells are sounded by means of a hammer actuated by an electric solenoid.

Operation of signals

Fog signals at stations where a continuous watch is maintained (identified in the Light Lists by the words "Resident Personnel") are sounded whenever the visibility decreases below a limit set for that particular station; typically, this might be two to five miles. The audible fog signals at certain stations are synchronized with the radio-beacon signals of these stations for distance-finding; see page 382(n).

Fog signals at locations where no continuous watch is maintained may not always be sounded promptly when fog conditions occur, or may operate erratically due to mechanical difficulties.

Where fog signals are operated continuously on a seasonal basis or throughout the year, this information will be found in the Light Lists.

FIG. 1606. Light structures rising out of the water are often protected by piles of rocks known as "rip-rap." Skippers should keep well clear as obstructions below the surface may extend far out. This is the light shown in the chart extract of fig. 1604—note there how the rip-rap is indicated around the light.

CAUTIONS IN USING FOG SIGNALS

Fog signals depend upon the transmission of sound through air. As aids to navigation, they have certain inherent limitations that *must* be considered. Sound travels through air in a variable and unpredictable manner. It has been established as fact that:

(a) Fog signals can be heard at greatly varying distances, and the distance at which such an aid can be heard may at any given instant vary with the bearing of the signal, and may be different on different occasions.

(b) Under certain conditions of the atmosphere, when a fog signal has a combination of high and low tones, it is not unusual for one of them to be heard but not the other. In the case of sirens which produce a varying tone, portions of the blast may not be heard.

(c) There are occasionally areas close to the signal in which it will not be heard. This is particularly true when the fog signal is screened by intervening land masses or other obstructions, or when the signal is on a high cliff.

(d) The apparent loudness of a fog signal may be greater at a distance than in the immediate vicinity.

(e) A patch of fog may exist at a short distance from a manned station but not be seen from it. Thus the signal may not be placed in operation.

(f) Some fog signals require a start-up interval.

(g) A fog signal may not be detected when the vessel's engines are in operation, but may be heard when they are stopped, or from a quieter location on deck.

Based on the above established facts, a mariner must *not* assume:

(1) That he is out of ordinary hearing distance from a fog signal because he fails to hear it.

(2) That because he hears a fog signal faintly, he is at a greater distance from it.

(3) That he is near to it because he hears it loudly.

(4) That the fog signal is not sounding because he does not hear it, even when in close proximity.

(5) That the detection distance and sound intensity under any one set of conditions is an infallible guide for any future occasion.

In summary, fog signals are valuable as warnings, but the boatman should not place implicit reliance upon them in navigating his vessel. They should be considered solely as warning devices.

Standby fog signals

Standby fog signals are sounded at some of the more important stations when the main signal is inoperative.

The standby signals may be of a different type and characteristic than the main signal. Details of such auxiliary apparatus, where they exist, are given in the Light Lists.

Lightships and Offshore Towers

Lightships are vessels of distinctive design and markings, equipped with lights, fog signals, and radiobeacons. They are anchored or moored at specific, charted locations to serve as aids to navigation; see fig. 1607.

Purpose

Lightships mark the entrances to important harbors, warn of dangerous shoals lying in much-frequented waters, and serve as departure marks for both ocean and coastwise traffic.

Lightships serve the same essential purposes as lighthouses. They take the form of vessels only because they are at locations where it is (or has been until recently) impracticable to build lighthouses. As will be noted later, modern construction technology has now made possible the replacement of all but a few of the traditional lightships with more efficient fixed structures.

LIGHTSHIPS

The hulls of lightships in U. S. waters are almost invariably painted red with the name of the station in large white letters on each side. All the signals—the light, fog signal, and radiobeacon—have distinctive characteristics so that the lightship may be identified under all conditions. As with lighthouses, details regarding these signals are shown briefly on charts and more completely in the Light Lists. A riding light on the forestay indicates the direction that the ship is heading, and since lightships ride to a single bow anchor, this also indicates the direction from which the current is flowing, whenever the current is stronger than the wind.

Modern U. S. lightships are self-propelled, capable of proceeding to and from their stations under their own power. All are diesel-powered and can use their main engines to either relieve the strain on their moorings during storms or work their way back to station if blown off by high winds and seas. Each lightship carries a crew of about 15 men.

FIG. 1607. Lightships are used to mark both offshore hazards and the entrance to major harbors. The entrance to the Golden Gate has been marked by lightships since 1898. The San Francisco Lightship is shown here anchored in 108 feet of water; her 450,000 candle-power light is 55 feet above the surface and can be seen 14 miles on clear nights. She is also equipped with two-tone diaphone fog signal and a radiobeacon.

Identification

A lightship underway to or from its station will fly the International Code flags "LO" signifying "lightship not at anchor on her station," fig. 1608. She will not show or sound any of the signals of a lightship, but will display the lights prescribed by the International or Inland Rules for a vessel of her class.

When on station at night, a lightship shows only the aid to navigation and riding lights. By day, lightships will display the International Code signal of the station whenever a vessel is in the vicinity and there are any indications that her crew fails to recognize the station, or whenever a vessel asks for information. The International Code signal for each lightship station is stated in the Light Lists.

Relief lightships

Whenever the regular lightship must be withdrawn from her station for maintenance, she is temporarily replaced with a *relief lightship*. These are painted the same colors as regular lightships, but have the word "RELIEF" on each side in lieu of a station name.

Relief lightships will generally exhibit lights and sound signals having the regular characteristics of the station. They may differ in outward appearance from the regular lightship in minor details. Changes in lightships are announced in advance by Notices to Mariners.

Station buoys

Station buoys, also referred to as "watch buoys," are used to mark the position of lightship stations. These buoys are located from several hundred yards to as much as a mile from the station as shown on the chart; the distance and direction are given in the Light Lists. They are *not* separately charted.

Station buoys serve as a substitute if the lightship is forced to seek shelter in extreme weather, and they aid in later returning the lightship to its correct position. They are always of an unlighted type and are marked with "LS" and the initials of the lightship station.

Cautions in using lightships

A skipper should set his course so as to pass a lightship with sufficient clearance to avoid the possibility of collision from any cause. It should be borne in mind that most lightships are anchored by a very long scope of chain and as a result the radius of their swinging circle is considerable. The charted position is the location of the anchor.

It must also be remembered that during extremely heavy weather lightships may be carried off station despite the best efforts of their crews, and perhaps without their knowledge. A navigator should not, therefore, implicitly rely on the position of a lightship during and immediately after severe storms. A lightship known to be off station will secure her light, fog signal, and radiobeacon, and will fly the International Code signal "LO."

A craft steering toward a radiobeacon on a lightship, "homing" on it, should exercise particular care to avoid collision. Sole reliance should *never* be placed on sighting the lightship or hearing her fog signal in time to prevent hitting her. The risk of collision will be lessened by ensuring that the radio bearing does not remain constant.

Skippers must also use care in passing lightships so as

FIG. 1608. A lightship flies the International Code flags "LO" when she is not on her station. These are seen above flying from the foremast. The vessel shown here is used as a temporary substitute for other lightships when those must return to port for maintenance, hence the name "RELIEF" in white letters on the red hull rather than the name of a specific station.

FIG. 1609. The old and the new in offshore aids to navigation. Lightships have been used since 1820, but in 1961 the Coast Guard started their replacement along the Atlantic Coast with tower structures. The fixed towers offer many advantages over lightships and will be constructed wherever hydrographic conditions permit. Frying Pan Shoals Light off the coast of North Carolina stands in 46 feet of water.

to not collide with the station buoy, remembering that it is unlighted and may be at a considerable distance from the lightship. Particular caution must be exercised in fog and at night.

OFFSHORE LIGHT TOWERS

Along the Atlantic Coast, lightships are being gradually replaced with offshore light structures, fig. 1609. The first of these was placed in operation in 1961 and others will be added until only a few lightships remain. On the Pacific Coast, lightships will remain in use as the greater depths of water make tower construction impractical.

Characteristics

A typical tower deckhouse is 60 feet above the water, 80 feet square, and supported by steel legs in pilings driven nearly 300 feet into the ocean bottom. The deckhouse accommodates living quarters, radiobeacon, and communications and oceanographic equipment. The top serves as a landing platform that will take the largest helicopters flown by the Coast Guard. On one corner of the deckhouse is a 32-foot radio tower supporting the radiobeacon antenna and a 3½-million candlepower light. At an elevation of 130 feet above the water, it is visible for 18 miles. The construction details of other towers will vary slightly, but all are of the same general type.

Advantages

Fixed offshore light stations have five major advantages over lightships:

(1) Lower operating costs. The annual operating, personnel, and maintenance expenses of a tower light station are only about one-third of those of a lightship.

(2) Greater light range. Greater luminous range is made possible by more efficient optics, and greater geographic range results from the increased height of the light above the water—some 50 to 70 feet higher than one on a lightship.

(3) Better fog signal projection. By eliminating the swinging to which a lightship is subject, fog signals may be projected specifically in the most useful directions under all circumstances.

(4) More accurate guidance for ships. The location of a tower light is fixed; it does not swing about the charted position and cannot be blown off station in violent storms.

(5) Longer life. Towers are expected to last 75 years, as compared with the average 50-year lifespan of lightships.

Unmanned light towers

In addition to the manned offshore light stations, the Coast Guard is also building unmanned light towers such as the one which replaced Brenton Reef Lightship at the entrance to Narragansett Bay.

Ranges and Directional Lights

Ranges and directional lights serve to indicate the centerline of a channel and thus aid in the safe piloting of a vessel. Although they are frequently used in connection with channels and other restricted waterways, they are not a part of the lateral system of buoyage and so were not covered in Chapter 15.

RANGES

A *range* consists of two fixed aids to navigation so positioned with respect to each other that when seen in line they indicate that the observer's craft *may* be in safe waters, fig. 1610. The aids may be lighted or unlighted as determined by the importance of the range, and may take a wide variety of physical appearances.

The conditional phrase "may be in safe waters" is used in the definition above since observation of the two markers in line is *not* an absolute determination of safety. A range is "safe" only within specific limits of distance from the front marker; a vessel too close or too far away may be in a dangerous area. The aids that comprise the range do not in themselves indicate the usable portion of the range; reference *must* be made to a chart of the

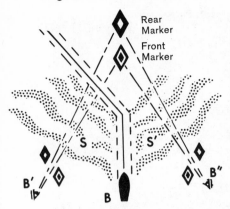

Rear Marker

Front Marker

FIG. 1610. The principle of range markers. A boat B follows a safe mid-channel course between shoals S and S' by aligning the front marker directly below the rear marker. If the range opens and the rear marker shows to the **left** of the front marker, the boat is off course, displaced toward B'. If the rear marker shows to the **right** of the front marker, she is displaced toward B". Ranges may be lighted or unlighted.

area and to other aids.

Ranges are described in the Light Lists by first giving the position of the front marker, usually in terms of geographic coordinates—latitude and longitude; and then stating the location of the rear marker in terms of direction and distance from the front marker. This direction, given in degrees and minutes, true, need not be used in ordinary navigation, but is useful in making checks of compass deviation. The rear daymark (and light, if used) is always higher than the one on the front aid.

Because of their fixed nature, and the accuracy with which a vessel can be positioned by using them, ranges are among the best aids to navigation. Preference should always be given to using a range when one is available; buoys should be referred to only in order to determine the beginning and end of the usable portion of the range.

Unlighted ranges

Although any two objects may be used as a range, the term is properly applied only to those pairs of structures built specifically for that purpose. Special shapes and markings will be used for the front and rear markers of a range for easier identification and more accurate alignment. Many different designs will be found in use today—front and rear daymarks of different shape, such as one round and the other diamond-shaped; both markers of the same overall shape, but with painted centers of different designs; and many others. To make ranges more easily identifiable, and easier to use, the Coast Guard has standardized on the use of rectangular daymarks, longer dimension vertical, painted in vertical stripes of contrasting colors, see page 292. The design of range daymarks will normally be described in the Light Lists.

Lighted ranges

Because of their importance and high accuracy in piloting, most range markers are equipped with lights to extend their usefulness through the hours of darkness. Entrance channels are frequently marked with range lights; the Delaware River on the Atlantic Coast and the Columbia River on the Pacific Coast are examples of this.

Range lights may be of any color used with aids to navigation—white, red, or green—and may show any characteristic. See fig. 1611. The principal requirement is that they be easily distinguished from shore backgrounds and from other lights. Front and rear lights will, however, often be of the same color (white is frequently used because of its greater visibility range), with different phase characteristics. Since both lights must be observed together for the proper steering of the craft, range lights will generally have

a greater "on" interval than will other lights. Range rear lights will normally be on more than their front counterparts. Fixed or occulting lights are typical for range rear aids, equal interval or quick flashing for range front lights.

Many range lights will be fitted with special lenses that result in a much greater intensity being shown on the range center line than off of it; the lights rapidly decrease in brilliance when observed from only a few degrees to either side. In some cases, the light will be visible only from on or very near to the range line; in other cases, a light of lesser intensity may be seen all around the horizon—this can be either from the main light source or from a small auxiliary "passing" light. Light is shown around the horizon when the front aid also serves to mark the side of a channel at a turn of direction.

Often range lights will be of such high intensity that they can be seen and used for piloting in the daytime, being of more value than the painted daymarks.

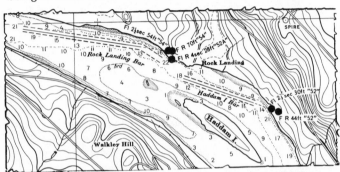

FIG. 1611. Lighted range markers are extensively used on the Connecticut River. When aligned by an observer in mid-channel, Rock Landing Range Front Light (flashing white, height 54 feet) shows below Rock Landing Range Rear Light (fixed red, height 70 feet). A similar range leads through Haddam Island Bar. Their daymarks are white diamonds with black centers. Details are given in the Light List.

DIRECTIONAL LIGHTS

The establishment of a range requires suitable locations for two aids, separated adequately both horizontally and vertically. In some areas, this may not be possible and a single light of special characteristics will be employed.

A *directional light* is a single light source fitted with a special lens so as to show a white light in a narrow beam along a desired direction, with red and green showing to either side. The width of the sectors will depend upon the local situation, but red will be seen if the pilot is to the right of the center line as he approaches the aid from seaward, and green if he is to the left of the desired track. A typical directional light, at Deer Island, Massachusetts, shows white for a sector of 2.4° with red and green showing for 8.5° to either side. Another directional light in Delaware Bay has a white beam width of 1° 40' with red and green sectors of 6½° to either side.

Directional lights will normally have an occulting or equal interval characteristic, so they are easily followed.

Caution regarding directional lights

A pilot should not place too great reliance on the various colors of a directional light for safe positional information. As noted for light sectors, the boundaries between colors are not sharp and clear; the light shades imperceptibly from one color to the other along the stated directional lines.

CHAPTER 17

GOVERNMENT PUBLICATIONS

The typical boatman undoubtedly thinks first of charts when considering the publications that are issued by governmental agencies to aid his safe boating. This is certainly a valid thought—so much so that another chapter is devoted entirely to charts—but he should not overlook the many other publications that are available to make his boating safer and more enjoyable. Generally, these are issued by the same governmental agencies as are charts. Such publications will be considered in this chapter.

PUBLISHING AGENCIES

Agencies of the Federal Government that issue publications valuable to the boatman include:

U.S. Coast & Geodetic Survey (now a part of the Environmental Science Services Administration, Department of Commerce).

United States Coast Guard (transferred in 1967 from the Treasury Department to the Department of Transportation).

U.S. Navy Department—the Naval Oceanographic Office and the Naval Observatory.

U.S. Army, Corps of Engineers (through its Lake Survey District and other District Offices).

The Weather Bureau (also a part of the Environmental Science Services Administration, Department of Commerce).

Government Printing Office

The Government Printing Office, an independent agency, does much of the actual printing of the publications prepared by the agencies listed above. The Superintendent of Documents is responsible for the sale of most of these publications, but not all of them. Unfortunately, there seems to be no rule for the determination of whether a publication is sold by the GPO, or by the preparing agency —for example: H.O. 9 can be purchased from the GPO, but H.O. 103 cannot be bought there, only from the Naval Oceanographic Office and its sales agents.

Publications that are sold by the GPO can be purchased by mail. The address is Superintendent of Documents, Government Printing Office, Washington, D.C. 20402. There is also a retail bookstore in the GPO building at North Capital and H Streets in Washington where over-the-counter purchases can be made. Personal checks for the purchase of publications are acceptable; they should be made payable to the "Superintendent of Documents."

State agencies

Publications of interest to boatmen are also prepared by many State agencies, so many that it is not possible to list them all in this book. Boatmen should check with local authorities in their own state and write ahead to other states when they expect to cruise into new waters. Information may be obtained that will add to safety and convenience, possibly avoiding legal embarrassment as well. "Ignorance is no excuse" applies both afloat and ashore!

The name of the state agency to be addressed will vary widely from state to state. Consult page **504** for the name and address of an office to which inquiries may be sent. Requests for information and literature should be as specific as possible.

SALES AGENTS

Various boating supply stores, marinas, and similar activities have been designated by governmental agencies as official *sales agents* for their publications. These agents accept responsibility for maintenance of adequate stocks of the various charts and documents of interest to mariners and boatmen in their respective areas.

Authorized sales agents may carry stocks of Coast & Geodetic Survey publications, Naval Oceanographic Office publications, Coast Guard publications, or combinations of two or three of these. It does *not* hold true that because an activity is an agent for one type of publication it will have those of other governmental agencies. Lake Survey charts and publications may be sold by local marinas and stores, but there is no formal system of sales agents.

Other information

Additional information on where to obtain certain specific government publications will be found on pages 439 and 497-499.

Coast & Geodetic Survey Publications

The Coast and Geodetic Survey (C&GS) is charged with the survey of the coasts, harbors, and tidal estuaries of the United States and its insular possessions. It issues the following publications relating to these waters as guides to navigation: Charts, Coast Pilots, Tide Tables, Tidal Current Tables, Tidal Current Charts, and chart catalogs.

The Coast and Geodetic Survey has now been combined with the Weather Bureau and the Central Radio Propagation Laboratory to comprise the Environmental Science Services Administration (ESSA) within the Department of Commerce.

TIDE TABLES

Tide Tables, fig. 1701, are of great value in determining the predicted height of the water at almost any place at any given time. These tables are calculated in advance and are published annually in four volumes, one of which covers the East Coast of North and South America and another the West Coast of these continents.

The Tide Tables give the predicted times and heights of high and low waters for each day of the year at a number of important points known as *reference stations*. The East Coast Tide Tables include 48 sets of detailed listings for such points as Portland, Boston, Sandy Hook, Baltimore, Miami, Pensacola, and Galveston. Additional

data are tabulated showing the differences in times and heights between these reference stations and thousands of other points, termed *subordinate stations*. From these tables, the tide at virtually any point along the coast can be easily computed.

The C&GS Tide Tables also include other useful data including tables of sunrise and sunset, reduction of local mean time to standard zone time, and moonrise and moonset.

The Tide Tables and their use in piloting are discussed at length in Chapter 20, pages 343–344(d).

TIDAL CURRENT TABLES

The Tidal Current Tables are in much the same format as the Tide Tables, see fig. 1702. However, instead of times of high and low waters, these tables give the times of maximum flood and ebb currents and times of the two slacks when current direction reverses. The times of slack water do *not* correspond to times of high and low tides, and the Tide Tables *cannot* be used to predict current situations. Velocity of the current at maximum strength is given in terms of knots (nautical miles per hour).

Tidal Current Tables are published in two volumes—Atlantic Coast of North America and Pacific Coast of North America and Asia. Included in each volume are tables from

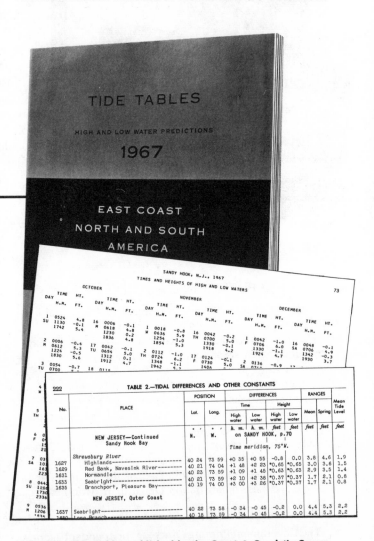

FIG. 1701 Tide Tables published by the Coast & Geodetic Survey provide necessary data for predicting height of tide at thousands of coastal points for any desired day and hour. Separate volumes are issued for the Atlantic-Gulf and Pacific Coasts.

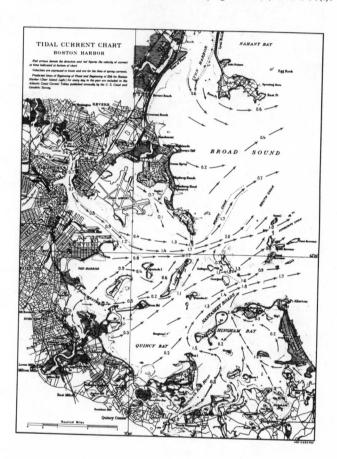

FIG. 1702 Tidal Current Tables are prepared in much the same format as the Tide Tables. A system of a limited number of reference points together with thousands of subordinate stations permits calculation of current strengths and slacks at virtually any location of navigational interest.

cially where tidal currents are complex, often flowing in opposite directions at the same stage of tide, a real advantage can be gained in consulting one of these charts. A few minutes' study may well be the means of carrying a favorable current through the entire passage, instead of needlessly bucking an opposing flow for much or all of the time. As is the case for all current predictions, it must be remembered that these charts indicate normal conditions; a strong wind from certain directions may have a decided influence on both the strength of currents and the times that maximums are reached.

The New York Harbor Tidal Current Charts are used in conjunction with the annual tide tables. All other Tidal Current Charts are used with the annual tidal current tables for their respective areas. See also pages 344(k) and 344(l).

FIG. 1703 Tidal Current Charts are available for a number of major bodies of water where such flows are of significance in piloting. A series of twelve charts, for hourly intervals in the cycle of ebb and flood, comprise each Tidal Current Chart.

which may be calculated current velocity at any intermediate time and the duration of slack water or weak currents.

Tidal Current Tables and their use in piloting are covered in detail in Chapter 20, pages 344(h) to 344(k).

TIDAL CURRENT CHARTS

Tidal Current Charts are available for eight bodies of water—Boston Harbor, Narragansett Bay to Nantucket Sound, Narragansett Bay, Long Island Sound and Block Island Sound, New York Harbor, Delaware Bay and River, San Francisco Bay, and Puget Sound (in two parts on separate charts). These are made up in sets of a series of twelve reproductions of the chart of the locality, each of which indicates graphically the direction and velocity of tidal currents for a specific hour with respect to the state of the tide or current prediction for a major reference station. Currents in the various passages are indicated with red arrows and velocities are noted at numerous points; see fig. 1703. By following through the sequence of charts, hourly changes in velocity and direction are easily seen. These charts make it possible to visualize just how tidal currents act in various passages and channels throughout every part of the entire twelve-hour-plus cycle.

Where currents run at considerable velocity, and espe-

COAST PILOTS

The amount of information that can be printed on nautical charts is limited by available space and the system of symbols that is used. Additional information is often needed for safe and convenient navigation. The Coast and Geodetic Survey publishes such information in the *Coast Pilots*. These are printed in book form, covering the coastline in eight separate volumes.

Each Coast Pilot, see fig. 1704, contains sailing directions

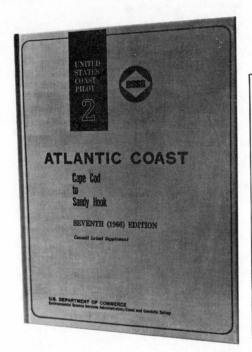

FIG. 1704 The Coast Pilot is issued in eight volumes for various sections of the coastline. Each includes sailing directions, courses and distances between ports; information on hazards and aids to navigation; data on facilities for supplies and repairs; and much other useful information that cannot be conveniently shown on nautical charts.

---

154   9. WESTERN LONG ISLAND SOUND

There are several marinas and boatyards in the harbor. Craft up to 12 tons can be hauled out for engine and hull repairs. Gasoline, diesel fuel, water, ice, storage facilities, lifts, and marine supplies are available. The town of Huntington maintains several launching ramps.

Lloyd Harbor extends westward from Huntington Bay nearly to Oyster Bay, from which it is separated by a narrow strip of beach at high water. Vessels drawing less than 7 feet can anchor just inside the entrance, where the depths are 7 to 11 feet. An abandoned light tower is about in the middle of the entrance.

Oyster Bay, on the south side of the sound about 5 miles westward of Eatons Neck Light, lies between Lloyd Neck and Rocky Point. The entrance and harbor are characterized by extensive shoals, boulder reefs, and broken ground making off from the shores. Vessels should proceed with caution if obliged to approach or cross shoal areas. The bay south of Cold Spring Harbor Light is a secure harbor, available for vessels of less than 18-foot draft. A fog signal is sounded at the light.

Lloyd Neck, between Huntington and Oyster Bays, is high and wooded, and has a high, yellow bluff on its north side 0.8 miles eastward of Lloyd Point. Many patches of boulders having least depths of 2 to 8 feet extend 0.2 to 0.5 mile offshore from **East Fort Point** to Lloyd Point. Small craft skirting this shore should keep well

Currents.—About 0.2 mile north of Cold Spring Harbor Light the velocity is about 0.5 knot; about 0.2 mile north of Cove Point, 1.2 miles southwestward, it is about 0.8 knot. For predictions, the Tidal Current Tables should be consulted.

Ice.—During severe winters ice has been known to extend the full length of the bay during part of January and February.

Plum Point, the easternmost point of Centre Island, is marked at its south end by a small stone tower; boat landings are on the southwest side of the point. A yacht club with a prominent flagstaff is about 0.3 mile west of Plum Point. The yacht club landing has depths of about 9 feet. See appendix for **storm warning display.**

Cooper Bluff, at the northeast end of Cove Neck is prominent. A boulder reef extends nearly 0.3 mile northward from Cove Point at the northwest end of **Cove Neck**, and is marked by a lighted buoy.

Cold Spring Harbor, the southeasterly end of Oyster Bay, extends about 2.3 miles southward of Cooper Bluff. The seminary on the hill of **West Neck**, on the east side of the harbor, is prominent. The harbor is free of dangers if the shores be given a berth of about 0.3 mile, the depths being 15 to 18 feet to near its head.

The village of **Cold Spring Harbor** is on the eastern shore near the head of the harbor. An oil company

---

between ports in its respective area, including recommended courses and distances. Channels, with their controlling depths, and all dangers and obstructions are fully described. Harbors and anchorages are listed, with information on those points at which facilities are available for boat supplies and marine repairs. Information regarding canals, bridges, docks, etc., which cannot be adequately expressed on charts due to limitations of space, is provided in full in the Coast Pilots. Information on the Intracoastal Waterways is contained in the various applicable volumes.

The various volumes of the Coast Pilot cover areas as follows:

> Atlantic Coast
> > No. 1 Eastport to Cape Cod
> > No. 2 Cape Cod to Sandy Hook
> > No. 3 Sandy Hook to Cape Henry
> > No. 4 Cape Henry to Key West
> > No. 5 Gulf of Mexico, Puerto Rico, and
> >   Virgin Islands
>
> Pacific Coast
> > No. 7 California, Oregon, Washington,
> >   and Hawaii
>
> Alaska
> > No. 8 Dixon Entrance to Cape Spencer
> > No. 9 Cape Spencer to Beaufort Sea
>
> Note: Currently there is no Volume No. 6.

Annual supplements are issued for each volume of the Coast Pilot. A volume for which a supplement has been issued should be used *only* in conjunction with the *latest* supplement. Each supplement is cumulative, complete in itself and superseding all prior supplements.

Annual supplements to the Coast Pilot are available without charge at local C&GS sales agents or from the Coast and Geodetic Survey, ESSA, Rockville, Md. 20852. On a

rotating basis, the C&GS reprints the various Coast Pilots to include all up-to-date data; the reprintings of any specific volume occur about every seven years.

CHART CATALOGS

The Coast and Geodetic Survey issues free *Chart Catalogs*, fig. 1705, in three volumes for the Atlantic and Pacific Coasts, including offshore islands, and for Alaska. These are actually small-scale outline charts with diagrams delineating the area covered by each nautical chart published by the C&GS. These catalogs are also sources of much additional information regarding charts and publications of other agencies, and the location of sales agents (shown both by a listing of the name and address of the agent and by a symbol on the chart-outline diagrams).

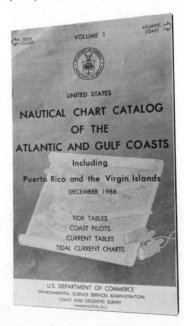

FIG. 1705 The Coast & Geodetic Survey issues catalogs of their nautical charts; these also include listings of other useful publications of the C&GS and other agencies. These catalogs show the area covered by each chart, the scale, price, etc. They are updated at intervals of 6 to 12 months.

C&GS OFFICES

Nautical charts and related publications of the Coast and Geodetic Survey can be purchased by mail (prepaid) or over-the-counter at offices in Washington, New York, and San Francisco. The complete address of these offices is shown in fig. 1706.

Other offices

Information concerning publications and activities of the Coast and Geodetic Survey may also be obtained from offices in Boston, Norfolk, New Orleans, Kansas City, Los Angeles, Portland (Oregon), Seattle, Anchorage (Alaska), and Honolulu. Addresses of these offices are listed in the Chart Catalogs.

⚓ Coast & Geodetic Survey, ESSA
Rockville, Md. 20852

⚓ Coast & Geodetic Survey, ESSA
Room 1407, Federal Office Building
90 Church Street
New York, N.Y. 10007

⚓ Coast & Geodetic Survey, ESSA
Room 121, Customhouse
San Francisco, Calif. 94111

FIG. 1706 If not available at local sales agents, publications and charts of the Coast & Geodetic Survey can be purchased by mail from one of the offices listed. A check or money order for the total price should accompany the order; the material will be sent postpaid.

Coast Guard Publications

The United States Coast Guard prepares a major navigational publication and a number of minor ones. All of these are worthy of a boatman's serious consideration.

LIGHT LISTS

The Light Lists are useful to any boatman, but particularly so to those who cruise into unfamiliar waters. These Lists provide more complete information concerning aids to navigation than can be conveniently shown on charts, see fig. 1707. They are *not* intended to be used in navigation in place of charts and Coast Pilots, and should not be so used. Charts should be consulted for the location of all aids to navigation. It may be dangerous to use aids to navigation without reference to charts.

The Light Lists describe, for the use of mariners, the lightships, lighthouses, lesser lights, buoys, and daybeacons maintained in all navigable waters of the United States by the Coast Guard and various private agencies. (In this usage, the Navy and all other non-USCG governmental organizations are considered to be "private agencies.") The data shown in the Lists includes the official name of the aid, the characteristics of its light, sound, and radio signals, its structural appearance, position, and other significant factors.

Light Lists are published in five volumes as follows:

Volume I—Atlantic Coast from St. Croix River, Maine to Little River, S.C.

Volume II—Atlantic and Gulf Coasts from Little River, S.C. to Rio Grande, Texas

Volume III—Pacific Coast and Pacific Islands

Volume IV—Great Lakes

Volume V—Mississippi River System

Within each volume, aids to navigation are listed by Coast Guard Districts in the following order: seacoast, major channels, Intracoastal Waterway, minor channel, and miscellaneous. Lighted and unlighted aids appear together in their geographic order, with amplifying data on the same page.

Seacoast aids are listed in sequence from north to south along the Atlantic Coast, from south to north and east to west along the Gulf Coast, and from south to north along the Pacific Coast. On the Atlantic and Gulf Coasts, aids along the Intracoastal Waterway are listed in the same sequence. For rivers and estuaries, the aids to navigation are shown from seaward to the head of navigation. Where an

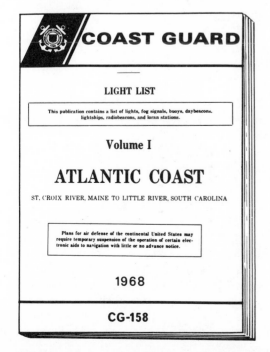

(1)	(2) Name		(3) Location		(4) Luminous Range	(5) Geographic Range	(6) Structure		(7)	
No.	Characteristic		Lat. N.	Long. W.	Intensity		Ht. above ground	Ht. above water	Remarks	Year
				MASSACHUSETTS					**FIRST DISTRICT**	
		SEACOAST								
53 *1390*	CAPE COD LIGHT............... Fl. W., 5ˢ Resident Personnel.		On highlands, on north-east side of cape. 42 02.4 70 03.7		20 300,000	20	White tower, covered way to dwelling. 66	183	RADIOBEACON: Antenna 170 feet 352° from light tower. See p. XX for method of operation. HORN, diaphragm; 1 blast ev 15ˢ (3ˢbl). 1798 – 1857	
56	*Nauset Lighted Whistle Buoy 4 ....* Fl. W., 4ˢ		In 126 feet 41 56.0 69 53.8		140	....	Red..........			
57 *1392*	**Nauset Beach Light**.............. Gp. Fl. W., 10ˢ 0.1ᶠl., 1.5ˢec. 0.1ᶠl., 1.5ˢec. 0.1ᶠl., 6.7ˢec. 3 flashes.		On beach at Eastham, east side of Cape Cod. 41 51.7 69 57.2		20 400,000	17	Conical tower, upper part red, lower part white. 48	114	Old tower, 18 feet high attached to cottage about ¼ mile south from present tower. 1839 – 1923	
58	*Chatham Lighted Whistle Buoy 6 ...* Fl. W., 4ˢ Chatham Buoy 2..................		In 102 feet .... 41 41.7 69 50.0 In 60 feet, about 1		160	....	Red.......... Red nun		White reflector.	

FIG. 1707 Light Lists, published by the U.S. Coast Guard, provide more detailed information on aids to navigation than can be shown on charts. Five volumes cover all coasts, the Great Lakes, and the Mississippi River system. Light Lists are to be used with, not as a substitute for, nautical charts.

aid serves both a channel leading in from sea and the ICW, it will be listed separately in both sequences.

All volumes of the USCG Light Lists are for sale by the Superintendent of Documents, Government Printing Office; the volume for the local area concerned is sold by many of the authorized chart and publication sales agents.

RULES OF THE ROAD

The Coast Guard issues a series of free pamphlets setting forth the Rules of the Road for various bodies of water. These include the general "Inland Rules" (Publication CG-169), fig. 1708, the "Great Lakes Rules" (CG-172), and the "Western Rivers Rules" (CG-184). The International Rules

FIG. 1709 The official U.S. Coast Guard Recreational Boating Guide contains excellent summaries of information relating to legally required equipment, other items that should be aboard a boat, registration and numbering, responsibilities of a skipper, and services rendered boatmen by the Coast Guard Auxiliary.

FIG. 1708 Separate pamphlets are issued by the U.S. Coast Guard covering Rules of the Road for Inland Waters, the Great Lakes, and the Western Rivers. The International Rules, used on the high seas, are included in the pamphlet covering Inland Rules.

of the Road, used on the open seas and outside of specified boundaries. at major ports, are included with the Inland Rules in CG-169 in a convenient parallel column format.

Copies of the Rules of the Road pamphlets may be obtained from Coast Guard Marine Inspection Offices in the major ports, or by writing to the Commandant (CHS), U.S. Coast Guard Headquarters, Washington, D.C. 20226.

RECREATIONAL BOATING GUIDE

An excellent collection of information on boat numbering, legal minimum equipment requirements, other equipment that should be carried, responsibilities when operat-

ing a boat, emergency procedures, and U.S. Coast Guard Auxiliary services is published as the *Official U.S. Coast Guard Recreational Boating Guide* (CG-340), fig. 1709.

This publication also contains an example of a boating accident report, a Distress Information Sheet, and guides to the safe loading capacity of small boats.

The USCG Recreational Boating Guide is revised periodically when required by changes in the applicable laws and regulations. Copies may be purchased by mail from the Superintendent of Documents, or frequently may be found for sale at marinas or boating supply stores; the price is 45¢.

OTHER USCG PUBLICATIONS

The Coast Guard issues a number of publications relating to the safety of navigation and covering such topics as aids to navigation, applicable rules and regulations, general safety matters, etc. See pages 497-498 for a more complete listing and information on where they may be obtained. Some of these are free, others are available for a nominal charge.

A USCG publication of more-than-usual interest is Ventilation Systems for Small Craft (CG-395). This free pamphlet explains the Coast Guard requirements for the ventilation of engine and fuel tank compartments on gasoline-powered boats.

Oceanographic Office Publications

The U.S. Naval Oceanographic Office (formerly the Hydrographic Office) is responsible for several publications of considerable value to boatmen.

Charts, publications, and other products of the Naval Oceanographic Office will be identified with a prefix to the individual chart or publication number as follows:

Nautical charts, publications, and other products used primarily for navigational purposes, and which are clearly not oceanographic in nature, will be identified with the letters "H.O." as a prefix to the chart or publication number as was done when such items were issued by the Hydrographic Office.

Oceanographic products, primarily publications, related to the dynamic nature of the oceans or the scientific aspects of oceanography will be identified with the letters "N.O.O." as a prefix to the publication or chart number.

BOWDITCH (H.O. 9)

The *American Practical Navigator*, originally written by Nathaniel Bowditch in 1799, and generally referred to simply as "Bowditch," is an extensive treatise on piloting, celestial navigation and other nautical matters. It is Publication No. H.O. 9, last revised in 1958 and reprinted with

H.O. Pub. No. 9

AMERICAN PRACTICAL NAVIGATOR

AN EPITOME OF NAVIGATION

ORIGINALLY BY
NATHANIEL BOWDITCH, LL.D.

1966—Corrected Print

PUBLISHED BY THE
U.S. NAVY HYDROGRAPHIC OFFICE
UNDER THE AUTHORITY OF THE
SECRETARY OF THE NAVY

U.S. GOVERNMENT PRINTING OFFICE
WASHINGTON : 1966

FIG. 1710 "Bowditch" is the name by which this popular and highly useful government publication is usually known. It contains a wealth of material on piloting, electronic and celestial navigation, and related topics. The mathematical tables contained in it are also available as a separate publication.

minor corrections in 1962 and 1966, see fig. 1710.

"Bowditch" has long been accepted as an authority on questions of piloting and navigation; a copy will be found useful on all but the smallest of boats. In addition to the lengthy text, the basic volume contains many mathematical tables as appendices. These tables alone are also available as a separate publication.

OTHER H.O. PUBLICATIONS

Other Oceanographic Office publications that may be found useful to a boatman include H.O. 117A, *Radio Navigation Aids;* H.O. 118A, *Radio Weather Aids;* and H.O. 103, *International Code of Signals, Visual* (see Chapter 26).

The Oceanographic Office publishes a series of *Sailing Directions* which provide supplementary information for foreign coasts and ports in a manner generally similar to the Coast Pilot for U.S. waters.

The *Lists of Lights* published by this agency likewise cover foreign waters and so are not duplicatory of the Coast Guard Light Lists. These are H.O. 111A through H.O. 116.

The Oceanographic Office's catalog of its charts is Publication No. H.O. 1N. It has an Introduction in three parts plus lists of charts subdivided into ten "regions." It may be purchased as a whole or separately by regions. Regions 0, 1, and 2 would be of the most interest to American boatmen. See fig. 1710a.

Other H.O. publications include a number of tables for the reduction of celestial observations, and tables and charts for plotting lines of position from Loran-A and Loran-C measurements. These are of interest only to those yachtsmen making extensive voyages on the high seas.

Additional Oceanographic Office publications are listed on page 499.

Obtaining Oceanographic Office Publications

Branch Offices of the Naval Oceanographic Office are located at Norfolk, Va.; Wilmington, Calif.; Honolulu, Hawaii; Rodman, C.Z.; and Yokosuka, Japan.

Charts and publications of the Naval Oceanographic Office are available for sale through authorized sales agents, and purchases should be made through these agents whenever possible. If not so available, charts may be purchased from the Branch Oceanographic Offices listed above, or by mail from the U.S. Naval Oceanographic Office, Washington, D.C. 20390, or from either of the Oceanographic Distribution Offices listed below. Mail orders from purchasers located west of the Mississippi River (except Gulf of Mexico and the Canal Zone area) should be sent to:

U. S. Naval Oceanographic Distribution Office, Clearfield, Utah 84016

Mail orders from all other localities should be sent to:

U.S. Naval Oceanographic Distribution Office, U.S. Naval Supply Depot, 5801 Tabor Ave., Philadelphia, Penna. 19120

Orders submitted to the U.S. Naval Oceanographic Office or to a Naval Oceanographic Distribution Office must be accompanied by a check or money order made payable to the "U.S. Naval Oceanographic Office" for the amount of the purchase. Material will be mailed at Government expense in regular printed-matter postal service. The added cost of requests for any special handling, such as air mail, special delivery, etc., must be borne by the purchaser.

Naval Observatory Publications

The U.S. Naval Observatory, Washington, D.C. publishes the *American Nautical Almanac.* This publication contains astronomical data necessary to boatmen who are concerned with celestial navigation, but is not needed for piloting. It can be purchased, in annual editions, from the Superintendent of Documents.

The Naval Observatory also participates in and assists the publication of other navigational documents such as the Tide Tables and celestial sight reduction tables, but it is not the agency directly responsible for them.

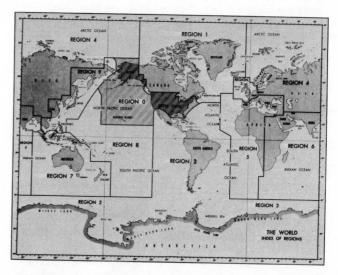

FIG. 1710a. The Oceanographic Office catalog indexes charts by regions. Of these, Region O (United States) is of particular interest.

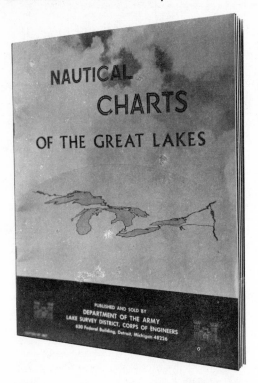

CORPS OF
ENGINEERS
U.S. ARMY

U. S. L A K E   S U R V E Y

GREAT LAKES PILOT
1967

BEARINGS ARE TRUE AND DISTANCES ARE EXPRESSED IN STATUTE MILES

The text of this Pilot has been edited and its publication supervised by the U.S. Lake Survey. It is a complete revision compiled from former Pilots; from surveys made by the U.S. Lake Survey; from publications of the U.S. Coast Guard; from information supplied by the Environmental Science Services Administration (U.S. Weather Bureau), the Department of Health, Education and Welfare, the St. Lawrence Seaway Development Corp., the New York State Department of Public Works, the Canadian Departments of Transport, of Public Works and of Energy, Mines and Resources (Mines and Technical Surveys), and the St. Lawrence Seaway Authority; and from revisory data related to the river and harbor improvements carried on in these waters, by the Corps of Engineers, U.S. Army.

FIG. 1711 The new U.S. Lake Survey chart catalog covers not only the Great Lakes, but also its outflow rivers, Lake Champlain, N.Y. State Barge Canal system, and Minnesota-Ontario border lakes.

FIG. 1712 The Great Lakes Pilot is a comprehensive volume prepared to supplement information given on charts published by the U.S. Lake Survey. It is revised annually and kept up-to-date by supplements issued monthly during the navigation season (May-November).

Army Engineers Publications

The Corps of Engineers of the U.S. Army has the responsibility for navigational and informational publications on the Great Lakes, major inland (non-tidal) rivers such as the Tennessee, Ohio, and Mississippi, and many lakes and reservoirs behind the large dams.

GREAT LAKES CHART CATALOGS

An excellent free catalog of Nautical Charts of the Great Lakes, fig. 1711, is available from the Lake Survey District, Corps of Engineers, 630 Federal Building, Detroit, Mich. 48226, where mail orders and counter sales of Lake Survey charts are handled. Lake Survey charts are also sold, over the counter only, at their sales offices in Sault Ste. Marie, Mich.; Buffalo, N.Y.; Cleveland, Ohio; Chicago, Ill., and Massena, N.Y.

Included in the waterways listed in the Lake Survey catalog, in addition to the Great Lakes and its outflow rivers, are Lake Champlain, the New York State Barge Canal System, and the Minnesota-Ontario Border Lakes. The catalog also supplies information on the Lake Survey's recreational chart series, designed especially for the operators of small pleasure boats, and other Lake Survey publications, such as the Great Lakes Pilot.

THE GREAT LAKES PILOT

For the Great Lakes and other waters covered by U.S. Lake Survey charts, the publication corresponding to the Coast Pilots is called the *Great Lakes Pilot,* fig. 1712. This is an annual publication, kept up to date during the navigation season by seven monthly supplements issued from May to November.

INTRACOASTAL WATERWAY BOOKLETS

The Army Engineers has prepared two paperbound booklets on the Intracoastal Waterway, which comes under its jurisdiction. These booklets contain descriptive material, photographs, small-scale charts, and tabulated data. Caution must be exercised, however, when using the distance tables as considerable differences exist between these publications and the C&GS charts of the Atlantic ICW. The Army Engineers use statute (not nautical) miles, and their zero point is at Trenton, N.J. rather than Norfolk, Va. Mileage differences will also be noted along the Gulf Intracoastal Waterway.

Unfortunately, these publications are *not* periodically updated, and they are of far less value than the corresponding volumes of the C&GS Coast Pilots with their annual supplements.

Bulletins on the Intracoastal Waterways are issued periodically by the Engineers' District Offices. Addresses of these offices are given on page 498.

RIVERS AND LAKES INFORMATION

Regulations relating to the use of many rivers and lakes (reservoirs), *Navigational Bulletins,* and *Notices to Navigation Interests* are issued by various offices of the Corps of Engineers, U.S. Army, as listed on page 439.   Other government publications relating to inland river and lake boating are also listed on that page, together with information as to where they may be obtained.

Weather Bureau Publications

The U.S. Weather Bureau, an element of ESSA, Department of Commerce, publishes *Daily Weather Maps* (see Chapter 12), but these are directly used by relatively few boatmen. Much greater reliance is placed on radio and television broadcasts of current weather conditions and predictions.

To assist mariners and boatmen in knowing when and where to listen for radio and TV weather broadcasts, the Weather Bureau publishes a series of *Coastal Warning Facilities Charts* in annual editions. These are discussed in more detail in pages 246-247 and 382(e)-(f).

Keeping Publications Up to Date

It is essential that certain navigational publications, as well as charts, be kept corrected and fully up to date with respect to the information contained in them. Incorrect, outdated information can be considerably more harmful than no information at all; a false sense of knowledge and confidence can easily lead to a dangerous situation.

Coast Pilots and Light Lists are the primary publications that need continual correction. Fortunately, the government has provided a convenient means for executing this most necessary function. The time and effort required are not great, provided a skipper keeps at it regularly and does not permit the work to build up a backlog.

NOTICE TO MARINERS

The U.S. Naval Oceanographic Office publishes a weekly *Notice to Mariners* which is prepared jointly with the Coast & Geodetic Survey and the Coast Guard; see fig. 1713. These pamphlets advise mariners of important matters affecting navigational safety, including new hydrographic discoveries, changes in channels and navigational aids, etc. Besides keeping mariners informed generally, the Notice to Mariners also provides information specifically useful for updating the latest editions of nautical charts and publications produced by the Naval Oceanographic Office, the Coast & Geodetic Survey, and the Coast Guard.

Each issue contains instructions on how it is to be used to correct charts and other publications. Certain supplementary information is published at the beginning of each year, and portions are repeated at mid-year or at quarterly intervals.

LOCAL NOTICES TO MARINERS

The Commander of each Coast Guard District issues *Local Notices to Mariners,* fig. 1714. These are usually better suited to the needs of boatmen who do not need information on remote or foreign waters. The Local Notices are reproduced and mailed from the respective District Headquarters, and corresponding items of information will reach boatmen several weeks in advance of the weekly Notices that are printed in Washington, D.C. and mailed from there.

Report all useful information

All boatmen are urged to cooperate with governmental agencies in keeping the buoyage system up to its highest

FIG. 1713 **Notice to Mariners is a free weekly publication used to correct charts and other navigational publications. A single volume now covers the major navigable waters of the world. Information is presented in the form of descriptive paragraphs, inserts for pasting on charts, and cut-outs for direct insertion in publications such as the Light Lists.**

efficiency and helpfulness by reporting any facts that may come to their attention concerning damage to aids, malfunctioning of lights, shifting of shoals and channels, new hazards, etc. Defects in navigational aids and new hazards should be reported to the nearest Coast Guard activity by the fastest means available, including radio if the situation is of sufficient urgency. Suggestions for the improvement of aids to navigation should be sent to the Commandant, U.S. Coast Guard, Washington, D.C. 20226.

Data concerning dangers to navigation, changes in shoals and channels, and similar information affecting charts or publications of the C&GS should be sent to the Director, Coast and Geodetic Survey, ESSA, Washington Science Center, Rockville, Maryland 20852.

DEPARTMENT OF TRANSPORTATION

CG-2535-PP
(Rev. 1-64)

UNITED STATES COAST GUARD

LOCAL NOTICE TO MARINERS

ISSUED BY: Commander, Seventh Coast Guard District Phone 350 - 5621
51 S. W. First Avenue, Miami, Florida 350 - 5622

SOUTH CAROLINA - SEACOAST: The U. S. Navy advises that controlled small arms and 40 MM firing, maximum ordinate 3,000 feet, will be conducted 9 through 15 April 1967 in the vicinity of 32-22N 79-43W and 32-12N 79-47W.

Controlled surface to surface and surface to air firing, maximum ordinate of 30,000 feet, will be conducted 9 through 15 April 1967 in the vicinity of 32-12N and 78-58W.

Charts: 1239, 1110, 1111, 1007, 1001

FLORIDA - GULF COAST: Consideration is being given to the following: Caloosa Lighted Bell Buoy 2 (LLNR 4398/5087) to be moved to a position about 2200 yards 190 degrees from San Carlos Bay Approach Light 4 (LLNR 5090.2).

Mariners having any objections to the above changes are requested to notify Commander, Seventh Coast Guard District, 51 S. W. First Avenue, Miami, Florida, 33130, before 31 July 1967.

Charts: 856SC, 1255 LLPgs. 571/642

FLORIDA - ST. LUCIE INLET: On or about 15 April 1967 the following changes will be made in aids to navigation:

St. Lucie Inlet Entrance Range Front Daybeacon, a vertical rectangular-shaped red daymark with a central white stripe, on a pile, 12 feet high, to be established in about 6 feet of water, 1730 yards 061 degrees from St. Lucie Crossover Range Front Light 4 (LLNR 6162).

St. Lucie Inlet Entrance Range Rear Daybeacon, a vertical rectangular-shaped red daymark with a central white stripe, on a dolphin, 20 feet high, to be established in about 5 feet of water, 250 yards 269 degrees from the front daybeacon.

Ref: LNM 13-67

Charts: 845SC, 855SC, 1247 LLPg. 619

REPORT DEFECTS IN AIDS TO NAVIGATION TO NEAREST COAST GUARD UNIT

DATE: 5 April 1967 NOTICE NO. 14-67

FIG. 1714 Local Notices to Mariners are published by each Coast Guard District on a "when required" basis, often several times per week. Information in Local Notices often reaches boatmen several weeks before it appears in weekly Notices from Washington. Check your local yacht club or marina for its file of Local Notices.

Quasi-Governmental Publications

In addition to the governmental agencies and their publications noted above, there are several activities that can be best described as "quasi-governmental." Publications issued by them are of considerable interest to boatmen.

RADIO TECHNICAL COMMISSION FOR MARINE SERVICES

This organization with the long name is for obvious reasons better known by its initials, RTCM. It includes representatives of governmental agencies such as the FCC, the Coast Guard, ESSA, Maritime Administration, and others; user organizations, such as ocean steamship operating groups, Great Lakes shipping interests, and the United States Power Squadrons; equipment manufacturers; labor organizations; and communications companies such as the Bell System. The RTCM does not have authority to make binding decisions, but it wields considerable influence through its function as a meeting place for the presentation and resolution of conflicting views and interests.

The RTCM publishes *Marine Radio Telephony,* a booklet presenting a simplified interpretation of the FCC Rules and Regulations relating to the use of radios on ships and boats. This small booklet can be most useful to a skipper with a set on board in the 2-3 Mc/s marine band. See fig. 2517.

The RTCM also publishes a companion operator's manual, *Maritime Mobile VHF-FM Radio Telephony—Usage in the United States.* This volume, as well as that for the 2-3 Mc/s marine band, may be purchased from the Executive Secretary, RTCM, P.O. Box 764, Washington, D.C. 20044.

NAVAL INSTITUTE PUBLICATIONS

The United States Naval Institute is not a governmental agency; rather it is a private association "for the advancement of professional, literary, and scientific knowledge in the Navy." One of its principal activities is the publication of books on naval and maritime matters.

The Naval Institute publishes a large number of books, but none will be more familiar to boatmen than *Dutton's Navigation and Piloting.* Like Bowditch, this volume has come to be an accepted authority on matters of piloting and navigation. Again like Bowditch, the current volume is an outgrowth of many years of development from an early work; the book was initially known as "Navigation and Nautical Astronomy" by Benjamin Dutton. This useful book can be purchased in boating supply and book stores, or directly by mail from the U.S. Naval Institute, Annapolis, Maryland, 21402. ⚓

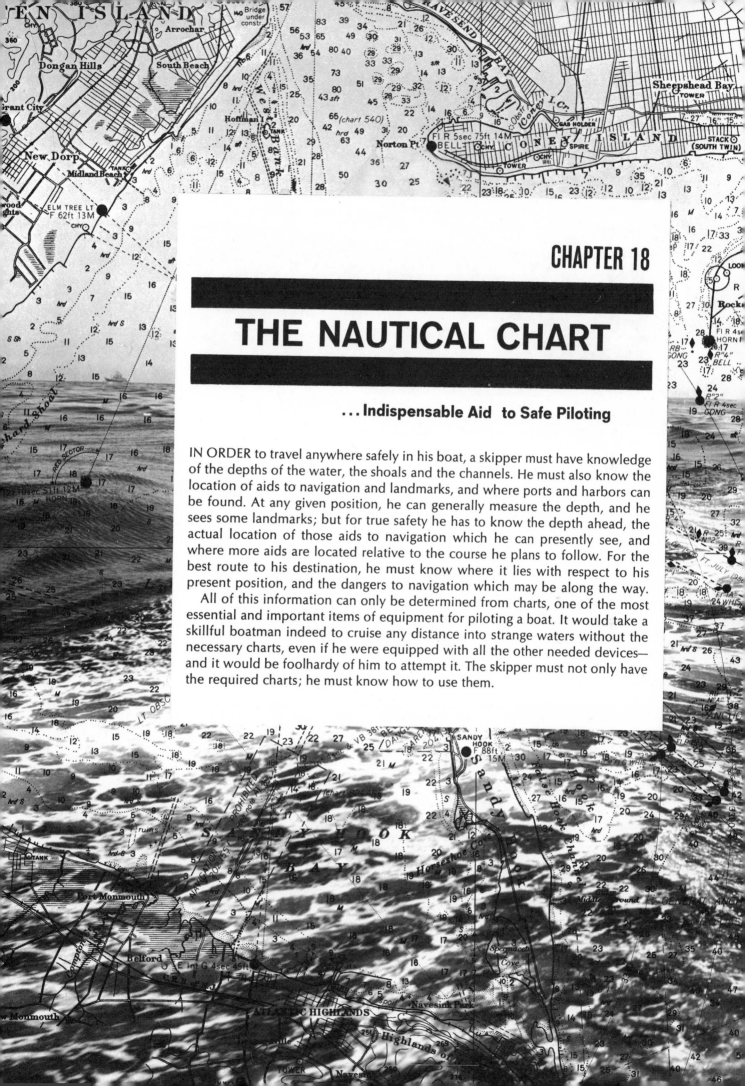

CHAPTER 18

THE NAUTICAL CHART

. . . Indispensable Aid to Safe Piloting

IN ORDER to travel anywhere safely in his boat, a skipper must have knowledge of the depths of the water, the shoals and the channels. He must also know the location of aids to navigation and landmarks, and where ports and harbors can be found. At any given position, he can generally measure the depth, and he sees some landmarks; but for true safety he has to know the depth ahead, the actual location of those aids to navigation which he can presently see, and where more aids are located relative to the course he plans to follow. For the best route to his destination, he must know where it lies with respect to his present position, and the dangers to navigation which may be along the way.

All of this information can only be determined from charts, one of the most essential and important items of equipment for piloting a boat. It would take a skillful boatman indeed to cruise any distance into strange waters without the necessary charts, even if he were equipped with all the other needed devices—and it would be foolhardy of him to attempt it. The skipper must not only have the required charts; he must know how to use them.

FIG. 1801 You are at Buoy "4" and the water is measured to be 18 feet deep, but what is the course to your destination, and how deep is the water along the way? Only a chart can give you this information —be sure that you have the right charts on board, and that you know how to use them.

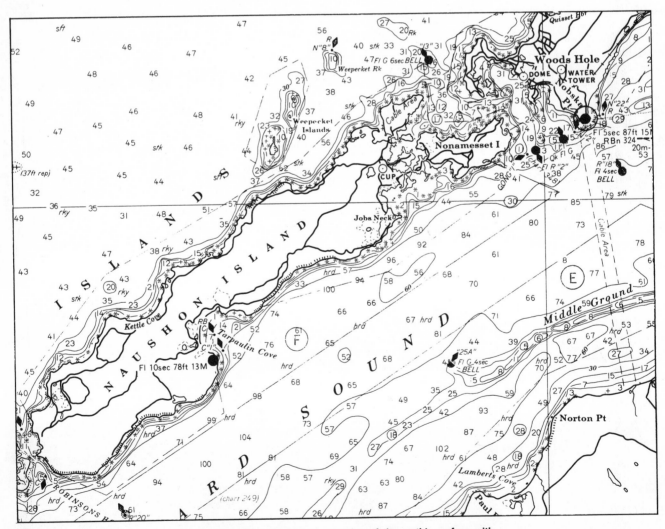

FIG. 1802 A nautical chart is a representation in miniature of a portion of the earth's surface with emphasis on natural and man-made features of particular interest to the navigator of a ship or boat.

CHARTS VS. MAPS

A *nautical chart,* fig. 1802, is a representation in miniature, on a plane surface, of a portion of the earth's surface emphasizing natural and man-made features of particular interest to a navigator. A map, fig. 1803, is a similar miniature representation for use on land in which the emphasis is on roads, cities, political boundaries, etc. For a boatman to refer to a chart as a "map" is to reveal his lack of nautical knowledge and experience.

A chart covers an area which is primarily water and includes such information as the depth of water, obstructions and other dangers to navigation, and the location and type of aids to navigation. Adjacent land areas are portrayed only in such detail as will aid a navigator—the shoreline, harbor facilities, prominent natural or manmade features, etc. Charts are printed on heavy-weight, durable paper so that they may be used as worksheets on which courses may be plotted and positions determined.

A basic requirement of a nautical chart is to provide the navigator with the proper information to enable him to make the *right* decision *in time to avoid danger.* Charts are prepared by various agencies of the Government to furnish the pilot or navigator with absolutely accurate representations of navigable bodies of water showing the depths, aids to navigation, shorelines, and other essential features. They differ from road maps both in the great amount of detailed information that they contain and in the precision with which they are constructed. The need for this accuracy can be appreciated when it is realized that an error of only a small amount in charting the position of a submerged obstruction could constitute a serious menace to navigation.

Several major oil companies produce a series of "cruising guides" which cover important boating areas, fig. 1804. These are useful in planning a nautical trip, but lack the detail, accuracy, and provision for revisions between printings (by means of Notices to Mariners) required for actual navigational use. Do *not* try to substitute them for official government charts.

GEOGRAPHIC COORDINATES

Charts will also show a grid of intersecting lines to aid in the description of a position on the water. These lines are the charted representations of a system of *geographic coordinates* which exist on the earth's surface, although in an unseen, imaginary sense like state boundaries.

The earth is nearly spherical in shape—it is slightly flattened along the polar axis, but the distortion is slight and

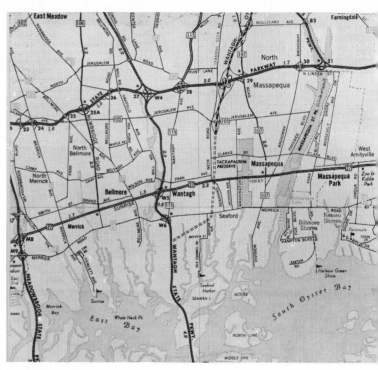

© General Drafting Co., Inc.

FIG. 1803 A map differs from a nautical chart in that the emphasis is on towns, roads, political boundaries, etc. It is designed primarily for motorists and should never be used for navigation.

FIG. 1804 The major oil companies issue "cruising guides" which may be of great value in planning a cruise, but should never be depended upon for the actual navigation of a boat.

need be of concern only to scientists, not boatmen. A *great circle,* fig. 1805a, is the line traced out on the surface of a sphere by a plane cutting through the sphere at its center. This is the largest circle that can be drawn on the surface of a sphere. A *small circle,* fig. 1805b, is one marked on the surface of a sphere by a plane that does not pass through its center.

Meridians and parallels

Geographic coordinates are defined by two sets of great and small circles. One is a set of great circles each of which passes through the north and south geographic poles— these are the *meridians of longitude,* fig. 1806. The other set is a series of circles each established by a plane cutting through the earth perpendicular to the polar axis. The

For greater precision in position definition, degrees may be subdivided into *minutes* (60 minutes = 1 degree) and *seconds* (60 seconds = 1 minute).

From figures 1808b and 1809, it will be seen that the meridians of longitude get closer together as one moves away from the equator in either direction, and eventually converge at the poles. Thus the distance on the earth's surface between adjacent meridians is not a fixed quantity but varies with latitude. On the other hand, the parallels of latitude are essentially equally spaced and the distance between successive parallels is nearly the same. One degree of latitude is, for all practical purposes, 60 nautical miles: and *one minute of latitude may be taken as one nautical mile,* a relationship which we will later see is quite useful.

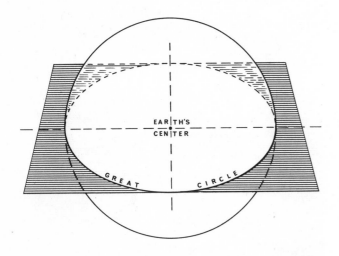

FIG. 1805 a   A GREAT CIRCLE is the line traced out on the surface of a sphere by a plane cutting through the center point of the sphere.
(From Dutton)

FIG. 1805 b   A SMALL CIRCLE is the line traced on the surface of a sphere by a plane which cuts through the sphere but does NOT pass through the center point of the sphere.

largest of these is midway between the poles and thus passes through the center of the earth, becoming a great circle; this is the *equator,* fig. 1807a. Other parallel planes form small circles which are known as the *parallels of latitude,* fig. 1807b.

Geographic coordinates are measured in terms of degrees (one degree is 1/360th of a complete circle). The meridian that passes through Greenwich, England is the reference for all measurements of longitude and is designated as the *prime meridian,* or *0°.* The longitude of any position on earth is described as —° East or West of Greenwich, to a maximum in either direction of 180°. The measurement can be thought of as either the angle at the north and south poles between the meridian of the place being described and the prime meridian, or as the arc along the equator between these meridians, fig. 1808a. The designation of "E" or "W" is an essential part of any statement of longitude, abbreviated as "long." or "λ" (the Greek letter lambda).

Parallels of latitude are measured in degrees North or South from the equator, from 0° at the equator to 90° at each pole. The designation of latitude (abbreviated "L") as "N" or "S" is necessary for a complete description of position, fig. 1808b.

FIG. 1806   MERIDIANS of LONGITUDE are formed on the earth's surface by great circles which pass through the North and South Poles.
(From Bowditch)

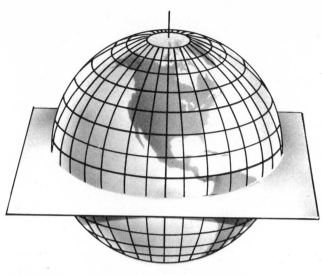

FIG. 1807 a The great circle that cuts through the earth perpendicular to the polar axis traces out the EQUATOR at the earth's surface.

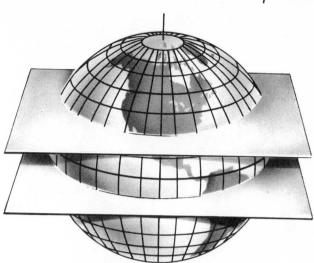

FIG. 1807 b PARALLELS of LATITUDE are the small circles formed at the earth's surface by planes perpendicular to the polar axis but not passing through the center of the earth. They are parallel to the plane of the Equator.

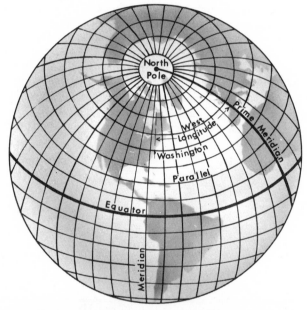

FIG. 1808 a Longitude is measured in degrees from the Prime Meridian (0°), which passes through Greenwich, England, East or West to a maximum of 180°. The designation of "E" or "W" is an essential part of any statement of longitude.

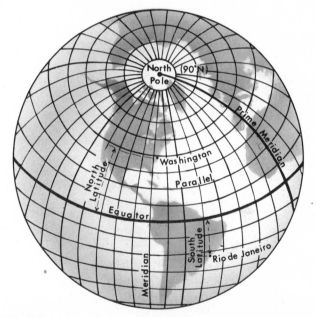

FIG. 1808 b Latitude is measured in either direction, North or South, from the Equator (0°) to the Poles (90°). Statements of latitude, abbreviated "L", must be labeled either "N" or "S" to be complete.

(From Bowditch)

CHART CONSTRUCTION

The construction of a chart for a portion of the earth's surface immediately produces the problem of representation of a spherical, three-dimensional surface on a plane, two-dimensional sheet of paper. Actually, it is impossible to accomplish this exactly. A certain amount of distortion is inevitable, but various methods, called *projections*, have been developed which provide practical and sufficiently accurate results.

The transfer of information from the sphere to the flat surface of the chart should be accomplished with as little distortion as possible in the shape and size of land and water areas, the angular relation of positions, the distance between points, and other more technical properties. Each of the different projections is superior to others in one or more of these qualities; none is superior in all characteristics. In all projections, as the area covered by the chart is decreased, the distortion diminishes, and the difference between various types of projections lessens.

Of the many techniques of projection that might be used, two are of primary interest to boatmen. The *Mercator projection* is an example of the most common; it is used for charts of ocean and coastal areas. The *polyconic projection* is employed for charts of the Great Lakes and inland rivers. The average skipper can quite safely navigate his boat using either type of chart without a deep knowledge of the techniques of projection. (For those who would know more of the various projection methods, see pages 329-332).

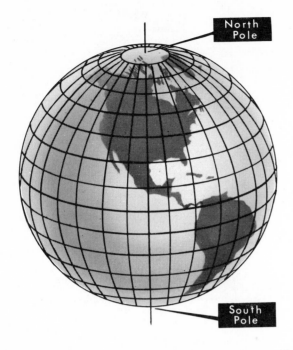

FIG. 1809 Meridians of longitude converge toward each other as one moves away from the Equator in the direction of either pole. All meridians meet at the North and South Poles.

DIRECTION

Direction is defined as the angle between a line connecting one point with another point and a base, or reference, line extending from the origin point toward the true or magnetic north pole; the angle is measured in degrees clockwise from the reference line. Thus direction on charts may be described as so many degrees "True" (T) or so many degrees "Magnetic" (M). The difference between these directions is "variation" and must be allowed for as described in Chapter 13. The principal difference in the use of charts on the Mercator projection and those on the polyconic projection lies in the techniques for measuring direction; this will be covered in Chapter 19 when the use of piloting instruments is considered.

Measurement of direction

To facilitate the measurement of direction, as in plotting bearings and laying out courses, most charts will have compass roses printed on them. A *compass rose,* fig. 1810, consists of two or three concentric circles, several inches in diameter and accurately subdivided. The outer circle has its zero at *true* north; this is emphasized with a star. The inner circle or circles are oriented to magnetic north. The middle circle, if there are three, is *magnetic* direction expressed in degrees, with an arrow printed over the zero point to indicate magnetic north. The innermost circle is also magnetic direction, but in terms of "points," and halves and quarters thereof; its use by modern boatmen will be limited. (One point = 11¼ degrees.) This innermost circle using the point system of subdivision may be omitted on some charts of the "small-craft" series.

The difference between the orientation of the two sets of circles is, of course, the magnetic variation at the loca-

tion of the compass rose. The amount of the variation and its direction (Easterly or Westerly) is given in words and figures in the center of the rose, together with a statement of the year that such variation existed and the annual rate of change. When using a chart in a year later than the date shown on the compass rose, it *may* be necessary to modify the variation shown by applying the annual rate of change. Such cases are, however, relatively rare as rates are quite small and differences of a small fraction of a degree may be ignored from a practical standpoint.

Each chart will have several compass roses printed on it at convenient locations where they will not conflict with navigational information. Roses printed on land areas may cause the elimination of topographical features in these regions.

Until a skipper has thoroughly mastered the handling of compass "errors," he should use only true directions and the true (outer) compass rose. Later, the magnetic rose may be used directly, thus simplifying computations.

Several cautions are necessary when measuring directions on charts. When large areas are covered, it is possible for the magnetic variation to differ for various portions of the chart. Check each chart when you first start to use it, and, to be sure, always use the compass rose nearest the area for which you are plotting. Depending upon the type and scale of the chart, graduations on the compass rose circles may be for intervals of 1°, 2°, or 5°. On some charts, the outer circle (true) is subdivided into units of 1° while the inner (magnetic) circle, being smaller, is subdivided into steps of 2°. Always check carefully to determine the interval between adjacent marks on each compass rose scale.

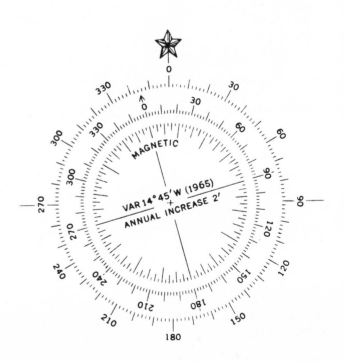

FIG. 1810 A compass rose graphically illustrates true and magnetic directions. The outer circle is in degrees with zero at true north. The inner circles are in degrees and "points" with their zero oriented to the magnetic north. Several will be found on each chart conveniently located for plotting courses and bearings.

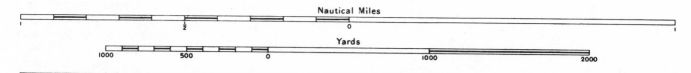

Nautical Miles

Yards

FIG. 1811 C&GS charts at scales of 1:80,000 or larger will have two sets of graphic scales. Each set consists of a scale of nautical miles and a scale of yards. On Intracoastal Waterway Charts, a scale of statute miles will also be shown.

DISTANCE

Distances on charts may be measured in statute or in nautical miles. The *statute (land) mile* of 5280 feet is the same as used on road maps; its use in boating is restricted to the Great Lakes and inland rivers. The *nautical mile*, 6076.1 feet in length, is used on charts of ocean and coastal waters. Only one type of mile will be used on any given chart. It is sometimes necessary to convert from one unit to the other. This is not difficult—*1 nautical mile = 1.15 statute miles,* or approximately 7 nautical miles equals 8 statute miles. In navigation, distances of up to a few miles or so may be expressed in yards, a unit which is the same no matter which "mile" is used on the chart.

SCALE

As a chart is a representation in miniature of an area of navigable water, actual distances must be "scaled down" to much shorter dimensions on paper. This reduction is termed the *scale* of the chart. The basic way of describing the scale of a chart is its so-called *natural scale,* an expression of the relationship between a given distance on the chart to the actual distance that it represents on the earth. This may be expressed as a ratio, 1:80,000 meaning that 1 unit on the chart represents 80,000 units on the actual land or water surface, or as a fraction $\frac{1}{80,000}$ with the same meaning.

The ratio of chart to actual distance can also be expressed as a *numerical* or *equivalent scale.* This is such a statement as "1 inch = 1.1 miles," another way of expressing a 1:80,000 scale. Equivalent scales are not as commonly used on nautical charts as on maps, but they may be encountered from time to time on such publications as cruising guides.

It is important that at all times the pilot have clearly fixed in his mind the scale of the chart then being used—in order that he will not misjudge the distance to aids to navigation, dangers, etc. Quite often in a day's cruise, a skipper will use charts of different scales, changing back and forth between small-scale coastal charts and larger-scale harbor charts. Unless he is keenly aware of the scale

of the chart being used at the moment, a pilot may find himself unexpectedly in a dangerous position.

Large-scale and small-scale

When chart scales are expressed fractionally, confusion sometimes results from the use of the terms "large-scale" and "small-scale." Since the number that is varied to change the scale is in the *denominator* of the fraction, as it gets larger, the fraction, and hence the scale, gets smaller. For example, $\frac{1}{80,000}$ is a smaller fraction than $\frac{1}{40,000}$, and thus a chart to the former scale is termed a smaller-scale chart. The terms "large-scale" and "small-scale" are relative and have no limiting definitions. Scales may be as large as 1:5,000 for detailed harbor charts, or as small as 1 to several million for charts of large areas of the world.

Charts at a scale of 1:80,000 or larger will normally carry, in addition to a statement of scale, two sets of *graphic scales,* fig. 1811, each subdivided into conveniently and commonly used units. Note that one basic unit is placed to the *left* of the scale's zero point and is subdivided more finely than is the main part of the scale. The use of these graphic scales will be covered in Chapter 19.

When using Mercator charts, the navigator can take advantage of the fact that one minute of the *latitude* scale on each *side* of the chart is essentially equal to one nautical mile. On charts of a scale smaller than 1:80,000, the latitude scale will be the only means of measuring distance.

A *logarithmic speed scale,* fig. 1812, is printed on all charts of 1:40,000 or larger scale. Its use is explained in Chapter 19.

SOURCES OF CHARTS

Who issues charts

Charts are prepared and issued by several agencies of the Federal Government. This is not duplication, however, as different areas and types of charts are the responsibility of each office. The majority of boatmen will use charts prepared by the Coast & Geodetic Survey of the Environ-

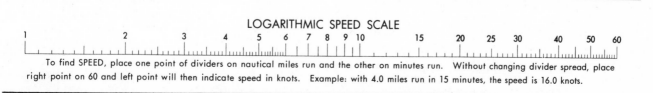

LOGARITHMIC SPEED SCALE

To find SPEED, place one point of dividers on nautical miles run and the other on minutes run. Without changing divider spread, place right point on 60 and left point will then indicate speed in knots. Example: with 4.0 miles run in 15 minutes, the speed is 16.0 knots.

FIG. 1812 C&GS charts of 1:40,000 or larger scale will have a LOGARITHMIC SPEED SCALE from which a graphic calculation of speed may be made if the time of run is measured between two known points. See Chapter 19 for a detailed discussion of its use.

mental Science Services Administration, Department of Commerce. C&GS charts cover the coastal waters of the United States, including harbors and rivers extending inland to the head of tidal action.

The Naval Oceanographic Office of the Department of Defense (formerly the Hydrographic Office) publishes charts of the high seas and foreign waters based on its own surveys and on charts originally produced by other countries. Boatmen will become familiar, for example, with HO charts when sailing to Bermuda or cruising in the Bahamas. (The designation "HO" was retained for charts and publications despite the change in the name of the agency.) Canadian waters, however, are charted by that nation's Hydrographic Service.

Charts of the Great Lakes and major inland rivers, such as the Ohio and the Mississippi, are issued by several activities of the U.S. Army Corps of Engineers. The Lake Survey District is the issuing agency for charts of the Great Lakes; their charts are identified by the letters "LS" preceding the chart numbers. Also available from the Army Engineers are charts for many of the inland lakes and canal systems. These are issued by various Division and District Offices.

Where to buy them

Charts may be purchased directly from the headquarters or field offices of the issuing agencies, or from retail sales agents. The government offices may be addressed as shown in fig. 1813. Sales agents are widely located in boating and shipping centers. Lists of sales agents for C&GS and HO charts are published in each Coast Pilot and periodically in Notices to Mariners as discussed in Chapter 17. Lake Survey charts are sold by designated offices of the Army Engineers as listed in their Chart Catalog and the Great Lakes Pilot. They are also unofficially sold by marinas and boating stores.

The cost of charts is amazingly little for the vast amount of information furnished to the navigator. The prices charged for charts include only a small part of the cost to the government for their production. Traditionally, it has been the duty of a country to aid safe navigation by publishing low-cost charts and nautical guides. Recent increases in chart prices have reflected only the general rise in costs, not a change in pricing policy.

C&GS and HO charts must be sold by agents at the price printed on them, a discount being allowed to the

---

CHART ISSUING AGENCIES

⚓ U.S. Coast and Geodetic Survey, ESSA
Rockville, Maryland 20852

⚓ U.S. Naval Oceanographic Office
Washington, D.C. 20390

⚓ U.S. Army Engineer District,
Lake Survey
630 Federal Building
Detroit, Michigan 48226

FIG. 1813 Information on nautical charts can be obtained by writing to the appropriate headquarters at the address shown above. Regional and District Offices may also be able to provide answers to questions on charts.

---

agent for his quantity purchases. Lake Survey charts are sold by the government offices at the printed price. When re-sold by boating stores, however, the price is usually marked up to a higher figure.

The prudent skipper carries on his boat a full set of charts covering the waters that he cruises, and he regularly replaces worn-out or outdated charts with new ones. Charts are among his best boating bargains!

Chart catalogs

Catalogs are available from issuing agencies which indicate the area covered by each chart, the scale used, and the price. These will be found useful when planning a cruise into unfamiliar boating waters.

The C&GS catalog is issued in three volumes, each a large, accordion-folded sheet; they are free. Volume 1 covers the U.S. Atlantic and Gulf coastal waters. Volume 2 is for the West Coast and Pacific Islands. Volume 3 covers the Alaskan Coast.

The HO chart catalog, publication number 1-N, is issued in "Regions" at a price of 25¢ each. Region "0" covers U.S. coastal waters; Region "2" includes the Bahamian and West Indian cruising areas as well as the waters bordering Central and South America.

The Lake Survey annually publishes its chart catalog covering the Great Lakes, Lake Champlain, the New York Barge Canal System, and other waters. It is available without charge upon request.

What Charts Show

Charts include a great amount of information and a boatman should carefully study each chart soon after he purchases it, certainly well before he must use it to safely navigate his craft.

BASIC INFORMATION

Located at some convenient place on the chart, where space is available, will be found the *general information block*, fig. 1814. Here is the chart title which is descriptive of the waters covered (the chart number will not appear

here, but rather in several places around the margins), a statement of the type of projection used and the scale, the unit of measurement of depth (feet or fathoms — one fathom equals six feet), and the datum plane for such soundings.

Elsewhere on the chart where there is space available (normally in land areas), other information will be found, such as the meaning of abbreviations used on this chart, special notes of caution regarding dangers, the units of measurement of heights and the reference plane from

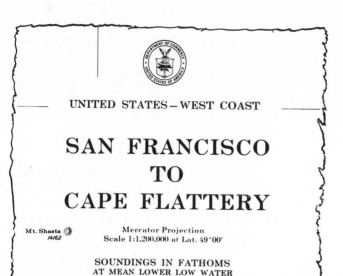

FIG. 1814 The title block shows the official name of the chart, the type of projection, scale, and datum and unit of measurement for depths. Printed nearby will be much valuable information—be sure to read all notes and data before using any chart.

which measured, tidal information, references to anchorage areas, and many other useful bits of data. *All* notes on charts should be read carefully and fully, as they may cover important information that cannot be graphically presented, or which may have come into existence since the chart was printed (rubber-stamped notes), fig. 1815.

Editions and revisions

The edition number and date appear in the margin at the lower left-hand corner; immediately following these figures will be the date of the latest revised printing, if any. Figures 1816a and b illustrate these two cases. The typical nautical chart is printed to supply the normal demand for one or two years; quantities are so limited to provide for bringing it up to date as frequently as practicable. Charts may be reprinted as-is when the stock runs low, but a revised printing is more likely. Revisions include all changes that have been printed in Notices to Mariners since the preceding issue of the chart. When major changes in hydrography occur, such as new surveys revealing significant differences between charted depths and actual conditions, a new edition is published; it, too, will include all other changes which have been made in aids to navigation, etc.

Special charts, for which there is an urgent need, are printed directly from smooth drafting without engraving; these are designated as "Provisional Charts" and are so labeled in the title block. A chart constructed from unverified information will be marked as a "Preliminary Chart."

It is of the utmost importance that only the latest edition of a chart be used. All new editions supersede older issues, which should be discarded. Between issues, charts should be corrected from information published in Notices to Mariners and other official documents. Many charts will show a third date rubber-stamped in the lower margin near the right-hand corner, fig. 1817. This is the date to which the chart has been hand-corrected by the issuing agency (Coast & Geodetic Survey, for example) for changes published in Notices to Mariners before it was sold and shipped. Local sales agents do *not* make further corrections to charts in their stocks. The purchaser should make

every effort to check all Notices subsequent to the number shown in the rubber-stamped marking and enter any applicable corrections. The safest chart is the one that is fully corrected up to date!

LATITUDE AND LONGITUDE SCALES

Nautical charts of the conventional type with the geographical north direction toward the top of the sheet will have latitude scales in each side border and longitude scales in the top and bottom borders. The meridians and parallels will be drawn across the chart as fine black lines at intervals of 2', 5', or 10' as determined by the scale of the particular chart.

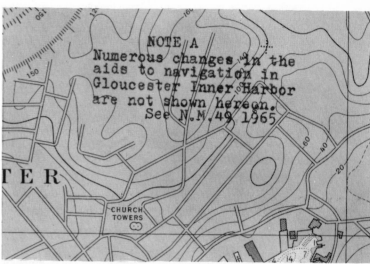

FIG. 1815 Charts may have rubber-stamped notes with information of great importance. These will usually concern changes which were too numerous for hand-correction. Check each chart you buy for such notes and read them carefully. This information will be incorporated into the chart in the next revised printing.

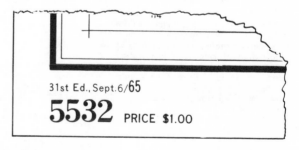

FIG. 1816 a The edition number and date are printed in the margin of each C&GS chart in the lower-left corner. Also shown here are the chart number and price.

FIG. 1816 b Between editions, revised printings are made of charts to include all changes that have been published in Notices to Mariners. Be safe—do not use obsolete charts!

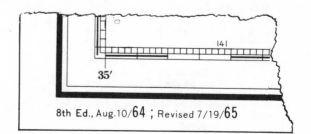

On C&GS charts having a scale larger than 1:49,000, such as on harbor charts, the subdivisions in the border scales are in terms of minutes and seconds of latitude and longitude, fig. 1818a.

On smaller-scale charts, the subdivisions are in minutes and fractions of minutes—charts at a scale of 1:80,000, such as 1210Tr, use minutes and tenths of minutes, fig. 1818b. Still smaller scale charts will use fifths or halves of minutes.

Where skewed projections are used, and north is not toward the top of the sheet, as on Intracoastal Waterway charts, the subdivisions of latitude and longitude are indicated along parallels and meridians at several convenient places.

USE OF COLOR

Nearly all charts use color, pages 292(h) and 292(i), to emphasize various features, and thus facilitate chart reading and interpretation. The number of different colors will vary with the agency publishing the chart and with its intended use. The Coast & Geodetic Survey makes use of five colors (and several shades of some of these) on their regular charts.

Land areas are shown in buff or yellowish color; water areas are white, the color of the paper, except for the shallower regions which are in blue. Areas that may be submerged at some tidal stages, but which uncover at others, are represented in green. Sand bars, mud flats,

coral reefs, and marshes are typical of such green areas on charts. On some charts, water areas that have been swept with wire drags to ensure the absence of isolated rocks or coral heads may be shown in a greenish half-tone with the depth of the sweep indicated. This shade of green is lighter than the solid color used for uncovering areas and no confusion should result.

Magenta, a purplish-red color, is used for many purposes; it was selected for its visibility under red light which is used on many vessels for reading charts during darkness because it does not destroy night vision as white light would. Red buoys are printed in this color, as are red daybeacon symbols. Lighted buoys of any color have a magenta disc superimposed over the dot portion of the symbol to enhance its identification as a lighted aid to navigation. This same scheme is used with lighthouses, lights, lighted ranges, etc. Caution and danger symbols and notes are printed in magenta; also compass roses and recommended courses where shown. Black, of course, is used for most symbols and the bulk of printed information.

LETTERING STYLES

In order to convey to the chart reader as much information as possible in the clearest form, a system has been adopted whereby certain classes of information are printed in one style of lettering and other classes in another style.

FIG. 1817 The issuing agencies hand-correct all charts (except for small-craft and certain other special editions) up to their date of sale. The last Notice to Mariners for which such corrections have been made is indicated by a rubber-stamp marking in the lower border near the right-hand corner.

FIG. 1817 a U.S. Coast and Geodetic Survey and Navy Department Oceanographic charts, as well as Light Lists and Coast Pilots, are corrected by Notices to Mariners. Illustrated is a typical extract showing a new marina and hydrography changes in Northport Harbor, Long Island, N.Y. Not all corrections require a reproduction from the chart affected (in this case No. 224). The amended section of chart shown is provided in the Notice as a loose insertion. The notes indicate which chart and Coast Pilot are affected.

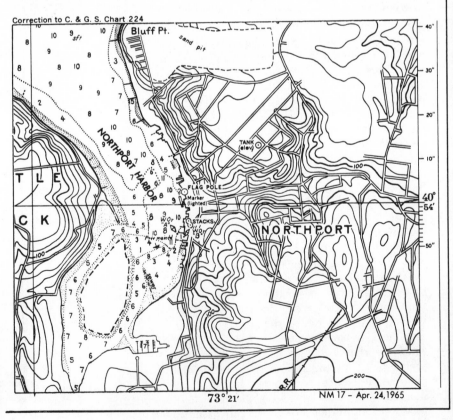

★ **(2295) LONG ISLAND SOUND—Northport Bay—Northport Harbor—Chart amendment.**—The accompanying reproduction of a portion of C. & G.S. Chart 224 shows a recently constructed marina and changes in hydrography in Northport Harbor. Approx. position: 40°54′ N., 73°21′ W.　　(N.M. 17/65.)

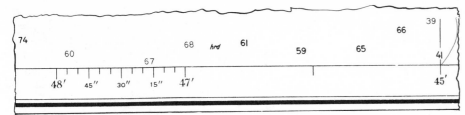

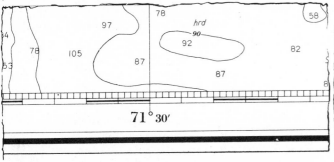

FIG. 1818(b) On charts with relatively small scales, the latitude and longitude border markings will be in minutes and fractions of minutes. On this 1:80,000 chart, meridians are drawn in every 10 minutes and the subdivisions are in minutes and tenths of minutes. On yet smaller scale charts, the smallest subdivision might be fifths, halves, or whole minutes of latitude and longitude.

By knowing what type of lettering is used for which class of information, one can more easily and quickly grasp the data being presented.

VERTICAL lettering is used for features which are dry at high water and are not affected by movement of the water, except for the height of the feature above the water, which may be changed by tidal action. See the use of vertical lettering for the power line towers and the bell fog signal in fig. 1819.

LEANING, or slanting, lettering *(such as this)* is used for water, underwater, and floating features, except depth figures. Note the use in fig. 1819 of leaning lettering for *"hrd S"* meaning a hard sand bottom at that point.

On smaller-scale charts, a small reef (covering and uncovering with tidal action) often cannot be distinguished by symbol from a small islet (always above water); the proper name for either might be "—— Rock." Following the standard of lettering, the feature in doubt is an islet if the name is in vertical letters, but is a reef if lettered in leaning characters.

Similarly, a piling visible above water at all tidal stages will be charted as "Pile," but one beneath the surface will be noted as *"subm pile."*

Periods after abbreviations are omitted in water and in land areas, but the lower-case *i* and *j* are dotted. Periods are used only where needed for clarity, as, for example, in certain notes.

WATER FEATURES

The information shown on charts is a combination of the natural features of the water and land areas and various selected man-made objects and features. Each item shown will have been carefully chosen for its value to those navigating vessels of all sizes.

Depths

The principal feature of concern to boatmen and mariners regarding water areas is the *depth*. For any system of

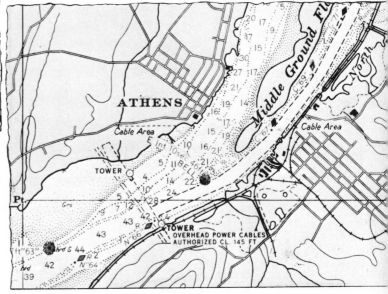

FIG. 1819 This chart excerpt illustrates the use of vertical lettering for features above water—"TOWERS," and leaning letters for underwater features—"hrd S", a hard sand bottom of the river at that point. Note also the designation of a CABLE AREA.

depth information, there must be a reference plane, or *datum*. This is obvious in coastal areas where depths may change hourly as a result of tidal action; it is likewise true in inland areas where lake or river levels may also change, though more slowly on a seasonal basis. Each chart will have printed on it a statement of the datum from which all depths, also called *soundings*, are measured. The choice of the reference plane is based on many factors, most of them technical, but the primary consideration is that of selecting a datum near to normal low-water levels.

Planes of reference

Different planes of reference are used on charts of various boating areas. For charts along the Atlantic seaboard, the Coast & Geodetic Survey uses *mean low water* as the datum for soundings. On the Pacific Coast, it is the *mean lower low water* that is used as a reference plane. (In some areas, one of the two daily low tides is markedly lower than the other—see Chapter 20 for a detailed discussion of tides.) Lake and river charts will generally use a datum which is based on past records of variations in level over many years. When entering strange waters, always be sure to check the chart for the statement of the datum used for depths.

Since by definition, "mean low water" is an average of low tide stages over a period of time, it can be seen that on approximately half the days individual low-water levels may be lower than the datum. This will result in actual depths being shallower than the charted figures. However, these variations are not often great enough to affect navigation. Many charts will have a small box with a tabulation of the extreme variations from charted depths that may be expected for various points, fig. 1820. Prolonged winds from certain directions, or persistent extremes of barometric pressure, may cause temporary local differences

TIDAL INFORMATION				
Place	Height referred to datum of soundings (MLW)			
	Mean High Water	Mean Tide Level	Mean Low Water	Extreme Low Water
	feet	feet	feet	feet
Wilmington, Del.	5.3	2.9	0.0	−4.0
Chester, Pa.	5.4	2.9	0.0	−4.0
Billingsport, N.J.	5.5	3.0	0.0	−4.5
Phila. Pier 9N., Pa.	5.8	3.1	0.0	−5.0

FIG. 1820 Coast and Harbor Charts will usually have information on the normal range of tides and the extreme variations from charted depths that may be expected. Check all newly-purchased charts for this important information.

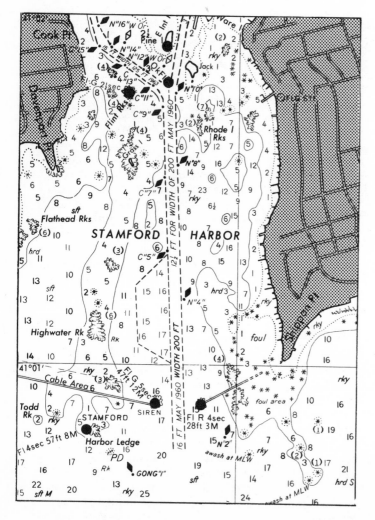

FIG. 1821 The side limits of "improved" (dredged) channels are marked by dashed lines. Information on the depth (and date of measurement) will often be printed between or alongside the dashed lines. In some cases, information on the width of the channel will also be shown.

from charted depths. *It must always be remembered that exceptional conditions may occur at which time the water may be much shallower than indicated on the chart.*

How depths are shown

Depth information is shown on the chart by many small printed figures. These indicate the depth at that point measured in units of feet or fathoms as stated in the basic information block of the chart. A few charts may mix these units of measurement, using feet in the shallower areas and fathoms offshore in deeper water; such charts, however, are relatively rare. The depth figures are only a small part of the many soundings taken by survey teams. Only the more significant and representative depths are selected for printing on the final chart.

The boatman can form some opinion of the characteristics of the bottom by noting the density of the depth information. Where depth figures are rather widely spaced, he can be assured of a reasonably flat or uniformly sloping bottom. Wherever the depths vary irregularly or abruptly, the figures will be more frequent and more closely spaced.

Fathom curves

Most charts will have *contour lines,* sometimes called *fathom curves,* connecting points of equal depth. Such lines will appear at certain depths as determined by the scale of the chart and the relative range of the depths. Typically, fathom curves are shown for 1, 2, 3 5, 10, and multiples of ten fathoms. Continuous solid lines or various combinations of dots and dashes are used to code the depth along each line, but it is often easier to learn a line's significance by inspection of the depth figures on either side of it.

On many charts, a blue tint is shown in water areas out to the curve that is considered to be the danger curve for that particular chart. In general, the 6-foot curve is considered the danger curve for small-craft and Intracoastal Waterway charts, the 12- or 18-foot curve for harbor charts, and the 30-foot curve for coast and general charts. (These types of charts are discussed in more detail on pages 326-328.) In some instances, the area between the 3-fathom and the 5- or 6-fathom curves may be tinted in a lighter shade of blue than the shallower areas. Thus it can be seen that while blue tint means shallow water, this symbolism does not have the same exact meaning on all charts. Check each chart that you use to determine at just what depth the coloring changes.

Charts on which no fathom curves are marked for water areas must be regarded with some suspicion and used with caution as this may indicate that soundings are too scarce to allow the lines to be drawn with accuracy.

Isolated soundings, shoaler than surrounding depths, should always be avoided, particularly if ringed around, as it is doubtful how closely the spot may have been examined and whether the least depth has been found.

Dredged channels

Dredged channels are shown on a chart by two dashed lines to represent the side limits of the improvement. The depth of the channel and the date on which such data were obtained will be shown within the lines or close alongside, see fig. 1821. A dredged basin will be similarly outlined with printed information on depths and date.

The depth shown, such as "6 feet 1965," is the controlling depth through the channel on the date shown but does not mean that this depth exists over the full width of the channel.

Channels are sometimes described on charts in terms of specific width as well as depth; for example, "8 feet for width of 100 feet." The printing of such depth information does not insure that it may not have subsequently changed due to either shoaling or further dredging. Such changes do occur, and therefore if your craft's draft is close to the depth shown for the channel, local information on existing conditions should be obtained if possible before entering.

Detailed information for many dredged channels is shown in tabular form on the applicable charts, with revisions of the data published in Notices to Mariners as changes occur.

Nature of the bottom

The nature of the bottom, such as sand, rocky, mud, grass, etc., or a more general description such as "hard" or "soft," will be indicated for many areas by means of abbreviations. This information is of value when anchoring, and advantage should be taken of it wherever it appears. The meanings of these and other abbreviations are usually given on the face of the chart near the basic identification block; many are self-evident, the more frequently encountered ones should be memorized.

The shoreline

The shoreline shown on charts is the mean high-water line except in marsh or mangrove areas where the outer edge of vegetation (berm line) is used. It is represented by a solid line which gradually decreases in width up streams and rivers. Unsurveyed shoreline, or shoreline connecting two surveys that do not join satisfactorily, is represented by a dashed line. The outer limits of marsh are indicated by a fine solid line. On some large-scale charts, a low-water line will be indicated by a single row of dots.

The region between the high- and low-water lines will be tinted green, and may be labeled "Grass," "Mud," "Sand," etc.

FEATURES OF LAND AREAS

Features and characteristics of land areas are shown on nautical charts in only such detail as will be of assistance to a navigator. Details are usually confined to those near the shoreline or of such a prominent nature as to be clearly seen for some distance offshore.

How topography is shown

The general topography of land areas will be indicated by contours, form lines, or hachures. *Contours* are lines connecting points of equal elevation. The specific height, usually measured in feet, of such contour lines may be shown by figures placed at suitable points along the lines. The interval of height between adjacent contours is uniform over any one chart.

Form lines, or *sketch contours,* are shown by broken lines and are approximations of contours intended to give an indication of terrain formations without exact information on height. They are used in areas where accurate data are not available in sufficient quantity to permit the exact location of contours. The interval between form lines is not necessarily uniform and no height figures are given.

Hachures are short lines, or groups of lines, indicating approximately the location of steep slopes. The lines follow generally the direction of the slope, the length of the lines indicating the height of the slope.

Cliffs, vegetation and the shore

Cliffs are represented by bands of irregular hachures. The symbol is not an exact "plan view," but rather somewhat of a "side elevation"; its extent is roughly proportional to the height of the cliff. For example, a perpendicular cliff of 100 feet height will be shown by a hachured band wider than one representing a cliff of 15 feet with

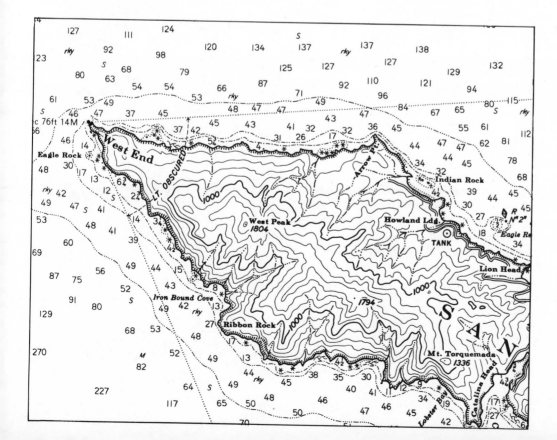

FIG. 1822 Information on the elevation of hills or mountain summits, or the tops of conspicuous landmarks, is often printed on a nautical chart. Heights are usually measured from Mean High Water.

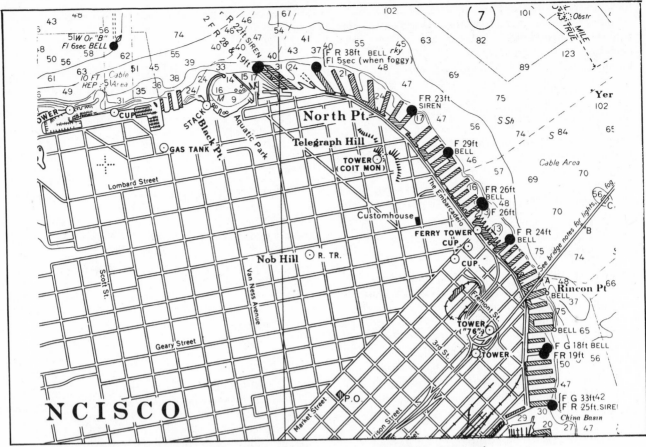

FIG. 1823 a On relatively large-scale charts, detailed information may be shown of the streets and buildings of a city or town, particularly near the waterfront. Some street names may be given, also the location of public buildings such as a customhouse and post office.

slope. According to the principles of "plan" drawing (viewing from directly above), a perpendicular cliff would be shown by one line only and could not be distinguished from an ordinary shoreline.

Spot elevations are normally given on nautical charts only for summits or the tops of conspicuous landmarks, fig. 1822. Heights are measured from mean high water.

The type of vegetation on land will sometimes be indicated by symbols or wording where such information may be of use to the mariner.

The nature of the shore is indicated by various symbols—rows of fine dots denote a sandy beach, small circles indicate gravel, irregular shapes mean boulders, etc.

MAN-MADE FEATURES

Man-made features on land will be shown in detail where they relate directly to water-borne traffic. Examples of these are piers, bridges, overhead power cables, and breakwaters. Other man-made features on land, such as built-up areas, roads, streets, etc., will be shown in some detail or will be generalized as determined by their usefulness to navigation and the scale of the chart. On large-scale charts, the actual network of streets will be exactly represented, with public buildings such as the post office and customs house individually identified, fig. 1823a. On less detailed charts, the town or city may be represented by a halftone shaded area for the approximate limits of the built-up area with major streets and roads shown by single heavy lines, see fig. 1823b. Prominent isolated objects, tanks, stacks, spires, etc., will be shown accurately

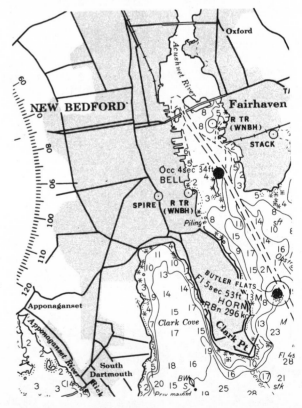

FIG. 1823 b On smaller-scale charts, cities, towns, and other built-up areas are generalized by "screening," a shading process that shows up as a darker, but not black, area. Only principal roads and streets are shown, these by a single, heavy solid line.

located in order that they may be used for taking bearings.

Specific descriptive names have been given to certain types of landmark objects for the purpose of standardizing terminology. Among the more often used are the following:

Building or **House**—the appropriate one of these terms is used when the entire structure is the landmark, rather than any individual feature of it.

Spire—a slender, pointed structure extending above a building. It is seldom less than two-thirds of the entire height of the structure, and its lines are rarely broken by intermediate structures. Spires are typically found on churches.

Dome—a large, rounded, hemispherical structure rising above a building; for example, the dome of the United States Capitol in Washington.

Cupola—a dome-shaped tower or turret rising from a building, generally small in comparison with the size of the building.

Chimney—a relatively small projection for conveying smoke from a building to the atmosphere. This term is used when the building is more prominent than the chimney, but a better bearing can be taken on the smaller feature.

Stack—a tall smokestack or chimney. This term is used when the stack is more prominent as a landmark than the accompanying buildings.

Flagpole—a single staff from which flags are displayed. This term is used when the pole is not attached to a building.

Flagstaff—a flagpole arising from a building.

Radio Tower—a tall pole or structure for elevating radio antennas.

Radio Mast—a relatively short pole or slender structure for elevating radio antennas; usually found in groups.

Tower—any structure with its base on the ground and high in proportion to its base, or that part of a structure higher than the rest, but having essentially vertical sides for the greater part of its height.

Lookout Station or **Watch Tower**—a tower surmounted by a small house from which a watch is regularly kept.

Tank—a water tank elevated high above ground by a tall skeleton framework. *Gas Tank* and *Oil Tank* are terms used for distinctive structures of specialized design.

Standpipe—a tall cylindrical structure whose height is several times its diameter.

Tree—an isolated, conspicuous tree useful as a navigational landmark.

When two similar objects are so located that separate landmark symbols cannot be used, the word "TWIN" is added to the identifying name or abbreviation. When only one of a group of similar objects is charted, a descriptive legend is added in parentheses; for example, ("TALLEST OF FOUR)" or "(NORTHEAST OF THREE)".

Radio broadcasting station (AM) antennas are shown on charts where they may be used for taking visual or radio bearings. The call letters and frequency are often shown adjacent to the symbol marking the location of the towers.

Symbols and Abbreviations

The vast amount of information to be shown on a chart, and the closeness with which many items appear, necessitate the extensive use of symbols and abbreviations. It is essential that a boatman have a high degree of familiarity with the symbols and abbreviations encountered on the charts that he uses. A skipper must be able to read and interpret his charts quickly and accurately; the safety of his boat may depend on this ability. Knowledge will come with use, but dependence upon a build-up from experience alone may be costly—specific study is recommended.

INTERNATIONAL STANDARDS

Symbols are conventional shapes and designs which indicate the presence of a certain feature or object at the location shown on the chart. No attempt is made at an accurate or detailed representation of the object, but the correct location is shown. Symbols and abbreviations used on charts prepared by the Coast & Geodetic Survey, the Naval Oceanographic Office, and the Army Engineers' Lake Survey have been standardized. These are published in a small pamphlet designated as Chart No. 1, available at 50¢ per copy. The same information is also printed on the reverse side of Training Chart No. 1210Tr. These standardized symbols and abbreviations are in general conformance with world-wide usage as adopted by the International Hydrographic Bureau.

The standardized symbols and abbreviations are shown in figures 1844 a-o; they are grouped into *classifications* and are *numbered* in accordance with Chart No. 1. In these designations, vertical figures indicate that the symbol or abbreviation is in conformity with the standards of the International Hydrographic Bureau. Slanting figures mean that the symbol or abbreviation shown either differs from that of the IHB or else that it does not appear in its standards; those items which differ from the IHB standard are underlined. Where letter designations are enclosed in parentheses, the symbol or abbreviation is in addition to those on the international list.

These standardized abbreviations will be used on all new charts or new editions by the Coast & Geodetic Survey, the Oceanographic Office, and the Lake Survey. Older charts may continue to show other symbols and abbreviations until they are next revised and brought into conformity with the standards.

Classification

In Chart No. 1, the standardized symbols and abbreviations are grouped into classifications as follows:

A—The Coast Line K—Lights
B—Coast Features L—Buoys and Beacons
C—The Land M—Radio Stations
D—Control Points N—Fog Signals
E—Units O—Dangers
F—Adjectives P—Various Limits
G—Harbors Q—Soundings
H—Topography R—Depth Contours
I—Buildings S—Quality of the Bottom
J—Miscellaneous T—Tides and Currents
Stations U—The Compass

Chart No. 1 also includes a table for the conversion of meters, fathoms, and feet.

BASIC SYMBOLS & ABBREVIATIONS

Simple inspection of many symbols will reveal a pattern or system to the way that they are formed. Knowledge of the general principles of chart symbols will facilitate learning of the details.

Buoys

Buoys, except mooring buoys, are shown by a diamond-shaped symbol and a small dot; the dot indicates the position of the buoy. To avoid interference with other features on the chart, it is often necessary to show the diamond shape at various angles to the dot; in some instances, the symbol might even appear "upside down." The symbol for a mooring buoy is number L22 in fig. 1844j; the small circle on the base line of the symbol indicates the position of the buoy.

A *black buoy* is shown as a solid black symbol without further identification of color. On charts using the normal number of colors, *red buoys* are shown in magenta; the

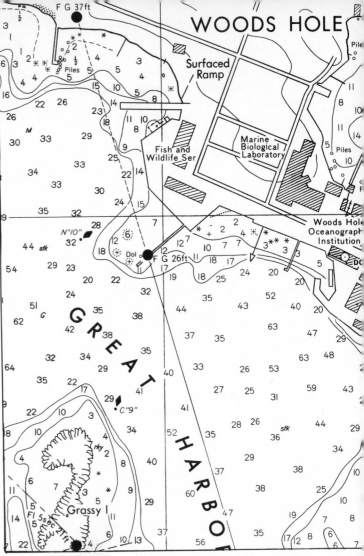

FIG. 1824 Ranges are excellent aids to navigation. They are charted by showing the front and rear markers with a line denoting the center of the range. This line is solid over the portion that is to be navigated, and dashed elsewhere.

FIG. 1825 This is a section from a "sailing chart." These charts, at scales of 1:600,000 or less, are the smallest scale series and cover long stretches of coastline. They are used by vessels approaching the coast from the high seas or when voyaging between distant coast ports.

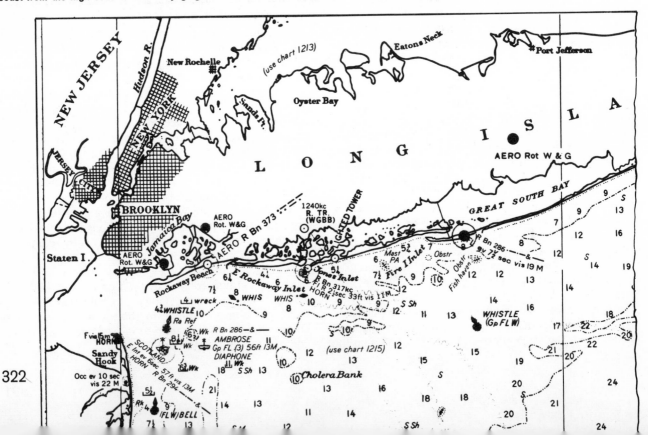

letter "R" may also be shown adjacent to the symbol. Other buoys are shown by open outline symbols with the color indicated by an appropriate abbreviation, such as "Y" for yellow, "W Or" for white and orange, etc. On charts without colors, red buoys are printed as open symbols with the identifying abbreviation "R."

A buoy symbol with a line across its shorter axis indicates a *horizontally banded buoy*. For a junction buoy, if colors are used, the upper half (away from the dot) will be red and the lower half black. This is true whether in actuality the uppermost band is red (as on a nun buoy) or black (as on a can buoy). The letters "RB" will appear near the symbol. Other kinds of horizontally banded buoys, such as white-and-orange *special purpose buoys,* will be shown by an open symbol with appropriate letters for the colors.

A buoy symbol with a line across its longer axis represents a *vertically striped buoy*. No colors will be used on this symbol; the colors of such a buoy will be indicated by abbreviations, usually "BW" for black and white.

The type and shape of *unlighted buoys* is often indicated by an abbreviation such as "C" for can, "N" for nun, or "S" for spar.

Lighted buoys are indicated by the placing of a small magenta disc over the dot which marks the buoy's position. The color and characteristics of the light are indicated by abbreviations near the symbol. Buoys equipped with a *reflector* to increase their detection by radar are often indicated by the abbreviation "Ra Ref" in addition to other identification.

Daybeacons

The symbol for *daybeacons,* unlighted aids to navigation, is a small triangle. In general, the same scheme for indicating color is used as for buoys except that two colors are not combined in a single symbol. The occasional red-and-black horizontally banded daybeacon is printed as an open symbol with the description of colors abbreviated, "RB."

Lighthouses

Lighthouses and lights are shown as black dots each with a small magenta disc as for lighted buoys. In addition to the color and characteristics of the light, there may be shown, in abbreviated form, information on the height of the light and its range of visibility (for a height of observer's eye of 15 feet above the water).

The type of *fog signal* on buoys, lights, and lighthouses so equipped will be indicated by a descriptive word or abbreviation adjacent to the chart symbol.

Identification by number

Buoys and lights are usually *numbered* (or less-frequently, designated with letters or combinations of letters and numbers). This identification is placed on the chart near the symbol and is enclosed in quotation marks to distinguish the figures from depth data or other numbers. Lighthouses and some major lights are named; the words

FIG. 1826 A small portion of C&GS Chart 1108. This is at a larger scale than Fig. 1825, but it still lacks many details. "General charts" should be used only for offshore navigation. Only major aids to navigation are shown. For comparison purposes, Figs. 1827 and 1828 show portions of this same area at progressively larger scales.

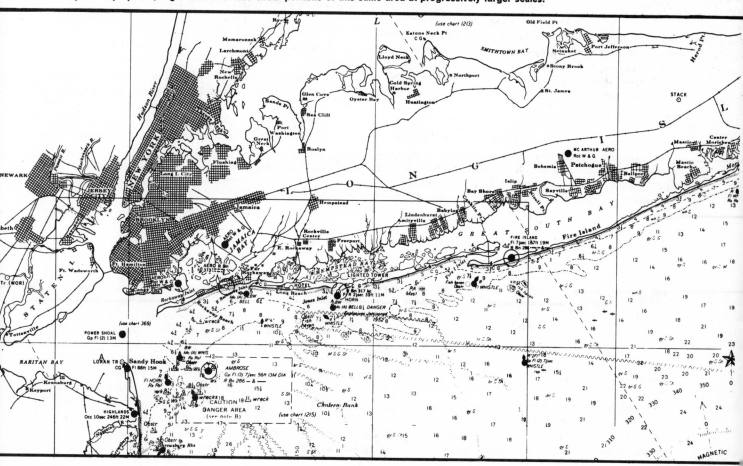

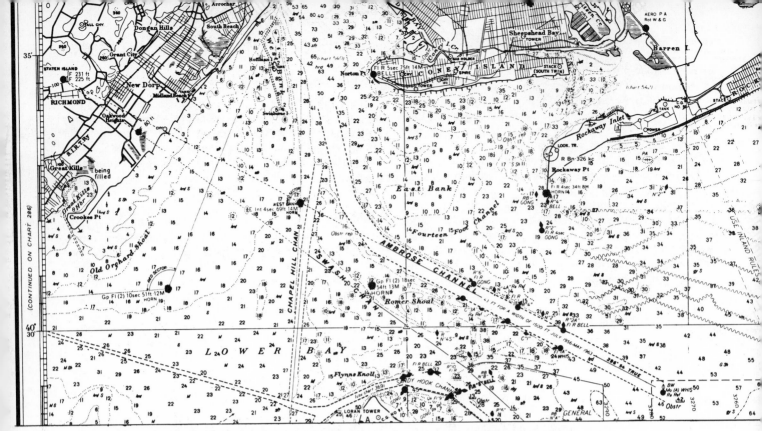

FIG. 1827 A portion of C&GS Chart 1215. "Coast charts," uusally at a scale of 1:80,000, are used for close-in coastwise navigation, entering and leaving harbors, and for cruising on some large inland bodies of water. The scale of this series is such that many more buoys and other aids to navigation can be shown. The depth of water is given in greater detail, the soundings being given in feet.

or abbreviations will be printed near the symbol where space permits.

Ranges

Ranges are indicated by the two symbols of the front and rear markers (lights or daybeacons), plus a line joining them and extending beyond. This line is solid over the distance for which the range is to be used for navigation; it continues on as a dashed line to the front marker and on to the rear marker, see fig. 1824.

Radiobeacons

Radiobeacons are indicated by a magenta circle around the basic symbol for the aid to navigation at which the beacon is located plus the abbreviation "R Bn." Aeronautical radiobeacons are shown only if they are useful for marine navigation; the same symbol is used and the iden-

tification "AERO" is added. The frequency, in kilocycles, is given, as is the identifying signal in dots and dashes of the Morse code. Aeronautical radio ranges use the same symbol as beacons plus "AERO R Rge."

Dangers to navigation

Symbols are also used for many types of *dangers to navigation*. Differentiation is made between rocks that are awash at times and those which remain below the surface at all tides, between visible wrecks and submerged ones, and between hazards which have been definitely located and those whose position is doubtful. There are a number of symbols and abbreviations for objects and areas dangerous to navigation. The prudent skipper will spend adequate time studying them, with the greatest emphasis being placed on those types commonly found in his home waters.

Chart "Series"

FOUR C & G S SERIES

As previously mentioned, charts are published in a wide range of scales. For general convenience of reference, the issuing agencies have classified charts into "series" as follows:

1. Sailing Charts—the smallest scale charts covering long stretches of coastline; for example, Cape Sable, Newfoundland to Cape Hatteras, N. C.; or the Gulf of Mexico; or San Francisco to Cape Flattery, Washington; see fig.

1825. The charts of this series are published at scales of 1:600,000 and smaller. Sailing charts are prepared for the use of the navigator in fixing his position as he approaches the coast from the open ocean, or when sailing between distant coast ports. They show the offshore soundings, the principal lights and outer buoys, and landmarks visible at great distances. Other than for ocean cruising races, the average boatman will have little use for charts in this series, except perhaps to plot the path of hurricanes and other tropical disturbances.

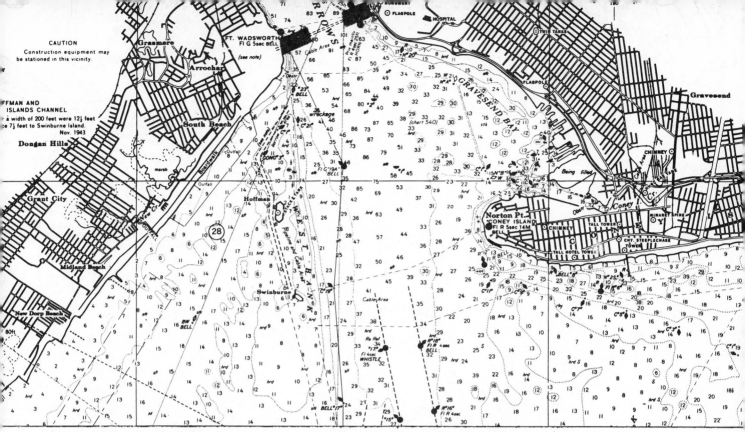

FIG. 1828 Portion of C&GS Chart 369. This extract shows some of the same area as the preceding three figures but at a greater scale and with more detail. "Harbor charts" at a scale of 1:40,000 or larger include all hazards and aids to navigation, some of which may have been omitted from smaller-scale charts. More details of features on land are also shown.

2. General Charts — the second series comprises charts with scales in the range of 1:100,000 to 1:600,000. These cover more limited areas, such as Cape May, N. J. to Cape Hatteras; or Mississippi River to Galveston Bay; or San Francisco to Point Arena, Calif. General charts are intended for coastwise navigation outside of offshore reefs and shoals when the vessel's course is mostly within sight of land and her position can be fixed by landmarks, lights, buoys, and soundings. Fig. 1826 is a portion of a general chart.

3. Coast Charts—this next larger scale series consists of charts for close-in coastwise navigation, for entering and leaving harbors, and for navigating large inland bodies of water. The scales used range from 1:50,000 to 1:100,000 with most at 1:80,000. See fig. 1827. Typical examples of coast charts are the widely-used training chart No. 1210Tr, and such navigational charts as the series of five which cover Chesapeake Bay or No. 5142 which takes the California boatman from Long Beach or Newport to Santa Catalina Island and back. The average boatman will use several charts from this series.

4. Harbor Charts — this is the largest-scale and most-detailed series, see fig. 1828. Scales will range from 1:40,000 to 1:5,000, with an occasional insert of even larger scale. The scale used for any specific chart is determined by the need for showing detail and by the desired area to be covered by a single sheet. Skippers of small craft will find this the most generally useful type of chart.

Stowage and use

C&GS charts in the four series above are printed by accurate techniques on highly durable paper. Individual charts will range in size from approximately 19x26 to 36x54 inches. As they are among the most important tools of the navigator, they should be given careful handling and proper stowage. If circumstances permit, they should be stowed flat or rolled, and in a dry place. Charts should never be folded if this can be avoided.

It is advisable that permanent corrections be made in ink so that they will not be inadvertently erased; all other lines and notations should be made lightly in pencil so that they may be erased when no longer applicable without removing permanent information or otherwise damaging the chart.

Lake Chart series

Charts of the Great Lakes published by the Lake Survey office of the Army Corps of Engineers are likewise grouped into series.

The *"general chart"* series includes one of all of the Great Lakes at a scale of 1:1,120,000, Chart No. 0. There are also separate charts for each lake at 1:500,000 or 1:400,000 scales; these are numbered 2, 3, 5, 7, and 9 from east to west.

Coast charts at a scale of 1:80,000 or 1:120,000 are designated with two-digit numbers, the first of which is the number of the general chart for that lake.

Harbor charts at scales of 1:60,000 to 1:5,000 comprise the most detailed series; these have three-digit numbers, the first two of which indicate the related coast chart. For example: Chart No. 2 covers all of Lake Ontario; Chart No. 23 is a coast chart from east of Sodus Bay, N. Y. to Rochester Harbor, N. Y.; and Chart No. 238 is the harbor chart of Rochester Harbor itself, see fig. 1829. (Note: an exception to this system occurs in upper Lake Michigan where the number series 701-706 is used for coast charts.)

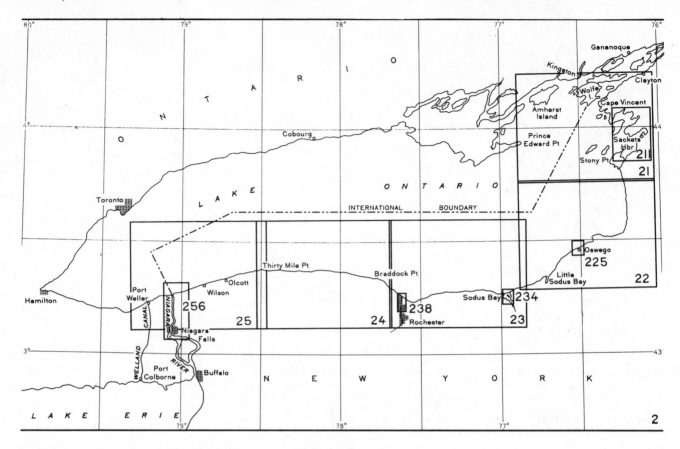

FIG. 1829 This page from the Lake Survey Chart Catalog illustrates the numbering system used in the Great Lakes and adjacent waters. Chart 2 covers all of Lake Ontario, Chart 23 a portion of the coast thereof, and Chart 238 a harbor within that portion. The charts are of a progressively larger scale, showing an increasing amount of detail.

SELECTING THE PROPER CHART

From a consideration of the four categories of charts discussed above, it will be noted that most boating areas will appear on two charts of different series, and that some will be covered by three or four charts of different scales. Such charts will vary widely in the extent of the area covered and the amount of detail shown. The selection of the proper chart to use is important.

The chart catalogs (fig. 1830 is an example of one published by the Coast & Geodetic Survey) indicate graphically the area covered by each chart. Also included is a listing giving the name, scale, and price of each chart. These catalogs provide a starting point for the selection of the proper charts for your cruise. In general, the closer you will be to shoal water and dangers to navigation, the larger you will want the scale of the chart that you are using.

What coast charts show

Coast charts show only the *major* hazards and aids to navigation, and give generalized information on depths. Some charts in this series will omit entirely any details on portions thereof which are covered by larger scale charts. For example, Narragansett Bay appears on Chart 1210, but no details at all are given, merely a small note "(Chart 353)." Other 1200 series coast charts include in their area coverage portions of the Atlantic Intracoastal Waterway, but the navigator is referred to the 800-SC ICW charts for all information on the inland route. Many coast charts include a small diagram outlining the areas covered by each larger scale chart—on No. 1210, this amounts to all or portions of 13 more-detailed charts.

What harbor charts show

Harbor charts will show more numerous soundings and *all* aids to navigation, and will permit the most accurate fixing of position from plotted bearings. The question may arise as to why ever select any but the largest-scale chart. The answer lies in the fact that as the scale is increased, the area that can be covered on a given size sheet of paper is proportionately reduced. Thus, for a cruise, many more charts of the harbor series would be required than from the coast series. Further, in some areas, continuous coverage from port to port is not possible from harbor charts alone. Another problem is that the increased number of larger-scale charts complicates the task of laying out a long run between ports.

The selection of the proper charts will usually result in a mixture of coast charts for the longer runs and harbor charts for entering ports and exploring up rivers and creeks. For some areas, one or more general charts, in addition to the coast and harbor charts, may be found useful. For example, the best route down Chesapeake Bay is more easily plotted on Charts 77 and 78 than on the series of coast charts 1226 to 1222. When you have a variety of charts on board, duplication of area coverage may result but the right chart is available for the various specific requirements.

In the margin of many charts, you will find helpful information regarding the next chart to use when you are going in a particular direction. This note will take the form of a statement such as "(Joins Chart 264)" or "(Continued on Chart 251)."

"SMALL-CRAFT" CHARTS

The charts in the four series just discussed are referred to as "conventional" charts and are intended for flat or rolled stowage. There is another category, a fifth series, which is of special interest to boatmen — these are the *Small-craft Charts* of the Coast & Geodetic Survey, designed for more convenient use in the limited space available on boats, and for folded stowage, fig. 1831. (See also color plate, page 292E.) The letters "SC" following the chart number identify charts published in this series.

The first chart in this series was 101-SC of the Potomac River. It was introduced in 1957 and immediately was popular beyond all expectations. Requests were soon received from hundreds of boatmen throughout the United States for similar coverage of their waters. The years since 1959 have seen a steadily increasing number of "SC" charts published, as well as revised editions for those already out. As of January 1966, there were 45 Small-craft editions published, with more in the planning stage.

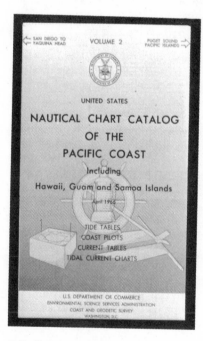

FIG. 1830 Chart Catalogs published by the various issuing agencies show the area coverage of each chart and greatly aid the skipper in the selection of the proper charts to be used in cruising unfamiliar waters. The title, scale, and prices are listed in tabular form. Shown here is one of the three volumes issued by the Coast & Geodetic Survey; all are available free upon request.

SC chart number groups

Small-craft Charts are listed in the C&GS Nautical Chart Catalog as they become available, and are placed in one of the following number groups:

1. 100-SC to 199-SC: Small-craft folios, consisting of three or four sheets printed front and back, accordion-folded, and bound in a suitable cover. (Size folded in cover 9" x 14¾".)

2. 600-SC to 699-SC: Small-craft route charts (rivers and narrow waterways).

800-SC to 899-SC: Small-craft route charts (Intracoastal Waterway).

Route charts consist of an accordion-folded single sheet printed front and back, and isued in a suitable jacket. (Size

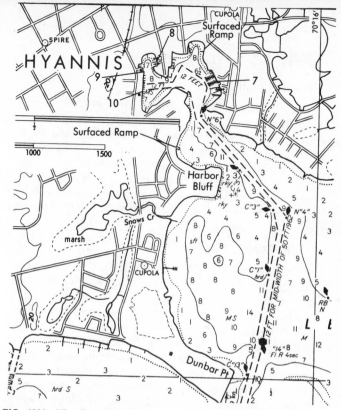

FIG. 1831 "Small-craft" Charts are a special series designed for the boatman. They are easier to use and stow, and contain added information of particular interest to the operators of power and sail boats. Included are data on boating facilities, tides and currents, weather broadcasts, etc.

folded in jacket 7¾" x 15½".)

3. 70-SC to 9500-SC (except for the number groups above): Small-craft area charts, generally conventional charts printed on a lighter-weight paper with additional information for small craft operators. They are folded once on a horizontal axis and then accordion-folded; they are issued in a protective jacket. (Size folded in jacket 7¾" x variable.)

Facilities data

A unique feature of these most-modern charts is the variety of data printed on the chart and its protective jacket, fig. 1832. No longer is it necessary to use other sources to locate repair yards and marinas; their locations are clearly marked on the chart, and the available services and supplies are tabulated on the jacket. A tide table for the year, current and marine weather information, rules of the road, signals, and warning notes are included for ready reference.

Small-craft charts make frequent use of "insets" to show such features as small creeks and harbors in greater detail. Fig. 1833 shows an inset from Chart 101-SC of the Potomac River.

Courses indicated

Many of the folio and route types of Small-craft charts will indicate a recommended track to be followed. The longer stretches of these tracks will be marked as to true or magnetic course (be sure to check which is used on that particular chart) and the distance in miles and tenths. Route charts of the Atlantic Intracoastal Waterway also have tick marks every five miles indicating the accumulated distance southward from Norfolk, Virginia to Florida, fig. 1834. Facilities along the ICW are numbered in accordance with the mileage at the point opposite the facility's location.

Revised annually

Small-craft charts are revised and reissued annually, usually to coincide with the start of the boating season in each locality. SC charts are *not* hand-corrected by the C&GS after they are printed and placed in stock. The skipper should keep his chart up-to-date between yearly editions by applying all critical changes as published in the local and weekly editions of Notices to Mariners—this is not a great chore, *if* you keep up with the changes and don't get behind!

OCEANOGRAPHIC OFFICE (HO) CHARTS

Charts of the Naval Oceanographic Office will be used by boatmen making long ocean voyages or visiting foreign waters (except Canada). In general, the presentation of information will not differ much from the more familiar C&GS charts, and few difficulties will be encountered. Symbols and abbreviations will be familiar to the coastal boatman, but land areas will be found to be tinted gray rather than buff. A standardized border has been adopted, and on charts with scales of 1:50,000 and larger, graphic scales of distances in yards and kilometers will be found in the right side and top borders respectively.

The Oceanographic Office issues special charts for the major ocean sailing races. These are regular editions of the applicable charts overprinted with additional information for the yachtsman, including the direct rhumb line, typical sailing tracks for seasonal winds, additional current data, and other useful items. The publication of these special charts is well-publicized in Notices to Mariners and boating periodicals.

It must be remembered that many HO charts are based on foreign surveys, fig. 1835. The authority for the charted information will always be given as will the date of the surveys. Check for this information, and apply appropriate judgment and caution when using charts of foreign waters; their accuracy and completeness will almost invariably be poor in comparison with C&GS charts of U.S. waters.

LAKE SURVEY CHARTS

As mentioned before, the polyconic method of projection is used for Army Engineer charts, and certain other small differences between these and C&GS charts will be noted. LS charts may use as many as four different shades of blue in denoting various depths of water nearest the shore—the deeper the shade, the shallower the water. Often courses and distances (in statute miles) will be shown for runs between important points.

FIG. 1832 Small-craft Charts are printed on lighter weight paper than those in the conventional series. These "SC" charts are then folded and placed in protective jackets. Some are bound-in (114-SC on the left) and others are merely slipped into their jackets (831-SC on the right).

The Lake Survey also issues special editions of charts for the small-craft operator. (See color plate, page 292D.) These are called "Recreational Craft Charts" and are issued in a bound volume of large-scale individual charts of special interest to boatmen.

INLAND RIVER CHARTS

Boatmen on inland rivers will use charts that are different in many respects from those used in coastal waters. Often these will be called "navigational maps" and be issued in book form with several pages covering successive stretches of a river.

Probably the most obvious difference is the usual lack of depth figures. In lieu of these, there will generally be a broken line designating the route to be followed. In order to make the best use of the paper sheet, each page may be oriented differently; north will seldom be toward the top, its actual direction being shown by an arrow. Some symbols may vary slightly in appearance from those on "salt water" charts, and additional ones may be used as required by local conditions. Distances are often designated in terms of statute miles upriver from a specified origin point.

More detailed information on river charts will be found in Chapter 28, particularly on pages 418, 424, and 430 to 437. A complete listing of where river charts and related publications can be obtained is presented on page 439.

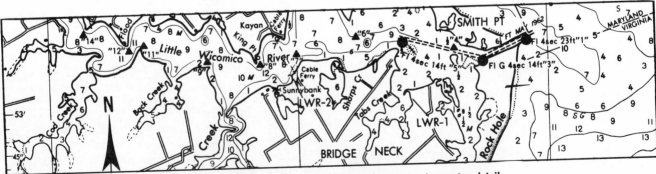

FIG. 1833 Insets are used liberally on Small-craft Charts to show local cruising areas in greater detail. This inset, No. 1 from Chart 101-SC, for the Little Wicomico River, is typical. Depths under six feet are tinted blue. Channel markers (black triangles in this reproduction) are in red and black on the original.

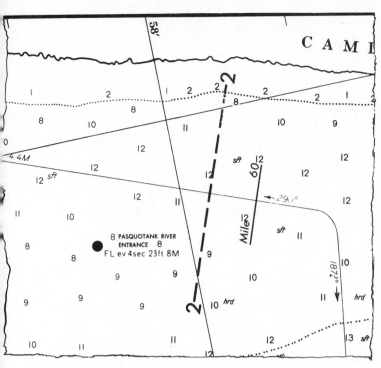

FIG. 1834 Charts of the Atlantic Intracoastal Waterway show a fine magenta line indicating the route to be followed. Tick marks are placed at five-mile intervals along this course line and are labeled with the accumulated mileage southward from Norfolk, Virginia. Passages over larger bodies of water may show information on true course and distance. The "2—2" line in the chart extract above is a matching indicator to facilitate shifting from one page of a small-craft chart to another.

CAUTIONS REGARDING USE

The production of charts is a major undertaking for the vast coastline and contiguous waterways of the United States. Our Atlantic coastline exceeds 24,500 nautical miles, the Gulf Coast 15,000 miles, the Pacific Coast 7,000 miles, and the Alaskan and Hawaiian shorelines total more than 30,000 nautical miles. The Coast & Geodetic Survey publishes more than 800 charts covering over two million square miles, and both of these figures continue to increase each year. In meeting its global responsibilities, the Naval Oceanographic Office puts out charts numbered in

the thousands, and there are, in addition, the many Army Engineer charts.

It can easily be seen that the task of keeping so many charts up-to-date is literally staggering. Surveys are constantly being made in new areas and must be rechecked in old areas. An extensive program of cooperative reporting by boatmen is used by the Coast & Geodetic Survey and the Lake Survey to supplement the information-gathering capability of the Government.

Every effort is made by the charting agencies to keep their products accurate and up-to-date with changing editions. Major disturbances of nature such as hurricanes along the Atlantic coast and earthquakes in the Pacific Northwest cause sudden and extensive changes in hydrography, and destroy aids to navigation. The everyday forces of wind and wave cause slower and less obvious changes in channels and shoals.

All boatmen must be alert to the possibility of changes in conditions and inaccuracies in charted information. Most charts will cite the authorities for the information presented and frequently the date of the information will be given. Use additional caution when the surveys date back many years.

FIG. 1835 Many charts issued by the Naval Oceanographic Office (HO Charts) are based on foreign surveys. This fact will be noted in the title block. Such charts should be used with caution, particularly if the surveys date back many years, as is often the case.

Chart Projections

The small craft skipper can safely navigate his boat without extensive knowledge of the various types of projection used in the preparation of charts. It is adequate to know that the projection of a spherical surface onto a plane surface inevitably results in some distortions; for small areas, these can be safely neglected.

As in almost any field, however, greater knowledge of the "how" and "why" will assist in understanding and using nautical charts. Hence the following paragraphs will provide additional detailed information on chart projections for those who would extend their knowledge in that direction.

The Mercator projection used in ocean and coastal waters and the polyconic projection used in inland lakes

and rivers have been mentioned earlier in this chapter. These, plus the gnomonic projection used in polar regions, will now be presented in more detail. There are many other systems of projection, but each has limited application and need not be considered here.

MERCATOR PROJECTION

The Mercator projection is often illustrated as a projection onto a cylinder. Actually, the chart is developed mathematically to allow for the known shape of the earth, which is not quite a true sphere. The meridians appear as straight, vertical lines, fig. 1836a. Here we have our first example of distortion, and it is quite obvious—the meridians no longer converge, but are now shown as being

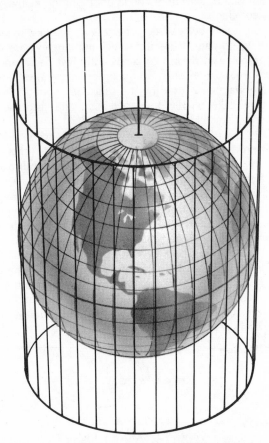

FIG. 1836 a   A Mercator projection starts with the placement of a cylinder around the earth parallel to the polar axis and touching the earth at the Equator. The meridians are projected out onto the cylinder and appear as a series of parallel straight lines when the cylinder is unrolled into a flat plane.

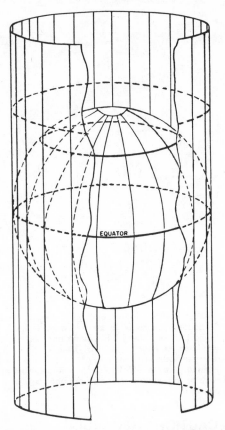

FIG. 1836 b   Parallels of latitude are projected onto the enveloping cylinder. They appear as parallel straight lines intersecting the meridians at right angles. The actual spacing of the meridians and parallels is adjusted to account for the true shape of the earth which is not an exact sphere. See text.

parallel to each other. This changes the representation of the shape of objects by stretching out their dimensions in an East-West direction.

To minimize the distortion of shape, one of the qualities that must be preserved as much as possible, there must be a stretching-out of dimensions in a North-South direction. The parallels of latitude appear as straight lines intersecting the meridians at right angles. Their spacing increases northward from the Equator, fig. 1836b, in accordance with a mathematical formula that recognizes the slightly oblate shape of the earth. This increase in spacing is not obvious in the case of charts of relatively small areas, such as in the harbor and coastal series, but it is quite apparent in Mercator projections of the world, fig. 1837, or of a large area such as covered by a sailing chart.

The Mercator projection is said to be "conformal," which means that angles are correctly represented and the scale is the same in all directions from any point.

By the Mercator technique of distortion, then counter-distortion, the shape of areas in high latitudes is correctly shown, but their size appears greater than that of similar areas in lower latitudes. An island, for example, in 60° latitude (Alaska) would appear considerably larger than an island of the same size located 25° above the equator (Florida). Its shape, however, would still be true to the actual proportions.

Advantages and disadvantages

The great value of the Mercator chart is that the meridians of longitude appear as straight lines all intersecting the parallels of latitude, also straight lines, at right angles to form an easily-used rectangular grid. Directions can be measured with reference to any meridian or any compass rose. The geographic coordinates of a position can easily be measured from the scales along the four borders of the chart. *We can draw upon a Mercator chart a straight line between two points and actually sail that course* by determining the compass direction between them; the heading is the same all along the line. Such a line is called a *rhumb* line. However, a great circle, the shortest distance between two points on the earth's surface, is a curved line on a Mercator chart; this is more difficult to calculate and plot. For moderate runs, the added distance of a rhumb line is insignificant, and this is the track that is used. Radio waves follow great circle paths and radio bearings on stations more than about 200 miles distant will require correction before being plotted on a Mercator chart.

The scale of a Mercator chart will vary with the distance away from the equator as a result of the N-S expansion. The change is unimportant on charts of small areas such as harbor and coastal charts, and the graphic scale may be used. The change in scale with latitude does become signi-

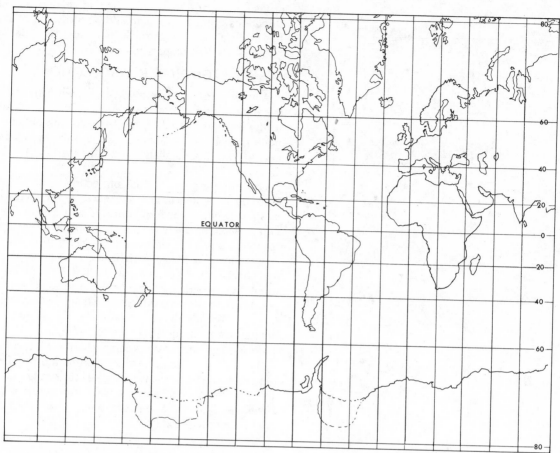

FIG. 1837 This Mercator projection of the world shows the considerable distortion in near-polar latitudes. Note that the spacing between parallels is not uniform, but increases as the distance from the Equator increases.

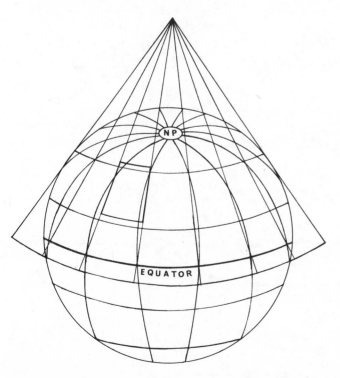

FIG. 1838 Polyconic projections are developed onto a series of cones tangent to the earth. Separate cones are used for each parallel of latitude. For clarity, the drawing above shows only one of these cones.

ficant, however, in charts covering greater areas, as on general and sailing charts. On such charts, it is necessary to measure distances using the latitude scale on either side margin, remembering that 1' of latitude is essentially 1 nautical mile. *Take care that distance is measured at a point on the latitude scale directly opposite the region of the chart being used. Never use the longitude scale at the top and bottom of the chart for measuring distance.*

POLYCONIC PROJECTION

Another form of chart construction is the *polyconic* projection. This method is based on the development of the earth's surface upon a series of cones, a different one being used for each parallel of latitude, fig. 1838. The vertex of the cone is at the point where a tangent to the earth at the specified latitude intersects the earth's axis extended. At the edges of the chart, the area between parallels is expanded to eliminate gaps.

The polyconic projection yields little distortion in shape, and relative sizes are more correctly preserved than in the Mercator projection. The scale is correct along any parallel and along the central meridian of the projection. Along other meridians, the scale increases with increased difference in longitude from the central meridian.

Parallels appear as nonconcentric arcs of circles and meridians as curved lines converging toward the pole, concave toward the central meridian, see fig. 1839. These characteristics contrast with the straight-line parallels and meridians of Mercator charts, and are the reasons why this

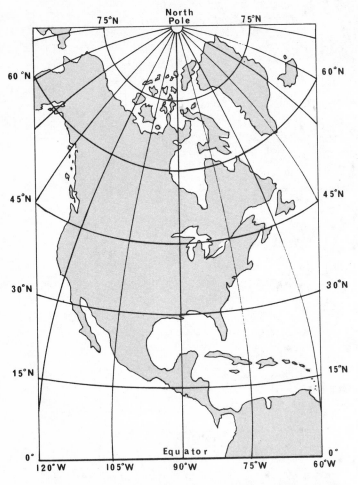

FIG. 1839 This polyconic projection of a large area emphasizes the curved characteristics of the parallels and meridians on this type of chart. Such curvatures exist on smaller area charts but are not so noticeable.

projection is not so widely used in marine navigation. Directions from any point should be measured relative to the meridian passing through that point; in actual practice, the nearest compass rose is used.

GNOMONIC PROJECTION

A *gnomonic* chart results when the meridians and parallels of latitude are projected onto a plane surface tangent to the earth at one point, fig. 1840. For the oblique case, meridians appear as straight lines converging toward the nearer pole; the parallels, except for the equator, appear as curves, fig. 1841.

Distortion is great, but this projection is used in special cases because of its unique advantage—*great circles appear as straight lines,* which of course is not so with the other two projections discussed above. Probably the easiest way to obtain a great circle track on a Mercator or polyconic chart is to draw it as a straight line on a gnomonic chart and then transfer points along the line to the other chart using the geographic coordinates for each point. The points so transferred are then connected with short rhumb lines and the result will approximate, closely enough, the great circle path, fig. 1842a and b.

A special case of gnomonic chart projection occurs when a geographic pole is selected as the point of tangency. Now all meridians will appear as straight lines, and the parallels as concentric circles. The result is a chart easily used for polar regions where ordinary Mercator charts cannot be used.

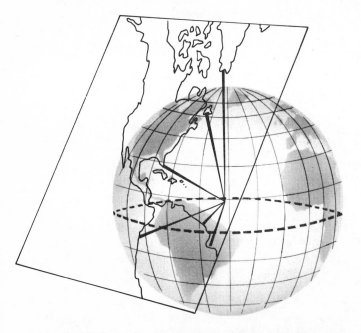

FIG. 1840 A Gnomonic projection is made by placing a plane surface tangent to the earth. Points on the earth's surface are then projected onto this plane. The point of tangency may be at any location.

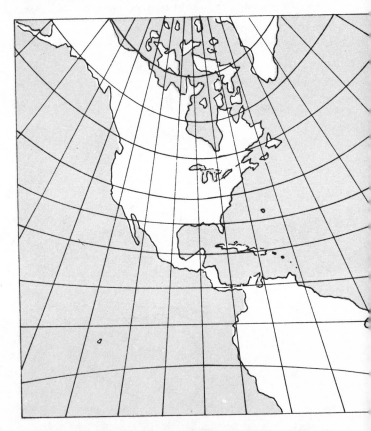

FIG. 1841 A chart made on the Gnomonic projection shows meridians as straight lines converging toward the nearer pole. The parallels, other than the Equator, appear as curves.

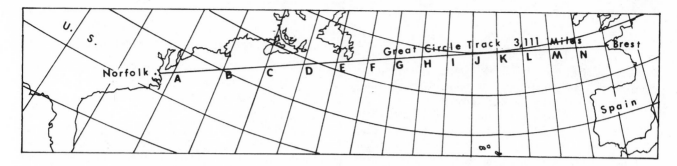

FIG. 1842 a A great circle provides the shortest distance between two points on the earth's surface, but is difficult to plot directly on a Mercator chart. An easier procedure is to draw it as a straight line on a Gnomonic chart, noting the latitude of each intersection of the track with a meridian.

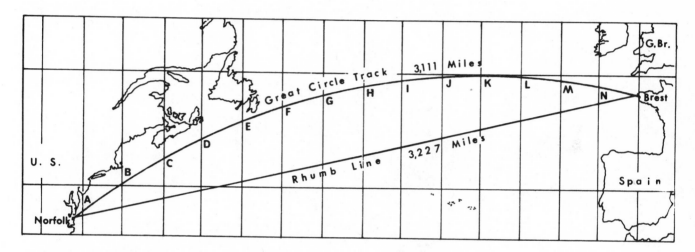

FIG. 1842 b Using the geographic coordinates of each point previously marked on the track, it is reconstructed on the Mercator chart by joining the points with short straight (rhumb) lines. This approximation can then be steered without great difficulty.

THE LAMBERT CONFORMAL PROJECTION

A projection can be made onto a single cone tangent to the earth at a single specified parallel of latitude; this is termed a *simple conic projection*. It is generally a poor projection as the scale is not correct except along the standard parallel. Areas not projected equally and correct angular relationships are not preserved.

The polyconic projection, previously considered, avoids some of these distortions, but only at the cost of the complexity of using a series of cones. Another technique to minimize the distortions of the simple conic projection is to have the cone *intersect* the earth's surface at two parallels. This general type is called a *conic projection with two standard parallels*.

If the spacing of the parallels is altered so that the distortion is the same along them as along the meridians, the projection becomes conformal, that is, the angular relationships are correctly represented, a highly desirable chart quality. This is known as the *Lambert conformal projection*. It is the most widely used conic projection,

although its use is more common among aviators than navigators. Its appearance is very much the same as the simple conic or polyconic projections. If the chart is not carried far beyond the standard parallels, and these are not a great distance apart, the distortion over the entire chart is small.

A straight line on this projection so nearly approximates a great circle that the two can be considered identical for most purposes of navigation. Radio bearings, from signals which are considered to travel great circle paths, can be plotted on a Lambert conformal chart without the correction needed when using a Mercator chart. This feature, gained without sacrificing conformality, has made this projection popular for aeronautical charts, since aircraft make much use of radio aids to navigation. It has made little headway in replacing the Mercator projection for marine navigation, except in high latitudes. In a slightly modified form, the Lambert conformal projection is sometimes used for polar charts.

PILOT CHARTS

No discussion of nautical charts would be complete without at least brief mention of a unique but valuable chart issued each month by the Naval Oceanographic Office. *Pilot Charts* present in graphic form information on ocean currents and weather probabilities for that month, plus other data of interest to a navigator. Timely articles are printed on the reverse side of each chart. They are issued in three editions—

> **(1) the North Atlantic Ocean,**
> **(2) the Greenland and Barents Seas,**
> **(3) the North Pacific Ocean.**

Fig. 1843 below, is a portion of the front side of a North Atlantic Pilot Chart.

NAUTICAL CHART MANUAL

Those desiring to know more about the basic essentials of nautical chart construction and details of the current charting practices of the Coast & Geodetic Survey might wish to purchase the "Nautical Chart Manual," 6th Edition. This 213-page manual is available from the Superintendent of Documents, U.S. Government Printing Office, Washington, D.C. 20402. The price is $6.75.

⚓

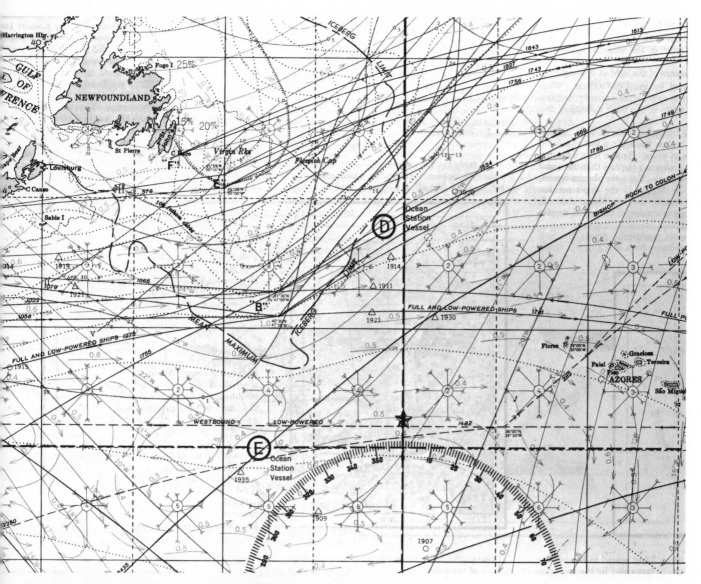

FIG. 1843 This is a small portion of the pilot chart of the North Atlantic for the month of May 1966. Dotted lines in blue on the original indicate the percentage of days in which fog can be expected for the month. The full lines represent the accepted tracks for full-powered and low-powered steamers. The wind rose (in blue on the original) in each 5-degree square shows the character of prevailing winds. Arrows fly with the wind. Length of the arrow gives percentage of the total number of observations in which the wind has blown from that point. The number of feathers shows the average force (Beaufort scale). Figures inside the circle give percentage of calms, light airs, and variable winds. Ocean station vessels (lettered red circles) supply meteorological information. The (red) long-short dashed line indicates extreme limit of ice. Outside this limit, triangles show where and when bergs have been sighted. Growlers are shown as small circles. Small (green) arrows indicate currents; velocity given in miles per day.

STANDARDIZED CHART SYMBOLS AND ABBREVIATIONS

The nautical chart can convey much or little to its user, depending upon the extent of his understanding of all those many small, odd shapes, marks, and lines. A great amount of information must be shown on a chart for safe navigation and, in many areas, there is little room for it. Thus, extensive use is made of *symbols* and *abbreviations*. To make chart reading easier, quicker, and surer, the various U.S. agencies that produce nautical charts have adopted a standardized system of abbreviations and symbols.

It is essential that a boatman have the ability to read and understand his charts rapidly and accurately. Knowledge of symbols and abbreviations is a "must" for this ability.

The standardized symbols and abbreviations are broadly grouped into classifications as follows:

A—The Coast Line
B—Coast Features
C—The Land
D—Control Points
E—Units
F—Adjectives
G—Harbors
H—Topography
I—Buildings
J—Miscellaneous Stations
K—Lights
L—Buoys and Beacons
M—Radio Stations
N—Fog Signals
O—Dangers
P—Various Limits
Q—Soundings
R—Depth Countours
S—Quality of the Bottom
T—Tides and Currents
U—The Compass

Most of the symbols used on nautical charts published by the Coast & Geodetic Survey and the Naval Oceanographic Office conform to the standards of the International Hydrographic Bureau (IHB), but a few do not. In the numbering of the symbols and abbreviations in fig. 1844 a to 1844(o) on this and the following pages, vertical figures indicate that

the designated symbol or abbreviation is in conformity with the IHB standards. Slanting figures mean that it either differs from the standard or does not appear in the international list. Where the figures are enclosed in *parentheses*, the symbol or abbreviation is in addition to those included in the IHB standards.

The symbols and abbreviations shown in fig. 1844 will be used on all CS and HO charts produced in the future. Cases may occur where older symbols still appear on charts that have not yet been revised and reissued in new editions.

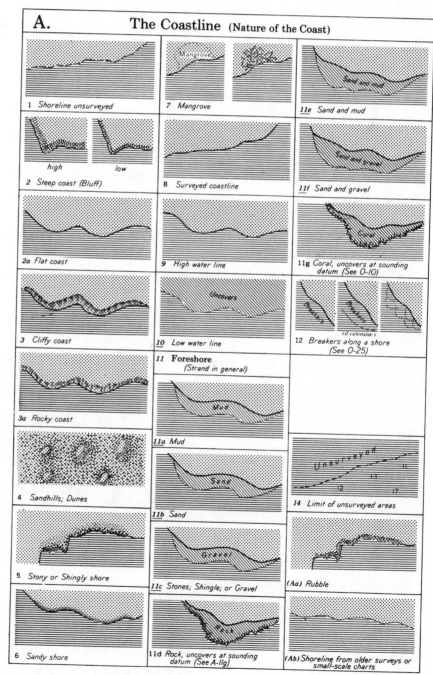

FIG. 1844 a   SYMBOLS—The coastline

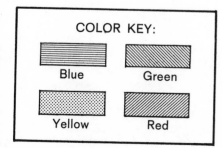

F. Adjectives, Adverbs and other abbreviations

1	gt	Great
2	lit	Little
3	lrg	Large
4	sml	Small
5		Outer
6		Inner
7	mid	Middle
8		Old
9	anc	Ancient
10		New
11	St	Saint
12	conspic	Conspicuous
13		Remarkable
14	D.. Destr	Destroyed
15		Projected
16	dist	Distant
17	abt	About
18		See chart
18a		See plan
19		Lighted, Luminous
20	sub	Submarine
21		Eventual
22	AERO	Aeronautical
23		Higher
24	exper	Experimental
25	discontd	Discontinued
26	prohib	Prohibited
27	explos	Explosive
28	estab	Established
29	elec	Electric
30	priv	Private, Privately
31	prom	Prominent
32	std	Standard
33	subm	Submerged
34	approx	Approximate
(Fa)	unverd	Unverified
(Fb)	AUTH	Authorized
(Fc)	CL	Clearance
(Fd)	maintd	Maintained
(Fe)	aband	Abandoned
(Ff)	cor	Corner
(Fg)	concr	Concrete
(Fh)	fl	Flood
(Fi)	extr	Extreme
(Fj)	mod	Moderate
(Fk)	bet	Between
(Fl)	1st	First
(Fm)	2nd	Second
(Fn)	3rd	Third
(Fo)	4th	Fourth

D. Control Points

1	△	Triangulation point (station)
2	⊙	Fixed point (landmark) (See L-63)
3	·256	Summit of height (Peak) (when not a landmark)
(Da)	◉256	Peak, accentuated by contours
(Db)	⊕256	Peak, accentuated by hachures
(Dc)		Peak, elevation not determined
(Dd)	⊙256	Peak, when a landmark
4	Obs Spot	Observation spot
5	BM	Bench mark
6	See View	View point
7		Datum point for grid of a plan
8	Astro	Graphical triangulation point / Astronomical
9	Tri	Triangulation
10	C of E	Corps of Engineers
(De)		Great trigonometrical survey station
12		Traverse station
13	Bdy. Mon	Boundary monument
(Df)	◇	International boundary monument

E. Units

1	hr	Hour
2	m: min	Minute (of time)
3	sec	Second (of time)
4	m	Meter
4a	dm	Decimeter
4b	cm	Centimeter
4c	mm	Millimeter
4d	m²	Square meter
4e	m³	Cubic meter
5	km	Kilometer
6	in	Inch
7	ft	Foot
8	yd	Yard
9	fm	Fathom
10	cbl	Cable length
11	M	Nautical mile
12	kn	Knot
12a	t	Ton
12b	cd	Candela (new candle)
13	lat	Latitude
14	long	Longitude
15	pub	Publication
16	Ed	Edition
17	corr	Correction
18	alt	Altitude
19	ht; elev	Height; Elevation
20	°	Degree
21	'	Minute (of arc)
22	"	Second (of arc)
23	No	Number
(Ea)	St. M	Statute mile
(Eb)	Msec	Microsecond

FIG. 1844 c Control points, units, adjectives, adverbs

B. Coast Features

1	G	Gulf
2	B	Bay
(Ba)	B	Bayou
3	Fd	Fjord
4	L	Loch; Lough; Lake
5	Cr	Creek
5a	C	Cove
6	In	Inlet
7	Str	Strait
8	Sd	Sound
9	Pass	Passage; Pass
10	Thoro	Thorofare
10a	Chan	Channel
10a		Narrows
11	Entr	Entrance
12	Est	Estuary
12a		Delta
13	Mth	Mouth
14	Rd	Road; Roadstead
15	Anch	Anchorage
16	Hbr	Harbor
16a	Hn	Haven
17	P	Port
(Bb)	P	Pond
18	I	Island
19	It	Islet
20	Arch	Archipelago
21	Pen	Peninsula
22	C	Cape
23	Prom	Promontory
24	Hd	Head; Headland
25	Pt	Point
26	Mt	Mountain; Mount
27	Rge	Range
27a		Valley
28		Summit
29	Pk	Peak
30	Vol	Volcano
31		Hill
32	Bld	Boulder
33	Ldg	Landing
34		Table-land (Plateau)
35	Rk	Rock
36		Isolated rock
(Bc)	Str	Stream
(Bd)	R	River
(Bf)	Slu	Slough
(Bg)	Lag	Lagoon
(Bg)	Apprs	Approaches
(Bh)	Rky	Rocky

C. The Land (Natural Features)

- 1 Contour lines (Contours)
- 1a Contour lines, approximate (Contours)
- 2 Hachures
- 2a Form lines, no definite interval
- 2b Shading
- 3 Glacier
- 4 Saltpans
- TREE / 5 Isolated trees
- 5a Deciduous or of unknown type
- 5b Coniferous
- 5c Palm tree
- 5d Nipa palm
- 5e Filao
- 5f Casuarina
- Cultivated
- 6 Cultivated fields
- 6a Grass; Grass fields
- 7 Rice; Paddy (rice) fields
- 7a Park; Garden
- 8 Bushes; Bushes
- 8a Tree plantation in general
- 9 Wooded; Deciduous woodland
- 10 Wooded; Coniferous woodland
- 10a Wooded; Woods in general
- 11 Tree top elevation (above height datum) 2560
- 12 Lava flow
- 13 River; Stream
- 14 Intermittent stream
- 15 Lake; Pond
- 16 Lagoon (Lag)
- Symbol used in small areas
- Swamp
- 17 Marsh, Swamp
- 18 Slough (Slu.)
- 19 Rapids
- 20 Waterfalls
- 21 Spring

FIG. 1844 b Features of the coast and natural features of the land

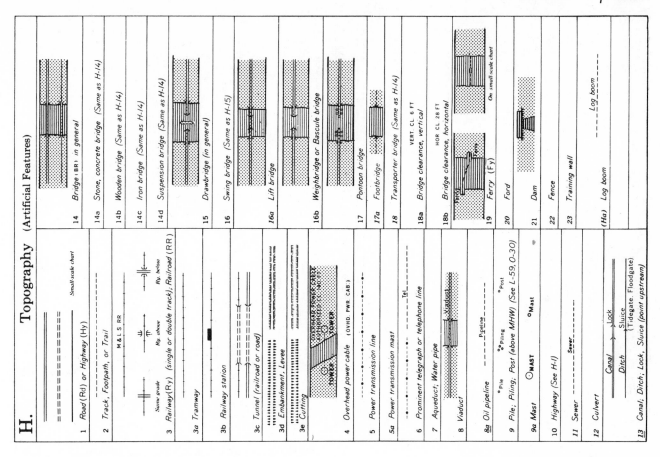

1844 e   Artificial features of topography

FIG. 1844 d   Ports and harbors

I. Buildings and Structures (continued)

No.	Abbrev.	Description
71		Gas tank; Gasometer
72	GAB °Gab	Gable
73		Wall
(Ii)	Ltd	Limited
(Ij)	Apt	Apartment
(Ik)	Cap	Capitol
(Il)	Co	Company
(Im)	Corp	Corporation
(In)	⊙	Landmark (conspicuous object)
(Io)	°	Landmark (position approx.)

J. Miscellaneous Stations

No.	Abbrev.	Description
1	Sta	Any kind of station
2	Sta	Station
3		Coast Guard station (Similar to LS. S.)
(Ja)	C.G. WALLIS SANDS	Coast Guard station (when landmark)
4	LOOK.TR	Lookout station; Watch tower
5		Lifeboat station
6	R.L.S.	Lifesaving station (See J-3)
7	Rkt. Sta	Rocket station
8	PIL. STA	Pilot station
9	Sig. Sta	Signal station
10	Sem	Semaphore
11	S. Sig. Sta	Storm signal station
12	W.B. SIG. STA	Weather signal station
(Jb)	W.B. SIG. STA	Weather Bureau signal station
13		Tide signal station
14		Stream signal station
15		Ice signal station
16		Time signal station
17		Time ball
18		Signal mast
19	FS °FP	Flagstaff;-Flagpole
20	F. TR	Flag tower
(Jc)	FS	Signal
21	Obsy	Observatory
22	Off	Office
(Jd)	BELL	Bell (on land)
(Je)	HECP	Harbor entrance control post

FIG. 1844 g   Other buildings and structures, and miscellaneous stations

FIG. 1844 f   Buildings and structures

I. Buildings and Structures (see General Remarks)

No.	Abbrev.	Description
1		City or Town (large scale)
(Ia)		City or Town (small scale)
2		Suburb
3	Vil	Village
3a		Buildings in general
4	Cas	Castle
5	□	House
6		Villa
7		Farm
8	Ch	Church
8a	Cath	Cathedral
8b	SPIRE Spire	Spire; Steeple
8c		Christian Shrine
9		Roman Catholic Church
10		Temple
11		Chapel
12		Mosque; Minaret
(Ib)		Moslem Shrine
13		Marabout
14	Pag	Pagoda
15		Buddhist Temple, Joss-House
15a		Shinto Shrine
16		Monastery; Convent
17		Calvary; Cross
17a		Cemetery, Non-Christian
18	Cem	Cemetery, Christian
18a		Tomb
19		Fort (actual shape charted)
20		Battery (Same as 1-19)
21		Barracks
22		Powder magazine
23	Airport	Airplane landing field
24	Airport	Airport, large scale (See P-13)
(Ic)		Airport, military (small scale)
(Id)		Airport, civil (small scale)
25		Mooring mast
26	King St St	Street
26a	Locust Ave Ave	Avenue
(Ie)	Grand Blvd Blvd	Boulevard
27	Tel	Telegraph
28	Tel.Off	Telegraph office
29	P.O.	Post office
30	Govt. Ho	Government house
31		Town hall
32	Hosp	Hospital
33		Slaughterhouse
34	Magz	Magazine
34a		Warehouse; Storehouse
35	MON °Mon	Monument
36	CUP °Cup	Cupola
37	ELEV °Elev	Elevator; Lift
(If)	Elev	Elevation; Elevated
38		Shed
39		Zinc roof
40	Ru	Ruins
41	TR Tr	Tower
42	WINDMILL	Windmill
43		Watermill
43a	WINDMOTOR	Windmotor
44	CHY °Chy	Chimney; Stack
45	SPIPE S'pipe	Water tower; Standpipe
46		Oil tank
47	Facty	Factory
48		Saw mill
49		Brick kiln
50		Mine, Quarry
51	Well	Well
52		Cistern
53	TANK °Tk	Tank
54		Noria
55		Fountain

K. Lights (continued)

69		Unwatched light
70	Occas	Occasional light
71	Irreg	Irregular light
72	Prov	Provisional light
73	Temp	Temporary light
(Kg)	D;Destr	Destroyed
74	Exting	Extinguished light
75		Faint light
76		Upper light
77		Lower light
78		Rear light
79		Front light
80	Vert	Vertical lights
81	Hor	Horizontal lights
(Kh)	VB	Vertical beam
(Ki)	RGE	Range
(Kj)	Exper	Experimental light
(Kk)	TRLB	Temporarily replaced by lighted buoy showing the same characteristics
(Kl)	TRUB	Temporarily replaced by unlighted buoy
(Km)	TLB	Temporary lighted buoy
(Kn)	TUB	Temporary unlighted buoy

L. Buoys and Beacons (see General Remarks)

1		Position of buoy
2	BELL	Bell buoy
3	GONG	Gong buoy
3a	WHIS	Whistle buoy
4		Can or Cylindrical buoy
5		Nun or Conical buoy
6		Spherical buoy
7	SP	Spar buoy
8		Pillar buoy
8a		Buoy with topmark (ball) (See L-70)
9		Barrel or Ton buoy
10		
(La)		Color unknown
(Lb)	FLOAT	Float
12	FLOAT	Lightfloat
13		Outer or Landfall buoy
14	BW	Fairway buoy (BWVS)
14a	BW	Mid-channel buoy (BWVS)
15		Starboard-hand buoy (entering from seaward)
16		Port-hand buoy (entering from seaward)
17	RBHB	Bifurcation buoy (RBHB)
18	RBHB	Junction buoy (RBHB)
19	RBHB	Isolated danger buoy (RBHB)
20	RBHB	Wreck buoy (RBHB or G)
20a	RBHB	Obstruction buoy (RBHB or G)
21		Telegraph-cable buoy
22		Mooring buoy (colors of mooring buoys never carried)
22a		Mooring
22b		Mooring buoy with telegraphic communications
22c		Mooring buoy with telephonic communications
23		Warping buoy
24		Quarantine buoy
25	Explos Anch	Explosive anchorage buoy
25a	AERO	Aeronautical anchorage buoy
26	Deviation	Compass adjustment buoy
27	BW	Fish trap buoy (BWHB)
27a	BW	Spoil ground buoy
28	BW	Anchorage buoy (marks limits)
29	Priv maintd	Private buoy (maintained by private interests, use with caution)

FIG. 1844 i   Other lights, buoys and beacons

FIG. 1844 h   Lights

K. Lights

1		Position of light
2	Lt	Light
(Ka)		Riprap surrounding light
3	Lt Ho	Lighthouse
4	AERO	Aeronautical light (See F-22)
4a		Marine and air navigation light
5	Bn	Light beacon
6		Light vessel; Lightship
8		Lantern
9		Street lamp
10	REF	Reflector
11	Ldg Lt	Leading light
12		Sector light
13		Directional light
14		Harbor light
15		Fishing light
16		Tidal light
17		Private light (maintained by private interests; to be used with caution)
21	F	Fixed light
22	Occ	Occulting light
23	Fl	Flashing light
24	Qk Fl	Quick flashing (scintillating) light
24a	I Qk Fl / Int Qk Fl	Interrupted quick flashing light
(Kb)	E Int	Equal interval (isophase) light
25a	S Fl	Short flashing light
26	Alt	Alternating light
27	Gp Occ	Group occulting light
28	Gp Fl	Group flashing light
28a	S-L Fl	Short-long flashing light
28b		Group short flashing light
29	F Fl	Fixed and flashing light
30	F Gp Fl	Fixed and group flashing light
31	Rot	Revolving or Rotating light
(Kbb)	Mo	Morse code
41		Period
42		Every
43		With
44		Visible (range)
(Kc)	M	Nautical mile (See E-11)
(Kd)	m; min	Minutes (See E-2)
(Ke)	sec	Seconds (See E-3)
45	Fl	Flash
46	Occ	Occultation
46a		Eclipse
47	Gp	Group
48	Occ	Intermittent light
49	SEC	Sector
50		Color of sector
51	Aux	Auxiliary light
52		Varied
61	Vi	Violet
62		Purple
63	Bu	Blue
64	G	Green
65	Or	Orange
66	R	Red
67	W	White
67a	Am	Amber
68	OBSC	Obscured light
(Kl)	Fog Det Lt	Fog detector light (See Nb)

M. Radio and Radar Stations

No.	Symbol	Description	No.	Symbol	Description
1	°R. Sta	Radio telegraph station	12	Racon	Radar responder beacon
2	°R. T	Radio telephone station	13	Ra Ref	Radar reflector (See Li)
3	R. Bn	Radiobeacon	14	Ra (conspic)	Radar conspicuous object
4	R. Bn	Circular radiobeacon	14a		Ramark
5	R.D	Directional radiobeacon; Radio range	15	D.F.S	Distance finding station (synchronized signals)
6		Rotating loop radiobeacon	(Mc)	AERO R. Bn 302	Aeronautical radiobeacon
7	R.D.F	Radio direction finding station	(Md)	AERO R. Rge 342	Aeronautical radio range
(Ma)	TELEM ANT	Telemetry antenna	(Me)	Ra Ref Calibration Bn	Radar calibration beacon
9	R. MAST	Radio mast	(Mf)	CONSOL Bn 190 Kc MMF	Consol (Consolan) station
	R. TR	Radio tower	(Mg)	Loran Sta Venice	Loran station (name)
(Mb)	TV TR	Television tower	(Mh)	LORAN TR SPRING ISLAND	Loran tower (name)
10	R. TR. (WBAL) 1090 Kc	Radio broadcasting station (commercial)	(Mi)	10	Radio calling-in point for traffic control
10a	°R. Sta	Q.T.G. Radio station			
11	Ra	Radar station			

N. Fog Signals

No.	Symbol	Description	No.	Symbol	Description
1	Fog Sig	Fog-signal station	12	HORN	Fog trumpet
2		Radio fog-signal station	13	HORN	Fog horn
3	GUN	Explosive fog signal	14	BELL	Fog bell
4		Submarine fog signal	15	WHIS	Fog whistle
5	SUB-BELL	Submarine fog bell (action of waves)	16	HORN	Reed horn
6	SUB-BELL	Submarine fog bell (mechanical)	17	GONG	Fog gong
7	SUB-OSC	Submarine oscillator	18		Submarine sound signal not connected to the shore (See N-5,6,7)
8	NAUTO	Nautophone	18a		Submarine sound signal connected to the shore (See N-5,6,7)
9	DIA	Diaphone	(Na)	HORN	Typhon
10	GUN	Fog gun	(Nb)	Fog Det Lt	Fog detector light (See Kf)
11	SIREN	Fog siren			

FIG. 1844 k   Radio and radar stations, fog signals

FIG. 1844 j   Buoys and beacons (continued)

L. Buoys and Beacons (continued)

No.	Symbol	Description	No.	Symbol	Description
30		Temporary buoy (See Kk,l,m,n)	55		Cardinal marking system
30a		Winter buoy	56	Deviation Bn	Compass adjustment beacon
31	HB	Horizontal stripes or bands	57		Topmarks (See L-9,70)
32	VS	Vertical stripes	58		Telegraph-cable (landing) beacon
33	Chec	Checkered	59	Piles	Piles (See O-30, H-9)
(Lc)	Diag	Diagonal buoy			Stakes
41	W	White		Stumps	Stumps (See O-30)
42	B	Black			Perches
43	R	Red	61	CAIRN / Cairn	Cairn
44	Y	Yellow	62		Painted patches
45	G	Green	63		Landmark (conspicuous object) (See D-2)
46	Br	Brown	(Lg)		Landmark (position approximate)
47	Gy	Gray	64	REF	Reflector
48	Bu	Blue	65	MARKER	Range targets, markers
(Ld)	Am	Amber	(Lh)	W Or / W Or	Special-purpose buoys
(Le)	Or	Orange	70	Note:	TOPMARKS on buoys and beacons may be shown on charts of foreign waters. The abbreviation for black is not shown adjacent to buoys or beacons.
51		Floating beacon			
52	RW Bn / W Bn / R Bn ; Bn ; Bn	Fixed beacon (unlighted or daybeacon); Black beacon; Color unknown			
(Lf)	MARKER	Private aid to navigation			
53	Bn	Beacon, in general (See L-52)	(Li)	Ra Ref	Radar reflector (See M-13)
54		Tower beacon			

Q. Soundings

No.	Symbol	Description
1	SD	Doubtful sounding
2	65̄	No bottom found
3		Out of position
4		Least depth in narrow channel
5	30 FEET APR 1958	Dredged channel (with controlling depth indicated)
6	24 FEET MAY 1958	Dredged area
7		Swept channel (See Q-9)
8		Drying or uncovering height in feet above chart (sounding) datum
9		Swept area, not adequately sounded (shown by green tint)
9a		Swept area adequately sounded (swept by wire drag to depth indicated)
10		Hair-line depths
10a	8₂ 19	Figures for ordinary soundings
11	8₂ 19	Soundings taken from foreign charts
12	8₂ 19	Soundings taken from older surveys or smaller scale charts
13	8₂ 19	Soundings taken by echo
14	8₂ 19	Sloping figures (See Q-12)
15	8₂ 19	Upright figures (See Q-10a)
16	(25) (2)	Bracketed figures (See O-1, 2)
17	6	Underlined sounding figures (See Q-8)
18	3₂ 6₁	Soundings expressed in fathoms and feet
(Qa)		Stream

P. Various Limits, etc.

1		Leading line, Range line
2		Transit
3		In line with
4		Limit of sector
5		Channel, Course, Track recommended (marked by buoys or beacons)(See P-21)
(Pa)		Alternate course
6		Leader cable
7		Submarine cable (power, telegraph, telephone, etc.)
7a	Cable Area	Submarine cable area
8	Pipeline	Submarine pipeline
8a	Pipeline Area	Submarine pipeline area
9	RESTRICTED AREA	Maritime limit in general
9a		Limit of restricted area
10		Limit of fishing zone (fish trap areas)
11		Limit of dumping ground, spoil ground (See P-9, G-13)
12		Anchorage limit
13		Limit of airport (See I-23, 24)
14		Limit of sovereignty (Territorial waters)
15		Customs boundary
16		International boundary (also State boundary)
17		Stream limit
18		Ice limit
19		Limit of tide
20		Limit of navigation
21	COURSE 095°00′ TRUE	Course recommended (not marked by buoys or beacons)(See P-5)
22		District or province limit
23		Reservation line
24	MARKERS MARKERS	Measured distance
25	PROHIBITED AREA	Prohibited area (See G-12)

FIG. 1844 m Various limits, and soundings

FIG. 1844-1 Dangers

O. Dangers

No.	Symbol	Description
1	⌀(25)	Rock which does not cover (elevation above MHW) (See general remarks)
	*Uncov 2 ft Uncov 2 ft *(2) (2)	
2		Rock which covers and uncovers, with height in feet above chart (sounding) datum
3		Rock awash at the level of chart (sounding) datum
	When rock of O-2 or O-3 is considered a danger to navigation (Same as O-26)	
4		Sunken rock with less than 6 feet of water over it (Same as O-26)
5		Sunken rock with between 6 and 33 ft of water over it (Same as O-26)
5a	(5) Rk	Shoal sounding on isolated rock (replaces symbol)
6		Sunken rock with more than 66 feet of water over it (Same as O-26)
	(2) Rk (2) Wk (2) Obstr	
6a		Sunken danger with depth cleared by wire drag (in feet or fathoms)
7		Reef of unknown extent
8	⌒ Sub Vol	Submarine volcano
9	Discol Water	Discolored water
10	Coral	Coral or Rocky reef, covered at sounding datum (See A-11d, 11g)

No.	Symbol	Description
11	⌀(25) Obstr	Wreck showing any portion of hull or superstructure above sounding datum
27	Obstruction	Obstruction
28	Wreck (See O-11 to 16)	
	Masts	Wreckage Wks
12		Wreck with only masts visible above sounding datum
13		Old symbols for wrecks
29	Wreckage	
29a		Wreck remains (dangerous only for anchoring)
13a		Wreck always partially submerged
30	Subm piles	Submerged piling (See H-9, L-59)
14		Sunken wreck which may be dangerous to surface navigation (See O-6a)
	Snags Stumps	
30a		Snags; Submerged stumps (See L-59)
15	(5) Wk	Wreck over which depth is known
31		Lesser depth, possible
16		Sunken wreck, not dangerous to surface navigation
32	Uncov Dres(See A-10; O-2, 10)	
33	Cov Covers (See O-2, 10)	
34	Uncov Uncovers (See A-10; O-2, 10)	
17	Foul	Foul ground
35	(3) Rep (1958)	Reported (with date)
	Eagle Rk (rep 1958)	Reported (with name and date)
18	Tide Rips Overfalls or Tide rips	Symbol used only in small areas
36	Discol Discolored (See O-9)	
37		Isolated danger
19	Eddies Eddies	Symbol used only in small areas
20	Kelp Kelp, Seaweed	Symbol used only in small areas
38		Limiting danger line
21	Bk Bank	
22	Shl Shoal	
39		Limit of rocky area
23	Rf Reef (See A-11d, 11g; O-10)	
23a	Ridge	
24	Le Ledge	
41	P A Position approximate	
42	P D Position doubtful	
43	E D Existence doubtful	
44	P Pos Position	
45	D Doubtful	
25	Breakers (See A-12)	
	Subm Crib Crib (above water)	
(Oa)	Crib	
26	Sunken rock (depth unknown)	
	Platform (lighted) HORN	
(Ob)		Offshore platform (unnamed)
	When rock is considered a danger to navigation	
	Hazel (lighted) HORN	
(Oc)		Offshore platform (named)

U. Compass

Compass Rose (VAR 14° 40' W (1963), ANNUAL INCREASE 2', MAGNETIC)

The outer circle is in degrees with zero at true north. The inner circles are in points and degrees with the arrow indicating magnetic north.

No.	Symbol	Meaning
1	N	North
2	E	East
3	S	South
4	W	West
5	NE	Northeast
6	SE	Southeast
7	SW	Southwest
8	NW	Northwest
9	N	Northern
10	E	Eastern
11	S	Southern
12	W	Western
21	brg	Bearing
22		True
23	mag	Magnetic
24	var	Variation
25		Annual change
25a		Annual change nil
26		Abnormal variation, Magnetic attraction
27	deg	Degrees (See E-20)
28	dev	Deviation

T. Tides and Currents

No.	Symbol	Meaning
1	HW	High water
1a	HHW	Higher high water
2	LW	Low water
(Ta)	LWD	Low water datum
2a	LLW	Lower low water
3	MTL	Mean tide level
4	MSL	Mean sea level
4a		Elevation of mean sea level above chart (sounding) datum
5		Chart datum (datum for sounding reduction)
6	Sp	Spring tide
7	Np	Neap tide
8	MHWS	Mean high water springs
8a	MHWN	Mean high water neaps
8b	MHHW	Mean higher high water
(Tb)	MHW	Mean high water
9	MLWS	Mean low water springs
9a	MLWN	Mean low water neaps
9b	MLLW	Mean lower low water
(Tc)	MLW	Mean low water
10	ISLW	Indian spring low water
11		High water full and change (vulgar establishment of the port)
12		Low water full and change
13		Mean establishment of the port
13a		Establishment of the port
14		Unit of height
15		Equinochial
16	Str.	Quarter; Quadrature
17		Stream
18		Current, general, with rate
19		Flood stream (current) with rate
20		Ebb stream (current) with rate
21		Tide gauge; Tidepole; Automatic tide gauge
23	vel.	Velocity, Rate
24	kn.	Knots
25	ht.	Height
26		Tide
27		New moon
28		Full moon
29		Ordinary
30		Syzygy
31	fl.	Flood
32		Ebb
33		Tidal stream diagram
34		Place for which tabulated tidal stream data are given
35		Range (of tide)
36		Phase lag
(Td)		Current diagram, with explanatory note

FIG. 1844 o   Tides and currents, the compass

FIG. 1844 n   Depth contours and tints, quality of the bottom

R. Depth Contours and Tints (see General Remarks)

Feet	Fathoms
0	0
6	1
12	2
18	3
24	4
30	5
36	6
60	10
120	20
180	30
240	40

Feet	Fathoms
300	50
600	100
1,200	200
1,800	300
2,400	400
3,000	500
6,000	1,000
12,000	2,000
18,000	3,000

Or continuous lines, with values

black) 5 ——— 100 (blue or

S. Quality of the Bottom

1		Ground
2	S	Sand
3	M	Mud; Muddy
4	Oz	Ooze
5	Ml	Marl
6	Cl	Clay
7	G	Gravel
8	Sn	Shingle
9	P	Pebbles
10	St	Stones
11	Rk; rky	Rock; Rocky
11a	Blds	Boulders
12	Ck	Chalk
12a	Ca	Calcareous
13	Qz	Quartz
13a		Schist
14	Co	Coral
(Sa)	Co Hd	Coral head
15	Mds	Madrepores
16	Vol	Volcanic
(Sb)	Vol Ash	Volcanic ash
17	La	Lava
18	Pm	Pumice
19	T	Tufa
20	Sc	Scoriae
21	Cn	Cinders
22	Mn	Manganese
23	Sh	Shells
24	Oys	Oysters
25	Ms	Mussels
26	Spg	Sponge
27		Kelp
28	Wd	Seaweed
29	Grs	Grass
		Seatangle
31		Spicules
32	Fr	Foraminifera
33	Gl	Globigerina
34	Di	Diatoms
35	Rd	Radiolaria
36	Pt	Pteropods
37	Po	Polyzoa
38		Cirripeda
38a		Fucus
38b		Mattes
39	fne	Fine
40	crs	Coarse
41	sft	Soft
42	hrd	Hard
43	stf	Stiff
44	sml	Small
45	lrg	Large
46	stk	Sticky
47	brk	Broken
47a	grd	Ground
48		Rotten
49		Streaky
50	spk	Speckled
51	gty	Gritty
52		Decayed
53	fly	Flinty
54	glac	Glacial
55		Tenacious
56	wh	White
57	bk	Black
58	vi	Violet
59	bu	Blue
60	gn	Green
61	yl	Yellow
62	or	Orange
63	rd	Red
64	br	Brown
65	ch	Chocolate
66	gy	Gray
67	lt	Light
68	dk	Dark
70		Varied
71		Uneven
76		Fresh water springs in sea-bed

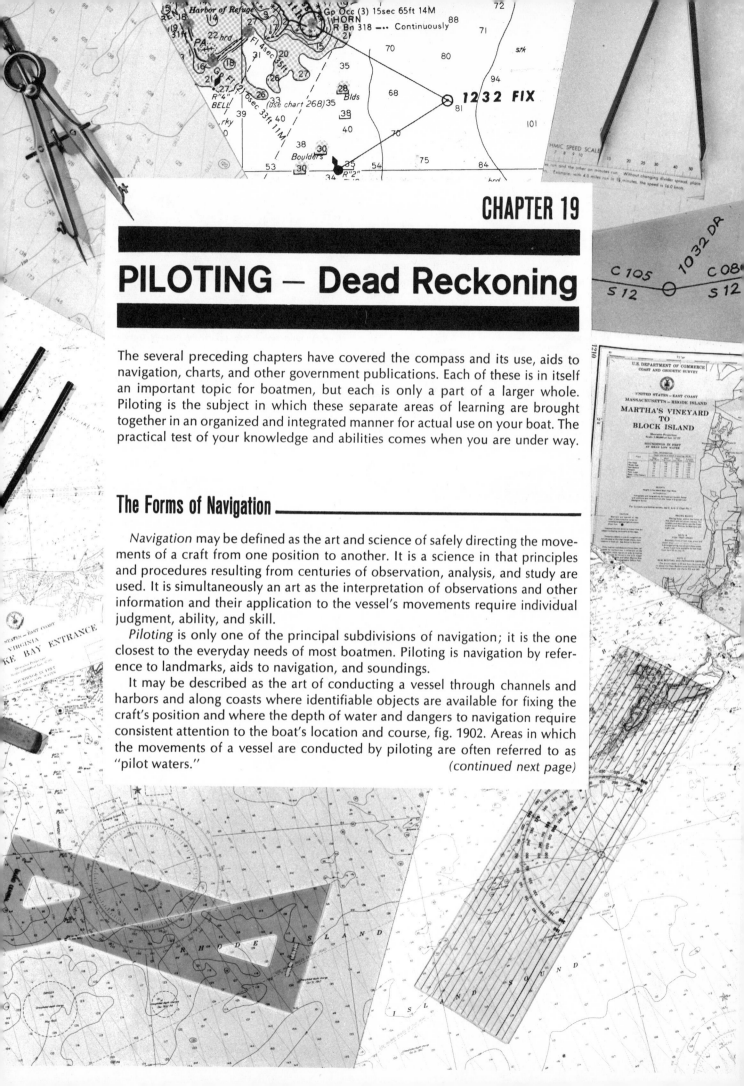

CHAPTER 19

PILOTING – Dead Reckoning

The several preceding chapters have covered the compass and its use, aids to navigation, charts, and other government publications. Each of these is in itself an important topic for boatmen, but each is only a part of a larger whole. Piloting is the subject in which these separate areas of learning are brought together in an organized and integrated manner for actual use on your boat. The practical test of your knowledge and abilities comes when you are under way.

The Forms of Navigation

Navigation may be defined as the art and science of safely directing the movements of a craft from one position to another. It is a science in that principles and procedures resulting from centuries of observation, analysis, and study are used. It is simultaneously an art as the interpretation of observations and other information and their application to the vessel's movements require individual judgment, ability, and skill.

Piloting is only one of the principal subdivisions of navigation; it is the one closest to the everyday needs of most boatmen. Piloting is navigation by reference to landmarks, aids to navigation, and soundings.

It may be described as the art of conducting a vessel through channels and harbors and along coasts where identifiable objects are available for fixing the craft's position and where the depth of water and dangers to navigation require consistent attention to the boat's location and course, fig. 1902. Areas in which the movements of a vessel are conducted by piloting are often referred to as "pilot waters."

(continued next page)

Dead Reckoning / CHAPTER 19

Along with piloting, the boatman will often use another form of navigation, *dead reckoning,* a procedure by which the craft's approximate location at any time is deduced from its movements since the last accurate determination of position.

Other subdivisions of navigation are *electronic,* which will be touched on briefly in the following chapters insofar as specific systems are applicable to small craft, and *celestial,* which will be left to more advanced students and texts.

The importance of piloting

Piloting is a most important part of navigation, and perhaps the form requiring the least study but the most experience and best judgment. It is used by boatmen in

FIG. 1902 Piloting, by reference to landmarks and aids to navigation, is most often done in waters restricted by shoals and other dangers and which are relatively heavily traveled by other boats.

FIG. 1901 Piloting is the principal form of navigation used by boatmen. It requires study and practice, but it often becomes one of the major sources of enjoyment in boating.   M. Rosenfeld.

rivers, bays, lakes, and close alongshore when on the open oceans. In such waters, the hazards to safe navigation may be quite frequent and the density of traffic quite high. The navigator of a craft of any size in pilot waters must have adequate training and knowledge; he must give his task close attention and constant alertness. Frequent determinations of position are usually essential, and changes in course or speed may be necessary at relatively short intervals.

The high seas vs. pilot waters

On the high seas, or well offshore in such large bodies of water as the Great Lakes, navigation can be more leisurely and relaxed. An error or uncertainty of position of a few miles will present no immediate hazard to the safety of the boat and its crew. But when one approaches the shore line, or the water shoals, a greater degree of accuracy is required. An error of only a few yards can result in running aground with certain embarrassment, and possibly much more serious consequences. The proximity of other craft requires constant knowledge of where the dangers lie and where one's own boat can be safely steered.

The enjoyment of piloting

Piloting can be "fun" for a boatman, but it will be most enjoyable when done without tension or anxiety; this happy state can be achieved only with a sound background of study and practice. The wise skipper "overnavigates" in times of fair weather so as to acquire the skill that will let him navigate his boat safely through fog or rain or night without fear or nervous strain.

The Dimensions of Piloting

The basic "dimensions" of piloting are direction, distance, and time. Other quantities which must be measured, calculated, or used, include speed, position, and depths and heights. A qualified pilot must have a ready understanding of how each of these dimensions is measured, expressed in units, used in calculations, and plotted on charts.

DIRECTION

Direction is the position of one point relative to another point without reference to the distance between them. As discussed earlier in the chapters on compasses and charts, modern navigation uses the system of angular measurement in which a complete circle is divided into 360 units called "degrees." Although each degree can in turn be subdivided into 60 minutes, the more common practice

in angular measurement in piloting is to use ordinary fractions such as $1/2$ and $1/4$, or decimal fractions in tenths.

True, magnetic, or compass

Directions are normally referred to a base line running from the origin point toward the geographic North Pole. Such directions can be measured on a chart with reference to the meridians of longitude and are called "true" directions. Measurements made with respect to the direction of the earth's magnetic field at that point are termed "magnetic" directions, and those referred to local magnetic conditions as measured by the craft's compass are designated "compass" directions, see fig. 1903. *It is of the utmost importance to always designate the reference used for directional measurement, true (T), magnetic (M), or compass (C).*

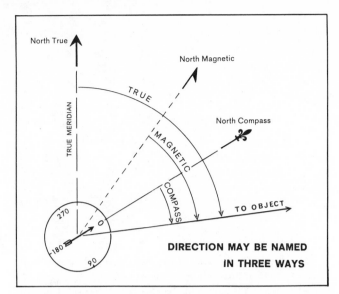

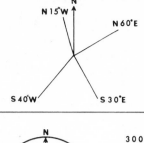

FIG. 1903 Direction is one of the basic "dimensions" of piloting. It can be measured with respect to True, Magnetic, or Compass North. Always be sure to designate the reference used.

Directions and angles

The basic system of measurement uses the reference direction as 0° (North) and measures clockwise through 90° (East), 180° (South), and 270° (West) around to 360° which is North again. Directions are expressed in three-digit form such as 005°, 030°, 150°, etc. Note that zeros are added before the figures denoting direction if necessary to make a three-digit number, for example, 005° or 030°, fig. 1904a. *Angles* which are *not* directions are expressed in one, two, or three digits as appropriate, 5°, 30°, 150°, etc., fig. 1904b.

Occasionally, directions will be expressed as so many degrees east or west of North or South, such as N30°E (030°), S20°E (160°), S40°W (220°), or N15°W (345°), fig. 1905. This form of expression, "direction in quadrant," is useful for some types of computations, but it is not employed for general navigational purposes.

Directions in the "point" system

The "point" system of angular measurement, so widely used in the days of sailing ships, has now fallen almost completely from practical use in navigation. It divided a complete circle into 32 points of 11¼ degrees each which could then be further subdivided fractionally. It is cumbersome to use and complicates calculations; with respect to the piloting of modern small craft, it is now of historical interest only.

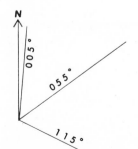

FIG. 1904a Directions are always designated by a *three-digit* number. Add zeros before a single or double-digit number as shown here.

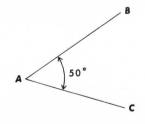

FIG. 1904b An angle between two directions, as distinguished from the directions themselves, is *not* expressed as a three-digit number. An angle such as BAC above is shown as simply 50°, not as 050°.

FIG. 1905 Directions may be described "in quadrant," but this technique is rarely used in modern boating. In this obsolete procedure, angles are measured in either direction from North or South to a maximum of 90°.

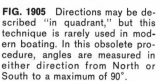
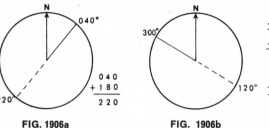

FIG. 1906a   **FIG. 1906b**

The *reciprocal* of a direction is simply the opposite direction, shown here as a broken line. To find a reciprocal, add 180° to the given direction. If the total exceeds 360°, subtract that amount. Alternatively, subtract 180° from the given direction if it is greater than that amount.

Reciprocals

For any given direction, there is its *reciprocal*. This latter direction is the direct opposite, differing by 180°. Thus the reciprocal of 030° is 210°, and the reciprocal of 300° is 120°. To find the reciprocal of any direction, simply add 180° if the given direction is less than the amount; or subtract 180°, if it exceeds that figure, as shown in fig. 1906.

DISTANCE

This is the second of the basic dimensions of piloting. *Distance* is defined as the spacial separation between two points without regard to the direction of one from the other. It is commonly thought of as the length of the shortest line that can be drawn between the two points.

Nautical and statute miles

The basic unit of distance in piloting is the *mile*, but, as noted in Chapter 18, there are two types of miles that a boatman may encounter. The *statute mile* is used on inland bodies of water such as the Mississippi River and its tributaries, the Great Lakes, etc. It is 5280 feet in length, the same "mile" that is so commonly used in measuring land distances.

On the high seas and connecting tidal waters, the unit of measurement is the *nautical mile* of 6076.1 feet. This "salt-water" mile is essentially equal to one minute of latitude, and this relationship is often used in navigation. Nautical miles are slightly longer than statute miles, and the comparison is usually taken as 7 nautical miles equals 8 statute miles. More accurately, the conversion of nautical miles into statute miles is done by using the factor of 1.15.

It is quite possible to cruise from an area using one kind of mile into waters where the other kind is used. Care must be exercised at such times to determine which type of mile is being used and so specify in calculations.

For shorter distances, a few miles or less, the unit of measurement may be the *yard*. This is the same unit of three feet as commonly used on land. Roughly, a nautical mile can be considered as being 2000 yards although this introduces a small error of about 1¼%. Feet are seldom used as a measure of horizontal distance in navigation.

TIME

The third basic dimension of piloting is *time*. Although the pilot does not need so accurate a knowledge of the exact time of day as does a celestial navigator, ability to determine the passage of time and to perform calculations with such *elapsed time* is essential. A boat should have aboard a clock or watch of reasonable time-keeping accuracy; a second one in reserve is desirable. For many practical problems in piloting, a stop watch will be found useful.

Units of time

The units of time used in boating are the everyday ones of *hours* of 60 *minutes* each. In piloting, measurements will not often be carried to the preciseness of *seconds* of time although decimal fractions of minutes may occasionally occur in calculations. Seconds and fractions of minutes may be used in competitive events such as races and predicted log contests, but seldom otherwise.

The 24-hour clock system

In navigation, including piloting, the time of day is expressed in a 24-hour system that eliminates the necessity for using the designations of "am" and "pm." Time is written in four-digit figures; the first two are the hour and the second pair represent the minutes. The day starts at 0001, one minute after midnight, 12:01 am in the old system. 0100 would be 1 am, 1000 is 10 am, and 1200 is noon. The second half of the day continues in the same pattern with 1300 being 1 pm, 1832 being 6:32 pm, etc., to 2400 for midnight. Time is spoken as "zero seven hundred" or "fifteen forty." The phrase "hours" should *not* be used. The times of 1000 and 2000 are correctly spoken as "ten hundred" and "twenty hundred," *not* as "one thousand" or "two thousand."

When performing arithmetic computations with time caution must always be exercised to remember that when "borrowing" or "carrying" there are *60* minutes in an hour, and not 100. As obvious and simple a matter as this may be, the mistake occurs all too often.

Time zones

A navigator in pilot waters must also be alert to *time zones*. Even in coastal or inland waters, it is possible to cruise from one zone to another resulting in the necessity for changing clocks, the plot on the chart, and the log; plus one's arrival time at the next port.

A further complication in time is the prevalence of "daylight time" in many boating areas during the summer months. Government publications are in standard time; local sources of information such as newspapers and radio broadcasts will undoubtedly use daylight time if it is in effect. Daylight time is one hour *later* than standard time. When going from standard time to daylight, *add* one hour; from daylight to standard, *subtract* one hour.

SPEED

No matter how fast or slow one's craft may be, speed is an essential dimension of piloting. *Speed* is defined as the number of units of distance that would be traveled in a specified unit of time.

The basic unit of speed is *miles per hour,* whether these be nautical or statute miles, as determined by location. A special name, *knot,* has been given to the nautical mile per hour. Note well that the word "knot" includes the element of time—to say "knots per hour" is not only incorrect, it is a mark of ignorance.

Conversion of knots and MPH

The conversion factors between statute miles per hour (MPH) and knots are the same as for the corresponding units of distance—1 knot = 1.15 MPH, or 7 knots roughly equals 8 MPH.

The unit "knot" may be abbreviated either as "kt." or "kn."; the former has a somewhat greater usage.

POSITION

The ability to describe accurately the position of his craft is an essential requirement for a pilot, and one that marks him as well qualified. To realize the importance and the difficulties of this seemingly simple task, one has only to listen to his radio on 2182 kc/s on a weekend afternoon during the boating season. The hesitant, inadequate, and inaccurate attempts by skippers to simply say where they are must surely irritate the Coast Guard and embarrass all competent boatmen!

Relative and geographic coordinates

Position may be described in relative terms or by geographic coordinates. When defined as a *relative position,* the location of the craft is described as being a certain distance and direction from a specified identifiable point such as a landmark or aid to navigation. A boat's position may be described with varying degrees of preciseness as determined by the accuracy of the data on which it is based. A skipper might say that he was "about two miles southwest of Brenton Reef Light"; or if he had the capability of being more precise, he could say, "I'm 2.2 miles, 230°. True from Brenton Reef Light," fig. 1907. In relative positioning, the distance may, of course, be essentially zero, as would be the case with a position report such as "I am at Lighted Whistle Buoy 2."

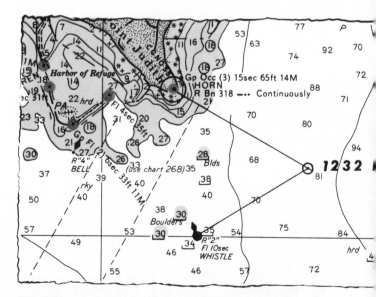

FIG. 1907 A boat's position may be described in "relative" terms. It is stated to be at a certain distance and direction from an identifiable object such as an aid to navigation. In this example, it would be "1.8 miles, 120 degrees True from Point Judith Light."

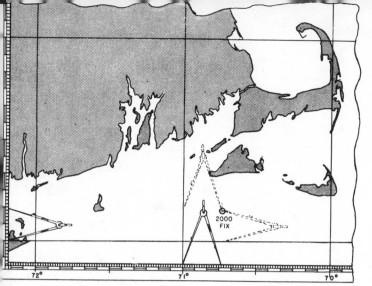

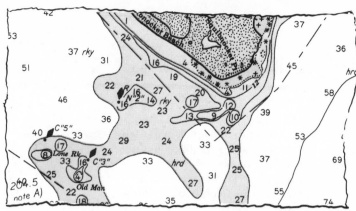

FIG. 1908 The position of a boat can be described in terms of "geographic coordinates." Using the subdivisions of the chart's borders, the latitude and longitude of the plotted position are measured and recorded. (from DUTTON'S NAVIGATION AND PILOTING)

FIG. 1909 Depth is a "dimension" of piloting that is often of the greatest importance to the safety of a boat and its crew. Be sure that you know whether the charted depths on the chart you are using are shown in feet or fathoms.

The preceding examples of position description have all used visible identifiable objects. It is also possible to state one's *geographic position* in terms of *latitude* and *longitude* using those nice straight, uniformly-spaced lines on charts which so unfortunately do not appear on the surface of the water. Using this procedure, the position is measured from the markings on either side and the top or bottom of the chart.

The units of measurement for geographic coordinates are *degrees* and *minutes,* but this degree is not quite the same unit as used in the measurement of direction, nor is this minute the same as the unit of time. Care must be used to avoid confusion between these units of position and other units with similar names. For precise position definition, one may use either *seconds* or *tenths of minutes* as determined by the chart being used. Typically, the smallest unit on the marginal scales of C&GS coast charts will be tenths of minutes, but for harbor charts it will be seconds; see page 325.

In a statement of geographic position, latitude is given first, before longitude, and the figures must be followed by "North" or "South" as appropriate. In U.S. waters, the latitude is, of course, always "North," even for the most unreconstructed "rebel." Similarly, longitude must be designated "East" or "West" to be complete; all U.S. waters are in West longitude, fig. 1908.

DEPTHS

The *depth* of the water is important both for the safety of a boat in preventing grounding and for navigational purposes. Thus, this vertical measurement from the surface of the water to the bottom is an essential dimension of piloting. Measurements may be made continuously or only occasionally as determined by the circumstances, but you can be sure that at some time or another on almost any cruise, knowledge of the depth will become critically important.

In pilot waters, depths will normally be measured in *feet.* In open ocean waters, the small craft operator may find himself on charts indicating depths in *fathoms* of six feet each. It is important to check each chart when purchased and again when used to note the unit of measurement of depth, fig. 1909.

In many areas, depths will fluctuate somewhat from the printed figures on charts due to tidal changes. Charts will indicate the *datum* used, the reference plane from which measurements were made. They will also indicate the normal range of tidal variations and the extreme low-water condition that must be considered.

HEIGHTS

The height, or elevation, of certain objects will be of concern to the pilot. The height of some landmarks and lighted aids to navigation may determine their range of visibility. Of more critical importance, however, are such vertical measurements as the clearance under a bridge, fig. 1910. *Heights,* or vertical dimensions upward from the surface of the water, are measured in *feet.* It should be noted that in tidal areas, the datum, or plane of reference, for heights is *not* the same as for depths. Examine each chart closely and note the datum from which heights are measured.

The usual datum for the measurement of heights is *mean high water.* This will be an imaginary plane surface above the mean low-water datum for depths by an amount equal to the *mean tide range;* the height of mean high water will usually be shown on a chart.

FIG. 1910 Charts will show the heights of bridges or other structures that will affect navigation. Heights are measured vertically in feet, usually from mean high water (MHW).

The Instruments of Piloting

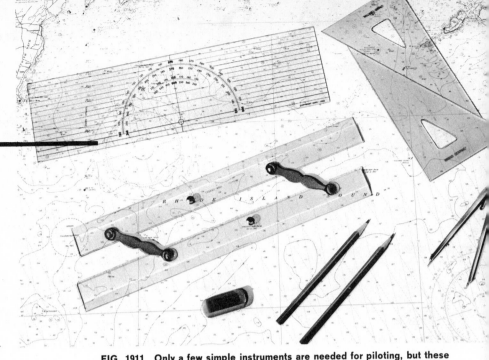

The practice of piloting in coastal and inland waters requires the use of a few simple tools or instruments, fig. 1911. These are not particularly expensive items, but they should be of good quality, well cared for, and used with the proper respect. A skilled man in any profession or trade is known by his tools, when that term is used in its broadest sense. A navigator may well be judged by his instruments and how he uses them.

FIG. 1911 Only a few simple instruments are needed for piloting, but these should be of good quality, used with respect, and properly maintained.

DIRECTION

Many instruments are used in the measurement of direction. Some are concerned with such measurement directly, and others with its measurement on a chart. Still other instruments are used to both measure direction from a chart and to plot directions from observations.

Determining Direction

The basic instrument on a boat for the determination of direction is a *compass*. With rare exceptions, this will be a *magnetic* compass as shown in fig. 1912 and described in Chapter 13. Directions obtained from this instrument will be "compass" directions and will require correction for deviation and variation as covered in that chapter.

A *gyro* compass is a complex device capable of indicating the true north direction without regard to magnetic conditions. However, its size, weight, electrical power requirements, and particularly its high cost, limit its use to the largest and most luxurious yachts. The average boatman must make do with a magnetic compass, but, properly used, this traditional piloting instrument will serve him well.

The compass is used primarily to determine the direction in which the craft is headed. Depending upon its location, and how it is mounted, the steering compass may also be used for determining the direction of other objects from the boat. Rough readings may be taken by sighting across the compass itself and estimating the reading of the compass card. More exact readings can be taken if a pair of *sight vanes* can be mounted on the compass as illustrated in fig. 1913. Sights taken with a steering compass are satisfactory as to accuracy, but are generally limited by physical considerations to objects forward of the beam.

Pelorus. A more flexible instrument for measuring the direction of objects from the boat is the *pelorus*, fig. 1914. This simple device consists of a set of sighting vanes mounted over a circular scale calibrated in degrees like a compass card. A means must be provided for mounting or temporarily locating the pelorus so that it may be properly oriented to the fore-and-aft center line of the boat. Peloruses may be purchased or made in the home workshop; see fig. 1915.

The circular scale of a pelorus is usually made so that it may be rotated to a desired position and there clamped in place. With the scale so set that 000° is dead ahead, over or parallel to the center line of the boat, the directions that are then measured are termed *relative bearings*.

FIG. 1912 A magnetic compass is the basic instrument for measuring direction on a boat. See Chapters 13 and 14 for detailed coverage of the compass.

FIG. 1913 The compass can be used to determine the direction from the boat to an object such as an aid to navigation. Greater accuracy will be obtained if *sight vanes* are used as shown here.

FIG. 1914 A *pelorus* is used to take bearings on objects from a boat. It consists of a set of sights mounted over an angular scale calibrated like a compass card.

The sight vanes placed on a compass, or those of a pelorus, may be replaced with a small telescope having cross-hairs. Greater accuracy will be achieved, but the telescope must be of low power in order to have a wide enough field of view to pick up and hold objects at a distance despite the movements of the boat.

Even greater flexibility of use can be obtained with one of several patented instruments now on the market. Each of these consists of a small magnetic compass conveniently mounted for holding in front of one's eyes, plus a set of sights and a prismatic optical system for simultaneously observing a distant object through the sights and reading the compass card. Internal lighting for night use is usually provided. Typical of these instruments is the Hand Bearing Compass (fig. 1916) with open sights. Fig. 1917 illustrates how some small compasses may be unshipped from their mounting and held at eye level to take a bearing.

Plotting directions

Once direction has been determined by compass, pelorus, or other device, it must be plotted on the chart. For this action, there are a number of instruments available. These same tools will be used when the problem is the determination of direction from the chart itself.

Course plotters. These are pieces of clear plastic, usually rectangular in shape, with one or more semi-circular angular scales marked thereon, see fig. 1918. The center of these scales is at or near the center of one of the longer sides of the plotter and is usually emphasized with a small circle or "bull's-eye." There are normally two main scales, one from 000° to 180° and the other from 180° to 360°; each is calibrated in degrees. There may also be smaller auxiliary scales offset 90° from the main scales. Lines are marked on the plotter parallel to the longer sides. Some instruments have distance marks along the edges corresponding to the more commonly-used chart scales.

Course plotters are used in the following manner:

1. *To determine the direction of a course or bearing from a given point,* place the plotter on the chart so that one of its longer sides is along the course or bearing line and slide the plotter until the bull's-eye is over a *meridian.* The true direction is then read on the scale where it is intersected by the meridian. Easterly courses are read on the scale that reads from 000° to 180°, and westerly courses are read on the other main scale, see fig. 1919.

These may be converted to compass directions or compass bearings, by numerically adding the heading of the boat as read from the steering compass at the instant of observation (subtract 360° from this sum if it exceeds that amount). A steady hand at the wheel is required, and the observer should call "Mark" at the time that he reads the pelorus so that the helmsman may simultaneously read the boat's compass. Alternatively, the helmsman may call a series of "marks" as he is on the prescribed heading, remaining silent if the boat falls off to either side. When using this technique, the observer takes his reading only when the helmsman is indicating that he is directly on the correct heading.

A second method of using a pelorus is to set the scale so that it matches the compass for the heading being steered. Readings then taken with the pelorus are directly compass bearings without further conversion. Two cautions must be observed — the craft must be directly on course at the time of observation; and, when correcting for *deviation,* the value used is that for the *heading* of the boat, *not* that for the observed direction. Because of these possible errors, particularly the latter one, this technique should be avoided, or used only with much practice and great care.

FIG. 1915 A pelorus may be purchased or it is easily made in a home workshop. A compass rose or card diagram such as Fig. 1310 or 1335 is cut out and mounted on a wooden or metallic base. A set of rotatable sighting vanes completes the pelorus.

FIG. 1916 A hand bearing compass has the advantage that it may easily be used from almost any place on a boat. Be careful, however, of using it near large masses of magnetic material that will introduce deviation errors.

FIG. 1917 Some compasses, like this Corsair, are so mounted (particularly on small boats) that they can be easily unshipped and held at eye-level for taking bearings. The same precautions regarding deviation must be observed as for a hand bearing compass.

If it is more convenient, the course or bearing may be lined up with one of the marked parallel lines rather than the edge of the course plotter. In measuring courses and bearings, it is not absolutely necessary to actually draw in the line connecting the two points, the plotter can be aligned using only the two points concerned. Usually, however, it will be found easier and safer to draw in the connecting line.

When the direction to be measured is within 20° or so of due North or South, it may be difficult to reach a meridian by sliding the course plotter across the chart. The small inner auxiliary scales have been included on the plotter for just such cases. Slide the plotter until the bull's-eye intersects a *parallel of latitude* line. The intersection of this line with the appropriate *auxiliary* scale indicates the direction of the course or bearing, see fig. 1920.

2. *To plot a specified direction (course or bearing) from a given point,* put a pencil on the origin point, keep one of the longer edges of the course plotter snug against the pencil, and slide the plotter around until the center bull's-

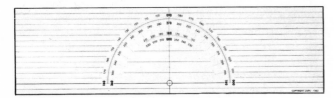

FIG. 1918 A *course plotter* is a single rectangular piece of transparent plastic ruled with circular scales and a set of lines parallel to its longer sides. Shown here is the model used by the U.S. Power Squadrons.

FIG. 1919 The course plotter is lined up with the course line along one of the longer sides, and then is moved until a meridian cuts through the "bull's eye." Direction can then be read from the appropriate main scale.

eye and the desired mark on the appropriate main scale both lie along the same meridian. With the plotter thus positioned, draw in the specified direction from the given point.

Alternatively, the plotter may first be positioned using the bull's-eye and scale markings without regard to the specified origin point. The plotter is then carefully slid up or down the meridian until one of the longer edges is over the origin point and then the direction line is drawn in.

For directions nearly North or South, one of the small auxiliary scales can be used in conjunction with a parallel of latitude.

3. *To extend a line* which must be longer than the length of the course plotter, place a pair of dividers, opened to three or four inches, tightly against the edge of the plotter and then slide the plotter along using the divider points as guides. Draw in the extension of the course or bearing line after the plotter has been advanced.

4. In piloting, it is sometimes necessary *to draw a new line parallel to an existing course or bearing line.* For such situations, the parallel lines marked on the course plotter may be used as guides.

Course protractors. Many pilots use a *course protractor,* fig. 1921, as their primary plotting tool. This instrument, with its moving parts, is not as easily used as the course plotter described above; but, when it is employed with care, it gives as satisfactory results.

In using the course protractor *to measure the direction of a course or bearing,* its center should be placed on the chart exactly over the specified origin point, such as the boat's position or an aid to navigation. The arm of the protractor is then swung around to the nearest compass rose on the chart, making the upper edge of the arm (which is in line with the center of the compass part of the course protractor) pass directly over the center of the compass rose.

Holding the course protractor arm firmly in this position, the compass part of the protractor is then turned around until the upper edge of the arm cuts across the same degree marking of the protractor compass as it does at the compass rose. The compass and the rose are now parallel. Holding the protractor compass firmly against the chart, the protractor arm is then moved around until its edge cuts across the second point involved in the course

FIG. 1920 If a meridian cannot be easily reached, as may be the case with courses within a few degrees of North or South, use the *auxiliary* inner scales and a *parallel* of latitude as shown here.

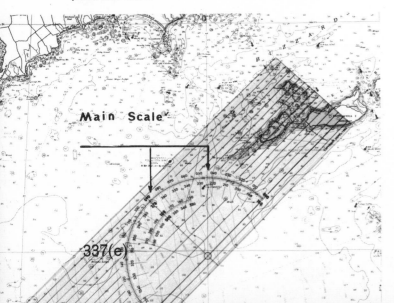

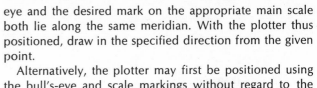

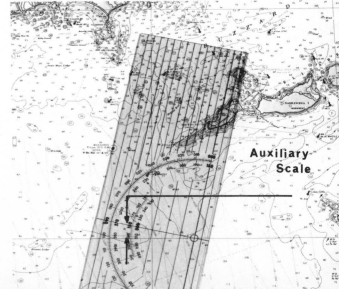

or bearing. The direction in degrees can then be read directly from the protractor compass scale.

To lay off a line in a specified direction from the given point, the protractor rose is first lined up with the compass rose on the chart as in the preceding instructions. Then the arm is rotated until the desired direction is indicated on the compass scale, and the line is drawn in; this line will have to be extended back to the origin point after the course protractor has been lifted off the chart.

Parallel rulers. A traditional instrument for measuring and plotting directions on charts is a set of *parallel rulers.* Their use on boats has declined somewhat in recent years, but they are still capable of giving good results if the navigator is careful to avoid slippage. Parallel rulers may be

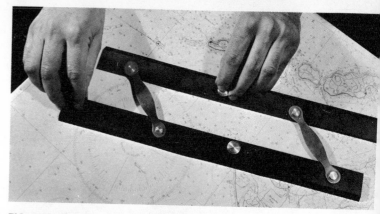

FIG. 1922 *Parallel rulers* are a traditional charting instrument. The two straightedges are kept in parallel alignment by the connecting links. Directions are transferred from one place to another by "walking" the rulers across the chart.

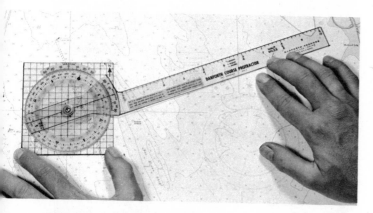

FIG. 1921 Some skippers prefer to use a *course protractor* as their primary plotting tool. It consists of two pieces of plastic movable with respect to each other.

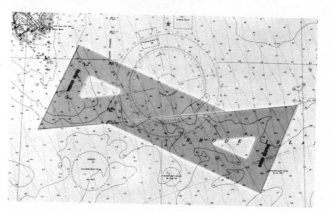

FIG. 1923 A pair of ordinary drawing triangles can be used for transferring a direction from one part of a chart to another, but not for great distances. See text for method of their use.

made of black (as shown in fig. 1922) or clear transparent plastic material. The two rulers are connected by metal linkages so that the edges always remain parallel. To measure the direction of a line, one ruler is lined up with the desired objects on the chart and then the pair is "walked" across the chart to the nearest compass rose by alternately holding one ruler and moving the other. To plot a line of stated direction, the process is essentially reversed; the procedure is started at the compass rose and worked to the desired origin point.

Drawing triangles. A pair of ordinary plastic *drawing triangles* can also be used for transferring a direction from one part of a chart to another, although not for very great distances. The two triangles need not be similar in size or shape. The two hypotenuses (longest sides) are placed together and one of the other sides of one triangle is lined up with the course or bearing line, or with the desired direction at the compass rose, fig. 1923. The other triangle is held firmly in place as a base, and the first one is slid along in contact with it, carrying the specified line to a new position while maintaining its direction. If necessary, the triangles may be alternately held and slid for moving somewhat greater distances.

Courser. One rather unique direction instrument, particularly useful in outboards or other situations of limited space, is a "Courser," a patented device consisting of a sheet of flexible plastic upon which are ruled a series of parallel lines, fig. 1924. One line is placed over the course or bearing to be measured and another will fall across or near the center of a compass rose on the chart. By slight adjustments to the Courser, directions can be read off the

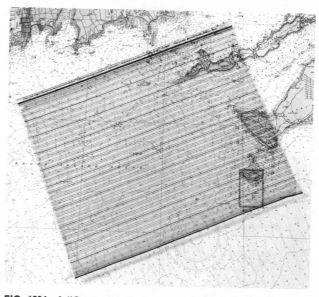

FIG. 1924 A "Courser" is a sheet of soft flexible transparent plastic on which parallel lines have been ruled. It is simple and convenient to use in smaller boats, and the accuracy obtained with it is adequate for such applications.

rose with sufficient accuracy for practical use in a small boat.

An ordinary *drawing protractor* may find some use aboard a boat for measuring angles, but it is not a highly useful instrument and can be omitted. A chart compass rose can always be used for angle measurement if this becomes necessary.

FIG. 1925 A *radar set* on a boat can measure the direction and distance to other boats, aids to navigation, prominent structures and terrain features, etc. The use of radar is covered more fully in Chapter 25.

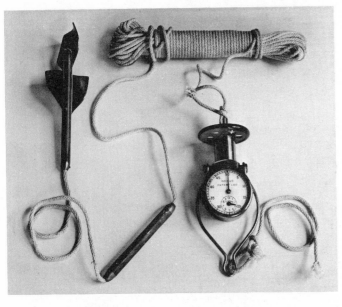

FIG. 1926 A *patent log*, used for determining distance run and speed. A log line connects the rotator to a registering device near the stern of the boat. The log line must be long enough to clear the wake as it is towed astern. In use, the rotator revolves as it is towed through the water, and the line transmits this rotary motion to the registering device which is calibrated so that the distance can be read directly from the dial.

FIG. 1927 A more modern patent log consists of a much smaller impeller mounted on the bottom of the boat connected to a dialed instrument for measuring speed and distance run through the water.

DISTANCE

Distance to an object can be measured directly by *radar*, fig. 1925; and distance traveled can be measured directly by a *summing log*, figs. 1926 and 1927. However, few boats are equipped with either of these items of equipment. Distance is usually measured in piloting by taking it from a chart.

Chart measurements for distance

Dividers. Distance is measured on a chart with a pair of *dividers*, fig. 1928a. The two arms of this small drafting instrument can be opened as desired, and the friction at the pivot is sufficient to hold them in place with the same separation between the points. Most dividers have some means for adjusting this friction; it should be enough to hold the arms in place, but not so much as to make opening or closing difficult. A special type of dividers has a center cross-piece (like the horizontal part of the capital letter "A") which can be rotated by a knurled knob to set and maintain the opening between the arms, fig. 1928b; thus the distance between the points cannot accidentally change. This type of dividers is particularly useful if kept set to some standard distance, such as one mile to the scale of the chart being used.

The dividers are first opened to the distance between the two points on the chart, then they are transferred without change to the chart's graphic scale, figs. 1929a and b. Note that the zero point on this scale is *not* at the left-hand end, but rather is one basic unit up the scale. This unit to the left of zero is more finely divided than are the remaining basic units. For the measurement of any distance, the right-hand point of the dividers is set on the basic unit mark that will result in the left-hand point falling somewhere on the more-finely-divided unit to the left of the zero. The distance measured is the sum of the basic units counted off to the right from the scale's zero point plus the fractional unit to the left from zero. In the illustration, the distance is 2½ units.

If the distance on the chart cannot be spanned with the dividers opened widely (about 60° is the maximum practical opening), set them at a convenient opening for a whole number of units on the graphic scale or latitude subdivisions, step this off the necessary number of times, then measure the odd remainder. The total distance is then the simple sum of the parts stepped off and measured separately, fig. 1930.

To mark off on the chart a desired distance, set the right point of the dividers on the nearest lower whole number of units, and the left point on the remaining fractional part of a unit measured leftward from zero on the scale. The dividers are now properly set for the specified distance at the scale of the chart being used and can be applied to the chart. If the distance is too great for one setting of the dividers, it may be stepped off in several increments.

Charts at a scale smaller than 1:80,000 will not have a graphic scale. In lieu thereof, distances are measured on the latitude scales at either side of the chart. Care should be taken to measure on these scales near the same latitude as the portion of the chart being used; in other words, move directly horizontally across the chart to either of its sides to use the scales.

With a little experience, dividers can be set and used

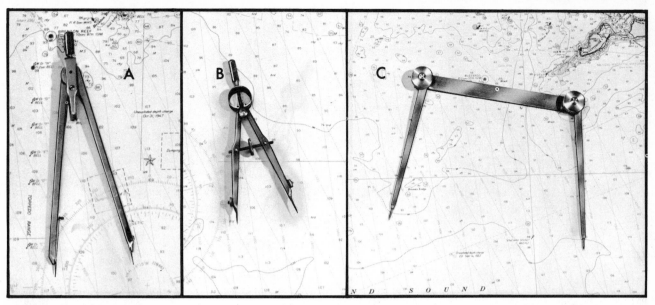

FIG. 1928 Dividers are used to measure distances on a chart. A—Friction at the pivot holds the arms to the desired opening. B—In this type of dividers, an adjustable center cross-arm maintains the separation between points and avoids accidental changes. C—Long-legged dividers enable the pilot to step off long runs on a chart, without "walking" them.

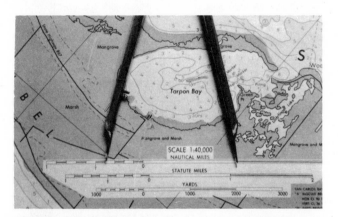

FIG. 1929 After the dividers have been set for the distance on the chart between the points concerned, they are moved to the graphic scale or latitude subdivisions at the edge of the chart. Distance is measured on these scales as described in the text.

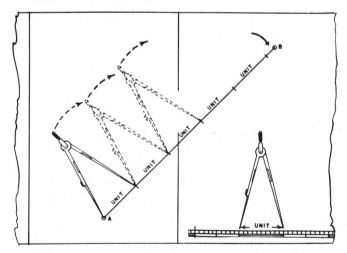

FIG. 1930 When a chart distance is too great to be measured with a single setting of the dividers, open the points to a convenient whole number of units. Step these along the chart for the required number of times and then measure any small left-over distance (arrow) in the usual manner. (Figs. 1908 and 1930 are based on DUTTON'S NAVIGATION AND PILOTING, copyright © 1957 and 1958 by U. S. Naval Institute, Annapolis, Maryland.)

With a little experience, dividers can be set and used with one hand. Making sure that the friction at the pivot is properly adjusted, practice this technique until it can be used with ease; such ability will add convenience and speed to your piloting work.

An instrument that looks much like a pair of dividers, except that a pencil lead or pen is substituted for one point, is called a *compass* (or *drawing compass* to distinguish it from a magnetic compass). This is used primarily for drawing arcs or circles.

Distance can also be measured across a chart with reduced, but generally acceptable, accuracy by using a *chart measurer*, fig. 1931. This device has a small wheel that is rolled along the chart; the wheel is internally geared to an indicating dial. Chart measurers will read distances directly in miles at various typical chart scales; separate models are available for charts using statute and nautical miles. They are particularly useful in measuring distances up rivers with many bends and changes of direction.

TIME

Every pilot, no matter how small his craft, should have a dependable and reasonably accurate timepiece. This can be a clock, wrist watch, or pocket watch. Long-term accuracy is of secondary importance in piloting, but short-term errors, those accumulated over the length of a day or half-day, should be small. A knowledge of the time of day within a few minutes will usually be sufficient. A clock, if used, should be mounted where it is clearly visible from the helm-seat or plotting table. If two clocks are used, be sure that they show the same time.

Elapsed time is usually of greater interest than *absolute* time. A stop watch will often be handy although it cannot be classed as a necessary instrument of piloting. Most stop watches have a second hand that makes one revolution for each minute, but there are some that sweep completely around in 30 seconds, and even a few that have a 10-second period. Know for sure the type of stop watch that you are using.

FIG. 1931 If a *chart measurer* is rolled across a chart, between two points, an indicating dial will show the distance directly for typical chart scales. It is especially useful in measuring distances on waterways with many bends and curves.

FIG. 1933 Many small boats are fitted with a simple device that measures speed by the pressure built up in a probe as a result of the movement of the boat through the water. Accuracy is quite good, but it must be remembered that it is speed through the water that is measured, and not speed made good over the bottom.

SPEED

Speed is a dimension that can be measured directly or calculated from knowledge of distance and time. Direct reading instruments are convenient, but they give only the relative speed through the water, and not the speed made good between two geographic points.

In years gone by, speed through the water was measured by use of a *chip log,* fig. 1932. More modern marine speedometers use the static pressure built up in a small tube by motion of the boat, fig. 1933, an impeller turned by the passing water, or a finger-like strut projecting below the bottom of the boat, fig. 1934. Many different models are available in a wide variety of speed ranges from those for sailboats to models reading high enough for fast speedboats.

Speed can be calculated from a knowledge of the distance covered and the elapsed time, to be discussed later in this chapter, or by the use of special calculating devices. These calculators are specialized adaptations of slide rules used for general mathematical calculations; they may be either linear or circular in form, figs. 1935a and b.

DEPTH

This most important dimension of piloting can be measured manually or electronically. A hand *lead line,* fig. 1936, is simple, accurate, and not subject to breakdowns. It does have the disadvantages, however, of being awkward to use, inconvenient in bad weather, and capable of giving only one or two readings per minute; a lead line can be used only at quite slow speeds.

Many small craft today are equipped with an *electronic depth sounder.* These devices can clearly, accurately, and most conveniently provide measurements of the depth of water beneath the boat. Moreover, soundings are indicated many times each second, so frequently that they appear to be a smooth, continuous measurement of depth. For more information on these relatively inexpensive but most useful piloting aids, see Chapter 25, pages 382g to 382i.

FIG. 1934 This speedometer, designed primarily for sailboats, is actuated by a strut or finger which projects below the bottom of the boat. A modern solid-state electronic instrument, it measures speed variations to 1/100 knot. An optional feature measures distance up to 999.9 nautical miles.

FIG. 1932 The old chip log, consisting of the log-chip, log-line, and log-glass. The log-chip is a thin piece of wood, weighted so that it will float vertically. The chip is thrown from the stern and the log-line is allowed to flow freely over the rail. The line is marked at intervals of 47 feet 3 inches, called "knots," and the number of knots that pass over the rail in the time that it takes the glass to empty is a direct measure of the speed.

FIG. 1934a Unipas-300, a versatile 12-volt solid-state navigational instrument, measures depth on 25- or 100-foot scales; speed, on various scales from 0-2.5 or 0-25 knots, with sensitivity as fine as .01 knot; and distance logged, in steps of .001 mile. Plug-in modules provide for twin-engine synchronization, wind-speed measurement, detection of gasoline vapors, and a battery check. At anchor, it will even measure current velocity.

MISCELLANEOUS PILOTING TOOLS

Among the most important of all piloting tools are the ordinary *pencils* and *erasers*. Pencils should be neither too hard nor too soft. If too hard, there will be a tendency to score into the chart paper; if too soft, smudging may result. A medium, or No. 2, pencil will often be found to be satisfactory, but personal preferences may cause some variation. Pencils should be kept well sharpened, and several should be handy to the piloting table.

FIG. 1935a Speed need not be measured directly; it may be calculated from a knowledge of distance and time. A circular calculator as shown here will make all speed-time-distance computations quickly and accurately.

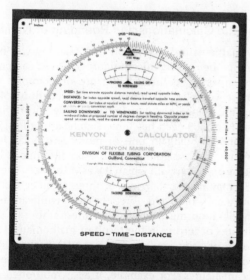

FIG. 1935b This calculator enables the pilot to solve 18 different types of navigational problems—speed-time-distance, conversions and measurement, and includes special aids for the sailboatman, even a plotting board on the reverse side.

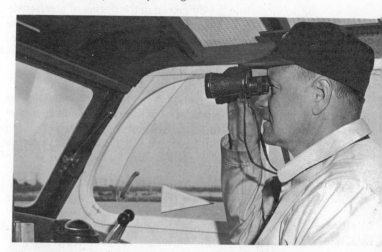

FIG. 1937 A good pair of binoculars is almost a necessity on a boat. The size most often recommended is designated "7 x 50." The eyepieces may be individually or centrally focused.

A soft eraser of the "Pink Pearl" type will be satisfactory for most erasures; an art gum eraser can be used for general chart cleaning.

Binoculars. A good pair of *binoculars* will be found essential for most piloting situations, fig. 1937. In selecting a pair of binoculars, it should be remembered that higher powers will result in greater magnification, bringing distant objects closer, but only at the cost of a more limited field of view. An adequate field of view is essential on small boats with their rapid and sometimes violent motion. Binoculars are designated by two figures, such as "6x30" or "10x50." The first figure indicates the power of magnification, the second is the diameter of the front lens in millimeters. This latter characteristic is important in night use. Most authorities recommend a 7x50 set of binoculars as best suited for marine use.

The binoculars may be individually focused (IF) for each eye, or centrally focused (CF) for both eyes, with a minor adjustment on one eyepiece to balance any difference between a person's two eyes. The choice between IF and CF glasses is a matter of personal preference.

Binoculars should be kept in their case when use is not imminent. When taken out, they should be carefully placed where they cannot be thrown from a table or ledge to the deck and damaged; protect your binoculars from any rough usage.

A boat should be equipped with several *flashlights* for emergency use. One of these should have a red lens or filter in order that it may be used to read charts and other printed matter at night without undue loss of night vision by a person who must both check the chart and act as helmsman or lookout.

FIG. 1936 Depth can be measured manually with a marked weighted line—a lead line. Markings can be of the traditional type with strips of leather and rags, or with modern direct-reading plastic tags.

MEASUREMENTS

In considering the measurement of various quantities in piloting, and the calculations in which they are used, some attention must first be given to standards of accuracy and precision. Statements of distance as 32 miles or 32.0 miles are not quite the same thing. The former merely says that to the best of observation and measurement the distance is not 31 nor 33 miles; the latter says that it is not 31.9 nor 32.1 miles. Note the difference in the degree of preciseness of these two statements of the same distance. Never write 32.0 for 32 unless your measurements are sufficiently precise to warrant such action.

STANDARD LIMITS OF ACCURACY

The navigation of various sizes of vessels naturally involves different standards of precision or accuracy as befitting the different conditions encountered. The piloting of small craft does not permit so high a degree of accuracy as on large ships that offer a more stable platform.

Direction

Direction is measured in small-craft navigation to the nearest whole degree. It is not reasonable to measure or calculate directions to a finer degree of precision when a boat is seldom steered with an accuracy closer than 2° or 3°.

Distance

Distances are normally expressed to the nearest tenth of a mile. This degree of precision, roughly 200 yards, is reasonable in consideration of the size of the craft and other measurement standards.

Time

Time is measured and calculated to the nearest minute. Fractions of a minute are rarely of any significance in routine piloting. In contests, however, time will be calculated to decimal fractions and used in terms of seconds.

Speed

Speed is calculated to the nearest tenth of a knot or mile-per-hour. It is seldom measurable to such fine units, but a calculation to the nearest tenth is not inconsistent with the expressed standards of accuracy of distance and time. This same degree of precision is used in calculations of current velocity.

Position

Geographic coordinates will be expressed to the nearest tenth of a minute of latitude and longitude, or to the nearest second, as determined by the scale of the chart. As explained in Chapter 18, latitude and longitude markings will be subdivided into minutes and seconds on the larger-scale charts (1:49,000 and larger) and in fractions of minutes on smaller-scale charts (1:50,000 and smaller).

Depths and heights of tide

Tidal variations in the depth of water are normally tabulated to the nearest tenth of a foot, fig. 1938; calculations are carried out to the same degree of precision. It must be recognized, however, that modifications to tidal action resulting from winds and atmospheric pressure variations make such a degree of precision hardly warranted.

PORTLAND, MAINE, 1966

TIMES AND HEIGHTS OF HIGH AND LOW WATERS

		OCTOBER					NOVEMBER			
DAY	TIME H.M.	HT. FT.	DAY	TIME H.M.	HT. FT.	DAY	TIME H.M.	HT. FT.	DAY	TIME H.M.
1 SA	0542 1148 1806	0.3 9.1 0.1	16 SU	0600 1212 1836	-1.0 10.9 -1.8	1 TU	0024 0618 1230 1854	8.3 0.8 9.4 -0.2	16 W	0118 0712 1330 2000
2 SU	0012 0612 1224 1836	8.7 0.5 9.1 0.1	17 M	0048 0648 1300 1924	9.8 -0.5 10.6 -1.3	2 W	0100 0654 1306 1936	8.1 0.9 9.3 -0.1	17 TH	0212 0806 1418 2048
3 M	0048 0648 1254 1918	8.5 0.7 9.1 0.1	18 TU	0142 0742 1354 2024	9.2 0.1 10.0 -0.8	3 TH	0148 0736 1354 2024	7.9 1.1 9.2 0.0	18 F	0306 0900 1512
4 TU	0124 0724 1336	8.2 0.9	19	0236	8.6	4				

FIG. 1938 **Heights of tides are tabulated in the tables of daily predictions to the nearest tenth of a foot. However, local conditions of wind and barometric pressure will often cause variations of greater magnitude.**

Arithmetic Calculations and Rounding of Numbers

Any mathematical expression of a quantity will have a certain number of "significant figures." These can perhaps be better explained through the use of examples rather than by a complicated definition. The quantity "4" has one significant figure; 4.0 or 14 has two significant figures; 5.12, 43.8, or 609 each has three significant figures, etc.

A quantity ending in one or more zeros may have a varying number of significant figures as determined by the degree of precision with which it was measured. The number 150 may have either two or three significant figures; 2000 may have one, two, three, or four significant figures.

Consideration must be given to the number of significant figures occurring in the result of mathematical calculations, especially multiplication and division. Results should not have an excessive and unwarranted number of significant figures. For example, if 83 is multiplied by 64, the result is 5312. But note that this quantity has four significant figures whereas each of the input quantities had only two significant figures. A more meaningful statement of the result would be 5310 or even 5300.

The process of reducing the number of significant figures is called "rounding." In order to have uniform results, rules have been established for the rounding of numbers.

1. If the digit to be rounded off is "4" or less, it is dropped or changed to a zero.

8.23 can be rounded to 8.2

432 can be rounded to 430

2. If the digit to be rounded off is "6" or larger, the preceding digit is raised to the next higher value and the rounded digit is dropped or changed to a zero.

8.27 can be rounded to 8.3

439 can be rounded to 440

3. If the digit to be rounded off is a "5," the rounding is to the nearest *even* value.

8.25 is rounded to 8.2

435 is rounded to 440

This rule may seem somewhat arbitrary, but it is followed

for consistency in results; it has the advantage that when two such rounded figures are added together and divided by two for an average, the result will not present a new need for rounding.

4. Rounding can be applied to more than one final digit; but all such rounding must be done in *one* step. For example: 6148 is rounded to 6100 in a single action; do not round 6148 to 6150, and then round 6150 to 6200.

In many of the statements of accuracy requirements in the preceding section, the phrase "to the nearest ———" has been used. Rounding is used to reduce various quantities to such limitations. For example: if you calculated the distance traveled in 48 minutes at 13 knots, you would get 1.04 miles. However, distance is normally stated to the nearest tenth of a mile, and so the proper expression for distance run would be 1.0 mile.

FIG. 1939 A Dead Reckoning plot should always be maintained when a boat is off-shore or cruising in large, open bodies of water.

M. Rosenfeld.

Dead Reckoning

When operating his boat offshore in large bodies of water, a pilot should have at all times at least a rough knowledge of his position on the chart. Basic to such knowledge is a technique of navigation known as *dead reckoning,* usually abbreviated to *DR.* This is the advancement of the boat's position on the chart from its last accurately determined location, using the course (or courses) steered and the speed (or speeds) through the water. No allowance is made for the effects of wind, waves, current, or steering errors.

Terms used in dead reckoning

At this point, we will deal with only those terms related to *dead reckoning.* Later, when the influence of current is being considered, additional terms will be introduced and defined.

The *DR track* (or *DR track line*) is the path that the boat is expected to follow (no current) represented on the chart by a line drawn from the last known position using courses and speeds through the water. The path the boat actually travels may be different due to one or more offsetting influences, to be considered later.

Course, abbreviated as "C" (but not to be confused with "C" as used to designate a compass direction), is the direction of the DR track line. Courses are normally plotted in terms of the true direction stated as a three-digit figure.

Heading is the direction in which the boat is pointed at any given time. The term is usually used in connection with the direction in which a boat must be steered in order to make good a desired path, allowing for various offsetting influences. Headings are often stated in terms of magnetic or compass directions.

Speed, abbreviated as "S," is the rate of travel through the water. This is the DR track speed; it is used, together with elapsed time, to determine *DR positions* along the track line.

The Basic Principles of Dead Reckoning

It is important that the pilot adhere to certain basic principles of dead reckoning.

1. A DR track is always started from a known position.

2. Only true courses steered are used for determining a DR track.

3. Only the speed through the water is used for determining distance traveled and a DR position along the track.

Although it may appear unusual to ignore the effects of a current that is known to exist, this is always done for reasons that will be established later.

The importance of dead reckoning

A DR track should always be plotted when navigating in large, open bodies of water. It is the primary representation of the path of the boat, the base to which other factors, such as the effect of current, are applied. Dead reckoning can be considered to be the basic method of navigation to which corrections and adjustments from other sources of information are applied.

At the same time, it must be remembered that this DR track is rarely a representation of the boat's actual progress. If there were no steering errors, speed errors, or external influences, the DR track could be used as a means of determining the craft's position at any time desired, as well as the ETA (Estimated Time of Arrival) at a stated destination. Despite the fact that this will rarely, if ever, be the case, a DR plot is highly desirable at all times as a safety measure in the event of unexpected variations in current, and it is most useful in the event of a sudden fog or other loss of visibility.

PLOTTING

Fundamental to the use of dead reckoning is the use of charts and plots of the craft's intended and actual positions.

FIG. 1940a The course is labeled above the line as shown here. The letter "C", followed by a space roughly equal to one character, and then the direction, in degrees True, as a three-digit number. Omit the degree symbol "°".

FIG. 1940b Speed is labeled below the course line. Write in the letter "S", a space, and the speed in knots or MPH as appropriate (but do not show the unit used).

Basic requirements

The basic requirements of plotting are *accuracy, neatness,* and *completeness.* All measurements taken from the chart must be made carefully, all direct observations must be made as accurately as conditions on a small craft will permit, and all calculations should be made in full and in writing. If time permits, each of these actions should be repeated as a check; errors can be costly!

Neatness in plotting is essential to avoid confusion of information on the chart. The drawing in on charts of excess or overly-long lines, or the scribbling of extraneous notes, may obscure small bits of vital information.

In addition to being neat, information on a chart must be complete. Often a pilot will have need to refer back to information that he placed on the chart hours, or even days, ago. It could be dangerous if he should have to rely on memory to supply part of the details. In some cases, the piloting duties may be shared among several persons; here it is obvious that all plotted information must be fully identified.

The use of standardized procedures for identifying information on charts will ensure neatness, completeness, and understandability to any person who uses it.

Labeling

Lines on charts should be drawn lightly and no longer than necessary. Be alert to the fact that a straightedge must be placed a slight distance off the desired position of the line to be drawn to allow for the thickness of the pencil point, no matter how finely it is sharpened.

The requirements of neatness and completeness combine to establish a need for *labeling*. To meet these requirements, certain rules and procedures have been established. The proper labeling of any plot is essential.

Immediately after any line is drawn on a chart, or any point is plotted, it should be labeled. The basic rules for labeling are:

1. The label for any *line* is placed *along* that line.

2. The label for any *point* should *not* be along any line; it should make such an angle with any line that its nature as the label of a point will be unmistakably clear.

The above basic rules are applied in the labeling of DR plots in the following manner:

1. The label indicating the direction of a DR track is placed *above* the track as a three-digit number preceded by the letter "C," fig. 1940a. Note that the degree symbol "°" is omitted.

2. The speed along the track is indicated by numerals

placed *under* the track line, usually directly beneath the direction label, fig. 1940b. The units, knots or MPH, are not shown. Never label distance along a track.

3. A known position at the start of a DR track, a *Fix,* to be discussed later, is shown as a circle across the track line. It is labeled with the time, in four-digit notation (24-hour clock system) followed by "FIX," fig. 1941.

4. A DR position along the track, calculated as a distance along the track at the specified speed through the water, is shown as a circle intersecting the track line; it is labeled with the time in four-digit notation plus the letters "DR," see fig. 1942.

Further applications of the basic rules of labeling will be given as additional piloting procedures and situations are introduced in subsequent chapters.

All lines on a chart should be erased when no longer needed to keep the chart clear. Erasures should be made as lightly as possible to avoid damage to the surface of the chart and its printed information.

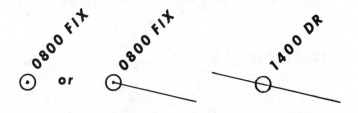

FIG. 1941 A known position of the boat is plotted as a dot with a small circle around it. If it is along a line, the dot will not show separately. Label the position with the time as a four-digit number in the 24-hour system plus the word "FIX".

FIG. 1942 A dead reckoning position along a track is plotted as a circle across the track line and labeled with the time followed by "DR".

D, T, AND S CALCULATIONS

As mentioned earlier, calculations involving distance (D), time (T), and speed (S) are often done by means of a small calculator. The use of such a device is perfectly acceptable, but the good pilot can accurately and quickly make his calculations without one, using only a simple set of equations and ordinary arithmetic. An ability to make arithmetical computations is necessary as a calculating device may not always be available.

The three basic equations are:

$$D = ST \qquad S = \frac{D}{T} \qquad T = \frac{D}{S}$$

Where D is distance in miles, T is time in *hours,* and S is speed in knots or miles per hour as determined by the type of mile being used. Note carefully that T is in hours in these basic equations. To use time in *minutes,* as is more normally the case, the equations are modified to read:

$$D = \frac{ST}{60} \qquad S = \frac{60D}{T} \qquad T = \frac{60D}{S}$$

Examples of the use of these practical equations may serve to make them clearer:

1. You are cruising at 14 knots; how far will you travel in 40 minutes?

$$D = \frac{ST}{60} \qquad D = \frac{14 \times 40}{60} = 9.3 \text{ miles}$$

Note that the calculated answer of 9.33 is rounded to

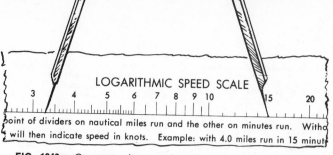

FIG. 1943a On some charts, a logarithmic speed scale may be used to graphically determine speed. First, set one point of your dividers on the scale division indicating the miles traveled, and the other on the number corresponding to the time in minutes.

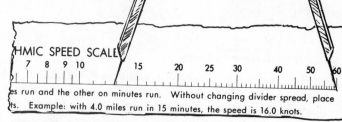

FIG. 1943b With the dividers maintaining the same spread, transfer them so that the right point is on the "60" of the scale (right end). The left point will indicate the speed in knots or MPH, as determined by the type of mile used.

the nearest tenth according to the rule for the degree of accuracy to be used in stating distance.

2. On one of the Great Lakes, it took you 40 minutes to travel 11 miles; what is your speed?

$$S = \frac{60D}{T} \qquad S = \frac{60 \times 11}{40} = 16.5 \text{ MPH}$$

3. You have 9½ miles to go to reach your destination, your cruising speed is 11 knots; how long will it take you to get there?

$$T = \frac{60D}{S} \qquad T = \frac{60 \times 9.5}{11} = 52 \text{ minutes}$$

Note again the rounding of results; the calculated answer of 51.8 minutes would be used as 52 minutes, except in contests where it would probably be used as 51 minutes 48 seconds.

The three practical equations of distance, time, and speed should be carefully memorized. Practice using them until you become thoroughly familiar with them and can obtain your answers to typical problems quickly and accurately.

Use of logarithmic scale on charts

Charts of the Coast and Geodetic Survey at scales of 1:40,000 and larger will have printed on them a *logarithmic speed scale.* *To find speed,* place one point of your dividers on the mark on the scale indicating the distance in nautical miles, and the other point on the number corresponding to the time in minutes, fig. 1943a. Without changing the spread between the divider arms, place the right point on the "60" at the right end of the scale; the left point will then indicate on the scale the speed in knots, see fig. 1943b.

This same logarithmic scale can also be used *to determine the time* required to cover a given distance at a specified speed (for situations not exceeding one hour). Set the two divider points on the scale marks representing speed in knots and distance in miles. Move the dividers, without changing the spread, until the right point is at "60" on the scale; the other point will indicate the time in minutes.

Likewise, *distance can be determined* from this logarithmic scale using knowledge of time and speed. Set the right point of the dividers on "60" and the left point at the mark on the scale corresponding to the speed in knots. Then, without changing the spread, move the right point to the mark on the scale representing the time in minutes; the left point will now indicate the distance in nautical miles.

CS charts will have instructions for determining speed printed beneath the logarithmic scale, but not the procedures for determining distance or time. In all cases, you must know two of the three quantities in order to determine the other.

Use of S-D-T calculators

It is not possible here to give detailed instructions for the operation of all models of speed-distance-time calculators. In general, such devices will have two or more scales, each logarithmically subdivided. The calculator will be set using two of the factors and the answer, the third factor, will be read off at an index mark.

If you have a calculator for S-D-T problems, read the instructions carefully and practice with it sufficiently, using simple, self-evident problems, to be sure of obtaining reliable results, even under the stress of difficult situations or emergencies.

SPEED CURVES

Although some boats may be equipped with marine speedometers, the more-often used method of determination of speed is through the use of engine speed as measured by the *tachometer* in revolutions per minute (RPM). A *speed curve* is prepared as a plot on cross-section (graph) paper of the boat's speed in knots or MPH for various engine speeds in RPM.

Factors affecting speed curves

The speed that a boat will achieve for a specified engine setting may be affected by several factors. The extent of each effect will vary with the size of the boat, type of hull, and other characteristics.

Load is a primary factor influencing a boat's speed. The number of persons aboard, the amount of fuel and water in the tanks, and the amount and location of other weights on board will affect the depth to which the hull sinks in the water and the angular trim. Both displacement and trim may be expected to have an effect on speed.

Another major factor affecting speed is the *underwater hull condition.* Fouling growth, such as barnacles or moss, increases the drag, the resistance to movement through the water, and slows the speed of the boat at any given engine RPM.

Whenever preparing speed data on a boat, the loading and underwater hull conditions at the time of the trials should be noted with the figures for RPM and speed. If a speed curve is made at the start of a boating season when the bottom is clean, it should be checked later on in the season if the boat is used in waters where fouling is a problem. A new speed curve may be required, or it may be possible to determine what small corrections can be applied to get a more accurate measure of speed. A good skipper also knows what speed differences he may expect from full tanks to half to nearly empty; the differences can be surprising in many boats.

Obtaining speed curves

Speed curves are obtained by making repeated runs over a known distance using different throttle settings and timing each run very accurately. Any reasonable distance can be used. Ordinarily, it should not be less than a half-mile in order that small timing errors will not excessively influence the results; it need not be more than a mile, to avoid excessive time and fuel requirements for the trials.

The run need not be an even half-mile or mile if the distance is accurately known. Do not depend upon floating aids to navigation — they may be slightly off-station, and, in any event, they have some scope on their anchor chains and will swing about under the effects of wind and current. Many areas will have *measured miles* (or half-miles), fig. 1944. These are accurately surveyed distances with each end marked by ranges. Use these courses whenever possible; they can be depended upon for accuracy and calculations are made easier by the even-mile distance. But do not let the absence of such a measured mile in your local waters keep you from having a speed curve for your boat. Use accurately charted wharves, fixed aids to navigation, points of land, etc.

In most speed trials, it will be necessary to run the known distance twice, once in each direction, in order to allow for the effects of current. Even in waters not affected by currents, it is advisable to make round-trip runs for each throttle setting to allow for wind effects.

For each *one-way* run, measure the time required; steer the boat carefully so that the most direct, the shortest run is made. Compute the speed for each run by the equations previously used. If a measured mile is used for the speed trials, speeds can be found easily by use of the table on page 463. If the measured distance is an exact half-mile, the tabulated speeds must be divided by two. Then average the *speeds* of each run of a pair at a given RPM to determine the true speed of the boat through the water. The strength of the current is one-half the difference between the speed in the two directions of any pair of runs. *Caution:* do *not* average together the *times* of a pair of runs to get a single time for use in the calculations; this will *not* give the correct value for speed through the water.

If time is measured with a regular clock or watch, be

RPM	N-S		S-N		Average Speed	Current
	Time	Speed	Time	Speed		
900	7m 54s	7.60	11m 25s	5.26	6.43	1.17
1100	6 53	8.72	9 14.2	6.50	7.61	1.11
1300	6 08.8	9.76	7 36.8	7.88	8.82	.94
1500	5 35.8	10.72	6 40.4	9.00	9.86	.86
1700	5 10.8	11.59	5 54.2	10.17	10.88	.71
1900	4 38.0	12.96	5 06.4	11.76	12.36	.60
2150	3 48.6	15.75	4 05.6	14.73	15.24	.51

FIG. 1945 Tabulated results of speed trials made for "Trident." Note that runs were made in each direction to account for the effect of current. Entries were made in the log as to fuel and water loads aboard and condition of the bottom of the hull.

careful in making the subtractions to get elapsed time. Remember that there are 60 seconds in each minute, not 100, and likewise 60 minutes in one hour. Most people are so used to decimal calculations that foolish errors are sometimes made when "borrowing" in the subtraction of clock times.

If one is willing to use a slightly more complex equation, the boat's speed through the water (or the strength of the current) can be found from a single calculation using the times of the two runs of each pair.

$$S = \frac{60D(Tu + Td)}{2TuTd} \qquad C = \frac{60D(Tu - Td)}{2TuTd}$$

Where S is speed through the water in knots or MPH
    C is current in knots or MPH
    Tu is time upstream, in minutes
    Td is time downstream, in minutes
    D is distance, in nautical or statute miles

In the preparation of a speed curve for a boat, sufficient pairs of runs should be made to provide points for a plot of speed versus RPM; some six or eight points will usually be enough for a satisfactory curve. With some types of hulls, there will be a break in the curve at a critical speed when the hull changes from displacement action to semi-planing action. At this portion of the curve, additional, more closely-spaced measurements may be required. For this reason, it is often a good idea to calculate speeds during runs and make a rough plot as you go along.

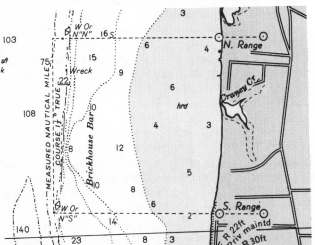

FIG. 1944 Many boating areas have *measured mile* courses established for making accurate speed trials. These will be shown on the chart of the area.

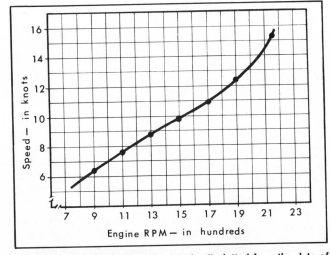

FIG. 1946 The speed curve for "Trident" plotted from the data of fig. 1945. This curve is truly accurate only for load and underwater hull conditions similar to those on the day of the trials.

It may also be found desirable to calculate the strength of the current for each pair of runs. It will probably be noted that the current values will vary during the speed trials, but such variations should be small and in a consistent direction, either steadily increasing or decreasing, or going through a slack period. The best results will normally be obtained if the trials are run at a time of minimum current.

Example of a Speed Curve

A set of speed trials was run for the motor yacht "Trident" over the measured mile off Kent Island in Chesapeake Bay, fig. 1944. This is an excellent course as it is marked both by buoys offshore and by ranges on land. The presence of the buoys aids in steering a straight run from one end of the course to the other; the ranges are used for greater accuracy in timing.

On this particular day, it was not convenient to wait for slack water, but a time was selected that would result in something less than maximum ebbing current. A table was set up in the log, and runs were made in each direction at speeds of normal interest from 900 RPM to 2150 RPM which was maximum for the 6-71 diesels.

The results of the runs are shown in fig. 1945. An entry was also made in the log that these trials were made with fuel tanks 0.35 full, the water tanks approximately 1/3 full, and a clean bottom. The column of the table marked "Current" is not necessary, but it serves as a "flag" to quickly expose any inconsistent data. Note that on these trials the current is decreasing at a reasonably consistent rate.

After the runs had been completed, a plot was made on cross-section paper of the boat's speed as a function of engine RPM. This resulted in the speed curve shown as fig. 1946.

DEAD RECKONING PLOTS

With knowledge of dead reckoning terms and principles, the rules for labeling points and lines, and the procedures for making calculations involving distance, time, and speed, it is possible to consider now the use of DR plots.

There are several specific rules for making and using DR plots.

1. A DR plot should be made when leaving a known position, fig. 1947.

2. A DR position should be shown whenever a change is made in course, fig. 1948a, or in speed, fig. 1948b.

3. A DR position should be plotted each hour on the hour, fig. 1949.

4. A new DR track should be started each time the boat's position is fixed. The old DR position for the same time as the fix should also be shown at the end of the old DR track, see fig. 1950.

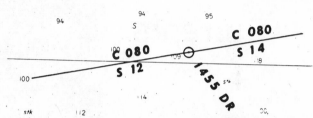

FIG. 1948b If a variation in speed is made without a change in direction, a DR position is plotted on the track and new labels of course and speed are entered following it.

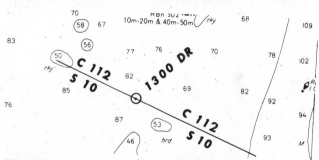

FIG. 1949 A DR position should be plotted each hour on the hour along the track even though there is no change in course or speed. These plots will keep the pilot informed of his progress and are useful in sudden emergencies.

FIG. 1950 Whenever the boat's position is fixed, such as by passage close by a buoy as shown here, a DR position is plotted for that time, calculated from speed and distance information. The fix is also plotted and a new DR track is started. The difference between the DR position and the Fix for the same time indicates the effect of offsetting influences such as current.

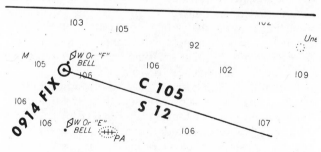

FIG. 1947 A dead reckoning plot is started when leaving a known position. The time of that position is plotted as a Fix; course and speed are labeled along the DR track.

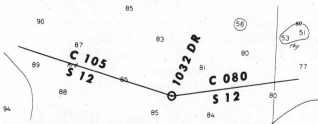

FIG. 1948a Whenever a change in course is made, a DR position is plotted for that time; the new course and speed are labeled along the new track.

CHAPTER 20

Tides and currents are of much interest and concern to the skipper who does his boating on coastal waters. Time invested in mastering their theory and practice will pay dividends in the form of increased safety, convenience, and economy. And too, there is the satisfaction of developing an ability to deal with natural phenomena that you can't change, but which can often be used to your advantage.

PILOTING —Tides and Currents

FIG. 2001 Boatmen in coastal regions must learn to cope with tidal conditions. The range from high water to low may be only inches, or it may be many feet.

Dead Reckoning and Currents

In the preceding chapter, it was noted that a dead reckoning plot is based upon the course steered and the boat's speed through the water. Even though offsetting factors were known to exist, they were *not* included in a DR plot. Thus, it can readily be seen that while a DR plot is a basic representation of a boat's motion, it fails to account for all existing circumstances.

Offsetting influences that will make the boat's actual path diverge from the DR track include current, leeway from wind and waves, and steering errors. Of these, the one that can be most easily and accurately handled is current. The extent of its effect will vary widely with the relative values of current strength and boat speed through the water, but often the influence of current can be a major factor in piloting.

Tides vs. Current

Perhaps at this point we should pause to make clear the proper meaning and use of several terms that are often loosely and incorrectly used. *Tide* is the rise and fall of the ocean level as a result of changes in the gravitational attraction between the earth, moon, and sun. It is a *vertical* motion only. *Current* is a *horizontal* motion of water from any cause. *Tidal current* is the flow of water from one point to another that results from a difference in tidal heights at those points. How often have you heard others say (or perhaps even said it yourself) that "The tide is certainly running strongly today!" This is not correct, for tides may be high or low, but they do not "run." Obviously, the correct expression would have been "The (tidal) current is certainly strong today." Remember—tide is vertical change; current is horizontal flow.

Tides

As tidal action is a primary cause of currents, let us consider it first, and save our consideration of currents for later. Actually, tides in themselves are important factors in the safe navigation of watercraft as will be discussed in the following pages.

Tides originate in the open oceans and seas, but are only noticeable and significant close to shore. The effect of tides will be observed along coastal beaches, in bays and sounds, and up rivers generally as far as the first rapids,

waterfall, or dam. Curiously, the effect of tides may be more noticeable a hundred miles up a river than it is at the river's mouth. Coastal regions in which the water levels are subject to tidal action are often referred to as "tidewater" areas.

Definition of Terms

In addition to the basic definition of tide as given above, certain other terms used in connection with tidal action must be defined. The *height of tide* at any specified time is the vertical measurement between the surface of the water and the *tidal datum* or reference plane. Do not confuse "height of tide" with "depth of water." The latter is the total distance from the surface to the bottom. The tidal datum for an area is selected so that the heights of tide are normally positive values, but the height can at times be a small negative number when the water level falls below the datum.

High water, or *high tide*, is the highest level reached by an ascending tide. Correspondingly, *low water*, or *low tide*, is the lowest level reached by a descending tide, fig. 2003. The difference between high and low waters is termed the *range* of the tide.

The change in tidal level does not occur at a uniform rate; starting from, say, low water, the level builds up slowly, then at an increasing rate which in turn tapers off as high water is reached. The decrease in tidal stage from high water to low follows a corresponding pattern of a slow buildup to a maximum rate roughly midway between stages followed by a decreasing rate. At both high and low tides, there will be periods of relatively no change in level; these are termed *stand*. *Mean sea level* is the average level of the open ocean and corresponds closely to mid-tide levels offshore.

TIDAL THEORY

Tidal action can be studied both from a theoretical view and in terms of actual conditions. It is perhaps best approached from an initial consideration of basic principles, with practical departures from theory being noted afterwards. As briefly mentioned earlier, tidal theory is based on the gravitational attraction between the earth on one hand, and the moon and sun on the other. In order to simplify the presentation of these effects, they will be described separately, although, of course, in actual practice, they both act simultaneously. Although the sun has a lesser effect on tides than the moon, its gravitational

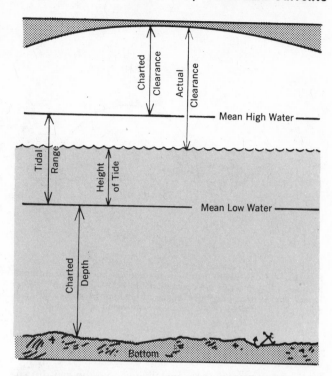

FIG. 2003   This diagram illustrates the relationship between some of the terms used to describe tidal conditions. Terms are defined in the text. Mean lower low water may be substituted for mean low water in some areas.

action is easier to visualize, and so it will be considered first.

Earth-Sun Effects

Each year the earth and the sun revolve around a common point located close to the center of the sun; for all practical considerations, the earth can be thought of as revolving around the sun. Just as a stone tied to the end of a string tends to sail off when a young boy whirls it about

FIG. 2002   The rise and fall of ocean tidal levels will cause a flow first into and then out of inland bodies of water such as bays, sounds, and the lower reaches of rivers. These tidal currents may have important effects on the piloting of boats in such waters.   (from Kodachrome by Wm. H. Koelbel)

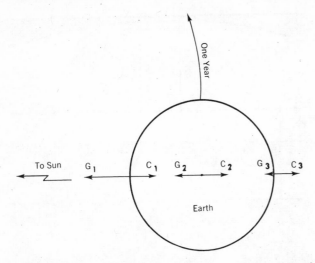

FIG. 2004 Tides result from the differences between centrifugal forces—C_1, C_2, and C_3—and gravitational forces—G_1, G_2, and G_3. The forces shown here are those of the interaction of earth and sun; corresponding forces result from the earth-moon relationship.

his head, so the earth tends to fly off into space. This is known as centrifugal force; it is designated as C in fig. 2004. (Remember that we are talking about the centrifugal force related to the sun-earth system, and not that of the day-night spinning of the earth on its axis.)

The earth is kept from flying off into space by the gravitational attraction of the sun, designated G in fig. 2004. Now, since the earth does not fly off into space, nor does it fall into the sun, C_2 and G_2 (at the center of the earth) must be equal.

Keeping mathematics at a minimum, we need only note that gravitational attraction varies inversely with the square of the distance between the objects, and centrifugal force varies directly with the radius of rotation—the distance from the sun in this case. Thus G_1 is greater than G_2 and G_3 is less. Likewise, C_1 is less than C_2 or C_3. With G_2 equal to C_2, there will be unbalanced forces at both sides—G_1 being greater than C_1 and C_3 being greater than G_3. These differences called SF_1 and SF_3 in fig. 2005, are the vertical tidal forces. Note that SF_1 points toward the sun and SF_3 away, and that SF_1 is essentially equal to SF_3.

Continuing our theoretical analysis, we can think of the earth as being a smooth sphere uniformly covered with water (no land areas). The two forces SF_1 and SF_3 will cause a flow of water toward their locations building up a bulge on either side of the earth in line with the earth-sun line; this is marked as "envelope" in fig. 2005. These points would accordingly experience a rising of the water level, a high tide. Between those two points, around the earth, the water would be drawn away, and such places would have a low tide.

As the earth turns on its axis, once in twenty-four hours, inside this envelope of water, each point on the earth's surface would then have two high and two low tides each day, following each other in alternate and regular succession.

Earth-Moon Effects

The moon is commonly thought of as revolving about the earth; actually, the two bodies revolve around a common point on a monthly cycle. This point is located about

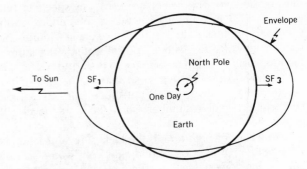

FIG. 2005 Inequalities of gravitational and centrifugal forces result in high tides on opposite sides of the earth at the same time, on the side away from the sun as well as the side toward it. Low tides will occur midway between these areas.

2900 miles from the center of the earth toward the moon (about 1100 miles deep inside the earth). By just the same logic as applied to the earth-sun system, a second set of tidal forces is developed. In explaining tidal forces in the earth-moon system, however, one must always remember to think of both the earth and the moon as revolving around a common point, rather than the moon merely going around the earth. It is only by the former concept that we can get the necessary centrifugal forces for tides on the earth.

Spring and Neap Tides

Let us now combine the earth-sun and earth-moon systems. Due to the fact that the moon is much closer to the earth (about 238,860 miles away), its tidal forces are approximately 2½ times greater than those of the sun (roughly 92,900,000 miles distant). The result is that the observed tide usually "follows the moon," but the action is somewhat modified by the sun's relative position. The two high and two low waters each day occur about 50 minutes later

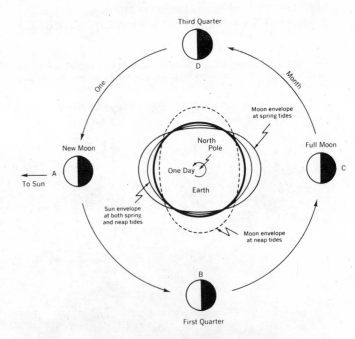

FIG. 2006 At new and full moon, combined gravitational "pull" of sun and moon acts to produce maximum effect; at these times, tidal ranges are greatest. At first and third quarters of the moon, the two gravitational forces partially offset each other and the net effect is at a minimum; tidal ranges are then least.

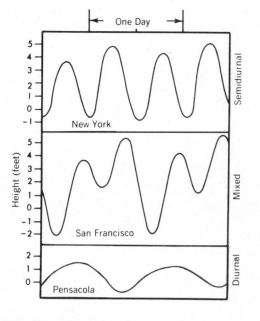

FIG. 2007 Characteristics of the daily cycle of tides vary widely at different places. Shown here are three basic types—from the top, semi-diurnal, mixed, and diurnal.

than the corresponding tides of the previous day.

In the course of any one month, the three bodies line up sun-moon-earth (position A in fig. 2006) and sun-earth-moon (position C). These are the times of the new and full moon, respectively. In both cases, the sun's effect (or "envelope") lines up with and reinforces the moon's effect, tending to result in greater-than-average tidal ranges (about 20%), called *spring tides*; note carefully that this name has nothing to do with the season of the year.

At positions B and D in fig. 2006, when the moon is at its first and third quarters, the tidal "bulge" due to the sun is at right angles to that caused by the moon (they are said to be "in *quadrature*"). The two tidal effects are in conflict and partially cancel each other, resulting in smaller-than-average ranges (again about 20%); these are *neap tides*.

It should also be noted that the tidal range of any given point varies from month to month, and from year to year. The monthly variation is due to the fact that the earth is not at the center of the moon's orbit. When the moon is closest to the earth, the lunar influence is at its maximum; tides at these times will have the greatest ranges. Conversely, when the moon is farthest from the earth, its effect, and tidal ranges, are the least.

In a similar manner, the yearly variations in the daily ranges of the tides are caused by the changing gravitational effects of the sun as that body's distance from the earth becomes greater or less.

ACTUAL TIDES

We have been considering the tidal forces and their envelope rather than the actual tide as we observe it in the sea. Why do they differ? The following are the main reasons:

1. Great masses of land, the continents, irregularly shaped and irregularly placed, act to interrupt, restrict, and reflect tidal movements.

2. Water, although generally appearing to flow freely, is actually a somewhat viscous substance and therefore

lags in its response to tidal forces.

3. Friction is present as the ocean waters "rub" against the ocean bottom.

4. The depth to the bottom of the sea, varying widely, influences the speed of the tidal motion horizontally.

5. The depths of the ocean areas and the restrictions of the continents often result in "basins" which have their own way of responding to tidal forces.

Although these reasons account for great differences between theoretical tidal forces and actual observed tides, there nevertheless remain definite, constant relationships between the two at any particular location. By observing the tide, and relating these observations with the movements of the sun, moon, and earth, these constant relationships can be determined. With this information, tides can be predicted for any future date at a given place.

Types of Tides

A tide which each day has two high waters approximately equal in height, and two low waters also about equal, is known as a *semidiurnal* type. This is the most common tide, and, in the United States, occurs along the east coast (fig. 2007, New York).

In a monthly cycle, the moon moves north and south of the Equator. Fig. 2008 illustrates the importance of this action to tides. Point A is under a bulge in the envelope. One half-day later, at point B, it is again under the bulge but the height is not as large as at A. This situation, combined with coastal characteristics, tends to give rise to a "twice daily" tide with unequal high and/or low waters in some areas. This is known as the *mixed* type of tide; see fig. 2007, San Francisco. The term "low water" may be modified to indicate the more pronounced of the two lows. This tidal stage is termed *lower low water* and is averaged to determine the *mean lower low water* (MLLW); this is used as the tidal datum in many areas subject to mixed tides. Likewise, the more significant of the higher tides is termed *higher high water*.

Now consider point C in fig. 2008. At this place, it is still under the bulge of the envelope. One half-day later, at point D, however, it is above the low part. Hence, the tidal forces tend to cause only one high and one low water each day (actually each 24 hours and 50 minutes approximately). This is the *diurnal* type, typified by Pensacola in fig. 2007.

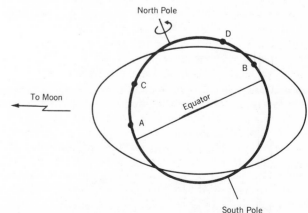

FIG. 2008 The moon travels north and south of the earth's equatorial plane. This change results in variations in the daily tidal cycle at any given location. Similar, but lesser, effects result from changes in the sun's position with respect to the earth.

Tides and Currents / CHAPTER 20

FIG. 2009 Watch out for falling tides! A prudent skipper knows not only the depth of water when he anchors, but also how it is going to change over the next 12 hours or so. In this river in Nova Scotia, the river bed will be exposed for about five hours; in the sixth hour the flood will rush in as a "bore" and rise 20 feet.
(from Kodachrome by Wm. H. Koelbel)

Whenever the moon is farthest north (as in fig. 2008) or south, there will be a tendency to have the diurnal or mixed type. When the moon lies over the Equator, we tend to have the semidiurnal type. These are *Equatorial tides* and the tendency toward producing inequality is then at a minimum.

The above theoretical considerations are, however, modified by many practical factors such as the general configuration of the coastline.

Special Tidal Situations

Peculiarities in the tide can be found almost everywhere, but none compare with those in the Bay of Fundy. Twice each day, the waters surge in and out of the Bay, producing, at Burntcoat Head, the highest tidal range in the world —a typical rise and fall of nearly 44 feet. At springs, according to Sailing Directions for Nova Scotia, it rises 51½ feet —on perigee springs, 53 feet.

This great range is often attributed to the funnel-like shape of the Bay, but this is not the main cause. Just as the water in a wash basin will slosh when you move your hand back and forth in just the right period of time, depending upon the depth of water and the shape of the basin, so the tide will attempt to oscillate water in bays in cycles of 12 hours and 25 minutes. It would be a coincidence indeed if a bay were of such a shape and depth as to have a complete oscillation with a period of exactly 12 hours and 25 minutes. A bay, however, can easily have a part of such an oscillation; such is the case in the Bay of Fundy.

A further factor in creating the large tidal ranges in the Bay of Fundy is the circumstance that they are controlled by the Gulf of Maine tides which, in turn, are controlled by the open ocean tides. The relationships between these tides are such as to exaggerate their ranges.

THE IMPORTANCE OF TIDES

A good knowledge of tidal action is essential for safe navigation. The skipper of a boat of any size will be faced many times with the need for knowledge of the time of high water and low water, and their probable heights. He may be faced with the desirability or necessity of crossing some shoal area, passable at certain tidal stages but not at others. He may be about to anchor, and the scope to pay out will be affected by the tide's range. He may be going to make fast to a pier or wharf in a strange harbor and will have need of tidal information if he is to adjust his lines properly for overnight.

Tidal effects on vertical clearances

The rise and fall of the tide will change the vertical clearance under fixed structures such as bridges or overhead power cables. These clearances are stated on charts and in Coast Pilots as heights measured from a datum which is *not* the same plane as used for depths and tidal predictions. The datum for heights is normally mean high water (MHW).

It will thus be necessary to determine the height of MHW above the tidal datum. On the East Coast, where the tidal datum is mean low water (MLW), the plane of mean high water is above MLW by the "mean range" which is listed in Table 2 of the Tide Tables, fig. 2010, for each reference and subordinate station.

On the West Coast, or in any area where the tidal datum is mean lower low water (MLLW), slightly more complicated calculations are required. Here, MHW is above the tidal datum by an amount equal to the sum of the "mean tide level" plus one-half of the "mean range"; both of these values appear in Table 2 for the West Coast.

If the tide level at any given moment is below MHW, the vertical clearance under a bridge or other fixed structure is then greater than the figures shown on the chart; but if the tide height is *above* the level of MHW, then the clearance is *less*. Calculate the vertical clearance in advance if you anticipate a tight situation, but *also* observe the clearance gauges usually found at bridges. Clearances will normally be greater than the charted MHW values, but will occasionally be less.

SOURCES OF TIDAL INFORMATION

The basic source of information on the time of high and low water, and their heights above (or below) the datum, is the *Tide Tables* published by the U.S. Coast and

Geodetic Survey, fig. 2010. Any predictions appearing in newspapers, or broadcast over radio and TV stations, will have been extracted from these tables. The cover jackets of charts in the small-craft series will also include excerpts from the Tide Tables as applicable to the area covered by the chart, fig. 2011.

Not to be overlooked is the possibility of "local knowledge." Never be hesitant to ask experienced local watermen when you are in unfamiliar waters and need information of any kind. The best of tables prepared by electronic computers sometimes cannot compare with a knowledge of what to expect that is based on years of local experience.

TIDE TABLES

The Coast and Geodetic Survey Tide Tables are of great value in determining the height of water at any place at a given time. These are calculated in advance and published annually. There are four volumes, one of which covers the East Coast of North and South America, and another the West Coast of these continents.

These Tables can usually be bought at any authorized sales agent for C&GS charts. The price for each volume is $2.00.

The Tide Tables give the predicted times and heights of high and low water for each day of the year at a number of important points known as *reference stations*. Portland, Boston, Newport, and Sandy Hook are examples of points for which detailed information is given in the East Coast Tables. Reference stations in the West Coast Tables include

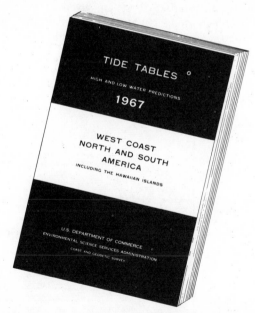

FIG. 2010 The Coast and Geodetic Survey uses modern electronic computing equipment to prepare advanced predictions of tidal levels at many points. These are published in the annual Tide Tables.

San Diego, the Golden Gate at San Francisco, and Aberdeen, Washington.

Additional data are tabulated showing the difference in times and heights between these reference stations and thousands of other points termed *subordinate stations*. From these tables, the tide at virtually any point of significance along the coasts can easily be computed. The West Coast Tide Tables contain predictions for reference sta-

tions and differences for about 1100 subordinate stations in North and South America.

The heights given in Tide Tables must, of course, be reckoned from some plane of reference, or tidal datum. From the discussion earlier in this chapter, it is evident that there are a number of different planes to which the heights might be referred. In actual practice, the predictions in the Tables are based on the same datum as that used in making the charts for any given locality. The datum used for the Atlantic Coast is *mean low water* (MLW), which is the average of *all* low-water levels. On the Pacific Coast, where the mixed type of tide is more prevalent, it is the average of the lower of the two low waters occurring each day (MLLW).

All of the factors that can be determined in advance are taken into account in tide predictions, but in the use of the tables, it must be remembered that certain other factors which have a pronounced influence on the height of tides, cannot be forecast months or years in advance. Such influences include barometric pressure and wind. In many areas, the effect of a prolonged gale of wind from a certain quarter is sometimes sufficient to offset all other factors. Tidal rivers may be affected by changes in the volume of water flowing down from the watershed. Normal seasonal variations of flow are allowed for in the predictions, but unexpected prolonged wet or dry spells may result in significant changes to the predictions of tidal heights. Intense rainfall upriver may result in changes to both the heights and times of tides; these effects may not appear downstream for several days.

Caution should therefore be exercised whenever using the Tide Tables, especially since low waters may at times go considerably lower than the level predicted.

Explanation of the Tables

Table 1 of the Tide Tables, fig. 2012, gives the predicted times and heights of high and low water at the main reference stations and is practically self-explanatory. Where no sign is given before the predicted height, the quantity is positive and is to be added to the depths as given on the chart. When the value is preceded by a minus (−) sign, the "heights" are to be *subtracted* from charted depths.

Time is given in the four-digit system from 0001 to 2400 (see page 337a). In many areas, caution must be exercised regarding *daylight time*. The Tide Tables are published in terms of local *standard* time, and a correction must be applied if you are in a DT locality.

While there are normally two high and two low tides each date, they are, on an average, nearly an hour later each succeeding day. Consequently, there will be instances when a high or low tide may skip a calendar day, as indicated by a blank space in the Tide Tables, fig. 2013. If it is a high tide, for example, that has been skipped, it will be noted that the previous corresponding high occurred late in the foregoing day, and the next one early in the following day; see the sequence for the late evening high tides of 1, 2, and 3 February in fig. 2013.

It may also be noted from a review of the Tide Tables that at some places there will be only one high and one low tide on some days, with the usual four tides on other days. This is not a diurnal tide situation, where a single high and low would occur every day. The condition considered here arises when the configuration of the land and the periods between successive tides are such that one tide is reflected back from the shore and alters the effect of the succeeding tide.

Sometimes the diurnal inequality (the difference in the height of the two high or two low waters of a day) is so increased as to cause only one low water each day. These tides are not unusual in the tropics and consequently are called *tropic tides*.

Table 2, Tidal Differences and Constants, fig. 2014, gives the information necessary to find the time and height of tide for thousands of subordinate stations by the application of simple corrections to the data given for the main reference stations. The name of the applicable reference station in each case is given in bold-face type at the head of the particular section in which the subordinate station is listed. The following information is given in separate columns of Table 2:

a. Latitude and longitude of the subordinate station.
b. Differences in time and height of high (and low) waters at the subordinate station and its designated reference station.
c. Mean and spring (or diurnal) tidal ranges.
d. Mean tide level.

Note carefully that the existence of a "minus tide" means that the actual depths of water will be *less* than the figures on the chart.

To determine the time of high or low water at any station in Table 2, use the column marked Differences, Time. This gives the hours and minutes to be added to (+) or subtracted from (−) the time of the respective high or low water at the reference station shown in bold-face type next *above* the listing of the subordinate station. Be careful in making calculations near midnight. The application of the time difference may result in crossing the line from one day to another. Simply add or subtract 24 hours as necessary.

The height of the tide at a station in Table 2 is determined by applying the height difference or ratio. A plus sign (+) indicates that the difference, in feet and tenths, is to be added to the height at the designated reference station for the same time; a minus sign (−) indicates that it should be subtracted.

Where height differences would give unsatisfactory predictions, ratios may be substituted for heights. Ratios are identified by an asterisk. These are given as a decimal fraction by which the height at the reference station is to be multiplied to determine the height at the subordinate station.

In the columns headed Ranges, the *mean range* is the difference in height between mean high water and mean low water. This figure is useful in many areas where it may

---

NEWPORT, R.I., 1966-1967

Times and Heights of High and Low Waters

Eastern Standard Time, For Daylight Saving Time Add 1 Hour

	APRIL 1966					MAY 1966					
DAY	TIME H.M.	HT. FT.	DAY	TIME H.M.	HT. FT.	DAY	TIME H.M.	HT. FT.	DAY	TIME H.M.	HT. FT.
1 F	0400 0954 1624 2218	3.6 −0.1 3.4 −0.4	16 SA	0436 1054 1700 2318	3.0 0.3 3.2 0.3	1 SU	0430 1030 1700 2312	3.7 −0.3 4.1 −0.5	16 M	0442 1018 1706 2312	3.0 0.3 3.6 0.3
2 SA	0454 1054 1718 2318	3.8 −0.4 3.8 −0.7	17 SU	0518 1118 1742 2348	3.1 0.2 3.4 0.1	2 M	0524 1118 1748	3.8 −0.5 4.4	17 TU	0524 1054 1748 2342	3.1 0.1 3.8 0.0
3 SU	0548 1148 1812	4.0 −0.7 4.2	18 M	0600 1148 1824	3.3 0.0 3.6	3 TU	0000 0612 1206 1836	−0.7 3.9 −0.7 4.6	18 W	0606 1130 1830	3.2 −0.1 4.0
4 M	0012 0636 1230 1900	−1.0 4.2 −0.9 4.5	19 TU	0018 0642 1218 1900	−0.1 3.3 −0.2 3.8	4 W	0048 0700 1248 1924	−0.8 3.9 −0.7 4.7	19 TH	0024 0648 1212 1906	−0.2 3.3 −0.2 4.2
5 TU	0106 0724 1318 1948	−1.1 4.2 −1.0 4.6	20 W	0048 0718 1248 1936	−0.3 3.4 −0.3 3.9	5 TH	0136 0748 1330	−0.8 3.8 −0.6	20 F	0100 0730 1254 1948	−0.3 3.3 −0.3 4.2

FIG. 2011 Small-craft charts give annual tidal predictions for reference stations covered by that chart. Information tabulated for marinas and other boating facilities includes tidal ranges at such locations and time differences from a reference station.

SEATTLE, WASHINGTON, 1967   101

TIMES AND HEIGHTS OF HIGH AND LOW WATERS

	OCTOBER					NOVEMBER					DECEMBER				
DAY	TIME H.M.	HT. FT.	DAY	TIME H.M.	HT. FT.	DAY	TIME H.M.	HT. FT.	DAY	TIME H.M.	HT. FT.	DAY	TIME H.M.	HT. FT.	DAY	TIME H.M.	HT. FT.
1 SU	0148 0830 1530 2124	9.1 0.4 11.5 4.2	16 M	0336 0930 1554 2212	9.4 2.8 11.0 2.3	1 W	0400 0936 1518 2212	10.9 4.1 12.0 −1.3	16 TH	0512 1018 1530 2230	10.8 6.4 10.4 −0.5	1 F	0512 1012 1512 2230	12.3 7.3 12.1 −3.5	16 SA	0554 1048 1506 2236	11.8 8.1 10.3 −1.4
2 M	0248 0918 1554 2200	9.8 0.7 11.7 2.7	17 TU	0424 1006 1612 2236	9.8 3.5 10.7 1.5	2 TH	0500 1030 1554 2254	11.7 5.0 12.0 −2.4	17 F	0548 1100 1548 2318	11.3 6.9 10.3 −0.9	2 SA	0606 1106 1554 2318	12.8 7.7 11.8 −3.6	17 SU	0624 1130 1536 2312	12.1 8.2 10.3 −1.6
3 TU	0348 1000 1618 2242	10.5 1.3 11.9 1.1	18 W	0506 1042 1624 2300	10.2 4.2 10.5 0.7	3 F	0554 1118 1630 2336	12.2 5.9 11.9 −3.0	18 SA	0630 1136 1612 2336	11.6 7.3 10.2 −1.2	3 SU	0654 1200 1636	13.0 7.9 11.4	18 M	0700 1212 1618 2348	12.3 8.2 10.2 −1.7
4 W	0448 1048 1648 2318	11.1 2.3 11.9 −0.3	19 TH	0548 1118 1642 2330	10.6 4.9 10.3 0.2	4 SA	0654 1206 1706	12.5 6.7 11.5	19 SU	0706 1218 1642	11.7 7.6 10.0	4 M	0006 0748 1300 1724	−3.3 13.0 7.9 10.8	19 TU	0736 1254 1654	12.5 8.1 10.0
5 TH	0548 1130	11.5 3.4	20 F	0624 1154	10.8 5.6	5 SU	0024 0754	−3.1 12.4	20 M	0012 0754	−1.2 11.8	5 TU	0048 0836	−2.5 12.9	20 W	0030 0812	−1.5 12.6
5 SU	0848 1530 2142	2.2 11.2 3.1	M	0748 1424 2054	2.5 11.8 1.9	W	0942 1506 2200	5.8 10.6 0.1	TH	0918 1430 2148	6.6 12.2 −2.8	F	1006 1436 2206	7.9 10.4 −1.0	SA	1006 1448 2218	8.4 11.8 −3.4
			31 TU	0300 0848 1448 2130	9.9 3.2 11.9 2.9							31 SU	0600 1100 1530 2306	13.0 8.3 11.5 −3.2			

TIME MERIDIAN 120° W. 0000 IS MIDNIGHT. 1200 IS NOON.
HEIGHTS ARE RECKONED FROM THE DATUM OF SOUNDINGS ON CHARTS OF THE LOCALITY WHICH IS MEAN LOWER LOW WATER.

FIG. 2012 Table 1 of the Tide Tables lists daily predictions of the time and height of high and low tides at selected reference stations.

	FEBRUARY				
DAY	TIME H.M.	HT. FT.	DAY	TIME H.M.	HT. FT.
1 W	0254 0918 1624 2300	4.0 12.5 1.3 8.9	16 TH	0248 0848 1600 2300	5.6 10.7 2.1 8.6
2 TH	0348 1000 1724	5.8 12.0 0.4	17 F	0342 0918 1654	6.9 10.3 1.6
3 F	0042 0500 1048 1824	9.4 7.3 11.5 −0.3	18 SA	0048 0448 1000 1754	9.1 7.9 10.0 1.0
4 SA	0218 0630 1136 1924	10.2 8.2 11.1 −0.8	19 SU	0218 0624 1042 1848	9.8 8.6 9.9 0.3
5 SU	0324 0800 1236 2024	11.1 8.4 10.7 −1.1	20 M	0312 0748 1148 1948	10.6 8.7 9.8 −0.4

FIG. 2013 An extract from Table 1 showing how a high tide may occasionally be omitted near midnght; see text for explanation. Similarly, a low tide near midnight may be skipped about once each two weeks.

TABLE 2.—TIDAL DIFFERENCES AND OTHER CONSTANTS

No.	PLACE	POSITION Lat.	POSITION Long.	DIFFERENCES Time High water	DIFFERENCES Time Low water	DIFFERENCES Height High water	DIFFERENCES Height Low water	RANGES Mean	RANGES Diurnal	Mean Tide Level
		° ′	° ′	h. m.	h. m.	feet	feet	feet	feet	feet
	WASHINGTON—Continued **Admiralty Inlet—Continued**	N.	W.	on PORT TOWNSEND, p.94						
				Time meridian, 120°W.						
897	Port Townsend (Point Hudson)--------	48 07	122 45	-0 04	-0 04	+0.3	+0.1	5.3	8.6	5.2
899	Marrowstone Point------------------	48 06	122 41	+0 09	+0 07	+0.5	0.0	5.6	8.8	5.3
901	Oak Bay----------------------------	48 01	122 43	+0 15	+0 29	+1.0	+0.1	6.0	9.4	5.6
	Hood Canal			on SEATTLE, p.98						
903	Port Ludlow------------------------	47 55	122 41	-0 27	-0 18	*0.88	*0.88	6.4	9.9	5.9
905	Port Gamble------------------------	47 51	122 35	-0 17	-0 17	*0.91	*0.91	6.7	10.3	6.2
907	Bangor Wharf-----------------------	47 45	122 44	-0 20	+0 04	-0.3	0.0	7.3	10.9	6.4
908	Zelatched Point, Dabob Bay---------	47 43	122 49	-0 10	-0 05	0.0	+0.1	7.5	11.3	6.6
909	Seabeck----------------------------	47 38	122 50	-0 03	+0 03	+0.3	+0.1	7.8	11.6	6.8
911	Union------------------------------	47 21	123 06	-0 09	+0 04	+0.4	0.0	8.0	11.7	6.8
	Puget Sound									
913	Point No Point---------------------	47 55	122 32	-0 16	-0 16	*0.92	*0.92	6.7	10.4	6.1
915	Port Madison-----------------------	47 42	122 32	-0 08	-0 08	+0.1	0.0	7.7	11.4	6.6
917	Poulsbo, Liberty Bay---------------	47 44	122 39	+0 02	+0 08	+0.6	+0.1	8.1	11.9	6.9
919	Brownsville, Port Orchard----------	47 39	122 37	+0 02	+0 08	+0.4	0.0	8.0	11.7	6.8
921	SEATTLE (Madison St.), Elliott Bay--	47 36	122 20	Daily predictions				7.6	11.3	6.6
923	Eighth Ave. South, Duwamish River---	47 32	122 19	+0 05	+0 07	-0.1	0.0	7.5	11.1	6.5
925	Port Blakely-----------------------	47 36	122 30	+0 02	+0 03	+0.2	0.0	7.8	11.5	6.7
927	Pleasant Beach, Rich Passage--------	47 36	122 32	+0 01	+0 07	+0.2	0.0	7.8	11.5	6.7
929	Bremerton, Port Orchard------------	47 33	122 38	+0 07	+0 12	+0.4	0.0	8.0	11.7	6.8
931	Tracyton, Dyes Inlet---------------	47 37	122 40	+0 30	+0 56	+1.0	0.0	8.6	12.3	7.1
933	South Colby, Yukon Harbor----------	47 31	122 32	+0 01	+0 07	+0.3	0.0	7.9	11.6	6.7
935	Des Moines-------------------------	47 24	122 20	+0 03	+0 09	+0.4	0.0	8.0	11.7	6.8
937	Burton, Quartermaster Harbor--------	47 23	122 28	+0 07	+0 13	+0.6	0.0	8.2	11.9	6.9
939	Gig Harbor-------------------------	47 20	122 35	+0 06	+0 14	+0.6	0.0	8.2	11.8	6.9
941	Tacoma, Commencement Bay------------	47 17	122 25	+0 07	+0 06	+0.5	0.0	8.1	11.8	6.8
943	Arletta, Hale Passage--------------	47 17	122 39	+0 23	+0 36	+1.7	0.0	9.3	13.0	7.4
945	Home, Von Geldern Cove, Carr Inlet--	47 16	122 45	+0 27	+0 39	+2.3	+0.2	9.7	13.6	7.8
947	Wauna, Carr Inlet------------------	47 23	122 38	+0 20	+0 36	+1.8	0.0	9.4	13.1	7.5
949	Steilacoom-------------------------	47 10	122 36	+0 22	+0 35	+1.8	0.0	9.4	13.1	7.5
951	Hyde Point, McNeil Island----------	47 12	122 39	+0 23	+0 41	+2.1	+0.2	9.5	13.4	7.7
953	Sequalitchew Creek, Nisqually Reach-	47 07	122 40	+0 24	+0 42	+2.1	+0.1	9.6	13.4	7.7
955	Longbranch, Filucy Bay-------------	47 13	122 45	+0 26	+0 39	+2.2	+0.1	9.7	13.5	7.7
957	Henderson Inlet--------------------	47 09	122 50	+0 27	+0 45	+2.6	+0.2	10.0	14.0	8.0
959	Vaughn, Case Inlet-----------------	47 20	122 46	+0 35	+0 47	+2.8	+0.2	10.2	14.1	8.1
961	Allyn, Case Inlet------------------	47 23	122 49	+0 27	+0 46	+2.8	+0.2	10.2	14.1	8.1
963	Walkers Landing, Pickering Passage--	47 17	122 56	+0 35	+0 47	+2.9	+0.2	10.3	14.3	8.1
965	Arcadia, Pickering Passage---------	47 12	122 56	+0 35	+0 54	+3.0	+0.2	10.4	14.4	8.2
967	Shelton, Oakland Bay---------------	47 13	123 05	+1 12	+1 54	+2.8	-0.2	10.6	14.2	7.9
969	Burns Point, Totten Inlet----------	47 07	123 03	+0 36	+0 54	+3.6	+0.2	11.0	15.0	8.5
971	Rocky Point, Eld Inlet-------------	47 04	123 01	+0 34	+0 52	+3.3	+0.3	10.6	14.7	8.4
973	Dofflemyer Point, Budd Inlet--------	47 08	122 54	+0 29	+0 47	+3.1	+0.2	10.5	14.4	8.2
975	Olympia, Budd Inlet----------------	47 03	122 54	+0 31	+0 46	+3.1	+0.2	10.5	14.4	8.2
	Possession Sound and Port Susan									
977	Mukilteo---------------------------	47 57	122 18	-0 08	-0 12	-0.3	-0.1	7.4	11.0	6.4
979	Everett----------------------------	47 59	122 13	-0 09	-0 11	-0.2	0.0	7.4	11.1	6.5
981	Tulalip----------------------------	48 04	122 17	+0 02	-0 02	0.0	0.0	7.6	11.2	6.6
982	Kayak Point------------------------	48 08	122 22	-0 04	-0 01	-0.4	-0.1	7.3	10.9	6.3
983	Stanwood,[1] Stillaguamish River------	48 14	122 22	+0 18	+2 10	*0.63	*0.29	5.7	7.4	3.6

*Ratio.
[1]The low water seldom falls below the chart datum.

FIG. 2014 Table 2—Tidal Differences and Other Constants. Data are given for hundreds of subordinate stations so that predictions can be made for almost any point of significance to navigation.

TIME FROM THE NEAREST HIGH WATER OR LOW WATER

Duration of rise or fall, see footnote. h.m.	h.m.	h.m.	h.m.	h.m.	h.m.	h.m.	h.m.	h.m.	h.m.	h.m.	h.m.	h.m.	h.m.	h.m.	h.m.
4 00	0 08	0 16	0 24	0 32	0 40	0 48	0 56	1 04	1 12	1 20	1 28	1 36	1 44	1 52	2 00
4 20	0 09	0 17	0 26	0 35	0 43	0 52	1 01	1 09	1 18	1 27	1 35	1 44	1 53	2 01	2 10
4 40	0 09	0 19	0 28	0 37	0 47	0 56	1 05	1 15	1 24	1 33	1 43	1 52	2 01	2 11	2 20
5 00	0 10	0 20	0 30	0 40	0 50	1 00	1 10	1 20	1 30	1 40	1 50	2 00	2 10	2 20	2 30
5 20	0 11	0 21	0 32	0 43	0 53	1 04	1 15	1 25	1 36	1 47	1 57	2 08	2 19	2 29	2 40
5 40	0 11	0 23	0 34	0 45	0 57	1 08	1 19	1 31	1 42	1 53	2 05	2 16	2 27	2 39	2 50
6 00	0 12	0 24	0 36	0 48	1 00	1 12	1 24	1 36	1 48	2 00	2 12	2 24	2 36	2 48	3 00
6 20	0 13	0 25	0 38	0 51	1 03	1 16	1 29	1 41	1 54	2 07	2 19	2 32	2 45	2 57	3 10
6 40	0 13	0 27	0 40	0 53	1 07	1 20	1 33	1 47	2 00	2 13	2 27	2 40	2 53	3 07	3 20
7 00	0 14	0 28	0 42	0 56	1 10	1 24	1 38	1 52	2 06	2 20	2 34	2 48	3 02	3 16	3 30
7 20	0 15	0 29	0 44	0 59	1 13	1 28	1 43	1 57	2 12	2 27	2 41	2 56	3 11	3 25	3 40
7 40	0 15	0 31	0 46	1 01	1 17	1 32	1 47	2 03	2 18	2 33	2 49	3 04	3 19	3 35	3 50
8 00	0 16	0 32	0 48	1 04	1 20	1 36	1 52	2 08	2 24	2 40	2 56	3 12	3 28	3 44	4 00
8 20	0 17	0 33	0 50	1 07	1 23	1 40	1 57	2 13	2 30	2 47	3 03	3 20	3 37	3 53	4 10
8 40	0 17	0 35	0 52	1 09	1 27	1 44	2 01	2 19	2 36	2 53	3 11	3 28	3 45	4 03	4 20
9 00	0 18	0 36	0 54	1 12	1 30	1 48	2 06	2 24	2 42	3 00	3 18	3 36	3 54	4 12	4 30
9 20	0 19	0 37	0 56	1 15	1 33	1 52	2 11	2 29	2 48	3 07	3 25	3 44	4 03	4 21	4 40
9 40	0 19	0 39	0 58	1 17	1 37	1 56	2 15	2 35	2 54	3 13	3 33	3 52	4 11	4 31	4 50
10 00	0 20	0 40	1 00	1 20	1 40	2 00	2 20	2 40	3 00	3 20	3 40	4 00	4 20	4 40	5 00
10 20	0 21	0 41	1 02	1 23	1 43	2 04	2 25	2 45	3 06	3 27	3 47	4 08	4 29	4 49	5 10
10 40	0 21	0 43	1 04	1 25	1 47	2 08	2 29	2 51	3 12	3 33	3 55	4 16	4 37	4 59	5 20

CORRECTION TO HEIGHT

Range of tide, see footnote. Ft.	Ft.	Ft.	Ft.	Ft.	Ft.	Ft.	Ft.	Ft.	Ft.	Ft.	Ft.	Ft.	Ft.	Ft.	Ft.
0.5	0.0	0.0	0.0	0.0	0.0	0.0	0.1	0.1	0.1	0.1	0.1	0.2	0.2	0.2	0.2
1.0	0.0	0.0	0.0	0.0	0.1	0.1	0.1	0.2	0.2	0.2	0.3	0.3	0.4	0.4	0.5
1.5	0.0	0.0	0.0	0.1	0.1	0.1	0.2	0.2	0.3	0.4	0.4	0.5	0.6	0.7	0.8
2.0	0.0	0.0	0.0	0.1	0.1	0.2	0.3	0.3	0.4	0.5	0.6	0.7	0.8	0.9	1.0
2.5	0.0	0.0	0.1	0.1	0.2	0.2	0.3	0.4	0.5	0.6	0.7	0.9	1.0	1.1	1.2
3.0	0.0	0.0	0.1	0.1	0.2	0.3	0.4	0.5	0.6	0.8	0.9	1.0	1.2	1.3	1.5
3.5	0.0	0.0	0.1	0.2	0.2	0.3	0.4	0.6	0.7	0.9	1.0	1.2	1.4	1.6	1.8
4.0	0.0	0.0	0.1	0.2	0.3	0.4	0.5	0.7	0.8	1.0	1.2	1.4	1.6	1.8	2.0
4.5	0.0	0.0	0.1	0.2	0.3	0.4	0.6	0.7	0.9	1.1	1.3	1.6	1.8	2.0	2.2
5.0	0.0	0.1	0.1	0.2	0.3	0.5	0.6	0.8	1.0	1.2	1.5	1.7	2.0	2.2	2.5
5.5	0.0	0.1	0.1	0.2	0.4	0.5	0.7	0.9	1.1	1.4	1.6	1.9	2.2	2.5	2.8
6.0	0.0	0.1	0.1	0.3	0.4	0.6	0.8	1.0	1.2	1.5	1.8	2.1	2.4	2.7	3.0
6.5	0.0	0.1	0.2	0.3	0.4	0.6	0.8	1.1	1.3	1.6	1.9	2.2	2.6	2.9	3.2
7.0	0.0	0.1	0.2	0.3	0.5	0.7	0.9	1.2	1.4	1.8	2.1	2.4	2.8	3.1	3.5
7.5	0.0	0.1	0.2	0.3	0.5	0.7	1.0	1.2	1.5	1.9	2.2	2.6	3.0	3.4	3.8
8.0	0.0	0.1	0.2	0.3	0.5	0.8	1.0	1.3	1.6	2.0	2.4	2.8	3.2	3.6	4.0
8.5	0.0	0.1	0.2	0.4	0.6	0.8	1.1	1.4	1.8	2.1	2.5	2.9	3.4	3.8	4.2
9.0	0.0	0.1	0.2	0.4	0.6	0.9	1.2	1.5	1.9	2.2	2.7	3.1	3.6	4.0	4.5
9.5	0.0	0.1	0.2	0.4	0.6	0.9	1.2	1.6	2.0	2.4	2.8	3.3	3.8	4.3	4.8
10.0	0.0	0.1	0.2	0.4	0.7	1.0	1.3	1.7	2.1	2.5	3.0	3.5	4.0	4.5	5.0
10.5	0.0	0.1	0.3	0.5	0.7	1.0	1.3	1.7	2.2	2.6	3.1	3.6	4.2	4.7	5.2
11.0	0.0	0.1	0.3	0.5	0.7	1.1	1.4	1.8	2.3	2.8	3.3	3.8	4.4	4.9	5.5
11.5	0.0	0.1	0.3	0.5	0.8	1.1	1.5	1.9	2.4	2.9	3.4	4.0	4.6	5.1	5.8
12.0	0.0	0.1	0.3	0.5	0.8	1.1	1.5	2.0	2.5	3.0	3.6	4.1	4.8	5.4	6.0
12.5	0.0	0.1	0.3	0.5	0.8	1.2	1.6	2.1	2.6	3.1	3.7	4.3	5.0	5.6	6.2
13.0	0.0	0.1	0.3	0.6	0.9	1.2	1.7	2.2	2.7	3.2	3.9	4.5	5.1	5.8	6.5
13.5	0.0	0.1	0.3	0.6	0.9	1.3	1.7	2.2	2.8	3.4	4.0	4.7	5.3	6.0	6.8
14.0	0.0	0.2	0.3	0.6	0.9	1.3	1.8	2.3	2.9	3.5	4.2	4.8	5.5	6.3	7.0
14.5	0.0	0.2	0.4	0.6	1.0	1.4	1.9	2.4	3.0	3.6	4.3	5.0	5.7	6.5	7.2
15.0	0.0	0.2	0.4	0.6	1.0	1.4	1.9	2.5	3.1	3.8	4.4	5.2	5.9	6.7	7.5
15.5	0.0	0.2	0.4	0.7	1.0	1.5	2.0	2.6	3.2	3.9	4.6	5.4	6.1	6.9	7.8
16.0	0.0	0.2	0.4	0.7	1.1	1.5	2.1	2.6	3.3	4.0	4.7	5.5	6.3	7.2	8.0
16.5	0.0	0.2	0.4	0.7	1.1	1.6	2.1	2.7	3.4	4.1	4.9	5.7	6.5	7.4	8.2
17.0	0.0	0.2	0.4	0.7	1.1	1.6	2.2	2.8	3.5	4.2	5.0	5.9	6.7	7.6	8.5
17.5	0.0	0.2	0.4	0.8	1.2	1.7	2.2	2.9	3.6	4.4	5.2	6.0	6.9	7.8	8.8
18.0	0.0	0.2	0.4	0.8	1.2	1.7	2.3	3.0	3.7	4.5	5.3	6.2	7.1	8.1	9.0
18.5	0.1	0.2	0.5	0.8	1.2	1.8	2.4	3.1	3.8	4.6	5.5	6.4	7.3	8.3	9.2
19.0	0.1	0.2	0.5	0.8	1.3	1.8	2.4	3.1	3.9	4.8	5.6	6.6	7.5	8.5	9.5
19.5	0.1	0.2	0.5	0.8	1.3	1.9	2.5	3.2	4.0	4.9	5.8	6.7	7.7	8.7	9.8
20.0	0.1	0.2	0.5	0.9	1.3	1.9	2.6	3.3	4.1	5.0	5.9	6.9	7.9	9.0	10.0

FIG. 2015 Table 3—Height of Tide at Any Time. This table is used in determining tide level at intermediate times between low and high waters.

be added to mean low water to get mean high water (MHW), the datum commonly used for the measurement of vertical heights above water, bridge and other vertical clearances, etc. The *spring range* is the average semidiurnal range occurring twice monthly when the moon is new or full. It is larger than the mean range where the type of tide is either semidiurnal or mixed, and is of no practical significance where the tide is of the diurnal type. Where this is the situation, the table gives the *diurnal range,* which is the difference in height between mean higher high water and mean lower low water.

Table 3, fig. 2015, is provided in order that detailed calculations can be made for the height of the tide at any desired moment between the times of high and low waters. It is equally usable for either reference stations in Table 1 or the subordinate stations of Table 2. Note that Table 3 is not a complete set of variations from one low to one high. Since the rise and fall are assumed to be symmetrical, only a half-table need be printed. Calculations are made from a high or low water, whichever is nearer to the specified time. In using Table 3, the nearest tabular values are used; interpolation is not necessary.

If the degree of precision of Table 3 is not required (it seldom is in practical piloting situations), a much simpler and quicker estimation can be made by using the following one-two-three rule of thumb. The tide may be assumed to rise or fall 1/12 of the full range during the first and sixth hours after high and low water stands, 2/12 during the second and fifth hours, and 3/12 during the third and fourth hours. The results obtained by this rule will suffice for essentially all situations and locations, but should be compared with Table 3 calculations as a check when entering new areas.

The table shown at the bottom of page 352p has been prepared from the above rule of thumb to supply multiplying factors for half-hour intervals of a rising or falling tide.

The Tide Tables also include four other minor tables which, although not directly related to tidal calculations, are often useful. Table 4 provides sunrise and sunset data at five-day intervals for various latitudes. Table 5 lists corrections to convert the local mean times of Table 4 to standard zone time. Table 6 tabulates times of moonrise and moonset for certain selected locations. Table 7 lists other useful astronomical data such as the phases of the moon, solar equinoxes and solstices, etc.

Each Table is preceded by informative material which should be read carefully prior to its use.

EXAMPLES OF TIDAL CALCULATIONS

The instructions in the Tide Tables should be fully adequate for the solution of any problem. However, examples will be worked out here for various situations as guides to the use of the various individual tables. Comments and cautions relating to the solution of practical problems involving the Tide Tables will also be given.

Example 1. Determination of the time and height of a high or low tide at a reference station.

Problem: What is the time and height of the evening low tide at Seattle on Sunday, 1 October 1967?

Solution: Using Table 1, fig. 2012, it will be seen directly that the evening low water occurs at 2124 Pacific Standard Time on this date and that the height is 4.2 feet above the tidal datum of mean lower low water.

Notes: a. Observe that if the date had been 3 November, the tide level at low water stand would have been a *minus* figure, —3.0 feet. At this time, the water level is predicted to be *below* the datum and actual depths will be *less* than those printed on the charts of this area.

b. Observe that if the date had been 4 November, there would have been no solution as the normal progression of the tides on a cycle of roughly 24 hours and 50 minutes has moved the normal evening low tide past midnight and into the next day. Thus, Saturday, 4 November has only three tides rather than the usual four.

c. It should be further noted that the reference stations are also listed in Table 2 and additional information is shown there. This table, fig. 2014, indicates, for reference stations as well as subordinate stations, the specific location for which predictions are given, the mean and spring (or diurnal) tidal ranges, and the mean tide level.

d. Remember to add one hour if you are in an area using daylight saving time.

Example 2. Determination of the time and height of a high or low tide at a subordinate station.

Problem: What is the time and height of the morning low water at Shelton on Oakland Bay, Puget Sound on Tuesday, 5 December 1967?

Solution: From the Index to Table 2 in the back of the Tide Tables, Shelton is found to be Subordinate Station No. 967. It is then located in Table 2 (fig. 2014). First, note that the Reference Station shown next *above* this place is "Seattle." Then note the time and height differences for Shelton for *low* waters; be sure to use the correct columns.

Th differences are then applied as follows:

Time		Height
00 48	At Seattle	—2.5 feet
1:54	Differences	—0.2
02 42	At Shelton	—2.7 feet

Thus, at Shelton on 5 December 1967, the predicted morning low water will occur at 0242 PST with a height of —2.7 feet (2.7 feet *below* the tidal datum).

Notes: a. If the date had been 5 October, the morning low water at Seattle for that date is at 1130. Adding the time difference of 1ʰ 54ᵐ would have resulted in a time prediction for Shelton of 1324, which is *not* a *morning* tide at the subordinate station. In this case, it would be necessary to use the low water at the reference station that occurs before midnight on the *preceding* day. At Seattle on *4* October, there is a low water at 2318; adding the time difference gives a morning low tide at Shelton of 0112 on *5* October.

b. Observe that if the subordinate station had been Port Gamble on Hood Canal, the height would be determined by multiplying the height at the reference station by the *ratio* of 0.91 rather than adding or subtracting a difference in feet. (Ratios may be either greater or less than 1.) Note also that here the time differences are *negative;* the high and low waters at the subordinate station occur *earlier* than at the reference station of Table 1.

c. The use of minus time differences with predictions of

FIG. 2016 Table 4—Local Mean Time of Sunrise and Sunset. Times are tabulated for various dates and latitudes, usually at intervals of 5 days and 2°; interpolation is used for exact dates and locations.

FIG. 2017 Table 5—Reduction of Local Mean Time to Standard Time. A correction, obtained from this table, is applied to the time of sunrise or sunset computed from Table 4 to get the time of the event in standard zone time. A further correction of one hour is needed for Daylight Saving Time.

Date	30° N. Rise	30° N. Set	32° N. Rise	32° N. Set	34° N. Rise	34° N. Set	36° N. Rise	36° N. Set	38° N. Rise	38° N. Set	40° N. Rise	40° N. Set
	h. m.	h. m.	h. m.	h. m.	h. m.	h. m.	h. m.	h. m.	h. m.	h. m.	h. m.	h. m.
Jan. 1	6 56	17 11	7 01	17 07	7 06	17 02	7 11	16 57	7 16	16 51	7 22	16 44
6	6 57	17 15	7 02	17 11	7 06	17 06	7 11	17 01	7 17	16 56	7 22	16 49
11	6 57	17 19	7 02	17 15	7 06	17 10	7 11	17 05	7 16	17 00	7 22	16 54
16	6 57	17 23	7 01	17 19	7 05	17 15	7 10	17 10	7 15	17 05	7 20	17 00
21	6 56	17 27	6 59	17 24	7 04	17 20	7 08	17 15	7 12	17 11	7 18	17 05
26	6 54	17 32	6 57	17 28	7 01	17 25	7 05	17 21	7 09	17 16	7 14	17 11
31	6 51	17 36	6 55	17 33	6 58	17 29	7 02	17 26	7 06	17 22	7 10	17 17
Feb. 5	6 48	17 40	6 51	17 37	6 54	17 34	6 58	17 31	7 01	17 27	7 05	17 23
10	6 45	17 44	6 47	17 42	6 50	17 39	6 53	17 36	6 56	17 33	7 00	17 29
15	6 41	17 48	6 43	17 46	6 45	17 44	6 48	17 41	6 50	17 39	6 54	17
20	6 36	17 52	6 38	17 50	6 40	17 48	6 42	17 46	6 44	17 44		16 52
25	6 31	17 56	6 32	17 55	6 34	17 53	6 36	17 51	6 39			16 47
											6 47	16 43
Mar. 2	6 26	17 59	6 27	17 58	6 28	17 57	6 29		6 48	16 44	6 52	16 39
7	6 20	18 03	6 22	18 02	6 22	18		16 47	6 53	16 42	6 58	16 37
12	6 14	18 06	6 14	18								
17	6 09	18 09			6 48	16 51	6 53	16 46	6 58	16 41	7 03	16 35
22	6 02				6 52	16 51	6 57	16 46	7 02	16 40	7 08	16 35
27		00	6 51	16 56	6 56	16 52	7 01	16 46	7 07	16 41	7 12	16 35
		17 01	6 54	16 58	6 59	16 53	7 04	16 48	7 10	16 42	7 16	16 36
	6 52	17 05	6 56	17 00	7 01	16 55	7 07	16 49	7 12	16 44	7 18	16 38
27	6 54	17 08	6 59	17 03	7 04	16 58	7 09	16 53	7 15	16 47	7 20	16 41
Jan. 1	6 56	17 11	7 01	17 07	7 06	17 01	7 11	16 56	7 16	16 50	7 22	16 44

Local mean time. To obtain standard time of rise or set, see Table 5.

Difference of longitude between local and standard meridian	Correction to local mean time to obtain standard time	Difference of longitude between local and standard meridian	Correction to local mean time to obtain standard time	Difference of longitude between local and standard meridian	Co to me to sta
° ′ ° ′	Minutes	° ′ ° ′	Minutes	°	
0 00 to 0 07	0	7 23 to 7 37	30	15	
0 08 to 0 22	1	7 38 to 7 52	31	30	
0 23 to 0 37	2	7 53 to 8 07	32	45	
0 38 to 0 52	3	8 08 to 8 22	33	60	
0 53 to 1 07	4	8 23 to 8 37	34	75	
1 08 to 1 22	5	8 38 to 8 52	35	90	
1 23 to 1 37	6	8 53 to 9 07	36	105	
1 38 to 1 52	7	9 08 to 9 22	37	120	
1 53 to 2 07	8	9 23 to 9 37	38	135	
2 08 to 2 22	9	9 38 to 9 52	39	150	
2 23 to 2 37	10	9 53 to 10 07	40	165	
2 38 to 2 52	11	10 08 to 10 22	41	180	
2 53 to 3 07	12	10 23 to 10 37	42		
3 08 to 3 22	13	10 38 to 10 52	43		
3 23 to 3 37	14	10 53 to 11 07	44		
3 38 to 3 52	15	11 08 to 11 22	55		
3 53 to 4 07	16	13 53 to 14 07	56		
4 08 to 4 00					
6 38 to 6 52	27	14 08 to 14 22	57		
6 53 to 7 07	28	14 23 to 14 37	58		
7 08 to 7 22	29	14 38 to 14 52	59		

If local meridian is east of standard meridian, subtract the c tion from local time.

If local meridian is west of standard meridian, add the corre to local time.

tides to occur shortly after midnight at the reference station may result in a change of date backward into the preceding day. Always be careful in making calculations close to 2400.

Example 3. Determination of the level of the tide at a reference station at a given time between high and low waters.

Problem: What is the height of the tide at Seattle at 1820 on Saturday, 2 December 1967?

Solution: From Table 1, we first note that the given time of 1820 falls between a high tide at 1554 and a low tide at 2318. We compute the time difference and range as follows:

Time	Height
23 18	11.8 feet
15 54	−3.6
7:24 time difference	15.4 feet range

Thus our desired tide level is on a falling tide whose range is 15.4 feet (since the low water height is a negative value, we are subtracting a minus number which is arithmetically equivalent to adding the numerical values).

The desired time is nearer to the time of the high water, so calculations will be made in Table 3, fig. 2015, using this starting point.

18 20	Desired time
15 54	Time of nearest high or low water
2:26	Difference

The given time is $2^h 26^m$ after the nearest high water. Table 3 is used to the nearest tabulated value; do not interpolate. Entering the *upper* part of the Table on the line for Duration of rise or fall of $7^h 20^m$, (nearest value to $7^h 24^m$), read across to the entry nearest $2^h 26^m$; this is $2^h 27^m$ in the tenth column from the left. Follow *down* this column into the *lower* part of Table 3 to the line for Range of Tide of 15.5 feet (nearest value to actual range of 15.4 feet). At the intersection of this line and column is found the correction to the height of the tide; in this case, 3.9 feet.

Since we have noted that in this example the tide is falling, and we are calculating from high water, the correction is subtracted from the height of high water: 11.8 − 3.9 = 7.9.

The predicted height of the tide at Seattle at 1820 PST on 2 December 1967 is 7.9 feet above the tidal datum.

Notes: a. Be sure that calculations are made for the right pair of high and low tides; be sure that the calculations are made for the *nearest* high or low water.

b. Be careful to apply the final correction to the nearest high or low water as used in its computation; do not apply it to the range; apply it in the right direction, down from a high, or up from a low.

Example 4. Determination of the height of tide at a subordinate station at a given time.

Problem: What is the height of the tide at Port Ludlow at 0930 on Saturday, 2 December 1967?

Solution: First, the times of the high and low waters on either side of the stated time must be calculated for the subordinate station using Tables 1 and 2. This is done as follows:

High water	06 06	At Seattle	12.8 feet
	−:27	difference/ratio	0.88
	05 39	At Point Ludlow	11.3 feet
Low water	11 06	At Seattle	7.7 feet
	−:18	difference/ratio	0.88
	10 48	At Point Ludlow	6.8 feet

Next, we calculate the time difference and range:

10 48		11.3
05 39		6.8
5:09 time difference		4.5 feet range

The time from the nearest high or low is calculated:

10 48
09 30
1:18 time from nearest low

With the data from the above calculations, enter Table 3 for a Duration of rise or fall of $5^h 09^m$ (use $5^h 00^m$), a time from nearest high or low of $1^h 18^m$ (use $1^h 20^m$), and a range of 4.5 feet. From these data, we find a correction to height of tide of 0.7 feet. We know that the tide is falling and that the nearest time of stand was the low water at 1048. From these facts, we can see that the correction is to be *added* to the low water height; 6.8 + 0.7 = 7.5.

The height of the tide at Port Ludlow at 0930 PST on 2 December 1967 is predicted to be 7.5 feet above the datum.

Note: Be sure to use the high and low tides occurring *at the subordinate station* on either side of the given time. It may be that in some instances with large time differences, a correction of times from the reference station to the subordinate station will show that you have selected the incorrect pair of tides; in this case select another high or low tide so that the pair used at the subordinate station will bracket the given time.

Example 5. Determination of the time of the tide reaching a given height at a reference station.

Problem: At what time on the afternoon of 4 October 1967 will the height of the rising tide reach 10 feet at Seattle?

Solution: This is essentially Example 3 in reverse. First, determine the range and duration of rise (or fall).

16 48	High water	11.9 feet
10 48	Low water	2.3
6:00	Duration	9.6 feet range

It is noted that the desired difference in height of tide is 11.9 − 10.0 = 1.9 feet. Enter the *lower* part of Table 3 on the line for a range of 9.5 feet (nearest value to 9.6) and find the column in which the correction nearest 1.9 feet is tabulated; in this case, the nearest value (2.0) is found in the ninth column from the left. Proceed *up* this column to the line in the upper part of the Table for a Duration of $6^h 00^m$ (here the exact value can be used). The time from nearest high or low found on this line is $1^h 48^m$. Since our desired level is nearer to high water than low, this time difference is subtracted from the time of high water; 1648 − 1:48 = 1500.

Thus the desired tidal height of 10 feet above datum is predicted to occur at 1500 PST on 4 October.

Note: A similar calculation can be made for a subordinate station by first determining the applicable high and low water times and heights at that station.

Example 6. Determination of vertical clearance.

Problem: What will be the vertical clearance under the fixed west span of the bridge across the Hood Canal near Port Gamble, Washington, at the time of morning high tide on 2 December 1967?

Solution: Chart 185-SC states the clearance to be 35 feet. The datum for heights is mean high water; the tidal datum is mean lower low water.

From Tables 1 and 2, we determine the predicted height of the tide at the specified time:

At Seattle	12.8 feet
ratio	0.91
At Port Gamble	11.6 feet

From Table 2, we calculate the height of mean high water for Port Gamble:

Mean tide level	6.2 feet
½ mean range	3.4
Mean high water	9.6 feet above tidal datum

The difference between predicted high water at the specified time and MHW is 11.6 − 9.6 = 2.0 feet. The tide is above MHW and the bridge clearance is reduced, 35 − 2.0 = 33 feet.

On the morning of 2 December 1967, the clearance at high tide under the fixed west span of the bridge across Hood Canal near Port Gamble is predicted to be 33 feet; this is *less* than the clearance printed on the chart.

ASTRONOMICAL DATA FROM THE TIDE TABLES

Table 4 gives sunrise and sunset information for various latitudes at five-day intervals. If more precise times are needed, interpolation can be used. Times are *local* meridian and must be corrected to standard zone time.

Example 7. Determination of the time of sunrise at a specified location.

Problem: What is the time of sunrise at Catalina Harbor, Santa Catalina Island on 12 February 1967?

Solution: From Table 2, we note that the latitude and longitude of the given point are 33° 26'N, 118° 30'W.

Fig. 2016 is an extract from Table 4; the applicable entries are set up as follows:

	32°N	34°N
Feb 10	0647	0650
Feb 15	0643	0645

Then we interpolate to the nearest minute vertically for the desired date:

	32°N	34°N
Feb 10	0647	0650
Feb 12	**0645**	**0648**
Feb 15	0643	0645

Next, interpolation is done horizontally for the latitude of the given point:

	32°N	**33° 26'N**	34°N
Feb 12	0645	**0647**	0648

This time of 0647 is local meridian time and must be corrected to zone time by Table 5, fig. 2017. The meridian of Pacific Standard Time is 120° W (from Table 1, bottom of any page).

$$\begin{array}{r} 120°\ 00' \\ 118°\ 30' \\ \hline 1°\ 30'\ \text{Longitude difference} \end{array}$$

From Table 5, the time correction for 1°30' is 6 minutes. Since Catalina Harbor is *east* of the zone meridian, the correction is *subtracted;* 0647 − 6ᵐ = 0641.

On the morning of 12 February 1967, the time of sunrise at Catalina Harbor is 0641 PST.

Notes: a. Interpolation can be done first horizontally for the latitude difference and then vertically for the desired date. The results may vary slightly due to rounding to the nearest minute, but the difference should not exceed one minute.

b. Calculations for the time of sunset are made in exactly the same manner.

c. Latitude and longitude data may be taken from a chart or any other source.

d. Times must be corrected for daylight time, if in effect.

Times of moonrise and moonset

Table 6 gives daily times for moonrise and moonset for selected points. Correction or interpolation for other points is *not* possible.

Currents

Current is the horizontal motion of water. This motion may be the result of any one of several factors, or of a combination of two or three. Although certain of these causes are of greater importance to a boatman than are others, he should have a general understanding of all.

TIDAL CURRENTS

Boatmen in coastal areas will be most affected by *tidal currents*. The rise and fall of tidal levels is a result of the flow of water to and from a given locality. This flow results in tidal current effects.

The normal type of tidal current, in bays and rivers, is the *reversing* current that flows alternately in one direction and then the opposite. Off-shore, tidal currents may be of the *rotary* type, flowing with little change in strength, but slowly and steadily changing direction.

A special form of tidal current is the *hydraulic* type such as flows in a waterway connecting two bodies of water. Differences in the time and height of the high and low waters of the two bays, sounds, etc., cause a flow from one to the other and back again. A typical example of hydraulic current is the flow through the Cape Cod Canal with Massachusetts Bay at one end and Buzzards Bay at the other.

Remember to use the terms correctly—tide is the *vertical* rise and fall of water levels; current is the *horizontal* flow of water.

FIG. 2018 The major ocean currents of interest to boatmen are the Gulf Stream off the East Coast and the California Current along the Pacific Coast.

OTHER TYPES OF CURRENT

Although most piloting situations involving current are concerned with tidal currents, there will be times when river, ocean, and wind-driven currents must be considered.

River currents

Boatmen on rivers above the head of tidal action must take into account *river currents*. (Where tidal influences are felt, river currents are merged into tidal currents and are not considered separately.) River currents will vary widely with the width and depth of the stream, the season of the year, recent rainfall in the river basin, etc.

Ocean currents

Off-shore piloting will frequently require knowledge and consideration of *ocean currents*. These result from regions of relatively constant winds such as the often-

mentioned "trade winds" and "prevailing westerlies." The rotation of the earth and variations in water density are also factors in the patterns of ocean currents.

The ocean currents of greatest interest to boatmen are the Gulf Stream and the California Current, fig. 2018. The *Gulf Stream* is a northerly and easterly flow of warm water along the Atlantic Coast of the United States. It is quite close to shore along the southern part of Florida, but moves progressively further to sea as it flows northward, where it both broadens and slows.

The *California Current* flows generally southward and a bit eastward along the Pacific Coast of Canada and the United States, turning sharply westward off Baja California (Mexico). It is a flow of colder water and, in general, is slower and less sharply defined than the Gulf Stream.

Wind-driven currents

In addition to the consistent ocean currents caused by sustained wind patterns, local *wind-driven currents* may be established by temporary conditions. The effect of wind blowing across the sea is to cause the surface water to move. The extent of the effect varies with many factors, but generally a steady wind for 12 hours or longer will result in a discernible current.

For a rough rule-of-thumb, the strength of a wind-driven current can be taken as 2% of the wind's velocity. The direction of the current will *not* be the same as that of the wind, a result of the earth's rotation. In the Northern Hemisphere, the current will be deflected to the right to a degree determined by the latitude and the depth of the water. The deflection may be as small as 15° in shallow coastal areas, or as great as 45° on the high seas; it is greater in the higher latitudes.

DEFINITIONS OF CURRENT TERMS

Currents have both strength and direction. The proper terms should be used in describing each of these characteristics.

The *set* of a current is the direction *toward* which it is flowing. A current that flows from North to South is termed a southerly current and has a set of 180°. (Note carefully the difference here from the manner in which wind direction is described—it is exactly the opposite: a wind from North to South is called a northerly wind with a direction of 000°.)

FIG. 2019 In some narrow passages, tidal currents are so strong that a lightly powered boat could not make headway against them, and must wait for slack water. Here, an auxiliary races through Cobscook Falls in Maine, propelled by a 10-knot "down-hill" current.
(Photograph courtesy Donald W. Gardner)

FIG. 2020 Table 1 of the Tidal Current Tables. Daily predictions are listed for the times and strengths of maximum flood and ebb currents, and the time of slack water, at major reference stations.

CHESAPEAKE BAY ENTRANCE, VA., 1967

F-FLOOD, DIR. 305 TRUE   E-EBB, DIR. 125 TRUE

SEPTEMBER

DAY	SLACK WATER TIME H.M.	MAXIMUM CURRENT TIME H.M.	VEL. KNOTS	DAY	SLACK WATER TIME H.M.	MAXIMUM CURRENT TIME H.M.	VEL. KNOTS
1 F	0400 0800 1542 2154	0030 0554 1224 1836	1.1E 0.4F 1.4E 1.1F	16 SA	0448 0942 1700 2254	0130 0718 1336 1954	1.3E 0.7F 1.6E 1.0F
2 SA	0436 0906 1630 2236	0118 0648 1312 1924	1.3E 0.6F 1.6E 1.3F	17 SU	0524 1030 1742 2324	0206 0754 1418 2024	1.3E 0.8F 1.6E 1.0F
3 SU	0512 1006 1718 2318	0200 0736 1400 2012	1.4E 0.8F 1.8E 1.4F	18 M	0554 1112 1824 2348	0242 0830 1454 2100	1.4E 0.9F 1.6E 0.9F
4 M	0554 1100 1806 2354	0236 0824 1442 2054	1.6E 1.1F 1.9E 1.4F	19 TU	0630 1148 1854	0318 0906 1530 2124	1.4E 0.9F 1.5E 0.9F
5 TU	0630 1148 1854	0318 0906 1530 2136	1.7E 1.2F 2.0E 1.4F	20 W	0012 0700 1224 1930	0342 0936 1606 2154	1.4E 1.0F 1.5E 0.8F
6 W	0036 0712 1242 1942	0400 0954 1618 2218	1.8E 1.4F 1.9E 1.4F	21 TH	0030 0730 1300 2006	0412 1006 1642 2224	1.3E 1.0F 1.4E 0.7F
7 TH	0112 0800 1336 2030	0442 1042 1712 2306	1.8E 1.4F 1.8E 1.2F	22 F	0054 0806 1336 2048	0442 1042 1718 2254	1.3E 1.0F 1.2E 0.6F

OCTOBER

DAY	SLACK WATER TIME H.M.	MAXIMUM CURRENT TIME H.M.	VEL. KNOTS	DAY	SLACK WATER TIME H.M.	MAXIMUM CURRENT TIME H.M.	VEL. KNOTS
1 SU	0400 0854 1612 2200	0042 0624 1248 1854	1.4E 0.8F 1.6E 1.2F	16 M	0454 1018 1718 2236	0136 0730 1354 1954	1.3E 0.9F 1.5E 0.8F
2 M	0436 0954 1700 2236	0124 0712 1336 1942	1.6E 1.1F 1.8E 1.3F	17 TU	0524 1054 1800 2300	0206 0806 1430 2024	1.4E 0.9F 1.5E 0.8F
3 TU	0518 1048 1748 2318	0206 0800 1424 2030	1.7E 1.3F 1.9E 1.4F	18 W	0554 1136 1830 2324	0242 0836 1506 2054	1.4E 1.0F 1.4E 0.7F
4 W	0600 1142 1836	0248 0848 1512 2112	1.9E 1.5F 2.0E 1.3F	19 TH	0624 1206 1906 2342	0306 0906 1542 2118	1.4E 1.1F 1.4E 0.7F
5 TH	0000 0648 1236 1924	0330 0936 1606 2154	1.9E 1.6F 1.9E 1.2F	20 F	0654 1242 1942	0336 0942 1618 2148	1.4E 1.1F 1.3E 0.6F
6 F	0036 0736 1330 2018	0418 1024 1654 2242	1.9E 1.6F 1.8E 1.1F	21 SA	0006 0730 1318 2024	0406 1012 1654 2224	1.3E 1.1F 1.2E 0.5F
7 SA	0118 0824 1424 2112	0506 1118 1748 2330	1.8E 1.5F 1.6E 0.9F	22 SU	0030 0806 1400 2106	0436 1054 1730 2300	1.3E 1.0F 1.1E 0.4F

The *drift* of a current is its velocity, normally in knots (except for river currents which will be in MPH). As noted in the preceding chapter, current drift is stated to the nearest tenth of a knot.

A tidal current is said to *flood* when it flows in from the sea and results in higher tidal stages. Conversely, a tidal current *ebbs* when the flow is seaward and water levels fall.

Slack vs. Stand

As these currents reverse, there are brief periods of no discernible flow, called *slack*, or *slack water*. The time of occurrence of slack is *not* the same as the time of *stand*, when the vertical rise or fall of tide has stopped. Tidal currents do *not* automatically slack and reverse direction when tide levels stand at high or low water.

High water at a given point simply means that the level there will not get any higher. Further up the bay or river, the tide will not have reached its maximum height and water must therefore continue to flow in so that it can continue to rise. The current can still be flooding after stand has been passed at our given point and the level has started to fall.

For example, let us consider the tides and currents on Chesapeake Bay. High tide occurs at Baltimore some 7 hours after it does at Smith Point, roughly half way up the 140 miles from Cape Henry at the entrance to Baltimore. On a certain day, high water occurs at 1126 at Smith Point, but slack water does not occur until 1304. The flooding current has thus continued for 1ʰ 38ᵐ after high water was reached.

Corresponding time intervals occur in the case of low water stand and the slack between ebb and flood currents.

In many places, the time lag between a low or high water stand and slack water is not a matter of minutes but hours. At The Narrows in New York Harbor, flood current continues for about 2 hours after high water is reached and the tide begins to fall, ebb for 2½ hours after low water stand. After slack, the current increases until mid-flood or mid-ebb, then gradually decreases. Where ebb and flood last for about six hours—as along the Atlantic seaboard—current will be strongest about three hours after

slack. Thus, the skipper who figures his passage out through The Narrows from the time of high water, rather than slack, will start about two and a half hours too soon and will run into a current at nearly its maximum strength.

NEED FOR KNOWLEDGE

Currents, primarily of the tidal type, will affect many boating situations. Currents will be a definite factor in piloting in tidal rivers, bays, and sounds. Coastal currents, resulting from waves striking the beaches at an angle, will often influence coastal piloting problems.

Effect on course and speed made good

A current directly in line with a boat's motion through the water will have a maximum effect on the speed made good, but with no off-course influence. The effect can be of real significance in figuring your ETA at your destination. It can even affect the safety of your craft and its crew if you have figured your fuel too closely and run into a bow-on current.

A current that is nearly at a right angle to your course through the water will have a maximum effect on the course made good and a minor effect on the distance you must travel to reach your destination. The off-course effect can be of great importance if there are shoals or other hazards near your desired track.

Knowledge of current set and drift can be applied to assist your cruising. Departure times can be selected to take advantage of favorable currents, or at least to minimize adverse effects. A 12-knot boat speed and a 2-knot current, reasonably typical situations, can combine to result in either a 10-knot or a 14-knot speed made good—the 40%

gain of a favorable current over an opposing one is significant both in terms of time en route and fuel consumed.

Even lesser currents have some significance. A half-knot current would hinder a swimmer and make rowing a boat noticeably more difficult. A one-knot current can seriously affect a sailboat in light breezes.

Difficult locations

In many boating areas, there will be locations where current conditions can be critical.

Numerous ocean inlets are difficult, or even dangerous, in certain combinations of current and onshore surf. In general, difficult surf conditions will be made more hazardous by an outward-flowing (ebbing) current. The topic of inlet seamanship is covered in more detail on pages 439a-439t.

There are a number of narrow bodies of water where the maximum current velocity is such as to make passage impossible at times for boats of limited power, and to seriously slow boats of greater engine power, fig. 2019. Such narrow passages are particularly characteristic of Pacific Northwest boating areas, but do occur elsewhere. Currents in New York City's East River reach a maximum of 4.6 knots, and at the Golden Gate of San Francisco velocities greater than 5 knots occur. Velocities of 3½ to 4 knots are common in much-traveled passages like Woods Hole, Mass., and Plum Gut, at the eastern end of Long Island, N. Y.

FIG. 2021 Table 2—Current Differences and Other Constants. Data are given for hundreds of subordinate stations so that predictions for current may be made for many points of navigational significance.

No.	PLACE	POSITION		TIME DIFFERENCES		VELOCITY RATIOS		MAXIMUM CURRENTS			
								Flood		Ebb	
		Lat.	Long.	Slack water	Maximum current	Maximum flood	Maximum ebb	Direction (true)	Average velocity	Direction (true)	Average velocity
		° ′ N.	° ′ W.	h. m.	h. m.			deg.	knots	deg.	knots
	CHESAPEAKE BAY—Continued			on CHESAPEAKE BAY ENTRANCE, p.64							
				Time meridian, 75° W.							
1151	Smith Point, 4.5 miles east of	37 53	76 09	+3 10	+3 15	0.7	0.5	350	0.7	165	0.8
1153	Smith Point Light, 6 miles north of	37 59	76 11	+3 50	+3 35	0.4	0.7	350	0.4	135	1.0
1155	Point Lookin	38 07	76 13	+4 35	+4 15	0.4	0.3	10	0.4	160	0.5
1157	Point No Point	38 09	76 14	+5 15	+5 10	0.4	0.4	355	0.4	150	0.6
				on BALTIMORE HARBOR APPROACH, p.70							
1158	Cedar Point, 3.2 miles east of	38 18	76 18	(*)	-3 10	0.2	0.8	30	0.2	175	0.6
1159	Cedar Point, 1.1 miles ENE. of	38 18	76 21	(¹)	-3 15	0.5	0.8	10	0.4	185	0.6
1160	Drum Point, 2.8 miles ENE. of	38 20	76 22	(*)	-2 55	0.2	0.5	335	0.2	185	0.4
1161	Cove Point, 0.6 mile NE. of	38 23	76 22	-3 00	-3 00	0.9	1.0	330	0.7	155	0.6
1162	Cove Point, 2.5 miles east of	38 23	76 20	-2 40	-2 45	0.6	0.8	310	0.5	155	0.6
1163	Cove Point, 3.3 miles east of	38 24	76 19	-3 35	-3 30	0.5	0.6	320	0.4	160	0.5
1164	Kenwood Beach, 1.5 miles NE. of	38 31	76 29	-2 20	-2 40	0.2	0.4	340	0.2	160	0.3
1165	James Island, 3.8 miles west of	38 31	76 25	(*)	(²)	0.5	0.4	0	0.4	190	0.3
1166	James Island, 2.5 miles WNW. of	38 32	76 24	-2 25	-2 40	0.5	0.6	0	0.4	175	0.5
1167	Sharps Island, 3.3 miles WNW. of	38 38	76 26	(*)	-1 45	0.5	0.4	345	0.4	185	0.3
1168	Holland Point, 1.6 miles east of	38 44	76 30	-1 10	-1 05	0.2	0.8	10	0.2	180	0.6
1169	Holland Point, 4.7 miles ENE. of	38 45	76 26	-1 00	-0 40	0.2	0.8	340	0.2	180	0.6
1170	Kent Point, 4 miles SW. of	38 48	76 26	-1 05	-1 05	0.6	0.6	25	0.5	210	0.5
1171	Horseshoe Point, 1.7 miles east of	38 50	76 27	-0 50	-0 55	0.6	0.6	5	0.5	200	0.5
1172	Bloody Pt. Bar Light, 0.6 mi. NW. of	38 50	76 24	-0 05	-0 15	0.9	0.6	35	0.7	190	0.5
1173	Thomas Pt. Shoal Lt., 1.8 mi. SW. of	38 52	76 28	-2 05	-2 20	0.5	0.4	340	0.4	190	0.3
1174	Thomas Pt. Shoal Lt., 0.4 mi. SE. of	38 54	76 26	-0 40	-0 45	0.9	1.1	10	0.7	185	0.9
1175	Tolly Point, 1.6 miles east of	38 56	76 25	-0 20	-0 20	0.6	0.9	355	0.5	190	0.7
1176	Chesapeake Bay Bridge, main channel	39 00	76 23	0 00	+0 10	0.9	1.1	25	0.7	230	0.9
1177	BALTIMORE HBR. APP. (off Sandy Point)	39 01	76 22	Daily predictions				25	0.8	190	0.8
1178	Love Point, 2.5 miles N. of	39 05	76 19	(³)	+0 05	0.8	0.5	55	0.6	240	0.4
1179	Craighill Channel, NE. of Mountain Pt.	39 05	76 24	+0 25	+0 35	0.8	0.9	350	0.6	175	0.7
1180	Craighill Angle, right outside quarter	39 08	76 23	+0 25	+0 25	0.6	0.6	345	0.5	170	0.5
1181	Sevenfoot Knoll Light, 0.8 mi. NE. of	39 10	76 24	+0 20	+0 35	0.5	0.2	345	0.4	160	0.2
1182	Swan Point, 2.1 miles west of	39 09	76 20	+1 10	+1 00	0.6	0.8	355	0.5	220	0.6
1183	Swan Point, 1.6 miles NW. of	39 10	76 18	+0 45	+0 50	0.8	0.9	20	0.6	215	0.7
1184	North Point, 2.5 miles NE. of	39 13	76 24	+1 10	+1 05	0.4	0.5	35	0.3	225	0.4
1185	Pooles Island, 4 miles SW. of	39 14	76 20	+1 00	+1 00	0.6	0.8	25	0.5	210	0.6
1186	Tolchester Beach, 0.4 mile WNW. of	39 13	76 15	+1 40	+1 35	0.9	1.1	15	0.7	225	0.9
1187	Pooles Island, 0.8 mile south of	39 16	76 16	+1 40	+1 20	0.9	1.2	60	0.7	255	1.0
1188	Pooles Island, 1.4 miles east of	39 17	76 14	+1 35	+1 30	1.0	1.5	30	0.8	215	1.2
1189	Robins Point, 0.7 mile ESE. of	39 18	76 16	+0 15	-0 15	1.4	1.0	25	1.1	210	0.8
1190	Worton Point, 1.1 miles NW. of	39 20	76 12	+1 40	+1 40	1.4	1.5	40	1.1	245	1.2
1191	Howell Point, 0.4 mile NNW. of	39 23	76 07	+1 25	+1 20	1.1	1.1	80	0.9	245	0.9
1192	Grove Point, 0.8 mile NW. of	39 24	76 03	+1 50	+1 50	1.0	1.0	60	0.8	235	0.8
1193	Turkey Point, 1.4 miles WSW. of	39 26	76 02	+1 25	+1 20	0.8	0.9	30	0.6	220	0.7
1194	Spesutie Island, channel north of	39 29	76 05	+1 45	+1 30	0.8	0.6	285	0.6	100	0.5
1195	Rocky Point, 0.5 mile west of	39 29	76 00	+2 15	+2 15	0.6	0.8	30	0.5	190	0.6
1196	Red Point, 0.2 mile W. of, Northeast R	39 32	75 59	+1 50	+1 40	0.9	0.6	----	0.7	----	0.5
1197	Havre de Grace, Susquehanna River	39 33	76 05	(⁴)	(⁴)	(⁴)	(⁴)	----	----	----	----

* Times of slack are indefinite.
¹ Flood begins, -3ʰ 25ᵐ; ebb begins, -2ʰ 35ᵐ.
² Maximum flood, -2ʰ 40ᵐ; maximum ebb, -1ʰ 45ᵐ.
³ Flood begins, -0ʰ 50ᵐ; ebb begins, +0ʰ 25ᵐ.
⁴ Tidal Current too weak and variable to be predicted.

TIDAL CURRENT PREDICTIONS

Without experience or official information, local current prediction is always risky. East of Badgers Island in Portsmouth, Maine, for example, the average ebb current flows at a maximum velocity of less than a half-knot. Yet, southwest of the same island, it averages 3.7 knots.

One rule is fairly safe for most locations—the ebb is stronger and lasts longer than the flood. Eighty percent of all reference stations on the Atlantic, Gulf, and Pacific coasts of the U.S. report currents stronger at the ebb. This is normal because river flow adds to the ebb, but hinders the flood.

On the Atlantic coast, expect to find two approximately equal flood currents and two similar ebb currents in a cycle of roughly 25 hours. On the Pacific coast, however, two floods and ebbs will differ markedly. On the Gulf coast, there may be just one flood and one ebb in 25 hours. In each case, these patterns are, of course, generally similar to tidal action in the respective areas.

Don't try to predict current velocity from the time that it takes a high tide to reach a given point from the sea's entrance. Dividing the distance from Cape Henry to Baltimore by the time that it takes high water to work its way up Chesapeake Bay gives a speed of 13 knots. True maximum flood current strength is only about one knot.

Another useful truism about tidal currents is that tidal currents at different places *cannot* be forecast from their tidal ranges. You would expect strong currents at Eastport, Maine, where the difference between successive high and low waters reaches as much as 20 feet. And you would be right; there are three-knot currents there. But Galveston, Texas, with only a two-foot range of tides has currents up to more than two knots. So has Miami with a three-foot range, and Charleston, S. C. with a six-foot range—these are stronger currents than Boston where the range is often more than 10 feet and as strong as at Anchorage, Alaska where it's as much as 35 feet from some highs to the next low.

A good forecasting rule for all oceans: expect strong tidal currents where two bays meet. The reason: tidal ranges and high water times in the two bodies of water are likely to be different.

For the coasting skipper, here is another tidal current fact that may be useful: near the beach, flood and ebb don't usually set to and from the land, but rather parallel with the coast. This is as true off New Jersey and Florida as it is off California and Oregon. A few miles offshore, however, and in some very large bays, the current behaves quite differently—the rotary current mentioned previously in this chapter.

TIDAL CURRENT TABLES

At any given place, current strength varies with the phases of the moon and its distance from the earth. It will be strongest when tidal ranges are greatest—near new and

TABLE A

Interval between slack and maximum current

Interval between slack and desired time (h. m.)	1 20	1 40	2 00	2 20	2 40	3 00	3 20	3 40	4 00	4 20	4 40	5 00	5 20	5 40
0 20	0.4	0.3	0.3	0.2	0.2	0.2	0.2	0.2	0.1	0.1	0.1	0.1	0.1	0.1
0 40	0.7	0.6	0.5	0.4	0.4	0.3	0.3	0.3	0.3	0.3	0.2	0.2	0.2	0.2
1 00	0.9	0.8	0.7	0.6	0.6	0.5	0.5	0.4	0.4	0.4	0.3	0.3	0.3	0.3
1 20	1.0	1.0	0.9	0.8	0.7	0.7	0.6	0.6	0.5	0.5	0.5	0.4	0.4	0.4
1 40		1.0	1.0	1.0	0.9	0.8	0.8	0.7	0.7	0.6	0.6	0.5	0.5	0.4
2 00			1.0	1.0	0.9	0.9	0.8	0.8	0.7	0.7	0.6	0.6	0.6	0.5
2 20				1.0	1.0	0.9	0.9	0.8	0.8	0.7	0.7	0.6	0.6	0.6
2 40					1.0	1.0	0.9	0.9	0.8	0.8	0.7	0.7	0.7	0.7
3 00						1.0	1.0	1.0	0.9	0.9	0.8	0.8	0.7	0.7
3 20							1.0	1.0	1.0	0.9	0.9	0.9	0.8	0.8
3 40								1.0	1.0	1.0	0.9	0.9	0.9	0.9
4 00									1.0	1.0	1.0	1.0	0.9	0.9
4 20										1.0	1.0	1.0	1.0	1.0
4 40											1.0	1.0	1.0	1.0
5 00												1.0	1.0	1.0
5 20													1.0	1.0
5 40														1.0

TABLE B

Interval between slack and maximum current

Interval between slack and desired time (h. m.)	1 20	1 40	2 00	2 20	2 40	3 00	3 20	3 40	4 00	4 20	4 40	5 00	5 20	5 40
0 20	0.5	0.4	0.4	0.3	0.3	0.3	0.3	0.3	0.2	0.2	0.2	0.2	0.2	0.2
0 40	0.8	0.7	0.6	0.5	0.5	0.5	0.4	0.4	0.4	0.4	0.3	0.3	0.3	0.3
1 00	0.9	0.8	0.8	0.7	0.7	0.6	0.6	0.5	0.5	0.5	0.4	0.4	0.4	0.4
1 20	1.0	1.0	0.9	0.8	0.8	0.7	0.7	0.6	0.6	0.6	0.5	0.5	0.5	0.5
1 40		1.0	1.0	0.9	0.8	0.8	0.7	0.7	0.7	0.6	0.6	0.6	0.6	0.6
2 00			1.0	1.0	0.9	0.9	0.9	0.8	0.8	0.7	0.7	0.7	0.7	0.6
2 20				1.0	1.0	1.0	0.9	0.9	0.9	0.8	0.8	0.8	0.7	0.7
2 40					1.0	1.0	1.0	0.9	0.9	0.9	0.8	0.8	0.8	0.7
3 00						1.0	1.0	1.0	0.9	0.9	0.9	0.9	0.8	0.8
3 20							1.0	1.0	1.0	1.0	0.9	0.9	0.9	0.9
3 40								1.0	1.0	1.0	1.0	0.9	0.9	0.9
4 00									1.0	1.0	1.0	1.0	0.9	0.9
4 20										1.0	1.0	1.0	1.0	1.0
4 40											1.0	1.0	1.0	1.0
5 00												1.0	1.0	1.0
5 20													1.0	1.0
5 40														1.0

FIG. 2022   Table 3—Velocity of Current at Any Time. Using the appropriate part, A or B, of this table, the velocity of the current at intermediate times between maximum strength and slack may be calculated for either a reference or a subordinate station.

DURATION OF WEAK CURRENT NEAR TIME OF SLACK WATER

Table A

Maximum current	Period with a velocity not more than—				
	0.1 knot	0.2 knot	0.3 knot	0.4 knot	0.5 knot
Knots	Minutes	Minutes	Minutes	Minutes	Minutes
1.0	23	46	70	94	120
1.5	15	31	46	62	78
2.0	11	23	35	46	58
3.0	8	15	23	31	38
4.0	6	11	17	23	29
5.0	5	9	14	18	23
6.0	4	8	11	15	19
7.0	3	7	10	13	16
8.0	3	6	9	11	14
9.0	3	5	8	10	13
10.0	2	5	7	9	11

Table B

Maximum current	Period with a velocity not more than—				
	0.1 knot	0.2 knot	0.3 knot	0.4 knot	0.5 knot
Knots	Minutes	Minutes	Minutes	Minutes	Minutes
1.0	13	28	46	66	89
1.5	8	18	28	39	52
2.0	6	13	20	28	36
3.0	4	8	13	18	22
4.0	3	6	9	13	17
5.0	3	5	8	10	13

FIG. 2023   Table 4—Duration of Slack. Although actual slack water is only a momentary event, current velocity is quite small for a significant period while the direction is reversing. Part A or B of this table is used in the same situations as for Table 3.

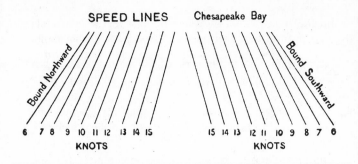

SPEED LINES   Chesapeake Bay

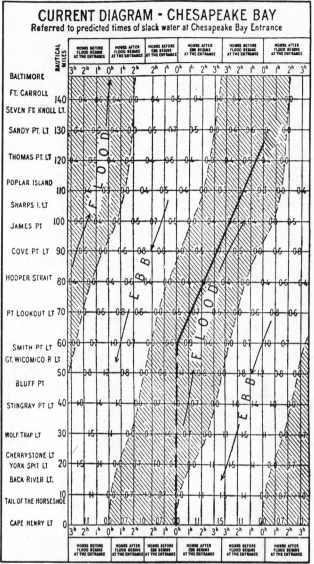

FIG. 2024. Tidal Current Diagrams from the Tidal Current Tables (East Coast volume only) provide a quick and simple way of determining the best speed and time of departure for a run up or down several of the major waterways subject to tidal currents.

full moon—and weakest when tidal ranges are least—near first and last quarters. Current velocity may vary as much as 40 percent above and below its average value.

The relationship between currents and tides makes possible the prediction of tidal currents. The Coast and Geodetic Survey publishes two volumes of predictions annually; one covers the Atlantic Coast of North America and the other the Pacific Coast of North America and Asia.

Each volume includes for its area, predictions of tidal currents in bays, sounds, and rivers, plus ocean currents such as the Gulf Stream. General information on wind-driven currents is also included although these, of course, result from temporary, local conditions and so cannot be predicted a year or more ahead. Your own past experience and "local knowledge," the advice of experienced watermen of the area, will be the best source of information regarding the effect of storm winds on local waters and their currents.

Tidal Current Tables are available at authorized sales agents for C&GS charts. The cost of each volume is $2.00.

Description of the Tables

The format and layout of the *Tidal Current Tables* is much the same as for the *Tide Tables* discussed earlier in this chapter. A system of reference stations, plus constants and differences for subordinate stations, is used to calculate the predictions for many points.

Table 1. There are 20 *reference stations* in the Atlantic Coast volume and 10 for the Pacific Coast. The Gulf of Mexico is included in the Atlantic Coast volume. For each station, there are tabulated the predicted times and strengths of maximum flood and ebb currents, plus the times of slack water. The direction of the flood and ebb currents is also listed, see fig. 2020.

Table 2. Time differences and velocity ratios are listed for hundreds of *subordinate stations*, fig. 2021. The location of these stations is described in terms of place names or position relative to identifiable points; the latitude and longitude are also given as an aid to their precise location. The direction and strength of typical maximum currents for each station are also tabulated. A number of subordinate stations will have only the footnoted entry "Current too weak and variable to be predicted." This information, even though negative in nature, is useful in planning a cruise.

Table 3. This table, fig. 2022, provides a convenient means for determination of the strength of the current at times intermediate between slack and maximum velocity. Use nearest tabulated values without interpolation.

Table 4. Although slack water is only a momentary event, there is a period of time on either side of slack during which the current is so weak as to be negligible

for practical piloting purposes. This period, naturally, varies with the maximum strength of the current, being longer for weak currents. Two sub-tables, fig. 2023, predict the duration of currents from 0.1 to 0.5 knot by tenths for normal reversing currents and for the hydraulic currents found at certain specified locations.

Table 5. For the Atlantic Coast only, information is given on rotary tidal currents at various offshore points of navigational interest. These points are described in terms of general location and specific geographic coordinates. Predictions of velocity and direction are referred to times after maximum flood at designated reference stations.

Current Diagrams

For a number of major tidal waterways of the United States, a *current diagram*, such as fig. 2024, is provided in the Tidal Current Tables. These give a graphic means of quickly and easily selecting a favorable time for traveling in either direction along these routes.

Time

The Tidal Current Tables list all predictions in *local standard time*. Be sure to make a conversion to daylight time if you are piloting in an area using such "fast" time; this is done by adding one hour to the tabulated times.

Cautions

As with tidal predictions, the data in the Tidal Current Tables may often be upset by sustained abnormal local conditions such as winds or rainfall. Use the current predictions with caution during and immediately after such weather abnormalities.

It should also be noted carefully that tidal current predictions are generally for a *spot location only;* the set and drift may be quite different only a mile or less away. This is at variance from predictions of high and low tides which can usually be used over fairly wide areas in the vicinity of the reference or secondary station.

EXAMPLES OF TIDAL CURRENT CALCULATIONS

The Tidal Current Tables contain all the information needed for the determination of such conditions as the time of maximum current and its strength, the time of slack water, the duration of slack (actually, the duration of the very weak current conditions), etc. Examples will be given of typical problems and their solution, plus comments and cautions to be used in connection with such situations.

Example 1. Determination of the time and strength of maximum current, and the time of slack, at a reference station.

Problem: What is the time and strength of the maximum ebb current at Chesapeake Bay Entrance during the afternoon of 17 October 1967?

Solution: As with the Tide Tables, the answer is available for a reference station by direct inspection. Fig. 2020 is a typical page from the Tidal Current Tables; we can see that the maximum ebb current on the specified afternoon is 1.5 knots setting 125° True; it is predicted to occur at 1430 EST.

Problem: What is the time of the first slack before ebb at this station on 17 October 1967?

Solution: Table 1 does not directly identify the slacks as being "slack before ebb" or "slack before flood"; this must be determined by comparison of the slack time with the nature of the next occurring maximum current.

From fig. 2020, we can see that the earliest slack that will be followed by an ebbing current at Chesapeake Bay Entrance on 17 October is predicted for 1054 EST.

Notes: a. Times obtained from the Tidal Current Tables are *standard;* add one hour for daylight time if in effect.

b. The set of the current for a reference station is found at the *top* of the page in Table 1; it is also given in Table 2 where further information, such as the geographic coordinates of the station, and the average velocity of maximum flood and ebb currents, is listed.

c. The normal day at Chesapeake Bay Entrance, where the tide is of the semi-diurnal type, will have four slacks

and four maximums. The tidal cycle of 24^h and 50^m will result in the occasional omission of a slack or maximum.

Example 2. Determination of the time and strength of maximum current, and the time of slack, at a subordinate station.

Problem: What is the time and strength of the morning flood current in Lynnhaven Inlet at the bridge on 21 September 1967?

Solution: Table 2, fig. 2021, gives time differences and velocity ratios to be applied to the predictions at the appropriate reference station. There is an Index to Table 2 in the rear of the Tidal Current Tables if it is needed to locate the given subordinate station.

In this problem, the time difference and velocity ratio are applied as follows:

10 06	at Chesapeake Bay Entrance	1.0 knot
−2:35	difference/ratio	0.6
07 31	at Lynnhaven Inlet	0.6 knot

The set (direction) of the current is also noted from the appropriate column of Table 2; in this case, it is 180° True.

Thus the predictions are for a maximum current of 0.6 knot setting 180° True at Lynnhaven Inlet bridge at 0731 EST on 21 September 1967.

Problem: What is the time of the first afternoon slack water at Lynnhaven Inlet bridge on 6 September 1967?

Solution: From Table 2, the time difference is found to be −2:05. This is applied to the time of slack at the reference station:

19 42	at Chesapeake Bay Entrance
−2:05	difference
17 37	at Lynnhaven Inlet bridge

The time of the first afternoon slack water at Lynnhaven Inlet bridge on 6 September 1967 is 1737 EST.

Notes: a. Observe that often there may be two separate time differences, one for slack and the other for maximum current, either flood or ebb. More complex situations with varied time differences will be shown by special footnotes to Table 2 where required. Note also that the velocity ratios may differ between ebb and flood.

b. Note that the direction of the current at a subordinate station must be taken from Table 2. It will nearly always differ from that at the reference station. No statement of current is complete without giving direction as well as strength.

c. The locations in Table 2 are usually a point some distance and direction from a landmark or aid to navigation. There may be several subordinate stations referred to the same base point (see subordinate stations 1117 to 1124, and 1149-1150 in fig. 2021); be sure to use the correct subordinate station.

Example 3. Determination of the current at an intermediate time at a reference station.

Problem: What is the velocity and set of the current at Chesapeake Bay Entrance at 1300 EST on 3 October 1967?

Solution: The time of slack and maximum current (ebb or flood) which bracket the desired time are found from Table 1. The interval between these times is determined, as is the interval between the desired time and the slack.

```
14 24
10 48
 3:36   interval, slack—maximum current
13 00
10 48
 2:12   interval, slack—desired time
```

With these time intervals, Table 3A is used to determine the ratio of the velocity of the current at the desired time to its maximum velocity. The nearest tabulated values are used, no interpolation. In this example, the ratio at the intersection of the line for $2^h 20^m$ and the column for $3^h 40^m$ is found to be 0.8. Multiply the maximum current by this decimal factor, $1.9 \times 0.8 = 1.5$.

From the times used, we note that the current is ebbing. From the top of Table 1, we determine that the direction is 125° True.

Thus, at 1300 EST on 3 October 1967, the current at Chesapeake Bay Entrance is predicted to have a velocity of 1.5 knots and be setting 125° True.

Notes: a. Except as specially indicated, use Table 3A, the upper portion of Table 3. The lower, B, portion is for use in designated waterways only.

b. Be sure that the interval is calculated between the desired time and the time of *slack,* whether or not this time is nearer to the given time than the time of maximum current.

c. Note that calculations of current velocity are rounded to the nearest tenth of a knot.

Example 4.   Determination of the current at an intermediate time at a subordinate station.

Problem: What is the velocity and set of the current at a point 5½ miles east of Stingray Point at 1700 EDT on 5 October 1967?

Solution: First, the predictions for slack and maximum current must be found for the subordinate station after converting 1700 EDT to 1600 EST for entering the Tables.

Slack		Maximum	
12 36 at Chesapeake Bay			
Entrance		16 06	1.9 knots, Ebb
+1:50 difference/ratio		+2:20	0.6
14 26 at subordinate station		18 26	1.1

With the information developed above, and the desired time, further calculations are made as follows:

```
18 26
14 26
 4:00   interval, slack—maximum current
16 00   (EST)
14 26
 1:34   interval, slack—desired time
```

Using Table 3A, fig. 2022, the velocity ratio is found to be 0.6; then $1.1 \times 0.6 = 0.7$. From Table 2, the direction is seen to be 180° True.

The current at 1700 EDT at a point 5½ miles east of Stingray Point on 5 October 1967 is predicted to be 0.7 knot setting 180° True.

Note: Calculations for the strength at an intermediate time of a hydraulic current, such as in the Cape Cod Canal or at Hell Gate in East River, New York City, are handled

exactly as above, except that the lower, B, part of Table 3 is used.

Example 5.   Determination of the duration of slack (weak current) at a designated point.

Problem: For how long will the current be less than 0.2 knot around the time of slack before flood on the morning of 6 September 1967 at Chesapeake Bay Entrance?

Solution: From Table 1, on the given date, the maximum currents on either side of this slack (at 0712) are 1.8 knots ebb at 0400 and 1.4 knots flood at 0954.

Using Table 4A, fig. 2023, the duration of current less than 0.2 knot is determined for each maximum; simple interpolation may be used for values of maximum current between the tabulated entries in the left-hand column of this table. The values found are 26 and 34 minutes; these are averaged as 30 minutes.

On 6 September 1967 at Chesapeake Bay Entrance, the predicted duration of a current less than 0.2 knot at the morning slack before ebb is 30 minutes, or from approximately 0659 until 0729.

Notes: a. If the maximum strengths of the ebb and flood currents are essentially the same, only one figure need be taken from Table 4.

b. Use the A or B portion of Table 4 in the same manner as for Table 3.

Example 6.   Use of a Tidal Current Diagram.

Problem: For an afternoon run up Chesapeake Bay from Smith Point to Sandy Point Light at 10 knots on 20 October 1967, what time should you depart from Smith Point for the most favorable current conditions?

Solution: We use the current diagram for Chesapeake Bay and a graphic solution, fig. 2024. Draw a line on the diagram parallel to the 10-knot northbound speed line so that it fits generally in the center of the shaded area marked "Flood." Project downward from the intersection of this line with the horizontal line marked Smith Point Light to the scale at the bottom of the diagram. The mark here will be seen to be "0ʰ after ebb begins at the entrance."

Referring to Table 1, it will be seen that on the given date, the afternoon slack before ebb occurs at 1242.

For a run up Chesapeake Bay to Sandy Point Light at 10 knots on the afternoon of 20 October 1967, it is predicted that the most favorable current conditions will be obtained if you leave Smith Point Light at about 1242 EST or 1342 EDT.

Notes: a. Similar solutions can be worked out for southbound trips, but it is likely that on longer runs you will be faced with both favorable and unfavorable current conditions. Selection of starting time may be made, however, to minimize adverse conditions.

b. Conditions shown on Tidal Current Diagrams are averages and for typical conditions; small variations should be expected in specific situations.

TIDAL CURRENT CHARTS

The Coast and Geodetic Survey also publishes a series of *Tidal Current Charts.* These are available for eight bodies of water, from Boston Harbor around to Puget Sound (see complete listing on page 299).

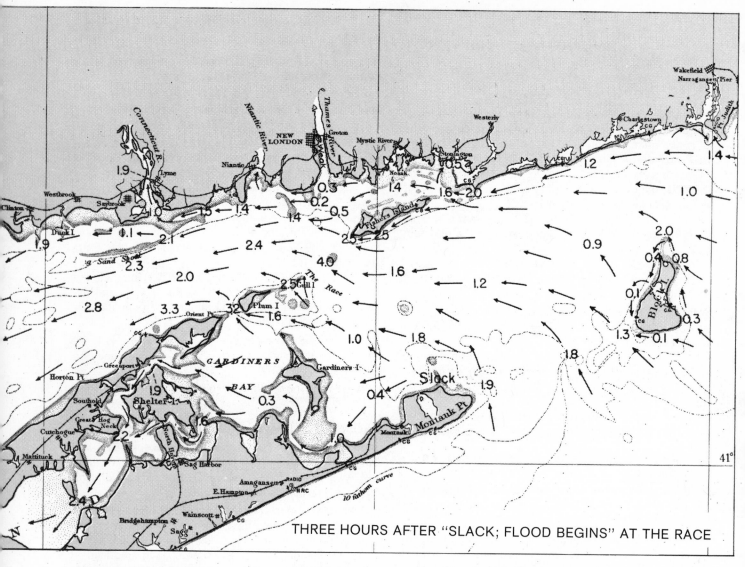

THREE HOURS AFTER "SLACK; FLOOD BEGINS" AT THE RACE

FIG. 2025 Tidal Current Charts are published for certain major bodies of water. Each is a set of 12 small-scale chartlets showing currents existing at hourly intervals throughout a complete cycle of flood and ebb.

Tidal Current Charts are made up in the form of a series of 12 reproductions of a small-scale chart of the area. Each of the charts depicts the direction and velocity of the current for a specific time in terms of hours after the predicted time of the beginning of flood or the beginning of ebb at the appropriate reference station. See fig. 2025. The currents in various passages and portions of the body of water are indicated by arrows and numbers. By following through the sequence of the charts, the hourly changes in strength and direction are easily seen.

These charts must be used with caution as tidal current strengths may vary widely between points separated by only a short distance.

Tidal Current Charts are periodically updated from new surveys and only the latest edition should be used.

RIVER CURRENTS

River currents, above tidal action, will consistently flow in one direction, but the velocity may vary widely. In some instances, information can be obtained from the U.S. Army Engineers, but usually your best source will be local personnel. Experience has shown, however, that such persons will more often than not overestimate current strength.

Usually, the strongest currents will occur in the deepest part of the channel. Near the banks, the current will be weaker; you may even find a counter-current running weakly in the opposite direction. In a bend of a river, expect the strongest current on the outside of the turn. Where a river narrows, or the flow is restricted by a shoal, an island, or man-made structure, the current will accelerate.

For further consideration of river current, refer to Chapter 29.

SUPPLEMENTARY SOURCES OF INFORMATION

The ultimate source of current information is your own eyesight and past experience, fig. 2026. These are most helpful even where there are predictions from the C&GS tables. As noted before, the tabular data are to be expected under "normal" conditions, and may be easily upset by unusual circumstances. Strong winds will, for example, drive water into or out of bays and modify tidal levels and currents.

◀ **0.6 KNOT**

Note (far left) how at 0.3 knot a wake is evident and the buoy inclines slightly. Doubling the velocity (0.6 knot, at left) increases the disturbance on both sides of the buoy. At 1.0 knot (below, left) it leans over and a whirlpool-like eddy has developed. Finally, at 2.2 knots (below), the wake has whitened. Buoy shapes affect the pattern and inclination.

2.2 KNOTS ▼

▲ **0.3 KNOT**

These photographs by Larry Riordan show clearly how buoys can be a helpful aid in estimating the direction and strength of current. Even though some data are available in Current Tables, predictions may be in error because of wind. Turbulence and eddies around a buoy increase with current velocity. In very strong currents, buoys may tow completely under.

1.0 KNOT ▶

FIG. 2026 Tidal current predictions are often upset by temporary local conditions of wind or rainfall. There is no substitute for an ability to interpret currents from visual observations. This excellent set of photographs shows visible indications on a buoy of currents of various strengths. Be careful; do not overestimate current velocity.

Currents and Piloting

One of the most interesting problems in small-craft piloting is the matter of currents, their effect upon boat speed, the determination of courses which must be steered to make good a desired path, and the time required to reach a destination. This is often know as *current sailing*.

Contrary to popular belief, the solution of current problems is really comparatively simple and does not require the use of higher mathematics to obtain results of practical accuracy. Indeed, when the fundamental principles have been mastered, the working out of current problems can be fun.

As a boat is propelled through the water, by oars, sails, or motor, and as it is steered, it moves with respect to the water. At the same time, the water may be moving with respect to the bottom and the shore as a result of current. The resultant motion of the boat is the net effect of these two motions combined, with regard to both velocity and direction. The actual track made good over the bottom will not be the same as the DR track, neither in terms of course nor speed.

The importance of tidal currents should not be underestimated. Unexpected current is always a threat to the skipper because it can carry his craft off course, possibly into dangerous waters. The risk is greater with slower boat speeds and under conditions of reduced visibility. A prediction of current effect can be added to a plot of a DR

track to obtain an *estimated position (EP)* plotted as a small square with a dot in the center, fig. 2027.

Leeway

Before proceeding further with current effects, let us here introduce, and then dispense with, the term *leeway*. By definition, leeway is the leeward (away from the wind)

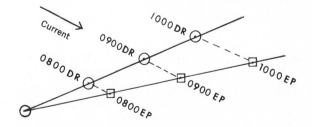

FIG. 2027 If the current is known, or can be estimated, a DR plot can be modified to show a series of Estimated Positions (EP) showing the effect of current.

motion of a vessel due to the wind. The term is most applicable to sailing craft, but it can be appreciable on larger motorboats and yachts. Its effect, however, need not be considered separately from current; the two may be lumped together, plus such factors as wave action on the boat, and the total offsetting influence termed "current."

Sailing Directions emphasize the necessity of taking such influences into account. A typical caution might read: "The directions 'steer' or 'make good' a course mean, without exception, to proceed from a point of origin along a track having the identical meridional angle as the designated course. Vessels following the directives must allow for every influence tending to cause deviation (not to be confused with compass deviation—Ed) from such track, and navigate so that the designated course is continuously being made good."

DEFINITION OF CURRENT SAILING TERMS

The terms "Course" and "Speed" were used in DR plots for the motion of the boat through the water without regard to current. Now this most important influence will be studied and additional terms must be introduced.

The *intended track* is the expected path of the boat, as plotted on a chart, after consideration has been given to the effect of current.

Track, abbreviated as TR, is the direction (true) of the intended track line.

Speed of advance, SOA, is the intended rate of travel along the intended track line.

It must be recognized that the intended track will not always be the actual track, and so two more terms are needed.

Course over the ground, COG, is the direction of the *actual* path of the boat, the track made good.

Speed over the ground, SOG, is the actual rate of travel along this track.

CURRENT SITUATIONS

A study of the effects of current resolves itself into two basic situations, as follows:

1. When the direction of the current, its *set,* is in the same direction as the boat's motion, or is in exactly the opposite direction.

2. When the direction of the current is at an angle to the boat's course, either a right or an oblique angle.

The first situation is, of course, the simplest and most easily solved. The velocity of the current, the *drift,* is added to, or subtracted from, the speed through the water to obtain the speed over the ground. The course over the ground (or intended track) is the same as the DR course—COG equals C, as does TR.

CURRENT DIAGRAMS

When the boat's motion and the set of the current form an angle with each other, the solution for the resultant course and speed is more complex, but still not difficult. Several methods may be used, but a graphic solution using a *current diagram* will usually be found to be the easiest to understand.

Basically, a current diagram represents the two component motions separately, as if they occurred independently and sequentially, which, of course, they do not. These diagrams can be drawn in terms of velocities or distances. The former is easier and is usually used; current diagrams in this book will be drawn in terms of velocities and labeled as shown in fig. 2028. If distances are plotted, be sure to use the same period of time for each component motion—one hour is commonly used since the units of distance will then be the same numerically as the units of speed.

Accuracy of current diagrams

The accuracy with which the resultant course and speed can be determined depends largely on the accuracy with which the current has been determined. Values of the current usually must be taken from tidal current tables or charts, or estimated by the skipper from visual observations; see fig. 2606.

Current diagrams may also be called "vector triangles of velocity," a profound title for a simple graphic procedure. The term "vector" in mathematics means a quantity that has both magnitude and direction. Directed quantities are important things. In current sailing, the directed quantities are the motions of the boat and the water (the current).

Vectors

A vector may be represented graphically by an arrow, a segment of a straight line with an arrowhead indicating the direction, and the length of the line scaled to the velocity, fig. 2029. If we specify that a certain unit of length is equal to a certain unit of speed—e.g., that 1 inch equals 1 knot—then two such vectors can represent graphically two different velocities. Any speed scale may be used, the larger the better for accuracy. The size of the available paper and working space will normally control the scale.

Current diagrams may be drawn on a chart either as part of the plot or separately. They may also be drawn on plain paper; in this case, it is wise to draw in a north line as the

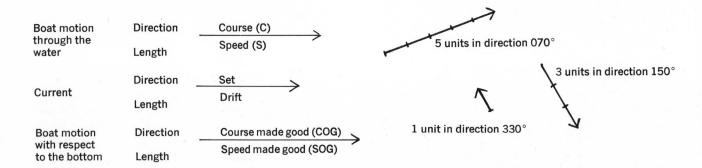

Boat motion through the water	Direction	Course (C)
	Length	Speed (S)
Current	Direction	Set
	Length	Drift
Boat motion with respect to the bottom	Direction	Course made good (COG)
	Length	Speed made good (SOG)

FIG. 2028 The component lines of a current diagram must always be correctly and completely labeled. Direction is shown above the line; velocity is noted below the line. Typical labels are shown above.

5 units in direction 070°

3 units in direction 150°

1 unit in direction 330°

FIG. 2029 A vector is a line representing a *directed quantity*. It has direction (shown by the arrowhead) and magnitude (length). Any convenient scale may be selected to indicate magnitude.

reference for measuring directions.

Since boats are subject to two distinct motions—the boat through the water, and the water with respect to the bottom—we will now consider how the resultant motion, or vector sum, is obtained by current diagrams.

Vector triangles

When the two motions are not in line with each other, they form two sides of a triangle, fig. 2030. Completing the triangle gives the third side which will be a vector representing the resultant motion or velocity. Thus, when any two velocity vectors are drawn to the same scale and form the sides of a velocity triangle, the third side will be the resultant velocity vector (the vector sum of the other two), and its direction and magnitude may be measured from the diagram.

It may be an aid to the visualization of the component motions if a time period of one hour is used and the points that are the corners of the triangle are considered as positions of the boat before and after certain motions, as follows:

O—the origin.

DR—the DR position of the boat as a result solely of its motion through the water.

W—the position of the boat solely as a result of the motion of the water.

P—the position (intended or actual) of the boat as a result of the combined action of the component motions.

(It should be noted that, in some cases, two of the above letters are applicable to a position; it is customary to use only one.)

"Tail-to-head" relationship. Note very carefully how the vectors for boat motion through the water and the current are drawn. These vectors are always drawn "tail-to-head," *not* so that both are directed out from the same source. (This rule applies only when one of the vectors is current; not when they both represent boat's motion.)

If both boat motion through the water and current are known, either may be drawn first from the origin; fig. 2031b will give the same resultant motion as fig. 2031a.

The four "Cases" of current problems

There are four typical current problems, different combinations of known and unknown factors. For convenience, we will call them Case 1, 2, etc.

CASE 1—Known: Boat's course (C) and speed (S) through the water; current set and drift.

To be determined: The intended (expected) track (TR) and speed of advance (SOA).

This is the determination of the effect of a known current if no allowance is made for its effect.

CASE 2—Known: Boat's course (C) and speed (S) through the water; the course (COG) and speed made good (SOG).

To be determined: The set and drift of the current.

This is the determination of the nature of an unknown current from observation of its effect.

CASE 3—Known: Boat's speed through the water (S), the set and drift of the current, and the intended track (TR).

To be determined: The course to be steered (C) and the speed of advance (SOA) along the intended track.

This is the determination of corrected course to be steered, but without regard for the effect on speed or ETA.

CASE 4—Known: The set and drift of the current, the intended track (TR), and the speed of advance desired (SOA).

To be determined: The course to be steered (C) and speed to be run through the water (S).

This is the "rendezvous" or "contest" case where the destination and the time of arrival are specified.

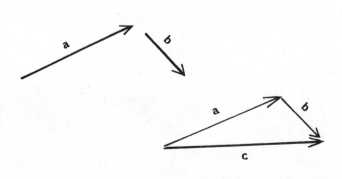

FIG. 2030 **Vectors may be combined graphically to determine the vector sum. Typically, vectors *a* and *b* above, representing component motions, are combined as vector *c*, the resultant motion of the two components.**

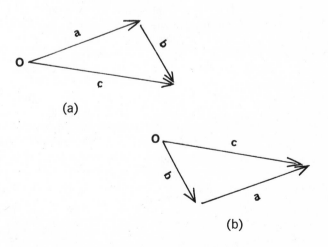

FIG. 2031 **The two vector triangles shown above appear to be different because in one vector *a* was drawn before vector *b*, and in the other, *b* was drawn before *a*. The resultant vector, *c*, however, is exactly the same for either procedure.**

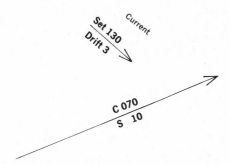

FIG. 2032 If a boat is traveling through the water on a course of 070°, and the current is setting in the direction 130°, it is obvious that the craft will be set off course to starboard. The question of how much, and the effect on speed over the bottom, is what must be determined. A current diagram will provide the answers.

Illustrative examples

Let us first consider **Case 1**—the effect of current on a boat's course and speed. If the set of the current is as shown in fig. 2032, then the boat will be set off to the right of the direction in which it is being steered. We will use a current diagram to determine the exact extent of this effect, the path the boat can be expected to follow and its speed (the intended track and speed of advance).

We first draw in a north line as a reference for measuring directions, fig. 2033a, and then the vector for the boat's speed through the water, O-DR, a line drawn from the origin in the direction 070° for a length of 10 units, fig. 2033b. Next we add the vector for current, DR-W, three units in the direction 130°, fig. 2033c. Note that we have remembered to observe the "tail-to-head" relationship rule. (Either of these two vectors could have been drawn first; the triangle would appear differently, but the result will be the same.) Because these vectors form two sides of a triangle of velocities, the third side O-W, fig. 2033d, is the resultant velocity at which the boat moves with respect to the bottom under the combined influences of its propulsion and the current. The point W can now be relabeled "P." The intended (or expected) track (TR) and the speed of advance (SOA) can be measured from the O-P line. In this example, it turns out that the boat can be expected to sail a course over the ground of 083° and to have a speed of advance of 11.8 knots. Note that the directions of these vectors are always plotted as *true* directions.

Summarizing briefly, we have drawn vectors to indicate independently the motion of the boat from two different influences, its own propulsion and the current. Actually, of course, the boat will *not* go first from O to DR and then on to P. All the time, it will travel directly along the intended track O-P. The boat is steered on course C, the direction of O-DR, but, due to the effect of current, it is expected to travel along the intended track O-P. This is the route that must be considered for shoals and other hazards to navigation.

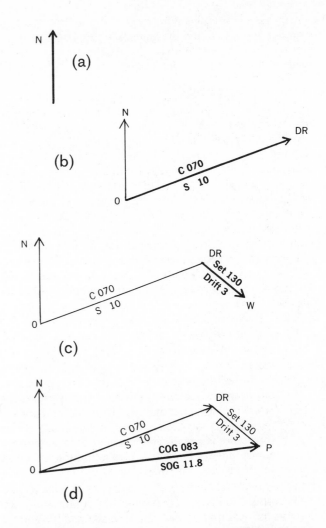

FIG. 2033 Current Diagram—CASE 1. These diagrams illustrate the step-by-step graphical solution: (a) the reference North line; (b) the vector for boat's motion through the water; (c) the vector for current, the motion of the water with respect to the bottom; and finally (d) the vector for the resultant motion of the boat with respect to the bottom.

Cruising men can never afford to ignore the effect of current. Down East, for example, in Maine waters big tidal ranges often cause baffling current conditions, compounded by unusual influences of headlands and river currents. Fog in such areas places a special premium on piloting skill.

FIG. 2034 Current Diagram—CASE 2. The prevailing current (actually the net effect of all offsetting influences) can be found graphically from a vector triangle of velocities.

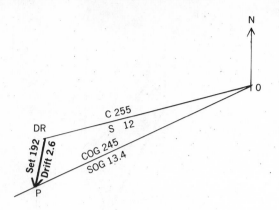

Now for a **Case 2** situation in which you know the course you have steered and the speed through the water from either the speed curve of your boat or a marine speedometer. It is also obvious to you that you did not arrive at your DR position. From your chart plot, you have been able to determine the course and speed over the ground. Current has acted to set you off your course—you desire to know its set and drift.

After again drawing a north reference line, plot vectors for your motion through the water—C 255°, S 12 knots; and your motion with respect to the bottom—COG 245°, SOG 13.4 knots. See fig. 2034. These vectors are both drawn outward from the origin, O, to points DR and P respectively. The "tail-to-head" rule is not applicable as neither of these vectors represents current. The action of the current has been to offset your boat from DR to P (which is also point W in this case), thus the set is the direction *from* DR *toward* P, and the drift is the length of this line in scale units.

In fig. 2034, the current is found to be setting 192° with a drift of 2.6 knots. This is the *average* current for the time period and location of the run from O to P for which the calculations were made; it is not the current at P. For the next leg of your cruise, these current values can be used as is, or modified as required by the passage of time and/or the continuing change in position of the boat.

Case 3 is a typical cruising situation—here, you know the track you desire to make good (TR 080°), you have decided to run at your normal cruising speed through the water (S 10 knots), and you have calculated (or estimated) the current's set (140°) and drift (4 knots). What you desire to know is the course to be steered (C) and the speed of advance (SOA) which can be used to figure your estimated time of arrival (ETA).

Draw in a north line and measure directions from it, fig. 2035a. Plot the current vector, O-W, at the specified direction and length, and a line (not a vector yet) in the direction of the intended track—this line should be of indefinite length at this time. From point W, swing an arc, with dividers or drawing compass, equal in length to the speed through the water in scale units. The point at which this arc intersects the intended track line is point P and the vector triangle has been completed. The direction of W-P is the course to be steered (C 060°); the length of the vector O-P is the speed over the ground (SOG 11.4) and from this the ETA can be calculated.

Let us look at the reasoning behind this graphic solution of Case 3. Again considering the component motions separately for the sake of simplicity, the boat is moved by current from O to W. It is to move from W at the specified speed through the water, but must get back on the intended track line; the problem is to find the point P on the track which is "S" units from point W. The solution is found by swinging an arc as described above.

Remember that all vectors are plotted as *true* directions, including C, the course to be steered in the preceding solution. This must be changed to a compass direction (course) for actual use at the helm.

In accordance with the principles of dead reckoning, it is desirable to plot the DR track even though a current is known to exist. This line, drawn from point O in the direction C and with a length of S scale units, forms a basis for consideration of possible hazards if the current is not as calculated or estimated, fig. 2035b.

FIG. 2035 Current Diagram—CASE 3. If you know your desired track, and have decided upon your speed through the water, a graphical solution (a) can be used to determine the course to be steered and the speed of advance. For safety's sake, a DR plot from the origin should be added as in (b).

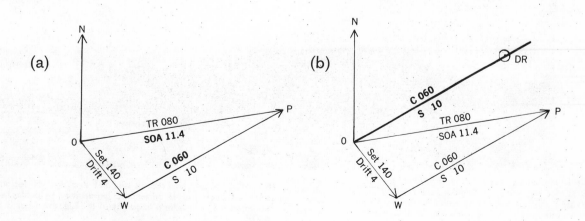

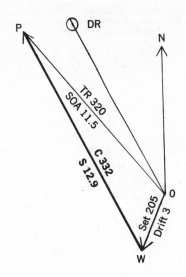

FIG. 2036 Current Diagram—CASE 4. This problem concerns the course to be steered and the speed at which to run in order to arrive at a specified destination at a predetermined time. This could be useful in a predicted log contest or in rendezvousing with another boat.

A **Case 4** situation is an interesting variation of Case 3—you desire to arrive at a specified point at a given time. It may be that you are competing in a predicted log contest, or merely that you have agreed to meet friends at that time and place. In addition to the data on current that you have, you have decided upon your track and your speed of advance. For fig. 2036, let us assume that the current sets 205° at 3 knots. You need to make good a track of 320°, and a quick distance-time-speed calculation sets your required speed of advance at 11.5 knots.

From the north reference line, draw the current vector O-W and the intended track vector O-P. Complete the triangle with the vector W-P which will give you the course to be steered (C 332 True) and the speed to run through the water (S 12.9) to arrive at the destination at the desired time. Line O-DR should be drawn in from the origin as a dead reckoning track for the sake of safety.

Solutions of Cases 1, 2, 3, and 4 using tabular data, rather than graphic plots, are given in pages 425 to 425(f).

These tables should not be used without a clear understanding of the fundamentals of current sailing, the component motions and their relationships to each other. These fundamentals, and the terms and symbols used, should be learned from simple graphic solutions as presented above.

FIG. 2037 Ability to estimate the set and drift of currents on a proposed course is of paramount importance to contestants in a predicted log race, where accuracy of the highest order is required to win.

CHAPTER 21

PILOTING—Position Determination

The art of piloting reaches its climax in *position determination*. Underway on a body of water of any size, where the safety of your boat and its crew is at stake, it's not "where you ought to be," or "where you think you are," but your knowledge of "where you are for sure" that counts. The development of an ability to determine your position quickly and accurately under a wide range of conditions should be one of your primary goals as a skipper.

The need for position determination

In three of the current sailing situations covered in the preceding chapter, the set and drift of the current were taken as known values. In everyday cruising, it is more than likely that the strength and direction of the actual current will be somewhat different from that calculated or estimated. Local wind conditions or abnormal rainfall will frequently upset tabular predictions; estimates based on visual observations of current will often be inaccurate unless the boatman has had considerable experience. Because of these uncertainties, current sailing solutions can be considered only as *estimates* of present positions and of future motions and positions.

Buoy positions are usually reliable; the Coast Guard expends much effort in keeping them on station and operating properly. They are, however, not infallible, and the position of a boat should be determined by other means as often as practicable.

Accurate position determination whenever the opportunity presents itself is essential in order that the safety of the craft can be verified, or corrective action taken promptly. By so doing, the true effects of the current may also become known. Further, such fixing of position makes possible the start of a new DR plot, fresher and more accurate than the old one.

Frequent position determination is an essential safety precaution. No matter how safe your boat is, no matter how experienced you are in boating, no matter how good the weather nor how calm the seas, emergencies can arise, and suddenly, too. Knowledge of where you are, extended from a *recent* position determination, can be of the greatest value when you must call for help. Or, if it is another boat that has trouble, you can set the most direct course to render assistance if you are sure of where you are.

THE SKIPPER'S RESPONSIBILITIES

It is the duty of a skipper to fix the position of his craft with such degree of precision and at such frequent intervals as is required by the proximity to hazards to safe navigation. This is an absolute requirement of the person in charge of the vessel, whether he is personally doing the piloting or this is being done by another person. He can assign the function, but he cannot delegate his responsibility.

The actual procedures in position determination will vary widely in practice. Proceeding down a narrow channel, positioning will be informal and a chart plot will not be maintained. But this does not mean that position de-

St. Petersburg Times Photo by Dan Hightower

FIG. 2101   The skipper of any boat is responsible for the safety of it and of all persons on board. He must be able to determine his position accurately, and do so as often as required by prevailing conditions.

termination is being omitted; indeed, it is being done essentially continuously by visual reference to the aids to navigation. On the other hand, during an open ocean passage, a plot will be maintained, but positions will be determined, other than by DR calculations, perhaps only three or four times each day.

Between the extremes cited above, there will be found the normal cruising situations in pilot waters. Cruising just offshore, or in the larger inland bodies of water, a skipper will usually maintain a plot of his track with periodic checks on its accuracy, perhaps every 15 or 20 minutes, perhaps at hourly intervals.

The ability to determine the position of his craft to an acceptable degree of accuracy under any condition of visibility is essential to safe boating. The absence of this ability, or any limitation on it, should restrict the extent of a person's boating activities, setting the boundaries of the water areas and weather conditions into which he will enter.

CHAPTER 21 / **Position Determination**

DEFINITION OF TERMS

A *line of position (LOP)* is a line, in actuality or drawn on a chart, at some point along which an observer is presumed to be located, fig. 2102. A LOP may result from observation or measurement; from visual, electronic, or celestial sources. It may be straight or curved; a circular LOP is sometimes referred to as a *circle of position*, fig.

2103. A line of position may be *advanced* (moved forward) or *retired* (moved backward) in time according to the movement of the vessel during the time interval involved. In piloting, the more usual situation will be the advancement of a previously taken LOP to the time of another LOP just taken.

A *bearing* is the direction of an object from the observer, expressed in degrees as a three-digit number—005°

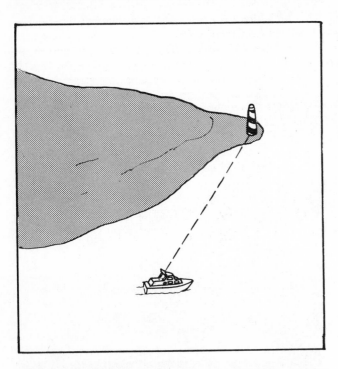

FIG. 2102 Position determination is based on "lines of position." These are lines, in actuality or on a chart, along which the observer is presumed to be located. A single line will not determine position, but it does tell the observer where he is *not* located, and such information is often useful.

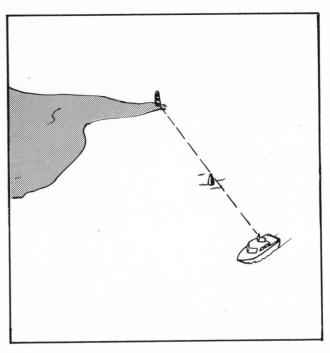

FIG. 2104 When two objects can be observed in line, an excellent line of position is established. Such "ranges" may have been set up with specific aids to navigation, or they may be any two identifiable objects such as ordinary navigational aids, landmarks, or natural or man-made features.

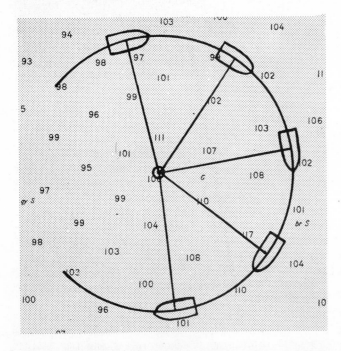

FIG. 2103 Lines of position may be curved as well as straight. A measurement of distance from an identified object yields a circular LOP. It may be plotted as a complete circle or as only a partial arc.

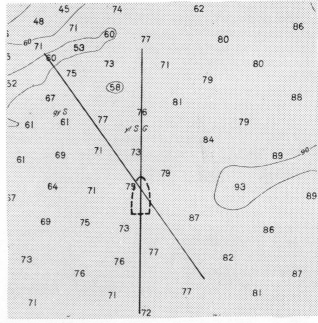

FIG. 2105 A "fix" is an accurately determined position for the observer and his craft. It is not based on any prior position, but is determined from currently observed lines of position or other data.

346

062°, 157°, etc. A *true bearing* is a bearing measured with reference to the true north direction as 000°. *Magnetic* and *compass bearings* are, respectively, observations with reference to the local magnetic north direction or to the craft's steering compass as it is affected by deviation at that moment. A *relative bearing* is a bearing measured with reference to the ship's heading—it is measured clockwise from the fore-and-aft line with 000° being dead ahead,

090° broad on the starboard beam, 180° dead astern, etc. (An older method of measuring relative bearings 180° to port or starboard is seldom used any more; it made calculations more complicated than necessary.)

A *range* consists of two objects that can be observed in line with each other and the observer, fig. 2104.

A *fix* is an accurately located position determined without reference to any prior position, fig. 2105. A *running fix* is a position that has been determined from LOPs at least one of which has been taken at a different time and advanced or retarded to the time of the other observation.

An *estimated position (EP)* is the best position obtainable short of a fix or good-quality running fix. It is the most probable position, determined from incomplete data, or from data of questionable accuracy.

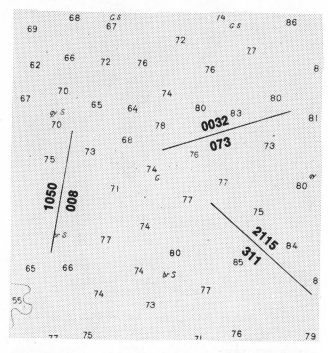

FIG. 2106 The correct labeling of lines of position is most important; unlabeled lines on a chart can only be a source of confusion. The time is always shown above the line (in 24-hour clock system) and direction below the line as a three-digit number without the "o" symbol.

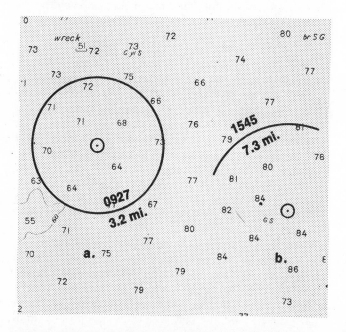

FIG. 2107 Circles of position are labeled in the same general manner as straight lines of position. The time is placed above the line and the distance below, as it would normally be viewed and read. Thus, the time may be "inside" or "outside" the circle as determined by the curvature of the arc.

Lines of Position

Lines of position are the basic elements of position determination. By definition, the observer, and his craft, are located somewhere along a LOP. If two LOPs intersect, the only position at which the vessel can be, and be on both lines, is their intersection. Thus, the usual fix is determined by the crossing of two lines of position.

Labeling

Since LOPs are also lines that are drawn on a chart, it is essential that they be labeled immediately, and that such labels conform to a standardized system. A label should contain all information necessary for identification, but nothing further that might cause confusion or clutter up the chart. The information to be recorded for each line of position is the time that it was observed or measured and its basic dimension, such as direction toward, or distance from, the object used.

A bearing is a LOP that has time and direction. Fig. 2106 shows several examples of correctly labeled bearings. Time is always shown *above* the line of the bearing, and direction *below* the line. Time is given as a four-digit figure in the 24-hour clock system. Directions are *true* and are written as a three-digit group with zeros prefixed as necessary.

A circle of position has dimensions of time and distance; it may be plotted as a complete circle, fig. 2107a, or merely as a partial circle, an arc, as in fig. 2107b. Time is labeled above the curved line and distance, with units, is shown below the line.

A range is a line of position whose direction is self-evident from the two points which define it. In this case, only time need be shown; it is placed above the line as for other LOPs; see fig. 2108.

Do not draw the line completely through the chart symbols for the two objects used as the range; this will avoid the necessity for subsequent erasure across the symbols. Draw the line neatly and no longer than necessary; it need not extend all the way to the front range marker or other object if the two features used to form the range are clearly evident.

A line of position that has been advanced (or retired) in time is labeled with *both* times above the line, the time of original observation or measurement and the time to which it has been advanced (or retired). The time of the original LOP is written first, followed by a dash and then

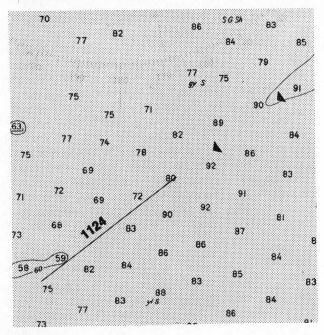

FIG. 2108 Since a range is based on the relationship between the two sighted objects, it is often used without a measurement of its actual direction. Ranges need be labeled only with the time of the observation.

the second time, fig. 2109.

Always label lines of position as soon as they are drawn. Unmarked lines on a chart can easily be a source of confusion. If labeling is put off until a later time, mistakes may be made.

FIXES

As previously defined, a fix is an accurately located position for a vessel. On many occasions in small-craft piloting, position will be established by passing close by an

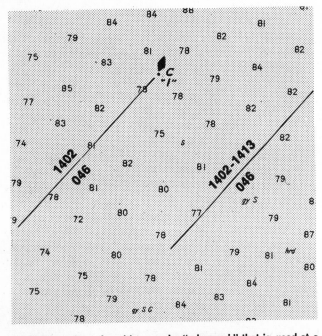

FIG. 2109 A line of position may be "advanced," that is, used at a later time than when it was observed if it is replotted to account for the movement of the boat since the time of observation. An advanced LOP is labeled with the original time and the time for which it is replotted. The direction, of course, remains the same.

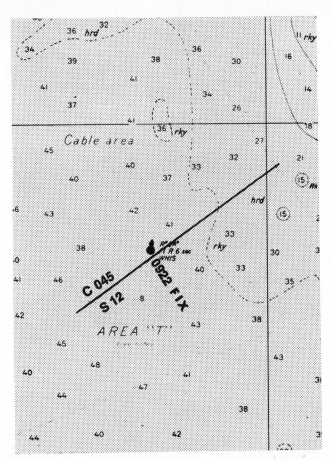

FIG. 2110 A simple, but excellent, determination of position occurs when a boat passes close alongside an aid to navigation or other identifiable point. A good pilot always notes the time of such an event on his chart.

identifiable object, usually an aid to navigation. This is, of course, a fix of the highest possible accuracy, and a skipper should always note the time of such an event on his chart plot, fig. 2110.

Fix from two LOPs

The typical fix obtained from lines of position will be the intersection of two such lines. It is important to consider the effect of the angle of intersection between the two LOPs on the accuracy of the position determination. Let us look first at the situation where the two lines cross at right angles, 90°, fig. 2111a. If there should be an error of, say, 2° in one LOP, the resulting fix from this mistake would be off only a short distance.

Consider now fig. 2111b in which the intersection angle is only 30°. An error of 2° in one LOP would result in a considerably greater change in the location of the intersection.

Two lines of position should intersect as nearly as possible at right angles; the angle of intersection should never be less than 60° nor more than 120° if this can be avoided.

Where there is no alternative, a fix from two lines of position intersecting at angles of 30° to 60° (120° to 150°) can be used, but only with caution. A position from two LOPs intersecting at less than 30° (more than 150°) is of too dubious accuracy for safe navigation. **Areas of uncertainty.** Lines of position will normally be stated as having a specific direction, such as 072°, 147°, etc. In actuality, there may be an uncertainty in each line of two or three, or even more, degrees. This condition can be shown graphically on the chart by additional lines drawn lightly on either side of the basic LOP; this should always be done if such uncertainty could mean the difference between a safe position and a hazardous one.

Lines of position from various sources and techniques will have different degrees of uncertainty. Only experience will give the pilot the ability to judge various methods and assign relative values of probable accuracy.

If two LOPs, each with its graphic representation of uncertainty, are drawn, the result is an *area of uncertainty* about the intersection of the lines of position; there is an element of doubt about the location of the fix. Figs. 2112a and b show how the angle of intersection alters this area of uncertainty and why it is desirable to have the LOPs cross as nearly as possible at 90°. Based on the mathematics of statistics and probability, the area of uncertainty is elliptical (circular if the LOPs cross at 90°) rather than the quadrilateral formed by the outside limiting lines for each bearing. In actual piloting, this distinction is more theoretical than practical. A detailed discussion of this topic, including the additional complexities that arise if one line of position can be considered to be more accu-

rate than the other, is beyond the scope of this book, but may be found in Bowditch, Chapter 29.

More than two LOPs

Since most lines of position obtained in small-craft piloting (except possibly ranges) are reasonably, but certainly not exactly, accurate, it is highly desirable to use more than two LOPs to reduce the uncertainty of position. There is no theoretical upper limit to the number of lines of position that can be used, but practical considerations with a boat underway will normally limit the pilot to three LOPs.

Ideally, since the observer is presumed to be on all three lines of position, they will intersect in a common point, fig. 2113a. The much more likely result is that when the observations are plotted, the lines will form a triangle, fig. 2113b.

The use of three LOPs results in a modification of the previously stated rule about the desirable intersection angle of the lines. For optimum results, the three lines should each differ in direction as closely as possible to 60° (or 120°), fig. 2114. In this configuration, an inaccuracy in any of the LOPs will result in the minimum net error of position.

An alternative technique to the above is to obtain two

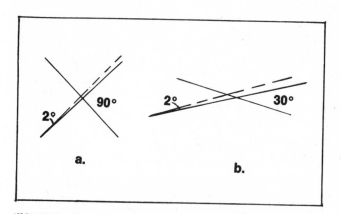

FIG. 2111 Lines of position taken from a small craft are seldom precisely accurate. Selection of an optimum angle of intersection between LOPs reduces the uncertainty of position. Shown here is the difference that a change of 2° in one LOP makes in the intersection point when the lines cross at 90° or at 30°.

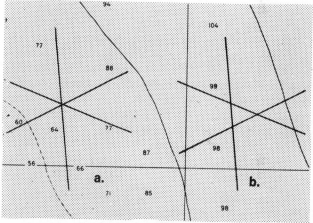

FIG. 2113 The use of more than two LOPs will enhance confidence in the resulting fix. Ideally, three lines of position will intersect at a common point, as in *a* above. More often in actual piloting, a triangle will be formed as shown in *b*. If the triangle is unreasonably large for the prevailing conditions, the observations should be checked or discarded.

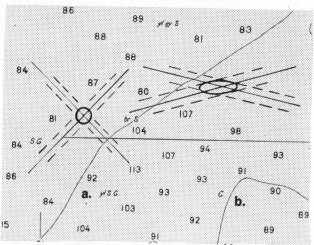

FIG. 2112 When each of two LOPs may have an inaccuracy of several degrees, there is an *area of uncertainty* around the intersection point. This is least, a circle, when the angle of intersection is 90°. Angles of 60° to 90° are satisfactory; those of 30° to 60° may be used with caution.

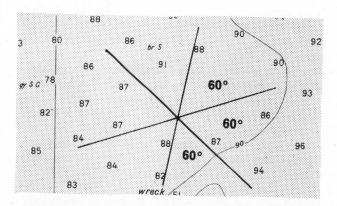

FIG. 2114 For an optimum set of three observations, the lines of position should cross at 60° to each other. This will seldom be exactly possible in actual piloting situations, but should be kept in mind as fundamentally desirable.

lines of position at nearly 90° to each other, and then a third LOP making an angle of approximately 45° with those of the original pair, figs. 2115a and b. This procedure has the advantage of providing an optimum two-LOP plot in the event that a change of visibility or other circumstance should suddenly prevent the third observation.

Triangles of position

As noted above, three lines of position will usually form a *triangle of position*. If this triangle is quite large, it is probable that there is a significant error in one or more of the LOPs, and a check should be made of the observations, calculations, and plotting.

If, however, the triangle is relatively small (and "relatively" will have to be defined in each situation as determined by the techniques used, the experience of the observer, the size of the boat, sea state, and other conditions), it can be assumed that no more than normal inaccuracies and uncertainties exist. In the everyday practice of piloting on boats, it is customary to use the center of the triangle of position, as estimated by eye, for the fix.

Labeling fixes

A fix is shown on a chart plot as a small circle with a dot in its center; it is labeled with the time followed by the letters "FIX"; see fig. 2116a. A running fix is labeled with the time and "R FIX"; fig. 2116b.

Often the dot in the center of the circle is not seen separately, as when the fix lies along a line or at the intersection of two lines. If the fix is obtained by passing close to a buoy or other aid to navigation, the dot or center of the chart symbol is used for the plot. The usual distance off, 50 to 100 yards or so, is not significant at typical chart scales; greater distances are estimated and the fix is plotted in the correct direction from the aid at a scaled distance.

THE VALUE OF A SINGLE LOP

The preceding discussion has centered on the use of two or more lines of position for obtaining a fix. While admittedly this is the most desirable situation, the value of a single LOP should not be overlooked.

Basically, a single line of position cannot tell a pilot where he is at the moment, but it can, within the limitations of its accuracy, tell him where he is *not*. If he is presumed to be somewhere along the LOP, then he cannot be at a position appreciably distant from the line. This information, although lacking in detail and negative in sense, may often be of value to a navigator concerned with the safety of his vessel.

A single line of position can frequently be combined with a DR position to obtain an "estimated position." This EP is the point along the LOP that is closest to the DR position for the same time. A line is drawn from the DR position perpendicular to the LOP until it intersects that line. The estimated position is marked with a small square and labeled with the time followed by "EP"; see fig. 2117a. Note that if a beam bearing is used, the EP will fall along the DR track line, fig. 2117b.

It is also possible to obtain an "estimated position with current" from a single LOP if the set and drift of the current have been determined from predictions or from its effect on the boat's course and speed made good. From

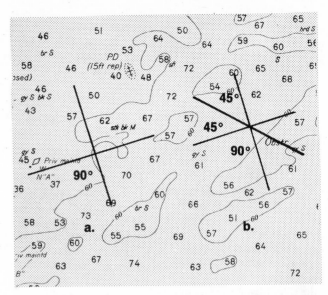

FIG. 2115 An alternative procedure for taking three observations is to select the first two objects so that their LOPs will cross at as near 90° as possible, a above. Then the third sight is taken so that its plotted LOP will cross the other two at approximately 45°, as in b above. If circumstances prevent the pilot from getting the third sight, he will still have a near-optimum two-LOP fix.

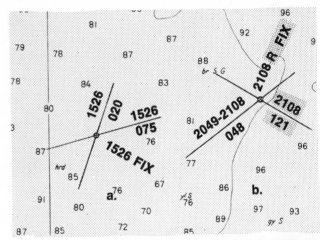

FIG. 2116 A *fix* is labeled with the time followed by "FIX" not written parallel to any line. A *running fix* is labeled with the time and "R FIX".

the DR position for the specified time, a line is drawn to scale to represent the effect of the current since the DR track was started from the last fix. This line is drawn in the direction of the set of the current and for a length equal to the "total drift," the distance found by multiplying the drift by the elapsed time since the last fix. This total drift line is labeled and from its end another line is drawn perpendicular to the LOP until it intersects that line; see fig. 2117c. The intersection is the *EP with current*; it is labeled in the same manner as before (the fact that current has been included is obvious from the plot).

In using an EP, make generous allowances for the uncertainty of the position; always err on the side of safety.

In some piloting situations, a single bearing on an object can be advanced and crossed with a later LOP on the same object. This will result in a running fix, not as desirable as a fix from two independent lines of position, but far better than a DR position or the pilot's "best guess."

Running fixes, and the use of a single LOP with depth measurements, will be discussed later in this chapter.

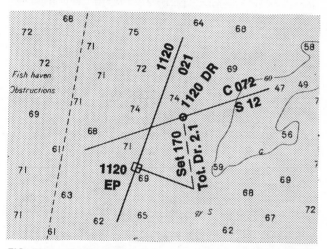

FIG. 2117 An *estimated position* can be obtained from a single line of position. It is the point on the LOP closest to the DR position for that time, see *a* above. If a beam bearing is used, the EP will fall along the DR track, as in *b* above.

FIG. 2117c If information about the current is available, an improved "estimated position with current" can be plotted. The offsetting effect of the current since the start of the DR track is calculated and plotted; the nearest point on the LOP from this current-influenced point is the EP.

FIG. 2118 A very simple, yet fully accurate method of taking bearings is to "aim" the boat directly at the sighted object and read the compass. Brief off-course swings for this purpose will not materially affect the DR plot but be sure that there are no hazards close alongside your course. Correct such compass bearings to true directions before plotting them.

Visual Observations

For the pilot of a typical motorboat or sailboat, the primary source of lines of position will be visual observations. These will include direct and relative bearings, ranges, and horizontal and vertical angle measurements. Correct identification of the sighted object is essential. Other methods and equipment may lead to LOPs such as those from radio direction finding, radar, and depth measurements, but these will normally be secondary to visual observations.

SIMPLE VISUAL BEARINGS

It will amaze the novice pilot (and perhaps some of the more experienced ones, too) how much navigational information can be obtained from the most simple of visual bearings, those directly ahead or broad on the beam.

Bearings dead ahead

Bearings taken directly ahead require no auxiliary equipment; the boat's steering compass will suffice. Only insignificant effects will be made on the DR track of a boat if the bow is momentarily swung off course and pointed toward an object on which it is desired to take a bearing. The craft should be held on this new heading long enough for the helmsman to properly line up on the object and for the compass to settle down and be read. This is normally a matter of less than a minute, perhaps only 20 or 30 seconds.

To use this technique, the pilot must be sure enough of his general location that the off-course swing can be made safely. But if such is the situation, he should not hesitate to use this quick and simple way of getting a line of position. The accuracy of bearings obtained by this method will normally be considerably greater than those of the more complex techniques to be discussed later.

The procedure of taking bearings dead ahead by "aiming" the boat at the object sighted upon has an additional advantage in that it can be accomplished by the helmsman alone, without the assistance of another person. Other methods will generally require the services of a second individual as the bearing-taker while the helmsman continues his normal duties, plus reading the steering compass at the time of the observation.

Beam bearings

If the observed aid to navigation or landmark is well around on either beam, it may not be feasible to make so great a deviation from the normal heading being steered in order to take a dead-ahead bearing. Or perhaps the limited width of the available deep water does not permit so large an excursion from the DR track. In this case, the other simple bearing technique may be used.

Determine some portion of the boat that is at a right angle to the fore-and-aft axis of the craft. Among the possibilities are bulkheads, seat backs, deck seams, etc. Sights taken along these features will determine when the observed object is directly abeam—a relative bearing of 090° or 270°.

The boat may be held on course and the passage of time awaited until sighting along the pre-selected portion of the boat indicates that the aid to navigation or other object is exactly broad on the beam. Its direction then is, of course, 90° greater or less than the direction read from the boat's compass at that moment.

If waiting until the object comes abeam in the normal course of events is not feasible or desirable, then the heading of the craft can sometimes be temporarily altered slightly as needed to bring the sighted object directly on the beam more quickly. Should such a temporary change of heading be made, the pilot must be sure that the 90° is added to, or subtracted from, the compass reading at the exact moment that the sighted object is abeam; do not use the normal base course.

Correction of compass bearings

The pilot should always remember that in either of these types of observations the bearings that are taken are *compass bearings*. It will be necessary to correct them for deviation and variation (see Chapter 13) and then plot them as *true* bearings. Any of the plotting instruments and techniques described in Chapter 19 may be used.

Beam bearings are obtained by adding 90° to or subtracting 90° from the boat's *true* heading. Be sure to correct the boat's compass heading for deviation and variation *first,* and *then* add the 90° if the observation was to starboard or subtract the 90° if the sighting was on the port beam. Do not use the direction of the bearing for entering the craft's deviation table; use the heading.

Plotting bearings

The direction measured by the visual observation is *from the boat toward the object.* When plotting is being done, the position of the boat is not known, but it is still possible to draw the line so that it will have the correct direction and lead toward, to, or through the chart symbol for the sighted object. The particular plotting instrument used will determine the exact procedures used.

It is also possible to plot a line of position outward from the sighted object by using the *reciprocal* of the corrected observed bearing. (In fact, this is the formally correct procedure, but it is usually by-passed in favor of the more direct technique mentioned in the paragraph above.) Here, caution must be taken to *first* correct the observed compass (or relative) bearing to a true direction, and then add or subtract 180° to obtain the reciprocal; do not reverse this sequence.

MORE SOPHISTICATED BEARINGS

The procedures just described above for bearings dead ahead and broad on the beam will suffice in many situations, but not in all. It may be neither safe nor convenient to alter the boat's heading for the purpose of taking a bearing.

Greater flexibility of navigation is obtained if bearings can be taken in any direction without a change in the normal heading of the craft. Such bearings will involve the use of the boat's compass, a pelorus or hand bearing compass, or some combination of these instruments.

Using the boat's compass

On many boats, it will be possible to take bearings directly over the steering compass, at least through a limited angle on either side of the bow. As determined by the construction of the compass, it may be feasible to sight directly over the card and get bearings of acceptable accu-

racy. On other models, a set of sighting vanes may be placed on the compass for greater precision in direction measurement. The directions in which bearings may be taken using the boat's steering compass will normally be limited by the nearby superstructure of the boat. Bearings taken using the boat's compass must be corrected for the deviation on the heading of the boat, *not* that for the bearing direction, and for the variation of the locality.

Using a hand-held compass

Direct visual bearings can also be taken using a hand-bearing compass, or even with the boat's compass if it is a model that has been designed for quick and easy dismounting with accurate remounting. It is normally not feasible to prepare a deviation table for such hand compass use because of the many different positions and circumstances connected with this procedure. Careful tests should be made to determine the locations about the boat, if any, at which a hand-held device can be used without deviation errors. These tests are best made from known positions by taking bearings on objects whose actual direction can be established from the chart. If deviation-free locations can be found on board, then correction will be required for magnetic variation only, to obtain true bearings for plotting.

Using a pelorus

Alternatively, a pelorus may be used to measure directions, usually as relative bearings. This instrument is, of course, not affected by magnetic disturbances on the boat and may be used at any location from which the desired object can be seen. The caution to be observed in this case is that the pelorus must be accurately aligned with the fore-and-aft axis, the keel-line, of the vessel. The correct positioning of the pelorus should be worked out for several locations on the boat so that sights may be taken on an object regardless of its relative position with respect to the boat.

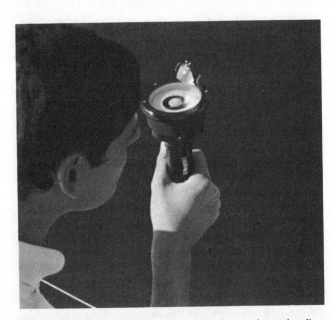

FIG. 2119 A hand bearing compass can be used to take direct readings on objects that cannot be sighted over the boat's steering compass. Before using such an instrument on your boat, however, make checks to find locations at which it will not be affected by local magnetic influences.

The scale of the pelorus can be aligned to the boat's heading and observations made directly in terms of compass bearings, but this procedure is generally less desirable than the technique of relative bearings to be described below. In all cases, the compass bearings must be converted to true bearings before plotting.

An exception to the above statement can be made in the case of an *experienced* pilot. It is possible to omit the step of correction from magnetic to true direction and plot in terms of magnetic bearings. This procedure, while appearing to be a handy short cut, has two pitfalls. First, it requires the use of the magnetic directions circle of the compass roses printed on the chart plus the use of a plotting instrument that determines direction from these compass roses rather than from the meridians and parallels; this rules out use of the convenient and accurate course plotter. Secondly, this technique requires the use of magnetic directions for all purposes, such as courses, ranges, set of current, etc., or else a confusing mixture of directions. Because of these two serious disadvantages, the possibility of plotting bearings as magnetic directions will be noted here, but will be discarded immediately in favor of the "old reliable" procedure of using only true directions on the chart.

RELATIVE BEARINGS

Relative bearings are those taken with respect to the vessel alone, without reference to geographic directions. Relative bearings offer some advantages, but also have some built-in problems.

The instrument for taking relative bearings is the pelorus. As noted before, it has the advantage of being usable anywhere on the boat if properly oriented. Its disadvantage is that close coordination is required between two persons, the bearing-taker and the helmsman. The heading of the boat at the instant of observation must be known, and direct communication between these two individuals is required.

To take a relative bearing, the scale of the pelorus is set with 000° dead ahead. The helmsman is alerted to the fact that a bearing is about to be taken; he concentrates on steady steering and continuously reads the compass. When the observation is made, the bearing-taker calls out "Mark," and reads the scale of the pelorus. (It is very helpful if the bearing-taker calls out "Stand by" a few seconds before his "Mark.") At the word "Mark," the helmsman notes the reading of the steering compass and calls it off to the observer or other person who will compute the bearing. If the compass should be swinging at the moment, so that an accurate reading cannot be taken, the helmsman calls out that information and the pelorus reading is discarded; another attempt is then made to take the bearing.

As noted in Chapter 19, an alternative technique is to have the helmsman call a series of "Marks" when, but only when, he has the boat directly on course. The bearing-taker makes his observation only when it is so indicated that the boat is on the specified heading.

When the relative bearing has been taken by either of the above techniques, it must be converted to a true bearing for plotting. This is done by adding the numerical values of the relative bearing and the *true* heading of the boat at the instant of observation. If the sum so obtained is more than 360°, that amount is subtracted. The true bearing can then be plotted and labeled.

If the true heading is not known for any reason, such as the boat's being momentarily off-course when the bearing was taken, it is, of course, necessary that it be determined before the addition of the preceding paragraph can be accomplished. *Always be sure to use the deviation value for the heading of the boat, and not for the bearing angle.* This is an often-made error, and one that must be continually guarded against.

In fig. 2121a, an observer on a boat heading 047° takes a relative bearing on a buoy of 062°. To determine the true bearing of this aid to navigation, these two numbers are added, 047° + 062° = 109°.

FIG. 2120 A pelorus eliminates the magnetic difficulties that may be experienced with a hand-held compass. It can be used at any point from which the target object can be seen. A pelorus must, however, be properly oriented to the fore-and-aft axis of the boat.

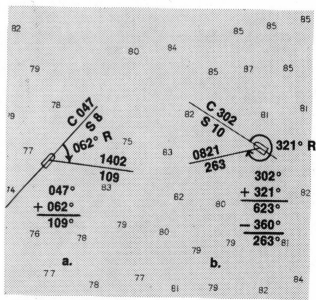

FIG. 2121 Relative bearings must be converted to true bearings before they are plotted. To do this, the relative bearing is added to the true heading of the craft at the moment of observation. If the sum exceeds 360°, that amount is subtracted.

In fig. 2121b, the boat is heading 306° by its compass when a relative bearing of 321° is measured. The variation is 6°W and the deviation (for the compass heading of 306°) is 2°E. The true heading of the boat is thus 306° − 6° + 2° = 302°. The sum of the relative bearing, 321° and the true heading 302° is 623°; therefore 360° is subtracted and a value of 263° is found to be the true bearing of the object.

If the pilot is so fortunate as to have multiple objects on which to take bearings, he should select the nearer ones (provided, of course, that desirable angles of intersection between the LOPs will result). An angular error of 1° will result in a lateral error of about 100 feet at a distance of one mile—at two miles, the *same* angular error will cause a lateral displacement of 200 feet; at three miles, 300 feet, etc.

RANGES

Lines of position from ranges are of exceptional value in position determination. They are free from all of the magnetic effects that might cause errors in bearings taken with a compass or a pelorus. Such LOPs are also easily obtained, much more so than those from bearings. Ranges can be absolutely accurate, as accurate as the charted positions of the two objects lined up in the observation. No matter how small the boat, how rough the water, or how poor the visibility, if you can see the objects come into line, you can plot a good line of position on your chart and so have half of an accurate fix.

Ranges can be classified into two groups. First, there are those that consist of two aids to navigation constructed specifically to serve as a range and are charted with a special symbol, see fig. 1824, page 322. The true direction of such ranges can be determined from the information in the Light List for the rear marker. Ranges are particularly useful in determining compass deviation because of their high accuracy.

It is not necessary, however, to have an especially constructed pair of aids to navigation in order to have a range. Any two objects that can be identified by sight and on the chart form a natural range and can be used in the same manner as one consisting of two formally established navigational aids. Among such objects are ordinary aids to navigation of all types; spires, radio towers, flagpoles, stacks, etc.; identifiable portions of bridges, such as center spans; and other prominent, isolated features; see fig. 2122. Caution should be exercised in using points of land as either a front or rear range mark; errors may be made in attempting to sight on the exact end of the point, particularly if it is of low elevation.

The taking of a LOP from a range requires no more than the observation of the time that the two objects came into line. The LOP is plotted on the chart by lining up the symbols for the two objects with a straightedge and drawing a light solid line over such portion of the chart where the LOP has significance. The line will normally not be drawn all the way back to the two objects that established the range. Its actual direction will not ordinarily need to be determined. The line should be labeled as soon as it is drawn on the chart.

This line of position can be crossed for a fix with another range, or with any other form of LOP. If such is not available at the time, the LOP from the range may often be advanced later and used as part of a running fix.

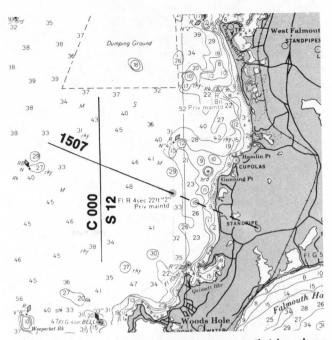

FIG. 2122 Pilots are not limited to those ranges that have been established as such by the Coast Guard or other authorities. Any two identifiable objects can be used. Here, a skipper northbound in Buzzards Bay can get an excellent line of position when light "2" lines up with the standpipe ashore.

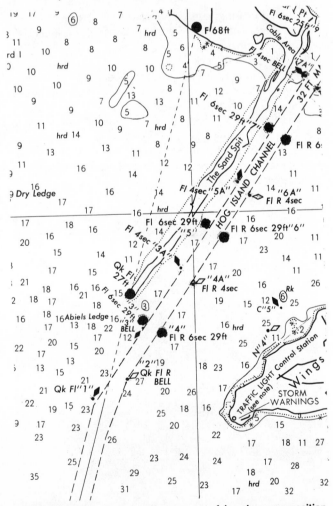

FIG. 2123 Ranges are excellent means of keeping your position centered in a channel, but caution must be exercised not to follow them beyond their proper limits. One or two buoys may be used to mark the beginning or end of a range-marked channel, the point at which to make a change of course.

Never pass up an opportunity to obtain a line of position from a range; there are none better. And there is no better fix than one obtained from the intersection of two ranges.

Ranges are often established by the Coast Guard or other authority to mark the center of important waterways, usually dredged channels or natural channels with hazards close on either side. When so established, the range center line will be printed on the chart, see fig. 1827, page 324. Such ranges will normally be used for direct steering rather than as a line of position, but there is no reason that they should not be used for the latter purpose if desired.

Two cautions should be observed in steering up or down a channel marked by a range. A vessel traveling in the opposite direction on the range will be on a collision course, or will pass too close aboard for comfort. Secondly, the beginning and end of the range, the ends of the solid portion of the line on the chart, must be noted carefully—a range can be followed for too great a distance on either end. Buoys will often be used to mark the spot at which to turn onto or off of the range line, fig. 2123. Always study your chart carefully when using a range.

HORIZONTAL ANGLES

A fix may also be obtained by measuring the two horizontal angles between the lines of sight to three identifiable objects, without a measurement of the relative or geographic direction to any of them. This procedure avoids the inaccuracies involved in relative or compass bearings. Such horizontal angles can be measured to a high degree of accuracy (as close as $1/2°$) with a sextant.

For plotting these horizontal angles, a *three-arm protractor*, fig. 2124, is the preferred instrument. Each side arm is set for the angle measured to its side of the line of sight to the center object. Then the instrument is moved about on the chart until the arms line up with the symbols for the

objects sighted upon in measuring the angles. There is a small hole in the center of the protractor through which a pencil point can be placed to mark the fix on the chart.

The same general technique can be used without a special instrument by drawing lines with the proper angles between them on a piece of transparent paper, fig. 2125. This is then moved about as before until the lines and points are properly related.

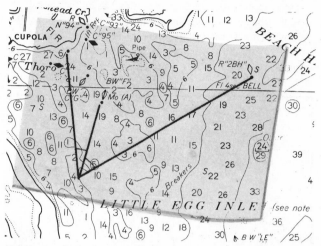

FIG. 2125 If a three-arm protractor is not available, the angles can be drawn on a sheet of transparent paper. This is then moved about on the chart until correctly positioned.

Some caution must be exercised in selecting the objects between which the angles are to be measured. Three points, not in a straight line, will all lie on the circumference of a specific circle, such as points X, Y, and Z in fig. 2126a. An angle measured between X and Y, or Y and Z, will be the same measured at A or B, or at any point on the circular arc from X around through A and B to Z. Thus,

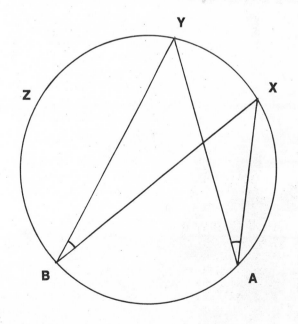

FIG. 2124 A three-arm protractor is a specialized plotting instrument used with the two-horizontal-angles technique of position determination. When the angles have been set, the arms are lined up with the appropriate chart symbols; then the position is marked with a pencil point through a hole in the center of the device.

FIG. 2126a In using the two-horizontal-angles method of positioning, the center of the three objects, Y in this illustration, should *not* be farther away from the observer than the other two. If this caution is neglected, the result may be an indeterminate solution called a "revolver," as shown above, where the boat may be at any point on a circle containing the three objects.

if the observer should be on the circle, his position will be indeterminate. This situation, known as a "revolver," can occur if the center object sighted upon is farther away from the observer than the other two. By selecting three objects so that they are essentially in line, or that the center one is closer to the observer, an indeterminate situation is avoided. (If the center object is closer, a circle still exists, but it curves away from the observer, and he could not possibly be on it.) See fig. 2126b.

A "revolver" should be avoided; but if one does develop, it can be made determinate by the addition of another LOP, such as a single bearing on one of the three objects, or on any other point.

This technique of using the two horizontal angles is not often used in practical piloting, but it does offer excellent results when high accuracy is needed. Fig. 2127 illustrates an instrument developed especially for the measurement of horizontal angles and bearings.

VERTICAL ANGLES

A circular line of position represents points at a constant distance from a specific object. Such distances are often found by the measurement of vertical angles with a marine sextant, or with a specialized device for such purposes alone.

The height of many natural and man-made features is

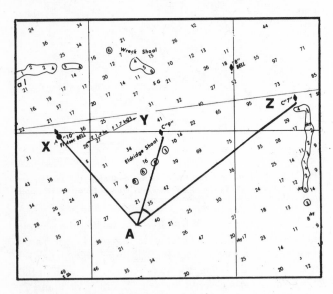

FIG. 2126b If the center object is on line with the other two, or is nearer to the observer, as Y is above, an indeterminate solution is avoided and a fix is found.

FIG. 2127 The Ilon position finder is a specialized instrument that determines a fix from a combination of the compass bearing to an object and the horizontal angle between that line of sight and the line to a second object.

FIG. 2128 A marine sextant, most commonly used for celestial navigation sights, may also be used in piloting for the measurement of vertical or horizontal angles.

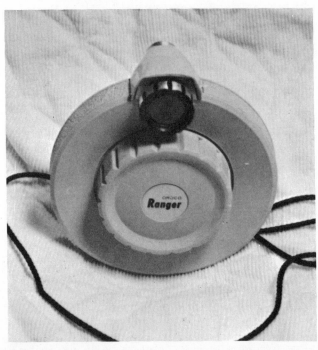

FIG. 2129 If a vertical or horizontal dimension of a distant object is known, this simple optical rangefinder can make an accurate measurement of the distance to it.

shown on charts. Such objects include lighthouses, bridges, radio towers, and generally similar features. Caution must be exercised to determine if the height shown is that above the structure's base on land or the vertical distance above the chart's datum for heights, usually mean high water. Frequently, a correction may be required for the tidal level at the time of observation, its difference from MHW, see Chapter 20. On such features as lighthouses, the height usually given is that of the *light,* not that of the top of the structure.

Using a sextant, the vertical angle is measured between the base and the top or other part of the structure, fig. 2128. This angle and the known height can be used to de-

termine the distance from the observer to the object. Solution can be had from plane geometry formulas, or from specially prepared tables such as Table 9 in Bowditch.

Special range finder instruments are now being marketed which use the principle of matching images much like the focusing mechanism of many cameras. It is still necessary, however, to know the height (or a horizontal dimension) of the object on which the observation is made. Fig. 2129 shows one such instrument.

DANGER BEARINGS AND ANGLES

The safety of navigation can often be insured without the establishment of a complete fix. As noted earlier, a single line of position has value—if it is of reasonable accuracy, it can assure you that you are somewhere along it and not elsewhere. A line of position can be chosen, in many piloting situations, that will keep a boat in safe water without precisely defining its position.

Danger bearings

A bearing line can be established so that positions on one side will assure the craft's being in safe waters, while a position on the other side may signify a hazardous situation; such a *danger bearing* is shown in fig. 2130. Here, a shoal, unmarked by any aid to navigation, lies offshore; the problem is to pass it safely. A lighthouse is observed on shore just beyond the shoal, and is identified on the chart. The danger bearing is a line from the lighthouse just tangent to the shoal on the safe side. This line is drawn on the chart and its direction is measured. The line is labeled with the direction preceded by the letters "DB." (No time is shown as it is not an actual observation.) For greater emphasis, short hachures may be added on the side toward the danger; and, if available, the use of a red pencil for this line is desirable to make it stand out from other lines on the chart.

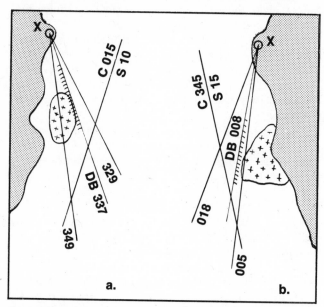

FIG. 2130 A *danger bearing* can be established so as to avoid an unmarked hazardous area. In *a* above, any bearing on object *X* that is more than 337° indicates a potentially hazardous position for the boat. In *b*, the reverse is true, bearing less than 008° are indications of possible danger if the craft continues on the same course.

As the boat approaches the hazardous area, a series of observations are made on the selected object. In the example shown in fig. 2130a, any bearing on the lighthouse *less* numerically than the danger bearing indicates a *safe* position; any bearing *greater* than the danger bearing indicates that the boat is in or approaching the shoal area if it continues on the same course. Should the danger area lie to starboard, rather than to port as in fig. 2130b, the "greater" and "less" factors above would be reversed.

Danger bearings cannot always be established for the safe passage of hazardous areas, but their use should be considered whenever conditions permit. It is necessary to have a prominent object, although it need not be an aid to navigation, that can be seen from the boat and positively identified on the chart. This object should lie beyond the danger area in the same general direction as the course of the boat as it approaches and passes the area to be avoided.

HORIZONTAL DANGER ANGLES

A horizontal angle measured between two identifiable fixed objects defines a circle of position. In fig. 2131, an observer at *X* or *Y* would measure the same angle between *A* and *B;* he would also measure the same angle at any point along that semi-circular arc. If the observer were on the other side of the center of the circle, at *X'* or *Y'*, or

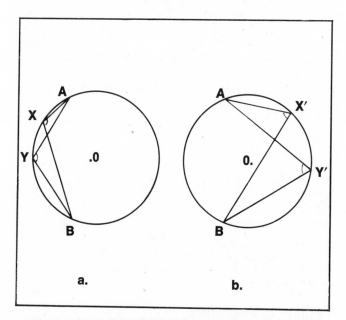

FIG. 2131a and b The various points at which there is a constant angle between the lines of sight to two objects form a circle. The angle between the lines to *A* and *B* is the same at *X* or *Y*. At points *X'* and *Y'*, the angle is likewise the same.

other point on that arc, a constant angle also would be observed. This angle, however, is not the same as that measured across the circle at X and Y. Note that the angle will be greater than 90° if the sighted objects are on the same side of the circle as the observer, as in fig. 2131a, and less than 90° if they are on the opposite side as in fig. 2131b.

Such a circle may be established to indicate the boundary between positions of safety and those of possible danger. When such a LOP is set up, the angle defined by the circle is termed the *horizontal danger angle*.

Fig. 2132 illustrates the use of a single horizontal danger angle to avoid an unmarked shoal area. The problem is to

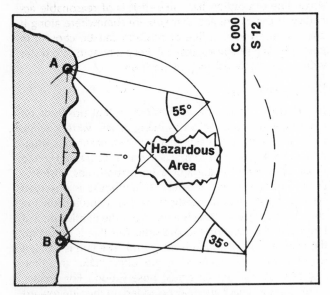

FIG. 2132 Horizontal angles between A and B are measured as the boat approaches the hazardous area. Any angle *less* than the *horizontal danger angle* of 55° indicates that the boat is in safe waters.

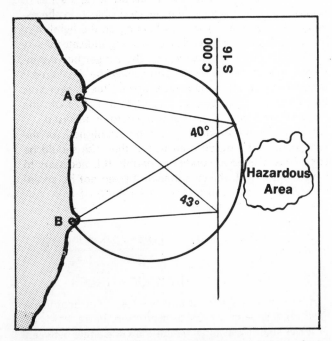

FIG. 2133 In this situation, it is desired to pass inshore of an unmarked hazardous area. The horizontal danger angle is established as before, but now the safe angular measurements are those greater than the horizontal danger angle.

stay sufficiently offshore to miss the hazard. The horizontal danger angle is found by drawing a circle that includes two prominent identifiable objects ashore, A and B in fig. 2132, and the shoal area. The circle is established by drawing a line between the sighted objects, and then drawing a second line at right angles to the first line at its midpoint. The center of the circle is found by trial-and-error along this second line so that the arc includes the desired points.

Lines are then drawn to A and B from any point on the circle near the shoal area and the angle between them is measured; in this example, it is 55°.

If the angle between the objects, measured from the boat as it approaches the area, is *less* than the horizontal danger angle, then the radius of the circle on which the boat is located is larger, and the boat is farther offshore in *safe* waters. On the other hand, if the measured horizontal angle is greater than the danger angle, the boat is closer in and may be in or approaching a hazardous area. The angle is preferably measured with a sextant, but it can be calculated from the difference between two compass or relative bearings.

Should the piloting situation require passage inshore of a shoal area, fig. 2133, a single horizontal danger angle can again be used. In this case, *safe* waters are indicated by angles *greater* than the danger angle.

Double horizontal danger angles

The two situations described above can be combined into *double horizontal danger angles* where the requirement is for a safe passage between two offshore hazardous areas. Fig. 2134 is essentially a combination of the two preceding illustrations. The principles are the same; here the safe horizontal angles are those *between* upper and lower danger limits.

Vertical danger angles

A circle of position, obtained from a vertical angle measurement, can also be used to mark the boundary between safe and hazardous waters. With a selected prominent object identified visually and on the chart, a circle is drawn using that object as the center and having a radius that will just include all of the hazardous area. The radius is measured from the chart and converted to a vertical angle by geometric formula or Table 9 in Bowditch. The danger circle is then labeled with the *vertical danger angle*. Fig. 2135 shows such a circular LOP outlining a shoal area.

As the boat approaches the dangerous area, a series of vertical angle measurements are taken on the selected object. Measurement of a vertical angle *less* than that specified as the vertical danger angle indicates that the observer is farther offshore, and consequently he is in *safe* waters.

Measurements of distance directly from an optical range finder can be substituted for vertical angles if such a device is on board.

Corresponding situations would prevail for safe passage inshore of a hazardous area, or between two danger areas, as was shown for horizontal danger angles.

Positioning Procedures

As mentioned earlier, the "basic" fix is obtained by crossing two lines of position. A third LOP is desirable, but this can be obtained in only a limited number of situations. It is assumed for the fix that the observations or measurements for these LOPs are made simultaneously, and this may often be the procedure on a naval ship or other large vessel. On small craft, however, the normal situation will be that of a single bearing-taker and one piece of equipment. Of necessity, therefore, observations will be taken sequentially rather than concurrently. If the observations are taken quickly, the distance traveled between them will be negligible, and adherence to the procedures to be described here will minimize the error from sequential observations.

As a result of the movement of the boat along its course, the observed bearing angles will be changing. Consider the relative *rate of change* of the bearing to each object to be sighted upon; those on the beam will be changing at a more rapid rate than those nearly dead ahead or astern; those on nearer objects will be changing more rapidly than those at greater distances.

For the most accurate determination of a fix from two lines of position, first take a sight on the object with the *least* rate of change, then on the other object, and finally a repeat on the first object. Use the second observation and the average of the first and third bearings (which are, of course, on the same object). If circumstances permit only one observation on each object, it is usually preferable to take the more rapidly changing bearing last and then make an immediate chart plot of both bearings.

If you are able to take observations on three objects, take them in descending order of rate of change of bearing and consider taking a repeat of the first bearing, if possible, for averaging as before.

The time of the fix should be that of the approximate middle of the series of observations. At typical boat cruising speeds and chart scales, a difference of a minute or two will not be significant. At 12 knots, a boat will travel 1/5 mile in one minute; on a 1:80,000 scale chart, this distance of approximately 400 yards is less than 3/16 inch.

Positioning standards of precision

As set forth in Chapter 19, there are generally accepted standards of precision in describing position of a vessel. If geographic coordinates are used, latitude and longitude, in that sequence, are stated to the nearest tenth of a minute on charts with scales of 1:50,000 or smaller, and to the nearest second on charts of larger scale.

If the position is stated with respect to some aid to navigation or landmark, direction from that point is given to the nearest degree (true) and distance is given to the nearest tenth of a mile.

THE RUNNING FIX

The lack of a second object on which to make an observation may at times prevent the immediate determination of the boat's position by a normal fix, even though one good line of position has been established. In such situations, a somewhat less accurate determination of position may be made by a *running fix (R Fix)*. In this technique there is one line of position at the time of the running fix and another from a different time, usually earlier. This latter LOP must be replotted from its position at the time of its measurement to account for the movement of the boat during the intervening time. The act of advancing the first LOP brings it to a common time with the second obser-

vation so that their intersection may be considered as a determination of position. It should be noted that this line so advanced (or retired) may have resulted from an observation on the *same* object as that used for the second sighting at the time of the running fix, or on a different object.

Advancing a line of position

A line of position is advanced as follows:
(1) A point is selected on the original LOP. This can be

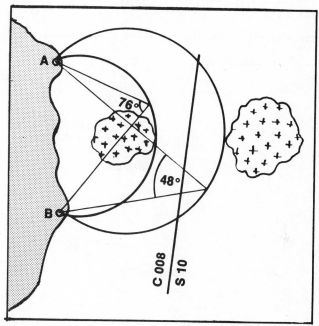

FIG. 2134 For passage between two unmarked hazardous areas, *double horizontal danger angles* may be used. This technique is essentially the combination of the two preceding situations; a safe passage is indicated by measurement of horizontal angles between specified upper and lower limits.

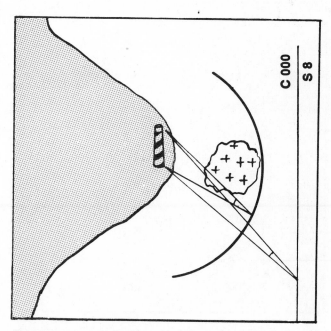

FIG. 2135 A measurement of vertical angle establishes a circle of position at a specific distance from a point. Such an angle can be calculated for an object of known height so as to insure that a boat does not get too close. Safe vertical angles are those *less* than the *vertical danger angle*.

the intersection of the line with the DR track, X in fig. 2136, or any point on the LOP, such as X'.

(2) The selected point is moved in an amount equal in distance and direction to the boat's motion during the time interval involved. This is most easily measured from the DR position at the time of observation to the DR position for the advanced time.

(3) The new LOP is drawn in through the advanced point parallel to the original LOP.

(4) The advanced LOP is labeled as soon as it is drawn: both times are shown above the line and the direction beneath it.

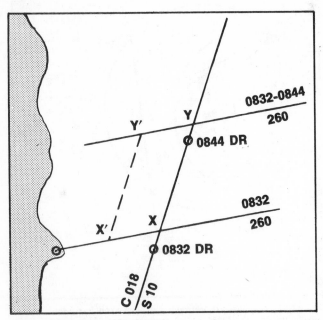

FIG. 2136 A line of position is *advanced* by moving forward any point on it an amount equal to the boat's motion during the time interval and re-drawing the line through this advanced point.

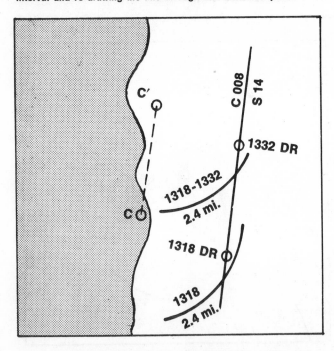

FIG. 2137 A circle of position, or circular LOP, is advanced by merely moving the center point an amount equal in direction and distance to the motion of the boat during the time interval, and redrawing the circle on the new center. In the illustration above, C = C' is equal to the spacing between the two DR positions.

Advancing a circular LOP

If the LOP to be advanced is circular, as would be the case with a distance measurement by vertical angle or range finder, the center of the circle is the point advanced by the procedure described above, fig. 2137. The circle or arc is redrawn using the new center, and is then labeled as for any other advanced LOP.

Advancing a LOP with course and/or speed changes

The advancement of the selected point on the initial LOP must take into account all changes in course and/or speed of the boat during the time interval. It is frequently a convenient procedure to calculate and plot the DR positions for the time of the initial observation and for the advanced time. The movement of the selected point on the initial LOP should parallel and equal a line drawn between these two DR positions. This technique is particularly useful if there has been more than one change in course and/or speed, fig. 2138.

Advancing a LOP with current

The advancement of a line of position may take into account current effects if they are adequately known or can be estimated. The selected point on the initial LOP is first advanced for DR speeds and courses, and then for the set and drift of the current, both calculations using the elapsed time interval between the two observations; see fig. 2139.

The accuracy of advanced LOPs

The accuracy of an advanced line of position can be only as good as the accuracy of the initial observation *decreased* by any errors or uncertainties in the navigator's data for the boat's course and speed (and current data, if used). Obviously, the longer the time interval over which

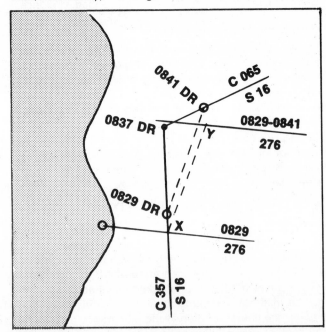

FIG. 2138 The advancement of a LOP must take into consideration all changes of course and/or speed during the time interval. The net effect can be determined by drawing a light line between the DR positions for the two times concerned. The selected point on the original LOP is advanced in the same direction and distance as this net effect line.

the sight is advanced, the greater the uncertainties become. The interval should, therefore, be the minimum possible, and, in piloting, should rarely exceed 30 minutes. (In navigation on the high seas, celestial lines of position are often advanced several hours, but the accuracy of positioning is less critical in these circumstances.)

The same criteria for the angle of intersection of lines of position apply to running fixes as were discussed previously for normal fixes. Running fixes involving three lines of positions (two of them advanced) are possible but are unusual in actual piloting practice.

Lines of position may be retired, moved back to an earlier time, in a similar manner. Such retrograde movement is, however, quite rare in piloting situations.

Running fixes and DR plots

The DR plot may be interrupted and restarted from a running fix if it is considered of reasonable accuracy. In all cases, however, a fix obtained from two or more essentially simultaneous observations or measurements is to be preferred over a running fix.

OBSERVATIONS ON A SINGLE OBJECT

In addition to the technique of the running fix using advanced lines of position, position information can be obtained from successive observations on a single object by means of several other more specialized procedures. These include: bow-and-beam bearings, doubling the angle on the bow, two bearings and run between, and two relative bearings.

Bow-and-beam bearings

Position determination is easily accomplished by the technique of taking two particular successive bearings on an object to one side or the other of the craft's course. The first bearing is taken when the object sighted upon

bears either 45° to starboard (RB 045°) or to port (RB 315°). The second bearings is taken when the same object is broad on the respective beam (RB 090° or 270°), fig. 2140. The time of each bearing having been noted, the time interval is found, and then the distance traveled between the two sightings is calculated using the boat's speed. Because of the nature of the triangle established by the two bearings and the course line, the boat is away from the sighted object at the time of the second (beam) bearing at the same distance as that traveled during the time interval. This distance is that traveled *over the bottom;* correction to the DR track should be made for any current or other offsetting influence if such information is known or can be estimated. Since there is a LOP (the beam bearing) and a distance, the position of the craft has been determined. It should be noted that this position is *not* necessarily the intersection of the second bearing and the course line; the craft may be off its intended track.

The principal advantage of this procedure is the ease with which it can be accomplished. Beam bearings are easily taken, and 45° relative bearings can be quickly set up using crude sights oriented with an ordinary plastic drafting triangle. On some boats, it may be possible to make the 45° sight over the steering compass. The bow-and-beam technique often can be done by the helmsman without assistance.

Doubling the angle on the bow

This is a more generalized application of the same principles as those involved in bow-and-beam bearings, in which a 45° angle was doubled to 90°. Geometric principles establish that whenever an angle on the bow is doubled, the distance from the position at which the second bearing is taken to the object sighted upon is equal to the distance traveled (over the bottom) during the time

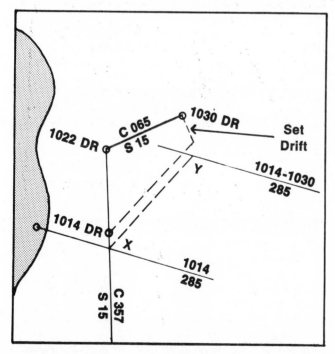

FIG. 2139 If the LOP is to be advanced with allowance for current, the same procedure as before is followed, except that a further movement is made from the second DR position to account for the current during the time interval and obtain an estimated position.

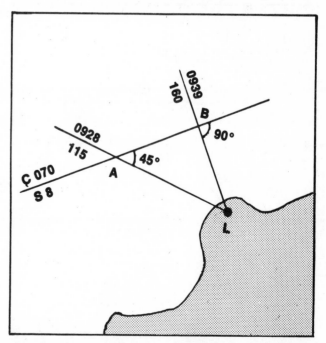

FIG. 2140 If a bearing is taken when an object bears 45° on either bow (RB = 045° or 315°), and again when the same object is broad on the beam (RB = 090° or 270°), the distance to the object at the time of the second bearing will be equal to the distance run (over the bottom) between the bearings; B-L = A-B.

interval between the two observations, fig. 2141. The angle referred to above is the relative bearing to starboard or to port. A relative bearing of, say 340° measured in the conventional manner, must be converted to an angle of 20° to port for the purpose of "doubling"; in this case, the doubled angle would be RB 320° (40° to port).

The doubling-of-the-bow-angle technique has the advantage of determining the boat's position *before* the sighted object is abeam. With information as to the boat's position at such an earlier moment, the course can be projected ahead on the chart. Should the craft be traveling too close to shore for passing a headland, a more adequate warning of the dangerous course will thus be in hand, and corrective action can be taken sooner.

This technique does, however, have a disadvantage in that it requires the possession and use of a pelorus or other instrument for measuring relative bearings with reasonable accuracy. Another disadvantage is that a second person is needed as a bearing-taker.

Two-bearings-and-run-between

With only a single object upon which sights can be taken, another method, known as "two-bearings-and-run-between" for lack of a better name, may be used. In this procedure, a bearing is taken on the object, the boat proceeds along her course, and a second bearing is taken after the angle has changed by at least 30°. This second bearing may be taken before or after the sighted object is passed abeam. From the times of each bearing, the time interval is calculated, and from this, the distance run is determined.

Both bearings are plotted, as is the course of the boat, fig. 2142. A pair of dividers is opened to the distance run between the two bearings and is then moved parallel to the course line until the points fall on the bearing lines.

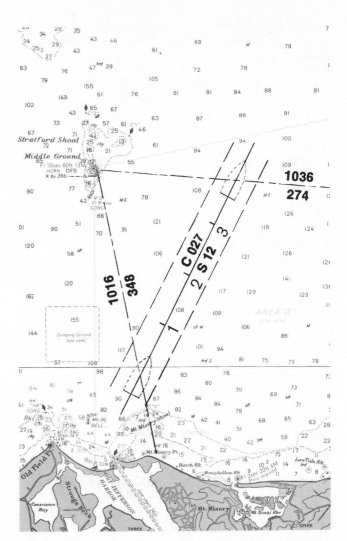

FIG. 2142 If two bearings are taken on a single object as the boat passes it, and are plotted on the chart, then only one point can be found on each LOP so that the course and distance made good will fit between these LOPs.

The divider points now indicate the positions of the boat at the times of the first and second bearings.

As before, the distance run must be that *over the bottom;* suitable corrections must be made for any current. The accuracy of this technique depends upon many factors: the accuracy of each of the two bearings, the accuracy of the calculation of the distance run over the bottom, and the accuracy with which the boat was steered during the interval between the two sightings. The net effect of this compounding of accuracies is to make the positions so determined somewhat less certain than the other techniques described above.

Two relative bearings

A more generalized solution from two relative bearings can be used if a copy of "Bowditch" is on board. Table 7 of that book uses two items of information—the angle between the course and the first bearing (the first relative bearing) and the difference between the course and the second bearing (the second relative bearing). Columns of the Table are in terms of the first item and lines are in terms of the second item above; the interval between tabular entries is two degrees in both cases.

For any combination of the two relative bearings within the limits of Table 7, two factors will be found. The first

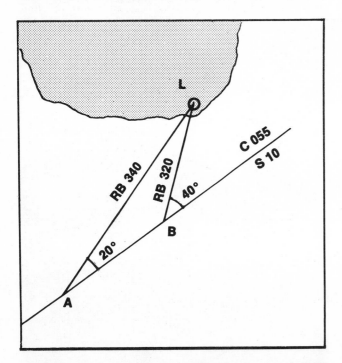

FIG. 2141 If two observations are made so that the second relative bearing is twice that of the first (as measured from the bow to either starboard or port), then the distance to the sighted object at the time of the second bearing is the same as the distance made good between the sightings; again, L-B = A-B.

number is a factor by which the distance run between the bearings is multiplied to obtain the distance away from the sighted object at the time of the second bearing. The second factor of the same entry in Table 7 is the multiplier to be used to determine the distance off when the object is abeam, assuming, of course, that the same course and speed are maintained. See fig. 2143.

Electronic Piloting

Although electronic navigation is essentially a topic in itself, and outside of the scope of piloting, brief mention will be made here of two techniques which have direct comparability and applicability to visual piloting.

RADIO BEARINGS AND DISTANCES

With relatively simple equipment, observations can be made of the direction to radio stations, even though such "objects" lie far beyond visual range, either as a result of night, fog, or simply great distance. See fig. 2144. Bearings can be taken on radiobeacons operated by the Coast Guard as aids to navigation; some aeronautical ranges and beacons operated by the FAA; on standard AM radio broadcast stations; and on stations in the 2-3 Mc/s marine band, including both shore and ship stations. In general, the desirability for use in radio direction finding is in descending order as listed above. Radio bearings can be taken under any condition of visibility, and on stations at ranges as great as hundreds of miles; accuracies will, of course, be more favorable with nearer stations.

Radio bearings are taken with a *radio direction finder*, usually referred to as an RDF. This item of electronic equipment is discussed more fully in Chapter 25, pages 382(j) to 382(n).

Using radio bearings

Radio bearings are plotted in essentially the same manner as visual bearings. They are not as sharp as visual observations, however; an accuracy of 2° to 3° is the best that can be expected, and this precision will be achieved only with experience. Accordingly, it is advisable to obtain three radio LOPs, and even so, the position so determined should not be considered as precise as one from visual bearings.

Accurate identification of the station being received is essential, and the exact location of the transmitting antenna must be plotted on the nautical chart if it is not already shown there.

Radio bearings taken on a station more than approximately 200 miles distant must be corrected if they are to be plotted on a Mercator chart. (The exact distance will vary with latitude and the relative position of the vessel and the radio station.) This correction is required because radio waves travel via the most direct route, a great circle path, and this does not plot as a straight line on a Mercator chart; see page 333. Table 1 in Bowditch provides the correction factor and instructions on how it should be applied. No correction is needed for nearer stations, or on stations at any distance if the plotting is done on a gnomonic chart.

Labeling RDF bearings and fixes

In view of the lesser accuracy of RDF bearings as com-

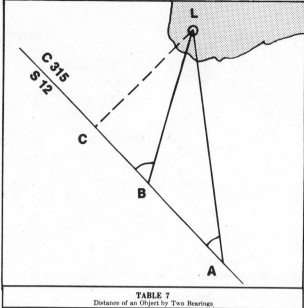

TABLE 7
Distance of an Object by Two Bearings

Difference between the course and second bearing	Difference between the course and first bearing												
	34°		36°		38°		40°		42°		44°		46°
44	3.22	2.24											
46	2.69	1.93	3.39	2.43									
48	2.31	1.72	2.83	2.10	3.55	2.63							
50	2.03	1.55	2.43	1.86	2.96	2.27	3.70	2.84					
52	1.81	1.43	2.13	1.68	2.54	2.01	3.09	2.44	3.85	3.04			
54	1.63	1.32	1.90	1.54	2.23	1.81	2.66	2.15	3.22	2.60	4.00	3.24	
56	1.49	1.24	1.72	1.42	1.99	1.65	2.33	1.93	2.77	2.29	3.34	2.77	4.14	3.43
58	1.37	1.17	1.57	1.33	1.80	1.53	2.08	1.76	2.43	2.06	2.87	2.44	3.46	2.93
60	1.28	1.10	1.45	1.25	1.64	1.42	1.88	1.63	2.17	1.88	2.52	2.18	2.97	2.57
62	1.19	1.05	1.34	1.18	1.51	1.34	1.72	1.52	1.96	1.73	2.25	1.98	2.61	2.30
64	1.12	1.01	1.25	1.13	1.40	1.26	1.58	1.42	1.79	1.61	2.03	1.83	2.33	2.09
66	1.06	0.96	1.18	1.07	1.31	1.20	1.47	1.34	1.65	1.51	1.85	1.69	2.10	1.92
68	1.00	0.93	1.11	1.03	1.23	1.14	1.37	1.27	1.53	1.42	1.71	1.58	1.92	1.78
70	0.95	0.89	1.05	0.99	1.16	1.09	1.29	1.21	1.43	1.34	1.58	1.49	1.77	1.66
72	0.91	0.86	1.00	0.95	1.10	1.05	1.21	1.15	1.34	1.27	1.48	1.41	1.64	1.56
74	0.87	0.84	0.95	0.92	1.05	1.01	1.15	1.10	1.26	1.21	1.39	1.34	1.53	1.47
76	0.84	0.81	0.91	0.89	1.00	0.97	1.09	1.06	1.20	1.16	1.31	1.27	1.44	1.40
78	0.80	0.79	0.88	0.86	0.96	0.94	1.04	1.02	1.14	1.11	1.24	1.22	1.36	1.33
80	0.78	0.77	0.85	0.84	0.92	0.91	1.00	0.98	1.09	1.07	1.18	1.16	1.28	1.27

FIG. 2143 Distance off at time of second bearing, **L-B,** and distance off when abeam, **L-C,** can be found by applying multiplying factors to the distance run, **A-B.** These factors for various pairs of angles will be found in Table 7 of Bowditch.

FIG. 2144 Radio direction finders (RDFs) can be used to take bearings on transmitters located a fraction of a mile, or several hundreds of miles, distant. Lines of position can be found at night, in fog, or when visibility is good but the station is too far away to be seen.

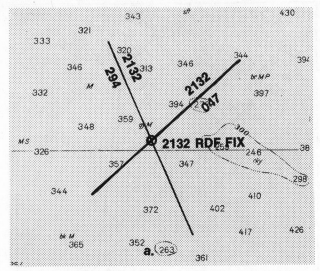

FIG. 2145a Because the accuracy of a fix derived from radio bearings is usually less than that of one obtained from visual observations, it should be labeled "RDF FIX".

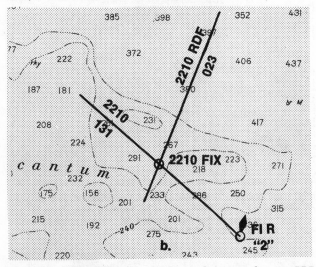

FIG.2145b If a combination of LOPs includes one from an RDF measurement, it may be well to add the letters "RDF" above the line where applicable.

Distance finding stations. At certain stations the radiobeacon and sound signal are synchronized for distance finding. The beginning of the ten-second radio dash and the beginning of the five-second blast of the fog signal are synchronized for this purpose. The ten-second radio dash and the long (5 second) blast of the fog signal commence at the same instant. Therefore, when within audible range of the sound signal, navigators on vessels with radio receivers capable of receiving the radiobeacon signals may readily determine their distance from the station by observing the time in seconds which elapsed between first hearing the beginning of the ten-second radio dash and the beginning of the five-second sound blast and dividing the result by 5.5 for nautical miles. The error of such observations should not exceed 10 percent.

The two seconds of silence preceding the long radio dash is a stand-by or warning signal as is also the one-second fog signal blast.

Observations for distance from these stations are not **restricted to vessels with direction finders,** but may be made by any vessel having a radio receiver capable of receiving in the band 285 to 325 kilocycles. An example of these synchronized signals follows:

	For 5 minutes	For 1 minute	
RBN	Off	48 Code	10 2 ■■■
		3 17 ■ 33	1 5 ■1 ■■ 5
FS	1 blast ev 20ˢ (3ˢbl)	■ Shows dash of RBN or blast of fog signal. Figures show seconds.	

If the interval between hearing the beginning of the long radio dash marking the end of the radiobeacon minute and the beginning of the long blast of the diaphone is 33 seconds, the observer is 33 + 5.5 = 6 miles from the light station.

FIG. 2146 Radiobeacons whose transmissions are periodically synchronized with the blasts of a fog signal are designated as *Distance Finding Stations (DFS)*. The Light Lists give detailed information on the synchronization pattern.

(1)	(2)	(3)	(4)	(5)	(6)		(7)
	Name	Location	Light or day-beacon above water	Candle-power	Structure, vessel, or buoy		
No.	Character and period of light	Latitude, N. Longitude, W.		Miles seen,	Top of lantern above ground	Established. Moved or rebuilt	Radiobeacon, fog signal, sectors and remarks
	(Duration in italics)	Deg. Min. Deg. Min.	Feet	in italics	Feet	Year	
FIRST DISTRICT		**MAINE**					
	GULF OF MAINE						
	Penobscot Bay						
	MONHEGAN ISLAND APPROACH						
168 3 J128	**MONHEGAN ISLAND LIGHT** Fl. W., 30ˢ (2.8ˢfl)	Near center of island.. 43 45.9 69 19.0	178	190,000 20	Gray conical tower covered way to white dwelling. 1824 47 1850		Within 3 miles of island the light is obscured between west and southwest.
169 4 J130	Manana Island Fog Signal Station... *Resident Personnel.*	On west side of island, close to Monhegan Island. 43 45.8 69 19.7	...	....	Brown brick house 1855 1870		**RADIOBEACON:** Antenna 2,880 feet 259° from Monhegan Island Light tower. **Distance finding station.** (See p. XVII for explanation.) **HORN,** diaphragm; *gp* of 3 blasts ev 60ˢ (2ˢbl-8ˢsi-2ˢbl-8ˢsi-2ˢbl-38ˢsi).

pared to visual sighting, and particularly those radio bearings taken on distant stations, it is desirable that the fix obtained from such lines of position be so identified. The location should be labeled with the time and "RDF FIX"; see fig. 2145a. If radio lines of position are mixed with visual bearings, the former may be identified by adding the letters "RDF" above the line following the time of observation, fig. 2145b.

Radio distance finding

Certain of the radiobeacons operated by the Coast Guard have the transmissions of their radio signals synchronized with the audible blasts of their fog signal. These are designated as *Distance Finding Stations.* The letters "DFS" will appear on the chart near the symbol for the basic aid to navigation, such as a lighthouse or major light. Aids to navigation operated as distance finding stations will be designated in the Light List as "DFS" in the remarks column and details of the exact synchronization scheme will be given, fig. 2146.

Because of the difference in the speed of travel of radio waves (essentially instantaneous over short distances) and the speed of sound (roughly 1100 feet per second) the two signals transmitted at the same instant will be received sequentially on a boat up to several miles distant. The distance from the aid to navigation, in nautical miles, to the observer can be calculated, to an accuracy of approximately 10%, by dividing the time difference, in seconds, between the arrival of the radio "beep" and the fog signal blast by 5.5.

The measurement of distance from the radiobeacon gives, of course, a circular line of position. This can be plotted and combined with a LOP from any other source or even with depth measurements. Because of the ±10% accuracy of the DFS technique, the result should be considered as an estimated position rather than a fix.

The use of this technique is confined to periods of reduced visibility when the fog signal is operating, and is limited to audible ranges of a few miles. Within these limitations, however, distance finding procedures of this type can be very useful.

RADAR BEARINGS AND DISTANCES

Radar is another item of electronic equipment that is covered in greater detail in Chapter 25, but which will be considered here in connection with piloting situations. Radar has unique advantages in that a single instrument can measure both direction and distance (range), and that these measurements can be accomplished under visibility conditions that would preclude visual observations.

Radar observations

Measurements of direction by radar are *not* as accurate as those by visual sightings, but radar will penetrate darkness; light and moderate rain without difficulty, and heavy rain with some reduction in effectiveness; fog; and other restrictions that would prohibit visual bearings or range measurements.

On the other hand, measurements of distance by radar can be quite accurate, much more so than such observations taken by vertical sextant angles or with simple optical range finders.

Use of radar information

Radar data are used in the same manner as information from visual observations. Lines of position are combined to obtain fixes—typical combinations include two bearings, a bearing with a distance measurement to the same or another object, or two distance measurements. A fix obtained by radar bearings and/or distance measurements is labeled with the time and "RAD FIX"; see fig. 2147.

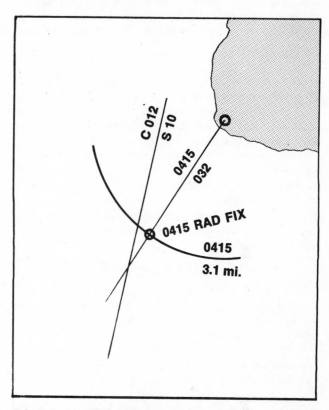

FIG. 2147 A fix obtained from radar lines of position is labeled on the chart as "RAD FIX". In the example above, a fix has been obtained on a single object by measurement of both bearing and distance.

When visibility conditions permit, a frequent combination, and an excellent one, is that of a visual bearing on an object and a radar measurement of distance to that same point.

Radar distance measurements also may be used in the same manner as distance determinations by vertical sextant angle to avoid a shoal area delineated by a circular LOP from a prominent object identifiable on the radarscope.

Radar observations on isolated objects such as buoys, offshore lighthouses, etc., usually are made without difficulty in identification of the object on the radarscope. When the radar target is on shore, however, some problems may be encountered in picking out the exact object on which the bearing and range information is to be obtained. Navigate with caution when using radar information from such objects. Even more so than other types of piloting, radar requires practice and the building up of experience. If you have a radar, use it often in non-critical times so that you can employ it and have the advantage of its unique capabilities when its use is essential. You must be capable of using it with competence and confidence when it is needed.

Depth Information in Piloting

Information on the depth of water under a vessel is usually considered to be merely a safety matter for the prevention of running aground. In actuality, such data can be of considerable value in piloting. The essential characteristic of depth information is the fact that although it cannot tell the pilot where he is, it can tell him *positively* where he is *not*. If an accurate measurement of depth gives a reading of 26 feet, you may be at any number of places where such is the depth, but you certainly are not at a position where the depth is significantly greater or less.

HOW DEPTH INFORMATION IS OBTAINED

Data on the depth of the water beneath a craft can be obtained manually or electronically. A hand lead line, see page 337(j), is a time-honored instrument of piloting, and every boat should have one of a length suitable for the waters usually sailed. It is accurate and dependable in use, although far from efficient or convenient. The modern-day trend is toward electronic depth sounders that can provide information at a much faster rate and with the convenience of reading a simple dial. They can also measure great depths that would be impracticable with a lead line. Electronic sounders are discussed in detail in Chapter 25, page 5 382(g) to 382(i).

USE OF DEPTH INFORMATION

In using depth information, regardless of how obtained, a correction for the height of tide may be required. The use of Tide Tables and the necessary calculations with their data are covered in Chapter 20.

Depth data can be combined with a line or lines of position obtained from other means to yield positional information. Under some circumstances, depth information alone may be of value in position determination.

Depth information and a single LOP

If the bottom of the body of water being navigated has some slope, and this slope is reasonably uniform, it may be possible to get positional information from a single LOP, typically a beam bearing, and a depth reading. The bearing line is plotted and then examined for a spot where the depth figure on the chart agrees with the measured depth as corrected for the tidal stage; be sure that there aren't several such depths along the LOP, fig. 2148. Such a location should be considered as an Estimated Position (EP) rather than a Fix.

Matching measured depths to the chart

In some instances, a rough estimate of the position of a boat can be obtained by matching a series of depth readings, appropriately corrected for the prevailing height of the tide, with depths printed on the chart. Depth readings are taken and recorded at regular time intervals, such as those corresponding to intervals of distance of one-tenth to one-half mile, as determined by the scale of the chart concerned, the density of printed depth figures, etc. (Electronic depth sounders can provide far more depth measurements than can be used.) These depths are marked on a piece of transparent paper at intervals determined by the scale of the chart, fig. 2149a. This piece of paper is then moved about on the chart, keeping the line of sound-

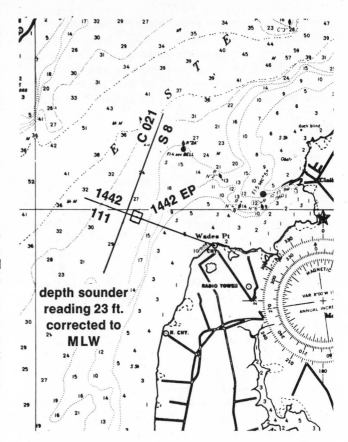

FIG. 2148 Depth information can often be used with a single LOP, such as a simple beam bearing, to determine an estimated position.

ings parallel to a line representing the course steered while they were being taken. A maximum degree of match is sought between the observed depths and the charted depths; exact concurrence should not be expected.

In the example shown here, the 60-foot depth as measured is aligned with the 10-fathom curve on the chart, and a search for a match is started. If the line of soundings is moved north of the position shown in fig. 2149b, the depths at the outer end would still be in general agreement, but the mismatch at the inshore end would generally show that the line was incorrectly placed. If the line were moved down the chart, keeping it parallel to the course sailed, then the 37-foot measurement near the inshore end would mismatch with the actual 48-foot depth. The matching found by the location shown in fig. 2149b is as close as may be expected, and this position of the line can be considered to fairly well indicate the track of the craft as the soundings were made.

Position determination by the use of depth data is not well suited to shorelines that are foul with offshore rocks, or areas that have varying, irregular depths. Nor can this technique be used where the depth is quite uniform with few or no variations. There are, however, many situations where it can, and should, be used.

Position checking by depth data

If an EP has been determined by some other method or combination of methods, consideration should be given to checking it by a depth measurement. Remember that confirmation cannot be positive, but that denial can be quite

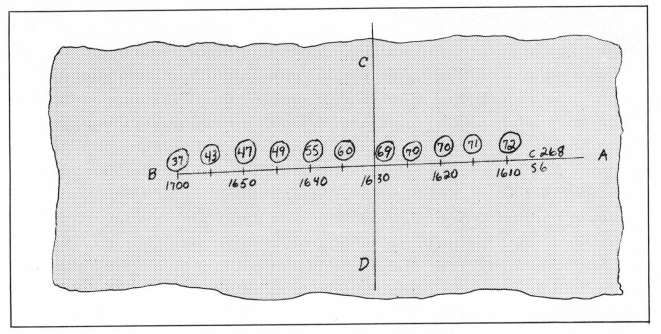

FIG. 2149a Position by a line (or chain) of soundings. The sound-ings are taken at regular intervals and plotted on transparent paper as shown.

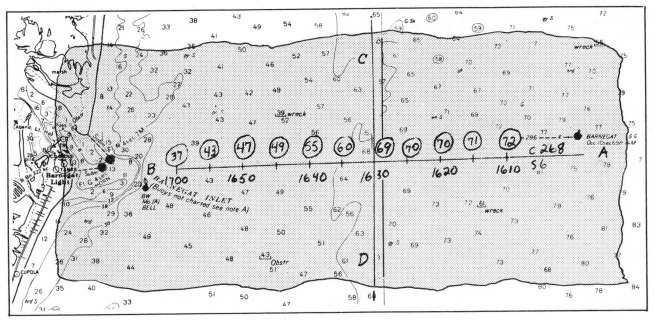

FIG. 2149b The paper is then moved about on the chart until meas-ured depths correspond with the charted depths.

certain if there is a significant difference between the depth at the boat's actual location and that charted for the estimated position. If such should be the case, a further verification of the estimated position is a necessity, per-haps even an urgent necessity!

Fathom curve sailing

When cruising along a coast that has a fairly uniformly sloping bottom offshore, piloting can often be simplified by an examination of the chart for a fathom curve that will keep the craft in safe waters generally and will avoid any specific hazards. The boat is then steered so as to keep the

reading of the electronic depth sounder within a few feet of the selected depth. If readings increase, the boat is gently steered toward shore; if they decrease, the wheel is put over a bit to edge farther offshore.

For the sake of safety, the chart should be checked for the *full* distance that this technique is to be used to be sure that there are no sudden changes in depth, or bends in the depth curve, that might result in an unexpectedly hazardous situation. For added safety, this examination of the chart should be carried beyond the intended end of fathom-curve sailing to prevent unexpected hazards from arising should your speed over the bottom be greater than anticipated.

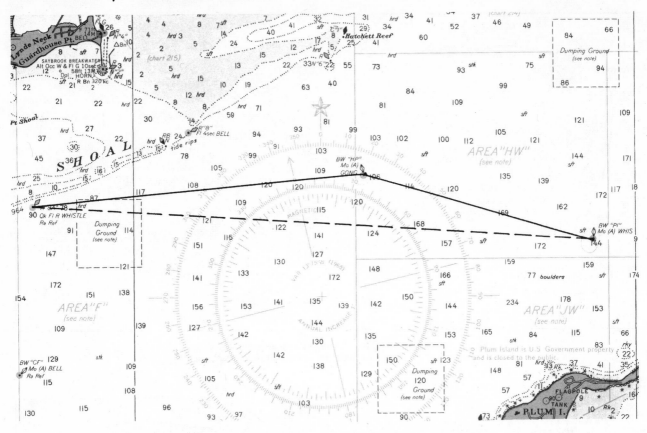

FIG. 2150 As a general rule, it is better practice to lay two short courses between buoys than one long one. This is especially true in thick weather.

Practice — and More Practice

Position determination is the part of piloting that truly cannot be learned "from the book." Study is important, it is essential, but the skipper must put into actual practice the various procedures and techniques. He must know the rules and principles involved, but he must also be able to apply them. Make a habit of "over-navigating" during daylight and good weather conditions so that you will be experienced and capable at night or in foul weather.

TABLE FOR FINDING HEIGHT OF TIDE ABOVE LOW WATER AT ANY HOUR OF THE EBB OR FLOOD		
FALLING TIDE Hours after high water	RISING TIDE Hours after low water	CONSTANT Rising or Falling
0	6	1.0
½	5½	0.98
1	5	0.92
1½	4½	0.84
2	4	0.75
2½	3½	0.63
3	3	0.50
3½	2½	0.38
4	2	0.26
4½	1½	0.16
5	1	0.08
5½	½	0.025

1. Find rise of tide for given day in Tide Tables (difference between heights of nearest high and low tides)
2. Enter column 1 or 2 on line corresponding to time for which height of tide is to be calculated
3. In column 3, find constant given for that time
4. Multiply constant obtained in (3) by total rise of tide (1)

Preceding pages in this chapter have provided all of the basic information required for the safe navigation of a boat in pilot waters —the dimensions and instruments of piloting, the procedures of dead reckoning, calculations involving tides and currents, and position determination. The material to be presented in this supplementary section extends beyond these fundamentals. These are techniques that will be useful in specialized situations, or which may provide a quicker or easier solution to a piloting problem. The material of this section might be considered as "graduate study" in small-craft piloting. These techniques should not be approached without a thorough understanding of Chapters 19 and 20, and the basic methods already discussed in Chapter 21. FIG. 2152 (left): Current problems, for example, may be solved with the aid of precomputed speed factors and course corrections—but first understand the principles.

PILOTING—Specialized Techniques

Current Problem Solutions from Tabulated Factors

When a boat moves in water that is in itself in motion with respect to the bottom as a result of current, two effects must be considered. One of these is the difference in speed over the bottom as compared with speed through the water. The other effect is the variation between the course steered and the path actually traveled.

THE VARIOUS CURRENT SAILING PROBLEMS

The effects mentioned above can be approached from several viewpoints:

(a) with a selected course and speed, together with a known or estimated current, *determining the track and speed of advance* that may be expected;

(b) with a desired track and speed to be run through the water, plus knowledge of the current, *determining the course to steer and the speed of advance* that may be expected; and

(c) with a desired track and speed of advance to be made good, and knowledge of the current, *determining the course to steer and the speed to run through the water.*

In all current situations, there are three pairs of direction and speed values—*boat with respect to the water, water with respect to the bottom,* and *boat with respect to the bottom.* For the solution of current sailing problems, in general, four of the above six quantities will be known (or estimated) and the other two are to be determined.

In Chapter 20, graphic solutions using vectors were used, see pages 338 to 344(r).

Such current problems can also be solved using data derived from an electronic digital computer. Solutions from these tables of data should not be attempted, however, without a thorough understanding of the relationships between the various quantities involved, as are shown in the graphic plots of Chapter 20. An understanding of the graphical procedure will reduce the chances of

misinterpreting the tables, or of using the factors incorrectly. For easier understanding, the same terms, abbreviations, and designations of problems (Case 1, Case 3, etc.) will be used here as in Chapter 20.

DISTANCE, TIME, AND SPEED CALCULATIONS

Where no current is present, the pilot's problem is a simple matter of *determining the time required to run a given distance in slack water.* Even where there is current, slack water speed (or speed through the water without reference to current) is a basic factor. The formulas for D, T, and S, see page 337(m), can be used, but the table of fig. 2151 is a handy means of achieving the same results. It was developed primarily for the cruising boatman who is interested in relatively long runs involving hours and minutes of time.

Slack water speed solutions

The use of fig. 2151 is simple, as the following examples will illustrate:

Example A. At 13 knots, how long does it take to go 36 miles?

Answer: Reading directly from the table, 2^h 46^m.

Example B. At 11 knots, how long does it take to go 43.6 miles?

Answer: Reading from the table—

to go 43. miles,	3^h 55^m
to go .6 miles,	3^m
to go 43.6 miles	3^h 58^m

Example C. At 14.3 knots, how long does it take to go 26.4 miles?

Answer: From the table, in the same manner as for Example B:

to go 26.4 miles at 14 knots,	1^h 53^m
to go 26.4 miles at 15 knots,	1^h 46^m
Difference in time for 1 knot,	7^m

Hence, to go 26.4 miles at 14.3 knots requires 1^h 53^m − (0.3 x 7^m) = 1^h 51^m.

SPEED—6 TO 27—IN MILES PER HOUR

DISTANCE—.1 TO 90—IN MILES

Dist. miles	6.0	7.0	8.0	9.0	10.0	11.0	12.0	13.0	14.0	15.0	16.0	17.0	18.0	19.0	20.0	21.0	22.0	23.0	24.0	25.0	26.0	27.0
.1	01	01	01	01	01	01	01	00	00	00	00	00	00	00	00	00	00	00	00	00	00	00
.2	02	02	02	01	01	01	01	01	01	01	01	01	01	01	01	01	01	01	01	00	00	00
.3	03	03	02	02	02	02	02	01	01	01	01	01	01	01	01	01	01	01	01	01	01	01
.4	04	03	03	03	02	02	02	02	02	02	02	01	01	01	01	01	01	01	01	01	01	01
.5	05	04	04	03	03	03	03	02	02	02	02	02	02	02	02	01	01	01	01	01	01	01
.6	06	05	05	04	04	03	03	03	03	02	02	02	02	02	02	02	02	02	02	01	01	01
.7	07	06	05	05	04	04	04	03	03	03	03	02	02	02	02	02	02	02	02	02	02	02
.8	08	07	06	05	05	04	04	04	03	03	03	03	03	03	02	02	02	02	02	02	02	02
.9	09	08	07	06	05	05	05	04	04	04	03	03	03	03	03	03	02	02	02	02	02	02
1.0	10	09	08	07	06	05	05	05	04	04	04	04	03	03	03	03	03	03	03	02	02	02
2.0	20	17	15	13	12	11	10	09	09	08	08	07	07	06	06	06	05	05	05	05	05	04
3.0	30	26	23	20	18	16	15	14	13	12	11	11	10	09	09	09	08	08	08	07	07	07
4.0	40	34	30	27	24	22	20	18	17	16	15	14	13	13	12	11	11	10	10	10	09	09
5.0	50	43	38	33	30	27	25	23	21	20	19	18	17	16	15	14	14	13	13	12	12	11
6.0	1 00	51	45	40	36	33	30	28	26	24	23	21	20	19	18	17	16	16	15	14	14	13
7.0	1 10	1 00	53	47	42	38	35	32	30	28	26	25	23	22	21	20	19	18	18	17	16	16
8.0	1 20	1 09	1 00	53	48	44	40	37	34	32	30	28	27	25	24	23	22	21	20	19	18	18
9.0	1 30	1 17	1 08	1 00	54	49	45	42	39	36	34	32	30	28	27	26	25	23	23	22	21	20
10.0	1 40	1 26	1 15	1 07	1 00	55	50	46	43	40	38	35	33	32	30	29	27	26	25	24	23	22
11.0	1 50	1 34	1 23	1 13	1 06	1 00	55	51	47	44	41	39	37	35	33	31	30	29	28	26	25	24
12.0	2 00	1 43	1 30	1 20	1 12	1 05	1 00	55	51	48	45	42	40	38	36	34	33	31	30	29	28	27
13.0	2 10	1 51	1 38	1 27	1 18	1 11	1 05	1 00	56	52	49	46	43	41	39	37	35	34	33	31	30	29
14.0	2 20	2 00	1 45	1 33	1 24	1 16	1 10	1 05	1 00	56	53	49	47	44	42	40	38	37	35	34	32	31
15.0	2 30	2 09	1 53	1 40	1 30	1 22	1 15	1 09	1 04	1 00	56	53	50	47	45	43	41	39	38	36	35	33
16.0	2 40	2 17	2 00	1 47	1 36	1 27	1 20	1 14	1 09	1 04	1 00	56	53	51	48	46	44	42	40	38	37	36
17.0	2 50	2 26	2 08	1 53	1 42	1 33	1 25	1 18	1 13	1 08	1 04	1 00	57	54	51	49	46	44	43	41	39	38
18.0	3 00	2 34	2 15	2 00	1 48	1 38	1 30	1 23	1 17	1 12	1 08	1 04	1 00	57	54	51	49	47	45	43	42	40
19.0	3 10	2 43	2 23	2 07	1 54	1 44	1 35	1 28	1 21	1 16	1 11	1 07	1 03	1 00	57	54	52	50	48	46	44	42
20.0	3 20	2 51	2 30	2 13	2 00	1 49	1 40	1 32	1 26	1 20	1 15	1 11	1 07	1 03	1 00	57	55	52	50	48	46	44
21.0	3 30	3 00	2 38	2 20	2 06	1 55	1 45	1 37	1 30	1 24	1 19	1 14	1 10	1 06	1 03	1 00	57	55	53	50	48	47
22.0	3 40	3 09	2 45	2 27	2 12	2 00	1 50	1 42	1 34	1 28	1 23	1 18	1 13	1 09	1 06	1 03	1 00	57	55	53	51	49
23.0	3 50	3 17	2 53	2 33	2 18	2 05	1 55	1 46	1 39	1 32	1 26	1 21	1 17	1 13	1 09	1 06	1 03	1 00	58	55	53	51
24.0	4 00	3 26	3 00	2 40	2 24	2 11	2 00	1 51	1 43	1 36	1 30	1 25	1 20	1 16	1 12	1 09	1 05	1 03	1 00	58	55	53
25.0	4 10	3 34	3 08	2 47	2 30	2 16	2 05	1 55	1 47	1 40	1 34	1 28	1 23	1 19	1 15	1 11	1 08	1 05	1 03	1 00	58	56
26.0	4 20	3 43	3 15	2 53	2 36	2 22	2 10	2 00	1 51	1 44	1 38	1 32	1 27	1 22	1 18	1 14	1 11	1 08	1 05	1 02	1 00	58
27.0	4 30	3 51	3 23	3 00	2 42	2 27	2 15	2 05	1 56	1 48	1 41	1 35	1 30	1 25	1 21	1 17	1 14	1 10	1 08	1 05	1 02	1 00
28.0	4 40	4 00	3 30	3 07	2 48	2 33	2 20	2 09	2 00	1 52	1 45	1 39	1 33	1 28	1 24	1 20	1 16	1 13	1 10	1 07	1 05	1 02
29.0	4 50	4 09	3 38	3 13	2 54	2 38	2 25	2 14	2 04	1 56	1 49	1 42	1 37	1 32	1 27	1 23	1 19	1 16	1 13	1 10	1 07	1 04
30.0	5 00	4 17	3 45	3 20	3 00	2 44	2 30	2 18	2 09	2 00	1 53	1 46	1 40	1 35	1 30	1 26	1 22	1 18	1 15	1 12	1 09	1 07
31.0	5 10	4 26	3 53	3 27	3 06	2 49	2 35	2 23	2 13	2 04	1 56	1 49	1 43	1 38	1 33	1 29	1 25	1 21	1 18	1 14	1 12	1 09
32.0	5 20	4 34	4 00	3 33	3 12	2 55	2 40	2 28	2 17	2 08	2 00	1 53	1 47	1 41	1 36	1 31	1 27	1 23	1 20	1 17	1 14	1 11
33.0	5 30	4 43	4 08	3 40	3 18	3 00	2 45	2 32	2 21	2 12	2 04	1 56	1 50	1 44	1 39	1 34	1 30	1 26	1 23	1 19	1 16	1 13
34.0	5 40	4 51	4 15	3 47	3 24	3 05	2 50	2 37	2 26	2 16	2 08	2 00	1 53	1 47	1 42	1 37	1 33	1 29	1 25	1 22	1 18	1 16
35.0	5 50	5 00	4 23	3 53	3 30	3 11	2 55	2 42	2 30	2 20	2 11	2 04	1 57	1 51	1 45	1 40	1 35	1 31	1 28	1 24	1 21	1 18
36.0	6 00	5 09	4 30	4 00	3 36	3 16	3 00	2 46	2 34	2 24	2 15	2 07	2 00	1 54	1 48	1 43	1 38	1 34	1 30	1 26	1 23	1 20
37.0	6 10	5 17	4 38	4 07	3 42	3 22	3 05	2 51	2 39	2 28	2 19	2 11	2 03	1 57	1 51	1 46	1 41	1 37	1 33	1 29	1 25	1 22
38.0	6 20	5 26	4 45	4 13	3 48	3 27	3 10	2 55	2 43	2 32	2 23	2 14	2 07	2 00	1 54	1 49	1 44	1 39	1 35	1 31	1 28	1 24
39.0	6 30	5 34	4 53	4 20	3 54	3 33	3 15	3 00	2 47	2 36	2 26	2 18	2 10	2 03	1 57	1 51	1 46	1 42	1 38	1 34	1 30	1 27
40.0	6 40	5 43	5 00	4 27	4 00	3 38	3 20	3 05	2 51	2 40	2 30	2 21	2 13	2 06	2 00	1 54	1 49	1 44	1 40	1 36	1 32	1 29
41.0	6 50	5 51	5 08	4 33	4 06	3 44	3 25	3 09	2 56	2 44	2 34	2 25	2 17	2 09	2 03	1 57	1 52	1 47	1 43	1 38	1 35	1 31
42.0	7 00	6 00	5 15	4 40	4 12	3 49	3 30	3 14	3 00	2 48	2 38	2 28	2 20	2 13	2 06	2 00	1 55	1 50	1 45	1 41	1 37	1 33
43.0	7 10	6 09	5 23	4 47	4 18	3 55	3 35	3 18	3 04	2 52	2 41	2 32	2 23	2 16	2 09	2 03	1 57	1 52	1 48	1 43	1 39	1 36
44.0	7 20	6 17	5 30	4 53	4 24	4 00	3 40	3 23	3 09	2 56	2 45	2 35	2 27	2 19	2 12	2 06	2 00	1 55	1 50	1 46	1 42	1 38
45.0	7 30	6 26	5 38	5 00	4 30	4 05	3 45	3 28	3 13	3 00	2 49	2 39	2 30	2 22	2 15	2 09	2 03	1 57	1 53	1 48	1 44	1 40
46.0	7 40	6 34	5 45	5 07	4 36	4 11	3 50	3 32	3 17	3 04	2 53	2 42	2 33	2 25	2 18	2 11	2 05	2 00	1 55	1 50	1 46	1 42
47.0	7 50	6 43	5 53	5 13	4 42	4 16	3 55	3 37	3 21	3 08	2 56	2 46	2 37	2 28	2 21	2 14	2 08	2 03	1 58	1 53	1 48	1 44
48.0	8 00	6 51	6 00	5 20	4 48	4 22	4 00	3 42	3 26	3 12	3 00	2 49	2 40	2 32	2 24	2 17	2 11	2 05	2 00	1 55	1 51	1 47
49.0	8 10	7 00	6 08	5 27	4 54	4 27	4 05	3 46	3 30	3 16	3 04	2 53	2 43	2 35	2 27	2 20	2 14	2 08	2 03	1 58	1 53	1 49
50.0	8 20	7 09	6 15	5 33	5 00	4 33	4 10	3 51	3 34	3 20	3 08	2 56	2 47	2 38	2 30	2 23	2 16	2 10	2 05	2 00	1 55	1 51
51.0	8 30	7 17	6 23	5 40	5 06	4 38	4 15	3 55	3 39	3 24	3 11	3 00	2 50	2 41	2 33	2 26	2 19	2 13	2 08	2 02	1 58	1 53
52.0	8 40	7 26	6 30	5 47	5 12	4 44	4 20	4 00	3 43	3 28	3 15	3 04	2 53	2 44	2 36	2 29	2 22	2 16	2 10	2 05	2 00	1 56
53.0	8 50	7 34	6 38	5 53	5 18	4 49	4 25	4 05	3 47	3 32	3 19	3 07	2 57	2 47	2 39	2 31	2 25	2 18	2 13	2 07	2 02	1 58
54.0	9 00	7 43	6 45	6 00	5 24	4 55	4 30	4 09	3 51	3 36	3 23	3 11	3 00	2 51	2 42	2 34	2 27	2 21	2 15	2 10	2 05	2 00
55.0	9 10	7 51	6 53	6 07	5 30	5 00	4 35	4 14	3 56	3 40	3 26	3 14	3 03	2.54	2 45	2 37	2 30	2 23	2 18	2 12	2 07	2 02
56.0	9 20	8 00	7 00	6 13	5 36	5 05	4 40	4 18	4 00	3 44	3 30	3 18	3 07	2 57	2 48	2 40	2 33	2 26	2 20	2 14	2 09	2 04
57.0	9 30	8 09	7 08	6 20	5 42	5 11	4 45	4 23	4 04	3 48	3 34	3 21	3 10	3 00	2 51	2 43	2 35	2 29	2 23	2 17	2 12	2 07
58.0	9 40	8 17	7 15	6 27	5 48	5 16	4 50	4 28	4 09	3 52	3 38	3 25	3 13	3 03	2 54	2 46	2 38	2 31	2 25	2 19	2 14	2 09
59.0	9 50	8 26	7 23	6 33	5 54	5 22	4 55	4 32	4 13	3 56	3 41	3 28	3 17	3 06	2 57	2 49	2 41	2 34	2 28	2 22	2 16	2 11
60.0	10 00	8 34	7 30	6 40	6 00	5 27	5 00	4 37	4 17	4 00	3 45	3 32	3 20	3 09	3 00	2 51	2 44	2 37	2 30	2 24	2 18	2 13
61.0	10 10	8 43	7 38	6 47	6 06	5 33	5 05	4 42	4 21	4 04	3 49	3 35	3 23	3 13	3 03	2 54	2 46	2 39	2 33	2 26	2 21	2 16
62.0	10 20	8 51	7 45	6 53	6 12	5 38	5 10	4 46	4 26	4 08	3 53	3 39	3 27	3 16	3 06	2 57	2 49	2 42	2 35	2 29	2 23	2 18
63.0	10 30	9 00	7 53	7 00	6 18	5 44	5 15	4 51	4 30	4 12	3 56	3 42	3 30	3 19	3 09	3 00	2 52	2 44	2 38	2 31	2 25	2 20
64.0	10 40	9 09	8 00	7 07	6 24	5 49	5 20	4 55	4 34	4 16	4 00	3 46	3 33	3 22	3 12	3 03	2 55	2 47	2 40	2 34	2 28	2 22
65.0	10 50	9 17	8 08	7 13	6 30	5 55	5 25	5 00	4 39	4 20	4 04	3 49	3 37	3 25	3 15	3 06	2 57	2 50	2 43	2 36	2 30	2 24
66.0	11 00	9 26	8 15	7 20	6 36	6 00	5 30	5 05	4 43	4 24	4 08	3 53	3 40	3 28	3 18	3 09	3 00	2 52	2 45	2 38	2 32	2 27
67.0	11 10	9 34	8 23	7 27	6 42	6 05	5 35	5 09	4 47	4 28	4 11	3 56	3 43	3 32	3 21	3 11	3 03	2 55	2 48	2 41	2 35	2 29
68.0	11 20	9 43	8 30	7 33	6 48	6 11	5 40	5 14	4 51	4 32	4 15	4 00	3 47	3 35	3 24	3 14	3 05	2 57	2 50	2 43	2 37	2 31
69.0	11 30	9 51	8 38	7 40	6 54	6 16	5 45	5 18	4 56	4 36	4 19	4 04	3 50	3 38	3 27	3 17	3 08	3 00	2 53	2 46	2 39	2 33
70.0	11 40	10 00	8 45	7 47	7 00	6 22	5 50	5 23	5 00	4 40	4 23	4 07	3 53	3 41	3 30	3 20	3 11	3 03	2 55	2 48	2 42	2 36
71.0	11 50	10 09	8 53	7 53	7 06	6 27	5 55	5 28	5 04	4 44	4 26	4 11	3 57	3 44	3 33	3 23	3 14	3 05	2 58	2 50	2 44	2 38
72.0	12 00	10 17	9 00	8 00	7 12	6 33	6 00	5 32	5 09	4 48	4 30	4 14	4 00	3 47	3 36	3 26	3 16	3 08	3 00	2 53	2 46	2 40
73.0	12 10	10 26	9 08	8 07	7 18	6 38	6 05	5 37	5 13	4 52	4 34	4 18	4 03	3 51	3 39	3 29	3 19	3 10	3 03	2 55	2 48	2 42
74.0	12 20	10 34	9 15	8 13	7 24	6 44	6 10	5 42	5 17	4 56	4 38	4 21	4 07	3 54	3 42	3 31	3 22	3 13	3 05	2 58	2 51	2 44
75.0	12 30	10 43	9 23	8 20	7 30	6 49	6 15	5 46	5 21	5 00	4 41	4 25	4 10	3 57	3 45	3 34	3 25	3 16	3 08	3 00	2 53	2 47
76.0	12 40	10 51	9 30	8 27	7 36	6 55	6 20	5 51	5 26	5 04	4 45	4 28	4 13	4 00	3 48	3 37	3 27	3 18	3 10	3 02	2 55	2 49
77.0	12 50	11 00	9 38	8 33	7 42	7 00	6 25	5 55	5 30	5 08	4 49	4 32	4 17	4 03	3 51	3 40	3 30	3 21	3 13	3 05	2 58	2 51
78.0	13 00	11 09	9 45	8 40	7 48	7 05	6 30	6 00	5 34	5 12	4 53	4 35	4 20	4 06	3 54	3 43	3 33	3 23	3 15	3 07	3 00	2 53
79.0	13 10	11 17	9 53	8 47	7 54	7 11	6 35	6 05	5 39	5 16	4 56	4 39	4 23	4 09	3 57	3 46	3 35	3 26	3 18	3 10	3 02	2 56
80.0	13 20	11 26	10 00	8 53	8 00	7 16	6 40	6 09	5 43	5 20	5 00	4 42	4 27	4 13	4 00	3 49	3 38	3 29	3 20	3 12	3 05	2 58
81.0	13 30	11 34	10 08	9 00	8 06	7 22	6 45	6 14	5 47	5 24	5 04	4 46	4 30	4 16	4 03	3 51	3 41	3 31	3 23	3 14	3 07	3 00
82.0	13 40	11 43	10 15	9 07	8 12	7 27	6 50	6 18	5 51	5 28	5 08	4 49	4 33	4 19	4 06	3 54	3 44	3 34	3 25	3 17	3 09	3 02
83.0	13 50	11 51	10 23	9 13	8 18	7 33	6 55	6 23	5 56	5 32	5 11	4 53	4 37	4 22	4 09	3 57	3 46	3 37	3 28	3 19	3 12	3 04
84.0	14 00	12 00	10 30	9 20	8 24	7 38	7 00	6 28	6 00	5 36	5 15	4 56	4 40	4 25	4 12	4 00	3 49	3 39	3 30	3 22	3 14	3 07
85.0	14 10	12 09	10 38	9 27	8 30	7 44	7 05	6 32	6 04	5 40	5 19	5 00	4 43	4 28	4 15	4 03	3 52	3 42	3 33	3 24	3 16	3 09
86.0	14 20	12 17	10 45	9 33	8 36	7 49	7 10	6 37	6 09	5 44	5 23	5 04	4 47	4 32	4 18	4 06	3 55	3 44	3 35	3 26	3 18	3 11
87.0	14 30	12 26	10 53	9 40	8 42	7 55	7 15	6 42	6 13	5 48	5 26	5 07	4 50	4 35	4 21	4 09	3 57	3 47	3 38	3 29	3 21	3 13
88.0	14 40	12 34	11 00	9 47	8 48	8 00	7 20	6 46	6 17	5 52	5 30	5 11	4 53	4 38	4 24	4 11	4 00	3 50	3 40	3 31	3 23	3 16
89.0	14 50	12 43	11 08	9 53	8 54	8 05	7 25	6 51	6 21	5 56	5 34	5 14	4 57	4 41	4 27	4 14	4 03	3 52	3 43	3 34	3 25	3 18
90.0	15 00	12 51	11 15	10 00	9 00	8 11	7 30	6 55	6 26	6 00	5 38	5 18	5 00	4 44	4 30	4 17	4 05	3 55	3 45	3 36	3 28	3 20

FIG. 2151 Time required to run a known distance at a specified speed. Time is shown in hours and minutes. Distances and speeds may be in nautical miles and knots, or in statute miles and MPH. Times for whole miles and fractions may be combined. See text.

The technique of interpolating between speeds in Example C is not precisely correct from a pure mathematics viewpoint. The error, if any, however, will be negligible in practical piloting situations, and the procedure is quite acceptable.

CURRENT PROBLEM SOLUTIONS

In solving current sailing problems with tabulated data, the pilot will still use the terminology developed in earlier chapters. For review, these terms are as follows:

Course (C)—the direction of the DR track, the direction the boat is steered through the water.

Speed (S)—the speed of the boat through the water, the DR track speed.

Set—the direction *toward* which the current is flowing.

Drift—the velocity of the current.

Track (TR)—the direction of the desired (expected) track line.

Speed of Advance (SOA)—the desired (expected) speed along the intended track line.

The terms *Course over the Ground (COG)* and *Speed over the Ground (SOG)* are used only with Case 2 problems which will not be considered in these tabular solutions.

Whenever distance and speed appear in the above definitions, and in the examples to follow, the units may be either statute miles and MPH, or nautical miles and knots.

Special terms

In the solution of current problems by tabulated factors, it is necessary to introduce certain additional terms not previously employed in the graphic solution of such problems.

$$\textit{Drift}, \text{ in percent} = \frac{\text{Drift} \times 100}{\text{Speed, or SOA, as specified}}$$

Relative set is the angle measured from the course steered (C), or from the desired (expected) track (TR), to the set of the current, measured either clockwise or counter-clockwise so that the angle is less than 180°. When measured in a *clockwise* direction, relative set is *positive;* when measured in a *counter-clockwise* direction, relative set is *negative.* In some cases, relative set will be figured with respect to course (C); in other cases, with respect to track (TR).

Fig. 2153 shows graphically the relationship of relative set and course change (CC) to the previously used terms of course, track, set, etc. for Case 1 problems.

Relative set is calculated as shown in the examples shown below:

Relative set = Set − Course, 180° or less to starboard or port.

Set	060	300
Course	−025	−340
Relative set	+035	−040

If (Set − C) is numerically greater than 180°, and positive, subtract 360° obtaining a *negative* relative set less than 180°.

Set	240
Course	−030
	+210
	−360
Relative set	−150

If (Set − C) is numerically greater than 180°, and negative, add 360°, obtaining a *positive* relative set less than 180°.

Set	060
Course	−300
	−240
	+360
Relative set	+120

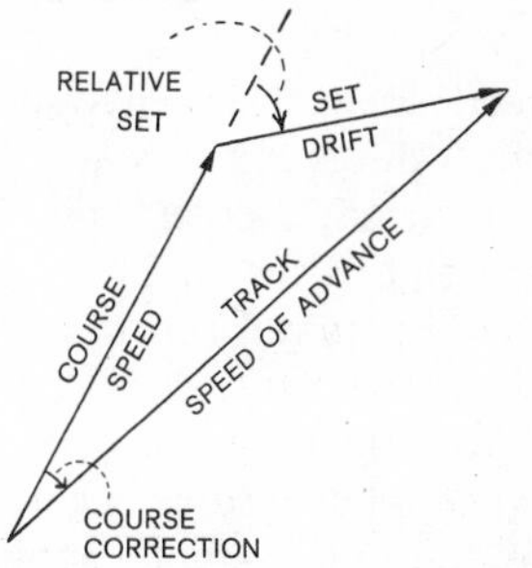

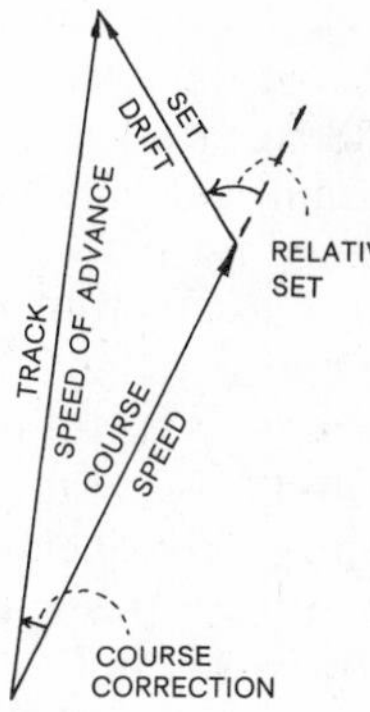

FIG. 2153 The tabular solution of current problems introduces two new terms—*relative set* and *course correction* (CC). The relationship of these terms to the more familiar directions and velocities are shown above for Case 1 problems.

Fig. 2154 and subsequent tables will yield a multiplying quantity, termed Speed Factor (SF), and an angle, called Course Change or Course Correction (CC). The use of these factors will be explained in connection with each of the three types of current problems to be solved by the tables.

Case 1 solutions by tabular factors

In Case 1, the pilot has selected the course that he will steer and the speed at which he will operate his boat with respect to the water (the engine rpm setting that he will use). He also has information on the set and drift of the current from predictions or visual observations. He desires to know *the direction of the path that the boat may be expected to follow with respect to the bottom (TR) and*

FIG. 2154 Case 1—To find Track and Speed of Advance from knowledge of Course and Speed through the water, plus relative set and percent drift. This table yields Speed Factors (SF) and Course Corrections (CC).

DRIFT—in percent of speed over water

Rel.	2		4		6		8		10		12		14		16		18		20	
Set	SF	CC	SF	CC	SF	CC	SF	CC	SF	CC	SF	CC	SF	CC	SF	CC	SF	CC	SF	CC
000	1.020	00	1.040	00	1.060	00	1.080	00	1.100	00	1.120	00	1.140	00	1.160	00	1.180	00	1.200	00
005	1.020	00	1.040	00	1.060	00	1.080	00	1.100	00	1.120	01	1.140	01	1.159	01	1.179	01	1.199	01
010	1.020	00	1.039	00	1.059	01	1.079	01	1.099	01	1.118	01	1.138	01	1.158	01	1.178	02	1.197	02
015	1.019	00	1.039	01	1.058	01	1.077	01	1.097	01	1.116	02	1.136	02	1.155	02	1.175	02	1.194	02
020	1.019	00	1.038	01	1.057	01	1.076	01	1.095	02	1.114	02	1.133	02	1.152	03	1.171	03	1.190	03
025	1.018	00	1.036	01	1.055	01	1.073	02	1.091	02	1.110	03	1.128	03	1.147	03	1.166	04	1.184	04
030	1.017	01	1.035	01	1.052	02	1.070	02	1.088	03	1.106	03	1.123	04	1.141	04	1.159	04	1.177	05
035	1.016	01	1.033	01	1.050	02	1.067	02	1.083	03	1.100	04	1.118	04	1.135	05	1.152	05	1.169	06
040	1.015	01	1.031	01	1.047	02	1.063	03	1.079	03	1.095	04	1.111	05	1.127	05	1.144	06	1.160	06
045	1.014	01	1.029	02	1.043	02	1.058	03	1.073	04	1.088	04	1.103	05	1.119	06	1.134	06	1.150	07
050	1.013	01	1.026	02	1.040	03	1.053	03	1.067	04	1.081	05	1.095	06	1.110	06	1.124	07	1.139	08
055	1.012	01	1.023	02	1.036	03	1.048	04	1.061	04	1.073	05	1.086	06	1.100	07	1.113	08	1.127	08
060	1.010	01	1.021	02	1.031	03	1.042	04	1.054	05	1.065	06	1.077	06	1.089	07	1.101	08	1.114	09
065	1.009	01	1.018	02	1.027	03	1.036	04	1.046	05	1.056	06	1.067	07	1.077	08	1.088	09	1.100	09
070	1.007	01	1.014	02	1.022	03	1.030	04	1.038	05	1.047	06	1.056	07	1.065	08	1.075	09	1.085	10
075	1.005	01	1.011	02	1.017	03	1.024	04	1.030	05	1.038	06	1.045	07	1.053	08	1.061	09	1.069	10
080	1.004	01	1.008	02	1.012	03	1.017	04	1.022	06	1.028	07	1.034	08	1.040	09	1.046	10	1.053	11
085	1.002	01	1.004	02	1.007	03	1.010	05	1.014	06	1.018	07	1.022	08	1.026	09	1.031	10	1.037	11
090	1.000	01	1.001	02	1.002	03	1.003	05	1.005	06	1.007	07	1.010	08	1.013	09	1.016	10	1.020	11
095	.998	01	.997	02	.997	03	.996	05	.996	06	.997	07	.998	08	.999	09	1.001	10	1.003	11
100	.997	01	.994	02	.991	03	.989	05	.988	06	.986	07	.985	08	.985	09	.985	10	.985	12
105	.995	01	.990	02	.986	03	.982	05	.979	06	.976	07	.973	08	.971	09	.969	10	.968	12
110	.993	01	.987	02	.981	03	.976	04	.970	06	.966	07	.961	08	.957	09	.954	10	.950	11
115	.992	01	.984	02	.976	03	.969	04	.962	05	.955	07	.949	08	.944	09	.938	10	.933	11
120	.990	01	.981	02	.971	03	.962	04	.954	05	.946	06	.938	07	.930	09	.923	10	.917	11
125	.989	01	.978	02	.967	03	.956	04	.946	05	.936	06	.927	07	.918	08	.909	09	.900	10
130	.987	01	.975	02	.963	03	.951	04	.939	05	.927	06	.916	07	.905	08	.895	09	.885	10
135	.986	01	.972	02	.959	03	.945	03	.932	04	.919	05	.906	06	.894	07	.882	08	.870	09
140	.985	01	.970	02	.955	02	.940	03	.926	04	.911	05	.897	06	.883	07	.870	08	.856	09
145	.984	01	.968	01	.951	02	.936	03	.920	04	.904	04	.889	05	.874	06	.859	07	.844	08
150	.983	01	.966	01	.949	02	.932	02	.915	03	.898	04	.882	05	.865	05	.849	06	.833	07
155	.982	00	.964	01	.946	02	.928	02	.910	03	.893	03	.875	04	.858	05	.840	05	.823	06
160	.981	00	.963	01	.944	01	.925	02	.907	02	.888	03	.870	03	.851	04	.833	04	.815	05
165	.981	00	.961	01	.942	01	.923	01	.904	02	.885	02	.866	02	.846	03	.827	03	.808	04
170	.980	00	.961	00	.941	01	.921	01	.902	01	.882	01	.862	02	.843	02	.823	02	.804	02
175	.980	00	.960	00	.940	00	.920	00	.900	01	.881	01	.861	01	.841	01	.821	01	.801	01
180	.980	00	.960	00	.940	00	.920	00	.900	00	.880	00	.860	00	.840	00	.820	00	.800	00

Rel.	22		24		26		28		30		32		34		36		38		40	
Set	SF	CC	SF	CC	SF	CC	SF	CC	SF	CC	SF	CC	SF	CC	SF	CC	SF	CC	SF	CC
000	1.220	00	1.240	00	1.260	00	1.280	00	1.300	00	1.320	00	1.340	00	1.360	00	1.380	00	1.400	00
005	1.219	01	1.239	01	1.259	01	1.279	01	1.299	01	1.319	01	1.339	01	1.359	01	1.379	01	1.399	01
010	1.217	02	1.237	02	1.257	02	1.277	02	1.296	02	1.316	02	1.336	03	1.356	03	1.376	03	1.396	03
015	1.214	03	1.233	03	1.253	03	1.273	03	1.292	03	1.312	04	1.331	04	1.351	04	1.371	04	1.390	04
020	1.209	04	1.228	04	1.247	04	1.267	04	1.286	05	1.305	05	1.325	05	1.344	05	1.363	05	1.383	06
025	1.203	04	1.222	05	1.241	05	1.259	05	1.278	06	1.297	06	1.316	06	1.335	07	1.354	07	1.373	07
030	1.196	05	1.214	06	1.232	06	1.250	06	1.269	07	1.287	07	1.306	07	1.324	08	1.343	08	1.361	08
035	1.187	06	1.204	07	1.222	07	1.240	07	1.258	08	1.275	08	1.293	09	1.311	09	1.329	09	1.347	10
040	1.177	07	1.194	07	1.211	08	1.228	08	1.245	09	1.262	09	1.279	10	1.297	10	1.314	11	1.331	11
045	1.166	08	1.182	08	1.198	09	1.214	09	1.231	10	1.247	10	1.263	11	1.280	11	1.297	12	1.314	12
050	1.154	08	1.169	09	1.184	10	1.199	10	1.215	11	1.230	11	1.246	12	1.262	13	1.278	13	1.294	14
055	1.141	09	1.155	10	1.169	11	1.183	11	1.198	12	1.212	12	1.227	13	1.242	14	1.257	14	1.272	15
060	1.126	10	1.139	11	1.152	11	1.166	12	1.179	13	1.193	13	1.206	14	1.220	15	1.235	15	1.249	16
065	1.111	10	1.123	11	1.135	12	1.147	13	1.159	14	1.172	14	1.184	15	1.197	16	1.211	17	1.224	17
070	1.095	11	1.105	12	1.116	13	1.127	14	1.138	14	1.149	15	1.161	16	1.173	17	1.185	18	1.197	18
075	1.078	11	1.087	12	1.096	13	1.106	14	1.116	15	1.126	16	1.136	17	1.147	18	1.158	18	1.169	19
080	1.061	12	1.068	13	1.076	14	1.084	15	1.093	16	1.102	17	1.111	18	1.120	18	1.130	19	1.140	20
085	1.042	12	1.049	13	1.055	14	1.062	15	1.069	16	1.076	17	1.084	18	1.092	19	1.100	20	1.109	21
090	1.024	12	1.028	13	1.033	15	1.038	16	1.044	17	1.050	18	1.056	19	1.063	20	1.070	21	1.077	22
095	1.005	13	1.008	14	1.011	15	1.015	16	1.019	17	1.023	18	1.028	19	1.033	20	1.038	21	1.044	22
100	.986	13	.987	14	.989	15	.991	16	.993	17	.996	18	.999	20	1.002	21	1.006	22	1.010	23
105	.967	13	.966	14	.966	15	.966	16	.967	17	.968	19	.969	20	.971	21	.973	22	.976	23
110	.948	13	.945	14	.943	15	.942	16	.941	17	.940	19	.940	20	.940	21	.940	22	.941	24
115	.929	12	.925	14	.921	15	.917	16	.915	17	.912	19	.910	20	.908	21	.907	22	.907	24
120	.910	12	.904	13	.899	15	.894	16	.889	17	.885	18	.881	20	.877	21	.874	22	.872	23
125	.892	12	.884	13	.877	14	.870	15	.864	17	.858	18	.852	19	.847	20	.842	22	.837	23
130	.875	11	.865	12	.856	13	.848	15	.839	16	.831	17	.824	18	.817	20	.810	21	.804	22
135	.859	10	.847	12	.837	13	.826	14	.816	15	.806	16	.797	18	.788	19	.779	20	.771	22
140	.843	10	.831	11	.818	12	.806	13	.794	14	.782	15	.771	16	.760	18	.750	19	.740	20
145	.829	09	.815	10	.801	11	.787	12	.774	13	.760	14	.747	15	.735	16	.722	18	.710	19
150	.817	08	.801	09	.786	10	.770	10	.755	11	.740	12	.726	14	.711	15	.697	16	.684	17
155	.806	07	.789	07	.772	08	.756	09	.739	10	.723	11	.707	12	.691	13	.675	14	.660	15
160	.797	05	.779	06	.761	07	.743	07	.725	08	.708	09	.690	10	.673	11	.656	11	.639	12
165	.790	04	.771	05	.752	05	.733	06	.714	06	.696	07	.677	07	.659	08	.641	09	.622	10
170	.784	03	.765	03	.745	03	.726	04	.706	04	.687	05	.668	05	.648	06	.629	06	.610	07
175	.781	01	.761	02	.741	02	.721	02	.702	02	.682	02	.662	03	.642	03	.622	03	.603	03
180	.780	00	.760	00	.740	00	.720	00	.700	00	.680	00	.660	00	.640	00	.620	00	.600	00

the speed of advance over the bottom (SOA) that will result from the current's effect.

Fig. 2154 can be used to solve the above problem. The tables of this figure are entered with the drift, in percent of speed through the water, at the top (columns labeled 2 to 40), and the relative set of the current (lines labeled 000° to 180° at the left side). The intersection of the appropriate column and line yields a Speed Factor (SF) and Course Change (CC).

In Case 1 problems, speed (S) is a known value; it is multiplied by SF to get the value for the speed of advance (SOA). In this type of current problem, the Course steered (C) is also a known value. Thus, "CC" is "Course Change," the angle by which the boat is set off course by the current. It is applied as follows:

Track (TR) = C + CC, when relative set is positive.

= C − CC, when relative set is negative.

Three examples will be used to illustrate the application of these tabular factors. Graphic plots of each example are shown as aids to understanding, but they are not required, and are not normally drawn.

Example D. (Fig. 2155)

Known: Course = 076° True
Speed = 8 knots
Set = 324°
Drift = 3 knots

To be determined: Track and Speed of Advance
Solution: Relative set = 324° − 076° = +248°
248° − 360° = −112°

$$\text{Percent drift} = \frac{3 \times 100}{8} = 38$$

From the table: for 110°, CC = 22°, SF = 0.940
for 115°, CC = 22°, SF = 0.907
by interpolation, for 112°, CC = 22°, SF = 0.927
Thus: Track = 076° − 22° = 054° True
Speed of Advance = 8 × 0.927
= 7.4 knots

Example E. (Fig. 2156)

Known: Course = 331° True
Speed = 9 knots
Set = 021°
Drift = 2.5 knots

To be determined: Track and Speed of Advance
Solution: Relative set = 021° − 331° = −310°
+360°
+050°

$$\text{Percent drift} = \frac{2.5 \times 100}{9} = 28$$

From the table: CC = 10°
SF = 1.199
Thus: Track 331° + 10° = 341°
Speed of Advance = 9 × 1.199
= 10.8 knots

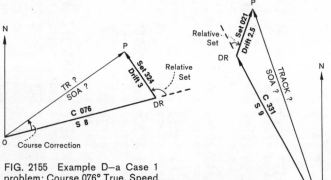

FIG. 2155 Example D—a Case 1 problem: Course 076° True, Speed 8 knots; Set 324°, Drift 3 knots. Find Track and Speed of Advance. See text for solution by tabular factors of fig. 2154.

FIG. 2156 Example E—a Case 1 problem with positive relative set. See text for solution.

Example F. (Fig. 2157)

Known: Course = 015° True
Speed = 10 knots
Set = 156°
Drift = 2 knots

To be determined:
Track and Speed of Advance
Solution:
Relative set = 156° − 015° = +141°

$$\text{Percent drift} = \frac{2 \times 100}{10} = 20$$

From the table: CC = 9
SF = 0.854
Thus: Track 015° + 9° = 024°
Speed of Advance = 10 × 0.854
= 8.5 knots

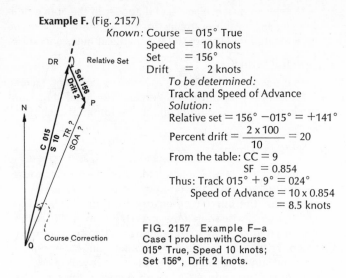

FIG. 2157 Example F—a Case 1 problem with Course 015° True, Speed 10 knots; Set 156°, Drift 2 knots.

Case 3 solutions by tabular factors

In Case 3 current sailing problems, the pilot has determined the direction of the track line that he desires to make good (TR) and has selected his rpm speed (S). He also has information on the set and drift of the current. He desires to determine what course he should steer through the water (C) and to know what speed of advance (SOA) will be achieved at this throttle setting.

In this Case (and in Case 4 problems to be examined later), relative set is the angle between the current and the desired track; see fig. 2158.

Relative set = Set − Track, 180° or less
to starboard or port.

As before, relative set is positive when measured clockwise and negative when measured counter-clockwise. Follow the same rules as for Case 1 if the subtraction gives you an angle greater than 180°.

Fig. 2159 may be used for the solution of this particular current sailing problem. As speed (S) is again a known quantity, it is multiplied by SF as before to obtain speed of advance (SOA).

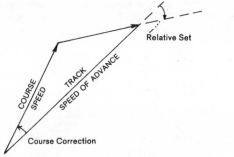

FIG. 2158 In Case 3 and 4 current sailing problems, the relative set is measured between the current and the intended track. The course correction remains as the angle between track and course as in Case 1.

In Case 3, the course to be steered (C) is a desired rather than a known value, and it must be determined by the application of a correction to the desired track (TR). Thus the tabulated angle "CC" is termed "Course Correction" and is used as follows:

Course to be steered (C)

= TR − CC, when the relative set is positive.

= TR + CC, when the relative set is negative.

Rel. Set	2	4	6	8	10	12	14	16	18	20	22	24	26	28	30	32	34	36	38	40
	SF CC	SF CC	SF CC	SF CC	SF CC	SF CC	SF CC	SF CC	SF CC	SF CC	SF CC	SF CC	SF CC	SF CC	SF CC	SF CC	SF CC	SF CC	SF CC	SF CC
000	1.020 00	1.040 00	1.060 00	1.080 00	1.100 00	1.120 00	1.140 00	1.160 00	1.180 00	1.200 00	1.220 00	1.240 00	1.260 00	1.280 00	1.300 00	1.320 00	1.340 00	1.360 00	1.380 00	1.400 00
005	1.020 00	1.040 00	1.060 00	1.080 00	1.100 00	1.119 01	1.139 01	1.159 01	1.179 01	1.199 01	1.219 01	1.239 01	1.259 01	1.279 01	1.299 01	1.318 02	1.338 02	1.358 02	1.378 02	1.398 02
010	1.020 00	1.039 00	1.059 01	1.079 01	1.098 01	1.118 01	1.138 01	1.157 01	1.177 01	1.196 01	1.216 02	1.235 02	1.255 02	1.275 03	1.294 03	1.314 03	1.333 03	1.353 04	1.372 04	1.392 04
020	1.019 01	1.037 01	1.056 01	1.075 01	1.096 01	1.115 02	1.135 02	1.154 02	1.173 03	1.192 03	1.211 03	1.230 04	1.249 04	1.268 04	1.287 04	1.306 05	1.325 05	1.343 05	1.362 06	1.381 06
025	1.018 01	1.036 01	1.054 01	1.072 01	1.090 02	1.107 03	1.125 03	1.143 04	1.160 04	1.178 05	1.195 05	1.212 06	1.230 06	1.247 07	1.264 07	1.281 08	1.298 08	1.315 09	1.331 09	1.348 10
030	1.017 01	1.034 01	1.052 02	1.068 02	1.085 03	1.102 03	1.119 04	1.135 05	1.152 05	1.168 06	1.184 06	1.201 07	1.217 07	1.233 08	1.248 09	1.264 09	1.280 10	1.295 11	1.311 11	1.326 12
035	1.016 01	1.033 01	1.049 02	1.064 03	1.080 03	1.096 04	1.111 05	1.127 05	1.142 06	1.157 07	1.172 07	1.187 08	1.202 09	1.216 09	1.231 10	1.245 11	1.259 11	1.273 12	1.287 13	1.301 13
040	1.015 01	1.030 01	1.045 02	1.060 03	1.075 04	1.089 04	1.103 05	1.117 06	1.131 07	1.145 07	1.158 08	1.172 09	1.185 10	1.198 10	1.211 11	1.224 12	1.236 13	1.249 13	1.261 14	1.273 15
045	1.014 01	1.028 02	1.042 02	1.055 03	1.068 04	1.081 05	1.094 06	1.107 06	1.119 07	1.131 08	1.143 09	1.155 10	1.167 11	1.178 11	1.189 12	1.200 13	1.211 14	1.222 15	1.232 16	1.242 16
050	1.013 01	1.025 02	1.038 03	1.050 04	1.061 04	1.073 05	1.084 06	1.095 07	1.106 08	1.117 09	1.127 09	1.137 11	1.147 11	1.157 12	1.166 13	1.175 14	1.184 15	1.193 16	1.201 17	1.209 18
055	1.011 01	1.022 02	1.033 03	1.043 04	1.054 05	1.064 05	1.074 07	1.083 08	1.092 08	1.101 09	1.110 10	1.118 11	1.126 12	1.134 13	1.141 14	1.149 15	1.155 16	1.162 17	1.168 18	1.174 19
060	1.010 01	1.019 02	1.029 03	1.038 04	1.046 05	1.055 06	1.063 07	1.070 08	1.078 09	1.085 10	1.092 11	1.098 12	1.104 13	1.110 14	1.116 15	1.121 16	1.126 17	1.130 18	1.134 19	1.138 20
065	1.008 01	1.016 02	1.024 03	1.031 04	1.038 05	1.045 06	1.051 07	1.057 08	1.063 09	1.068 10	1.073 12	1.077 13	1.082 13	1.086 15	1.089 16	1.092 17	1.095 18	1.097 19	1.099 20	1.101 21
070	1.007 01	1.013 02	1.019 03	1.025 04	1.030 05	1.035 06	1.039 08	1.043 09	1.047 10	1.051 11	1.054 12	1.056 13	1.059 14	1.061 15	1.062 16	1.063 17	1.064 19	1.064 20	1.064 21	1.063 22
075	1.005 01	1.010 02	1.014 03	1.018 04	1.021 06	1.024 07	1.027 08	1.029 09	1.031 10	1.033 11	1.034 12	1.035 13	1.035 15	1.035 16	1.035 17	1.034 18	1.033 19	1.031 20	1.029 22	1.026 23
080	1.003 01	1.006 02	1.009 03	1.011 05	1.013 06	1.014 07	1.015 08	1.015 09	1.015 10	1.015 11	1.014 13	1.013 14	1.012 15	1.010 16	1.007 17	1.005 18	1.001 20	.998 21	.993 22	.989 23
085	1.002 01	1.003 02	1.003 03	1.004 05	1.004 06	1.003 07	1.002 08	1.001 09	.999 10	.997 11	.995 13	.992 14	.989 15	.985 16	.980 17	.976 19	.971 20	.965 21	.959 22	.952 23
090	1.000 00	.999 02	.998 03	.997 05	.995 06	.993 07	.990 08	.987 09	.984 10	.980 12	.976 13	.971 14	.966 15	.960 16	.954 17	.947 19	.940 20	.933 21	.925 22	.917 23
095	.998 01	.996 02	.993 03	.990 05	.986 06	.982 07	.978 08	.973 09	.968 10	.963 11	.957 13	.950 14	.943 15	.936 16	.928 17	.920 19	.911 20	.902 21	.892 22	.882 23
100	.996 01	.992 02	.988 03	.983 05	.978 06	.972 07	.966 08	.960 09	.953 10	.946 11	.938 13	.930 14	.922 15	.913 16	.903 17	.893 18	.883 20	.873 21	.861 22	.850 23
110	.995 01	.989 02	.983 03	.976 04	.969 06	.962 07	.955 08	.947 09	.938 10	.929 11	.920 12	.911 13	.901 14	.890 16	.879 17	.868 18	.857 19	.844 20	.832 22	.819 23
120	.993 01	.986 02	.978 03	.970 04	.961 05	.953 06	.943 08	.934 09	.924 10	.914 11	.903 12	.892 13	.881 14	.869 15	.857 16	.844 17	.831 19	.818 20	.804 21	.790 22
125	.991 01	.982 02	.973 03	.964 04	.954 05	.943 06	.933 07	.922 08	.911 09	.899 10	.887 12	.875 13	.862 14	.849 15	.836 16	.822 17	.808 18	.793 19	.778 20	.763 21
135	.990 01	.979 02	.969 03	.958 04	.946 05	.935 06	.923 07	.910 08	.898 09	.885 10	.872 11	.858 12	.844 13	.830 14	.816 15	.801 16	.786 17	.770 18	.754 19	.738 20
145	.988 01	.977 02	.964 03	.952 04	.939 05	.926 06	.913 07	.900 08	.886 08	.872 09	.857 10	.843 11	.828 12	.813 13	.797 14	.781 15	.765 16	.749 17	.732 18	.715 19
155	.987 01	.974 02	.960 03	.947 04	.933 04	.919 05	.904 06	.890 07	.875 08	.860 09	.844 10	.829 11	.813 11	.797 12	.780 13	.764 14	.747 15	.730 16	.712 17	.695 18
165	.986 01	.971 02	.957 02	.942 03	.927 04	.912 05	.896 06	.880 06	.865 07	.849 08	.832 09	.816 10	.799 11	.782 11	.765 12	.748 13	.730 14	.712 15	.695 16	.676 16
175	.985 01	.969 01	.953 02	.937 03	.921 04	.905 04	.889 05	.872 06	.855 07	.838 07	.821 08	.804 09	.787 10	.769 10	.751 11	.733 12	.715 13	.697 13	.679 14	.660 15
185	.984 01	.967 01	.950 02	.933 03	.916 03	.899 04	.882 05	.865 05	.847 06	.830 07	.812 07	.794 08	.776 09	.758 09	.739 10	.721 11	.702 11	.684 12	.665 13	.646 14
195	.983 01	.965 01	.948 02	.930 02	.912 03	.894 03	.876 04	.858 05	.840 05	.822 06	.803 06	.785 07	.766 07	.748 08	.729 09	.710 09	.691 10	.672 10	.653 11	.633 12
205	.982 01	.964 01	.945 01	.927 02	.908 02	.890 03	.871 03	.853 04	.834 04	.815 05	.796 05	.777 06	.758 06	.739 07	.720 07	.701 08	.681 08	.662 09	.643 09	.623 10
215	.981 00	.962 01	.943 01	.924 02	.905 02	.886 02	.867 03	.848 03	.829 04	.810 04	.790 04	.771 05	.752 05	.732 05	.713 06	.693 06	.674 07	.654 07	.634 07	.615 08
225	.981 00	.961 01	.942 01	.923 01	.903 01	.884 02	.864 02	.845 02	.825 03	.805 03	.786 03	.766 04	.747 04	.727 04	.707 04	.687 05	.668 05	.648 05	.628 06	.608 06
235	.980 00	.961 00	.941 01	.921 01	.901 01	.882 01	.862 01	.842 02	.822 02	.802 02	.783 02	.763 02	.743 03	.723 03	.703 03	.683 03	.663 03	.644 04	.624 04	.604 04
245	.980 00	.960 00	.940 00	.920 00	.900 00	.880 01	.860 01	.841 01	.821 01	.801 01	.781 01	.761 01	.741 01	.721 01	.701 01	.681 01	.661 02	.641 02	.621 02	.601 02
255	.980 00	.960 00	.940 00	.920 00	.900 00	.880 00	.860 00	.840 01	.820 00	.800 00	.780 01	.760 00	.740 00	.720 00	.700 00	.680 00	.660 00	.640 00	.620 00	.600 00

FIG. 2159 Case 3—To find Course to be steered and Speed of Advance from knowledge of desired Track and Speed through the water, plus relative set and percent drift. This table yields Speed Factors (SF) and Course Corrections (CC) to be applied as shown in text.

In other words, the course correction is toward the current.

Again, three examples will be used to illustrate the application of the tabular factors; these will actually be the same situations as the previous examples, but with different known and unknown elements.

Example G. (Fig. 2160)

Known: Track = 054° True
Speed = 8 knots
Set = 324°
Drift = 3 knots

To be determined: Course and Speed of Advance

Solution: Relative set = 324° − 054° = 270°
−360°
−090°

Percent drift = $\dfrac{3 \times 100}{8}$ = 38

From the table: CC = 22°
SF = 0.925

Thus: Course = 054° + 22° = 076°
Speed of Advance = 8 x 0.925
= 7.4 knots

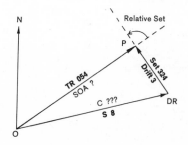

FIG. 2160 Example G—a Case 3 problem: Track 054° True; Speed 8 knots; Set 324°, Drift 3 knots. Desired: Course and Speed of Advance. See text for solution by tabular factors of fig. 2159.

Example H. (Fig. 2161)

Known: Track = 341° True
Speed = 9 knots
Set = 021°
Drift = 2.5 knots

To be determined:
Course and Speed of Advance

Solution:
Relative set = 021° − 341° = −320°
+360°
+040°

Percent drift = $\dfrac{2.5 \times 100}{9}$ = 28

From the table: CC = 10°
SF = 1.198

Thus: Course 341° − 10° = 331°
Speed of Advance = 9 x 1.198
= 10.8 knots

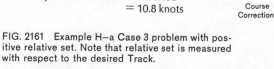

FIG. 2161 Example H—a Case 3 problem with positive relative set. Note that relative set is measured with respect to the desired Track.

Example I. (Fig. 2162)

Known: Track = 024° True
Speed = 10 knots
Set = 156°
Drift = 2 knots

To be determined:
Course and Speed of Advance

Solution:
Relative set = 156° − 024° = +132°

Percent drift = $\dfrac{2 \times 100}{10}$ = 20

From the table: for 130°, CC = 9°, SF = .860
for 135°, CC = 8°, SF = .849
by interpolation, for 132°, CC = 9°, SF = .856

Thus: Course = 024° − 9° = 015°
Speed of Advance = 10 x 0.856
= 8.6 knots

FIG. 2162 Example I—a Case 3 problem with desired Track 024° True; Speed 10 knots; Set 156°, Drift 2 knots. To be determined: Course to be steered and Speed of Advance.

353 (d)

DRIFT—in percent of speed of advance

RELATIVE SET—000 TO 180

Rel.	2		4		6		8		10		12		14		16		18		20	
Set	SF	CC	SF	CC	SF	CC	SF	CC	SF	CC	SF	CC	SF	CC	SF	CC	SF	CC	SF	CC
000	.980	00	.960	00	.940	00	.920	00	.900	00	.880	00	.860	00	.840	00	.820	00	.800	00
005	.980	00	.960	00	.940	00	.920	00	.900	01	.881	01	.861	01	.841	01	.821	01	.801	01
010	.980	00	.961	00	.941	01	.921	01	.902	01	.882	01	.862	02	.843	02	.823	02	.804	02
015	.981	00	.961	01	.942	01	.923	01	.904	02	.885	02	.866	02	.846	03	.827	03	.808	04
020	.981	00	.963	01	.944	01	.925	02	.907	02	.888	03	.870	03	.851	04	.833	04	.815	05
025	.982	00	.964	01	.946	02	.928	02	.910	03	.893	03	.875	04	.858	05	.840	05	.823	06
030	.983	01	.966	01	.949	02	.932	02	.915	03	.898	04	.882	05	.865	05	.849	06	.833	07
035	.984	01	.968	01	.951	02	.936	03	.920	04	.904	04	.889	05	.874	06	.859	07	.844	08
040	.985	01	.970	02	.955	02	.940	03	.926	04	.911	05	.897	06	.883	07	.870	08	.856	09
045	.986	01	.972	02	.959	03	.945	03	.932	04	.919	05	.906	06	.894	07	.882	08	.870	09
050	.987	01	.975	02	.963	03	.951	04	.939	05	.927	06	.916	07	.905	08	.895	09	.885	10
055	.989	01	.978	02	.967	03	.956	04	.946	05	.936	06	.927	07	.918	08	.909	09	.900	10
060	.990	01	.981	02	.971	03	.962	04	.954	05	.946	06	.938	07	.930	09	.923	10	.917	11
065	.992	01	.984	02	.976	03	.969	04	.962	05	.955	07	.949	08	.944	09	.938	10	.933	11
070	.993	01	.987	02	.981	03	.976	04	.970	06	.966	07	.961	08	.957	09	.954	10	.950	11
075	.995	01	.990	02	.986	03	.982	05	.979	06	.976	07	.973	08	.971	09	.969	10	.968	12
080	.997	01	.994	02	.991	03	.989	05	.988	06	.986	07	.985	08	.985	09	.985	10	.985	12
085	.998	01	.997	02	.997	03	.996	05	.996	06	.997	07	.998	08	.999	09	1.001	10	1.003	11
090	1.000	01	1.001	02	1.002	03	1.003	05	1.005	06	1.007	07	1.010	08	1.013	09	1.016	10	1.020	11
095	1.002	01	1.004	02	1.007	03	1.010	05	1.014	06	1.018	07	1.022	08	1.026	09	1.031	10	1.037	11
100	1.004	01	1.008	02	1.012	03	1.017	04	1.022	06	1.028	07	1.034	08	1.040	09	1.046	10	1.053	11
105	1.005	01	1.011	02	1.017	03	1.024	04	1.030	05	1.038	06	1.045	07	1.053	08	1.061	09	1.069	10
110	1.007	01	1.014	02	1.022	03	1.030	04	1.038	05	1.047	06	1.056	07	1.065	08	1.075	09	1.085	10
115	1.009	01	1.018	02	1.027	03	1.036	04	1.046	05	1.056	06	1.067	07	1.077	08	1.088	09	1.100	09
120	1.010	01	1.021	02	1.031	03	1.042	04	1.054	05	1.065	06	1.077	06	1.089	07	1.101	08	1.114	09
125	1.012	01	1.023	02	1.036	03	1.048	04	1.061	04	1.073	05	1.086	06	1.100	07	1.113	08	1.127	08
130	1.013	01	1.026	02	1.040	03	1.053	03	1.067	04	1.081	05	1.095	06	1.110	06	1.124	07	1.139	08
135	1.014	01	1.029	02	1.043	02	1.058	03	1.073	04	1.088	04	1.103	05	1.119	06	1.134	06	1.150	07
140	1.015	01	1.031	01	1.047	02	1.063	03	1.079	03	1.095	04	1.111	05	1.127	05	1.144	06	1.160	06
145	1.016	01	1.033	01	1.050	02	1.067	02	1.083	03	1.100	04	1.118	04	1.135	05	1.152	05	1.169	06
150	1.017	01	1.035	01	1.052	02	1.070	02	1.088	03	1.106	03	1.123	04	1.141	04	1.159	04	1.177	05
155	1.018	00	1.036	01	1.055	01	1.073	02	1.091	02	1.110	03	1.128	03	1.147	03	1.166	04	1.184	04
160	1.019	00	1.038	01	1.057	01	1.076	01	1.095	02	1.114	02	1.133	02	1.152	03	1.171	03	1.190	03
165	1.019	00	1.039	01	1.058	01	1.077	01	1.097	01	1.116	02	1.136	02	1.155	02	1.175	02	1.194	02
170	1.020	00	1.039	00	1.059	01	1.079	01	1.099	01	1.118	01	1.138	01	1.158	01	1.178	02	1.197	02
175	1.020	00	1.040	00	1.060	00	1.080	00	1.100	00	1.120	01	1.140	01	1.159	01	1.179	01	1.199	01
180	1.020	00	1.040	00	1.060	00	1.080	00	1.100	00	1.120	00	1.140	00	1.160	00	1.180	00	1.200	00

Rel.	22		24		26		28		30		32		34		36		38		4
Set	SF	CC	SF	CC	SF	CC	SF	CC	SF	CC	SF	CC	SF	CC	SF	CC	SF	CC	SF
000	.780	00	.760	00	.740	00	.720	00	.700	00	.680	00	.660	00	.640	00	.620	00	.60
005	.781	01	.761	02	.741	02	.721	02	.702	02	.682	02	.662	03	.642	03	.622	03	.60
010	.784	03	.765	03	.745	03	.726	04	.706	04	.687	05	.668	05	.648	06	.629	06	.61
015	.790	04	.771	05	.752	05	.733	06	.714	06	.696	07	.677	07	.659	08	.641	09	.62
020	.797	05	.779	06	.761	07	.743	07	.725	08	.708	09	.690	10	.673	11	.656	11	.63
025	.806	07	.789	07	.772	08	.756	09	.739	10	.723	11	.707	12	.691	13	.675	14	.66
030	.817	08	.801	09	.786	10	.770	10	.755	11	.740	12	.726	14	.711	15	.697	16	.68
035	.829	09	.815	10	.801	11	.787	12	.774	13	.760	14	.747	15	.735	16	.722	18	.71
040	.843	10	.831	11	.818	12	.806	13	.794	14	.782	15	.771	16	.760	18	.750	19	.74
045	.859	10	.847	12	.837	13	.826	14	.816	15	.806	16	.797	18	.788	19	.779	20	.77
050	.875	11	.865	12	.856	13	.848	15	.839	16	.831	17	.824	18	.817	20	.810	21	.80
055	.892	12	.884	13	.877	14	.870	15	.864	17	.858	18	.852	19	.847	20	.842	22	.83
060	.910	12	.904	13	.899	15	.894	16	.889	17	.885	18	.881	20	.877	21	.874	22	.87
065	.929	12	.925	14	.921	15	.917	16	.915	17	.912	19	.910	20	.908	21	.907	22	.90
070	.948	13	.945	14	.943	15	.942	16	.941	17	.940	19	.940	20	.940	21	.940	22	.94
075	.967	13	.966	14	.966	15	.966	16	.967	17	.968	19	.969	20	.971	21	.973	22	.97
080	.986	13	.987	14	.989	15	.991	16	.993	17	.996	18	.999	20	1.002	21	1.006	22	1.0
085	1.005	13	1.008	14	1.011	15	1.015	16	1.019	17	1.023	18	1.028	19	1.033	20	1.038	21	1.04
090	1.024	12	1.028	13	1.033	15	1.038	16	1.044	17	1.050	18	1.056	19	1.063	20	1.070	21	1.07
095	1.042	12	1.049	13	1.055	14	1.062	15	1.069	16	1.076	17	1.084	18	1.092	19	1.100	20	1.10
100	1.061	12	1.068	13	1.076	14	1.084	15	1.093	16	1.102	17	1.111	18	1.120	18	1.130	19	1.14
105	1.078	11	1.087	12	1.096	13	1.106	14	1.116	15	1.126	16	1.136	17	1.147	18	1.158	18	1.16
110	1.095	11	1.105	12	1.116	13	1.127	14	1.138	14	1.149	15	1.161	16	1.173	17	1.185	18	1.19
115	1.111	10	1.123	11	1.135	12	1.147	13	1.159	14	1.172	14	1.184	15	1.197	16	1.211	17	1.22
120	1.126	10	1.139	11	1.152	11	1.166	12	1.179	13	1.193	13	1.206	14	1.220	15	1.235	15	1.24
125	1.141	09	1.155	10	1.169	11	1.183	11	1.198	12	1.212	12	1.227	13	1.242	14	1.257	14	1.27
130	1.154	08	1.169	09	1.184	10	1.199	10	1.215	11	1.230	11	1.246	12	1.262	13	1.278	13	1.29
135	1.166	08	1.182	08	1.198	09	1.214	09	1.231	10	1.247	10	1.263	11	1.280	11	1.297	12	1.31
140	1.177	07	1.194	07	1.211	08	1.228	08	1.245	09	1.262	09	1.279	10	1.297	10	1.314	11	1.33
145	1.187	06	1.204	07	1.222	07	1.240	07	1.258	08	1.275	08	1.293	09	1.311	09	1.329	09	1.34
150	1.196	05	1.214	06	1.232	06	1.250	06	1.269	07	1.287	07	1.306	07	1.324	08	1.343	08	1.36
155	1.203	04	1.222	05	1.241	05	1.259	05	1.278	06	1.297	06	1.316	06	1.335	07	1.354	07	1.37
160	1.209	04	1.228	04	1.247	04	1.267	04	1.286	05	1.305	05	1.325	05	1.344	05	1.363	05	1.38
165	1.214	03	1.233	03	1.253	03	1.273	03	1.292	03	1.312	04	1.331	04	1.351	04	1.371	04	1.39
170	1.217	02	1.237	02	1.257	02	1.277	02	1.296	02	1.316	02	1.336	03	1.356	03	1.376	03	1.39
175	1.219	01	1.239	01	1.259	01	1.279	01	1.299	01	1.319	01	1.339	01	1.359	01	1.379	01	1.39
180	1.220	00	1.240	00	1.260	00	1.280	00	1.300	00	1.320	00	1.340	00	1.360	00	1.380	00	1.40

FIG. 2163 Tabulation of Speed Factors (SF) and Course Corrections (CC) for the solution of Case 4 current sailing problems. Be careful to use the proper set of tabular factors for a Case 1, 3, or 4 problem; there is a separate table for each Case.

It might be supposed that the course corrections and speed factors above would be the same as those found in the preceding table and used in the examples for Case 1, but a careful comparison of the tables will reveal that this is not so. To illustrate, let us suppose that the drift is 20 percent and the relative set is 90°. Using the table of fig. 2154 for Case 1, we find that the current sets us off course by 11°. From the table of fig. 2159, however, we find that we must alter course 12° to compensate for the same current situation.

Also, when the course is not corrected, the speed factor is 1.020, which means that our speed of advance is two percent greater than our speed through the water (but, of course, it isn't getting us where we want to be). If, as in Case 3, we do "crab" into the current by the required 12°, the speed factor is 0.980, meaning that our actual speed of advance is two percent less than our speed through the water. Obviously, the two cases, and their respective tabulated factors, are different.

Case 4 solutions by tabular factors

This is a variation of Case 3 in which the pilot knows both where he wants to go and when he desires to arrive. Thus he has a desired track (TR) and speed of advance (SOA) in addition to the known or estimated set and drift of the current. He needs to determine *the course to be steered (C) and the necessary speed through the water (S).*

Fig. 2163 enables the pilot to determine these desired quantities without the construction of a vector diagram. Instead, he uses another set of course corrections (CC) and speed factors (SF). These factors are not the same as in either of the preceding tables and must be used for Case 4 problems only.

The speed to be run through the water (S) is determined by multiplying the desired speed of advance (SOA) by the tabular factor SF. The course to be steered is found by adding the correction angle CC to, or subtracting it from, the track (TR) in the same manner as for Case 3.

Course to be steered (C)

= TR − CC, when the relative set is positive.

= TR + CC, when the relative set is negative.

The same basic examples as before will be used, but again with different combinations of known and unknown elements.

Example J. (Fig. 2164)

Known: Track = 054° True

SOA = 7.4 knots

Set = 324°

Drift = 3 knots

To be determined: Course and Speed

Solution: Relative set = 324° − 054° = 270°

−360°

−090°

Percent drift $= \frac{3 \times 100}{7.4} = 40$

From the table: CC = 22°

SF = 1.077

Thus: Course = 054° + 22° = 076°

Speed = 7.4 x 1.077 = 8 knots

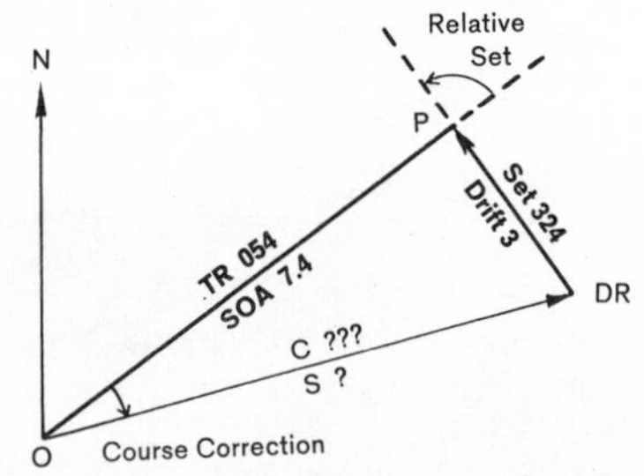

FIG. 2164 Example J—a Case 4 problem: Track 054° True, Speed of Advance 7.4 knots; Set 324°, Drift 3 knots. To be found: Course to be steered and Speed to be run through the water. See text for solution by tabular factors of fig. 2163.

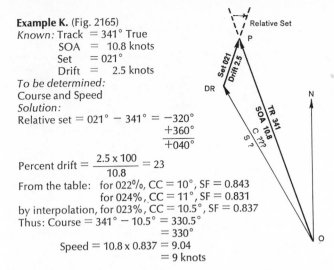

Example K. (Fig. 2165)
Known: Track = 341° True
    SOA = 10.8 knots
    Set = 021°
    Drift = 2.5 knots
To be determined:
Course and Speed
Solution:
Relative set = 021° − 341° = −320°
            +360°
            +040°

Percent drift = $\frac{2.5 \times 100}{10.8}$ = 23

From the table: for 022%, CC = 10°, SF = 0.843
        for 024%, CC = 11°, SF = 0.831
by interpolation, for 023%, CC = 10.5°, SF = 0.837
Thus: Course = 341° − 10.5° = 330.5°
            = 330°
    Speed = 10.8 × 0.837 = 9.04
            = 9 knots

FIG. 2165 Example K—a Case 4 problem in which both the Track and Speed of Advance are specified. The Course to be steered and the Speed to be run through the water are the values to be found by the application of tabulated course correction and speed factor.

FIG. 2166 Example L—a Case 4 problem to be solved by use of the factors from fig. 2163. Given: Track 024° True, Speed of Advance 8.6 knots; Set 156°, Drift 2 knots. To be found: Course and Speed.

Example L. (Fig. 2166)
Known: Track = 024° True
    SOA = 8.6 knots
    Set = 156°
    Drift = 2 knots
To be determined:
Course and Speed
Solution:
Relative set = 156° − 024° = +132°

Percent drift = $\frac{2 \times 100}{8.6}$ = 23

From the table, by double interpolation,
    for 132°/23% : CC = 8.3°
            SF = 1.167
Thus: Course = 024° − 8.3° = 015.3°
            = 015°
    Speed = 8.6 × 1.167 = 10 knots

PILOTING IN CURRENTS: GENERAL RESUME OF THE THREE CASES		CASE 1	CASE 3	CASE 4
KNOWN: Set and Drift, plus		Course	Track	Track
		Speed Through Water	Speed Through Water	Speed of Advance
DESIRED:		Speed of Advance	Speed of Advance	Speed Through Water
		Track	Course	Course
Calculate Before Using Table	% Drift	Drift X 100 / Speed Through Water	Drift X 100 / Speed Through Water	Drift X 100 / Speed of Advance
	Relative Set	SET—COURSE (180° or less to port or starboard)	SET—TRACK (180° or less to port or starboard)	SET—TRACK (180° or less to port or starboard)
Read from table, interpolating, if necessary	SF	Speed factor	Speed factor	Speed factor
	CC	Course Change	Course Correction	Course Correction
ANSWERS		Speed of Advance = (Speed through water) X SF	Speed of Advance = (Speed through water) X SF	Speed Through Water = (Speed of Advance) X SF
	If Rel. Set is positive (to St'bd.)	TRACK = COURSE + CC	COURSE = TRACK − CC	COURSE = TRACK − CC
	If Rel. Set is negative (to Port)	TRACK = COURSE − CC	COURSE = TRACK + CC	COURSE = TRACK + CC

Summary of tabular factor solutions

Fig. 2167 is a consolidated presentation of the procedures used in the solution of current sailing problems using tabulated factors of course and speed corrections. The numbering of the cases corresponds to the basic presentation of current problems in Chapter 20 and the examples above.

In all of the cases presented here, the set and drift of the current were considered to be known values, as determined from the Tidal Current Tables or Charts, or from visual observations. Thus, Case 2 of the current sailing problems—the determination of the characteristics of an unknown current from the measurement of its effects—is omitted from this tabular technique.

FIG. 2167 Summary of the procedures for the solution of certain current sailing problems by the use of pre-computed factors and corrections.

Specialized Positioning Procedures

In addition to the generally used procedures for position determination previously described in this chapter, there are other, more specialized, techniques. These should not be scorned as "short cuts"; they will provide valid position information and fixes under the particular circumstances that permit their use.

COMBINATIONS OF RELATIVE BEARINGS

The bow-and-beam-bearings technique has already been described, fig. 2140. This was a particular set of two relative bearings, 045° and 090° (or 315° and 270°). It was included there because of its basic simplicity and the ease with which such a pair of bearings could be obtained. There are other combinations of relative bearings, not so easily obtained, but quite easily used.

Special pairs of bearings

The following sets of bearings have such a relationship to each other that the run between the first bearing and the second will nearly equal the distance away from the sighted object when it is passed abeam:

20°-30°, 21°-32°, 22°-34°, 23°-36°, 24°-39°, 25°-41°, 27°-46°, 29°-51°, 30°-54°, 31°-56°, 32°-59°, 34°-64°, 35°-67°, 36°-69°, 37°-71°, 38°-74°, 39°-77°, 40°-79°, 41°-81°, 43°-86°, 44°-88°.

There are also additional pairs of angles that could theoretically be used, but these involve half-degrees and have been omitted here as such precision is not usually obtainable on small craft.

It should be noted that these are pairs of relative bearings to port as well as to starboard. In the table above, "20°-30°" can be either relative bearings 020° and 030°, or 340° and 330°; "31°-56°" can be either RB 031° and 056°, or RB 329° and 304°; etc.

The 7/8th rule

If observations are made when the relative bearings are 30° and 60° on either bow, simple calculations will give *two* useful items of information. The distance run between the two bearings is equal to the distance to the object at the time of the second bearing (doubling the angle on the bow). Also, this same distance, fig. 2168, multiplied by $7/8$ is the distance that the craft will be off from the sighted object when it is broad on the beam, provided that course and speed are not changed.

The 7/10th rule

A situation comparable to the preceding rule is that which exists when the two relative bearings are $22\frac{1}{2}°$ and $45°$ to port or starboard (assuming that bearings can be taken to a half-degree). In this case, as before, the distance away from the sighted object at the time of the second bearing is equal to the distance run between bearings, but the multiplier is 7/10 to determine the distance off the sighted object when it is abeam.

THREE BEARINGS AND RUN BETWEEN

The technique of using *two* bearings and the run between them was illustrated in fig. 2142. The positional information derived from this procedure was dependent upon the assumption that the course and speed made good with respect to the bottom during the run between bearings was accurately known. Along strange coasts, without current predictions or means of estimating current effects, this assumption is often of doubtful validity.

By taking a *third* bearing and timing a second run (between the second and third bearings), enough additional known factors are entered into the problem so that no assumption need be made about the course made good nor the actual speed over the bottom. All that is required for this technique is a prominent object or mark on shore, plus the means for taking bearings and measuring time intervals.

As soon as you spot the object, "X" in fig. 2169, take a bearing on it and note the exact time; record both items of information. Plot the bearing line on your chart, line XA in fig. 2169(a). Next, when the object is exactly broad on the beam, note the time. Plot this line of position on the chart. Later, when the bearing to X has changed enough to give a good angle of intersection, take a third bearing and again note the time carefully. Plot this line, XC. Be sure that throughout this procedure you are maintaining a steady course and speed through the water.

Since you have recorded the time of each bearing, you can determine the two elapsed times, and compute the *ratio* between these intervals.

For example, if you ran for $32\frac{1}{2}$ minutes between the first and second (beam) bearings, and then for $22\frac{1}{2}$ minutes more to the third bearing, the ratio would be $32\frac{1}{2}/22\frac{1}{2}$, which can be reduced to 6.5/4.5.

Through a convenient point, B, on the beam bearing line, draw a light "construction" line in the direction of your course (C) as steered. Using point "B" as the reference or zero point, measure off to each side, along the construction line, distances proportional to the ratio of the time intervals using any convenient scale, fig. 2169(b).

Erect perpendiculars to the construction line at the spots determined by these proportionate distances. These lines, drawn at $90°$ angles to the construction line, intersect the bearing lines XA and XC at points A′ and C′ respectively, fig. 2169(c).

Connect points A′ and C′ with a line and you have your answer. Line A′-C′ is the course you are making good and

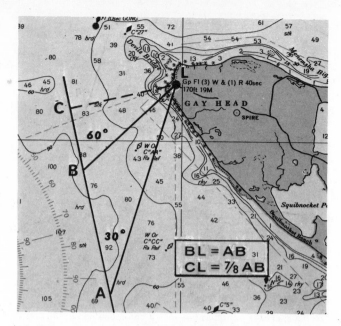

FIG. 2168 If observations are made when the relative bearings of a fixed object are 30° and 60°, and the distance made good between these observations is calculated, the pilot can determine his distance from the object both at the time of the second bearing and when it is abeam by the "⅞th Rule."

it includes all effects of current, wind, steering errors, etc. Point A′ was your position at the time of the first bearing and point C′ at the time of the third bearing.

It is because we are using a *ratio,* and not speed, that the accuracy of speed over the bottom as affected by current need not be known by the pilot in order to determine his course and position. Actually, the true speed over the bottom can be found easily. The distance from point A′ to point C′ can be determined from the chart scale, the elapsed time is the sum of the two intervals; thus the speed being made good can be calculated.

This simple graphic solution shows plainly whether you are making good your intended track, or whether you are being set off shore or on shore. It helps you to determine whether your course parallels the beach and therefore is valuable along a poorly marked coast.

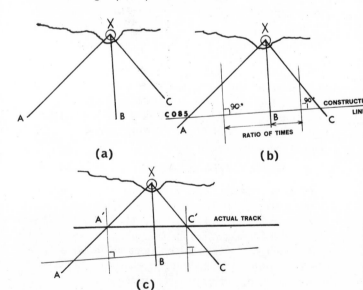

FIG. 2169 The actual track of a boat under unknown conditions of current can be determined by taking three bearings on a single object. See text for details of this technique.

Relative Motion

The easiest way to acquire what is often called a "sailor's eye" is to learn the simple, but basic, principles of *relative motion*. The term "relative motion" scares some people, but it is really quite a simple subject to master. It is also one of the most useful skills that a boatman can acquire as it gives quick and accurate answers to problems involving moving vessels.

For example, you find that your motorboat is converging on another boat that has the right of way. If you hold your present course and speed, will you clear her? Or your sailboat is beating to windward on a port tack, and you find a boat coming in on the starboard tack. Will you cross safely ahead, or must you pass astern? Or you have laid a course for a buoy, making allowance for the current. Have you made the right allowance? Relative motion will give you the answers to all such questions.

When a boat is under way, its movement across the water is termed *actual motion*. If it is anchored, the movements of another craft appear in their actual relationship to the earth's surface; you are observing that boat's actual motion. But if you get under way, the movement of the other boat appears to be different because you are now observing *relative motion*. Some objects, especially moving ones, seem to be doing things that are not actually happening; elements of what may be almost an optical illusion can exist.

Let us suppose that you are under way and proceeding north at 5 knots up a marked channel. You sight another boat coming directly toward you; this other craft is also making 5 knots. The two boats are converging at a *relative speed* of 10 knots which is simply the sum of your speed and his. Both craft are passing the stationary channel markers at the same actual speed, but the distance between them is lessening at a rate which is the sum of the individual speeds.

As the other boat approaches, you recognize the skipper as a friend and turn around to join him on his southerly course. As soon as the boats are alongside each other on the same course and at the same speed, *relative motion* ceases to exist because the other boat stays in the same place relative to your boat. Only *actual motion* remains—that of your boat past the buoys and over the bottom. If the other craft develops engine trouble and slows down, there is again relative motion between the two vessels. He will appear to be moving aft because of his reduced speed. Thus, the rule may be stated as follows: *relative motion is present only when the actual movements of two or more objects are not the same.*

Relative bearings

The bearing of an object is usually taken as a relative bearing; these were discussed in pages 352a, b. See fig. 2170. With practice, the relative bearing of an object can be estimated within five or ten degrees. It must be remembered that a change in course of your own boat will change the relative bearings of all objects around it. Thus, if you are on a course of 050° True and sight an object bearing 090° relative, the true bearing of that object will be 140°, fig. 2171a. Come left to a course of 020°, and although the true bearing will remain unchanged at 140°, the rela-

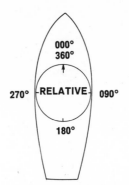

FIG. 2170 In determining relative motion in small-craft piloting, much use is made of relative bearings measured clockwise from 000° dead ahead.

tive bearing will now become 120°, fig. 2171b.

In small craft piloting, approximations will usually suffice in relative motion problems and special instruments are not needed. A steady hand at the wheel or tiller, a clear eye, and a rough mental diagram are all that are needed. A pelorus can be used, but seldom is, in actual practice.

TO CROSS OR NOT TO CROSS

When determining the relative motion of another boat, it is necessary either to convert relative bearings to compass (or true) bearings, or to maintain a steady course. In practice, it is easier to maintain a steady course, with the result that any change in relative bearing will be the result of a change in the positions of the boats relative to each other, rather than the result of the changing course of your craft. Since the desired information is the changing positions of the boats relative to each other, the actual value of the relative bearing is of far less importance than the direction and rate of change, if any.

Collision bearings

What we want to know in any crossing or converging situation is: will we cross ahead of, or astern of, the other boat, or will we hit her? Because the two boats are considered relative to each other, it is convenient to think of one's own boat as stationary—relative to the other boat. Thus, we have three basic situations:

1. The relative bearing of the other boat moves ahead (toward the bow), or
2. The relative bearing of the other boat moves aft, or
3. The relative bearing of the other boat remains constant.

Fig. 2172a illustrates the first situation, that of a boat passing ahead. This illustration indicates the actual successive positions of the two boats. Fig. 2172b represents

FIG. 2171 If a boat's heading changes, the relative bearing of an object is changed by the same amount. From the situation in *a* below to that in *b*, the true heading of the boat has changed from 050° to 020°; the relative bearing has changed by the same amount, from 090° to 120°. (Note that the sum of the heading and the relative bearing remains constant.)

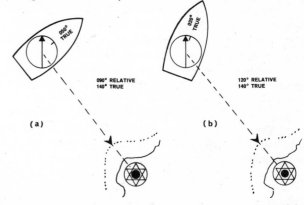

(a)   (b)

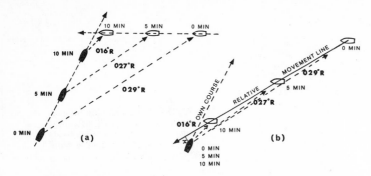

FIG. 2172 The positions of two boats are shown for three intervals of time separated by five minutes each. In *a*, the actual positions of each craft are shown. In *b*, the motion of the other boat is shown *relative* to our craft. In both cases, the relative bearings move forward on our boat and the other craft will cross ahead of us. The distance *x* is the separation at the *point of closest approach.*

the same situation shown in terms of motion relative to our own boat as stationary. The bearing change is then more clearly seen.

The line connecting the positions of the other boat in fig. 2172b is the *line of relative movement,* the relative course and relative distance traveled by the other boat in relationship to our boat. Provided both boats maintain course and speed, it is a straight line. In this situation, when the line of relative motion is extended, it passes the bow of our "stationary" boat; therefore, the other boat following that line relative to us will cross ahead. The distance "*x*" fig. 2172b is the distance apart that the two boats will be at the *closest point of approach* (CPA).

The second case, in which the relative bearing moves aft, is the opposite of the first situation. The relative mo-

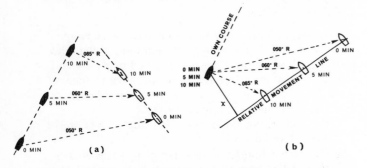

FIG. 2173 In this crossing situation, the relative bearings move aft, and the other boat will pass astern of us (we will pass ahead of her). The actual successive positions of each craft are shown in *a*, and relative motion is shown in *b*.

tion line passes astern, and so will the other boat. Figs. 2173a and b illustrate this situation.

If the relative bearing does not change, the line of relative motion will pass through our boat's position, the distance "*x*" is zero, and the two boats will collide unless one or both changes course or speed. See figs. 2174a and b.

It is important to note that figs. 2172-2174 are intended to illustrate situations rather than actual chart plots on a boat. The position of the other craft could not be plotted unless distance as well as bearing information was available, and this is unlikely unless your boat has radar. The significance here is that *bearing information only,* which is available to any pilot, will by its change, if any, tell him whether he will pass ahead, astern, or "through" the other craft. The closest point of approach can be determined only if an actual plot based on distances is made, but lack of this information is not significant.

Rules for crossing situations

The foregoing discussion, formulated into rules, results in the following procedures for a crossing situation:

1. Maintain a reasonably steady course and speed.
2. Observe the relative bearing of the other boat only when you are on your specified compass course. You must be on the *same* course each time you take a relative bearing.
3. Watch the other boat for changes in course or speed which would obviously upset the relative motion conditions.
4. (a) If the relative bearing moves ahead, the other boat will pass ahead.
   (b) If the relative bearing moves aft, the other craft will pass astern.
   (c) If the relative bearing is steady, there is a dangerous possibility of collision.

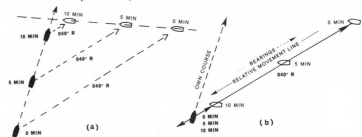

FIG. 2174 Here is a crossing situation in which the relative bearing does *not* change! A collision will result if both craft maintain course and speed. Note that in *b* the line of relative movement passes *through* our boat and the value of *x* is reduced to zero.

Offsetting effects of current or wind

There is another useful application of relative motion in the case of allowances for offsetting the effects of current and/or wind.

In fig. 2175, the boat has been put on a course that her skipper believes will put her close aboard the buoy marking the shoal. At the time of the first bearing, "0" minutes, the buoy bears 340° relative. Five minutes later, the relative bearing has changed to 350°. It is clear from this change that the boat is being set down more than expected and that the relative movement line of the buoy will pass ahead of the boat, i.e., the boat will pass on the shoal side of the buoy. If the bearings on the buoy remained steady, the boat would pass close to it; and if the bearings shifted gradually away from the bow, the skipper would know that he would clear the shoal safely.

In fig. 2175a, the problem is shown in terms of the boat moving relative to the buoy. In fig. 2175b, the boat is considered to be stationary and the relative movement line is that of the buoy. Note that the relative movement lines in the two representations are parallel, equal, and opposite.

FIG. 2175 Relative motion considerations are also applicable when the other "craft" is stationary, such as a buoy. The change, if any, of the relative bearings on the object can be used to determine on which side of it you will pass. In *a* and *b* below, the motion is considered relative to the buoy and to your boat, respectively.

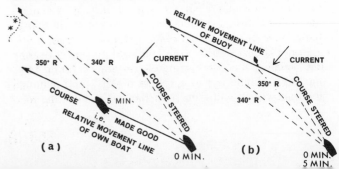

The Maneuvering Board

Since 1920, the U.S. Naval Oceanographic Office (formerly the Hydrographic Office) has published a plotting sheet known as the *Maneuvering Board (H.O. 2665)*. This device is used by all maritime services for the solution of relative motion problems. Complicated movements of large task forces, as well as the tracking of a single ship, are plotted on maneuvering boards to facilitate the solution of problems of interception and the determination of the course and speed of radar contacts.

Use on boats

Here we will consider a few of the simpler, though useful, applications of the maneuvering board, using only the plotting sheet, parallel rulers or equivalent, and a pair of dividers. For the fortunate yachtsman who has radar aboard, however, the applications are increased ten-fold.

Description of the sheet

To observe the physical appearance of a maneuvering board, examine fig. 2176 which shows one reduced about 40% from its original size of approximately 12 inches square. On it is printed, in green, a large circle with bearing lines radiating outward from the center every 10 degrees, and 10 concentric circles ½ inch apart to indicate speed or distance. At the right and left sides are lines of scale with numbered marks spaced equal to the distance between the concentric circles. Thus, a speed line drawn out to the fifth circle could indicate 5, 10, 15, 20, or 25 knots as determined by your choice of scale.

At the bottom of the sheet are three lines divided into logarithmic scales for use in solving time, distance, and speed problems. If two of these quantities are known, the third may be found by drawing a line between the known values on the appropriate scales, and finding the answer at the intersection of this line with the third scale.

In fig. 2177, observe the solution to three problems: (1) if you run 6 miles in 30 minutes, your speed is 12 knots; (2) to run 6 miles at 12 knots will require 30 minutes; or (3) running at 12 knots for 30 minutes, you will cover 6 miles. Distance, time, speed—knowing two, you can quickly, easily, and accurately solve for the third. This alone makes the maneuvering board a handy device, but it is only a small sample of its usefulness.

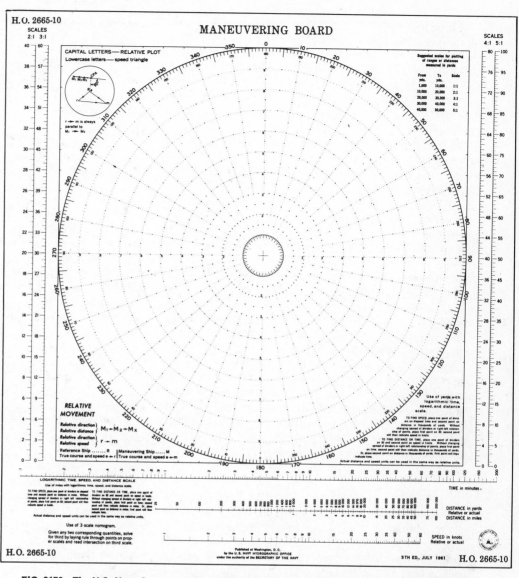

FIG. 2176 The U.S. Navy Oceanographic Office (formerly the Hydrographic Office) publishes pads of a useful plotting sheet known as a *maneuvering board*. These sheets are particularly handy when plotting situations or relative motion.

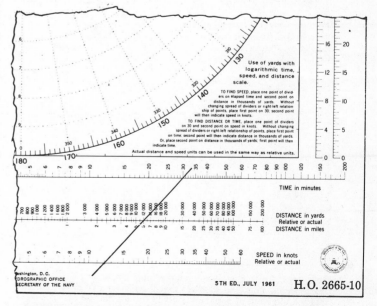

FIG. 2177 Extract from a maneuvering board showing the logarithmic distance-time-speed scales. The problem illustrated by the line drawn across the scales is discussed in the text.

The bearing lines and circles of distance facilitate the plotting of positions of other craft or objects relative to the boat on which the maneuvering board is being used. These radial lines and concentric circles can also be used for vector diagrams with lines drawn to represent actual and relative motion. Each vector, according to its length and direction, depicts a statement of fact in the problem. For example: a vector line to indicate a course of 040° and a speed of 5 knots would be drawn outward along the 40° bearing line to a length of 5 units, i.e., to the fifth circle. If the speed is greater than 10 units (knots or MPH), use is made of the 2:1, 3:1, 4:1, or 5:1 scales at the sides of the chart.

A vector line indicates graphically the direction and velocity of an element of the problem, such as the course and speed of your boat, another boat, the wind, or the current. In some instances, the vector will not be drawn from the center of the sheet, but its direction is always measured with reference to the center point and the outer circular scale.

Points on diagrams of positions are labeled with upper-case (capital) letters; points on vector diagrams are labeled with lower-case letters.

Maneuvering boards come in pads of 50 sheets. Each sheet is printed on both sides, and the paper is sufficiently heavy that both sides may be used. The fifth edition of H.O. 2665 includes condensed instructions in each of the four corners, outside the circular scale. The pad comes with a cover sheet on which is printed a "sample problem" but this, unfortunately, is a problem of interest to naval task force commanders, not boatmen.

USE OF THE MANEUVERING BOARD

The H.O. 2665 sheets may well be used for plots of the relative motion of two vessels in a crossing situation as shown in figs. 2172-2174. These sheets are particularly useful on board radar-equipped craft where distance as well as bearing can be measured. Fig. 2178, for example, is a re-plot of fig. 2173b on a maneuvering board sheet.

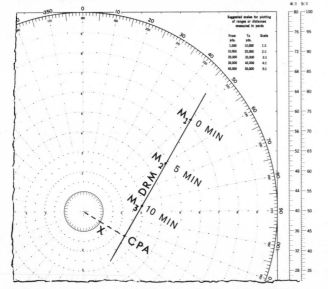

FIG. 2178 This is a re-plot of the situation of fig. 2173b on a Maneuvering Board sheet. Note that the plot has been rotated so that the direction of one's own boat is toward the top of the sheet (RB 000° dead ahead). The direction of relative motion (DRM) can be readily taken from the sheet, and the point of closest approach (CPA) and "miss distance" easily determined.

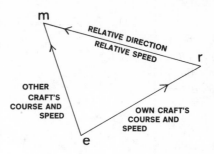

FIG. 2179 A vector triangle of relative motion. The course and speed of your own craft is plotted as *e - r* and the apparent (relative) motion of the other craft as *r - m*. The triangle can be closed with the line *e - m* which is the *actual* course and speed of the other craft.

From a plot such as fig. 2178, with successive relative positions of the other craft plotted at recorded times, the direction of relative movement (DRM) and speed of relative movement (SRM) can be found. SRM is determined from the logarithmic scales at the bottom of the sheet using distance and time as the known factors. Knowing these relative motion quantities, and the course and speed of your own boat, a *vector triangle* can be used to determine the *actual* course and speed of the other craft. The relationships between these quantities are shown in fig. 2179. Point e, always at the center of the maneuvering board, represents earth, the reference for actual motion. Point r is the outer end of the speed vector, *e-r*, for the *reference* craft (your boat). The vector *r-m* represents the relative motion of the *maneuvering* (other) craft. By completing the triangle with the vector *e-m*, always outward from the point e at the center, the actual course and speed of the other boat are found. When such a vector triangle is drawn on a maneuvering board sheet, as in fig. 2180, the actual course can be read directly from the outer circular scale, and the actual speed can be read from the convenient concentric circles of the sheet, remembering to apply the same scale factor as used in plotting the speed of your own boat.

True wind problem

Fig. 2181 illustrates what is called a *true wind problem*.

Situation: Your sailboat is close-hauled on true course 080°, speed 5 knots. The apparent (relative) wind is coming over the starboard side from 125° true with a velocity of 15 knots.

Problem: You want to sail your boat as close to the wind as possible, say at an angle of 45° off the true wind. You wish to know the direction and velocity of the *actual* wind so as to be able to determine whether you can lay the mark on the next tack, and the best course that you will be able to make to windward.

Solution: Draw your course and speed vector, *e-r*, along the bearing line for 080° outward from the center for 2½ circles (5 knots at a scale of 2:1). From point r, draw a line for the relative wind in the direction *toward* which the wind is traveling; use parallel rulers or another plotting instrument to transfer this direction from the bearing line out to the point r. With dividers, measure off the length for 15 knots along the 2:1 scale at the left side of the chart; lay off this distance along the relative wind line and so obtain the vector for that element of the problem. Where this vector ends is point w.

Next, draw a line from point e at the center to point w;

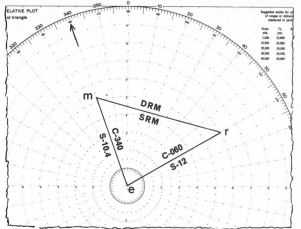

FIG. 2180 This is a re-plot of the preceding illustration on a Maneuvering Board sheet. The actual course of the other craft can be read directly from the outer scale of figures and the speed from the concentric rings; note that in this example the speed ratio is 2:1, each circle represents 2 knots or MPH.

this vector, e-w, represents the direction and velocity of the *true wind*. Since wind direction is never expressed in terms of where it is going (blowing toward), we look directly across the board and see that it is blowing *from* 142°. The velocity of 12 knots is read directly from the circles, the sixth circle at a scale of 2:1. Now it can be seen that the motion of your boat through the water has caused the apparent wind to come from a direction 17° counter-clockwise from its true direction. (The actual wind velocity is seen to be less than the apparent velocity, but this information is not pertinent to this particular problem.)

To determine our course for sailing at an angle of 45° to the actual wind on the next, port, tack, it is merely a matter of adding 45° to the true wind direction of 142° to get 187°.

Current sailing problems

One problem common to both sail boats and motor boats is that of choosing the correct course in traversing an area where the current will set the craft off her intended track if allowances are not made. In fig. 2182 we have the graphic solution of two questions. What is the current doing? What course do we take to correct for it?

Assume that your boat is on course 320° at a speed of 6 knots to pass close aboard a light vessel that now, at 0800, is dead ahead, 9 miles distant. As you progress through the water on your specified course, you notice that the light vessel appears to be moving to your left. This indicates that a current is at work on your port side.

To learn the set and drift of the current, and the course needed to correct for it: Plot the 0800 position of the light vessel from you—320°, 9 miles. Fix your present position and determine from the chart the new relative position of the light vessel. In fig. 2182 this is 310° and 7 miles; label this position with the time, 0829.

Now, draw in your boat's course and speed vector, e-r, of 320° and 6 knots, using a 2:1 scale ratio and the third circle. Note that the same scale ratio does not have to be used for both distance and speeds; it must, however, be constant within either category.

With parallel rulers or other plotting instrument, transfer the direction of the line of relative movement between the two plots of the light vessel's position to point r and draw in a line to some convenient length. After measuring the distance "traveled" by the light vessel, solve for its relative speed using the distance-time-speed logarithmic

scales. In this case, 2.4 miles in 29 minutes gives 5.2 knots.

Using the speed scale factor of 2:1, the speed of 5.2 knots is laid off along the line drawn from r. The point so found is labeled m and a line drawn *from m* to e at the center represents the set and drift of the current. This is found to be 080° and 3 knots.

With this information, we can now determine a new course to correct for the effect of the current. Remembering that our vessel *never* leaves the center of the maneuvering board, we must make the light vessel "come to us." A line drawn from the 0829 position of the light vessel, the broken line in fig. 2182, is the line that we wish the light vessel to follow on its way to us.

Parallel a line to this, starting at a convenient distance out, beyond the third circle (6 knots at our 2:1 speed scale), and draw toward point m in the same direction as the intended track of the light vessel; this is line a-m in the illustration. Where this relative movement line crosses the third circle is the course to steer for a speed of 6 knots —287°. It should be noted that there are many possible

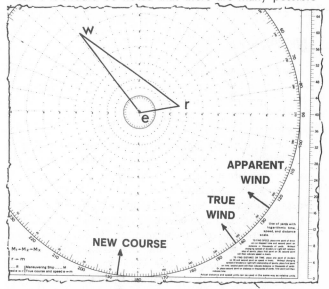

FIG. 2181 The maneuvering board can be used to determine the velocity and direction of the true wind to aid in setting a new course on the next tack. See the text for details of this technique.

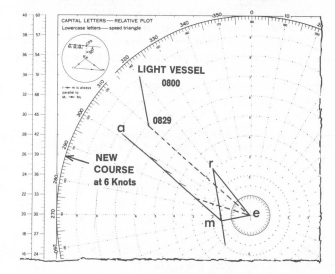

FIG. 2182 In this problem, a maneuvering board sheet enables the pilot to determine the current setting the boat off the desired track. It is also possible to graphically determine the necessary new course to be steered for any given speed.

combinations of courses and speeds available along this line, and that any increase in speed would bring a lesser course change, and vice versa. For example: looking out along the line *a-m*, we would find that for 8 knots, the course would be 293°; for 10 knots, 297°; for 12 knots, 299°.

Other uses for the maneuvering board

The examples above have barely touched on the many uses of the maneuvering board sheets. There are many more applications—all interesting, but of lesser direct use in small-craft boating. Those interested in this topic in more detail can satisfy their curiosity in the many pages of *Bowditch* and *Dutton* devoted to the maneuvering board and its uses.

A pad of 50 maneuvering boards (H.O. 2665-10) may be obtained almost anywhere that Oceanographic Office publications are sold. The cost is only a few cents for each sheet, a small price to pay for safety and interesting, easy piloting!

Longshore Piloting

There are a number of specialized techniques that might well be a part of every skipper's piloting skills. Their practicability has been thoroughly tested.

DELIBERATE OFFSET OF COURSE

One of these specialized piloting techniques is used in making a landfall. The essence of it is this—lay your course, *not* for your objective, but decidedly to one side to allow for possible inaccuracies in the offsetting effect of the current, or to account for possible uncertainties of position. The advantage of this procedure lies in the fact that should you not arrive at your destination at the scheduled time, you have a near-certainty, rather than considerable doubt, as to which way you should turn to reach your objective.

The technique is best explained by use of an example.

Situation

Let us assume that you have been fishing somewhere in the area between Block Island and Martha's Vineyard. After several hours of trolling, drifting, and just circling around, your position is quite problematical. Just as you decide that your fishing luck has run out for the day and it is time to head for Block Island Harbor, fog sets in to make the situation more interesting.

Your best "guesstimate," in the absence of any positional information, is that you are somewhere to the east of bell buoy "1", marked as point *B* in fig. 2183; you believe that you are somewhere in the vicinity of point *A* on the chart.

Solution with deliberate offset of course

It's a good plan to lay your course for the off-lying bell buoy—as a matter of fact, that's what they are there for—but even if there were no such buoy, there can be merit in laying the course decidedly off to one side of the ultimate objective, Block Island Harbor.

Suppose you lay your course AB to the bell buoy and miss it by ⅛ mile to the north. When you pick up the 3-fathom (18-foot) curve, at *C,* you know you are north of

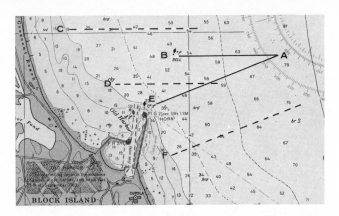

FIG. 2183 If you are caught in a fog somewhere offshore in the vicinity of point A, the inclination might be to head directly for the harbor entrance at E. It is much safer, however, to deliberately head for a point more to the north on a course that will take you past the bell buoy at B. The text explains why.

the harbor—a fact confirmed by the realization that you would have picked it up much sooner if you were south of the harbor entrance.

Had you missed it by ⅛ mile to the south, and picked up the 3-fathom curve at *D,* you could still follow the curve southeastward to buoy C "3". Even if your position were ¼ mile south of *A* when you laid your course westward, you would still pick up the 3-fathom curve at the harbor entrance.

You find added assurance of your general position above the harbor entrance when you find depths holding generally at 3 fathoms on your course southeastward. If your calculations were completely wrong and you ran southeastward from any point below the harbor entrance, depths would increase.

Solution without deliberate offset of course

Consider, however, what could happen if you missed your objective E by ¼ mile to the south if the course had been laid direct to buoy C "3". Picking up the 3-fathom curve at F, you could not be sure whether you were north or south of the entrance.

Your first conclusion might be that, since you have run a few minutes overtime before reaching the 3-fathom curve, you are north of the harbor. But don't forget that you didn't accurately know your starting point. Suppose you had been several minutes eastward of where you thought you were when the fog set in. In this event, the additional few minutes running time before reaching 18-foot depths is reasonable.

On the assumption that you are indeed somewhat to the north of the harbor, you turn south, proceeding slowly and carefully. A few minutes pass, but still no buoy or harbor entrance. How far to continue? That buoy may be just ahead, obscured by the fog. On the other hand, doubt creeps in. You couldn't have been that far off in your reckoning—or could you? So there you are, in a fog—literally and figuratively.

General procedures

In the first example above (where we laid a course for the bell) the intended track was laid about ⅜ mile to the north of the objective (the harbor entrance). How much deliberate offset of course is made in any given case varies within limits determined by what you feel would be a maximum error under the circumstances. On a long run in from offshore, making a landfall on a beach that trends in a straight line for miles in either direction with few marks of identification even if visibility is good, you may prefer to make an allowance of a mile or more. It adds little to the total run, but eliminates much uncertainty. But don't use this technique blindly, without regard to possible dangers that may line the beach. Study the chart carefully and adapt the procedure to the situation at hand.

Crossing the Gulf Stream

This same procedure may be used in crossing the Gulf Stream. Rather than attempting to make an exact allowance for the distance you will be set northward, a somewhat overly-generous allowance is made, with the knowledge that if you don't pick up your target landmark after the allotted passage time, you have only to turn northward. It can be comforting to know the proper direction in which to turn, rather than to have to make a choice with perhaps a 50-50 chance of being wrong.

The same technique can be used in recrossing the Gulf Stream on your westward passage back to Florida. Again, over-allow for the northward offsetting influence of the Stream and plan to turn northward as you approach the coast if you see no identifiable landmarks.

NIGHT PILOTING BY TIMETABLE

Another specialized piloting technique that will go far toward increasing the pleasure of nighttime piloting is the establishment of a "timetable" for your particular cruise.

Preparing the timetable

When you anticipate a night run, don't wait until you are on your way before studying out courses, distances, running times, etc. Go over the entire trip in advance and acquaint yourself thoroughly with the separate legs of the cruise, the aids to navigation that you will pass, the characteristics of the lights, and other items of piloting interest.

Then set up a timetable, assuming that you will leave your point of departure at exactly 0000, and note in orderly fashion the predicted time of arrival abeam of every light and buoy on both sides of your intended track. Alongside each entry, show the characteristics of the navigational aid and the compass course at the time. You can also enter into your timetable the approximate times that major lights can be expected to become visible.

Using the timetable

Invest in an alarm clock or watch with a luminous dial and set it for 12 o'clock when you start your run from the point of departure on which your predetermined timetable is based. Then as the flashing, occulting, or other lights successively wink over the horizon, you won't have to dash below to puzzle out characteristics and identify each in turn. The elapsed time from your start will clue you as to the identity of the aid to navigation.

The timetable will aid you in knowing where you are at any time, what light you just passed, what the characteristics will be of the next light to appear, and when that should happen. The use of elapsed time, rather than actual clock time, allows flexibility in the starting time; it is not necessary to revise your entire timetable if you take your departure earlier or later than originally planned. If any discrepancy creeps in consistently between when events should happen and when they actually do, the hands of the clock or watch can be shifted as needed.

NIGHT COASTWISE PILOTING
BY SHORE LIGHTS

For night piloting alongshore, the lights of towns and settlements along the beach can be used to estimate distances offshore. An experienced boatman reports that he has been able to maintain a course approximately 5½ miles offshore going down the Jersey coast simply by keeping in sight of the reflected glow in the sky above lights in towns along the shore.

The appearance of direct rays of light would be a signal indicating that the distance offshore was decreasing to 5 miles or less, whereupon it would be advisable to haul off until only the reflected glow was visible once more. The objective of keeping so far offshore was to avoid the extensive areas of fish net stakes, and yet not lose contact with land.

The distance that the direct rays will be seen will be determined by the height of the observer's eye, and should be determined by the individual skipper for his own boat. The principles involved, however, remain the same for all craft.

FOLLOWING THE BEACH

Elsewhere, we have considered how a boat may be piloted along a coast by following a constant depth, or fathom curve. It is possible, however, that the sounder might be inoperative or not available for some other reason. It is well to have another means of following the shoreline approximately when visibility conditions permit the observation of objects on the beach.

Let's say that you wish to parallel the Jersey or Long Island beach (or any average coast where there are no hills or mountains ashore to stand out prominently at long range). Fig. 2184 shows such a coastline. From the deck of a typical small boat at sea, you will be unable to see the beach if you are more than about 4½ miles offshore, due to the earth's curvature. If you can just make out the beach, you are approximately 4 miles out. This, naturally, will not hold true if there is haze or fog.

FIG. 2184 With just a little effort, you can determine for your height of eye on your boat the distances offshore at which you can see the beach and certain features of the buildings. Your distances shouldn't vary much from those shown here for a typical boat.

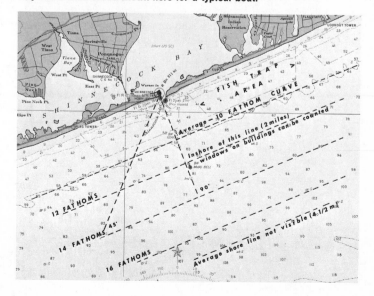

Specialized Piloting Techniques / CHAPTER 21

Distance off by visibility of details

Now as you follow the coast, you will probably trend in closer without realizing that you are off your intended track. Buildings appear, and you find that you can distinguish detail enough to make out individual windows of houses. This means that you are roughly within 2 miles of the beach.

Thus, you have established two limits, by keeping within sight of the beach, but far enough off that you cannot count windows, you are averaging 2 to 4 miles offshore. Meticulous pilots may object that this is too loose, but there are many cruises that do not require any higher degree of precision.

Check for your height-of-eye

The 2-mile distance at which windows can be counted will not vary with the observer's height of eye. This is a matter of distance and detail. The 4- to 4½-mile limits of visibility for the beach itself, however, are subject to variation from one boat to another. These are average figures; establish more exact distances for your own craft by using the bow-and-beam bearings technique or any other positioning procedure.

A NEW POSITION FINDER

Earlier in this chapter, we considered a positioning technique using two horizontal angles between the lines of sight to three identifiable objects. See figs. 2124-2126. Although this is a standard method, it has not been widely used on small boats because a sextant is normally required to measure the angles and a three-arm protractor to plot them accurately. As a sextant would be a relatively large investment for this use only, those who do not venture onto the high seas and use celestial navigation do not normally have one aboard.

The Weems Position-Finder is a combination instrument that can be used both to measure the angles and do the chart plotting. It eliminates the need for a sextant for making observations, and the attendant steps of reading angles from the sextant scale and setting these values on the protractor. This results in a saving of time, effort, and risk of error. As the observations are taken, the arms of this instrument are locked in position, and the device becomes, in effect, a three-arm protractor with the angles already set. The actual values of the angles need never be known. The solution is entirely independent of the compass or other instruments. The optical principle employed is shown in fig. 2185.

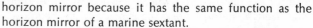

FIG. 2187 The position-finder in place on a chart. The arms are set directly as the observations are made, and no angles need be read in order to determine the fix. The three arms are aligned with the chart symbols for the objects sighted upon; the observer's position is at the center of the instrument.

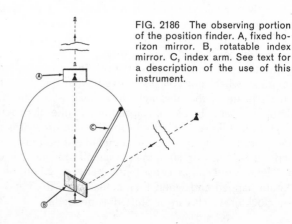

The observing portion of the device, fig. 2186, consists of a fixed horizon mirror, A, in which the reflected image of one object is seen immediately below the true image of the center object viewed over the top of the mirror. This is called a horizon mirror because it has the same function as the horizon mirror of a marine sextant.

The rotatable index mirror, B, is moved by the index arm, C, to reflect the image of the right or left object into the fixed mirror. By viewing through the slot in the center of this mirror, it is possible to use this one mirror for both the right and left angles. This is not possible with a sextant, where the index mirror is offset and can be used for only one horizontal angle at a time.

The plotting portion of the position-finder consists of three arms, pivoted at one center point, at which a pencil mark can be made through a hole onto the chart. The center arm is permanently located with an etched centerline at 90° to the plane of the horizontal mirror. The two movable arms can be locked in position during the observations, avoiding the need for any reading of scales and subsequent setting of the arms before plotting. The inside edges of the movable arms are used for plotting.

Using the position-finder

Three objects are selected that can be identified visually and on the chart. The procedure is to measure the angle between the line of sight to the center object and those to the right-hand and left-hand objects. The two angles cannot be measured simultaneously. If it is apparent that one angle is changing at a more rapid rate than the other, the angle changing more slowly should be measured first and the angle changing more rapidly last; otherwise, it is not important which angle is measured first.

Each angle is measured in accordance with the detailed instructions furnished with the instrument. As the angles are measured, the movable arms are locked into place. The instrument is then transferred to the chart and used as a conventional three-arm protractor, lining up each arm with the respective chart symbol and marking the position with a pencil through the hole in the center of the device. Fig. 2187 shows the Position-Finder in place on a chart.

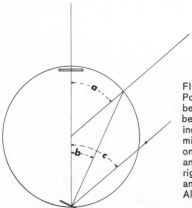

FIG. 2185 Optical principle of Position Finder. Angle *a* is angle between two objects on shore being observed. Angle *b* is amount index arm, and therefore index mirror, is turned. This is always one-half of angle *a*. Angle *c* is angle of light rays coming from right hand object to index mirror and reflected to horizon mirror. Always the same as angle *a*.

FIG. 2186 The observing portion of the position finder. A, fixed horizon mirror. B, rotatable index mirror. C, index arm. See text for a description of the use of this instrument.

ECHO PILOTING

An approximate method of determining distance, in passages or other bodies of water where there are sheer cliffs that will produce echoes, is to sound a short blast of the whistle or horn, and time, preferably with a stop watch, the interval before the echo is received.

Divide this interval in seconds by two (because the sound has to travel to the shore and return as the echo), and multiply that figure by 1100, a rough value for the speed of sound in air in feet per second. (Actually, at 32°F, the speed is 1088 feet per second and at 72°F it is 1132 fps, but the figure of 1100 is close enough for the accuracy of the timing method used.)

For example, you sound a short blast on your horn and time the interval until the return of the echo as five seconds. Half of this time is 2½ seconds; multiply by 1100, and you have 2650 feet or a distance off of slightly less than one-half nautical mile.

This is sometimes called "dog-bark navigation" and is used to a limited extent in the inside passage to Alaska on the British Columbia coast. If an echo can be received from both shores, a vessel can be kept in the approximate middle of the passage by holding such a course that an echo will be received simultaneously from both sides.

THE RULE-OF-SIXTY

Another useful specialized piloting technique is the *Rule-of-Sixty*. It provides a simple, practical way of changing course to clear an off-lying danger area without a lot of chart work. Again, the technique is best explained with an example.

Let's assume in this case that you have come out of Portsmouth Harbor and are running a southerly course down the coast to Cape Ann. See fig. 2188. Somewhere out off Newburyport you pick up dead ahead the light on Straitsmouth Island, marked C in the figure. Your course made good along the line AC has been 164° True. A bell buoy has been placed a mile and a half eastward of the light to mark a number of rocks and ledges that must be cleared. It is obvious that you must make a change of course for safety. The problem is how much?

Instead of getting out the chart and plotting a position and a new course to clear the bell buoy, you can apply the Rule-of-Sixty and get a new course with a simple mental calculation. You know from the chart or Light List that the light on Straitsmouth Island is visible for 8 miles, assuming good visibility. (With less than perfect visibility, you will have to establish your distance from the light by other means. But on this night, the visibility is good and you can accept the distance as 8 miles when the light appears on the horizon.)

The procedure is to divide 60 (the rule) by 8 (the distance); the result is 7.5. Since you want to clear the light by a mile and a half, you multiply 7.5 by 1.5 and get 11.25. This is rounded to 11, and is the number of degrees that you must change your course. Thus, your new course is 164° − 11° = 153° True. Long before you need to be concerned about the rocks and ledges, you will pick up the bell buoy north of Flat Ground and then the light on the bell buoy at D.

Although this technique is quite valid and acceptable as a specialized procedure, it should not be considered a full

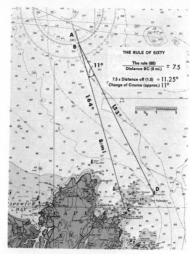

FIG. 2188 The Rule of Sixty can guide you in determining how much to change course to clear an obstacle seen ahead at a known distance. The rule can be applied without making a chart plot of the situation.

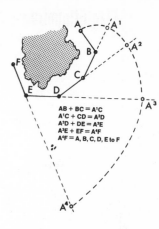

FIG. 2189 The length of the several straight courses required to pass around a point of land can be added graphically and measured all at one time, rather than measuring them separately and adding the distances numerically.

substitute for the basic and conventional procedure of accurately determining your position and plotting a revised course. There may be circumstances where the Rule-of-Sixty will be useful, such as on a single-handed passage or under conditions too rough for accurate plotting, but consider it a "secondary" method rather than a first-choice method.

DETERMINING THE DISTANCE AROUND A HEADLAND

A pilot may be confronted with the problem of determining the total distance to be covered when rounding a headland or point of land in a series of short, straight courses. There is a graphic method that will give a quick and accurate solution.

In fig. 2189, the boat is at A. You want to know the total run to F on the other side of the point if you proceed to B, then C, D, and E in turn.

In the figure, lines are drawn from point to point, but after you become familiar with the technique, you can merely swing the legs of your dividers from point to point so as to ensure that the invisible line determined by the points will be far enough offshore to be safe.

Step-by-step procedures

The starting point is A; use a pair of dividers and measure the distance to B. Keep the dividers' leg point that is at B on that point, and swing the other leg around from A to the right until it touches the broken line extended backwards from C to B at A^1. Hold this dividers' point on A^1, and extend the other leg from B to C.

Now hold the point at C fast and swing the other point around from A^1 until it touches the broken line extended backward from D to C at A^2. Hold this point fast at A^2 and open the dividers further, as before, until the point at C reaches to D.

This same step-by-step procedure is repeated to find A^3 and A^4. When the dividers have been finally extended from A^4 to F, they are set to measure the total distance around the headland using the chart's graphic scale or latitude markings.

This technique saves much time and is more accurate than the usual procedure of measuring each leg separately and adding the distance together to get the total run.

Fig. 2201
Mastless motor boat. Aft, US or USPS ensign (not yacht ensign). Forward, yacht club burgee, Squadron pennant or USCG Aux. blue ensign.

Fig. 2202 *(above)*
Typical outboard cruiser or open boat, with temporary staff placed on forward deck. Same flags at bow and stern as Fig. 2201 (except USCG Aux. blue ensign). At deck staff may be flown an officer's flag, a private signal or the USCG Aux. blue ensign.

Fig. 2203 *(left)*
Mastless cruiser with temporary staff on deck. Same flags as Fig. 2202.

Chapter 22

FLAG ETIQUETTE

How to fly your flags afloat—

Where and when to fly them—

Flag, pennant or burgee, which?—

Origin of the national and yacht ensigns—

Flags for masts ashore—

Etiquette in foreign waters

Fig. 2204
Cruiser with bow and stern staffs, with signal mast and yardarm. At bow, Squadron pennant or club burgee. Aft, US ensign or USPS ensign. At main truck, officer's flag or private signal. At starboard yardarm, USPS ensign (if not flown aft), absent flag or guest flag.

Fig. 2205
Typical mastless outboard boat. Same flags as Fig. 2201.

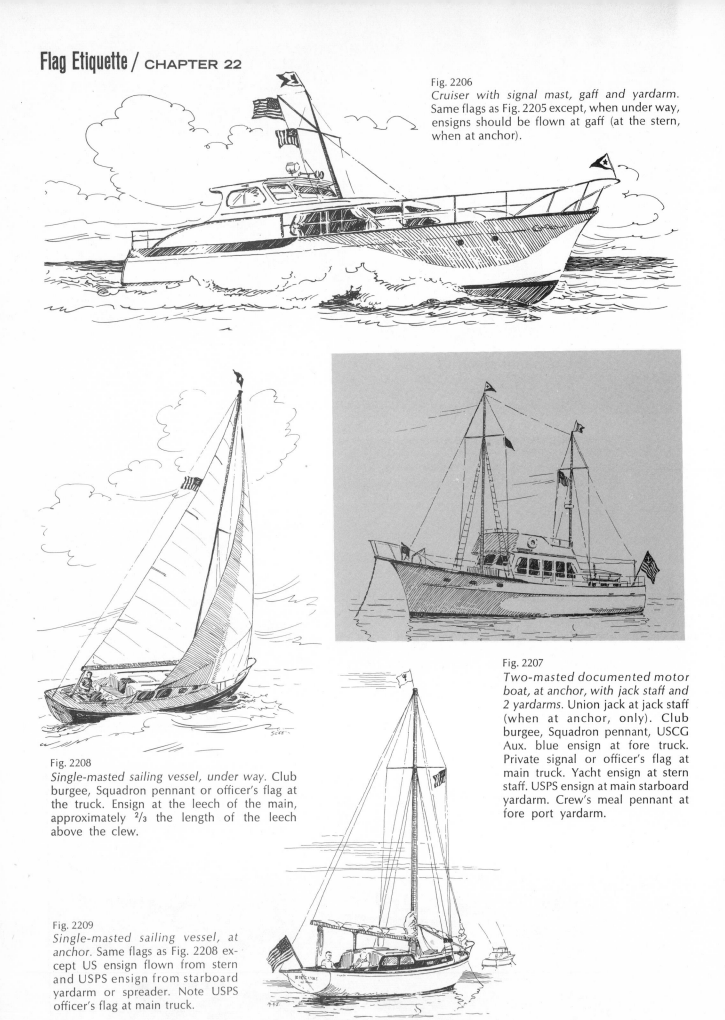

Fig. 2206
Cruiser with signal mast, gaff and yardarm. Same flags as Fig. 2205 except, when under way, ensigns should be flown at gaff (at the stern, when at anchor).

Fig. 2207
Two-masted documented motor boat, at anchor, with jack staff and 2 yardarms. Union jack at jack staff (when at anchor, only). Club burgee, Squadron pennant, USCG Aux. blue ensign at fore truck. Private signal or officer's flag at main truck. Yacht ensign at stern staff. USPS ensign at main starboard yardarm. Crew's meal pennant at fore port yardarm.

Fig. 2208
Single-masted sailing vessel, under way. Club burgee, Squadron pennant or officer's flag at the truck. Ensign at the leech of the main, approximately ²/₃ the length of the leech above the clew.

Fig. 2209
Single-masted sailing vessel, at anchor. Same flags as Fig. 2208 except US ensign flown from stern and USPS ensign from starboard yardarm or spreader. Note USPS officer's flag at main truck.

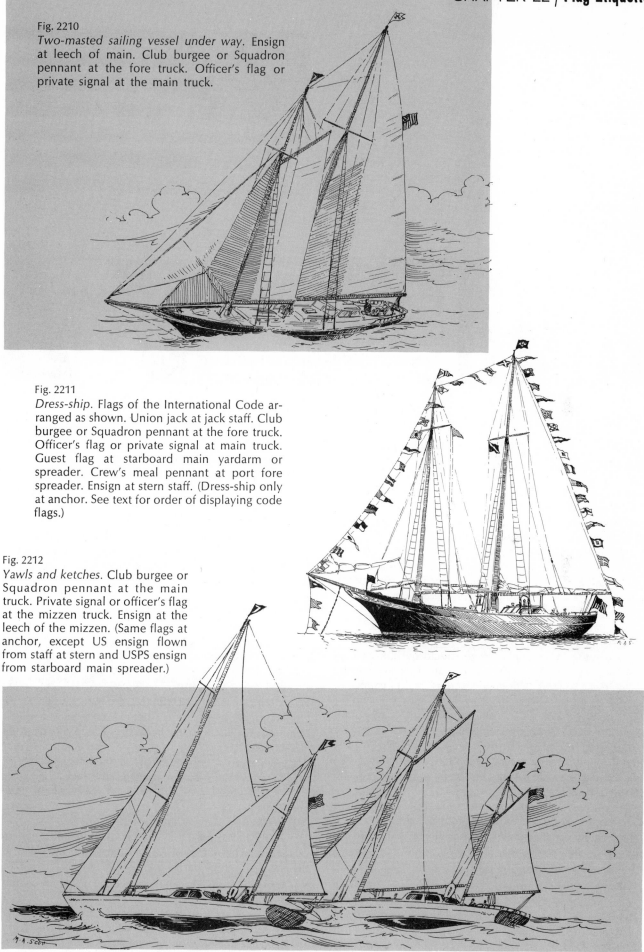

Fig. 2210
Two-masted sailing vessel under way. Ensign at leech of main. Club burgee or Squadron pennant at the fore truck. Officer's flag or private signal at the main truck.

Fig. 2211
Dress-ship. Flags of the International Code arranged as shown. Union jack at jack staff. Club burgee or Squadron pennant at the fore truck. Officer's flag or private signal at main truck. Guest flag at starboard main yardarm or spreader. Crew's meal pennant at port fore spreader. Ensign at stern staff. (Dress-ship only at anchor. See text for order of displaying code flags.)

Fig. 2212
Yawls and ketches. Club burgee or Squadron pennant at the main truck. Private signal or officer's flag at the mizzen truck. Ensign at the leech of the mizzen. (Same flags at anchor, except US ensign flown from staff at stern and USPS ensign from starboard main spreader.)

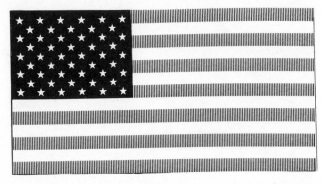

U.S. ENSIGN

U.S. ENSIGN, the one and only U.S. National flag, proper for all yachts, without reservation. Old Glory, the flag with 50 stars and 13 stripes. Flown, when at anchor, at the stern staff. When under way in inland waters, and when meeting or passing other vessels on the high seas, weather and rig permitting, by: motor yachts at the stern staff; by motor yachts with mast and gaff at the gaff.

Marconi-rigged sailboats, when under sail, fly the ensign at the leech of the mainsail, or when there's more than

U.S. POWER SQUADRON ENSIGN

U.S. YACHT ENSIGN

U.S. COAST GUARD AUXILIARY ENSIGN

one mast, at the leech of the aftermost sail, approximately ²/₃ the length of the leech above the clew.

Gaff-rigged sailboats, when under sail, fly the ensign at the peak of the mainsail gaff, or when there's more than one mast, at the peak of the aftermost gaff. In the case of a schooner with Marconi main and gaff foresail, the ensign flies from the leech of the mainsail.

Under power alone, or when at anchor or made fast, the ensign should be flown from the stern staff of all sailboats. *(The English practice is to fly the ensign at a stern staff, on all sailing craft at anchor, under way, under sail and under power.)*

On yawls and ketches, the ensign is flown from the mizzen.

At 8 A.M., the national ensign should be hoisted first, followed by the USPS ensign (if you are a member of the U.S. Power Squadrons in good standing, and in command of the boat), the yacht club burgee, officer's flag, and/or private signal. For C.G. Auxiliary vessels the same order holds, but C.G. Auxiliary blue ensign and officer's flag are substituted for yacht club flags. Flags are hoisted smartly, but lowered ceremoniously. Flag officer's flags, though displayed day and night, may be temporarily lowered and hoisted at colors.

At U.S.P.S., C.G. Auxiliary, or club rendezvous, marine parades, etc., on order of the Commanding Officer, flags may be flown after sundown but must be lowered at or before midnight, as ordered.

U.S. POWER SQUADRONS ENSIGN is flown as an outward and visible signal to other craft that the boat is commanded by a member of the USPS in good standing, one who is an able seaman, with a knowledge of things nautical, and competent to handle his craft.

Flown from the stern staff (or gaff under way) or from

starboard yard arm (the latter preferred) at the option of the member, on motor craft under way and on both motor and sailing craft at anchor.

On sailing vessels under way it's flown at leech of the Marconi's main or at the mainsail gaff peak (aftermost mast on vessels with more than two masts).

U.S. YACHT ENSIGN, by custom and by rulings of government authorities, may be flown on yachts of all sizes in place of the U.S. Ensign. Strictly speaking, the Yacht Ensign is not the American flag. Originally the flying of the Yacht Ensign was restricted to documented vessels of a special classification. However, all such restrictions have now been removed. Most Yacht Clubs now provide in their club by-laws that the Yacht Ensign be flown from the stern staff of power vessels, both at anchor and underway; at the stern on sailing craft when at anchor and at the leech of the mainsail when underway.   (See page IX a)

U.S. COAST GUARD AUXILIARY ENSIGN, known as the "Blue Ensign" is flown only from 8 A.M. to sunset when a qualified Auxiliarist is in charge of an approved facility. Here's how:

- [ ] On a vessel without a mast—at the bow staff.
- [ ] On a vessel with one mast—at the truck.
- [ ] On a vessel with two or more masts—at the main truck.
- [ ] NEVER in place of the national ensign.

The USPS ensign may be flown at its proper location on boats displaying the U.S.C.G. Aux. ensign to indicate that the owner is a member of both organizations.

YACHT CLUB BURGEE, generally triangular in shape, sometimes swallow tail.

Flown from the bow staff of mastless and single-masted vessels (foremost truck of vessels with two or more masts); at the main truck of yawls and ketches.

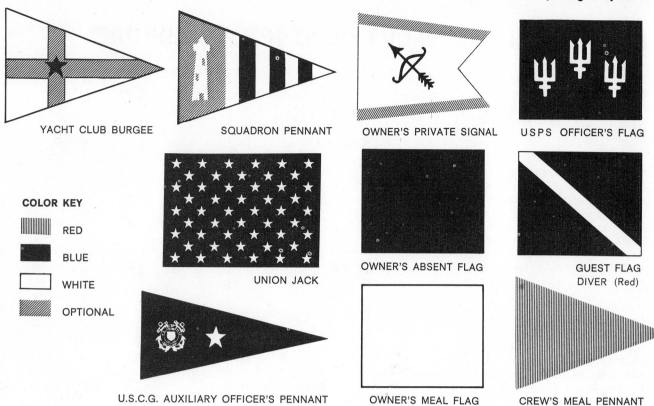

YACHT CLUB BURGEE

SQUADRON PENNANT

OWNER'S PRIVATE SIGNAL

USPS OFFICER'S FLAG

COLOR KEY

RED

BLUE

WHITE

OPTIONAL

UNION JACK

OWNER'S ABSENT FLAG

GUEST FLAG
DIVER (Red)

U.S.C.G. AUXILIARY OFFICER'S PENNANT

OWNER'S MEAL FLAG

CREW'S MEAL PENNANT

Burgee may be flown under way and at anchor. It is, however, permissible to substitute the private signal for the burgee on single-masted yachts without bow staff when under way.

SQUADRON PENNANT. A distinguishing Squadron pennant which has been approved by the District and authorized by the U.S. Power Squadrons' Governing Board, may be flown between morning and evening colors, in place of and instead of the club burgee.

NOTE: Color reproductions of all Squadron pennants will be found on the end papers of this book.

OWNER'S PRIVATE SIGNAL, generally swallow tail in shape, sometimes rectangular or pennant, flown from masthead of single-masted motor boats, at the main truck of motor boats with two masts, at the main truck of single-masted sailing vessels when under way and at the aftermost truck of sailing yachts with two or more masts. Mastless motor yachts may display, on a staff erected on the superstructure, the flag designated by this code to be flown from the truck of single-masted yachts.

OFFICER'S FLAG, rectangular in shape, blue (with white design) for senior officer(s); red for next lower in rank; white (with blue design) for lower rank. Other officer's flag (except fleet captain) may be swallow tail or triangular in shape, as provided in the regulations of those organizations making provisions for such flags. Flown in place of private signal on all rigs of motor and sailing vessels except on single-masted sailing vessels, when it is flown in place of burgee at truck.

UNION JACK, a rectangular blue flag with 50 white stars. The Union Jack may be displayed *only* at the jackstaff on sailing yachts and at the jackstaff on motor yachts with more than one mast, between morning and evening colors,

and only while at anchor on Sundays or holidays, or when dressing ship. The Union Jack shall never be substituted for or replace the club burgee.

ABSENT FLAG, rectangular blue flag, flown during owner's absence in daylight hours. Flown from starboard yardarm, starboard main spreader or equivalent, provided USPS ensign is not flown at this hoist, with a USPS member in command. (Replaced at night, at anchor, by blue light.)

GUEST FLAG, a rectangular blue flag, crossed diagonally by a white stripe, flown during daylight, when owner is absent but guests are on board. Flown from the starboard yardarm, starboard main spreader or equivalent, provided USPS ensign is not being flown from this hoist. Guest flag should also be flown when owner is absent but a member of his family is aboard.

U.S.C.G. AUXILIARY OFFICER'S PENNANT, or a past officer's burgee (same design except swallow-tail shape), flies day and night when officer is on board. On a vessel without a mast, flown at the bow staff in lieu of the Auxiliary flag. On a vessel with one mast, at starboard spreader. On a vessel with two or more masts, at main starboard spreader.

Only *one* officer's pennant or burgee may be flown at one time. An incumbent officer's pennant takes precedence. When the Blue Ensign is displayed, it is improper to hoist a guest, owner absent, meal, cocktail, or novelty flag.

OWNER'S MEAL FLAG, a white rectangular flag, flown at anchor, during daylight meal hours of owners, from the main starboard spreader or yardarm, if the USPS ensign is not at this hoist. (Replaced by white light at night.)

CREW'S MEAL PENNANT, red, flown during daylight, at anchor, during the meal hours of the crew at the fore port yardarm or spreader.

FLYING FLAGS AT YACHT CLUB HOISTS ASHORE

These diagrams illustrate how flags can be displayed for a variety of situations and on different types of yacht club masts and poles.

NOTES: The flag of the Senior Club Officer present on the club grounds or aboard his boat in the club anchorage, or Storm Signal flags can be substituted for the International Code Flags shown in the diagrams, except in the case illustrated at bottom left. The diagrams show hoists as if you were standing ashore facing seaward.

If only a Yacht Club single pole with no yard or gaff, only the U.S. Flag should be flown, at the truck.

If a pole with yardarm only, the U.S. Flag should be flown at truck, Club burgee at starboard yardarm, USPS Ensign or other organizational flag may be flown at port yardarm during activities ashore of such organization.

On national holidays and on days of special yachting significance, it is permissible to fly the flags of the International Code.

The code for "flying flags ashore at Yacht Clubs" may be followed for flags flown ashore at the homes of yachtsmen.

Signal flags, such as storm and weather flags, etc. should be flown from a conspicuous hoist.

Flags of yachting organizations should not be flown from commercial establishments, except by special permission.

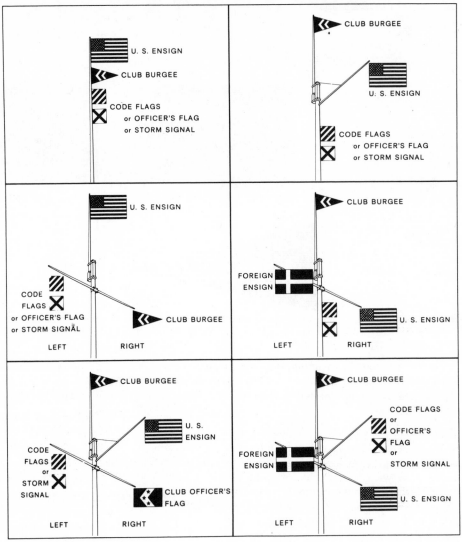

Source: U. S. Navy Dept. Code & Signal Section

About Pennants

Pennant or Burgee. Adrift in a foggy sea of semantics, a sea lawyer could easily founder, groping for the right terms to describe those bits of bunting he flies from the truck and bow staff. Basically, there are four shapes his signals may take—rectangular, triangular, rectangular swallow-tailed, and triangular swallow-tailed. What to call them? Pennants or burgees?

We can't go far wrong if we think of a *pennant* as a flag smaller at the fly than at the hoist which is (1) commonly pointed, triangular (2) often truncated, as in some Navy signals (3) sometimes swallow-tailed (4) occasionally a long thin streamer.

The *burgee* we might regard as a swallow-tailed flag which is (1) often rectangular (2) may be pennant-shaped (3) by popular usage, the identifying signal of a yacht club, regardless of shape.

Naval Reserve Pennants. There are two types of Naval Reserve pennant. (See illustrations, pages ix-b and ix-c.) The *Naval Reserve Yacht Pennant* is displayed at the fore truck by yachts and vessels commanded or owned by Naval Reserve Officers, designated by the Secretary of the Navy as suitable for service as naval auxiliaries in time of war. The *Naval Reserve Yacht Owners Distinguishing Pennant* is a personal flag flown, preferably at the fore truck, on yachts owned by, or under the command of, individuals who donated yachts or other craft for use by the Navy during World War II. Those awarded this pennant are not necessarily members of the U.S. Naval Reserve.

Racing Pennant. A distinctive pennant has been designed by the Sea Cliff (N.Y.) Yacht Club as an identifying signal for racing boats. The field is blue, with white fluorescent strip in the middle, and red anchor superimposed. Cruising yachts carry it at the starboard spreader; smaller boats fly it from the leech of the mainsail. It aids race committees in distinguishing contesting boats; other boats, hopefully, will give them a wide berth. It is suggested that other clubs follow Sea Cliff's lead, standardizing on the design illustrated below.

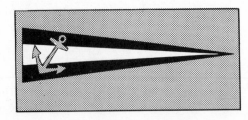

"And yet, though silent, it speaks to us—speaks to us of the past, of the men and women who went before us, and of the records they wrote upon it." —PRESIDENT WILSON

The Flag of Your Country

THE FLYING of flags and colors on motor craft, sailing and other yachts is governed largely by custom. Few, if any, laws or government regulations have ever been enacted on this subject. Mention has seldom if ever been made by Congress in all of its years, of any requirements for the flying of any flag on numbered, undocumented or unlicensed vessels or yachts. Documented yachts are expected to fly the yacht ensign but the enforcement of even this regulation is questionable.

A review or a brief history of the United States National Flag should permit one to better understand some of the fundamentals on which many of the customs of flags and colors are based, especially their evolution for use on the water.

The origin and early history of the use of national flags is very indefinite. This is especially true of the national ensign of the United States. Early Colonial and American history makes very little mention of our flag or flags. Our Navy seems to have begun the use of the Stars and Stripes immediately after the Continental Congress had passed an Act in June, 1777, establishing the Stars and Stripes as the flag of this country. However, it was not until 1895 or some 30 years after the close of the Civil War, that the United States cavalry was given the right to carry the Stars and Stripes as the national standard. It was in 1841 that the infantry first used the national colors. Not until 1876 did the Marines carry the Stars and Stripes.

As the Navy made use of the national flag from the beginning and the other branches of the U.S. government were slow in adopting it, it emphasizes that the Stars and Stripes as the national ensign is a flag of the sea and its right to be flown from yachts is clearly established.

On the subject of the origin and development of the flag from which the Stars and Stripes has been evolved, accounts are too conflicting to warrant placing much credence in them. Prince Edward, afterwards Edward I of England, about the middle of the last half of the 13th century, adopted the Red Cross of St. George, on a white field, as the national flag of England. After James VI of Scotland ascended the throne of England in 1603, as James I, he was much annoyed by the wrangling between the masters of English and Scotch ships when they met at sea as to which one should dip its colors to the other. Therefore, in 1606, he stopped this annoyance and to help unite the two kingdoms into one country, combined the two crosses into a new flag, which subsequently became known as the Union

Jack. This he required all vessels of both countries to carry at their mainmast. A century later when the two countries agreed upon their union, a national agreement required the union of the crosses to be used on flags, banners, standards, and ensigns both at sea and on land.

Near the beginning of the revolution, General Washington assigned to the various officers as a distinction of rank, ribbons varying in color and these were worn by them until something more formal was designed. There were practically no flags or colors although some of the individual companies of the Colonial Army are supposed to have brought with them those which they had previously used. Later General Washington urged the various Colonels to provide for their regiments colors of such design as might appeal to them. This was frequently done and in many instances, some designs of 13 units were used to represent the 13 colonies.

Some of the colonies adopted flags of their own. Massachusetts adopted the Pine Tree, with the motto An Appeal to Heaven. Rhode Island selected one having an anchor and the word Hope and within the canton a union of 13 white stars on a blue field, said to be the first flag on which the 13 colonies were represented by 13 stars.

South Carolina's flag has an interesting history. In September 1775, the Committee of Safety of Charleston instructed Colonel William Moultrie to take possession of Fort Johnson on James Island, which he did. The uniforms of their troops were blue with a silver increscent in the cap. Soon realizing that a flag was needed, he improvised one having a blue field with a white increscent in the canton. This was the flag which sergeant Jasper so gallantly rescued on June 28, 1776, when the fort of palmetto logs on Sullivans Island was attacked by the British Fleet under Admiral Sir Peter Parker. It was under this flag that the Declaration of Independence was read to the people of Charleston on August 8, 1776. When the state came to officially adopt a flag, it took the one which Colonel Moultrie had designed and in recognition of the good services of the palmetto logs, placed upon it a palmetto tree.

While our first flag act was adopted June 14, 1777, by resolution of the Continental Congress and reading as follows: "Resolved, That the flag of the United States be thirteen stripes, alternate red and white; that the union be thirteen stars, white in a blue field, representing a new constellation" yet there is nothing to show that the Revolutionary Army ever carried any flags furnished by the American Congress. Those which were carried were purely personal, each made by or for some officer, company or regiment, and represented the sentiments of the makers. However, the United States Navy began to use the flag immediately after it was authorized by the Continental Congress.

History records only one Stars and Stripes that was carried by the American Army during the Revolutionary War. It was carried by the North Carolina Militia at the Battle of Guilford Courthouse, March 15, 1781, but the stripes were blue and red and the union had a white field with 13 eight-pointed stars. There is also another flag hanging in the State House at Annapolis, which it is claimed was carried by the Third Maryland Regiment in 1781. It has 13 five-pointed stars, one in the center, and 12 arranged in the form of a circle around it. In both of these cases, the flags were purely personal, not official.

The Stars and Stripes preserved in the State House of Boston is claimed to have flown over Fort Independence during the American Revolution but was not carried by the Army. In 1863 each battery of artillery and each company of cavalry was allowed to carry a small flag consisting of Stars and Stripes but that privilege was revoked at the end of the Civil War. The U.S. Marines did not carry the Stars and Stripes as national colors until 1876, yet those which they carried as such in the Mexican and Civil Wars had an eagle in the union.

In none of the three acts adopting the United States national flag is there any mention as to how the stars should be arranged or how many points they should have. In one of the first flags, the stars were sometimes arranged in a circle or with one star in the center and the remaining 12 either in the form of a circle or hollow square, or three horizontal rows of 4, 5 and 4 stars respectively. In a later flag, they were also arranged in several different orders, three horizontal rows of five each or three vertical rows of five each; sometimes in the quincunx order as was the flag that floated over Fort McHenry when Key wrote the Star Spangled Banner.

Apparently about 1841, when the United States Infantry was first given the right to carry the Stars and Stripes, there was a desire on the part of some to preserve their old national colors in the union of the new flag. One of these had an eagle with a bunch of arrows in one claw and the Indian pipe of peace in the other with 13 stars above and a like number below. During the Mexican War, the Fourth Indiana Volunteers carried a flag having in the union an eagle standing on a segment of the globe with a bunch of arrows in one claw, as though intending to conquer the earth.

Near the beginning of the 20th Century, the different departments of our National Government appointed representatives to confer and see if they could not bring order out of chaos. The proportions of Naval flags and Army colors were quite different, the former being much longer in proportion to its height, the latter being much shorter to avoid interfering with the color or standard bearer. It was decided to leave the Army colors alone but to fly the Naval flag from flagstaffs and from Government buildings.

Accordingly, following the recommendations of this committee, President Taft, in 1912, issued an executive order defining minutely the proportions and other details of the Stars and Stripes, at the same time approving a cus-

tom which had existed in the Navy of placing on their small boats flags having only 13 stars instead of the full complement. The use of only 13 stars on our small or boat flags was discontinued by an executive order of President Wilson, dated May 29, 1916, and now all flags, colors, etc., used by the United States Government are required to have their full complement of 50 stars. In all of the discussion by the conference it does not appear that there was any mention whatsoever of the yacht ensign or the rights or duties of yachts or any other vessels to fly any particular flag.

From the foregoing it will be seen that the United States has only one flag. The use of the yacht ensign is misleading. England has, by law, created a flag for its navy, another for its merchant service, another for yachts and another for its land forces; each is a national flag and entitled to the position and courtesy due the colors of a nation. But, in the United States, wherever, whenever and for whatever purpose the national colors are flown, there is but one flag to fly.

The place of honor for the national colors on land and sea is as follows: on land on a straight mast, at the head; on a mast with a gaff, at the gaff. At sea and at anchor on a steam or motor vessel, at the flag staff aft; on vessels under sail, at the peak; and on vessels with a gaff, at this gaff when under way.

There has never been passed a law compelling boats to fly the national flag or none at all from the place of honor. It has probably never been contemplated that a loyal citizen would ever do otherwise. Yet, we are free to do as we

The American flag is flying here, properly, from the gaff at a yacht club station. The club burgee is at the masthead.

M. Rosenfeld.

like and in the use of this freedom there has grown the custom of flying the yacht ensign at the point of honor at shore stations and aboard yachts. There are today ardent yachtsmen in high places who believe this custom aboard yachts should be continued.

The yacht ensign had its beginning on August 7, 1848, when the Congress passed "an act to authorize the Secretary of the Treasury to license yachts and for other purposes" providing for the enrollment and licensing of yachts and exempting them from entering and clearing at Custom-houses. The third paragraph of the act provided "that all such licensed yachts shall *use a signal* of the form, size and colors prescribed by the Secretary of the Navy." (This paragraph has been subsequently reenacted as Sec. 4215 Revised Statutes of the United States.) The Secretary of the Navy acted promptly, and on August 26, 1848, he requested the New York Yacht Club to submit a design for this signal. The design they submitted on January 9, 1849, was the then adopted American ensign, which carried thirteen stars in a circle in the blue field and the thirteen red and white stripes (the Betsy Ross flag), in which they placed a fouled anchor in the center of the circle of stars. The Secretary of the Navy accepted the suggestion of the New York Yacht Club and authorized the adoption of the design.

It is the design of the yacht "signal" that has resulted in the present confusion because its similarity in appearance to the national ensign promptly led yachtsmen to fly the "signal" now known as the yacht ensign in place of the national ensign and the custom has grown until at present nearly all pleasure craft, from outboard speedsters up, are flying the "signal" as an ensign. The yacht ensign was created only as a signal for yachts enrolled and licensed (documented) and exempted them from entering and clearing at Custom-houses. Presumably it was to be flown in addition to the national ensign on documented yachts. To fly it from a club mast ashore signifies nothing.

Under present law it is the general rule that "the ownership of a vessel determines its national character." Several cases bear upon this and explain also how else a vessel's nationality may be proved.

In one called the Merritt (17 Wall 582, 21 L.Ed. 682) Mr. Justice Hunt, writing for the U.S. Supreme Court in October 1873, observed that "The documents a vessel carries furnish the only evidence of her nationality."

In the 1880's, U.S. v. Seagrist (27 F. Cas. No. 16,245) held that the register of a vessel, while proper evidence of nationality, is not indispensable, and the flag and ownership of the vessel may be proved by *any* competent evidence.

In 1894 in St. Clair v. United States (154 U.S. 134) the Supreme Court ruled not only that the "certificate of the vessel's registry, and its carrying the American flag, was admissible in evidence," but that "such evidence made, at least, a *prima facie* case . . . of the nationality of the vessel. . . ." This means that such evidence is sufficient to prove the points for which it is introduced unless it is contradicted by other evidence.

Conclusion: Generally the nationality of a vessel is determined by the nationality of her owner. Her papers or her flag may indicate otherwise, however, but neither is conclusive on the issue. Both elements are entitled to prima facie weight—that is, they will stand unless overcome by other evidence. Obviously there are no exclusive ways

Never fly the American flag from the masthead of a mast equipped with a gaff, as illustrated here. Just as on a ship, the gaff, even though lower in height, is the place of honor.

to prove this matter in a court of law; all material and relevant evidence on the issue will be allowed.

DRESSING SHIP

On national holidays, at regattas, and on other special occasions, yachts often dress ship with International Code signal flags. Flag officers' flags, club burgees, and national flags are not used. The ship is dressed at 8:00 A.M. and remains so dressed from morning to evening colors. (While at anchor only.) See fig. 2211, page 357.

In dressing ship, the yacht ensign is hoisted at the peak or staff aft, and the jack at the jackstaff. Then a rainbow of flags of the International Code is arranged, reaching from the waterline forward to the waterline aft, by way of the bowsprit end to the foretop masthead, then across to the main topmast, and down to the main boom end, allowing several flags to touch the water line from both the bowsprit end and the main boom end. To keep the flags in position, a weight should be attached to the end of each line. Where there is no bowsprit, flags will start at the stem-head. Flags and pennants should be bent on alternately, rather than in any indiscriminate manner. Since there are twice as many letter flags as numeral pennants, it is good practice, as in the Navy, to follow a sequence of two flags, one pennant, etc., etc., throughout. In order to effect a degree of uniformity in yacht procedure, the following arrangement has been proposed:

Starting from forward, AB2, UJ1, KE3, GH6, IV5, FL4, DM7, PO Third Repeater, RN First Repeater, STo (zero), CX9, WQ8, ZY Second Repeater.

The arrangement here proposed is designed to effect a harmonious color pattern throughout.

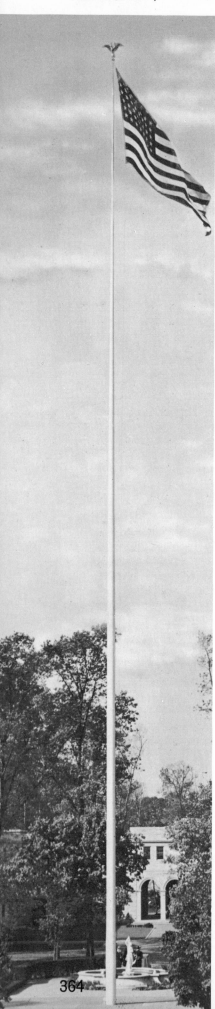

The Evolution of the United States Flag

GRAND UNION:
Before the American Revolution, the Colonies used a flag with a British ensign as the canton, plus 13 alternate red and white stripes signifying the original Colonies.

GADSDEN FLAG:
Even before 1776, there were those who resented anything in our flag resembling the British ensign. The Gadsden flag was developed about this time with a coiled rattlesnake on a yellow field with the words "Don't Tread On Me." Other flags used by some of the Colonies carried such slogans as "Liberty or Death."

BUNKER HILL FLAG:
In the New England area, the pine tree of Maine was the popular flag emblem. This appeared on the banner hoisted by the Colonies at Bunker Hill. It showed a red background with the pine tree in the canton. Another was the British blue ensign with a pine tree in the canton.

FIRST "STARS AND STRIPES":
Congress passed the first flag resolution on June 14 (now flag day), 1777. The battle of Bennington in August of the same year is believed to mark the first display of Old Glory with 13 stars and 13 stripes, with 11 stars arranged in a semi-circle and one in each corner. The 76 denotes the year of Independence.

COWPENS FLAG:
This flag, consisting of 12 white stars in a circle with one in the center, with 13 alternate red and white stripes, was first carried in the battle of Cowpens, January 1781.

BETSY ROSS FLAG:
The legend has it that Betsy Ross of Philadelphia was asked in 1776 to design a national flag suggested by General Washington. She is credited with making the stars 5-pointed and arranging them in a circle on the national flag.

FLAG OF 1795:
This flag had 15 stripes and 15 stars indicating the 15 States at that time. Five new stars were added during the five years this flag flew, but no additional stripes. This flag is credited with being the first official flag to fly over the Capitol in Washington.

FLAG OF THE CONFEDERACY:
Of the four Confederate flags, the one shown was most popular and best known; it consisted of a blue cross arranged diagonally across a red field. On the cross were 13 stars.

FLAG OF 1912:
Two stars were added to the flag when this design became offical, representing the new States of Arizona and New Mexico. The stars were arranged in six rows of 8 stars each and remained unchanged for 47 years.

OLD GLORY OF TODAY:
With the admission of the 49th and 50th States, Alaska and Hawaii, 2 more stars were added to the flag, making a total of 50, arranged in 5 rows of 6 stars each and 4 rows of 5 stars each. The flag became official on July 4, 1960.

The United States ensign proudly flies from the tallest single-masted, unguyed flagpole in the world (172 ft.) at the United States Merchant Marine Academy, Kings Point, N. Y.

Suggested Flag Ceremonies and Etiquette at Yacht Club and Squadron Meetings

FLAG CEREMONIES AT SQUADRON MEETINGS

It is better to place the flags with ceremony than to consider them merely a part of the decorations and equipment.

The route of march in advancing the colors will depend upon the size and layout of the meeting place, width of aisles, etc. In the following it is assumed that the flag of the United States and the USPS flag are to used, mounted on staffs, and with stands properly located in advance.

In small or congested rooms the following is recommended.

The bearer of the flag of the United States stands at the right side of the room, as viewed by the audience, with the bearer of the USPS flag on the opposite side of the room, in the open space between the first rows of chairs and the speaker's platform. If there is no raised platform for the head table or speaker, the bearers of the U.S. and USPS flags take positions opposite from the positions indicated (see paragraph 4 Display of Flags at Squadron Meetings).

The Commander raps his gavel for order, and as soon as obtained announces "We will now have the presentation of the colors. All please rise and stand at attention."

As soon as this is accomplished the Commander orders, "Color Guard—Present the colors." The Color Guard, on the order, marches in opposite directions across the room in front of the speaker's platform. At the center point and just before passing, each comes to a distinct stop facing each other. The bearer of the USPS flag dips his flag slightly and as soon as his flag is back up in carrying position both bearers continue their march and place the flags in their respective stands.

As soon as each flag is placed both bearers step back and come to the position of breast salute, facing the flag of the United States.

Referring back in the above, as soon as the bearers start their march across the room, the Commander orders all present "Breast Salute."

As soon as the bearers have come to the position of breast salute as above, the Commander orders "Two." (Second count of the salute routine.) On this order all present return to the position of attention and the color bearers retire.

The Commander then raps his gavel and orders all present "Be seated" or calls for the Invocation, after which he seats the audience.

If a larger hall is used or more formal ceremonies are desired, the flags may be marched up the center aisle or right aisle. If in single file, with the United States flag in the lead, if abreast with the U.S. flag on the right of marchers.

If marching up the center aisle, at the point where the cleared space between the front seats and the table is reached, the bearer of the USPS flag stops momentarily and allows the bearer of the U.S. flag to cross in front of him. The flag dip is used only when the flags meet from opposite directions as in the first method above.

The Commander follows the same sequence of orders as for the first method above.

COLOR RETIRING CEREMONIES

Color retiring ceremonies may properly and easily be followed at all formal business meetings, where there is a definite moment of official closing. It is not recommended at social gatherings.

Color retiring ceremonies are as follows:

Just before declaring the meeting adjourned the Commander gives the order "Color Guard, stand by to retire the colors." On receiving this order, the Color Guard advances and stands directly in front of their respective colors. When both are in position the Commander orders "Attention" and all present rise and stand at attention. When this is accomplished the Commander orders "Color Guard, secure the colors."

Each color bearer at this command removes his flag from the stand and together do an about-face to face the audience, and then hoist the flags to carry position.

As soon as this is accomplished the Commander orders "Breast salute" and all present except the color bearers comply. As soon as the position of breast salute is accomplished, the color bearers step off together to retrace their presentation march. If the first method described for presenting colors is used, the dipping ceremony is repeated just before they cross in the center of the room. In this method, as soon as the colors reach the side of the room, or if the aisle method is used, as soon as the colors pass from sight or reach the back of the room, the Commander orders "Two" and all present return to the position of attention.

The Commander may now order the meeting adjourned, or may seat the audience first if there are to be informal activities following.

On a shore mast equipped with gaff, at yacht clubs and similar marine installations such as marinas, USPS and USCG Auxiliary shore headquarters, etc., the U.S. Ensign should be flown from the gaff, the position of honor. The illustration above, made from a poster issued by the U.S. Government, shows Old Glory flying from the gaff. Even though there may be positions at a greater height above the ground, yet the flying of the ensign from the gaff is not a violation of the statutes that "no flag should be displayed 'above' the U.S. Ensign."

USPS CODE OF FLAG ETIQUETTE FOR U.S. BOATS IN FOREIGN WATERS

Motor Boats*

MASTLESS VESSELS (with bow and stern staffs)

Foreign national flag at bow staff.
Own ensign at stern staff.

ONE-MAST MOTOR VESSELS (with yard-arm)

Foreign national flag at bow staff.
Own ensign at stern staff.
Club flag at starboard yard-arm.
Private signal or flag officer's flag at masthead.

TWO-MAST MOTOR VESSELS

Underway:—

Club pennant at bow staff.
Foreign national flag at fore-truck.
Private or flag officer's flag at main-truck.
Own ensign at stern staff.

At anchor or dock:—

The practice outlined above for two-mast motor vessels under way is also correct when at anchor, or at a dock.

Sailing Vessels

SLOOPS AND CUTTERS

Own ensign at peak when under sail and at stern staff when at anchor or under power.
Club signal at masthead when at anchor.
Private signal at masthead when underway.
Flag officer's flag in place of club flag or private signal.
Foreign flag on forestay at anchor, and forestay or forward starboard shroud one-third mast height when underway.

YAWLS AND KETCHES

Own ensign at mizzen peak when under sail and at stern staff when at anchor or under power.
Club pennant at main-truck.
Private signal at mizzen-truck.
Flag officer's flag in place of private signal.
Foreign flag on forestay at anchor, and forestay or forward starboard shroud one-third mast height when underway.

SCHOONERS OF TWO OR MORE MASTS

Own ensign at after peak when under sail and at stern staff when at anchor or under power.
Club signal at fore-truck at anchor.
Private signal at main-truck.
Flag officer's flag at main-truck in place of private signal.
Foreign flag at bow staff or forestay at anchor, and fore-truck or forward starboard shroud while underway.

All Vessels

Hoist your own ensign first and lower last if you are shorthanded.

Show your own colors if entering or leaving port before 8:00 A.M. or after sunset, but do not pay honors except from 8:00 A.M. to sunset.

---

* NOTE: Motor boats with a gaff should fly their own ensign at gaff while underway, but at stern staff while at anchor or tied to a dock.

DISPLAY OF FLAGS AT YACHT CLUB AND SQUADRON MEETINGS

1. The flag of the United States should be displayed either from a staff, or flat against the wall above and behind the speaker's table.

2. The flag of the United States should never be draped or laid over anything except a casket, at which time special rules apply.

3. When displayed flat against a wall it should be fastened along the upper edge only, with the union to the flag's right, to the left as viewed by the audience. This applies whether the flag is hung with stripes vertical or horizontal. The horizontal position of the stripes is preferable.

4.* When displayed on a staff indoors, in an enclosure where there is no platform at the head of the room, the U.S. ensign is stood at the right of the audience; but if there is a platform, the U.S. ensign is displayed on a staff at the left of the audience, namely, at the right of the speaker. The USPS ensign, if also displayed, is stood at

* See USPS Officers Manual.

the left of the audience where there is no platform, and at the right of the audience (left of the speaker) if there is a platform. If the Canadian ensign is also to be so displayed, it should be at the right of the audience where there is no platform, and at the right of the speaker where there is a platform but just inboard of the U.S. ensign.

5. If the flag of the United States, and another, are displayed with crossed staffs, as at the head of a room, the flag of the United States should be at the flag's right, to left as viewed by the audience, and with its staff in front of the other.

6. If the flag of the United States is displayed with other flags in a group, from staffs, it should be in the center and slightly higher or in front of the other flags.

7. If the USPS flag is to be displayed flat against a wall, it is hung as prescribed for the Flag of the United States, as in paragraph 3 above, but on the opposite wall.

DISPLAY OF STATE FLAGS

Any citizen of any state, according to P/C William B. Matthews Jr., Boating Administrator for the State of Maryland, may fly the flag of that state unless it is specifically prohibited by law. On a *vessel with one or more masts,* the State flag is flown at the main truck in place of the private signal, officer's flag or Coast Guard Auxiliary ensign. On a *mastless boat,* the State flag would be flown at

the bow staff in place of a club burgee. It should be understood that, when a State flag displaces a Coast Guard Auxiliary ensign at the truck, an Auxiliary officer cannot fly his officer's pennant from the starboard yardarm. When the State flag at the truck displaces the flag of an officer of a yacht club or the USPS, he cannot fly his officer's flag at any hoist.

Honoring Other National Flags

Just as a certain code of etiquette has been adopted to govern the display of flags by American yachts on the waterways of our own nation, so too there is a certain accepted procedure to which pleasure boats should properly adhere when they cross international boundaries into the waters of another nation.

There are only a limited number of positions from which flags may be properly displayed on motor boats and consequently when a foreign flag is to be flown, it must displace one of the flags commonly flown in home waters.

The United States Power Squadrons has adopted a code of flag etiquette which might well be followed by all American pleasure craft cruising in foreign waters.

MOTOR BOATS

For the purposes of this flag code, motor boats may be divided into three general groups: (1) mastless vessels, having bow and stern staffs only; (2) single-masted motor vessels, with yardarm; and (3) vessels with two masts.

Mastless vessels. A motor boat having only bow and stern staffs, if in home waters, would fly the yacht club burgee forward and her own ensign aft. In foreign waters, she must obviously keep her own ensign at the place of honor aft. Therefore she has no alternative but to display the national flag of the foreign country which she is visiting at the bow staff in place of her own club burgee. Under no circumstances should she try to fly both flags from one staff at the same time. That principle holds consistently true throughout all flag etiquette.

Motor vessels with one mast. Considering next the motor vessel with one mast and yardarm—possibly the most common of all arrangements aboard cruising motor boats—her own ensign remains at the stern staff and her private signal or officer's flag at the masthead. Her club flag, flown at the bow staff in home waters, is now displayed at the starboard yardarm, giving way to the foreign national flag, which is properly displayed at the bow staff.

Motor vessels with two masts. Some of the larger motor craft have two masts. Assuming that the mainmast has no gaff, then the practice is as follows. Her own ensign is at the stern staff as usual, and her private signal or officer's flag stays at the main truck. The club pennant goes to the bow staff, making way for the foreign national flag at the fore truck. This is correct practice whether the vessel is under way or lying at anchor, or at a dock.

The only variation of this procedure for two-masted vessels is found when the mainmast is equipped with a gaff. In such cases, the gaff takes precedence over the stern staff as the position of honor when the vessel is under way. Therefore the vessel's own ensign flies at the gaff instead of the stern staff when under way. However, when she comes to anchor or ties up to a dock, then the ensign should appear at the stern staff just as it would in vessels without a gaff both at anchor and under way.

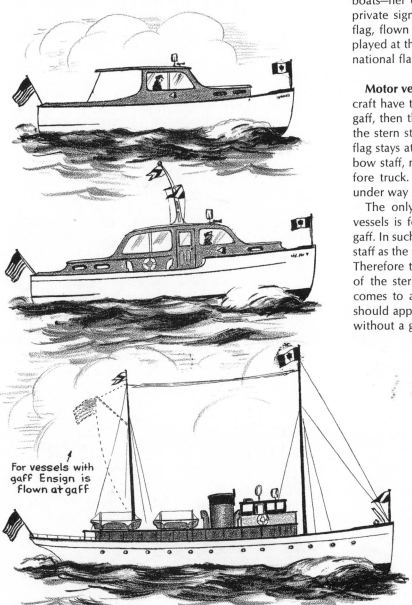

For vessels with gaff Ensign is flown at gaff

NOTE:—National flags should never be flown at a yard arm for any reason. Correct method of flying a foreign flag (illustrated in this article) applies only when waters of that nation are entered.

Ashore, it is common practice among U. S. yacht clubs on the border to fly the Canadian flag at the masthead, with the U.S. flag at the gaff, when they have Canadian entries in races or Canadian flag officers officially in the club house.

Flag Etiquette / CHAPTER 22

SAILING VESSELS

Sailing vessels can also be divided into general classifications, insofar as the display of flags is concerned. This classification is based on the arrangement of their masts, and is as follows: (1) sloops and cutters; (2) yawls and ketches; and (3) schooners, whether they have two masts or more.

Sloops and cutters have only one mast, the basic distinction being that the cutter's mast is further aft. Sailing vessels of this type show their own ensign at the peak when under sail, but at the stern staff when at anchor or under power. Most sailboats today have the jib-headed (Marconi) rig. Since such a rig has no gaff, the ensign is flown from the leech of the sail in a position which would correspond with the peak if there were a gaff.

Sloops and cutters fly the club signal when at anchor only, from the masthead. When under way, the private signal takes the place of the club pennant at the masthead. In the event that the owner is a club officer, then his officer's flag is flown instead of the club flag at anchor or the private signal when under way. All of this practice is identical whether the vessel is in home waters or abroad.

There is no need to displace any of these flags when going abroad. In foreign waters, the sloop or cutter flies the foreign ensign from her forestay when at anchor, and from the forestay or from the forward starboard shroud (one-third mast height) when under way.

Yawls and ketches have two masts, the larger of which is forward. Their ensign flies at the mizzen peak when under sail, at the stern staff when at anchor or running under power without sails. The club pennant is at the main truck, private signal at the mizzen truck. If the owner is a flag officer of a club, the officer's flag flies at the mizzen truck in place of the private signal. Again, this part of flag practice is identical for home or foreign waters.

To take care of the foreign flag, yawls and ketches, like sloops and cutters, fly it on the forestay when at anchor, and on the forestay or forward starboard shroud (one-third mast height) when under way.

Schooners. The third category of sailing vessels embraces schooners, having two masts or more. Perhaps the best way to show the distinction between the practice in home and foreign waters for them is to outline first the procedure in home waters and then point out the differences in practice when abroad.

At home, the schooner has her own ensign at the after peak when under sail, but at the stern staff when at anchor or under power, without sails set. The club signal is at the fore truck, private signal at the main truck. The flag officer's flag would be flown in place of the private signal at the main truck.

Now, when the schooner is in foreign waters, the practice is the same except that the club signal is flown at the fore truck when at anchor only, (not when under way.) Also, when at anchor, the foreign flag is flown at the bow staff or forestay, but when under way the foreign flag should be at the fore truck or the forward starboard shroud.

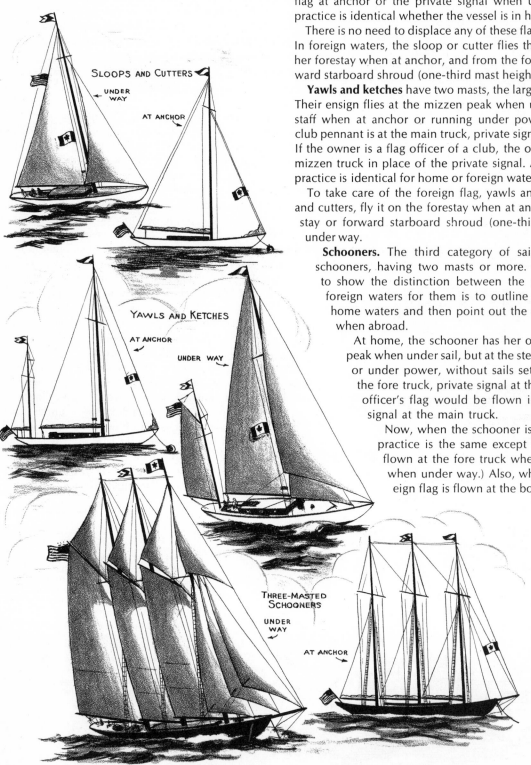

SLOOPS AND CUTTERS
UNDER WAY
AT ANCHOR

YAWLS AND KETCHES
AT ANCHOR
UNDER WAY

THREE-MASTED SCHOONERS
UNDER WAY
AT ANCHOR

See page 364(b) for tabulation of USPS code of flag etiquette for boats in foreign waters, and page ix(a) for complete flag code adopted by the USPS.

Many boatmen spend their time afloat with little or no thought to the customs and etiquette of yachting. This is regrettable, for their activities can be more enjoyable both to themselves and to others with some knowledge and practice of doing things "the proper way."

A *custom* is defined in one dictionary as "the habitual practice; the usual way of doing a thing in given circumstances." Such long-standing practices and procedures have usually developed out of trial and error over many years into the "best," or "safest," or "most appropriate" method. By adhering to yachting customs, a boatman is benefiting from long years of others' experience — to defy custom is really to miss a fine opportunity. A love of boats and the water should be accompanied by respect for the traditions and long-established customs of the sea.

Etiquette has been described as "a prescribed or accepted code of usage as established for any occasion." Since recreational boating is a purely voluntary activity, let us drop the "prescribed" aspect of that description and emphasize the "accepted" qualities of the usages. If etiquette were regarded as no more than blind adherence to certain set conventionalities and amenities of social life, there might be sound reasons why one could question the need for, or desirability of, conforming to relatively rigid rules of conduct.

Just as soon, however, as one realizes that these principles of etiquette are not mere arbitrary laws demanding conformity on the part of all individuals— that they are basically the natural expressions of those who instinctively conduct themselves in a sincerely considerate manner toward all others, regardless of rank or race—it becomes quite obvious why anyone should seek to follow the practices that distinguish the true gentleman and yachtsman.

YACHTING CUSTOMS and ETIQUETTE

CHAPTER 23

Customs in general

In the varied relationships of people in many walks of life, a natural body of customs and accepted procedures inevitably develops to govern such relationships. Nowhere is this better exemplified than in the various branches of government service. In the departments that are concerned with diplomacy and statesmanship, observance of the correct form is inextricably woven into the act itself. In the military services, it is safe to say that efficient functioning could not be achieved without the many established customs and procedures.

Customs in Boating

The direct application of all naval customs and forms of etiquette to boating activities would be quite inappropriate and quickly rejected by most boatmen. There are, however, many customs and items of service etiquette that can be used as-is or modified for the circumstances of non-military small craft. Other boating customs derive directly from the ways of the sea and seafaring men.

Customs and Etiquette / CHAPTER 23

The Skipper

By custom and by law, the skipper of a craft has the sole ultimate responsibility and authority aboard, especially in emergencies. These are spelled out in some detail in Chapter 7; here it is enough to note that these duties and powers have developed over the years, first as desirable and necessary practices, then as customs, and finally, in many cases, into legal requirements.

Leadership

Even on non-military and non-commercial small craft leadership is an important requirement. Getting things done by a willing and happy crew is a large step forward in putting the "pleasure" into pleasure boating. Proper attention to customs and etiquette provides a basis for effective leadership.

Leadership is said to be largely a matter of intelligent and just administration of authority. Knowledge along technical lines and of practical matters does not automatically provide the capability for leadership. This involves a study and cultivation of such qualities as self-control, judgment, courage, earnestness, sympathy, and loyalty, to name just a few of the many necessary attributes. One of the best methods of acquiring these qualities is to consciously take stock of one's own shortcomings with a view toward eliminating deficiencies and developing the desired characteristics—do this rather than demand in one's crew a degree of perfection that one has not himself attained.

Discipline

Leadership and discipline, including self-discipline, are logically considered in conjunction with each other—they are inseparable. Given a group of individuals in which all have the qualities of leadership developed to a greater or lesser degree, discipline will give each person an appreciation of the authority and responsibilities of their appointed or elected leader. Consequently, they will each work at assigned tasks in mutual cooperation, and will not waste time or mental effort in envy of their superior's position. The leader, in turn, will have the ability to inspire his subordinates to self-development and the voluntary

FIG. 2301 By law as well as long-established custom, the skipper of a boat has the sole ultimate responsibility and authority for the actions of the craft and the safety of all those aboard.

acceptance of higher responsibilities. It is an error for any leader to believe that he can grow no more; the effective leader grows as well as the men he leads.

It should be quickly apparent that the principles above have great applicability to the world of boating. The yacht club, Power Squadron, or unit of the Coast Guard Auxiliary that reflects an understanding of these ideas will flourish. Of all places, there is none where the demand for capable leadership and discipline is more vital than aboard a vessel, whether it be a large yacht, an ocean-racing sailboat, or a motorboat of any size. The skipper has, and must have, the final authority; he must be equal to that responsibility. If he is worthy of his trust as a "leader," he will get the cooperation of his crew by "leading" and not by driving.

PERSONAL SALUTES

Hand salutes are not often given by civilian boatmen, although they may be used in some formal ceremonies. In a way, this lack of personal saluting is unfortunate, for what better way is there to say "thank you" to a cooperative bridge tender or to the skipper of a boat that slowed down in passing you than to give him a snappy—but not exaggerated—hand salute. Its meaning will never be misunderstood and it will often be much appreciated. It is more of a show of appreciation than merely a wave of the hand in greeting.

Origins

The practice of hand salutes is believed to have had its origins at least as far back as the days of the Romans, when the raising of one's hand, palm forward, was a gesture to show that no dagger was concealed in it. The native American Indians used much the same gesture to indicate a lack of harmful intent. Today, happily, we have other motives when showing respect for superiors.

Uncovering the head also dates back to ancient days. Certain types of headgear, however, were not easily removed, and so the present day salute evolved as a gesture in which the hand is raised to the visor of the cap in much the same manner as if the visor of a helmet were going to be lifted.

Exchanging salutes

Etiquette prescribes that in ceremonies a person junior in rank or seniority should salute first. It is emphasized that this deference to superiors does not imply an admission of inferiority, no more than one could logically be accused of cowardice when displaying a wholesome respect for laws. Those who might take the attitude that a salute is undemocratic should recognize that such an act is merely an extension of the courtesies of everyday life. The salute, thus understood, becomes an opportunity to respect the authority an official represents with no thought of personal inferiority.

BOARDING AND LEAVING GOVERNMENT SHIPS

It is not inappropriate for a civilian boatman in an organizational uniform, or even in informal clothing but wearing a uniform or visored cap, to observe the proper naval etiquette when boarding and leaving a ship of the Navy, Coast Guard, Coast & Geodetic Survey, or other gov-

FIG. 2302 Of all places, there is none where the demand for capable leadership and discipline is more vital than aboard an ocean-racing sailboat. The skipper must have final authority.

ernmental agency. He can be assured that his actions will be promptly and properly responded to by the personnel of the watch.

Procedures

When reaching the upper platform of the gangway or accommodation ladder, the person about to board, and before stepping aboard, should stop, then turn toward the stern of the vessel and salute the national ensign. He then turns back to the Officer of the Deck (O.O.D.), salutes, and says: "Request permission to come aboard, sir." The O.O.D. returns both salutes as they are given and with the second one says "Permission granted."

When leaving the vessel, the individual first salutes the Officer of the Deck and says: Request permission to leave ship, sir." The O.O.D. returns the salute and grants permission. At the top of the gangway or other platform, the departing person stops, faces aft, and salutes the U.S. Flag; the O.O.D. returns this salute also, but says nothing.

If the individual is *not* wearing a cap, the *salutes* are *omitted,* but the request for permission to board or depart is made as noted above.

DAILY COLOR CEREMONIES

If a boatman is at a yacht club, or a military or naval base, where formal morning and evening color ceremonies are held, he should follow the actions of local personnel who are not in formation. If he is outdoors when the flag is raised or lowered, and he is wearing a uniform or visored cap, he should face the flag and give a hand salute, holding it until the ceremony is completed. If he is wearing a civilian hat, this should be removed and held over the left breast. If no headgear is worn, the right hand should be placed over the left breast. This is the "breast salute." Women not in uniform stand at attention and give the

breast salute. Automobiles are stopped and personnel remain inside.

The above rules do not, of course, apply if the boatman is engaged in hoisting or lowering his own colors. He should complete his actions and then, if the official ceremonies have not ended, he should stand at attention, and salute if appropriate.

On official occasions, the same salutes as above are given for the playing of the Star Spangled Banner or national anthem of another country.

Yachting Etiquette

Etiquette in yachting takes many forms, but all are essentially the act of showing consideration and courtesy to others. The range of correct etiquette extends from simple everyday actions to formal daily routines and official ceremonies.

Boarding another boat

The etiquette to be observed when coming on board another person's boat is derived from that explained above for boarding a naval vessel. Salutes are seldom exchanged, but a simple request for permission to come aboard is always in good taste. An occasion for saluting might be if the individual boarding were wearing a uniform cap and the craft were that of the commodore of the yacht club or the commander of a Power Squadron.

When leaving another's boat, the naval form of requesting permission is not used. A simple statement of thanks for the hospitality or best wishes for a pleasant cruise is sufficient.

SALUTES BETWEEN VESSELS

In formal ceremonies such as a rendezvous of a yacht club or Power Squadron, the fleet of boats present may pass in review before the flagship of the commodore or USPS commander. In such cases, each craft will salute as it passes. In other isolated instances, joining a club cruise or passing a ship with a high public official embarked, salutes may be exchanged between vessels.

Dipping the ensign in salute

Federal law prohibits dipping the Flag of the United States (the 50-star flag) to any person or thing, and only government vessels are permitted to dip the national ensign in reply to a dip.

The law does, however, permit organizational or institutional flags to be dipped. Thus the U.S. Power Squadrons Ensign, when flown from stern or gaff, may be dipped to salute another craft, or dipped in reply to a dip.

The status of the Yacht Ensign (13 stars in a circle around an anchor on a blue field) is not spelled out clearly, but since the law specifically covers only the Flag of the United States, the assumption has been made that the Yacht Ensign may be dipped.

In a fleet review of a unit of the Power Squadrons, the USPS Ensign should be flown from the stern staff or gaff if a suitable size flag is available. In this way, the flag dipped would be that of the organization holding the review.

All vessels in any review, flying either the USPS or Yacht Ensign at the stern or gaff, should dip that flag when their

FIG. 2303 "Dressing ship" is an old custom applicable to yachts as well as to naval and merchant vessels. This is done only on special occasions and the proper procedures must be followed to be correct.

YACHT ROUTINES

The following regulations, particularly applicable to a consideration of yachting etiquette, are taken from that portion of the New York Yacht Club code entitled *Yacht Routine*. These deal with salutes, boats (meaning tenders and dinghies), and general courtesies. Other sections, not given here, relate primarily to the display of flags, signaling, and lights.

The routines of other yacht clubs may be considerably less formal and detailed than that which follows, but whatever routines are used they are likely to have been derived from the procedures of the New York Yacht Club.

Salutes

All salutes shall be made by dipping the ensign once, lowering the ensign to the dip and hoisting it when the salute is returned. All salutes shall be returned.

Whistles shall never be used in saluting.

Guns may be used to call attention to signals, but their use otherwise shall be avoided as much as possible.

Vessels of the United States and foreign navies shall be saluted.

When a flag officer of the Club comes to anchor, he shall be saluted by all yachts present, except where there is a senior flag officer present.

When a yacht comes to anchor where a flag officer is present, such officer shall be saluted. A junior flag officer anchoring in the presence of a senior shall salute.

Yachts passing shall salute, the junior saluting first.

All salutes shall be answered in kind.

A yacht acting as Race Committee boat should neither salute nor be saluted while displaying the Committee flag.

Boats

Upon entering and leaving boats, deference is shown seniors by juniors entering first and leaving last.

When in boats, flag officers display their flags, captains (owners) their private signals, and members (non-owners) the club burgee. When on duty, the fleet captain and race committee display their distinctive flags. The flag of the senior officer embarked takes precedence. A flag officer embarked in a boat not displaying his distinctive flag should be considered as present in an unofficial capacity.

When two boats are approaching the same gangway or landing stage, flag officers shall have the right of way in order of seniority.

Whenever possible, boat booms shall be rigged in at night. Otherwise, a white light shall be shown at the end. All boats made fast to the stern of a yacht at anchor shall show a white light at night.

Courtesies

When a flag officer makes an official visit, his flag, if senior to that of the yacht visited, shall be displayed in place of the burgee while he is on board.

A yacht may display the personal flag of a national, state, or local official when such individual is on board, or the national ensign of a distinguished foreign visitor. This flag should be displayed in place of the private signal or officer's flag for the President of the United States, and in place of the burgee for all other officials and visitors.

On Independence Day, and when ordered on other occasions, a yacht shall, when at anchor and the weather

bow comes abreast of the stern of the flagship and return it to full height when their stern clears the bow of the flagship.

On this occasion, the Flag of the United States should *not* be flown, but if it is, *do not dip it* and use only the hand salute described below. Do not dip any flag other than the flag being flown at the stern staff or the gaff (including the equivalent position on a Marconi sail).

Hand saluting

When a vessel is officially reviewing a parade of other vessels, the senior officer present stands on the deck of the reviewing ship with his staff in formation behind him. Only he gives the hand salute in return to salutes rendered him.

On a boat passing in review, if the skipper has his crew and guests in formation behind him, only he gives the hand salute. If the crew and guests are in uniform and standing at attention at the rail facing the reviewing boat as they pass, they all give the hand salute. The criterion is whether or not the other persons aboard are in formation. If in formation, only the skipper salutes; but if not in formation, all salute.

For both situations, the hand salute is given as the flag is dipped and is held until it is raised again.

Gun salutes

Guns should not be used in salutes between yachts unless ordered by a national authority or by the senior officer present.

FIG. 2304 Cruising will usually take a boatman well away from familiar home waters. He should be alert to the peculiarities of local customs and should conform to the way in which things are done at the club or harbor he is visiting.

permits, *dress ship* from morning to evening colors. See pages 357 and 363.

After joining the Squadron during the Annual Cruise, a yacht shall request permission before leaving.

Cruising

When cruising away from home waters, the wise skipper keeps a sharp eye out for local customs. It is a mark of courtesy to conform to local procedures and practices.

While visiting at a yacht club of which you are not a member, observe the actions and routines of the local owner-members, and particularly the club officers. This is especially important with respect to evening colors. Not all clubs strictly calculate the daily time of sunset, and some may be earlier than you would normally expect.

If you will be off your boat at the time of evening colors—in the clubhouse for dinner, for example—be sure to take down your flags before you leave your craft.

Be a good neighbor

Consideration of the other skipper is an important element of yachting etiquette. Don't anchor too close to another boat so as to give cause for concern for the safety of both craft; consider the state of the tide and the effect of its range on the radius about which you will swing. Use a guest mooring only with permission; tie up to a fuel pier only briefly.

In the evening hours at an anchorage, don't disturb your neighbors on other boats. Sound travels exceptionally well across water and many cruising boatmen turn in early for dawn departures. Keep voices down and play radios only at low levels. If you should be one of the early departees, leave with an absolute minimum of noise.

Be a good neighbor in other ways, too. Don't throw

trash and garbage overboard. Secure flapping halyards; they can be a most annoying source of noise for some distance. When coming into or leaving an anchorage area, do so at a dead slow speed to keep your wake and wash at an absolute minimum.

Passing other boats

A faster boat overtaking and passing a slower one in a narrow channel should slow down *sufficiently* to cause no damage or discomfort. Often overlooked is the fact that it may be necessary for the *slower* boat itself to reduce speed. If that boat is making, say, 8 knots, the faster boat can only slow down to about 10 knots in order to have enough speed differential left to get past. At this speed, the passing boat may unavoidably make a wake that is uncomfortable to the other craft. In such cases, the overtaken boat should slow to 4 or 5 knots to allow herself to be passed at 6 or 7 knots with little wake.

If adequate depths of water extend outward on one or both sides of the course, it is the courteous thing for the passing boat to swing well out to a safe side to minimize the discomfort of the overtaken boat.

Proper etiquette calls for power boats to pass sailing craft astern or well to leeward.

GUESTS ABOARD

If you are invited to go cruising for a day, a weekend, or a more extended period, there are many things to be considered—clothes, promptness, gifts, aids, noise, smoking, privacy, and time.

FIG. 2305 Whenever circumstances such as the depth of water permit, power boats should observe the proper etiquette of passing sailboats on their lee side or crossing under their stern. Consideration of the other skipper is a mark of a good yachtsman. The wake must always be kept down to a reasonable level.

Take a minimum of *clothes*, packed in collapsible containers, or at least in suitcases that will nest inside each other when empty—storage space is severely limited aboard boats. Bring one outfit of "city clothes" for use at those places ashore requiring such dress. Bring two bathing suits if you plan to do much swimming—at times, things dry slowly around a boat. For additional comments on boating clothing and shoes, see Chapter 24.

For the *stowage of clothing* you bring aboard, the skipper may assign a special locker which he has cleared for your convenience. Don't scatter gear and clothing all over the boat. Use the locker provided, keep it orderly, and thus help the skipper keep things shipshape.

When a *sailing time* is given, be there ahead of time. The skipper generally chooses a time with a purpose in mind—the tides and currents, normal weather patterns, the length of the planned run, etc.

Meal times are set for the convenience of the galley hand. It is inconsiderate for a tardy guest to delay meals. In any event, it is bad manners to be late for a meal.

Rising and *bedtimes* are a matter of convenience to everyone aboard because of the generally limited washing and toilet facilities. Get up promptly when the skipper or paid hands are heard moving about. Use the head as expeditiously as possible, make up your bunk, stow any loose gear about the cabin, and appear on deck. When the skipper suggests that it is time to retire for the evening, take the hint and bed down.

Noise on a boat seems to amplify, so walk and speak softly and your shipmates will be glad you're aboard.

Smoking is stopped, of course, when gasoline is to be taken aboard, but care is the order of the day even when smoking is permissible. A carelessly flicked cigarette ash or butt has started many a fire in a chair, awning, or compartment. Cigars leave a particularly unpleasant after-odor and should be enjoyed only in the open air.

Many small particles—pipe tobacco and ashes, peanut shells, bits of potato chips, crumbs, etc.—have a way of getting into cracks, crevices and corners, and there defying the ordinary cleaning facilities found on a boat. Use care with all of these things.

Privacy becomes valuable on a protracted cruise. Part of every day should be set aside for getting away from everyone else aboard. Your cruisemates will be more glad of your company if it is not constant.

Should occasions arise where you board the boat from a *dinghy*, or have an opportunity to use the skipper's dinghy (with his permission, of course) use care in coming alongside. Unship oarlocks which could scar the boat's planking, and stow oars in the boat; never leave them in the oarlocks.

Gifts are certainly not expected, but are always acceptable. Be sure, however, that they are appropriate for boating—if in doubt, make it liquid and consumable. When invited on board for a day or a week, ask what you can bring. If the owner wants to provide all of the food and drink, the guest might take the cruising party ashore for a good dinner at the first port of call. Buying part of the fuel is looked upon as a partial charter by some government agencies, but bringing food or liquid refreshment is not so regarded.

Assistance on board a boat can be useful, or it can do more harm than good. If you don't know what to do, sit down out of the way and be quiet. Always keep out of the line of vision of the helmsman and be particularly quiet and unobtrusive when the craft is being docked or undocked.

If being on board is not a new experience, or you wish to learn to be more useful, you may ask what you can do to help. Ask, however, when things are calm and uneventful; don't ask in the midst of getting under way or coming alongside a pier.

Above all, if you are assigned to do something, do exactly that. If you think that the instructions were wrong, say so, but don't go off on your own when the skipper thinks that you are doing what he asked.

FIG. 2306 Having guests aboard for a day's cruise or longer period can add to a boat owner's enjoyment of his recreation by sharing his enjoyment with others. Guests can do their part by "fitting in" with the routine of the craft.

FIG. 2307 Guests aboard for a cruise may offer their assistance in the operation of the craft or in the daily chores. They should not, however, tackle work without the skipper's knowledge and should work under proper supervision.

CHAPTER 24

BOATING CLOTHING and UNIFORMS

FIG. 2401 Many boatmen find an informal visored cloth cap the most practical form of headgear afloat. It is comfortable, provides good shade for the eyes, and stays on well in a breeze. Club emblems, but no insignia of rank, may be worn on such caps.

(Photograph by Frank Rohr)

The subject of "clothing and uniforms" encompasses both the matter of wearing or not wearing a uniform and that of safe, sensible apparel for today's boating. In each of these areas rather strong differences of opinion will be found to exist.

When it comes to clothing, most boatmen have rather strong convictions as to whether or not they should, or must, abide by any arbitrary set of regulations. The spokesmen of one faction argue that they go afloat for pleasure and relaxation, and propose to dress as they please—for comfort and practicability. The other group advocates strict adherence to all the proprieties, frowning on those who do not conform to the dictates of etiquette, whether it be in dress, the display of flags, or other areas.

Who is right? Actually neither, in the sense that the other would be wrong. There is room for differences of opinion, and no logical reason why each group and individual should not be entitled to his own position and actions.

Good taste

Few boatmen would deliberately violate the principles of good taste in regard to dress aboard their craft. In some cases, it is merely a matter of not realizing that such principles exist. Errors are often made in the use of various devices and insignia worn on uniforms, and in the choice of articles of uniforms themselves. Generally these practices would be corrected if the wearer knew that he was in error.

One thing is certain. The clothing that might be appropriate and acceptable in one situation may be decidedly in bad taste in another. It would be hard to say who would be more uncomfortable—the outboarder in shorts at a yacht club dinner party or the commodore in spotless whites tinkering with a balky engine under a blazing sun.

Origins of present-day clothing

The clothing that is worn while boating today has developed over the years from the quite stiff and formal uniforms of the late 1800's and early years of this century. The steady trend toward smaller, owner-operated craft has taken its toll on the rigid customs of yachting circles—the "dressing for dinner" routine. The establishment of many small, much less formal yacht clubs and boating clubs has likewise supported the gradual change to a more informal mode of attire. A third factor is the general trend of modern life to an easier, more casual mood.

These developments all combine to make a full yachting uniform something of a rarity aboard present-day craft or at typical yacht clubs.

Yacht Club Uniforms

Essentially all yacht clubs provide in their by-laws for uniforms and insignia of rank. In actual practice, however, there will be found a wide variance in the degree to which such apparel is worn. In a very few clubs, the officers, many members who are boat owners, and even some non-owner members have uniforms and will wear them on formal occasions. Hardly ever will full uniforms be worn while cruising or at every-day activities around the clubhouse. It should be noted, though, that members are not required to have uniforms; their purchase and use are purely optional.

Uniforms in typical clubs

In most yacht and boating clubs, the officers will own uniforms, but few members will have them. Rare indeed in these clubs would be a uniform on a member who did not own a boat.

In the smaller and even less formal clubs, the uniforms of officers and members may be limited by general agreement and custom to the wearing of a uniform cap only, worn with any boating clothes of good taste. This is not "wrong" although it may be viewed with disfavor by older, more tradition-minded yachtsmen. It is well in tune with the informality of modern life and family-style boating, particularly outboarding.

When uniforms are worn

Yacht and boating club uniforms are typically worn only on special occasions, although it is quite reasonable to wear a uniform cap with regular clothing while engaged in ordinary activities while afloat or at the club piers. Formal occasions for uniform wearing might include the ceremonies at the beginning of a new season, the installation of officers, holiday regattas, and the like. The best guidance at any club regarding the wearing or non-wearing of the full uniform or cap only is the policy adhered to by the majority of the officers and members.

On board and under way, the cap will probably be the only item of uniform worn on owner-operated boats. On larger craft where there are paid hands to take care of the operation of the yacht, a uniform for the owner would seem to be in far better taste, as well as more sensible, than on a small boat where the owner-captain must break out his own anchor, swab his own deck, and attend to numerous other chores both clean and dirty.

Derivation of the uniform

On one point, at least, there can be little argument. For the occasions where a uniform is appropriate, it should certainly follow the style prescribed by yacht clubs as correct. For authority, no better source can be found than the code to which the New York Yacht Club has adhered for many years. While there may be minor deviations in the practices of other clubs, the N.Y.Y.C. rules are the basic form on which the others are patterned.

Basic uniforms

The service dress uniform prescribed for yacht club officers and members is normally a double-breasted sack coat of navy blue or white cloth, serge or flannel, with trousers of the same material or of white drill. The cap is of navy blue cloth and has a patent leather visor, black chin strap, and black buttons. The white cap is of the same style with a fixed or removable cover. White shirts with black or dark ties are appropriate; some clubs have ties of their own design. White or black shoes are worn to match the trousers; boating shoes are not worn with a uniform except under limited circumstances afloat when advisable for safety.

Cap emblems

There are a number of styles of yachting caps offered by the manufacturers of uniforms. In every case, an emblem or device will be found on the front of the band over the visor. This identifies the club to which the individual belongs and indicates his status in the club. See figures 2402(a), (b), (c), (d). The central part of the device will be an enameled metal or silk embroidered disc showing the distinctive emblem of the club, basically its burgee. This is placed at the intersection of two crossed fouled anchors in gold embroidery.

Insignia of rank

If the yachtsman holds the office of commodore, there will be three gold stars around the anchors, one at the top and one at each side. See fig. 2402(a).

COMMODORE ★ ★ ★
Trefoil with 4 additional black stripes; 3 gold stars within loops.

VICE COMMODORE ★ ★
Trefoil with 3 additional black stripes; 2 gold stars within side loops.

REAR COMMODORE ★
Trefoil with 2 additional black stripes; 1 gold star in center loop.

FIG. 2402(a) Yacht club officers are distinguished by insignia on sleeve and cap. Stars of current officers are gold, those of past officers, when used, are silver.
(All insignia illustrations courtesy Commodore Uniform Company, Inc.)

The vice-commodore of the club, next lower in rank, has the same device except that he is entitled to two stars, one on each side of the anchors.

The third-ranking officer, the rear commodore, rates one star, placed above the device the same as the top star of the commodore.

Members and staff officers

The N.Y.Y.C. code prescribes that captains (owners of boats) and ex-flag officers rate only the two gold fouled anchors without the gold stars of incumbent officers. In some clubs, however, this practice is modified to authorize past officers to wear silver stars of the same number and in the same locations.

In most yacht clubs, a member who is not a boat owner uses a cap device with a *single* fouled anchor placed vertically, fig. 2402(c). Some clubs, however, omit this separate insignia and allow the wearing of two crossed fouled anchors for all members not holding office.

Other officers of a club (often referred to as "staff officers") are distinguished by certain symbols in gold placed above the regular cap emblem, fig. 2402(b). A fleet captain, for example, is identified by a horizontally placed anchor. The secretary is entitled to a maple leaf; the treasurer, an acorn; the measurer, a short bar; and a member of the race committee, a half-inch anchor placed vertically. A fleet surgeon is identified by a red cross.

Variations exist in some clubs—the letter M for the measurer; the letters RC for race committeemen.

Sleeve insignia

Rank and status are also indicated by stripes on each sleeve of the uniform coat, fig. 2402(a). On blue uniforms, the stripes are black; on white coats, they are white.

A commodore wears five stripes of mohair braid, the upper one taking the shape of what is known as a trefoil—this might be described as a triple loop, one part vertical and the others horizontal. In each loop of the trefoil, the commodore wears a gilt star. Regulations, of course, prescribe the width of the braid, how far from the cuff the

lower stripe is and how far apart the others are, the size of the stars, etc.

The vice-commodore wears four stripes, the upper one being a trefoil, and there are two stars, one in each horizontal loop.

The rear-commodore has three stripes with one star in the upper loop of the trefoil formed by the top stripe.

Boat owners and staff officers are entitled to two stripes, the upper one having the trefoil; they, of course, have no stars. Members not owning boats wear a single stripe which has the trefoil.

Ex-flag officers continue to wear the stripes designating their former rank, but omit the stars that they were entitled to while holding office.

No gold braid

Note particularly that in all of the uniform descriptions above there is *no* mention of *gold braid* for the yachtsman, whether member, owner, or officer. The only gold permissible is the gold fouled anchors of the cap device, the stars on cap and sleeve, and the insignia of the staff officers.

The yachtsman does *not* wear a gold chin strap on his cap, nor is there any sanction for the wearing of gold embroidery on the cap visor as is worn by senior Navy and Coast Guard officers—the so-called "scrambled eggs." This has been seen in some boating circles in recent years, but is entirely incorrect and improper for a boatman.

Formal dress

In some of the older clubs, the uniform regulations prescribe a mess jacket for the most formal occasions. This might be compared with a tuxedo or dinner jacket of civilian dress. The yacht club mess jacket is single-breasted, of blue undress worsted, with rolling collar made with a long roll, and pointed lapels. It is trimmed with black silk braid and appropriate collar and sleeve ornaments.

In most clubs, however, the more formal uniform will consist of the regular service dress coat with a bow tie substituted for the usual four-in-hand tie.

STAFF OFFICERS' INSIGNIA

FIG. 2402(b) Cap insignia worn by staff officers are illustrated at the right. Sleeve insignia is shown above—trefoil with one additional black stripe, and insignia of officer in the center loop (in this case the gold anchor of the Race Committee).

RACE COMMITTEE

FLEET CAPTAIN

FLEET SURGEON

SECRETARY

TREASURER

MEASURER

Blazers

A relatively recent development in boating clothing is the wearing of a blazer jacket with matching or contrasting slacks. This is a comfortable and attractive alternative to the full club uniform except on formal occasions. It has been widely adopted and its use continues to spread.

Blazers are dark blue, two- or three-button style, single-breasted with a left upper and two lower patch pockets. Either black or gilt buttons may be prescribed by the club's rules for the front and sleeves of the jacket.

A patch of the club burgee on crossed fouled anchors, or other design derived from the club insignia, is worn on the upper left pocket. The blazer is not, however, an item of uniform and thus no insignia of rank is worn on the sleeve or elsewhere on the blazer. The club uniform cap should be worn with the blazer only if authorized by the club's rules.

UNIFORMS OF PAID CREW

The uniform regulations of the New York Yacht Club, from whence most other clubs' procedures are derived, include a complete set of descriptions of uniforms for various *paid* crew members. Crews, in general, are much smaller today than they were in the days of very large sail and steam yachts when the regulations were originally drafted, but logical adaptations to current conditions can easily be made.

Rare indeed will be the yacht paid captain—"sailing master" in NYYC terminology—in blue uniform with four gold sleeve stripes, or chief engineer with three red stripes, overseeing a crew of mates, assistant engineers, boatswains, oilers, coxswains, and launchmen. If blue crew uniforms are seen, it will be noted that the trefoil device of club members is not worn by professionals.

The typical work and cruising uniform of paid crew is khaki. Blue coats and trousers may be worn in port or for more formal occasions. White uniforms may be worn in warm or hot climates.

Caps for paid crew

The cap is the distinguishing device of the professional. See fig. 2402(d). The use of gold for the chin strap is as proper for the paid crewmen as it is improper for the owner. Further, the insignia above the gold strap is always quite different. There is no single accepted design for the cap ornament for the professional. Many owners have adopted an embroidered design consisting of their club burgee and their personal flag crossed and partially surrounded by a gold wreath. Others use a more simple design of crossed clear anchors (*not* the fouled anchors of the owner's emblem) within a plain gold circle. Engineering personnel would wear a three-bladed propeller in lieu of the anchors.

Skippers and mates of charter fishing boats may be seen using the last design described above with or without the word "captain" or "mate" embroidered in gold above the circle.

CLUB UNIFORMS IN GENERAL

Having read all of the above, one might reach the conclusion that most boatmen own a wardrobe full of uniforms and never relax in anything less formal. That, how-

ever, is not at all true. While the formal occasions mentioned contribute in large measure to the general good fellowship and enjoyment found in yachting circles, if the sport were ever to lose its basic character as a freedom from shore-based conventions, it would very rapidly lose some of its virtues, and most likely many of its followers.

OWNER - CLUB MEMBER

MEMBER (non-owner)

OWNER (non-member)

FIG. 2402(c) While practice varies among yacht clubs, the cap and sleeve insignia illustrated here satisfy the dictates of etiquette. Above—the boat-owning yacht club member has a trefoil with one additional black stripe on the sleeve; the member who owns no boat has the trefoil without additional stripes.

CAP INSIGNIA FOR YACHTING PROFESSIONALS

FIG. 2402(d) Traditionally correct devices for paid hands aboard yachts. Crossed flags in gold wreath may be used, at the yacht owner's discretion, by professional officers and crewmen. Crossed anchors in gold wreath often designate the paid captain. Crossed anchors (in circle) are worn by deck officers, propeller in circle by engineer officers. Lettering in gold wreath (below) is self-explanatory.

FIG. 2403 Officers and members of the U.S. Power Squadrons may wear a variety of uniforms for different climates and occasions. Uniform "C" shown here with long-sleeve white shirt, black tie, and long white trousers is typical of those worn at outdoor summer ceremonies such as flag-raisings. The Sea Explorer Scouts forming the color guard are not a part of the USPS, but many Squadrons do sponsor such units.
(Photograph by Frank P. Beauchamp)

USPS Uniforms

Although the United States Power Squadrons is not a military organization, it has a rather full set of uniforms, winter and summer, formal and informal. These are not required to be worn by all members, and many do not, but they are authorized and specified if desired. Most officers will wear uniforms for meetings, rendezvous ceremonies, and other special occasions. Uniforms are not generally worn to various USPS educational classes.

Uniform combinations

The USPS uniforms range from informal white Bermuda shorts worn with open-neck, short-sleeve shirt to regular dark blue coat and trousers that can be worn with four-in-hand tie during the day or with bow tie for evening events. In between are uniforms consisting of the short-sleeve shirt and long white trousers, or a long-sleeve white shirt and black tie worn with the same trousers. See fig. 2403. The blue uniform coat may also be combined with white trousers for more formal affairs in warm climates. Although not a part of the uniform series, there is a USPS blazer that may be worn for many occasions.

Insignia of rank

Officer's rank in the United States Power Squadrons is indicated on the uniform coat by sleeve braid and embroidered insignia. A varying number of black stripes, up to four, is used as on yacht club uniforms, but in addition there are three different widths of braid used in combination. The long-sleeved white shirt also carries the sleeve insignia but not the braid.

Uniform cap

As with yacht clubs, there is a uniform cap that is worn both with the various uniforms and by itself with informal boating clothes. The rank of various local, District, and National officers is also indicated on the cap. A USPS cap ornament may be worn on non-uniform boating caps, but in such cases no insignia of rank is shown.

Further information

Details of the USPS uniforms and insignia of rank are spelled out in the by-laws of that organization and are illustrated in the officers' manual. A table of information on officers' sleeve braid and insignia, cap insignia, and flags will be found on page 495.

Coast Guard Auxiliary Uniforms

The uniforms worn by officers and members of the Coast Guard Auxiliary have evolved through several distinct phases over recent years. The uniforms are now more "military" than "yachting" although the organization remains basically civilian in nature. Its supervision and administration by the regular Coast Guard does not change the Auxiliary's non-military status. The title of "Commodore" in various combinations remains in use also as a carry-over from earlier days.

Uniform combinations

The uniforms of the USCGAux—and that is the correct abbreviation, not USCGA—include a "service dress" in blue, khaki, and combination (blue coat with white trousers); working uniforms in blue and khaki (with boating shoes optional); and tropical whites. Members of the Auxiliary would not, of course, need all of these uniforms, only those appropriate to their area and normal duties. A black bow tie may be worn with the combination service dress uniform for formal evening events. There are also uniform jackets, raincoats, and overcoats.

Insignia of rank

The rank of various officers is now indicated by sleeve braid, shoulder boards, and pin-on insignia, all patterned after those worn by regular Coast Guard officers, but with differences designed to distinguish the Auxiliarist.

Braid on sleeves and shoulder boards is of silver rather than gold and is worn in stripes, half-stripes, and broad stripes in a series comparable to those worn by Ensigns to Rear Admirals of the Coast Guard and Navy. The Auxiliary, however, does not use rank titles like those of the regular and reserve services. Braid is prescribed for the office held rather than for rank titles. Sleeve braid rings go only half-way around each sleeve.

Shoulder boards worn with khaki uniforms carry the same number of stripes as the sleeves of blue coats; these are also used with the overcoat. Shoulder boards of the most senior officers are solid silver braid with one or two stars as appropriate.

The Auxiliary shield is worn above the stripes of both shoulder boards and sleeve rings.

Collar insignia, worn on the khaki and blue shirts, consist of the same series of designs used for officers of the Armed Forces, but with a letter "A" in blue or red super-

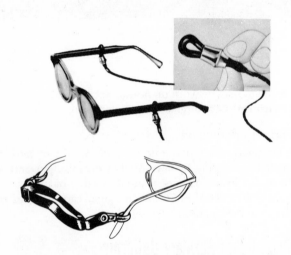

FIG. 2404 Eyeglasses, if accidentally dropped overboard, are likely to be lost. To prevent this, "keeper" cords or holders are available. Light flotation devices may also be attached to the frames.
(Courtesy Commodore Uniform Company, Inc.)

imposed. Similar insignia in slightly larger size are worn on the uniform raincoat.

Rank insignia of the Coast Guard Auxiliary are illustrated on page x.

Uniform caps

Officers and members of the Auxiliary wear frame caps similar to those used by regular officers; white and khaki covers are used—the blue cover is no longer used by the Coast Guard and Navy.

The chin straps of members' frame caps are black, those of officers are silver. Visor ornamentation in silver is worn on the caps of senior officers.

A "working cap" of boating style is authorized in blue and khaki. The fore-and-aft "garrison" cap has been reduced to an optional item only.

INFORMAL CLOTHING

Informal boating clothing varies widely with the individual, the area, and the activities engaged in. Essentially the only degree of uniformity exists at the two extremes—

top and bottom, cap and shoes. In between, the individual is "on his own," guided only by good sense and good taste. "Gag" or extreme uniforms and clothing do not meet the latter criterion and should be avoided.

Caps

The yachtsman who is particular to wear the correct style of yachting cap on formal occasions may often go hatless in the summer time. The sun is strong around the water, however, and protection of some kind for head and eyes is usually necessary, which probably gives rise to the custom of wearing the yachting cap even when other parts of the uniform are omitted. See fig. 2401.

When informal boating caps of the visored style, often referred to as "flat-top" or "flight deck" type, are worn, the careful skipper adds no organizational or rank insignia except as prescribed by the organization concerned.

Especially among the sailing enthusiasts a white cloth hat with wide brim all around, frequently with green underneath or with a green transparent visor, is popular.

Sun glasses

Sun glasses are widely used afloat to prevent eye strain from sun glare. Glasses with Polaroid lenses are among the best as they are particularly efficient in glare reduction.

Those individuals who must wear glasses with prescription lenses for distant vision will find it highly desirable to have a pair made with the prescription in tinted glass. The tint must be dark enough to cope adequately with the extreme degrees of brightness found on and near the water. Persons using bifocals for both near and distant vision correction will also find the use of tinted glass most desirable while afloat.

Regular eyeglasses or sun glasses must be protected from accidental loss overboard. See fig. 2404. A keeper chain or cord can be worn around the back of the person's neck, or a light flotation device can be attached to the frames to keep them from sinking if dropped into the water.

Foot-gear

Shoes that cannot be relied upon to give you a sure, slip-proof footing on a wet or slippery deck are highly dangerous on a boat. Coupled with this is the necessity of using a type of sole and heel that will not scratch fine decks.

For all-around use afloat, the best informal footwear available is a sneaker type of shoe with cloth uppers and soles of special material and designs that can be depended upon to give a grip on a wet, heeling deck. Slits in the soles of Sperry Topsiders, Randy Boatshus, and others provide an effective "squeegee" action. For more dressy occasions, shoes with leather uppers, but the same non-slip soles, are available.

Cork soles and special designs are available that will not pick up grit and sand when worn ashore, to be tracked back on deck when returning to the boat. Ordinary sneakers or tennis shoes may be worn provided they do not have a smooth sole that would permit slipping on a wet deck. Crepe-soled shoes, though comfortable, are doubtful items on a boat.

Women may wear much the same footgear as men. High heels, obviously, have no place on a boat.

BAGGAGE

Closely related to clothing for boatmen is the luggage that they and their guests use to bring aboard such apparel and related personal items. Storage space always seems to be at a premium on boats, and baggage should be soft and collapsible if possible. Canvas duffel bags are probably the most practical luggage, but other types that will fold and stow flat can be used.

IN SUMMARY

Summing up on the question of what to wear while boating, it would seem reasonable to say that if the occasion requires the use of a uniform, then the uniform should be correct in detail according to the regulations and customs of the organization concerned. If, on the other hand, the clothing is being chosen for informal wear, comfort and utility would seem to be the major considerations.

FIG. 2405 **Foul weather gear is essential for most boatmen, especially those on sailing craft. It should provide full protection from wind-driven rain and spray. The type shown above is of international orange color to provide the greatest visibility should the wearer fall overboard. Matching boots with non-slip soles complete the outfit.**

FIG. 2406 **A flotation jacket is comfortable, light weight and functional, serving not only as a practical garment but providing buoyancy like a life preserver if the wearer should fall overboard.**
(Courtesy Commodore Uniform Company, Inc.)

Foul-weather gear

Wet weather clothing is essential afloat. You may have a closed-in deckhouse for protection while under way, but there will be occasions when you must go on deck regardless of rain to make fast to a pier, handle an anchor, or pick up a mooring.

Oilskin slickers and sou'westers were the traditional heavy-weather garments, but now foul-weather gear is made of more modern materials and in a variety of styles. See fig. 2405. Articles are available that are light-weight and comfortable to wear. Check your boating store or mail order catalog for the protective clothing best suited to your boating activities.

The secret of greater comfort is to put on foul-weather gear *before* you get wet. It is equally effective in keeping moisture *in* as well as out if you delay in donning it until after you are partially or thoroughly wet.

Clothing for warmth

Boating activities are often extended into months of chilly weather. Special parka-style coats with hood attached are made for yachtsmen, where warmth and light weight, together with wind- and water-resistant qualities, are prime requisites. These are made of soft waterproof canvas or synthetic material, backed up with a lining for warmth.

A recent development is the flotation jacket which will not only provide warmth on deck but also a considerable measure of buoyancy should the wearer fall overboard. See fig. 2406.

Don't mix uniforms

Since the insignia and devices used by yacht clubs differ from those prescribed for the USPS, it is evident that breaches of etiquette would result from wearing, at the same time, articles associated with two different organizations. This might be compared with wearing two socks that were not mates, or a brown shoe and a black one. For example, fouled anchors belong on the cap of an amateur yachtsman, the member of a yacht club. In the center of these anchors belong the yacht club insignia, not the USPS emblem. Again, the sleeve braid with trefoil identifies the member of a yacht club; USPS insignia of rank or merit marks would definitely be improper in combination with such braid.

Similarly, items of the USCGAux uniform, or rank insignia of that organization, should never be mixed with USPS or yacht club apparel or insignia.

The key to correct practice, of course, is to wear the insignia of only one organization at any one time. And, naturally, to avoid the use of any uniform item or insignia to which you are not entitled.

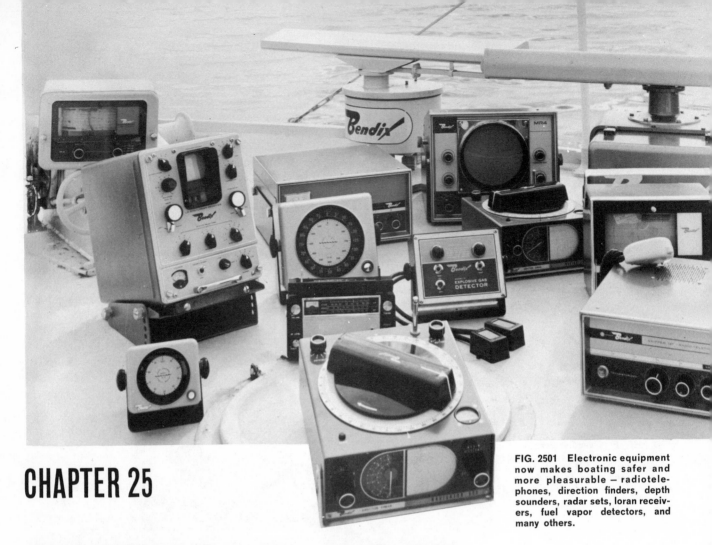

FIG. 2501 Electronic equipment now makes boating safer and more pleasurable — radiotelephones, direction finders, depth sounders, radar sets, loran receivers, fuel vapor detectors, and many others.

CHAPTER 25

ELECTRONIC EQUIPMENT AND ITS USE

THE EVER-INCREASING variety of electronic equipment that is available for small craft places on all boatmen the burden of knowing more about this subject. "Electricity" and "electronics" are generally mysterious topics to the average person on the water; you can't see or feel them, but you know that they exist from their effects. The typical boatman shrinks from technical details on electricity and electronics, yet if he fails to put them to work for him on his boat, he is seriously neglecting valuable assistance easily available to him.

The owner of a boat of any size should know four things about electronic equipment—(1) what items are available for his craft, see fig. 2501, (2) how, in very general terms, such equipment operates, (3) how it should be used for greatest effectiveness, and (4) what he should and should not do regarding its maintenance. Such knowledge and understanding will mean not only greater safety on the water, but also increased convenience and pleasure. There is no intention or expectation of making an electronics technician out of Mr. Average Boatman, but he will be surprised how much can be understood and how much better his equipment will serve his requirements when used with greater knowledge of its capabilities and limitations. Technical language will be kept at a minimum in this chapter; only enough details will be included as are needed to make the necessary explanations.

"Electrical" and "electronic" are terms often used in an overlapping manner. In this chapter, *electronic* will be the term applied to equipment primarily employing tubes and transistors. *Electrical* equipment will be considered to include such things as motors, generators, lights, etc. The items of electronic equipment to be covered here are radiotelephones, direction finders, depth sounders, radar, loran, consolan, automatic steering devices, and several minor items.

Electrical Systems

Electrical power must be considered briefly before electronic equipment for this is the life-blood of such devices as radios, direction finders, and the like. Although a few transistorized items may operate from self-contained batteries, the bulk of electronic equipment is powered from the boat's electrical system. With many of today's outboard motors having generators or alternators, there is almost no lower limit to the size of boat which can have one or more electronic devices, but the total load must not exceed the electrical system's capacity.

Voltages

Electronic equipment is available for input voltages of 6, 12, 32, or 115, the first three being for direct current (DC) systems, and the last for alternating current (AC) operation. By far the most popular voltage is 12; its primary advantages are the widest selection of items and generally the lowest cost.

Six-volt systems are regarded today as obsolete; the lower voltage requires higher currents for the same power, and this results in heavier wiring or excessive voltage drops

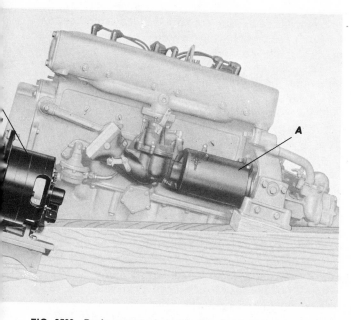

FIG. 2502 Basic source of electrical power for operation of electronic equipment is a generator (A) or alternator (B) driven by main engine. Most electrical systems are 12-volts DC; some older boats have 6-volt. Larger craft may use 32 volts.

between the battery and the load. The use of 32-volt equipment has the advantage of requiring even smaller currents for a given load than do 12-volt systems, but many items such as low and medium power radios, depth sounders, etc., are largely unavailable in this voltage rating. A 32-volt electrical system also has the disadvantage of requiring a larger and more expensive battery.

The current popularity of 12-volt systems in automobiles makes economical the use of such generators, batteries, and regulators on boats. Equipment powered by 115 volts AC can be used, but the primary power must be continuously generated as AC cannot be stored in batteries as can DC. Thus, except where specifically mentioned as being different, it will be assumed throughout this chapter that

items of electronic equipment being discussed are powered from a 12-volt DC electrical system.

Generators and Alternators

On essentially all boats, the basic source of electrical power will be a generator or an alternator driven by a main engine. See fig. 2502. The difference between these electrical devices is technical and the boat owner need not concern himself with them, except to know that the alternator is the more modern of the two and has the advantage of a greater output at low engine rpm. The external result is the same with both devices: a DC voltage somewhat greater than that of the battery (about 14 volts for a 12-volt system) so that energy can be put into the battery against its natural tendency to discharge into a completed circuit.

The flow of electricity from the generator or alternator into the battery will be through a *voltage regulator*. This device prevents the generator from charging at a rate in excess of its capacity, prevents the battery from being overcharged, and cuts out the generator from the circuit when the engine is not running in order to prevent the generator from acting as a load on the battery and running it down. For more on the operation of such generators and alternators, see books and pamphlets on engine electrical systems.

For boats that are in port with people aboard for a considerable portion of the time, it may be necessary to install a *charger*. This electrical device takes 115-volt AC shore power, *transforms* it to a lower voltage, and then *rectifies* it to DC. Thus as energy is taken from the boat's battery, it is replaced from shore power and the battery is completely or partially protected from becoming discharged.

Storage Batteries

Fortunately, DC electrical energy can be stored in batteries, and electronic equipment can be used without the operation of the main engine. See fig. 2503. There are several types of storage batteries that might be used in a boat but cost, that most practical of considerations, eliminates all but the lead-acid type used in automobiles.

In connection with electronic equipment, the basic question may be stated as "Is there enough storage capac-

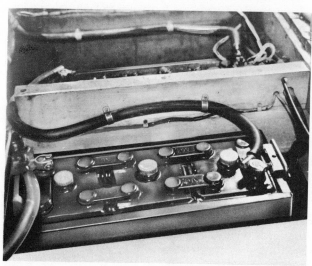

FIG. 2503 Direct current (DC) electrical energy can be stored in a battery. Boats commonly use automobile-type lead-acid batteries.

ity in the boat's electrical system for me to add this new equipment?" Capacity is measured in *ampere-hours*—the product of current drain in amperes multiplied by time in hours. This must be computed for all electrical loads, lights, motors, pumps, etc., as well as for electronic equipment. And there must be enough left over to start the main engine if only one set of batteries is installed! If the estimate of demand exceeds capacity (or if this has been found out the hard way!), a larger battery is needed. The installation of a larger battery may or may not require a larger generator and new regulator. The ratio of running time to idle time will determine this.

Wiring

If the generator and battery are the heart of a boat's electrical system, then the wires supplying the power to the electronic equipment are the veins and arteries. The wires must be heavy enough, of sufficient cross-sectional area, to carry the current of the loads connected to that

Fig. 2504
RECOMMENDED WIRE GAUGE SIZES
12-Volt Systems

Distance in feet—Source to Load

Current in Amps	10 or less	15	20	30	40	50
5	14	14	12	12	10	8
10	12	12	10	8	6	6
15	10	10	8	6	6	4
20	10	8	6	6	4	2
30	8	6	6	4	2	2

FIG. 2504 Table indicates minimum size of wire for various combinations of current and distance, based on voltage drop of not more than ½-volt in wiring exclusive of connectors. Distances are measured along path followed by wires. For 6-volt systems, substract 2 from each gauge number; for 32-volt systems, 4 may be added, but do not use wire smaller than 14-gauge for any circuit.

circuit. Adequate size is determined by two factors: heating effect and voltage drop. The passage of current through a wire increases its temperature; obviously it must not become so hot that it is a fire hazard. As a general rule of thumb, a wire should not become appreciably warm to the touch when carrying its full load.

The voltage drop problem is the more common one. The heating losses just mentioned result in a lower voltage being delivered to the load than is put into the wire at the generator/battery end. The voltage drop increases with a greater load, being directly proportional to the current in the wire. If the conductors are not of adequate size, the voltage delivered may be too low to operate the electronic device or other load efficiently.

Most, but not all, boats are delivered with wiring adequate for the installed equipment. The problem normally arises as additional accessories are installed. The solution requires either the replacement of existing wires with larger conductors, or the installation of additional main circuits back to the battery (assuming, always, that the various load combinations have been calculated and the

battery capacity is adequate).

The *gauge number* of wire runs opposite to its size; the larger the wire, the smaller the gauge number. Wires of smaller diameter than 14 gauge should not be used for any purpose in a boat's electrical system; most circuits should have heavier wire. The voltage drop is proportional to the length of the circuit between source and load. The longer the circuit, the larger the wire must be to prevent an excessive drop. Figure 2504 provides information to determine the minimum size of wire to be used for various loads and lengths of circuits in a 12-volt system. The insulation of wiring used on boats should be suitable for the damp conditions which will be found below decks; thermoplastic insulation, type T or TW, is best.

Switches, Fuses, Circuit Breakers

Of the utmost importance in the electrical system providing power to the boat's electronic equipment are the various protective devices, including *switches, fuses,* and *circuit breakers.* Every marine electrical system should have a *main distribution center* where there are switches and overload protective devices. In addition to the switches on the individual pieces of electronic gear which are used to turn them on and off in regular operation, the various loads should be connected together into several *branch circuits,* each with a protective element and a means of shutting off power. This is necessary in order that a short-circuit or other failure on one branch circuit will not require turning off all electrical power.

The combining of loads into branch circuits should be carefully considered, as should the selection of the existing circuit to which a new accessory is to be connected. Loads which are likely to be used at the same time should be connected to different branch circuits; likewise, the loads that are most vital to the boat's safety should be connected to different branch circuits.

Further, there should be a *master switch* by means of which all electrical power can be cut off in case of fire, for working on the electrical system, or when the boat is to be left unattended. An excellent type of master switch is an enclosed, explosion-proof, heavy-duty switch which can be mounted directly at the battery and operated remotely from the instrument panel by means of a cable such as is used on engine chokes and throttles.

Overload protection may be by means of either fuses or circuit breakers. Fuses are less expensive initially, but are a one-time-use device. The cartridge type which fits into clips is preferred over the screw-in plug type often found on shore. The cartridge type is less subject to loosening under vibration, with resulting poor contact. On circuits with motors, be sure to use a "slow-blow" type of fuse in order to withstand the initial starting current surge without going to an overly large capacity fuse for the wiring to be protected. Circuit breakers are a greater initial expense, but there are no spares to be bought and carried aboard as there are with fuses. Many types of circuit breakers can be tripped manually and thus can additionally serve as switches.

With this consideration of electrical systems as the primary power source, we can now turn our attention to the actual items of electronic equipment suitable for use on recreational small craft, and desirable for greater safety and convenience.

Radiotelephones

When the subject of electronic equipment for boats arises, the first thought probably will be "radio." See fig. 2505. The principal purpose of a radio on any recreational boat is *safety*. Certain other uses are authorized, but by law these are secondary to safety communications.

Safety Communications

A boat's radio may be used to summon assistance in a wide variety of situations. A leak may have started, involving risk of sinking; the motor may have failed in the face of worsening weather; or there may have been illness or injury to some person aboard. The possibilities of radio's adding to the safety of a boat and its crew are virtually unlimited.

There are many stations listening on the distress frequency — Coast Guard shore facilities, lighthouses, and craft of all sizes, plus many commercial stations on shore. In addition, the regulations of the Federal Communications Commission (FCC) require that a listening watch be maintained when the radio equipment of a boat is turned on but is not actively being used to communicate with another station. Thus there is a high degree of likelihood — a near certainty—that someone (probably many) will hear your distress call and either come to your assistance or get help for you.

Operational Communications

In addition to its safety value, a radio on a boat may be used for contacts with other boats for "operational" communications. The large number of marine band stations, and the few radio channels available, have made it necessary for the government to impose severe restrictions on the use of radios. As defined by the FCC, operational communications are limited to matters relating to "navigation, movement, and management." *Navigation* includes the actual piloting of a vessel, while *movement* relates to future moves of the boat such as might occur during a club cruise. Radio messages of the *management* category pertain to the obtaining of fuel, dockage, repairs, etc., and are limited to matters too urgent to permit handling by slower means of communication.

Business Communications

A third type of operational radio traffic is called "business communications," but this is limited to commercial and government craft, and so need not be considered here. Note that for talking between recreational boats, the *only* permitted kinds of radio transmission are *safety* and *operational* communications as narrowly defined by the FCC. Social and personal conversations between boats — any "superfluous" communications—are strictly prohibited.

Ship-to-shore Communications

In most areas of the United States, a radio on a boat also makes possible contact with various commercial shore stations on channels designated for that purpose. Through these stations, the boat becomes part of the nationwide telephone system; calls may be placed to, or received from, any home or business telephone. The restrictions placed on boat-to-boat contacts do not apply on these channels; calls placed through a "Marine Operator" may

FIG. 2505 A radiotelephone, properly selected, installed, and used, can provide safety and operational communications to other boats, the Coast Guard, and to shore stations.

be of a personal or social nature. The charges for ship-to-shore calls are quite reasonable — the regular land telephone rates from the location of the shore station plus a dollar or two depending upon the position of the boat.

Frequency Bands

Radiotelephones for ships and boats operate on two frequency bands. Generally speaking, these can be called medium frequency (MF) and very high frequency (VHF). (We say "generally speaking" because many MF sets will also cover some high frequency (HF) channels, but these are quite different from VHF.) Equipment operating in the Citizens Band may also be used on boats; these sets, however, are not in the "maritime service" as established by the FCC and must be considered separately.

Probably 98% or more of the radios now on boats operate in the MF band, on frequencies between 2 and 3 megacycles. (One megacycle (Mc/s) equals 1,000 kilocycles (kc/s).) The discussion which follows will be focused on MF equipment; VHF will be discussed later.

Choosing a Set

The selection of a radiotelephone is much like that of a new automobile—there are many manufacturers and many models. A number of factors must be weighed in determining which is the right set for your boat.

Almost certainly, the first question that will be asked is "How powerful a set should I get?" A decision should be based on the intended use of the boat and its radio, and on the electrical power available on board. See fig. 2506. The legal power limits are 15 watts to 150 watts (400 watts is permitted for coastal ship-to-shore contacts). These are input powers to the final amplifier stage of the transmitter.

Choosing a too-powerful set for the electrical system of your boat will only lead to trouble, while placing too much emphasis on economy and picking a radio of insufficient power will surely result in disappointment. The battery drain may be roughly calculated as follows: multiply the transmitter input power rating by 3 for a transistorized set or by 4½ for a vacuum tube set. This will give the approximate drain on the boat's electrical system when the transmitter is on the air. Divide this power in watts by the voltage of the electrical system and you will have the drain in amperes. This is, of course, the maximum, and not the average, drain, but the wiring and the battery capacity must be adequate for the greatest load to be imposed. The average load will be less; how much less is determined by the ratio of transmitting time to listening time. The above calculations are intended to give only a rough indication of maximum battery drain. When considering any specific radio, consult the advertising literature or instruction book to learn the specific primary power requirements of that set.

Power and Range

"How far can I talk with a transmitter of a certain power?" Unfortunately, there is no clear and specific answer. The limitations result much more from the degree of congestion on the radio channels than on transmitter power. Very roughly, the following daytime ranges over salt water might be expected under average interference conditions:

20 watts	30 miles
35 watts	40 miles
65 watts	50 miles
150 watts	65 miles

At night, signals will be heard at greater distances, but the interference level rises correspondingly as additional stations come within reception range. Transmission over fresh water will reduce operating range, and if land areas lie between the two stations, an even greater reduction will occur.

The setting of a marine radio to the desired frequency is simplicity itself; all tuning is done at the time that the set is installed. Thereafter, the boat owner merely turns a selector knob to the desired channel or pushes the proper button. Most marine radiotelephones have from four to eight channels, the larger number being found on the more powerful and more expensive sets. Thus the boat owner must determine his requirements for different channels and use this as the second factor in selecting the radio for his boat.

Number of Channels

The legal minimum number of channels, set by the FCC, is three—these are the 2182 kc/s distress and calling channel plus two working frequencies. The boat owner may also want to have the ability to talk with the Coast Guard on their frequency of 2670 kc/s, and with one or more marine operators. Except for the boat that travels very widely, six channels will probably prove sufficient. Excess channel capability in your set is not harmful, but it does add to the purchase price without being of any value to you.

Antenna and Ground

The overall radio installation includes an antenna and ground system as well as the basic set. These are important

FIG. 2506 Select antenna of good quality, as large as can be safely mounted. Install clear of other metallic objects, as high as possible.

FIG. 2507 Marine radios come in wide variety. This 150-watt unit, maximum power for inland waters, has eight channels and provision for remote operation. "Squelch" control silences normal background noise.

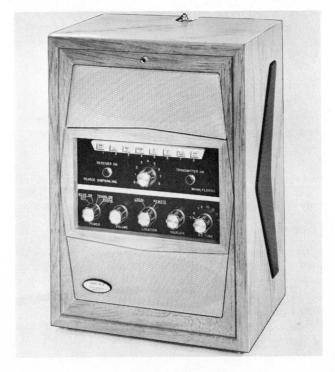

FIG. 2508 Although range is not as great, VHF (Very High Frequency) reception is relatively free from static and man-made electrical noises. VHF channels are less congested, interference between stations rare.

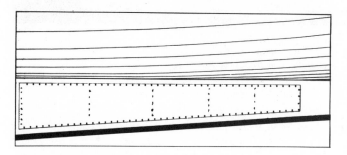

FIG. 2509 Copper sheet secured to wooden keel provides adequate ground; consult service technician as to size. On carvel hulls, ground plate may be attached to planking.

items and deserve careful consideration. An antenna for a boat should be as large as can be properly mounted and of high quality. See fig. 2506. The ground system must have an adequate size plate properly installed. See fig. 2509. Money invested in the best possible antenna and ground system will pay off in results far more than if it had been spent for greater transmitter power.

The VHF Band

The characteristics of the VHF band, 156-162 Mc/s, are in general the reverse of the MF band discussed above. There is little congestion on the various channels, but the range is quite limited. The principal advantage is more reliable communication with almost interference-free reception. The normal range is only about 20 miles, but it is unchanged whether by day or night. There is also a desirable freedom from static caused by lightning and local electrical noises since VHF sets use frequency modulation (FM). See fig. 2507.

In the past, the major obstacle to VHF installations has been their greater cost. Now, however, sets are on the market at prices comparable to those of 2-3 Mc/s equipment. This development should expedite the move to the more technically desirable VHF channels. In recent years, the Coast Guard has greatly expanded the number of its boats and shore stations that can operate on VHF as

well as MF. Thus there is now some coverage for emergency calls and this will continue to grow but, for the foreseeable future, MF (2182 kc/s) offers the better chance of getting assistance when it is needed.

Installation and Maintenance

Radio equipment may be physically installed and electrically connected by the boat owner or any person. Before it is put on the air, however, the set must be checked out by a person holding a first or second class license who will make certain tests required by the FCC rules. Radio installations on gasoline-powered boats will generally require some form of ignition noise suppression or shielding; this is a job for a technician. With regard to maintenance, an unlicensed person is limited to matters which will not affect the quality of the signal on the air. For example, he can replace bad fuses, tubes, etc., but cannot change crystals or adjust antenna loading.

RADIO LICENSES

With over 100,000 marine radio stations operating on a very few channels in the 2-3 Mc/s band, the need for licensing and regulations can easily be seen. The FCC issues its Rules and Regulations in various "Parts," of which "Part 83—Stations on Shipboard in the Maritime Service" is applicable to recreational boats.

To control the use of radio stations, holding down interference and making possible emergency and essential communications, a system of licenses is used. Recognizing that harmful interference could result from either malfunctioning equipment or from misuse of a properly operating set, licenses are required for both the station (see fig. 2510) and the person operating it. Although it is termed a station license, the FCC authorization is essentially concerned with the transmitting component only. The set owner need not concern himself with the many technical requirements for equipment provided that he has a set that is "type accepted."

The Station License

To obtain a station license, an individual must be a citizen of the United States. (If the applicant is a corporation, the situation is more complex; see Section 83.23 of the FCC Rules.) Application is made on Form 502 which is either mailed to the FCC, Gettysburg, Penna. 17325, or taken to one of the more than 30 FCC field offices. The fee for a station license is $10 for the five-year term. The actual issuance of the license will take perhaps as long as 30 days, but if the application is personally taken to an FCC office, you will be given an interim authorization which will permit immediate use of your set; the fee for station license plus interim authorization is $13.

Radio station licenses are issued in the name of the *owner* and the *vessel*. A station license is not automatically transferred to another person upon sale of the boat, nor may a license be moved with the radio set to a new craft owned by the same person. A simple change in the name of the boat or licensee (but not a change in ownership), or his address does *not* require license modification. Just send a letter to the FCC advising them of the change; a copy of this letter must be posted with the license. Neither modification of license nor letter is required for a change

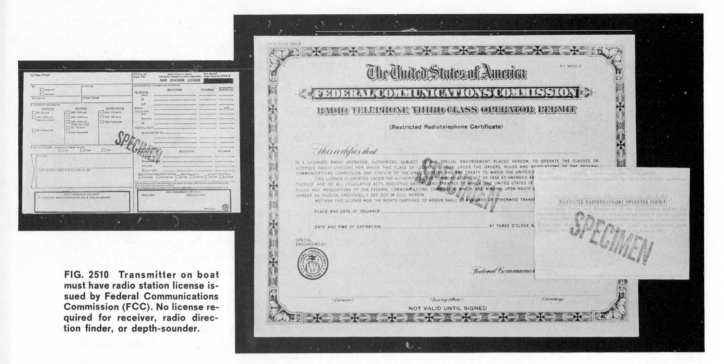

FIG. 2510 Transmitter on boat must have radio station license issued by Federal Communications Commission (FCC). No license required for receiver, radio direction finder, or depth-sounder.

FIG. 2511 In addition to station license, person in charge of set must have operator's permit. Either Restricted Radiotelephone Operator Permit or Third Class Radiotelephone Operator Permit is satisfactory for voluntarily equipped boat.

in type-approved equipment operating in the same frequency band. If VHF is to be added to a 2-3 Mc/s station, a modification is needed.

The regulations require that a station license be conspicuously posted aboard the vessel. At the end of its five-year term, it must be renewed if continued operation of the station is desired. Form 405-B is used for renewal; it should be sent to Gettysburg with a $4 renewal fee before the expiration of the license. If, but only if, timely application for renewal has been made, operation may continue even should the renewed license not be received before the expiration date. If the use of the radio station is permanently discontinued at any time, the license must be returned to the FCC in Washington for cancellation.

The Operator's Permit

A personal license is required for the operation of any marine band radio station. The average boatman will obtain either a *Restricted Radiotelephone Operator Permit* or a *Third Class Radiotelephone Operator Permit*. See fig. 2511. Higher class licenses are available for persons with technical training and experience, but they are needed only for making tuning adjustments and repairs. An unlicensed person may talk into the microphone of a radio, but a licensed operator must be present and responsible for the use of the station.

With certain specified exceptions, an applicant for any grade of license must be a U.S. citizen. A Restricted Permit is obtained by submitting an application on FCC Form 753. This form contains all necessary instructions, including where to mail it; there is no need to appear in person at any FCC office. The permit is issued, without test or examination, by "declaration." The applicant must be at least 14 years old and "certify" that he (1) can receive and transmit spoken messages in the English language; (2) can keep a rough log in English, or in a foreign language translatable into English; (3) is familiar with the applicable laws, treaty provisions, rules, and regulations; and (4) understands his responsibility to keep currently informed of the regulations, etc. The Restricted Permit, fee $2, is valid for the lifetime of the person to whom issued, unless, of course, it is suspended or revoked.

For the Third Class Operator Permit, there is no age limit, but an examination is required. This test is nontechnical, covering only operating rules and procedures; questions are all of the multiple-choice type. You will find the examination not at all difficult if you prepare yourself for it properly. A free Study Guide is available from FCC offices. The privileges of this higher class of license are currently no greater than those of the Restricted Permit, but it has become a matter of pride for many boat owners to qualify for it and post it on their boat. Boats carrying more than six passengers for hire, however, are "compulsorily equipped" and must have a crewman with at least a Third Class Permit. The fee for a Third Class Permit is $3, and it is issued for a five-year term.

If your radio operator permit is lost, or becomes so mutilated that it is illegible, you should immediately apply for a duplicate. Use the same form as for the original application, and include a $2 fee regardless of the grade of the permit. The circumstances must be clearly stated and, if the license has been lost, you must certify that a reasonable search has been made. Continued operation is authorized if a signed copy of the application for a duplicate is posted. Should a lost license be found later, either it or the duplicate must be sent at once to the FCC for cancellation.

FIG. 2512 The FCC Rules require that a radio transmitter be secure against use by unauthorized persons. A set in an exposed location, as above, can be fitted with a key-operated switch for its electrical power. Physical security may also be used, such as a lock for the panel door in fig. 2513.

RADIO OPERATING RULES

Hand in hand with licensing, radio operating rules have been established to bring order out of chaos on the air and reduce the interference that would inevitably result from the overcrowded conditions on the few frequencies available. Actually, the legally required procedures are only a bare minimum and must be supplemented with voluntary procedures for the most efficient communications.

As stated before, radio communications (other than ship-shore telephone calls) must be necessary and of a "safety" or "operational" nature. Even within these limitations, a system of priorities has been established to make sure that the more important messages get through. First, of course, are *distress* calls and related follow-up messages; these are identified by the signal "Mayday" and receive "absolute priority" over other communications. Second are *urgent* messages; these are defined as relating to the safety of a ship, aircraft, or other vessel, or of some person on board or in sight. Urgent communications are identified by the signal "Pan." In third place on the priority list are *safety* messages, those concerning the safety of navigation or giving important weather warnings; these transmissions are identified by the safety signal, "Security."

The system of priorities has been established to ensure that the message that *has* to get through does so without delay. No station or operator has any exclusive rights to any frequency; the nature of his traffic determines whether he should transmit or keep silent. One of the most important FCC regulations requires that an operator *listen before transmitting* to ensure that he will not interfere with the communications of others, and particularly not with distress or other priority traffic. See fig. 2518.

2182 kc/s for Calling and Distress

The most important channel in the MF band is 2182 kc/s —the International Radiotelephone Distress Frequency. In order to keep one channel relatively clear of traffic so that even a weak distress call can be heard, the use of this frequency is limited to distress traffic and the initial contact between vessels. This latter use as a "Calling Frequency" is permitted to ensure that when a station is not working on another channel, it is listening on 2182 kc/s for calls. Thus many stations are constantly monitoring the distress frequency and a call for help is much more likely to be heard.

Listening on 2182 kc/s is not only a logical procedure, it is legally required. A "voluntarily equipped" boat need not have its radio turned on, but if it is, it must be tuned to the distress and calling frequency when not being actively used on another channel. A "compulsorily equipped" boat must have its radio on and tuned to 2182 kc/s when not communicating on another frequency.

FIG. 2513 Radio station license must be posted near equipment. On voluntarily-equipped boats, an Operator Permit may be posted. Alternatively, a Restricted Permit or a Verification Card for a Third Class Permit may be carried in one's personal possession.

Ship-to-ship and Ship-to-shore Channels

The second group of frequencies covers the ship-to-ship "working" channels. After making their initial contact on 2182 kc/s, stations desiring to communicate with each other must shift from the calling channel to a working frequency. These frequencies are:

2638 kc/s . . . . All areas
2003 kc/s . . . . Great lakes only
2830 kc/s . . . . Gulf of Mexico only
2738 kc/s . . . . All areas other than Great
                       Lakes and Gulf of Mexico
2142 kc/s . . . . Pacific Coast south of 42°
                       North latitude; daytime only.

For ship-to-shore calls, a third series of channels is provided. These assignments will vary for the different Marine

Operators located along the coasts and the Great Lakes. The channels for your area can be found in Part 83 of the FCC Rules.

On the Great Lakes and adjacent waters, the various frequencies are normally referred to by "channel numbers"; in Canada, some are designated by "range numbers." Those most used are:

2182 kc/s	Channel 51	Range 1
2003 kc/s	Channel 52	Range 4
2638 kc/s	Channel 54	
2670 kc/s	Channel 56	

Legal Requirements

Legal operation of a radio station aboard a boat requires four things. First, a license for the station, properly posted.

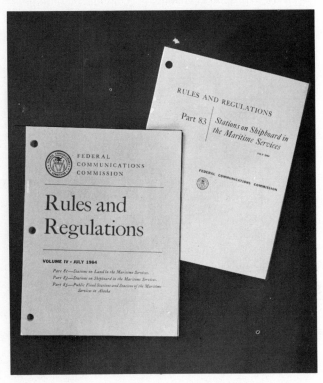

FIG. 2514 Every radio station licensed in Marine Service must have current copy of Part 83, FCC Rules and Regulations. See text for details.

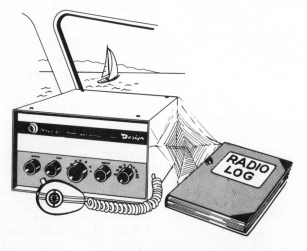

FIG. 2515 Every radio station on a boat must have radio log. Requirements are simple, but don't neglect them!

Second, an operator's license. This may be posted, or a Restricted Permit or a Verification Card for a Third Class Permit may be carried on one's person. Third, a station log. Fourth, an up-to-date copy of Part 83 of the FCC Rules on board or in a secure place on shore.

Part 83 will be found with two other parts in Volume IV of the FCC Rules and Regulations. See fig. 2514. This volume may be purchased by mail from the Superintendent of Documents, Government Printing Office, Washington, D. C. 20402. The price is $2 which includes a subscription to changes to this volume as issued. Changes are mailed in the form of reprinted pages; it is a simple task to remove old pages and insert new ones.

The Radio Log

Log keeping for a radio station on a voluntarily equipped boat has been made much easier than it used to be, but don't let this simplification stop you from meeting the present minimum requirements of the FCC. See fig. 2515. Each page of the log must show the name of the vessel and the radio call sign; each entry must be signed by the person making it. Entries are required for all distress calls heard or transmitted, for all urgent and safety communications transmitted, and any information related to maritime safety. The log must also show the time of starting and ending a listening watch on 2182 kc/s, *but remember that the keeping of such a watch is not mandatory on recreational boats.*

All installation, service, and maintenance work performed on the radio equipment must be logged. It is *not* necessary to make entries for ordinary communications to other boats, the Coast Guard, or shore stations. Logs must be retained for one year following the last entry, except for unusual circumstances described in the Rules. Logs must be made available for inspection upon request from any authorized FCC representative. Inspection of the station by such an official must be permitted at any reasonable hour, and at such frequent intervals as may be determined necessary in the discretion of the FCC.

Rules Governing Transmissions

Transmissions on the calling channel must be limited to the securing of an agreement as to the working frequency to be used, and this may not take longer than two minutes. Any one calling transmission must not take longer than 30 seconds and, if no reply is heard, you must wait two minutes before calling again. Another two minutes must separate a second and a third attempt to make contact and, if these fail, a delay of 15 minutes is required before a new calling cycle can be started (the 15 minutes may be reduced to 3 if other stations will not receive interference from the calls).

Once contact is made on a working frequency, the exchange of transmissions (between boats) must (1) be of a legally proper nature, (2) be of the minimum length possible, and (3) not exceed three minutes in length. After concluding the contact, neither boat shall re-contact the other until 10 minutes have elapsed. The stations may, however, communicate with others during this time. These time limitations do not apply in emergency situations, nor do they apply to ship-shore telephone calls.

The Communications Act of 1934, together with the FCC Rules, strictly prohibit the use on the air of any language which is "obscene, indecent, or profane." This is watched as closely as possible by various government monitoring stations and violators have been taken into court a number of times. Special, more severe, penalties are specifically provided for this offense.

Procedure for Station Identification

The FCC has established certain procedures to be followed in identifying your station on the air. Such identification must be given in the English language by stating the official call sign. Phonetic words for the letters may be used but are not legally required; any understandable word may be employed, but use of the international aviation and military alphabet is recommended. See fig. 2516. If the station is operating under an interim authorization, it will not have received its call sign. In this case, identification must be made by announcing the name of the craft *and the name of the licensee.* The licensee's name is required because of the great number of boats with identical or similarly sounding names. It is often erroneously omitted, but this is a violation subject to penalties.

Radio stations must be identified, as a minimum, at the beginning and end of an exchange of transmissions with another station, but identification of *each* transmission is *not* required. If both 2182 kc/s and a working frequency are used, the beginning and ending identification is required on each frequency. The station's call sign or interim identification must be made with each transmission for any other purpose, such as a test. If the exchange of transmissions exceeds 15 minutes (which would be legal only on ship-to-shore telephone calls) the station must identify itself at least once each 15 minutes.

Secrecy Requirements

The Communications Act of 1934 and the Rules of the FCC protect the *secrecy* of communications. No person may divulge to another person, except the addressee or his authorized agent, any knowledge gained from receiving or intercepting radio transmissions not addressed to himself, *nor shall he use such knowledge for his own benefit.* This basic point of law should be carefully noted by all who operate radios on boats. It does not apply to distress communications nor to broadcasts for the general use of the public, but it does apply to *all* other conversations heard on the air. It could even be construed to apply to the fellow who listened to find out where the fish were biting and then moving in on the good spots.

OPERATING PROCEDURES

The FCC Rules contain only a few instances of specific operating procedures, chiefly in connection with emergency communications. The various examples of operating procedures given below are in conformance with the regulations, but go further than the legal requirements; they are offered as examples of good practices on the air. See fig. 2517.

How to Make a Call

Listen carefully to make sure that the channel you want to use is not busy. If it is busy, you will hear voices, or from most public shore stations, an intermittent busy tone. Except in a safety emergency, don't interrupt.

Standard Phonetic Spelling Alphabet

A	ALFA	**N**	NOVEMBER
B	BRAVO	**O**	OSCAR
C	CHARLIE	**P**	PAPA
D	DELTA	**Q**	QUEBEC
E	ECHO	**R**	ROMEO
F	FOXTROT	**S**	SIERRA
G	GOLF	**T**	TANGO
H	HOTEL	**U**	UNIFORM
I	INDIA	**V**	VICTOR
J	JULIETT	**W**	WHISKEY
K	KILO	**X**	X-RAY
L	LIMA	**Y**	YANKEE
M	MIKE	**Z**	ZULU

FIG. 2516 When receiving conditions are poor, use phonetic equivalents for individual letters in spelling out difficult words such as name of boat or person.

When the conversation is to take place on a ship-to-ship frequency—unless you have reached an agreement in advance as to the time and frequency, establish contact on 2182 kc/s and then shift to the agreed-upon intership channel.

When the conversation is to take place through a commercial shore station—make your initial contact on a working frequency of that station; this will speed your call.

Both of these practices are designed to relieve the load on 2182 kc/s so that its utility for safety purposes will not be jeopardized.

Steps to Follow in Making a Call (other than a Distress, Urgency, or Safety Call)

Boat-to-boat calls—Listen to make sure 2182 kc/s is not busy. If it is free, put your transmitter on the air and say—

"(Name of boat called) This is (Name of your boat and call sign), Over." To avoid confusion, always observe the proper sequence of call signs—state the name or call sign of the *other station first,* then give your own identification after saying 'This is'—don't reverse the sequence.

(If necessary, the identification of the station called, and your boat's name and call sign may each be given two or three times, but not more; the entire calling transmission must not take longer than 30 seconds.)

Listen for a reply. If no contact is made, repeat the above after an interval of at least two minutes. After establishing contact switch to the agreed upon intership working channel. One exchange of communications shall not exceed three minutes after establishing contact on the working frequency. After conversation is completed, say—

"This is (name of your boat and call sign), Out."
You shall not establish contact thereafter with the same boat until 10 minutes has elapsed.

Ship-to-shore Service

Listen to make sure that the working channel you wish to use is not busy. See fig. 2518. If it is clear, put your transmitter on the air and say—

"(Location) Marine Operator This is (Name of your boat and call sign), Over."

Listen for a reply. If no contact is made, repeat after an interval of at least two minutes.

When the Marine Operator answers, say—

"This is (Name of your boat and call sign) calling (telephone number desired), Over."

After the telephone conversation is completed, say—

"This is (Name and call sign of your boat), Out."

How to Receive a Call

Your boat can be reached only when your receiver is turned on and tuned to the frequency over which you expect to receive calls.

The receiver you use to maintain watch on 2182 kc/s

FIG. 2518 To minimize interference, FCC has established strict rules. Listen before transmitting and do not interfere with communications in progress. Keep contacts short and observe time limitations.

FIG. 2517 Booklet "Marine Radio Telephony" contains extracts from FCC Rules plus explanations to make them easily understood. Available from Radio Technical Commission for Marine Services, c/o FCC, Washington, D.C.

will assure that you get calls addressed to you by other boats. For calls from public shore stations, you will generally need to keep a receiver tuned to a working frequency of the station for that area. It is urged that you have one receiver for watch-keeping and a second one to ensure that you can be reached by a public shore station over a working channel. This will help to keep 2182 kc/s free for its primary purpose of securing help.

Steps in Receiving a Call

Boat-to-boat calls—When you hear your boat called, put your transmitter on the air and say—

"(Name of boat that called) This is (Name of your boat and call sign), Over."

Switch to the agreed upon intership channel. After the conversation is completed, say—

"This is (Name of your boat and call sign), Out."

Shore-to-ship calls—When you hear the name of your boat called, put your transmitter on the air and say—

"(Name of station that called) This is (Name of your boat and call sign), Over."

After the conversation is completed, say—

"This is (Name of your boat and call sign), Out."

FIG. 2519 RADIOTELEPHONE ALARM SIGNAL (two alternate audio tones of different pitch) attracts attention to boats in trouble. Some larger radios now have built-in generator for this signal; separate units available for other sets.

Distress, Urgency, Safety

In an emergency as a part of the marine safety and communications system, you have help on 2182 kc/s at your fingertips wherever you may be.

Only when grave and imminent danger threatens your boat and immediate help is required, use the distress procedure — radiotelephone alarm signal (if available) and MAYDAY. Transmitted on 2182 kc/s, it should be heard by many boats, as well as by the Coast Guard and public shore stations within range.

FIG. 2520 Prudent skipper tunes in latest weather bulletins before plotting day's course, especially when considering long run offshore.

The *Radiotelephone Alarm Signal* consists of two audio tones, of different pitch, transmitted alternately. The purpose of this signal is to attract the attention of persons on watch, and, at some stations, to actuate automatic devices giving an alarm. It shall be used *only* to announce that a distress call or message is about to follow. (Exception: it may be used with the Urgency Signal in two specified instances. See FCC Rules.) Coast Guard shore radio stations are now equipped with devices to generate this signal, and such devices are now being built into some larger models of boat radios. See fig. 2519.

The Distress Procedure—"Mayday"—2182 kc/s

Distress communications include the following actions:

1. The RADIOTELEPHONE ALARM SIGNAL (whenever possible) followed by—
2. The DISTRESS SIGNAL "MAYDAY."
3. The DISTRESS MESSAGE.
4. Acknowledgment of Receipt of Distress Message.
5. Further Distress Messages and other communications.
6. Transmission of the Distress Procedure by a boat or shore station not itself in distress.
7. Termination of Distress Situation.

The DISTRESS CALL consists of:

—the Distress Signal MAYDAY, spoken three times;
—the words THIS IS;
—the identification (name and call sign) of the craft in distress, spoken three times.

The DISTRESS MESSAGE follows immediately and consists of:

—the Distress Signal MAYDAY, spoken three times;
—the identification of the craft;
—particulars of its position (latitude and longitude, or true bearing and distance in miles from a known geographical position);
—the nature of the distress and the kind of assistance desired;

—any other information that might facilitate the rescue; especially a description of the boat: length, color, type, etc.; and the number of persons aboard; OVER.

Example of Distress Procedure

"(Alarm Signal, if available, for one minute). Mayday, Mayday, Mayday This is Yacht Blue Duck, WZ 1234, Yacht Blue Duck, WZ 1234, Yacht Blue Duck, WZ 1234:

Mayday, Yacht Blue Duck, WZ 1234, 133 degrees true, 12 miles from Montauk Point. Struck submerged object, taking on water fast, engine disabled, estimate cannot stay afloat more than one hour. Four persons on board. Blue Duck is 26-foot cabin cruiser, white hull. Maintaining watch on 2182 kc/s. This is Yacht Blue Duck, WZ 1234, Over."

General Rules for Distress

With your life at stake, you have a far better chance by following the correct procedure, but the provisions of the International Radio Regulations authorize a vessel in distress to use *any means* at its disposal to attract attention, make known its position, and obtain help.

Stay on 2182 kc/s; but if no answer to a distress call is received, repeat it on any other available frequency on which attention might be attracted.

Speak slowly and distinctly. Use phonetic words for letters when necessary, especially when giving the letters of your call sign.

You may be requested to transmit a "long count" or other suitable signals to permit direction finding stations to determine your position; always end your transmission with the name and call sign of your boat.

If you have to abandon ship, the radio transmitter should be locked on the air, if considered necessary and conditions permit. The purpose of this is to locate you by radio direction finding bearings. If you have already been visually located, do not lock your transmitter on the air as the signal would interfere with rescue operations.

All vessels having knowledge of distress traffic, and

which cannot themselves assist, are *forbidden* to transmit on the frequency of the distress traffic; but they should listen and follow the situation until it is evident that assistance is being provided. Always listen before transmitting. It is *unlawful* for any radio operator to *willfully* or *maliciously interfere with* or cause interference to *any radio communication* or *signal*. No person shall knowingly transmit, or cause to be transmitted, any *false* or *fraudulent signal of distress* or *communication* relating thereto.

Radio Silence

The signal "Seelonce Mayday" has been adopted internationally to control transmissions on the distress frequency, telling all other stations to leave the air and maintain radio silence. The companion signal "Seelonce Feenee" indicates the end of radio silence and permission to resume normal operations.

If You Hear a MAYDAY Call

If you are not in distress, but hear a "Mayday" call, this is what you should do:

1. *Listen—Do Not Transmit.*
2. Try to determine if you are the craft in the best position to take action, or if some other vessel is better located or better equipped.
3. *If* yours is the logical boat to render assistance, reply to the distress message as follows:

"(Name of craft in distress) This is (Name of your boat and call sign), Received Mayday (your position, your course and speed toward the scene of the distress, and your estimated time of arrival), Over."

4. If yours is not the logical boat to take action, maintain radio silence, but continue to monitor the frequency closely for any further developments—make an entry in your radio log of the Mayday call and your actions.

When another station retransmits a distress message, the words "Mayday Relay" must be spoken three times before station identification.

Test Transmissions

The FCC Rules are very specific and strict with regard to testing on the air. Always remember, when making tests, to take every precaution not to cause interference.

Listen before testing, to make sure that the frequency on which you intend to transmit is not busy; if it is in use, you must obtain the consent of the stations concerned before proceeding. If the air is clear, put your transmitter on the air and say—

"This is (name of your boat and call sign) Test."

If you hear no station tell you to "Wait," you may proceed, saying "Testing" followed by a number count or other phraseology that will not confuse listeners.

The test signals must be brief—not more than 10 seconds.

At the end of the test, announce the name and call sign of your boat, and your general location.

Tests shall not be repeated on 2182 kc/s until after a wait of at least five minutes; on other frequencies, a pause of one minute is sufficient.

Weather Reports

When aboard your boat, you can keep up to date on weather and other marine information by listening to the working frequencies of public or U.S. government shore stations. See fig. 2520. Coast Guard stations transmit weather and other information on 2670 kc/s after a preliminary announcement on 2182 kc/s.

The U.S. Weather Bureau publishes a series of *Coastal Warning Facilities Charts* at only 10¢ each. In addition to showing where weather warnings are displayed day and night, these charts give the frequency and schedules of radio (AM and FM) and TV stations broadcasting weather reports and forecasts. See fig. 1243 on page 246.

Don't take chances—the information on weather conditions is there—get it.

VIOLATIONS AND PENALTIES

Hopefully, you will never be in violation of the FCC Rules and will have no need for knowledge of the procedures and penalties involved. Yet things do not always work out that way, so it is just as well to be informed.

If you receive a citation of violation from the FCC, you must reply in duplicate within 10 days, to the office that issued the citation. See fig. 2522. If a complete reply cannot be given in that time, an interim reply must be sent and supplemented as soon as possible. If for reasons beyond your control, you cannot reply at all within 10 days, do so at the earliest date practicable, and fully support your reasons for the delay. Each letter to the FCC must be complete and contain all the facts without cross-reference to other correspondence. The answer must contain a full explanation of the incident and describe the actions taken to prevent a recurrence of it. If personnel errors are involved, your reply must state the name and license number of the operator concerned.

You may be lucky, however, and receive a "warning notice" rather than a citation. In this instance, no reply is required. The FCC form that you receive will indicate whether or not an answer is necessary. If one is required, don't get yourself into further trouble by failing to answer *within 10 days.*

Revocation and Suspension of License

A station license may be revoked for any one of a number of specified violations of the Communications Act or the FCC Rules. Operator licenses and permits normally are not revoked but are suspended for varying periods of time.

FIG. 2522 If you receive citation for violation of FCC Rules and Regulations, submit written reply within ten days. No reply required if you receive "warning," rather than citation.

Notice of suspension must be given in writing and is not effective until 15 days after receipt. Within this period, you can apply for a hearing, and this automatically defers the suspension until after the hearing has been held and the FCC has ruled.

Fines Imposed

In addition to the revocation or suspension of licenses, the FCC can prosecute violators in the Federal District

Courts. Any violation of the Communications Act may be punished by a fine of not more than $10,000, or imprisonment for not more than one year, or both. A second offense, not necessarily a repeat of the first, increases the maximum limit on the prison term to two years. For a violation of any FCC rule, regulation restriction, or condition, or of any treaty provision, a court may additionally impose a fine of not more than $500 for *each and every day* during which the violation occurred.

Administrative Forfeitures

To avoid the delays, costs, and general cumbersomeness of formal court prosecutions, the FCC has the authority to levy its own "administrative forfeitures," actually small fines, for 12 specified violations. These fines are in addition to any other penalties that may be imposed by law.

Among these twelve, the violations of principal concern to the operators of radio stations of boats are:

—Transmission of any unauthorized communications on a distress or calling frequency.

—Failure to identify the station at the times and in the manner prescribed by the Rules.

—Interference with a distress call or distress communications.

—Operation of a station without a valid permit or license of the proper grade.

—Transmission of any false call contrary to the Rules.

—Failure to respond to official communications from the FCC.

The maximum forfeiture for a single violation, or a series of violations all falling within a single category as listed above, is $100. If, however, more than one category is involved, the maximum liability is raised to $500 for a station licensee, or $400 for an individual operator. It should be noted that the term "operator" may be applied to any person using the equipment, whether or not licensed by the FCC. In some cases, if two different persons are involved, forfeitures may be assessed against both the station licensee and the person who was operating the station.

The procedures for the imposition of these administrative fines have been kept simple, yet ample protection is afforded to the rights of individuals. Upon receipt of a "notice of apparent liability for forfeiture," the addressed person has open to him three courses of action. He can pay the fine and so close the incident; or he may, within 30 days, submit a written statement to the FCC giving reasons why he should be allowed to pay a lesser fine, or none at all; or he may request an interview with an FCC official. These last two courses of action can be combined, submitting both an explanation and a request for an interview. If either or both of these actions are taken, the FCC will review all of the information relative to the case, and make a final determination.

There is no judicial appeal from the FCC's ruling, and you had best pay up as there are established procedures for turning over cases of non-payment to a District Attorney for prosecution.

Depth Sounders

Depth sounders (fig. 2523) closely rival radiotelephones as the most popular item of electronic equipment for boats; they have a wide range of use—lakes, rivers, bays, and off-shore. Your sounder can be one of the most interesting and useful devices on your boat.

Depth sounders are a modern replacement for the hand-held lead line used for uncounted centuries to determine the depth of water beneath a ship. This electronic device furnishes a vastly greater amount of information, and does it with much greater ease, especially in nasty weather. It provides safety as well as convenience in boating, and so is doubly advantageous to have on board.

How Depth is Measured

Depth is determined by measuring the round-trip time for a pulse of ultrasonic energy to travel from the boat to the bottom of the water and be reflected back to the point of origin. See fig. 2524. The frequency of the audio pulses generally lies between 50,000 and 200,000 cycles per second, too high to be heard by human ears. Their average velocity through the water is approximately 4800 feet per second; slight variations in speed will occur between salt and fresh water and with different temperatures. The resulting small errors, however, can be safely ignored for the relatively shallow depths of interest to the operators of recreational boats.

Probably the greatest advantage of the electronic device over the hand-held lead line is the essentially continuous nature of the information furnished. Depth sounders vary

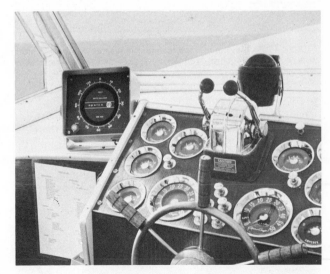

FIG. 2523 Depth sounders are popular on all waters. This compact, inexpensive device gives many indications of depth each second.

widely in the rate at which readings are taken, but in all cases many more soundings are taken than could be accomplished by hand. Current equipment takes readings at rates between 1 and 30 *each second*.

Components of a Depth Sounder

The major components of a depth sounder are a source of energy (transmitter), a means of sending out the pulses and picking up the echoes (transducer), a receiver to amplify the weak echoes, and a visual presentation of the information. See fig. 2525. The transducer usually takes the form of a round block of hard ceramic material several inches in diameter and an inch or so thick. In many cases, it is given an oblong, streamline shape to reduce drag.

The visual presentation of information on the depth of the water is accomplished by either an "indicator" or a "recorder." The indicator provides a non-permanent indication of the depth, in most cases by the use of a flashing light, although in a few units an ordinary electric meter is used with a suitably calibrated dial. The flashing light is mounted on the end of an arm which rotates around a scale much like the second hand of a clock, only much faster. The zero of the scale is usually at the top of the dial and a flash of light occurs there when the outgoing pulse leaves the transducer on the boat's bottom. A second flash

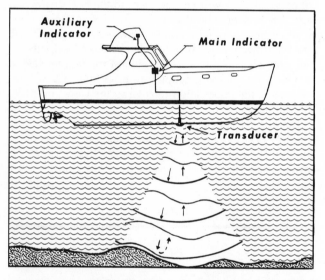

FIG. 2524 An electronic depth sounder measures depth by sending pulses of high frequency sound waves, reflected back from bottom. Distance measured by time taken by pulses for round-trip.

occurs when the pulse is received back at the transducer, having been reflected back from the bottom of the water. The deeper the water, the longer it will take for the echo to return to the boat; the longer this takes, the farther the arm will have rotated around the dial. (Fig. 2526.) Thus the scale of depths increases clockwise around the face of the indicator.

FIG. 2525 Typical depth sounder consists of two units, transducer on bottom of boat and electronics package with indicator near helmsman. Model shown has calibrated meter with two ranges.

Principle of the Depth Sounder Illustrated

An example may make this clearer. If the sounder has a depth range of 240 feet, at full scale the sound pulses will have traveled a round-trip distance of 480 feet. Taking the speed of sound in water at 4800 feet per second, the round-trip will have taken 1/10 second. Therefore the arm carrying the flashing light must make one full rotation in 1/10 second; this is 10 rps or 600 rpm.

If the depth is only, say, 80 feet, the echo will cause the light to flash when the arm has made only 1/3 of a full revolution, and the flash will occur at a position corresponding to four o'clock on a clock dial. In many models, it is possible to detect greater than full-scale depths by turning up the sensitivity control until a flash is seen on the "second trip around" of the rotating arm. Using the same sounder as in the preceding example, if the water was known to be quite deep, and a weak reading of 60 feet was seen with the sensitivity control well advanced, it could mean an actual depth of 300 feet (full scale plus 60 feet). Some models are now calibrated with two sets of numbers around the dial for first and second revolutions of the flashing light. Caution is essential to avoid reading the depth as much greater than is actually the case.

With the recording type of sounder, a permanent record is made of the depths, and notations as to the boat's position can be made directly on the paper tape. See fig. 2527. The paper moves horizontally from a supply roll to a take-up spool at the rate of one inch in several minutes. A dry method of chemically marking the paper is normally used to avoid the messiness of ink. A recording type of depth sounder has some advantages, but this type is more expensive. Some models are now available with both flashing light indicator and a permanent paper tape record of the depths.

Correction to "Zero" Depth

If you have a sounder on your boat, you must know its "zero" depth. In most instances, the transducer is mounted on the hull several feet below the water surface and, as

FIG. 2526 On this sounder, indicator shows flash of light at "O" on scale and another opposite depth.

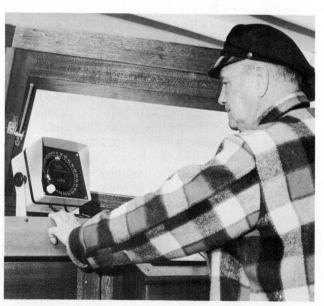

FIG. 2527 With recording type of sounder, depth is measured many times each second and presented as series of dots on scaled tape.

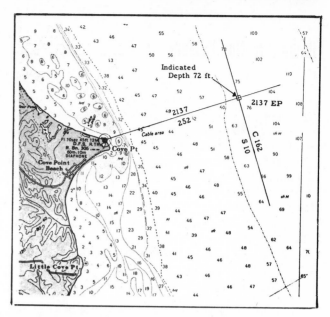

FIG. 2528 Navigator notes that Cove Point Light is abeam at 2137 but can get no other line of position. Depth sounder showing depth of 72 feet gives Estimated Position (EP).

depths are measured from the transducer, the indications will be neither the depth of water from the surface nor the depth beneath the keel of the boat. On some models, the zero flash can be offset on the dial to its depth below the surface, then the indicated depths are correspondingly increased to show directly the full distance between the water surface and the bottom without need for adding a correction. This is advantageous when the sounder is used for navigation.

The nature of the bottom of the body of water will have an effect on the appearance of the flash which indicates the depth. Learn how to determine roughly the nature of the bottom by the characteristics of the flashing light; a surprising amount of information can be obtained. Sharp, clear indications mean a hard bottom. Conversely, broad and fuzzy flashes indicate a soft, muddy bottom. Multiple flashes, each fairly sharp, can result from rocky bottoms; the ultrasonic pulses are reflected more or less horizontally to adjacent rocks before being returned upward. The added time delays for these sideward bounces make them show up as if they were at greater depths. Additional flashes at multiples of the least depth indicated may result, in shallow water with a hard bottom, from pulses being reflected downward again by the craft's hull following the first round-trip. Two or even three round-trips may occur; the cure for this is to turn back the sensitivity control until only the first indication is seen. In *all* cases of multiple flashes, play it safe and assume that the minimum reading is the true depth! As the depth indication flash will always have some width, be sure to read the "trailing" edge, or least indicated depth. This is the correct value.

Application in Piloting

The primary application of an electronic depth sounder is to assist in the safe navigation of the boat in unfamiliar waters. It can provide much useful information, but must be used with care as *it makes no predictions ahead.*

Information on the depth of water is reassuring in itself; furthermore, it can be used to assist in determining the

boat's position. It can be used to make rough position data somewhat more exact. For example, if only a single line of position (LOP) is available, an estimated position (EP) can often be obtained from the additional knowledge of the depth of the water. See fig. 2528. This requires a fairly uniform sloping bottom and some knowledge of the state of the tide. Many times, a rough EP can be obtained from indications of an abrupt change in depth.

A line of soundings can sometimes be matched with chart figures to locate the boat's track. See pages 352(o) and 411. This is most easily done on depth recorders, but is also possible on indicating types by logging depths at regular time intervals. Depths are plotted on a strip of paper with their distance apart matched to the scale of the chart and the speed of the boat. The paper strip is moved about on the chart parallel to the boat's course until the depths match. This technique is not possible in all locations and should be used with caution lest an erroneous conclusion as to the boat's position lead to danger. Often in conditions of low visibility, a boat can be navigated to a desired destination by using the depth sounder to follow along a path of roughly constant depths. This is the technique of "following a fathom curve."

A depth sounder may also be used navigationally in a negative sense. If your depth indication agrees with the charted depth for your estimated position, you may, *or may not,* be there; the same depth figures occur in many places on any chart. If, however, your sounder shows a considerably different value than that charted for your DR (dead reckoning) position, it is an almost sure indication that your DR is *not* correct. Thus, while a depth sounder cannot positively confirm a DR plot, it can surely call it wrong.

The location of fish with a depth sounder is possible, but you may be disappointed with your results at first. Experience is required and you will improve with practice. Detection will generally be limited to schools of fish or quite large single fish. The echoes are quite weak and the sensitivity control will have to be advanced.

Radio Direction Finders

On the seacoasts of the United States, and on the Great Lakes and other large inland bodies of water, a *radio direction finder* (RDF) is an important piece of electronic equipment. See fig. 2529. Primarily installed as a safety item, it can also be a great convenience to the boat operator. It is the primary radio aid to navigation for small craft.

A complete radio direction finding system consists of four components:

1. One or more radio transmitters at known locations.
2. An RDF set on the boat.
3. Charts covering both the location of the transmitters and the area of operation of the boat.
4. A person who knows the operation of the system.

To be fully effective, the RDF system must be used with competence and confidence — an incorrect radio bearing can lead to disaster; a correct bearing that is ignored because of mistrust can be equally disastrous.

Special RDF Features

Basically, an RDF is a radio receiver with two additional features. First and vitally important is the directional antenna. Usually, this antenna is rotatable so that the set may be secured firmly in a convenient location. The directional antenna employed with an RDF set is an improved version of the simple loop used on portable receivers, the directional characteristics of which are familiar to most boatmen. This antenna may take the form of a loop a foot or so in diameter or it may appear as a plastic bar measuring about an inch square by some six inches in length. Both types will be mounted on top of the set; either will do the job.

FIG. 2529 When visibility is poor, RDF can help fix position, or navigator may "home in" on transmitter near his destination.

As the antenna is rotated through 360°, these directional antennas show two positions of maximum signal strength and two positions of minimum sensitivity called "nulls." With properly balanced construction and no local interfering objects, the two maximum signal positions will be separated by 180°, as will be the nulls which are found 90° in either direction from the maximums. It is characteristic of these antennas that the maximum signal points are broad and poorly defined, while the nulls are marked and precise. For this reason, the nulls are used for direction finding.

The second special feature of RDFs is a visual null indicator. While the operator can judge by ear the position of the antenna at minimum signal with fair accuracy, a more precise bearing can be obtained by observing a visual indicator. This is normally a small electric meter, read for either a maximum or minimum deflection of its needle in accordance with the instructions for the particular set being used.

FIG. 2530 Radiobeacon charts are published in Light Lists. As reproduced here, not to be used for navigation. The frequency, identification signal, and schedule of operation are shown on this chart.

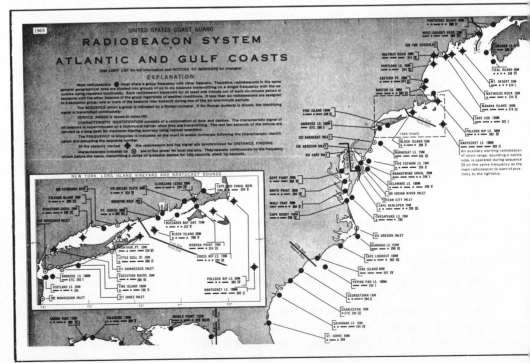

(1)	(2)	(3)	(4)	(5)	(6)		(7)
	Name	Location	Light or day-beacon above water	Candle-power	Structure, vessel, or buoy		Radiobeacon, fog signal, sectors and remarks
No.	Character and period of light	Latitude, N. Longitude, W.			Top of lantern above ground	Established Moved or rebuilt	
	(Duration in italics)	Deg. Min. Deg. Min.	Feet	*Miles seen, in italics*	Feet	Year	
			FLORIDA				SEVENTH DISTRICT
	SEACOAST						
4388 J3060	**DRY TORTUGAS LIGHT** ..... Fl. W., *20ˢ (1ˢ fl)* Resident Personnel.	On Loggerhead Key... 24 38.0 82 55.2	151	1,500,000 *19*	Conical tower, lower half white, upper half black. 157	1826 1858	**RADIOBEACON:** Antenna 365 feet 233° from light tower. See p. XVII for method of operation.
	Tortugas Sea Buoy 8	In 21 feet, at southwest end of shoal making off Garden	...	....	Red; 1st-cl. nun		

FIG. 2531 The location of the antenna of a radiobeacon is shown in the Light List under the listing of the basic aid to navigation with which it is associated.

RDF Frequency Bands

Radio direction finders normally cover three frequency bands: a low frequency (LF) beacon band, the standard AM radio broadcast band, and the 2-3 Mc/s MF communications band. The LF beacon band is of primary interest for the marine radiobeacons operated by the Coast Guard on frequencies between 285 and 325 kc/s at locations along or just off our coastlines and the Great Lakes. See fig. 2530. Aeronautical beacons, somewhat lower and higher in frequency, are also within the tuning range of these sets and can be used for direction finding. (These aero beacons, or "ranges" as they are called, are an excellent source of weather information at 15 and 45 minutes past each hour.)

Coverage of the standard AM radio broadcast band is desirable because of the large number of stations on which bearings can be taken. It should be noted, however, that the accuracy of bearings on this band will not be quite as good as it will on the LF beacon band. The 2-3 Mc/s marine band is generally used only for special purposes such as "homing" since the accuracy of bearings is still less on these higher frequencies.

A direction finder can readily double as an entertainment receiver, particularly if it is of the low-drain transistor type. Coverage of the marine band permits the RDF to be used to monitor a second communications channel when the radiotelephone's receiver is tuned to 2182 kc/s. Usually, a direction finder is tunable to any frequency in the band rather than being crystal-controlled on spot channels. This characteristic permits the monitoring of frequencies to which the boat's radio is not tuned. The pre-tuned spot-frequency feature may also be present on the more expensive models to permit more accurate tuning and quicker frequency changes.

Precise knowledge is required of the antenna location of the radiobeacon or other type of station. For the low frequency band, the locations of Coast Guard operated beacons are shown on standard navigation charts and are listed in Light Lists published by the U.S. Coast Guard. (Fig. 2531.) The *Coastal Warning Facilities Charts* previously described list many broadcast band radio station antenna locations by latitude and longitude. If not already shown

FIG. 2532 For accurate RDF bearings, you must have table of radio deviation corrections. RDF shown here has built-in sighting vanes for visual bearings, or separate pelorus may be used.

on your area's nautical charts, these locations may be plotted from this information. Aeronautical radio ranges and beacons are similarly listed and may be plotted if not already shown on your charts.

Marine Radiobeacons

Marine radiobeacons are divided into four classes according to their power and normal reliable range:

Class A .... 200 miles
Class B .... 100 miles
Class C .... 20 miles
Class D .... 10 miles
    (marker beacons)

A few of the primary beacons, and the short-range markers, operate continuously. The others are "sequenced"; up to six beacons operating in turn on the same frequency, each being on the air for one minute and then off while the others take their turn. The sequence of operation can be determined from the charts or by reference to the Light List. It is indicated by a Roman numeral immediately following the frequency; if no Roman numeral is shown, the beacon operates continuously.

Radio Deviation

All RDFs are subject to local deviation errors caused by the reflection of the radio signals by nearby wires and other metallic objects. This is generally similar to the effect of masses of iron on a magnetic compass. One important difference, however, is that the radio bearing errors vary with respect to the *relative* bearing angle; the heading of the boat is not the deciding factor as it is with compass deviation. A table, or curve, must be prepared to show the corrections for RDF error on various relative bearings. Separate tables will generally be required for each of the frequency bands.

Determining RDF Deviation Error

RDF deviation errors are determined by comparison of observed radio bearings with known correct bearings. Either of two methods may be used. The simplest is to take radio bearings on a radiobeacon or other type of transmitting antenna within sight, at the same time having another person take direct visual bearings. See fig. 2532. The difference between these readings is the radio deviation error. If no radio station is within sight, take radio bearings from a known location and compare them with correct bearings as taken from a chart. Avoid doing this while made fast to the club pier; erroneous readings may result from reflections caused by adjacent boats. In both cases, the deviation corrections have the same numerical value as the errors, but with the opposite sign.

Calibration readings should be taken of a strong local station which is received clearly without interference. A complete deviation correction table, preferably in steps of not more than 15°, should be prepared for the low frequency band. Then spot checks can be made to determine if the same corrections will apply on higher frequency bands or if separate tables must be made for each band. Correction tables should be checked at least annually, and additionally if the direction finder is relocated on the boat or major changes are made in the electrical wiring, rigging, etc.

Direct and Reciprocal Bearings

Due to the technical characteristics of a loop antenna, two nulls can be found 180° apart. In most situations, the navigator's general knowledge of his approximate position will suffice to eliminate the reverse reading. If this is not

FIG. 2534 Taking radio bearing, antenna is rotated to locate null, angle read from scale. Reading, normally, is a relative bearing.

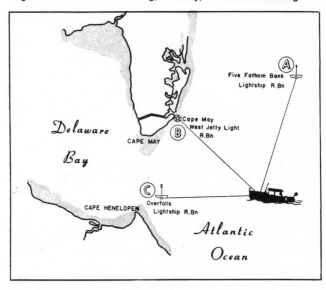

FIG. 2535 Boat shown here could determine position by bearings on any two radiobeacons at "A," "B" and "C." Better fix would be obtained by using all three beacons.

possible, or to be absolutely sure, special measures can be taken. Nearly all direction finders have either an integral auxiliary "sense" antenna or a connection terminal for an external antenna. By operating a switch, this antenna is connected into the circuit to change the directional characteristics to a single null and single maximum pattern. Simple procedures will then indicate which of the previous nulls is the direct bearing and which is the reciprocal reading. (The sense antenna is not left in the circuit all the time as more precise readings are obtained from the loop alone.)

Always use a portable RDF set from the same position on the boat; a change in location may require a completely new deviation table. See fig. 2533. As an RDF contains strong magnets in the speaker and meter, be sure to keep it at least several feet away from the boat's compass, both while in and out of use.

FIG. 2533 To ensure accuracy always use portable RDF from same position. Do NOT, however, place it too close to compass. Speaker magnet may affect it; three feet is safe minimum separation.

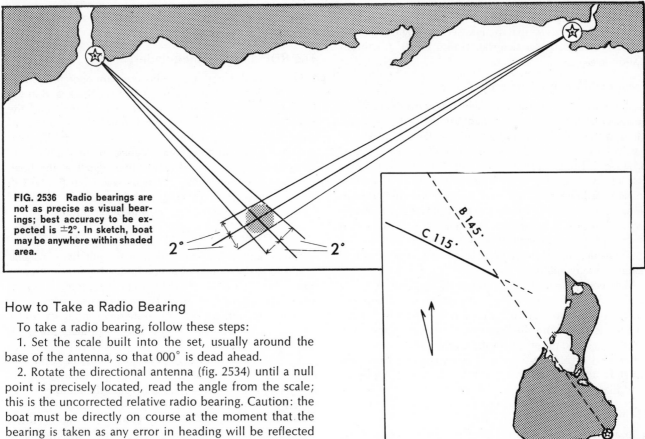

FIG. 2536 Radio bearings are not as precise as visual bearings; best accuracy to be expected is ±2°. In sketch, boat may be anywhere within shaded area.

FIG. 2537 Using single radio bearing, skipper notes bearing of 145° on Southeast Pt., Block Island, will bring him safely to Great Salt Pond. He holds his 115° heading, taking frequent radio bearings. When they increase to 145°, he changes course and homes on signal to entrance buoy.

How to Take a Radio Bearing

To take a radio bearing, follow these steps:

1. Set the scale built into the set, usually around the base of the antenna, so that 000° is dead ahead.

2. Rotate the directional antenna (fig. 2534) until a null point is precisely located, read the angle from the scale; this is the uncorrected relative radio bearing. Caution: the boat must be directly on course at the moment that the bearing is taken as any error in heading will be reflected in the resultant radio bearing.

3. If there is any doubt as to whether the reading just taken is the direct or reciprocal bearing, use the sense antenna to identify it. If the reading is the reciprocal, do *not* add or subtract 180°, take a new bearing.

4. Having determined the direct bearing angle, apply the proper deviation correction; the sum is the corrected relative radio bearing.

5. Add the boat's *true* heading, subtracting 360° if the sum exceeds that amount; this is now the true radio bearing from the boat, plot in the same manner as a visual bearing.

The above steps outline in basic terms the correct procedures to be followed in taking a radio bearing. In the use of any particular RDF set, however, the manufacturer's manual should be studied and the instructions followed closely.

Plotting the Radio Bearing

If the transmitting station is more than 200 miles away, and the plotting is to be done on a Mercator chart, a further correction is necessary before plotting. This small correction is required because the great circle path along which radio waves travel does not plot as a straight line on this type of chart. The amount of correction, and the procedure for applying it, can be found in Table 1 of Bowditch.

Radio bearings are plotted in the same manner as visual bearings, and the use of an RDF requires the same degree of piloting knowledge and plotting skill. Radio bearings do not have as high a degree of precision as visual bearings, and for this reason a three-bearing fix is desirable. See fig. 2535. The best probable accuracy for radio bearings is on the order of plus or minus 2°, and some experience and

practice are required to reach this precision. In situations involving close proximity to dangerous waters, a careful navigator will draw additional lines 2° to either side of the corrected bearing; these will indicate graphically the probable limits of his position; see fig. 2536.

Position-finding by Radio Bearings

Radio bearings can also be used in any of the other forms of position plotting—bow and beam bearings, doubling the angle, danger angles, etc. If only a single radio bearing can be obtained, it is possible to combine this with a visual bearing, an astronomical line of position, or a depth reading to determine an estimated position. (Fig. 2537.) Remember that this EP will be no better than the accuracy of the poorest method used, and navigate accordingly.

In order to ensure the most accurate position from radio bearings:

1. Take bearings from as strong signals as possible.

2. Use the low frequency band in preference to higher frequencies.

3. Avoid taking bearings on radio stations located inland, particularly those behind coastal hills or mountains.

4. Take three or more bearings on different stations if possible; make sure that you identify the station correctly

and know the location of the transmitting antenna.

5. Take bearings so that the intersection angle is at least 30°, preferably 90° for two-station fixes or 60° for three-station fixes.

Factors Affecting Accuracy

There are two circumstances which tend to degrade the accuracy of radio bearings. "Night effect" is the term applied to the fact that all radio bearings taken at night, but particularly those made near sunset and sunrise, show a broader and sometimes shifting null. This makes less precise any bearing taken at these times, and efforts should be made to take bearings under these conditions only on stations less than 30 to 40 miles distant. If this is not possible, the next best procedure is to take a series of readings on each station and average them for a mean reading; but still consider the accuracy to be less than that of a reading taken in the daytime.

The second special circumstance of lessened accuracy comes into effect when the radio waves travel approximately parallel to a coastline for any appreciable portion of the distance from the transmitting station to the RDF. There is a bending effect on the signals which can be as much as 10°, pulling the waves in toward the land. Fortunately, the effect is to make the boat appear closer to land than it actually is.

Homing with an RDF

In addition to determination of the position of a boat, an RDF can be used in several other interesting ways. When the directional antenna is set on 000° relative, the craft may be directed toward a radio station by steering so as to keep the signal strength at the deepest point of the null. One RDF model has a direct-reading meter which shows the helmsman whether he is to the right or left of his course. This homing procedure provides a simple navigational technique for getting into port when visibility conditions are bad or other navigational aids are not available; but be sure that the direct course doesn't lead into shoal water or other dangerous areas. It also makes possible the steering of the most direct course to the scene of a distress situation.

These applications usually make use of signals in the 2-3 Mc/s marine communications band. Here the accuracy of radio bearings is less than on lower frequency bands, but the homing process works satisfactorily because the signal strength gets stronger as the source is approached. Caution must be exercised not to run directly into the source of the signals (this may seem like rather obvious advice, but it has happened!).

The RDF as a Distance-finder

Certain of the marine radiobeacons are operated as *Distance Finding Stations* (shown as DFS on charts and in the Light List). For these stations, fog sound signals and the radio signals are periodically synchronized. Due to the difference in the speed of travel of these two signals, the radio pulse is heard before the sound signal. The time difference, in seconds, of the arrival of the two signals at the boat, divided by 5.5, gives the distance away from the DFS in nautical miles with an accuracy of about 10%. Consult the Light List to learn the exact scheme of synchronism.

Use and Care of an RDF

Throughout any consideration of the purchase, installation, and use of a radio direction finder, it must be remembered that such an item of electronic equipment is first of all a safety device. Any other planned use, such as an auxiliary receiver, is a bonus feature only, and must not be allowed to detract from readiness for its primary use when needed.

An RDF should be used often in periods of good visibility so as to gain familiarity with its operation under circumstances permitting visual checks on the radio bearings which are obtained. Frequent practice reduces the personal error component of the total error in radio bearings, thus improving the overall accuracy. If these procedures are followed, there is every reason for a boat owner to trust his RDF to bring him safely into port under any conditions of visibility.

Automatic Radio Direction Finders

An automatic radio direction finder (ADF) indicates on a dial the direction to a transmitter once it has been tuned in—no swinging of a loop, no 180° ambiguity.

ADFs cover the same frequency bands as manual RDFs and use the same types of transmitting stations. They are, of course, more complex in circuitry and thus more expensive. The antenna is continuously rotated, either mechanically or electronically, whenever the set is turned on. Often such equipment is a fixed installation with a remote antenna, but portable models are available.

The advantages of ADFs lie in their ease and speed of operation. They are, however, subject to the same radio deviation as manual RDFs and a correction table must be prepared.

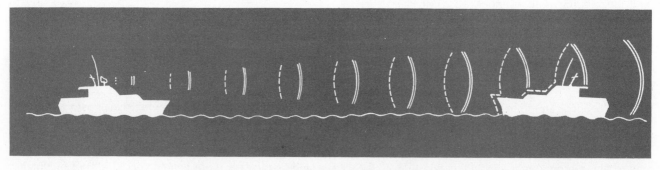

FIG. 2539 A marine radar set operates by sending brief pulses of super high frequency radio waves, reflected back by other ships, navigational aids and land masses. Sketch shows pulse traveling outward and echo returning. Speed is so great echoes are received before next pulse is transmitted.

FIG. 2540 Most radars have two major sections. Shown is antenna and upper electronics unit containing transmitter and portion of receiver. Antenna must be mounted high to have clear "look" in all directions.

Radar

Radar is an excellent means of marine navigation and is used on vessels of all sizes down to boats about 30 feet in length. Although size, power requirements, and cost limit its use on recreational boats, its capabilities and limitations should be known to all boatmen for their own safety when cruising on waters navigated by radar-equipped vessels.

Radar Principles

A radar set sends out brief pulses of super-high frequency radio waves that are reflected by objects at a distance. The time that it takes for the pulse to go out and the echo to return is a measure of the distance to the reflecting object. See fig. 2539. In broad principles, this is the same technique as previously described for depth sounders, except that transmission is through air rather than water, and radio waves have been substituted for ultrasonic pulses. A refinement has been made in that the radar pulses are sent out in a very narrow beam which can be pointed in any direction around the horizon and used to determine direction as well as distance.

Components of a Radar Set

The major components of a radar set are:

1. The *transmitter* which generates the radio waves; it includes the *modulator* which causes the energy to be sent out in brief pulses.

2. The *antenna* which radiates the pulses and collects the returning echoes. See fig. 2540. The antenna is highly directional in its horizontal characteristics, but 8 to 10 times wider vertically. The beam pattern can be thought of as being like a fan turned up on edge. The beam's narrow horizontal directivity gives it a fairly good angle-measuring capability, while its broadness in the vertical plane helps keep the beam on an object despite any rolling or pitching of the vessel.

3. The *receiver* which detects the returned reflections and amplifies them to a usable strength. See fig. 2541.

4. The *indicator* which provides a visual display of objects sending back reflections.

Radars operate at frequencies far above the usual radio communications bands. At such super-high frequencies, radar pulses act much like light waves in that they travel in essentially straight lines. They travel at the speed of light, 186,000 miles per second. For each nautical mile of distance to the target, only a fraction more than 12 microseconds are required for the round-trip of the outgoing pulse and the returned echo. Pulses, each of which lasts for only a fraction of a microsecond (one millionth of a second), are sent out at a rate of from 600 to 4000 each second depending upon the design of the equipment. The directional antenna rotates at a rate of one revolution in about 4 seconds. The round-trip time for a pulse is so short that the antenna has not appreciably moved before the reflection is returned.

The Plan Position Indicator (PPI)

Marine navigational radars use a Plan Position Indicator (PPI) type of display. A circular cathode ray tube of a special type from 5 to 20 inches in diameter is used. See fig. 2542. The center of the face represents the position of the radar-equipped vessel and the presentation is roughly like that of a navigational chart.

A bright radial line on the face of the tube represents the radar beam; it rotates in synchronism with the antenna. Reflections show up as points or patches of light depending upon the size of the echo-producing object. The persistence of the screen is such that the points and patches of light do not completely fade out before the antenna has made another rotation and they are restored to brilliance. Thus the picture on the radarscope is repainted every few seconds.

Radar Range Scales

The relative bearing of an object is indicated directly on the screen; a position corresponding to the "12" on a clock face is directly ahead. The distance to the object is proportional to the distance from the center of the screen to the point of light which is the echo. On most radars, concentric circles of light are used as range markers to make the estimation of distances both easier and more accurate. All radar sets have multiple range scales which may be selected to suit the purpose for which the radar is being used. Longer range scales provide coverage of greater areas, but at a cost of less detail and poorer definition.

Radar sets have both a maximum and a minimum range, each of which is of importance in the operation of the equipment. The maximum range is determined by the transmitter power and the receiver sensitivity, provided, of course, that the antenna is at a sufficient height above water that the range is not limited by the distance to the horizon. See fig. 2543. (The radar pulses normally travel with just a slight amount of bending; thus the radar horizon is about 15% farther away than the visual horizon.)

Because a radar pulse has a definite duration, and therefore occupies a definite length in space as it moves outward from the antenna, there is a minimum range within which objects cannot be detected. This minimum range, usually between 20 and 50 yards, is important when maneuvering in close quarters, as when passing buoys at the side of a narrow channel.

Units for Small Craft

Radar sets for small craft usually consist of two units. Modern design of the components makes it possible to combine the antenna, transmitter, and a portion of the receiver into a single unit installed on a mast or on the pilothouse. This unit, usually weighing between 60 and 120 pounds, should be located as high as possible in order to avoid limiting the range of the set. The antenna should have an unobstructed "look" in all directions. The remainder of the receiver and the indicator are located near the helmsman's position. Improved design techniques have resulted in indicator units so small that they may be fitted into a pilothouse in any number of positions.

Because radar sets radiate radio frequency energy, they must be licensed by the FCC, but this is not difficult to do for commercially produced equipment. No license is required to operate a radar, but for its installation and maintenance, the technician must have a second- or first-class radio operator's license with a special "ship radar" en-

dorsement. The owner and station licensee of a marine radar installation is responsible that only a properly licensed individual does all of the technical work on the equipment.

Principal Applications

Radars have two principal applications aboard ships and small craft. They are often thought of primarily as anti-collision devices, but are even more often used to assist in the piloting of the vessel.

Radar was originally conceived for the detection and tracking of ships and aircraft. It offers an excellent means of extending the coverage of a visual lookout, especially at night and under conditions of reduced visibility. This greater range of detection affords more time for a ship to maneuver to avoid another craft or an obstacle.

Radar serves another valuable function in the piloting of a vessel approaching a coastline or traveling in confined waters. It has real advantages even in the daytime, and, of course, becomes particularly helpful at night or in fog.

Fixes by Radar

The daytime advantages of radar stem from its ability to measure distance. Often a landmark or navigation aid can be seen and a visual bearing easily obtained. If, however, only one such object can be seen, only a single line of position is obtained and a fix is not possible. With a measurement of distance by radar, a fix becomes possible. See fig. 2544. The bearing could have been made by radar simultaneously with the range measurement, but a visual bearing is more precise and should be used if possible. The capability of getting a fix from a single object is often of great importance to the navigator.

Fixes may also be obtained in low visibility situations—from a single radar bearing and range measurement, from crossed bearings (fig. 2545—but this is not too accurate due to the finite width of the radar beam), and preferably from distance measurements to two or more points that can be identified on both the radar screen and the chart. More than two ranges or bearings should be taken and plotted to prevent the possibility of a false fix which might occur if one of the echoes on the scope were incorrectly

FIG. 2541 (Left) Lower section of radar set contains remainder of receiver, indicator, and all operating controls, located within easy view of helmsman, but not too close to compass.

FIG. 2542 (Right) Marine radars present information on ships, buoys, shorelines, etc. as patches of light on face of PPI scope. Radar-equipped boat is at center of scope.

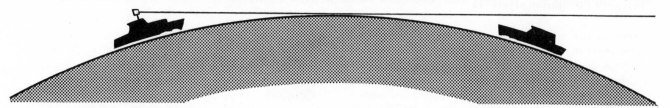

FIG. 2543 Maximum range of radar set on small craft is more likely to be limited by antenna height than by transmitter power. Radar waves bend slightly but distance to radar horizon is only 15% greater than to optical horizon.

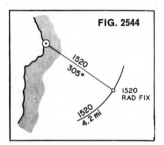

FIG. 2544

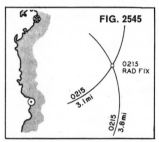

FIG. 2545

FIG. 2544 Radar fix may be obtained from single object, using both distance and bearing measurements. Navigator must be sure he has correctly identified object on both radar scope and chart.

FIG. 2545 Getting navigational fix by plotting distance to two identifiable objects as measured by radar. Radar measurements of distance provide more accurate fix than do radar bearings. Ranges to more than two objects are desirable.

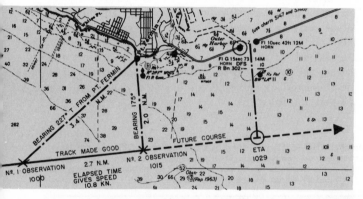

FIG. 2546 For greatest benefit, radar information must be plotted. Here two successive measurements of bearing and range of a fixed point on shore provide data to plot track and speed made good by radar-equipped boat. Track can be projected ahead to give estimated time of arrival (ETA) at any point. Effect of currents may be determined by comparison of heading and slack-water speed with track and speed made good.

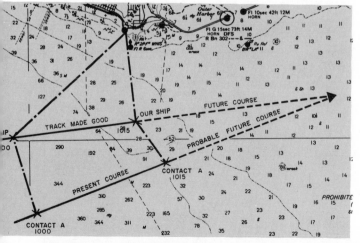

FIG. 2547 Because radar is changing position with your boat, you cannot depend upon appearance of radar-scope to give indication of course and speed of another vessel. It is necessary to make radar plot. Shown are track and speed of your vessel as established in fig. 2546, plus actual track and speed of another craft based on two successive radar measurements of relative bearing and distance. Both tracks may be projected ahead to evaluate possibility of collision should neither craft change course or speed.

identified. In all cases, the use of radar lines of position and fixes is the same as for visual plotting, giving due consideration to the lesser accuracy of bearing information. See figs. 2546 and 2547 for additional illustrations of radar plotting.

Coastline Pictures on the PPI

The use of radar to determine a vessel's approximate position from observation of the presentation of a coastline on a radarscope is not a safe procedure. The image seen on the PPI will often vary appreciably from the appearance of a chart. This is true despite some widely publicized photographs of radar screens showing such distinctive patterns as New York harbor appearing nearly identical with the actual scene. Because the radar beam, as narrow (1° to 4°) as it is, does have a finite width, and because the pulse, as brief (0.1 to 0.5 microsecond) as it is, does have a definite length in space, the picture on a radar PPI scope is not an exact replica of the land area or other object returning the echoes. Normally, radar echoes will be returned from buildings, hills, etc., some distance inland from the shorelines shown on charts.

Passive Radar Reflectors

The motorboat owner who does not have a radar can still do something to increase his safety in relation to this item of electronic equipment. He can equip his craft with a *passive radar reflector*. See fig. 2548. This simple and inexpensive item consists of thin lightweight metal sheets, or areas of fine-mesh metal screening, arranged in mutually perpendicular planes. These may fold for storage, but must remain rigid with respect to each other when opened for use. A relatively small reflector with each metal surface only about two feet square will provide a radar reflection as strong as that from a medium-sized steel ship. The echo from the wooden hull of a small craft is so weak as to be easily overlooked in the echoes from the waves if a reflector is not used. With a passive reflector hoisted as high as possible, the operator of a small craft can be sure that his boat will be detected on the radar screens of passing ships. Often Coast Guard or other rescue craft searching for a boat in distress are radar-equipped; the use of a passive radar reflector greatly increases the chances of being quickly spotted.

Electronic Navigation Systems

There are two electronic navigation systems which will be of interest to boatmen. These are *Consolan* and *Loran*. In general, the advantages of one are the disadvantages of the other, and vice versa. Consolan requires only simple, inexpensive equipment on the boat (indeed, if you have a good RDF, nothing else will be required except charts or tables), but this system is useful only in limited areas. Loran stations are many and widespread, but the receiving equipment required is rather expensive and its operation is somewhat more complex.

CONSOLAN

A Consolan station sends out a pattern of dots and dashes, the relative number and sequence of which will provide a line of position. See fig. 2549. (Strictly speaking, "Consolan" applies to stations with two antenna towers, and "Consol" to stations with three towers; to the boatman on the receiving end, there is no difference, and Consolan will be used as the inclusive term.) The pattern is repeated every 20° to 30°, and the boatman must know his approximate position in order to recognize which sector he is in, but this should present no practical difficulty.

For the proper reception of the dots and dashes, it is almost essential that the receiver or direction finder be equipped with a beat frequency oscillator (BFO), and most RDFs are now so designed. Good selectivity is also necessary to prevent interference from other signals on nearby frequencies. It is not necessary that the RDF have a meter (visual null indicator), but if it does, this feature can also be of use in receiving Consolan signals.

Consolan signals are easily used by boatmen, but there are only two stations—at San Francisco, call letters SFI, frequency 192 kc/s; and at Nantucket, TUK, 194 kc/s. These are frequencies just below the marine radiobeacon band, but within range of most RDFs. The lack of stations is a limitation, but it is not as great as it might seem as Consolan signals can be received at distances as much as 1500 miles. On the other hand, there are two zones within reception range where the signals are not usable. The first covers an area within 30 to 50 miles of the station in all directions, and the other extends outward to all distances for about 20° on either side of a line running through the antenna towers. See fig. 49 for an illustration of the dot and dash sectors, and the sectors of unreliability.

Consolan signals are heard in cycles of 75 seconds each. First the station identification letters are transmitted in Morse code for 7½ seconds, then there is a 2½-second silent period, followed by 30 seconds of dots and dashes, 2½ seconds of silence, another 30 seconds of dots and dashes, and a final 2½-second silent period; the cycle is then repeated. Operation is continuous day and night, fair weather and foul.

FIG. 2549 Portion of Consolan chart (HO 16510) published by Oceanographic Office of the Navy. Consolan bearings are not dependent on compass, on steering, or on an antenna, and can be picked up farther out than regular radio bearings (up to approximately 800 miles). Information on Consolan is published in HO 117 (A and B), Radio Navigational Aids.

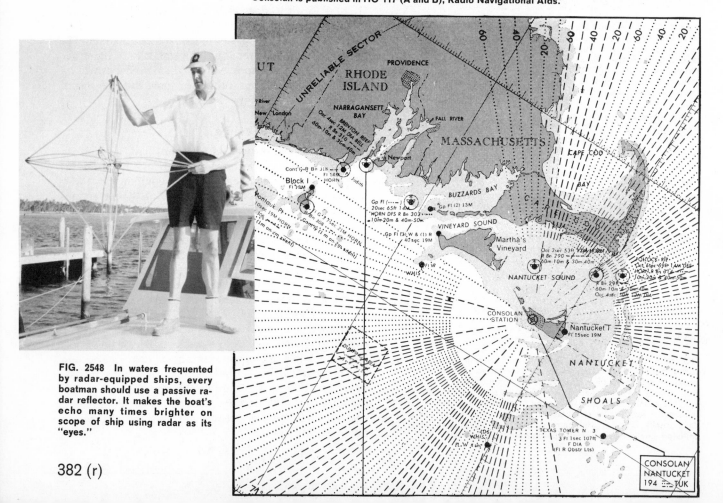

FIG. 2548 In waters frequented by radar-equipped ships, every boatman should use a passive radar reflector. It makes the boat's echo many times brighter on scope of ship using radar as its "eyes."

Finding a Line of Position

A line of position (LOP) is found by determining whether dots or dashes are heard first in each 30-second period, and how many of each there are (all 30-second periods are alike at any position). There is always a total of 60 dashes and dots in each 30 seconds of transmission, but the transition from one to the other is blurred into a brief period of continuous signal known as the *equisignal*. Count the dashes that can be heard distinctly, and do likewise for the dots; subtract the total of these from 60 to determine the ones lost in the equisignal. Divide these lost counts equally between dots and dashes, and add them to those counted. For example:

Dashes counted (first heard) 15
Dots counted 39
    Total 54
Remainder not heard 60 − 54 = 6
Corrected number of dashes 15 + 3 = 18
Corrected number of dots 39 + 3 = 42

Since dashes were heard before dots, you are in a dash sector with a count of 18. Care must be exercised when you are near the border between sectors; you may hear all dots or all dashes with an equisignal. Consult H.O. 117A for guidance in computing the correct dot or dash count.

Determination of the LOP may be made from either tables (fig. 2550) or directly from certain charts. H.O. 117A (117B for West Coast) includes information of Consolan station locations, frequencies, etc., plus tables giving true bearings for each number of dots and dashes in all sectors. These are great circle bearings from the station and must be corrected for plotting on Mercator charts; tables of such corrections are in H.O. 117A and B or Bowditch may be used.

To avoid the trouble of determining the LOP from tables and then plotting it, special charts are available for the East and West Coasts showing Consolan lines.

Accuracy of Consolan LOPs

The accuracy of Consolan LOPs will vary with the receiver's position with respect to the station as well as with the care with which the counting of dots and dashes is done. The greatest accuracy is achieved at right angles to the line through the antenna towers; also daytime reception will usually be somewhat more accurate than at night. In all cases, accuracy will be better than 1°, and often better than ½° if the counting has been done carefully. However, at distances of hundreds of miles, these small angular errors represent uncertainties of position of up to 10 miles. Thus, Consolan is an excellent offshore navigation system, but is not to be used when nearing a coastline.

It is unfortunate that the scarcity of Consolan stations prevents the obtaining of two or more lines of position from this electronic navigation system, and thus a "Consolan Fix." However, an LOP derived from Consolan signals can, of course, be combined with other positional information for the determination of a fix or EP.

LORAN

Loran is the basic navigation system for ocean-going ships. Its coverage is extensive and includes all offshore boating areas. Loran is a passive system; there is no transmitter aboard the vessel, but a relatively complex and ex-

Count of Dashes					7600.2	Nantuck
0	10.5	29.8	49.6	73.6		
1	10.4	29.6	49.5	73.3		
2	10.2	29.5	49.3	73.1		
3	10.0	29.3	49.1	72.9		
4	9.9	29.1	48.9	72.6		
5	9.7	29.0	48.8	72.4		
6	9.5	28.8	48.6	72.2		
7	9.4	28.7	48.4	71.9		
8	9.2	28.5	48.2	71.7		
9	9.0	28.3	48.1	71.5		
10	8.9	28.2	47.9	71.3		
11	8.7	28.0	47.7	71.0		
12	8.5	27.9	47.5	70.8		
13	8.4	27.7	47.4	70.6		
14	8.2	27.5	47.2	70.3		

Count of Dots					7600.3	Nantucket Con	True Bear
0	20.2	39.5	60.7	91.4	138.6		16
1	20.1	39.3	60.5	91.1	138.9		16
2	19.9	39.1	60.3	90.7	139.3		16
3	19.7	39.0	60.1	90.3	139.7		16
4	19.6	38.8	59.9	89.9	140.1		17
5	19.4	38.7	59.7	89.5	140.5		17
6	19.3	38.5	59.5	89.2	140.8		17
7	19.1	38.3	59.3	88.8	141.2		17
8	18.9	38.2	59.1	88.5	141.5		17
9	18.8	38.0	58.9	88.1	141.9		17
10	18.6	37.9	58.7	87.7	142.3		17
11	18.5	37.7					17

FIG. 2550 Excerpts from tables of Consolan bearings from Oceanographic Office publication 117A. Note several bearings are given for each dot or dash count. You must know roughly where you are in relation to transmitting station to select proper bearing.

FIG. 2551 Here navigator uses special radio receiver to pick up loran signals. Loran, simple to operate, provides quick fixes of good accuracy. One reading gives line of position from special chart or tables. Another on second pair of signals gives information for loran fix.

pensive receiver is required. See fig. 2551. Loran is a valuable supplement to celestial navigation, particularly when weather prevents the taking of sights.

Loran stations operate on frequencies between 1750 and 1950 kc/s. A pair of transmitters send out pulses of radio waves which are received on board the vessel. The difference in time of arrival of the pulses from each station is measured electronically, and this information is used to determine a line of position. The pulses are not sent out simultaneously, but are synchronized in a predetermined manner. A second pair of pulses is used to determine another LOP and the result is a Loran fix. Normally, one station is common to each of the two pairs; it is called the "master" and the others are "slaves."

Loran has different day and night ranges because of the radio frequencies involved. Daytime reception using "ground waves" is the most accurate and average ranges are about 500 miles. This can be extended by the use of "sky waves" to as much as 1200 miles as determined by the power of the transmitter. Reception at night, also using sky waves, may extend out to 1400 miles, but with lessened accuracy. Range is considerably reduced when the radio waves must cross over land.

Accuracy of Loran LOPs

The accuracy of a Loran LOP varies over the coverage area of the pair of stations being used; it is greatest near the base line (line between the two stations) or base line extended. Ground wave LOPs should give a fix within 1½ miles accuracy over 80% of the normal coverage area. The accuracy when using sky waves will be degraded to a position uncertainty of from 5 to 7 miles. These accuracies are not affected as much by the passage of the pulses over land as for other systems which determine the direction of arrival of the radio waves.

A line of position can usually be determined in about two minutes; training in the use of a Loran receiver is required, but skill is soon acquired with practice. Loran stations must be accurately identified and the controls of the receiver manipulated properly to measure the time difference in arrival of the pulses. Thereafter, the position may be obtained from tables or plotted directly on readily available charts. As with other navigational techniques, three LOPs will give a better fix than two; coverage is such as to make this possible in many areas.

Automatic Steering Devices

Automatic steering devices are electrical or electro-hydraulic equipment used to hold a boat on a predetermined heading. They are often, but erroneously, referred to as "automatic pilots"; they do no part of the piloting of a boat.

In lieu of the direct application of human muscle power to the steering mechanism of a boat, electric or hydraulic motors may be used to move the rudder to the desired angle and to hold it there. See fig. 2552. The control of these motors may be made automatic by the addition of a direction-sensing element and suitable electronic amplifiers. Either magnetic or gyroscopic compasses can be used to sense heading changes, but the former is nearly always used because of its lower cost.

Most automatic steering devices have controls which allow temporary manual over-riding of the automatic controls with the boat returning to the preset heading when the over-ride switch is released. This permits brief course changes to avoid obstructions or other boats without having to reset the desired heading. Local control boxes on long cords make possible the maneuvering of the boat while away from the normal helm position. This control of the craft, however, does not include throttle changes or forward-reverse shifting.

The use of automatic steering devices is simple. They do much to relieve boredom and fatigue on long, straight stretches. The device can, under most circumstances, steer

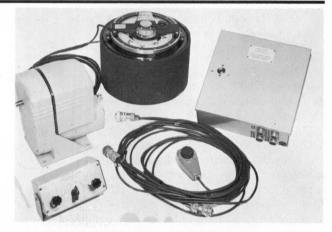

FIG. 2552 Automatic steering mechanism can do better job than human helmsman! Components are shown—magnetic compass with sensing attachments, electronic amplifier, steering motor, and control boxes.

a straighter course than a human helmsman. The disadvantage in this equipment lies in its misuse, excessive reliance on the device and failure to keep a person at the helm as a lookout ready to take over immediately if a dangerous situation should develop. It must also be remembered that the sensing element is usually no more "intelligent" than a magnetic compass; it is subject to all of the same outside corrupting influences such as tools, portable radios, beer cans, etc., if they are placed too close.

Citizens Band Radio

Citizens Band (CB) radio operations must be considered separately from those of the 2-3 Mc/s and VHF bands as they come under an entirely different set of FCC Rules. The CB sets are relatively inexpensive, easy to install, and simple to operate. See fig. 2553.

The Citizens Radio Service (CRS) is unique; it is not intended to duplicate any other radio service. It is *not* a substitute for the safety features of the regular marine radio service in the 2-3 Mc/s band, nor for the ship-to-shore connections into the public telephone system. Likewise, it is *not* a new type of hobby or amateur service for casual contacts at great distances. The CRS has its own particular functions and these do not overlap or conflict with other established services. As the result of widespread misuse of CB sets, the FCC, in April 1965, tightened its rules to control CRS operations more strictly.

Citizens Band communications can relate to either the business or social activities of the licensee, but they must be "necessary"—messages which could be sent by other means, or which need not be sent at all, are not permitted by FCC regulations. CB stations may not, of course, be used to further any illegal activity.

CB LICENSES

Licenses for stations in the Citizens Band have been made as easy as possible to obtain, and operator permits are not required at all. There are only a minimum of legal restrictions on the applicant and the equipment. To get a station license, a person must be a U.S. citizen and at least 18 years old. Licenses may also be issued to corporations provided that they meet certain rules regarding the U.S. citizenship of their officers and owners or members. Licenses may not be transferred to another person; prompt report by letter is required for a change in address (but not for a change in approved equipment). Licenses are good for 5 years; renewal requires the same form and fee.

Application for a CB station license is made on Form 505 available from any FCC office. A portion of the application is returned as the station license, and this must be received before the equipment can be used. A check or money order for $8 must accompany each application for a station license, which may, at no additional cost, include any number of sets owned by the same individual or organization.

In licensing equipment to be used on the Citizens Band, the FCC primarily envisions separate complete communications systems to meet the needs of individual licensees. This system would normally communicate within itself, and contacts with other stations heard on the air would be the exception rather than the normal mode of operation. In this connection, a "station" is all of the equipment used by a licensee in his system, and a "unit" is the term applied to a particular transmitter-receiver combination. Thus a *station* normally consists of at least two *units,* although it may consist of many more. Only in well-justified instances will the FCC license a single-unit station in the Citizens Band. The planned use of a Class D set by a boat owner belonging to a group operating a CB system would be an example of justification for licensing a single unit.

AUTHORIZED CHANNELS

The FCC has authorized 23 channels for the Citizens Band; they are generally referred to by channel number rather than frequency in megacycles. Any of them may be used by any licensee *for communications between units of one station.* For contacts between different stations, *only* channels 9 through 14, plus 23, may be used. Various efforts have been made to standardize the use of certain

FIG. 2553 Citizens Band radios find many applications in boating, car, home or summer cottage. Model shown is specially designed for marine use.

channels for specific purposes, but all such actions are unofficial and do not have the force of law or regulation. Because individual sets are generally limited in the number of channels on which they can transmit without being returned to a shop for retuning, some local coordination is necessary, either to ensure the feasibility of intercommunication between stations where it is legally permissible, or conversely to reduce interference between stations without mutual interests.

Class D stations in the Citizens Band are limited to 5 watts input power and, without special approval, an antenna must not extend more than 20 feet above the building on which it is mounted. With these restrictions, the usual reliable range is on the order of five miles, but may extend to 15 miles or more. These are groundwave ranges; skywave transmission of CB signals will often occur and cause signals to be heard at distances of several thousand miles despite their low power. The FCC Rules prohibit exchanges between stations at distances of more than 150 miles.

OPERATING PROCEDURES

Operation of a Citizens Band station is quite simple. No specific operating procedures need be learned and used; no log is required. However, there are regulations which must be known and obeyed.

The FCC Rules require that *all* communications be restricted to the *minimum practicable transmission time,* but no time limits are placed on intercommunications between units of the same station. Between different stations, however, an exchange must be limited to a maximum of 5 minutes; after its completion, both stations must remain off the air for an additional 5 minutes, monitoring the frequency just used. A station called during this waiting period may break silence to advise the other station to stand-by. Avoidance of this waiting period by changing to another channel is prohibited.

Station identification must be given at the beginning and end of each exchange of transmissions on each frequency used. If the contact continues for more than 15 minutes (legal only between units of the same station), identification must be made at least each 15 minutes. The Rules

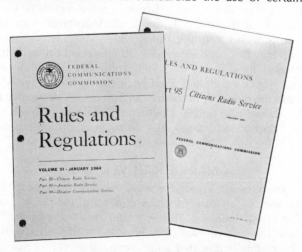

FIG. 2554 Each CB licensee must have on hand CURRENT copy of Part 95 of FCC Rules and Regulations. See text for details.

specifically require that *each letter and digit* of the call sign must be transmitted separately and distinctly. For example, 2951 must be said as "two nine five one." not as "twenty-nine fifty-one"; and 4500 as "four five zero zero," not as "forty-five hundred." Only standard phonetic alphabets may be used for the letters of the call sign.

The CB Rules now provide priority for transmissions involving the immediate safety of life of persons or protection of property. Under such conditions, the regulations restricting inter-station contacts to certain channels, limiting the durations of exchanges, etc., are waived, provided that a report is made to the FCC after the emergency is over. There are no priorities for other types of communications.

The usual prohibitions against profane, obscene, and indecent language apply to the Citizens Band. Plain language must be used, except that abbreviations and normal operating signals (such as the "10" Code) are permitted, provided that a list of such signals and their meaning is kept in the station records. Although no operator permit is required, CB stations may be operated only by the licensee, members of his immediate family, his employees, and certain other individuals specifically authorized in the regulations. CB stations may *not* be operated by a person who has had his own license revoked or has surrendered it for cancellation as the result of rule violations. The licensee must remember that he retains full responsibility for all use of all units of his station. The same system of administrative forfeitures (small fines) that applies to marine band radio operations is also applicable to CB.

The FCC now requires that a CB licensee have a *current* copy of the applicable Rules, now Part 95. See fig. 2554. The only practicable way of complying is to purchase a copy of the FCC Rules and Regulations, Volume VI, from the Superintendent of Documents, Government Printing Office, Washington, D. C. 20402. The price of $1.25 includes a subscription to the mailing service for changes as they are issued.

Miscellaneous Electronic Equipment

There are many small items of electronic equipment that can be installed on a boat for the greater safety and convenience of the owner and his guests. The boatman should consider each for possible installation on his craft, not forgetting that each item will usually add a bit to the load on the battery and electrical wiring.

FUEL VAPOR DETECTORS

A *fuel vapor detector* is considered by many boatmen to be an essential piece of safety equipment aboard any craft using gasoline as fuel. See fig. 2555. These devices provide a visual warning of the build-up of any dangerous concentration of fuel vapors in the bilges. Frequently, such a device also provides an audible alarm in addition to the visual warning.

The installation of a fuel vapor detector is not difficult electrically or mechanically, but it is essential that it be done correctly. The location of the detector unit is important if the maximum safety benefit is to be obtained. Have your installation checked by a surveyor or safety inspector from your insurance company. Even the best fuel vapor detector is no substitute for electric bilge blowers, forced ventilation fans that pull air and fumes out of the lower parts of your boat's interior.

AUXILIARY RECEIVERS

If your boat does not have a direction finder that can be used as an *auxiliary receiver,* the boat owner should consider the purchase of one of several compact and lightweight receivers that are available at a reasonable price. See fig. 2556. This additional receiver can serve the functions previously mentioned of monitoring a second communications channel or of backing up the regular receiver in case of its failure. If the auxiliary receiver is of the transistorized type, the added battery drain is negligible, or it may be operated from its self-contained dry batteries. Models are available with either continuous tuning or several crystal-controlled fixed frequencies. This latter type lacks the flexibility of the former, but has the advantage of quick and sure tuning. These small receivers, if they have self-contained batteries, may be taken ashore on a beach or in the dinghy if you leave your boat for any reason.

MARINE CONVERTERS

The growing use of electrical equipment on boats has resulted in a steadily increasing demand for power from the craft's batteries. The generator or alternator on the boat's engine will suffice to keep the batteries charged if the engine is operated a large enough percentage of the time that the electrical equipment is in use. There is no way to state a general figure as to what proportion of the

FIG. 2555 Fuel vapor detector, properly installed and used, will warn of explosive vapors in bilge. Models available with audible alarm and visual indicator.

FIG. 2556 With auxiliary receiver, second marine band channel may be monitored, or you can listen to frequency for which your radio-telephone does not have a crystal. Model shown operates from self-contained batteries.

FIG. 2557 Boat batteries are normally charged by generator or alternator driven by main engine. At dockside, marine converter keeps batteries up by converting shoreside AC power to DC at proper voltage for boat's electrical system.

time is required as individual conditions will vary too widely.

It you are one of the boat owners who finds that all too often his battery is down so far that it won't start the engine, then you are a candidate for a *marine converter*. See fig. 2557. This relatively simple electrical device converts the 115-volt AC dockside electricity into the 6, 12, or 32 volts DC required for the boat's electrical system. It is essentially a continuous-duty battery-charger with control circuits to permit it to operate safely left unattended.

INVERTERS

It may seem a bit contradictory to immediately discuss a means of getting 115-volt AC electrical power from the boat's low voltage DC system just after having considered the reverse process, but there is a reason. There is no way to store AC in a battery, and if AC is needed when under way, the only means of getting it (without installing an engine-driven auxiliary generating plant) is to "invert" the DC power from the batteries into AC.

Alternating current aboard a boat of any size is useful for the powering of television or hi-fi sets, tape recorders, electric razors, electric mixers or other small household appliances. Small inverters are available using vibrators or transistors and these will quietly and efficiently supply you with small amounts of "shore-type" electricity. These DC to AC converters are *not* suitable for use with electrical devices whose function is to produce heat, such as toasters and irons; the power required for such items is beyond the capacity of inverters.

AUXILIARY GENERATING PLANTS

Inverters using vibrators or transistors are usually limited to a power rating of not more than 250 watts. If greater amounts of 115-volt AC power are required for cooking, air conditioning, or heating, the installation of a small

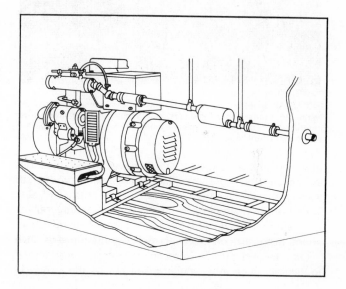

FIG. 2558 Inverters can change DC electrical power of boat's batteries to 115-volts AC for operation of shore-type electrical equipment, up to a few hundred watts. For heavier loads, install auxiliary electric plant driven by its own gasoline or diesel engine. (Diagram from Technical Bulletin T-021, Installation of Onan Marine Generating Plants.)

auxiliary generating plant should be considered. See fig. 2558. These units are available in sizes from 500 watts to 10 kilowatts or more, with either gasoline or diesel engines to match the type of fuel used in the main engines.

Calculation of the size of generator you will need is not difficult as nearly all items of electrical equipment are plainly rated in watts of power consumed. Be careful, however, about loads that are not constant. For example, an electric refrigerator unit may consume only about 100 watts *average* power since it does not run continuously, but while it is running it may require 400 watts, and the momentary starting load will be even greater. Be generous and be safer; install an electric plant with an adequate excess or reserve capacity. You will soon think of more electrical and electronic gear to add to your boat.

INTERCOM SYSTEMS

While most people think of a boat as being too small and compact to have internal communications problems, there are numerous possible applications for simple intercom systems. See fig. 2559. The interior of many larger cruisers, particularly those of the double-cabin type, are so divided that voices do not carry well from one compartment to another. A simple three-station intercom system connecting the bridge, forward cabin, and after cabin will

Then you can have constant contact between the person at the boat's controls and the person raising or lowering the anchor, or handling the docking lines. Just try to get up a badly fouled anchor without communicating with the helmsman, and you will quickly appreciate this small electronic device.

RUDDER POSITION INDICATORS

A simple and inexpensive, but very useful, item is a *rudder position indicator*. See fig. 2560. These are standard equipment of large vessels and tugboats, but are seldom found on recreational boats. This small degree of use probably results from a lack of knowledge of the availability of the device and how it works. A small unit is in-

FIG. 2559 Small intercom system permits easy communication between all areas aboard cruisers and yachts. Master unit shown controls five substations, including one on foredeck, useful when anchoring or docking.

FIG. 2560 Rudder position indicators are always found on large ships and tugs, infrequently on small craft. They deserve wider use. Knowledge of rudder angle helps when docking, undocking, entering canal locks, etc.

make possible easy conversation between these locations and save many steps. On a boat with a small crew, such as a couple living aboard by themselves, a quick and easy means of internal communications is truly a safety item as the helmsman need not leave the controls or divert his attention to carry on a conversation or summon assistance.

On a larger boat, the intercom system can be extended to include a unit in a weather-proof box on the foredeck.

stalled at the rudder post and wires are run forward to a meter located within easy view of the helmsman. This meter is calibrated in degrees of right or left rudder. A quick glance will instantly tell the exact position of the rudder at that moment; such information is of considerable value when getting under way or docking with little steerageway. Once you have and use one of these electronic items, you will never be without it.

New Unit of Frequency Measurement

The familiar units of radio frequency measurement—cycles, kilocycles, and megacycles—are being gradually replaced with new units. Scientific organizations are now using the term "Hertz" to replace "cycles per second." This new unit is named for a pioneer in the field of radio waves, Heinrich Hertz, 1857-1894. (Did you know that the familiar units of Ohms, Amperes, Volts, Watts, and many others were all derived from the names of persons who developed early theories and laws of electricity?) The FCC has accepted the definition of "Hertz," abbreviated as "Hz," and this unit along with kilohertz (kHz) and megahertz (MHz) may be found in increasing use.

INTERNATIONAL FLAGS AND PENNANTS

ALPHABET FLAGS			NUMERAL PENNANTS
Alfa — Diver Down; Keep Clear	**K**ilo — Desire to Communicate	**U**niform — Standing into Danger	1
Bravo — Dangerous Cargo	**L**ima — Stop Instantly	**V**ictor — Require Assistance	2
Charlie — Yes	**M**ike — I Am Stopped	**W**his-key — Require Medical Assistance	3
Delta — Keep Clear	**N**ovem-ber — No	**X**ray — Stop Your Intention	4
Echo — Altering Course to Starboard	**O**scar — Man Overboard	**Y**ankee — Am Dragging Anchor	5
Foxtrot — Disabled	**P**apa — About to Sail	**Z**ulu — Shore Stations	6
Golf — Want a Pilot	**Q**uebec — Request Pratique	**REPEATERS** 1st Repeat	7
Hotel — Pilot on Board	**R**omeo — Require a Tug	2nd Repeat	8
India — Altering Course to Port	**S**ierra — Engines Going Astern	3rd Repeat	9
Juliett — On Fire; Keep Clear	**T**ango — Keep Clear of Me	CODE — Code and Answering Pennant (Decimal Point)	0

NOTE: From revised International Code of Signals effective 1 April 1969.

How International Code Flags are Used in Signaling

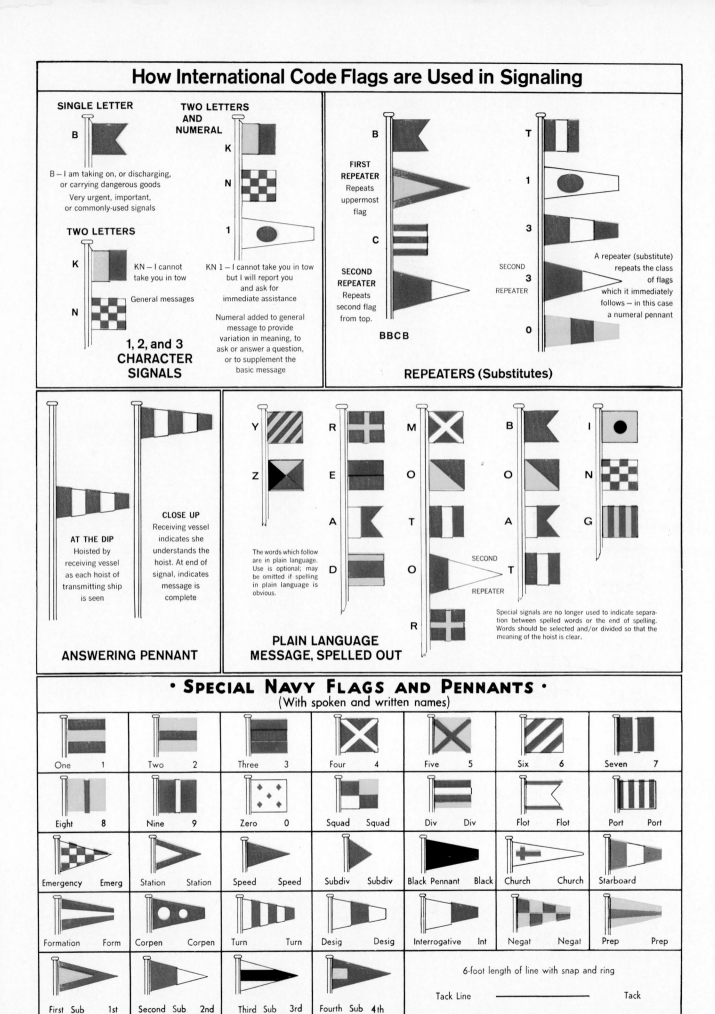

SINGLE LETTER

B

B – I am taking on, or discharging, or carrying dangerous goods

Very urgent, important, or commonly-used signals

TWO LETTERS AND NUMERAL

K
N
1

KN 1 – I cannot take you in tow but I will report you and ask for immediate assistance

Numeral added to general message to provide variation in meaning, to ask or answer a question, or to supplement the basic message

TWO LETTERS

K
N

KN – I cannot take you in tow

General messages

1, 2, and 3 CHARACTER SIGNALS

REPEATERS (Substitutes)

B

FIRST REPEATER Repeats uppermost flag

C

SECOND REPEATER Repeats second flag from top.

BBCB

T
1
3
3

SECOND REPEATER

0

A repeater (substitute) repeats the class of flags which it immediately follows – in this case a numeral pennant

ANSWERING PENNANT

AT THE DIP Hoisted by receiving vessel as each hoist of transmitting ship is seen

CLOSE UP Receiving vessel indicates she understands the hoist. At end of signal, indicates message is complete

PLAIN LANGUAGE MESSAGE, SPELLED OUT

Y
Z

R
E
A
D

M
O
T
O
R

B
O
A
T

I
N
G

The words which follow are in plain language. Use is optional; may be omitted if spelling in plain language is obvious.

SECOND REPEATER

Special signals are no longer used to indicate separation between spelled words or the end of spelling. Words should be selected and/or divided so that the meaning of the hoist is clear.

• SPECIAL NAVY FLAGS AND PENNANTS •
(With spoken and written names)

One 1	Two 2	Three 3	Four 4	Five 5	Six 6	Seven 7
Eight 8	Nine 9	Zero 0	Squad Squad	Div Div	Flot Flot	Port Port
Emergency Emerg	Station Station	Speed Speed	Subdiv Subdiv	Black Pennant Black	Church Church	Starboard
Formation Form	Corpen Corpen	Turn Turn	Desig Desig	Interrogative Int	Negat Negat	Prep Prep
First Sub 1st	Second Sub 2nd	Third Sub 3rd	Fourth Sub 4th			

6-foot length of line with snap and ring

Tack Line ——————— Tack

See also page 383

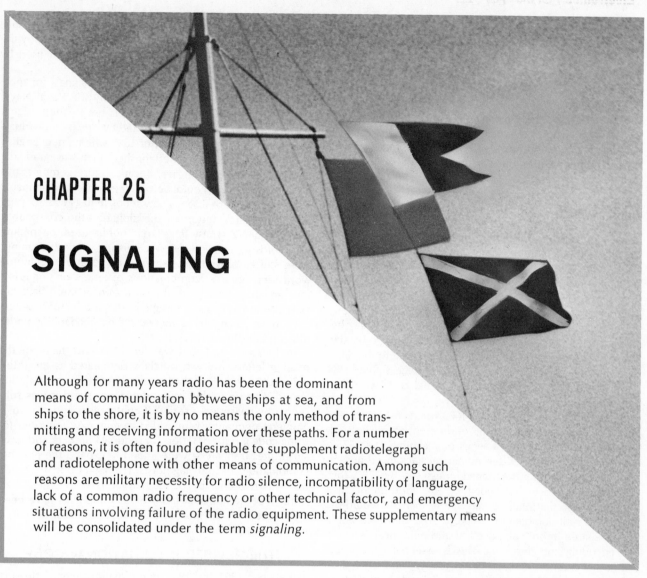

CHAPTER 26

SIGNALING

Although for many years radio has been the dominant means of communication between ships at sea, and from ships to the shore, it is by no means the only method of transmitting and receiving information over these paths. For a number of reasons, it is often found desirable to supplement radiotelegraph and radiotelephone with other means of communication. Among such reasons are military necessity for radio silence, incompatibility of language, lack of a common radio frequency or other technical factor, and emergency situations involving failure of the radio equipment. These supplementary means will be consolidated under the term *signaling*.

FIG. 2601 Aboard this vessel arriving in a U.S. port, the two-letter International Code flag signal AM (Alfa Mike) at the masthead signifies "Have you a doctor?" and the single-letter Q (Quebec) at the starboard yardarm is flown to "request pratique." (Rosenfeld photo)

The forms of signaling

The principal forms of signaling are: (1) flag-hoist, (2) flashing light, and (3) semaphore. These are all visual means; signaling by audible methods, such as by Morse code on the boat's horn, is of little practical use. Sound signals as used in the Rules of the Road are covered elsewhere and will not be repeated here.

VISUAL SIGNALING

Visual signaling should not be a new or strange concept to the average boatman, although he probably lacks the detailed knowledge to read such signals. The yachtsman crossing a busy harbor will certainly see many ships flying signal flags; and should it be a naval harbor, such as Hampton Roads or San Diego, he will undoubtedly also see flashing signal lights, and perhaps sailors sending semaphore.

The value of visual signaling

The time taken to acquire a rudimentary knowledge of visual signaling can be of value to a boatman in at least two ways. Not the least of these is the pleasure and satisfaction of knowing what is going on and being able to explain it to the other crew members and guests aboard his boat. Merchant ships, fig. 2602, will be flying signal flags indicating the presence of a pilot aboard, the handling of dangerous cargoes, an imminent sailing, and other interesting facts. Naval and Coast Guard vessels, fig. 2603, probably will be flying many more flags, some signifying simple facts like those noted above, and others signaling more complex naval messages and maneuvers. Being able to read and know the meaning of at least a portion of these signal flags, or other types of signals, will give the boatman a greater sense of "belonging" to the maritime world around him.

Signaling / CHAPTER 26

The greater value, however, in a knowledge of signaling lies in the added margin of safety that it can provide. So much dependence is placed today on the boat's radio-telephone that one often overlooks the possibility of its not being available when needed. It need not be an electronic failure that precludes your communicating with another craft; it could be merely a lack of a common frequency or type of modulation. Radio will undoubtedly remain your primary means of boat-to-boat and boat-to-shore communications, but don't overlook the added possibilities of signaling.

Signal Codes

For more than two thousand years, information and orders have been communicated between ships by means of flags. In the days of the ancient Greeks and Romans, battles were begun by the hoisting of streamers of various colors. These were first raised on the vessel carrying the commander of the naval force—hence the term "flagship."

The development of modern flag-hoist signaling may be said to date from 1340 when the British Navy officially listed two signals—one for all captains to come to the flagship and the other that the enemy had been sighted. By 1530, the French Navy was using a signal code with five meanings.

Signal books first appeared in 1673 when an English system was established using flags of different colors hoisted at various places to give a series of meanings. The 1738 French signal code used ten numerical flags in groups of three for transmitting prearranged messages. By 1780, this technique had been expanded by the addition of two "repeaters" so that only 12 flags, rather than 30, would be needed for all combinations, 000 to 999. The code book was prepared in both alphabetical and numerical sections for encoding and decoding. This is essentially the same format as is used for signal books today. The French system also provided for the relaying of signals to the more distant ships in a formation, again just as is currently done in naval forces at sea.

The first American flag code was proposed in 1797 employing numeral pennants and repeaters for 290 signals, and in 1802 a modified version was adopted for use by the Continental Navy. Flag-hoist signaling has been used by the American Navy continuously since then.

In 1817, the British adopted a code of signals for merchant ships different from that used by the Royal Navy. In other countries, non-naval vessels used various signal systems that usually were published by private individuals or groups. These prevailed until 1857 when a new English "commercial code" was established that was gradually adopted by other countries. Because more combinations were needed than could be obtained with ten pennants in combinations of three, a new set of 18 flags was adopted and named after letters of the alphabet—the consonants, less X, Y, and Z. These flags could not be used for spelling out words as the vowels were missing; coded meanings were still employed for geographical locations, common words and phrases, combinations of letters or single letters, and numbers. More than a dozen of these flags are still used in the original design as adopted in 1857; others have been changed to increase their readability under difficult conditions of visibility.

In 1897, the alphabet was filled out with flags for the missing letters and was officially designated as the International Code of Signals. Experience with this code during World War I revealed many deficiencies, and it was subsequently revised in a series of conferences and meetings. Numeral pennants were added to eliminate the need for using code groups of letters for sending numbers, and three substitutes (repeaters) were added to expand the possible combinations of four-flag hoists. The 1930 Code was made truly international by being standardized in official versions in seven languages. Since 1955, the flags have been associated with the phonetic alphabet now so widely used in radio-telephone communications.

THE REVISED INTERNATIONAL CODE

Between 1961 and 1964 an international committee met periodically and drew up a new Code of Signals. The revised Code is intended primarily for situations related to the safety of navigation and persons, especially where language difficulties arise. Official versions of the new Code are now published in nine languages. It is suitable for transmission by *all* means of communications, including radiotelephony.

H.O. 102

The revised International Code of Signals became effective on 1 April 1969. For American use, it has been published by the Naval Oceanographic Office as H.O. 102. This new volume replaces both the old H.O. 103 used for visual signaling and H.O. 104 used for radio. The book can be purchased from local sales agents, or it can be ordered by mail from the U.S. Naval Oceanographic Office, Washington, D.C. 20390.

H.O. 102 includes both general procedures applicable to all forms of communication and specific rules for flag signaling, flashing light signaling, sound signaling, radiotelegraphy, radiotelephony, and signaling by hand flags, using either semaphore or the Morse code.

Principles of coding

The revised Code is based on the principle that each

FIG. 2602 Merchant ships are often seen flying a single flag from the International Code of Signals. This vessel has the "H" flag hoisted to signify that there is a pilot aboard. The "G" flag would have indicated a request for a pilot. All of the alphabet flags have a special meaning when flown singly as well as when used in groups of two or more.

FIG. 2603 Naval and Coast Guard ships make much use of signal flags for communicating with other vessels. Each flag represents a letter, number or special meaning. Government ships always hoist the flags of their call letters when entering or leaving port.

signal will have a complete meaning. It thus omits the vocabulary method that was a part of the old Code. The Geographical Section, not being considered essential, was dropped. By these means, it was possible to reduce considerably the volume of the Code and achieve greater simplicity.

The signals used consist of: (1) single-letter signals allocated to meanings which are very urgent, important, of very common use; (2) two-letter signals for general messages; and (3) three-letter signals (all beginning with "M") for medical messages.

In certain cases, *complements* are used—an added numeral following the basic two-letter signal. Complements express: (1) variations in the meaning of a basic signal; (2) questions and answers related to the meaning of the basic signal; and (3) supplementary, specific, or more detailed meanings.

Spelling

When names must be sent, or other words for which there are no signal groups in the International Code, they must be spelled out. The signal group YZ *may* be used to indicate that the groups which follow are plain language words rather than code signals; it can, however, be omitted if the spelling is obvious. The "alphabetical signals" formerly used have been discontinued.

Special procedures

The International Code of Signals provides special procedures for many purposes such as signaling time, courses and bearings, geographical coordinates, etc. The details of these procedures are too lengthy for inclusion in this book; the boatman needing such knowledge will find it in full in H.O. 102. This volume is a "must" for a boatman who may need to communicate with foreign ships or shore stations; it is a necessity for any skipper who carries a full set of signal flags and uses them to communicate with other yachts or with Naval and Coast Guard vessels. It is an interesting book to have aboard even if such signaling is not contemplated.

The problem of compiling a code from which expressions in any one of nine languages might be taken was a difficult one, and certain principles must be followed in its use. These are outlined in the instructions in H.O. 102 and should be read carefully before attempting to use the code itself. Otherwise, because of the form used, erroneous interpretations might be placed on a message sent in code.

Typical code signals from H.O. 102

The simple single-letter signal codes are shown beneath the flags on page 383. Typical two-letter groups are listed in fig. 2615.

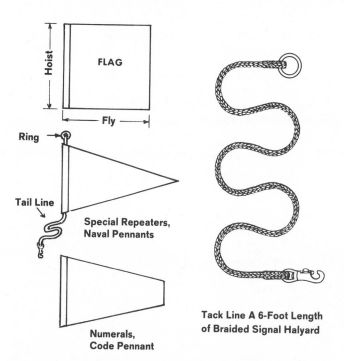

FIG. 2604 Flags and pennants of the International Code of Signals are joined together with snaps and rings. The "tail line" extending below each flag provides the spacing beween them in each group; the "tack line" provides a greater spacing between two groups hoisted on the same halyard.

387

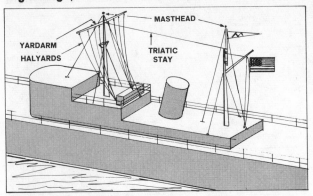

FIG. 2605 Signal flags are normally hoisted on halyards rising to the yardarms. In some situations, particularly on naval vessels, hoists may be made at more than one location simultaneously. See text for sequence in which such multiple hoists are read.

Flag-hoist Signaling

The set of international code flags prescribed for flag-hoist signaling consists of 26 alphabetical flags, 10 numeral pennants, three substitutes, and the answering pennant. The names "substitute" and "repeater" are used interchangeably in publications on flag-hoist signaling. In either case, they are pennants that are employed as replacements for flags (or pennants) already used once in a hoist, since there is only one of each letter or number in a set.

Five standardized colors are used for signal flags—red, white, blue, yellow, and black. Most of the flags are of two colors, selected and arranged for maximum contrast. Two flags are of a single solid color, several use three colors, and one uses four colors. Each flag and pennant has a piece of line sewn into its hoist edge, extending slightly above the cloth to a metal ring, and for several inches below the cloth ending in a snap hook. This "tail line"

provides the spacing between the flags of a hoist; the combination of snaps and rings permits the rapid joining together of the individual flags and their connection onto a signal halyard. See fig. 2604.

The flags and pennants of the International Code are shown in full color on page 383. Also indicated here are the meanings of the flags when flown singly. Of these, probably the most often seen will be the "B" flag, displayed while a ship is carrying or handling an explosive cargo, and the "H" flag flown when a pilot is on board.

Special naval flags and pennants

The boatman may sometimes see vessels of the U. S. Navy and Coast Guard flying signals that include flags and pennants not found in the International Code. The Navy uses a set of *numeral flags* as well as the regular pennants for numbers. In addition, special flags and pennants have been adopted for naval formations and maneuvers.

The U. S. Navy uses the three substitutes of the International Code and has added its own fourth substitute.

The special naval flags and pennants are shown in color at the bottom of page 384.

FLAG SIGNALING PROCEDURES

Signal flags are flown singly and in combinations of two or more; see page 384. Flags and pennants may be mixed as required.

When signaling by means of the flags and pennants of the International Code, it is advisable to show only a single *hoist* at a time. A hoist means one or more *groups* displayed from a single halyard. The signal is read from the top down. Each group of letters and/or numerals constitute a separate signal; when several groups are used on a single hoist, they must, of course, be separated to convey the correct meaning. A *tackline,* a six-foot length of line with a snap hook in one end and a ring in the other, is used as a spacer to separate the groups.

FIG. 2606 Flag hoists are read from the top flag down. If there should be more than one halyard in use from the same yardarm at the same time, the hoists are read from outboard inward as shown above.

TYPICAL SIGNALS FROM A YACHT CLUB SIGNAL CODE

A — The course will be _____.
H — Communicate with me via radiotelephone.
L — Come within hail.
Q — Race will finish off _____.
T — Send club launch.
BF — Anchor for night at _____.
CQ — Captains and guests are invited on board this yacht at _____.
CZ — Congratulations, well done.
DC — Mail for you ashore at _____.
IR — Monday
JQ — 0730
NG — Bangor, Maine
SG — Newport, R. I.
AQP — N.N.E.
ARU — S.W.

FIG. 2607 In a typical yacht club signal code, single letters will consist of special, racing, and emergency signals; two-letter groups will represent general and designating signals, and days of the week and hours of the day; three-letter groups are compass signals.

Signals should be kept flying until acknowledged. There are occasions when more than one hoist need be displayed simultaneously; in such cases, an order of sequence must be followed in order to interpret the message correctly. The hoists are read in the following order: (1) masthead, (2) triatic stay, (3) starboard yardarm, and (4) port yardarm, fig. 2605.

In cases where more than one hoist is flown from a yardarm, they are read from outboard inward, fig. 2606. When a vessel displays more than one hoist from a triatic stay, they are read from the foremost one aft.

The terms *superior* and *inferior* are often used in relation to signals. A signal is superior to another if hoisted

FIG. 2608 On boats equipped with a full set of signal flags and pennants, a flag chest or locker may be built in, with letter or name plates to identify code flags in their individual pigeonholes.

before the latter, either in point of time or hoist. If hoisted after, it is inferior.

Obviously, a visual signal is going to fail in its purpose if it is not clearly visible. For that reason, signals should always be flown where they can be seen best by the receiving vessel or shore station. This means that each flag must stand out clearly, not fouled by the halyard, sails, etc.

Signal groups

If every message transmitted by flag signals had to be spelled out letter by letter, it is obvious that the procedure would become impossibly lengthy, wasting much time and effort. Many typical messages have been given two-letter signals in the revised Code. One of the first steps in gaining proficiency in visual signaling is to become thoroughly familiar with the code book. With such knowledge, one will naturally frame his messages so as to use phrasing for which code groups have been provided, lessening the number of words that must be spelled out.

Calling and answering

When calling a particular vessel, her signal letters are hoisted superior to the message that is to follow. Otherwise, in the absence of such signal letters, the message would be understood to be addressed to all vessels in sight of the signal. If the vessel's signal letters are not

known, she can be requested to hoist them by displaying the code letter group CS and hoisting your own signal letters at the same time. As another alternative, display of the code group YQ would convey the message: "I wish to signal to the vessel on bearing indicated from me." This signal would, of course, be accompanied with another hoist indicating the bearing concerned so as to distinguish between several vessels that might be within sight.

In order to understand the procedure followed in answering a signal, there are several terms that should be explained. A signal is said to be *at the dip* when it is hoisted only about half as high as the halyard will permit. It is said to be *close up* when it has been hoisted as high as possible. See page 384 center left.

In receiving signals, the vessel or vessels addressed should hoist the answering pennant at the dip when each hoist is seen, closing up to indicate that the signal is understood. Then when the hoist on the transmitting ship is hauled down, the answering pennant on the receiving vessel is lowered to the dip again so as to be ready to acknowledge the next hoist in a similar manner when that one is understood. This continues until the message is completed, at which time the answering pennant alone is hoisted aboard the transmitting ship; this signal is acknowledged by the receiving ship as before, after which the answering pennants are hauled down.

When a hoist can not be clearly distinguished, the answering pennant is kept at the dip on the receiving ship and a signal is hoisted to convey the reason for the difficulty. If, on the other hand, the signal can be distinguished but not understood, the letters ZL are hoisted.

Substitutes or Repeaters

With every set of code flags there are included three *substitutes*. These permit the repetition of a signal flag in a group without carrying extra sets of flags. In the procedures of the International Code, substitutes repeat the same *class* of flag that precedes them; that is, following alphabetical flags they repeat them, but if used with numeral pennants they repeat such pennants.

Considering then only the class of flag directly preceding the substitute, the first substitute repeats the top such flag; the second substitute, the second flag from the top; and the third substitute, the third flag from the top. An answering pennant used as a decimal point is disregarded. For example: if the signal were T1330, the hoist would be: T, 1, 3, second substitute, 0. See the illustration on page 384, upper right. A particular substitute is never used more than once in the same group. If the signal were BBCB, the hoist would read: B, first substitute, C, second substitute. Note that the first substitute has been used once in place of the second letter and cannot be used again. However, as used it represented the letter B, and so it can be repeated by use of the second substitute; see page 384.

Naval procedures

Flag-hoist signaling procedures between Naval and Coast Guard vessels will vary from that used by merchant ships and yachts. These differences stem from the different and special requirements of naval formations and maneuvers. They need not cause any concern to boatmen, however, for in communications with non-naval craft, these vessels will use International Code procedures.

YACHT CLUB SIGNAL CODES

Many yacht clubs have adopted signal codes of their own that are not in conformity with the International Code. The purpose of the signals prescribed in such codes is principally to provide a means of communication between craft of the club's fleet. These local codes permit quicker and easier signaling for matters of particular interest to that group. See fig. 2607.

While the codes do vary between different clubs, there is a tendency toward standardization of both the signals and the procedures. The interpretation of club signals will generally require the availability of that club's signal code as published in its year book.

Most clubs provide that when using the club code the burgee is hoisted over the code flags; the absence of the burgee indicating that the hoist should be read from the International Code of Signals. In other cases, the procedures provide that the three signal flags YV 1 can be hoisted to indicate specifically that the International Code is being used, its absence indicating the use of the club code. It is necessary to know the procedures of the particular club concerned.

General yachting uses of signal flags

Most boats will not carry a full set of signal flags and pennants, fig. 2608, but may carry one or more for special use under certain conditions.

The flying of the single flag "Q" when returning from a foreign port is correct and desirable in accordance with its International Code meaning "My vessel is healthy and I request free pratique." See fig. 2601. *Pratique* is the formal term for permission to use a port.

The code flag "T" is often seen flying on boats at yacht club moorings. Its meaning at such times is a request for "transportation"—a call for the club launch to come alongside and pick up passengers for shore. This is not in accordance with the International Code of Signals, but has general acceptance and understanding through wide usage.

Another single code-flag signal is the flying of the letter "M" to signify "Doctor on board"; this differs from the revised International Code meaning. Not yet in general use, its value is gradually being recognized and the practice is spreading. While most, if not all, doctors look to their boating hours as a time "to get away from it all," knowledge that a boat has a doctor on board is of great importance should an accident happen within sight; it is to be hoped that the practice of flying the "M" flag will be adopted by more and more physicians and surgeons.

SPECIAL FLAGS

Many flags will be seen on boats that undoubtedly "signal" a meaning, but nonetheless will not be found in any signal code, International or yacht club.

The more official of these flags include the owner absent, guest aboard, and meal flags described on page 359. Next in line would come the cocktail flag, the meaning of which is never in doubt, closely followed by a newer flag bearing a foaming mug of beer. For the non-alcoholically inclined, there is now a flag decorated with a pot of coffee, obviously inviting the beholder to "come on over and have one."

Boats operating out of sport-fishing ports will often be seen flying flags bearing the likeness of various game fish, indicating their catch for that day. Unhappily, you may also see boats flying the "skunk" flag signifying "no luck today."

A special flag that must be strictly honored is the "diver down" flag—rectangular red with a single white diagonal stripe. Keep well away from any boat or float displaying this signal.

There seems to be an ever-expanding list of what might be called "comic" flags. These are not particularly in good taste in yachting circles, but as they can be considered as signaling information, their existence will be noted here. Among such flags are the ball-and-chain (wife aboard), witch-on-a-broom (wife not on board), battle-axe (mother-in-law aboard), and two sleeping rabbits (do not disturb). See fig. 2609.

There is also the skull-and-crossed-bones "pirate" flag that is often seen, but which apparently has no standardized meaning, if indeed it has any meaning beyond its decorative (?) value.

BATTLE-AXE
MOTHER-IN-LAW ABOARD

SKUNK
(NO FISH CAUGHT)

COCKTAIL

COFFEE

BALL & CHAIN
WIFE ABOARD

WITCH—
WIFE ASHORE

BEER

BUNNIES—SLUMBER
DO NOT DISTURB

FIG. 2609 Many boats will be seen flying the so-called "novelty" or "gag" flags. While in somewhat questionable taste in strict yachting circles, it must be admitted that, properly used, they do "signal" information to other craft.

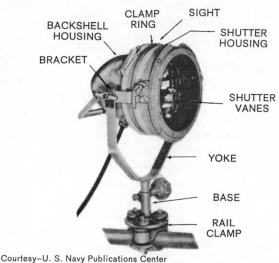

BACKSHELL HOUSING
CLAMP RING
SIGHT
BRACKET
SHUTTER HOUSING
SHUTTER VANES
YOKE
BASE
RAIL CLAMP

Courtesy—U. S. Navy Publications Center

FIG. 2610 For short-range signaling, naval vessels will use small searchlights not much larger than those found on motorboats. The flashes of light are formed by opening and closing shutter vanes in front of the light source. The Navy also uses several larger sizes of signal searchlights up to 36-inch carbon-arc lights.

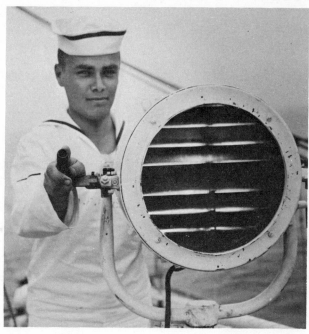

Courtesy—United States Coast Guard

Flashing Light Signaling

Signaling by short and long flashes of light is widely used by naval forces. It is much faster than hoists of code flags and has a much greater range than semaphore signaling. It maintains the radio silence sometimes needed for security.

Navy vessels may use small or large signal searchlights, yardarm or masthead lights, or special security devices. For normal ranges from one ship to another, a small search-light about the size of those mounted on medium-sized boats will be used, fig. 2610. These lights will be bright enough for signaling during the day or night. To communicate over greater distances, which may be several miles or more, large and powerful arc-light searchlights will be found on major naval vessels.

Searchlights of all sizes are normally used to communicate with another specific vessel or with a shore station. For signaling to all ships around a harbor or in a formation at sea, use will be made of the yardarm or masthead blinker lights, less powerful but capable of being read

NONDIRECTIONAL BLINKER LIGHTS

FIG. 2611 For non-directional flashing light signaling, a vessel may be equipped with yardarm blinker lights. They may also be located as a pair at a masthead. With these lights the range over which signals can be sent is much less than that of a searchlight.

from any direction, fig. 2611. Security can be achieved by using cones over the signal searchlight to restrict the light pattern, or by using infrared devices that require special receiving equipment to read the signals being sent.

Small-craft use

Flashing light signaling is useful also to boatmen. It has the advantage of needing little or no special equipment; an ordinary flashlight is usually used as the signaling light. There is, however, the disadvantage that a knowledge of the Morse code is required.

Generally, flashing light signals from a boat are limited to nighttime use by the low power of the light source. The boat's searchlight cannot be turned on and off fast enough for the practical transmission of Morse code dots and dashes—the Navy's signal searchlights are left on continuously during use, with shutters being rapidly opened and closed to make the short and long flashes of light. The short but definite time for the filament of a boat's search-light to come up to brilliance and die out is too great for message sending, but would be satisfactory for such special use as the three shorts, three longs, and three shorts of an SOS signal. (••• — — — •••)

THE INTERNATIONAL MORSE CODE

As noted above, the International Morse Code of *dots* and *dashes* is used for flashing light signaling. The flashes and the spaces between them are defined in terms of *units* —a *dot* is *one* unit long; a *dash* is *three* units; the space between the dots and dashes of a single character (letter or number) is one unit long, between characters it is three units, and between words or groups it is five units in length. The length of a "unit" is roughly set by the skill of the operator and the speed at which he can transmit accurately; it is always well to transmit somewhat more slowly than one's maximum capability to minimize errors and, in

A	•—	J	•———	R	•—•
B	—•••	K	—•—	S	•••
C	—•—•	L	•—••	T	—
D	—••	M	——	U	••—
E	•	N	—•	V	•••—
F	••—•	O	———	W	•——
G	——•	P	•——•	X	—••—
H	••••	Q	——•—	Y	—•——
I	••			Z	——••

1	•————	2	••———	3	•••——
4	••••—	5	•••••	6	—••••
7	——•••	8	———••	9	————•
				0	—————

Period •—•—•—
Comma ——••——
Interrogative •—• ——•— (RQ)
Distress Call •••———••• (SOS)
From —•• (DE)
Invitation to transmit (go ahead) —•— (K)
Wait •—••• (AS)
Error •••••••• (EEEE etc.)
Received •—• (R)
End of each message •—•—• (AR)

NOTE:
A dash is equal to three dots.
The space between parts of the same letter is equal to one dot.
The space between two letters is equal to three dots.
The space between two words is equal to five dots.

FIG. 2612 The International Morse Code, with certain simple procedure signals.

case of doubt, it is better to exaggerate slightly the lengths of dashes and spaces than it is to shorten them.

The letters of the alphabet, numbers, and punctuation marks are signaled in Morse code by combinations of dots and dashes. Letters have from one to four components, numbers have five, and punctuation symbols have six. The basic Morse code is shown in fig. 2612.

Time is required to memorize the Morse code characters for the letters, numbers, and simple punctuation marks; but it *can* be done by anyone, and it is well worth the effort required. Once learned, and occasionally used, it will not be forgotten and may prove extremely valuable some day in an emergency.

FLASHING LIGHT PROCEDURES

Formal procedures have been prescribed for the establishment and carrying out of communications by flashing light. The boatman need know only the barest fundamentals, enough for emergencies, leaving the full details, as described in H.O. 102, to the professional signalman.

Establishing contact

A vessel desiring to establish flashing light communications with another trains its light on the other and sends the other's call letters, if known, or the signal AA, AA, etc. (•—•—, •—•—, etc.). This is discontinued when the vessel called answers.

TTTTT, etc. (—————, etc.) is the signal used to answer the above call; it is discontinued when the first ship stops calling.

Procedure signals

Certain letters and combination of letters have been given special procedural meanings. They are, in effect, brief messages in themselves. Some of the more basic signals are given below with their meanings; the bar over the letters means that they are run together and transmitted as a single character.

T (—) is the single dash flash signifying the receipt of each word or code group in a message.

R (•—•) means "Message received."

EEEEEE, etc. (••••••, etc.) is the erase sign, signifying that a mistake has been made. It is answered by the receiving ship with the same signal. When answered, the sending ship repeats the *last word or group sent correctly* and then goes ahead with the rest of the message.

RQ Interrogative, or "The significance of the previous group should be read as a question."

C Affirmative, or "The significance of the previous group should be read in the affirmative."

N Negative, or "The significance of the previous group should be read in the negative. When used with voice transmissions, the procedure signal is 'NO'."

"C" and "N" (or "NO") can be used singly to indicate an affirmative or negative statement or reply. When "N" (or "NO") or "RQ" are used to change an affirmative signal into a negative statement or a question, they are sent after the main signal.

OK Acknowledging a correct repetition, or "It is correct."

CS "What is the name or identity signal of your vessel (or station)?"

DE "From" (used to precede the name or identity signal of the calling station.

RPT Repeat signal: "I repeat" or "Repeat what you have sent" or "Repeat what you have received."

Many of the above procedure signals may be used with means of communication other than flashing light. When used by voice, the letters are spoken from the phonetic alphabet, except for "NO" which is spoken as the word.

Using the repeat sign

When the repeat sign is sent singly, it means "Repeat all of the last message." It can be used in conjunction with the signs AA, AB, WA, or WB and an identifying word or the signals AA, AB, BN, WA, and WB plus an identifying group or groups (or word or words) to request the repetition of a portion of a message.

AA All after . . .
AB All before . . .
BN All between . . . and . . .

WA   The word or group after . . .
WB   The word or group before . . .
For example:
RPT alone means to repeat the entire message.
RPT AA RED means "Repeat all after the word Red."
RPT AB MJ means "Repeat all before the group MJ."
RPT WA EY means "Repeat the group after the group EY."
RPT WB BOY means "Repeat the word before the word Boy."
RPT BN FR TX means "Repeat the groups between the groups FR and TX."

Repeat signs are not to be used when a message is not understood or when a message as decoded is unintelligible. In such cases, suitable signals taken from the Code are to be used.

Use of International Code groups

YV is the international code group indicator, used in messages transmitted by Morse-code as the first group of the coded text and signifies that the message that follows consists of code groups, not plain language.

FLASHING LIGHT SIGNALING BY BOATS

Although the average boatman may have little regular use for flashing light signaling, this means of communications may prove of great value in emergencies. Take, for example, the situation in which a boat is aground at night. It may be unsafe for another boat to approach close enough for shouting back and forth across the gap between them—there may be uncertainty as to where the shoal water lies, or the other craft may draw considerably more water and thus have to stand off at a distance. Knowledge of the Morse code, being able to receive as well as send, will permit the exchange of vital information using nothing more than an ordinary flashlight. Knowledge of plain language is used and numbers are spelled out.

Use of the signal YV (or "INTERCO" by voice) and groups from the International Code of Signals will provide a means of getting around a language barrier.

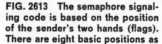

Courtesy—United States Coast Guard

FIG. 2613   The semaphore signaling code is based on the position of the sender's two hands (flags). There are eight basic positions as shown; for any character, one hand is at a position and the other hand is at one of the seven remaining positions.

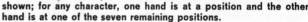

Semaphore Signaling

Semaphore signaling may make a boatman think of his Boy Scout days, but actually this means of communication is used more at sea than on land. A pair of skilled naval signalmen "talking" rapidly back and forth with semaphore flags is an interesting sight and a thoroughly practical one.

Semaphore signaling is normally done with a pair of hand flags for greater visibility. Such flags can be omitted for signaling over short distances, although the use of handkerchiefs, rags, etc. will aid in the reading of the signals.

The semaphore alphabet

Information is transmitted in semaphore signaling by the position of the sender's two hands. For each character, each hand will be in one of eight possible positions, vertically up or down, straight out to either side, or at positions midway between, fig. 2613.

The semaphore alphabet is shown in fig. 2614. The *break sign* (or *front*, as shown in the illustration) is most important; it is used between words and, without a pause, between double letters appearing in a word. In semaphore plain language is used and numbers are spelled out.

SEMAPHORE PROCEDURES

The desire to communicate by semaphore is indicated by sending the signal K 1 by any means. The other ship hoists the answering pennant at the dip to acknowledge the signal, and closes it up when she is ready to receive. If unable to communicate by semaphore, the reply is the signal YS 1. For simple boating situations, it is sufficient to use the attention sign, waving both arms from straight out to vertically upward.

Each letter is sent distinctly with the sender's flags (or hands) moving directly from the positions of one letter to those of the next, and then dropping to the break (front) position at the end of the word. The sender then waits for the receiver to send "C" indicating that the word has been received and the message should be continued. At the end of the message, the signal AR is sent; if at any time a mistake is made, a series of Es is made, then the *full last word sent correctly* is retransmitted followed by the word in which the error was made and the rest of the message.

SEMAPHORE SIGNALING BY BOATMEN

Semaphore signaling has its advantages and its disadvantages for use from recreational boats. It permits communications over greater distances than a voice will carry, even when amplified through a loud-hailer; it is effective where wind or breakers would drown out sound. A typical use of semaphore might be from a stranded boat to a Coast Guard rescue craft that could not approach close enough for shouting back and forth.

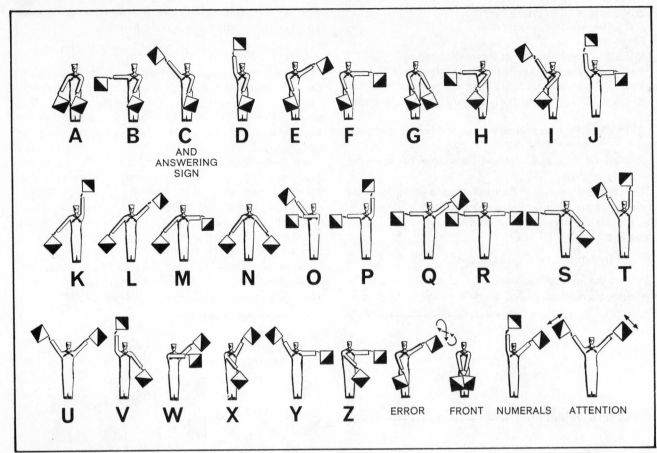

FIG. 2614 The Semaphore Signaling Code.

Courtesy: U. S. Navy Training Publications Center

Semaphore requires no special equipment, as does flag-hoist signaling. It is probably more satisfactory for day use than flashing light. On the other hand, it requires learning a new code and regular practice to develop *any* degree of competence. Another disadvantage is that it is not usable for communications at night.

Even though a boatman does not develop a full qualification in semaphore signaling, a knowledge of the letter "R" is often useful. "R" has wide recognition (as "Roger" on radiotelephone circuits) as meaning "received and understood." The semaphore "R" — both arms stretched straight out to the sides—is a simple, but highly effective, way of signaling to another person that you "got the message." Clearly and distinctly given, it is a much more satisfactory means of acknowledging information or instructions than a careless wave of one hand.

Sound Signaling

Signaling by sound using the boat's horn or whistle is possible, but has severe limitations.

Sound signaling should be used only with the greatest of caution, due to the confusion that it might create with passing or fog signals. A good rule for boatmen would be to become familiar with its principles and procedures, but never to use it except in emergencies or situations in which one was certain that no misunderstandings could possibly arise from its use.

A sound signal should be as brief as possible, and, except in an emergency, communications should be limited to the single-letter signals. In fog or on inland waters, where traffic is heavy, sound signals must be kept to an absolute minimum.

SOUND SIGNALING PROCEDURES

The Morse code is used for signaling by sound, with calling and answering procedures generally similar to those used for flashing light. The receiving craft makes no signal as the message is sent unless a character is missed in which case the repeat signal RPT is immediately signaled. When the message is completed, the sending ship signals $\overline{AR}$; if the message has been fully received, the other ship acknowledges by sending R.

Further details on signaling by sound will be found in H.O. 102.

**Two-letter groups
from the International Code of Signals.**

(Effective 1 April 1969.)

AE	I must abandon my vessel.	**PD**	Your navigation light(s) is (are) not visible.
CJ	Do you require assistance?	**PT**	What is the state of the tide?
CN	I am unable to give assistance.	**QX**	I request permission to anchor.
JI	Are you aground?	**RY**	You should proceed at slow speed while passing me (or vessels making this signal).
JL	You are running the risk of going aground.		
JW	I have sprung a leak.	**UF**	You should follow pilot boat (or vessel indicated).
KN	I cannot take you in tow.	**UO**	You must not enter harbor.
LN	Light (name follows) has been extinguished.	**UT**	Where are you bound for?
LO	I am not in my correct position. (To be used by a lightship.)	**YK**	I am unable to answer your signal.
		YX	I wish to communicate by radiotelephony on frequency indicated.
LR	Bar is not dangerous.		
LS	Bar is dangerous.	**ZM**	You should send (or speak) more slowly.
MF	Course to reach me is . . .	**ZP**	My last signal was incorrect. I will repeat it correctly.
MG	You should steer course . . .		
NF	You are running into danger.	**ZQ**	Your signal appears incorrectly coded. You should check and repeat the whole.
NG	You are in a dangerous position.		

FIG. 2615

Signaling and the Boatman

Knowledge and ability in signaling can bring both added pleasure and safety to a boatman. Pleasure can be had from being able to recognize and understand simple flag hoists or other visual signals. Safety will surely result from being able to use such methods of communications in an emergency, his or someone else's. Visual signals can often mean the difference between the communication of vitally necessary information, even though slowly and tediously, and no communication at all. Such signals are particularly valuable when one's boat has no radio, or the set on board fails to work when needed.

The more knowledge and ability in signaling the better, but expertness is neither expected nor needed. Simple knowledge of the code flags, the Morse alphabet, or the semaphore code, plus the rudiments of procedure, are all that are required. The boatman should make the effort to learn the fundamentals of signaling, and he should keep in practice. Some day when least expected, it could mean a great difference to all on board his boat.

Seamanship in Breaking Inlets

CHAPTER XXVII

ILLUSTRATED BY LESTER FAGANS

FOR a motor boat to proceed in safety at sea and to carry its passengers and crew in security and comfort from port to port along the coast, such a craft must possess certain hull characteristics. These are:

1. Stability   3. Propulsion   5. Strength
2. Buoyancy   4. Steering   6. Endurance

In the modern well-designed motor boat all of these six items of construction characteristics were designed and inbuilt into the craft by its creators when its lines were laid down on the drafting board. The elastic limits of safety in each case have been mathematically and accurately computed and are known with a proven degree of exactitude by test. Knowing that the boat would roll and might even capsize in violent sea conditions when immersed in her native element, her creators placed within her hull an invisible but powerful mechanical servant —her righting arm. Sufficient length and weight were given to this physical force to insure that the boat would return to an even keel in her struggles to constantly stabilize herself at sea and to withstand the ordinary rigors of wave formations, consideration having been given to the individual motor boat's size.

In these articles we are not concerned with ordinary wave conditions of the so-called trochoidal type met commonly off shore and far at sea but rather with the confused maelstrom found during a summer on-shore gale or strong wind before any breaking coastal inlet. The deceiving appearance of these seas, from an off-shore aspect, might overwhelm the unwary, the novice or the careless should he enter them in his boat unprepared or inexperienced. Under these conditions and upon entry into such surf, should a single one of the elements of boat construction enumerated above fail or become destroyed as a result of poor seamanship or inexperience, it is almost axiomatic that the destruction of the remaining five elements will rapidly follow and the boat and its crew may be lost.

The characteristics listed above are set down in order of importance as related to surf running in broken water and it becomes obvious, upon inspection, that the first requisite for a motor boat's safe passage through a breaking inlet is the *preservation of the boat's stability*. In other words, the boat must be handled with that degree of seamanship, as she drives through the racing inlet, that will insure that she will remain in an upright position.

Little that is comprehensive and authentic as to collective detail covering the many and varied phases of this subject's widely scattered components has been written. An effective treatise of all of them would be material for volumes. In our consideration of the subject as a whole we must keep in mind that all inlet conditions vary greatly and the speed, shape, cadence, and height

A Master Surfman Discusses the Technique of

Handling Motor Boats in Breaking Seas

with which the seas crash onward to the land in violent crescendo are largely governed by the great compressive influence of bottom contour, bottom declivity and bottom channels.

It is difficult, therefore, to set down didactic direction for the guidance of the seaman when he enters broken water before a coastal inlet with his motor boat. The manufacturing of a norm of explanation must be approached with caution on account of the ever-changing wave behavior encountered in the field's dissimilar scope and the seamanship requirements and surf practices that are required by the many varied types of motor boat hull construction and speeds. The truth is that there is no norm. Safety and success in running broken surf depends almost wholly on the individual motor boat captain's brand of seamanship as suited to the particular hull under him.

In order to correctly evaluate most of the known components of adequate seamanship in breaking inlets, in relation to our research, we are forced to use applicable portions of the knowledge and experience of the master surfman, the naval architect and the engineer. Such a combination of human avocations fertilized in the brain of one individual during a single lifetime is rare indeed. No scientific studies, of record, of wave formations, heights, velocities, currents and counter-currents in any breaking inlet have ever been made.

We do know, however, from the collective experience of those who have spent their lives in surf, that as these great trochoids approach the beach from the sea, owing to the influence of bottom declivity, friction and compression are initiated and the sea wave rushing along at some 40 knots starts to decelerate but that its crest starts to climb and may reach a height of 50 to 60 feet with a crest speed of 25 to 30 or more knots, in some cases.

Imagine, then, in an ordinary on-shore gale, the difficulty of safe passage that confronts the motor boat captain as he lies before a breaking coastal inlet contemplating the cadence of the seas. Heaving in the trough in a hull whose water-planes, projected rudder area and shaft torque were designed for maximum efficiency at some 15 knots in the long and regular swells at sea, he now reflects, as he watches, that the ability of the same boat to now turn Mr. Hyde and carry him through the racing white mass off there to leeward, rests with his skill as a seaman, the strength and endurance of his boat and the integrity of his power and gear under stress.

Sensitive to the realization that when his boat was built her designers created her to go to sea and that it was not intended that she should cruise in steep, short seas whose height of crest might attain some 50 feet and roar along at a speed of 30 to 35 knots, he realizes that his boat was built as a compromise of naval architecture. He knows that the hiatus of difference between the required characteristics of the motor cruiser and those of the professional surf-boat were too great for the engineer's art to successfully bridge.

One of the illustrations shows a motor surf boat used commonly on both European and American coasts. It is impossible, in breaking surf, to destroy this motor boat's stability or impair her buoyancy—provided she is not holed. The illustration demonstrates her general hull lines; a future illustration will show the extent of her water-tight integrity—she is self-bailing and self-righting. Should sea water in any tonnage enter the motor boat in either of her open compartments that are exposed to the sea (passenger space forward and cockpit aft) these compartments would immediately free themselves through

When heavy seas are breaking on an inlet bar, the thing to avoid at all costs is a broach.
Here a sea has caught the boat on the port quarter and she is starting to go into a broach.

With nothing to hold her stern up to the sea, the boat illustrated on the previous page is shown here swinging broadside into broach. In this position, water will start to pour over the deck and coaming into the cockpit. When necessary to enter an inlet through heavy seas, it is imperative to keep the boat square before the seas, and avoid breaking crests

freeing ports that are provided along her sides in the way of these spaces. Her deck under these compartments is water-tight and extremely strong. There is one case of record in which one of these boats, crossing a bad bar in extremely boisterous weather and bad surf conditions, rolled over three times and yet brought her crew through, hurt but alive.

In her short 36 feet of length she has six transverse bulkheads and two longitudinal ones. She has tremendous strength and weight (12 tons) in comparison with the ordinary motor boat of similar dimensions. She has a bar keel made up of two tons of cast lead. The boat has generous beam, 10 feet 8 inches. She is rather deeper than similar motor boats of her length, 5 feet 6 inch draft; she has moderate power for her size, 100 h.p., direct connected internal combustion engine. Her oak ribs are about half the distance on center as are those of the ordinary motor boat's frames and about 100 percent larger in size. Through heavy cypress planking she is put together with wood screws and her cost of construction with gear is in excess of $30,000—quite a price for a 36-foot boat with a speed of 9 knots. There is no boat in the world that is her equal or her better in surf, breaking or surging. She is sharp on both ends and her controls are water-tight.

Her items of equipment are simply but efficiently arranged and it is pertinent to note that her twin drogue pawls are mounted *on the center line aft;* more will be heard of this arrangement later. The boat has positive stability under any sea conditions and even though, with inexpert handling, she may turn over, she most surely will come back to an upright position as a result of the placement of her heavy bar keel and consequent low center of gravity. Her entire bottom is completely watertight with the exception of her machinery space and she has buoyancy voids even above the water line, a cross section of which will be shown later on. To sink her she would have to be holed through about 80 percent of her bottom.

For the motor boat yachtsman or small boat operator it is obvious that it is neither desirable or possible to own or attempt to build a motor boat of the type described above. The cost of construction alone is prohibitive and the boat's ability to perform successfully in surf has been obtained by great sacrifice of other important seagoing qualities that are commonly found in comfortable and

able boats of similar dimensions. Considerations of weight, economy, maneuverability, speed and leg-room would prohibit ownership of such a craft either as a yacht or workboat. Further than this, the boat is extremely lively at sea owing to her rapid and whip-like gyrations from one roll to another since the low and concentrated placement of her heavy keel results in an unnaturally low center of hull gravity which produces an extremely short rolling period.

For the average motor boat owner the designer is put to the task of creating a motor boat whose stability, while not the equal of the motor surf-boat, or positive under all of the conditions met in broken surf, is sufficient to insure the safety of the boat at sea under all wave conditions, provided she is handled with a reasonably good degree of seamanship, and will successfully cope with unfavorable wave conditions and even dangerous ones for a reasonable period of time.

It becomes apparent now that the motor boat owner who may, through emergency or other uncontrollable circumstance at sea, be forced to attempt passage of a breaking inlet in his boat, should understand something of, or sufficient of, the nature of the stability in the craft under him since his boat's stability plays so great a part in her performance the moment she enters the outer edge of the breakers.

Consider now the diagram illustrating the stern view of a motor boat rolling freely, easily and deeply in a seaway—actually the boat's action simulates that of a pendulum. Like the pendulum her hull has been set in motion by some exterior force. In this case the physical energy that is stored up in the sea waves has spent a portion of its force against the sides and bottom of her hull and precipitated motion in the form of rotation similar to that of the pendulum.

In the case of the pendulum the mechanical couple of force that is stored up between the suspended weight and the pivoted pendulum (which is capable of oscillation) has produced rotation, when an exterior force, such as the touch of a finger, has initiated motion. Now in a motor boat hull there exists a similar couple of forces which also produce rotation, the result and manifestation of which is rolling, the degree of the roll being controlled by the boat's center of gravity in relation to the boat's center of buoyancy.

Referring again to the diagram (right) of a boat rolling freely in a seaway, B is the center of buoyancy if the boat were in an upright position and immersed in still water. B' represents the boat's new center of buoyancy as related to the new position she assumed in a deep starboard roll from her original vertical state. CG is the center of gravity of the boat's mass. CG-M is called the motor boat's metacentric height and is a measure of her initial stability or safety against capsizing. The higher M is above CG the greater will be the value of the righting arm and consequently the greater will be the tendency of the boat to right herself. GZ is the righting arm and the greater the length of this line, the greater will be the couple of forces tending to right or capsize the boat. Arrow W pointing downward through CG is the thrust of gravity tending to force the boat back to an even keel. Arrow W' pointing upward through B' is the center of the force of buoyancy and tends to lift the boat back to even keel—the force of buoyancy lift being centered through B'.

Now it is axiomatic that as long as the vertical line drawn through B' intersects the line BM above CG, the center of gravity, the boat is in a stable condition and will return to an even keel. Since the force of gravity acting through the arrow W is downward and the lift of buoyancy concentrated through the point B' is upward, a mechanical couple of forces is set up and will produce rotation in the direction of the arrow above the sketch at D. If, however, the vertical through B' should intersect the line B-CG below CG, the couple will produce rotation in the opposite direction than shown in the diagram at D, and the boat will capsize or, in surf, will go into a broach. This is clearly illustrated in the diagram showing the boat on her beam ends.

Preserve the Stability

It is apparent from the foregoing that the motor boat captain entering a coastal inlet where white crests are seen to be breaking must first *know what he is trying to accomplish* if he is to bring his boat and crew through it safely. His first consideration, then, in this direction, is the *preservation of the stability of his boat*. In the accomplishment of this, his personal skill as an able seaman is so intertwined and bound up with his boat's construction characteristics and her resultant behavior in boisterous surf that it is extremely difficult, or impossible, to separate the two.

That the boat must be kept squarely before the seas now as she approaches the outer breakers is an obvious mandate of good seamanship—that both of her bilges must rest squarely immersed on the back of the sea that will carry

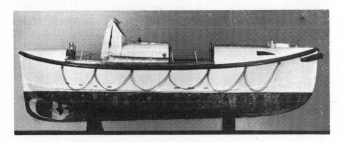

A modern motor surf boat. Unless she is holed, it is impossible to destroy her stability or impair her buoyancy

her through the inlet is an imperative necessity for insurance that her rudder will act instantly and that her propeller will not beat the air. That her bulwarks must not dip into the spume so that she takes sea water aboard which would immediately affect her *stability* and buoyancy is a consideration of major import.

Her speed must now be carefully gauged. The boat must not be allowed to approach a crest, for once she

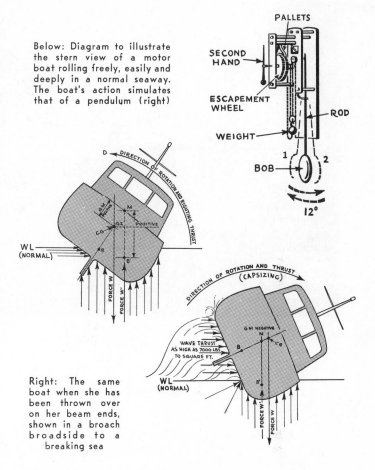

Below: Diagram to illustrate the stern view of a motor boat rolling freely, easily and deeply in a normal seaway. The boat's action simulates that of a pendulum (right)

Right: The same boat when she has been thrown over on her beam ends, shown in a broach broadside to a breaking sea

climbs near one of these racing tufts of scud there is no power on earth that will stop her run—neither must she be allowed to slowly slide downwards towards the slatch or hollows—if she should be overwhelmed in the trough the forces of hundreds of tons of sea water might tear her apart—the seas must be kept breaking ahead and astern of her at all costs.

The above are all considerations of the master seaman in broken surf. They are closely allied to all effort to preserve the motor boat's stability in a breaking inlet. Yet there are other important construction characteristics inbuilt into motor boats, the effect of which bears considerably on the performance of the small boat in surf. These effects must be explored fully before further considering methods of inlet seamanship. A concise understanding of all of the collective purpose of these details must be had in order that the dictates of good seamanship in breaking inlets may be more readily applied at the proper time.

Buoyancy! The submarine chasers of World War I withstood the incredible pounding of the short steep seas of the English Channel

A Discussion of the Differences in Handling

Various Types of Boat, Depending on Their Design

And the Speeds At Which They Can Be Driven

BUOYANCY is defined, according to Webster, as the resultant upward pressure of a fluid on an immersed object floating on the surface of a still liquid. When 35 cubic feet of water are displaced by any motor boat hull floating in salt water, sufficient buoyancy exists under the boat to support one ton of weight. Boats of generous beam and draft, with bottom area distributed over a large area of water, are usually found to be not only the most stable boats but also the buoyant ones.

The modern motor boat, therefore, with a good turn of speed, comes into its own in breaking surf in this respect and among the motor boats of the work boat class probably the Jersey beach fishing skiff from 18 to 40 feet in length, when properly handled, has no peer in breaking inlets. What this type of hull might lack in length of water planes underway it gains in freeboard and beam, the fullness of which, in most cases, is carried from the hull's point of entry of wetted surface, in operation, in almost a straight line to the stern.

Beyond this, these motor boats are powered with high horsepower for their size and tonnage which, transmitted to the propeller shaft, results in the production of tre-

mendous shaft torque. This becomes a large stabilizing influence in an open surf-boat which depends largely on its natural buoyancy and freeboard for its preservation in breaking seas, where safe and stable flotation together with sufficient fairness of hull contour must be depended upon to cope with the high wave speeds that are encountered at the entrance of coastal inlets in moderate on-shore gales. The upward thrust of buoyancy in these motor boat hulls at an immersion of 3 feet is roughly 192 pounds to the immersed square foot.

Now the location of the position of the center of buoyancy in any hull has a great influence on the manner in which she is handled in steep or breaking seas. The position of this center is largely controlled by the motor boat's designed water planes underway, the location and extent of her hull weights (machinery, equipment, etc.), her general dimensions, hull contour and shaft torque. There are other considerations affecting the location of her center of buoyancy but these are the main ones that concern us here.

Notice, now, the illustration showing a longitudinal section of the ordinary round-bilged surf boat whose dimen-

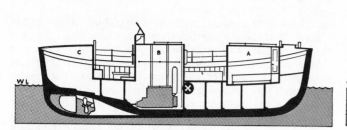

Longitudinal section of the ordinary round-bilged surf boat. The center of buoyancy is about where spotted. Numerous watertight compartments would serve to localize any threat to buoyancy by the entrance of water

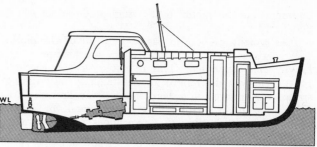

Above: Section of a conventional round-bilge slow-speed cruiser (10 knots). In steep seas she is handled like the surf boat (left, above) but, because she has no watertight compartmentation, great care must be exercised to prevent entrance of sea water into hull

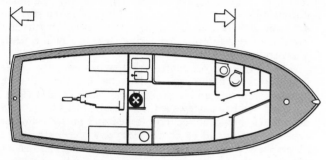

Center of buoyancy, longitudinally and transversely, falls about at point X, somewhat abaft of amidships when underway

Much of the reserve buoyancy forward in newer, faster semi-displacement types of hull is gained by flare (shaded area, above, left) and sheer (black area "A", above right). Buoyancy aft is great due to extreme beam at the transom. Note, in the plan at left and drawing below, how her water planes underway differ from those of slower types of hull. The slow and fast types call for different methods of handling

sions are roughly 36 feet by 10 feet 6 inches by 5 feet 6 inches. Compare this with the illustration showing a typical section of the conventionally arranged and designed motor boat hull of similar dimensions with the exception of somewhat smaller beam and slightly less draft. Each hull is equipped with about 100 h.p. at 1000 r.p.m. motors. In both of these motor boats the center of buoyancy is in about the same locational plane and since the power and speed of both hulls are about equal (9-10 knots), it is evident that in steep seas both motor boats should be handled with about the same method of sea-

manship, due allowance being made for the great strength of the professional motor surf boat.

It is mandatory, for safe seamanship, that each boat of the type described should have the full length of its water planes in immersion at all times, regardless of sea condition, so that the center of buoyancy of each will remain as near as possible to its designed location. The center of buoyancy in all motor boats of the type described is approximately about the midship section, transversely and longitudinally, and your hull's greatest flotation effort therefore is centered through her midship section aided by the reserve

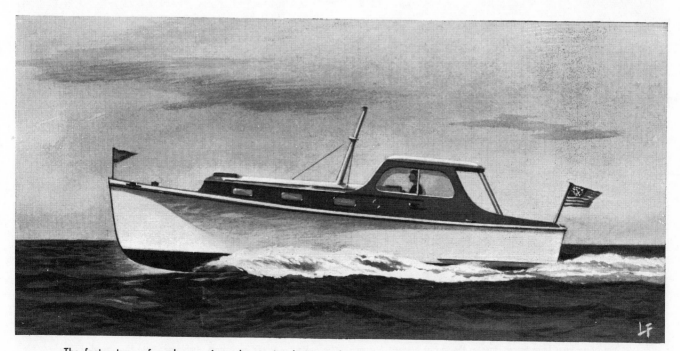

The faster type of modern cruiser, due to its design and speed, must be handled differently from the surf boat

buoyancy on the motor boat's ends produced by sheer and flare.

It is worthy of note in passing that all of the motor surf boat's areas of natural buoyancy are profusely and heavily compartmented. This, of course, gives to the hull great rigidity and strength in withstanding the crushing strains encountered in a boisterous seaway and also enhances the motor boat's ability to withstand for an indefinite length of time the tremendous pounding with which cycloidal seas will punish a small motor boat. She will wear out her crew before she tires herself.

The great boon, however, of this profuse compartmentation is her security from the hazard of free surface should a leak develop in any portion of her bottom. In this case, such an entering volume of seawater, that would otherwise surge at will over her bilges creating a hazard to her buoyancy and a threat to her stability through its rapidly shifting weight, is immediately localized by the water-tight compartments constructed within her bilges. If half of her bottom were ripped out she would still float on her water-tight decks with the aid of her secured reserve buoyancy from the water line to the top of her deck erections.

Should her passenger well forward and her cockpit aft become filled by a sweeping sea she would immediately free herself, for both spaces are self-bailing. No sea water can enter her bilges through any topside source since all her deck erections are water-tight against 100 pounds pressure and any apertures in her deck structures are secured by heavy dogs setting her hatch door knife-edges deeply in heavy rubber. There are no deck transoms or skylights installed. Any hatches are made of heavy bronze screwed into heavy recess rings installed in her deck. This motor boat was designed and built to steam *out of* a breaking inlet and into the face of seas that may reach 40 feet in height whose crest speed might exceed 30 knots. She is homely as a hedge fence but she is perfection in buoyancy, stability and security; even with lubberly hand-

ling she is practically indestructible as she waddles her way through the breakers.

Look for a moment at the illustration of the motor boat with no watertight compartmentation. In the event that a cross sea either ripped her skylight open or tore the hatches from their coamings on either her trunk cabin or cockpit deck and three or four tons of sea water entered the hull, disaster would surely follow in the violence of the breakers. With the first roll that the boat took this uncontrolled mass of seawater, surging about the interior of the hull, would immediately seek the lowest level of the hull's depression, the boat would be hove down on its beam ends, and the chances are that the boat would never again be able to rise since her propeller would be jerked out of the water, her rudder control totally lost, her buoyancy invaded and her stability destroyed, which would insure her capsize. She has, of course, no bilge compartmentation and in the case of an uncontrollable leak developing in steep or broken seas the seawater would course through the entire length and breadth of her interior, rendering her, to say the least, uncontrollable.

The moral is, of course, that whenever you enter broken seas with this type of boat be sure that all deck hatches, transoms and vents are well secured and tight; all deck appurtenances such as anchors, life buoys and deck boxes should be securely lashed and no loose line or ends of lines should be above decks *any place*. It should all be stowed securely below—any loose line left about the decks or cockpit might end up in one of your screws. Any loose gear that might come adrift might go through your transom.

Extreme care and judgment as to the time of entry into the breakers should be used with these round-bilged slow boats. In an inlet that is breaking white across its entire width such an entry should only be made in the most pressing emergency and then only if the motor boat is equipped with an efficiently built drogue. Never attempt

Do not allow your boat to get close to the top of a crest. She might be hurled over the crest and pitch-poled into the trough below

to tow swamped dinghies or the ends of unsecured lines over the stern of your boat—you may not be able to get rid of the dink when you anticipated you should and it may be that the tender might board your boat and either kill some one or so damage the gear of your boat that you might lose control of her. This has actually happened.

A heavy or light line towed over the stern will always float and most certainly will find its way into your propeller in heavy surf. It is impossible either to see or anticipate what an unsecured bight of line hanging over your stern will do next or what direction it may take. It is also impossible to keep a strain on such a line for the reason that you are constantly engaged in the rapid manipulation of your throttle, to keep the seas breaking either ahead or astern of her and you are using radical and frequently large degrees of rudder angle in an attempt to keep her squarely before the seas.

Seas Have a Regular Cadence

It is true that all breaking seas before a coastal inlet during a strong onshore breeze have a regular cadence and, as the bottom slope starts to slow down the great ocean trochoids and build up their crests, smaller waves form after the passage of the large ones. Usually the smaller seas form in well defined locations and appear in regular cadence after several large seas have passed. If you are going to enter the surf you should do so at a time when you are sure of operating and maneuvering your way through the inlet in an area of seas of this type, keeping a close eye on the color of the water ahead of you and attempting, as best you can, to keep your boat in the darkest green of the water and measuring the break of the crests both ahead and astern of you.

The sea crests must be kept breaking ahead and astern of your boat for if you allow a sea to break aboard your motor boat, she might survive one such break if she were extremely well constructed and did not fill but it is difficult to imagine she would live through the second one to come aboard. Do not allow your boat to gather speed that might become uncontrollable. In this respect you must keep a close watch on the vertical movement of your bow and stern. Should your stern start to rise under you and your bow begin to descend, slow down your motor and let the sea roll under the total length of your immersed water planes and let it break ahead of you.

Do not try to ride the back of a sea with a full bilged boat; your hull was not designed to be efficient at the wave speed with which the sea is travelling and your torque is too low in value to give you much effective rudder control. If your stern begins to descend rapidly and your bow starts to rise, increase your r.p.m. and do so radically immediately; this is a sure sign that you are falling back into the trough and should your boat be sucked into the counter-current *travelling in the opposite direction than that of the crests* a sea may break on your boat at any time. Such counter-currents exist in the hollows of these steep seas and more will be heard of them later.

Using the Drogue As a Brake

Should your boat begin to run and you feel that you cannot stop her by closing the throttle, do not attempt to reverse her if seas are very bad; you may kite your stern around to port in an instant and hopelessly broach her. Use your drogue to break her. Keep your drogue lines clear and free and when you give the word to set the drogue keep everyone clear of the stern except the drogue tender. When your drogue "roots," its towline will straighten out like an iron bar and sing like a bow-string. Your boat will immediately start to slow down and you may find that by keeping your drogue rooted (set) and blasting your power wide open you have better control of her.

If you do not find this to be so, trip your drogue by simply releasing the tow line and the drogue will spill the instant it feels the touch of the trip line on its apex. Do not allow your boat to get close to the top of any crest; wave speed in this type of cycloidal sea is highest just before the crest is reached and in this position not even a drogue will stop her. Your boat might be hurled over the crest and pitch-poled (see the illustration) into the trough below. When you arrive in less boisterous water, slow down your boat and get your drogue aboard by slacking out on your tow line and heaving in on your trip line while you are going slowly ahead.

Remember that all of the foregoing are the usual tactics applied in breaking surf by experienced surfmen in *full displacement, round bilged* and normally slow boats. You could not apply this practice successfully to modern, well designed semi-displacement and fairly fast types of hull; all surf running in broken seas simply amounts to keeping a motor boat's center of buoyancy somewhere near its designed position in an attempt to preserve her stability and this is accomplished by keeping the boat, while she is maneuvering through breaking surf, on her designed water planes underway. The designed wetted surfaces of the modern motor cruiser differ greatly from those of the slow round-bilged boat in respect to length, breadth, contour and depth.

Handling the Modern Motor Boat

Now let us consider the modern type of motor boat. From simple inspection of the illustration of this type, it immediately becomes apparent that to attempt to handle boats of this type in breaking seas in a similar manner to those boats of the slow round-bilged types which we have discussed would be only to tempt fate. We first note that as a result of carrying out her lines of flotation in almost a straight line from her widest breadth somewhat forward of amidships to the stern her center of buoyancy underway has been shifted from the amidships section and falls somewhere abaft of the center section of the boat, somewhere about the point X. From an inspection of the illustrations, we note that the length of the modern boat's immersed water-planes is considerably shorter but that she has relatively greater beam than her slower type sister. We see that much of the reserve buoyancy in the newer type of hull forward is gained by deck sheer, flare and contour; her buoyancy aft is very great on account of her extreme beam at the transom. The exact length of her designed and operational water-planes underway is governed primarily by her trim and amount of shaft torque applied at her strut or struts.

It is well to remember here that, when you are about to enter breaking seas with your semi-displacement type hull, this is not the time to start monkeying with your normal trim. This statement is made *all books and articles on the subject to the contrary notwithstanding*. As you have found your boat's trim to be correct at sea under normal conditions—so it should remain when you start through a breaking inlet. Do not go shifting weights to the stern; by so doing you might slow down your boat at a time when all of the speed you can possibly get out of the hull might be the only requisite for a safe passage through the inlet. Once your correct trim has been established both by design and your own experience with your boat, let the boat alone. There are very definite reasons for the foregoing statement as applied to the modern semi-displacement type motor boat.

Throttle the Key to Control

The one variable over which you have direct and manual control, which will determine whether or not you shall keep your boat immersed fairly on its designed water-planes during your passage through the inlet is the *amount of shaft torque* (turning effort) that is applied to your shaft through the manipulation of your engine throttle. Your degree of judgment in the handling of your throttle and your dexterity and sensitivity to the urge of your helm are now the factors that are going to see you safely through the tumbling seas about you. Remember that your stern controls your bow and that your rudder's greatest point of efficiency is reached only as the highest shaft torque is applied to your screw and your rudder is fed a literal wall of hydraulic pressure surrounding both sides of its vertical surfaces against which its motion becomes effective at the instantaneous touch of your hand.

Again you must watch the seas closely and patiently before you attempt to enter the area of breakers. Judge, if you can, the speed of the slowest of the seas and make a decision as to whether or not you can handle your hull at the speed that the smallest groups of waves to leeward are traveling. You know from past experience with your hull, before a following sea, just about how much of a run your boat will take before she starts to become unmanageable. If you should decide that there is any element of doubt as to your ability to handle your craft at the speed with which the inlet seas are crashing onward to the land do not, under any conditions, attempt to enter the inlet. It is by far better to go to sea and spend a miserable night hove to than risk loss of life. Ordinarily, a hull whose designed full power is produced between 12 and 16 knots will stand a run in a seaway of about 17 to 22 knots before she starts to become difficult to control, provided she is not pounding. Twin screw boats will do somewhat better than this in steep seas that are traveling from astern.

When you have decided to enter the breakers, have streamed

your drogue, and selected your point of entry on the back (seaward side) of one of the smallest and slowest of the seas, approach the surf as near as possible at the speed of the sea that is going to take you through the inlet. Your drogue tow line should be secured over the center line of your transom; your trip line can be made fast to any cleat or samson post about the quarter—it does not matter as long as your lines have no chance of fouling. Mentally measure the length of the sea you are about to ride and so manipulate your throttle and rudder that your eventual position upon it will place you squarely on its horizontal center with your stern directly before the following seas.

Keep Clear of Breaking Crests

Watch her now and note her behavior as you gather speed; there is a possibility that you might ride the sea, if you have made a selection in the right group of seas, clear through the inlet without it showing any tendency to break. Should the sea show a proclivity to gather sufficient speed and accelerate itself to the point of breaking keep its crest well ahead of your bows. Take a quick glance astern now and then and note your position with respect to the sea that is breaking over your quarter. Should you find your boat uncomfortably close to the one that is breaking astern open your throttles immediately—don't wait until you can feel the suction of the slatch (undertow) pulling your hull back into the yawning hollow that lays just beyond your stern. Remember that that suction is travelling in a reverse direction to your own forward motion and there is a possibility that you might lose rudder control if you allow your boat to slide down the back of the sea and too close to this hollow vortex.

As you gather speed on your opened throttles and regain your correct and safe position on the sea's back, attempt to synchronize your speed to that of the sea as you race through; should your hull show a tendency to dip either gunwale or become tender at the quarters to the sea action racing from the direction of the stern slow her down again and straighten her up with your helm immediately. When she straightens up again and regains her normal position gun her again and keep her scudding along resting squarely on the full length of her normal water planes.

Breaking a Run

When she is out before it again and should she show a tendency to run and you feel that she might get out of control due to the great speed which you are now making, set your drogue immediately by simply releasing the trip line; by manipulation of your throttles, in bursts if necessary, keep sufficient torque applied to your shafts to guarantee you steerage in attempting to keep her squarely before the seas. As the drogue breaks her run and pulls you back from the crest, cautiously open your throttles without tripping the drogue. You may find that you have better control of her by keeping your drogue set and blasting the full discharge of her fast-

turning screws into her rudders. In twin screw installations this is often found to be the case for your keel, held in the vise-like mechanical center of the slip-streams of both screws, now resists any tendency of the flying seas to broach her.

As she roars along, approaching the quiet water which can now be seen on the other side of the breakers, her speed seems to increase—20 . . . 21 . . . 22 knots the speed indicator clocks, her motors thundering under you, while the drogue digs a valley in the breakers astern and the tow rope sings in the spume. This is a thrill supreme. Its only equal in the world perhaps is the performance of the beach boys *riding the forward face* of the steeply breaking surf before the Waikiki Beach Hotel. Like the surfboard of the aborigine some of these modern hulls, intelligently handled and properly powered, are marvels in breaking surf.

Secure the Dinghy Aboard

Before closing this part of the discussion, it may be well to mention a word of caution regarding the towing of tenders upon the entrance to a coastal inlet under the conditions previously described. If the tender cannot be taken aboard and lashed down securely, bottom up, it is by far safer to cast the tender adrift and lose it rather than to attempt to tow it through the breakers. Once you enter the breakers you have no control over its gyrations whatsoever; your attention is necessarily bent in the direction of keeping your boat in a stable condition and it is impossible for a crew member to exercise any control of it at all while your boat is charging through the surf. A towed tender may capsize, interfere with your drogue lines or actually come aboard of your boat. There is a case of record in which a fisherman (200 tons and 92 feet in length) towing a heavy seine boat, in which a large seine was being carried, while crossing a badly breaking bar on the southeastern coast of the United States, was broached and beached with a loss of six of her crew. This happened as a result of the seine boat boarding the ship, due to the unequal speeds of the two craft in the breakers, killing the engineer and two of the crew members on deck, while the seine fouled the vessel's screw and the ship became helpless in heavily breaking seas. She was beached ultimately with the loss of three more of her crew from the decks.

Should the tender capsize, it would immediately act as a stern anchor as a result of which your motor boat would be immediately swept by a sea and the water-tight integrity of your hull would be instantly invaded, to say the least. If it should foul your drogue lines it might take charge of the operation of the drogue and set it at a time when such an occurrence might result in disastrous disadvantage to your motor boat, laboring in the breakers, or, vice-versa, it might release the drogue at a time when operation advantage might require that the drogue be set and deeply rooted. A tender, therefore, should either be brought aboard and securely lashed bottom side up to the deck or if this is impractical the tender should be cast adrift.

The modern fast sea skiff is among the ablest of small boats in breaking inlets

How Waves Are Generated—The Trochoidal Type

Of the Open Sea and the Breaking Cycloid in Shallow

Water on the Coastal Shelf and at Inlet Bars

AS a motor boat skipper, you are not likely to get into difficulty with your craft in steep, following seas until the speed of those seas approaches and exceeds the speed of your boat.

Sea speed and wave height in breaking inlets depend largely on the depth of breaking, depth to the bottom, rapidity and degree of bottom compression, depth and disposition of bottom obstructions, and state of the tide and currents. Sea contour and shape, in conjunction with the foregoing, are in the main controlled by direction and force of the winds; angular approach of the swells to the inlet bars; and the direction and positional relation of bars (when a number of them are present) to the

are present or where multiple bars extend in divergent directions. To go back to the beginning, sea waves, in general, are creatures begot from the winds over the oceans. Their speed and direction at sea are directly dependent upon the speed and direction of the winds. In a Western Ocean winter gale, as a result of the wind's blowing heavily in one direction for several days, storm waves of over 1,000 feet in length with wave speeds of 71.6 feet per second (about 42.5 to 43 knots) are commonly met by large express passenger vessels. Progress of even the largest and most powerful of these ships is seriously hampered, if not stopped, by these graybacks— trochoidal seas.

The cycloidal type of wave breaking on a bar. Hitting it obliquely, it starts to break where it first feels the effect of shoaling. Note especially the steepness of the crest

others, plus the direction and dimensions of bottom channels.

Knowing the speed of the wind and with an intimate knowledge of local bottom conditions, the type of breaker, approximate wave height and wave speed can be predicted with a fair degree of accuracy in individual localities. However, the statement contained in Part One of this series regarding the futility of attempting to prescribe didactic directions for the motor boat man about to enter breaking seas before a shallow coastal inlet is still true. The bottom approach to every inlet varies widely as to depth, declivity, bottom contour, number of bars and their position in relation to each other and bottom obstructions.

The most difficult of these coastal inlets to run before steeply peaked seas are those where outer and inner bars

It is a common occurrence for these great ships to be forced to heave to in the heavy gusts and the largest of the seas. Hull strains encountered in storm waves reaching heights of 37 to 44 feet are such that even the largest of these powerful vessels might suffer severe damage if not navigated with caution. A ship is but an extended steel girder and it *is* possible to bend it.

The waves of such a storm area at sea travel rapidly out of the locality of the gale and approach the land after a passage of many hundreds of miles in the form of swells. That these swells travel great distances in a relatively short time can be attested by any boatman who has observed the heavy swells outside of the breaker line and surf pounding on the Jersey beaches 650 to 1,000 miles in advance of a tropical hurricane the center of which might be located in the West Indies, a couple of days previous to the actual arrival of the gale itself.

Where such a storm changes its direction, the tendency of these trochoidal swells, as they advance toward the beach, is to decrease both in length and height. As they arrive at the outer inlet coastal bars in rapid succession, even with no storm winds driving them onward, their speed and volume are still considerable and thus, even in fine cruising weather beyond the breaker line, extremely heavy surf may be seen pounding the beaches while high, confused breakers assault the inlet jetties. Should the storm continue in the direction in which the swells have approached the land, such inlets become impassable except to the professional surf-boat.

Basically, then, breaking seas in coastal inlets are precipitated by winds either of the local area variety or may be caused by those of some distant storm area. The characteristics, contour, speed and condition of wave heights before a breaking coastal inlet, however, are another matter.

For his own safety the cruising motor boat man should learn to identify the two primary classes into which sea waves fall. See illustrations. The storm sea that we described in the first part of this series, racing at 30 or more knots beyond the 90-fathom curve and attaining

are met at sea as well as before breaking inlets. These are creatures of wide shoal water areas where shoalness exercises a great effect in the steepening of wave crests and the shortening of seas into vicious cycloids as the result of the wind's blowing over the sea for a prolonged period in one direction. Southern reaches of the North Sea and the westerly portion of the English Channel are world famous for their creation of breakers of this type for sustained periods. Such waves, like their inlet cousins (of the breaker type) are dangerous to small boats. Equally, they constitute a hazard to large ocean freighters. Owing to the length of these vessels, they may be forced to straddle three to four such seas, thereby setting up within hull structures severe sagging and hogging strains under which their collective girder strength might buckle.

With regard to the above, in passing, it is interesting to note the record of the American submarine chaser of World War I in those tumultuous breakers in the English Channel and North Sea during the winters of 1917 and '18. The chaser itself was probably an accident of birth—she was never meant to be a surf boat—but she acquitted herself in those distant and seething breakers as probably the greatest motor surf-boat of all time.

Deep-sea wind waves, as they advance to the shore,

In steep seas, the boat must be kept away from the crests. With sufficient power, this skiff can ride the back of one sea right through the inlet

wave heights of over 40 feet, are generated from swells of the trochoidal type as a result of wind pressure in some distant or local area. They attain great lengths but seldom break except under the influence of storm winds and become confused only as a result of winds of hurricane force; in gusts or squalls, they become dangerous to large ships. It is possible to find these trochoidal type swells present in a delightful cruising area, beyond the beach line, where no wind is apparent. Should you find such a situation you had best watch your barometer for these swells may easily portend difficulty for your boat upon return to your inlet if such return is to be delayed more than three to six hours. Slopes approaching the peaks of such sea waves are long and gradual.

In the second or cycloidal type of sea wave, with which we are mainly concerned, it is well to know that these

do not progress landward as phalanxes of motional regularity or in consistent direction. In the course of their travel, they may either lose or gain some of the speed of transmission, and they may approach the beach from divergent directions. Since they advance over great distances from the locality of their origin they may travel either in the same direction in which the winds were moving that generated them or, having passed through areas where swells advancing from other localities were met, they may take on a new direction. It is entirely possible, therefore, that an observer on the beach may, at times, behold heavy breakers crashing into an inlet entrance against the prevailing local winds. In other words the direction of the prevailing off-shore winds in the locality in which the motor boat captain might be cruising offers no assurance that he will not be confronted

Coast Guardsmen are experienced in the handling of boats in heavy weather. At Yaquina Bay, Ore., this 52' motor lifeboat goes out on routine winter patrol

with badly breaking inlet conditions upon his return to his particular inlet.

Ordinarily, any motor boat operator who must return to his home port through any coastal inlet should keep himself generally informed as to over-all weather conditions, even those existing far at sea, as a hedge against what he can expect for inlet sea conditions between the time of his departure from the jetties and the time of his return. Lacking such knowledge, he should consult his barometer frequently and should any deviation from its ordinary height be observed he must view this occurrence as a cause for caution.

From storm areas trochoidal seas and swells move in the direction of the land in groups or, as some observers have put it, in trains of swells. Deep-water waves advancing on the land from any wind area are not uniform as to wave height, wave period or speed. As they approach and pass over the coastal shelf their entire complexion as to contour and characteristic rapidly changes to that of the shorter-period steep cycloid, owing to the influence of rapid bottom shoaling and other various bottom conditions and obstructions peculiar to the locality.

A 1,000-foot storm wave, for instance, after it crosses the 100-fathom curve, begins a rapid process of slow-down mainly owing to bottom friction and the compression of declivity but it starts to build up in height and steepness, as a result of decreased depth and compression, from a wave speed of some 42.4 knots and a wave period of 14.0 seconds (passing of two successive crests by a fixed point) until it finally crashes into the outer bar of a coastal inlet perhaps reduced in length to some 400 to 600 feet and slowed down to a speed of 26.8 to 32.7 knots. The wave period has now been shortened to, roughly, 11 seconds. A lot can happen in a period of 11 seconds to a motor boat operating in breakers — you have little time to change your mind.

Two-hundred-foot sea waves (typical of a mid-August blow in northern latitudes) approach the inlet bars at a speed of about 20 knots and with a shortened wave period of about 6.2 seconds. In the case of the 1,000-foot wave pounding into any coastal inlet bar at a wave speed of 42 knots such a confused sea and steep breakers would result as to definitely preclude inlet navigation to small boats. The inlet would be impassable. Were it possible to place a 35-foot motor boat on the back (seaward side) of one of these roaring cycloids, its captain would find that his bow had risen some 45 to 50 degrees from its normal horizontal plane. The motor boat would probably go into a reverse pitchpole and upend backwards as a result of its fore and aft stability being destroyed. Of course, it would be entirely unmanageable as a result of the excess of wave speed over that of its own top hull speed.

In the latter case, considering the breaking effect of the 200-foot wave, depending on bottom depths, number and related positions of inlet bars, bottom declivity and channel contour, the inlet would very likely be passable, but extremely dangerous. Such seas are fast enough to produce breakers of the so-called plunging type which, owing to their speed, height, shortness of wave period and steepness, are capable of producing chaotic conditions to confront the small boat operator contemplating entrance through them.

Even sea waves of 100 feet in length with a surface speed of 13.4 knots and a wave period of 4.4 seconds, passing over a bar whose submerged depth is 15 feet, have been known to produce a plunging type breaker with a height of 14 feet, almost equal to the depth. Now a 15-foot breaker with another one 4.4 seconds behind it is a dangerous proposition to the small boat captain who finds himself scudding before it. If he ever needs that old propeller torque blasting its solid and uninterrupted stream of water down onto his rudder surfaces, he

Confused inlet conditions are created when seas strike a bar at several angles. In some cases it is impossible to keep a boat squarely before the sea

needs it now! Should you consider this statement slightly extravagant, just go up to the gutters on your roof and visualize what would happen to a 5- or 6-ton mass of wooden construction, capable of being moved in four directions at once but advancing at a speed of 15 to 20 knots over the ground, should it be hurled down from such a height. Do not forget in a situation of this type that, unless your boat is expertly handled, you may have a portion or all of the speed of translation here to contend with (speed of the wave plus the speed of the boat).

Factors Affecting Breaker Height

Breaker height, it has now been seen, depends on the height of deep water waves approaching the coast, the depth of the water over bars which they must pass before coursing into an inlet, the strength of local winds (at times), and general bottom topography. Tides, state of the tide and currents also affect their height in a contributory sense. Practically the same components govern their speed with the exception that influence of currents and the state of tide has a more pronounced effect on the speeds of breakers *before inlets* than they do on height. The *depth* of breaking also influences their speed. Any or all of these components might operate in conjunction before inlets whose contour and general topography or bar condition produces them all. On the other hand, but a single one or two of them might be present and yet produce the greatest of breaker confusion.

Direction and contour of the breakers meeting bottom bars from the sea are often governed largely by the angular approach of the ocean waves to such bars as they meet before inlets. Should the swells arrive in an oblique direction to that of the submarine bars, that end of the swell which makes first contact with these obstructions will break sharply over the bar end and the remaining portion of the wave may swing about the bar, in a wide turn, refracting as it breaks against the remaining length of bar. We have already seen that bottom channels, the shape of submarine shelves and bottom obstructions such as ledges and heavy boulders lying in diverse directions also contribute their influence to the contour of inlet breakers.

Effect of Outer and Inner Bars

Now knowing all of the foregoing it would seem reasonable to conclude that the most hazardous inlet conditions that the entering motor boat captain might expect to meet will be encountered before inlets where outer and inner bars are present on the ocean's floor. A submerged outer bar lying at a depth of 35 to 40 feet upon impact of such seas immediately slows down the first portion of the onrushing trochoid to a speed of probably 20 to 22 knots and at the same time bottom compression deflects a large portion of its volume upwards and the wave "breaks" upon the surface of the sea. When it peaks up to the point that its top becomes unstable, the wind whips off its crest and the wall of solid water, now risen to a height of 18 to 20 feet, crashes into the trough.

Its crest having been formed and its contour well defined, the breaker, driven on by the remainder of its initial sea-speed, now roars across the intervening space of sea until it again begins to feel the shoaling over the inner bar and the compression of its shallower declivity. As a result of this further compression or squeeze and the wave's meeting the inner bar at a different angle of approach and contact, a perfect welter of confusion now exists on the surface of the sea and it may well be possible that the observing motor boat man offshore would not be able to find *any safe path* or channel through such confused breakers before the inlet jetties.

Where Channels Are Oblique to the Sea

Years ago, before it was protected by a jetty, Jones Inlet was a notorious example of this type of breaker confusion, resulting, in a driving southeaster, from the presence of outer bars lying on the ocean's floor in divergent directions, thus forcing the seas to meet them at different angles of approach. Even in quite mild weather where ocean swells were present and were rolling in

here at speeds varying between 12 and 15 knots, passage of such an inlet channel was difficult and even hazardous. No small boat operator should enter such an area without a reliable local pilot unless he possesses an intimate knowledge of the bottom contour of the vicinity in which he proposes to operate in breakers. Low-powered motor boats, small boats with hydroplane-type bottoms, outboard-driven boats with low freeboard and flat bottom sections, and small sailboats should use extreme caution in attempting to navigate in such areas. Their operators should be watchful of weather conditions and cognizant of local forecasts. It should be pointed out here that where a winding and angular channel presents itself as the only navigable path through confused breakers, high freeboard in motorboat construction is a prime essential, high propeller torque is a vital necessity, and instantly responsive engine power in large amounts must be available. Almost any type of sailboat in breakers is a bad risk.

Breaker cadence before such inlets as these is entirely unrecognizable during the times of a heavy on-shore blow. The changing direction of the channel and the presence of the outer bar in angular relation to the inner obstruction (bar) simply destroy the contour and recognizable profiles of any wave trains between the two bars under the influence of heavy, onshore winds.

Breaker Cadence Destroyed

The entrance to Scituate Harbor on the coast of Massachusetts is a similar locality in which breaker cadence disappears and becomes unrecognizable in any wind that is blowing hard from the eastward, onshore. The same effect that was produced before Jones Inlet in relation to the destruction of well-defined breaker and swell cadences is repeated before the jetties at Scituate, however, from differing bottom conditions. Though the channel before the jetties at Scituate runs in lengths that are fairly straight, the bottom that surrounds this pathway through the gradually rising ocean floor is strewn with giant boulders and long and irregular bottom ledges lying close to the channel edges, scattered in all directions in a wide area of open sea before the inlet. These ledges are barely submerged, during periods of low water, and under the influence of a driving easterly, across the full sweep of Massachusetts Bay, a mass of breaking and white confusion is produced that may easily awe even the hardiest local professionals.

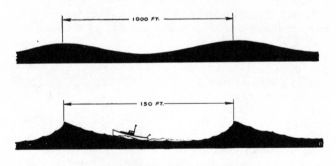

A trochoidal sea (upper)
and cycloidal type (lower)

Watch Surface Swells

So—get out your chart, irrespective of the direction of the local wind as you lie before a breaking inlet—watching. Remember: the breakers hold their secrets well, and the winds that blow before these breaking inlets are fickle indeed. During the summer months on the Atlantic seaboard they have been recorded as changing as many as twenty times in twenty-four hours. So, when you lie around fishing before one of these inlets, keep one eye peeled on the nature of the surface swells as they lazily roll in from over the horizon, and the other on your barometer. Don't wait "until it starts to get rough." An inspection of your bottom chart may assist you in making the correct decision, right now.

(Use the chart for all the information it can give you, but remember that channels and shoals shift so fast at many inlets that buoys cannot be indicated on the chart, and buoys at times may not mark the best water.—Ed.)

Leaving the "I-love-you" (1—4—3) flash of lonely Minot's over the quarter and picking up the long, piercing fingers of the Highland about a point off the starboard bow and coursing it down until we bring it abaft the beam a few degrees, we turn west and south down past the booming beaches of the southerly side of Cape Cod—the natives call it "the back side." Down over the shoals we run, wind northwest, force 2, and picking up a little, barometer slowly rising. She's making good time—getting a little push from the light northwester and rolling easily in the swells that seems to be coming from a general northerly direction. We cross the gulley (Hudson River Canyon) and seem to lose some of the swell. In the early hours of the morning Atlantic City Light stabs through the loom of the half-twilight in staccato sweepings and gleams, between periods, in friendly beckoning. Swell rising somewhat now, as we roll along over the coastal shelf.

Use Judgment Before Entering

The beach line into which Atlantic City Inlet cuts its long length of passage runs roughly in a north-northeast and south-southwest direction. Ordinarily therefore, a northwester, even though it may be blowing force 3 to 4, may not compel the small boat captain to seek shelter on any course to the northward provided he just clears the seaward end of the fish trap stakes in his progress up the beach. Should he mistakenly reason, however, that *since the wind is off the beach* either Atlantic City or Manasquan would offer convenient shelter in the event of the wind's hardening, he will be well warned to inspect bar conditions off both inlets before attempting entrance. In a moderately fresh offshore breeze, where strong flooding tides or currents run heavily against the wind, breaker heights and speeds build up in certain long inlets that, at times, may preclude passage of such channels even to the professional surf-boat man. Under such weather conditions, even in the upper reaches of Atlantic City Inlet, half a mile from the entrance and well inside, breakers clear and solid may be observed going over the railroad structure.

In spite of assurances by local professionals and beach captains that this popular inlet is never impassable to those who possess an intimate knowledge of local bar conditions, this simply is not so. The inlet is a long and dangerous one and, owing to the duration of time that the motor boat captain must spend traversing its extended length through the short steep breakers, his boat may take a severe drubbing before she rides her last sea on through the other side of the bridge structure. In this inlet one must make the correct decision first; you cannot turn around when you are half way through it, should you decide you cannot control your boat in the steepness and speed with which the breakers are roaring up the inlet, or as you see the light buoy dip its lantern. The beach over there on the westerly side of the inlet is very hard and you have a long way to go to find a worse spot to be in, if you attempt to turn the bow of your boat into the breakers.

Where the Beach Is Steep

A few miles up the beach, to the northward, lies another artful Charybdis jutting her jettied fingers out into the surf—Manasquan. An ebb tide and the arrival of heavy sea swells off the inlet bar here simply create a havoc of white confusion; heavy wind need not be present. However, as opposed to the bottom topography off Scituate, which destroys the cadence and natural contour of sea swells on their arrival over the shoals, before Manasquan the average motor boat man can recognize the swells arriving in their trains and groups even in moderately boisterous weather. Beach declivity here is steep, and high-speed breakers start to build up in height about the 30-foot curve. From that point shoreward the wedge of rapidly shoaling bottom accelerates their tendency to climb until, at less than $\frac{1}{8}$ mile to seaward of the jetties, breakers of 8 to 10 feet in height have been observed with speeds over the bottom of about 14 to 15 knots in weather off the beach that might be considered moderately good cruising weather, offshore. Even if you were able to pass successfully through these seas, with a period of less than 5 seconds and a degree of steepness that would probably put the bows of your boat at an angle of about 35 to 40 degrees from her normal horizontal plane, the seas as they pass over the 16-foot shelf crossing the mouth of the inlet drop abruptly down into 7 feet of channel depth between the jetties and roar up the alley formed by the stone buttresses, their hollows sometimes exposing the bottom of the inlet between crests. Any boat, if she did not become unmanageable before her nose got inside the stone breakers, would be smashed here, on contact with the bottom, in seas like this.

If you intend to do any inlet running in bad weather, look to your gear. Confidence in the craft under you is the supreme requisite.

Sailboats and auxiliaries, as a rule, should be kept out of breaking inlets. The Friendship sloop (above) does fairly well in breakers up to five or six feet in height

Approaching the bar, look for the dark water, indicating the best depth, and keep out of the white water of the breakers

Some Thoughts on Bottom Design;

Effect of Currents on Breakers;

Use of Oil and the Drogue;

Handling a Skiff in the Breakers;

Suggestions for Sailing Craft

Much information has been made available to the motor boat man, both scientific and practical, concerning static surf conditions on open beaches and procedures for safe landing through them. Men have made professions of the surf's mastery and many texts are replete with knowledge of such tactics. Not so the inlet, however. Breakers, both of the coastal variety and those surging before a coastal inlet, offer difficult situations for the procurement of exact scientific data, since this is attended by considerable risk.

The motor boat captain must not confuse recommended practices for landing through beach surf with the running of coastal inlets before which white water is surging. Static surf conditions on open beaches are widely dissimilar to the almost organized confusion of wild breakers coursing over an inlet bar. Neither is the regularity of surf or the cadence of its swells affected by so many unseen but compelling components of force, and factors of form, speed, height and direction, as is the inlet breaker.

Never attempt to back your boat into a breaking inlet. Were you to try this in a modern semi-displacement hull, your quarter would be seized by the seas and you would be broached long before your beam was parallel to them. Should you escape this situation and ultimately find your bows facing the breakers, you would immediately lose steering control; if you attempted to gun your motor to give you sufficient rudder effect to hold her head up to the breakers, you would either plunge her nose under a breaker or stave in your bows.

Oil, before a badly breaking inlet, is valueless. The action of bottom declivity in forcing seas to break at such precipitous heights allows the wind to get under their crests and scatter the crest spume in all directions. The shortness of the breaker period continuously breaks the hold of the oil's viscosity upon the surface and scatters the oil with the spume in all directions. The use of oil in breakers on the coastal shelf is another matter and has much to recommend it, since the breaker period is much longer. This is particularly true where towing operations are imminent or in progress. Placing a tow line aboard a disabled boat or taking the crew off a distressed craft is often facilitated by using an oil slick to windward. If you think, however, that the condition of the breaking inlet is so bad as to warrant the use of oil, stay out of it if possible. Go to sea and heave her to, if necessary, for there never was a boat built, that was capable of keeping the sea, that will not heave to on some quarter and in some direction.

Do not attempt to tow another boat (especially a sailboat) through a breaking inlet. Collision is almost a certainty.

The use of a surf line as an aid in entering a breaking inlet is attended with danger to those who might be tending the line. Should you attempt to hold your boat's head up with such an arrangement you might jerk the samson post out of her or shatter the bow section. Cross seas or current might fling the stern of your boat across the jetties, for you have no control of her at the end of a line. Unlike beach surf, the direction of breaking seas before a coastal inlet is by no means constant. Remember that high surf on open beaches is influenced and precipitated to a much greater degree than are the breakers before a coastal inlet by the local direction of the winds. Surf in beach localities is usually at its greatest height during the course of an on-shore gale or high wind. The steepness of these beach breakers is ordinarily governed by declivity, the length of the swell train as it arrives on the beach from the ocean, and the length of time the wind has been blowing in force in one direction. The cadence of such beach surf is usually much more regular and discernible.

We have discussed elsewhere the proclivity of Manasquan to break with no wind present in its vicinity or with the wind blowing off the beach, yet precipitating breakers before its entrance of such short period and height as to preclude safe passage through it in an ordinary motor boat. Likewise, before Atlantic City, combinations of bottom topography, channel contour, tides, currents and obstructions produce collateral effects on breakers that the surfman operating on an open beach may never meet.

A three or four-knot current flowing in heavy volume out of a narrow inlet and funneled into a restricted opening will bore into the base of a concaved on-rushing breaker and all but stop the turbulent water there. At the same time it tends to force the crest higher while the residual speed of the breaker drives that crest on over its stalled hollow, which may have reversed its direction now in obedience to the current's influence. Rising in great height to the point of instability, it crashes down into the trough—this, every 4.5 seconds. Add to this the natural flow of recession—for the pounding breakers ascending the bar must find their way back to the sea—and you can see why counter-currents in the trough may travel in a direction directly opposite to that of the breaker's crest.

In surf on open beaches where such currents exist in lesser extent it is called undertow. You can feel it seething about your ankles as your feet sink into the beach sands. As the current flows back in recession to the sea, it undermines the sand that bears the weight of your body. Should you advance too close to the breaker zone the undertow might seize your body and draw it into the vortex of the pounding surf.

In heavy breakers before a coastal inlet you can feel that current clutching at your boat's bottom. The laboring exhaust will warn you as it changes its note. With one eye watching the seas over the side you can see her slow down and feel a tension peak in the hull vibrating under you. Naturally, therefore, the best position for your boat as you enter the breaker zone is about the horizontal center of the sea's broad back. Should you ever sense the clutch of that counter-current, *open your throttle wide, instantly.* You understand, now, why we said that plenty of power *must* be available at the touch of your finger tips.

If you have a drogue set, trip it right now. Every drogueman that knows his business always carries a sharp, heavy knife or has an axe within reach. She may labor a little in the twenty seconds (that seem an hour) it takes to claw her way clear, but keep forcing her. As she shakes herself free and you feel the tension on her hull slacken a bit, be careful to close the throttle some. If you approach the top of the crest where the speed of the breaker is highest, you risk being hurled over in a pitchpole.

In inlet areas where the range of the tide may vary between 6 and 12 or more feet the state of the tide exerts a strong influence on the breakers. Here, between the two extremes of tide, there exists a varied condition of sea contour, speed and height. This may be due to differing degrees of beach declivity being presented to the breakers between the two tide depths or to the increased or lessened effect of bottom obstructions before the inlet. In approaches to those inlets where the bottom has no submerged obstructions such as bars, ledges or both scattered about and where the degree of beach declivity is almost plateau-like, breakers of less steepness can usually be expected at low water than at higher states of the tide. Scituate and Manasquan are both affected by rapid rise of the ocean floor at high stages of the tide. Before Scituate, though, this characteristic is complicated by the presence of large ledges and huge boulders, lying all over the bottom.

The effect on an inlet breaker's wave period and its height produced by currents flowing into it, across it or in a direction oblique to it is always greatest when the current is at its maximum strength in either direction. No general rules can be laid down for the guidance of the motor boatman confronted with the confusion of white water created where steep breakers and cross seas tear about the inlet's mouth as a result of such

The sketch below illustrates how waves of the open sea, encountering shallow water on bars at the entrance to inlets, may form breakers which must be avoided at all costs by the boatman running an inlet. At A and B, at the crests, the velocity is the highest—in this case, 22 knots for waves that are advancing with a speed, at C and D, of 15 knots. At E a swell is shown starting to peak up as it

feels the effect of the beach declivity, G. At F, the direction of currents of recession and the undertow is reversed, with a speed of 2 to 3 knots. The boat is shown with drogue set, the tow line attached to a bridle at the large end. The trip line to the smaller aft end is slack, and if the boat must gain speed to escape a breaker astern, the trip line will be hauled in to upset the drogue

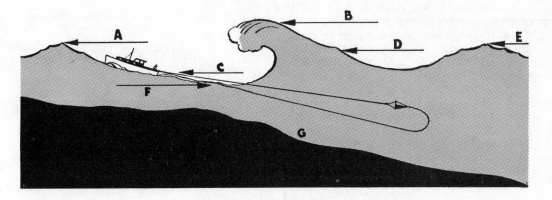

bottom topography, current and tidal effects. Safe passage of the inlet *must* take all of these considerations into account. It is mandatory to enter the breakers at a time when the wave period is at its greatest length and the lessened wave heights are at their lowest value of steepness. This period occurs about twenty minutes before reversal of the tides in either direction. We cannot separate the effect of any single one of these varied components on inlet breakers. We must consider them collectively, since we are dealing with a complicated collateral result on a fluid substance that moves in all directions at the whim of winds, tides and currents. Wave cadence, in most cases at this time, seems to be more regular and discernible.

It is of interest to record here a few impact pressures of inlet breakers accurately obtained as a result of dynamometer tests in shoal water areas, in pounds per square foot.

Height of breaker	Pressure per sq. foot (pounds)
4-foot	406 lbs.
6 "	3,000 "
10 "	4,562 "
20 "	6,083 "

The height of one of the highest cycloidal type breakers was recorded in the North Sea—43 feet. Sea trochoids will *also* break under the lash of prolonged winds of gale force or the hurricane. Bars they meet far off shore will produce breaking seas. The Pacific probably produces the highest of such breakers for over the long reaches or fetch of that ocean, winds blow for thousands of miles in one direction for protracted periods, commonly building up crest lengths of over 1,000 feet during the winter period. The Columbia River bar, during periods of high on-shore winds or protracted gales in the same direction, commonly produces breakers of between 55 and 60 feet in height. These prohibit the passage of 10,000-ton ships. Green water descending on a ship of this size in such tonnage as a breaker that high would produce would tear apart any assembled structure similar to a ship floating on the ocean's surface, with the exception of a sphere—*contour* again.

The highest sea trochoid, whose height was ever accurately computed, was observed by the navigating officer of the USS Ramapo during a protracted gale in the North Pacific during the winter season of 1933. The method of computation and circumstances under which the observation was made were recorded in Naval Institute Proceedings some years ago. In the English Channel strong currents alone have been known to produce breakers some 25 feet in height and about 250-270 feet in length. They can give the staunchest steel ship an astonishing punishment. A series of unending breakers of such dimensions assaulting the hull structure of a ship or boat about its forward flat keel sections with trip-hammer blows, delivering a wallop of about 4,500 pounds per square foot every 7.7 seconds, has been a fatal test for many a ship at sea, of either wooden or steel construction.

Looking back at the table showing the force of breakers crashing against any flat surface at an angle of 90 degrees, one marvels that any kind of vessel can withstand the impact of such blows. The answer lies in the designer's dexterity to fashion hull contour so it will deflect such blows and distribute the force of impact, or divert it from the hull. Sturdiness of hull structure is also paramount. Demands for speed and comfort tend to interfere, at times, with the accomplishment of such a purpose. Often the designer, as a result, has been forced to compromise, and to deviate from the age-old principle of the strongest type of construction ever known—spherical or ring-type.

The frigate United States, built about 1800, is an example of this kind of construction. Were she to be placed in a drydock and you viewed her from astern you could trace around her stern section a perfect circle. Her bulwarks were given tumble-home; even the vital sections of her decks were heavily cambered, thus completing a connected circle. Her broad stern sections (transom) and her bows show pronounced curvature. Her transom was curved outboard to break the force of following seas and to prevent her from being pooped in high breakers or seas. Her bows were fined up only enough to give her deflective entrance to the impact of waves. Ships of such construction as this made a tremendous fuss as they swept through the seas. Their bulbous underbodies set up large areas of submerged frictional resistance end eddy currents. They were exasperatingly slow in light airs and threw stern waves as high as a house when driven by the gale. All this is granted, but they cruised the seven seas both in high latitudes and low; few, if any, were ever lost as a result of destruction by sea waves.

A wooden ship of this type of ring construction even circumnavigated the Polar ice pack—around the top of the world. Her entire hull structure was forced above the surface of the sea time and again by the crushing action of the heaviest ice known to man. Yet she lived to *sail* her intrepid crew home in safety. There was not one inch of area about the weather surfaces of these old veterans that the full force of a breaker could clutch at to obtain leverage to start an opening as a lever to

In the sketch above, drawn to scale, the bottom lines of a World War I subchaser are shown. There was no flat spot anywhere in the hulls of these remarkably able boats

Two views of the hull of a comparatively modern type of semi-displacement motor boat, showing the flared bow sections forward and the underbody aft designed for good cruising speeds

An older type of full displacement cruiser, showing the roundness of lines, both in profile and section. The dotted lines show how nearly her midship section approaches a semicircle

weaken her hull structure. Unlike their more modern sisters with sweeping, graceful speed lines, their bottoms were of such contour as to make them sufficiently stable in high seas and give enormous strength in breakers. They were built about the postulate that they *must* weather any gale in any ocean.

Those were strong ships but their manner of construction could not be applied with success to modern motor boats nor could their "system" of curvature cope with demands for speed in present day motor-driven craft. About the only relic of this example of floating construction left in modern motor boat building may be observed under the turtle deck of the modern motor surf boat. Here speed has necessarily been sacrificed. You cannot have both, and your brand of seamanship plus your ability to utilize to advantage the highly contoured surfaces of your craft in breakers must take the place of the great strength of connected ring construction. Remember that the professional motor surf boat was built to steam out of any breaking inlet where she can find sufficient depth for her propeller, and for effective steering. Your pleasure boat was never designed to do this, so look over inlet conditions before you go to sea.. You can always get authentic reports on bar conditions—don't take a chance and "try it."

Perhaps the most successful compromise of modern motor boat construction in respect to contour-build and retained ring strength was, again, the little American chaser of World War I. Coupled with these qualities was the dependable placement of continuous high torque and its position under her quarter. There was not a flat spot in her entire hull structure (see illustration of the chaser's bottom); she had a modified degree of flare forward and her deck, to complete the connected circle of ring construction, was cambered.

Yet she possessed considerable speed. The placement of her balanced rudder was so expert in relation to her screws that there was no possible position she might assume in the breakers that could deprive her of effective rudder control. Her enormous delivery of torque was available on her shafts 2.5 seconds after the demand for it was rung down. So great was the effect of her high torque on rudder surfaces that the unwary quartermaster was often shocked to attention by having the helm jerked from his hands, when either of her two wing motors were started, despite the fact that her rudder operating linkage passed through a system of gearing.

Some Aspects of Bottom Design

Now of the various resistances which oppose a motor boat's progress through the water, those of greatest detriment and ever-present obstruction to the designer are frictional resistance and wave-making. To the motor boat captain, struggling in steep breakers, where either of these twin elements is present in exaggerated degree, both work as a double-edged hindrance to safe passage through breaking seas. The frictional wake which is the result of the confluence of the two is usually greater in velocity in full displacement type hulls about the center section of the boat; it may be defined as water having forward motion in the direction in which your craft is traveling. Where it is observed at the stern of your boat, surging about in high turbulence, your propellers are being forced to deliver their power in water that already has forward motion. This results in high slip and propeller thrust losses. Since it interferes with instantaneous delivery of high torque in breakers the designer has resorted to streamlining of bottom sections. Any abrupt termination of hull contour or poorly faired bottom sections handicap you in breakers. In part, the designer is relying on your knowledge of seamanship and good sense in the handling of your craft in breakers in his admonishment of *never pounding* any of your streamlined bottom sections. Such contour has been necessary to produce the speed that *you* demanded.

In the evolution of boat contour, the designer has evolved a hull form whose bottom section, limits of wetted surface (underway), and stern profiles are highly streamlined. These are aimed at decreasing the length of frictional resistance and minimizing effects of frictional wake. Thus additional speed is gained for less weight of horsepower. Greater comfort, extra stability athwartship, and roominess aft also result from carrying out much of the boat's full beam almost to the stern. To the extent that a design is intended for greater speed, a higher caliber of seamanship is called for when handling the boat in rough, breaking seas.

As we study the modern motor boat's underbody (see illustration) we note that the patterned ends of her wide quarter are somewhat flatter in section than the steeper curves of her runs forward. Viewing her forward, from the forefoot knuckle to the top of her

stem post, the graceful curves of her bow flares are pleasing. By the stern we note her broad transom is brought in at the bilge in a sharp but graceful turn. Her rudders look small for the job but the propellers just ahead of the rudder post look business-like. Many elements of her design reveal a similarity to the famous Jersey beach skiff which, intelligently handled, is one of the most able of modern boats in inlet or beach breakers.

Handling a Skiff

The skiffman well realizes the necessity of keeping his stern squarely before the break of the seas when he enters the breakers. He learned the hard way and he knows that if his boat should become tender at the quarters as a result of inattention or lack of realization of his position, as he roars along on the back of a sea, the submerged portion of his transom and waterline section of his planking aft will instantly produce rudder effect. Since the projected area in friction against the sea in that portion of his hull is far greater than that of his rudders, he can only expect the breakers to seize that portion of his hull and throw him into a broach.

He is deeply conscious of the presence and force of the pressure wave surging along at his bottom's entrance to the sea just forward of his 'midship section and he uses his controls to keep the force of that pressure wave constant and surging evenly down over the outer surfaces of his bottom planking *in a fore and aft direction. He never pounds it.* To do so would immediately destroy the continuity of the stabilizing effect of his high and continuous torque; in exaggeration it might even fracture a plank. It's risky, and *bad* seamanship.

He can feel the force of that pressure wave through the soles of his shoes and he can judge its degree by the vibrations of his hull as his reflexes tell him to move his throttle ahead slightly when they decrease and to ease it back a bit if the rumblings beneath him become excessive.

He rarely uses his drogue for he is not the fool to get caught out there when the breakers are high before the inlet. But, should his boat start to run, its pretty to see his "drugman" go to work and break her out of it. He knows his boat is so constructed aft that she'll stand the whipping strain of that shattering jerk of the drogueline as the drogueman spins off the turns of the trip and the tow-line's red markers fly in the spume—ripping out of the sea as his 2-inch drogueline takes the entire load of his roaring motor's output plus the speed of the breaker's advance.

His skiff now broken out of her run, the Jerseyman knows he cannot ease off and allow a following sea to assault the broad face of his transom. His racing hull now being in a high state of tension, a breaker packing a two-ton wallop reaching his transom might demolish the whole after section of his boat. The chaser's transom was concaved outboard; a sea just couldn't hit it a solid jolt. Not so his skiff, however—so he runs from the breaker and holds her where the tumbling sea cannot reach him.

Dodge the Cross Seas

Contour construction in small boats in breaking inlets is a mighty important element of design for none better than the Jerseyman realizes those sweeping sections of bow flare forward become flat when faced with the impact of the sea as it attempts to pound them. Should he see a cross sea tearing across his course he'll slow her down or dodge it if he senses that his bows are on a collision bearing with it, for you might as well hit the jetty full tilt as collide with that breaker.

Such cross seas are grave risks to motor boats with bow cockpits, whether or not these are supposed to be self-bailing.

It will be gleaned, as the reader follows through the text, that drogues and their use assume an important stature at times of emergency in breakers. Reference to the *details* of their use and the manner of *adaptation* of the different types of drogues to specific types of hulls have been left unexplained—largely for the reason that pages of explanation might divert the attention of the reader from the subject at hand. Limitations of space might not do that field of seamanship full justice in a discussion where so many elements of boat construction and sea condition are fused together and must be separated in part and then placed back together again for the purposes of full understanding. The amateur boatman has a long voyage to make on the course we have set here. It must not be complicated any more than necessary. Use of drogues and their adaptation is simply another field of seamanship.

In these days of great, responsive and dependable power, able and staunch motor craft and rapid, accurate, reliable weather and bar forecasts, the use of a drogue in breakers is all but a lost art. Only a few of the older beach denizens are left now who were expert in their use. Yet it is a great comfort to have one aboard suited to your own particular boat both in inlet breakers and for the purpose of lying to it in bad weather at sea.

Forward Cockpits

Before leaving the subject of handling modern motor boats in breaking seas, perhaps a word should be said concerning the vulnerability of open forward cockpits. It is not meant to infer that motor boats of such construction must always be restricted from entrance to the breakers before a coastal inlet. However it seems rather a contradiction of good seagoing sense to otherwise construct a boat whose strength, hull contour, and power are equal to the challenge of the breakers and then to vitiate these good qualities by placing in vulnerable ends a deep, open compartment capable (if filled) of throwing the craft into an immediate broach. Rarely do forward cockpits have adequate means of freeing themselves as fast as demands of safe operation in breakers press upon such a craft. Remember that breaking seas may be encountered in other waters than those of coastal inlets. They may occur at any place on the coastal shelf where the force of wind, depth of water, and combinaton or strength of currents are conducive to their formation.

Flat Surfaces Vulnerable

Looking back over the taffrail, we have also noted the vulnerability of flat-surfaced structures exposed to waves and weather. We know something of the force *in tons* that assaults these non-contoured weather surfaces. Therefore, if you plan a cruise along the coast, see to it that you have a stout hatch that can be battened down over your forward cockpit—or at least carry aboard materials from which you can quickly construct a suitable cover, if conditions necessitate your bringing the boat's head into heavy seas.

Among the modern materials that have found increasing use in boat construction is flat sheet plywood. Primarily, of course, it is used in the hulls of small craft that are not expected to run breaking inlets. It also lends itself to use in bulkheads, interior joiner work, etc. Properly framed, it has tremendous strength—as in decks, which can often be made stronger than those planked in the conventional manner. But it certainly should not be expected, in either hulls or superstructure, to be able to withstand the full impact of breaking seas, if used in the form of flat surfaces with inadequate framing to back it.

Remember—if you are confronted with the necessity of running breakers before a coastal inlet—every portion of the weather surfaces of your ship becomes a strength member. Collectively, they must be tied into your main framing in a secure and rigid fashion—your deck carlins, cabin sides and bulwarks, weather bulkheads and transoms—flat deckhouse structures, even your cabin and cockpit decks all bear their proportion of the sea-load in the breaker. The breakers will *always* attack the weakest link in the construction chain of your motor boat *first*.

Fast Boat Runs Bahia Honda

We have mentioned that the amount of punishment some of these well built modern high-speed motor boats will take in breakers is little short of amazing when handled with confidence and the certainty of experience. As a case in point, it might be recalled that some years ago, running the inlet off Bahia Honda with an injured sailor aboard, in one of the more modern, strong, high-speed motor boats a little over 38 feet in length and capable of a speed of about 28 knots with her two big engines full out, on her passage through the inlet she turned completely over in a period of (as near as could be calculated) 2.5 seconds. She righted herself inside the breakers on the inlet side of the bar and came up with her crew in the cockpit and with her port motor still pounding out its 3200 r.p.m. Her two-man crew had been lashed on short bights to her cockpit stanchions previous to her entry into the breakers. The injured sailor had been lashed to the cabin floor.

It looked like only a 50-50 chance, as her crew watched on the seaward side of the breaker line, and from what could be seen of the breakers in the darkness through the flying spume of the gale, the inlet breakers appeared to be about seven to eight feet in height but their period was extremely short. The sailor's life was at stake

and the chance had to be taken. If the boat had a drogue aboard and set when she laid down on her port side and started to run, her mad speed might have been broken and stopped but, like the Dutchman's anchor, old faithful Charlie wasn't there that time. This boat was capable of an honest 28 knots. Her engines, at the time she entered the outer breakers, were not quite full out and she was being handled by a sailor who had spent many years of his life in small boats in the breakers. You can imagine the speed those inlet seas were making!

A few days later the boat was hauled out—the couplings connecting both engines to the tailshafts were checked for alignment, both machines carefully gone over, holding down bolts and all framing in the way of her power plant was checked. Except for three of her six tailshaft flange bolts on the starboard coupling that were found to have slacked up and were only hand-tight, there was nothing amiss with her power plant. A tight wire was run over her hull and she was carefully trammed by two experts both in her center section and at her ends. Her hull was as fair as the day she first met the sea. The only evidence of the mauling she took and damage sustained in her wild passage through Honda was the tearing from their flanges of two 1¼-inch pipe stanchions that supported and stiffened her cabin top. These two were badly twisted. She had no forward cockpit.

The Auxiliary in Breakers

The difficulties in breakers of the sail boat with auxiliary engine are complicated by the general contour of both its submerged and exposed body plan, its rigging and lofty sparring. In any coastal inlet where breakers are present over three feet in height in conjunction with strong winds blowing on the land, a breaker length of roughly 100 feet and wave periods of less than five seconds, entrance may be attended with extreme difficulty and should only be attempted in extreme emergency, with the auxiliary type of boat. Unless such a boat, contemplating the entrance of a coastal inlet where breakers are seething across its mouth, is extremely high-powered, has a body and topside form that will easily assimilate a sea speed in excess of 15 knots, has very short ends and is very moderately sparred, she should not attempt any such entrance. Rather she should be taken to sea and hove to even in the face of worsening weather; her chance for survival is far better.

It should be borne in mind that the inlet breaker is no respecter of size and great length of hull. A 90-foot Gloucesterman, probably one of the most able types of small sailing vessels afloat, in consideration of its heavy power installation, rig and hull contour, excepting perhaps the world famous Ramsgate trawler and Dutch Pilot boat, found this out one night in a roaring southeaster and a snowstorm while attempting to enter Cold Spring Inlet on the Jersey coast. With the wind almost dead astern, force 5, and approaching the narrow entrance to the inlet under power and bare poles, excepting a rag of riding trysail set flying on the main, she took a heavy squall just off the entrance to the jetties. A cross sea struck her under the flare of her port bow and forced her bows to starboard and slowed her down; she was then pooped by a following breaker, losing her dog-house over the wheel box. Her starboard nest of dories went by the board across the deck and demolished her fish pens as they went, tearing loose from the chainplates her forward, port side, mainmast shroud. The vessel now being in a deep port roll, the wind from astern, driving at her lofty spars and rigging, simply took charge of her steering arrangements and directed her course squarely at 90 degrees to the direction of the gale (while the ship was making an estimated speed of better than 15 knots) into the immovable bulk of the north jetty. She rode clear to the top of the jetty before the cold stone stopped her mad run.

Auxiliaries Need Sea Room

Many qualified and authoritative persons have written, in a general sense, of the hazards connected with the driving of such auxiliary craft before high following seas and winds of gale force from astern. Every experienced captain of such motor-sail boats senses this danger. The wise sailor, therefore, even though he may be entirely uninitiated or have no conception whatever of the forces at work aloft and those acting on his hull, will watch his chance and, using his power if necessary, will bring his bows to the seas at the earliest opportunity before he dismasts his vessel or she is hopelessly pooped or broached. This can only be done where sea room is available. It cannot be accomplished where the captain of such a boat is threatened with loss of control of his ship in a breaking inlet.

Maneuvering through a breaking coastal inlet the captain of the strictly motor-driven craft has none of these problems to deal with. A clear understanding, however, of the effect of the elements of construction, general contour of hull form and the possibilities of lofty rig leverages must be possessed by the operator of an auxiliary. He should realize how these components are so closely connected with the difficulties of handling his straining hull in breakers before high winds, and, in particular, when his hull is cramped for sea room and maneuvering space when an attempt is made to force her through the narrow channel of a breaking inlet.

Now as the size and lateral plane of auxiliary craft are reduced, the general ratio of the combined qualities of weatherliness, in such types, falls off in almost direct proportion to the degree in size to which the boat is reduced. In other words, it does not necessarily follow, because a big auxiliary might be an able craft in breakers on the coastal shelf, that a smaller vessel of similar design will retain her ability to keep the sea and handle reliably under identical sea conditions.

How Size Affects Craft of Similar Design

In moderate weather and reasonably smooth going, an exact counterpart of the larger craft but only half her size might possibly outclass her larger sister in ability to work to windward under sail, would probably be fast in stays and possess the general rapid response to her helm which the overall design of her larger counterpart makes possible. However, when the smaller version is brought before heavy seas, alternately breaking, or where it is necessary to bring her bows head to the seas in an attempt to heave her to—the abilities of the larger auxiliary and her diminutive counterpart company.

To begin with, the righting moments of such small craft when heeled at any angle of inclination near the crest of a breaker are far less than when such a boat is making headway on her normal water planes. Consequently, this factor of tenderness augmented by the gyrations of lofty rigging weights, reeling aloft under the influence of high windage, creates a situation where extreme watchfullness, in heavy breakers, becomes the pass-word of safety. Despite their other attributes of speed, grace and quick response to rudder motion in moderate weather, there is no heaving-to of these ships, with the wheel hard down in a becket, and going below to a pinochle game. By reason of their short keels and resultant quickness in stays, they are also quick under boisterous sea conditions and must be constantly "handled." Resorting to the use of power, before high following breakers, is liable to complicate the situation and in most cases combinations of motor and canvas should only be used when such boats are riding head-to or just off the seas, or to aid in bringing them head to the seas. Despite all of the above (since such motor-sail craft must always be "handled") they must have sea-room, and the forcing of one of these sensitive craft into the tumultuous confines of a breaking inlet channel is fraught with danger to the boat and its crew.

The Underbody Design

Answering the constant demands for speed, speed and more speed out of such motor auxiliaries particularly on windward legs and in stays, the designer has constantly cut away at the bottom sections of these boats until in some cases there is little evidence of such a boat's keel sections left, and the forefoot has all but disappeared. This has to be done in the interest of reducing the amount of frictional area in contact with the sea, an elimination of frictional wake and eddy-making, and, where a boat's forefoot has disappeared, a lessening of the slowing effects of lee bow surge and rapidity of motion in stays. That the designer has achieved his objective there is not the least doubt, but such success has been bought at the cost of creating a craft whose action under power in almost any type of cycloid, unless handled with extreme care, does not emulate, in any sense, the predictable action of a modern motor boat in heavy following breakers before high winds.

There are few boats of any type devoid of forefoot or forefoot gripe, that will "hang on" when hove to or lie without fretfulness to the end of a drogue line in heavy cycloids. This applies equally to both motor and sailing vessels, and combinations of the two. Boats of such construction all evince a tendency to pivot on the after sections of their keel while their bows are at the whim of

surface forces of the sea and are shoved higher and yon by them, making the boat uncomfortable when stemming breakers and resulting in the necessity of having to "sail" such craft constantly. Before the breakers and running, this tendency is exaggerated in the opposite direction, for now the boat's stern, which is the first portion of the ship's bulk to feel the force and direction of the waves from astern, seems to want to proceed off in one direction unmindful of the fact that it might be pushing the overhanging and lightly displaced bows off in another direction. There are several components of hull shape, sectional displacement and rigging plan that are responsible for this alarming tendency of such craft before steep breakers and high winds from astern. They are difficult to separate.

Tendency to Broach

Auxiliary craft whose straight keel section is but a third or less of their waterline length seem to be more prone to this yawing proclivity before heavy breaking seas and are more likely to be thrown into a broach than are their long, straight-keeled and extended-forefoot sisters. As a result of their deep draft aft and the pulling aft of concentrated keel weights (aft of designed centers of buoyancy) to offset the tendency of their sail plans to depress shallow bows, the inertia built up in that section of the vessel where displacement is greatest and weights are heaviest tends to follow the natural physical law of proceeding in a straight line. Unfortunately, this submerged section of the ship about the keel knuckle and slightly forward of it, feels the violence of the breakers least while the exposed topsides (transom) of the vessel, directly above the keel knuckle, are first to meet the onslaught of breakers and to be attacked from diverse directions. At sea, such forces tearing at the hull produce wild twisting strains. In the narrow confines of an inlet channel, if the breakers are more than four feet high, her actions are likely to be so unpredictable as to make the passage difficult, if not hazardous. You just could not get power enough in her to control her and, under power alone, she could never hope to approach the performance of the modern motor boat in breakers. The inlet just is no place for her.

In my opinion, about the ablest thing in a small auxiliary that has been produced in this country that will stay with you in breakers of up to about six feet in height is the Friendship sloop. Her keel, though sloping, runs her full length; she has short ends, and she'll waddle through small breakers like the professional surfboat. There *are* sailboats in the world that will run breakers—the planing type sailboats of the South Sea natives which, like the modern semi-displacement motor boat, has none of the foregoing complications of contour to beset them in the breakers. These native craft attain speeds of 15 knots and higher sailing against the wind.

Keep the Auxiliary Out of Breaking Inlets

When you attempt to make a motor boat out of the average auxiliary, and take her through a badly breaking inlet, you are forcing your vessel into a situation which her creators never intended she should be pushed into. If you want to run breakers, tell your architect. What he designs for you will have few of the characteristics of the auxiliary.

We have pointed out the restlessness of this type of ship when you attempt to heave it to in breakers on the coastal shelf. She *will* heave to and she *will* lay to a drogue line, but you can't put the gyro-pilot on her when the wind is force 6 and the seas are 5 and breaking. She won't do the thinking, for that lies in the department of your seamanship and good judgment.

Many sailboat rudders are relatively inefficient. Under sail, the bottom third of such rudders is the position where their greatest projected area should be placed. That section of the rudder, however, is often cut away to preserve contour and reduce eddy-making. Under power, it is the vertical center section of the rudder directly abaft the discharge from your wheel where such rudders should be given their greatest lateral area. But here steering control has been reduced by the cutting away of the rudder blade to make room for the propeller. If you run your shaft out through either of the bilges you are faced with a worse situation in the breakers for then you have the directional effect of your wheel to fight and you do not have the influence of high shaft torque to mitigate the effect of any of these constructional deficiencies. Your power, of necessity, is low. She just doesn't belong in breaking inlets.

CHAPTER XXVIII

• # River Piloting

Piloting on Our Fresh-Water Inland Waterways Can

Be a Rewarding Experience—a Pleasant Change,

for the Salt-Water Boatman, from Coastal Cruising.

Chart of the principal navigable waterways in the eastern half of the United States. The Mississippi River System, including its tributaries, constitutes a network of more than 12,000 miles navigable by pleasure craft.

LEGEND

— IMPROVED INTRACOASTAL WATERWAY
• • • OPEN BAY WATER
▪▪▪ AUTHORIZED FOR IMPROVEMENT
— PRINCIPAL IMPROVED CONNECTING WATERWAYS

From Booklet "The Gulf Intracoastal Waterway"

A typical river scene on the Ohio, made from the Kentucky side below Louisville. Deep water favors the outside of the bend.

For the cruising yachtsman who has never laid his course inland, there are surprises in store. Many a coastal boatman is likely to regard the inland waterways as little better than glorified "canals" to be used only as links between large bodies of salt water. Cruising them for their own sake might never occur to him, and canalling, in his mind, is synonymous with "ditch-crawling."

As a matter of fact, some of the finest cruising this country affords can be found on the vast network of interconnected rivers and lakes which give access to areas far removed from tidal waters. Throughout the United States there are nearly 30,000 miles of improved inland waterways. The Mississippi River system alone embraces more than 12,000 miles of waterways navigable by small craft —the largest network of navigable inland waterways, in fact, in all the world. Of these 12,000 miles, the greater part provides depths of better than 6 feet. Using the Mississippi, the Great Lakes, the New York State Barge Canal and other waterways linking these with the Atlantic and Gulf Intracoastal Waterways, the boatman can circumnavigate the entire eastern portion of the United States, a cruise of more than 5,000 miles. Only a comparatively small portion of this would be in the open sea, although the Great Lakes, of course, are sizable bodies of water, comparable to the ocean insofar as small boat cruising is concerned.

While rivers as a rule seldom offer great open expanses common to the coast where the usual techniques of piloting are called into play, they do demand unique piloting skills. On the rivers, local lore often outweighs some of the fundamental piloting principles which are the coastal pilot's law. Ever-changing conditions on the rivers put a premium on local knowledge and elevate river navigation to the status of an art.

One of the first things to impress the salt water boatman on his cruise inland is the perpetual change of scenery as he threads mile after scenic mile of sinuous cross-country course—over hills, into the valleys, through farmlands, forests and cities. Basically the transition is one from salt water to fresh, from tidal to nontidal waters. "Fresh" water does not necessarily imply clear, pure water. In the Missouri, river water is freighted with silt that clogs water strainers and wears out strut bearings and shafts. But in Lake Champlain, you can stop in mid-lake and top off your fresh water tanks.

Because inland water may be designated as non-tidal, it does not follow that there are no fluctuations in level. On the coast we are accustomed to daily changes in height —normally two highs and two lows each day. Inland, the variation in rivers is more apt to be of a seasonal nature, as spring freshets, loaded with debris, flood down from the headwaters, overflow banks, and course down to the sea at surprising velocities. At St. Louis, the seasonal fluctuation in river level from flood conditions in the late winter and early spring to normal levels in the late summer and fall may range from 40 to 50 feet. And in some of the navigable streams, sudden hard rains may raise the level several feet in a matter of hours.

In the passes at the mouth of the Mississippi, there is generally one high and one low water in 24 hours, with a range of about 18 inches. At New Orleans the diurnal range of the tide during low water stages averages about

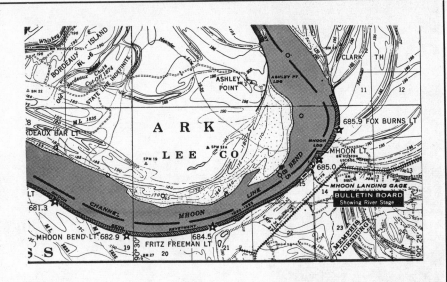

Section of a typical Mississippi River chart. On the original, the shaded areas appear in blue tint. Channel lines, lights and mileages are printed in red. River stages, or heights, are given on the bulletin boards, locations of which are indicated on the chart in red. Note the revetment which Army Engineers have constructed on the outside of the bend to protect the bank from erosion. Small circles are 1 statute mile apart. Parallels of latitude and meridians of longitude appear, but no compass rose, as used on coastal charts. New charts in sheet form are now available for the Upper Mississippi River, replacing older bound books.

9 inches, with no periodic tide at high river stages. Current in this area is negligible from a piloting standpoint. High water stages occur around April, low in October, with extreme differences in level up to 21 feet.

In the larger lakes, a strong wind will lower levels to windward and pile up the water to leeward. Lake levels vary from year to year and show a seasonal rise and fall as well, low in the winter, high in the summer. Barometric pressure also exerts an influence on lake levels, sometimes causing a sudden temporary oscillation of considerable magnitude. This lake phenomenon is called a seiche.

Usually the cruise inland from the coast does mean a change from exposed to sheltered waters. That, however, is purely relative. While it is true that you can cruise hundreds of miles continuously on streams where shelter from bad weather is seldom more distant than the nearest bank, the larger lakes must be treated with respect. Lake Superior, for example, is the largest body of fresh water in the world. Deep, with rock-ribbed coasts and subject to storm and fog as well, it presents a challenge to even

AIDS TO NAVIGATION

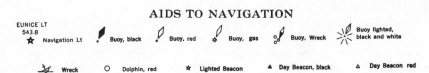

Symbols used on Mississippi River charts. Navigation lights, black buoys and red buoys are in red on original. Solid red distinguishes black buoys—open red, red buoys.

HYDROGRAPHIC

Hydrographic notations from the legend given in a book of Mississippi River charts. Miles above Head of Passes in red on the original, the river gage in red and black. Most river charts show few soundings, if any. Black arrow is used to indicate direction of current flow, as in illustration at right.

TYPICAL CROSSING CHANNEL

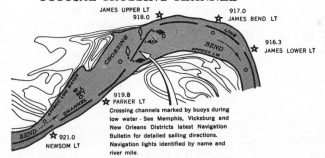

Typical crossing channel, as illustrated in chart book, Cairo to Gulf of Mexico. Note how channel sweeps toward outside of bend. Channel line, lights and mileages in red on original.

Photograph from T.V.A., Knoxville

Locks and dams make rivers navigable by changing levels in successive stages. Here a group of cruisers on the Tennessee ascend to a higher level, as they pass through Wilson Dam Lock in Alabama. Coiling lines, the crew make ready to sail out of the lock.

the saltiest pilot. Lake Erie, though smaller than Superior, is comparatively shallow. In a gale of wind, seas cannot shape up in the normal pattern of ocean waves. Consequently, they are short and steep, frequently breaking in heavy squalls. Even New York's Lake Oneida, only 20 miles in length, can build up seas that will test the ability of an offshore boat.

Broadly speaking, river currents, though they may fluctuate in velocity, will trend always in one direction—from headwaters to mouth. Despite this, tidal rivers connecting with the sea may feel the effect of tidal conditions at the mouth, backing the water up so that the cruiser can take advantage of a favorable current going upstream when tidal conditions are right. On the Hudson, for example, a 10-mile cruiser, starting at The Battery at the beginning of the flood, can carry a favorable current all the way to Albany, 150 miles inland. Tides, here, even this far inland, may range in excess of 6 feet, yet at Newburgh and West Point far down the river, the mean range will be only half that.

Shoaling is a serious problem in most rivers. Spring floods build up current velocities, stir up silt in river bottoms, wash more down from the banks, and carry this load in suspension to be deposited in the form of mud flats and sand bars that present navigational hazards by closing off channels. The Connecticut River on the East Coast is a good example of this, where heavy expenditures are required annually to keep channels dredged to project depths. In the Mississippi, a jellied mass of muck called flocculation is deposited as a sediment on the river bed to a depth of 10 or 15 feet. Deep-draft vessels plow through

it, and high water stages of the river flush it out into the Gulf so Army Engineers do not bother to dredge it at low water stages.

Often where a river discharges into a bay or sound, current velocities are no longer sufficient to hold the silt in suspension and a bar or shoal is built up across the river mouth, much as creeks and streams behave when they flow into the ocean, creating an obstacle against free passage into open water, unless a channel is dredged and protected by breakwaters. On bars of this kind, bad seas may build up in strong currents opposed by the wind. As a matter of fact, at the confluence of some rivers, disturbed surface conditions may be encountered, even where there is seemingly no wind to account for it.

River currents have been the subject of extensive studies and their vagaries are of utmost importance to the masters of deep-draft commercial craft. The surface current acting on a small pleasure boat may in fact be actually contrary to that which grips the keel of a large ship near the river bottom. Even with respect to surface currents alone, there is a variation from bank to mid-stream. Friction of the banks and bottom retards velocity. The skipper of the commercial boat—where fuel costs and hours of operation are of vital import—knows this as he carries the strength of a mid-river current downstream with him. Returning he runs close under the bank to escape the strength of flow opposing him—even turning slightly into coves behind points to take advantage of the counter-current that tends opposite to the trend of the river's flow.

Perhaps the factors which the professional pilot weighs so carefully are less significant to the small boatman.

419

A lone cruiser passes out of one of the highest lift locks in the nation, having been raised 80 feet at Fort Loudon Lock as she proceeds up the Tennessee toward Knoxville, Tenn.

Nevertheless, the pleasure boatman can profitably take a leaf from the river pilot's log and cut his running time and fuel bills merely by running courses that make elemental factors work for him, rather than against him.

Again, speaking broadly, unless there is something in the bottom contour or man-made structures to alter them, river channels have a natural trend somewhat akin to the configurations in creeks along the marshes of our coasts, where the flow of water tends to carry across the stream on the outside of bends, scouring out a natural channel at the outside while depositing a bar on the points.

Study a river chart which gives the depths (those of the Coast & Geodetic Survey do) and notice the trend. Then when you are piloting a river where the navigational "maps" give no clue to depths (as in the Ohio and Mississippi) you can begin to develop an instinct with regard to interpretation of the river's natural course. Try to visualize the whole picture, if you can, as it would appear to you if you were looking down on the river *and* your boat from a plane. This way you will be less likely to run straight courses from buoy to buoy, cutting corners, with obvious risk of piling up on a point. You will appreciate better the problems of the agency which buoys the waterway, where a pair of buoys are used to mark a point and the channel edge opposite, with a similar pair abreast of the next point. Between the two points the river may be taking a natural curve and a mid-channel course would be represented, not by a straight line between the two pairs of buoys, but by a curved line conforming roughly to the trend of the river as a whole.

Gradually developing this sense of perspective, you'll be more acutely conscious of the actual track you make good over the bottom relative to nearby shoals and side limits of the channels. Where currents do occasionally flow diagonally across your

course, you will allow for them instinctively and look astern frequently to help maintain that sense of position.

As you glance astern in unfamiliar waters, your wake will provide a clue to the safety of your course. When the natural sequence of waves in your wake is broken, there must be something to disturb it. As it rolls off into shallow water, the smooth undulation will give way to a sharper formation, even cresting on the flats in miniature "breakers." When they encounter a reef or flooded area where submerged stumps lie close to the surface, the wake will show the difference. But when that short peaked unnatural wake closes up toward your stern, sheer off . . . . fast!—away from the side where the telltale wake builds up.

On some river charts, even the curves showing the topography ashore supply clues to what may be expected in the river itself. Frequently contour curves crowded close together on land at the water's edge indicate a cliff rising sheer from the surface, with prospects of good depths close under such a bank. The cliff or hill, as the case may be, may at the same time provide a prominent landmark as a guide to steer by.

Piloting the rivers and canals, encountering bridges, locks and guard gates in rapid succession, you will soon acquire a new awareness of controlling vertical and horizontal clearances. On tidewater you were, no doubt, acutely conscious of depths as a critical consideration. Navigating a waterway where you normally could be assured a 6-foot depth, you automatically exercised extra caution around inlets where rapid shifting of the

Cruiser entering Kentucky Dam Lock. Note striping on wall.

shoals might cut your controlling depth to a couple of feet. On the rivers, you will have the clearance overhead on your mind. There may be places on some streams where a fixed bridge will arbitrarily determine your "head of navigation." Beyond that point, your cruising may be restricted to an exploratory trip in the dinghy.

On some of our principal waterways—the New York State Barge Canal System, for example—overhead clearance is restricted to 15½ feet. Masts on auxiliaries must be unstepped and carried on deck, and outriggers and radiotelephone antennas hinged down out of the way. Commercial craft are built with regard for limiting clearance under bridges and in locks. Superstructures are kept low and pilot houses may even be made retractable, to lower for passage under bridges. Fixed overhead power cables are generally high enough to provide clearance for masted vessels, and this clearance is noted on the chart. High water stages on the rivers naturally cut overhead clearances under bridges by the amount of rise above normal pool levels. Chart books for the Ohio give examples of how to calculate existing clearances at open river stages from the vertical clearances at normal pool stage, and at 1936 high water stage, shown on the charts.

Signals for the opening of drawbridges, lift bridges, etc., are not uniform in all waters so it will be necessary to consult local regulations. For the Great Lakes area, for example, they

Two big tows pass on the Mississippi at Vicksburg bridge.

Photograph by George Yater

The wandering Ohio from the campus of Hanover College

Five cruisers, bound upstream, leave Pickwick Dam Lock located in southern Tennessee. Note the long guide wall.

are covered in detail in the Great Lakes Pilot. Elsewhere, as on the Illinois Waterway, information may be had from Army Engineer District Offices. On the New York Barge Canal, the signal is three short distinct blasts of the whistle.

Before the days of locks and dams, many of our rivers were unnavigable. Water coursing down valleys at the land's natural gradient, dropping perhaps hundreds of feet in a score of miles, runs too fast and encounters too many natural obstacles. To overcome them, engineers dam the natural waterways at strategic spots, creating a series of "pools" or levels that may be likened to a stairway. Good examples of how closely these can resemble a flight of stairs will be found at places like Waterford, N. Y., and the Rideau Canal at Ottawa, where vessels descend or ascend a series of locks in quick succession.

To a river pilot, the term "pool stage" indicates the height of water in a pool at any given time with reference to the datum for that pool. On the rivers pool stages are posted on conspicuous bulletin boards along the river banks so as to be easily read from passing vessels. Locations of the bulletin boards are given on the river charts. On the Ohio, gage readings are displayed at the powerhouses of the dams. These indicate depths of the pool impounded by the dam next below. A depth of 9 feet is uniformly taken to indicate the pool at normal elevation. A reading of 8.7 feet would indicate that the lower pool at the dam is 0.3 foot below normal elevation. These readings are preceded by the letters NP (normal pool) in white on a green background.

Photograph courtesy J. D. Tennison, Jr.

At Mile 715.0 on the Lower Mississippi River, just a few miles below Memphis, pleasure craft anchor on the back side of a bar in slack water with complete protection from the wake of passing towboats. There are many such bars along the Mississippi from Baton Rouge on north. The river boatman will find them a snug haven for anchorage at night or during severe weather.

Locks and Dams, and the Part They Play in Making Rivers Navigable. The Proper Handling of Pleasure Craft in Passing Through Locks, and Some Special Problems of Meeting and Passing Commercial Traffic in Narrow Canals and Congested Waterways.

Photograph from Corps of Engineers, U. S. Army

A fleet of pleasure craft, locking through together, almost fill all of the available space in a lock chamber of the Inner Harbor Navigation Canal Lock in New Orleans, as they head east on the Gulf Intracoastal Waterway. Gates recess into the lock walls.

Dams on our inland waterways, without locks, would restrict river cruising to the individual pools and prevent through navigation except to small craft light enough to be portaged around the dams. Locks, in conjunction with the dams, provide the means for watercraft to move from level to level. Locks vary in size but since they must invariably handle commercial traffic, their limiting dimensions offer no restriction to the movement of pleasure craft. On the New York State Barge Canal, a tanker will almost fill a lock, with little space to spare.

Locks are practically water-tight chambers with gates at each end. Valves are provided to admit water as re-

quired. When a vessel is about to be locked upstream to a higher level, the upstream gate is closed, the downstream gate opened, and the water stands at the lower level. The vessel enters the lock through the open gates at the lower end, the gates close behind her and water is valved in until the chamber is full to the upstream level. Now the upstream gate is opened, and the boat is free to resume her course upstream. Locking down is naturally the reverse of this procedure.

Signals are provided for vessels approaching a lock (commonly a long and a short blast) answered by signals from the lock tender. The river boatman should familiarize himself with the special signals applicable to the particular waterway he is using. The Army Engineers at Pittsburgh publish an informative little illustrated leaflet entitled "Locking Through," which sets forth, in a nutshell, the main essentials as they apply to the Ohio.

On the Ohio, vessels sound a long and short blast on the whistle from a distance of not more than one mile from the lock. (On the New York State Barge Canal, they signal with three distinct blasts.) When approaching a lock, boats must wait for the lockmaster's signal before entering. When bound downstream, stay in the clear at least 400 feet upstream from the end of the guide wall leading along the bank into the lock. Approach through the buoyed channel directly toward the lock and keep clear of spillway sections of the dam. Be particularly careful not to obstruct the movement of any large commercial craft that may be leaving the lock. When bound upstream, keep well clear of the turbulent water invariably found below a dam.

On the Mississippi, signs are painted on the river face of the guide wall warning small craft not to pass a given point until signalled by the lock attendant. Near this sign a signal cord is placed. Small craft may use this to alert lock attendants, in lieu of signals used on other waters.

Traffic signal lights at the Ohio locks resemble those you find on the highway—red, amber and green, vertically arranged. Flashing red warns: do not enter, stand clear. Flashing amber signifies: approach, but under full control. Flashing green gives you the all-clear signal to enter. (On N. Y. State Canals, a fixed green light gives clearance to

enter; fixed red requires the vessel to wait. U. S. and commercial vessels take precedence; pleasure boats may be locked through with commercial craft if a safe distance may be maintained between them.)

Where locks are in pairs (landward and riverward) the lockmaster on the Ohio may also use an air horn, the significance of his blasts as follows: 1 long, enter landward lock; 2 long, enter riverward lock; 1 short, leave landward lock; 2 short, leave riverward lock.

The Secretary of the Army has established an order of priority with respect to the handling of traffic at locks, giving precedence in this order: 1, U. S. military craft; 2, mail boats; 3, commercial passenger craft; 4, commercial tows; 5, commercial fishermen; and 6, pleasure boats. This means that small pleasure craft may sometimes have to wait to be locked through with other vessels. In deciding on an order of precedence, the lockmaster also takes into account whether vessels of the same class are arriving at landward or riverward locks, and whether they are bound upstream or downstream.

The concrete walls of locks are usually rough and dirty. Consequently a boat will need adequate fender protection. Ordinary cylindrical fenders will pick up dirt and roll on the wall to smear the topsides. Fender boards, consisting of a plank (2-by-6 perhaps, several feet long) suspended horizontally outside the usual fenders, work well amidships or aft where sides are reasonably straight. Bags of hay have the same objection as cylindrical fenders, except

A view of the wickets at one of the Ohio River movable dams. Wickets are held in an upright position during low water stages of the river. At high water, they can be lowered, creating a navigable pass which river boats use without locking.

Photograph from J. M. Wallace

Photograph from Corps of Engineers, U. S. Army

At Mile 633 on the Mississippi, Army Engineers' equipment works on bank protection. Such floating equipment should be passed with caution. Day signal (extreme right) is a black-and-white vertically striped ball over a red ball; at night, equipment of this kind will show three red lights in vertical line.

Photograph from N. Y. State Department of Public Works

A westbound tug and barge (pushed ahead) enter the empty Erie Canal Lock No. 4, where they will be raised 34½ feet to the upper level. Propellers on large commercial craft throw a lot of water astern—something for small craft to watch.

on heavily flared bows at the edge of deck where they flatten down and work pretty well. Auto tires wrapped with burlap would be ideal except that their use is illegal in some canals. As you can't be sure which side of a lock you'll be using, it's wise to fender both sides.

Another essential in locking is adequate line. How heavy it is to be depends on the size of boat; how long depends on the depth of the locks. Good ½″ manila is generally

adequate for average sized cruisers. In general, each line (bow and stern) will have to be at least twice as long as the depth of lock. The object of this is to permit your running the bight of a line around a bollard on the top of the lock wall, using it double. Then, on the lower level, when you're read to cast off, you can haul the line in without assistance from above. At Little Falls, N. Y., the drop is roughly 40 feet, so 100 feet is not too much for

Reproduction of a portion of an Ohio River chart. Arrow (top) indicates true north, seldom at top of chart. Arrow at left indicates direction of river flow. Note symbols for cans and nuns (see legend, next page). Location of bulletin board showing river gages is shown on chart.

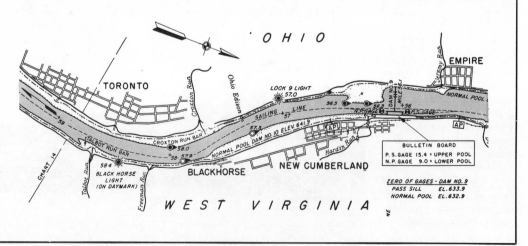

the length of each of the two lock lines in such cases.

Ladders are often recessed into lock walls and on some canals small craft by choice will follow the ladder up, rung by rung, with boat hook or lock lines. On the Ohio, this is frowned upon and boats are requested not to use the ladders. In addition to big bollards along the top of the lock wall, some locks have other recessed posts at intervals in the walls in vertical line. Locking up, lines can be cleared successively from lower posts and transferred to higher ones within reach. In other locks, floating mooring hooks move up and down to follow the pool levels.

Rising or falling, stand by your lock lines at all times and tend them carefully. This requires a hand forward and another aft, though with only two aboard the helmsman could handle the after line. One of the most dangerous practices is to make fast to a bollard above and then secure to a bitt or cleat on deck. If the level drops, your craft is "hung," with risk of serious damage.

Entering and leaving locks, it's always imperative to throttle down and keep the boat under complete control. This is especially true when locking through with other boats. Sometimes, on fleet cruises, it will be necessary to tie up two abreast at each lock wall. This is entirely feasible as long as all boats are intelligently handled. On sail-away cruises to New York from the plant of a western New York State boatbuilder, fleets of twenty or more were handled successfully without damage to any.

Occasionally one hears cautions concerning the possibility of a boat's being tossed about as water boils into locks from the open valves. Actually, lock tenders on our inland waters are careful to control this flow, and there is little cause for apprehension on this score. With a light craft, however, some thought should be given to placement in a lock when passing through with large commercial craft. A light hull, directly astern of a powerful tug, can take quite a tossing around when her big wheel starts to throw the water astern.

There are various kinds of locks, all of which accomplish the same end of effecting a change of level. Gates may swing or roll back and in cases are hoisted in vertical lift, permitting traffic to pass through under the gate. Such is the case at Little Falls, N. Y. On the Trent Waterway in Canada, a hydraulic lock lifts the boat in a water-filled chamber and in another instance a marine railway actually hauls the boat out to get her up over a hill. Through passage on a waterway like the Trent, then, is obviously

U.S. Light	
Daymark	
Temporary buoys:	
Can (black)	
Nun (red)	
Permanent type buoy	
Can (black)	
Nun (red)	
Flasher buoys:	
Can (white flash)	
Nun (red flash)	
Radar buoy	
Gage	
Arrival Point	
for Lockages	
General bank line	
Water's edge at	
pool stage	
Bar, with less than	
project 9' depth	
at pool stage	
Aerial crossings:	
Power	
Telephone	
Seaplane Base	

Legend of symbols used on navigation charts of the Ohio River. Some of these are illustrated on the chart shown on preceding page.

limited to craft within the capacity of the ways to haul. At Troy, N. Y., a Federally operated time lock opens only at stated intervals—on the hour—occasionally causing a slight delay in lockage.

Lock permits, obtainable without charge from the Superintendent of Operation and Maintenance, State Department of Public Works, Albany, N. Y., are required to navigate the New York State Barge Canal. On Western Rivers, no special permission or clearance is required for passage through the locks. There are regulations to be observed, however, and copies of these should be obtained from Army Engineer Offices at Chicago or St. Louis.

The point made by Army Engineers as to the necessity

Photographs by Corps of Engineers, U. S. Army

Longest vessels in the world are not the big ocean liners but the tows on Western Rivers made up of barges propelled by a towboat at the stern. Length often exceeds 1000 feet. They should always be passed with great care, especially at bends.

West of Rochester the New York State Barge Canal passes through a rock cut. Speed limit is 6 statute miles per hour.

At Lockport, New York, lock tenders open the gates for craft ready to lock down. The locks here are double.

for caution when approaching locks is well taken. They emphasize the importance of following the buoyed channel closely. Some years ago, a cruiser bound down the Hudson missed the lock at Troy, which lies far over on the east bank, and went *over* the dam. By rare good fortune, she was able to continue her cruise to New York under her own power. Looking down the river from above the dam, it's virtually impossible to see any break in the water's surface, yet there's no excuse for such an occurrence if one pays attention to the buoys as indicated on the chart.

Actually, there are times and places when it is proper to go *over* a dam, strange as that may sound. On the Ohio, they use a movable type of dam having a lock chamber on one side and "bear traps" on the other. In the middle, between them, there are movable wickets which can be held in an upright position during low water stages and lowered at times of high water. When the wickets are up, traffic necessarily passes through the lock. With the wickets down, at high water, boats run through the navigable pass, over the dam, without locking. By day, it is important to watch the bulletin boards at the locks to know whether the lock or the navigable pass is to be used. By night, distinguishing lights are used on the guide walls. When the navigable pass is being used, the gage reading on the powerhouse bulletin board shows the depth of water over the pass sill at the dam. The reading is in white on a scarlet background, and is preceded by the word PASS.

One point that needs careful watching is the strong current set when bear traps are open. These bear traps are devices used to regulate pool levels within certain limits without having to lower the wickets in the navigable pass. In your passage downstream, while waiting for a lock to open, the set may tend to draw you away from the lock approach toward the dam.

One other caution—approach each lock with care and heed the signals at every one. The fact that the navigable pass is in use at one dam is no assurance that it will be at the next.

Be on guard against current set anywhere near a spillway.

Not all waterways are merely improved versions of natural rivers and lakes. Artificial land cuts are often used to connect navigable waterways and provide continuous passage between major bodies of water. Lake Champlain is accessible from the upper reaches of the Hudson only because of a 24-mile land cut connecting the two. A dredged land cut is also encountered at the western end of the Erie Canal to connect Lake Erie with mid-state rivers.

Narrow cuts of this kind pose problems of their own. A typical earth section of dredged canal might have a bottom width of only 75 feet, at the surface perhaps 125 feet, and a depth, let's say, of 12 feet. If normal cruising speeds were maintained through such sections, the bank would be quickly washed down into the channel and maintenance problems would be aggravated. Consequently in such artificial waterways, speed limits are rigidly enforced. In New York canals, the limit is 6 statute mph in the land lines, 10 mph in canalized rivers and lake sections. It's wise to heed the regulations as lock keepers use their phone connections between locks to check on running times.

Some of the land lines are cut through solid rock, perhaps only 100 feet or less in width. This makes a virtual trough with ragged walls of blasted rock. Anyone who has ever run in company with other craft in a confined channel like this knows full well how the wakes of a group of boats may synchronize at times and build up out of all proportion to that of a single craft running alone. Unless serious thought is given to maintenance of moderate speed, regardless of legal limits, small craft can get out of control under such conditions and yaw exactly as they would in a steep swell over an inlet bar. We've seen it happen, with damage to the boat, when the boat's run was ultimately checked by the rock walls.

Most of our inland waterways handle considerable commercial traffic. In a narrow dredged cut a big tug or tanker requires the better part of the channel. As she approaches, you'll see a sizable bow wave built up, practically running ahead of her, and the water drawn away by suction to lower the level at both her sides amidships. Give such traffic as wide a berth as safety with respect to channel widths permits.

Tugs with tows astern in narrow waterways present a real problem to approaching small craft. Fortunately, most of the "towing" today is done by pushing scows and barges ahead of the tug. This keeps the whole tow under better control as a single unit. In times past we have, however, seen a single file of a dozen or more pleasure boats following the right hand edge of a channel, start to pass a tug with tow astern at a bend. The first boats would get through nicely with

A pleasure steamer locking through one of the TVA locks.

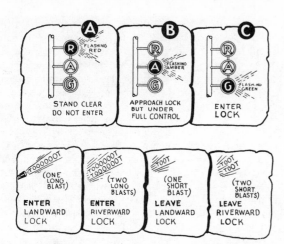

A FLASHING RED	**B** FLASHING AMBER	**C** FLASH. NO GREEN
R A G	R A G	R A G
STAND CLEAR DO NOT ENTER	APPROACH LOCK BUT UNDER FULL CONTROL	ENTER LOCK

T-O-O-O-O-O-T (ONE LONG BLAST)	T-O-O-O-O-O-T T-O-O-O-O-O-T (TWO LONG BLASTS)	TOOT (ONE SHORT BLAST)	TOOT TOOT (TWO SHORT BLASTS)
ENTER LANDWARD LOCK	**ENTER** RIVERWARD LOCK	**LEAVE** LANDWARD LOCK	**LEAVE** RIVERWARD LOCK

Signal lights and air horn signals used on the Western Rivers to control traffic at locks. (From "Locking Through," prepared by Army Engineers, St. Louis.)

ample passing room but the swinging barges would gradually cut down the passing room to starboard to such an extent that boats bringing up the rear would be forced to pass to port. Even with the tow ahead, this swinging effect must be taken into account at narrow bends so it's generally wise to pass on the inside of the bends.

Big rafts of barges bunched together on the Mississippi in one vast tow may cover many acres in extent. The prudent pleasure boat pilot will appreciate the problems of handling such colossal floats and never jeopardize their activities, regardless of any considerations of right of way. Integrated tows are often made up of a bowpiece, a group of square-ended barges, and a towboat (at the stern) lashed together in one streamlined unit 1000 feet or more in length. At night, to an observer in a small boat, the towboat's lights may be more conspicuous than those on the tow far out ahead. Consequently, special caution is indicated when attempting to run the rivers at night, even though the river itself be so well lighted as to make this feasible. When commercial traffic is using powerful searchlights their blinding beams may make it impossible for the small boatman to see anything at all. Shore lights add to the difficulty, because of reflections in the water. Then, too, in some rivers, especially in flood, there's the hazard of floating and partially submerged debris.

On all the rivers, recreational craft should give commercial tows a wide berth. In particular they should stay away from the front of tows when under way. If you happen to stall in such a spot, it might be impossible for the tow to stop or steer clear. With the way she carries, a commercial tow may at times travel half a mile or more before she can come to a full stop.

The need for keeping a boat under control on approach to locks has already been mentioned. The same applies to bridges, especially when strong currents tend to sweep a boat down toward the bridge structure. This takes on increased significance when vessels must wait to allow a bridge to open after signalling. Unless care is exercised the current may carry a boat down and put her in a position from which it may be virtually impossible to extricate her without twin-screw power. It is on this principle that Western River Rules grant right of way to a "descending" vessel (one proceeding downstream) since the "ascending" vessel is under far better control. Difficulty of maneuvering is aggravated when vessels are trying to handle tows.

River currents sometimes attain such speed that navigation upstream is unfeasible though capably handled boats may safely be taken down. Such is the case in the Galop Rapids of the St. Lawrence where the velocity may run around 12-13 mph. Some river boats have power enough to ascend certain rapids. As a general rule, it is best to avoid them by using canals and locks that by-pass them, unless the skipper has local knowledge or engages the services of a local pilot.

From Kodachrome by Wm. H. Koelbel

A guard gate on the Champlain Canal. Gates of this kind can be lowered when work is being done on the locks below.

Photograph courtesy J. D. Tennison, Jr.

Just below the Memphis bridges, vessels work over a wreck caused when a barge got out of control in the river current and sank after striking bridge piers at high water. Day signal (double frustums of a cone, base to base, in vertical line) indicating vessel at work on wreck, is prominently displayed.

Guntersville (Ala.) Yacht Club on TVA's Guntersville Lake.

Photograph from TVA

Finding an Anchorage or Mooring for Overnight Stops on the Rivers. River Charts and How They Differ from Those of Coastal Waters. Local Knowledge for Boatmen Running the Mississippi River.

PROBLEMS of where to tie up or anchor for the night are always with us when cruising, whether on coastal or inland waters. On coastal waters, it may be essentially a matter of finding a sheltered cove or basin to avoid risk of a rough night in an exposed anchorage. As a rule on the rivers, shelter from blows is closer at hand, yet there are areas great enough in expanse to work up sizable seas, especially with the wind opposing the current. Then too, there is the matter of finding protection in narrow waterways from passing river traffic and the wake it throws. Finally, there's always the question of personal preference as to whether one seeks the seclusion of quiet anchorages off the beaten track or prefers the activity usually associated with cities and centers of population.

The development in recent years of new marinas on some of the inland waterways—the TVA, for example—has been of great help in this respect. Not only do they provide a place to tie up for the night, but fuel supplies and other necessities are generally available at the marina or near at hand.

On the Tennessee River, safety harbors and landings have been provided for use in case of bad weather, mechanical failure or other contingencies. Their locations are shown on the charts. Safety harbors are usually coves off the navigable channel. Direction boards on shore define the entrance, and cross boards mark the upper limits.

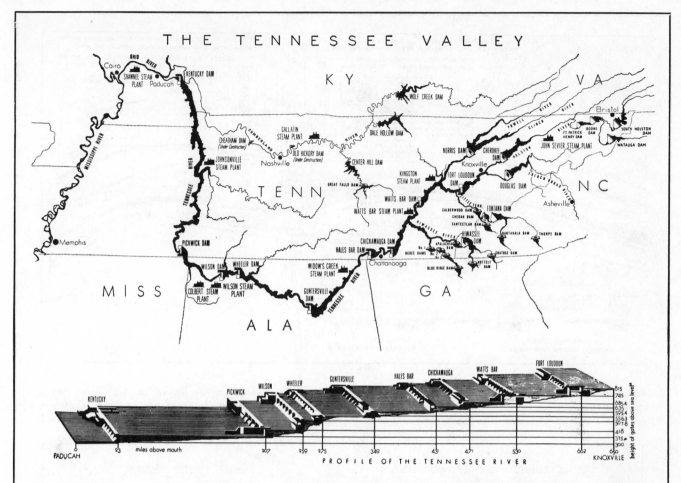

THE TENNESSEE VALLEY

Map of the Tennessee Valley showing location of dams in the TVA system. Dams impound water, creating vast lakes for recreational boating, while locks permit through traffic to by-pass dams on cruises throughout the system. Potential flood waters are stored in wet seasons, released in dry seasons, and minimum depth of 9 feet is maintained for navigation.

Safety landings are areas where banks have been cleared of stumps, boulders and snags, so vessels may land safely. Upper and lower limits are marked by direction boards—white if a 9′ depth is available at all pool stages; orange if the depth is 9′ at all except low water stages of the river.

The New York State Barge Canal provides terminals at intervals along the route, though these may be occupied by commercial craft. Of concrete, the terminals require adequate fendering when used by small pleasure craft. In order to allow for the seasonal range in levels, or stages, on Western rivers, most yacht clubs are afloat,

on strings of barges, necessitating a long climb up the river bank at low-water stages to get to town.

Frequently a glance at the chart (or navigational map) will reveal a likely place to anchor for the night. A widening of the river may offer an opportunity to get out of the reach of traffic, a small tributary or slough may invite exploration (with caution, sounding as you go), or the natural configuration of river banks and bars may provide a natural harbor with complete protection. Islands in mid-river frequently leave a secondary channel fine for small craft of easy draft, while heavy-draft commercial

Photograph from Joliet Assn. of Commerce

The Illinois Waterway provides a navigable connecting waterway between the Great Lakes at Chicago on Lake Michigan to Grafton, Ill., on the Mississippi by way of the Chicago, Des Plaines and Illinois Rivers. View at left shows a tow passing through bridges at Joliet, Illinois.

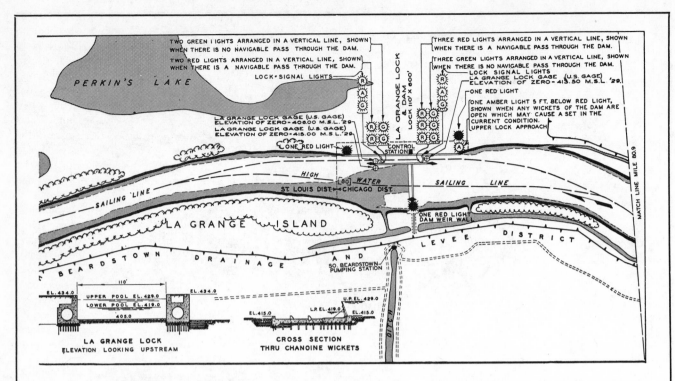

TWO GREEN LIGHTS ARRANGED IN A VERTICAL LINE, SHOWN WHEN THERE IS NO NAVIGABLE PASS THROUGH THE DAM.

TWO RED LIGHTS ARRANGED IN A VERTICAL LINE, SHOWN WHEN THERE IS A NAVIGABLE PASS THROUGH THE DAM.

LOCK-SIGNAL LIGHTS

THREE RED LIGHTS ARRANGED IN A VERTICAL LINE, SHOWN WHEN THERE IS A NAVIGABLE PASS THROUGH THE DAM.

THREE GREEN LIGHTS ARRANGED IN A VERTICAL LINE, SHOWN WHEN THERE IS NO NAVIGABLE PASS THROUGH THE DAM.

LOCK SIGNAL LIGHTS

LA GRANGE LOCK GAGE (U.S. GAGE) ELEVATION OF ZERO-413.50 M.S.L. '29.

ONE RED LIGHT

ONE AMBER LIGHT 5 FT. BELOW RED LIGHT, SHOWN WHEN ANY WICKETS OF THE DAM ARE OPEN WHICH MAY CAUSE A SET IN THE CURRENT CONDITION. UPPER LOCK APPROACH

PERKIN'S LAKE

LA GRANGE LOCK & DAM LOCK 110' X 600'

LA GRANGE LOCK GAGE (U.S. GAGE) ELEVATION OF ZERO-406.00 M.S.L.'29 LA GRANGE LOCK GAGE (U.S. GAGE) ELEVATION OF ZERO-415.00 M.S.L.'29

ONE RED LIGHT

CONTROL STATION

SAILING LINE

SAILING LINE

HIGH [80] WATER ST. LOUIS DIST.-CHICAGO DIST.

MATCH LINE MILE 80.9

LA GRANGE ISLAND

ONE RED LIGHT DAM WEIR WALL

LEVEE DISTRICT

BEARDSTOWN DRAINAGE AND

SO. BEARDSTOWN PUMPING STATION

EL. 434.0   110'   EL. 434.0
UPPER POOL EL. 429.0
LOWER POOL EL. 419.0
405.0

U.P.EL. 429.0
EL. 415.0   L.P. EL. 419.0   EL. 415.0

LA GRANGE LOCK
ELEVATION LOOKING UPSTREAM

CROSS SECTION
THRU CHANOINE WICKETS

Extract from one of the Illinois Waterway charts. With wicket-type dams which can be lowered at high-water stages, traffic uses the navigable pass through the dam, indicated by "high water sailing line." System of lights, explained on chart, shows whether lock or navigable pass is to be used. Below, the symbols. Lights and nun buoys in red on original.

LEGEND OF SYMBOLS

GENERAL

SHORE LINE ────────

LEVEE

9-FOOT CONTOUR ────────────

MILES FROM GRAFTON ──────── [50]

VERTICAL BRIDGE CLEARANCE FOR 80 FOOT HORIZONTAL CLEARANCE

MOVABLE TYPE BRIDGE, NO OPERATING MACHINERY INSTALLED

U.S. GAGE

AIDS TO NAVIGATION

FLASHING POST LIGHT IN PEORIA LAKE ────────

POST LIGHT ────────

FLOAT LIGHT ────────

DAYMARK ────────

BLACK (CAN) BUOY ────────

RED (NUN) BUOY ────────

BRIDGE CLEARANCE GAGE ────────

FLASHING SIGNAL LIGHTS ON BRIDGE ────────

traffic is confined to the main channel. When a river cuts a channel behind a section of bank, a "towhead" is formed. Sometimes these are filled in at the upper end by river deposits, forming a natural protected anchorage in the lower end. At times you can get behind a pile dike, a type of structure used on rivers to protect banks from washing away. The dike juts out into the river and, by tying up to one of the piles just inside the outer end, on the downstream side, you have protection not only from passing traffic but from floating debris as well. When entering sloughs between islands in search of an anchorage, beware of submerged wing dams at the upstream end. To be safe, enter and leave from the downstream end.

In some cases sufficient protection for an overnight anchorage can be obtained behind a mid-river bar. Occasionally one can find a tiny cove (like Partridge Harbor on Lake Champlain) where there's room for only a few boats, and no room to swing at anchor, so you anchor the bow off and run a stern line to the nearest tree ashore.

One trick they use on Western rivers is the so-called river hitch. To tie up to a bank for the night, the boat's bow is held up to the bank with power while a line is run to a nearby tree. Then a sapling is cut, 15 to 20 feet long, and lashed from bank to stern to hold the stern off. Another line ashore holds the stern in.

As a rule when tying up for the night on inland rivers, lines need not be laid with allowance for the tidal range common on the coasts. On tidal rivers, it is of course a factor (6-foot range at Albany) and even on the inland rivers there's always the chance of a change in level with hard rainstorms, etc. It pays to observe the practices of local craft and to be guided accordingly. Tied to a barge or float which will itself rise and fall with changing levels, the boatman need provide only such slack in lines as may be required for comfort if a passing craft happens to throw a disturbing wake.

The character of the bottom varies widely on inland waterways. Especially in their lower courses, river bottoms are often soft mud, pointing to the desirability of carrying, in your complement of ground tackle, at least one anchor with broad flukes of a design that will dig down till it reaches good holding bottom. In such spots, the anchor with spidery arms and flukes will cut through and provide no holding power at all, whereas on a hard bottom the same anchor might be highly efficient. When you get into rocky bottoms or areas infested with roots and snags, you will want to resort to one of the tricks for being prepared to recover the anchor if fouled. One easy way is to use a light line from the anchor crown long enough to reach the surface, where the end of line is buoyed. If the anchor snags, pick up the buoy and raise the anchor with the trip line, crown first. Some anchors are provided with slip rings, shear pins or other device to make them snag-proof.

On the subject of anchoring, there's a point to bear in mind when piloting in bodies of water like Lake Champlain. Along some shores, which may be particularly inviting because of their scenic attractions, you may find a depth of a couple of hundred feet running up to sheer cliff shores. If your power fails, your anchor would be of little use in such depths, and if the breeze is toward those cliffs you're on a bad lee shore.

When anchoring on the big rivers near a sand bar or island, or, for that matter, when beaching the boat to go ashore in such a place, a good rule to follow is to pick the downstream rather than the upper end. If an anchor drags or if for any reason you get aground on the upstream end, it's practically like being on a lee shore except that in this case the current, instead of the wind, is constantly working to drive you harder aground. Water at the downstream end is likely to be quieter and the eddies encountered there may help to free a grounded boat. Grounding hard on the rivers may be more troublesome than it is on tidewater, where the next rising tide will generally free a craft without any other assistance.

One of the points likely to strike the tidewater boatman most forcefully when he takes to the Western rivers is the radical difference between river charts and the Coast and Geodetic Survey charts to which he is accustomed. River charts are commonly in the form of books of "navigational maps," each page covering successive short stretches of the river in strip form. A typical example is the bound volume prepared by the Mississippi River Commission, Vicksburg, Miss., to cover the Mississippi from Cairo, Ill., to the Gulf of Mexico. This is on a scale of 1:62,500 (approximately 1 inch to the mile). All of the soundings (with a few exceptions) and detailed positions of rocks, reefs, ledges and shoals so familiar on

A view of the upstream side of Alton Lock and Dam No. 26 on the Mississippi River above St. Louis, Missouri. Note the double locks (extreme left). The landward lock of the pair is considerably larger than the riverward lock. Signals indicate which to use.

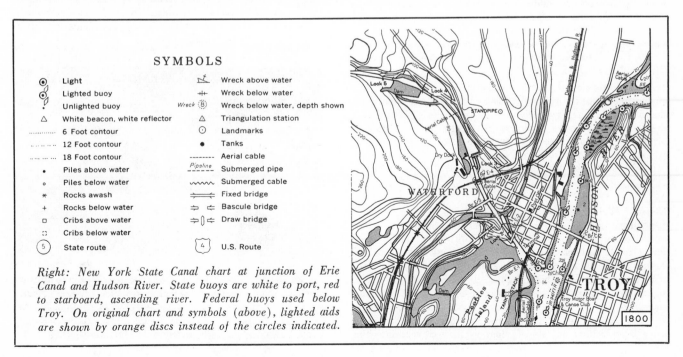

Right: New York State Canal chart at junction of Erie Canal and Hudson River. State buoys are white to port, red to starboard, ascending river. Federal buoys used below Troy. On original chart and symbols (above), lighted aids are shown by orange discs instead of the circles indicated.

431

coastal charts are omitted. In their place the course of the river is traced in blue tint between heavy black lines which delineate the banks. A broken red line is used to indicate the channel line. Navigation lights are denoted by a red star with white dot in the center together with a number which designates its distance upstream above a fixed reference point—in this case A.H.P., "Above the Head of Passes." The Head of Passes is the point not far above the mouth where the river splits into separate channels leading through the delta into the Gulf. Mileages are given in red every five miles, with red circles at one-mile intervals. Mileages above and below the Head of Passes are printed in red. A detailed table is given in the book, listing in alphabetical order all towns, cities, bridges, mouths of rivers, and other important features adjacent to the main channel, with distances (AHP) in miles and map numbers on which the features appear.

Before starting a cruise on the lower Mississippi, the pilot should make a careful study of the legend which appears on the inside front cover of the chart book. Symbols used to designate the various aids to navigation are given, with abbreviations, topographic and hydrographic features, and an illustration of a typical crossing channel (the latter marked by buoys during periods of low water). Charts are on the polyconic projection and elevations refer to mean level.

On the Illinois Waterway

The book of charts for the Illinois Waterway is prepared by the Chicago District of the Army Engineers. A page of general information in this volume covers practically everything the pilot needs to know in navigating the waterway as he follows his charts. Attention should be paid to the legend of symbols, which differ in some respects from those found on coastal charts. The main channel is shown in white, shoal areas in blue tint. The "sailing line" is indicated by a broken line, the miles from Grafton in brackets in black. Scale is 1 inch to 1000 feet.

Aids to navigation include post lights or range lights with fixed white lights, and some flashing lights. Daymarks are white diamonds on posts without lights. Red nuns are found on the left edge of the channel, black cans on the right edge, proceeding downstream. Detailed information on the operation and lighting of bridges and locks and locking regulations are all given in the Illinois Waterway chart book.

Charts for the Middle and Upper Mississippi from Cairo to Minneapolis (also prepared by the Chicago District of the Army Engineers) resemble those for the lower river except that they are done in black and white with no color to help distinguish significant features. Mileages are reckoned above Cairo. A separate book is available for the Mississippi from Cairo at the mouth of the Ohio to Grafton at the mouth of the Illinois Waterway.

A small booklet of charts for Navigation Pools 25 and 26 of the Mississippi River and Illinois Waterway (published by the St. Louis Engineer Office) is distinguished primarily by the fact that it shows hazard areas (under 6-foot depth) in bright red shading, harbors or anchorage areas with an anchor symbol, and the availability of fuel, water, railways, launching ramps, repairs and docking facilities at specified locations.

When the salt water pilot turns to the book of charts of New York State Canals (published by the U. S. Lake Survey, Detroit, Mich.) he finds himself on more familiar ground. Land areas are tinted a light buff, channels in white, depths of 12 feet or less in a light blue tint with dotted depth curves for 1 and 2 fathoms and distinct black lines delineating the banks. Here, too, are the buoy symbols (diamond and dot) with orange disc signifying lights. Buoys and other aids on shore have their identifying numbers given and rough scattered soundings appear to give the pilot a good idea as to whether he dare venture out of the channel to seek an anchorage in some bend behind an island. Buoy symbols appear in white to port and red to starboard, entering from seaward, to correspond with the white and red lights they carry at night. Even rocks and wrecks are indicated with symbols similar to those used on coastal charts. The scale in this series of charts, with a few exceptions, is 1:21,120 (3 inches to the mile). Reference plane is normal pool level. Arrows indicating direction of current flow, used on other river charts, do not appear on those of New York waterways.

Tennessee Easy to Navigate

Commercial towboat pilots consider the Tennessee River channel to be one of the best marked and easiest to navigate of all the inland waterways. The Tennessee itself is navigable for cruisers for 650 continuous miles from Paducah, Kentucky, to Knoxville, Tenn. The channel is marked with buoys, lights and dayboards so that it can be navigated both day and night. Locks in each of the nine main stream dams are open 24 hours a day every day and may be used without charge. Pleasure boats are locked through with commercial tows when there is room, or are entitled to separate lockage at the end of each hour. In addition to the main navigation channels, there are about 225 miles of feeder channels, marked by buoys and dayboards, which are used by recreational craft.

Navigation charts are available in two sizes for the entire length of the Tennessee, as well as navigation maps for the thirteen major tributary reservoirs, from the Tennessee Valley Authority, Knoxville, Tenn. The charts, on scales of 1 inch to the mile, and 1 inch to the half-mile, are multi-colored, showing sailing lines and aids to navigation, including buoys, lights, daymarks, safety harbors, hazards, and depths of water at all reservoir pool stages. Other important features are highways, railroads, bridges, wire crossings, terminals, docks, piers, landings and towns. Many private boat docks offering a variety of services and accommodations are scattered along the 10,000 miles of TVA shoreline. A survey of these is available in a folder from the TVA Information Office at Knoxville. Bound sets of charts of the Tennessee are also available from District Engineers at Cincinnati, Nashville and Louisville.

Charts of the Ohio River, in the form of bound sets of continuous multilith charts, are available from District Engineers at Pittsburgh, Huntington and Louisville. There are three sets—Pittsburgh to Powhatan Point, Ohio; Powhatan Point to Aberdeen, Ohio; and Aberdeen to Cairo, Ill. On a scale of one inch to 2000 feet, they show sailing lines, lights, daymarks, arrival point markers for locks, normal pool elevations, mouths of tributary systems, location of bars, channel buoys, bridges, aerial crossings, seaplane bases, docks, terminals, landings, and navigation structures. No soundings are given. Mileages zero at Pittsburgh.

At River Mile 775 AHP in Tennessee on the Mississippi a towboat with 23 barges passes a channel dredge. Small craft are advised to pass such dredges with caution and to avoid areas upstream from the dredge and floating discharge pipe line which usually extends several hundreds of feet.

In addition to these, there is also a set of photolithographic charts of the Ohio from Pittsburgh to the mouth in 281 sheets, on a scale of one inch to 600 feet. These show topographic features, sailing lines, 5-foot contours, high water, low water, normal pool lines, bench marks, etc.

A detailed list of all charts of the Ohio and its navigable tributaries—the Allegheny, Big Sandy, Cumberland, Green, Barren, Nolin, Rough, Kanawha, Kentucky, White and Eel— is available from the Division Engineer, Ohio River Division, in Cincinnati. This list is in the form of a mimeographed Division Bulletin and contains much other valuable data on navigation of the Ohio.

Missing from the river map is the compass rose of coastal charts which enables the pilot to lay a compass course and determine true and magnetic bearings and courses. River charts generally show instead a simple arrow to indicate true north, and on strip charts north may not necessarily be at the top of the page. On charts of the Lower Mississippi, parallels of latitude and meridians of longitude are given. The compass is little used on river boats and the binoculars take its place to aid the pilot in sighting from one navigational aid to the next. In fog, this means that pleasure boat traffic comes pretty much to a standstill, though the big commercial craft carry on using radar for their eyes. This is not to imply that the compass can be dispensed with on all rivers and lakes. In the lower reaches of larger tidal rivers, like the Connecticut, compass courses are occasionally laid in fog, and on the Great Lakes where straight-line courses of 100 miles or more are not unusual, the compass is an indispensable accessory.

Charts of the Great Lakes

Piloting problems on the Great Lakes are much the same as they are along the coast because of the great expanse of water involved. Charts of the Great Lakes, published by the U. S. Lake Survey, are excellent, covering features of the navigable waters in great detail. They show depths of water (the lesser depths in blue tint), safe channels, submerged reefs and shoals, aids to navigation, adjacent shorelines with topographic features and landmarks, types of bottom, and much additional related information. Scales of the charts vary from as large as 1:2.500 to 1:20,000 for harbor charts and insets, down to 1:80,000 to 1:130,000 for coast charts, and 1:400,000 or 500,000 for general charts of individual lakes. Smallest scale used is the general chart of all the Great Lakes, at 1:1,200,000. For close work on the rivers, the scale varies from 1:15,000 to 1:40,000.

On Lake charts, the familiar compass rose is available, showing in magenta tint both true and magnetic directions, with the variation stated. In parts of the Lakes, variation reduces to zero, where, except for deviation, which is always with us, magnetic and true courses are alike. Elsewhere on the Lakes, great deposits of iron ore in the earth produce a strong local attraction, most pronounced along the north shore of Lake Superior where variation has been observed to change from 26° to 7° in a distance of 650 feet.

Most Lake charts are on the polyconic projection and show some of the principal courses between ports, giving the course in degrees true with the distances in statute miles. Comparative elevations are referred to mean tide as calculated at New York.

To supplement the information available on Lake charts, cruising boatmen should have a copy of the Great Lakes Pilot (published by the U. S. Lake Survey, Detroit). Corresponding to the Coast Pilots used on coastal waters, it provides detailed information which cannot be given on the charts. Included are full descriptions of the waters charted, laws and regulations governing navigation, bridge clearances, signals for locks and bridges, dimensions and capacities of marine railways, and weather information. Purchasers of the Pilot get, free, seven monthly supplements (May-November) to keep the Pilot up to date.

The Army Engineers at Vicksburg, Miss., publish an informative pamphlet, "Mississippi River Navigation," which contains not only a great deal of interesting background information on navigation of the Mississippi, but also a few pages with explicit instructions "For Part-Time Pilots," the pleasure boatmen who are using the great river in increasing numbers.

Among other things, the Engineers caution against regarding the Mississippi with insufficient respect. The lower river, they point out, is very large, with low-water widths of ½ mile and bankfull widths up to 9000 feet. These bankfull stages generally occur between December and July, most frequently in March or April. Low-water stages occur in the fall months, October and November.

Lake Pepin typifies the kind of exposed area that may be encountered even on the upper river. This lake, a broadening of the river proper, is 21 miles long and up to 2½ miles in width. Sizable seas build up in such areas. Current velocities on the Mississippi average 4 to 6 mph. At extreme high stages of the river, velocities may be even greater in the narrower sections. At low and medium stages velocities range from 2 to 2½ mph.

River Engineers call special attention to the many kinds of floating equipment constantly at work on construction and maintenance projects along the river. Hydraulic pipeline dredges may have long lengths of floating pipeline which must be avoided. Bank protection equipment carried on barges may extend several hundred feet from shore into the stream, frequently in the swiftest part of the current. Small craft should keep well clear of all such equipment because of the hazard of being swept under it. As a matter of fact, on all waters, river traffic should exercise caution and consideration when passing dredges and similar equipment, slowing down to avoid doing damage with the wake. Army Engineers have prepared regulations governing lights and day signals displayed by all types of craft working on river projects, and the passing of such equipment by other vessels. These will be found in full detail in one section of the Pilot Rules for Western Rivers.

Though in some areas small craft do tie up to the river banks, the Engineers urge caution here, too. Avoid, they advise, vertical banks which may be in a stage of active caving. Exposed tree roots in the banks should be viewed with suspicion as a possible evidence of recent erosion. Such areas obviously are places to avoid when seeking a place to tie up along the bank. Rock riprap can be rough on a boat's bottom.

As for navigation of the river itself, the Engineers point out, too, that sand bars encountered during periods of low water may be quite unstable. Consequently, caution should be exercised in using them for camping or swimming. Floating and partially submerged debris, such as tree trunks and branches, constitute a navigational hazard for small craft, requiring a sharp lookout at all times. The same applies to piloting in the shallower areas, to avoid submerged stumps and snags. Floating debris is generally at its worst in the spring months under flood conditions, when high water and drifting logs may also shift buoys from their charted locations.

River currents sometimes flow so fast that buoys are towed under, leaving only a V-shaped eddy on the surface to reveal their location. Coastal boatmen have sometimes experienced this condition at inlets. Sometimes the top of the buoy will be visible to a boat bound upstream, or the wake of a passing boat may expose it momentarily.

The V-shaped surface eddy left by a buoy partially or totally submerged in a strong current will necessarily point upstream, as the wake divides downstream from the buoy. Any surface wake like this is to be mistrusted, as a submerged obstacle may lurk beneath. This is not to be confused with the condition where two currents meet at the downstream end of a middle bar where converging surface eddies may also show as a V shape, pointing downstream.

One of the major aids to navigation along the Mississippi is the light on shore. In this view, illustrating the position of a typical light used for marking bends and upper and lower ends of crossings, the steamer Mississippi approaches Four Mile Bayou Light, River Mile 728 A.H.P. Number board visible just above the light shows the mileage on the river side.

Piloting on the Mississippi River. Aids to Navigation on the Rivers.

Light Lists and Other Publications of Interest to the River Boatman.

Some Special Rules of the Road Applicable to River Cruising.

ON its meandering way to the Gulf, the Mississippi winds and twists and bends in a sinuous course that adds many miles to the airline distance. The river is eternally changing, and Army Engineers are everlastingly at work to maintain and improve the navigable channels. Sometimes, a single loop in the river will necessitate a 10-mile run to gain one mile on the route south.

At some of the bends, when the river goes on a rampage under flood conditions, it will cut a channel across the narrow neck of land, forming what is called a chute and creating an island from what was once a peninsula. With-

out local knowledge it is usually wise to avoid the chutes and stick to the main channel. To save distance and straighten navigable channels, the Army Engineers have dredged cut-offs, like the chutes, and these become the new navigable channel.

This constant changing of the Mississippi's course, both by nature and by dredging, has left old channels as dead-end arms of the new, and elsewhere, by closing them off, has created horseshoe-shaped ("oxbow") lakes with no connection with the new channel. River piloting always demands close attention to the chart to avoid being shunted

Extract from the Mississippi River Light List, showing some of the lights and daymarks on the Illinois Waterway. Distances are given in statute miles, above Grafton. These agree with mileages given on aids to navigation. Note the data given on visibility of directional lights.

Name of aid Character and period of light	Number of miles from Grafton	Bank or side of channel	Remarks
GRIST ISLAND BEND DAYMARK	258.9	Left	
Grist Island Light Fl. W., 2 sec.	258.8	Right	Visible 360° with 3° directional light oriented downstream.
Barry Island Light Fl. W., 2 sec.	256.0	Right	Visible 360° with 3° directional light oriented upstream.
Heule Light Fl. W., 2 sec.	255.1	Right	3° directional light oriented downstream; daymark.
C., R. I. & P. Ry Bridge, vertical lift. Clearances: Horizontal, 141 feet; vertical, closed 19.9 feet, open 47.5 feet, above pool stage.	254.1		
ROCK ISLAND BRIDGE DAYMARK	254.1	Left	Painted on bridge pier.

into one of the unnavigable arms, or a dead-end heading.

On the Mississippi, as on most rivers, the deepest water and the fastest current are usually found on the outside of bends, at the end of dikes and along the steep banks. As a rule, gently shelving shores should be given a wide berth. Always be wary of unusual surface conditions, especially at high water. A smooth slick or a line or broken water may reveal the presence of a submerged dike or wing dam, used to control the direction of flow of river current. As these wing dams are often submerged even at normal river stages, they constitute a real hazard unless close attention is paid to the chart.

No flat statement can be made as to the relative depth of water indicated by certain sets of surface conditions. This requires a river sense the pilot must develop with experience. On the one hand, where there is a chop in the channel there may be areas of relatively smooth slicks over the bars, especially if there is any weed growth present. As against this, there will be combinations of wind-current conditions where the channel will be comparatively smooth with ripples to reveal the bars. In some narrow river channels, with wind against the current, a small sea builds up in which the larger waves disclose the deeper water, growing progressively smaller until there is no sea at all on the bars at channel's edge. But under any given set of conditions, the boatman with an eye peeled for natural signs will, with the aid of his chart and the buoys, quickly learn to read the signs the river has for those eager to understand its secrets.

Boatmen running the rivers bring back widely conflicting reports of hazards encountered, or the absence of them. Perhaps this may be attributed to the fact that one made his cruise in the early spring, encountering high water, flood conditions, racing currents and drifting trees pos-ing a constant threat to propellers, even to hulls. Another, no doubt, has made his trip under ideal conditions in September or October, possibly as the first leg of a cruise down to the Gulf and Florida for the winter season. With water levels at a low stage and currents at reasonable velocities, no obstacles have been encountered on the entire cruise from Lakes to Gulf. There is that much difference in seasonal conditions. River navigation at extreme flood stages, as a rule, is not to be recommended without the services of an experienced pilot.

A typical example of this conflict in reports of conditions observed is the story of "sand boils" in the Mississippi caused by sand piling up on the river bed. One reports these whirlpool-like disturbances so violent that they practically throw the boat out of control. Others, in more favorable months, find them no worse than surface eddies felt at the helm, but certainly with no element of danger for a boat. (For a swimmer, it might be otherwise.)

Some river boatmen have reported underwater bearings ruined, jackets filled with silt, and water pump gears worn out at the end of one river run. Others have observed no difficulty whatever on this score. As a general rule, as in all other places where waters are laden with silt, the logical course is to provide, in advance, what protection is available in the form of effective water strainers, fresh water cooling systems, cutless type underwater bearings, and pump impellers of a type that will handle mud and sand better than bronze gears.

Discounting all the stories of violent current disturbances, the fact remains, of course, that current is a real factor to be reckoned with on the rivers. When one stream of some velocity flows out into another, a small boat crossing the current at the mouth will feel the effect of this set and will probably have to allow

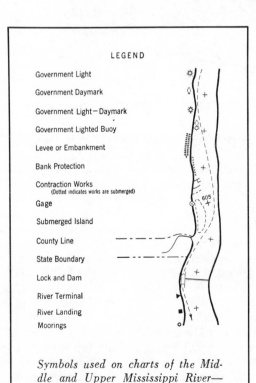

LEGEND

Government Light

Government Daymark

Government Light – Daymark

Government Lighted Buoy

Levee or Embankment

Bank Protection

Contraction Works
(Dotted indicates works are submerged)

Gage

Submerged Island

County Line

State Boundary

Lock and Dam

River Terminal

River Landing

Moorings

Symbols used on charts of the Middle and Upper Mississippi River—Cairo to Minneapolis—all in black and white, no distinguishing colors.

A fleet of pleasure craft heading downstream on the Mississippi River after leaving the lock chamber at Harvey Lock, on the west bank at New Orleans. About two dozen craft have passed through at one time in a single locking. Note the towboats standing by waiting their turn to enter lock. Gate (lower right corner) is closed; other (center) is open.

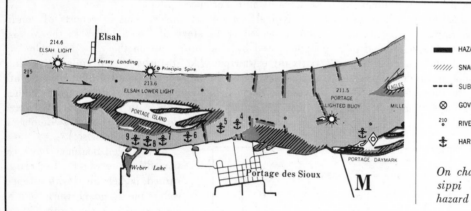

LEGEND

▬▬ HAZARD AREA (LESS THAN 6 FT BELOW EL 418.0 POOL 26)

///// SNAG, STUMPS, AND UNDERWATER HAZARDS

---- SUBMERGED GOVERNMENT DIKE

⊗ GOVERNMENT GAGE

210 RIVER MILEAGE

⚓ HARBOR OR TIE UP POINT

On charts of Pools 25 and 26 (Mississippi River and Illinois Waterway) hazard areas are shown in bright red.

somewhat by heading up into it. Pilots of heavy commercial craft are keenly aware of the way they carry with the current under their vessel. To the small boat operator it's a factor of relatively less importance, yet significant enough to be remembered at all times.

Since conditions on the river are in a constant state of flux, with channels changing and levels fluctuating, the river boatman should keep posted on the latest available data at all times. Just as the coastal boatman has his *Notices to Mariners* to turn to for authoritative information, so, too, the river boatman can refer to the *Navigation Bulletins* issued by the district offices of the Army Engineers at Memphis, Vicksburg and New Orleans. They show latest sailing directions, locations of navigational aids such as lights, buoys, etc., and similar up-to-date information required by the river pilot. For the Ohio, there are *Notices to Navigation Interests,* available from the Engineer Office at Pittsburgh.

Detailed information on rules and regulations applicable to the Mississippi may always be obtained from the Commander of the 2nd Coast Guard District at St. Louis.

One of the most helpful aids to the river pilot is the Light List, published by the U.S. Coast Guard. In it all lights, buoys and aids to navigation are tabulated, together with the river mileage (in statute miles to the nearest tenth) as reckoned from a zero point which may be at or near the mouth, as in the case of the Mississippi, or some other logical reference point, such as Pittsburgh on the Ohio. For the Lower Mississippi, a designation of Mile 104 AHP would be interpreted as 104 statute miles "Above the Head of Passes."

Aids to navigation along the river banks are conspicuously marked with mileages which correspond to the distances from the zero reference tabulated in the Light List. It is always an easy matter, therefore, to get a "fix." All you need do is read the mileage as posted on one of the light structures ashore, and compare with the mileage figures given on the chart. These lighted aids, of various shapes, are painted white and have names which appear on the charts and in the Light Lists as well. The mileage figures take the place of the odd and even numbers that are characteristic of buoys on coastal waters. They are a

Portion of U.S. Lake Survey Chart No. 43 (Saint Claire River) scale 1:40,000, drawn on the polyconic projection, in which distortion is very small and relative sizes are correctly preserved. Depths are referred to the sloping surface of the river at specified lake levels above mean tide at New York. Note the International Boundary, in mid-stream, and separate channels around the flats for traffic upstream and downstream. River traffic here is heavy. Illustration is to the same scale as the chart itself.

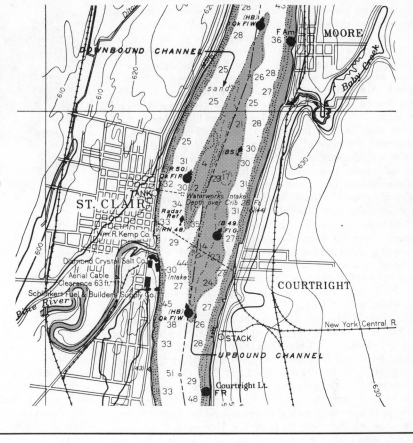

A light and mileage board, showing the river mile. Note the wake of the strong river current flowing past the piles of the dike. Currents are a factor to be reckoned with in river piloting.

distinct convenience in computing boat speeds and figuring the total day's run from the log.

In the larger rivers, it is usually feasible to run close to shore to identify the aid from the Light List, then head for the next, picking it up with binoculars if necessary. In closer work on some narrower rivers, as previously cautioned, it may be wise to ease around bends to follow the channel trend as delineated by the buoys rather than running straight from aid to aid. With no aids to serve as guides, the safest practice usually is to favor the center, keeping at least one-quarter of the river's width off the bank.

Designation of the banks of a river may at first be confusing. Left and right banks are named relative to your course *downstream*. The left bank, in river terminology, is the left bank as you face downstream; the right bank to your right facing downstream. On the New York State Barge Canal, however, when regulations refer to the "starboard" side of the canal, they mean the right hand side entering from Waterford. Thus the starboard side of the Champlain Canal is the east side; but on the

Erie Canal, the north side becomes the starboard side.

Most lights on the Mississippi River System show through 360°—visible, that is, all around the horizon. In some cases, however, directional aids project the light in one direction only. Some of these directional aids supplement the power of a 360° light by increasing the candlepower in one direction only. The arc through which the directional beam is visible varies with the navigational need of the locality. A concentrated beam may be used in a long narrow reach, but a wider spread in a more open area where conditions are less critical.

Generally speaking, lights on the Western Rivers are placed strategically at the upper and lower ends of crossings as marks to steer by, with additional lights between as required by conditions. Where there are no crossings, lights are used along the banks as passing lights. Reference to the chart will indicate how the light is to be used.

Daymarks on the Mississippi are usually white diamond shapes with number board at the top to designate the mileage. In the center, a red triangle is used for left bank aids (descending the river) and a vertical black rectangle for right (descending) bank aids. Daymarks have a reflector at each of the four corners, red on the left bank, white on the right bank. Daymarks among the trees on shore may take the form of two white boards crossed in the form of an X.

The coastal boatman will have no difficulty whatever with buoyage systems on the rivers. In the main, they will follow the same basic principle which puts black can-type buoys to port and red nun-type buoys to starboard when entering from seaward. Sometimes, as on the Mississippi, buoys will be topped with white for improved visibility, to show up against shore backgrounds.

Buoys on the Mississippi carry reflectors similar to those used on shore aids—red on the left bank, white on the right bank. Buoys marking wrecks show a quick flashing light, white or red on the left (descending) side of the channel, white or green on the right (descending) side. On buoys marking channel junctions or obstructions, the light characteristic is an interrupted quick flash (5 flashes 10 times a minute). Generally in mid-channel these lights will be white; red if toward the left side of the channel; and green if toward the right. As on the coast, the red-and-black horizontally banded buoy is used to mark junctions and obstructions. If found near the edge of a channel, it should be passed with caution, taking soundings to determine which is the proper side.

In all cases, buoys should be followed with reference to whatever charts or navigational maps may be available, as deviations from the conventional system of buoyage will be found in some rivers. On the New York State Barge Canal, for example, buoys are alike in shape on both sides of the channel. Entering from seaward, red buoys with red lights are on the starboard hand, but white buoys with white lights are found on the port hand. When craft are anchored at night along the side of the canal marked by red navigation lights, New York state authorities require the use of a red, rather than white, anchor light.

The chart, invariably, will prevent confusion and misunderstanding in following any system of buoyage. Symbols for can and nun buoys on Ohio River charts will seem particularly strange to coastal boatmen (See illustration, Part Two, from the legend.) In the Great Lakes Light List, Canadian buoys are specially identified by the letter C. Except for minor differences in design, the system of buoyage used in Canadian waters is in agreement with that adopted by the United States.

On some of the rivers, notably the Hudson and the Connecticut, where channels through flats in the river are stabilized and maintained by dredging, ranges on shore marked by conspicuous squares and diamonds are of great aid to the pilot in staying inside the limits of a narrow channel. Aligning the front and rear ranges, the pilot can hold his course in mid-channel, despite even heavy cross winds that might otherwise tend to set him off on the shoal to leeward.

Special River Rules

If the coastal boatman cruises far inland, his course will inevitably lead him into waters where Pilot Rules for traffic afloat—the Rules of the Road—differ from those to which he is accustomed. Consequently he should study in detail the rules applicable to the particular waters he uses.

On the coast, vessels operate mainly under two sets of rules —the International Rules when outside the boundaries prescribed for the high seas (even though this be just outside the inlet or off the beach), and the Inland Rules for waters inside these boundaries, with certain exceptions. It is these exceptions which require attention. For example, on the Great Lakes and their connecting and tributary waters as far east as Montreal, and the St. Marys River, vessels are subject to the Great Lakes Rules. On the Mississippi River system, with its tributaries, between its source and the Huey P. Long Bridge, ten miles above New Orleans (including part of the Atchafalaya River), and the Red River of the North, they are subject to the Pilot Rules for Western Rivers.

Elsewhere, the specific differences in rules under the four jurisdictions have been treated at length (see "How Pilot Rules Differ," *Piloting, Seamanship and Small Boat Handling*, Chapter IV). It is outside the scope of this series to repeat them here. In broad principle, Western River Rules are largely in general agreement with International Rules. However, it is interesting to point up a few of the outstanding differences encountered on the rivers.

We have already called attention to one Western River rule for vessels meeting in narrow channels, which gives right of way to a vessel bound downstream. Here is an example of a

Photograph courtesy J. D. Tennison, Jr.

A typical Mississippi river bank riprapped with cement to protect banks against erosion. Boatmen must use care near such banks due to risk of damage to the boat's bottom.

special rule having particular significance to the river pilot. The ascending (burdened) vessel, bound upstream, must sound the first passing signal, but vessels pass on the side determined by the (privileged) descending vessel.

Ascending vessels, on the Western Rivers, stop if necessary below the entrance of narrow channels to allow descending vessels to pass through. At the confluence of two rivers, the vessel having the other to port gives the first signal.

Bends in rivers, insofar as floating traffic is concerned, may be compared with blind corners on the road. Western River Rules provide that when a vessel could not be seen at a distance of 600 yards, three distinct blasts are to be sounded on the whistle. This warning signal must be answered by any approaching vessel within hearing around the bend, and the vessels exchange the usual passing signals only when they come within sight of each other. (On waters other than Western Rivers, the warning signal at a bend is a long, or prolonged, blast.)

When a steam vessel leaves her dock or anchorage, she gives the same signal (three distinct blasts) as prescribed for steam vessels nearing a bend.

Commercial craft on Western Rivers use a special amber visual signal synchronized with their passing whistle signal blasts. Motorboats are exempt from this rule. On both the Western Rivers and Great Lakes passing whistle signals are given in all weathers, regardless of visibility.

The fog signal for power-driven vessels under way on the Rivers is 3 distinct blasts every minute (2 of equal length, followed by a longer one). Sailing vessels give the same fog signals as power-driven vessels, but use the fog horn.

When towing, power-driven vessels sound 3 distinct blasts of equal length, at intervals of not more than 1 minute. Steamers lying to during fog or thick weather, when another vessel is heard approaching, give 1 tap on the bell if lying at the right bank, 2 taps if lying at the left bank, at 1-minute intervals.

One other fundamental difference, peculiar to Western River rules, requires a privileged vessel to hold her course, but not her speed. When risk of collision exists, all power-driven vessels reduce speed or stop if necessary.

If in cruising the Great Lakes and northern rivers, you should cross the International Boundary into Canada, bear in mind that there are customs and immigration regulations to be observed.

For detailed information on rules of the road, right of way, whistle signals, fog signals, lights for all types of craft and other pertinent regulations, the boatman is referred to the Pilot Rules, available free from Coast Guard Marine Inspection Offices in principal ports, or the Commandant (CHS), U.S. Coast Guard, Washington, D.C.

PUBLICATIONS OF INTEREST TO RIVER PILOTS

One of the best single sources of information concerning charts of inland waters and other publications on river piloting is the Mississippi River Commission, Corps of Engineers, U. S. Army, P.O. Box 80, Vicksburg, Miss. They publish a comprehensive mimeographed list of offices which issue charts of the various sections of the Mississippi, Missouri, Ohio and other tributaries, the Illinois Waterway, Great Lakes, etc. This list also includes mention of many publications of the Coast Guard and other government agencies. A Division Bulletin listing in detail all charts of the Ohio and its tributaries is prepared by the Division Engineer, Ohio River Division, P.O. Box 1159, Cincinnati 1, Ohio.

RIVER CHARTS, as well as the indispensable **NAVIGATION BULLETINS** and **NOTICES TO NAVIGATION INTERESTS** are distributed by the various offices of the Corps of Engineers, U. S. Army. in the areas over which they have jurisdiction. They are located at:

Memphis District—P.O. Box 97, Memphis 1, Tenn.
Vicksburg District—P.O. Box 60, Vicksburg, Miss.
New Orleans District—Foot of Prytania Street, New Orleans, La.
St. Louis District—420 Locust St., St. Louis 2, Mo.
Rock Island District—Clock Tower Building, Rock Island, Ill.
St. Paul District—U. S. Post Office & Customhouse, 180 E. Kellogg Blvd., St. Paul 1, Minn.
Missouri River Division—Farm Credit Bldg., 206 So. 19th St., Omaha 1, Neb.
Chicago District—475 Merchandise Mart, Merchandise Mart Plaza, Chicago 54, Ill.
North Central Division—536 So. Clark St., Chicago 5, Ill.
Ohio River Division—P.O. Box 1159, Cincinnati 1, Ohio.
Pittsburgh District—925 New Federal Bldg., Pittsburgh, Pa.
Huntington District—237 Fourth Ave., P.O. Box 2127, Huntington 18, W. Va.
Louisville District—830 West Broadway, P.O. Box 59, Louisville 1, Ky.
Nashville District—306 Federal Office Bldg., P.O. Box 1070, Nashville 1, Tenn.
Southwestern Division—1114 Commerce St., Dallas 2, Texas.
Galveston District—606 Santa Fe Bldg., Galveston, Texas.
Mobile District—2301 Grant St., Mobile 7, Ala.

CHARTS—Tennessee River—Available from the Tennessee Valley Authority, Maps and Engineering Records Section, 102A Union Building, Knoxville, Tennessee. Bound sets available from District Engineers at Cincinnati, Nashville and Louisville.

CHARTS—Great Lakes and connecting rivers, Lake Champlain, New York Canals and Minnesota-Ontario Border Lakes (including some Canadian waters). U. S. Lake Survey, Corps of Engineers, U. S. Army, 630 Federal Building, Detroit 26, Mich.

CHARTS—Canadian Waters. Hydrographic Chart Distribution, Canadian Hydrographic Service, Department of Mines and Technical Surveys, 615 Booth St., Ottawa, Canada.

CHARTS—Coastal Waters and Intracoastal Waterway, New York to Florida. Also Coast Pilots, Tide Tables and Current Tables, all for coastal waters. U. S. Coast & Geodetic Survey, Washington 25, D. C. (The Coast Pilot for the Gulf Coast contains much valuable data on the Mississippi River System.)

NOTICE TO MARINERS—Data for up-to-date corrections to coastal charts, Coast Pilots, etc. U. S. Oceanographic Office, Navy Department, Washington, D. C. (Local daily notices available from Commanders of the various Coast Guard Districts. For the Mississippi, from St. Louis and New Orleans offices.)

LIGHT LISTS—Separate volumes for Mississippi River System, Great Lakes, and coastal waters. Superintendent of Documents, Government Printing Office, Washington 25, D. C., and local Coast Guard offices at St. Louis and New Orleans.

GREAT LAKES PILOT—U. S. Lake Survey, Corps of Engineers, U. S. Army, 630 Federal Building, Detroit 26, Mich.

YACHTSMAN'S GUIDE TO THE GREAT LAKES—Seaport Publishing Co., 843 Delray Ave., S.E., Grand Rapids 6, Mich.

RULES OF THE ROAD—Separate volumes for Inland Waters of Atlantic and Pacific Coasts and Gulf of Mexico; Great Lakes; and Western Rivers. U. S. Coast Guard Headquarters, Washington 25, D. C. For Western Rivers, available also from local Coast Guard offices at St. Louis and New Orleans.

REGULATIONS to Govern the Use, Administration and Navigation of the Ohio River, Mississippi River above Cairo, Ill. and Their Tributaries—District Engineer, St. Louis, Mo. (Also available at any lock.)

RULES AND REGULATIONS to Govern the Operation of Drawbridges Crossing the Mississippi River and All Its Tributaries and Outlets—District Engineer, Chicago, Ill.

RULES AND REGULATIONS Governing Navigation and Use of the New York State Canal System—Superintendent of Operation and Maintenance, State Department of Public Works, Albany, N. Y.

NEW YORK STATE CANALS AND WATERWAYS—Official map, with condensed information on canal system, navigational aids, pleasure boat regulations, data on locks, etc. Superintendent of Operation and Maintenance, State Department of Public Works, Albany, N. Y.

CRUISING GUIDE BOOK for the New York State Barge Canal System and Connecting Navigable Canadian Lakes, Rivers and Waterways—Cruising Guidebook, 146 Sheridan Ave., Albany, N. Y.

MISSISSIPPI RIVER NAVIGATION—Division Engineer, Lower Mississippi Valley Division, Corps of Engineers, U. S. Army, P. O. Box 80, Vicksburg, Miss.

LOCKING THROUGH—Things you should know if you use navigation locks, District Engineer, St. Louis, Mo. Also available from other District Engineers.

OHIO RIVER HANDBOOK—Piloting information, statistics, lore and legend pertaining to the Ohio and its tributaries. Young & Klein, Inc., 1351 Spring Lawn Ave., Cincinnati 23, Ohio.

YOUR OHIO—Pamphlet of general interest. Corps of Engineers, Ohio Division.

RADIO AIDS TO NAVIGATION, GREAT LAKES—U. S. Coast Guard, 9th District, Main Post Office Building, Cleveland 13, Ohio.

INLAND WATERWAY GUIDE, Great Lakes Edition—Inland Waterway Guide, Inc., 101 North Andrews Ave., Fort Lauderdale, Fla.

RECREATION IN TVA LAKES—Tabulates boat docks and related services, with map. Information Office, Tennessee Valley Authority, Knoxville, Tenn.

BOATING AND FISHING GUIDE to the Great Lakes of the South—The Nashville Tennessean, Nashville, Tenn.

MAP, PRINCIPAL WATERWAYS OF THE UNITED STATES—Chief of Engineers, Department of the Army, Operations Division, Civil Works, Washington 25, D. C.

CHARTING THE GREAT LAKES—The story of the United States Lake Survey, United States Lake Survey, 630 Federal Bldg., Detroit 26, Mich.

CRUISING GUIDES AND CHARTS AND HARBOR BOOKLETS—Several of the large oil companies offer useful publications dealing with the inland waterways. Texaco Waterways Service, 135 E. 42nd St., New York 17, N. Y.; Gulf Tourgide Bureau, Box 8056, Philadelphia 1, Pa. (east of Mississippi); Mobil Touring Service, Mobil Oil Co., 150 E. 42nd St., New York, N. Y.; Esso Touring Service, 15 W. 51st St., New York 19, N. Y.

NAVIGATION LOCKS AND DAMS, MISSISSIPPI RIVER—District Engineer, St. Louis, Mo.

TIPS ON RIVER SAFETY—District Engineer, St. Louis, Mo.

MISSISSIPPI RIVER, CHAIN OF ROCKS CANAL AND LOCKS—District Engineer, St. Louis, Mo.

THE GULF INTRACOASTAL WATERWAY—District Engineer, Vicksburg, Miss. (Charts from same source.) More complete pamphlet available from Superintendent of Documents, Washington 25, D. C.

YOUR KEY TO THE LOCK—U. S. Army Engineer District, Corps of Engineers, Room 322, Federal Building, P. O. Box 991, Albany 1, N. Y. Pamphlet prepared for the guidance of yachtsmen passing through the Federal Lock at Troy, N. Y.

From "Your Key to the Lock"

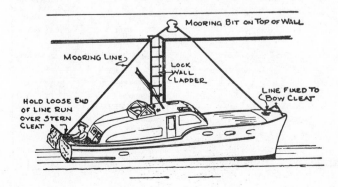

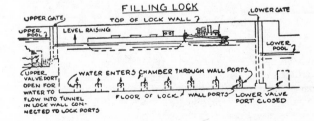

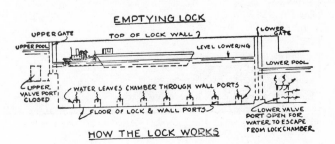

HOW THE LOCK WORKS

439

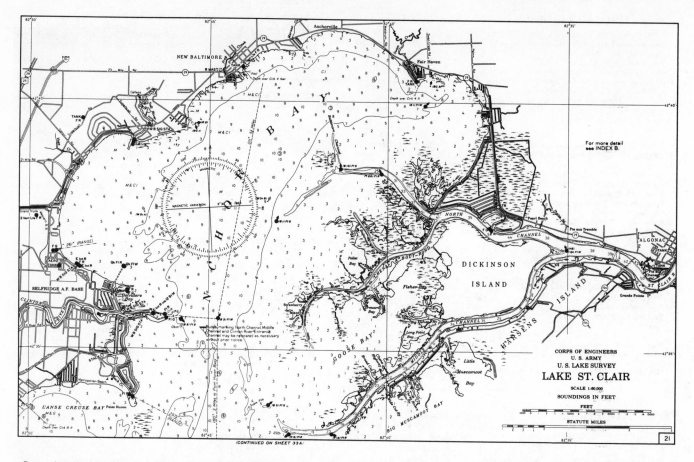

Reproductions (reduced more than half) of two typical pages from the U. S. Lake Survey Recreational Chart Series No. 400 covering the Detroit River, Lake St. Clair and the St. Clair River. Charts of this kind are prepared for the express purpose of providing the boatman with a maximum of navigational information in convenient form. In these volumes, data are included which is not available on other chart series. In the original, Lake St. Clair (above) is shown on a scale of 1:60,000; Belle Isle and a portion of the Detroit River (below) 1:15,000. On the original, two tints of blue are used to define limits of the shoaler areas (up to one and two fathoms), thus emphasizing navigable deep-water channels which appear in white, with soundings in feet in black figures. Land areas are tinted light yellow.

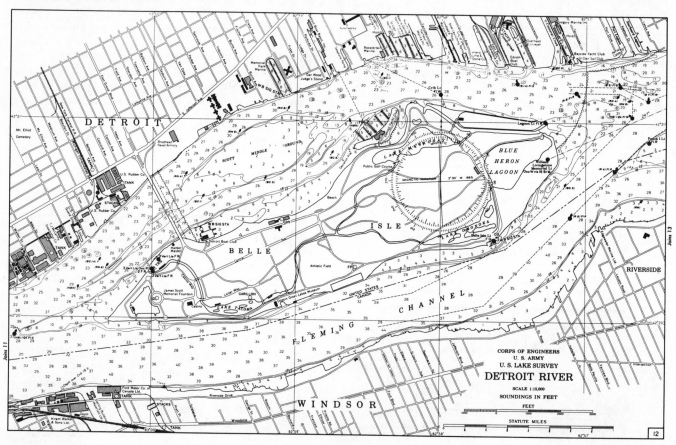

Outboard Seamanship

As in any workable partnership, it is essential that the components—in this case, boat and motor—can get along together. Within that boundary the boatman must determine 1) what he needs from 2) what is available within his budget.

For the new boatman especially, it is a deranging problem to sift the bag of brightly colored, boldly worded, attention-grabbing brochures, flyers, throw-aways; to disengage himself from the pouring of claims; to stand beyond the flood of "bigger and better," "mostest," and "fastest"; to de-

CHAPTER XXIX

cide what he wants a boat for and, on the basis of competent knowledge, what he wants in a boat.

Now, if it is speed you want—and certainly the sensation of a planing hull streaking over the water is one of outboarding's pleasures—be sure to acquire the boat, motor and combina-

tion thereof that will give you maximum safe performance even at high speed ranges. Too heavy a motor—too heavy, that is, for the particular boat—will cause the boat to squat at the stern and keep the bow pointed acutely celestial. Too light a motor, conversely, will cause the boat to perform sluggishly.

Bear in mind when determining horsepower that a boat which makes 15 mph with a 7½-hp motor won't necessarily make 30 with a 15. The better boats are designed for certain speeds with certain power; exceed that plan and you will perhaps do no more than burn fuel and dangerously overload your craft's transom.

Apart from consulting with competent dealers and others with experience, you can obtain reliable advice from the Outboard Boating Club of America's (OBC) "capacity recommendation plate" affixed to the hulls of some outboard boats. It gives the maximum horsepower and load the boat is designed to take.

If your boat lacks such a plate, ask the dealer for recommendations, or request them directly from the builder. Following these limitations will help avoid two common causes of accidents: over-powering and overloading!

TYPES OF BOATS

There is a wide array of boats from which to choose, from 4-hp car-top prams to buxom cruisers able to take two of the highest horsepower motors available. There are dinghies, skiffs, canoes, runabouts and utilities. There are special rigs like Sea Sleds, modified motor-catamarans and outboard-powered houseboats.

Your first question: What are you going to use your outboard boat for. Fishing? Family cruising? Skiing? Beach picnics? Skindiving? Photogra-

Proper trim is important. In illustration above, boat lists heavily to port. Weight should be distributed to keep boat on even keel, as shown below.

phy? Speed? Combinations of any of these? Narrow your choice and you've practically decided on your type boat. A fisherman doesn't want to troll in a hydroplane designed to zoom at 50 mph!

Your second question: In what kind of water are you going to use the boat? Salt or fresh? Large, open bays and lakes, or shallow, sheltered rivers? The shoal-draft boat you drive on placid ponds may not stand you in good stead on open, rough waters.

Here is a brief rundown on the types of outboards available. Hulls break down into two basics: displacement and planing. Displacement boats cruise *through* the water, planing hulls lift and skim *over* the surface.

Often it is difficult to make a sharp distinction between "displacement" and "planing" types of hulls. Planing hulls receive a large part of their support at speed from the dynamic reaction of the water against the bottom, and part from buoyancy which diminishes with increased speed, but never quite disappears at any speed. Generally, planing begins when the water breaks cleanly away at the chines and transom. In these days of high horsepower, many cruisers are actually planing hulls. Practically all runabouts plane, of course.

Flat bottom (displacement type) hulls. Usually rowboats or skiffs 14′ to 18′; used for fishing or utility purposes on shallow streams and small, protected lakes. They are not fast, are generally heavy and roomy. (Some light, flat bottom boats plane and are fast.)

Round bottom (displacement) hulls. Dinghies, tenders, car-top craft, occasionally runabouts 12′ to 18′. These hulls at low speeds are often more easily driven and maneuvered than the flat-bottom craft. (Many fast, light, round bottom boats will also plane.)

Hydroplane (planing) hulls. Generally used for racing. Bottom, which is flat, may be "stepped," i.e., divided into two levels, about amidships. The resultant notch reduces wetted surface, increasing speed.

Vee-bottom hulls. Commonly used for runabouts, utilities and cruisers when speed is a factor. Forward undersection is usually deep "V" in shape. Bottom flattens toward amidships, until at the stern it becomes broad and flat.

A utility and a runabout, in effect, are practically interchangeable terms. Both craft function about the same, are

about the same size, take about the same horsepower, etc. The runabout, however, is generally considered to be a bit faster and more luxuriously equipped than a utility of comparable size.

Now, it you've made your choice, here are a couple of tips before actually buying. Take the boat and motor for a trial spin to see how they operate together and in various water conditions. Never buy a boat, especially a used boat, when it is in the water without first having her hauled. Check to see that bottom, frames, planking and fastenings are sound. If you are inexperienced, have a competent person examine the rig.

UNDER THE LAW

Be sure you and your boat comply with federal, state and local boating laws. You will have to check the laws of your community yourself (OBC publishes a round-up of state laws; federal laws are obtainable from the Coast Guard).

Determine if your boat must be numbered. Under the Federal Boating Act of 1958, all boats regardless of length (but not documented) that carry an engine of *more* than 10 hp, and are used on navigable (federal) waters, must be numbered. Some states, enacting legislation under the federal act but varying from the hp specification, require that all boats carrying *any* propulsive machinery be numbered. Where states have not assumed the numbering function, the Coast Guard is doing the job, following the "more-than-10-hp" guide.

FITTING HER OUT

Begin by installing the motor properly—manufacturer's diagrams will

Heavy 22-foot runabout above can safely carry two large (60 hp here) motors. Even one of these would overpower small outboard below.

Photographs from Mercury Outboard Motors

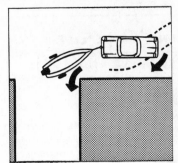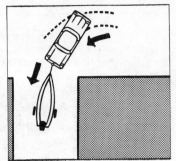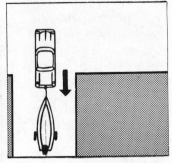

Remember, trailer always backs in direction opposite to that of car. Driver swings close to launching ramp (left), then cuts car away from ramp, placing trailer at angle to ramp and driveway, cuts wheels of car to left (center), backs slowly into ramp as trailer moves to right. Driver straightens wheel after "jackknifing" car-and-trailer until both are in line, then backs slowly down ramp.

help here. Generally the task is to seat the motor squarely on the center of the transom and to securely tighten the bracket screws (motor angle will be discussed later). Some motor makes provide special transom plates for mounting, and you may prefer using a transom pad beneath the clamps to reduce vibration and prevent the wood from being marred. A length of chain through the motor bracket and around a transom knee will prevent the motor from being lost overboard.

Next, let's buy our required equipment. The skipper has much leeway as to brand and type of equipment he'll carry in this category, provided it meets legal requirements. For life-saving devices, for example, he can purchase cushions or jackets or ring buoys—provided each is Coast Guard approved. He must, of course, have one such device for each person aboard. OBC strongly recommends life jackets for children and non-swimmers. and that these persons wear them at all times when aboard.

Make sure your passengers know where the life-saving devices are—keep them accessible!—and how they are used, before you get under way. A buoyant cushion, incidentally, is used by slipping the left arm through one of the loops and the right leg through the other (reverse this for left-handers). The wearer then holds the cushion against his chest with the bridled arm, keeping the other arm and both legs free for swimming.

If your hull is even partially enclosed, the law requires that you carry a fire extinguisher. Place it where it can be grabbed quickly! Extinguishers of the vaporizing liquid type, particularly carbon tetrachloride, can no longer be installed on boats. Those manufactured before December, 1958, however, and already installed and

serviceable, can be used until January 1962.

Even if you plan absolutely never to use your boat at night, you should install the lights prescribed for your class boat. Engine trouble, fuel problems or unexpectedly fine fishing may keep you out longer than you intended. Two lights are required (Inland Rules) for outboards up to 26′: a combination red and green light on the bow, and a white stern light, visible all around the horizon (360°) for at least two miles.

Outboards between 16 and 26 feet must carry a horn, or a hand-, mouth- or power-whistle audible for at least ½ mile. This device can be used both for passing whistle signals and fog signals.

The equipment required by law does not cover all that is required by boating's exigencies. The law, for instance, says nothing about carrying an extra propeller, but if your motor should slam into some hefty debris, disabling the propeller, the situation would demand a spare. An anchor with enough line (at least ⅜″ nylon or ½″ manilla

for most outboards), a compass, enough fuel, a well-equipped tool box, a first-aid kit, flashlight, distress flares and smoke signals, are some of the items a prudent skipper will demand. The accompanying equipment list gives a complete rundown.

Don't pass over an oar, or paddle, on your list, even if it presents a stowage problem. An oar may turn out to be all you have for motive power at one time or another, and can be used to swing the bow around should you go aground. Not infrequently, an extended oar handle is used to help a person who has fallen overboard to get back to the boat.

ON THE ROAD

Trailers, like boats and motors, come in many varieties. They are produced variously equipped with electric winches, adjustable keel rollers, finger-tip controls for loading and launching, etc. Your problem, as before, is to get the right combination—this time the right trailer for your boat and motor.

You must have a trailer able to

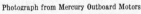

Although this runabout demonstrates great carrying capacity, she should never carry so many passengers. Overloading is dangerous practice in small craft. No one should be permitted on forward deck while under way.

carry the weight of your motor(s), the boat, *and the gear stowed in the boat.* This last factor is too often overlooked in making calculations. That done, check the prospective trailer's load capacity, found usually on a plate affixed to the trailer. If the load to be carried (some builders underestimate the weight of their boats, so check carefully) is within 100 pounds of the trailer's listed weight capacity, buy the *next larger* model! Don't mislead yourself here, though, and purchase a huge trailer for a modest-size boat. The trailer must fit the hull!

Remember, a trailer, like any dry-land cradle, is an unnatural place for a boat, so you must baby the craft all you can. Make the trailer bed as comfortable as possible. See that it fits the contours of the hull (special trailers are made for the modified catamaran type of outboard). Plenty of padding and bracing may be needed. Treat the boat right on the trailer and you'll get sought-for results in the water. There must not be a "sag" in the hull or a "hook" (in the stern, from too short a trailer). Such things may change the shape of your boat permanently, affecting your speed in the water and handling of the boat.

One type of trailer—often referred to as the full-keel support type—rests the boat on a boom or series of adjustable rollers. Another kind supports the boat with cradles, usually one forward and one aft. A boat kept too long on such a cradle, though, as for winter storage, tends to sag.

If you trailer the boat with the motor clamped to the transom, be sure the clamps are tight and the lower unit is secured to the transom or to the trailer frame, this last step to prevent the motor from tilting forward during sudden stops.

Be sure, too, that your trailer is adequately supporting the weight of the motor. In some instances it may be necessary to relocate trailer wheels closer to the rear, thus providing more direct support and at the same time keeping the load weight heavier—by 50 to 60 pounds—at the trailer front.

With the center of gravity located somewhat forward, towing will be smoother. Also, when you disconnect the trailer from the car you will be able to walk away with it—even when the trailer's loaded!

A bumper hitch will serve if you are trailering a light rig. For the heavier jobs, though, use a hitch that

EQUIPMENT CHECK LIST

FOR SKIPPER, CREW AND BOAT

POWER:
Two outboard motors, one with generator
Set of engine controls
Two propellers
Tachometer with throw-switch
Two 12-volt batteries
Two battery boxes

NAVIGATION:
Charts • Light list • Log book
Pair of lucite parallel rules
Pair of dividers
Pair of 7 x 50 binoculars
Lead line
Coast Pilots
USPS textbook: Piloting, Seamanship and Small Boat Handling
Inland Waterway Guide
Oil company cruising charts
Compass
Plenty of paper, pens and pencils
Watch with second hand

GROUND TACKLE:
8-pound standard Danforth anchor
12-pound Hi-Tensile Danforth
Two 100-foot lengths of ⅜″ nylon
Two 5-foot lengths of ¼″ galvanized chain
Four ¼″ galvanized shackles
Four ⅜″ galvanized thimbles

REQUIRED:
Freon-type air horn with refill
2½-pound dry chemical fire extinguisher
Four approved life jackets
Four Coast Guard-approved buoyant cushions
Properly functioning running lights with spare bulbs, fuses
State registration certificate
State numbers properly mounted

SAFETY EQUIPMENT:
First-aid kit
Flares, day and night
Electric bilge pump
Manual bilge pump
12-foot oar • Boat hook
Portable radio
Two spare propellers
Cotter pins for propeller hubs
Hand flashlight

Hand lantern
Two extra spark plugs

MOORING:
Four 25-foot lengths of ⅜″ nylon
One 50-foot length of ⅜″ nylon
Three plastic-foam fenders
Six fender locks

CLOTHING:
Two pair of foul-weather suits
Two pair of boating shoes
Two ski parkas
Sun glasses • Towels • Warm socks
Chinos • Bathing suits • Underwear
Sweaters • Caps • Gloves
Shirts, warm and summery
Set of thermal underwear

SLEEPING:
Sheets • Pillows • Warm blankets
Alarm clock

TOOLS:
Fiberglass tool-tackle box
Several sharp pen knives
Set of regular screwdrivers
Set of Phillips screwdrivers
Interchangeable-headed hammer
Pliers, regular and long-nosed
Boat tape
Spark plug remover and gauge
Sandpaper and emery cloth
Various types of oil and graphite
Assortment of screws and bolts with nuts and washers
Wrenches, socket and open end
Wood filler
Waterproof sealer
Extra fuses
Extra "keys" for tanks

GALLEY:
Stainless steel ice pick
Alcohol
Cigarettes • Matches • Lighter fluid
Copper wool • Soap • Soap dish
Assorted pots and pans
Spice containers
Plastic plates and cups
Stainless-steel eating utensils
Aluminum foil
Can and bottle openers
Stainless steel cleaner

HEAD:
Toilet paper • Comb
Sun tan lotion • Insect repellent
Tooth brush • Tooth paste

MISCELLANEOUS:
Swab • Bucket • Sponges
Camera • Plastic wrap • Film
Bilge cleaner • Ash trays

ALL THE EQUIPMENT LISTED ABOVE IS CARRIED ABOARD ONE PARTICULAR BOAT, A 22-FOOT EXPRESS CRUISER POWERED BY TWO OUTBOARD MOTORS. BECAUSE THE BOAT IS REPRESENTATIVE OF A GREAT MANY CRAFT IN USE TODAY, THE LIST SERVES AS AN EXCELLENT REFERENCE FOR THOSE SEEKING AN EQUIPMENT GUIDE.

fits directly to the car's frame—a frame hitch. It's a good idea, too, to cover the motor while trailering to keep dust out. Remove the cover at journey's end so condensation does not cause damage.

Keep trailer tires correctly inflated.

Keep trailer lights and reflectors working properly.

Make sure your insurance covers your boat and motor while being trailered.

Know and comply with the trailer laws that obtain in the areas you use. Often, these laws vary from state to state.

For launching, you'll probably use one of the many hard-topped ramps available. Occasionally, you may launch from a natural site. In this case, choose an area with a gently sloping shore but with ground hard enough to give ample tire traction. You can increase traction by slightly deflating the tires—but remember this when you start homeward. Stop at the first place for air.

Maneuvering your trailered boat into the water takes practice: beginners often come to a stalemate when car and trailer are "V"-ed before the water. Have someone shout instructions while you back onto the launching ramp at a 90° angle to the water.

Remember that in backing if you want the trailer to go to the right, you turn the steering wheel to the left, and vice versa.

Don't back the trailer into the water immediately. When in position on the ramp, stop and 1) release any tie downs and 2) tilt the motor so it doesn't hit any obstacle. Now back the trailer slowly, making sure the water doesn't reach the car's hubcaps.

Unlock the bow winch and secure a line to the bow. Push the boat off the trailer into the water, always holding the bow line so the boat does not float away. Unlock the trailer winch cable and with the bow line ease the boat into position for boarding.

GETTING ABOARD

If you are boarding from a beach, climb in over the bow when practical. When boarding from a float or low pier, step aboard as nearly amidships as possible. Bend so your weight is kept low, thus helping to keep the boat stable. Grasp the gunwale (the boat's side rails) for balance. In a small outboard, do not step on a gunwale or you'll flip the craft.

Do not carry bulky supplies while boarding. If you are alone, place the supplies where you can get at them from aboard. Or have someone hand them to you.

FUELING

A half pint of gasoline has the destructive power of five sticks of dynamite. When you fuel, you deal with at least several gallons of gasoline. So take every precaution—take nothing for granted!

It is wise, for instance, to remove portable fuel tanks from the boat when possible and take them ashore to fill. Extinguish all flames and close all electrical circuits. Warn everyone aboard and everyone about that there'll be no smoking.

Make sure the gas pump hose nozzle is in contact with the rim of the fill tank opening to prevent generating a spark of static electricity, which might ignite the gas.

Watch your fuel mixture now, both as to gas-oil ratio and the physical mixing of the two. Both are important to the smooth operation of the motors. Afterwards, make sure the lid of the tank is on tight to prevent leakage.

If your outboard carries fuel tanks which would be impractical to remove for fueling—anything larger than a 6-gallon tank would probably be impractical to remove—or permanently installed fuel tanks, your fueling procedures closely follow those for inboards. Before taking on fuel, close all doors, hatches, windows, etc., to keep gasoline vapors from getting below. After fueling, open all doors, hatches, etc., and allow enough time for ventilation to clear these areas before starting the motors.

The mixing of gasoline and oil for large portable tanks and for permanently installed tanks can be done in several ways—all of which are time-consuming but, outboard motor engineers agree, extremely important, even more so than getting the exact gas-oil ratio.

One method is to use a metal (for grounding gas hose nozzle) funnel, preferably with a screen filter, which is inserted into the fill pipe or tank and into which can be poured the gas and oil at the same time, apportioning the oil at a slow rate and allowing the stream of gasoline to thoroughly blend with the oil.

A second method is to mix the gasoline and oil in a separate 5- or 6-gallon can (with pouring spout) and then pour from this into your fuel tanks.

Some gasoline companies are supplying their marinas with outboard pumps that serve up fuel already mixed. A dial regulates the ratio, according to your needs.

Do not, as should already be clear, pour the oil directly into the tank—it will not mix!

Check the fuel system now for leakage. Moreover, if you've spilled any gasoline, carefully wipe the area with a rag (which should then be disposed of) and hose down with fresh water, when possible.

Remember to thoroughly ventilate the boat before starting the motor. It is essential that you be alert for gasoline vapors. These vapors, heavier than air, crawl into the lower portions of the boat and wait, stubbornly and menacingly! A bilge blower, especially on an outboard cruiser, may be a prudent investment.

MOTOR ANGLE

For best motor performance, the drive of the propeller should be in a line parallel to the keel of the boat and parallel to the flat surface of the water. This means you must set your motor at a 90° angle (or very close to it) to the water, straight up and down. If the propeller is tilted away from the stern—assuming a vertical transom—the bow of the boat tends to rise too high while the stern squats. If the propeller is tilted toward the stern, pushing it up, the bow tends to nose too deep, plowing its way unnecessarily.

TRIM

The number of seats in a boat is no indication of the number of persons she can carry safely. Overloading, as has been pointed out, is a frequent cause of boating accidents. One of the best ways to avoid overloading is by planning how many people you will take—within the limits of your boat's capacity—and inviting *just so many*, no more!

Before discussing trim it would be well for readers to realize that the factors involved become more critical as boat size and weight decrease.

Have all weight evenly distributed (passengers seated toward the centerline of the boat and not hanging over the gunwales) so the boat will trim properly—slightly down by the stern; never down at the bow—and perform as she was designed to do. If the load is concentrated forward or aft, the boat will needlessly plow or drag, respectively, reducing your safety margin and increasing your fuel consumption.

Trim your boat as well as possible before getting under way. It is dangerous for passengers to change places or move around in a boat (except in a large outboard cruiser) that is scooting along briskly. If such movement becomes essential, stop or slow the craft first, remembering in rough weather to keep enough momentum to retain steerage control and to keep the boat headed into waves and wind. Have the person who must move keep low and near the boat's centerline.

To this point we have dealt with such preliminary matters as choosing the outboard boat, motor and trailer, and fitting out the craft. Now we're ready to take the outboarder for a spin—the real test of the things he has bought and the things he should know.

Your boat gets its directional "orders" from the stern. That outboard motor at the transom does more than provide propulsion: it acts as a rudder, pushing the transom in the direction of the drive and thus pointing the bow the opposite way. Remote control steering, however, that is, a steering wheel generally near the bow with cable installation aft to the motor, permits you to steer your boat in the manner of an automobile: turn the wheel to starboard (right) and your boat will head to starboard, turn to port and it will go to port. But let the boat-automobile simile end there. The pivoting action of a boat is not like the turning action of a car, and leaving or getting into a slip or float will quickly point up the distinctions.

Make a final check before getting under way. Do you have enough fuel? Are your passengers seated properly? Have you told them about the life-sav-ing devices, their location and their use? Is the way ahead or astern, as the case may be, clear?

Getting under way with an electric starting motor is as easy as pressing a button or turning a key. Once the motor is running, allow enough time for it to warm up before casting off. Listen carefully now, and from now on, to the running motor. Familiarity with that sound so that you detect even slight changes in it will enable you to pick up faults which may develop, such as worn plugs, improperly adjusted carburetor, wrong size propeller for the particular load or job, insufficient or contaminated fuel, and so on.

When the motor is running smoothly and the lines are free, ease the shift into gear and proceed slowly. Remember this about speed: the slower your boat is going the less room it needs to turn or stop, but your boat must be in gear—forward or reverse—for you to have steerage way. Guide your throttle accordingly.

UNDER WAY

Exercise your knowledge of the Rules of the Road now, tempered by good sense, right of way or no! Small craft should stand off as far as possible from large yachts and commercial ships. Watch their wakes with vigilant care. Don't count on such ships to look out

---

A BOAT HAS NO BRAKES

Many persons who have not handled a boat have the misconception that one can be maneuvered and stopped as easily as an automobile. But a boat has no brakes. The new boat owner should practice landings and leaving of docks as often as possible. Work on steering too.

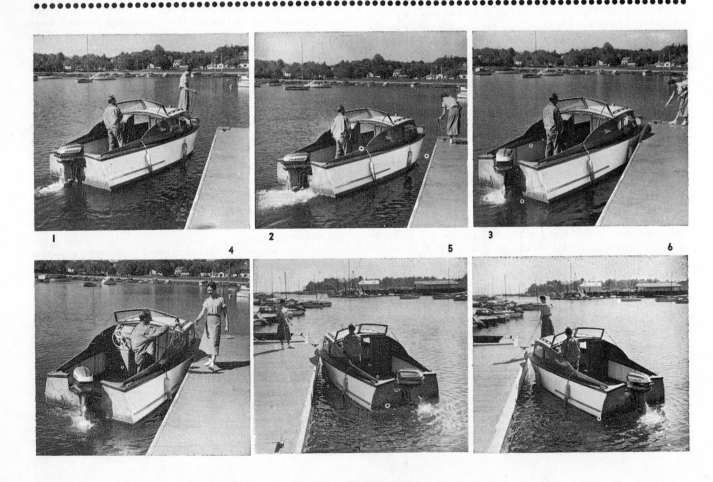

1 2 3

4 5 6

for you; they need more room to stop, are more difficult to turn, and sometimes have "blind spots"—areas which are obscure or entirely blocked to the helmsman. Never assume the pilot of a vessel sees you: stay clear.

It is courteous and incumbent, too, to tend to your own wake and wash so as not to cause damage to other craft. You are legally responsible for the damage caused by your wake or waves.

Should you come upon a tow in the bend of a river. or a tow maneuvering near shore, note whether the tow is swinging to port or starboard, and give it the room it needs.

You should not bring your boat near a moored vessel. If circumstances make it necessary to do so, be exceedingly wary. Strong river currents moving under a moored barge can pull a boat under. Moreover, cross currents, that is, a current that is running at about a right angle to your course, require great caution. When you get into such a situation, give any object, floating or made fast, an extra wide berth.

WATCH THE WEATHER

Keep your mind on your course and boat handling but keep an eye on the weather. even if this morning's weathercast was for blue skies. Learn to recognize threatening cloud formations. Train yourself to be sensitive to shifts in wind direction; a shift in the wind often presages a change in the weather. And know and observe official storm warnings.

CARRY AN ANCHOR

In boating be prepared to do things you may not have planned to do. Anchoring, for instance. Always carry an anchor aboard, properly rigged with plenty of line and accessibly stowed.

In rough waters, anchoring will generally hold your bow into the wind or waves, a desirable effect to stay safest and driest, provided your boat is properly trimmed. A boat down at the bow while at anchor will not head into the wind. (We use "wind" here as a convenience. Actually, the direction and force of the current may have more effect on the position the boat will take at anchor than the wind alone. Experience along these lines is the best teacher.)

One auxiliary use of an anchor is to help get your boat clear should you run it aground. If a small boat is available or if the nearby water is sufficiently shallow so that you can wade, carry the anchor as far out as the line will permit—the farther the better—either from the bow or from the stern, wherever the deeper water is. A strong pull on the anchor line now will usually get the boat free.

Always check the water's depth, by chart, line or paddle, before letting go the anchor. Anchoring in relatively

Important part of your job in deriving peak performance from boat is getting right propeller for job. Number of blades, diameter and pitch are factors to consider. Here outboarder uses dial device on variable pitch propeller to change pitch to one most suitable for boat's load and planned activity this time out. Check propeller frequently for nicks, dents and out-of-pitch blades. These should be corrected as speed, fuel consumption and smoothness of operation are affected by propeller's action.

APPROACHING AND LEAVING A FLOAT WITH AN OUTBOARD

The outboard boat has true "power steering" in that the direction of thrust of the motor, and not a ruddder, guides the boat. As a result, outboard craft are exceptionally maneuverable. They handle easily in reverse because the boat follows the motor, making especially easy the maneuvers for approaching and leaving a float. With twin engines, one can be driven ahead and the other astern to provide an efficient means of turning in restricted waters. The technique of handling a single-screw outboard when approaching (Figures 1-4) and leaving (Figures 5-8) is illustrated here.

1. *Float is approached at an angle, with crew member ready to get bow line ashore. Fenders should be out.*

2. *Crewman takes line ashore and makes it fast to cleat on float.*

3. *Driver puts motor into reverse, turning his wheel to bring stern in.*

4. *Forward line will hold fast as motor brings it dockside. Stern line is then made fast to another cleat.*

5. *In leaving float when it is not practical to steer dead ahead, stern line is taken in while bow line is still fast to float. Motor is reversed and turned away from float.*

6. *Crewman releases bow line and steps aboard while taking in line.*

7. *As bow line is cast off, driver brings his wheel about to straighten boat, continuing in reverse until well clear.*

8. *With both lines in, driver switches gear to forward and pulls ahead, making certain stern is safe in case he should swing to port.*

7

8

Photographs from Evinrude Motors

deep water is inefficient; don't do it except in emergencies.

The type of anchor—or anchors, for a spare, heavier "hook" is worth springing for—you carry depends on the size of your boat, the kind of bottom in which you will generally anchor, and various other conditions. Coil the anchor rode (line) neatly for running, before you lower the anchor, and keep your feet out of the coils. Secure the bitter (inboard) end of the rode to a cleat, this apart from the hitch you make to stop the rode from running out (and check that the anchor is fast to the rode).

Don't throw the anchor overboard; lower it, and slowly so it doesn't arc into your hull. Don't lower it, however, until the boat's headway is stopped. Come up into the wind or current, whichever is strongest. Wait until the bow is over the spot where you want the anchor to lie. Then, when all headway is off and just before the boat makes sternway (drifts backwards), lower the anchor until the crown hits the bottom. You'll feel the gentle thud.

With the anchor on the bottom and the boat reversing slowly, let out the rode. As a general rule, pay out a scope of approximately six or seven times the depth of water. The longer the scope the better the anchor's holding power. Be sure, though, that you have room enough to swing around the amount of feet you've payed out.

You won't want to anchor too close to another craft. Privacy and safety are comforts skippers cherish.

In heavy weather you'll want to let out as much scope as possible. The length of the anchor rode is even more important in holding power than the weight of the anchor. A lightweight anchor with a long rode will hold in many cases where a heavy anchor with a short scope will drag.

CAUSES OF ACCIDENTS

Various studies have shown the following to be major causes of accidents:

1) Overloading, overpowering and improper trim.

2) High speed turns, particularly in rough water.

3) Failure to keep a sharp lookout for obstructions.

4) Going out in bad weather.

5) Standing in a moving boat.

6) Having too much weight too high on the boat, as when someone sits on the deck of a small outboard.

7) Leaks in the fuel system.

8) Going too far off shore.

Top: Boat at left is burdened vessel. She slows, yields right of way, and goes astern of privileged boat on right.

Center: Boatmen are cautioned against wearing cushions as life preservers, as shown. Straps are intended to be grasped. If arms are slipped through straps and cushion is held across chest, person will float face up.

Left: Like other boatmen, outboarders should have a working knowledge of piloting aids, buoyage systems, and navigational instruments. This will promote safety afloat and widen the range of boating activities.

Each of these factors—and others not listed here—can and should be avoided. A carefully matched boat, motor, propeller, etc., operated in accordance with the law and with courtesy, will go a long way toward eliminating accidents and even distressing moments. But some possibility always remains. You should be prepared to act in an emergency.

One of the leading causes of death in boating accidents is drowning. Many of these fatalities result from people falling overboard. As the skipper of your boat you have a responsibility to *know how* to rescue such a person. You should practice the maneuvers involved in accomplishing this. A ring buoy with line attached can be used as a simulated victim. Practice enough so you'll be able to act almost instinctively should the need arise; the minutes saved can be a life saved.

The Outboard Boating Club of America suggests that you adopt the following rescue procedure:

As soon as someone falls overboard, maneuver the boat's stern away from him. Shift into neutral (cut the motor if you do not have a gearshift) and throw a ring buoy or buoyant cushion near him . . . *near* him, don't conk him with it. See that you are clear of the overboard person now before engaging the propeller.

Circle around quickly, selecting the course that will allow you to get to the person while the boat heads into the wind or waves. Approach him slowly, now, taking care to come alongside and not over the victim. Stop the motor before attempting to take him aboard.

When alongside, extend a paddle or boat hook to him, or toss him one end of a line. Lead him around to the stern, where freeboard is lowest, if there is enough space at the transom for him to get aboard without injuring himself on the motor. On many outboards the transom is cramped with motor, fuel tanks, junction boxes, etc., so that it would be necessary to help the victim aboard over the side, as far aft as possible. In either case, the use of a boarding ladder will help matters. To avoid capsize when he is boarding, passengers should help trim the boat by shifting their weight.

On very small outboards without remote controls, it may be practical to remove the motor and take the man-overboard in over the transom. When helping a person aboard, hold him under the armpits and lift.

If the person has sunk from sight, probe gently beneath the surface with a paddle. Dive for him only if you are an experienced swimmer, and then just as a last resort.

OTHER EMERGENCIES

Stay with the boat if it capsizes! Almost invariably the temptation is to swim to shore, and almost invariably the shore is farther than it appears. Many outboard boats will float, even if filled with water. Aluminum and fiberglass boats usually have built-in flotation tanks. (Flotation tanks of wood or metal must be watertight, or they become a hazard. Sailboats with such tanks sometimes test them during the season by "sinking" the craft.) Some boats are fitted with materials like Styrofoam to give reserve buoyancy. And life jackets for persons in the water, of course, will provide much safety.

If your boat gets caught in a squall or in heavy seas, slow down immediately, maintaining only enough power to head the boat into or at a slight angle to the wind and waves. Have everyone don life preservers, yourself included. Don't try to smash your boat through the waves at high speed in an attempt to get home; you're inviting disaster. Rather, take the seas as gently as possible on the bow. The hull may pound, and the waves may toss up a lot of spray, but you'll have your best point of control over the boat. Should the craft get caught broadside in a trough, you run the risk of capsize.

If you find it difficult to keep the boat headed into the seas, or if the motor quits, some kind of drag, like a heavy anchor or a bucket, payed out with a long scope from the bow, may help in keeping the boat from falling into a trough. Some boats, though relatively few, carry sea anchors for this purpose, but opinions as to their effectiveness vary. As a rule, one would expect to use such a rig only in a storm at sea where there is plenty of sea room—not a situation the outboarder is likely to encounter. In heavy weather and where the motor can be idled, it is best to keep the motor going so it can be used instantly to keep the boat under control. Idling it will minimize fuel consumption.

Keep enough weight at the stern in stormy weather to hold the propeller in the water. Because the motor, as was pointed out earlier, serves as a rudder apart from providing propulsive power, you will have no helm control when the propeller leaves the water.

Whenever safely possible, of course, get to a protected harbor rather than attempt to ride out a storm. But don't let your haste disturb your judgment. Try to avoid taking large

waves on the stern; they can swamp the craft, though self-bailing wells aft reduce this potential. There's risk, too, of pitchpoling (turning end over end) in a heavy following sea, by being driven too fast before it. You may have to use reverse to check your speed.

If you must turn in a heavy sea watch for a lull in the wave formations in which to do it, so you won't get caught broadside in a trough by an approaching wave.

Always cross a large wave, or wake, at about a right angle. This lets you retain the best possible control over your boat.

Should your fuel supply run out—manually choking the motor will get the last few drops from the fuel tank—or should you be in need of other assistance, there are several distress signals that can be used. These include waving a white flag (a shirt or towel will serve), shooting smoke or flare signals, sending repeated blasts on a horn or whistle, lowering and raising both arms over your head and down to your sides, or flying an ensign upside down.

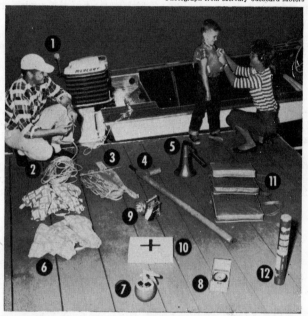

As a starter your equipment should include at least these dozen items: 1) proper running lights; 2) 50 feet of extra line; 3) anchor and line; 4) bilge pump; 5) horn; 6) life jacket for each passenger aboard; 7) fire extinguisher; 8) compass; 9) hand lantern; 10) first-aid kit; 11) buoyant cushions, and 12) safety flares. You'll add to these later.

MOORING AND DOCKING

You've made a short, practice run now and are ready to return. When making a landing, proceed slowly. Your wake won't disturb other moored vessels; you'll be better able to gauge the effects of wind, wave or current upon your boat; you can easily avoid mooring buoys, frequently found in berthing areas; and, if your motor is of the gearshift type, the throttle will be closed enough for shifting gears.

If the water is shoal in your landing area, put the motor on "release" so it will kick up if anything is hit, or, lacking such a device, have someone stand by the motor, ready to tilt it up at your command.

In landing at natural areas, try to select a sandy beach with little surf breaking. What from the boat appears to be a gentle, undulating surf may from the beach be a boiling tempest breaking over an acute land slope.

Close the beach (bring the boat in) at a right angle. Tilt up the motor before it strikes bottom, and haul the boat up the beach as far as possible—allowing for tide—so it will not be battered nor broached by waves.

In bringing your boat alongside a pier or up to a mooring,

watch the wind. Do not land on the weather side of the pier unless necessary. A crowded gas dock, though, often makes it necessary. Bear in mind, in such a situation, that the wind will be nudging your craft into the pier, so maneuver and use your reverse gear as needed to keep your boat clear. Also, come into the pier at an angle that will permit you to lie alongside at least a boat length away, permitting the wind to move you next to the pier. See that your boat is properly fendered before you come up to the pier, and don't cut your motor(s) until you're safely secured.

When making a preferable landing, on the lee side of a pier, head your boat into the wind or current, thus retaining better control.

From whichever side you approach, turn the craft before it reaches the pier so that it comes parallel to the structure. If you have a gearshift, use reverse to stop headway, then shift to neutral and make the landing with the motor still running.

If you do not have a gearshift, throttle down to a low speed, pivot the motor 180° (which gives you the equivalent of reverse), and get a bow line to the pier. Using this as a spring, the stern can be brought in, if necessary, by going forward slowly with the propeller turned *away* from the pier. Once the boat is alongside, secure a stern line.

MAKING FAST

An eye spliced into one end of each dock line makes it easy to quickly throw them over a bollard or around a cleat. In other situations, a couple of fast and handy knots to know and use are the clove hitch and bowline.

Generally you'll want to use at least a bow and stern line to make fast. Under certain conditions of wind and current, it may be desirable to tie with a bow line only, allowing your boat to float away from the pier; but if the boat's going to be left untended, put out a stern anchor. A change in the wind or current may bring your boat bumping into the pier.

In tidal waters, allow enough line for rise and fall. You may otherwise return to find your boat lynched unceremoniously out of the water, if the cleats have not let go.

A block (pulley) and weight arrangement, a shackle and cable setup on pilings, etc., will allow the lines and thus the boat to ride the tide. Where such an arrangement is lacking, run the bow and stern lines several bollards (or equivalent) away from the boat so that the lines are at about 45° angles to the boat. This allows considerable flexibility for tidal variation.

IN GENERAL

Keep your boat's speed under control at all times. Don't show off. Respect the rights, and comforts, of others afloat: slow down not only when your boat's in danger but when it's a matter of courtesy to others. When passing other craft in the same or opposite direction, give them a wide berth. Never attempt to "hose-down" those aboard another boat. When passing by or through an anchorage, throttle down to your lowest speed and keep an acutely alert lookout for moorings, swimmers, debris, etc.

If you are going off shore or for a relatively long cruise even on inland waters, make those at home familiar with your plans, in as much detail as possible. Should trouble develop, you'll find the Coast Guard most welcomely cooperative, ready to render assistance. The more they know about your plans and boat, the more help they can be.

Your actions on the water can do much to fight against the restricting legislation that inevitably will be proposed from time to time concerning boats and boatmen. And remember, your speed may be prima facie evidence of your guilt.

Mercury Outboard Motors

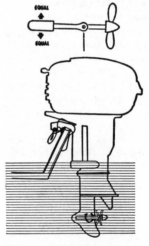

Part of the job in becoming a boatman is learning the language inherent to the sport. Illustration above gives many of the commonly used terms you'll want to know and use.

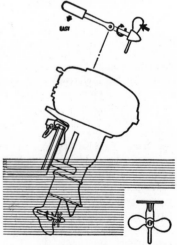

Below: If motor is tilted with lower unit toward transom, effective blade pitch on port side is practically zero, but increased on starboard side. Result easier steering to starboard and harder turning to port. With thrust not parallel to water line, stern will rise and bow will trim too low. Opposite effect results when motor is tilted aft.

Above: For easy steering and proper trim, adjust the motor vertically on the transom with cavitation plate parallel to the water flow, as illustrated. In this position, propeller blades take an equal bite on the water on each side of the center line.

To insure safety, check your boat and motor against these curves and formulas, designed to prevent over-powering and overloading. A check list to use for trouble-shooting the motor; thoughts on propeller choice and additional miscellaneous equipment; safety suggestions; and a quiz to test your outboarding knowledge.

Twin-motor installation, *increasingly popular on today's outboards, provides plenty of power and safety margin besides: if one motor quits the other will get boat in. Tachometer is helpful instrument to keep motors synchronized for most efficient operation.*

THIS series on outboarding, readers may recall, placed much emphasis on the matching of boat and motor. If the boat doesn't have an OBC (Outboard Boating Club of America) plate listing the hull's load and power limits, part one pointed out, it was suggested that you get sound advice on the matter. Here now is a way for you to determine those limits yourself.

For horsepower, simple multiplication and a look at the graph (right) will render the *maximum* horsepower that can be safely used on the boat in question. This horsepower can be derived from a single engine or as a total from a twin installation. Either way, it is an uppermost limit, a sort of safety belt that all boatmen are encouraged to use.

THE HORSEPOWER CURVE

The first step, the simple arithmetic we talked about, is to multiply the hull's overall length by its maximum width *at the stern.* Length is measured from the stem to the transom on a straight line parallel to the keel. Don't include extensions like outboard brackets, fins, etc., in the measurement.

The second step is to take the product of the length-times-width problem (if fractions are involved use the nearest integer, or whole number) and find this figure along the vertical axis (left edge) of the graph. Enter here and follow the horizontal line to where it intersects the curve. Now follow down to the bottom. The figure you reach at the bottom scale is the maximum horsepower for that particular hull.

If the intersection falls between figures, the one at the right is taken as the maximum horsepower for the hull.

Example: The length-width product of a 14½-foot hull with a maximum transom width of 5 feet is 72.5. Enter the side of the graph at 73 and follow the horizontal line to its intersection with the curve. Reading this point of intersection along the bottom of the graph gives us a figure somewhere between 55 and 60. Because it is between ratings, we take the figure to the right of the intersection, so that 60 is our answer. The *maximum* power then that we can use on our 14½-footer is 60 horsepower, in the form of either a single 60-hp engine or two 30s.

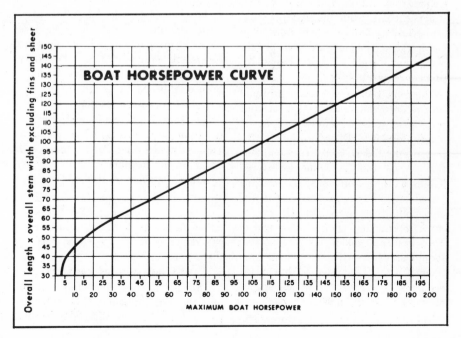

BOAT HORSEPOWER CURVE

Overall length x overall stern width excluding fins and sheer

MAXIMUM BOAT HORSEPOWER

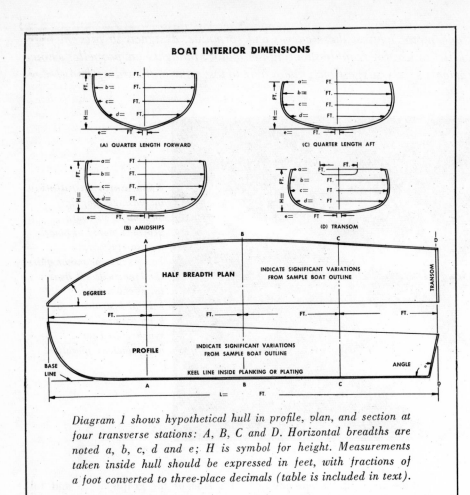

BOAT INTERIOR DIMENSIONS

(A) QUARTER LENGTH FORWARD

(C) QUARTER LENGTH AFT

(B) AMIDSHIPS

(D) TRANSOM

HALF BREADTH PLAN

INDICATE SIGNIFICANT VARIATIONS FROM SAMPLE BOAT OUTLINE

DEGREES

TRANSOM

PROFILE

INDICATE SIGNIFICANT VARIATIONS FROM SAMPLE BOAT OUTLINE

BASE LINE

KEEL LINE INSIDE PLANKING OR PLATING

ANGLE

L=   FT.

Diagram 1 shows hypothetical hull in profile, plan, and section at four transverse stations: A, B, C and D. Horizontal breadths are noted a, b, c, d and e; H is symbol for height. Measurements taken inside hull should be expressed in feet, with fractions of a foot converted to three-place decimals (table is included in text).

A SAFE LOAD

Determining the load limit—that is, the *maximum* combined weight of passengers, engine and miscellaneous equipment a given hull can safely carry—is not quite so simple. The OBC, it is true, has provided us with a formula for the job, namely Maximum Weight Capacity = Cubic Capacity × 12.5 lbs. per cu. ft., but the equation contains *two* unknowns. We must find Cubic Capacity before we can solve for Maximum Weight Capacity. Follow the procedure carefully.

Diagram 1 shows a hypothetical hull in profile, plan, and section at four transverse stations. These are: A, ¼ length forward; B, amidships; C, ¼ length aft; and D, at the transom. Sections A, B and C divide the overall length, L, into four equal parts. Horizontal breadths are measured at top, a, and bottom, e, of height, H, and at three intermediate points: b, c and d. Measurements taken inside the hull should be expressed in feet, with fractions of a foot converted to three-place decimals (see Table A for conversions of fractions to decimals).

There are two steps now before working out the final equation. These are 1) computing areas of sections which will permit us to 2) compute cubic capacity.

AREAS OF SECTIONS

Areas of Sections A, B and C are each found separately by using the formula:

$$Area = \frac{H}{12}(a+4b+2c+4d+e).$$

On the theory that excessive freeboard in proportion to beam does not necessarily contribute to a hull's safety, maximum values (see Table B) have been established for height, H.

CUBIC CAPACITY

The formula to compute Cubic Capacity of the hull is based on the areas (found in step one) for Sections A, B and C in the formula:

Cubic Capacity of Hull =

$$\frac{L}{12}(4A+2B+4C).$$

Areas A, B and C are in square feet; the cubic capacity in cubic feet, to three places.

MAXIMUM WEIGHT CAPACITY

This is the final step, and requires only the multiplication of the cubic capacity by the factor 12.5. The original equation, you'll perhaps remember, is:

Maximum Weight Capacity = Cubic Capacity × 12.5 lbs. per cu. ft. The result is an overall total in pounds, expressing to the nearest integer the safe maximum weight capacity of a given hull. But remember, a boat safely loaded and safely powered still has its limits, which is where seamanship and competent boat handling come into use.

For full information on boat horsepower and weight capacities, flotation, standardized dimension of outboard boats and motors, ventilation, fuel systems, steering systems, lighting for small boats, safety equipment, trailer facts, fire protection standards and many other details of recommended practices for outboards, readers may consult the Engineering Manual published by the Outboard Industry Associations, 307 North Michigan Ave., Chicago 1, Illinois.

★ ★ ★

TROUBLE SHOOTING THE OUTBOARD

MOTOR WON'T START:
Fuel tank empty
Fuel line closed
Fuel tank air vent closed
Motor not primed or choked
Low speed carburetor needle valve needs adjusting
Spark plug improperly gapped, cracked, fouled or lose
Magneto points improperly gapped; coil or condenser weak
Improper fuel mixture

MOTOR MISSES:
Pinched or kinked fuel line
Fouled spark plugs
Carburetor needs adjustment and/ or cleaning
Fuel filter needs cleaning
Improper fuel mixture
Frayed lead wire insulation

MOTOR LOSES POWER:
Carburetor needs adjustment
Fuel line not clear
Wrong type spark plugs
Motor overheating, check cooling system

EXCESSIVE VIBRATION:
Carburetor needs adjustment
Propeller bent, broken or fouled
Spark plug not firing
Clamp screws or other device loose

MOTOR OVERHEATS:
Water pump defective
Water intake clogged

★ ★ ★

ADDED FLOTATION

Still another step can be taken to assure the safety of your passengers and your boating rig: built-in flotation. This can take the form of air chambers or of the addition of some buoyant material, in either case, of sufficient quantity to support the weight even if the boat is entirely submerged.

A note to the OBC, 307 North Michigan Ave., Chicago, Ill., will bring you information on how you can determine the amount of flotation you need for your craft. First, however, you might try writing directly to your boatbuilder; he may already have done the computation involved.

WHAT PROP?

Your outboard motor, carefully selected under the foregoing considerations discussed in this series, may or may not come with a propeller. Either way, you want to be sure to turn the right wheel for the job your boat and motor must do.

Propeller manufacturers, and some outboard motor manufacturers, make a wide range of wheels for you to choose from. Ask their advice before buying. The choice, say, for a 16' to

TABLE A
Conversion of Inches to Decimals in Feet

Inches (or fractions)	Decimals in Feet	Inches (or fractions)	Decimals in Feet
1/8"	.010'	3"	.250'
1/4"	.021'	4"	.333'
3/8"	.031'	5"	.417'
1/2"	.042'	6"	.500'
5/8"	.052'	7"	.583'
3/4"	.062'	8"	.667'
7/8"	.073'	9"	.750'
1"	.083'	10"	.833'
2"	.167'	11"	.917'

18' runabout might go from a 2-bladed propeller with a pitch ratio (pitch divided by diameter) of 1.3 for a high-speed, lightweight rig to a 3- or 4-bladed propeller with a pitch ratio of .8 for a heavily loaded, slow speed craft. Fuel economy and boat performance will be markedly affected by propeller selection.

ELECTRONIC EQUIPMENT

Much of the electronic equipment previously held to be suitable only for yachts and their kin is now designed and produced for use in the smaller boat, including the outboard. Chief items in this equipment are the radiotelephone, depth finder and direction finder. Their price, bulk and weight have all been put into a range that will appeal to the outboarder, especially in the light of the equipments' various uses.

MISCELLANEOUS EQUIPMENT

Many of the points to be made here, readers will observe, have been dealt with in preceding parts. They are repeated, briefly, because of their significance.

The fire extinguisher(s) you use aboard the boat must be of a Coast Guard-approved type. If there's any doubt as to the approval status of the particular extinguisher, check with your local Coast Guard Inspection Office.

Of the approved types now on the market you'd do well to buy a carbon dioxide, dry chemical or foam extinguisher. The vaporizing liquid type, both those that must be pumped and those with stored pressure, will not be accepted as approved after January 1, 1962.

Check your extinguisher regularly, and recharge or refill as needed.

Lifesaving devices too must be of an approved type. The choice ranges from preservers and cushions to ring buoys and vests. The buoyant materials used in these devices include kapok, cork, balsawood, and vinyl-covered fibrous glass.

Take care that you have enough of these devices (one for each person aboard) and that their location and use is common knowledge—*before* you get under way!

Fire prevention of course is the responsibility of everyone

aboard but it is the special province of the skipper. In that capacity you must insist upon certain rules—and see to it that they are followed. You must, for instance, see that all cigarettes are out when approaching a gas dock. And you must see that none of your passengers forgets the smoking moratorium during the fueling process.

Most outboards are equipped with portable tanks. If they are of six-gallons or less in capacity, remove them from the craft for fueling. And see that they are made secure when in the boat. Ventilation, leakage and spill, of course, are all things you'll have to watch vigilantly.

Outboards with permanent fuel tanks should conform with approved inboard practice, running fill pipes to decks outside the coaming and venting outside the hull. Fill pipes should extend almost to the bottom of the tank, and not terminate at the top of the tank.

Permanent or portable, ground the gas hose nozzle to the fill pipe when fueling. This prevents static electricity from generating a spark which, in turn, might ignite gasoline fumes and blast boat and passengers out of the running.

IN CASE OF AN ACCIDENT

If you are involved in a boating accident on the navigable waters of the United States you are required by law to stop and give whatever help you can, without seriously endangering your boat or passengers. You must also identify yourself and your boat to any person injured or to the owner of any property damaged.

You must file a written accident report if there is 1) loss

TABLE B
Maximum Allowable Height for a Transverse Section

Beam of Section	Max. Height	Beam of Section	Max. Height
Up to 4.042'	1.583'	5.710' to 6.042'	2.083'
4.043' to 4.375'	1.667'	6.043' to 6.375'	2.167'
4.376' to 4.709'	1.750'	6.376' to 6.709'	2.250'
4.710' to 5.042'	1.833'	6.710' to 7.042'	2.333'
5.043' to 5.375'	1.917'	7.043' to 7.375'	2.417'
5.376' to 5.709'	2.000'	7.376' to 7.709'	2.500'

NOTE:—The maximum allowable height (H) is based on **width** (a) for that section on the Interior Dimensions. If the actual height of the section is **less** than the maximum allowable height, use the **actual height**. If the actual height of the section is **more** than the maximum allowable height, use the **maximum allowable height**.

of life, 2) injury causing a person to remain incapacitated for more than 72 hours, or 3) physical damage to property (including vessels) in excess of $100. If in doubt, report!

If you're in trouble while afloat, you'll find the Coast Guard, other boatmen and professional seamen ready to do what they can. To help the Guard assist you, the following steps are recommended:

1) Let somebody know your plans for the day including destination, intended stops en route, and estimated time of return. At the first opportunity notify those concerned of any change in plans.

2) Don't use MAYDAY in voice radio distress communications unless immediate assistance is required.

To get help when it's needed, of course, you'll want to know and carry some of the recognized distress signals. Apart from the radiotelephone, perhaps the most valuable distress aid available, there are a host of other devices. Flares, a continuous sounding with a whistle or horn, the raising and lowering of outstretched arms to each side, and so on, are some examples.

YOUR RESPONSIBILITIES

When you are admonished to know the Rules of the Road you should be aware that there are four different sets of such rules in effect according to your boating locality. These are: 1) Inland, 2) Great Lakes, 3) Western Rivers and 4) International. Copies of the rules you're interested in can be secured from your local Coast Guard office.

Hints on understanding the Inland Rules appear in the CG booklet *Recreational Boating Guide*, for sale by the Superintendent of Documents, U.S. Government Printing Office, Washington 25, D.C., at 40 cents a copy. The section is worth quoting here:

"Note that in these rules, 'steam vessel' includes *any* vessel propelled by machinery.

"If you are equipped with both machinery and sail, the *only* time you are considered as a sailing vessel under the rules is when you are propelled by sail alone. (Note: If you carry an engine of more than 10 hp—or less where states have so specified—you are required to have a registration number.)

"Risk of collision can, when circumstances permit, be ascertained by carefully watching the compass bearing of an approaching vessel. If the bearing does not appreciably change, such risk should be deemed to exist.

"The law says that in obeying and construing these rules due regard shall be had to all dangers of navigation and collision and to any special circumstances which may render a departure from the rules necessary in order to avoid immediate danger.

"The rules of the road apply alike to the small pleasure craft and large commercial ships such as ocean liners or freighters. However, the large vessel with her great length and tremendous weight requires a great deal more room to maneuver; because her turning circle is large, her stopping distance is relatively great, and often her deep draft restricts her to little variance from channel courses. Common sense dictates that operating a small pleasure craft too close to the large oceangoing vessel or a tug with tow may be dangerous."

QUIZ FOR OUTBOARD BOATMEN

1) Outboard boats on federal waterways are not required to follow the same Rules of the Road that apply to large commercial steamers.

2) A tacking sailboat always has right of way over an outboard boat.

3) Outboarders may disregard federal regulations that concern "steam vessels."

4) Outboard boats under way on federal waters must carry their registration certificates aboard.

5) Outboard boats powered by engines of 10 hp or less when used on federal waters are always required to be registered.

6) Money paid for boat registration fees is deductible from federal income taxes.

7) Sailboats with auxiliary outboard motors, used on federal waters, always must be registered.

8) Sailboats propelled by sail alone and used on federal waters are never required to be registered.

9) Outboard boats are required by law to have sufficient flotation to keep the boat afloat should it fill with water.

10) The proper propeller for a particular hull, motor and job helps achieve best boat performance.

11) Depth sounders are not suitable for use on outboard boats.

12) Life-saving equipment, like cushions, used on an outboard boat need not be Coast Guard-approved.

13) Liquid-type fire extinguishers have been CG-approved since January 1, 1962.

14) Fire extinguishers on an outboard boat should be kept in some remote place aboard, well out of the way of wind and water which may come aboard.

15) Portable fuel tanks should never be removed from the boat for filling.

16) You are not responsible for any damage caused by your boat's wake or waves.

17) In case of capsize, promptly swim as far from the boat as possible.

18) Only one set of Rules of the Road is in effect in the United States.

19) If your outboard boat is equipped with sail also, it is under the Rules considered a sailing vessel only when it is propelled by sail alone.

20) If you use both an outboard motor and a sail to propel your boat you are under the Rules considered a sailing vessel.

21) The Rules invariably require a large commercial vessel to keep clear of an outboard craft.

22) A boat propelled by oars must keep clear of an outboard boat.

23) You may anchor your outboard in a channel to fish, providing you keep clear of traffic.

24) A boating accident in which no one is killed need not be reported.

25) Any outboard hull is suited for the highest-powered stock outboard motor.

26) High-powered outboard motors on small, light hulls provide greatest speed and safety.

27) When under way at high speed give *all* your attention to your own safety.

28) Maintain your course and speed when passing another vessel close aboard.

29) Under all circumstances, maintain your course and speed when you have the right of way.

30) When an outboard boat turns, its stern swings in a direction opposite to the desired change in course.

31) Once your anchor is "holding bottom" the length of the anchor rode payed out is unimportant.

32) Wise practice to help assure proper anchor holding is to pay out anchor rode at least five times the depth of the water.

33) If you run aground you should attempt to get the anchor into deep water as far from the boat as possible.

34) The outboard motor(s) serves as a rudder on an outboard boat.

35) Maneuvering an outboard boat is relatively more difficult with two motors than with one.

36) The Coast Guard themselves can impose no penalty for the reckless operation of a boat on federal waters.

37) A bow line about 8 feet long and a stern line about 6 feet long, both made ready for landings, are always of sufficient size.

38) The bitter end of your anchor rode should be made fast when anchoring.

39) When anchoring, throw the anchor as far from the boat as possible.

40) Lower the anchor into the water, don't drop it.

41) Give the boat sternway after the anchor sets to test the anchor's holding power.

42) When attempting to get a person into the boat from the water, the boat's engine(s) should be kept running.

43) In a squall give the boat plenty of speed through the water.

44) When in a storm and heavy sea, stop your boat's engine(s) and drift.

45) Usually try to cross a large wave at about a right angle.

46) Because an unexpected delay might change your schedule, don't tell friends or relatives what your estimated time of arrival is, especially when making lengthy cruises or going off shore.

47) Don't equip your boat with running lights if you don't expect to run at night.

48) A compass is not required by federal law to be aboard an outboard boat.

49) Some states now issue boat registration numbers.

50) Some states now have jurisdiction over the federal waters within their state boundaries, concerning the equipment carried by and the inspection of boats operated upon those waters.

51) Boats exempted from their state's federally approved numbering provisions must apply to the Coast Guard for a number.

52) All violations of the Federal Motorboat Act of 1940 are punishable by a fine of not more than $2000.

53) Fog horns should not be used in place of a whistle.

54) The permanent seats in your new boat are an indication of how many persons that boat may safely carry.

55) It is preferable for safety's sake to have your outboard boat trim slightly by the stern rather than by the bow, when underway.

56) When adjusting trim underway by the relocation of passengers, never slow boat speed.

57) Your boat's freeboard is not a factor in determining the number of passengers you can safely carry.

58) The buoyancy of Coast Guard-approved kapok cushions remains unaffected when sat upon frequently.

59) It is desirable to paint the underbody of a boat moored in salt water with an anti-fouling paint, whether the boat is wood, fiberglass or metal.

60) At open throttle a 2-cycle outboard motor of 20 horsepower will consume less fuel than a 4-cycle inboard engine of 20 horsepower.

61) The improper mixing of oil and gasoline is apt to cause spark plug fouling on an outboard motor.

62) Gasoline spilled in a wet bilge, because it mixes with bilge water, loses its explosion potential.

63) Federal law requires U.S. pleasure boats underway to display the U.S. flag.

64) Speed limits posted on the water by the U.S. Corps of Army Engineers must be obeyed by boatmen.

65) A hull that makes 15 mph with a 7½-hp outboard motor will make 30 mph with a 15-hp outboard motor.

66) It is wise to carry a paddle or pair of oars of sufficient length (relative to the size of the boat) aboard an outboard boat.

67) Federal law requires all boat trailers to exhibit back-up lights.

68) Federal law specifies no minimum age for boat operators on federal waters.

69) A siren may be substituted for the whistle required by Pilot Rules for fog signals given by "steam vessels."

70) To insure sufficient ventilation when filling the permanent fuel tanks on your outboard boat, open all windows, hatches and doors.

ANSWERS TO QUIZ QUESTIONS

Compare your answers with these: Questions 4, 6, 10, 19, 30, 32, 33, 34, 38, 40, 41, 45, 48, 49, 53, 55, 59, 61, 64, 66, 68 and 69 are true. All others are false.

THE log book is the official record of your boat's cruise. The data therein forms an important accessory to piloting as well, not only on the particular cruise in question but for all other trips over the same or approximately the same routes. The data recorded in the log book also may be a contribution to the general fund of knowledge concerning waters used for motor-boat cruising; therefore, the facts and figures entered in the log book should be accurate and conclusive. In the case of large sea-going vessels the entries in the log are frequently referred to as evidence in legal actions.

While there are numerous forms of log books available, most of these are not well suited for motorboat use; rather, they are designed to meet the needs of larger vessels. The log sheet shown with this chapter has been designed especially to meet the needs of both small and large cruising boats whose owners are interested in coastwise cruising and proper piloting. The column headings are self-explanatory and may be kept as completely as desired.

In Column B the names of the important marks, buoys, aids to navigation, etc., which are passed on one's cruise are entered and the time of passing same is listed opposite each in Column A with the distance off in Column E.

The next three columns are used for listing the courses to the next object which is to be passed. If one is dealing in "true" compass courses this data is listed in Column H. If magnetic courses are preferred these should be entered in

CHAPTER XXX

Keep a Log

Column G with the courses corrected for the variation and deviation of the boat's own compass in Column F and the distance to the next objective in Column I. A deviation table for the boat's compass should be available so that it will be possible to determine the compass course from the magnetic course.

The data for columns J and M should be worked out from the chart and listed in advance of starting the cruise or at least before starting on the particular leg of the run in question.

The actual rpm of the motor should be listed in Column J. If the rpms are changed, the time of so changing should be recorded by using a new line on the log sheet.

Column K is for the estimated speed that the boat is making over the bottom which is a far different thing than her speed through the water. This is where the Skipper's real ability and knowledge of his own boat begin to come in. It considers such data as rpm of the motor, direction and force of the wind, set and drift of the current, and condition of the sea, and of course the load which the boat is carrying, condition of her underbody, etc., etc. Experience only can teach one how to apply these varying factors as they affect each boat differently, but constant observation of them will make a Skipper very adept in a short time.

Naturally before one starts on a cruise he has determined his boat's speed at different rpms of the motor. He has become familiar with the tide and current tables published by the government and can determine the effect of a tidal current on a boat's course. The amount which the wind and waves help or retard a boat on her course is something which must also be determined by experience. But this is valuable information and the cruising man should take time to gather all possible data on this subject.

From the Column I and Column K data it will be easy to compute the time which the boat should be abeam of the next object, Column M. Calculate the data for Column M with greatest accuracy and care. It is important especially in the fog or should fog shut down on you after you have made your departure from the last object. The safety of your boat and crew may depend upon how carefully you have worked this out.

The actual time on the course, Column N, is simply the difference between the clock time when you are actually

TABLE I

CLOUD FORMATIONS AND SYMBOLS

CIRRUS, (Ci.)—Detached clouds, delicate and fibrous looking, taking the form of feathers, generally of a white color, sometimes arranged in belts which cross a portion of the sky in great circles, and, by an effect of perspective, converging toward one or two opposite points of the horizon.

CIRRO-STRATUS, (Ci.-S.)—A thin, whitish sheet, sometimes completely covering the sky and only giving it a whitish appearance, or at others presenting, more or less distinctly, a formation like a tangled web. This sheet often produces halos around the sun and moon.

CIRRO-CUMULUS, (Ci.-Cu.)—Small globular masses or white flakes, having no shadows, or only very slight shadows, arranged in groups and often in lines.

ALTO-CUMULUS, (A.-Cu.)—Rather large globular masses, white or grayish, partially shaded, arranged in groups or lines, and often so closely packed that their edges appear confused. The detached masses are generally larger and more compact at the center of the group; at the margin they form into finer flakes. They often spread themselves out in lines in one or two directions.

ALTO-STRATUS, (A.-S.)—A thick sheet of a gray or bluish color, showing a brilliant patch in the neighborhood of the sun or moon, and which, without causing halos, may give rise to coronœ. This form goes through all the changes like the Cirro-Stratus, but its altitude is only half so great.

STRATO-CUMULUS, (S.-Cu.)—Large globular masses or rolls of dark cloud, frequently covering the whole sky, especially in winter, and occasionally giving it a wavy appearance. The layer of Strato-Cumulus is not, as a rule, very thick, and patches of blue sky are often visible through the intervening spaces. All sorts of transitions between this form and the Alto-Cumulus are noticeable. It may be distinguished from Nimbus by its globular or rolled appearance and also because it does not bring rain.

NIMBUS, (N.)—Rain clouds; a thick layer of dark clouds, without shape and with ragged edges, from which continued rain or snow generally falls. Through the openings of these clouds an upper layer of Cirro-Stratus or Alto-Stratus may almost invariably be seen. If the layer of Nimbus separates into shreds or if small loose clouds are visible floating at a low level underneath a large Nimbus, they may be described as Fracto-Nimbus (Fr.-N.), the "scud" of sailors.

CUMULUS, (Cu.)—Woolpack clouds; thick clouds of which the upper surface is domeshaped and exhibits protuberances, while the base is horizontal. When these clouds are opposite the sun the surfaces usually presented to the observer have a greater brilliance than the margins of the protuberances. When the light falls aslant, they give deep shadows; when, on the contrary, the clouds are on the same side as the sun, they appear dark, with bright edges. The true Cumulus has clear superior and inferior limits. It is often broken up by strong winds, and the detached portions undergo continual changes. These may be distinguished by the name of Fracto-Cumulus (Fr.-Cu.).

CUMULO-NIMBUS, (Cu.-N.)—The thunder-cloud or shower-cloud; heavy masses of clouds rising in the form of mountains, turrets, or anvils, generally having a sheet or screen of fibrous appearance above, and a mass of clouds similar to Nimbus underneath. From the base there usually fall local showers of rain or of snow (occasionally hail or soft hail).

STRATUS, (S.)—A horizontal sheet of lifted fog; when this sheet is broken up into irregular shreds by the wind or by the summits of mountains, it may be distinguished by the name of Fracto-Stratus (Fr.-S.).

FRACTO-STRATUS, (Fr.-S.)—A horizontal sheet of lifted fog broken into irregular shreds by wind or the summits of mountains, is distinguished by the name of Fracto-Stratus (Fr.-S.).

FRACTO-CUMULUS, (Fr.-Cu.)—Cumulus, when broken up by strong winds, undergo continual changes. These are distinguished by the name of Fracto-Cumulus (Fr.-Cu.).

Amount of Clouds

In the scale for the amount of clouds 0 represents a sky which is cloudless and 10 a sky which is completely overcast.

Table I, which describes various cloud formations. Amount of clouds is recorded by figures from 0 to 10

TABLE II — MODIFIED BEAUFORT WIND SCALE

Code Figure	Beaufort's Scale	Effect on Sea	Velocity (Knots)	Terms Used in U. S. Weather Bureau Forecasts
0	CALM	Sea like a mirror	Less than 1	Calm
1	LIGHT AIR	Ripples—no foam crests	1–3	Light
2	LIGHT BREEZE	Small wavelets, crests have a glassy appearance and do not break	4–6	Do.
3	GENTLE BREEZE	Large wavelets, crests begin to break. Scattered whitecaps	7–10	Gentle
4	MODERATE BREEZE	Small waves becoming longer. Frequent whitecaps	11–16	Moderate
5	FRESH BREEZE	Moderate waves, taking a more pronounced long form; many whitecaps, some spray	17–21	Fresh
6	STRONG BREEZE	Large waves begin to form; extensive whitecaps everywhere, some spray	22–27	Strong
7	MODERATE GALE	Sea heaps up and white foam from breaking waves begins to be blown in streaks along the direction of the wind	28–33	Do.
8	FRESH GALE	Moderately high waves of greater length; edges of crests break into spindrift. The foam is blown in well-marked streaks along the direction of the wind	34–40	Do.
9	STRONG GALE	High waves. Dense streaks of foam along the direction of the wind. Spray may affect visibility. Sea begins to roll	41–47	Gale
10	WHOLE GALE	Very high waves. The surface of the sea takes on a white appearance. The rolling of the sea becomes heavy and shocklike. Visibility is affected	48–55	Do.
11	STORM	Exceptionally high waves. Small and medium sized ships are lost to view for long periods	56–63	Whole Gale
12	HURRICANE	The air is filled with foam and spray. Sea completely white with driving spray; visibility very seriously affected	64–71	Hurricane
13	HURRICANE		72–80	Do.
14	HURRICANE		81–89	Do.
15	HURRICANE		90–99	Do.
16	HURRICANE		100–109	Do.
17	HURRICANE		110–118	Do.

abeam of the object and the entry in Column A. The actual speed, Column O, is also easily computed from Columns I and N, after reaching the object. By comparing the entries in Columns K and O, or Columns L and N, the Skipper will know how good he has been in estimating the effect of the many varying factors on the speed of his boat. In estimating the time he should be at the next object, Column M, he can make due allowance for the amount which his estimate was in error.

The data to be entered at the bottom are physical observations which are worth recording from time to time. Tables I, II, IV and V give a convenient code for listing such data. Data on the estimated set and drift of the current can be obtained from the government current tables.

As an illustration of the proper keeping of the log we will consider a cruise made on Long Island Sound, July 4, from Manhasset Bay, N. Y., to New London, Connecticut, a distance of about 100 miles. Data on the speed of the boat is shown in Table VII and the deviation on easterly and northerly courses in Table VI.

We elect to run our motor at 1400 rpm which gives us a boat speed of exactly 10 miles per hour through the water. We take our departure from Gangway bell buoy number 27 off the entrance to Manhasset Bay at exactly noon, Eastern Standard Time. Our tide table shows us that it will be high water at nearby Willets Pt. at 1242. There is a fresh westerly wind blowing which we estimate to be about 15 miles per hour. This wind is nearly directly astern of us and it kicks up quite a chop. The sky overhead is cloudless, the barometer reads 30.22 and the thermometer 80 degrees.

We elect to run down the Sound, keeping close to the north shore of Long Island until we reach Orient Shoal and then cruise diagonally across the Sound to the entrance of the Thames River. This route will be a little longer than if we should go down the center of the Sound, yet we will be in sight of land at all times with many aids to navigation available as a check on our position should fog shut down on us.

Previous to the start of our cruise we have drawn the courses we are to follow on Coast and Geodetic Survey charts numbers

Table II, which supplies data concerning the force of wind and described in various commonly used forms

1211, 1212 and 1213. We have made these courses pass close to a number of fixed aids to navigation so that the greatest distance between marks is less than 15 miles. We have scaled the distance between the various marks and have entered this data in Columns B and I, with the distance off when abeam in Column E. In scaling from these charts, we do it in nautical miles as there is no statute mile scale on the charts. We convert statute miles by multiplying the distances in nautical miles by 1.15.

In advance, we have also calculated the various magnetic courses between marks and have listed these in Column G, and have applied the deviation of our compass, Table VI, to get our compass courses which we have listed in Column F.

From the known speeds of our boat, Table VII, it should now be an easy matter to determine in advance the time we should be abeam of each of the marks listed in Column B, except for two major conditions which we can not forecast in advance. While we do know that we are going to take our departure from Gangway bell at 1200 on July fourth, yet we have no way of determining in advance what the direction of the wind or condition of the sea will be on that day. Both of these elements might help or retard our progress.

They should always be taken into account, insofar as possible.

The other condition which might develop to change any pre-arranged time schedule is fog. While we have decided to run our motor at 1400 rpm, which gives us a boat speed of 10 miles per hour, should fog shut in on us, the law requires, and safety makes it essential, that we slow down. So if fog comes, our motor will be run at 1000 rpm which is equivalent to a boat speed of 8 miles per hour.

A bad blow might also make it necessary to cut down our engine speed but at this season of the year this is unlikely. On the other hand should head winds be met, the engine might be speeded up slightly to keep our boat speed at 10 miles an hour.

Yet in spite of these unknowns of wind, sea and fog it would

NAMES, ADDRESS, AND TITLES OF GUESTS ABOARD. Mate: W.H. Koelbel; Deckhand: Dan Schrader; George Rupprecht

Guests: W.F. Bailey, Marybelle Johnson, Ruth B. Smith

A CLOCK TIME	B PLACE ABEAM BUOY, LANDMARK OR VESSEL PASSED	C TO PORT OR STARBOARD	D COMPASS BEARING TO PLACE ABEAM	E DISTANCE OFF MILES	F COURSE STEERED	G MAGNETIC	H TRUE	DISTANCE MILES	J MOTOR R.P.M.	K ESTIMATED SPEED M.P.H.	L ESTIMATED TIME TO NEXT OBJECTIVE	M WOULD BE ABEAM NEXT OBJECTIVE AT	N ACTUAL TIME BETWEEN OBJECTIVES	O ACTUAL SPEED BETWEEN OBJECTIVES	P DEPTH	Q BOTTOM	R REMARKS
12 00	Gangway Bell #27	S		0	051	045		1.3	1400	9.68	8	12 08	8	9.68			
12 08	Execution Light	P		0	079	079		5.75	"	9.72	35	12 43	34	10.12			
12 42	Matinicock Bell #21	S		0	079	079		8.6	"	10.16	51	13 34	51	10.10			
13 33	Lloyds Bell #15	S		0	084	090		4.8	"	10.4	28	14 02	28	10.28			
14 01	Eatons Point Can #13	S		.25	092	098		14.4	"	10.16	1:25	15 27	1:25	10.18			
15 26	Old Field Point Gong 11a	S		.3N	092	098		8.05	"	10.25	47	16 14	48	10.05			
16 14	Black Can #9	S		0	092	098		7.3	"	10.50	42	16 56	44	9.96			
16 58	Herod Point Shoal Can #7	S		.3N	092	098		6.3	"	10.50	36	17 32	37	10.20			Dirt in fuel
17 35	Roanoke Shoal Can #5	S		0	079	079		14.6	"	10.65	1:22	18 54	1:22	10.68			Rain
18 57	Hortons Point Light	S		.7N	071	068		7.3	"	10.0	42	19 36	54	9.94			
19 41	Orient Point Shoal Can #3	S		.6N	071	068		12.8	1000	9.0	1:25	21 01	28	8.72			Mist
21 09	Bartletts Reef Whistle #2A	P		0	071	068		3.35	1000	8.65	23	21 24	38	5.29	65	sft	Mist
21 47	Sarah Ledge Gong	P		0	019	011		3.05	1000	10.00	18	21 42	29	6.32	45	sft	Mist to fog
22 16	New London, Burr's Dock	P		0					1400								Fog

FUEL — In Tanks at Start 100 galls — At Finish 20 galls — Took Aboard — Used 80

FRESH WATER — In Tanks at Start 50 galls — In Tanks at Finish 42 galls — Took Aboard

RUNNING LIGHTS — Lit at 19 40 — Extinguished at 22 20

HIGH WATER (time) 12 42 at (place) Willetts Point — DAYS RUN 97.60 +3.5 miles

LOW WATER (time) 17 30 at (place) New London — TOTAL CRUISE RUN

OWNER F.W. Horenburger

Time 12 20 — Wind Force 4 — Direction W

Current: Set SW — Drift (+ or — m.p.h.) 0.32 — State of Sea 6

Weather b — Clouds 0 — Visibility 0

Barometer 30.22 — Temperature 80°

be well to work out in advance the expected time of arrival at the various points and enter this data in Column M. Then as we proceed down the Sound slight adjustments in these times may be made to correct for any of these conditions unknown at the present moment. Such necessary changes should be small under normal conditions.

But before we can pre-determine these times of passing the various points there is just one more variable which must be taken into consideration—the tides and currents. The current may have a great effect on our speed. But fortunately the Government supplies us with sufficient data on currents to permit us to pretty accurately estimate their effect on our speed. It's a fascinating subject so we will now figure in advance what the effect of the tidal current all the way down the Sound should be on our boat and then later, while we are underway, we'll see how good our estimates have been.

Since we are operating on Eastern Standard Time we can use the times in the Current Tables directly. We find that the Current Diagrams of Long Island Sound refer to the conditions existing in The Race, Long Island Sound, and the two periods of the current cycle listed in tabular form are headed "Slack Flood Begins," and "Slack Ebb Begins."

The tidal current charts are lithographed reproductions showing by means of lines, arrows, and figures, the story of the current for every hour of a complete twelve-hour cycle. A separate chart is printed for each hour and these are referenced to the stage of the cycle called Slack Flood Begins and Slack Ebb Begins, which are tabulated.

Slack Flood Begins as per current diagrams is at 0722 on July 4 and since we plan to start at noon we can use as our first chart the one headed "Five Hours After Slack Flood Begins at The Race." While this is actually 22 minutes later than our schedule we can, for all practical purposes, ignore that one-third hour difference. As a matter of actual fact there would be a barely perceptible difference in the vicinity of Execution Light, although nearer The Race where currents are much stronger than at Gangway Bell. Since we are not concerned with the conditions existing there at the moment we will not worry about it now.

Our first course to Execution Light is 045 degrees and the drift is found to be 0.4 knot and the set practically 225 degrees, or directly opposing our progress. On the inside cover of our Tidal Current Charts appears a correction table which gives a factor by which current velocities are to be multiplied to suit the conditions on any one cycle of the tide. Our maximum predicted flood velocity is 2.9 knots, and the maximum ebb 3.3 knots. The table indicates that for 2.9 knots flood we apply a correction factor which, in this case, happens to be 0.7. Therefore, every current figure which we shall use throughout must be multiplied by 0.7 to give its correct value for the day and time and then by 1.15 to convert to statute miles.

Similarly, on July fourth the time 1314 is given as the Slack Ebb Begins. We can reference all of the rest of our problems to that figure. We find also that the maximum ebb is at 1623 and the predicted velocity on that particular flow is 3.3 knots.

Now, going back to the 0.4 knot found in our first course, we apply 0.7 and se-

cure 0.28 knot and since we are doing all of our problems in statute miles, this turns out to be 0.32 mile against us. Our unit speed of 10 miles will accordingly be reduced to 9.68 miles. In order to learn how long a period of time will be required to cover a distance of 1.30 miles we can apply a formula involving time, speed, and distance in various ways so that any one factor can be found when the other two are known.

Elapsed time = Seconds in an hour multiplied by distance and divided by speed

$$\text{or} \quad \frac{3{,}600 \times 1.3}{9.68} = 8 \text{ minutes } 03 \text{ seconds}$$

therefore, the time required to reach Execution Rock will be 8 minutes. We can discard the seconds as being ultra precise which, after all, is not required. To solve for the other factors in the formula it may be rewritten as follows:

Speed = seconds in an hour multiplied by distance, and divided by the elapsed time in seconds

or: Distance = Elapsed time in seconds multiplied by speed (mph) and divided by seconds in hour.

With these three formulas the problem can be solved in any of its variations. It may also be applied by using minutes instead of seconds, but this has the disadvantage of giving results in minutes and decimals of a minute, which is a less convenient unit. While these formulas have been introduced to indicate the method of solving the time and speed problems, it is very much simpler to locate a table which gives the speed in miles per hour for any reasonable combination of minutes and seconds for a mile. A simple multiplication will then give the time for greater distances. Further times and speeds in this problem will, therefore, be taken from such a table.

We can continue the same current diagram for about one hour. For the second course, to Matinicock bell buoy number 21, our distance by chart is 5.75 miles and we find that on this run two current figures apply, one of 0.4 knot and one of 0.3 knot. Using a mean of 0.35 and multiplying by the correction factor of 0.7 and by 1.15 to reduce to statute miles we get 0.28 mile opposed. Our net speed, therefore, will be 9.72 mph. From

TABLE III

STANDARD ABBREVIATIONS USED ON CHARTS

Relating to Lights

Lt. Light, L.H. Lighthouse, REF. Reflector, F Fixed, Occ Occulting, Fl Flashing, QK Fl Quick Flashing, I Qk Interrupted Quick, Alt Alternating, Gp Occ Group Occulting, Gp Fl Group Flashing, S-L Short-long, F Fl Fixed and flashing, F Gp Fl Fixed and group flashing, Rot. rotating, min. minutes, sec. seconds, M. nautical mile, Gp. group, SEC. sector, Vi. violet, Bu. Blue, G. green, Or. orange, R. red, W. white, Am. amber, OBSC. obscured, (U) unwatched, Occas. occasional, Irreg. irregular, Temp. temporary, Vert. vertical, Hor. horizontal, D destroyed, Exting. extinguished, V.B. vertical beam, Exper. experimental, R. range, AERO aeronautical.

Relating to Buoys and Beacons

C Can, N Nun, Sp Spherical, S Spar, Quar. Quarantine, Priv. maintd. Maintained by private interests, H.B. Horizontal bands, V.S. Vertical stripes, Chec. checkered, W. white, B. black, R. red, Y. yellow, G. green, Br. brown, Gy. gray, T.B. temporary buoy, Bn. beacon, REF. Reflector.

Relating to Fog Signals

Fog Sig. Fog signal station, SUB-BELL Submarine fog bell, SUB-OSC. Submarine oscillator, NAUTO. Nautophone, DIA. Diaphone, SIREN

Fog siren, HORN Fog trumpet or fog horn, BELL Fog bell, WHIS. Fog whistle, REED Reed horn, D.F.S. Distance finding station, GUN Fog gun.

Relating to Bottoms

Grd. ground, S. sand, M. mud, Oz. ooze, Ml. marl, Cl. Clay, G. gravel, Sh. shingle, P. pebbles, St. stones, Sp. specks, Rk. rock, Bld. boulder, Ck. chalk, Qz quartz, Co. coral, Co. Hd. coral head, Md. madropore, Vol. Ash. volcanic ash, La, lava, Pm. pumice, T. tufa, Sc. scorice, Cn. cinders, Mn. manganese, Sh. shells, Oys. oysters, Ms. mussels, Spg. sponge, Grs. grass, Wd. weeds, Fr. foraminifera, Gl. globigerina, Di. diatom, Rd. radiolaria, Pt. pteropod, Po. polyzoa, fne. fine, crs. coarse, sft. soft, hrd. hard, stf. stiff, sml. small, lrg. large, stk. sticky, brk. broken, rky. rocky, spk. speckled, gry. gritty, fly. flinty, glac. glacial, wh. white, bk. black, bu. blue, gn. green, yl. yellow, rd. red, br. brown, gy. gray, lt. light, dk. dark, Ca. calcareous.

Relating to Dangers

Bk. bank, Shl. Shoal, Rf. reef, Le. ledge, Obstr. obstruction, Wk. wreck, Wks. wreckage, cov. covers, uncov. uncovers, Rep. reported, Discol. discolored, P.A. position approximate, P.D. position doubtful, E.D. existence doubtful, Pos. position.

When examining a chart we find symbols used which abbreviate features of the lights, buoys, fog signals and nature of bottom our table we find this is equivalent to 370 seconds per mile. For 5.75 miles, therefore, 2127 seconds or 35 minutes 27 seconds to cover the 5.75 miles, giving the predicted time of 1243.

TABLE IV
STATE OF SEA SYMBOLS

State of Sea—The state of the sea is expressed by the following system of symbols:

B. — Broken or irregular sea.	M. — Moderate sea or swell.
C. — Choppy, short, or cross sea.	R. — Rough sea.
G. — Ground swell.	S. — Smooth sea.
H. — Heavy sea.	T. — Tide-rips *
L. — Long rolling sea.	

* Tide-rips—Agitation of the surface water caused by the tide passing swiftly over a shoal.

We have still not run out of our first chart of current diagrams which we have been using so continue our computations in the same manner. The current strength is falling so that our speed will not be retarded as strongly for we are approaching the slack water condition and soon will find the current helping us. On the run to Lloyds of 8.6 miles, which will consume more than 50 minutes, we pass out of the first hour and must use the next current diagram sheet headed "Slack Ebb Begins at The Race." Here we find that somewhere between the two charts we have passed through the slack period of the tide. At the start of the leg a current of minus 0.3 gradually stops and runs the other way with greater strength of plus 0.5. We assume, therefore, that a mean of these helped us throughout and our speed has picked up to 10.16 miles, after applying correction factors. This is equivalent to 354 seconds per mile, for 8.6 miles or a total of 3044 seconds, equal to 50 minutes 44 seconds. We are due at Lloyds bell, therefore, at 1334.

The next course carries us to the can buoy off Eaton's Point, a distance of 4.8 miles. Our first estimate of speed indicates about 29 minutes so the Slack Ebb Begins diagram still applies. Our course has changed to 090 degrees and the current set inshore is approximately 090 degrees also. Notice that near shore the current runs counter to the main axis of the Sound. The figure 0.5 knot can reasonably be assumed to apply throughout and this becomes when translated to miles and corrected 0.4 mile. Our speed, therefore, will be 10.4 miles. This requires 346 seconds per mile or for 4.8 miles, a total of 1661 seconds or 27 minutes 41 seconds, say 28 minutes. We are due at Eaton's at 1402.

The next run is a long one, 14.40 miles to the black gong buoy off Old Field Point. The currents on this run are favorable but weak. No definite figures appear, so that we must estimate the probable strength. Further out in the Sound it seems to be about 0.4 knot or slightly more. On our second course we can perhaps estimate a strength of 0.2 knot, which we shall do. This corrected current equals only 0.16 mile, so our speed is computed at 10.16 mph. This is equivalent to 354 seconds per mile or 5098 seconds total equal to 1 hour and 25 minutes. We have progressed thus far in our journey to beyond Old Field Point and by now the time has advanced so that we can use the chart for "Two Hours After Slack Ebb Begins at The Race." Our next course, 098 degrees, carries us to black can number 9 near Rocky Point. A weak current which may be estimated at perhaps 0.3 knot or 0.25 mile helps us and for the next forty odd minutes we will be in it. For our speed 10.25 miles, we require 351 seconds per mile or 2826 seconds or 47 minutes for this leg of 8.05 miles. This brings us to 1614 and we must, therefore, use the "Three Hours After Slack Ebb Begins" diagram for the next hour.

The distance to Herod Point Shoal, can number 7, is 7.30 miles. The current strength along the course selected is about 0.6 knot equivalent when corrected to 0.48 mile, let's say 0.5 mile favorable. Our speed then is 10.5 miles or 343 seconds per mile. It will require 2504 seconds or 41 minutes 44 seconds for the leg, so we set our time down as 42 minutes more, which brings us to Herod Point at 1656. A short run of 6.30 miles

to Roanoke Shoal, can number 5, can be figured at the same current strength and the data for this run works out to be 36 minutes required, due at 1732. At this buoy our courses are changed to a more northerly direction to keep more or less parallel to the shore to Horton's Point. While the light itself is on the shore, our course is laid to a point 0.7 mile offshore. We advance to the next current chart. the one called "Four Hours After Slack Ebb Begins" and while current strengths inshore are only about half of what they are further out in the stream our preference of course keeps us closer to shore. No figures are given along the projected line of our course. The figure 0.6 appears off Roanoke Point, but the figures offshore are greater, running to 1–2 knots. The great volume of water in the Sound is flowing out through the narrower channels of The Race where the current really flows fast. It is safe to assume, therefore, that the strength here will be somewhat greater than 0.6 so let us assume 0.8 knot which in miles is 0.65 mile. Our speed, therefore, is 10.65 miles and will require 338 seconds per mile or a total of 4935 seconds, one hour and 22 minutes, so that we will be abeam of Horton's Point at 1854.

Our next leg takes us to can number 3 off Orient Shoal. We notice that we have now passed out of the scope of the tidal diagram we have been using and since our current tables give us the fact that Slack Flood Begins is at 1922, we accordingly turn to the first chart in the booklet and regard that as being the conditions existing at 1922. We have laid out our cruise only as far as Horton's Point and during the run to Orient Point will be in the conditions indicated. We notice now that the current is no longer favorable but opposed to our progress. And since we are at the edge of the current strength and also some few minutes ahead of the current time of the chart, we can assume slack water for this course and figure our speed at 10 miles without allowances of any kind. The distance of 7.05 miles is accordingly covered in 42 minutes 18 seconds at the rate of 360 seconds per mile, which brings us to Orient Point at 1936.

TABLE V
WEATHER SYMBOLS

Weather—To designate the weather a series of symbols devised by the late Admiral Beaufort is employed. The system is as follows:

b. — Clear blue sky.	r. — Rainy weather, or continuous rain.
d. — Drizzling, or light rain.	
f. — Fog, or foggy weather.	s. — Snow, snowy or snow falling.
g. — Gloomy, or stormy-looking.	
h. — Hail.	t. — Thunder.
l. — Lightning.	u. — Ugly appearances or threatening weather.
m. — Misty weather.	
p. — Passing showers of rain.	w. — Wet, or heavy dew.
q. — Squally weather.	z. — Hazy.

To indicate great intensity of any feature its symbol may be underlined; thus, r., heavy rain.

The same diagram will serve further for the course to Bartlett's Reef bell. This is 12.8 miles distant and will take us about an hour and a quarter. By examining the next chart, "One Hour After Slack Flood Begins," we see that during the later part of this leg we will be opposed by stronger currents and for at least a part of the time by as much as 2.1 knots. The early parts of the run will be opposed by currents of 0.4 and 1.0 knot and, further, our course now will be somewhat diagonally through the current flow and no longer head on to it. We find 0.3, 1.0, 2.1 and 1.6; an average of these is 1.25, and in miles and corrected it is equal to 1.0 mile. Our course is 067 degrees and the set of the current is 270 degrees. We find that while there is a difference of about 22½ degrees in the directions there is not sufficient difference to alter the effect of the current and estimate that our speed throughout the run will be 9 miles—or 400 seconds per mile. For 12.80 miles we will require 5120 seconds or 1 hour 25 minutes and 20 seconds. We are due at Bartlett's Reef bell at 2101.

From Bartlett's to Sarah Ledge gong is 3.35 miles, and conditions on chart "Two Hours After Slack Flood Begins" apply. Current strength is given as 1.7 knots equivalent to 1.35 miles so that our speed will be reduced to 8.65 miles or 416 seconds per mile. For 3.35 miles this equals 1394 seconds or 23 minutes and 14 seconds. Our schedule will then show us due at Sarah Ledge at 2124 almost within sight of our destination. Our last leg will be a run of 3.05 miles up the Thames River to Burr's Landing in New London. Since the current in the river is weak, we again estimate our full 10-mile speed and find at 360 seconds per mile, we will consume 1098 seconds or 18 minutes 18 seconds to complete our journey. We should finish our trip at 2142 if everything goes as per schedule and there are no untoward events to delay or upset the schedule. Our time table is completed and our estimates all entered in the log. Remember that all of these studies have been made prior to our actual cruise of July 4. Wind, weather and uncertainty will now get in their good work and upset our calculations during the course of the cruise.

TABLE VI
DEVIATION OF COMPASS
(From Deviation Card)

Magnetic (Degrees)	Deviation (Degrees)
011	8W
045	6W
068	3W
079	0
090	6E
098	6E

Now let us carry out the keeping of the log during the course of our actual run and see how closely correct our estimates were. Our departure from Gangway bell is made at exactly 1200 as planned. We adjust our speed to 1400 revolutions and prepare to enjoy an exhilarating trip. A moderate westerly breeze and a slight chop lend zest to the action of the boat. Our revolutions are watched carefully and the mate is at the wheel while the skipper prepares to keep the log. The short run to Execution is made exactly on time. At the light we square away from the course down the Sound and find the wind more on the stern. The sun shines brightly so the cook and guests go up on the forward deck to catch some sun tan. The mate steers a careful course; due to the following sea this work requires close attention. Soon the bell off Matinicock appears and is sighted by the guests forward. At the time when it is abeam we find ourselves a minute ahead of schedule, having passed the buoy at 1242. This increase in speed is due to the effect of the following wind and sea. We notice the strength of wind is less and also that the sea is smoother. It is less difficult to steer and the motion of the boat is quieter. Lloyd's Bell appears and is passed at 1333, indicating that we are running closely to schedule, but are ahead by the minute gained in the first leg. The sea becomes quieter and the wind drops still more until soon it is gone and the water is calm. Before long Eaton's Point can appears which is passed at 1401 still one minute ahead of schedule. The mate has been steering for two hours and is now relieved by the skipper who takes over the wheel while the mate keeps the log.

A long run to Old Field Point, almost 14½ miles, is made without incident; the weather gets warmer as the temperature has gone up from 80 to 85 degrees. Before long the gong buoy off Old Field Point comes abeam and is left astern at 1526, still ahead of time. The wind is now coming in a bit more from the south and is so recorded. The course is still 098 degrees and for 8.05 miles to can number 9 near Rocky Point the cruise continues; we arrive there at 1614 and note we have lost the minute and are back on schedule. Apparently the allowance for current was too generous. Here the mate and skipper relieve each other again after a two hour trick at the wheel. We continue

toward can number 7 at Herod Point, course still the same, wind becoming noticeably stronger from the south and we notice a little sea making up. Since we are under the lee of the land it is not uncomfortable. We pass Herod Point can at 1658 and find we have lost still another minute. Wind has increased and we roll pretty heavily in the beam sea and notice that the engine no longer runs steadily. There are interruptions in its rhythm and soon it pops a couple of times and hesitates. The trouble is quickly diagnosed as foreign matter in the fuel and since the boat is equipped with dual gasoline strainers, the skipper goes below and switches the flow to the clean strainer and removes the sediment and dirt from the other. All is well again and we roll along, reaching Roanoke Shoal can 5 at 1735. We find we have lost further time due to the trouble with the fuel and further due to lack of attention to the steering while the engine was cutting up. The weather also has been clouding over and by now we have large masses of heavy cumulo-nimbus clouds. It has become hazy and squally so the oilskins have been brought out in anticipation of showers. The watch is changed again at 1800. While it has clouded over visibility has not been impaired and we make our Horton Point Light on shore. We are abeam of it at 1857, three minutes behind schedule, no doubt due to a lesser current strength than anticipated. It now starts to rain so oilers are put on. There is a moderate sea with a reduced wind, but still misty. Sunset at 1940 and running lights go on. Orient Shoal can 3 is difficult to find as it is getting dark, we are behind schedule by several minutes and it is still misty with reduced visibility. We finally find it at 1941 and are now 5 minutes behind our schedule.

TABLE VII
SPEED OF BOAT

R.P.M.	M.P.H.
1000	8.0
1100	8.5
1200	9.1
1300	9.6
1400	10.0
1500	10.9

The next run will take us diagonally across the Sound to Bartlett's Bell some 12.8 miles and almost an hour and a half further. The misty condition continues, although it is not yet sufficiently thick to require a reduction in speed. We are running more slowly due to the stronger current opposed to us and after relief at the wheel at 8 o'clock we find the cook has the evening meal ready. The course is held carefully and a watch is kept for the light on the buoy. We find a flashing white considerably to starboard of our course and change to examine it more closely. It turns out to be the steamer lane buoy which was on our plotted course but the current has headed us off to the westward more than we anticipated; we make a little greater allowance and at 2109 we are abeam of Bartlett's Reef flashing red whistle. We have lost still more time on our schedule and are now eight minutes behind. The mist is getting thicker and shortly becomes a genuine fog. We reduce our speed to 1000 revolutions and go ahead at 8 miles. Wind has eased off to easterly and very light so that the sea is calm and everything would be perfect except for the fog. We hold our course, but are uncertain as to the effect of the current which is setting us to the westward towards the reef. We decide to check our position and stop the engine so that we may take a sounding. Skipper takes the wheel while the mate makes a cast and reports almost eleven fathoms, 65 feet. We locate the point on our chart which agrees with this depth and once more resume our journey. (If a definite course or similar line of position is not available, a chain of soundings might be required.) Before long we find the gong buoy at Sarah's Ledge. We hear it and pick our way toward it by the sound of its several gongs which make it so easy to recognize. Slowing down and with time lost for sounding we are quite far behind schedule as it is now 2147.

Changing our course up the Thames River we soon lose sight of Sarah Ledge and still find ourselves in a dense fog. While holding our course at 1000 revolutions we are fairly certain of our position, but after some minutes on this course feel that it is advisable to obtain a check by another sounding. Once again the engine is stopped and a cast of the lead is made, this time showing only 45 feet, 7½ fathoms. We locate this spot on the chart and find that it checks with our course. We continue with more confidence and as we get up the river we find a slight lifting of the fog which permits us to locate Burr's dock, our destination. We arrive here at 2216 some 34 minutes behind our original schedule, tired and weary from the long journey and the difficulties of coming through the fog. Guests are rowed ashore and delivered to the taxi driver while the crew returns aboard to get a good night's rest. We observe that the schedule, as prepared in advance, was followed fairly closely until the fog shut in and delayed us. Currents were not always up to the strength anticipated and did not help as much as expected. It indicates, however, that close schedules are entirely practical and can be adhered to very closely in all normal weather conditions. Keeping a log forms one of the most interesting and educational features of cruising.

Table VIII (right), boat speed over a measured 1-mile course can be picked out by inspection. For example, if it takes 4 minutes and 19 seconds to run a statute mile (5280-foot) course, the boat's speed is 13.9 statute miles per hour. If the course were a nautical mile (6080 feet), the speed is 13.9 knots (nautical miles per hour). (The international nautical mile, recently adopted by the Coast Guard, is taken to be 6076.1 feet.)

TABLE I—SPEED OVER A MEASURED MILE

Sec.	1 min.	2 min.	3 min.	4 min.	5 min.	6 min.	7 min.	8 min.	9 mid.	10 min.	11 min.	12 min.
0	60.000	30.000	20.000	15.000	12.000	10.000	8.571	7.500	6.667	6.000	5.455	5.000
1	59.016	29.752	19.890	14.938	11.960	9.972	8.551	7.484	6.654	5.990	5.446	4.993
2	58.064	29.508	19.780	14.876	11.921	9.945	8.531	7.469	6.642	5.980	5.438	4.986
3	57.143	29.268	19.672	14.815	11.881	9.917	8.511	7.453	6.630	5.970	5.430	4.979
4	56.250	29.032	19.565	14.754	11.842	9.890	8.491	7.438	6.618	5.960	5.422	4.972
5	55.384	28.800	19.459	14.694	11.803	9.863	8.471	7.423	6.606	5.950	5.414	4.965
6	54.545	28.571	19.355	14.634	11.765	9.836	8.451	7.407	6.593	5.941	5.405	4.959
7	53.731	28.346	19.251	14.575	11.726	9.809	8.431	7.392	6.581	5.931	5.397	4.952
8	52.941	28.125	19.149	14.516	11.688	9.783	8.411	7.377	6.569	5.921	5.389	4.945
9	52.174	27.907	19.048	14.458	11.650	9.756	8.392	7.362	6.557	5.911	5.381	4.938
10	51.428	27.692	18.947	14.400	11.613	9.730	8.372	7.347	6.545	5.902	5.373	4.931
11	50.704	27.481	18.848	14.343	11.576	9.704	8.363	7.332	6.534	5.892	5.365	4.925
12	50.000	27.273	18.750	14.286	11.538	9.677	8.333	7.317	6.522	5.882	5.357	4.918
13	49.315	27.068	18.653	14.229	11.502	9.651	8.314	7.302	6.510	5.873	5.349	4.911
14	48.648	26.866	18.557	14.173	11.465	9.626	8.295	7.287	6.498	5.863	5.341	4.905
15	48.000	26.667	18.461	14.118	11.429	9.600	8.276	7.273	6.486	5.854	5.333	4.898
16	47.368	26.471	18.367	14.062	11.392	9.574	8.257	7.258	6.475	5.844	5.325	4.891
17	46.753	26.277	18.274	14.008	11.356	9.549	8.238	7.243	6.463	5.835	5.318	4.885
18	46.154	26.087	18.182	13.953	11.321	9.524	8.219	7.229	6.452	5.825	5.310	4.878
19	45.570	25.899	18.090	13.900	11.285	9.499	8.200	7.214	6.440	5.816	5.302	4.871
20	45.000	25.714	18.000	13.846	11.250	9.474	8.182	7.200	6.429	5.806	5.294	4.865
21	44.444	25.532	17.910	13.793	11.215	9.449	8.163	7.186	6.417	5.797	5.286	4.858
22	43.902	25.352	17.822	13.740	11.180	9.424	8.145	7.171	6.406	5.788	5.278	4.852
23	43.373	25.175	17.734	13.688	11.146	9.399	8.126	7.157	6.394	5.778	5.270	4.845
24	42.857	25.000	17.647	13.636	11.111	9.375	8.108	7.143	6.383	5.769	5.263	4.839
25	42.353	24.828	17.561	13.585	11.077	9.351	8.090	7.129	6.372	5.760	5.255	4.832
26	41.860	24.658	17.476	13.534	11.043	9.326	8.072	7.115	6.360	5.751	5.248	4.826
27	41.379	24.490	17.391	13.483	11.009	9.302	8.054	7.101	6.349	5.742	5.240	4.819
28	40.909	24.324	17.308	13.433	10.976	9.278	8.036	7.087	6.338	5.732	5.233	4.813
29	40.450	24.161	17.225	13.383	10.942	9.254	8.018	7.073	6.327	5.723	5.225	4.806
30	40.000	24.000	17.143	13.333	10.909	9.231	8.000	7.059	6.316	5.714	5.217	4.800
31	39.561	23.841	17.062	13.284	10.876	9.207	7.982	7.045	6.305	5.705	5.210	4.794
32	39.130	23.684	16.981	13.235	10.843	9.184	7.965	7.031	6.294	5.696	5.202	4.787
33	38.710	23.529	16.901	13.187	10.811	9.160	7.947	7.018	6.283	5.687	5.195	4.781
34	38.298	23.377	16.822	13.139	10.778	9.137	7.930	7.004	6.272	5.678	5.187	4.774
35	37.895	23.226	16.744	13.091	10.746	9.114	7.912	6.990	6.261	5.669	5.180	4.768
36	37.500	23.077	16.667	13.043	10.714	9.091	7.895	6.977	6.250	5.660	5.172	4.762
37	37.113	22.930	16.590	12.996	10.682	9.068	7.877	6.963	6.239	5.651	5.165	4.756
38	36.735	22.785	16.514	12.950	10.651	9.045	7.860	6.950	6.228	5.643	5.158	4.749
39	36.364	22.642	16.438	12.903	10.619	9.023	7.843	6.936	6.218	5.634	5.150	4.743
40	36.000	22.500	16.364	12.857	10.588	9.000	7.826	6.923	6.207	5.625	5.143	4.737
41	35.644	22.360	16.290	12.811	10.557	8.978	7.809	6.910	6.196	5.616	5.136	4.731
42	35.294	22.222	16.216	12.766	10.526	8.955	7.792	6.897	6.186	5.607	5.128	4.724
43	34.951	22.086	16.143	12.721	10.496	8.933	7.775	6.883	6.175	5.599	5.121	4.718
44	34.615	21.951	16.071	12.676	10.465	8.911	7.759	6.870	6.164	5.590	5.114	4.712
45	34.286	21.818	16.000	12.632	10.435	8.889	7.742	6.857	6.154	5.581	5.106	4.706
46	33.962	21.687	15.929	12.587	10.405	8.867	7.725	6.844	6.143	5.573	5.099	4.700
47	33.644	21.557	15.859	12.544	10.375	8.845	7.709	6.831	6.133	5.564	5.092	4.693
48	33.333	21.429	15.789	12.500	10.345	8.824	7.692	6.818	6.122	5.556	5.085	4.687
49	33.028	21.302	15.721	12.457	10.315	8.802	7.676	6.805	6.112	5.547	5.078	4.681
50	32.727	21.176	15.652	12.414	10.286	8.780	7.660	6.792	6.102	5.538	5.070	4.675
51	32.432	21.053	15.584	12.371	10.256	8.759	7.643	6.780	6.091	5.530	5.063	4.669
52	32.143	20.930	15.517	12.329	10.227	8.738	7.627	6.767	6.081	5.531	5.056	4.663
53	31.858	20.809	15.451	12.287	10.198	8.717	7.611	6.754	6.071	5.513	5.049	4.657
54	31.579	20.690	15.385	12.245	10.169	8.696	7.595	6.742	6.061	5.505	5.042	4.651
55	31.304	20.571	15.319	12.203	10.141	8.675	7.579	6.729	6.050	5.496	5.035	4.645
56	31.034	20.455	15.254	12.162	10.112	8.654	7.563	6.716	6.040	5.488	5.028	4.639
57	30.769	20.339	16.190	12.121	10.084	8.633	7.547	6.704	6.030	5.479	5.021	4.633
58	30.508	20.225	15.126	12.081	10.056	8.612	7.531	6.691	6.020	5.471	5.014	4.627
59	30.202	20.112	15.063	12.040	10.028	8.592	7.516	6.679	6.010	5.463	5.007	4.621

TABLE IX SCALE OF VISIBILITY (Record number in log)	
Scale Number	Prominent Objects Not Visible At
0	50 yards
1	200 yards
2	500 yards
3	½ mile
4	1 mile
5	2 miles
6	4 miles
7	7 miles
8	20 miles
9	More than 20 miles

Table IX (left) gives a scale for visibility of objects at sea, using numbers which can be recorded in the log.

Table X (right) indicates how the state of the sea can be recorded by numbers.

(See also page 462)

TABLE X STATE OF THE SEA (Using Numerals instead of letters. See Table B)		
Scale Number	Description Of Sea	Height Of Wave
0	Calm	0 or less than 1 foot
1	Smooth	1 to 2 feet
2	Slight	2 to 3 feet
3	Moderate	3 to 5 feet
4	Rough	5 to 8 feet
5	Very rough	8 to 12 feet
6	High	12 to 20 feet
7	Very high	20 to 40 feet
8	Precipitous	40 feet or more
9	Confused	Record chief direction

SHIP'S BELL TIME

Ship's bell time originated in sailing ship days, when the crew of a vessel was divided into Port and Starboard Watches, each on duty four hours, then off four hours.

One stroke on the ship's bell indicates the first half hour of the watch. Then an additional bell is struck for each succeeding half hour. Thus 8 bells indicates the end of a four-hour watch. This is repeated each watch. When the time calls for two or more strokes, they are sounded in groups of two.

The first five watches are as follows: First Watch 2000 to 2400; Middle Watch 2400 to 0400; Morning Watch 0400 to 0800; Forenoon Watch 0800 to 1200; and Afternoon Watch 1200 to 1600. The next

4 hours are divided into two Dog Watches; The First Dog Watch 1600 to 1800; and the * Second Dog Watch, 1800 to 2000. By means of the Dog Watches, the watches can be changed every day, so that each watch gets a turn of eight hours rest at night. Otherwise each member of the crew would be on duty the same hours every day.

―――――――――

* In the Second Dog Watch, to indicate that a new watch has taken over, the sequence of bells is varied as follows: 1 Bell, 1830; 2 Bells, 1900; 3 Bells, 1930; 8 Bells, 2000. The ship's clock of course repeats the sequence of 1 to 8 bells every four hours day and night without variation.

Bells, and How Struck	First Watch	Middle Watch	Morning Watch	Forenoon Watch	Afternoon Watch	First Dog Watch	Second Dog Watch
1 Bell (.)	2030	0030	0430	0830	1230	1630	—
2 Bells (..)	2100	0100	0500	0900	1300	1700	—
3 Bells (.. .)	2130	0130	0530	0930	1330	1730	—
4 Bells (.. ..)	2200	0200	0600	1000	1400	1800	—
5 Bells (.. .. .)	2230	0230	0630	1030	1430	—	*1830
6 Bells (.. .. ..)	2300	0300	0700	1100	1500	—	*1900
7 Bells (.. .. .. .)	2330	0330	0730	1130	1530	—	*1930
8 Bells (.. .. .. ..)	2400(M)	0400	0800	1200(N)	1600	—	*2000

NOTE: See 24-hour clock system, p. 337(a). — (M) Midnight   (N) Noon — * See text for sequence of bells in Second Dog Watch.

GUN SALUTES AS MILITARY HONORS
(See also page 371)

Rank	Guns at Arrival	Guns at Departure	Ruffles and Flourishes
President	21	21	4
President of foreign republic or a foreign sovereign	21	21	4
Member of a royal family	21	21	4
Former President	21	21	4
Vice-President	..	19	4
Secretary of State on board a vessel of the Navy representing the President	..	19	4
Ambassador	..	19	4
Secretary of Defense	19	19	4
Deputy Secretary of Defense	19	19	4
Assistant Secretaries of Defense	17	17	4
Secretary of the Navy	19	19	4
Secretary of the Army	19	19	4
Assistant Secretary of the Navy	17	17	4
Cabinet Officer	..	19	4
Chief Justice	..	17	4
Governor General, United States Islands	..	19	4
Governor of state, territory or United States Islands	..	19	4
President pro tempore of the Senate	..	19	4
Speaker of the House of Representatives	..	17	4
Committee of Congress	..	17	4
Envoy Extraordinary	..	15	3
Assistant Secretary of the Army	..	15	3
Minister resident or "diplomatic representative"	..	13	2
Charge d'affairs	..	11	1
Consul general	..	11	..
Consul	..	7	..
Vice-consul or consular agent (where he is the only representative of the United States)	..	5	..
Admiral and General	..	17	4
Vice-Admiral and Lieutenant General	..	15	3
Rear Admiral and Major General	..	13	2
Commodore and Brigadier General	..	11	1

DISTANCE OF VISIBILITY AT SEA

Elevation of Eye (Feet)	0.8	3	7	12	19	27	49	76
Horizon Distance (Nautical Miles)	1	2	3	4	5	6	8	10

UNITED STATES COAST GUARD AUXILIARY
FLAG CODE CONFIGURATIONS

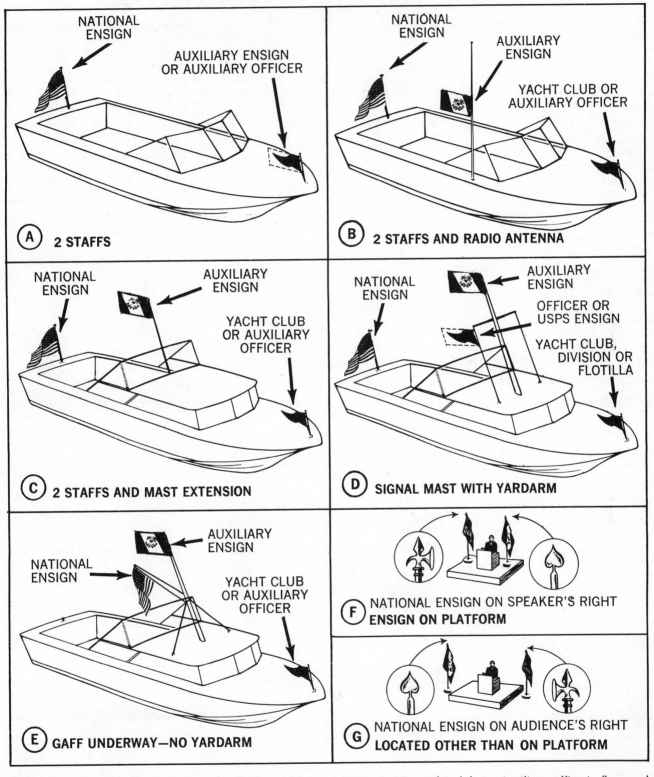

A 2 STAFFS

NATIONAL ENSIGN

AUXILIARY ENSIGN OR AUXILIARY OFFICER

B 2 STAFFS AND RADIO ANTENNA

NATIONAL ENSIGN

AUXILIARY ENSIGN

YACHT CLUB OR AUXILIARY OFFICER

C 2 STAFFS AND MAST EXTENSION

NATIONAL ENSIGN

AUXILIARY ENSIGN

YACHT CLUB OR AUXILIARY OFFICER

D SIGNAL MAST WITH YARDARM

NATIONAL ENSIGN

AUXILIARY ENSIGN

OFFICER OR USPS ENSIGN

YACHT CLUB, DIVISION OR FLOTILLA

E GAFF UNDERWAY—NO YARDARM

AUXILIARY ENSIGN

NATIONAL ENSIGN

YACHT CLUB OR AUXILIARY OFFICER

F NATIONAL ENSIGN ON SPEAKER'S RIGHT **ENSIGN ON PLATFORM**

G NATIONAL ENSIGN ON AUDIENCE'S RIGHT **LOCATED OTHER THAN ON PLATFORM**

The information on page 496 has been drafted to show in tabular form what the United States Coast Guard Auxiliary has approved as a flag code for power vessels. The problem would be simplified if there were no diversification of sizes and types of boats, thus providing a uniform number and arrangement of positions at which the flags might be displayed. To illustrate typical configurations on small craft for the display of the national ensign, Auxiliary ensign, USPS ensign, yacht club or Auxiliary officer's flag, and division or flotilla pennant, the chart above provides a key for the respective types, depending on what staffs, yardarms and halyards may be available. In addition to configurations shown for boats, figures F and G illustrate correct procedure when the national and Auxiliary ensigns are displayed at meetings ashore, the practice depending on whether or not the ensign is located on the platform.

CHAPTER XXXI

Nautical Dictionary

Illustrations by Meredith A. Scott

A

ABACK. The position of the sails when the wind presses their surface toward the mast, tending to force the vessel astern.

ABAFT. Toward the stern.

ABEAM. On the side of the vessel, amidships, or at right angles.

ABOARD. Within, on board the vessel.

ABOUT. To go on the opposite tack.

ABREAST. Alongside of. Side by side.

A-COCK-BILL. The position of the yards of a ship when they are topped up at an angle with the deck. The position of an anchor when it hangs to the cathead.

ADRIFT. Broken from moorings or fasts.

AFLOAT. Resting on the surface of the water.

AFORE. Forward. The opposite of abaft.

AFT. Near the stern.

AGROUND. Touching the bottom.

AHEAD. In the direction of the vessel's bow. *Wind ahead* is from the direction toward which the vessel's head points.

AHULL. When a vessel lies with her sails furled and her helm lashed alee.

ALEE. When the helm is in the opposite direction from that in which the wind blows.

ALL-ABACK. When all the sails are aback. (*See Aback.*)

ALL HANDS. The entire crew.

ALL IN THE WIND. When all the sails are shaking.

ALOFT. Above the deck.

AMIDSHIPS. In the centre of the vessel; either with reference to her length or to her breadth.

ANCHOR. An iron instrument which, when dropped to the bottom, holds the vessel.

ANCHOR-WATCH. (*See Watch.*)

APEAK. When the cable is hove taut so as to bring the vessel over her anchor.

APRON. A timber fixed behind the lower part of the stem above the fore end of the keel.

ARM. YARD-ARM. The extremity of a yard. Also, the lower part of an anchor, crossing the shank, and terminating in the flukes.

ARMING. A piece of tallow put in the cavity and over the bottom of a lead-line.

ASTERN. In the direction of the stern. The opposite of ahead.

ATHWART. Across.

Athwart-ships. Across the line of the vessel's keel.

Athwart-hawse. Across the direction of a vessel's head. Across her cable.

ATHWART-SHIPS. Across the length of a vessel. The opposite to fore-and-aft.

ATRIP. The position of the anchor when it is raised clear of the ground.

AVAST. To stop; "Avast heaving!"

AWEATHER. When the helm is put in the direction from which the wind blows.

AWEIGH. The same as atrip.

AWNING. A covering of canvas over a vessel's deck, or over a boat, to keep off sun or rain.

AYE. Yes; and is always used in lieu therefor at sea, as "Aye, aye, sir," meaning "I understand."

B

BACK. To back an anchor, is to carry out a smaller one ahead of the one by which the vessel rides, to take off some of the strain.

To back a sail, is to throw it aback. (*See Aback.*)

To back and fill, is to alternately back and fill the sails.

To back water, is to push on the oars, to give a boat sternway.

BACKSTAYS. Rigging running from the masthead to the vessel's side, slanting a little aft, or to the deck near the stern.

BAG. A sail bags when the leech is taut, and the canvas slack.

BALANCE-REEF. The closest reef, and makes the sail triangular, or nearly so.

BALD-HEADED. Said of a schooner having no topmasts.

BAIL. To bail a boat, is to throw water out of her. (Also *bale.*)

BALLAST. Heavy material, as iron, lead, or stone, placed in the bottom of the hold, to keep a vessel steady.

To freshen ballast, is to shift it. *Shingle ballast is coarse gravel.*

BALLOON JIB. A large triangular head-sail used in light and moderate weather, with a free wind.

BANK. A boat is *double banked* when two oars, one opposite the other, are pulled by men seated on the same thwart.

BAR. A bank or shoal. *Capstan-bars* are heavy pieces of wood by which the capstan is worked.

BARE-POLES. The condition of a vessel when she has no sail set.

BARGE. A large double-banked boat, usually used by the commander of a vessel in the navy.

BARK, OR BARQUE. A three-masted vessel, having her fore and main masts rigged like a ship's, and her mizzen mast like the main mast of a schooner, with no sail upon it but a spanker, and gaff topsail.

BARNACLE. A shell-fish often found on a vessel's bottom.

BATTENS. Thin strips of wood put around the hatches, to keep the tarpaulin down. Also, put upon rigging to keep it from chafing. A large batten widened at the end, and put upon rigging, is called a *scotchman.* Battens are often used on yachts on the leech of a mainsail to make it set flat.

BEACON. A post or buoy placed over a shoal or bank to warn vessels of danger. Also a signalmark on land.

BEAMS. Strong pieces of timber stretching across the vessel, to support the decks.

On the weather or lee beam, is in a direction to windward or leeward, at right angles with the keel.

On beam-ends. The situation of a vessel when turned over so that her beams are inclined toward the vertical.

BEAR. An object *bears* so and so, when it is in such direction from the person looking.

To bear down upon a vessel, is to approach her from the windward.

To bear a hand. To make haste.

BEARING. The direction of an object from the person looking. The *bearings* of a vessel are the widest part of her below the plank-sheer. That part of her hull which is on the water-line when she is at anchor and in her proper trim.

BEATING. Going toward the direction of the wind, by alternate tacks.

BECALM. To intercept the wind. A vessel

to windward is said to *becalm* another. So one sail *becalms* another. A highland has the same effect. (See blanket.)

BECKET. A piece of rope placed so as to confine a spar or another rope. A handle made of rope, in the form of a circle; the handle of a chest is called a *becket*.

BEES. Pieces of plank bolted to the outer end of the bowsprit, to reeve the foretopmast stays through.

BEFORE THE WIND. Said of a sailing vessel when the wind is coming from aft, over the stern.

BELAY. To make a rope or line fast by turns around a pin or coil, without hitching or seizing it.

BELOW. Beneath, or under, the deck. One *goes below* when going down into the cabin.

BEND. To make fast.

To bend a sail, is to make it fast to the spar.

To bend a cable, is to make it fast to the anchor.

A bend, is a knot by which one rope is made fast to another.

BENDS. The strongest part of a vessel's side, to which the beams, knees, and foothooks are bolted. The part between the water's edge and the bulwarks.

BERTH. The place where a vessel lies. The place in which a person sleeps.

BETWEEN DECKS. The space between any two decks of a ship.

BIBBS. Pieces of timber bolted to the hounds of a mast, to support the trestle-trees.

BIGHT. The double part of a rope when it is folded. Any part of a rope may be called the bight, except the ends. Also, a bend in the shore, making a small bay or inlet.

———— • ————

The language of the sea is spiced with terms and phrases so trenchant and vigorous that "salty talk" is no idle figure of speech. Our nautical terminology of today has been handed down from an era of "iron men and wooden ships," when wind-bellied canvas drove tall-sparred vessels to the ends of the Seven Seas. Often the boatman using nautical terms as they are commonly applied today, fails to grasp the significance of their original derivations. While the barbed expletives and commands that flew so freely across the decks of ancient windjammers would scarcely be appropriate aboard a modern yacht (and quickly be recognized as affectations when so used), an understanding of the jargon of the sea is certainly an aid to fuller appreciation of its literature. If this nautical dictionary aids in such an understanding, and helps the reader to add a dash of salt to his nautical talk, while avoiding such affectation, it will have served its purpose well. The definitions are necessarily brief; all could be amplified if space permitted.

BILGE. That part of the floor of a ship upon which she would rest if aground; being the part near the keel which is more in a horizontal than a perpendicular line.

Bilge ways. Pieces of timber bolted together and placed under the bilge, in launching.

Bilged. When the bilge is broken in.

Bilge Water. Water which settles in the bilge.

Bilge. The largest circumference of a cask.

BILGEWAYS. Timbers placed beneath a vessel when building.

BILL. The point at the extremity of a fluke of an anchor.

BINNACLE. A receptacle placed near the helm, containing the compass, etc.

BITTS. Perpendicular pieces of timber going through the deck, to secure ropes to. The cables are fastened to them, if there is no windlass. There are also *bitts* to secure the windlass, and on each side of the heel of the bowsprit.

BITTER, OR BITTER-END. The inboard end of an anchor cable secured to the bitt, or below decks to some strong structural member.

BLADE. The flat part of an oar which goes into the water.

BLANKET. A vessel to windward of another is said to blanket the leeward vessel when she takes the wind from the latter's sails, due to their relative positions.

BLOCK. A piece of wood with sheaves, or wheels, through which the running rigging passes, to add to the purchase.

BLUFF. A vessel which is full and square forward.

BOARD. The stretch a vessel makes upon one tack, when she is beating.

Stern-board. When a vessel goes stern foremost.

By the board. When the masts of a vessel fall over the side.

BOAT-HOOK. An iron hook with a long staff.

BOATSWAIN. A ship's officer who has charge of the rigging and who calls the crew to duty.

BOBSTAYS. Used to confine the bowsprit to the stem or cutwater.

BOLSTERS. Pieces of soft wood, covered with canvas, placed on the trestle-trees, for the eyes of the rigging to rest upon.

BOLTS. Cylindrical bars of iron, copper, or composition, used to secure the different parts of a vessel.

BOLT-ROPE. The rope which goes round a sail, and to which the canvas is sewed.

BONNET. An additional piece of canvas attached to the foot of a jib by lacings.

BOOBY HATCH. A raised small hatch.

BOOM. A spar used to extend the foot of a fore-and-aft sail or studdingsail.

Boom-horse. A curved metal fitting made into the boom band, on which a sheet-block travels.

Boom-irons. Iron rings on the yards, through which the studdingsail booms traverse.

BOOMKIN. A short spar projecting from the stern, to which a sheet block is secured, for an overhanging boom.

BOTTOMRY. A term in marine law referring to mortgaging on ships.

BOUND. Refers to destination or condition of vessel. (Outward bound, fogbound.)

BOW. The rounded part of a vessel, forward.

BOWER. A working anchor, the cable of which is bent and reeved through the hawsehole.

Best bower is the larger of the two bowers.

BOWLINE. A rope leading forward from the leech of a square sail, to keep the leech well out when sailing close-hauled. A vessel is said to be *on a bowline*, or *on a taut bowline*, when she is close-hauled. Also a knot tied in the end of a line to form a loop that will not slip.

Bowline-bird. The span on the leech of the sail to which the bowline is toggled.

BOWSE. To pull upon a tackle.

BOWSPRIT. A large, strong spar, standing from the bows of a vessel.

BOX-HAULING. Wearing a vessel by backing the head sails.

BOX. To box the compass, is to repeat the thirty-two points of the compass in order.

BRACE. A rope by which a yard is turned about.

To brace a yard, is to turn it about horizontally.

To brace up, is to lay the yard more fore-and-aft.

To brace in, is to lay it nearer square.

To brace to, is to brace the head yards a little aback, in tacking or wearing.

BRACKISH. Said of a mixture of fresh water and salt sea water.

BRAILS. Ropes by which the foot or lower corners of fore-and-aft sails are hauled up.

BRAKE. The handle of a ship's pump.

BREAK. To break bulk, is to begin to unload.

To break ground, is to lift the anchor from the bottom.

To break shear, is when a vessel, at anchor, in tending, is forced the wrong way by the wind or current, so that she does not lie well to keep clear of her anchor.

BREAKER. A small cask containing water.

Breakers. Waves broken by ledges or shoals.

BREAST-FAST. A rope used to confine a vessel broadside to a wharf, or to some other vessel.

BREAST-HOOKS. Knees in the forward part of a vessel, across the stem, to secure the bows.

BREAST-ROPE. A rope passed round a man in the chains, while sounding.

BREECH. The outside angle of a knee-timber. The after end of a gun.

BREECHING. A strong rope used to secure the breech of a gun to the ship's side.

BRIDLE. Spans of rope attached to the leeches of square sails to which the bowlines are made fast. *Bridle-port.* The foremost port, used for stowing the anchors.

BRIG. A square-rigged vessel, with two masts. An *hermaphrodite brig* is rigged on the foremast like a brig and on the mainmast like a schooner.

BRING TO. The act of stopping a sailing vessel by bringing her head up into the wind.

BROACH-TO. To slew round when running before the wind.

BROADSIDE. The whole side of a vessel.

BROKEN-BACK. When a vessel is so strained as to droop at each end.

BUCKLERS. Blocks of wood made to fit in the hawse-holes, or holes in the half-ports, when at sea. Those in the hawse-holes are sometimes called *hawse-blocks.*

BULK. The whole cargo when stowed. *Stowed in bulk,* is when goods are stowed loose, instead of being stowed in casks or bags.

BUNK. Bed on board ship.

BULKHEAD. Strong partitions in the hold of a vessel at regular lengths, to prevent water filling all parts of the vessel in case of accident.

Temporary partitions of boards to separate different parts of a vessel.

BULL. A sailor's term for a small keg, holding a gallon or two.

BULLS EYE. A small piece of stout wood with a hole in the centre for a stay or rope to reeve through, without a sheave, and with a groove round it for the strap, which is usually of iron. Also, a piece of thick glass inserted in the deck to let in light.

BULWARKS. Wood work around a vessel above deck, fastened to stanchions.

BUM-BOATS. Boats which lie alongside a vessel in port with provisions, fruit, etc., to sell.

BUMPKIN. Pieces of timber projecting from the vessel to board the fore tack to; also from each quarter, for the main brace-blocks.

BUNT. The middle of a sail.

BUNTING. Thin woolen stuff of which, flags are made.

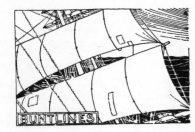

BUNTLINES. Ropes used for hauling up the body of a sail.

BUOY. A floating cask, or piece of wood, attached by a rope to an anchor, to show its position. Also, floated over a shoal, or other dangerous place as a beacon.

To stream a buoy, is dropping it into the water before letting go the anchor.

A buoy is said to *watch,* when it floats upon the surface of the water.

BURGEE. A small flag, either pointed or swallowtail.

BURTON. A tackle, rove in a particular manner.

A single Spanish burton has three single blocks, or two single blocks and a hook in the bight of one of the running parts.

A double Spanish burton has three double blocks.

BUSH. The center piece of a wooden sheave in a block.

BUTT. The end of a plank where it unites with the end of another.

Scuttle-butt. A cask with a hole cut in its bilge, and kept on deck to hold water.

BUTTOCK. That part of the convexity of a vessel abaft, under the stern, contained between the counter above and the after part of the bilge below, and between the quarter on the side and the stern-post.

BY. *By the Head.* When the head of a vessel is lower in the water than her stern. If her stern is lower, she is *by the stern. By the Wind.* Close-hauled.

C

CABLE. A large, strong rope, made fast by the anchor, by which the vessel is secured. A cable is usually 120 fathoms in length.

CABOOSE. A house on deck, where the cooking is done. Commonly called the *Galley.*

CALL. Bos'n's call used for piping orders.

CAMBER. A curvature upwards.

CAN-HOOKS. Slings with flat hooks at each end, used for hoisting barrels or light casks, the hooks being placed round the chimes, and the purchase hooked to the centre of the slings.

CANT-TIMBERS. Timbers at both ends of a vessel, raised obliquely from the keel.

Lower Half Cants. Those parts of frames situated forward and abaft the square frames or the floor timbers which cross the keel.

CANVAS. The cloth of which sails are made.

CAP. A thick, strong block of wood with two holes through it, one square and the other round, used to confine together the head of one mast and the lower part of the mast next above it.

CAPSIZE. To overturn.

CAPSTAN. A machine placed perpendicularly on the deck, used for heaving or hoisting.

CARDINAL POINTS. The four main points of the compass.

CAREEN. To heave a vessel down upon her side. To lie over, when sailing on the wind.

CARLINGS. Pieces of timber running between the beams.

CARRICK-BEND. A kind of knot. *Carrick bitts* are the windlass bitts.

CARRY-AWAY. To break a spar, or part a rope.

CARRY ON. To carry all sail possible.

CARVEL. Smooth-planked, as distinguished from lapstrake.

CAST. To pay a vessel's head off, in getting under way, on the tack she is to start upon. To *cast off* a line is to let it go.

CAT. The tackle used to hoist the anchor up to the cat-head. *Cat-block,* the block of this tackle.

CAT BOAT. A sailboat having one mast, well forward, and no headsails.

CAT-HARPIN. An iron leg used to confine the upper part of the rigging to the mast.

CAT-HEAD. Large timbers projecting from the vessel's side, to which the anchor is secured.

CAT'S-PAW. A kind of hitch made in a rope. A light current of air on the surface of the water.

CAULK. To fill the seams of a vessel with oakum or caulking cotton.

CEILING. The inside sheathing of a vessel.

CENTERBOARD. A pivoted board or metal plate, housed in a trunk, which can be lowered to reduce a sailboat's tendency to make leeway when tacking.

CHAFE. To rub the surface. *Chafing-gear* is the stuff put upon rigging and spars to prevent chafing.

CHAINS. Strong links or plates of iron, the lower ends of which are bolted through the ship's side to the timbers. Their upper ends are secured to the bottom of the dead-eyes in the channels. The chain cable of a vessel is called familiarly her *chain*.

Rudder-chains lead from the outer and upper end of the rudder to the quarters.

CHAIN-PLATES. Plates of iron bolted to the side of a ship, to which the chains and dead-eyes of the lower rigging are connected.

CHAMFER. To take off the edge, or bevel the plank.

CHANNELS. Broad pieces of plank bolted edgewise to the outside of a vessel. Used in narrow vessels for spreading the lower rigging.

CHARTER PARTY. A contract in marine law.

CHECK. To stop or impede, as to check the cable from paying out.

CHEEKS. The projections on each side of a mast, upon which the trestle-trees rest. The sides of the shell of a block.

CHINE LOG. Longitudinal member used at the intersection of sides and bottom of flat or V-bottom boats.

CHINSE. To drive oakum into seams.

CHIPS. Nickname for ship's carpenter.

CHOCKS. Wedges used to secure anything with, or to rest upon. The long boat rests upon two *chocks*, when it is stowed. *Chock-a-block*. When the lower block of a tackle is run close up to the upper one, so that you can hoist no higher. This is also called *two-blocks*.

CISTERN. An apartment in the hold of a vessel, having a pipe leading out through the side, with a sea-cock, by which water may be let in.

CLAMPS. Thick planks on the inside of vessels, to support the ends of beams.

CLAWING OFF. To work off close-hauled from lee shore.

CLEAR. A vessel clears from a port when necessary papers are put in order at the custom house, preparatory to sailing. Lines or rigging are cleared when tangled gear is straightened out. Land is cleared when left as a vessel sails. The bilge is cleared when pumped out.

CLEAT. A piece of wood used in different parts of a vessel to belay ropes to.

CLEW. The lower corner of square sails, and the after corner of fore-and-aft sails.

CLEWLINE. A rope that hauls up the clew of a square sail.

CLINCH. A half-hitch, stopped to its own part.

CLINKER. Lapstrake planking, in which planks overlap at the edges, as distinguished from carvel (smooth).

CLOSE-HAULED. When a vessel is sailing as close to the wind as she will go.

CLOSE-REEFED. When all the reefs are taken in.

CLOVE-HITCH. Two half-hitches round a spar or other rope.

CLOVE-HOOK. An iron clasp, in two parts, moving upon the same pivot, and overlapping.

CLUBBING. Drifting down a current with an anchor out.

COAL TAR. Tar made from bituminous coal.

COAMINGS. Raised work around the hatches, to prevent water going into the hold.

COAT. *Mast-coat* is a piece of canvas, tarred or painted, placed around a mast or

bowsprit, where it enters the deck to keep out water.

COCK-BILL. To cock-bill a yard or anchor. (See *A-cock-bill*.)

COCKPIT. An apartment in a vessel of war, used by the surgeon during an action. A space or well, sunken below the sheer line. Usually aft, but small *forward cockpits* are also in common use on motor cruisers.

CODE SIGNALS. Flag signals for speaking at sea.

CODLINE. An eighteen thread line.

COIL. To lay a rope up in a circle, with one turn or fake over another.

A coil is a quantity of rope laid up in this manner.

COLLAR. An eye in the end or bight of a shroud or stay, to go over the mast-head.

COLLIER. A vessel used in coal trade.

COMPANION. A wooden covering over the staircase to a cabin.

Companion-way, the staircase to the cabin. *Companion ladder*. Leading from the poop to the main deck.

COMPASS. The instrument which shows the course of a vessel.

COMPOSITE. A vessel with iron or metal frame and wooden skin.

CONNING, or CUNNING. Directing the helmsman in steering a vessel.

CORINTHIAN. Amateur.

COUNTER. That part of a vessel between the bottom of the stern and the wing-transom and buttock. *Counter-timbers* are short timbers put in to strengthen the counter.

COURSES. The common term for the sails that hang from a ship's lower yards. The foresail is called the *fore course* and the mainsail the *main course*.

COXSWAIN. The person who steers a boat and has charge of her.

CRAB. To catch a crab is to catch the oar in the water by feathering it too soon.

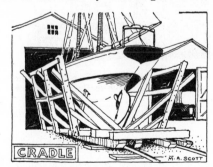

CRADLE. A frame to hold a vessel upright when hauling her up.

CRAFT. A general term applied to any collection of small vessels.

CRANES. Pieces of iron or timber at the vessel's sides, used to stow boats or spars upon. A machine used for hoisting.

CRANK. A vessel which is inclined to lean over a great deal and cannot bear much sail.

CRANSE IRON. A cap or ring at end of bowsprit.

CREEPER. An iron instrument, with four claws, used for dragging the bottom of a harbor or river.

CRINGLE. A short piece of rope with each end spliced into the bolt-rope of a sail confining an iron ring or thimble.

CROSS-BARS. Round bars of iron, bent at each end, used to turn the shank of an anchor.

CROSS-JACK. The cross-jack yard is the lower yard on the mizzen mast.

CROSS-PAWL. Pieces of timber that keep a vessel together while in frame.

CROSS-PIECE. A piece of timber connecting two bitts.

CROSS-SPALES. Pieces of timber placed across a vessel, and nailed to the frames, to keep the sides together until the knees are bolted.

CROSS-TREES. Pieces of oak supported by the cheeks and trestle-trees at the mastheads, to sustain the tops on the lower mast, and to spread the rigging at the topmasthead.

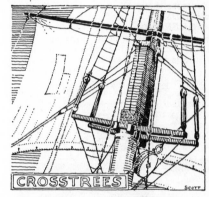

CROW-FOOT. A number of small lines rove through the euvrou to suspend an awning by.

CROWN of an anchor, is the place where the arms are joined to the shank.

To crown a knot, is to pass the strands over and under each other above the knot.

CRUTCH. A knee or piece of knee-timber, placed inside of a vessel to secure the heels of the cant-timbers abaft. Also the chock upon which the spanker-boom rests when the sail is not set.

CUCKOLD'S NECK. A knot by which a rope is secured to a spar, the two parts of the rope crossing each other, and seized together.

CUDDY. A cabin in the fore part of a boat.

CUT-WATER. The foremost part of a vessel's bow, which projects forward of the bows.

CUTTER. A small boat. Also, a kind of sloop.

D

DAVY JONES. The Spirit of the sea. *Davy Jones' Locker* is the bottom of the sea.

DAVITS. Pieces of timber or iron, with sheaves or blocks at their ends, projecting over a vessel's sides or stern, to hoist up boats. Also, a spar with a roller or sheave at its end, used for fishing the anchor, called a *fish-davit.*

DEAD EYE. A circular block of wood, with holes through it, for the lanyards of rigging to reeve through, without sheaves, and with a groove round it for an iron strap.

DEAD-LIGHTS. Ports placed in the cabin windows.

DEAD RECKONING. A reckoning kept by observing a vessel's courses and distances by the log.

DEAD-RISING, or *RISING-LINE.* Those parts of a vessel's floor, throughout her length, where the floor-timbers terminate upon the lower futtock.

DEAD-WATER. The eddy under a vessel's counter when in motion.

DEAD-WOOD. Blocks of timber, laid upon each end of the keel, where the vessel narrows.

DECK. The planked floor of a vessel, resting upon the beams.

DECK-STOPPER. A stopper used for securing the cable forward of the windlass or capstan, while it is being overhauled.

DEEP-SEA-LEAD. The lead used in sounding at great depths.

DEPARTURE. The easting or westing made by a vessel. The bearing of an object on the coast from which a vessel commences dead reckoning.

DERELICT. A vessel forsaken on the high seas.

DERRICK. A single spar, supported by stays and guys, to which a purchase is attached, used to unload vessels, and for hoisting heavy objects.

DINGHY. A small open boat.

DISPLACEMENT. The weight of water displaced by any vessel.

DOG. A short iron bar, with a fang or teeth at one end, and a ring at the other. Used for a purchase, the fang being placed against a beam or knee, and the block of a tackle hooked to the ring.

DOG-VANE. A small vane, usually made of bunting, to show the direction of the wind.

DOG-WATCHES. Half watches of two hours each, from 4 to 6 and 6 to 8 P.M.

DOLPHIN. A rope or strap around a mast to support the puddening, where the lower yards rest in the slings. Also, a spar or buoy, to which vessels may bend their cables.

DOLPHIN - STRIKER. The martingale boom, a spar projecting down from the bowsprit cap to spread the martingale stays which run out to the jib boom and counteract the strain of head stays.

DOUSE. To lower suddenly.

DOWNHAUL. A rope used to haul down jibs, staysails, and studdingsails.

DRAFT. The depth of water which a vessel requires to float her.

DRAG. A machine with a bag net, used for dragging on the bottom for anything lost. A sea anchor to keep the head of the vessel to the wind, in bad weather.

DRAW. A sail *draws* when it is filled by the wind.

DRIFTS. Pieces in the sheer-draught where the rails are cut off.

DRIVE. To scud before a gale, or to drift in a current.

DRIVER. The fifth mast of a six-masted schooner. Also the small fore-and-aft spanker sail set at the stern of a full-rigged ship.

DROP. The depth of a sail, from head to foot, amidships.

DRUM-HEAD. The top of the capstan.

DUB. To reduce the end of a timber.

DUCK. A kind of cloth, lighter and finer than canvas; used for small sails.

DUNNAGE. Loose material, placed on the bottom of the hold, above the ballast, to stow cargo.

E

EARING. A rope attached to the cringle of a sail, by which it is bent or reefed.

EBB. The reflux of the tide.

EDDY. A circular motion in the water caused by the meeting of opposite currents.

ELBOW. Two crosses in a hawse.

ENSIGN. The flag carried by a ship as the insignia of her nationality.

EQUINOX. The time the sun crosses the equator.

EVEN-KEEL. The position of a vessel when she is so trimmed that the sits evenly upon the water, neither end being down more than the other.

EUVROU. A piece of wood, by which the legs of the crow-foot to an awning are extended.

EYE. The circular part of a shroud or stay, where it goes over a mast.

Eye-bolt. A long iron bar, having an eye at one end, driven through a vessel's deck or side into a timber or beam, with the eye remaining out, to hook a tackle to. If there is a ring through this eye, it is called a *ring-bolt.*

An Eye-splice is a kind of splice made with the end of a rope.

Eyelet-hole. A hole made in a sail for cringle or roband to go through.

The Eyes of a vessel. The extreme forward part.

F

FACE-PIECES. Pieces of wood wrought on the fore part of the knee of the head.

FACING. Letting one piece of timber into another with a rabbet.

FAG. A rope is *fagged* when the end is untwisted.

FAIR-LEADER. A strip of board or plank or metal, with holes in it, for running rigging to lead through. Also, a block or thimble used for the same purpose.

FAKE. A turn of rope in a coil. To *fake* (or *flake*) *down* is to coil a line down with ends overlapping so it will run freely without fouling.

FALL. That part of a tackle to which the power is applied in hoisting.

FALSE KEEL. A supplementary keel, bolted to the main keel on the outside, to give a vessel more draft.

FANCY-LINE. A line rove through a block at the jaws of a gaff, used as a downhaul. Also, a line used for cross-hauling the lee topping-lift.

FASHION-PIECES. The aftermost timbers, forming the shape of the stern.

STERN FASTS

FAST. A rope by which a vessel is secured. There are *bow, breast, quarter,* and *stern* fasts.

FATHOM. Six feet.

FEATHER. *To feather an oar* in rowing, is to turn the blade horizontally with the top forward as it comes out of the water, so as not to take the wind or dip up water.

FEATHER-EDGED. Planks which have one edge thicker than another.

FENDERS. Pieces of rope or wood hung over the side of a vessel or boat, to protect it from chafing. The fenders of small boats and yachts are usually made of canvas and stuffed with cork.

FID. A block of wood or iron, placed through the hole in the heel of a mast, and resting on the trestle-trees of the mast below. This supports the mast. Also, a wooden pin, tapered, used in splicing rigging, etc.

FIDDLE-BLOCK. A long shell, with one sheave over the other, the lower smaller than the upper.

FIFE-RAIL. The rail around a mast.

FIGURE-HEAD. A carved head or full-length figure, over the cut-water.

FISH. To raise the flukes of an anchor upon the gunwale. Also, to strengthen a spar when sprung or weakened, by fastening on other pieces.

FISH-DAVIT. The davit used for fishing an anchor.

FISH-HOOK. A hook with a pennant, to the end of which the fish-tackle is hooked.

FISH-TACKLE. The tackle used for fishing an anchor.

FLARE. When a vessel's sides go out from the perpendicular. The opposite to *tumbling-in.*

FLAT. A sheet is said to be hauled *flat,* when it is hauled down close.

Flat-aback, when a sail is blown with its after surface toward the stern.

FLAW. A gust of wind.

FLEET. To come up on a tackle and draw the blocks apart, for another pull, after they have been hauled *two-blocks.*

Also, to shift the position of a block or fall, so as to haul to more advantage.

FLEMISH-HORSE. An additional foot-rope at the ends of top-sail yards.

FLOOR. The bottom of a vessel, on each side of the keelson.

FIGUREHEAD

FLOOR TIMBERS. Timbers of a vessel placed across the keel.

FLOWING SHEET. When a vessel has the wind free, and the sheets are eased off.

FLUKES. The broad triangular plates at the extremity of the arms of an anchor, terminating in a point called the *bill.*

FLUSH. Level with.

FLY. That part of a flag which extends from the Union to the extreme end.

FOOT. The lower end of a mast or sail.

FOOT-ROPE. A rope upon which to stand when reefing or furling sail.

FOOT-WALING. The inside planks or lining of a vessel, over the floor-timbers.

FORE. Used to distinguish the forward part of a vessel, or things forward of amidships: as *fore mast, fore hatch.* The opposite to *aft* or *after.*

FORE-AND-AFT. Lengthwise with the vessel. The opposite to *athwartships.*

FORECASTLE. That part of the upper deck forward of the foremast; or, forward of the after part of the fore channels. Also, the forward part of the vessel, under the deck, where the sailors live.

FORE-FOOT. A piece of timber at the forward extremity of the keel, upon which the lower end of the stem rests.

FORE-LOCK. A flat piece of iron, driven through the end of a bolt, to prevent its drawing.

FORE MAST. The forward mast of a vessel.

FORE-REACH. To shoot ahead, as when going in stays.

FORE-RUNNER. A piece of rag, terminating the stray-line of the log-line.

FORGE. *To forge ahead,* to shoot ahead; as, in coming to anchor, or when going in stays.

FORWARD. In front of.

FOTHER OR FODDER. To draw a sail,

filled with oakum, under a vessel's bottom, to stop a leak.

FOUL. The opposite of clear.

FOUL ANCHOR. When the cable has a turn around the anchor.

FOUL HAWSE. When the two cables are crossed or twisted, beyond the stem.

FOUNDER. When a vessel fills with water and sinks.

FOX. Made by twisting together two or more ropeyarns.

A Spanish fox is made by untwisting a single warn and laying it up the contrary way.

FRAME. Skeleton of a vessel.

FRAP. To pass ropes around a sail to keep it from blowing loose. Also, to draw ropes around a vessel which is weakened, to keep her together.

FLOWING SHEET

FREE. A vessel is going *free,* when she has a fair wind. A vessel is *free,* when the water has been pumped out of her.

FREEBOARD. That portion of a vessel out of water.

FRESHEN. To relieve a rope, by moving its place; as, to *freshen the nip* of a stay, is to shift it so as to prevent its chafing through. *To freshen ballast,* is to alter its position.

FRENCH-FAKE. To coil a rope with each fake outside of the other, beginning in the middle. If there are to be riding fakes, they begin outside and go in. This is a *Flemish coil.*

FOOTROPES

FULL-AND-BY. Sailing close-hauled on a wind. The order given to keep the sails full and at the same time close to the wind.

FURL. To roll a sail up snugly on a yard or boom, and secure it.

FUTTOCK-PLATES. Iron plates crossing the sides of the toprim perpendicularly. The dead-eyes of the topmast rigging are fitted to their upper ends, and the futtock-shrouds to their lower ends.

FUTTOCK-SHROUDS. Short shrouds, leading from the lower ends of the futtock-plates to the bend around the lower mast, just below the top.

FUTTOCK-STAFF. A short piece of wood or iron, seized across the upper part of the rigging, to which the cat-harpin legs are secured.

FUTTOCK-TIMBERS. Timbers between the floor and navel timbers, and the top-timbers. There are two—the *lower,* which is over the floor, and the *middle,* which is over the navel timber. The navel timber is sometimes called the *ground futtock.*

FULL AND BY STARB'D TACK

GAFF TOPSAIL

G

GAFF. A spar, to which the head of a fore-and-aft sail is bent.

GAFF-TOPSAIL. A light sail set over a gaff, the foot being spread by it.

GAGE. The depth of water of a vessel. Also, the position as to another vessel, as having the *weather* or *lee gage.*

GALLEY. The place where the cooking is done.

GALLOWS-BITTS. A strong frame raised amidships, to support spare spars, etc.

GAMMONING. The lashing by which the bowsprit is secured to the cutwater.

GANG CASKS. Small casks, used for bringing water on board in boats.

GANGWAY. That part of a vessel's side, amidships, where people pass in and out of the vessel.

GARBOARD-STRAKE. The planks next the keel, on each side.

GARLAND. A large rope, strap or grommet, lashed to a spar when hoisting it on board.

GARNET. A purchase on the mainstay, for hoisting.

GASKETS. Ropes or piece of canvas, used to secure a sail when it is furled.

GEAR. A general term, meaning rigging.

GIG. Usually, the officers' boat.

GIMBALS. The brass ring in which a compass sets to keep it level.

GIMBLET. To turn an anchor around by its stock. To turn anything around on its end.

GIRTLINE. A rope rove through a single block aloft, making a whip purchase. (Also known as a gantline.)

GIVE WAY! An order to men in a boat to pull with more force, or to begin pulling. The same as, *Lay out on your oars!* or *Lay out!*

GOB-LINE or *GAUB-LINE.* A rope leading from the martingale inboard. The same as *back-rope.*

GOOSE-NECK. An iron ring fitted to the end of a yard or boom.

GORES. The angles at one or both ends of cloths that increase the breadth or depth of a sail.

GORING-CLOTHS. Pieces cut obliquely and put in to add to the breadth of a sail.

GRAFTING. Covering a rope by weaving yarns together.

GRAINS. An iron with four or more barbed points, used for striking small fish.

GRANNY KNOT. A square knot improperly tied.

GRAPNEL. A small anchor with several claws.

GRAPPLING IRONS. Crooked irons, used to seize and hold vessels fast.

GRATING. Open lattice work of wood. Used principally to cover hatches in good weather; also to let in light and air.

GREAVE. To clean a ship's bottom by burning.

GRIPE. The outside timber of the forefoot, under water, fastened to the lower stem-piece. A vessel *gripes* when she tends to come up into the wind.

GRIPES. Bars of iron, with lanyards, rings, and clews, by which a boat is lashed to the ring-bolts of the deck. Those for a quarter-boat are made of long strips of canvas, going round her and set taut by a lanyard.

GROMMET. A ring formed of rope, by laying around a single strand.

GROUND TACKLE. General term for anchors, cables, warps, springs, etc.; anything used in securing a vessel at anchor.

GUN-TACKLE PURCHASE. A purchase made by two single blocks.

GUNWALE. The upper rail of a boat or vessel.

GUY. A rope attached to anything to steady it, and bear it one way or another in hoisting.

GYBE. To change the position of the sails of a fore-and-aft vessel from one side to the other without going in stays.

H

HAIL. To speak or call to another vessel, or to men in a different part of the ship.

HALYARDS. Ropes or tackles used for hoisting and lowering yards, gaffs, and sails.

HALYARD

HAMMOCK. A piece of canvas, suspended by each end, in which seamen sleep.

HAND. To *hand* a sail is to *furl* it. *Bear-a-hand;* make haste. *Lend-a-hand;* assist. *Hand-over-hand:* hauling rapidly on a rope, by putting one hand before the other alternately.

HAND-LEAD. A small lead, used for sounding in rivers and harbors.

HANDSOMELY. Slowly, carefully. As "Lower handsomely!"

HANDSPIKE. A long wooden bar, used for heaving at the windlass.

HANDY BILLY. A watch-tackle.

HANKS. Rings or hoops of wood, rope, or iron, around a stay.

HARPINGS. The fore part of the wales, which encompass the bows of a vessel, and are fastened to the stem.

HARPOON. A spear used for striking whales and other fish.

HATCH, or *HATCHWAY.* An opening in the deck to afford a passage up and down. The coverings over these openings are called *hatches.*

HATCH-BAR. An iron bar, going across the hatches to keep them down.

HAUL. *Haul her wind,* when a vessel comes up close upon the wind.

HAWSE-HOLE. The hole in the bows through which the anchor cable runs.

HAWSE-PIECES. Timbers through which the hawse-holes are cut.

HARPOON

HAWSE-BLOCK. A block of wood fitted into a hawse-hole when at sea.

HAWSER. A large rope used for various purposes, as warping, for a spring, etc.

HAWSER-LAID, or *CABLE-LAID* rope, is rope laid, with nine strands, against the sun.

HAWSE HOLE

HAZE. Punishing a man by keeping him unnecessarily at some disagreeable work.

HEAD. The work at the prow of a vessel. If it is a carved figure, it is called a *figure-head;* if simple carved work, bending over and out, a *billet-head;* and if bending in, like the head of a violin, a *fiddle-head.* Also, the upper end of a mast, called the *mast-head.* On pleasure boats, the toilet compartment is referred to as the head.

HEAD-SAILS. All sails that set forward of the fore-mast.

HEART. A block of wood in the shape of a heart, for stays to reeve through.

HEART-YARNS. The center yarns of a strand.

HEAVE SHORT. To heave in on the cable until the vessel is nearly over her anchor.

HEAVE-TO. To put a vessel in the position of lying-to.

HEAVE IN STAYS. To go about, tacking.

HEAVER. A short wooden bar, tapering at each end, used as a purchase.

HEEL. The after part of the keel. The lower end of the mast or boom. Also, the lower end of the stern-post. *To heel,* is to careen on one side.

HEELING. The square part of the lower end of a mast, through which the fid-hole is made.

HELM. The machinery by which a vessel is steered, including the rudder, tiller, wheel, etc.

HELM-PORT. The hole in the counter through which the rudder head passes.

HIGH AND DRY. The situation of a vessel when she is aground, above water mark.

HITCH. The manner of fastening ropes.

HOG. A flat, rough broom, used for scrubbing the bottom of a vessel.

HOGGED. Said of a vessel which, as a result of strain, droops at each end.

HOLD. The interior of a vessel, where the cargo is stowed.

HOLD WATER. To stop the progress of a boat by keeping the oar-blades in the water.

HOLY-STONE. A large stone, used for cleaning a ship's decks.

LABOR

HOME. The sheets of a sail are said to be *home,* when the clews are hauled chock out to the sheave-holes. An anchor *comes home* when it is loosened from the ground and is hove in.

HEAD SAILS

HOOD. A covering for a companion hatch, skylight, etc.

HOOD-ENDS or **HOODING-ENDS.** The ends of the planks which fit into the rabbets of the stem or stern-post.

HOOK-AND-BUTT. The scarfing, or laying the ends of timbers over each other.

HORNS. The jaws and booms and gaffs. Also, the ends of crosstrees.

HOUNDS. Projections at the mast-head serving as shoulders for the trestle-trees to rest upon.

HOUSE. *To house* a mast, is to lower it about half its length, and secure it by lashing its heels to the mast below. *To house a gun,* is to run it in clear of the port and secure it.

HOUSING, or **HOUSE-LINE.** A small rope made of three small yarns, and used for seizings.

HULL. The body of a vessel.

I

IRONS. A ship is *in irons,* when, in tacking, she will not bear away one way or the other.

J

JACK. A common term for the *jack-cross-trees.*

JACK-BLOCK. A block used in sending topgallant masts up and down.

JACK-CROSS-TREES. Iron cross-trees at the head of the long topgallant masts.

JACK-STAFF. A short staff, raised at the bowsprit cap, upon which the Union Jack is hoisted.

JACK-STAYS. Ropes stretched taut along a yard to bend the head of the sail to. Also, long strips of wood or iron, used for the same purpose.

JACK-SCREW. A purchase, used for stowing cotton.

JACOB'S LADDER. A ladder made of rope, with wooden steps.

JAWS. The inner ends of booms or gaffs, hollowed to go around the mast.

JEWEL-BLOCKS. Single blocks at the yard-arms, through which the studdingsail halyards lead.

ward. *The Flying-jib* sets outside of the jib.

JIB-BOOM. The boom, rigged out beyond the bowsprit, to which the tack of the jib is lashed.

JIGGER. A small tackle, used about decks or aloft. Small sail set aft on yawls and ketches. Gaff sail on fourth mast of large schooners.

JIB. A triangular sail set on a stay, for-

HELM

JOLLY-BOAT. A small boat, usually hoisted at the stern, on coasting vessels.

JURY-MAST. A temporary mast, rigged at sea, in place of one lost.

K

KECKLING. Old rope wound around cables, to keep them from chafing.

KEDGE. A small anchor, used for warping. *To kedge,* is to warp a vessel ahead.

KEEL. The lowest and principal timber of a vessel, running fore-and-aft the entire length, and supporting the frame. It is composed of several pieces, placed lengthwise, scarfed and bolted together.

KEEL-HAUL. To haul a man under a vessel's bottom, by ropes at the yard-arms on each side. Formerly practised as a punishment in ships of war.

KEELSON. A timber placed over the keel on the floor-timbers, and running parallel with it.

KETCH. A vessel with two masts, the smaller one aft, stepped forward of the rudder post.

KEVEL, or **CAVIL.** A piece of wood, bolted to a timber or stanchion, used for belaying ropes to.

KEVEL-HEADS. Timber-heads, used as kevels.

KINK. A twist in a rope.

KNEES. Crooked pieces of timber, having two arms, used to connect the beams of a vessel with her timbers.

KNIGHT-HEADS. The timbers next the stem on each side, and continued high enough to form a support for the bowsprit.

KNITTLES, or **NETTLES.** The halves of two adjoining yarns in a rope, twisted together, for pointing or grafting. Also, small line used for seizings and for hammock clews.

KNOT. A unit of speed (not distance) equivalent to one nautical mile per hour. The expression "knots per hour" is incorrect.

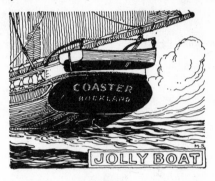

COASTER ROCKLAND

JOLLY BOAT

L

LABOR. A vessel is said to labor when she rolls or pitches heavily.

LACING. Rope used to lash a sail to a spar, or bonnet to a sail.

LAND-FALL. Making land. *A good land-fall,* is when a vessel makes the land as intended.

LAND HO! The cry used when land is first seen when coming from sea.

LANYARDS. Ropes rove through dead-eyes for setting up rigging. Also a rope made fast to anything to secure it.

LARBOARD. The old term for the port or left-hand side of a vessel.

LATCHINGS. Loops on the head rope of a bonnet, by which it is laced to the foot of the sail.

LATITUDE. Distance north or south of the equator.

LAUNCH. A large boat. The *Long-boat.*

LAY. To come or to go; as, *Lay aloft! Lay forward! Lay aft!* Also, the direction in which the strands of a rope are twisted; as, from left to right, or from right to left.

LEACH LINE. A rope used for hauling up the leach of a sail.

LEAD. A piece of lead, in the shape of a cone or pyramid, with a small hole at the base, and a line attached to the upper end, used for sounding. The hole in the base is greased so as to get at the formation of the bottom.

LEADING-WIND. A fair wind. Applied to a wind abeam or quartering.

LEDGES. Small pieces of timber placed athwart-ships under the decks, between the beams.

LEADING WIND

LEE-BOARD

LEE. The side opposite to that from which the wind blows; if a vessel has the wind on her starboard side, that will be the *weather,* and the port will be the *lee* side.

Lee helm is the condition, in a sailing vessel, when the helm must be kept to leeward to hold a boat on her course. This means the rudder is on the windward side, tending to bring the bow up into the wind. (See weather helm.)

A lee shore is the shore upon which the wind is blowing.

LIE-TO

Under the lee of anything, is when you have that between you and the wind.

By the lee. A vessel, going free, when she has fallen off so much as to bring the wind around her stern, and to take her sails aback on the other side.

LEE-BOARD. A board fitted to the lee side of flat-bottomed crafts, to prevent their drifting to leeward.

LUG SAIL

LEEWAY. What a vessel loses by drifting to leeward. When sailing close-hauled with all sail set, there should be little leeway.

LEECH, or **LEACH.** The border or edge of a square sail, at the sides. In a fore and aft sail, the after edge.

LEEWARD. The lee side. In a direction opposite to that from which the wind blows, which is called *windward.* The opposite of *lee* is *weather,* and of *leeward* is *windward.*

LIBERTY. Leave to go ashore.

LIE-TO, is to stop the progress of a vessel at sea, either by counter-bracing the yards, or by reducing sail so that she will make little or no headway, but will merely come to and fall off by the counteraction of the sails and helm.

LIFE-LINES. Ropes carried along yards, booms, etc., or at any part of the vessel, to hold on by.

LIFT. A rope or tackle, going from the yard-arms to the mast-head, to support and move the yard. Also, a term applied to the sails when the wind strikes them on the leeches and raises them slightly.

LIGHTER. A craft, used in loading and unloading vessels.

LIMBERS, or **LIMBERHOLES.** Holes cut in the lower part of the floor-timbers, each side of the keel, so as to allow water to flow fore-and-aft. *Limber-boards* are placed over the limbers to keep dirt from choking the limber-holes, and are movable. *Limber-chain.* A chain or small wire-rope rove fore-and-aft through the limbers, to clear them if necessary. *Limber-streak.* The streak of foot-waling nearest the keelson.

LIST. The inclination of a vessel to one side; as, a *list* to port, or a *list* to starboard.

LOCKER. A chest or box, to stow things in. *Chain-locker.* Where the chain cables are kept. *Boatswain's locker.* Where tools and small stuff for working upon rigging are kept.

LOG-BOOK. A journal kept by the chief officer, in which the position of the vessel, winds, weather, courses, distances, and everything of importance that occurs, is noted down.

LOG. An instrument for determining the speed of a vessel.

LONG BOAT. The largest boat in a merchant vessel.

LONGITUDE. Distance east or west of meridian of Greenwich.

LOOF. That part of a vessel where the planks begin to bend as they approach the stern.

LOOM. That part of an oar which is within the row-lock. Also, to appear above the surface of the water; to appear larger than natural, as in a fog.

LOOSE-FOOTED. A sail (fore and aft) not secured along the foot to a boom.

LUBBER. A greenhorn aboard a ship. *Lubber Line,* the fore-and-aft line of a compass.

LUFF. To put the helm so as to bring the ship up nearer the wind. Also, the round part of a vessel's bow. The forward leech of fore-and-aft sails.
Keep your luff! etc. Order to luff.

LUFF-TACKLE. A purchase composed of a double and single block.
Luff-upon-luff. A luff-tackle applied to the fall of another.

LUGGER. A small vessel carrying lug-sails.

LUG-SAIL. A sail used in boats and small vessels, bent to a yard which hangs obliquely to the mast.

LURCH. The sudden rolling of a vessel to one side.

MARKS

M

MADE. A *made mast* or *block* is one composed of different pieces. A ship's lower mast is usually a made spar, her topmast is a whole spar.

MAIN. In all vessels it applies to the principal mast and sail.

MAKE. To *make sail* is to set it. To *make fast* is to secure a line to a bitt, cleat, etc.

MALLET. A small maul, made of wood; as, *caulking-mallet; also, serving-mallet,* used in putting service on a rope.

MANILLA. A fibre grown in the Philippines.

MAN-ROPES. Ropes used in going up and down a vessel's side.

MARCONI RIG. Uses tall triangular jib-headed sails, as distinguished from the gaff rig.

MARKS. The markings of a lead line to show depths at a glance or by feeling.

MARL. To wind or twist a small line or rope around another.

MARLINE. Small two-stranded stuff, used for marling. A finer kind of spunyarn.

MARLING-HITCH. A hitch used in marling.

MARLINGSPIKE. An iron pin, sharpened at one end, and having a hole in the other for a lanyard.

MARRY. To join ropes together by a worming over both.

MARTINGALE. A short, perpendicular spar, under the bowsprit end, used for guying the head-stays. Sometimes called a dolphin striker.

MAST. A spar set upright from the deck, to support rigging, yards, and sails.

MASTER. The commander of a vessel.

MAT. Made of strands of old rope, and used to prevent chafing.

MATE. An officer ranking next to the master.

MATTHEW WALKER. A stopper knot which takes its name from the originator.

MESSENGER. A rope used for heaving in a cable by the capstan.

MIDSHIPS. The timbers at the broadest part of the vessel.

MILE. A nautical mile is 1-60 of a degree of latitude, generally 6,080 feet.

MISS-STAYS. To fail of going about from one tack to another.

MIZZEN-MAST. The aftermost mast of a ship. The spanker is sometimes called the *mizzen.*

NEAP TIDES

MONKEY BLOCK. A small single block strapped with a swivel.

MOON-SAIL. A small sail sometimes carried in light winds, above a skysail.

MOORING. Commonly, the anchor, chain, buoy, pennant, etc., by which a boat is permanently anchored in one location.

MOP. A cloth broom used on board vessels.

MOULDS. The patterns by which the frames of a vessel are worked out.

MOUSE. To put turns of rope-yarn or spunyarn around the end of a hook and its standing part when it is hooked to anything, so as to prevent its slipping out.

MOUSING. A knot or puddening, made of yarns, and placed on the outside of a rope.

MUFFLE. Oars are muffled by putting mats or canvas around their looms in the row-locks.

N

NAVIGATION. The art of conducting a ship from port to port.

NEAP TIDES. Tides that occur near the moon's quadrature, when the range is less than average.

NEAPED. The situation of a vessel when she is aground at the height of the spring tides.

NEAR. Close to the wind.

NEST. Dories, or small boats, are nested when stowed one inside the other.

NETTING. Network of rope or small lines. Used for stowing away sails or hammocks.

NIP. A short turn in a rope.

NOCK. The forward upper end of a sail that sets with a boom.

NUN-BUOY. A buoy tapering at each end.

NUT. Projections on each side of the shank of an anchor, to secure the stock to its place.

O

OAKUM. Stuff made by picking rope-yarns to pieces. Used for caulking, and other purposes.

OAR. A long wooden instrument with a flat blade at one end, used for propelling boats.

NUN BUOY

OFF-AND-ON. To stand on different tacks towards and from the land.

OFF THE WIND. Said of a boat sailing with sheets eased (slacked off.) She is *on the wind* when close-hauled.

OFFING. Distance from the shore.

OUT-HAUL. A rope used for hauling out the clew of a sail.

OUT-RIGGER. A spar rigged out to windward from the tops or cross-trees, to spread the breast-backstays.

OVERHAUL. To overhaul a tackle, is to let go the fall and pull on the leading parts so as to separate the blocks. *To overhaul a rope,* is generally to pull a part through a block so as to make slack. *To overhaul rigging,* is to examine it.

P

PAINTER. A rope attached to the bows of a boat, used for making her fast.

PALM. A piece of leather fitted over the hand, with an iron for the head of a needle to press against in sewing canvas. Also, the fluke of an anchor.

PARBUCKLE. To hoist or lower a spar or cask by single ropes passed around it.

PENNANT

M. S.

PARCEL. To wind tarred canvas around a rope (called *parcelling.*)

PARRAL. The rope by which a yard is confined to the mast at its center.

PART. To break a rope or chain.

PARTNERS. A frame-work of short timber fitted to the hole in a deck to receive the lower end of a mast or pump, etc.

PAZAREE. A rope attached to the clew of the foresail and rove through a block on the swinging boom. Used for guying the clews out when before the wind.

PAUNCH MAT. A thick mat, placed at the slings of a yard or elsewhere.

PAWL. A short bar of iron, which prevents the capstan or windlass from turning back.

PAY-OFF. When a vessel's head falls off from the wind. *To pay.* To cover over with tar or pitch. *To pay out.* To slack up a cable or rope, and let it run out.

PEAK. The upper outer corner of a sail attached to a gaff.

PENDANT OR PENNANT. A long narrow piece of bunting, carried at the masthead. *Broad pennant,* is a square piece, carried in the same way, in a commodore's vessel. *Pennant.* A rope to which a purchase is hooked. A long strap fitted at one end to a yard or masthead, with a hook or block at the other end, for a brace to reeve through, or to hook a tackle to.

PILLOW. A block which supports the inner end of the bowsprit.

PIN. The axis on which a sheave turns. Also, a short piece of wood or iron to belay ropes to.

PINCH. To hold a sailboat so close to the wind that sails shiver.

OFFING

PINK-STERN. When a vessel has a high, narrow stern, pointed at the end.

PINNACE. A boat, in size between a launch and the cutter.

PINTLE. A metal bolt, used for hanging a rudder.

PITCH. A resin taken from pine, and used for filling up the seams of a vessel.

PLANKS. Thick, strong boards, used for covering the sides and decks of vessels.

PLUG. A piece of wood, fitted into a hole in a vessel or boat, so as to let in or keep out water.

PINK STERN

POINT. To take the end of a rope and work it over with knittles.

POLE. Applied to the highest mast of a ship, as *sky-sail pole.*

POOP. A deck raised over the after part of the spar deck.

POPPETS. Perpendicular pieces of timber fixed to the fore-and-aft part of the bilge-ways when launching.

PORT. The left side of a vessel as you look forward.

PORT OR PORT-HOLE. Holes in the side of a vessel. Also, holes in the bow of a vessel by which to load and unload large timber, etc., too long to go through the hatches.

PORTOISE. The gunwale. The yards are *a-portoise* when they rest on the gunwale.

PRAYER BOOK. A small, flat holystone used in narrow places.

PREVENTER. An additional rope or spar, used as a support.

PRICKER. A small marling spike, used in sail-making, rigging, etc.

PUDDENING. A quantity of yarns, matting, or oakum, used to prevent chafing.

PUMP-BRAKE. The handle to the pump.

PURCHASE. A mechanical power which increases the force applied.

Q

QUADRANT. An instrument used in navigation.

QUARTER. The part of a vessel's side between the after part of the main chains and the stern. The *quarter* of a yard is between the slings and the yard-arm.

QUARTER-BLOCK. A block fitted under the quarters of a yard on each side of the slings, for the clewlines and sheets to reeve through.

QUARTER-DECK. That part of the upper deck abaft the mainmast.

QUARTER-MASTER. A petty officer, who attends the helm and binnacle, watches for signals, etc.

QUICK-WORK. That part of a vessel's side which is above the chainwales and decks.

QUILTING. A coating about a vessel, outside, formed of ropes woven together.

QUOIN. A wooden wedge for the breach of a gun to rest upon.

R

RABBET. A grove to receive the edge of a plank in ship building.

RACE. A strong, rippling tide.

RACK. To seize two ropes together, with cross-turns. Also, a *fair-leader* for running rigging.

RACK-BLOCK. A course of blocks made from one piece of wood, for fair-leaders.

RAIL. Top of the bulwarks (topsides above the deck).

RAKE. The inclination of a mast from the perpendicular.

RAMLINE. A line used in mast-making to get a straight middle line on a spar.

RANGE OF CABLE. A quantity of cable, ready for letting go the anchor or paying out.

In piloting, a *range* consists of two objects in line, used as an aid in steering a course. *Range of tide* is the amount of its rise and fall.

RATLINES. Lines running across the shrouds, horizontally, and used, in going aloft, as a ladder.

RATTLE-DOWN RIGGING. To put ratlines upon rigging. It is still called rattling

down, though rigging is now rattled *up,* beginning at the lowest.

RAZEE. A vessel of war which has had one deck cut down.

REACH. A sailing vessel reaches when the wind is, roughly, abeam. With the wind on the quarter, it is a *broad reach.* It is a *close reach* when the wind is just forward of the beam, but the vessel is not close-hauled.

READY ABOUT. The order to stand by to tack ship.

REEF. To reduce a sail by taking in upon its head, if a square sail, and its foot, if a fore-and-aft sail.

REEF-BAND. A band of stout canvas sewed on the sail across, with points in it, and earrings at each end for reefing.

REEF-TACKLE. A tackle used on a square sail to haul the middle of each leech up toward the yard, so that the sail may be easily reefed. Also, on fore-and-aft vessels, to haul out the foot of the sail.

REEVE. To pass the end of a rope through a block, or an aperture.

RELIEVING TACKLE. A tackle hooked to the tiller, to steer by in case of accident to the wheel or tiller-ropes.

RENDER. To pass a rope through a place. A rope is said to *render* or not, as it goes freely.

RIB-BANDS. Long, narrow, flexible pieces of timber nailed to the outside of the ribs so as to encompass the vessel lengthwise.

RIBS. The timbers of a vessel.

RIDE AT ANCHOR. To lie at anchor. Also, to bend or bear down by main strength and weight.

RIDERS. Interior timbers placed occasionally opposite the principal ones, to which they are bolted, reaching from the keelson to the beams of the lower deck. Also, casks forming the second tier in a vessel's hold.

RIGGING. The general term for all the ropes of a vessel. Also, the common term for the shrouds with their ratlines; as, the *main rigging, mizzen rigging,* etc.

RIGHT. To *right* the helm, is to put it amidships.

RING. The iron ring at the upper end of an anchor, to which the cable is bent.

RING-BOLT. An eye-bolt with a ring through the eye.

RING-TAIL. A small sail, shaped like a jib, set abaft the spanker in light winds.

ROACH. A curve in the foot of a square sail, by which the clews are brought below the middle of the foot. The *roach* of a fore-and-aft sail is in its forward leech.

ROAD, or *ROADSTEAD.* An anchorage at a distance from the shore.

ROLLING TACKLE. Tackles used to steady the yards in a heavy sea. Also, used on smoke stacks of steamers to keep them steady.

ROPE. Generally speaking, rope is cordage of greater than one-inch circumference. The term has often been abused, as a piece of rope when put to use on a vessel becomes a line, in most cases. Among the relatively few ropes, properly speaking, are bolt ropes, foot ropes, bell ropes, bucket ropes, man ropes, yard ropes, back ropes, and top ropes.

ROPE-YARN. A thread of hemp, or other stuff, of which a rope is made.

ROUGH-TREE. An unfinished spar.

ROUND IN. To haul in on a rope.

ROUND UP. To haul up on a tackle.

ROUNDING. A service of rope, hove around a spar or larger rope.

ROWLOCKS. The receptacles for the oars in rowing.

ROYAL. A light sail next above a top-gallant sail.

ROYAL YARD. The yard from which the royal is set. The fourth from the deck.

RUBBER. A small instrument used to rub or flatten down the seams of a sail in sail-making.

RUDDER. That by which a vessel or boat is steered, attached to the stern-post.

RULES OF THE ROAD. The international regulations for preventing collisions at sea.

RUN. The after part of a vessel's bottom, which rises and narrows in approaching the stern-post. *By the run.* To let go *by the run,* is to let go altogether, instead of gradually.

RUNG-HEADS. The upper ends of the floor-timbers.

RUNNER. A rope to increase the power of a tackle. It is rove through a single block, and a tackle is hooked to each end, or to one end, the other being fast.

RUNNING RIGGING. The ropes that reeve through blocks, and are pulled and hauled, such as braces, halyards, etc.; in contrast to the *standing rigging,* the ends of which are securely seized, such as stays, shrouds, etc.

S

SADDLES. Pieces of wood hollowed out to fit on the yards to which they are nailed, having a hollow in the upper part for the boom to rest in.

SAG. To *sag to leeward,* is to drift off bodily to leeward.

SAILS are of two kinds: *square. sails,* which hang from yards, their foot lying across the line of the keel, as the courses, topsails, etc.; and *fore-and-aft-sails,* which set upon gaffs, booms, etc., their foot running with the line of the keel.

SAILS FORE AND AFT AND SQUARE

SAIL HO! The cry used when a sail is discovered at sea.

SAMSON POST. A single bitt in the bow of a small boat.

SAVE-ALL. A small sail sometimes set under the foot of a lower sail, often called a *catch-all.*

SCANTLING. A term applied to any piece of timber, with regard to its breadth and thickness, when reduced to the standard size.

SCARF. To join pieces of timber at their ends by shaving them down and overlapping them.

SCHOONER. A vessel with two or more masts. A *fore-and-aft* schooner has only fore-and-aft sails. *A topsail schooner* carries a square fore topsail, and frequently, topgallant sail and royal schooners are now built with two, three, four, and many with five masts.

SCORE. A groove in a block or dead-eye.

SCOTCHMAN. A large batten placed over the turnings-in of rigging, to prevent chafing.

SCRAPER. A small, triangular iron instrument, with a handle fitted to its centre, used for scraping decks, masts, etc.

SCROWL. A piece of timber bolted to the knees of the head, in place of a figure-head.

SCUD. To drive before a gale, with no sail, or only enough to steady the vessel.

SCHOONER

Also, low, thin, clouds that fly swiftly before the wind.

SCULL. A short oar. *To scull,* is to impel a boat by one oar at the stern.

SCUPPERS. Holes cut in the water-ways for the water to run from the decks.

SCUTTLE. A hole cut in a vessel's deck, as, a hatchway. Also, a hole cut in any part of a vessel. *To scuttle,* is to cut or bore holes in a vessel to make her sink.

SEA. Waves (collectively) caused by wind blowing at the time and place of observation. (See *swell.*)

SEAMS. The intervals between planks in a vessel's deck or side.

SEIZE. To fasten ropes together by turns of small stuff, to secure hooks, etc.

SEIZINGS. The fastenings of ropes that are seized together.

SELVAGEE. A skein of rope-yarns or spunyarn, marled together. Used as a neat strap.

SENNIT, or **SINNIT.** A braid, formed by plaiting rope-yarns or spunyarn together.

SERVE. To wind small stuff, as rope-yarns, spunyarn, etc., around a rope, to keep it from chafing. It is wound and hove round taut by a serving-board or mallet.

SET. To *set up rigging,* is to tighten it.

SEXTANT. The instrument used in determining altitudes of heavenly bodies.

SHACKLES. Links in a chain cable fitted with a movable bolt so that the chain can be separated.

SHANK. The main piece in an anchor; the stock is made fast at one end, and the arms at the other.

SHANK-PAINTER. A strong rope by which the lower part of the shank of an anchor is secured to the ship's side.

SHARP UP. Yards when braced as near fore-and-aft as possible.

SHEATHING. A casing or covering on the bottom of a vessel.

SHEARS. Two or more spars, raised at angles and lashed together near their upper ends, used for lowering or hoisting heavy objects.

SHEAR HULK. An old vessel fitted with shears, etc., and used for taking out and putting in the spars of other vessels.

SHEAVE. The wheel in a block upon which the rope runs. *Sheave-hole,* the place cut in a block for the ropes to reeve through.

SHEEP-SHANK. A hitch or bend, used to shorten a rope temporarily.

SHEEPSHANK

SHEER, or **SHEER-STRAKE.** The line of plank on a vessel's side, running fore-and-aft under the gunwale. Also, a vessel's position when riding by a single anchor.

SHEETS. Ropes used in working a sail, to keep the clew down to its place. With square sails, the sheets run through each yard-arm. With boom sails, they haul the sails to the desired positions.

SHEET ANCHOR. A vessel's largest anchor.

SHELL. The case of a block.

SHIP. A vessel with three or four masts, with tops and yards. To enter on board a vessel. To fix anything in its proper place, such as *ship* shape.

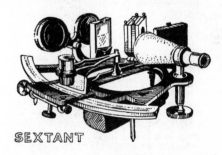

SEXTANT

SHIVER. To shake the wind out of a sail by bracing it so that the wind strikes upon the leech.

SHOE. A piece of wood used for the bill of an anchor to rest upon. Also, for the heels of shears, etc. Also added to a vessel's keel to give her more draft.

SHOE-BLOCK. A block with two sheaves, one above the other, the one horizontal and the other perpendicular.

SHORE. A prop or stanchion, placed under a beam. To *shore,* to prop up.

SHORT BOARD. Same as a short tack or leg. A long board is a long tack.

SHORTEN. One shortens sail when he takes in canvas to reduce the area of sail set.

SHROUDS. Ropes on each side of a vessel, reaching from the mast-heads to the vessel's sides, to support the masts.

SILLS. Pieces of timber put in horizontally between the frames to form and secure openings.

SISTER BLOCK. A long piece of wood with two sheaves in it, one above the other, with a score between them for a seizing, and a groove around the block, lengthwise. Two blocks of same size attached to a ring usually used for jib-halyards, etc.

SKEG. Timbers used to deepen the after part of a keel, or a metal or wood extension of the keel protecting the propeller, and often supporting the rudder.

SHIP

SPINNAKER

SPARS. The general term for masts, yards, booms, gaffs, etc.

SPEAK. One speaks a vessel when communicating with her at sea.

SPEAKING TRUMPET. A trumpet for conveying orders on board a vessel.

SPELL. The common term for a portion of time given to any work. *To spell,* is to relieve another.

SPENCER. A fore-and-aft sail, set with a gaff and no boom, and hoisting from a small mast called a *spencer-mast,* just abaft the fore and main masts.

SPILL. To shake the wind out of a sail.

SPILLING LINE. A rope used for spilling a sail. Used in bad weather.

SPLICE. To join two ropes together by interweaving their strands.

SPINNAKER. A light sail of great spread used on yachts when running before the wind.

SPIRIT COMPASS. The modern style of compass.

SPOON-DRIFT. Water swept from the tops of the waves by the violence of the wind, and driven along before it, covering the surface of the sea.

SPRAY. An occasional sprinkling dashed from the top of a wave by the wind.

SPREADERS. Arms of metal or wood used to spread shrouds or stays and give better support to a mast.

SPRING. To crack or split a mast. *To spring a leak,* is to begin to leak. *To spring a luff,* is to force a vessel close to the wind, in sailing.

A *spring line* is one used at a dock to keep a vessel from moving ahead or astern.

SPRING-STAY. A horizontal stay running between mastheads of a schooner.

SPRING TIDES. The highest and lowest course of tides, occurring every new and full moon.

SPRIT. A small boom or gaff, used with sails in small boats. The lower end rests in a becket or snotter by the foot of the mast, and the other end spreads and raises the outer upper corner of the sail, crossing it diagonally. A sail so rigged is called a *sprit-sail.*

SPRIT-SAIL-YARD. A yard lashed across the bowsprit or knightheads, and used to spread the guys of the jib and flying jibboom.

SPUNYARN. A rope formed by twisting together two or three rope-yarns.

SPURLING LINE. A line communicating between the tiller and tell-tale.

SPURS. Pieces of timber fixed on the bilge-ways, their upper ends being bolted to the vessel's sides above the water. Also, curved pieces of timber, serving as half beams, to support the decks where the whole beams cannot be placed.

SPUR-SHOES. Large pieces of timber that come abaft the pump-well.

SQUARE. Yards are *squared* when they are horizontal and at right angles with the

---

SKIN. The part of a sail which is outside and covers the rest when it is furled. Also, the sides of the hold; as, an article is said to be stowed *next to the skin.*

SKYSAIL. A light sail next above the royal.

SKY-SCRAPER. A skysail when it is triangular.

SLABLINE. A small line used to haul up the foot of a course.

SLACK. The part of a rope or sail that hangs down loose. *Slack in stays,* is sail of a vessel when she works slowly in tacking.

SLEEPERS. The knees that connect the transoms to the after timbers on the ship's quarter.

SLING. To set in ropes, so as to put on a tackle to hoist or lower it.

SLINGS. The ropes used for securing the centre of a yard to the mast. Also, a large rope fitted so as to go around anything which is to be hoisted or lowered.

SLIP. To let go a cable and stand out to sea. To *slip the anchor.*

SLIP-ROPE. A rope bent to the cable outside the hawse-hole, and brought in on the weather quarter, when ready to slip the anchor.

SLOPS. A name given to ready-made clothing supplied by the captain.

SLOOP. A small vessel with one mast.

SLOOP OF WAR. A vessel of any rig, mounting between 18 and 32 guns.

SMALL STUFF. Spun-yarn, marline, and the smallest kinds of rope, such as ratline, etc.

SNAKE. To pass small stuff across a seizing, with marling hitches at the outer turns.

SNATCH-BLOCK. A single block, with an opening in its side below the sheave, or at the bottom, to receive the bight of a rope.

SNOTTER. A rope going over a yard-arm, with an eye, to bend a tripping-line to in sending down topgallant and royal yards, and other spars.

SNUB. To check a rope suddenly.

SNYING. A curved plank edgewise, to work in the bows of a vessel.

SO! An order to stop hauling upon any-thing when it has come to its right position.

SOLE. A piece of timber fastened to the foot of the rudder, to make it level with the false keel.

SOUND. To get the depth of water by a lead and line. The pumps are *sounded* by an iron *sounding rod,* marked with a scale of feet and inches.

SPAN. A rope with both ends made fast, so a purchase can be hooked to its bight.

SPANKER. The after sail of a ship or bark.

keel. Squaring by the lifts makes them horizontal; and by the braces, makes them at right angles with the vessel's line. *To square a yard,* means to bring it in square by the braces.

SQUARE-SAIL. A temporary sail, set at the fore-mast of a schooner or the main-mast of a sloop, when going before the wind.

STAFF. A pole or mast, used to hoist flags upon.

STABILITY. Stiffness of a vessel.

STANCHIONS. Upright posts of wood or iron, placed so as to support the beams of a vessel. Also, upright pieces of timber, placed at intervals along the sides of a vessel, to support the bulwarks and rail, reaching down to the bends, by the side of the timbers, to which they are bolted. Also, any fixed, upright support.

STAND. The interval during which the tide is neither rising nor falling.

STAND BY! To be prepared to act at once.

STANDING. The *standing part* of a rope is that which is fast, the opposite to the

STARBOARD

hauling part. The *standing part* of a tackle is that part which is made fast to the blocks and between that and the next sheave, the opposite to the hauling and leading parts.

STANDING RIGGING. That part of a vessel's rigging which is made fast to the sides.

STARBOARD. The right side of a vessel, looking forward.

STEEVE

START. A sheet is started when it is eased off.

STATION BILL. A list showing the station of every man, in case of accident.

STAY. To tack a vessel, or put her about, so that the wind, from being on one side, is brought upon the other, around the vessel's head. *To stay a mast,* is to incline it forward or aft, or to one side or the other, by the stays and backstays. A mast is said to be *stayed* too much forward or aft, or too much to port, etc.

STAYS. Large ropes, used to support masts, and leading from the head of one mast down to another, or to some part of the vessel. Those which lead forward are called *fore-and-aft stays;* and those which lead down to the vessel's sides, *back-stays.*

In stays or *hove in stays,* a vessel when she is *staying,* or going from one tack to the other.

STAYSAIL. A triangular fore-and-aft sail set from a stay.

STEADY! To keep the helm as it is.

STEERAGE. That part of the between-decks which is just forward of the cabin.

STEEVE. A bowsprit *steeves* more or less, as it is raised more or less from the horizontal. The *steeve* is the angle it makes with the horizon. Also, a long, heavy spar, with a place to fit a block at one end, and used in stowing cargo, which need be stowed close.

STEM. A piece of timber reaching from the forward end of the keel, to which it is scarfed, up to the bowsprit and to which the two sides of the vessel are secured.

STEP. A block of wood secured to the keel, into which the heel of the mast is placed.

STERN. The after end of a vessel.

STERNWAY. The motion of a vessel when going stern foremost.

STERN-FRAME. The frame composed of the stern-post transom and the fashion-pieces.

STERN-POST. The aftermost timber in a vessel, reaching from the after end of the keel to the deck. The stem and stern-post are the two extremes of a vessel's frame. The rudder is attached to the stern-post.

STERN-SHEETS. The after part of a boat, abaft the rowers, where the passengers sit.

STEVEDORE. A man who loads and unloads cargoes of vessels.

STIFF. The quality of a vessel which enables her to carry a great deal of sail without lying over much on her side. The opposite to *crank.*

STIRRUPS. Ropes with thimbles at their ends, through which the foot-ropes are rove, and by which they are kept up towards the yards.

STERN

STOCK. A beam of wood or a bar of iron, secured to the upper end of the shank of an anchor, at right angles with the arms. An iron stock usually goes with a key, and unships.

STOCKS. The frame upon which a vessel is built.

STOOLS. Small channels for the dead-eyes of the backstays.

STOPPER. A stout rope with a knot at one end, and sometimes a hook at the other, used for various purposes about decks; as, making fast a cable, so as to overhaul.

STOPPER BOLTS. Ring-bolts to which the deck stoppers are secured.

STOP. A fastening of small stuff. Also, small projections on the outside of the checks of a lower mast, at the upper parts of the hounds.

STOPWATER. A soft wood dowel driven in a hole bored through the joint between the keel and an adjoining timber, such as the stern to prevent leakage.

STOVE. A vessel is stove when her hull is smashed in from the outside.

STOW. To pack the cargo.

STRAND. A number of rope-yarns twisted together. Three, four, or nine strands twisted together form a rope. A rope is *stranded* when one of its strands is parted or broken. A vessel is *stranded* when she is driven on shore.

STRAP. Rope or iron around a block to keep its parts together.

STREAK, or *STRAKE.* Planks running fore and aft on the outside of a vessel.

STREAM. The *stream anchor* is one used for warping, etc., and sometimes as a lighter anchor to moor by, with a hawser. It is smaller than the *bowers,* and larger than the *kedges.*

STRETCHERS. Pieces of wood placed across a boat's bottom, inside, for the oars-

STUDDING SAILS

men to press their feet against, when rowing. Also, cross pieces placed between a boat's sides to keep them apart when hoisted up and griped.

STRIKE. To lower sail or colors.

STRIP. To dismantle.

STUDDINGSAILS. Light sails set outside the square sails, on booms rigged out for that purpose. They are only carried with a fair wind and in moderate weather.

SUED, or *SEWED.* The condition of a ship when she is high and dry on shore.

SUPPORTERS. The knee-timbers under the cat-heads.

SURF. The breaking of the sea upon the shore.

SURGE. A large, swelling wave. To *surge* a rope or cable, is to slack it up suddenly where it renders around a pin, or around the windlass or capstan.

SWAB. A mop, formed of old rope, used for cleaning and drying decks.

SWAY. To hoist up.

SWEEP. To drag the bottom. Also, large oars, used in small vessels to force them ahead.

SWELL. Wave movements caused by wind blowing at some point remote from that of observation, or by winds which have blown at the point of observation previous to the time of observation. (See *sea.*)

SWIFT. To bring two shrouds or stays close together by ropes.

SWIFTER. The forward shroud to a lower mast. Also, ropes used to confine the capstan bars to their places when shipped.

SWIG. The mode of hauling upon the bight of a rope when its lower end is fast.

SWIVEL. A long link of iron, used in chain cables, made so as to turn upon an axis intended to keep the turns out of a chain.

SYPHERING. Lapping the edges of planks over each other for a bulk-head.

T

TABLING. Letting one beam-piece into another. Also, the broad hem on the borders of sails, to which the bolt-rope is sewed.

TACK. To put a ship about, so that from having the wind on one side it is brought around on the other by the way of her head. The opposite of *wearing.*

A vessel is on the *starboard tack,* or has her *starboard tacks on board,* when she has the wind on her starboard side.

The rope or tackle by which the weather clew of a course is hauled forward and down.

The *tack* of a fore-and-aft sail is the rope that keeps down the lower forward clew; and of a studdingsail, the lower outer clew. The tack of the lower studdingsail is called the *outhaul.* Also, that part of a sail to which the tack is attached.

TACKLE. A purchase; formed by a rope rove through one or more blocks.

TAFFRAIL. The rail around a ship's stern.

TAIL. A rope spliced into the end of a block and used for making it fast to rigging or spars is called a *tail-block.* A ship is said to *tail* up or down stream, when at anchor, according as her stern swings up or down with the tide; the opposite to *heading* one way or another.

TAIL-TACKLE. A watch-tackle.

TAIL ON! To take hold of a rope and pull.

TAR. A liquid gum, taken from pine and fir trees, and used for caulking, and to put upon yarns in rope-making, and upon standing rigging, to protect it from the weather.

TARPAULIN. A piece of canvas, covered with tar, used for covering hatches, boats, etc. Also, the name commonly given to a sailor's hat when made of tarred or painted cloth.

TAUT. Tight, snug.

TELL-TALE. A compass hanging from the beams of the cabin, by which the heading of a vessel may be known at any time. Also, an instrument connected with the steering apparatus, and traversing so that the position of the rudder can be determined.

TEND. To watch a vessel at anchor at the turn of tides, and cast her by the helm, and some sail, if necessary, so as to keep turns out of the cables.

TENDER. A top-heavy vessel, with insufficient stability, is said to be tender.

TENON. The heel of a mast, made to fit into the step.

THICK-AND-THIN BLOCK. A block having one sheave larger than the other. Sometimes used for quarter-blocks.

THIMBLE. An iron ring, having its rim concave on the outside for a rope or strap to fit snugly.

THOLE-PINS. Pins in the gunwale of a boat, between which an oar is held when pulling.

THROAT. The inner end of a gaff, where it widens and hollows in to fit the mast. Also, the hollow part of a knee. The *throat* brails, halyards, etc., are those that hoist or haul up the gaff or sail near the throat. Also, the angle where the arm of an anchor is joined to the shank.

THRUM. To stick short strands of yarn through a mat or canvas, to make a rough surface.

THWARTS. The seats going across a boat, upon which the oarsmen sit.

TIDE. To *tide up or down* a river or harbor, is to work up or down with a fair tide and head wind or calm, coming to anchor when the tide turns.

TIDE RODE. When a vessel, at anchor, swings by the force of the tide. Opposite to *wind-rode.*

TIER. A range of casks. Also, the range of the fakes of a cable or hawser.

The *cable tier* is the place in a hold or between decks where the cables are stowed.

TILLER. A bar of wood or iron, put into the head of the rudder, by which it is moved.

TIMBER. A general term for all large pieces of wood used in ship-building. Also, more particularly, long pieces of wood in a curved form, bending outward, and running from the keel up, on each side, forming the *ribs* of a vessel. The keel, stem, stern-posts and timbers form a vessel's outer frame.

TIMBER-HEADS. The ends of the timbers that come above the deck. Used for belaying hawsers and large ropes.

TOGGLE. A pin placed through the bight or eye of a rope, block-strap, or bolt, to keep it in its place, or to put the bight or eye of another rope upon, securing them together.

TOMPION. A bung or plug placed in the mouth of a cannon.

TOP. A platform placed over the head of a lower mast, resting on the trestle-trees, to spread the rigging, and for the convenience of men aloft. To *top* up a yard or boom, is to raise up one end of it by hoisting on the lift.

TOP-BLOCK. A large iron-bound block, hooked into a bolt under the lower cap, and used for the top-rope to reeve through in sending up and down topmasts.

TOP-LIGHT. A signal lantern carried to the top.

TOP-LINING. Lining on the after part of sails, to prevent chafing against the top-rim.

TOPMAST. The second mast above the deck. Next above the lower mast.

TOPGALLANT MAST. The third mast above the deck.

TOP-ROPE. The rope used for sending topmasts up and down.

TOPSAIL. The second sail above the deck.

TOPGALLANT SAIL. The third sail above the deck.

TOPSIDES. Sides of a vessel between the water line and the rail.

TOPPING LIFT. A lift used for topping up the end of a boom.

TOP-TIMBERS. The highest timbers on a vessel's side, being above the futtocks.

TOSS. To throw an oar out of the rowlock, and raise it perpendicularly on its end, and lay it down in the boat, with its blade forward.

TOUCH. A sail is said to *touch,* when the wind strikes the leech so as to shake it a little.

Luff and touch her! To bring the vessel up and see how near she will go to the wind.

TOW. To draw a vessel along in the water.

TRAIN-TACKLE. The tackle used for running guns in and out.

TRANSOMS. Pieces of timber going across the stern-post, to which they are bolted. Raised platforms in small vessels and yachts, used for seats, etc.

TRANSOM-KNEES. Knees bolted to the transoms and after timbers.

TRAVELLER. An iron ring, fitted so as to slip up and down rigging.

TREENAILS, or **TRUNNELS.** Long wooden pins, used for nailing a plank to a timber.

TREND. The lower end of the shank of an anchor, being the same distance on the shank from the throat that the arm measures from the throat to the bill.

TRESTLE-TREES. Two strong pieces of timber, placed horizontally and fore-and-aft on opposite sides of a mast-head, to support the cross-trees and top, and for the fid of the mast above to rest upon.

TRIATIC STAY. A rope secured at each end to the heads of the fore and main masts, with thimbles spliced into its bight, to hook the stay tackles to.

TRICE. To haul up by means of a rope.

TRICK. The time allotted to a man to stand at the helm. A *trick* at the wheel.

TRIM. The conditions of a vessel, with reference to her cargo and ballast. A vessel is *trimmed* by the head or by the stern. *In ballast trim,* is when she has only ballast on board. Also, to arrange the sails with reference to the wind.

TRIP. To raise an anchor clear of the bottom.

TRIPPING LINE. A line used for tripping a spar in sending it down.

TROUGH. A vessel lies *in the trough* of the sea when down in the hollow between crests.

TRUCK. A circular piece of wood, placed at the head of the masts of a vessel. It has small holes or sheaves in it for signal halyards to be rove through. Also, the wheel of a gun-carriage.

TRUNNIONS. The arms on each side of a cannon by which it rests upon the carriage, and on which, as an axis, it is elevated or depressed.

TRUSS. The rope by which the centre of a lower yard is kept in toward the mast.

TRYSAIL. A fore-and-aft sail, set with a boom and gaff, and hoisting on a small mast abaft the lower mast, called a *trysail-mast.* This name is generally confined to the sail so carried at the mainmast of a full-rigged brig; those carried at the foremast and at the mainmast of a ship or bark being called *spencers,* and those that are at the mizzenmast of a ship or bark, *spankers.*

TUMBLING HOME. A ship's sides when they fall in above the bends. The opposite of *wall-sided.*

TURK'S HEAD. An ornamental knot.

TURN. Passing a rope around a pin or kevel, to keep it fast. Also, two crosses in a cable. *To turn in* or *turn out,* nautical terms for going to rest in a berth or hammock, and getting up. *Turn up!* The order given to send the men up from between decks.

TYE. A rope connected with a yard, to the other end of which a tackle is attached for hoisting.

TYPHOON. A hurricane in the Eastern seas.

U

UNBEND. To cast off or to untie.

UNION. The upper inner corner of an ensign. The rest of the flag is called the *fly.* The *union* of the U. S. ensign is a blue field with white stars and the *fly* is composed of alternate white and red stripes.

Union-down. The situation of a flag when it is hoisted upside down, bringing the union down instead of up. Used as a signal of distress.

Union-jack. A small flag, containing only the union, without the fly, usually hoisted at the bowsprit-cap.

UNMOOR. To heave up one anchor so that the vessel may ride at a single anchor.

V

VANE. A fly at the mast-head, revolving on a spindle, to show the direction of the wind.

VANG. A rope leading from the peak of the gaff of a fore-and-aft sail to the rail on each side, used for steadying the gaff.

VEER. The wind when it changes. Also, to slack a cable and let it run out.

To veer and haul, is to haul and slack alternately, until the vessel gets headway.

VIOL. A larger messenger sometimes used in weighing an anchor by a capstan. Also, the block through which the messenger passes.

W

WAIST. That part of the upper deck between the quarter-deck and forecastle.

Waisters. Green hands, or broken-down seamen, placed in the waist of a man-of-war,

WAKE. The track or path a vessel leaves behind her when sailing.

WALES. Strong planks in a vessel's sides, running her entire length fore-and-aft.

WALL. A knot put on the end of a rope.

WALL-SIDED. A vessel is *wall-sided* when her sides run up perpendicularly from the bends. The opposite to *tumbling home* or *flaring out*.

WARD-ROOM. The room in a vessel of war in which the commissioned officers live.

WARE, or *WEAR*. To turn a vessel around, so that, from having the wind on one side, the wind will be on the other side, carrying her stern around by the wind. In *tacking*, the same result is produced by carrying a vessel's head around by the wind.

WARP. To move a vessel from one place to another by means of a rope made fast to some fixed object, or to a kedge. A *warp* is a rope used for warping. If the warp is bent to a kedge which is let go, and the vessel is hove ahead by the capstan or windlass, it would be called *kedging*.

WASH-BOARD. Light pieces of board placed above the gunwale of a boat.

WATCH. A division of time on board ship. There are seven watches in a day reckoning from 12 M. round through the 24 hours, five of them being of four hours each, and the two others, called *dog watches*, of two hours each, viz., from 4 to 6, and from 6 to 8 P. M. Also, a certain portion of ship's company, appointed to stand a given length of time. In the merchant service all hands are divided into two watches, port and starboard, with a mate to command each. A *buoy* is said to *watch* when it floats on the surface.

WATCH-AND-WATCH. The arrangement by which the watches are alternated every other four hours. In distinction from keeping all hands during one or more watches.

Anchor watch, a small watch of one or two men, kept while in port.

WATCH HO! WATCH! The cry of the man that heaves the deep-sea-lead.

WATCH-TACKLE. A small luff purchase with a short fall, the double block having a tail to it and the single one a hook. Used about deck.

WATER SAIL. A *save-all*, set under the swinging-boom.

WATER-WAYS. Long pieces of timber, running fore-and-aft on both sides, connecting the deck with the vessel's sides. The scuppers run through them to let the water off.

WAY. Movement of a vessel through the water. Technically, she is *under way* when not at anchor, aground, or made fast to the shore, but commonly way is interpreted as progress through the water—*headway*, when going forward; and *sternway* when going astern, backward. To clarify terms often confused, it might be said that one *weighs anchor* preparatory to getting *under way*.

WEAR. To bring a vessel on the other tack by swinging her around before the wind.

WEATHER. In the direction from which the wind blows.

A ship carries a *weather helm* when she tends to come up into the wind.

Weather gage. A vessel has the *weather gage* of another when she is to windward of her.

A *weatherly ship*, is one that works well to windward, making but little leeway.

WHISKERS

WEATHER-BITT. To take an additional turn with a cable round the windlass-end.

WEATHER ROLL. The roll which a ship makes to windward.

WEIGH. To lift up, as, to weigh an anchor or a mast.

WELL FOUND. A vessel is well found when well equipped.

WHEEL. The instrument attached to the rudder by which a vessel is steered.

WHIP. A purchase formed by a rope rove through a single block. *To whip*, is to hoist by a whip. Also to secure the end of a rope from fagging by seizing of twine. *Whip-upon-whip.* One whip applied to the fall of another.

WHISKERS. The cross-trees to a bowsprit.

WINCH. A purchase formed by a horizontal spindle or shaft with a wheel or crank at the end.

WINDLASS. The machine used to weigh the anchor.

WIND-RODE. The situation of a vessel at anchor when she swings and rides by the force of the wind, instead of by the tide or current.

WINDWARD. The direction from which the wind blows, as distinguished from leeward. The weather side of a ship is the windward side.

WING. That part of the hold or between-decks which is next the side.

WINGERS. Casks stowed in the wings of a vessel.

WING-AND-WING

WING-AND-WING. The situation of a fore-and-aft vessel when she is going dead before the wind, with her foresail on one side and her mainsail on the other.

WITHE or *WYTHE*. An iron band fitted on the end of a boom or mast, with a ring or eye to it, through which another boom or mast or rigging is made fast.

WOOLD. To wind a piece of rope around a spar.

WORK. A vessel works when otherwise rigid members of the construction loosen up. She *works to windward* when gaining ground against the wind by successive tacks.

WORK UP. To draw the yarns from old rigging and make them into spunyarn, foxes, sennit, etc. Also, a phrase for keeping a crew constantly at work upon the needless matters, and in all weathers, and beyond their usual hours, for punishment.

WORM. To fill up between the lays of a rope with small stuff wound around spirally. Stuff so wound round is called *worming*.

WRING. To bend or strain a mast by setting the rigging up too taut.

WRING-BOLTS. Bolts that secure the planks to the timbers.

WRING-STAVES. Strong pieces of plank used with the wring-bolts.

Y

YACHT. A vessel of recreation or state.

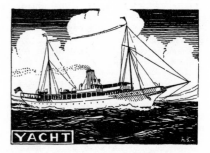

YACHT

YARD. A long piece of timber, tapering slightly toward the ends, and hung by the centre to a mast, to spread the square sails upon.

YARD-ARM. The extremities of a yard.

YARD-ARM AND YARD-ARM. The situation of two vessels, lying alongside each other so that their yard-arms cross or touch.

YAW. The motion of a vessel when she goes off her course.

YAWL

YAWL. A vessel with two masts, the small one aft, stepped abaft the rudder post.

YELLOW FLAG. Signifies vessels in quarantine.

YEOMAN. A man employed in a vessel of war to take charge of a store-room; as, boatswain's yeoman the man that has charge of the stores, of rigging, etc.

YOKE. A piece of wood placed across the head of a boat's rudder with a rope attached to each end, by which the boat is steered.

CHAPTER XXXII
Navigation and Piloting Hints

When piloting, try to visualize from the chart how landmarks, channels, obstructions, and navigational aids will appear when you pick them up.

+

Do you have difficulty with the identification of buoys? Remember the letters BPOE—*b*lack buoys, on the *p*ort side, with *o*dd numbers, *e*ntering harbors.

+

Entering strange inlets, use the buoys with caution. Bars shift continually. Breakers reveal the shoal spots.

+

If you are running a compass course, corrected for predetermined deviation, be sure that all principal iron and steel objects are in the position they occupied when the deviation was calculated.

+

Know your speed on a measured course. Estimated speeds are invariably flattering . . . and unreliable in piloting.

+

Your outboard boat, if it was designed primarily as an outboard, must carry the equipment specified by law, like any other motor boat. The fact that it may be shorter than sixteen feet does not excuse it.

+

Check your side-light screens to see that they do not shine across the bow. Red must be visible only on the port side, green to starboard.

+

Too much emphasis cannot be placed on the value of ranges in navigating difficult waterways. If there are no established marks to serve as guides, pick natural landmarks with the aid of the chart.

+

Aside from the possibility of being stopped by some watchful inspector, sea-going ethics prescribe that whistle signals be answered, promptly.

+

Blind corners, where a river or creek makes a sharp bend, call for caution. Best to throttle down and sound a long warning whistle blast.

+

Stern lights are often mounted on the aft end of the canopy top. Under way, the stern settles and the light is obscured to approaching boats at close range. A foot of brass pipe will raise it high enough to be visible all around, as the law requires.

+

A well used chart adds much to the satisfaction of cruising. Thorough study of the one showing your local waters may reveal a good many interesting features that would escape the keenest observer.

+

To steer a straight course, when stuck without a compass, tow a sinker or weight from a light line made fast amidships. Any deviation from a straight course will show as the line moves away from a center point on the taffrail.

+

Coming to anchor in a strange harbor, it's always good practice to check your position by reference to buoys or landmarks on the chart.

+

If another boat approaches your course from any point in the area covered by your green light (dead ahead to two points abaft the starboard beam) give way to her. She has the right of way.

+

When the inboard scupper of a self-bailing cockpit runs below the water line, permitting water to back in, push a thin stick through the hole until it projects outside the planking. Vacuum behind the stick will draw the water out.

+

If your compass is electrically lighted, be sure that the wires are twisted around each other. Current flowing through straight wires might be the source of a large compass error.

+

An anchor frequently gets such a bite that a man cannot break it. When that happens, heave up short on the line till it stands straight up and down and take a turn around the bitt. Then go ahead with the power a few yards.

+

Surface rips will often be produced by deep-lying reefs or obstructions. If they are of consequence to boatmen, the chart or Coast Pilot will give necessary information.

+

Running at night, keep a lookout astern. Helps a lot in keeping your bearings under certain conditions of visibility.

+

Small or illegible numbers will not pass Government inspection. See that they are at least three inches high and keep on the right side of the law.

+

Boats with right hand propellers frequently have a slight tendency to run to port when going ahead with the rudder set for a straight course. This is caused by a difference in thrust exerted by the upper and lower blades.

+

Ripples, eddies and surface colors tell a story of their own. Watch them in channels you know and you'll profit by them in strange waterways.

+

Twin-screw engine installations are most effective when the motors turn in opposite directions. Maneuvering qualities are best when the tops of the propeller blades turn outward from the center.

+

Before making fast to a tidewater dock, consider the stage and range of the tide. Then make due allowance so the boat isn't hung or swamped with the rise and fall.

+

Docking a boat with right hand wheel is facilitated if she is brought up port side to dock or float. The propeller, reversing, throws the stern toward the dock, instead of away from it.

+

The essence of good seamanship is preparedness. The ablest skipper, like an adept at chess, anticipates the next move and is ready to meet it.

+

New boats occasionally suffer a temporary loss of speed shortly after launching. Bottom planks swelling as they absorb water squeeze out seam fillers, leaving ridges which create resistance. Smoothing the seams will correct this condition.

+

In case of grounding, quick action with the reverse often saves the day. Chances are she'll back off as the wake rolls under the boat.

+

Blisters on paint jobs are caused by moisture in the wood. The sun, in drawing out the water, takes the paint with it. To avoid this, paint only on thoroughly dry surfaces.

+

Night running develops confidence. And tests your powers of observation. Limited range of vision alters the perspective.

+

When dinghies and other equipment are carried on deck, they should be lashed securely, even in smooth water. The wash of a fast boat can create as much disturbance as a good sized sea.

+

A small amount of canvas on a motor boat will steady her a lot offshore in a beam sea.

+

Water will stop an alcohol blaze—but not gasoline. Keep your extinguishers freshly filled and know how to use them. That will take all the hazard out of fire.

+

A drag, like a bucket or sea anchor, towed astern, is useful in a bad following sea. Helps to prevent broaching to.

+

Shoal water affects a boat's speed and control—even though the keel doesn't actually strike bottom.

+

In waters littered with drift, reasonable attention to the course ahead will often save a haulout to repair a crippled wheel.

+

Running a doubtful channel on a windy day, favor the windward side. In case of grounding, it might be hard to work off a leeward shoal.

+

If you ever carry "paying guests," remember that you are then operating the boat for hire and require a license. It is awarded without cost.

481

Bucking a heavy head sea, it's often helpful to meet the waves quartering somewhat on the bow. Depends, of course, on the boat and the sea.

✛

There's a thrill in spectacular landings —but a bill if your reverse gear lets you down.

✛

A wise boatman will observe, and glean bits of experience from all sources. A large part of that skill you admire in men who have a way with the helm of a yacht, has been picked up among the fishermen.

✛

Visibility varies with atmospheric conditions. Sometimes it is possible to see clearly objects normally below the horizon. Refraction of light rays causes this.

✛

Never leave poles or boat hooks on deck where they may be stepped on. Rolling under foot, they might give some one a ducking.

✛

River sailing is intriguing. One always wonders what lies just around the bend ahead.

✛

Grass and weed can be thrown from an anchor line before getting it on deck. Swish the line up and down before the grass is clear of the water.

✛

When laying up for the winter, frame the cover if possible to keep it away from the hull. Complete circulation of air, inside and out, will promote a sweet, clean condition through the winter months.

✛

Blocking under a boat shored up out of water should be so placed as to simulate conditions as nearly as possible when the hull is waterborne. Stresses concentrated at certain points should be avoided.

✛

Riding out a gale at anchor or towing under strenuous conditions, it's not a bad idea to wrap canvas around lines where they rub on chocks or rails. The chafing gear will take the wear and save the rope.

✛

Making fast to a cleat, let the strain of the line come on the cleat first, rather than on the last turn of rope. Otherwise, it might be hard to free with a heavy strain on it.

✛

Ring buoys are sometimes lashed too well. When needed, they are wanted quick. Light lashings or hooks will hold them in place, yet leave them free for instant use.

✛

In selecting equipment, utility is a more vital consideration than beauty or finish. A chromium plated pump that won't pump isn't a pump.

✛

Have a spare tiller aboard, so arranged that the boat can be handled with it direct—irrespective of any failure in any part of the regular steering mechanism.

Wet lines in closed lockers are a prolific source of trouble. Dry them thoroughly before stowing whenever possible.

✛

In a pinch, ordinary soap will temporarily seal a gas line leak.

✛

Lines should always be neatly coiled down. Aside from ship-shape appearance, it's desirable that they always be ready for immediate use.

✛

A strainer in the gas line will trap more dirt than a carburetor can swallow.

✛

Getting under way, be sure you haven't left a line trailing overboard. Propellers have a strange attraction for them.

✛

Water pump suction sometimes collapses the intake hose and stops circulation. A short length is enough to stop vibration, and the walls should be strong.

✛

Old plugs in a motor spell poor economy. A good fat spark from a clean new plug with the right gap will cut down fuel cost and improve engine performance.

✛

If you haven't been able to locate the source of that persistent vibration, or if you suspect your motor of inefficiency, have your propeller checked for pitch. A bent blade could be responsible . . . and it's easily fixed.

✛

Anchoring on a foul bottom, attach a short buoyed trip line to the crown. A pull on it will release the flukes if caught under a rock or ledge.

✛

Dock lines require renewal just as much as other rope used aboard. It takes a stout line to withstand the surge created by a passing boat or the strain of a violent gale of wind.

✛

Electrolytic action destroys iron used near brass or bronze in salt water. Zinc in contact with the iron will take the action and save the iron.

✛

Don't run with a slipping clutch. Simple adjustments are always provided and taking up a notch or two will save the gear.

✛

In changing wheels, remember that propellers may be right-handed or left-handed. Looking forward at the driving face of the blades from aft, a right-handed wheel swings clockwise.

✛

A few minutes are well spent occasionally in going over all nuts and bolts on the engine with a wrench. Lag screws holding the motor down are particularly prone to loosen up with vibration.

✛

Some engines suffer more from over-overhauling than from neglect. Modern engines don't have to be pulled down every year. Keep your motor clean and leave it alone when it's running right.

There is a happy medium in the choice of anchor line. Given strength enough, thin lines will hold better in deep water than thick, buoyant ones.

✛

Thin ice will often damage a hull more than a thick coating. "Window-pane" ice, an eighth of an inch thick, cuts cedar like a sharp chisel. Sheet copper at the water line will protect the hull.

✛

If you foul your propeller with grass or other debris, it's not always necessary to go overboard or haul the boat out to clear it. Reversing will often do the trick.

✛

A hull afloat soaks up an amazing weight of water. With cruisers, that's not so vital. But if you own a fast runabout, and want to take home the silverware from regattas, hoist the hull clear of the water whenever it's not in service.

✛

When the soft purr of the exhaust suddenly takes on a dry, hollow note, check up on the water circulation. It's likely that the water has failed.

✛

It is not regarded as good form to fly the burgees of more than one club at a time, even though you may be a member of each.

✛

Neglect will ruin a storage battery. Add enough distilled water occasionally to keep the plates covered with liquid at all times.

✛

In general practice, boat steering wheels turn with the boat's head, as in automobiles. The opposite method is likely to be confusing, except to some old tug skippers.

✛

Before letting an anchor go, make sure the line is clear and ready to run without fouling. One foot caught in the coils might create an embarrassing situation.

✛

In heaving a line, hold it in such a manner that the end uncoils itself naturally from the outside. Otherwise it's likely to snarl up and fall short.

✛

Colors should be flown from eight in the morning till sundown. Club burgee at the forward staff, owner's private signal at the masthead, and ensign aft.

✛

Boarding ladders are all right over-side at anchor. But they ought to be stowed when the boat is under way.

✛

Gasoline tanks should be provided with tight fillers to the deck.

✛

Motors run best with the switch on. Just before the expiring battery gives its last gasp from futile cranking, check up on this small, but important, detail.

✛

As a rough basis of estimating, the height of sea waves, in feet, is generally reckoned at half the velocity of the wind in miles per hour.

New lines have a mean habit of twisting themselves into hard kinks. They can be worked out by towing the line astern, one end made fast to the after bitt.

+

In greater numbers every year, boatmen are keeping their craft in commission all winter. If you do, keep jackets and water lines drained to prevent bursting from the expansion caused by freezing.

+

When using a compass with considerable deviation and it is desired to steer a compass course to make good a certain magnetic course, an appreciable error will be introduced if the deviation is taken from the usual table under compass heading of ship; several interpolations are necessary to eliminate this error.

+

In taking vertical sextant angles where large tidal ranges exist, it is well to remember that the height of lighthouses above high water, as stated in the Light List, should be corrected for tide.

+

The taking of bearings of distant objects which have been sighted by binoculars will be greatly facilitated by noting cloud formations directly over or near the object observed.

+

On a rocky coast it should be borne in mind that the lead of the surveying vessel may have missed a rising head. Except where surveys have been made in great detail, only a survey with a wire drag is sure to have caught every rock.

+

In taking vertical sextant angles the object observed should be close to the shore line for the best results. The sextant angle will be in error if the object is situated far inland from the shore.

+

A vessel with an object one point on the bow will pass it abeam at about one-fifth of the distance away at the time of the first bearing.

+

A check on the patent log may be obtained occasionally when spar buoys are standing upright, denoting little or no current.

+

A sounding taken at the same time as an observation for a line of position will, under certain conditions, prove of great value in giving an approximate position on the line.

+

At times of distant haze a better horizon is often secured by reducing the height of eye.

+

In planning to enter a strange port, the mariner should give careful previous study to the chart, sailing directions, and tide tables; and should select the most suitable marks for use, providing substitutes in case those selected can not be recognized with absolute certainty.

+

To prevent kinks in the patent log line when hauling it in, pass the inboard end across the deck and stream it as the line comes in.

+

Never be too positive as to your ship's position, for overconfidence has led many an experienced and skillful navigator into distressing disaster.

+

Where available, ranges should be marked on the chart to be used either to lead clear of dangers or to check the deviation of the compass.

+

A single line of position will at times furnish the mariner with valuable information. For instance, if it points toward the coast, it marks the bearing of a definite point on the shore; or if it parallels the coast, it clearly indicates the distance off.

+

When determining a ship's position by cross bearings, objects should be selected with not less than 30° nor more than 150° between them. Near objects are preferable to those at a distance, keeping in mind the disadvantage of very near landmarks which may change rapidly in bearing.

+

When plotting the position of a ship with three correctly observed cross bearings an intersection will not result if the compass error used is incorrect. The ship's true position is within the triangle formed by bearings only when she is within the triangle formed by the objects themselves, otherwise her position lies outside the triangle formed by the bearings.

+

A vessel's run from a point with an object bearing 26½° forward of the beam until it bears 26½° abaft the beam is equal to the distance from the object when abeam.

+

A vessel's distance from an object abeam is five times the distance run between its bearing 1 point forward of the beam and its bearing abeam, current excepted.

+

An excellent substitute for the three-armed protractor (station pointer), with which to lay off horizontal sextant angles for position, will be found in a piece of fairly stiff transparent paper. Place the paper over the chart compass rose and lay off the angles from the center of rose and then use in the same way as the protractor.

+

There are three methods by which, without obtaining the precise position, the navigator may assure himself that he is clear of any particular danger. They are: (1) By following a range. (2) By using the danger angle. (3) By using the danger bearing.

When piloting during thick weather it is often desirable to estimate the vessel's position by echo from a bold shore or echo board. A convenient approximation is to point off one place in the number of seconds elapsed from sounding of ship's whistle until echo is heard. This will be the distance off in miles and tenths of miles.

+

In taking a bearing on the tangent of an island or point, an error will be introduced if the shore is shelving and the tide is above the chart datum. What may appear as a long point at low water disappears with the rise of tide. This error is emphasized where there is a great tidal range.

+

When steaming along a well-charted coast in overcast weather, the error of the compass may be obtained by fixing the position by sextant angles between three suitable objects. Another observer at the same moment should carefully note the compass bearing of a distant, well-defined, and charted object. With the position plotted with a three-armed protractor (station pointer) or tracing paper, the true bearing of the distant object is readily taken from the chart, and when compared with the compass bearing furnishes the error. Lights may be used at night.

+

If a vessel, with an object at a certain bearing on the bow, steams until the angle of the bearing is doubled, the distance run during the doubling of the angle is the distance off at the last bearing. Thus, if the angle is 30° and a vessel runs until the object bears 60° on the bow, covering 10 miles, she is 10 miles from the object when it bears 60°; current excepted.

+

The distance at which a light will be passed when abeam may be ascertained at the time it first appears on the horizon by the use of Table 3, Bowditch, using the light's bearing from the bow as a course and its visibility, corrected for height of eye, as the distance. In the departure column will be found the distance off when abeam. The distance to be run until light is abeam will be found in the latitude column. It is assumed that the course is made good and that weather conditions render visibility normal.

+

The distance from any object of a known height may be ascertained by multiplying the height in feet by 0.565 and dividing the result by the number of minutes in the vertical sextant angle of the object. The quotient will be the distance off in nautical miles and decimals of a mile.

+

Navigators may ascertain the distance they will pass a charted object abeam by use of the following bearing combinations. The bearings are from the bow. The distance run between them is the distance the object will be passed abeam, current excepted:
22°—34°, 27°—46°, 32°—59°. 40°—79°

When locating a ship's position by sextant angles, using three charted objects, a condition arises where this method fails. A circle can always be drawn through three points, and when the ship happens to be on this circle, the position is indeterminate and another object must be selected.

+

Radio bearings near sunrise or sunset are not always reliable.

+

Compass deviations can be conveniently and reliably checked when at anchor, or when steaming along a coast, by taking bearings of a range consisting of two conspicuous well-charted objects. The distance between the objects should be greater than the ship's distance from the nearer object.

+

In piloting, the vessel's position should be fixed at all times, even when entering ports considered safe and easy of access, and should be constantly checked, using those marks whose identity has been established beyond doubt.

+

A change in engine rpm does not always necessarily mean engine trouble. Check the depth of water. You may be crossing a shoal. Sometimes boat speed will be reduced, the trim changed and rpm affected, even though the keel is not in fact touching bottom.

+

Mariners are cautioned when plotting bearings received from a radiocompass station to use the position of the receiver ashore, and when plotting bearings obtained by a direction finder aboard ship to use the position of the transmitter of the sending station. In some cases the transmitter and the receiver are a considerable distance from each other.

+

When a vessel sights a known light her distance off in miles, when abeam, may be anticipated approximately by multiplying the number of degrees the light bears on the bow by the visibility (corrected for height of eye), and dividing this product by 60.

+

In determining accurately the distance off a light by any method where two bearings of one object with the run between are taken and when current or heavy wind exists, the course made good and the distance over the bottom must be known and used.

+

Radiobeacons are operated continuously during thick and foggy weather. Vessels approaching port from seaward or steaming along a coast may infer that the visibility conditions ahead are poor if, by listening in, the beacon in that quarter is found to be working. This should be done at a time other than its scheduled clear-weather operating period, and they sometimes operate upon request for tests. Certain stations pause during thick weather to listen in. (See H. O. No. 205 for schedules.)

Fog at sea is principally caused by three conditions, namely, (1) by calm or comparatively still air which fosters the radiation fogs, (2) by warm or moist winds blowing over a cold sea surface, and (3) by cold winds, either wet or dry, blowing over the warm sea surface.

A temperature fall of 2° F. is often sufficient to produce a fog; a corresponding rise, to dispel it.

+

On approaching land during a fog the nearest radiocompass station should be requested to furnish bearings.

+

In light fog or drizzling rain an iceberg may be visible 1 to 3 miles; in dense fog it can not be seen more than 100 yards ahead of the ship. On a clear, starlit night a lookout will not pick up an iceberg at a distance greater than one-fourth of a mile, unless its position is definitely known.

+

In a light fog it may be assumed that a man aloft will sight an iceberg sooner than one on deck; in a dense fog, however, the latter will probably catch the first evidence of a berg by the breaking of the sea at its base or by growlers and fragments of ice from it.

+

Radio bearings crossing intervening land should be mistrusted.

+

Near the lee side of lofty islands the weather is generally clear as far as fog, mist and low clouds are concerned. Therefore in making a landfall in thick weather better visibility may be experienced if approach is made from leeward.

+

Moderate speed in a fog is held by the courts to be: "Such a rate of speed as will enable a vessel, after discovering another vessel meeting her, to stop and reverse her engines in sufficient time to prevent any collision from taking place."

+

Entire dependence can never be placed on fog signals, because with no apparent reason large zones of silence often occur at varying directions and different distances from the origin of sound.

+

Set of current is the direction toward which it flows; the direction of wind from whence it blows.

+

The flood tide may be running in a harbor and the water falling at the piers; conversely, the ebb may be running in the stream and the water rising at the piers.

+

A vessel proceeding against the tide, especially the ebb, in a tidal river will gain an advantage by favoring the bank.

+

Current arrows on pilot charts indicate averages; actual currents may be encountered that differ widely, even opposite to the charted arrows.

In estimating current when vessel is in ballast, leeway should be carefully allowed for.

+

The mariner is enabled to note the set of the current at night by the establishment of riding lights on the forestays of lightships.

+

A vessel in light trim may not encounter the same current as a deep-draft vessels. The current is usually greater on the surface than at the bottom. The flood in the Hudson River off New York has its greatest velocity at mid-depth.

+

In navigating the lower reaches of tidal rivers the ebb near the surface will be found to be stronger and will last longer than the flood; near the bottom the duration of flood and ebb become approximately equal. Wind, barometric pressure, and recent rains over regions contiguous to the upper river, all affect flow and duration of tidal current.

+

In a bay with a narrow entrance through which great quantities of tidal water must pass each tide, the maximum velocity at the entrance may be expected at about high and low water. The flood and ebb current at such points is found to begin about 3 hours after low water and high water, respectively.

+

When the water is fairly homogeneous and the depth is great, the surface movement is deflected about 45° to the right of the wind's direction of travel in the Northern Hemisphere, and 45° to the left in the Southern Hemisphere.

+

The best water of a river or natural channel may be expected in the center of the stream of the straight reaches and at the outside of the bends; the swiftest current will usually be found along the line of the best water.

+

After currents are generated, in the Northern Hemisphere, the conformation of the bottom tends to deflect them to the right around islands and shoals and to the left around basins and deeps.

+

The flood tide in an estuary makes earlier at the bottom than at the surface. This variation is more marked in midstream than at the sides. Hence a deep-draft vessel will probably swing to the flood before a light-draft vessel does in the same vicinity. The ebb makes at about the same time at the surface as at the bottom.

+

When a large-scale harbor chart is not available, a workable substitute may be constructed from the information given on a small-scale chart. Divide the desired harbor area of the small-scale chart into a convenient number of equal squares and transfer the shoreline, as an enlargement, to a plain sheet of desirable size likewise ruled in similar squares. Add soundings, contours, landmarks, etc., in their relative positions. Check the accuracy of the plan by bearings and distances and construct a scale of distances.

A liquid compass should be shielded from the sun, especially when in the Tropics.

+

If a compass is unshipped for any purpose, check the lubber's line upon replacement, to be sure it is on the fore-and-aft line.

+

It is advisable to keep chronometers away from positions where severe shocks are liable to occur, such as the constant slamming of a door.

+

A watch officer obliged to look at a chart on a dark night may, with advantage, close one eye when the light is turned on and when again in darkness open the closed eye. The vision will be improved by this expedient, which lessens the temporary blindness caused by the light.

+

When adjusting compasses or ascertaining deviation by known bearings of terrestrial objects, distant objects are preferable to those near at hand.

+

Excessive rolling or pitching due to synchronism may be checked by changing the course or speed, at times very slightly.

+

Swells are waves propagated by wind at a distance, or may be caused by a wind that previously was blowing in the locality; while the waves set up by wind prevailing are called, collectively, sea.

+

Wind blowing over smooth water has less wave-producing power than when blowing over water already in motion.

+

Any marked change from diurnal variation in the barometer readings within the Tropics is a sign indicative of an atmospheric disturbance; caution should be exercised during the hurricane season.

+

The velocity of the wind is dependent upon the steepness of the barometric gradient rather than on the reading of the barometer; that is, there may be little or no wind with a reading of 29.00 inches, yet on another occasion a wind of hurricane force may be blowing with a reading of 29.70 inches. The distance between the isobars controls the wind force; the closer they are the steeper the gradient and the stronger the wind.

If the wind shifts to the right in the Northern Hemisphere the vessel is in the right-hand or dangerous semicircle of the depression; to the left, she is in the left-hand or navigable semicircle.

+

According to the Buys Ballot's law, when facing the wind, the barometer will be lower on the right hand than on the left in the Northern, and vice versa in the Southern Hemisphere.

+

If the wind does not shift, but continues to blow steadily with increasing force, and with a falling barometer, it may be assumed that the vessel is on or near a storm track.

+

Waves reach their greatest development in the rear quadrant of the dangerous or right semicircle of the Northern and the left semicircle of the Southern Hemisphere.

+

When in front of a hurricane but not very near the center, the vortex bears with an average of 10 points to the right when facing the wind in the Northern Hemisphere, but a larger allowance must be made when in the rear quadrants. When directly in front of a hurricane the wind does not change in direction.

+

Vessels anchored or moored under high land should be prepared for sudden and violent squalls which sweep down the mountains. The cold, heavy air of the heights seeks the lower levels with destructive force in many ports of the world.

+

Oil has the greatest modifying effect on deep-water waves.

+

Changes in wave formation may be an indication of shoaling water for waves close up and heighten when running from deep into shoal water. A deeply laden vessel in heavy weather would be safer in avoiding, if possible, the position of abrupt changes in depths, as the seas running from deeper water feel the bottom, rise and become sharper.

+

The length of waves due to wind increases with the distance from the weather shore (fetch). The longest fetch is in the waters of the higher latitudes of the Southern Hemisphere, hence in that region are experienced the longest seas.

Wreckage and floating objects which eventually sink beneath the surface through loss of buoyancy will continue to the bottom, regardless of the greater density and pressure, at increasing depths, so long as their weight exceeds the weight of water they displace.

+

A vessel's draft in salt water is roughly one-quarter of an inch per foot less than in fresh water.

+

The area of a vessel's waterplane in square feet (that is, the area of a deck everywhere flush with the water line) divided by 420 will give roughly the number of tons required to increase the mean draft 1 inch.

+

Sound travels at about 1,132 feet per second in air, at 68½° F.; about 4,794 feet per second through water, at 66° F.

+

Icebergs in the North Atlantic float with about one-ninth of their mass out of water.

+

The earth moves left-handed around the sun; that is, toward the right when facing that body in the southern sky. As a result the sun seems to work correspondingly eastward among the fixed stars as a background, and at sunset new constellations appear in the east from month to month and the old ones disappear in the west.

+

When the declination of the sun is 0° (on the Equator) the days and nights are of equal length (12 hours) the world over, except in extreme polar regions.

+

When the sun is 0° declination about March 21 and September 22, it rises in true east and sets in true west throughout the world, except in the polar regions.

+

About June 21 the sun reaches its highest point of northern declination, 23° 27'. This is the longest day of the year for the Northern Hemisphere. At the North Pole this day the sun's path is everywhere parallel to the horizon and 23° 27' in altitude.

+

When the star Mizar of the Great Bear and the star Ruchbah of Cassiopeia, which are in line with Polaris, are either above or below that star, the latter is bearing north true, and the error of the compass may be easily obtained.

CHAPTER XXXIII — Right or Wrong?

The following quiz was used originally to qualify students of the Seamanship Training Corp for seamanship certificates. Test yourself, marking the statements true or false, and compare with answers on page 487. Credit for each correct answer, 7 points. For each incorrect answer, deduct 4 points. No credit for unanswered questions. Passing grade 700 points.

1. Broad on the starboard bow means the same as 4 points on starboard bow.

2. The clew of a sail is that edge nearest the mast.

3. A yawl has her mainmast stepped forward of the rudder post.

4. The names of the sails of a two masted schooner from forward are: jib, mainsail, mizzen.

5. The names of the sails of a ketch from forward are: jib, mainsail, mizzen.

6. The expression "10 knots per hour" is correct.

7. The wind backed from east to south, through southeast.

8. The weather side is the high side when sailing close hauled.

9. When one sails downwind and he wishes to get the sail on the other side of the boat, he generally jibes.

10. Grapnels are generally used for permanent moorings at a club anchorage.

11. Spring tides are those that take place in the Spring.

12. A fix refers to repairing the engine.

13. Hard a lee is the command to heave the anchor.

14. A sheet bend may be used for bending two lines together for towing purposes.

15. The bowline should not be used where there is danger that the loop may slip.

16. Towing a manila line astern is a good method of taking the kinks out of it.

17. Wet manila line should be stowed immediately.

18. Yachts of less than 300 tons are not required to carry any licensed officers.

19. The federal government specifies what equipment sailing yachts without motors are required to carry.

20. Sailing yachts with motors are required to carry certain equipment specified by the federal government.

21. For a 30-foot motor boat, an ordinary mouth whistle will pass government inspection as the whistle required by the rules.

22. A dinghy towed astern or carried on deck will pass as life-saving equipment.

23. The government requires that an anchor, compass, anchor line and pump must be carried on board.

24. Motor or sailing vessels of 16 tons or more (not carrying passengers for hire) are required to be documented.

25. The boat which has the right of way is known as the privileged vessel.

26. It is the duty of the right of way vessel to hold her course.

27. The burdened vessel should always keep clear of the privileged vessel.

28. Answering one blast of the whistle with one blast is known as giving a cross signal.

29. In case of collision between two vessels, there is no obligation for them to stand by each other to render assistance.

30. The danger zone is from dead ahead to two points aft of the port beam.

31. A sailing vessel (close hauled) on the starboard tack has the right of way over one on the port tack.

32. A sailing vessel which is running free must keep out of the way of the one which is close hauled.

33. A 25 foot auxiliary under sail alone carries only a combination red-and-green light.

34. A 25 foot sail boat without any engine carries no fixed white lights.

35. A 25 foot motor boat carries a white bow light with red and green side lights and a 32 point white light.

36. A 16 foot sail boat on Long Island Sound carries a white light only and this to be shown in time to prevent collision.

37. A red side light seen in your danger zone is an indication that your boat is a burdened one and must give way.

38. When both red and green side lights are visible, it is an indication that the other vessel will pass clear of you.

39. Lights on boats must be lighted one-half hour before sundown.

40. Buoys are always located exactly as shown on the chart.

41. Red buoys are numbered with even numbers.

42. Black buoys are numbered with odd numbers.

43. Buoys painted with black and white vertical stripes are not numbered.

44. Red buoys are left on your port hand on leaving a harbor.

45. If a buoy on a chart is marked S4, you should leave it on your starboard side on entering a harbor.

46. An alternating light is one which changes color, that is, shows alternately white and red or green in various combinations.

47. A 45 foot motor boat should never carry more than one anchor.

48. When anchoring, you should be safe if the scope used is equal to twice the depth of the water.

49. A sea anchor is used for anchoring at sea.

50. The compass rose printed on charts indicates deviation.

51. Depths of water are always indicated on charts in fathoms.

52. The water is never shallower than is indicated on the chart.

53. Charts indicate the depths at mean high water.

54. The direction of an arrow shown on the chart indicates the best possible course.

55. The North Pole of the compass points toward geographic north.

56. The compass card is divided into 360 points.

57. The cardinal points are N, NE, E, SE, S, SW, W, NW.

58. The reverse course of 315 degrees is 45 degrees.

59. Deviation is the angular difference between true north and a free needle suspended at the point in question.

60. Variation is determined by referring to the compass rose on the chart.

61. The amount of variation is the same or approximately the same at all points on the earth's surface.

62. True courses are those referred to the true north or to the true compass rose on the chart.

63. Magnetic courses are those referred to the magnetic north or to the magnetic compass rose on the chart.

64. Easterly variation occurs when magnetic north is to the east of the true North.

65. Westerly deviation occurs when the compass north is to the west of the magnetic north.

66. If the compass on one's boat has one point westerly deviation on a northerly course, it will have the same deviation on all courses.

67. Variation at Portland, Maine, and New York City is 15 degrees westerly.

68. Correcting a course means changing from magnetic to true by applying variation or changing from compass to magnetic by applying deviation, or changing from compass to true by applying both variation and deviation.

69. Uncorrecting a course means changing from true to magnetic by applying deviation or changing from magnetic to compass by applying deviation or changing from true to compass by applying variation.

70. Correct easterly errors clockwise.

71. Correct westerly errors counter-clockwise.

72. Uncorrect westerly errors counter-clockwise.

73. Uncorrect easterly errors clockwise.

74. In determining the deviation of your compass by putting your boat over a course, the magnetic direction of which as determined by the chart is SW and your compass indicates SW ¼ W, the deviation will be ¼ point W.

75. Magnetic direction by chart is NE x E, your compass indicates N x E ½ E, then deviation is 3½ points westerly.

76. With a magnetic course SW, variation one point E, the true course will be SW x W.

77. With a true course of 225 degrees and a variation of 11¼ degrees west, the magnetic course will be 236 degrees, 15 minutes.

78. With a magnetic course SW x W ½ W, variation one point E, deviation ½ point E, the true course is W x S ½ S.

79. With a true course of 106 degrees, 52 minutes, 30 seconds; variation 10 degrees, 56 minutes west; deviation 4 degrees, 06 seconds E; the magnetic course will be 117 degrees, 48 minutes, 30 seconds.

80. With a true course of 70 degrees, 18 minutes, 45 seconds; variation one point W; deviation ¾ point W; the compass course will be E.

81. Rudder is as effective when boat is going astern as it is when going ahead.

82. With rudder hard right, single right hand screw, when starting to back, the boat will generally back to starboard.

83. In turning, the bow swings the greater amount.

84. If a boat is drifting with wind or current, a course may be directed by her rudder.

85. In turning around in a narrow canal, where it is not possible to make a complete turn in one swing, it is better to turn to starboard when going ahead.

86. The painter of the dinghy towed astern should be given no attention upon making a landing.

87. As a general rule in a single screw boat, the bow tends to swing to port.

88. Most modern small sailing craft are gaff rigged.

89. Both the centerboard and keel of a sail boat tend to give it leeway.

90. A lee helm is preferable to a weather helm on a sailing craft.

91. The CE should be located slightly forward of C L P.

92. A boat with a lee helm tends to swing up into the wind more readily than one with weather helm.

93. If your sailing vessel were heading into the wind and you should hear two blasts on the fog horn ahead of you, you would know that a sailing vessel on the port tack might be crossing your bow from your port to your starboard.

94. In a fog, if you heard a rapid ringing of a bell, you would know that it was a boat at anchor or aground.

95. In a fog, if you heard one long blast followed by two short blasts on a whistle, it would indicate a vessel with a tow or one not under control.

96. A motor boat gives her fog signal on a fog horn.

97. Two strips of leather on the lead line indicates two fathoms.

98. Five strips of leather on a lead line indicates five fathoms.

99. Ten fathoms on the lead line is marked by a red rag.

100. Fathoms which correspond with the depths marked on the lead line are called marks.

101. The intermediate fathoms which do not correspond with the depths marked on the lead line are called deeps.

102. The patent log always indicates distance in nautical miles.

103. The time of high water at Sandy Hook may be determined from the Tide Tables.

104. The characteristics of Execution Light should be obtained from the Coast Pilot.

105. Piloting is defined as a science of navigation without the use of physical landmarks.

106. In dead reckoning, the position of buoys and lighthouses is made use of at frequent intervals.

107. Two of the more common methods of locating one's position or determining a fix, are: cross bearings, and two bearings and a run between.

108. If a light bears 4 points off the bow at 10 A.M. and is abeam at 10:45 A.M. and the speed of the boat is 12 m.p.h., the boat will be 9 miles off the light at 10:45 A.M.

109. Course SE, bearing of light at 8:00 P.M. E; at 9:00 P.M. NE; speed of boat 10 m.p.h., then the boat will be 9 miles off the light at 9.00 P.M.

110. If an object is 26½° off the bow at noon and 45° at 12:30 P.M. with a speed of 8 knots, then the object will be 4 miles off when abeam.

111. The International Flag Code consists of 26 flags representing letters, 10 flags representing numerals, 3 repeater flags and an answering pennant.

112. Time is signaled by four numeral pennants preceded by and joined with the letter T.

113. Numbers are signaled by the pennants and require no further signal to indicate that they represent numbers.

114. The N flag means yes in the International Code.

115. The C flag means no.

116. The International flag signal of distress is the code flags N. C.

117. The first repeater always repeats the first flag, reading from the top down, of that class of flag that immediately precedes the repeater.

118. The code flag over E means that the letters that follow are spelling.

119. The code flag over G means that the spelling is completed.

120. The U. S. ships' calls begin with the N flag, the K flag or the W flag.

121. The Z flag is used to call shore stations.

122. The Coast Guard indicates to you that this is the best place to land, by a man on shore beckoning in the day time and two torches burning close together at night.

123. One black ball shown from a steamer indicates that she is taking explosives aboard.

124. The signal for a submarine in distress is a red smoke bomb.

125. Upon seeing a red smoke bomb, it should be reported to the Coast Guard without delay.

126. The NE storm warning signal is two square red flags with black square centers.

127. The day mark for a fishing vessel on inland waters is a basket in the rigging displayed in the direction from the anchor ball towards nets or gear.

128. Ship's bell time strikes 8 bells at 12, 3 and 8 o'clock.

129. Storms which develop in the southwest are usually quickly followed by clearing.

130. To expect clearing weather, the wind should veer.

131. The forces of the wind are expressed by the Beaufort scale, numbers 0 to 12.

132. A spring line is used for towing in heavy weather.

133. If you suspected local attraction as the cause of your compass error, you would check this in the Coast Pilot.

134. Range is a term having to do with all of the following: (1) The alignment of navigation lights to indicate a channel, (2) Measurement of the vertical movement of tide between high and low water, (3) The white lights on a vessel's masts which indicate her course, (4) Running out all anchor cable for cleaning. (Only one T. or F. for answer required.)

135. You see a vessel sailing with the wind abeam. She is sailing full and by.

136. Because of the gravitational influence of the moon and sun, acting on the earth, every locality along the Coast has two high and two low tides every 24 hours.

137. A line-throwing gun is used by the Coast Guard in life saving.

138. In heavy weather, it is preferable to find shelter under a windward shore rather than under a lee shore.

139. A sea painter is a line used on vessels when handling life boats.

140. Drift refers to the velocity of a tidal current.

141. The U. S. flag and Yacht Club burgee should be flown during daylight, that is, from dawn to dusk.

142. No penalty can be imposed for personal injury or property damage caused by operating a boat recklessly.

143. Going through a yacht anchorage at high speed or close to a boat at anchor or underway indicates that you are a good seaman. (Credit 6 points.)

(Answers below)

Answers to True-or-False Quiz

1. True	17. False	33. False	49. False	65. True	81. False	97. True	113. True	129. True
2. False	18. True	34. False	50. False	66. False	82. False	98. False	114. False	130. True
3. True	19. False	35. False	51. False	67. False	83. False	99. False	115. False	131. True
4. False	20. True	36. False	52. False	68. True	84. False	100. True	116. True	132. False
5. True	21. False	37. True	53. False	69. False	85. True	101. True	117. True	133. True
6. False	22. False	38. False	54. False	70. True	86. False	102. False	118. True	134. True
7. False	23. False	39. False	55. False	71. True	87. True	103. True	119. True	135. False
8. True	24. False	40. False	56. False	72. False	88. False	104. False	120. True	136. False
9. True	25. True	41. True	57. False	73. True	89. False	105. False	121. True	137. True
10. False	26. True	42. True	58. False	74. True	90. False	106. False	122. False	138. True
11. False	27. True	43. True	59. False	75. False	91. True	107. True	123. False	139. True
12. False	28. False	44. True	60. True	76. True	92. False	108. True	124. True	140. True
13. False	29. False	45. True	61. False	77. True	93. True	109. False	125. True	141. False
14. True	30. False	46. True	62. True	78. True	94. True	110. True	126. False	142. False
15. False	31. True	47. False	63. True	79. True	95. True	111. True	127. True	143. False
16. True	32. True	48. False	64. True	80. True	96. False	112. True	128. False	

How Well Do You Know the Rules of the Road?

Try these Questions
Asked by
the Coast Guard
When
Renewing Licenses
for Deck Officers

RECOGNIZING that a solid understanding of rules of the road governing traffic afloat is essential to hold collisions to a minimum, the Coast Guard has modified requirements for renewal of deck officers' licenses.

When such officers have not seen active service for three years, they must pass an examination. Those who have been in active service or have held a position closely associated with ship operation during that three-year period must submit an affidavit that they have, within the preceding three months, read the Rules of the Road, and must demonstrate their knowledge of how to apply them.

This "demonstration of knowledge" takes the form of an "exercise," not an examination, in which the officer answers multiple-choice questions, published in the Coast Guard's Navigation and Vessel Inspection Circular No. 7-60. When answering, the officer may refer to published Rules of the Road. There is no minimum passing grade, but each question must be answered correctly before the license will be renewed. This may necessitate re-checking with the Rules where incorrect answers have been given.

There are four groups of questions, covering the separate jurisdictions —International, Inland, Great Lakes, and Western Rivers. The applicant is tested only on rules applicable to the waters he sails.

Because the rules are of equal importance to pleasure boatmen, even though they need no license, extracts from the several sets of questions are published on pages 490a-490f, in four parts. Those given below (Part I) are based on the Inland Rules. In lieu of answers, the Coast Guard cites in each case the appropriate rule to be found in *Rules of the Road, International, Inland—CG 169.*

PART ONE—INLAND RULES

The day signal sketched indicates that the vessel is:
(a) Handling buoys, (b) Anchored, (c) Dredging,
(d) Engaged in hydrographic survey.
(See Pilot Rule 80.25)

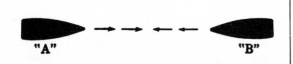

If you were in charge of navigation of "A", you should:
(a) Blow one blast, (b) Blow two blasts, (c) Hold course and speed, letting "B" take avoiding action, (d) Stop in all cases.
(See Article 18, Rule 1)

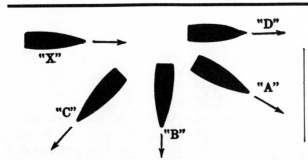

At different times, vessel "X" was navigated with respect to the four vessels sketched. Which one was she obligated to give way to?
(a) "A" ("A" is overtaking "X"), (b) "B", (c) "C", (d) "D" ("X" is overtaking "D").

(See Article 24)

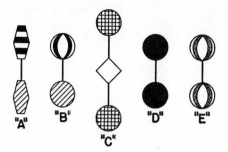

"A"   "B"   "C"   "D"   "E"

Match the signals sketched above with the class of vessel denoted:

(a) Suction dredge underway and engaged in dredging *(See Pilot Rule 80.21)*, (b) Engaged in hydrographic survey *(See Pilot Rule 80.33)*, (c) Towing a submerged object *(See Pilot Rule 80.18)*, (d) Handling navigation aid *(See Pilot Rule 80.33a)*, (e) Laying cables or pipes *(See Pilot Rule 80.22)*.

Whistle signals to indicate course changes have a duration of:

(a) One second, (b) Two seconds, (c) Three seconds, (d) Four seconds.
(See Pilot Rule 80.03)

The Rule of Special Circumstance would apply when meeting *all but one* of the following—To which one would it *not* apply?

(a) When meeting several vessels at one time, (b) When meeting a tug with tow bound downstream in a heavy current, (c) When meeting a vessel unable to maneuver in accordance with the Rules, (d) When encountering a vessel engaged in laying cable, (e) When meeting a vessel end on or nearly end on.

(See Article 27)

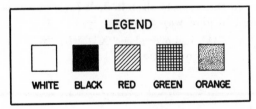

LEGEND

WHITE   BLACK   RED   GREEN   ORANGE

The vessel with lights shown as sketched above seen in inland waters would be:

(a) Dredging, (b) Laying mats, (c) Fishing, (d) Not under command, (e) A pilot vessel.
(See Article 9)

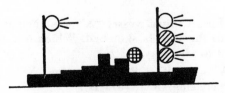

The vessel showing lights as sketched above would be:

(a) Towing a submerged object, (b) Not under command, (c) A self-propelled suction dredge, (d) Laying telegraph cable.

(See Pilot Rule 80.21)

Moderate speed in fog is generally interpreted to mean ability to stop within which of the following fractions of the range of visibility:

(a) One-fourth, (b) One-half, (c) Two-thirds, (d) Three-fourths.

A steam vessel under way in fog but stopped and having no way upon her blows on her whistle:

(a) One prolonged blast every two minutes, (b) Two prolonged blasts every two minutes, (c) One prolonged blast every minute, (d) One short blast every minute.
(See Article 15)

On overtaking another vessel, before passing her on her port side you must:

(a) Blow one short blast and be answered by one short blast, (b) Blow two short blasts and be answered by two short blasts, (c) Blow one short blast, (d) Blow two short blasts.

(See Article 18, Rule VIII)

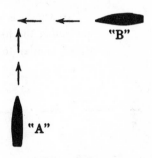

"B"

"A"

If you were in charge of navigation of "A" (above) you should *not*:

(a) Go under stern of "B", (b) Back down on engines, (c) Stop, (d) Cross ahead of "B".

(See Article 22)

If you were in charge of navigation of "B", *(sketch above)* you should:

(a) Go under stern of "A", (b) Back down on engines, (c) Stop, (d) Hold course and speed.

(See Article 21)

When collision cannot be avoided by "A" alone *(sketch above)* "B" must:

(a) Cross under "A"s stern, (b) Back down, (c) Hold course and speed under all circumstances, (d) Take such action as will best aid to avert collision.

(See Article 27)

Rowing boats under sail or oars must show:

(a) Side lights, (b) Mast lights, (c) Stern light, (d) A white light in time to prevent collision.

(See Article 7)

In fog, an anchored vessel must ring the bell every:

(a) Minute for five seconds, (b) Two minutes for five seconds, (c) Three minutes for ten seconds.

(See Article 15)

Risk of collision can best be determined by:

(a) Checking the distance of an approaching vessel, (b) Carefully watching the compass bearing of an approaching vessel, (c) Watching the other vessel for any signals he may give, (d) Observing the range of the approaching vessel's masts or mast lights.

(See Preliminary to Steering & Sailing Rules)

Match the fog signals listed with the class of vessel denoted:

(a) A prolonged blast of the whistle every minute, (b) A blast of the fog horn every minute, (c) A rapid ringing of the bell for 5 seconds every minute, (d) Two blasts of the fog horn every minute, (e) Three blasts of the fog horn, (f) One prolonged blast followed by two short blasts.

A. a steam vessel towing, B. a sailing vessel on the starboard tack, C. a sailing vessel on the port tack, D. a sailing vessel with the wind abaft the beam, E. a steam vessel under way, F. a vessel at anchor.

(See Article 15)

Nearing a bend where the channel around the bend is obscured a vessel should blow on the whistle:

(a) A short blast, (b) A long blast, (c) Two long blasts, (d) Three long blasts.

(See Article 18, Rule 5)

A vessel signifies intention to pass a dredge by blowing:

(a) One short blast, (b) Two short blasts, (c) Three short blasts, (d) One long blast.

(See Pilot Rule 80.26)

"My engines are going full speed astern" is indicated on the whistle by:

(a) One short blast, (b) Two short blasts, (c) Three short blasts, (d) Four short blasts.

(See Article 28)

PART TWO

INTERNATIONAL RULES

Part One was concerned only with Inland Rules of the Road. Officers navigating the high seas would be given questions from the International Rules, similar to those below. (Refer to *Rules of the Road—CG 169*.)

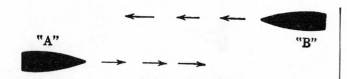

Vessel "A":

(a) Can continue on course and speed, (b) Must alter course to left, (c) Must alter course to right, (d) Must back down.

(See Rule 18 (a))

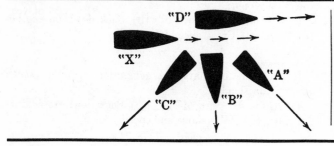

At different times, vessel "X" was navigated with respect to the vessels sketched. Which one was she obligated to give way to?

(a) "A" ("A" has overtaken "X"), (b) "B", (c) "C", (d) "D" ("X" is overtaking "D")

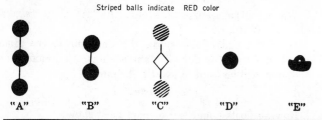

Striped balls indicate RED color

Match the day signals sketched with the class of vessel denoted:

(a) Trawler *(See Rule 9)*, (b) Vessel aground *(See Rule 11)*, (c) Vessel at anchor *(See Rule 11)*, (d) Vessel not under command *(See Rule 4)*, (e) Vessel tending a navigational aid *(See Rule 4)*.

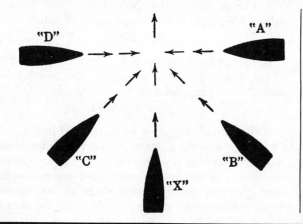

At different times, vessel "X" was navigated with respect to the vessels sketched. Which one was she obligated to give way to?

(a) "A", (b) "B" ("B" is overtaking "X"), (c) "C" ("C" is overtaking "X"), (d) "D".

INTERNATIONAL RULES OF THE ROAD

In fog, a bell forward and a gong aft must be sounded by anchored vessels whose length is over:
(a) 200 feet, (b) 250 feet, (c) 300 feet, (d) 350 feet.
(See Rule 15)

Vessels towed make fog signals on:
(a) Fog horn or whistle, (b) Whistle only, (c) Fog horn only, (d) Bell, (e) Gong.
(See Rule 15)

Match each fog signal with the vessel which would sound it:
Signals: (a) One prolonged blast on whistle, (b) A blast consisting of a series of several alternate notes of higher and lower pitch, (c) Three blasts on the fog-horn, (d) Two prolonged blasts on the whistle, (e) One prolonged and three short blasts on the whistle, (f) One prolonged and two short blasts on the whistle.
Ships: A. Vessel towing, B. Fishing vessel, C. Sailing vessel, wind abaft the beam, D. Power driven vessel underway, E. Vessel towed, F. Power driven vessel underway but stopped and making no way through the water.
(See Rule 15)

Match each fog signal with the vessel which would sound it:
Signals: (a) Two blasts on the fog-horn, (b) One prolonged and two short blasts on the whistle, (c) A rapid ringing of a bell following by the sounding of a gong, (d) One blast on the whistle followed by the ringing of a bell, (e) One blast on the fog-horn, (f) A rapid ringing of the bell preceded and followed by three strokes on the bell.
Ships: A. A sailing vessel on the starboard tack, B. A fishing vessel of 20 tons or upward, C. A vessel aground, D. An anchored vessel over 350' in length, E. A vessel picking up a navigation mark, F. A sailing vessel on the port tack.
(See Rule 15)

Match each of the sound signals given with its proper meaning:
Sound Signal: (a) One short blast on the whistle, (b) Two short blasts on the whistle, (c) Three short blasts on the whistle, (d) Five or more short and rapid blasts on the whistle.
Meaning: A. I am altering course to port, B. My engines are going astern, C. I am altering course to starboard, D. I am in doubt whether you are taking sufficient action to avert collision.
(See Rule 28)

If, at night, you sighted the towboat sketched you should see looking from abeam:
(a) Two white lights in a vertical line and a red side light, (b) Three white lights in a vertical line, (c) A red side light, (d) Three white lights in a vertical line and a red side light.
(See Rule 3)

A vessel is under way when she is:
(a) At anchor, (b) Aground, (c) Made fast to shore, (d) None of the above.
(See Rule 1)

One of the following statements is correct if A and B (below) are in sight of one another:
(a) "A" and "B" should each alter course to the right, each blowing one short blast on the whistle, (b) "A" and "B" should each alter course to the right. No whistle signals need be sounded, (c) "A" or "B" should blow one blast and wait for a response before altering course.
(See Rule 18 and Rule 28)

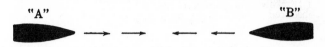

The day signal of a basket is displayed by:
(a) Dredges, (b) Trawlers, (c) Cable-layers, (d) Boats tending divers.
(See Rule 9)

A sailing vessel of 20 tons or upward under way makes her fog signal on a:
(a) Bell, (b) Gong, (c) Whistle, (d) Fog horn.
(See Rule 15)

In a narrow channel, power-driven vessels shall whenever possible:
(a) Stay in the middle, (b) Keep to the left, (c) Keep to the right.
(See Rule 25)

Match the lights sketched below with the class of vessel denoted:
(a) Cable layer *(See Rule 4)*, (b) Power driven Pilot vessel *(See Rule 8)*, (c) Fishing vessel *(See Rule 9)*, (d) Not under command *(See Rule 4)*.

Solid black disc indicates RED light

Approaching an anchorage in fog, you hear one short, one prolonged, and one short blast in that sequence on a ship's whistle. This indicates a vessel:
(a) Towing, (b) Not under command, (c) Anchored, and warning you of her position, (d) Just getting underway from the anchorage, (e) Stopped.
(See Rule 15)

In fog, a power-driven vessel, hearing forward of the beam another vessel which cannot be seen, must wherever possible:
(a) Put the engines on standby, (b) Reduce to one-half speed, (c) Reduce to slow speed, (d) Stop her engines.
(See Rule 16)

Whistle signals to denote course changes must be sounded:
(a) In fog, (b) When vessels are in sight of one another, (c) When you can be reasonably sure of hearing the other vessel's acknowledgement, (d) Every time you alter course.
(See Rule 28)

MATCH the signal to be used between pilot and engineer with its meaning:

(a) 1 bell, (b) 2 bells, (c) 3 bells, (d) 4 bells.

A. all right, B. check, C. back, D. stop.

(See Pilot Rule 90.15 (d))

On overtaking another vessel, before passing her on her port side you must:

(a) Blow one distinct blast and be answered by one distinct blast, (b) Blow two distinct blasts and be answered by two distinct blasts, (c) Blow one distinct blast, (d) Blow two distinct blasts.

(See Pilot Rule 90.8)

A steam vessel hearing, apparently not more than four points from right ahead, the fog signal of another vessel shall at once reduce her speed to:

(a) Slow ahead, (b) Zero, (c) Bare steerageway.

(See Rule 15)

A sailing vessel under way makes her fog signal on:

(a) Bell, (b) Gong, (c) Whistle, (d) Fog horn.

(See Rule 14)

Approaching a bend where the channel around the bend is obscured a steam vessel should blow on the whistle:

(a) One distinct blast, (b) Several short and rapid blasts, not less than five, (c) One blast of at least 8 seconds duration, (d) Three long blasts.

(See Pilot Rule 90.6)

Match the vessel with the fog signal.

(a) Four bells at intervals of one minute, sounded in the same manner in which four bells are struck in indicating time, (b) One blast on the fog horn every minute, (c) At intervals of not more than 2 minutes a rapid ringing of the bell for from 3 to 5 seconds and, in addition, at intervals of not more than 3 minutes one short blast, two long blasts, and one short blast in quick succession on the whistle, (d) A screeching or Modoc whistle for from 3 to 5 seconds every minute, (e) Three distinct blasts of the whistle every minute.

A. a steam vessel underway, B. a steamer with a raft in tow, C. a sailing vessel on the starboard tack, D. a steam vessel aground in or near a channel or fairway, E. a vessel in tow.

(See Rule 14)

Incorrectly answering a two blast signal with one blast, or incorrectly answering a one blast signal with two blasts is known as:

(a) Reverse signals, (b) Reciprocal signals, (c) Cross signals, (d) Danger signals.

(See Pilot Rule 90.3)

When passing within 200 feet of a Coast Guard vessel servicing an aid to navigation, maximum speed is:

(a) 1 mph, (b) 3 mph, (c) 5 mph, (d) 7 mph.

(See Pilot Rule 90.15a)

A vessel of 600 feet in length is at anchor. She must display in addition to four anchor lights, a white light at least every —— feet along the deck:

(a) 50, (b) 75, (c) 100, (d) 125.

(See Rule 9)

The passing signal when two steam vessels are meeting in a narrow channel with a current should first be sounded by:

(a) The ascending steamer, (b) The descending steamer, (c) Either vessel, (d) The faster steamer.

(See Rule 24 Pilot Rule 90.5)

In fog, a steam vessel underway, excepting only a steam vessel with raft in tow, shall sound at intervals of not more than —— minute(s) —— distinct blast(s) of her whistle:

(a) one, one; (b) two, one; (c) one, two; (d) one, three.

(See Rule 14)

Two red lights in a vertical line one over the other indicate a vessel that is:

(a) Not under command, (b) In distress, (c) Fishing, (d) Servicing aids to navigation.

(See Rule 30)

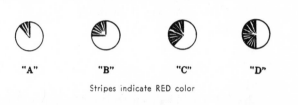

"A"   "B"   "C"   "D"

Stripes indicate RED color

Which of the circles shown has a *red* sector which best shows the arc of visibility of the red side light?

Two black balls in a vertical line indicate a vessel that is:

(a) In distress, (b) Not under command, (c) Fishing, (d) Servicing aids to navigation.

(See Rule 30)

In the situation sketched, one distinct blast by "B" means:

(a) I am directing my course to starboard, (b) I intend to hold course and speed and cross your bow, (c) I intend to go under your stern, (d) You should direct your course to starboard.

(See Pilot Rule 90.10)

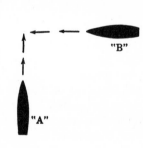

Which of the circles sketched below has a *white* sector which best represents the arc of visibility of the foremast light?

(See Rule 3 (a))

"A"   "B"   "C"   "D"

Part Four — WESTERN RIVERS

In previous installments, specimen questions were published from the Inland, International and Great Lakes rules of the road as used by the U.S. Coast Guard when renewing licenses for deck officers. We conclude, below, with questions from the Western River Rules. No operator's licenses are required on boats used exclusively for pleasure but these questions serve as a refresher to test your familiarity with the rules. Where appropriate citations are given in italics, see publication Rules of the Road, Western Rivers (U.S.C.G. 184).

If an overtaking vessel blows two distinct blasts and you think it dangerous for her to pass you:

(a) Blow one short blast, (b) Blow two short blasts, (c) Blow four or more short and rapid blasts, (d) Do not answer.

(See Rule Numbered 22)

If in overtaking another vessel as sketched at left you occasionally saw her mast lights and green side lights:

(a) The other vessel must keep clear of you, (b) You and the other vessel share equally the responsibility for keeping clear, (c) You should assume that it is your duty to keep clear, (d) You must alter course to the left.

(See Rule Numbered 22)

When underway, sail vessels and vessels towed make fog signals on the:

(a) Bell, (b) Whistle or fog horn, (c) Whistle, (d) Fog horn.

(See Rule Numbered 15)

In fog, an anchored vessel must ring the bell every:

(a) Minute for five seconds, (b) Two minutes for three seconds, (c) Three minutes for ten seconds, (d) Four minutes for five seconds.

(See Rule Numbered 15)

The two white lights displayed, as sketched at right, would indicate at night that the vessel is:

(a) Not under command, (b) Over 150 feet in length and is at anchor, (c) Under 150 feet in length and is at anchor, (d) A pilot vessel.

(See Rule Numbered 13)

Passing within 200 feet of floating plants in channels, maximum speed is:

(a) 3 mph, (b) 4 mph, (c) 5 mph, (d) 6 mph.

(See Western Rivers Pilot Rule 95.61)

If an ascending steamer makes no signal by the time a descending, approaching steamer is within one-half mile, the descending steamer blows first:

(a) One distinct blast. (b) Two distinct blasts, (c) Four or more short and rapid blasts, (d) One long blast.

(See Rule Numbered 18)

If the pilot of a descending steam vessel deems it unsafe to take the side indicated by a two blast signal given by an approaching, ascending steam vessel, he shall immediately signify that fact by sounding:

(a) One distinct blast, (b) Two distinct blasts, (c) Three distinct blasts, (d) Four or more short and rapid blasts.

(See Rule Numbered 18)

The two vessels sketched above, are governed by which of the following rules:

(a) Overtaking, (b) Meeting end on, (c) Crossing, (d) Approaching.

(See Rule Numbered 19)

When temporarily moored to the right bank in fog, a steamer hears a fog signal of an approaching vessel. The temporarily moored vessel should sound at intervals not to exceed one minute:

(a) One blast of the whistle, (b) Two blasts of the whistle, (c) One tap of the bell, (d) Two taps of the bell.

(See Rule Numbered 15)

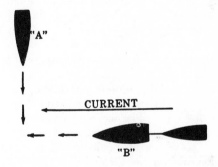

Steam vessel "B" (above) towing with the current has the right of way, and intends to cross the bow of "A." "B" should blow:

(a) One distinct blast of her whistle, (b) Two distinct blasts of her whistle, (c) Three distinct blasts of her whistle, (d) Four short and rapid blasts of her whistle.

(See Rule Numbered 19)

In fog, a steam vessel underway *without* a tow sounds at intervals not more than one minute:

(a) One long blast, (b) Three distinct blasts, (c) Two blasts of equal length, followed by a longer blast, (d) A longer blast followed by two blasts of equal length.

(See Rule Numbered 15)

In fog, a steam vessel underway and *towing* another vessel or vessels sounds at intervals of not more than one minute:

(a) One distinct blast of the whistle, (b) Two distinct blasts of the whistle, (c) Three distinct blasts of the whistle, (d) Four short and rapid blasts of the whistle.

(See Rule Numbered 15)

A vessel intending to pass a dredge first blows:

(a) One distinct blast, (b) Three distinct blasts, (c) Four short and rapid blasts, (d) One long blast.

(See Western Rivers Pilot Rule 95.60)

RULES FOR SMALL PASSENGER VESSELS

(See also pages 15 and 23)

Rules and regulations for small passenger vessels were prescribed under the Act of May 10, 1956, (Public Law 519) and their provisions made effective as of June 1, 1958. (Copies of the new rules and regulations (CG-323) may be purchased from U. S. Coast Guard Headquarters, Washington 25, D. C.)

Under this act a "passenger-carrying vessel" means any vessel which carries *more than six passengers* and which is:

(1) Propelled in whole or in part by steam or by any form of mechanical or electrical power and is of 15 gross tons or less; or

(2) Propelled in whole or in part by steam or by any form of mechanical or electrical power and is of more than 15 gross tons and less than 100 gross tons and not more than 65 feet in length measured from end to end over the deck excluding sheer; or

(3) Propelled by sail and is of 700 gross tons or less; or

(4) Non self-propelled and is of 100 gross tons or less.

A few exceptions are made, including: certain foreign vessels; vessels operating on non-navigable waters of the United States; vessels laid up and out of commission; public vessels; and lifeboats.

Vessels subject to the act must be inspected by the Officer in Charge, Marine Inspection, U. S. Coast Guard, from whom applications for inspection are obtained.

Certificates of inspection are valid for three years. They describe the area in which the vessel may operate; minimum crew required; maximum number of passengers; minimum lifesaving and firefighting equipment required, etc.

Effective June 1, 1959, no person holding only a "motorboat operator's license" is permitted to operate vessels subject to this law. The scope of licenses issued under the act varies according to the waters plied. For offshore waters, an "ocean operator's license" is issued. Within the coastline and on the Great Lakes, the license is an "operator's license" (illustrated herewith). Licenses are valid for 5 years; application is to be made on Coast Guard Form CG-866, to the nearest U. S. Coast Guard Officer in Charge, Marine Inspection.

Of particular interest to yachtsmen and boatmen who use their craft exclusively for pleasure is the definition, in the regulations, of a passenger. "A passenger is every person other than the master and the members of the crew or other persons employed or engaged in any capacity on board a vessel in the business of that vessel." (There are, however, certain exceptions, for example: aboard vessels on international voyages, children under one year of age; the owner or his representative; members of a paid crew; employees of the owner or charterer; and persons aboard tugs and towboats not over 50 gross tons who have not contributed for their carriage.) Most important exception, insofar as the yachtsman is concerned, is the following: *"any guest on board a vessel which is being used exclusively for pleasure purposes who has not contributed any consideration, directly or indirectly, for his carriage."*

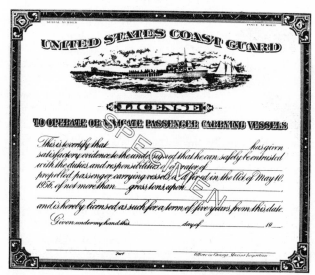

The type of license now issued by the Coast Guard to operators of small passenger vessels (carrying more than six passengers) within the coastline and on the Great Lakes

---

Notice of Arrival on Coastwise Cruises

There is a little-known law on the statute books (C.F.R. Title 33, Chapter I, Part 124, Section 124.10) which requires foreign vessels and documented vessels of the United States (not numbered boats) navigating the "high seas" on coastwise cruises to give 24 hours' notice of their time of arrival to the Captain of the Port at their next intended port of call.

Bodies of water like Long Island Sound and Chesapeake Bay are excluded from the act's definition of "high seas" but waters of the open sea below the low-water mark (as, for example, offshore along the Jersey beach) are included.

This is basically a safety and security measure to control entrance of commercial vessels into U.S. ports. For a time, the law was invoked occasionally against documented yachts, but now they are specifically exempted (Fed. Reg. Document 60-7063, July 29, 1960) in an amendment which exempts, among several types of vessels, "United States yachts, arriving at a United States port or place from a port or place outside the United States, or destined from one port or place in the United States to another port or place in the United States."

Bilge Ventilation

Gasoline in its liquid and vapor states is potentially dangerous, but this fact need *not* make recreational boating hazardous. All that is required is a respect for its potential, combined with safe boat construction and sensible operating procedures. To enjoy safe boating, one need only follow Coast Guard regulations and good common sense.

WHEN REQUIRED

The "proper and efficient" ventilation of boat bilges was established as a requirement by the Motorboat Act of 1940 for all boats employing volatile fuels (gasoline) with certain limited exceptions. These are:

(1) Boats constructed before the effective date of the Act, 25 April 1940.

(2) Boats of "open" construction.

Open construction defined

The Coast Guard has prepared a set of specifications to guide the boat owner as to whether his craft meets the definition of "open construction." To qualify for exemption from the bilge ventilation regulations, the boat must meet *all* of the following conditions.

(1) As a minimum, engine and fuel tank compartments must have 15 square inches of open area directly exposed to the atmosphere for each cubic foot of *net* compartment volume. (Net volume is found by determining total volume and then subtracting the volume occupied by the engine, tanks, other accessories, etc.)

(2) Fuel and engine compartments must have at least one square inch of open area per cubic foot within one inch of the compartment bilge level, or floor, so that vapors (which are heavier than air) can drain out into open areas.

(3) There must be no long or narrow unventilated spaces accessible from the engine or fuel tank compartments into which a fire could spread, unless the space meets requirements of item 4 below.

(4) Long, narrow compartments, such as side panels, if joining engine or fuel tank compartments and not serving as ducts, must have at least 15 square inches of open area per cubic foot through frequent openings along the compartment's full length.

Be safe—be sure

If your craft does not meet one or more of the specifications above, or if there is *any* doubt, *play it safe and provide an adequate ventilation system.* To err on the safe side will not be costly; it may save a great deal, perhaps even a life.

Diesel-powered boats

Diesel fuel does not come within the Coast Guard's definition of a "volatile" fuel, and thus bilge ventilation legal requirements are not applicable. It is, however, a sensible step to provide essentially the same ventilation system for your boat even if it is diesel-powered.

VENTILATION FUNDAMENTALS

If a boat will entrap fumes, i.e., it is not an "open" boat, it is required to have at least two ventilator ducts fitted with cowls at their openings to the atmosphere.

The ventilators, ducts, and cowls must be installed so that they provide for efficient removal of explosive or flammable gases from bilges of *each* engine and fuel tank compartment. Intake ducting must be installed to extend from the cowls to at least midway to the bilge or at least below the level of the carburetor air intake. Exhaust ducting must be installed to extend from the lower portion of the bilge to the cowls in the open atmosphere. Ducts should not be installed so low in the bilge that they could become obstructed by a normal accumulation of bilge water.

Cowls attached to intake and exhaust ducts should be located and trimmed for maximum effectiveness, and so as to prevent recirculation of fumes through the bilges.

ACTIONS OF 1966-67

The Coast Guard in 1966 and 1967 took action to implement much more stringently existing laws and regulations regarding "proper and efficient" bilge ventilation. The law did not change, only the interpretation and enforcement thereof. The tightened regulations are for the safety of the craft and those aboard—a wise skipper cheerfully complies and does more than meet minimum requirements.

ACCEPTABLE VENTILATION SYSTEMS

No foolproof ventilation system has been developed. The efficiency of various shaped cowls and ducts, the size and location of components, the capacity of mechanical blowers, and the choice of materials are all related to safety. There is no such thing as a ventilation system "approved by the Coast Guard." There has been, however, a great deal of study and thought, some testing, and years of experience upon which to base requirements. These have led to the conclusion that, *as a minimum,* fresh air must be ducted into *each* engine and fuel tank compartment, and dangerous fumes ducted out of the craft.

To create a flow through the ducting system, at least when underway or when there is a wind, cowls (scoops) or other fittings of equal effectiveness are needed on all ducts. A wind-actuated rotary exhauster or mechanical blower is considered equivalent to a cowl on an exhaust duct.

Ducts required

If it wasn't clear before, there's no mistaking it now: *ducts* are a necessary part of the ventilation system. A mere hole in the hull won't do; that's a vent, not a ventilator. "Vents," the Coast Guard explains, "are openings that permit venting, or escape of gasses due to pressure differential. Ventilators are openings that must be fitted with *cowls* to direct the flow of air and vapors in or out of *ducts* that channel movement of air for the actual displacement of fumes from the space being ventilated."

Ducting materials

For safety and long life, ducts should be made of nonferrous, galvanized ferrous, or sturdy high-temperature-resistant non-metallic materials. Ducts should be routed clear of, and protected from, contact with hot engine surfaces. Text continued on page 494(d)

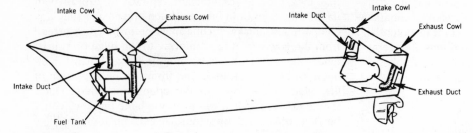

STERN-DRIVE RUNABOUT—Note that all engine and fuel tank compartments need to be efficiently ventilated. Hence, not only the engine area aft should be ducted, but the fuel compartment forward also. As on all installations, an electric exhaust blower is recommended, to be installed externally if it is not of the sealed or arcless type.

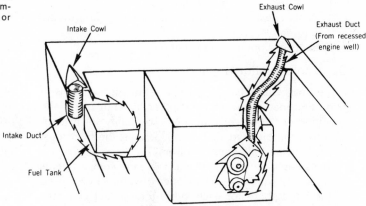

STERN-DRIVE INSTALLATION—Be sure the cowls are arranged to prevent the exhaust being picked up by the intake. If you can't spread them sufficiently apart horizontally (4 feet), to achieve this you probably can work it out by arranging one higher than the other. Where a power-driven exhaust blower is used in a *separate* duct, its duct may terminate in a flush fitting without a cowl. If the blower is in a natural ventilation duct, a cowl must be used and located so as to be in a normal suction situation.

INSTALLATION WHERE TRANSOM FUEL TANK IS USED—The requirements remain the same: at least two cowl-fitted ventilators properly ducted and of sufficient capacity.

INSTALLATION WHERE AFT SEAT IS USED—Where the fuel tank is under a stern seat, ventilate as illustrated in the diagram. It's a good idea to be sure you can get to the tank quickly, if for nothing else, to inspect it. Hinge the seat if it is not already so constructed.

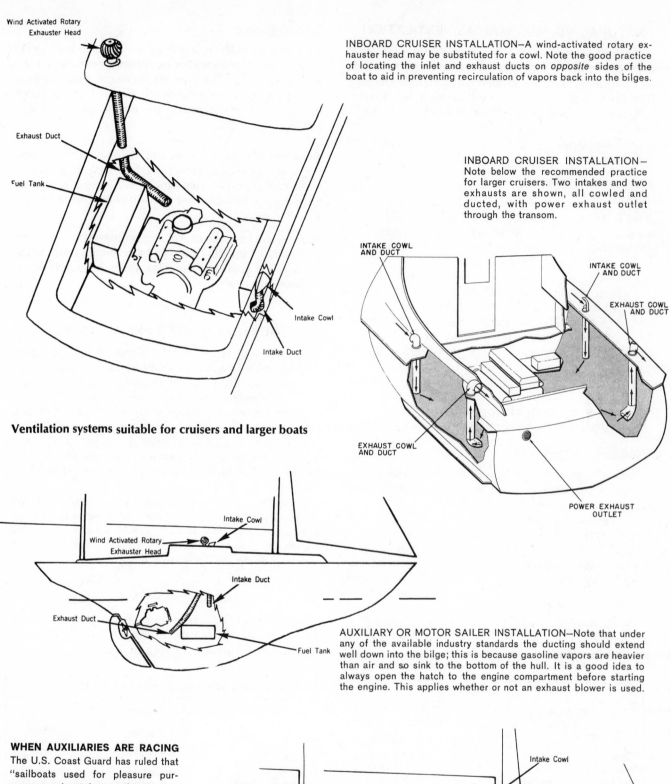

Wind Activated Rotary
Exhauster Head

Exhaust Duct

Fuel Tank

Intake Cowl

Intake Duct

INBOARD CRUISER INSTALLATION—A wind-activated rotary exhauster head may be substituted for a cowl. Note the good practice of locating the inlet and exhaust ducts on *opposite* sides of the boat to aid in preventing recirculation of vapors back into the bilges.

INBOARD CRUISER INSTALLATION—
Note below the recommended practice for larger cruisers. Two intakes and two exhausts are shown, all cowled and ducted, with power exhaust outlet through the transom.

INTAKE COWL
AND DUCT

INTAKE COWL
AND DUCT

EXHAUST COWL
AND DUCT

EXHAUST COWL
AND DUCT

POWER EXHAUST
OUTLET

Ventilation systems suitable for cruisers and larger boats

Intake Cowl

Wind Activated Rotary
Exhauster Head

Intake Duct

Exhaust Duct

Fuel Tank

AUXILIARY OR MOTOR SAILER INSTALLATION—Note that under any of the available industry standards the ducting should extend well down into the bilge; this is because gasoline vapors are heavier than air and so sink to the bottom of the hull. It is a good idea to always open the hatch to the engine compartment before starting the engine. This applies whether or not an exhaust blower is used.

WHEN AUXILIARIES ARE RACING

The U.S. Coast Guard has ruled that "sailboats used for pleasure purposes need not be ventilated when under sail alone and may block off cowls and ducts leading to engine and fuel compartments when under sail alone."

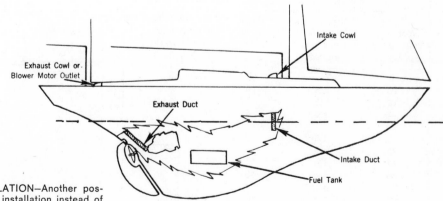

Intake Cowl

Exhaust Cowl or
Blower Motor Outlet

Exhaust Duct

Intake Duct

Fuel Tank

AUXILIARY OR MOTOR SAILER INSTALLATION—Another possible ventilation arrangement is the midship installation instead of the fore and aft one as above.

NATURAL VS. MECHANICAL VENTILATION

The systems described above provide for ventilation without mechanical assistance. The efficiency of a "natural" ventilation system is greatest when there is a breeze from forward of the beam. This will normally occur when underway or at anchor, and some of the time when in a slip. Although less efficient when the wind is abaft the beam, some scouring effect in bilges may be expected even then.

Mechanical blowers

To provide a positive means of exhausting vapors when there is little or no movement of air, and especially before starting engines when risk of explosion is greatest, mechanical blowers are *recommended* for engine spaces. This is not, however, a legal requirement.

It is suggested that ducting separate from the natural ventilation system be installed for mechanical blowers. Exhaust blowers should be of the sealed or arcless type, and, if located within the compartment being ventilated, be positioned as high as possible. Blower fan blades or impellers should be non-sparking; if installed in the exhaust duct of the natural ventilation system, they should not interfere with functioning of the duct as a natural ventilator.

Exterior terminations of separate power exhaust ducts may be fitted with flush louvered fittings instead of cowls.

Positioning of cowls

Normally, the intake cowl will face forward in an area of free airflow underway, and the exhaust cowl will face aft where a suction effect can be expected.

The two cowls, or sets of cowls, should be located with respect to each other, horizontally and/or vertically, so as to prevent return of fumes removed from any space to the same or any other space. Intake cowls should be positioned to avoid pick-up of vapors from fueling operations.

Air for carburetors

Openings into the engine compartment for entry of air to the carburetor are in addition to requirements of the ventilation system.

Size of ducts

Ventilation must be adequate for the size and design of the craft. There should be no constriction in the ducting system that is smaller than the minimum cross-sectional area required for reasonable efficiency. Where a stated size of duct is not available, the next *larger* size should be used.

Small motorboats. To determine the minimum crosssectional area of the cowls and ducts for motorboats having small engine and/or fuel tank compartments, see Table 10-1, which is based on *net* compartment volume (as previously defined).

Cruisers and larger boats. For most cruisers and other large motorboats, Table 10-2, which is based on the craft's beam, is a practical guide for determination of the minimum size of ducts and cowls.

GENERAL SAFETY PRECAUTIONS

Ventilation systems are *not* designed to remove vapors in large quantities such as might be caused by breaks in fuel lines, leaking tanks, or dripping carburetors. If gas odors are detected, repairs are generally needed.

Before starting the engine, especially on calm days and on boats without a power ventilation system, the engine compartment should be opened to dissipate any vapors that may be present. The smaller the compartment, the quicker an explosive mixture of gasoline vapors can develop.

Regardless of the ventilation system installed, always open hatches and use your nose to detect any gasoline odors. Even the slightest trace should warn you to search for the cause and to ventilate the compartment thoroughly before pressing the starter switch.

PASSENGER-CARRYING VESSELS

Vessels that carry more than six passengers *for hire* are subject to special regulations. Consult the nearest Coast Guard Marine Inspection Office for details.

TABLE 10·1			
	One *intake* and One Exhaust System		Two *Intake* and Two Exhaust Systems
Net volume (cu. ft.)	Minimum inside diameter for each duct (inches)	Area sq. in. for cowl	Minimum inside diameter for each duct (inches)
Up to 8	2	3	
10	2¼	4	
12	2½	5	
14	3¾	6	
17	3	7	
20	3¼	8	2½
23	3½	10	2½
27	3¾	11	3
30	4	13	3
35	4¼	14	3
39	4½	16	3
43	4¾	19	3
48	5	20	3

TABLE 10-2—*Two* Intake and *Two* Exhaust Systems		
Vessel beam (feet)	Minimum inside diameter for each duct (inches)	(Area square inches)
7	3	7
8	3¼	8
9	3½	9
10	3½	10
11	3¾	11
12	4	12
13	4¼	13
14	4¼	14
15	4½	15
16	4½	16
17	4½	17
18	5	18
19	5	19

INSIGNIA AND FLAGS OF U.S. POWER SQUADRON OFFICERS

(For illustration of U.S.P.S. flags in color, See page ix-e)

(NATIONAL OFFICERS)

#	OFFICE	RANK	SLEEVE INSIGNIA	CAP INSIGNIA	SLEEVE BRAID	FLAG
1	Chief Commander	C/C	3 Gold Crossed Tridents (1¼ in.)	3 Gold Crossed Tridents (2 in.)	1-Two inch 3-Half inch (Spaced ¼ in. apart)	Blue Rectangular 3 Crossed White Tridents (12 inch)
2	Executive Officer	V/C	2 Gold Crossed Tridents (1¼ in.)	2 Gold Crossed Tridents (2 in.)	1-Two inch 2-Half inch (Spaced ½ in. apart)	Red Rectangular 2 Crossed White Tridents (12 inch)
2	Director of Education	V/C	Same as above	Same as above	Same as above	Same as above
2	Administrative Officer	V/C	Same as above	Same as above	Same as above	Same as above
2	Secretary	V/C	Same as above	Same as above	Same as above	Same as above
2	Treasurer	V/C	Same as above	Same as above	Same as above	Same as above
3	As Defined in By-Laws	R/C	One Gold Trident (1¼ in.)	One Gold Trident (2 inch)	1-Two inch 1-Half inch (½ in. Apart)	White Rectangular One Blue Trident (12 inch)
4	As Defined in By-Laws	Stf/C	One Gold Trident (1¼ in.) without Cross Bar and with Interposed Circle	Same as for Rear Commander but without Cross Bar	1-Two inch	White Rectangular One Blue Trident (12 inch) without Cross Bar but with Interposed Circle
5	Flag Lieutenant	F/Lt	Two Gold Crossed Speaking Trumpets ¾ inch long	Two Gold Crossed Speaking Trumpets ¾ inch long	1-Two inch	White Swallowtail Two Blue Crossed Speaking Trumpets (12 in.)
6	Chaplain and Aides to Chief Commander	Aides C/C	Gold Binocular ½ inch across	Gold Binocular ½ inch across	1-Two inch	White Swallowtail Blue Binocular 8 inches in length
	General Member of Governing Board		One Gold Scallop Shell, ½ inch wide with base down	One Gold Scallop Shell, ½ inch wide with base down	1-Two inch	None

(DISTRICT OFFICERS)

#	OFFICE	RANK	SLEEVE INSIGNIA	CAP INSIGNIA	BRAID	FLAG
7	District Commander	D/C	3 Gold Delta Tridents (1 inch) arranged as Squadron Cdr.	3 Gold Delta Tridents (5/8 in.) arranged same as Squadron Cdr.	1-One inch 3-Half inch (Spaced ¼ in. Apart)	Blue Rectangular — 3 White Delta Tridents (10 inch) arranged same as Squadron Commander.
8	District Executive Officer	D/Lt/C	2 Gold Delta Tridents (1 inch) arranged same as Squadron Lt/C	2 Gold Delta Tridents (5/8 in.) arranged same as Squadron Lt/C	1-One inch 2-Half inch (Spaced ½ in. Apart)	Red Rectangular — 2 White Delta Tridents (10 inch) arranged same as Squadron Lt, Commander
8	District Administrative Officer	D/Lt/C	Same as above	Same as above	Same as above	Same as above
8	District Educational Officer	D/Lt/C	Same as above	Same as above	Same as above	Same as above
9	District Secretary	D/1st/Lt	One Gold Delta Trident (one inch)	One Gold Delta Trident (5/8 inch)	1-One inch 1-Half inch (Spaced ½ in. Apart)	White Rectangular — One Blue Delta Trident (10 inch)
9	District Treasurer	D/1st/Lt	Same as above	Same as above	Same as above	Same as above
9	Other elected Officers and/or Elected Committee Chairmen	D/1st/Lt	Same as above	Same as above	Same as above	Same as above
11	Flag Lieutenant	D/F/Lt	2 Crossed Red Speaking Trumpets (5/8 inch)	2 Crossed Red Speaking Trumpets (5/8 inch)	1-One inch	White Swallowtail — Two Crossed Red Speaking Trumpets (10 in.)
10	Appointed Officers Other than Chaplain and Aides to D/C	D/Lt	One Red Delta Trident (One inch)	One Red Delta Trident (5/8 inch)	Same as above	White Swallowtail — One Red Delta Trident (10 inch)
12	Chaplain and Aides to District Commander	Aide/D/C	Red Binocular ½ inch across	Red Binocular ½ inch across	Same as above	White Swallowtail Red Binocular (8 inch)

(SQUADRON OFFICERS)

#	OFFICE	RANK	SLEEVE INSIGNIA	CAP INSIGNIA	BRAID (Spaced Half-Inch Apart)	FLAG
13	Commander	Cdr.	3 Gold Tridents (¾ inch) placed at traditional angle	3 Gold Tridents (Half inch) traditionally arranged	4 Half Inch	Blue Rectangular 3 White Tridents (8 inch) Traditionally arranged
14	Executive Officer	Lt/C	2 Gold Tridents (¾ inch) traditionally arranged	2 Gold Tridents (Half Inch) traditionally arranged	3 Half Inch	Red Rectangular 2 White Tridents (8 inch) traditionally arranged
14	Educational Officer	Lt/C	Same as above	Same as above	Same as above	Same as above
15	Elected First Lieutenant	1st/Lt	One Gold Trident (¾ inch)	One Gold Trident (Half inch)	2 Half Inch	White Rectangular One Blue Trident (8 inch)
15	Secretary	1st/Lt	Same as above	Same as above	Same as above	Same as above
15	Treasurer	1st/Lt	Same as above	Same as above	Same as above	Same as above
17	Flag Lieutenant	F/Lt	One Red Speaking Trumpet (Half inch) placed vertically	One Red Speaking Trumpet (Half inch) placed vertically	One Half Inch	White Swallowtail — Red Speaking Trumpet (8 inch) placed vertically
16	Lieutenant	Lieut.	One Red Trident ¾ inch	One Red Trident (Half inch)	Same as above	White Swallowtail — One Red Trident (8 inch)
16	Chaplain	Lieut.	Same as above	Same as above	Same as above	Same as above

UNITED STATES COAST GUARD AUXILIARY FLAG CODE FOR POWER VESSELS

FLAG	NATIONAL ENSIGN	COAST GUARD ENSIGN	AUX. ENSIGN	AUX. OFFICER PENNANT OR BURGEE	YACHT ENSIGN	USPS ENSIGN	USPS OFFICER FLAG	YACHT CLUB PENNANT OR UNIT	YACHT CLUB OFFICER FLAG	HOUSE FLAG	GAG FLAGS — MEAL, ETC.
FACILITY NORMAL CONDITION — FLOWN (STATUS 1)	STERN STAFF OR GAFF (Note #1)	NO	TRUCK — BOW STAFF (Note #2) (Note #14)	STB'D. YARD — BOW STAFF (Note #3) (Note #6)	(Note #4)	STB'D. YARD ONLY (Note #5)	(Note #6)	BOW STAFF (Note #10)	STB'D. YARD (Note #6)	NO (Note #7)	NO (Note #8)
UNDER ORDERS — FLOWN (STATUS 2)	STERN STAFF OR GAFF (Note #1)	NO	TRUCK — BOW STAFF (Note #2) (Note #14)	STBD. YARD — BOW STAFF (Note #3) (Note #15)	NO (Note #15)	NO (Note #15)	NO (Note #15)	NO (Note #15)	NO (Note #15)	NO (Note #7)	NO (Note #8)
UNDER ORDERS USCG OFFICER ABOARD — FLOWN (STATUS 3)	STERN STAFF OR GAFF (Note #1)	TRUCK (Note #16)	NO (Note #16)	NO (Note #16)	NO (Note #16)	NO (Note #16)	NO (Note #16)	NO (Note #16)	NO (Note #16)	NO (Note #7)	NO (Note #8)
HOURS FLOWN	0800 TO SUNSET	DAY AND NIGHT UNDER ORDERS (Note #13)	DAY AND NIGHT (Note #9)	OFFICER ABOARD DAY AND NIGHT	0800 TO SUNSET (Note #4)	0800 TO SUNSET Note #5	DAY AND NIGHT (Note #6)	0800 TO SUNSET (Note #11)	DAY AND NIGHT (Note #12)	(Note #7)	NO

NOTES

#1 **The National Ensign** shall be flown from the stern staff on a power boat except when the vessel is equipped with a gaff, in which case the ensign is flown from the stern staff at anchor, and the gaff when underway.

#2 **Auxiliary Ensign**
(a) Shall be flown from the main truck when the vessel is equipped with a mast(s).
(b) Without a mast, from the bow staff.

#3 **Auxiliary Officer**—Pennant or burgee shall be flown from the starboard yardarm when the vessel is equipped with a signal mast. If the vessel has no mast, it may be flown in lieu of the Auxiliary ensign from the bow staff. The pennant of a current officer shall take precedence over his own higher ranking past officer's burgee. However, as a matter of courtesy to a visiting officer, display the highest ranking officer flag (pennant or burgee).

#4 **The Yacht Ensign**
(a) The flying of the yacht ensign on any yacht, numbered or documented, is neither mandatory nor forbidden.
(b) A documented yacht operating under official orders, becomes a Government vessel, and Government vessels may not fly the "Yacht ensign."
(c) All facilities not documented shall fly the U.S. ensign, whenever the Auxiliary ensign is flown.

#5 **USPS Ensign**—This is the only "service" organization recognized by this code. The USPS ensign may be flown only from the starboard yardarm of a signal mast, never from the stern staff or gaff. On facilities flying the Auxiliary ensign, this position of honor is reserved for the national ensign.

#6 **Officer Flags**—Auxiliary, USPS, yacht or boat club, either pennants or burgees, are flown from the starboard yardarm, except as noted in #3. Only one of these flags may be flown at a time.

#7 **House Flag**—The owner's private signal known as a house flag is correctly flown at the truck between morning and evening colors; therefore, it cannot be flown at the same time as the Auxiliary ensign.

#8 **Gag Flags**—Because of the quasi-official status of an Auxiliary facility, cocktail flags, ball-and-chain, or other humorous flags shall not be flown when the Auxiliary ensign is flown. Other flags, such as crew's pennant, owner's meal flag, guest flag, absent flag, also shall not be flown with the Auxiliary ensign.

#9 **The Auxiliary Ensign**—may be flown day and night on currently inspected facilities displaying decal, while in commission.

#10 **The Yacht Club Pennant**—can be flown from the bow staff.

#11 **The Yacht Club Pennant, Flotilla, or Division, Unit Flags**—shall be flown from 0800 to sunset.

#12 **Yacht Club Officer Flags**—shall be displayed day and night.

#13 **The Coast Guard Ensign**—shall be flown day and night while the facility is under orders with a Coast Guard officer aboard.

#14 **No Signal Mast**—When a boat is equipped with a bow and stern staff, and does not have a signal mast, but has a radio antenna, the Auxiliary ensign may be properly displayed by substituting the antenna for a signal mast. The height of the uppermost portion of the hoist of the Auxiliary ensign should be affixed at a point approximately $2/3$ the height of the antenna. No additional antennas or outriggers may be utilized.

#15 **A Facility Under Official Orders (STATUS 2)** shall be permitted to fly the Auxiliary officer's pennant or burgee, in addition to the U.S. and Auxiliary ensigns. All other flags—yacht ensign, USPS ensign, yacht club pennants, officer flags, flotilla, division, etc. shall not be flown.

#16 **Coast Guard Officer Aboard Facilities Under Orders (STATUS 3)** the Coast Guard Ensign substitutes for the Auxiliary ensign; all other flags except the national ensign shall be taken down. This includes Auxiliary officer pennants or burgees, yacht ensign, unit flags, USPS ensign, yacht or boat club flags, etc.—only two flags shall be permitted—the national ensign and the Coast Guard ensign.

SEE UNITED STATES COAST GUARD AUXILIARY FLAGS IN FULL COLOR, Page IX-F
AND ILLUSTRATIONS, Page 463

Where To Obtain Charts, Cruising Information, And Other Publications

CHARTS OF VARIOUS WATERWAYS

Charts, U. S. Coastal Waters—Charts of coastal waters such as the Atlantic, Pacific and Gulf Coasts, the Hudson River as far north as Troy, and the Atlantic and Gulf Intracoastal Waterways, are published by the United States Coast & Geodetic Survey, Washington Science Center, Rockville, Md., 20852, and are available from them, their distribution offices, or any of their sales agents, listed semi-annually in the Oceanographic Office Notice to Mariners.

Charts, Great Lakes—Charts of the Great Lakes and connecting rivers, Lake Champlain, New York State Canals, Lake of the Woods, and Rainy Lake are available from the U. S. Lake Survey, 630 Federal Bldg., Detroit, Mich. 48226. They also publish a catalog of charts issued by that office.

Charts, New York State Canals—A bound booklet of charts of the New York State canals (Champlain, Erie, Oswego, and Cayuga-Seneca), east of Lyons, is available from the U. S. Lake Survey, 630 Federal Bldg., Detroit, Mich. 48226.

Charts, Mississippi River and Tributaries—(*Middle & Upper Mississippi River; Cairo, Ill. to Minneapolis, Minn.*)
(*Middle Mississippi River; Cairo, Ill. to Grafton, Ill.*)
(*Mississippi River from Cairo, Ill. to Gulf of Mexico*)
(*Small Boat Navigation Chart; Alton, Ill. to Clarksville on the Mississippi River and Grafton, Ill., to LaGrange, Ill. on the Illinois River*)
(*Illinois Waterways; from Grafton, Ill. to Lake Michigan at Chicago and Calumet Harbors*)
U. S. Army Engineer District, 906 Olive Street, St. Louis, Missouri, 63101.

The offices listed below will supply exhaustive lists of available charts, detailing sources, prices, scales, and exact sections covered.

Mississippi River and connecting waterways, north of Ohio River—U. S. Army Engineer Division, North Central, 536 South Clark St., Chicago, Ill. 60605.

Mississippi River and tributaries, below Ohio River—Mississippi River Commission, P.O. Box 80, Vicksburg, Miss. 39181. This office also has a free booklet, "Mississippi River Navigation," discussing history, development and navigation of the river.

Ohio River and tributaries; Pittsburgh, Pa., to the Mississippi River—U. S. Army Engineer Division, P.O. Box 1159, Cincinnati, Ohio 45201.

Tennessee and Cumberland Rivers—U. S. Army Engineer District, P. O. Box 1070, Nashville, Tenn. 37202. Another general information source for the Tennessee is the Tennessee Valley Authority, Maps and Engineering Records Section, 102A Union Bldg., Knoxville, Tenn.

Missouri River and tributaries—U. S. Army Engineer District, 6012 U. S. Post Office and Court House, Omaha, Neb. 68102.

Charts, Canadian Waters—Charts of Canadian waters are available from Hydrographic Chart Distribution, Canadian Hydrographic Service, Department of Mines and Technical Surveys, 615 Booth St., Ottawa, Canada. These include charts of Canadian coastal waters; Canadian sections of the Great Lakes including Georgian Bay; the St. Lawrence River; Richelieu River; Ottawa River; The Rideau Waterway; and other Canadian lakes, canals, etc.

Prices and details are given in a Coastal and Inland Waters Catalog; indexes of charts for any area in Canada are available free from the address above.

Charts, Foreign Waters—These are published by the U. S. Naval Oceanographic Office, Washington, D. C. 20390, and are available through any of the sales agents listed twice a year in Notice to Mariners, published by the U. S. Naval Oceanographic Office. A general catalog and ten regional catalogs are available.

NOTICE TO MARINERS

Notice to Mariners—This is a weekly pamphlet published by the U. S. Naval Oceanographic Office, Washington, D. C. 20390. Is is issued so mariners may keep nautical charts and Coast Pilots up to date. Twice a year the Notices contain lists of Branch Oceanographic offices; U. S. Coast Guard District offices; U. S. Coast & Geodetic Survey District offices; U. S. Engineer offices; agents for the sale of Oceanographic Office charts and publications; data on all publications of the Oceanographic Office; data on the various Coast Pilots, Tide Tables, Current Tables and Tidal Current Charts sold by the U. S. Coast & Geodetic Survey; data on U. S. Coast Guard Light Lists; and a list of agents for the sale of Coast and Geodetic Survey and Coast Guard publications.

Local Notices, of interest primarily within the limits of each of the Coast Guard Districts, are issued by Commanders of the respective districts, and are available from their district offices.

COAST PILOTS

Coast Pilots—For coastal waters, and the Atlantic and Gulf Intracoastal Waterways, these are published by the U. S. Coast and Geodetic Survey, Washington Science Center, Rockville, Md. 20852, and are available from them, their distribution offices, or sales agents as listed semi-annually in Notice to Mariners. These volumes supplement the information given on charts, with detailed descriptions of routes, courses, distances, depths, harbors, sources of supplies, tides, currents, weather, list of yacht clubs, facilities for repairs, etc.

For the Great Lakes and other waters covered by U. S. Lake Survey charts, the publication corresponding to the Coast Pilot is called the Great Lakes Pilot. This is an annual publication, kept up-to-date during the navigation season by seven monthly supplements issued from May to November. It is obtained from the U. S. Lake Survey, 630 Federal Bldg., Detroit, Mich. 48226.

For Canadian waters—available from Hydrographic Chart Distribution, Canadian Hydrographic Office, Dept. of Mines and Technical Surveys, 615 Booth St., Ottawa, Canada. Details are given in the Coastal and Inland Waters Catalog available from Hydrographic Chart Distribution at the address given above. A descriptive list of Pilots and Sailing Directions is also available.

LIGHT LISTS

Light Lists—These are published by the U. S. Coast Guard and are for sale by the Superintendent of Documents, Washington, D. C. 20402, or any of the Coast Guard sales agents listed semi-annually in the Oceanographic Office Notice to Mariners. They describe lighted aids, radio beacons, fog signals, unlighted buoys, and daymarks. Vol. I covers Atlantic Coast from St. Croix River, Me., to Little River, S. C. Vol. II, Atlantic and Gulf Coasts from Little River, S. C., to Rio Grande River, Tex., and the Antilles. Vol. III, Pacific Coast and Islands. Vol. IV, Great Lakes. Vol. V, Mississippi River.

TIDE AND CURRENT TABLES

Tide Tables, Current Tables and Tidal Current Charts—These are also publications of the U. S. Coast & Geodetic Survey, Washington Science Center, Rockville, Md. 20852, and may be obtained from them, their distribution offices, or from any of their sales agents listed semi-annually in Notice to Mariners.

RULES OF THE ROAD

Rules of the Road—Rules of the Road are published for three areas, namely: C.G. No. 169—Certain inland waters of the Atlantic and Pacific coasts and of the coast of the Gulf of Mexico; C.G. No. 172—The Great Lakes and their connecting tributary waters and the St. Mary's River; and C.G. No. 184—The Western Rivers and the Red River of the North. They are published by the U. S. Coast Guard and copies may be obtained from Coast Guard Marine Inspection Offices in principal ports, or the Commandant (CHS), U. S. Coast Guard, Washington, D. C. 20226.

Handbook of Boating Laws—in four editions for Southern, Northeastern, North Central and Western states. Lists state requirements for registering, numbering, equipment and small boat operation; fuel tax laws; boat trailer laws; and applicable federal regulations. Available from Outboard Boating Club, 333 N. Michigan Ave., Chicago, Ill. 60601.

NEW YORK STATE CANALS

Rules and Regulations Covering Navigation and Use of the New York State Canal System—A booklet by this title is published by and is available from New York State Dept. of Public Works, Division of Operation and Maintenance, Albany, N. Y. It contains a description of the New York Canal System, and regulations pertaining to use of the canal. Applications for free season permits to use the canals should be made to the same office.

Canal Guide Book for the New York State Barge Canal System and Connecting Navigable Waterways—A booklet of great value in cruising the Hudson River, Lake Champlain, New York State canals, and connecting Canadian waterways, including the St. Lawrence River and parts of Lake Erie and Lake Ontario. Lists sources of supplies such as fuel, oil, engine repairs, fresh water, provisions, anchorage and dockage. Available from Cruising Guide Book, 146 Sheridan Avenue, Albany, N. Y. 12210.

The Northwest Passage—Cruise kit and guide book, with charts, for Hudson River, Champlain Canal and Lake Champlain. Division of Motor Boats, New York Conservation Dept., Albany, N. Y. 12226.

The Grand Canal—Cruise kit and guide book, with charts, for Erie Canal, Oswego Canal, and the Cayuga Seneca Canals. Division of Motor Boats (address above).

INTRACOASTAL WATERWAYS

Waterway Guide—A publication detailing for the yachtsman a vast amount of information concerning the inland waterways. The Northern Edition covers the coast from Maine to New York; the Middle Atlantic Edition from New York to Sea Island, Ga.; the Southern Edition from Sea Island, Ga., to Florida and Gulf Coast to New Orleans; the Great Lakes Edition from New York to the Great Lakes with connecting Canadian canals and rivers. Available from Waterway Guide, Inc., P. O. Box 2586, Jacksonville, Florida 32203.

Intracoastal Waterway Booklets—Comprehensive descriptions of the Intracoastal Waterway, with data on navigation, charts, distances, etc. Prepared by Corps of Engineers, U. S. Army, and sold by Superintendent of Documents, Washington, D. C. 20402. In two sections: (1) Atlantic Section, Boston to Key West, (2) Gulf Section, Key West to Brownsville, Tex.

Intracoastal Waterway Bulletins—Frequent bulletins giving latest information on the condition of the Intracoastal Waterway are published by the Corps of Engineers. These are available from the following District Offices of the Army Engineers: Foot of Front St., Norfolk, Va. 23510; P. O. Box 1890, Wilmington, N. C. 28402; P. O. Box 905, Charleston, S. C. 29402; P. O. Box 889, Savannah, Ga. 31402; P. O. Box 4970, Jacksonville, Fla. 32201; P. O. Box 1169, Mobile, Ala. 36601; P. O. Box 1229, Galveston, Tex. 77551.

OTHER CRUISING PUBLICATIONS

Cruising Charts, Guides and Booklets—Some of the large oil companies provide free cruising services for yachtsmen. These companies will go to considerable length to provide such items as cruising charts from which the itinerary can be planned, harbor booklets showing the facilities available in all the principal ports, mimeographed outlines of various cruises containing a digest of up-to-date information on the waterways involved, etc. Sources for this kind of material include: Texaco Waterways Service, 135 E. 42nd St., New York 17, N. Y.; Gulf Tourgide Bureau, Box 8056, Philadelphia 1, Pa. (east of Mississippi); Mobil Touring Service, Mobil Oil Co., 150 E. 42nd St., New York 17, N. Y.; Esso Touring Service, 15 W. 51st St., New York 19, N. Y.

The Yachtsman's Guide and Nautical Calendar—A valuable handbook of boating and cruising information—tide and current tables, coast pilot data, charts, courses, distance tables, yacht club directory, buoyage, nautical terms, flag etiquette, knots and splices, piloting hints, etc. Published annually by Motor Boating, 959 Eighth Ave., New York, N. Y. 10019.

Cruising Guide to the New England Coast—Descriptions of harbors, anchorages, and waterways by Fessenden Blanchard. Includes Hudson River, Long Island Sound and the New Brunswick coast. Available from Sailing Book Service, 34 Oak Ave., Tuckahoe, N. Y. 10707.

Cruising Guide to the Southern Coast—Blanchard's guide to the Intracoastal Waterway—Norfolk to New Orleans, including other Florida waterways. Sailing Book Service (address above).

Cruising Guide to the Chesapeake—Another Blanchard guide, with a wealth of information on Chesapeake Bay. Sailing Book Service (address above).

Yachtsman's Guide to Northern Harbors—Harbors, boat basins and services around Long Island, and seacoast of New England. Seaport Publishing Co., 843 Delray Ave., S.E., Grand Rapids 6, Mich.

Guide for Cruising Maryland Waters—Prepared by Maryland Dept. of Tidewater Fisheries. Twenty full-color charts, with more than 200 courses and distances plotted. Maryland Board of Natural Resources, State Office Bldg., Annapolis, Md. Available from the same address is the booklet Maryland Marine Facilities.

Chesapeake Bay Country—With map in color of Chesapeake Bay country and tributaries, indexed marine facilities, and fishing grounds, Dept. of Tidewater Fisheries, Annapolis, Md. Boating Handbook for Maryland Waters also available.

Boating Atlas of Tidewater Virginia—An atlas of 53 charts in full color covering the ocean front, lower Chesapeake Bay, the James, York, Rappahannock and Potomac Rivers. Includes buoyage system, rules of the road, location of marine facilities, state and Coast Guard regulations, notes from the Coast Pilot, Tide Tables, safety suggestions, and a course protractor. Distributed by Paxton Co., 1019 Main St., Norfolk, Va.

Florida Boating—Pamphlet giving data on waterways, charts, Florida boat registration, and water safety regulations, fishing licenses, area maps and information, plus a directory of marine facilities throughout the state. Available from Florida Development Commission, Carlton Bldg., Tallahassee, Fla.

Yachtsman's Guide to the Great Lakes—Harbors, services, supplies on the Great Lakes, St. Lawrence, Richelieu and Hudson Rivers, Lake Champlain, and New York State Barge Canal. Seaport Publishing Co., 843 Delray Ave., S. E., Grand Rapids, Mich. 49506.

Cruising the Georgian Bay—Cruising information, with 23 pages of Ontario Government Aerial Survey Maps and tabulations of services and facilities at ports. Bellhaven House, 12 Dyas Road, Don Mills, Ontario.

Cruising the North Channel—Covers the waterway between Manitoulin Island and the north shore of Lake Huron. Bellhaven House, see address above.

Cruising the Trent-Severn Waterway—A cruising guide, including rules and regulations, supply points and services, mileages and general data. British Book Service, see address above.

Trailer Boating Where the North Begins—Written especially for the small boatman, and includes the Muskoka, Parry Sound, and Lake-of-Bays areas of Ontario. Bellhaven House, see address above.

Harbor Guide to the Upper Mississippi River—From Minneapolis to St. Louis, including St. Croix River. Covers harbors (services and location), cities and towns (population, transportation, shopping centers, tourist interest), locks and dams, mileage charts, source of navigation charts, history of river. Available from Mildred Quimby, 801 South Michigan, Prairie du Chien, Wisconsin.

Yachtsman's Guide to the Bahamas—A complete guide book for a cruise in the Bahamas. The data it contains is much like the information found in Coast Pilots. The Customs and Immigration information will be found especially valuable to those who have never cruised to foreign waters. Available from Tropic Isle Publishers, Inc., P. O. Box 613, Coral Gables, Fla. 33134.

Yachtsman's Guide to the Caribbean—Island, port and anchorage charts on courses from Florida through the Bahamas to the Greater Antilles and the Leeward and Windward Islands; lists of facilities, refueling places, customs and port formalities on all islands in the Caribbean. Seaport Publishing Co., 843 Delray Ave. S. E., Grand Rapids, Mich. 49506.

The Alluring Antilles—This cruising guide provides accurate, precise and ample information about every island in the West Indies. D. Van Nostrand Co., Inc., 120 Alexander St., Princeton, N. J. 08540.

Virgin Islands—Eggleston's descriptions of islands, harbors, people, history, passages, and facilities. Illustrated. Sailing Book Service, 34 Oak Avenue, Tuckahoe, N. Y. 10707.

U. S. COAST GUARD PUBLICATIONS

Recreational Boating Guide—CG-340. 77 pp. Information on boat numbering; legal minimum equipment requirements; other equipment you should carry; responsibilities when operating; aids to navigation; hints on safety afloat; emergency procedures; and U. S. Coast Guard Auxiliary services. Contains copies of Federal Boating Act of 1958, and the Motorboat Act of April 25, 1940; sample of Application for Number form; Boating Accident Report; and Radio Distress Information Sheet. Superintendent of Documents, Government Printing Office, Washington, D. C. 20402.

Pleasure Craft—CG-290. Digest of boating laws and regulations. Numbering. Boating accidents. Sales to aliens. Law enforcement. Documentation. C. G. approved equipment. Equipment requirements. Suggestions for safety. U. S. Coast Guard offices.

Aids to Marine Navigation of the United States—U. S. Coast Guard publication CG-193. Illustrated. 32 pages. U. S. Coast Guard, Washington, D. C. 20226. Basic principles underlying the marking of coasts and waterways with lighthouses, lightships, fog signals, radiobeacons, loran, and buoys. Treats primarily of the manner in which the physical characteristics of various aids to navigation serve the mariner.

Marine Radiobeacons—U. S. Coast Guard. 16 pp. Obtainable from U. S. Coast Guard, Washington, D. C. 20226. Instructional pamphlet for the beginner studying navigation.

Ocean Electronic Navigational Aids—U. S. Coast Guard pamphlet CG 157-1. 73 pp. Loran, radiobeacon and radarbeacon systems; and loran, radio direction finder and radar ship equipment. Available from Superintendent of Documents, Washington, D. C. 20402.

Rules and Regulations for Uninspected Vessels—U. S. Coast Guard. 16 pages. Copies may be obtained from District Coast Guard Offices. Requirements for all vessels not subject to inspection, including those subject to the Motorboat Act of April 25, 1940. Every motorboat owner should obtain a copy. Refer to CG-258.

Rules and Regulations for Numbering Undocumented Vessels—U. S. Coast Guard publication CG-267. Available from District Coast Guard Offices or the Commandant (CHS), U. S. Coast Guard, Washington, D. C. 20226.

Rules and Regulations for Small Passenger Vessels—U. S. Coast Guard publication CG-323. Requirements for vessels carrying more than six passengers. Available from District Coast Guard Offices, or the Commandant, U. S. Coast Guard, Washington, D. C., 20226.

Manual for Lifeboatmen and Able Seamen—Illustrated. 63 pages. Obtainable from the U. S. Coast Guard, Washington, D. C. 20226. Lifeboats, life rafts, life floats, buoyant apparatus, davits, and releasing gear are described. Refer to C.G. 175.

GASOLINE TAX REFUNDS

Gasoline Tax Refunds—Some states allow a refund, in whole or in part, of the gasoline tax when the fuel is used for boat purposes. However, the regulations differ greatly and it would be well for the yachtsman to become familiar with these regulations in advance. The Texaco Waterways Service, 135 E. 42nd Street, New York 17, N. Y.; and Mobil Oil Co., Inc., Marine Retail Dept., 150 E. 42nd St., New York 17, N. Y., issue Bulletins describing these regulations.

MISCELLANEOUS PUBLICATIONS
OF THE OCEANOGRAPHIC OFFICE

The Oceanographic Office produces charts and Sailing Directions (Pilots) and lists of lights of all oceans and seas, and of foreign coasts and islands and harbors, but only general charts of the coasts of the United States.

Information on Oceanographic Office Charts and Publications. H. O. Pub. 1-N. Catalog listing some of the more popular index charts, world charts, general nautical charts, magnetic charts, pilot charts, bathymetric charts, special charts, plotting charts, oceanographic and bottom sediment charts, aeronautical charts, loran charts, published by the U. S. Navy Oceanographic Office, with information on H. O. nautical, aeronautical and oceanographic publications. Free Introduction, Part I, is a general listing.

Sailing Directions are books supplementing the nautical charts issued by the Oceanographic Office. They contain descriptions of coast lines, harbors, dangers, aids, port facilities, and other data which cannot be conveniently shown on charts.

Notice to Mariners containing corrections to nautical charts and publications are issued weekly by the Oceanographic Office, Branch Oceanographic Offices, and United States Consulates.

Daily Memorandum carries a synopsis of the latest information relating to dangers and aids to navigation, including reports of drifting buoys, wreckage, and other hazards together with advance items that will appear in the Notice to Mariners. The Daily Memorandum is issued locally by the Branch Oceanographic Offices and the most urgent of the reports are also broadcast by radio under the title, Government Hydro All Ships and Stations, and rebroadcast locally.

Pilot Charts of the North Atlantic Ocean, North Pacific Ocean are issued monthly. These present information on average winds and currents, percentages of gales and calms, and other hydrographic data of a varied nature.

H.O. Pilot Charts

#576 Atlas of Pilot Charts—South Atlantic Ocean and Central American Waters.
#577 Atlas of Pilot Charts—South Pacific, Indian Oceans.
#1400 Pilot Chart of the North Atlantic Ocean (Monthly).
#1401 Pilot Chart of the North Pacific Ocean (Monthly).

H.O. Lists of Lights and Fog Signals

Light Lists published by the Oceanographic Office give detailed descriptions of navigational lights and fog signals, and mention signals of various kinds operated at lighthouses.

Vol. I covers the Coast of North and South America (only the seacoast lights of the United States), the West Indies, and the Hawaiian Islands.

Vol. II covers islands of the Pacific and Indian Oceans, Australia, Asia, and the East Coast of Africa.

Vol. III covers the West Coasts of Europe and Africa, the Mediterranean Sea, Black Sea, and the Sea of Azov.

Vol. IV covers the British Islands, English Channel, and North Sea.

Vol. V covers Norway, Iceland, and Arctic Ocean.

Vol. VI covers the Baltic Sea with Kattegat, Belts and Sound, and Gulf of Bothnia.

Volumes I, II, III, are revised and reissued annually and Volumes IV, V, VI at less frequent intervals. Volumes IV, V, VI are corrected by annual supplements containing changes that have taken place during the year or years since the books were published. These supplements are mailed free of charge to purchasers of the books. Weekly corrections to the Light Lists are published in the section, Corrections to H.O. Light Lists, at the end of the Notice to Mariners. This section includes minor corrections not appearing in the main body of the Notice.

Other H. O. Publications of the Oceanographic Office

Chart #1—Nautical Chart Symbols and Abbreviations.

#9 American Practical Navigator. Originally by Nathaniel Bowditch, LL.D. etc. Revised (Including the Useful Tables.)
#234 Breakers and Surf; Principles in Forecasting.
#601 Wind, Sea, and Swell: Theory of Relations in Forecasting.

#602 Wind Waves at Sea, Breakers and Surf.
#102 International Code of Signals.
#117 Radio Navigational Aids. Marine Direction-Finding Stations, Radiobeacons, Time Signals, Navigational Warnings, Distress Signals, Medical Advice and Quarantine Stations, Loran, Consol, and Regulations Governing the Use of Radio in Territorial Waters.
#118 Radio Weather Aids. General weather information, broadcast schedules, international index numbers with locations of stations, key groups, and call signs.
#151 Tables of Distances Between Ports.
#2100 World Star Chart.
#2102D Star Finder and Identifier (AN Type).
#226 Handbook of Magnetic Compass Adjustment and Compensation.

WEATHER

Weather Forecasting—U. S. Department of Commerce, Weather Bureau. Illustrated. 40 pages. Generally accepted facts and theories of meteorology and some of the principles of weather forecasting, in popular style. Atmospheric Pressure, Circulation of the Atmosphere, Weather Forecasting, and An Atmospheric Survey, concerning the gathering of information by the Weather Bureau stations for weather maps. Superintendent of Documents, Washington, D. C. 20402.

The Hurricane—United States Department of Commerce, Weather Bureau. Illustrated. 22 pages. An interesting paper dealing solely with the hurricane. The general information contained in this publication should be known by all who go to sea. Superintendent of Documents, Washington, D. C. 20402.

Circular R. W. B. 1151 Preparation and Use of Weather Maps at Sea—U. S. Department of Commerce, Weather Bureau. Illustrated. 100 pages. The Ship's weather observation, Radio weather message and its uses, Radio weather bulletins, Preparation of weather maps, Weather types, Tropical storms. Drawing inferences from weather map.

The Daily Weather Map—United States Department of Commerce, Weather Bureau. Five weather maps of the United States are included, data for which are prepared from observations taken daily at hundreds of stations throughout North America. A complete explanation of the maps, including all symbols and tables used in plotting the data appears on the reverse side of the Sunday map only. Superintendent of Documents, Washington, D. C. 20402.

MISCELLANEOUS PUBLICATIONS

Rules of the Nautical Road—U. S. Naval Institute, Annapolis, Md. Revised edition by Lt. Alfred Prunski, U.S.C.G., of the textbook by Captain Raymond F. Farwell, U.S.N.R., designed to show new changes in International Rules which took effect January 1, 1954. Gives comparison with up-to-date Inland Rules and Pilot Rules. Includes interpretations of rules by courts.

The American Nautical Almanac—United States Naval Observatory. Copies purchased from the Superintendent of Documents. A compact publication containing all the ephemeris material essential to the solution of problems of navigational position. Contains a Star Chart which shows the position of the stars used in navigation. Instructions for its use are included. The Star Chart may be purchased separately. (Star Chart in larger form may be purchased from Oceanographic Office sales agents.)

Tide and Current Investigations of the Coast and Geodetic Survey—U. S. Coast and Geodetic Survey, Washington, D. C. 20230. Illustrated. 50 pages. Types and forms of tides, earthquake waves, tidal currents, and wind currents.

First Aid—Supt. of Documents, Washington, D. C. 20402. Illustrated. 160 pages. This is one of the best first aid manuals obtainable. Only first aid instruction is given.

Miscellaneous Publication No. 9. The Ship's Medicine Chest and First Aid at Sea—United States Public Health Service. Illustrated. 498 pages. Prepared especially for seafaring people. An excellent treatise. Sections included give special instruction for emergency treatment, and First Aid by Radio. (Superintendent of Documents, Washington, D. C. 20402.)

Magnetic Poles and the Compass—U. S. Coast and Geodetic Survey. Superintendent of Documents, Washington, D. C. 20402.

TEXT OF THE MOTORBOAT ACT OF APRIL 25, 1940

As Amended to June 15, 1959 (46 U.S.C. 526-526u)

An act to amend laws for preventing collisions of vessels, to regulate equipment of certain motorboats on the navigable waters of the United States, and for other purposes

Be it enacted by the Senate and House of Representatives of the United States of America in Congress assembled, That the word "motorboat" where used in this Act shall include every vessel propelled by machinery and not more than sixty-five feet in length except tugboats and towboats propelled by steam. The length* shall be measured from end to end over the deck, excluding sheer: *Provided,* That the engine, boiler, or other operating machinery shall be subject to inspection by the Coast Guard, and to its approval of the design thereof, on all said motorboats, which are more than forty feet in length, and which are propelled by machinery driven by steam. *(46 U.S.C. 526.)*

Classes of Motorboats

Sec. 2. Motorboats subject to the provisions of this Act shall be divided into four classes as follows:

Class A. Less than sixteen feet in length.

Class 1. Sixteen feet or over and less than twenty-six feet in length.

Class 2. Twenty-six feet or over and less than forty feet in length.

Class 3. Forty feet or over and not more than sixty-five feet in length. *(46 U.S.C. 526a.)*

Lights

Sec. 3. Every motorboat in all weathers from sunset to sunrise shall carry and exhibit the following lights when under way, and during such time no other lights which may be mistaken for those prescribed shall be exhibited:

(a) Every motorboat of classes A and 1 shall carry the following lights:

First. A bright white light aft to show all around the horizon.

Second. A combined lantern in the fore part of the vessel and lower than the white light aft, showing green to starboard and red to port, so fixed as to throw the light from right ahead to two points abaft the beam on their respective sides.

(b) Every motorboat of classes 2 and 3 shall carry the following lights:

First. A bright white light in the fore part of the vessel as near the stem as practicable, so constructed as to show an unbroken light over an arc of the horizon of twenty points of the compass, so fixed as to throw the light ten points on each side of the vessel; namely, from right ahead to two points abaft the beam on either side.

Second. A bright white light aft to show all around the horizon and higher than the white light forward.

Third. On the starboard side a green light so constructed as to show an unbroken light over an arc of the horizon of ten points of the compass, so fixed as to throw the light from right ahead to two points abaft the beam on the starboard side. On the port side a red light so constructed as to show an unbroken light over an arc of the horizon of ten points of the compass, so fixed as to throw the light from right ahead to two points abaft the beam on the port side. The said side lights shall be fitted with inboard screens of sufficient height so set as to prevent these lights from being seen across the bow.

(c) Motorboats of classes A and 1 when propelled by sail alone shall carry the combined lantern, but not the white light aft, prescribed by this section. Motorboats of classes 2 and 3, when so propelled, shall carry the colored side lights, suitably screened, but not the white lights, prescribed by this section. **Motorboats of all classes, when so propelled, shall carry, ready at hand, a lantern or flashlight showing a white light which shall be exhibited in sufficient time to avert collision.

(d) Every white light prescribed by this section shall be of such character as to be visible at a distance of at least two miles. Every colored light prescribed by this section shall be of such character as to be visible at a distance of at least one mile. The word "visible" in this Act, when applied to lights, shall mean visible on a dark night with clear atmosphere.

(e) When propelled by sail and machinery any motorboat shall carry the lights required by this section for a motorboat propelled by machinery only.

(f) Any motorboat may carry and exhibit the lights required by the Regulations for Preventing Collisions at Sea, 1948, Act of October 11, 1951 (65 Stat. 406-420; 33 U.S.C. 147-147d), as amended, in lieu of the lights required by this section. *(46 U.S.C. 526b.) (Amended by Act of June 4, 1956.)*

Whistle, Bell and Life Preservers

Sec. 4. Every motorboat of class 1, 2, or 3, shall be provided with an efficient whistle or other sound-producing mechanical appliance. *(46 U.S.C. 526c.)*

Sec. 5. Every motorboat of class 2 or 3 shall be provided with an efficient bell. *(46 U.S.C. 526d.)*

Sec. 6. Every motorboat subject to any of the provisions of this Act and also all vessels propelled by machinery other than by steam more than sixty-five feet in length shall carry at least one life preserver, or life belt, or ring buoy, or other device of the sort prescribed by the regulations of the Commandant of the Coast Guard, for each person on board, so placed as to be readily accessible: *Provided,* That every such motorboat and every such vessel propelled by machinery other than by steam more than sixty-five feet in length carrying passengers for hire shall carry so placed as to be readily accessible at least one life preserver of the sort prescribed by the regulations of the Commandant of the Coast Guard, for each person on board. *(46 U.S.C. 526e.)*

Licensed Operator

Sec. 7. No such motorboat, and no other vessel of fifteen gross tons or less propelled by machinery other than steam, while carrying passengers for hire, shall be operated or navigated except in charge of a person duly licensed for such service by the Secretary of the department in which the Coast Guard is operating. Whenever any person applies to be licensed as operator of any motorboat, or of any other vessel of fifteen gross tons or less propelled by machinery, carrying passengers for hire, the Secretary shall make diligent inquiry as to his character, and shall carefully examine the applicant orally as well as the proofs which he presents in support of his claim, and if the Secretary is satisfied that his capacity, experience, habits of living, and character are such to warrant the belief that he can safely be entrusted with the duties and responsibilities of the station for which he makes application, the Secretary shall grant him a license authorizing him to discharge such duties on any such motorboat, or on any other vessel of fifteen gross tons or less propelled by machinery, carrying passengers for hire, for the term of five years. Such license shall be subject to suspension or revocation on the same grounds and in the same manner with like procedure as is provided in the case of suspension or revocation of license of officers under the provisions of section 4450 of the Revised Statutes, as amended (U.S.C. 1952 edition, title 46, sec. 239): *Provided,* That motorboats and other vessels of fifteen gross tons or less propelled by machinery shall not be required to carry licensed officers except as required in this Act: *And provided further,* That licenses herein prescribed shall not be required of motorboats or of any other vessels of fifteen gross tons or less propelled by machinery engaged in fishing contests previously arranged and announced. *(46 U.S.C. 526f.) (Amended by Act of May 10, 1956.)*

Fire Extinguishers

Sec. 8. Every motorboat and also every vessel propelled by machinery other than by steam more than sixty-five feet in length shall be provided with such number, size, and type of fire extinguishers, capable of promptly and effectually extinguishing burning gasoline, as may be prescribed by the regulations of the Commandant of the Coast Guard, which fire extinguishers shall be at all times kept in condition for immediate and effective use and shall be so placed as to be readily accessible. *(46 U.S.C. 526g.)*

Racing Outboards Exempt

Sec. 9. The provisions of sections 4, 5, and 8 of this Act shall not apply to motorboats propelled by outboard motors while competing in any race previously arranged and announced or, if such boats be designed and intended solely for racing, while engaged in such navigation as is incidental to the tuning up of the boats and engines for the race. *(46 U.S.C. 526h.)*

Flame Arresters

Sec. 10. Every motorboat and also every vessel propelled by machinery other than by steam more than sixty-five feet in length shall have the carburetor or carburetors of every engine therein (except outboard motors) using gasoline as fuel, equipped with such efficient flame arrester, backfire trap, or other similar device

---

*NOTE—The expression "length shall be measured from end to end over the deck excluding sheer" has been interpreted to mean a straight line measurement of the overall length from the foremost part of the vessel to the aftermost part of the vessel. Bowsprits, boomkins, rudders, outboard motor brackets, and similar fittings or attachments are not to be included in the measurement. Length shall be stated in feet and inches.

** Now carry 12-pt. white light aft.

as may be prescribed by the regulations of the Commandant of the Coast Guard: *Provided,* That this section shall apply only to such motorboats or vessls, the construction of which or the replacement of the engine or engines of which is commenced subsequent to the passage of this Act.

Ventilation of Bilges

Sec. 11. Every such motorboat and every such vessel, except open boats, using as fuel any liquid of a volatile nature, shall be provided with such means as may be prescribed by regulations of the Commandant of the Coast Guard for properly and efficiently ventilating the bilges of the engine and fuel tank compartments so as to remove any explosive or inflammable gases: *Provided,* That this section shall apply only to such motorboats or vessels, the construction or decking over of which is commenced subsequent to the passage of this Act.

Pilot Rules Not Required

Sec. 12. Motorboats shall not be required to carry on board copies of the pilot rules.

Negligent Operation

Sec. 13. (a) No person shall operate any motorboat or any vessel in a reckless or negligent manner so as to endanger the life, limb, or property of any person. To "operate" means to navigate or otherwise use a motorboat or a vessel.

(b) In the case of collision, accident, or other casualty involving a motorboat or other vessel subject to this Act, it shall be the duty of the operator, if and so far as he can do so without serious danger to his own vessel, or persons aboard, to render such assistance as may be practicable and necessary to other persons affected by the collision, accident, or casualty in order to save them from danger caused by the collision, accident, or casualty. He shall also give his name, address, and identification of his vessel to any person injured and to the owner of any property damaged. The duties imposed by this subsection shall be in addition to any duties otherwise provided by law.

(c) In the case of collision, accident, or other casualty involving a motorboat or other vessel subject to this Act, the operator thereof, if the collision, accident, or other casualty results in death or injury to any person, or damage to property in excess of $100, shall file with the Secretary of the Department within which the Coast Guard is operating, unless such operator is required to file an accident report with the State under section 3 (c) (6) of the Federal Boating Act of 1958, a full description of the collision, accident, or other casualty, including such information as the Secretary may by regulation require.

(46 U.S.C. 526l.) (Amended by Act of September 2, 1958.)

Penalty for Negligent Operation

Sec. 14. Any person who shall operate any motorboat or any vessel in a reckless or negligent manner so as to endanger the life, limb, or property of any person shall be deemed guilty of a misdemeanor and on conviction thereof by any court of competent jurisdiction shall be punished by a fine not exceeding $2,000, or by imprisonment for a term of not exceeding one year, or by both such fine and imprisonment, at the discretion of the court. *(46 U.S.C. 526m.)*

Authority to Arrest

Sec. 15. Any officer of the United States authorized to enforce the navigation laws of the United States, shall have power and authority to swear out process and to arrest and take into custody, with or without process, any person who may commit any act or offense prohibited by section 13, or who may violate any provision of said section: *Provided,* That no person shall be arrested without process for any offense not committed in the presence of some one of the aforesaid officials: *Provided further,* That whenever an arrest is made under the provisions of this Act, the person so arrested shall be brought forthwith before a commissioner, judge, or court of the United States for examination of the offense alleged against him, and such commissioner, judge, or court shall proceed in respect thereto as authorized by law in cases of crimes against the United States. *(46 U.S.C. 526n.)*

Penalties for Other Violations

Sec. 16. If any motorboat or vessel subject to any of the provisions of this Act is operated or navigated in violation of this Act or any regulation issued thereunder, the owner or operator, either one or both of them, shall, in addition to any other penalty prescribed by law be liable to a penalty of $100: *Provided,* That in the case of motorboats or vessels subject to the provisions of this Act carrying passengers for hire, a penalty of $200 shall be imposed on the owner or operator, either one or both of them, thereof for any violation of section 6, 7, or 8 of this Act or of

any regulations pertaining thereto. For any penalty incurred under this section the motorboat or vessel shall be liable and may be proceeded against by way of libel in the district court of any district in which said motorboat or vessel may be found.

(46 U.S.C. 526o.) (Amended by Act of September 2, 1958.)

Regulations and Enforcement

Sec. 17. The Commandant of the Coast Guard shall establish all necessary regulations required to carry out in the most effective manner all of the provisions of this Act, and such regulations shall have the force of law. The Commandant of the Coast Guard or any officer of the Coast Guard authorized by the Commandant may, upon application therefor, remit or mitigate any fine, penalty, or forfeiture incurred under this Act or any regulation thereunder relating to motorboats or vessels, except the penalties provided for in section 14 hereunder. The Commandant of the Coast Guard shall establish such regulations as may be necessary to secure the enforcement of the provisions of this Act by any officer of the United States authorized to enforce the navigation laws of the United States. *(46 U.S.C. 526p.)*

Sec. 18. The proviso contained in the last paragraph of section 2 of the Act of May 11, 1918 (40 Stat. 549; 46 U.S.C. 223), shall apply also with like force and effect to motorboats as defined in this Act.

Motorboats as defined in this Act are hereby exempted from the provisions of Revised Statutes 4399, as amended (48 Stat. 125; 46 U.S.C. 361). *(46 U.S.C. 526q.)*

When Act Takes Effect

Sec. 19. This Act shall take effect upon its approval as to all of the sections hereof except sections 6, 7, and 8, which sections shall take effect one year from the date of said approval, and for a period of one year from the date of approval of this Act sections 5, 6, and 7 of the Motorboat Act of June 9, 1910 (Public, Numbered 201, Sixty-first Congress; 36 Stat. 462), shall continue in full force and effect, except that from and after the date of the approval of this Act the Secretary of Commerce shall have authority to remit or mitigate all fines or penalties heretofore or hereafter incurred or imposed under sections 5 and 6 of the Motorboat Act of June 9, 1910. Except as hereinabove expressly provided, the Motorboat Act of June 9, 1910, above referred to, is repealed upon the approval of this Act and as to sections 5, 6, and 7 of said Act hereinabove continued the said sections are hereby repealed effective one year from the date of approval of this Act. Nothing in this Act shall be deemed to alter or amend section 4417a of the Revised Statutes (U.S.C., 1934 edition, Supp. IV, title 46, sec. 391a), the Act of August 26, 1935 (U.S.C., 1934 edition, Supp. IV, ch. 7A, secs. 178 and 179), the Act of June 20, 1936 (U.S.C., 1934 edition, Supp. IV, title 46, sec. 367), or repeal Acts of Congress or treaties embodying or revising international rules for preventing collisions at sea. *(46 U.S.C. 526r.)*

Sec. 20. There are hereby authorized to be appropriated such sums as may be necessary to carry out the provisions of this Act. *(46 U.S.C. 526s.)*

Section 21 (Numbering Certificate) Repealed

(NOTE.—The following section 21 is repealed, effective April 1, 1960, by Act of September 2, 1958.)

Sec. 21. The provisions of section 210 of title II of the Anti-Smuggling Act, approved August 5, 1935 (49 Stat. 526; U.S.C., 1934 edition, Supp. IV, title 46, sec. 288), requiring a certificate of award of a number to be kept at all times on board of the vessel to which the number has been awarded shall not apply to any vessel not exceeding seventeen feet in length measured from end to end over the deck, excluding sheer, or to any vessel whose design of fittings are such that the carrying of the certificate of award of the number on such vessel would render such certificate imperfect, illegible, or would otherwise tend to destroy its usefulness as a means of ready identification. *(46 U.S.C. 526t.)*

Application of Act

Sec. 22. (a) This Act shall apply to every motorboat or vessel on the navigable waters of the United States, its Territories and the District of Columbia, and every motorboat or vessel owned in a State and using the high seas.

(b) As used in this Act—

The term 'State' means a State of the United States, a Territory of the United States, and the District of Columbia.
(46 U.S.C. 526u.) (Added by Act of September 2, 1958.)

Approved: April 25, 1940 (as amended 1946 Reorganization Plan No. 3, July 16, 1946; 1950 Reorganization Plan No. 26, July 31. 1950; May 10, 1956, June 4, 1956, September 2, 1958).

TEXT OF THE FEDERAL BOATING ACT OF 1958

Public Law 85-911 85th Congress, H. R. 11078
September 2, 1958

An act to promote boating safety on the navigable waters of the United States, its Territories, and the District of Columbia; to provide coordination and cooperation with the States in the interest of uniformity of boating laws: and for other purposes.

Be it enacted by the Senate and House of Representatives of the United States of America in Congress assembled, That this Act may be cited as the "Federal Boating Act of 1958".

Definitions

SEC. 2. As used in sections 3 to 5, inclusive, and sections 7 to 13, inclusive, of this Act—

(1) The term "undocumented vessel" means any vessel which is not required to have, and does not have, a valid marine document issued by the Bureau of Customs.

(2) The word "vessel" includes every description of watercraft, other than a seaplane on the water, used or capable of being used as a means of transportation on water.

(3) The word "Secretary" means the Secretary of the Department in which the Coast Guard is operating.

(4) The word "owner" means the person who claims lawful possession of a vessel by virtue of legal title or equitable interest therein which entitles him to such possession.

(5) The term "State" means a State of the United States, a Territory of the United States, and the District of Columbia.

Numbering of Vessels

SEC. 3. (a) Every undocumented vessel propelled by machinery of more than 10 horsepower, whether or not such machinery is the principal source of propulsion, using the navigable water of the United States, its Territories and the District of Columbia, and every such vessel owned in a State and using the high seas, shall be numbered in accordance with this Act, except—

(1) foreign vessels temporarily using the navigable waters of the United States, its Territories and the District of Columbia;

(2) public vessels of the United States;

(3) State and municipal vessels;

(4) ships' lifeboats; and

(5) vessels designated by the Secretary under section 7 (b) of this Act.

(b) The owner of an undocumented vessel required to be numbered under subsection (a) of this section shall secure a number for such vessel in the State in which it is principally used, in accordance with the State numbering system approved by the Secretary in accordance with subsection (c) of this section, or if no such numbering system has been approved by the Secretary for the State where such vessel is principally used, shall secure a number for such vessel in accordance with subsection (d) of this section.

(c) The Secretary shall establish an overall numbering system for the numbering of vessels required to be numbered under subsection (a) of this section. He shall approve any State system for numbering vessels which is submitted to him which meets the standards set forth below:

(1) The system of numbering shall be in accordance with the overall system of numbering established by the Secretary.

(2) The certificate of number and the number awarded shall be valid for a period not exceeding three years, unless canceled or surrendered, and may be renewed for additional periods.

(3) The number awarded shall be required to be painted on, or attached to, each side of the bow of the vessel for which it was issued, and shall be of such size, color, and type, as may be prescribed by the Secretary. No other number shall be permitted to be carried on the bow of such vessel.

(4) The certificate of number shall be pocket size and shall be required to be at all times available for inspection on the vessel for which issued, whenever such vessel is in use.

(5) The owner shall be required to furnish to a designated State official, notice of the transfer of all or any part of his interest in any numbered vessel, and of the destruction or abandonment of such vessel, within a reasonable time thereof. The owner shall be required to notify a designated State official of any change in his address within a reasonable time of such change.

(6) The State shall require that reports be made to it of accidents involving vessels numbered by it under its numbering system, and shall compile and transmit to the Secretary such statistics on such accidents.

(7) The State shall recognize the validity of a number awarded to any vessel by another State under a numbering system approved by the Secretary under this Act, or awarded a number by the Secretary, for a period of at least ninety days.

(8) In the case of a State having its numbering system approved after April 1, 1960, such State shall accept and recognize any valid certificate of number awarded under subsection (d) of this section for so long as such certificate would otherwise be valid under such subsection (d), except that where such a certificate would remain valid for more than one year after the date when such State's numbering system was approved, the State may accept and recognize the validity of such certificate for a lesser period, but such period shall not end sooner than one year from the date of approval of such system.

(9) The State may exempt any vessel or class of vessels from the numbering provisions of its system if such vessel or class of vessels has been made exempt from the numbering provisions of section 3 (d) by the Secretary under section 7 (b) of this Act.

(10) The States may charge fees in connection with the award of certificates of number and renewals thereof.

(11) The States may require that the operator of a vessel required to be numbered hereunder shall hold a valid safety certificate to be issued under such terms and conditions as may be provided by State law.

(d) The owner of an undocumented vessel required to be numbered under subsection (a) of this section who uses his vessel principally in a State which does not have a numbering system approved by the Secretary under subsection (c) of this section, shall make application to the Secretary, and upon payment of the fee established under section 5, such owner shall be granted a certificate of number containing the number awarded such vessel by the Secretary.

Certificate Valid Three Years

(e) The certificate of number initially awarded to an owner under subsection (d) of this section shall be valid for three years from the date of the owner's birthday next occurring after the date the certificate of number is issued, unless surrendered or canceled pursuant to regulations of the Secretary. If at the end of such period such ownership has remained unchanged, such owner shall, upon application and payment of the fee established under section 5 of this Act, be granted a renewal of such certificate of number for an additional three-year period.

(f) The number awarded under subsection (c) or (d) of this section shall be painted on, or attached to, each side of the bow of the vessel for which it was issued, and shall be of such size, color, and type as may be prescribed by the Secretary. No other number shall be carried on the bow of such vessel.

(g) The certificate of number granted under subsection (c) or (d) of this section shall be pocket size and shall be required to be at all times available for inspection on the vessel for which issued whenever such vessel is in use, and shall constitute a document in lieu of a marine document that sets forth an official number issued by the Bureau of Customs.

(h) Whenever the Secretary determines that a State is not administering its approved system for numbering vessels in accordance with the standards set forth under subsection (c) of this section, he may withdraw such approval. The Secretary shall not withdraw his approval of a State system of numbering until he has given notice in writing to the State setting forth specifically wherein the State has failed to maintain such standards.

SEC. 4. The owner of any vessel numbered under section 3 (d) of this Act shall furnish to the Secretary notice of the transfer of all or any part of his interest in any numbered vessel, and of the destruction, or abandonment of such vessel, within a reasonable time thereof. The owner shall notify the Secretary of any change in his address within a reasonable time of such change.

SEC. 5. The Secretary may prescribe reasonable fees or charges for the numbering of a vessel, or renewal thereof, under subsections (d) and (e) of section 3 of this Act.

Motorboat Act Amended

SEC. 6. (a) Section 13 of the Act entitled "An Act to amend laws for preventing collisions of vessels, to regulate equipment of certain motorboats on the navigable waters of the United States, and for other purposes", approved April 25, 1940 (46 U. S. C. 526l), is amended to read as follows:

"SEC. 13. (a) No person shall operate any motorboat or any vessel in a reckless or negligent manner so as to endanger the life, limb, or property of any person. To 'operate' means to navigate or otherwise use a motorboat or a vessel.

"(b) In the case of collision, accident, or other casualty involving a motorboat or other vessel subject to this Act, it shall be the duty of the operator, if and so far as he can do so without serious danger to his own vessel, or persons aboard, to render such assistance as may be practicable and necessary to other persons affected by the collision, accident, or casualty in order to save them from danger caused by the collision, accident, or casualty. He shall also give his name, address, and identification of his vessel to any person injured and to the owner of any property damaged. The duties imposed by this subsection shall be in addition to any duties otherwise provided by law.

"(c) In the case of collision, accident, or other casualty involving a motorboat or other vessel subject to this Act, the operator thereof, if the collision, accident, or other casualty results in death or injury to any person, or damage to property in excess of $100, shall file with the Secretary of the Department within which the Coast Guard is operating, unless such operator is required to file an accident report with the State under section 3 (c) (6) of the Federal Boating Act of 1958, a full description of the collision, accident, or other casualty, including such information as the Secretary may by regulation require."

(b) Section 16 of such Act of April 25, 1940 (46 U. S. C. 526o), is amended by striking out "than that contained in section 14 of this Act".

(c) Such Act of April 25, 1940 (46 U. S. C. 526–526t), is further amended by adding at the end thereof the following new section:

"SEC. 22. (a) This Act shall apply to every motorboat or vessel on the navigable waters of the United States, its Territories and the District of Columbia, and every motorboat or vessel owned in a State and using the high seas.

"(b) As used in this Act—

"The term 'State' means a State of the United States, a Territory of the United States, and the District of Columbia."

SEC. 7. (a) The Secretary shall make such rules and regulations as may be necessary to carry out the provisions of this Act: *Provided,* That such rules and regulations shall be submitted to the Speaker of the House and the President of the Senate when Congress is in session, and shall not become effective until sixty days thereafter.

(b) The Secretary may, from time to time, and for such periods as he may prescribe, exempt any vessel or class of vessels from the numbering provisions of subsection (d) of section 3 of this Act.

Violations and Penalties

SEC. 8. (a) Whoever being the owner of a vessel required to be numbered under this Act, violates section 3 or 4 of this Act, or regulations established by the Secretary under section 7 of this Act, shall be liable to a penalty of $50 for each violation. Whoever operates a vessel in violation of section 3 of this Act, or regulations established by the Secretary under section 7 of this Act, shall be liable to a penalty of $50 for each violation.

(b) The Secretary may assess and collect any penalty incurred under this Act or any regulations prescribed pursuant to section 7 of this Act. The Secretary may, in his discretion, remit or mitigate any penalty imposed under this section, or discontinue prosecution therefor on such terms as he may deem proper.

(c) Commissioned, warrant, and petty officers of the Coast Guard may board any vessel required to be numbered under this Act at any time such vessel is found upon the navigable waters of the United States, its Territories and the District of Columbia, or on the high seas, address inquiries to those on board, require appropriate proof of identification therefrom, examine the certificate of number issued under this Act, or in the absence of such certificate require appropriate proof of identification of the owner of the vessel, and, in addition, examine such vessel for compliance with this Act, the Act of April 25, 1940, as amended, and the applicable rules of the road.

SEC. 9. It is hereby declared to be the policy of Congress to encourage uniformity of boating laws, rules, and regulations as among the several States and the Federal Government to the fullest extent practicable, subject to reasonable exceptions arising out of local conditions. In the interest of fostering the development, use, and enjoyment of all the waters of the United States it is further declared to be the policy of the Congress hereby to encourage the highest degree of reciprocity and comity among the several jurisdictions. The Secretary, acting under the authority of section 141 of title 14 of the United States Code, shall to the greatest possible extent enter into agreements and other arrangements with the States to insure that there shall be the fullest possible cooperation in the enforcement of both State and Federal statutes, rules, and regulations relating to recreational boating.

Publication of Accident Reports

SEC. 10. The Secretary is authorized and directed to compile, analyze, and publish, either in summary or detailed form, the information obtained by him from the accident reports transmitted to him under section 3 (c) (6) of this Act, and under section 13 (c) of the Act entitled "An Act to amend laws for preventing collisions of vessels, to regulate equipment of certain motorboats on the navigable waters of the United States, and for other purposes", approved April 25, 1940 (46 U. S. C. 526l), together with such findings concerning the causes of such accidents and such recommendations for their prevention as he may deem necessary. Such information shall be made available for public inspection in such manner as the Secretary may deem practicable.

SEC. 11. (a) Except section 3 (d), this Act shall take effect on the date of its enactment.

(b) Section 3 (d) of this Act shall take effect April 1, 1960.

SEC. 12. The Act entitled "An Act to require numbering and recording of undocumented vessels", approved June 7, 1918, as amended (46 U. S. C. 288), and section 21 of the Act entitled "An Act to amend laws for preventing collisions of vessels, to regulate equipment of certain motorboats on the navigable waters of the United States, and for other purposes", approved April 25, 1940, as amended (46 U. S. C. 526t), shall not be applicable in any State having a numbering system approved by the Secretary under section 3 (c) of this Act. Such Act of June 7, 1918, and such section 21 of the Act of April 25, 1940, are repealed effective April 1, 1960.

Law Enforcement

SEC. 13. The applicability and the jurisdiction for enforcement, upon the navigable waters of the United States, its Territories and the District of Columbia, of the laws of the United States and of any State which require the numbering and otherwise regulate the use of undocumented vessels, shall be as follows:

(1) Such laws of the United States shall be applicable and enforced on such waters by law enforcement officers of the United States.

(2) Such laws of any State in a State having a numbering system approved by the Secretary under section 3 (c) of this Act shall be applicable and enforced on such waters by law enforcement officers of the State or by law enforcement officers of the appropriate subdivisions of the State.

(3) Nothing herein shall preclude enforcement of State or Federal laws pursuant to agreements or other arrangements entered into between the Secretary and any State within the contemplation of section 9 of this Act.

(4) Nothing herein shall interfere with, abrogate or limit the jurisdiction of any State: *Provided, however,* That the Secretary shall not approve any State system for numbering which does not fully comply with the standards set forth in section 3 (c).

Approved September 2, 1958.

WHERE TO APPLY FOR NUMBERING CERTIFICATES

The Federal Boating Act of 1958 called for the registration and numbering of all motorboats over a specified horsepower for identification, with a provision that the individual state should have jurisdiction in all cases where their state legislation would conform to the standard established by the federal act. Approval by the U. S. Coast Guard is required in each case.

By July 1966, the Coast Guard had officially approved the numbering systems of all states except Alaska, New Hampshire, Washington, and Washington, D. C. In these jurisdictions application forms for Coast Guard registration numbers may be obtained through local post offices or any Coast Guard facility. In Guam and Puerto Rico, application should be made to the Officer in Charge, Marine Inspection, U. S. Coast Guard.

Boats principally used in states having an approved number-ing law are numbered exclusively by the state; Coast Guard numbers are obsolete. In compliance with the Federal Act all of these state laws grant 90-day reciprocity to out-of-state boats awarded numbers pursuant to Federal law or a federally approved state numbering system.

The Outboard Boating Club of America (333 No. Michigan Ave., Chicago 1, Ill.) has compiled all available information on state boating laws in handbooks for various regions of the country. These include not only the registration and numbering requirements, but also all related laws on equipment, operation, use of trailers, etc., which readers are urged to obtain.

Given below are extracts from OBC data, listing agencies responsible for boat numbering laws.

ALABAMA Department of Conservation, State Administrative Building, Montgomery, Alabama 36104.

ALASKA Department of Natural Resources, Division of Lands, 344-6th Avenue, Anchorage, Alaska 99501. The State of Alaska has no pleasure boating laws. The State Department of Natural Resources can answer general questions about boating in the State.

ARIZONA Motor Vehicle Division, Arizona Highway Department, 1739 West Jackson, Phoenix, Arizona 85007.

ARKANSAS Revenue Department, State Capitol Building, Little Rock, Arkansas 72201

CALIFORNIA Department of Harbors and Watercraft, 1416-9th Street, Room 1336, Sacramento, California 95814.

COLORADO Game, Fish & Parks Department, 6060 Broadway, Denver, Colorado 80216.

CONNECTICUT Boating Safety Commission, Department of Agriculture & Natural Resources, State Office Building, Hartford, Connecticut 06115.

DELAWARE Small Boat Safety Division, Commission of Shell Fisheries, P. O. Box 512, Lewes, Delaware 19958.

FLORIDA State Board of Conservation, 107 West Gaines Street, Tallahassee, Florida 32304.

GEORGIA State Game and Fish Commission, 401 State Capitol, Atlanta, Georgia 30334.

HAWAII Harbors Division, Department of Transportation, Box 397, Honolulu, Hawaii 96809.

IDAHO Motor Vehicle Division, Department of Law Enforcement, P. O. Box 34, Boise, Idaho.

ILLINOIS Conservation Department, 400 South Spring Street, Springfield, Illinois 62706.

INDIANA Department of Natural Resources, 605 State Office Building, Indianapolis, Indiana 46209.

IOWA State Conservation Commission, East 7th & Court Avenues, Des Moines, Iowa 50308.

KANSAS Fish & Game Commission, Pratt, Kansas 67124.

KENTUCKY Department of Public Safety, Division of Boating, Frankfort, Kentucky 40601.

LOUISIANA Wild Life & Fisheries Commission, Wild Life & Fisheries Building, 400 Royal Street, New Orleans, Louisiana 70130.

MAINE Bureau of Watercraft Registration and Safety, State Office Building, Augusta, Maine 04330.

MARYLAND Department of Chesapeake Bay Affairs, State Office Building, Annapolis, Maryland 21404.

MASSACHUSETTS Division of Motorboats, 100 Nashua Street, Boston, Massachusetts 02114.

MICHIGAN Department of State, Mutual Building, Lansing, Michigan 48918.

MINNESOTA Department of Conservation, 625 North Robert Street, St. Paul, Minnesota 55101.

MISSISSIPPI Boat and Water Safety Commission, 605 West Capitol Street, Jackson, Mississippi 39203.

MISSOURI Boat Commission, P. O. Box 603, Jefferson City, Missouri 65101.

MONTANA State Board of Equalization, Capitol Building, Helena, Montana 59601.

NEBRASKA State Game, Forestation & Parks Commission, Lincoln, Nebraska 68509.

NEVADA Fish & Game Commission, Box 678, Reno, Nevada 89504.

NEW HAMPSHIRE Division of Motor Vehicles, Department of Safety, 85 Loudon Road, Concord, New Hampshire 03301. The State of New Hampshire registers powerboats operated on inland or nontidal waters. As this registration system does not comply with the Federal Boating Act of 1958, the Coast Guard has retained the responsibility for registering and numbering undocumented vessels with more than 10 horsepower chiefly used on navigable waters of the United States within the territorial limits of New Hampshire.

NEW JERSEY Bureau of Navigation, Department of Conservation & Economic Development, Box 1889, Trenton, New Jersey 08625.

NEW MEXICO State Park and Recreation Commission, P. O. Box 1147, Santa Fe, New Mexico 87501.

NEW YORK Division of Motorboats, State Conservation Department, New York State Campus, 1220 Washington Avenue, Albany, New York 12201.

NORTH CAROLINA Wildlife Resources Commission, Box 2919, Raleigh, North Carolina 27602.

NORTH DAKOTA State Game & Fish Department, Bismarck, North Dakota 58501.

OHIO Watercraft Division, Department of Natural Resources, 802 Ohio Departments Building, Columbus, Ohio 43215.

OKLAHOMA Boat & Motor Licensing Division, Industrial Development & Park Department, Room 500, Will Rogers Building, Oklahoma City, Oklahoma 73105.

OREGON State Marine Board, State Agriculture Building, 635 Capitol Street, N.E., Salem, Oregon 97310.

PENNSYLVANIA Miscellaneous License Division, Pennsylvania Dept. of Revenue, Harrisburg, Pennsylvania 17127.

RHODE ISLAND Registry of Motor Vehicles, Executive Department, State Capitol Building, Providence, Rhode Island 02903.

SOUTH CAROLINA Wildlife Resources Department, P. O. Box 167, Columbia, South Carolina 29202.

SOUTH DAKOTA Department of Game, Fish & Parks, State Office Building, Pierre, South Dakota 57501.

TENNESSEE Game & Fish Commission, 706 Church Street, Doctors Building, Nashville, Tennessee 37203.

TEXAS Highway Department, Motor Vehicle Division, 40th & Jackson, Austin, Texas 78703.

UTAH Boating Division, Utah State Park & Recreation Commission, 132 South Second West, Salt Lake City, Utah 84101.

VERMONT Marine Division, Department of Public Safety, Montpelier, Vermont 05602.

VIRGINIA Game & Inland Fisheries Commission, P. O. Box 1642, Richmond, Virginia 23213.

WASHINGTON Washington State Parks and Recreation Commission, 522 South Franklin, P. O. Box 1128, Olympia, Washington 98502. The State of Washington does not have a boat registration and numbering law. This is handled by the U. S. Coast Guard on navigable waters of the United States within the territorial limits of Washington. The State Parks Department does operate quite a number of marine parks and can answer general questions about boating in the State.

WEST VIRGINIA Department of Natural Resources, State Office Building, Charleston, West Virginia 25305.

WISCONSIN Conservation Department, P. O. Box 450, Madison, Wisconsin 53701.

WYOMING Game & Fish Commission, P. O. Box 1589, Cheyenne, Wyoming 82001.

DIST. OF COLOMBIA Metropolitan Police Department, Harbor Precinct, 550 Maine Avenue, S.W., Washington, D. C. 20024.

PUERTO RICO Puerto Rico has no pleasure boating laws. Boat registration and numbering on navigable waters of the United States are handled by the U. S. Coast Guard.

VIRGIN ISLANDS Department of Commerce, Marine & Aviation Services, Charlotte Amalie, St. Thomas Island, Virgin Islands.

REGULATIONS DRAFTED BY THE UNITED STATES COAST GUARD

TO IMPLEMENT THE FEDERAL BOATING ACT OF 1958

(Effective March 10, 1959)

PART 170—GENERAL PROVISIONS
Authority and Purpose

§ 170.01–1 *Purpose of regulations.* The regulations in this subchapter provide:

(a) Standards for numbering under the Federal Boating Act of 1958.

(b) Requirements with respect to statistical information under the Federal Boating Act of 1958 and the Act of April 25, 1940, as amended.

(c) Requirements with respect to "Boating Accident Reports" and accident statistics.

§ 170.01–5 *Assignment of functions.* By virtue of the authority vested in the Commandant of the Coast Guard by the Secretary of the Treasury in Treasury Department Order No. 167–32, dated September 23, 1958 (23 F. R. 7605), the regulations in this subchapter are prescribed to carry out the intent and purpose of the Federal Boating Act of 1958, and the Act of April 25, 1940, as amended (46 U. S. C. 526–526t).

Application

§ 170.05–1 *Scope.* The regulations in this subchapter are applicable in the United States, its Territories, and the District of Columbia.

§ 170.05–5 *Vessels subject to the requirements of this subchapter.* Except as specifically noted, this subchapter shall be applicable to undocumented vessels.

Definitions of Terms

§ 170.10–1 *Commandant.* This term means the Commandant of the U. S. Coast Guard.

§ 170.10–5 *Coast Guard District Commander.* This term means an officer of the Coast Guard designated as such by the Commandant to command all Coast Guard activities within his district.

§ 170.10–10 *Horsepower.* This term means the rated horsepower of the machine at maximum operating RPM.

§ 170.10–15. *Length.* As set forth in section 1 of the Act of April 25, 1940, as amended (46 U. S. C. 526), this term means the length of the vessel "measured from end to end over the deck excluding sheer."

§ 170.10–20 *Machinery.* This term includes inboard and outboard engines and all other types of motors or mechanical devices capable of propelling vessels.

§ 170.10–25 *Officer in Charge, Marine Inspection.* This term means any person from the civilian or military branch of the Coast Guard designated as such by the Commandant and who, under the superintendence and direction of the Coast Guard District Commander, is in charge of an inspection zone.

§ 170.10–30 *Operate.* As set forth in subsection 13 (a) of the Act of April 25, 1940, as amended (46 U. S. C. 526 *l*), this term "means to navigate or otherwise use a motorboat or a vessel."

§ 170.10–35 *Operator.* This term means the person who operates or who has charge of the navigation or use of a motorboat or a vessel.

§ 170.10–40 *Owner.* As set forth in subsection 2 (4) of the Federal Boating Act of 1958, this term "means the person who claims lawful possession of a vessel by virtue of legal title or equitable interest therein which entitles him to such possession."

§ 170.10–45 *Ships' lifeboats.* This term means lifeboats used solely for life-saving purposes and does not include dinghies, tenders, speedboats, or other types of craft carried aboard a vessel and used for other than lifesaving purposes.

§ 170.10–50 *State.* As set forth in subsection 2 (5) of the Federal Boating Act of 1958, this term "means a State of the United States, a Territory of the United States, and the District of Columbia."

§ 170.10–55 *Ten horsepower.* As used in subsection 3 (a) of the Federal Boating Act of 1958, this term means the aggregate of all propellant machinery on a vessel.

§ 170.10–60 *Undocumented vessel.* As set forth in subsection 2 (1) of the Federal Boating Act of 1958, this term means "any vessel which is not required to have, and does not have, a valid marine document issued by the Bureau of Customs."

§ 170.10–65 *Vessel.* As set forth in subsection 2 (2) of the Federal Boating Act of 1958, this term "includes every description of water craft, other than a seaplane on the water, used or capable of being used as a means of transportation on water." This definition includes, but is not limited to, motorboats, sailboats, rowboats, canoes, ships, tugs, towboats, ferries, cargo vessels, passenger vessels, tank vessels, fishing vessels, charter boats, party boats, barges, scows, etc.

Appeals and Judicial Review

§ 170.15–1 *Judicial review or relief.* Nothing in this subchapter shall be so construed as to prevent any party from seeking a judicial review by, or relief in, an appropriate Court of law. This applies to any standard or regulation in this subchapter or to any decision or action taken pursuant thereto by the Coast Guard. If any provision of the regulations in this subchapter is held invalid, the validity of the remainder of this subchapter shall not be affected thereby.

§ 170.15–5 *Right of administrative appeal.* (a) Any person aggrieved by a decision or action taken by the Coast Guard under the regulations in this subchapter has a right to an administrative appeal therefrom. An appeal from a decision or action initially made or performed by an enforcing officer may be made to his commanding officer. Any decision or action of such commanding officer may be appealed to the Coast Guard District Commander of the district in which the action was taken or decision was made. A further appeal may be made to the Commandant, U. S. Coast Guard, from the decision of the District Commander.

(b) No special form is required, but such appeal shall set forth the decision or action appealed from and the reasons why it should be set aside or revised. Arrangements may be made for presenting an appeal in person.

§ 170.15–10 *Time limits.* (a) Any appeal to a Coast Guard District Commander shall be made in writing within 30 days after the decision or action appealed from shall have been rendered or taken.

(b) Any appeal to the Commandant shall be made in writing within 30 days after the decision or action appealed from shall have been rendered or taken.

§ 170.15–15 *Decision on appeal.* Pending the determination of an appeal, the decision or action appealed from shall remain in effect.

§ 170.15–20 *Initial decisions or actions of the Commandant.* Any person aggrieved by any decision or action initiated by the Commandant may request a review by writing to the Commandant within 30 days after the decision or action has been rendered or taken. Such a request shall set forth the decision or action desired to be reviewed and the reasons why it should be set aside or revised.

§ 170.15–25 *Reports and assessments of penalties for violations.* The reports of violations, assessment, collection, mitigation or remission of civil penalties shall be in accordance with §§ 2.50–20 to 2.50–30, inclusive, of Subchapter A (Procedures Applicable to the Public) of this chapter.

3. Subchapter S is amended by inserting a new Part 171, reading as follows:

PART 171—STANDARDS FOR NUMBERING

General

§ 171.01–1 *Vessels to be numbered.* (a) Certain undocumented vessels are required to be numbered by subsection 3 (a) of the Federal Boating Act of 1958, which reads as follows:

Every undocumented vessel propelled by machinery of more than 10 horsepower, whether or not such machinery is the principal source of propulsion, using the navigable waters of the United States, its Territories and the District of Columbia, and every such vessel owned in a State and using the high seas, shall be numbered in accordance with this Act, except—

(1) Foreign vessels temporarily using the navigable waters of the United States, its Territories and the District of Columbia;

(2) Public vessels of the United States;

(3) State and municipal vessels;

(4) Ships' lifeboats; and

(5) Vessels designated by the Secretary under section 7 (b) of this Act.

(b) Nothing in this section shall prohibit the numbering of any undocumented vessel, which may be propelled by machinery, upon request of the owner.

§ 171.01–5 *Exemptions.* Pursuant to subsections 3 (a) (5) and 7 (b) of the Federal Boating Act of 1958, the following are exempt from the requirement to be numbered:

(a) Undocumented vessels used exclusively for racing.

(b) Undocumented vessels operating under valid temporary certificates of number.

§ 171.01–10 *Determining horsepower of machinery.* (a) In general, for existing and new equipment, the manufacturer's rated horsepower at a stated maximum operating RPM as set forth on the nameplate attached to the engine, or as stamped on the engine, or as described in a "book of instructions" or other literature issued for such engine will be accepted as prima facie evidence of the horsepower of the machinery in question. In event the machinery does not have marked thereon or accompanying it any literature or tag setting forth the manufacturer's rated horsepower, or should the Coast Guard dispute the manufacturer's rated horsepower, then the Coast Guard's listing of horsepower will be accepted as prima facie evidence of the horsepower.

(b) In the event the owner or operator of a power propelled vessel disagrees with the findings of the Coast Guard as to horsepower, it shall be the responsibility of such owner or operator to prove to the satisfaction of the Coast Guard what is the actual horsepower of the propelling machinery.

Vessel Identification

§ 171.05–1 *Numbering pattern to be used.* (a) The numbers issued pursuant to the Federal Boating Act of 1958 shall be in accordance with the pattern described in this section.

(b) The number shall be divided into parts. The first part shall consist of the symbols identifying the State of principal use, followed by a combination of numerals and letters which furnish individual vessel identification. The group of digits appearing between letters shall be separated from those letters by hyphens or equivalent spaces. As examples: AL–001–AA, or AK 99 AZ.

(c) The first part of the number shall be an abbreviation in capital letters of the State. The abbreviations of the States are as follows:

Alabama—AL	North Carolina—NC
Alaska—AK	North Dakota—ND
Arizona—AZ	Nebraska—NB
Arkansas—AR	Nevada—NV
California—CF	New Hampshire—NH
Colorado—CL	New Jersey—NJ
Connecticut—CT	New Mexico—NM
Delaware—DL	New York—NY
Florida—FL	Ohio—OH
Georgia—GA	Oklahoma—OK
Hawaii—HA	Oregon—OR
Idaho—ID	Pennsylvania—PA
Illinois—IL	Rhode Island—RI
Indiana—IN	South Carolina—SC
Iowa—IA	South Dakota—SD
Kansas—KA	Tennessee—TN
Kentucky—KY	Texas—TX
Louisiana—LA	Utah—UT
Maine—ME	Virginia—VA
Massachusetts—MS	Vermont—VT
Maryland—MD	Washington—WN
Michigan—MC	West Virginia—WV
Minnesota—MN	Wyoming—WY
Mississippi—MI	Wisconsin—WS
Missouri—MO	District of Columbia—DC
Montana—MT	

(d) The remainder of the boat number shall consist of not more than four arabic numerals and two capital letters or not more than three arabic numerals and three capital letters, in sequence, separated by a hyphen or equivalent space, in accordance with the serials, numerically and alphabetically.

(1) As examples of the first alternative:

State designator	Maximum of 4 digits; numerical group	Maximum of 2 letters; alphabetical group
NY	1	A
NY	83	A B
NY	345	T R
NY	9999	Z Z

(2) As example of the second alternative:

State designator	Maximum of 3 digits; numerical group	Maximum of 3 letters; alphabetical group
NC	1	A
NC	83	A B
NC	345	P F
NC	999	Z Z Z

(e) Since the letters "I", "O" and "Q" may be mistaken for arabic numerals, all letter sequences using "I", "O" and "Q" shall be omitted. Objectionable words formed by the use of two or three letters will not be used.

(Sec. 3 (c), 72 Stat. 1754)

§ 171.05–5 *Display of number on vessel.* (a) Subsection 3 (f) of the Federal Boating Act of 1958 requires in part that "the number awarded * * * shall be painted on, or attached to, each side of the bow of the vessel for which it was issued * * *".

(b) The numbers shall be placed on each side of the forward half of the vessel in such position as to provide clear legibility for identification. The numbers shall read from left to right and shall be in block characters of good proportion not less than 3 inches in height. The numbers shall be of a color which will contrast with the color of the background and so maintained as to be clearly visible and legible; i. e., dark numbers on a light background, or light numbers on a dark background.

(Sec. 3 (c) (3), (f), 72 Stat. 1754, 1755)

(c) Subsection 3 (f) of the Federal Boating Act of 1958 also provides "no other number shall be carried on the bow of such vessel."

§ 171.05–10 *Numbering livery boats.* (a) The numbering requirement of this part shall apply to livery boats.

(b) The certificate of number of a livery boat shall be plainly marked, "livery boat."

(c) The description of the motor and type of fuel will be omitted from the certificate of number in any case where the motor is not rented with the boat.

§ 171.05–15 *Numbering of manufacturers' and dealers' boats.* (a) Numbering requirements of this part shall apply to boats operated by manufacturers and dealers.

(b) The description of the boat will be omitted from the certificate of number since the numbers and the certificates of number awarded may be transferred from one boat to another. In lieu of the description, the word "manufacturer" or "dealer,"

as appropriate, will be plainly marked on each certificate.

(c) The manufacturer or dealer may have the number awarded printed upon or attached to a removable sign or signs to be temporarily but firmly mounted upon or attached to the boat being demonstrated or tested so long as the display meets the requirements in § 171.05–5.

Application for Number

§ 171.10–1 *To whom made.* (a) On and after April 1, 1960, the owner of any vessel required to be numbered and principally used in a State which has not assumed the functions of numbering under the Federal Boating Act of 1958 shall prior to its use apply to the U. S. Coast Guard for a number for such vessel.

(b) An undocumented vessel principally used in a State which has assumed the functions of numbering under the Federal Boating Act of 1958 will not be numbered by the Coast Guard.

§ 171.10–2 An amendment (March 15, 1960) describes procedures for making application for a Coast Guard number. Applications (Forms CG–3876 and CG–3876A) are available at all First Class and Second Class Post Offices and at designated Third and Fourth Class Post Offices in those states in which undocumented vessels must be numbered by the Coast Guard.

§ 171.10–5 *Application requirements.* The application for a number shall include the following:

(a) Name and address of owner.

(b) Date of birth of owner.

(c) Present citizenship of owner.

(d) State in which the vessel is principally used.

(e) Present number (if any).

(f) Hull material (wood, steel, aluminum, plastic, other).

(g) Type of propulsion (outboard, inboard, other).

(h) Type of fuel (gas, diesel, other).

(i) Length of vessel.

(j) Make and year built (if known).

(k) Statement as to use (pleasure, livery, dealer, manufacturer, commercial-passenger, commercial-fishing, commercial-other).

(1) A certification of ownership by the applicant.

(m) Signature of owner.

§ 171.10–15 *State in which vessel is principally used.* (a) For the purposes of numbering, the statement of the owner with respect to the State in which the vessel is to be principally used, as set forth in the application for number, will be accepted, prima facie, as true.

(b) If the vessel is to be principally used on the high seas, then it shall be assigned a number for the State in which the vessel is usually docked, moored, housed, or garaged.

§ 171.10–20 *Application for renewal of number.* An application for renewal of a certificate of number shall be made by the owner on an application therefor which must be received by the Coast Guard within a period consisting of the last 90 days before the expiration date on the certificate of number and the same number will be issued upon renewal. Any application not so received shall be treated in the same manner as an original application except that the same number may be reissued if the application is received within one year from date of expiration.

§ 171.10–25 *Lost or destroyed certificate of number.* (a) If a certificate of number is lost or destroyed, the owner within 15 days shall notify the Commandant (MVI–10), U. S. Coast Guard, Washington 25, D. C. The notification shall be in writing and shall describe the circumstances of the loss or destruction.

(b) If an application for a duplicate certificate of number (Form CG–3919) (see § 171.10–30) is submitted without delay, it may also provide the written notification required by paragraph (a) of this section.

§ 171.10–30 *Duplicate certificate of number.* An amendment (March 15, 1960) describes procedure for making application for a duplicate certificate when the original is lost or destroyed. Two-part applications (Forms CG–3919 and CG–3919A) are available at post offices as described in § 171.10–2. Completed application forms are submitted to the post office, where a special fee stamp is bought and attached.

Ownership

§ 171.13–1 *Claim of ownership.* (a) The certified statement of ownership on the application for number shall be the minimum requirement for proof of ownership acceptable to the Coast Guard.

§ 171.13–5 *Liens.* Liens of all kinds, including reservations or transfers of title to secure debts or claims, will be disregarded in determining ownership under this subpart. A lienholder who acquires possession and title by virtue of default in the terms of the lien instrument, or any other person who acquires ownership through any such action of a lienholder, may apply for a number and shall attach to such application a signed statement explaining the fact in detail.

Certificate of Number

§ 171.15–1 *Information required on certificate.* The certificate of number shall include the following:

(a) Name and address of owner.

(b) Date of birth of owner.

(c) Present citizenship of owner.

(d) State in which the vessel is principally used.

(e) Present number (if any).

(f) Hull material (wood, steel aluminum, plastic, other).

(g) Type of propulsion (outboard, inboard, other).

(h) Type of fuel (gas, diesel, other).

(i) Length of vessel.

(j) Make and year built (if known).

(k) Statement as to use (pleasure, livery, dealer, manufacturer, commercial-passenger, commercial-fishing, commercial-other).

(l) A certification of ownership by the applicant.

(m) Signature of owner.

(n) Number awarded to vessel.

(o) Expiration date of certificate.

(p) Notice to the owner that he shall report within 15 days changes of ownership or address, and destruction or abandonment of vessel.

(q) Notice to the owner that the operator shall:

(1) Always carry this certificate on vessel when in use.

(2) Report every accident involving injury or death to persons, or property damage over $100.

(3) Stop and render aid or assistance if involved in boating accident.

§ 171.15–5 *Size and characteristics of certificate.* The certificate of number shall be pocket size (approximately 2½″ x 3½″) and water resistant.

§ 171.15–10 (a) *Temporary certificate.* Pending the issuance of the original certificate of number, the owner of the vessel will be furnished a temporary certificate of number valid for 60 days from date of issue. This temporary certificate shall be carried on board when the vessel is being operated.

Two amendments, paragraphs (b) and (c), (March 15, 1960) identify temporary certificates and require that they be postmarked to be valid.

§ 171.15–15 *Period of validity of certificate.* The original certificate of number initially awarded by the Coast Guard shall be valid for a period ending 3 years from the anniversary of the date of birth of the applicant next succeeding the issuance of the certificate. Each renewal shall be valid for a period ending 3 years from the date of expiration of the certificate so renewed. A certificate issued to other than an individual shall expire 3 years from date of issuance.

§ 171.15–20 *Notification of changes required.* (a) When the owner of a Coast Guard numbered vessel changes the State in which the vessel is principally used, he shall within 90 days surrender the certificate of number to the Coast Guard. The owner shall also apply for another original number to the office issuing numbers for that State.

(b) When the owner of a Coast Guard numbered vessel changes his address from that shown on his certificate, but does not change the State in which the vessel is principally used, he shall notify in writing the Commandant (MVI–10), U. S. Coast Guard, Washington 25, D. C., of his new address within a period not to exceed 15 days from such change. This written notification should be on Form CG–3920 (change of address notice), which is available upon request from any Post Office which handles applications for certificates of numbers (see § 171.10–2), or from any Coast Guard Marine Inspection Office.

(c) When a Coast Guard numbered vessel is lost, destroyed, abandoned, or transferred to another person, the certificate of number issued for the vessel shall be surrendered to the Commandant (MVI–10), U. S. Coast Guard, Washington 25, D. C., within a period not to exceed 15 days after such event. When the numbered vessel is lost, destroyed, abandoned, or transferred to another person, the owner shall within 15 days notify in writing the Commandant (MVI–10), U. S. Coast Guard, Washington 25, D. C., of the change in the status of the vessel. This written notification should be on Form CG–3921 (Notification of change in status of vessel), which is available upon request from any Post Office which handles applications for certificates of numbers (see § 171.10–2), or from any Coast Guard Marine Inspection Office. If the certificate of number is lost or destroyed, a description of such circumstances shall be reported as required by § 171.10–25.

(d) The application for number by a new owner of a vessel shall, for purposes of fee, be regarded as an original application for number, but where the vessel will continue in use in the same State of principal use, the new number shall be identical with the previous one, except where a lienholder acquires title and lawful possession by virtue of his lien, in which case a new number shall be issued.

(e) A change of motor is not required to be reported to the Coast Guard.

§ 171.15–25 *One certificate for each vessel.* The intent of this subpart is that the owner of an undocumented vessel shall not have more than one valid number or valid certificate of number for any one vessel at any time. Therefore, the owner will violate the regulations if he retains more than one valid certificate of number for any one vessel.

§ 171.15–30 *Cancellation of certificate and voiding of number.* (a) Subsection 3 (e) of the Federal Boating Act of 1958 authorizes the cancellation of certificates of number, thereby voiding the numbers issued. This means that a certificate may be canceled and number voided by proper authority even though such action occurs before the expiration date on the certificate and such certificate is not surrendered to the issuing office.

(b) Certain causes for cancellation of certificates and voiding of numbers are:

(1) Surrender of certificate for cancellation.

(2) Issuance of a new number for the same vessel.

(3) Issuance of a marine document by the Bureau of Customs for the same vessel.

(4) False or fraudulent certification in an application for number.

(c) In the absence of an application for renewal as provided in § 171.10–20 a number is automatically void on the date of expiration as shown on the certificate of number.

Fees and Charges

§ 171.17–1 *Fees.* (a) The fees charged by the U. S. Coast Guard are based upon the estimated cost of the administration of the Coast Guard's numbering system.

(b) The fees are as follows:

(1) Original numbering—$3.00.

(2) Reissue of lost or destroyed certificate of number—$1.00.

(3) Renewal of number—$3.00.

§ 171.17–5 *Method of Payment.* (a) The fee for original numbering shall be paid by purchase of a special fee stamp from any Post Office which sells the special fee stamps. (See § 171.10–2)

(b) The fee for reissue of lost or destroyed certificate of number (duplicate certificate of number) shall be paid by purchase of a special fee stamp from any Post Office which sells the special fee stamps. (See § 171.10–30)

(c) No application for an original certificate of number or for a duplicate certificate of number will be processed without an appropriate special fee stamp attached thereto. No special fee stamps shall be sold prior to April 1, 1960.

(d) The fee for renewal of number is payable to the U. S. Coast Guard and shall accompany the application.

Availability of Records

§ 171.20–1 *Enforcement or assistance programs.* Upon request, information on ownership and identity of Coast Guard numbered vessels shall be available to Federal, State, and local officials, as needed, in any enforcement or assistance programs.

§ 171.20–5. *Disclosure of information.*

(a) The records pertaining to the numbering of undocumented vessels pursuant to this part are considered to be public records.

(b) Information based on such Coast Guard records may be released upon oral or written inquiry, subject only to reasonable restrictions necessary to carry on the business of the office. The Coast Guard may permit excerpts to be made or the copying or reproduction thereof by a private individual or concern authorized by the Coast Guard. The fees and charges for copying, certifying, or searching of records for information shall be assessed in accordance with 33 CFR 1.25.

4. The title for Part 172 is amended to read:

PART 172
NUMBERING REQUIREMENTS UNDER ACT OF JUNE 7, 1918

5. Part 172 is amended by adding at the end thereof a new Subpart 172.25, reading as follows:

Termination Requirements

§ 172.25–1 *Effective termination dates of numbering laws.* Effective April 1, 1960, the Act of June 7, 1918, as amended, and section 21 of the Act of April 25, 1940, are repealed by section 12 of the Federal Boating Act of 1958. In addition, these laws shall cease to be applicable prior to April 1, 1960, in any State when such State has assumed the functions of numbering under the Federal Boating Act of 1958.

§ 172.25–5 *Effective termination dates for regulations in this part.* (a) No certificate of award of number will be issued nor numbers assigned to vessels pursuant to this part on and after April 1, 1960.

(b) The regulations prescribed under the Act of June 7, 1918, as amended, shall cease to be applicable in any State when such State has assumed the functions of numbering under the Federal Boating Act of 1958.

§ 172.25–10 *Interim use of certificates of award of number and numbers awarded.* Pending receipt of a certificate of number under the Federal Boating Act of 1958, for which application has been made and proof thereof retained, the owner of every vessel of more than 10 horsepower with a valid certificate of award of number on March 31, 1960, shall retain such number and certificate for temporary identification until renumbered pursuant to the Federal Boating Act of 1958.

6. Subchapter S is amended by inserting a new Part 173, reading as follows:

PART 173—BOATING ACCIDENTS, REPORTS, AND STATISTICAL INFORMATION

Boating Accidents

§ 173.01–1 *General.* (a) The provisions of this subpart shall apply (1) to all uninspected motorboats and (2) to all other uninspected vessels used for pleasure or recreational purposes. Uninspected vessels, other than motorboats, used for commercial purposes are not included.

(b) The provisions in this subpart are applicable in the United States, its Territories, and the District of Columbia, as well as to every such vessel which is owned in a State, Territory, or the District of Columbia and using the high seas.

§ 173.01–5 *Reportable boating accidents.* (a) Subsection 13 (c) of the Act of April 25, 1940, as amended (46 U. S. C. 526l), reads as follows:

In the case of collision, accident, or other casualty involving a motorboat or other vessel subject to this Act, the operator thereof, if the collision, accident, or other casualty results in death or injury to any person, or damage to property in excess of $100, shall file with the Secretary of the Department within which the Coast Guard is operating, unless such operator is required to file an accident report with the

State under section 3 (c) (6) of the Federal Boating Act of 1958, a full description of the collision, accident, or other casualty, including such information as the Secretary may by regulation require.

(b) For the purpose of this subpart a "boating accident" means a collision, accident or other casualty involving (1) an uninspected motorboat or (2) any other uninspected vessel used for pleasure or recreational purposes.

(c) A vessel subject to this subpart is considered to be involved in a "boating accident" whenever the occurrence results in damage by or to the vessel or its equipment; in injury or loss of life to any person, or in the disappearance of any person from on board under circumstances which indicate the possibility of death or injury. A "boating accident" includes, but is not limited to, capsizing, collision, foundering, flooding, fire, explosion and the disappearance of a vessel other than by theft.

(d) A report is required whenever a vessel subject to this subpart is involved in a "boating accident" which results in any one or more of the following:

(1) Loss of life.

(2) Injury causing any person to remain incapacitated for a period in excess of 72 hours.

(3) Actual physical damage to property (including vessels) in excess of $100.

§ 173.01–10 *Written report required.* (a) Whenever death results from a boating accident, a written report shall be submitted within 48 hours. For every other reportable boating accident a written report shall be submitted within five (5) days after such accident.

(b) The operator(s) of the boat(s) shall prepare and submit the written report(s) to the Coast Guard Officer in Charge, Marine Inspection, nearest to the place where such accident occurred or nearest to the port of first arrival after such accident, unless such operator is required to file an accident report with a State under subsection 3 (c) (6) of the Federal Boating Act of 1958.

(c) Every written report shall contain the following information:

(1) The numbers and/or names of vessels involved.

(2) The locality where the accident occurred.

(3) The time and date when the accident occurred.

(4) Weather and sea conditions at time of accident.

(5) The name, address, age, and boat operating experience of the operator of the reporting vessel.

(6) The names and addresses of operators of other vessels involved.

(7) The names and address of the owners of vessels or property involved.

(8) The names and addresses of any person or persons injured or killed.

(9) The nature and extent of injury to any person or persons.

(10) A description of damage to property (including vessels) and estimated cost of repairs.

(11) A description of the accident (including opinions as to the causes).

(12) The length, propulsion, horsepower, fuel and construction of the reporting vessel.

(13) Names and addresses of known witnesses.

(d) The Coast Guard Form CG-3865 (Boating Accident Report) may be used for the written report required by this section.

§ 173.05–1 *Required reports.* The Coast Guard will obtain, compile, analyze, and publish periodic reports in a uniform manner with respect to vessels having currently valid certificates of number, and with respect to boating accidents.

§ 173.05–5 *Reports with respect to numbered vessels.* The Coast Guard will compile statistics on numbered vessels as of March 31, June 30, September 30, and December 31 of each year. This information includes as of the reporting date:

(a) The total number of all valid certificates of number outstanding.

(b) The total number of valid certificates of number held by vessels numbered under subsection 3 (a) of the Federal Boating Act of 1958.

(c) The total numbers of valid certificates of number held by vessels described by class, type, and construction.

§ 173.05–10 *Reports with respect to boating accidents.* The Coast Guard will compile statistics on boating accidents reported during each quarter, ending on March 31, June 30, September 30, and December 31 of each year. This information will include:

(a) The total number of boating accidents reported during each such period.

(b) The totals of boating accidents reported during each such period, grouped according to the cause, nature, and results and including the class, type, and construction of vessels involved.

(c) The totals of boating accidents reported during each such period by vessels required to be numbered under subsection 3 (a) of the Federal Boating Act of 1958 according to vessels described by class, type, and construction.

Availability of Information

§ 173.10–1 *"Boating Accident Reports".* (a) The "Boating Accident Reports" are intended to furnish the information necessary for the Coast Guard to make findings of causes of accidents and recommendations for their prevention, and to compile information for use in making statistical reports.

(b) Except as provided in paragraph (c), individual "Boating Accident Reports," or copies of or excerpts therefrom, will not be released.

(c) "Boating Accident Reports" may be available for additional statistical studies, on the condition that information from individual reports shall not be disclosed, and subject to prior arrangements and reasonable restrictions necessary in the carrying on of the business of the office.

§ 173.10–5 *Statistical records and statistical reports.* After information has been released or published, the statistical records and statistical reports obtained and compiled by the Coast Guard, as distinguished from the individual "Boating Accident Reports" described in § 173.10–1, shall be made available for inspection and use by the public during normal office hours subject to reasonable restrictions necessary in the carrying on of the business of the office.

Dated: December 19, 1958.

[SEAL]   J. A. HIRSHFIELD,
Rear Admiral, U. S. Coast Guard,
Acting Commandant.

[F. R. Doc. 58–10628; Filed, Dec. 24, 1958; 8:45 a. m.]

PILOTING, SEAMANSHIP
AND SMALL BOAT HANDLING

1969-70 Edition

Motor Boating Ideal Series—Volume V

GENERAL INDEX

(See Definitions of Nautical Terms, Pages 464-480 and Contents, Pages vi and vii)

NOTE:—Page numbers in the 1969-70 edition of this book remain the same as in earlier editions. Additional new material is folioed by the use of letters, a, b, c, etc.

In a textbook such as **Piloting, Seamanship and Small Boat Handling,** its value to the student, and to all readers for reference purposes, is immeasurably enhanced by a comprehensive general index.

In line with this objective, our index has been enlarged from year to year with succeeding editions. In this 1969-70 edition, for example, it has been expanded again, now totaling approximately 2500 references.

Where multiple listings make it desirable, the reader may turn to a basic head, such as compass, flags, lights, etc., and conveniently find the particular phase of the subject in question. Concerned with variation of the compass, for example, he may find it as a sub-head under the broad listing of "compass," or may turn directly to "variation" where various aspects of variation are, in turn, sub-headed. Generous use of cross-references has been made throughout. Listings start on page 510.

515(657)

Q

R

T

*Note:-Although this page is numbered "523," yet by actual count it is in reality page No. "689" (695, if a 2-page unfolioed color insert and 4 pages of end-papers, in color, are included). This difference is due to the fact that there are 166 lettered pages, such as 78a, 78b, etc. The reason for this is that, as new material is added to new editions, such new pages are given folio numbers corresponding to those of the existing allied subjects plus letters. By this method the basic page numbers remain unchanged and references in student outlines, etc., do not go out-of-date.

 MT. CLEMENS
 MUSKEGON
 NARRAGANSETT BAY
 NEPTUNE
 NEWARK BAY
 NEW BRITAIN
 NEW HAVEN
 NEW LONDON

 NEW ORLEANS
 NEWPORT
 NEW RIVER
 NEW YORK
 NIAGARA
 NOBSCOT
 NOR-MAC
 NORTHEAST RIVER

 NORTH. NEW JERSEY
 NORTH RIVER
 NORWALK
 NORWICH
 OAKLAND
 OAK ORCHARD
 OAK RIDGE
 OCALA

 OKINAWA
 OLD COLONY
 OLD FIELD POINT
 OLYMPIA
 ORANGE
 ORLANDO
 OSHKOSH
 PAINESVILLE

 PALISADES
 PALM BEACH
 PASADENA
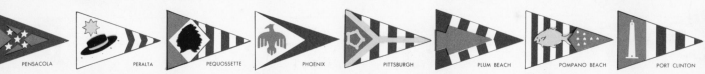 PATAPSCO RIVER
 PATCHOGUE BAY
 PATUXENT RIVER
 PECONIC BAY
 PEEKSKILL

 PENSACOLA
 PERALTA
 PEQUOSSETTE
 PHOENIX
 PITTSBURGH
 PLUM BEACH
 POMPANO BEACH
 PORT CLINTON

 PORT HURON
 PORTSMOUTH
 POSSESSION SOUND
 POTOMAC RIVER
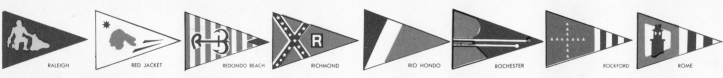 POVERTY BAY
 PYMATUNING
 QUAD CITY
 QUINCY

 RALEIGH
 RED JACKET
 REDONDO BEACH
 RICHMOND
 RIO HONDO
 ROCHESTER
 ROCKFORD
 ROME

 ROWAYTON
 SACANDAGA
 SADDLE RIVER
 SAGINAW BAY
 ST. ANDREW BAY
 ST. JOSEPH
 ST. LAWRENCE

 ST. PAUL
 ST. PETERSBURG
 SALISBURY
 SALT CREEK
 SAN ANTONIO
 SAN DIEGO
 SANDUSKY
SAN FERNANDO VALLEY

 SAN FRANCISCO
SAN GABRIEL VALLEY
SAN LUIS REY
SANTA BARBARA
SANTA CLARA
SANTA MONICA BAY
SANTANA
SARASOTA